HANDBOOK
OF
PERSONALITY
PSYCHOLOGY

Edited by

ROBERT HOGAN

JOHN JOHNSON

STEPHEN BRIGGS

ACADEMIC PRESS

HANDBOOK OF PERSONALITY PSYCHOLOGY

HANDBOOK OF PERSONALITY PSYCHOLOGY

Edited by

ROBERT HOGAN

UNIVERSITY OF TULSA
TULSA, OKLAHOMA

JOHN JOHNSON

PENNSYLVANIA STATE UNIVERSITY
DUBOIS, PENNSYLVANIA

STEPHEN BRIGGS

UNIVERSITY OF TULSA
TULSA, OKLAHOMA

ACADEMIC PRESS

SAN DIEGO   LONDON   BOSTON   NEW YORK   SYDNEY   TOKYO   TORONTO

This book is printed on acid-free paper. ⊗

Academic Press,
525 B Street, Suite 1900, San Diego, California 92101-4495, USA
http://www.apnet.com

Academic Press Limited
24-28 Oval Road, London NW1 7DX, UK
http://www.hbuk.co.uk/ap/

Library of Congress Cataloging-in-Publication Data

Handbook of personality psychology / edited by Robert Hogan, John
    Johnson, Stephen Briggs.
          p.   cm.
    Includes index.
    ISBN 0-12-134645-5 (hard). -- ISNB 0-12-134646-3 (soft)
    1. Personality.   I. Hogan, Robert.   II. Johnson, John (John A.)
III. Briggs, Stephen R.
BF698.H3345   1995
155.2--dc20   94-39181
                                                       CIP

PRINTED IN THE UNITED STATES OF AMERICA
97 98 99 00   01   02 EB   9   8   7   6   5   4   3   2

Contents

Part I Introduction
Nature of Personality Psychology

Chapter 1 A Conceptual History of Personality Psychology
Dan P. McAdams

CHAPTER 14 **EVOLUTIONARY PERSPECTIVES ON PERSONALITY TRAITS**
ARNOLD H. BUSS

CHAPTER 15 **GENETICS, TEMPERAMENT, AND PERSONALITY**
DAVID C. ROWE

CHAPTER 16 **PSYCHOPHYSIOLOGICAL APPROACHES TO PERSONALITY**
RUSSELL G. GEEN

Part V SOCIAL DETERMINANTS OF PERSONALITY

Chapter 23 Internal Inhibitions and Controls
Edwin I. Megargee

Part VII Personality and the Self

Chapter 24 Congruence of Others' and Self-Judgments of Personality
David C. Funder
C. Randall Colvin

CHAPTER 28 PERSONALITY STRUCTURE: THE RETURN OF THE BIG FIVE
JERRY S. WIGGINS
PAUL D. TRAPNELL

CHAPTER 29 EXTRAVERSION AND ITS POSITIVE EMOTIONAL CORE
DAVID WATSON
LEE ANNA CLARK

CHAPTER 30 AGREEABLENESS: A DIMENSION OF PERSONALITY
WILLIAM G. GRAZIANO
NANCY H. EISENBERG

CHAPTER 31 CONCEPTIONS AND CORRELATES OF OPENNESS TO EXPERIENCE
ROBERT R. MCCRAE
PAUL T. COSTA, JR.

CHAPTER 32 CONSCIENTIOUSNESS AND INTEGRITY AT WORK
JOYCE HOGAN
DENIZ S. ONES

PART VIII APPLIED PSYCHOLOGY

CHAPTER 33 PERSONALITY, INTERACTIVE RELATIONS, AND
APPLIED PSYCHOLOGY
WILLIAM F. CHAPLIN

Contributors

Numbers in parentheses indicate the pages on which the authors' contributions begin.

James R. Averill (513) Department of Psychology, University of Massachusetts, Amherst, Massachusetts 01003

Roy F. Baumeister (681) Department of Psychology, Case Western Reserve University, Cleveland, Ohio 44106

Arnold H. Buss (345) Department of Psychology, University of Texas, Austin, Texas 78712

David M. Buss (317) Department of Psychology, University of Texas, Austin, Texas 78712

William F. Chaplin (873) Department of Psychology, University of Alabama, Tuscaloosa, Alabama 35487

Lee Anna Clark (767) Department of Psychology, University of Iowa, Iowa City, Iowa 52242

C. Randall Colvin (617) Department of Psychology, Northeastern University, Boston, Massachusetts 02115

Paul T. Costa, Jr. (269, 825) NIA-NIH Gerontology Research Center, Baltimore, Maryland 21224

Laurie Couch (465) Department of Psychology, Fort Hays State University, Hays, Kansas 67601

Rebecca A. Eder (209) St. Louis Children's Hospital, St. Louis, Missouri 63110

Nancy H. Eisenberg (795) Department of Psychology, Arizona State University, Tempe, Arizona 85287

Robert A. Emmons (485) Department of Psychology, University of California, Davis, California 95616

John F. Finch (143) Department of Psychology, Texas A&M University, College Station, Texas 77843

Bram Fridhandler (543) California Pacific Medical Center and University of California, San Francisco, San Francisco, California 94143

David C. Funder (617) Department of Psychology, University of California, Riverside, California 92521

Stella Garcia (167) Department of Psychology, University of Texas at San Antonio, San Antonio, Texas 76010

Russell G. Geen (387) Department of Psychology, University of Missouri, Columbia, Missouri 65211

William G. Graziano (795) Department of Psychology, Texas A&M University, College Station, Texas 77843

Charles F. Halverson, Jr. (241) University of Georgia, Athens, Georgia 30602

Reid Hastie (711) University of Colorado, Boulder, Colorado 80309

Sean Hayes (543) Department of Psychology, Pepperdine University, Malibu, California 90263

Ravenna Helson (291) Institute of Personality and Social Research, University of California at Berkeley, Berkeley, California 94720

Joyce Hogan (849) University of Tulsa, Tulsa, Oklahoma 74104

William Ickes (167) Department of Psychology, University of Texas at Arlington, Arlington, Texas 76010

Oliver P. John (649) Department of Psychology, University of California, Berkeley, Berkeley, California 94704

John A. Johnson (73) DuBois Campus, Pennsylvania State University, DuBois, Pennsylvania 15801

Warren H. Jones (465) Department of Psychology, University of Tennessee, Knoxville, Tennessee 37996

John F. Kihlstrom (711) Department of Psychology, Yale University, New Haven, Connecticut 06520

Michael J. Lambert (947) Psychology Department, Brigham Young University, Provo, Utah 84602

James T. Lamiell (117) Department of Psychology, Georgetown University, Washington, District of Columbia 20057

Jane Loevinger (199) Department of Psychology, Washington University, St. Louis, Missouri 63130

Dan P. McAdams (3) School of Education and Social Policy, Northwestern University, Evanston, Illinois 60208

Robert R. McCrae (269, 825) NIA-NIH Gerontology Research Center, Baltimore, Maryland 21224

Sarah C. Mangelsdorf (209) Department of Psychology, University of Illinois, Urbana-Champaign, Champaign, Illinois 61820

Edwin I. Megargee (581) Department of Psychology, Florida State University, Tallahassee, Florida 32306

Leslie C. Morey (919) Department of Psychology, Vanderbilt University, Nashville, Tennessee 37240

Deniz S. Ones (849) University of Minnesota, Minneapolis, Minnesota 55455

Jennifer Pals (291) Institute of Personality and Social Research, University of California at Berkeley, Berkeley, California 94720

Delroy L. Paulhus (543) Department of Psychology, University of British Columbia, Vancouver, British Columbia V6T 1Z4, Canada

Thomas F. Pettigrew (417) Stevenson College, University of California, Santa Cruz, California 95064

Richard W. Robins (649) Department of Psychology, University of California, Davis, Davis, California 95616

David C. Rowe (367) School of Family and Consumer Resources, University of Arizona, Tucson, Arizona 85721

William McKinley Runyan (41) School of Social Welfare, University of California at Berkeley, Berkeley, California 94720

Susan Scott (465) Department of Psychology, University of Tulsa, Tulsa, Oklahoma 74104

Timothy W. Smith (891) Department of Psychology, University of Utah, Salt Lake City, Utah 84112

Mark Snyder (167) Department of Psychology, University of Minnesota, Minneapolis, Minnesota 55455

Marjorie Solomon (291) Institute of Personality and Social Research, University of California at Berkeley, Berkeley, California 94720

Edwin C. Supplee (947) , Tripler Regional Medical Center, Honolulu, HI 96859

Paul D. Trapnell (737) Department of Psychology, University of British Columbia, Vancouver, British Columbia V6T 1Z4, Canada

Harry C. Triandis (439) Department of Psychology, University of Illinois, Urbana-Champaign, Champaign, Illinois 61820

Karen S. Wampler (241) Texas Tech University, Lubbock, Texas 79409

David Watson (767) Department of Psychology, University of Iowa, Iowa City, Iowa 52242

Stephen G. West (143) Department of Psychology, Arizona State University, Tempe, Arizona 85287

Deborah J. Wiebe (891) Department of Psychology, University of Utah, Salt Lake City, Utah 84112

Jerry S. Wiggins (95, 737) Department of Psychology, University of British Columbia, Vancouver, British Columbia V6T 1Z4, Canada

PREFACE

This Handbook was conceived in the early 1980s, during a time when personality psychology was under heavy attack as a scientifically worthless endeavor. Researchers had trouble publishing in mainstream journals or getting grant proposals funded, and the discipline seemed in danger of disappearing from the intellectual radar scope.

Such a state of affairs seems very strange given that: (1) the conclusions reached by anthropology, criminology, economics, history, political science—indeed, all the social sciences—depend heavily on assumptions about human nature; (2) scholars in these fields rarely examine their psychological assumptions; and (3) personality psychology is the one discipline that takes the self-conscious evaluation of human nature as its central intellectual task. This point highlights the significance of personality psychology in modern social science.

It is hard to imagine a more important topic. Despite the overwhelming significance of the topic, personality psychology, as noted above, almost disappeared in the 1970s and early 1980s. The reasons were varied, but the biggest problem was the enthusiasm of American psychology for behaviorism. Behaviorism is the antithesis of personality psychology; it argues that what people do depends primarily on their social circumstances. It also denies that there are stable structures inside people that can explain their behavior.

Behaviorism is a useful methodology for training animals to perform, but as a model of human nature it is seriously inadequate. The problem is that it ignores evolutionary theory, one of the most important developments in the history of science. Evolutionary theory, combined with human behavior genetics, reveals sensible and reproducible evidence for stable tendencies within individuals.

Over the past 10 years personality psychology has made a remarkable comeback. There are probably two reasons for this. First, social psychologists have discovered individual differences and have learned that, by incorporating personality measures in their experiments, they get better results. Second, industrial/organizational psychology has discovered that well-constructed measures of personality predict occupational performance as well as cognitive measures, but they do not yield the adverse impact of cognitive tests.

This Handbook celebrates the rebirth of personality psychology, and in so doing, it has two unique features. First, the chapters, which cover every subfield in personality psychology, were written by the best-known and best-qualified people in the discipline. Second, the chapters were written with students in mind; the authors were asked not to write for one another but to write in a way that would be accessible to intelligent nonpsychologists. In my judgment they have succeeded remarkably well.

Robert Hogan

PART I

INTRODUCTION

NATURE OF PERSONALITY PSYCHOLOGY

CHAPTER 1

A CONCEPTUAL HISTORY OF PERSONALITY PSYCHOLOGY

DAN P. MCADAMS

NORTHWESTERN UNIVERSITY

A history is an interpretation of the past in light of what followed. It is a *story* about how events and changes *led up to* a subsequent state of affairs. If that subsequent state of affairs is the current state of affairs, then the historian must make sense of how the past may have led up to the present. The prevailing view of the present, therefore, influences how the past is to be seen. If recent reviews are any indication, there appear to be increasingly positive signs concerning the present health of personality psychology (D. M. Buss, 1991; Craik, 1993; Digman, 1990; McAdams, 1994; Pervin, 1985, 1990; Singer & Kolligan, 1987; Wiggins & Pincus, 1992). This history, therefore, begins with a mildly optimistic perception of the current state of affairs in personality.

When the present is seen in relatively optimistic terms, narratives of the past are likely to manifest themes of either *progress* or *rebirth*. Both are apparent in this history, though they are tempered by themes of stagnation and disorganization as well. The theme of progress is a favorite in histories of science, for most people assume that science moves forward, toward greater understanding and truth. From the current vantage point, some progress in the history of personality psychology can be seen, but the progress appears uneven and fitful. Sanford (1963) warns that the research activity of psychologists at any particular time may not accurately reflect main ideas in the field. Other reviewers have noted that the field of personality psychology is especially prone to conceptual and methodological fads (Sechrest, 1976). A challenge for this history, therefore, is to discern broad conceptual trends as they have evolved over time. As such this account is highly selective, passing over many ephemeral fads as well as many substantive contributions to the field that simply cannot be included in the short space given for such a daunting exposition. Finally, this is a *recent* history of personality psychology, concentrating on the twentieth century, and it is heavily weighted toward concept trends and developments in America.

I. PERSONALITY PSYCHOLOGY'S UNIQUE FEATURES: HOLISM, MOTIVATION, AND INDIVIDUAL DIFFERENCES

Personality psychology became an identifiable discipline in the social sciences in the 1930s. During that decade a number of separate lines of inquiry came together, culminating in the highly integrative programs for the field generated by Allport (1937), Murray (1938), and Lewin (1935). The first issue of the journal *Character and Personality* appeared in 1932. The journal aimed to join German studies of character with British and American studies of individual differences in persons, incorporating case studies, correlational surveys, experiments, and theoretical discussions. McDougall (1932) wrote the lead article, exploring various meanings of the terms "character" and "personality." Early contributors included Adler, Jung, Spearman, Frenkel-Brunswik, Rosenzweig, and MacKinnon.

The publication of Allport's (1937) *Personality: A Psychological Interpretation* marked the formal arrival of personality on the scene of social science. Although textbooks on mental hygiene, abnormal psychology, and character and personality had appeared in earlier years (e.g., Bagby, 1928; Bruce, 1908; Jastrow, 1915; Roback, 1927), Allport's was the first to articulate a grand vision for the field of personality and to place it within the context of historical and contemporary scholarship in the arts and sciences. (Stagner's [1937] textbook in personality, written from an experimental/behaviorist point of view, appeared in the same year, but its historical influence has not been nearly as great as that of Allport's.) Allport viewed personality psychology as the study of the individual person. He defined personality as "the dynamic organization within the individual of those psychophysical systems that determine his unique adjustments to his environment"—a definition that, shorn of its sexist language, is still serviceable today. Allport later (1961) changed "unique adjustments to his environment" to "characteristic behavior and thought."

From the beginning, personality psychology was a dissident field in the context of American experimental psychology (Hall & Lindzey, 1957). Whereas American psychology tended toward the elementaristic, personality was holistic, taking the *whole person* as the primary unit of study. Whereas American learning theory focused on the relations between external stimuli and publicly observable responses in rats and other animals, personality concerned itself with the problem of human motivation, conceived in terms of unobservable dynamics and promptings from within. Whereas experimental psychologists searched for universal laws applicable to all individuals, personality focused on how people were different from each other as well as how they were alike. In addition, personality psychology invited collaborations with a wide variety of disciplines lying outside the mainstream of American experimental psychology. These included psychoanalysis and other depth psychologies, German characterology, mental testing, and abnormal psychology.

With its triple emphasis on the whole person, motivation, and individual differences, personality psychology has always held a rather tenuous and ambiguous status in American psychology. On the one hand, some have proclaimed that proper personality theory is (or should be) nothing less than integrative psychological theory at the highest level, placing personality at the center of all of psychology (e.g., G. S. Klein & Krech, 1951; McCurdy, 1965). On the other hand, some have suggested that the discipline is so amorphous that it should be abolished, or allowed to fade away (Blake & Mouton, 1959). Both extremes are problematic in that they fail to affirm a separate identity for the field of personality psychology: it is either nothing or everything (which is also nothing). This historical account affirms an identity for personality psychology as a discipline that has its own distinguishing features. Three of these are the emphases on (1) the whole person, (2) motivation and dynamics, and (3) individual differences.

II. HISTORICAL ROOTS: BEFORE THE 1930s

A. The Whole Person

Before Allport, a distinguished group of European scholars championed the whole person as a unit of scientific study. Relatedly, these scholars tended to conceptualize persons themselves as *striving toward wholeness,* toward unity and purpose in their lives. Comte (1852) envisioned a new science, which he named *la morale,* dedicated to the examination of the individual person as both "a cause and consequence of society" (Allport, 1954, p. 8). In Comte's view, the person is more than a biological and a cultural being. The person is a uniquely patterned moral agent existing as a unified and directed whole. *La morale* could be viewed from either a biological or a social/cultural perspective, but the identity of the new science was also to transcend these two views. Writes Allport (1954), "what Comte was seeking was a science of personality—unfortunately some years before such a science was possible" (p. 8).

Dilthey (1900/1976) argued for a purely human life science, divorced from the objective approaches of the natural sciences. Rejecting virtually all canons of conventional scientific methodology, his psychology of *Verstehen* set as its goal the empathic understanding of the inner unity of the individual life. Somewhat less radical was the *personalistic* psychology of Stern (1924), premised on the assumption that the person is a "multiform dynamic unity." Closer to the mainstream in academic psychology was McDougall's (1908) view that whereas personality may be seen in terms of a number of different instincts and sentiments, the master sentiment is *self-regard,* which makes for the unity of self, or what McDougall called *character.*

Both James (1890) and Freud (1923/1961) left room in their writings for the person's strivings toward unity and wholeness. For James the *self-as-me* (the objective self or self-concept)—in its material, social, and spiritual aspects—encompasses all that the person understands to be "me" and "mine." By contrast, James' *self-as-I* (the subjective self or ego) is a fleeting state, a person's moment of consciousness, destined to slip instantaneously away into a rushing stream. For Freud, "the I" (*das Ich*, or ego) is a unifying agent of sorts, working to effect compromises among conflicting forces within the person and between the person and the environment, with the final goal of reducing anxiety and promoting effective, reality-based functioning. When wholeness or unity is destroyed, the person is bound to suffer problems.

B. The Problem of Motivation

Hall and Lindzey (1957) write that personality theorists have traditionally assigned a crucial role to the motivation processes. More than most other fields in the social sciences, personality psychology concerns itself with the internal springs of human action. This orientation is evident even in textbooks written before Allport (1937): "It is surely in the springs of human action, if anywhere, that the key to the problem of personality is to be found" (Garnett, 1928, p. 14).

Conceptualizations of human motivation may be broadly classed into those emphasizing (1) biological constructs such as drives, instincts, and brain rewards, and (2) cognitive processes such as expectancies, values, schemas, and attributions (Geen, Beatty, & Arkin, 1984). In the early years of this century, personality theories tended to draw on the former class, invoking various biological or quasi-biological explanations for why people ultimately do what they do. Therefore, Freud (1905/1953, 1920/1955) argued that biologically anchored drives concerning sexuality and aggression provide the energy and the direction for much of human behavior, though their manifestations are disguised through the defensive machinations of the ego and the generally antagonistic demands of the social world. McDougall (1908) presented a more differentiated theory of motivation, suggesting that human behavior is energized and guided by 12 instincts and five "nonspecific innate tendencies." Major instincts include those concerned with reproduction, food seeking, construction (building things), and gregariousness. Whereas Freud's Eros and death instincts are generally viewed to be irrational and at odds with the demands of social life, McDougall saw instinctive activity as complexly patterned, reality-based behavior that is sustained until some natural goal is achieved. For McDougall, instinctive behavior is socially adaptive and situationally malleable.

McDougall's (1908) concept of *sentiment* represents an attempt to move toward the cognitive pole of motivational theorizing. Similar in meaning to the contemporary term "value," a sentiment develops when the mental image of an object or activity in the environment becomes associated with one or more instincts. People form sentiments with regard to concrete objects (one's favorite book), collectivities (church, gang), and abstractions (qualities of honesty, courage) (Hogan, 1976). At the most abstract level, Spranger (1928) offered a more thoroughly cognitive approach to human motivation in positing six central value types in personality. Men and women are primarily motivated by their allegiance to either theoretical, social, political, artistic, economic, or religious values—a typology captured in Allport and Vernon's (1931) measure, "A Study of Values." Whereas biological drives seem to "push" behavior in an efficient-cause manner, values seem to "pull" behavior toward certain goal states, suggesting something more of a teleological or final-cause explanation of human motivation (Rychlak, 1981).

C. Differences among People

Western conceptualizations of individual differences in personality can be traced back at least 2,000 years to the ancient typologies of Hippocrates and Galen. The behavioral characterization of the sanguine, phlegmatic, melancholic, and choleric has proven an amazingly durable contribution to psychological theorizing, brought forward to modern times by Kant, Wundt, and, in the twentieth century, Eysenck (1973), who reconceptualizes the types along the dimensions extraversion and neuroticism. Posterity has been less kind to the ancient belief that blood, bile, and phlegm are the physiological underpinnings of these behavioral types, but the somatotype theories of Kretschmer (1921) and Sheldon (1940) retain a biological emphasis, as have numerous theories of human "temperament." Much of the groundwork for differential psychology was laid before the 1930s, extending back to the pioneering work of Galton on mental testing and Binet on intelligence, the invention of correlation and factor analysis, and the emergence of formal test theory and the psychometric movement in the United States and Britain (see Anastasi, 1958, 1976; Jackson & Paunonen, 1980, for reviews). Spurred by the mobilization of large military forces for World War I, psychologists began to invent self-report, multi-item tests to assess individual differences in personality functioning. A fore-runner to the MMPI, Woodworth's (1919) Personal Data Sheet was used to screen out men who were unfit for military service because of personality maladjustment. Bernreuter (1931) developed the first multitrait personality inventory, containing scales to assess neuroticism, introversion, dominance, self-sufficiency, confidence, and sociability.

III. THE FORMATION OF SYSTEMS: 1930–1950

A. Allport's Psychology of the Individual

Allport's (1937) vision for personality psychology was a humanistic alternative to the prevailing mechanistic paradigms of stimulus–response psychology in the 1930s. In addition, it was an optimistic antidote to Freudian determinism and the growing emphasis, in clinical writings, on human pathology. In his autobiography, Allport (1968) states that he wished to create a field of study centered on an image of man "that would allow us to test in full whatever democratic and humane potentialities he might possess" (p. 394). Toward the end of the Great Depression in Europe and America and on the eve of World War II, Allport wrote *Personality* in the spirit of social reform and the hope for a better world. Allport's text was cosmopolitan, erudite, and steeped in old-world European scholarship. But it was also profoundly American, in its unabashed optimism and egalitarian tone.

Allport presented an eclectic array of concepts and hypotheses, loosely tied to one dominant theme: the person is a unique whole. It is somewhat ironic that in the history of personality psychology the central theme of the seminal textbook in the field has remained the most controversial and hotly disputed aspect of Allport's legacy, as if the field's *raison d'etre* doubles as its perpetual nemesis. How can a science of the person assume that each person is unique? If science seeks lawfulness across persons (nomothetics), then how can it make sense of, even leave room for, the uniqueness of the individual (idiographics)? Many, if not most, personality psychologists have traditionally objected to Allport's insistence that personality psychology must focus on the uniqueness of the individual case (e.g., Holt, 1962). But they have been kinder, at least in their rhetoric if not in their research, when it comes to Allport's insistence that personality psychologists concern themselves with the person's wholeness.

In Allport's own theorizing, the person's wholeness and unity are probably best captured in his concept of self, or the *proprium*. The "proprium includes all aspects of personality that make for inward unity" (Allport, 1955, p. 40). Eight different aspects of the proprium can be identified, each emerging at a particular point in the development of the person. In their developmental order of emergence, these are (1) the sense of bodily self, (2) self-identity, (3) self-esteem, (4) self-extension, (5) self-image, (6) self-as-rational-coper, (7) propriate strivings toward life goals, and (8) a unifying sense of self-as-knower, or the sense of the totality of the person as a process that is continually changing and becoming.

In Allport's view, both human motivation and individual differences are accounted for by traits. For Allport, a trait is "a neuropsychic structure having the capacity to render many stimuli functionally equivalent, and to initiate and guide equivalent (meaningfully consistent) forms of adaptive and expressive behavior" (1961, p. 347). Allport held that traits are real, causal entities that correspond to as yet unknown neurophysiological structures. They are not mere descriptive categories of functionally equivalent behaviors. Rejecting the distinction between motive and trait, Allport insisted that traits have motivational features, serving to energize, direct, and select behavior. Despite popular misconceptions, however, Allport did not argue that traits make for extraordinarily high cross-situational generality in human behavior (Zuroff, 1986). A single person may be characterized by contradictory traits. Furthermore, behavior is always a function of the situation, in that "the ever changing nature of traits and their close dependence upon the fluid conditions of the environment forbid a conception that is over-rigid or over-simple" (Allport, 1937, p. 312).

B. Murray's Personology

After the death of Prince in 1928, Murray became the director of the Harvard Psychological Clinic, and for the next decade he commanded a remarkable intellectual expedition, rallying together scholars from a wide variety of disciplines under the banner of personology (Robinson, 1992; Shneidman, 1981; White, 1981, 1987). Like Allport, Murray championed a science of the whole person. But if Allport's vision was steeped in the Enlightenment, Murray's personology was born of Romanticism (Shweder, 1984). Whereas Allport viewed the human mind as potentially rational and orderly, Murray focused his attention on that which is relatively irrational, passionate, and laden with conflict and emotion. Murray sought to bring the insights of Freud and (especially) Jung toward the center of academic psychology. His eclectic theory blends psychoanalytic ideas with strands from McDougall and Lewin and themes from the study of literature, mythology, and medicine. While Murray was just as committed as Allport to conceiving persons as integrated wholes, he was less sanguine about the possibility that personality is a unified and self-consistent totality. There is nothing like a proprium in Murray's personology. Instead a typical personality is

> a flow of powerful subjective life, conscious and unconscious: a whispering gallery in which voices echo from the distant past; a gulf stream of fantasies with floating memories of past events, currents of contending complexes, plots and counterplots, hopeful intimations and ideals . . . . A personality is a full congress of orators and pressure-groups, of children, demagogues, communists, isolationists, war-mongers, mugwumps, grafters, log-rollers, lobbyists, Caesars and Christs, Machiavels and Judases, Tories and Promethean revolutionists.
>
> *(Murray, 1940, pp. 160–161)*

Murray and his colleagues set forth the basic principles of personology in the landmark volume, *Explorations in Personality* (1938). Among the more influential concepts are *need, press, thema,* and *unity thema.* The primary motivational constructs in Murray's system are the 20 or so psychogenic needs, such as the needs for achievement, affiliation, dominance, play, and succorance. Each need stands for a force "which organizes perception, apperception, intellection, conation and action in such a way as to transform in a certain direction an existing, unsatisfying situation" (Murray, 1938, p. 123). A press is an environmental situation that functions as an opportunity for or obstacle to the expression of a particular need. The person's subjective perception of the situation is termed the "beta press"; the objective nature of the situation is the "alpha press." A thema is a recurrent need–press interaction. A unity thema is a dominant pattern of related needs and press (plural) which organizes or gives meaning to a large portion of the individual's life. Ultimately derived from infantile experience, a unity thema may be viewed as the central, organizing motif of a person's biography.

C. Lewin's Field Theory

Both Allport and Murray assumed that behavior is a function of the interaction of the person and the environment (Ekehammer, 1974; Zuroff, 1986). But Lewin was more explicit about the interaction. In *A Dynamic Theory of Personality,* Lewin (1935) conceived both the person and the environment as differentiated aspects of an integrated *life space.* The life space contains the totality of possible facts which are capable of determining the behavior of an individual at a given moment. Strongly influenced by the Gestalt theories of Wertheimer and Kohler, Lewin viewed the person-in-the-environment as a contemporaneous gestalt—a field of forces that assumes a characteristic form at a particular moment in time. All of the determinants of behavior at a given moment are in the field at the moment. Thus, Lewin's approach, in contrast to Allport and Murray, tends to deemphasize developmental constructs. Whereas Murray (1938) said that "the history of the organism *is* the organism" (p. 39) and Allport (1937) spoke of stages in the development of the proprium, Lewin advocated an ahistorical analysis of person–situation interactions.

Lewin viewed human motivation in terms of energy transformations in a dynamic field. Energy is released when the person attempts to return to equilibrium after the onset of a state of tension. The person experiences *tension* when one part of the inner-personal region is thrown out of balance vis-à-vis other parts. This is caused by the arousal of a need—generally defined as either (1) a physiological condition (e.g., hunger), (2) a desire for something, or (3) an intention to do something. A *valence* is the value of a particular region of the environment for a person. A region of positive valence is one that contains a goal object which will reduce tension when the person enters the region. Therefore, valences become coordinated with needs, in a way not unlike Murray's characterization of the need–press thema. Lewin's conceptualizations of energy, tension, need, and valence paved the way for subsequent expectancy-value theories of motivation, as in Atkinson (1964) and Rotter (1954).

D. The Integration of Psychoanalysis and Learning Theory

While Allport and Murray labored on behalf of personality at Harvard and Lewin founded research programs at Cornell (1933–1935) and the University of Iowa (1933–1945), a group of social scientists at Yale's Institute of Human Relations were working to bring about closer collaboration among the fields of psychology, psychiatry, sociology, and anthropology. Hull's (1943) learning theory served as the overarching conceptual framework while psychoanalysis and social anthropology provided data, ideas, and agendas for empirical research and theoretical syntheses. N. E. Miller and Dollard (1941; Dollard & Miller, 1950) sought to reformulate psychoanalysis in learning-theory terms. They believed that all significant human behavior is *learned* in particular social, cultural, and historical contexts. Learning involves four fundamental factors. First, learning is motivated by *drives,* conceptualized as strong internal stimuli that propel behavior. Learned drives are social needs that are ultimately derived from primary physiological drives, like hunger and thirst. Second, learning is given direction and guidance cues, which are stimuli in the environment that provide information concerning what the organism should attend to and how the organism should respond. Third, learning involves a *response:* propelled by drive and guided by *cue,* the organism acts. Such action leads to a reduction in drive, which in itself is rewarding and thus constitutes *reinforcement,* the fourth and final component of learning. There can be no reinforcement without some kind of drive reduction.

Miller and Dollard translated a number of classic Freudian ideas into the more objective and operational language of drive, cue, response, and reinforcement. For instance, they substituted for Freud's "pleasure principle" the principle of reinforcement, understood as the reduction of a primary or learned drive. The psychoanalytic concept of "transference" was seen as a special case of stimulus generalization. "Repression" became inhibition. "Anxiety" was viewed as a learned, secondary drive, acquired through repeated experiences of pain (a primary drive itself) and threatened pain. Psychosexual development was explained according to principles of learning and conditioning applied to the realms of feeding and weaning, cleanliness training, early sex training, and the socialization of a child's anger. These translations became central concepts in the important longitudinal investigation of child rearing and personality launched by Sears, Maccoby, and Levin (1957) and the cross-cultural studies of Whiting and Child (1953).

E. Factor Theories

Relying on factor analysis, Cattell (1946, 1950) developed a comprehensive system of personality that resembles in various features conceptualizations from McDougall, Freud, Lewin, Murray, and Allport. For Cattell, the central problem in personality psychology is the prediction of behavior. Indeed, he defined personality quite generally as "that which permits a prediction of what a person will do in a given situation" (1950, p. 2). If prediction is to be accurate, then the psychologist must obtain quantitative information on a great many variables at many different levels, weigh and scale the information appropriately, and combine the information into a specification equation. The *specification equation* is a linear combination of quantitative indices of certain traits, roles, and states, each weighted according to its relevance *in the present situation.* Thus, the interactional nature of behavior—that behavior is a function of the person interacting with the environment—is given mathematical form in Cattell's specification equation. Like Allport, Cattell viewed the trait as a central personality variable. For Cattell, a trait is a mental structure that may be inferred from observable behavior to account for regularity and consistency in behavior. Surface traits represent clusters of manifest variables that appear to go together; source traits are the underlying factors that determine the multiple surface manifestations. Traits may also be divided into three general categories with respect to their content and function: *dynamic* traits, which set the individual into action to accomplish a goal; *ability* traits, which concern the effectiveness with which the individual reaches a goal; and *temperament* traits, which concern such stylistic aspects of responding as speed, energy, and emotional reactivity.

Other factor theories were developed by Guilford (1959; Guilford & Zimmerman, 1949) and Eysenck (1952). Eysenck's conceptualization has become increasingly influential over the past 30 years. Eysenck divides personality into three very broad traits, existing as higher order factors in the analysis of responses from thousands of subjects on hundreds of self-report questionnaire items. The three dimensions are extraversion–introversion, neuroticism, and psychoticism. Eysenck hypothesizes that all three are grounded in particular neurophysiological patternings and that individual differences in each are substantially influenced by one's genetic makeup.

F. Dominant Trends in the Grand Systems

Between 1930 and 1950 a number of personality psychologists developed grand systems for understanding the whole person and predicting what the person will do. In addition to Allport, Murray, Lewin, Miller and Dollard, Cattell, Guilford, and Eysenck, broad systems of personality were proposed by Murphy (1947), Angyal (1941), Lecky (1945), and the psychoanalytic ego psychologists such as Erikson (1950) and Hartmann (1939), as well as the neo-Freudian perspectives from Fromm (1941), Horney (1939), Rank (1945), and M. Klein (1948). Amidst the rich diversity, a few consistent trends in these conceptual systems may still be discerned.

First, most of the personality systems created in the 1930s and 1940s were based on the assumption that the person may be seen from many different perspectives and on many different levels. Most of the systems, therefore, proposed multiple constructs organized on multiple levels. For Allport, Murray, and Cattell no single trait, need, attitude, or sentiment is to be seen as the "key" to personality. Rather, various constructs are organized in complex hierarchies (Murray, Cattell) or idiographic patterns unique to the individual (Allport). Despite the plethora of variables and levels, however, many of the systems make a second important claim—that the person may still be viewed as a unified and organized totality. Such constructs as proprium (Allport), unity thema (Murray), and dynamic lattice (Cattell) attempt to account for the potentially integrated and holistic nature of human personality. "Self" and "ego" are parallel constructs proposed by Lecky (1945) and the ego psychologists, respectively. Most personality systems from this era are either explicitly or implicitly organismic in that they emphasize the consistency and coherence of normal personality and view the individual organism as an organized and complexly structured whole.

A third trend involves motivation. Many of the systems propose some variation of tension reduction as a theory of human motivation. This is most appparent in Miller and Dollard, but it is also prominent in Cattell's concept of erg, Lewin's view of dynamics in the life space, and Murray's concept of a need as transforming "in a certain direction an existing, unsatisfying situation." The general view is that organisms seek some sort of equilibrium, drives or needs increase tension, and the organism is motivated to act upon drives or needs in order to reduce tension, which is ultimately satisfying or reinforcing. The emphasis on tension reduction is most apparent in the work of the two psychologists who, in the overall, were probably the most influential general theorists during this time: Freud and Hull.

Finally, many systems conceived of personality development in terms of learning in society, or what might be termed socialization. The individual begins as an unsocialized and assumedly self-centered creature, but over time he or she learns how to be an effective and relatively cooperative member of a complex social world. With the exceptions of Eysenck and Cattell, the personality systems of the time placed a great deal of stock in Lockean environmentalism—the person is a product of his or her environment; traits, motives, sentiments, and attitudes are learned in the environment. The most important learning occurs in childhood, especially in the family. Development is continuous and relatively gradual, a product of basic principles of learning that remain pretty much the same across the entire life span.

IV. THE ELABORATION OF CONSTRUCTS: 1950–1970

Psychologists returned to their university settings at the end of World War II to face what would become the greatest expansion in higher education in the history of American society. Large numbers of war veterans returned to or entered college, many taking advantage of the GI Bill. Universities scrambled to keep up with burgeoning enrollments, building new laboratories, classrooms, and residence halls and enlarging their departments well beyond their prewar size. Like most other university departments, psychology departments grew in size and diversity. Federal funding for psychological research became much more plentiful, stimulating and promoting a multitude of applied and basic research programs across the country. The expansion brought with it increasing specialization. Fewer and fewer psychologists saw themselves as "generalists." Rather they were now "developmental psychologists," "social psychologists," or "physiological psychologists," not simply "psychologists." After World War II, psychology expanded with exuberance into many nonacademic settings, as witnessed by the tremendous growth of clinical psychology and other "applied" subdisciplines, the boom in psychotherapies and various forms of counseling and behavior change, the expansion of psychology into the schools, and the growing professionalization of a field whose primary roots were in academia.

Within academic psychology, certain traditions of scholarship seemed to ride the crest of the general expansion while others risked being washed away. Stimulated by exciting new theories (e.g., Festinger, 1954; Heider, 1958) and bold laboratory simulations (e.g., Asch, 1951; Milgram, 1963), experimental social psychology enjoyed something of a golden age through the mid-1960s. By contrast, personality psychology seemed to flounder. As a whole, personality psychology was generalist by nature in an age of specialization, sympathetic to correlational approaches for research in an era that glorified the experimental method, and interested in differences among people during a time when social psychology was suggesting that, in some ways, everybody is pretty much the same. And to the extent that people might be "different," they are likely to be different, some seemed to suggest, in ways related to pathology—a province of the growing discipline of clinical psychology. Between 1950 and 1970, personality psychology witnessed a gradual erosion of its identity within psychology as a whole. As one reviewer put it a few years later, personality psychology can be spelled in one of two ways: c-l-i-n-i-c-a-l or s-o-c-i-a-l (Sechrest, 1976).

After the war, personality psychologists settled down to do hypothesis-testing research. Through conventional nomothetic methods, they sought to articulate some of the key personality constructs embedded in the grand theories. In order to do this, they often had to disembed those constructs. In order to focus on a single personality construct, the researcher might have to pull it out of its theoretical context. Once the construct was out, it was sometimes difficult to fit it back in.

A. The Focus on Constructs and Their Measurement

As World War II was coming to an end, the editorial board of *Character and Personality* announced its first "editorial reorientation" since the journal's inception in 1932. Anticipating the postwar return of psychologists to universities and the coming increase in subsmissions for publication, the board decided that the journal should shift from its rather eclectic role—incorporating a wide range of articles, from theoretical essays to case studies to research reports—to one focused more exclusively on empirical research. They wrote, "appropriate methodological, histori-cal, and theoretical contributions will continue to be accepted, but the major empha-sis will be placed upon reports of original, empirical, and, as far as material permits, significant experimental investigations, without restriction as to technicality of pre-sentation" (Zener, 1945, p. 1). The journal was also to change its name to the *Journal of Personality*. This editorial change was indicative of a broader shift that became very apparent in the years to come: personality psychology was becoming more self-consciously empirical.

The shift is apparent in one of the early and important postwar textbooks in the field: McClelland's (1951) *Personality*. Like Allport and Murray, McClelland argued that the personality psychologist should be concerned with the whole person. As if to underscore his point, McClelland made good use of an extensive case study—the case of Karl—in the text. However, McClelland's vision for the field of personality psychology in 1951 was quite different from that promoted by the grand theorists a few years before, as is evident in the following passage from the book's Preface:

> Working with concrete lives like this [the case of Karl], as they proceed through the theoretical discussions in this book, should prevent students or anyone else from gaining the impression that I am trying to present "a system" or "a theory" of personality. No one knows enough at present to build a theory. Rather what is needed and what I have tried to do is to find a number of constructs in terms

of which we can collect data about personality, perhaps with the ultimate hope of building a theory.

(McClelland, 1951, p. xiv)

The history of personality psychology between the years 1950 and 1970 is aptly foreshadowed in McClelland's words. The time for building theories was over. Rather, personality psychologists were now to identify key constructs in terms of which data might be collected and analyzed. The promise was that construct elaboration would increase psychologists' knowledge of different parts of the person. Once psychologists knew more about the parts, they would be able to put together better grand theories about the whole.

Many of the classic contributions to the literature on personality psychology in the 1950s and 1960s concern problems and issues in the measurement of constructs. Cronbach and Meehl (1955) struggled with the question of how personality psychologists might determine the worth and validity of a given measure designed to assess individual differences on such psychologically meaningful but ultimately hypothetical dimensions as "intelligence," "extraversion," "ego strength," and the like. Such dimensions, which are indeed the staple of virtually all personality theories ever invented, cannot be directly observed but exist instead as open concepts (Meehl, 1977) or "constructs" whose workings can be known only by the network of laws in which they occur (Hogan, 1988).

Along with Loevinger (1957), Cronbach and Meehl presented guidelines for the establishment of *construct validity* in psychological research. The process of construct validation is essentially that of hypothesis testing in science—a dynamic process through which constructs become further defined and articulated as new findings and new measures accumulate over time. Campbell and Fiske (1959) zeroed in on two derivatives of construct validity—*convergent* and *discriminant* validity. Different measures of the same construct should be highly correlated whereas measures of constructs that purport to be different should indeed be uncorrelated. Thus, measures of constructs should measure what they claim to measure, and nothing else. The emphasis on convergent and discriminant validity reflected a general concern that personality psychologists clarify and make more precise the meanings of their constructs.

The 1950s and 1960s saw the construction and refinement of a number of omnibus personality inventories designed to measure many different constructs at once. The clinically oriented MMPI, whose scales were derived solely from empirical-key coding, remained the most popular self-report inventory. Newer measures for assessing individual differences in normal populations, however, employed more eclectic scale construction strategies, drawing explicitly, in some cases, upon personality theory. Popular inventories developed during this time include the California Psychological Inventory (CPI; Gough, 1957), Cattell's (1957) Sixteen Personality Factor Questionnaire (16PF), and two measures of Murray's needs: Edwards' (1957) Personal Preference Schedule (EPPS) and Jackson's (1970) Personality Research Form (PRF).

Amidst the flurry of activity in test construction and validation, two measurement controversies rose to the fore: clinical versus statistical prediction (Meehl, 1954; Sawyer, 1966) and the problem of response styles (Christie & Lindauer, 1963; Edwards, 1957; Jackson & Messick, 1958). The latter preoccupied a great number of researchers for many years, producing a voluminous literature in personality journals and books. At stake was the validity of self-report scales designed to assess individual differences in personality constructs. Do these scales assess the content variables they claim to assess or do they instead tap general test-taking styles that cut across a wide variety of content domains? The controversy was never fully resolved, but some of the most compelling evidence for the content integrity of personality tests was summoned forth by Block (1965), who, for example, demonstrated that the factor structure of the MMPI remained essentially unchanged whether or not one controls for the social desirability of the items. People primarily respond to the content of the items, regardless of their rated desirability. Nonetheless, test developers came to pay closer attention to the potential problem of social desirability and sought to mitigate or control for response bias when possible (Jackson, 1971; Wiggins, 1973).

B. Popular Constructs of the 1950s and 1960s

Four personality constructs that received a tremendous amount of empirical attention during this time are authoritarianism, achievement motivation, anxiety, and field independence. Each of the four attracted creative and dedicated investigators who developed ambitious research programs anchored to specific measurement procedures. Thus, the constructs were generally well conceived, well operationalized, and boldly marketed to the scientific community at large. Each of the constructs generated empirical findings and new theoretical ideas that spoke to central issues and problems in personality functioning. In at least two of the cases (authoritarianism and achievement motivation), psychologists extended their inquiries into the realms of societal structures, economics, and history.

The most important reasons for the popularity of these four, however, may reside in the nature of American society in the 1950s and 1960s. Each of the four constructs reflects prevalent concerns and preoccupations among middle-class Americans of the day. Fresh from the great victory of World War II, Americans moved optimistically forward as the world's preeminent role models of economic and technological success driven by individual know-how and dedicated teamwork. Democracy had triumphed over authoritarian dictatorships. The community of free-thinking individualists had proven stronger, more efficient, and more flexible than the rigidly hierarchical systems that oppressed the many for the (short-term) benefit of the few. Yet these optimistic assessments of America's role and destiny lived alongside more pessimistic viewpoints that decried mindless conformity and rigid authoritarianism and warned of a smoldering cultural uneasiness in the 1950s (Sarason, 1988). A central cultural tension was that between the *individual and the group*. In *The Lonely Crowd,* Riesman (1950) explored the intractable problems of group life among the "inner directed" and the "outer directed" members of American postwar society. Kenniston (1963) wrote to youth's alienation from the traditional groupings and institutions of America on the eve of the social upheavals of the late 1960s. Erikson (1959) spoke of identity crises in modern industrial societies, imploring youth to live boldly within a dialectic between conformity to and rejection of the status quo.

Within the cultural context of middle-class America in the 1950s and early 1960s, the *authoritarian personality* (Adorno, Frenkel-Brunswik, Levinson, & Sanford, 1950) represented an idealized type—a character syndrome personifying German Nazism, over which free-thinking American individualists had assumedly triumphed, only to encounter again in the guise of American bigotry and racism, portrayed in increasingly stark relief as the civil rights movement grew. By contrast, the *need for achievement* (McClelland, 1961; McClelland, Atkinson, Clark, & Lowell, 1953) enjoyed middle-class society's unambivalent blessing in the 1950s as Americans worked hard to consolidate their position as the number-one economic power in the world. A personality construct that celebrated entrepreneurship and innovation resonated well with the values and goals of corporate America.

Anxiety was the price Americans had to pay for living in a postwar, newly nuclearized age. Although this third personality construct is traditionally found at the center of many different systems and theories of personality, both ancient and modern, its salience as a research topic in the 1950s and 1960s (e.g., Sarason & Mandler, 1952; Spielberger, 1966; Taylor, 1953) may have reflected some of the cultural concerns captured in the verse of W. H. Auden, when he christened the middle part of the twentieth century "the age of anxiety." Finally, the construct of *field independence* (Witkin, 1950) considers the perceptual problem of individual figure and common ground. To what extent can the individual divorce the embedding context from the embedded phenomenon? Those who are able to interpret reality in a decontextualized, inner-directed manner are deemed field independent. By contrast, those who view phenomena in context—those whose perceptions are more outer directed—are considered be field dependent. The polarities of individual and group, figure and ground, and self and context reflect a cultural tension that, in America, is probably as old as de Tocqueville's nineteenth century appraisal of American life. Yet the tension seemed to grow stronger and more salient after World War II, subtly influencing the questions asked and answers sought by American personality psychologists.

C. Conceptual Trends

Three general trends may be discerned in the history of personality psychology between approximately 1950 and 1970. These are (1) the *splitting of the whole person* into decontextualized dispositional constructs, (2) the *downfall of tension reduction* as an organizing idea in human motivation, and (3) the emergence of *cognitive* approaches to understanding the person. With respect to the first, postwar personality psychologists borrowed liberally from the grand theories of the previous generation to identify important individual-difference variables for hypothesis-testing research. But, with few exceptions, they abandoned the spirit of those earlier integrative attempts. To paraphrase McClelland's (1951) text, "nobody knew enough" yet to conceptualize the whole person within a single meaningful framework. By the end of the 1960s, Allport, Murray, and Lewin were generally viewed as heroic but rather naive pioneers, and their quests to understand the whole person were considered anachronistic in an era of precise measurements, no-nonsense factor analysis, and tough experimental designs (Fiske, 1971). There was reason to believe, furthermore, that the general concept of a "whole person" might itself be an anachronism. Sociologists like Goffman (1959) argued that much of life is mere role playing and impression management in response to situational demands and that no unifying and unified core of the person need be considered in understanding what people do and think. Similarly, many social psychologists and social-learning theorists were beginning to suggest that the nature of situations, not the person, is the primary determinant of how a person will behave.

By the end of the 1960s, the stage was set for an ideological battle between the "trait psychologists" and the "situationists." The former sought to account for behavior in terms of personality constructs, like achievement motivation and field independence; the latter focused on the exigencies of the environment. For both camps, however, the whole person was no longer a factor to be considered, for the first group had split him into little pieces and the second had disregarded him completely. Of course, there were important exceptions to this trend. White (1952, 1963) and his colleagues carried on the personological tradition of Murray in their idiographic "studies of lives." Block (1971) and others at the University of California (Barron, 1969; MacKinnon, 1965) sought to discern individual differences in *patterns* of traits in the same person evolving over time.

One of the unifying themes in the grand theories of the 1930s and 1940s was the central role of tension reduction in human motivation. In the 1950s, however, the concept received a series of fierce blows from a number of different directions. While no single knockout punch was ever delivered, by 1970 the referee was about to call the fight. Research on animals began to suggest that motivation often does not involve any detectable decrease in tension or drive. For instance, Sheffield, Wolff, and Backer (1951) reported that male rats would cross an electric grid to copulate with a receptive female even though they were always interrupted before orgasm so there was no drive reduction. Harlow, Harlow and Meyer (1950) found that rhesus monkeys would work to disentangle a mechanical puzzle even in the absence of primary drive reduction. Closer to home, White (1959) composed a devastating critique of tension reduction in human behavior and argued for a reconceptualization of motivation along the lines of mastery and competence. Bowlby (1969) substituted cybernetics and modern ethology for oral libidinal discharge to explain the development of mother–infant attachment. Psychoanalysts began to disregard Freud's "metapsychology" for its outdated emphasis on erotic and aggressive drives, energy transfers, and cathexis (Eagle, 1984; Guntrip, 1971).

As many observers have noted, psychology as a whole was beginning to experience the cognitive revolution. The gradual erosion of the doctrine of tension reduction was part of a larger transformation in American psychology from a mechanistic, drive-oriented, stimulus–response viewpoint to a more cognitive model of human behavior and experience emphasizing information processing, image making, and the subjective construction of meaning (Singer & Singer, 1972). Kelly's (1955) personal construct psychology was a harbinger of cognitive things to come. For Kelly, the person is a quasi-scientist seeking to predict and control his or her world. Each person seeks to make sense of reality through the use of bipolar cognitive categories, or personal constructs. To know the whole person is to comprehend the vicissitudes and nuances of his or her construct system; to comprehend individual differences is to compare and contrast the structures, and to a lesser extent contents, of different persons' construct systems. In a somewhat similar vein, G. A. Miller, Galanter, and Pribram (1960) employed the language of cybernetics to explain how behavior is rather more guided by rational plans and goals than driven by blind instinct. In the 1960s, more and more personality psychologists were beginning to couch their explanations for human behavior in cognitive terms.

V. DOUBT AND A RENEWAL OF CONFIDENCE: 1970 TO THE PRESENT

In 1951, McClelland claimed that personality psychologists did not "know much" yet, but the tenor of his text was extremely hopeful, and the reader was still able to conclude that greater knowledge might be just around the corner. Sears's (1950) chapter on personality in the first *Annual Review of Psychology* is similarly cautious but optimistic, as is true of MacKinnon (1951), Bronfenbrenner (1953), and Nuttin (1955). Signs of discontent, however, began to appear in the mid-to-late 1950s as reviewers seemed to become increasingly frustrated about contradictory empirical results, nagging peccadillos in personality measurement, and the field's overall lack of coherence. By the late 1960s, personality psychology was being called "a disconcerting sprawl" (Adelson, 1969; Sanford, 1963) of "well controlled studies that are virtually irrelevant to the questions they are supposed to answer" (Rorer & Widiger, 1983), yielding results that are "inconsequential, trivial, and even pointless" (Sechrest, 1976).

The rising tide of discontent culminated in the publication of a few extraordinarily influential critiques of the field—Carlson (1971), Fiske (1974), and Mischel (1968, 1973)—and the spread of a general view that personality psychology was experiencing a major crisis. In the 1970s some even suggested that the field was dead. Outside academia, furthermore, certain social and cultural changes seemed to create a less than hospitable scene for personality psychology. Social upheavals in the late 1960s and early 1970s cast serious doubt on the adequacy of traditional frameworks for identifying "types" of people and stable individual differences. Both in clinical work and in the study of normal persons, personality diagnosis and assessment could be viewed as mere "labelling" by an unempathic and out-of-touch establishment (Goffman, 1961; Rosenhan, 1973). The antiwar, civil rights, and women's movements all sensitized Americans to the pervasive influence of culture and environment on human behavior and experience—influence experienced in the contexts of family, class, ethnicity, race, and nation-state. The implicit message was this: The person is a product—even a victim—of social context; therefore, one should focus on context rather than person—on social influence rather than individuality. In addition, some came to see traditional personality psychology as dominated by an Anglo-masculine world view. One could reasonably argue in 1970 that the only whole persons whom personality psychologists ever studied anyway were upper middle-class, white males.

A. The Decade of Doubt

In an article entitled "Where is the Person in Personality Research?" Carlson (1971) suggested that personality psychology had lost its center. Sampling 226 articles published in two major personality journals in the late 1960s, Carlson found not a single study that fulfilled the promises of Allport and Murray concerning personality's commitment to the investigation of the whole person. Rather, the prototypical study was a contrived laboratory experiment or a simple correlational investigation of a large group of college men, about whom the researchers collected only a few pieces of information and with whom the researchers spent, on the average, less than an hour. Virtually abandoned were inquiries into (a) the organization of personality, (b) the stability of personality, (c) problems of the mature individual, (d) psychosexuality, (e) striving for personal goals, and (f) the development and power of friendship or love. She concluded:

> Personality psychology would seem to be paying an exorbitant price in potential knowledge for the security afforded by preserving norms of convenience and methodological orthodoxy. Must these important, unanswered questions be left to literature and psychiatry?
>
> (p. 207)

Carlson implied that personality psychologists had lost their way during the era of construct elaboration. Research and theorizing had become so narrow that personality psychologists were no longer able to address the central questions of the field posed by the grand theorists. By contrast, Fiske (1974) suggested that personality psychology had gone about as far as it could go. From Fiske's even more pessimistic outlook, personality psychology had begun to reach the limits of what a scientific study of the person could conceivably achieve. The constructs of personality are inevitably linked to the conventions of everyday language, Fiske claimed. Meanings are bound to be ambiguous, like language. No truly cumulative knowledge base can be built on the shifting sands of personality conceptualizations.

The most influential critique, however, was delivered by Mischel. In *Personality and Assessment* (1968), Mischel's highly selective review concluded that personality dispositions, typically measured via paper-and-pencil tests and questionnaires, account for very little of the variance in human behavior. For the most part, there is very little cross-situational generality in behavior, Mischel argued. Instead, human action tends to be dictated by situationally specific factors. Individual differences in situations are more effective predictors of behavior than are individual differences in traits. Mischel raised the possibility that the only place that traits may truly exist is in the mind of the personality psychologist. Thus, personality psychologists may be guilty of committing a fundamental attributional error by imposing broad categories concerning internal dispositions to explain (and predict) the behavior of others, when in fact that behavior is better explained by factors specific to the situation.

The critiques of Carlson, Fiske, and Mischel ushered in a decade of doubt in the history of personality psychology. Many personality psychologists began to doubt the credibility of the entire enterprise of studying persons; others seemed to become highly defensive, hastily dismissing the critiques as overly simplistic or idealistic lamentations. Over the course of the decade, an increasing number of journal articles considered the mounting crisis of confidence. It is important to note, however, that there was more than one crisis during this time, for the critiques are very different from each other. Neither Fiske nor Mischel seems especially concerned with the question, "Where is the person?" And Carlson seems to suggest that personality psychologists could recapture the prize of the whole person if they would only summon up the will of yesteryear and thereby release the creative energies that lie trapped beneath the norms of methodological orthodoxy.

It is also interesting to note that only one of the critiques was ever seriously addressed by personality psychologists during the 1970s and 1980s. Mischel's indictment of trait psychology ultimately met with a barrage of countercriticism, stimulating a lengthy "debate" about the relative contributions of traits and situations in the prediction of behavior (Alker, 1972; D. J. Bem & Allen, 1974; Block, 1977; Bowers, 1973; Chaplin & Goldberg, 1984; Cheek, 1982; Ekehammer, 1974; Endler & Magnusson, 1976; Epstein, 1979, 1984; Funder & Ozer, 1983; Hogan, DeSoto, & Solano, 1977; Kenrick & Stringfield, 1980; Lamiell, 1981; McClelland, 1981; Mischel & Peake, 1982; Ozer, 1986; Rushton, Brainerd, & Pressley, 1983; Snyder, 1983; West, 1983). What is intriguing to note here is that personality psychologists sought to settle the debate on primarily *empirical* grounds, much in the spirit of Mischel's original critique. This is to say that researchers designed new studies and collected new data to determine (a) the extent to which individual differences in traits and situations *are* able to predict behavior and (b) the extent to which people's behavior can be seen to be consistent over time and across different situations. Like Mischel, they proceeded in a pragmatic and empirical fashion.

In an effort to improve the predictive power of traditional trait measures, certain personality psychologists have championed (a) moderator variables and (b) aggregation. With respect to the first, D. J. Bem and Allen (1974) and others have suggested that predictions of behavior can be enhanced when assessments of a person's level on a given trait measure are coupled with assessments of the extent to which the given trait is relevant, salient, or important for the person. The latter assessment is conceived as a moderator variable. The argument suggests that only when a trait is relevant, salient, or important for the person may individual differences in the trait be predictive of behavior. In other words, personality psychologists can predict some of the people some of the time. A number of other moderator approaches have been developed, such as Snyder's (1983) position that the personality variable of self-monitoring serves as a general moderator. According to Snyder, individual differences in personality traits are especially predictive of behavior among persons who are low in self-monitoring. These are the people who are relatively oblivious to the demands of situations and, therefore, more likely to act in accord with inner dispositions. Epstein (1979, 1984) has championed the judicious use of aggregation in personality studies to increase predictive power. In Epstein's view, trait measures are bound to do a poor job in predicting the single act because the single act is not a reliable index of behavioral trends. When functionally similar acts are aggregated over time and across situations, reliability is enhanced and personality trait measures are able to do a better job of predicting behavior.

The trait–situation debate appeared to die down in the 1980s as many psychologists settled on a compromise position that most of them suggested they had advocated all along. Though major differences in emphasis are still apparent, many personality psychologists now seem to agree that behavior is a function of both traits (or internal dispositional variables in general) and situations: that the person and the environment *interact* to produce behavior. Though Interactionism is nothing new (see Lewin, 1935), the perception among many reviewers is that personality psychologists are now more explicitly interactionist in their thinking and in their research designs (Kenrick & Funder, 1988). The less sanguine view, however, is that a lot of time and energy have been wasted marshalling empirical support for various ideological positions. Rorer and Widiger (1983) assert that a "great deal of nonsense has been written on the trait–situation topic, and as far as we can tell all the data that have been collected are irrelevant to solving the problem, which is conceptual" (p. 446).

This is not to suggest that the trait–situation controversy has been a mindless exercise in number crunching. Many of the contributions have been well conceived and ingeniously designed. But the controversy has not directly produced the broad conceptual advances in personality psychology that some observers of the field believe are needed (Carlson, 1984; Helson & Mitchell, 1978). Furthermore, the empirical activity has tended not to speak directly to the concerns raised by Carlson's (1971) and Fiske's (1974) critiques, which were much more conceptual in nature and, it is probably fair to say, more challenging.

Nonetheless, personality psychology appeared to move through the 1980s and into the 1990s with a renewed optimism and vigor (Hogan & Jones, 1985; Maddi, 1984; West, 1983). Although the serious doubts raised in the previous decade had not been put to rest, researchers and theorists in the field seemed to have found a new confidence and credibility. Signs of renewal are increasingly manifest in many different places today. With respect to research methodology, personality psychologists appear to be employing a wider range of approaches, including naturalistic strategies for experience sampling (Hormuth, 1986), behavioral genetic methods

(Plomin, 1986), structural equation models (Judd, Jessor, & Donovan, 1986), and various qualitative methodologies (Helson, 1982; Mendelsohn, 1985; Runyan, 1982; Wrightsman, 1981). With respect to research topics, personality psychologists have broadened their inquiries to incorporate important issues in health psychology (Jemmott, 1987; Kobasa, 1985; Suls & Rittenhouse, 1987) and life-span development (Eichorn, Clausen, Haan, Honzik, & Mussen, 1981; Wrightsman, 1988; Zucker, Rabin, Aronoff, & Frank, 1992), and they have made important contributions in studies of the quality of personal relationships (Duck, 1986; Hendrick & Hendrick, 1986), loneliness and shyness (Briggs, 1985; Shaver & Rubenstein, 1980), gender and sex roles (S. L. Bem, 1981; Cook, 1985; Franz & Stewart, 1994), optimal experience (Csikszentmihalyi, 1982; Privette, 1983), adaptation to life changes (Stewart & Healy, 1985), and the biological bases of personality (A. H. Buss & Plomin, 1984; D. M. Buss, 1984, 1991; Revelle, 1995). An increasing number of research projects integrate perspectives from both personality and social psychology (Blass, 1984). And within psychology in general today interest in individual differences in persons appears to be increasing.

B. The Whole Person

A renewed emphasis on the whole person in contemporary personality psychology is perhaps most evident in the burgeoning theoretical and research literature on the self (Honess & Yardley, 1987; Lapsley & Power, 1988; Loevinger & Knoll, 1983; Schlener 1985; Shaver, 1985). The concept of self has traditionally served as a rallying point for those psychologists inclined to view persons as wholes and disposed to ask questions about how persons find unity and coherence in their lives. In recent years, the self has been rediscovered in a number of new guises, including those of "schema" (Markus, 1977), "prototype" (Kuiper & Derry, 1981), "theory" (Berzonsky, 1988; Epstein, 1973), and "story" (Gergen & Gergen, 1983; McAdams, 1985). In psychoanalytic circles, the emergence of Kohut's (1977) self-psychology is an important conceptual development.

Some of the most fruitful theorizing about the self comes from the interface of cognitive developmental psychology and personality (Loevinger, 1987). Blasi (1988), Damon and Hart (1982), and Kegan (1982) have formulated developmental theories of the self that draw on the tradition of structural developmentalism as epitomized in the writings of Piaget and Kohlberg. These stage theories seek to chart the self's development from a simple and undifferentiated structure to increasing autonomy, differentiation, and integration. Compared to the developmental formulations of the 1930s and 1940s, these tend to place less emphasis on basic principles of learning and the socialization of the individual in a particular cultural system.

The most influential scheme of this kind for personality psychology is Loevinger's (1976) conception of ego development, which has been carefully operationalized through a sentence completion test. For Loevinger, the ego is one's overall framework of meaning for interpreting experience, encompassing aspects of character development and impulse control, interpersonal style, conscious preoccupations, and cognitive complexity. In the earliest (immature) stages of ego development, the person adopts a simplistic, global, and egocentric framework for understanding experience: the impulsive and self-protective stages. In the middle stages, one's framework of meaning is more differentiated and integrated and less egocentric, but reality is now apprehended in stereotypic, banal, and highly conventional ways: the conformist and conformist/conscientious stages. At the highest stages (conscientious, autonomous, or integrated), one comes to question the simple dictates of convention, and one's understanding of a range of issues becomes more highly differentiated and integrated so that contradiction and ambiguity become tolerable and the individuality of others is accepted, even "cherished." Persons at the highest stages manifest a rich inner life and complex understanding of self as an evolving whole in a social and historical context. Few people reach the highest stages; most "stop" developing somewhere in the middle. In Loevinger's developmental typology, one's terminal stage of ego development is *the* major individual difference variable of personality.

Although some theories of the self provide integrative frameworks for viewing the person as a unified and unifying whole, others suggest a multiplicity in self and identity. Horowitz (1979) presents a clinically anchored scheme of multiple selves or "states of mind." Markus and Nurius (1986) conceptualize the person in terms of a wide assortment of "possible selves," each functioning as a semiautonomous structure containing information concerning what the person believes he or she might be or fears to be. Similarly, Higgins (1987) has developed a theory of "self-discrepancy" in which various "actual selves," "ideal selves," and "ought selves" coexist in a confederacy of me's. Rosenberg and Gara (1985) have underscored the multiplicity of personal identity. Borrowing from deconstructionist literary theory, Sampson (1985) suggests that psychologists should consider the possibility that the self need not be unified or coherent. Instead, he argues for a "decentralized, nonequilibrium ideal, whose very being hinges on continuous becoming" (Sampson, 1985, p. 1203). In a somewhat similar vein, Shotter and Gergen (1989) have suggested that the self is to be viewed as a set of dynamic texts that are constructed and negotiated through social interaction, no single text serving as an integrative core.

McAdams (1985, 1993) also views self in textual terms but argues that, beginning in late adolescence and young adulthood, a person strives to create unity and purpose in life through the conscious and unconscious formulation of a single, dominant text—a dynamic and internalized *life story,* or personal myth, that integrates one's reconstructed past, perceived present, and anticipated future while situating the person in a social niche and in historical time. The motivational content of a person's self-defining life story is organized along the "thematic lines" of *agency* (power/achievement/autonomy) and *communion* (love/intimacy/care) (Bakan, 1966; Wiggins, 1991). The story displays a characteristic "narrative tone" (ranging from comic or romantic optimism to tragic or ironic pessimism), a unique quality of personal "imagery," pivotal scenes (called "nuclear episodes"), main characters in the guise of idealized self-personifications (called "imagoes"), and an anticipated story ending that serves to "leave something behind" for the next generation (the "generativity script"). McAdams' narrative conception of the self draws from Adler's (1927) concept of the "guiding fiction" and Sartre's notion of the "true novel" (Charme, 1984) in human living, and it connects to a growing literature on the importance of narrative in human lives and personality (e.g., Baumeister, Stilwell, & Wotman, 1992; Bruner, 1986, 1990; Gregg, 1991; Hermans, Kempen, & van Loon, 1992; Howard, 1991; Polkinghorne, 1988; Rosenwald & Ochberg, 1992; Sarbin, 1986; Spence, 1982).

C. Motivation

Recent years have continued the trend away from tension-reduction theories of human motivation and toward cognitive approaches for understanding the dynamics of action. In the 1970s, Weiner reconceptualized achievement motivation in cognitive attributional terms (Weiner, 1980). Depression and learned helplessness have been interpreted from the standpoint of dysfunctional attributional styles (Abramson, Seligman, & Teasdale, 1978) and faulty schemata (Beck, 1976). More recently, personality psychologists have proposed a host of cognitive variables to account for the goal-directed, inner-motivated features of human behavior (see Cantor & Kihlström, 1985), "personal strivings" (Emmons, 1986), and "personal projects (Palys & Little, 1983). Deci and Ryan (1985) have developed a "cognitive evaluation theory of intrinsic motivation" positing a basic human desire to feel competent and self-determining. Carver and Scheier (1981) have sought to explain motivation in terms of a hierarchy of control systems and feedback loops.

Tomkins' (1987) *script theory* represents an ambitious attempt to integrate certain cognitive themes within a theory of motivation and personality that places prime emphasis on affect. Tomkins identifies approximately 10 primary affects, such as joy, excitement, sadness, and anger. Izard (1977) has articulated a very similar view. Each of these affects has served an adaptive function throughout human evolution, and each is associated with a particular physiological response, including a corresponding set of facial expressions. In Tomkins' view, affects are the primary motivators of human behavior, amplifying biological drives and providing life's goals with the emotional coloring that makes them worthy of pursuit. Tomkins views the person as a playwright who fashions his or her personal drama from the earliest weeks of life. The most basic component of the drama is the "scene," which is viewed as an idealized recollection of a specific happening or event in one's life which contains at least one affect and one object of that affect. A "script" is a set of rules for interpreting, creating, enhancing, or defending against a family of related scenes (Carlson, 1988). The process of connecting scenes into a meaningful pattern is called "psychological magnification"—a process that works differently for different sorts of scripts and affect patterns. Understanding the unique patterning of human motivation in an individual's life involves an intensive analysis of the recurrent affects, critical scenes, scripts, and different modes of psychological magnification that the person manifests across the life span.

The evolutionary theme in Tomkins' script theory is developed more fully in Hogan's (1987) *socioanalytic theory* of personality. Socioanalytic theory ties together strands of evolutionary biology, psychoanalysis, and sociological role theory. Human beings have evolved to live in small groups that are variously organized into status hierarchies. In this context, the two central motivational tendencies in human behavior are toward seeking acceptance and seeking status in social groups. As Hogan puts it, "getting along and getting ahead are the two great problems in life that each person must solve" (Hogan, Jones, & Cheek, 1985). The two great problems are always addressed and resolved in the context of ritualized social interaction. Following Mead (1934) and Goffman (1959), Hogan views social behavior as an elaborate game, governed by rules and conventions, scripted into roles and routines, and mastered by the most skillful managers of impressions. Through role playing and impression management the individual finds a part to play in society, a social identity that specifies a recognized niche in the community. This is not to trivialize social behavior. Rather, the striving for status and acceptance through ritualized social interaction is an unconscious, central, genetic tendency for all human beings:

> . . . self-presentation and impression management are not trivial party games. They are fundamental processes, rooted in our history as group-living animals. They are archaic, powerful, compulsive tendencies that are closely tied to our chances for survival and reproductive success.
>
> (*Hogan et al., 1985, p. 181*)

Tomkins' script theory and Hogan's socioanalytic theory are indicative of the growing interest in personality psychology today in the concepts of affect and instinct. Zajonc (1980) and Rychlak (1988) have argued that the first step in the apprehension of any event or experience is a basic affective judgment—that emotional preferences precede, and are more basic than, cognitive inferences. Other theorists have sought to integrate cognitive and affective approaches (Izard, 1977; Singer & Kolligan, 1987). The concept of biological instincts has attained a new respectability, as expressed in ethological conceptions like Bowlby's (1969) attachment theory—which has been expanded in creative ways to organize research and theory on human love and adaptation (e.g., Hazan & Shaver, 1987)—and in provocative speculations about the application of sociobiological viewpoints to personality and social psychology (D. M. Buss, 1984; Cunningham, 1981).

D. Differences among People

Personality psychologists have come back to traits. Now that the trait–situation controversy has subsided, a steady stream of research findings have documented impressive longitudinal consistency in a number of important individual difference variables (e.g., Conley, 1985; Costa, McCrae, & Arenberg 1980). New ways of understanding traits have also been proposed. In their "act-frequency approach" to personality, D. M. Buss and Craik (1984) conceive of traits as summary categories containing discrete and representative behavioral acts. Different act members of a trait family differ in their "prototypicality." Those closest to the "center" of the family are "best examples" of a given trait, as the act "talking to a stranger" might function as an especially prototypical example for extraversion. Those acts on the periphery are less representative and likely to shade into other adjacent trait categories.

In the 1980s, personality psychologists expressed a great deal of interest in formulating a single systematic taxonomy for personality traits. Such a framework might identify a finite set of central, most salient, or highest-order personality traits and/or place various traits into a conceptually appealing order. Expanding upon the early work of Leary (1957), Wiggins and Broughton (1985) refined a circumplex model of traits organized according to the orthogonal axes of strength (e.g., dominant–submissive) and warmth (e.g., agreeable–quarrelsome). Eysenck (1973) has proposed his own circumplex, organized according to extraversion–introversion and neuroticism–stability. Covering the same conceptual space as Eysenck, Gray (1987) suggests that anxiety and impulsivity represent two primary and physiologically grounded orthogonal dimensions in personality, each tilted 45° to Eysenck's pair. Another increasingly influential system for conceptualizing individual differences comes from the longitudinal investigations of Block (1971, 1993; Funder, Parke, Tomlinson-Keasey, & Widaman, 1993) employing the California Q Set. Two major dimensions underlying the various personality types and developmental trajectories identified by Block and his colleagues are ego resiliency and ego control.

At the current time, the most influential formulation of individual differences in personality is the "Big Five" trait taxonomy. Building on the early work of Fiske (1949), Norman (1963), and Tupes and Christal (1961), a number of personality psychologists have proposed that the universe of trait dimensions can be reduced to approximately five basic bipolar categories (Digman, 1990; Goldberg, 1981, 1993; John, 1990; McCrae, 1992; McCrae & Costa, 1987). Different factor-analytic studies have cut the pie in slightly different ways, but a representative breakdown is that of McCrae and Costa (1987), who identify the five as (1) extraversion–introversion (E) (2) neuroticism (N), (3) openness to experience (O), (4) agreeableness–antagonism (A), and (5) conscientiousness–undirectedness (C). Goldberg's painstaking lexical analyses suggest that these five dimensions are encoded in language. At least in the case of English, these five may serve as the grand organizing dimensions with respect to which virtually all trait labels for describing general nonconditional individual differences in human behavior and experience can be construed.

VI. CONCLUSIONS: PROGRESS AND STAGNATION

In conclusion, the history of personality psychology in the twentieth century may be broadly viewed from the standpoint of conceptual progress and stagnation. The field of personality has traditionally emphasized the study of the whole person, the dynamics of human motivation, and the identification and measurement of individual differences among persons. How much conceptual progress has been made in each of these three areas?

First, significant progress may be seen in the conceptualization of human motivation. The decline of general drive-reduction theories and the emergence of highly differentiated cognitive–affective approaches to understanding the dynamics of action appear to represent a major conceptual advance. The recent formulations of Tomkins (1987), Izard (1977), Hogan (1987), McClelland (1985), and Bowlby (1969) draw upon some of the best ideas from modern cognitive psychology while grounding motivational theory in human evolution and emotional dynamics. These theories do not simply "leave room for" the less-than-rational emotions and instinctual tendencies. Rather they portray human motivation in complex cognitive–affective–instinctual terms and, in the cases of Tomkins and Hogan, provide a very compelling sociocultural context within which to understand the dynamics of human behavior and social interaction.

In the area of individual differences, *moderate* progress may be observed. The empirical elaboration of personality constructs beginning in the 1950s, the subsequent trait–situation debate, and the recent flurry of research on broad personality dispositions have combined to enrich and broaden psychologists' understanding of key personality traits while underscoring their limitations and their situationally specific manifestations. Those who complained that the only good way to organize the plethora of possible personality traits was that provided by the alphabet (London & Exner, 1978) may now take heart in the emergence of circumplex models and the Big Five as compelling organizing schemes. Although the efforts to order trait dimensions deserve resounding applause, one begins to be concerned in this area about creeping conceptual imperialism. Psychologists should not be too quick to assimilate every conceptual scheme under the sun to the Big Five framework. Simply reducing the person to five trait scores will not satisfy those who seek a more differentiated portrait for comprehending individual differences. Furthermore, the Big Five dimensions do not directly address many issues with which personality psychologists have traditionally been concerned—issues such as personality dynamics, personality development, life changes, life histories, identity and the development of self, and the relation between the person on the one hand and society, culture, and history on the other (McAdams, 1992).

Finally, it is disappointing to note that little progress appears to have been made in the conceptualization of the whole person. The reemergence of the self as a viable construct in personality psychology is surely a positive development in this regard. But with the possible exception of Loevinger's theory of ego development, self theories have yet to provide the breadth and depth necessary to integrate disparate conceptual strands in comprehending the whole person. The hope of Allport and Murray that personality psychology would someday provide a coherent way of understanding the whole person has not yet been realized. The grand theories of the 1930s and 1940s have not proven adequate to the task, though they continue to provide insights and guidelines. More recent theorizing about the person has been more limited in scope, with the possible exception of Tomkins (1987), whose multifaceted theory still needs to be systematized and fleshed out before it can expect to gain wide appeal. The field of personality still suffers from the lack of a persuasive integrative framework for understanding the person as a differentiated and integrated dynamic whole living in a complex social context. It was largely the generation of such encompassing frameworks in the 1930s and 1940s that established personality psychology's reputation as that of a dissident field. As the grand theories came to be rejected, the field of personality seemed to become more conventional, losing its unique status as the dissenting champion of the whole person. Perhaps any integrative conceptual framework for comprehending the whole person is doomed to be rejected sooner or later. But until the field of personality begins again to generate such candidates for rejection, it will fall somewhat short of fulfilling the promise of its pioneers.

ACKNOWLEDGMENT

I thank Rae Carlson, Jonathan Cheek, Bob Hogan, John Johnson, Jane Loevinger, Dave McClelland, Bob Nicolay, and Mac Runyan for their gracious and extensive comments on early drafts of this chapter. The preparation of the manuscript was aided by a grant from The Spencer Foundation. Correspondence should be addressed to Dan P. McAdams, Graduate Program in Human Development and Social Policy, Northwestern University, 2115 North Campus Drive, Evanston, IL 60208.

REFERENCES

Abramson, L. Y., Seligman, M. E. P., & Teasdale, J. D. (1978). Learned helplessness in humans: Critique and reformulation. *Journal of Abnormal Psychology, 87,* 49–74.

Adelson, J. (1969). Personality. *Annual Review of Psychology, 20,* 217–252.

Adler, A. (1927). *The practice and theory of individual psychology.* New York: Harcourt Brace World.

Adorno, T. W., Frenkel-Brunswik, E., Levinson, D. J., & Sanford, R. N. (1950). *The authoritarian personality.* New York: Harper & Brothers.

Alker, H. A. (1972). Is personality situationally specific or intrapsychically consistent? *Journal of Personality, 40,* 1–15.

Allport, G. W. (1937). *Personality: A psychological interpretation.* New York: Henry Holt.

Allport, G. W. (1954). The historical background of modern social psychology. In G. Lindzey (Ed.), *Handbook of social psychology* (Vol. 1, pp. 3–56). Cambridge, MA: Addison-Wesley.

Allport, G. W. (1955). *Becoming: Basic considerations for a psychology of personality.* New Haven, CT: Yale University Press.

Allport, G. W. (1961). *Pattern and growth in personality.* New York: Holt, Rinehart & Winston.

Allport, G. W. (1968). An autobiography. In G. W. Allport (Ed.), *The person in psychology* (pp. 376–409). Boston: Beacon Press.

Allport, G. W., & Vernon, P. E. (1931). A test for personal values. *Journal of Abnormal and Social Psychology, 25,* 368–372.

Anastasi, A. (1958). *Differential psychology* (3rd ed.). New York: Macmillan.

Anastasi, A. (1976). *Psychological testing* (4th ed.). New York: Macmillan.

Angyal, A. (1941). *Foundations for a science of personality.* New York: Commonwealth Fund.

Asch, S. E. (1951). Effects of group pressure upon the modification and distortion of judgments. In H. Guetzkow (Ed.), *Groups, leadership, and men* (pp. 177–190). Pittsburgh, PA: Carnegie Press.

Atkinson, J. W. (1964). *An introduction to motivation.* New York: Van Nostrand-Reinhold.

Bagby, E. (1928). *The psychology of personality.* New York: Henry Holt.

Bakan, D. (1966). *The duality of human existence: Isolation and communion in Western man.* Boston: Beacon Press.

Barron, F. (1969). *Creative person and creative process.* New York: Holt, Rinehart & Winston.

Baumeister, R. F., Stilwell, A., & Wotman, S. R. (1990). Victim and perpetrator accounts of interpersonal conflict: Autobiographical narratives about anger. *Journal of Personality and Social Psychology, 59,* 994–1005.

Beck, A. T. (1976). *Cognitive therapy and the emotional disorders.* New York: International Universities Press.

Bem, D. J., & Allen, A. (1974). On predicting some of the people some of the time: The search for cross-situational consistencies in behavior. *Psychological Review, 81,* 506–520.

Bem, S. L. (1981). Gender schema theory: A cognitive account of sex typing. *Psychological Review, 88,* 354–364.

Bernreuter, R. G. (1931). *The personality inventory.* Stanford, CA: Stanford University Press.

Berzonsky, M. D. (1988). Self-theorists, identity status, and social cognition. In D. K. Lapsley & F. C. Power (Eds.), *Self, ego, and identity: Integrative approaches* (pp. 243–262). New York: Springer-Verlag.

Blake, R. R., & Mouton, J. S. (1959). Personality. *Annual Review of Psychology, 10,* 203–232.

Blasi, A. (1988). Identity and the development of the self. In D. K. Lapsley & F. C. Power (Eds.), *Self, ego, and identity: Integrative approaches* (pp. 226–242). New York: Springer-Verlag.

Blass, T. (1984). Social psychology and personality: Toward a convergence. *Journal of Personality and Social Psychology, 47,* 1013–1027.

Block, J. (1965). *The challenge of response sets: Unconfounding meaning, acquiescence, and social desirability in the MMPI.* New York: Appleton-Century-Crofts.

Block, J. (1971). *Lives through time.* Berkeley, CA: Bancroft Books.

Block, J. (1977). Advancing the psychology of personality: Paradigmatic shift or improving the quality of research? In D. Magnusson & N. S. Endler (Eds.), *Personality at the crossroads: Current issues in interactional psychology.* Hillsdale, NJ: Erlbaum.

Block, J. (1993). Studying personality the long way. In D. C. Funder, R. D. Parke, C. Tomlinson-Keasey, & K. Widaman (Eds.), *Studying lives through time: Personality and development* (pp. 9–44). Washington, DC: American Psychological Association.

Bowers, K. S. (1973). Situationism in psychology: An analysis and a critique. *Psychological Review, 80,* 307–336.

Bowlby, J. (1969). *Attachment and loss: Vol. 1. Attachment.* New York: Basic Books.

Briggs, S. R. (1985). A trait account of social shyness. *Review of Personality and Social Psychology, 6,* 35–64.

Bronfenbrenner, U. (1953). Personality. *Annual Review of Psychology, 4,* 157–182.

Bruce, H. A. (1908). *The riddle of personality.* New York: Moffat, Yard.

Bruner, J. (1986). *Actual minds, possible worlds.* Cambridge, MA: Harvard University Press.

Bruner, J. (1990). *Acts of meaning.* Cambridge, MA: Harvard University Press.

Buss, A. H., & Plomin, R. (1984). *Temperament: Early developing personality traits.* Hillsdale, NJ: Erlbaum.

Buss, D. M. (1984). Evolutionary biology and personality psychology: Toward a conception of human nature and individual differences. *American Psychologist, 39,* 361–377.

Buss, D. M. (1991). Evolutionary personality psychology. *Annual Review of Psychology, 42,* 459–491.

Buss, D. M., & Craik, K. H. (1984). Acts, dispositions, and personality. *Progress in Experimental Personality Research, 13,* 241–301.

Campbell, D. T., & Fiske, D. W. (1959). Convergent and discriminant validation by the multitrait-multimethod matrix. *Psychological Bulletin, 56,* 81–105.

Cantor, N., & Kihlström, J. F. (1985). Social intelligence: The cognitive basis of personality. *Review of Personality and Social Psychology, 6,* 15–34.

Carlson, R. (1971). Where is the person in personality research? *Psychological Bulletin, 75,* 203–219.

Carlson, R. (1984). What's social about social psychology? Where's the person in personality research? *Journal of Personality and Social Psychology, 47,* 1304–1309.

Carlson, R. (1988). Exemplary lives: The use of psychobiography for theory development. *Journal of Personality, 56,* 105–138.

Carver, C. S., & Scheier, M. F. (1981). A control systems approach to behavioral self-regulation. *Review of Personality and Social Psychology, 2,* 107–140.

Cattell, R. B. (1946). *Description and measurement of personality.* New York: World Book.

Cattell, R. B. (1950). *Personality: A systematic, theoretical, and factual study.* New York: McGraw-Hill.

Cattell, R. B. (1957). *Personality and motivation structure and measurement.* New York: World Book.

Chaplin, W. F., & Goldberg, L. R. (1984). A failure to replicate the Bem and Allen study of individual differences in cross-situational consistency. *Journal of Personality and Social Psychology, 47,* 1074–1090.

Charme, S. L. (1984). *Meaning and myth in the study of lives.* Philadelphia: University of Pennsylvania Press.

Cheek, J. M. (1982). Aggregation, moderator variables, and the validity of personality tests. *Journal of Personality and Social Psychology, 43,* 1254–1269.

Christie, R., & Lindauer, F. (1963). Personality structure. *Annual Review of Psychology, 14,* 201–230.

Comte, A. (1852). *The positive polity.* London: Longmans, Green.

Conley, J. J. (1985). Longitudinal stability of personality traits: A multi-trait-multimethod-multioccasion analysis. *Journal of Personality and Social Psychology, 19,* 1266–1282.

Cook, E. P. (1985). *Psychological androgyny.* New York: Pergamon.

Costa, P. T., Jr., McCrae, R. R., & Arenberg, P. (1980). Enduring dispositions in adult males. *Journal of Personality and Social Psychology, 38,* 793–800.

Craik, K. H. (1993). The 1937 Allport and Stagner texts in personality psychology. In K. H. Craik, R. Hogan, & R. N. Wolfe (Eds.), *Fifty years of personality psychology* (pp. 3–20). New York: Plenum Press.

Cronbach, L. J., & Meehl, P. E. (1955). Construct validity in psychological tests. *Psychological Bulletin, 52,* 281–302.

Csikszentmihalyi, M. (1982). Toward a psychology of optimal experience. *Review of Personality and Social Psychology, 3,* 13–36.

Cunningham, M. R. (1981). Sociobiology as a supplementary paradigm for social psychological research. *Review of Personality and Social Psychology, 2,* 69–106.

Damon, W., & Hart, D. (1982). The development of self-understanding from infancy through adolescence. *Child Development, 53,* 841–864.

Deci, E. L., & Ryan, R. M. (1985). *Intrinsic motivation and self-determination in human behavior.* New York: Plenum Press.

Digman, J. M. (1990). Personality structure: Emergence of the five-factor model. *Annual Review of Psychology, 41,* 417–440.

Dilthey, W. (1976). The development of hermeneutics. In H. P. Rickman (Ed.), *W. Dilthey: Selected writings.* Cambridge, England: Cambridge University Press. (Original work published 1900).

Dollard, J., & Miller, N. E. (1950). *Personality and psychotherapy.* New York: McGraw-Hill.

Duck, S. (1986). *Human relationships: An introduction to social psychology.* London: Sage.

Eagle, M. N. (1984). *Recent developments in psychoanalysis: A critical evaluation.* New York: McGraw-Hill.

Edwards, A. L. (1957). *The Edwards personal preference schedule.* New York: The Psychological Corporation.

Eichorn, D. H., Clausen, J. A., Haan, N., Honzik, M. P., & Mussen, P. H. (1981). *Present and past in middle life.* New York: Academic Press.

Ekehammer, B. (1974). Interactionism in personality from an historical perspective. *Psychological Bulletin, 81,* 1026–1048.

Emmons, R. A. (1986). Personal strivings: An approach to personality and subjective well-being. *Journal of Personality and Social Psychology, 51,* 1058–1068.

Endler, N. S., & Magnusson, D. (1976). Toward an interactional psychology of personality. *Psychological Bulletin, 83,* 956–974.

Epstein, S. (1973). The self-concept revisited: Or a theory of a theory. *American Psychologist, 28,* 404–416.

Epstein, S. (1979). The stability of behavior: 1. On predicting most of the people much of the time. *Journal of Personality and Social Psychology, 77,* 1097–1126.

Epstein, S. (1984). The stability of behavior across time and situations. In R. A. Zucker, J. Aronoff, & A. I. Rabin (Eds.), *Personality and the prediction of behavior* (pp. 209–268). New York: Academic Press.

Erikson, E. H. (1950). *Childhood and society.* New York: Norton.

Erikson, E. H. (1959). Identity and the life cycle: Selected papers. *Psychological Issues, 1*(1), 5–165.

Eysenck, H. J. (1952). *The scientific study of personality.* London: Routledge & Kegan Paul.

Eysenck, H. J. (1973). *Eysenck on extraversion.* New York: Wiley.

Festinger, L. (1954). A theory of social comparison processes. *Human Relations, 7,* 117–140.

Fiske, D. W. (1949). Consistency of the factorial structures of personality ratings from different sources. *Journal of Abnormal and Social Psychology, 44,* 329–344.

Fiske, D. W. (1971). *Measuring the concepts of personality.* Chicago: Aldine.

Fiske, D. W. (1974). The limits of the conventional science of personality. *Journal of Personality, 42,* 1–11.

Franz, C., & Stewart, A. J. (Eds.). (1994). *Women creating lives.* Boulder, CO: Westview Press.

Freud, S. (1953). Three essays on the theory of sexuality. In J. Strachey (Ed. and Trans.), *The standard edition of the complete psychological works of Sigmund Freud* (Vol. 7, pp. 126–243). London: Hogarth Press. (Original work published 1905).

Freud, S. (1955). Beyond the pleasure principle. In J. Strachey (Ed. and Trans.), *The standard edition of the complete psychological works of Sigmund Freud* (Vol. 18, pp. 3–64). London: Hogarth Press. (Original work published 1920).

Freud, S. (1961). The ego and the id. In J. Strachey (Ed. and Trans.), *The standard edition of the complete psychological works of Sigmund Freud* (Vol. 19, pp. 12–66). London: Hogarth Press. (Original work published 1923).

Fromm, E. (1941). *Escape from freedom.* New York: Farrar & Rinehart.

Funder, D. C., & Ozer, D. J. (1983). Behavior as a function of the situation. *Journal of Personality and Social Psychology, 44,* 107–112.

Funder, D. C., Parke, R. D., Tomlinson-Keasey, C., & Widaman, K. (Eds.). (1993). *Studying lives through time: Personality and development.* Washington, DC: American Psychological Association.

Garnett, A. C. (1928). *Instinct and personality.* New York: Dodd, Mead.

Geen, R., Beatty, W. W., & Arkin, R. M. (1984). *Human motivation: Physiological, behavioral, and social approaches.* Boston: Allyn & Bacon.

Gergen, K. J., & Gergen, M. M. (1983). Narratives of the self. In T. R. Sarbin & K. E. Scheibe (Eds.), *Studies in social identity.* New York: Praeger.

Goffman, E. (1959). *The presentation of self in everyday life.* Garden City, NY: Doubleday.

Goffman, E. (1961). *Asylums.* Garden City, NY: Doubleday.

Goldberg, L. R. (1981). Language and individual differences: The search for universals in personality lexicons. *Review of Personality and Social Psychology, 2,* 141–166.

Goldberg, L. R. (1993). The structure of phenotypic personality traits. *American Psychologist, 48,* 26–34.

Gough, H. G. (1957). *California psychological inventory: Manual.* Palo Alto, CA: Consulting Psychologists Press.

Gray, J. A. (1987). Perspectives on anxiety and impulsivity: A commentary. *Journal of Research in Personality, 21,* 493–509.

Gregg, G. S. (1991). *Self-representation: Life narrative studies in identity and ideology.* New York: Greenwood Press.

Guilford, J. P. (1959). *Personality.* New York: McGraw-Hill.

Guilford, J. P., & Zimmerman, W. S. (1949). *The Guilford-Zimmerman temperament survey.* Beverly Hills, CA: Sheridan Supply Co.

Guntrip, H. (1971). *Psychoanalytic theory, therapy, and the self.* New York: Basic Books.

Hall, C. S., & Lindzey, G. (1957). *Theories of personality.* New York: Wiley.

Harlow, H. F., Harlow, M. K., & Meyer, D. R. (1950). Learning motivated by a manipulation drive. *Journal of Experimental Psychology, 40,* 228–234.

Hartmann, H. (1939). *Ego psychology and the problem of adaptation.* New York: International Universities Press.

Hazan, C., & Shaver, P. (1987). Romantic love conceptualized as an attachment process. *Journal of Personality and Social Psychology, 52,* 511–524.

Heider, F. (1958). *The psychology of interpersonal relations.* New York: Wiley.

Helson, R. (1982). Critics and their texts: An approach to Jung's theory of cognition and personality. *Journal of Personality and Social Psychology, 43,* 409–418.

Helson, R., & Mitchell, V. (1978). Personality. *Annual Review of Psychology, 29,* 555–586.

Hendrick, C., & Hendrick, S. (1986). A theory and method of love. *Journal of Personality and Social Psychology, 50,* 392–402.

Hermans, J. J. M., Kempen, H. J. G., & van Loon, R. J. P. (1992). The dialogical self: Beyond individualism and rationalism. *American Psychologist, 47,* 23–33.

Higgins, E. T. (1987). Self-discrepancy: A theory relating self and affect. *Psychological Review, 94,* 319–340.

Hogan, R. (1976). *Personality theory: The personological tradition.* Englewood Cliffs, NJ: Prentice-Hall.

Hogan, R. (1987). Personality psychology: Back to basics. In J. Aronoff, A. I. Rabin, & R. A. Zucker (Eds.), *The emergence of personality* (pp. 79–104). New York: Springer.

Hogan, R. (1988). The meaning of personality test scores. *American Psychologist, 43,* 621–626.

Hogan, R., DeSoto, C. B., & Solano, C. (1977). Traits, tests, and personality research. *American Psychologist, 32,* 255–264.

Hogan, R., & Jones, W. H. (Eds.). (1985). *Perspectives in personality* (Vol. 1). Greenwich, CT: JAI Press.

Hogan, R., Jones, W. H., & Cheek, J. M. (1985). Socioanalytic theory: An alternative to armadillo psychology. In B. R. Schlenker (Ed.), *The self and social life* (pp. 175–198). New York: McGraw-Hill.

Holt, R. R. (1962). Individuality and generalization in the psychology of personality: An evaluation. *Journal of Personality, 30,* 377–402.

Honess, T., & Yardley, K. (Eds.). (1987). *Self and identity: Perspectives across the lifespan.* London: Routledge & Kegan Paul.

Hormuth, S. E. (1986). The sampling of experiences *in situ. Journal of Personality, 54,* 262–293.

Horney, K. (1939). *New ways in psychoanalysis.* New York: Norton.

Horowitz, M. J. (1979). *States of mind.* New York: Plenum Press.

Howard. G. S. (1991). Culture tales: A narrative approach to thinking, cross-cultural psychology, and psychotherapy. *American Psychologist, 46,* 187–197.

Hull, C. L. (1943). *Principles of behavior.* New York: Appleton-Century-Crofts.

Izard, C. E. (1977). *Human emotions.* New York: Plenum Press.

Jackson, D. N. (1970). A sequential system for personality scale development. In C. D. Spielberger (Ed.), *Current topics in clinical and community psychology* (Vol. 2, pp. 61–96). New York: Academic Press.

Jackson, D. N. (1971). The dynamics of structured personality tests. *Psychological Review, 78,* 229–248.

Jackson, D. N., & Messick, S. (1958). Content and style in personality assessment. *Psychological Bulletin, 55,* 243–252.

Jackson, D. N., & Paunonen, S. V. (1980). Personality structure and assessment. *Annual Review of Psychology, 31,* 503–552.

James, W. (1890). *Principles of psychology.* New York: Holt.

Jastrow, J. (1915). *Character and temperament.* New York: Appleton.

Jemmott, J. B., III. (1987). Social motives and susceptibility to disease: Stalking individual differences in health risks. *Journal of Personality, 55,* 267–298.

John, O. P. (1990). The "Big Five" factor taxonomy: Dimensions of personality in the natural language and in questionnaires. In L. Pervin (Ed.), *Handbook of personality theory and research* (pp. 66–100). New York: Guilford Press.

Judd, C. M., Jessor, R., & Donovan, J. E. (1986). Structural equation models and personality research. *Journal of Personality, 54,* 149–198.

Kegan, R. (1982). *The evolving self: Problem and process in human development.* Cambridge, MA: Harvard University Press.

Kelly, G. (1955). *The psychology of personal constructs.* New York: Norton.

Kenniston, K. (1963). Inburn: An American Ishmael. In R. W. White (Ed.), *The study of lives* (pp. 40–71). New York: Atherton Press.

Kenrick, D. T., & Funder, D. C. (1988). Profiting from controversy: Lessons from the person-situation debate. *American Psychologist, 43,* 23–34.

Kenrick, D. T., & Stringfield, D. O. (1980). Personality traits and the eye of the beholder: Crossing some traditional philosophical boundaries in the search for consistency in all the people. *Psychological Review, 87,* 88–104.

Klein, G. S., & Krech, D. (1951). The problem of personality and its theory. *Journal of Personality, 20,* 2–23.

Klein, M. (1948). *Contributions to psychoanalysis: 1921–1945.* London: Hogarth Press.

Kobasa, S. C. (1985). Personality and health: Specifying and strengthening the conceptual links. *Review of Personality and Social Psychology, 6,* 291–311.

Kohut, H. (1977). *The restoration of the self.* New York: International Universities Press.

Kretschmer, E. (1921). *Physique and character.* Berlin: Springer.

Kuiper, N. A., & Derry, P. A. (1981). The self as cognitive prototype: An application to person perception and depression. In N. Cantor & J. F. Kihlström (Eds.), *Personality cognition, and social interaction* (pp. 214–232). Hillsdale, NJ: Erlbaum.

Lamiell, J. T. (1981). Toward an idiothetic psychology of personality. *American Psychologist, 36,* 276–289.

Lapsley, D. R., & Power, F. C. (Eds.). (1988). *Self, ego, and identity: Integrative approaches.* New York: Springer-Verlag.

Leary, T. (1957). *Interpersonal diagnosis of personality.* New York: Ronald Press.

Lecky, P. (1945). *Self-consistency.* New York: Island Press.

Lewin, E. (1935). *A dynamic theory of personality.* New York: McGraw-Hill.

Loevinger, J. (1957). Objective tests as instruments of psychological theory. *Psychological Reports, 3,* 635–694.

Loevinger, J. (1976). *Ego development.* San Francisco: Jossey-Bass.

Loevinger, J. (1987). *Paradigms of personality.* San Francisco: Jossey-Bass.

Loevinger, J., & Knoll, E. (1983). Personality: Stages, traits, and the self. *Annual Review of Psychology, 34,* 195–222.

London, H., & Exner, J. E., Jr. (Eds.). (1978). *Dimensions of personality.* New York: Wiley.

MacKinnon, D. W. (1951). Personality. *Annual Review of Psychology, 2,* 113–136.

MacKinnon, D. W. (1965). Personality and the realization of creative potential. *American Psychologist, 20,* 273–281.

Maddi, S. R. (1984). Personology for the 1980s. In R. A. Zucker, J. Aronoff, & A. I. Rabin (Eds.), *Personality and the prediction of behavior* (pp. 7–41). New York: Academic Press.

Markus, H. (1977). Self-schemata and processing information about the self. *Journal of Personality and Social Psychology, 35,* 63–78.

Markus, H., & Nurius, P. (1986). Possible selves. *American Psychologist, 41,* 954–969.

McAdams, D. P. (1985). *Power, intimacy, and the life story: Personological inquiries into identity.* New York: Guilford Press.

McAdams, D. P. (1992). The five-factor model in personality: A critical appraisal. *Journal of Personality, 60,* 329–361.

McAdams, D. P. (1993). *The stories we live by: Personal myths and the making of the self.* New York: Morrow.

McAdams, D. P. (1994). *The person: An introduction to personality psychology* (2nd ed.). Fort Worth, TX: Harcourt Brace.

McClelland, D. C. (1951). *Personality.* New York: Holt, Rinehart & Winston.

McClelland, D. C. (1961). *The achieving society.* New York: Van Nostrand.

McClelland, D. C. (1981). Is personality consistent? In A. I. Rabin, J. Aronoff, A. M. Barclay, & R. A. Zucker (Eds.), *Further explorations in personality* (pp. 87–113). New York: Wiley.

McClelland, D. C. (1985). *Human motivation.* Glenview, IL: Scott, Foresman.

McClelland, D. C., Atkinson, J. W., Clark, R. A., & Lowell, E. L. (1953). *The achievement motive.* New York: Appleton-Century-Crofts.

McCrae, R. R. (Ed.). (1992). *The five-factor model: A special issue of the Journal of Personality.* Durham, NC: Duke University Press.

McCrae, R. R., & Costa, P. T., Jr. (1987). Validation of the five factor model of personality across instruments and observers. *Journal of Personality and Social Psychology, 52,* 81–90.

McCurdy, H. G. (1965). *Personality and science: A search for self-awareness.* Princeton, NJ: Van Nostrand.

McDougall, W. (1908). *Social psychology.* London: Methuen.

McDougall, W. (1932). Of the words character and personality. *Character and Personality, 1,* 3–16.

Mead, G. H. (1934). *Mind, self, and society.* Chicago: University of Chicago Press.

Meehl, P. E. (1954). *Clinical vs. statistical prediction: A theoretical analysis and a review of the evidence.* Minneapolis: University of Minnesota Press.

Meehl, P. E. (1977). Specific etiology and other forms of strong influence: Some quantitative meanings. *Journal of Medicine and Philosophy, 2,* 33–53.

Mendelsohn, G. (1985). La Dame aux Camelias and La Traviata: A study of dramatic transformations in the light of biography. In R. Hogan & W. H. Jones (Eds.), *Perspectives in personality* (Vol. 1, pp. 271–303). Greenwich, CT: JAI Press.

Milgram, S. (1963). Behavioral study of obedience. *Journal of Abnormal and Social Psychology, 67,* 371–378.

Miller, G. A., Galanter, E., & Pribram, K. H. (1960). *Plans and the structure of behavior.* New York: Holt, Rinehart & Winston.

Miller, N. E., & Dollard, J. (1941). *Social learning and imitation.* New Haven, CT: Yale University Press.

Mischel, W. (1968). *Personality and assessment.* New York: Wiley.

Mischel, W. (1973). Toward a cognitive social learning reconceptualization of personality. *Psychological Review, 80,* 252–283.

Mischel, W., & Peake, P. K. (1982). Beyond Déja Vu in the search for cross-situational consistency. *Psychological Review, 89,* 730–755.

Murphy, G. (1947). *Personality: A biosocial approach to origins and structure.* New York: Harper and Brothers.

Murray, H. A. (1938). *Explorations in personality.* New York: Oxford University Press.

Murray, H. A. (1940). What should psychologists do about psychoanalysis? *Journal of Abnormal and Social Psychology, 35,* 150–175.

Norman, W. T. (1963). Toward an adequate taxonomy of personality attributes: Replicated factor structure in peer nomination personality ratings. *Journal of Abnormal and Social Psychology, 66,* 574–583.

Nuttin, J. (1955). Personality. *Annual Review of Psychology, 6,* 161–186.

Ozer, D. J. (1986). *Consistency in personality: A methodological framework.* New York: Springer-Verlag.

Palys, T. S., & Little, B. R. (1983). Perceived life satisfaction and the organization of personal project systems. *Journal of Personality and Social Psychology, 44,* 1221–1230.

Pervin, L. A. (1985). Personality: Current controversies, issues, and directions. *Annual Review of Psychology, 36,* 83–114.

Pervin, L. A. (1990). Personality theory and research: Prospects for the future. In L. A. Pervin (Ed.), *Handbook of personality theory and research* (pp. 723–727). New York: Guilford Press.

Plomin, R. (1986). Behavioral genetic methods. *Journal of Personality, 54,* 226–261.

Polkinghorne, D. (1988). *Narrative knowing and the human sciences.* Albany, NY: SUNY Press.

Privette, G. (1983). Peak experience, peak performance, and flow: A comparative analysis of positive human experience. *Journal of Personality and Social Psychology, 45,* 1361–1368.

Rank, O. (1945). *Will therapy and truth and reality.* New York: Knopf.

Revelle, W. (1995). Personality processes. In L. W. Porter and M. R. Rosenzweig (Eds.), *Annual review of psychology* (Vol. 46, pp. 295–328). Palo Alto, CA: Annual Reviews, Inc.

Riesman, D. (1950). *The lonely crowd.* New Haven, CT: Yale University Press.

Roback, A. A. (1927). *The psychology of character.* London: Kegan Paul.

Robinson, F. (1992). *Love's story told: A life of Henry A. Murray.* Cambridge, MA: Harvard University Press.

Rorer, L. G., & Widiger, T. A. (1983). Personality structure and assessment. *Annual Review of Psychology 34,* 431–463.

Rosenberg, S., & Gara, M. A. (1985). The multiplicity of personal identity. *Review of Personality and Social Psychology, 6,* 87–114.

Rosenhan, D. L. (1973). On being sane in insane places. *Science, 179,* 250–258.

Rosenwald, G. C., & Ochberg, R. L. (Eds.). (1992). *Storied lives: the cultural politics of self-understanding.* New Haven, CT: Yale University Press.

Rotter, J. B. (1954). *Social learning and clinical psychology.* Englewood Cliffs, NJ: Prentice-Hall.

Runyan, W. M. (1982). *Life histories and psychobiography: Explorations in theory and method.* New York: Oxford University Press.

Rushton, J. P., Brainerd, C. J., & Pressley, M. (1983). Behavioral development and construct validity: The principle of aggregation. *Psychological Bulletin, 94,* 18–38.

Rychlak, J. E. (1981). *Personality and psychotherapy* (2nd ed.). Boston: Houghton Miflin.

Rychlak, J. E. (1988). *The psychology of rigorous humanism* (2nd ed.). New York: New York University Press.

Sampson, E. E. (1985). The decentralization of identity: Toward a revised concept of personal and social order. *American Psychologist, 40,* 1203–1211.

Sanford, R. N. (1963). Personality: Its place in psychology. In S. Koch (Ed.), *Psychology: A study of a science* (Vol. 5, pp. 488–592). New York: McGraw-Hill.

Sarason, S. B. (1988). *The making of an American psychologist: An autobiography.* San Francisco: Jossey-Bass.

Sarason, S. B., & Mandler, G. (1952). Some correlates of test anxiety. *Journal of Abnormal and Social Psychology, 47,* 810–817.

Sarbin, T. (Ed.). (1986). *Narrative psychology: The storied nature of human conduct.* New York: Praeger.

Sawyer, J. (1966). Measurement and prediction, clinical *and* statistical. *Psychological Bulletin, 66,* 178–200.

Schlenker, B. R. (Ed.). (1985). *The self and social life.* New York: McGraw-Hill.

Sears, R. R. (1950). Personality. *Annual Review of Psychology, 1,* 105–118.

Sears, R. R., Maccoby, E. E., & Levin, H. (1957). *Patterns of child rearing.* Evanston, IL: Row Peterson.

Sechrest, L. (1976). Personality. *Annual Review of Psychology, 27,* 1–27.

Shaver, P. (Ed.). (1985). *Self, situations, and social behavior: Review of personality and social psychology* (Vol. 6). Beverly Hills, CA: Sage.

Shaver, P., & Rubenstein, C. (1980). Childhood attachment experience and adult loneliness. *Review of Personality and Social Psychology, 1,* 42–73.

Sheffield, F. D., Wolff, J. J., & Backer, R. (1951). Reward value of copulation without sex drive reduction. *Journal of Comparative and Physiological Psychology, 44,* 3–8.

Sheldon, W. H. (1940). *The varieties of human physique: An introduction to constitutional psychology.* New York: Harper.

Shneidman, E. S. (Ed.). (1981). *Endeavors in psychology: Selections from the personology of Henry A. Murray.* New York: Harper & Row.

Shotter, J., & Gergen, K. (Eds.). (1989). *Texts of identity.* London: Sage.

Shweder, R. A. (1984). Anthropology's romantic rebellion against the enlightenment, or there's more to thinking than reason and evidence. In R. A. Shweder & R. A. Levine (Eds.), *Culture theory: Essays on mind, self, and emotion* (pp. 27–66). Cambridge, England: Cambridge University Press.

Singer, J. L., & Kolligan, J., Jr. (1987). Personality: Developments in the study of private experience. *Annual Review of Psychology, 38,* 533–574.

Singer, J. L., & Singer, D. G. (1972). Personality. *Annual Review of Psychology, 23,* 375–412.

Snyder, M. (1983). The influence of individuals on situations: Implications for understanding the links between personality and social behavior. *Journal of Personality, 51,* 497–516.

Spence, D. (1982). *Narrative truth and historical truth.* New York: Norton.

Spielberger, C. D. (1966). The effects of anxiety on complex learning and academic achievement. In C. D. Spielberger (Ed.), *Anxiety and behavior.* New York: Academic Press.

Spranger, E. (1928). *Types of men.* Halle: Niemeyer.

Stagner, R. (1937). *Psychology of personality.* New York: McGraw-Hill.

Stern, W. (1924). *Die menschliche Persönlichkeit.* Leipzig, Germany: J. A. Barth.

Stewart, A. J., & Healy, J. M., Jr. (1985). Personality and adaptation to change. In R. Hogan & W. H. Jones (Eds.), *Perspectives in personality* (Vol. 1, pp. 117–144). Greenwich, CT: JAI Press.

Suls, J., & Rittenhouse, J. D. (Eds.). (1987). *Personality and physical health: A special issue of the Journal of Personality.* Durham, NC: Duke University Press.

Taylor, J. (1953). A personality scale of manifest anxiety. *Journal of Abnormal and Social Psychology, 48,* 285–290.

Tomkins, S. S. (1987). Script theory. In J. Aronoff, A. I. Rabin, & R. A. Zucker (Eds.), *The emergence of personality* (pp. 147–216). New York: Springer.

Tupes, E. C., & Christal, R. E. (1961). *Recurrent personality factors based on trait ratings. U.S. Air Force Systems Command, Aeronautical Systems Division, Technical Report,* No. 61–97.

Weiner, B. (1980). *Human motivation.* New York: Holt, Rinehart & Winston.

West, S. G. (1983). Personality and prediction: An introduction. *Journal of Personality, 51,* 275–285.

White, R. W. (1952). *Lives in progress* (1st ed.). New York: Holt, Rinehart & Winston.

White, R. W. (1959). Motivation reconsidered: The concept of competence. *Psychological Review, 66,* 297–333.

White, R. W. (Ed.). (1963). *The study of lives.* New York: Atherton Press.

White, R. W. (1981). Exploring personality the long way: The study of lives. In A. I. Rabin, J. Aronoff, A. M. Barclay, & R. A. Zucker (Eds.), *Further explorations in personality* (pp. 3–19). New York: Wiley.

White, R. W. (1987). *A memoir: Seeking the shape of personality.* Marlborough, NH: The Homestead Press.

Whiting, J. W. M., & Child, I. L. (1953). *Child training and personality: A cross-cultural study.* New Haven, CT: Yale University Press.

Wiggins, J. S. (1973). *Personality and prediction: Principles of personality assessment.* Reading, MA: Addison.

Wiggins, J. S. (1991). Agency and communion as conceptual coordinates for the understanding and measurement of interpersonal behavior. In D. Cicchetti & W. Grove (Eds.), *Thinking clearly about psychology: Essays in honor of Paul Everett Meehl* (pp. 89–113). Minneapolis: University of Minnesota Press.

Wiggins, J. S., & Broughton, R. (1985). The interpersonal circle: A structural model for the integration of personality research. In R. Hogan & W. H. Jones (Eds.), *Perspectives in personality* (Vol. 1, pp. 1–47). Greenwich, CT: JAI Press.

Wiggins, J. S., & Pincus, A. L. (1992). Personality: Structure and assessment. *Annual Review of Psychology, 43,* 473–504.

Witkin, H. A. (1950). Individual differences in ease of perception of embedded figures. *Journal of Personality, 19,* 1–15.

Woodworth, R. S. (1919). *Personal data sheet.* Chicago: Stoelting.

Wrightsman, L. S. (1981). Personal documents as data in conceptualizing adult personality development. *Personality and Social Psychology Bulletin, 7,* 367–385.

Wrightsman, L. S. (1988). *Personality development in adulthood.* Newbury Park, CA: Sage.

Zajonc, R. B. (1980). Feeling and thinking: Preferences need no inferences. *American Psychologist, 35,* 151–175.

Zener, K. (1945). A note concerning editorial reorientation. *Journal of Personality, 14,* 1–2.

Zucker, R. A., Rabin, A. I., Aronoff, J., & Frank, S. (Eds.). (1992). *Personality structure in the life course.* New York: Springer.

Zuroff, D. C. (1986). Was Gordon Allport a trait theorist? *Jorunal of Personality and Social Psychology, 51,* 993–1000.

STUDYING LIVES

PSYCHOBIOGRAPHY AND THE CONCEPTUAL STRUCTURE OF PERSONALITY PSYCHOLOGY

WILLIAM MCKINLEY RUNYAN

UNIVERSITY OF CALIFORNIA AT BERKELEY

I. INTRODUCTION

There is a puzzling history in the relationships between personality psychology and the study of individual lives. Most simply, the study of individual persons and lives was one of the central concerns and motivating agendas for founders of the field such as Gordon Allport (1937) and Henry Murray (1938), but was then lost sight of in the 1950s and 1960s (with some exceptions, as in the work of Robert White [1952] or Erik Erikson [1958]), as far greater attention was given to psychometric concerns and the experimental study of particular processes.

This was a remarkable turn of events in the constitution and changing definition of the field. Major texts of the period, such as Hall and Lindzey's *Theories of Personality* (1957), which as the most widely used text eventually sold more than 700,000 copies, and Walter Mischel's *Personality and Assessment* (1968), gave almost no attention to the study of individual persons or lives. Hall and Lindzey argued that the fruitfulness of personality theories "is to be judged primarily by how effectively they serve as a spur to research" (p. 27), while Mischel argued for the superiority of experimentally based social learning and cognitive theories over trait and psychodynamic approaches for the prediction and modification of behavior. Note that an improved understanding of individual persons was not a significant criterion in either of these influential formulations of the field.

How did the study of individual persons and lives fall by the wayside? It seems to have been due to a combination of changing intellectual fashions about what it means to "be scientific," personal and temperamental preferences for particular kinds of research, the kinds of graduate students attracted to the field in the growing competition with clinical psychology after World War II, patterns of funding and grant support, and institutional processes determining who was or was not hired and promoted at Harvard, Stanford, Yale, Berkeley, and other major universities around the country. Precisely how all this unfolded, however, remains somewhat obscure and needs to be illuminated through more detailed research on the intellectual and institutional history of personality psychology. In any case, there has been a remarkable resurgence of interest in recent years in the study of individual lives and in psychobiography among personality psychologists (e.g., Alexander, 1990; Anderson, 1981a, 1988; Cohler, 1988; Elms, 1988a, 1988b, 1994; McAdams, 1990; McAdams & Ochberg, 1988a; Runyan, 1982, 1988a, 1988b, 1994).

This chapter is intended to help reintegrate or reweave the study of lives back into the fabric of personality psychology. The objective is not to stomp out other forms of research, or to argue that personality psychology should be nothing but the study of lives, but rather, to argue that the study of persons or lives is *one* of the central objectives of the field. A discipline of psychology which does not contribute to a better understanding of persons is pretty pathetic. Particularly pathetic is a personality psychology which fails to do so. My hope is to contribute to an emerging "gestalt shift" in personality psychology, so that the study of persons and lives is again seen as one of its central objectives.

The objectives of this chapter are to reexamine, perhaps even help rehabilitate, the study of lives in the field of personality psychology and to examine how the study of lives is related to quantitative and experimental research traditions.

The second section will explore the conceptual structure of personality psychology and argue for a conception of the field in terms of the four objectives of developing general theories of personality, analyzing individual and group differences, studying specific processes or classes of behavior, and, finally, studying individual lives. The third section discusses the concept of progress as a way of addressing methodological and epistemological problems in the study of individual lives. The fourth section will explore relationships between the study of lives and quantitative and experimental traditions of research in personality. The fifth section examines the uses of a "hard" to "soft" continuum for understanding relationships among a variety of traditions, objectives, and methods in personality psychology. I will argue that thriving interdisciplinary syntheses at the hard end of psychology, such as cognitive science and neuroscience, might well be supplemented by a synthesis at the soft end of psychology, with the study of lives in social, cultural, and historical contexts as one leading candidate for such a soft synthesis.

II. THE CONCEPTUAL STRUCTURE OF PERSONALITY PSYCHOLOGY

It is very difficult to get a conceptual grasp on the structure of the field of personality psychology due to the enormous range of things going on within it. What common ground, if any, is there between theories of psychosexual stages, factor-analytic studies of questionnaire responses, experimental studies of aggression, assessment and prediction studies, behavior genetics, and psychobiography? How to understand the structure of a field which includes such apparently bewildering diversity?

A first common way of organizing the field of personality psychology is in terms of major theoretical orientations or traditions, such as psychoanalysis, behaviorism or learning theory, trait and psychometric approaches, and humanistic psychology. These are the "Big Four," which are almost always discussed, while other traditions sometimes discussed are culture and personality, behavior genetics and sociobiology, the study of lives, and cognitive approaches to personality. This approach is frequently used in undergraduate personality courses and is adopted in undergraduate texts such as Liebert and Spiegler's *Personality: Strategies and Issues* (1987), Pervin's *Personality: Theory, Assessment, and Research* (1980), and Peterson's *Personality* (1988). A variant of this is a biographical analysis of the work of major theorists in the field, such as with Hall and Lindzey's *Theories of Personality* (1957, and subsequent editions) and Monte's *Beneath the Mask: An Introduction to Theories of Personality* (1987).

A second way of dividing up the field is in terms of core conceptual issues which cut across theoretical orientations, including topics such as the structure of personality, the dynamics of personality, development of personality, assessment of personality, and the change of personality. This strategy was used by Gordon Allport in his foundational text *Personality: A Psychological Interpretation* (1937), and is used in the preface to the more than 40 volumes of the Wiley Series on Personality Processes.

A third way of dividing up the field is in terms of different methodological traditions or techniques. The most influential version of this is probably by Lee Cronbach, who in "The Two Disciplines of Scientific Psychology" (1957) and "Beyond the Two Disciplines of Scientific Psychology" (1975) argued that the field of psychology could be seen as developing along an experimental tradition and a quantitative-correlational tradition, which needed to be integrated into a more comprehensive interactional tradition, examining the interaction of individual differences with responses to experimental and situational conditions. These correlational, experimental, and interactional research designs have all been important in personality psychology, along with longitudinal, cross-cultural, archival, and case study methods. Another approach to conceptualizing the field of personality from a methodological perspective is provided in Kenneth Craik's (1986) analysis of the history of personality psychology in terms of the rise, fall, and resurrection of seven different methodological traditions, which he identifies as biographical/archival, field studies, laboratory methods, naturalistic observational assessment, observer judgments, personality scales and inventories, and projective techniques.

A fourth way of dividing up the field of personality is in terms of empirical research on substantive processes and classes of behavior, such as aggression, sexual behavior, creativity, altruism, anxiety, psychopathology, locus of control, delay of gratification, achievement motivation, and stress and coping. Many textbooks combine a discussion of four or five major theoretical traditions with a number of specific personality processes (e.g., Mischel, 1981; Phares, 1988; Wiggins, Renner, Clore, & Rose, 1976). Textbooks are, of course, also organized according to various combinations of these four principles, such as a discussion of four theories followed by a set of substantive processes, or a review of four or five major theoretical orientations with research and applications discussed under each; or theory, empirical research, and applications may be placed in separate sections; and so on.

In this chapter I want to propose a fifth way of conceptualizing the structure of personality psychology; one which cuts across the prior conceptual frameworks and which raises intriguing questions about the degree of interrelatedness of the disparate intellectual enterprises which constitute the field. If successful, this framework may bring into view aspects of the structure of the field not previously visible.

The central idea is that the field of personality psychology is concerned with four major tasks or objectives: (1) developing general theories of personality, (2) studying individual and group differences, (3) analyzing specific processes and classes of behavior, and (4) understanding individual persons and lives.

The relationships between these four objectives, and the development of each of them over time, are outlined in Figure 1. Starting with the top row, General theory, we can trace the development of a number of the major theoretical programs in personality psychology, beginning with psychoanalysis around 1900 with the publication of Freud's *Interpretation of Dreams* (1900/1958); behaviorism around 1913 with John B. Watson's "Psychology as the Behaviorist Views It"; culture and personality in the 1930s with Margaret Mead, Ruth Benedict, Edward Sapir, and others; the psychometric approach in the 1940s with the early publications of Hans Eysenck and R. B. Cattell; the humanistic-phenomenological approach of Carl Rogers and Abraham Maslow; cognitive approaches with the work of George Kelley in 1955, but then more extensively with cognitive-experimentalists such as Mischel, Bandura, Cantor, and Kihlström; and work in behavior genetics and sociobiology becoming more prominent in the 1970s and 1980s with E. O. Wilson, Arnold Buss, David Buss, and others. It should be emphasized that these historical datings are highly approximate, but the primary point is to outline the historical emergence of each theoretical tradition and then be able to raise questions about its relations to developments in studies of individual and group differences, of specific processes and classes of behavior, and of individual persons and lives, as represented in the bottom three rows of Figure 1.

The second row, that of studying individual and group differences, is represented with a sample of relatively influential programs of this type, such as studies of intelligence by Binet, Terman, Wechsler, Eysenck, Howard Gardner, and others;

General
Theory

	Psychoanalytic					
		Behavioral	Culture & personality	Psychometric		
					Humanistic	
						Cognitive
		Biological				Behavior genetic & Sociobiological

Individual & group differences

Intelligence:	Binet	Terman		Wechsler	Eysenck	H. Gardner
Psychopathology:	Kraepelin			DSM-I Menninger		DSM-III
Personality traits, dimensions, types:	Introversion–Extraversion	Murray	MMPI	Meehl CPI Cattell Wiggins	"Big 5"	
				Q-sort Block		
Group differences: (gender, age, race, class, culture, historical period)				Cronbach Eysenck authoritarian personality act frequency		

Specific processes & classes of behavior

dreams   honesty   achievement   social cognition
slips   motivation   stress & coping
jokes   frustration &   altruism   self-monitoring
anxiety   phobias   aggression   creativity   goal-seeking
                                          sexual   delay of   drug use
                                          behavior gratification   suicide
                                 anti-Semitism   symptoms

Individual persons and lives

Self-understanding:	Freud's case studies:		Case Studies in	DSM-III
Clinical patients:	Dora, Little Hans, Rat Man,		Behavior Modification	Casebook
Research subjects:	Dr. Schreber, et al.	"Earnst"	Lives in Letters	Cocaine
			Progress from Jenny	Users
Biographical figures:	Leonardo da Vinci			

Dostoevsky   The Early Mental   Hitler   Young Man Luther
Moses   Traits of 300   Gandhi   H. James
                Geniuses   George III Wilson   Stalin
                                                        E. Dickinson
                     Melville   Van Gogh, etc.

       1900   1940   1980

FIGURE 1   The history of four interrelated types of inquiry in personality psychology.

studies in psychodiagnostic categories, as with Kraepelin, Karl Menninger, and the *Diagnostic and Statistical Manual* (DSM-I, DSM-III); studies of personality traits, dimensions, and types, as with studies of extroversion–introversion by Jung and others, Henry Murray's studies of needs, development of the MMPI, Meehl's analysis of clinical versus statistical prediction, Gough's California Psychological Inventory (CPI); the work of Cattell, Eysenck, Block, Cronbach, Wiggins, and others on personality measurement, and recent discussion of the "Big Five" dimensions of personality. The study of group differences according to gender, age, race, social class, culture, and historical period may also be included in this row, but for purposes of simplicity in the diagram, I have focused on studies of individual differences.

The third row is concerned with studies of specific processes and classes of behavior, as with a set of phenomena examined in psychoanalysis, including dreams, slips, jokes, and anxiety; the study of phobias studied by Watson and other later behaviorists; the famous study of "honesty" by Hartshorne and May (1928); the study of frustration and aggression at Yale by Dollard, Doob, Miller, Mowrer, and Sears (1939); the study of sexual behavior by Kinsey and colleagues (1948, 1953);

the study of anti-Semitism in conjunction with research on the authoritarian personality; the study of achievement motivation by McClelland, Atkinson, Clark, and Lowell (1953); studies of creativity at the Institute of Personality Assessment and Research, U.C. Berkeley, by Donald MacKinnon (1978), Frank Barron (1969), Ravenna Helson (1984–1985), and others; studies of delay of gratification by Walter Mischel in the 1960s and later (Mischel, 1966); and a variety of other more recent studies of different classes of behavior. The items noted on the chart are obviously only selections from a much larger set.

The bottom row deals with studies of individual persons and lives, which have been divided into the four subgroups of studies in self-understanding, of clinical patients, of research subjects, and of biographical figures. A few of the items included in the diagram are Freud's famous clinical case studies of Dora, Little Hans, the Rat Man, and Dr. Schreber et al.; Freud's psychobiographical analyses of Leonardo da Vinci, Dostoevsky, and Moses; the study of intelligence in 300 historical geniuses by Catherine Cox (1926) in association with Lewis Terman; the case study of "Earnst" written by Robert White in Henry Murray's *Explorations in Personality* (1938), the study of Adolf Hitler by the O.S.S. in World World II, and many other subsequent psychobiographies; Henry Murray's studies of Herman Melville; the study of three normal lives in *Lives in Progress* (White, 1952); Gordon Allport's analysis of *Letters from Jenny* (1965); the influential edited collection of *Case Studies in Behavior Modification* (Ullmann & Krasner, 1965); Erik Erikson's psychobiographical studies of *Young Man Luther* (1958) and *Gandhi's Truth* (1969); a personality research study of nine *Cocaine Users* (Spotts & Shontz, 1980); case studies in the DSM-III casebook; and psychobiographical studies of Henry James, Joseph Stalin, Emily Dickinson, Vincent Van Gogh, and many others (see Gilmore, 1984; Runyan, 1982, 1988a, 1988b).

Although methodological approaches are not explicitly included in this diagram, it may be noted that different methodological approaches tend to be associated with particular objectives, and thus with particular rows in the chart. Most simply, the bottom row of studying individual persons and lives tends to rely on case study, archival, historical, and interpretive methods; the third row, of studying specific processes and classes of behavior, tends to rely more heavily on experimental methods; while the second row, of studying individual and group differences, tends to rely more on psychometric, correlational, and factor-analytic methods. The top row, general theory, may draw on varying combinations of methodological approaches.

This conceptual partitioning of the field of personality psychology into four different objectives or streams of work is useful from a number of different perspectives. First, it makes clear some of the very different kinds of objectives pursued by different investigators. It is across these lines that different individuals and groups in personality psychology sometimes have little interest in, respect for, or even knowledge of each other's research. These differences have led at times to severe criticisms of each other's work, such as experimentalists being unhappy with the relatively grand or untestable claims of general theorists or, conversely, of general theorists being uninterested in the more microexperimental studies of specific behaviors or the quantitative measurements of particular dimensions. Some such analysis of the internal lines of division and criticisms within the field is necessary for understanding its intellectual and interpersonal structure.

A second issue suggested by this diagram is that of the fascinating epistemological question of the very possibility of knowledge in each of these four enterprises. What kinds of knowledge are and are not possible in each of these four lines of inquiry, from developing general theory down to studying individual lives? The third section of this paper will focus on the issue of intellectual progress in the study of individual lives, but similar questions may be raised about each of the other levels.

Third, laying out the historical evolution of work within each of these four tasks raises interesting empirical and historical questions about what connections there are between them over time. What influence has the development of general theory had upon the study of specific individual and group differences, upon specific processes and classes of behavior, or upon the study of individual lives? How, for example, has psychoanalysis as a general theory had an influence upon diagnostic classifications, upon the study of specific classes of behavior such as dreams, jokes, or psychiatric symptoms, or upon the study of individual lives such as Leonardo da Vinci or Martin Luther? In turn, what influence has research at each of these three levels had upon the development of psychoanalytic theory? Or, to take an example from the individual and group difference level, how have the diagnostic categories in the *Diagnostic and Statistical Manual* (DSM-IV) been influenced by advances in psychoanalytic theory, behavioral theory, cognitive theory, and biological theory (Millon & Klerman, 1986)? How have diagnostic categories such as schizophrenia and borderline disorders been related to the study of specific symptoms or clusters of symptoms and to the interpretation of individual clinical or historical figures? In short, a whole research agenda is opened up by examining the existence or degree of interconnectedness or not between research within each of these four partially independent streams of work.

At a minimum, this conceptualization of the structure of personality psychology in terms of four distinct tasks or objectives and their relationships to each other is *one* of the useful ways of conceptualizing the structure of the field of personality, along with the previously discussed conceptualizations in terms of theoretical orientations, core conceptual issues, methods, and classes of substantive phenomena. My hunch is that this conceptualization reveals something fundamental about the structure of the field, although I will only begin to be able to argue that here.

III. PROGRESS IN PSYCHOBIOGRAPHICAL INQUIRY

Work in psychobiography has developed not only within psychology, but also within psychoanalysis and psychiatry, history, political science, literature, and an assortment of other fields including religion, the history of science, and so on. The field of psychobiography is traditionally defined as beginning with Freud's *Leonardo da Vinci and a Memory of His Childhood* (1910/1957), with a number of the earliest psychobiographies summarized in Dooley's "Psychoanalytic Studies of Genius" (1916).

I have reviewed the intellectual and institutional growth of work in psychobiography and psychohistory elsewhere (Runyan, 1988a), including a quantitative analysis of the growth of publications in the field and a review of professional organizations, specialty journals, conferences, academic courses, and dissertations in the field, so I will not repeat that broader survey here. I will, however, discuss several developments within personality psychology. The study of individual lives was championed by Henry Murray (1938, 1981), Gordon Allport (1937, 1942, 1965), Robert White (1952, 1963, 1972), and others at Harvard beginning in the 1930s. Although there were earlier academic psychologists involved in psychobiography, such as Morton Prince's *Psychology of the Kaiser: A Study of His Sentiments and His Obsession* (1915) and "Roosevelt as Analyzed by the New Psychology" (1912), and G. Stanley Hall's *Jesus, the Christ, in the Light of Psychology* (1917), these were isolated works that fell on infertile soil, leaving no continuous legacy. In contrast, the personological and study of lives tradition begun by Murray, Allport, and White has had an enduring impact. Later personality psychologists working within the personological and study of lives tradition include Alan Elms with psychobiographical studies of Allport (1972), Freud (1980), Skinner (1981), Murray (1987), and others; James Anderson with methodological writings on psychobiography (1981b) and on William James (1981a) and Henry Murray (1988); Robert Stolorow and George Atwood on personality theorists (1979); Peter Newton on Samuel Johnson (1984); Ravenna Helson on E. Nisbet (1984–1985); Gerald Mendelsohn on Verdi (1985); Rae Carlson in applying Silvan Tomkins' script theory (1981); myself on conceptual and methodological issues (1982, 1983, 1988a,b); Irving Alexander on Freud, Jung, and Harry Stack Sullivan (1990); and Dan McAdams on Yukio Mishima (1985).

In *Life Histories and Psychobiography: Explorations in Theory and Method* (Runyan, 1982), I attempted to provide a critical review of basic methodological and conceptual problems encountered in the intensive study of individual lives, whether in the form of biographies, psychobiographies, or clinical case studies. This included a review of psychological literature on the case study method, idiographic methods, and psychobiography. The discussion of psychobiography analyzed issues such as the kinds of evidence needed for a psychobiographical interpretation, the critical evaluation of alternative psychobiographical explanations, the dangers of psychological reductionism, the extent to which adult personality and behavior can or cannot be explained by childhood experience, the problems of attempting to "reconstruct" early life events, the trans-historical and cross-cultural applicability of psychological theory, and finally, the relative contributions of psychoanalytic and non-psychoanalytic theory to psychobiography. The relations of psychobiography to the wider field of psychohistory, as well as to other hybrid disciplines such as political psychology, historical psychology, and psychological anthropology, are analyzed in *Psychology and Historical Interpretation* (Runyan, 1988a).

The recent resurgence of interest in the study of lives among personality psychologists is well represented in a special issue of the *Journal of Personality* on "Psychobiography and Life Narratives" (McAdams & Ochberg, 1988b), also published as a book with the same title (McAdams & Ochberg, 1988a). As stated in the Introduction,

> Today, personality psychologists seem less ashamed than they did 20 years ago to admit that the subject of their study is human lives. . . . Once again, it is okay to study the "whole person." Better, contemporary personologists insist, as did pioneers like Gordon Allport and Henry Murray, that such an endeavor is the personologist's *raison d'être*. (McAdams, 1988a, p. 1)

Two further indicators of the integration of the study of lives back into personality psychology are a general personality textbook, *The Person: An Introduction to Personality Psychology* (McAdams, 1990), which gives substantial attention to individual life stories and psychobiography, and a recent book on *Personology: Content and Method in Personality Assessment and Psychobiography* (Alexander, 1990), which contains psychobiographical interpretations of Freud, Jung, and Harry Stack Sullivan, suggests principles for psychobiographical interpretation, and outlines a teaching format for integrating personality assessment with the study of individual lives. An important recent book on psychobiography is *Uncovering Lives: The Uneasy Alliance of Biography and Psychology* (Elms, 1994), which provides practical methodological advice and contains fascinating psychobiographical portraits of psychologists such as B. F. Skinner, Freud, Jung, and Gordon Allport, as well as of selected science fiction writers and political figures.

Either explicitly or implicitly, many psychologists still have a number of objections to the detailed study of individuals. We have been trained to think about social science in a way which makes the study of individuals seem somehow trivial, irrelevant, or misguided. Typical concerns are that the study of individuals is not rigorous enough, is too subjective, is not generalizable enough, or is not sufficiently scientific. I will briefly review a number of these criticisms and respond to them.

Perhaps the most widespread criticism of studies of particular lives is that it is difficult to generalize from them. Staub (1980) suggests that "if we *focus* on the uniqueness of every human being, we cannot generalize from one person to another. Since the aim of science is to discover laws or principles—applicable at least to some, if not to all people—what we will learn will not contribute to a science of psychology" (p. 3). Allport's summary of such criticisms is that "We'd have to generalize to other people or else we'd have nothing of any scientific value" (Allport, 1962, p. 406).

These criticisms seem to be based on the unwarranted assumption that the goal of personality psychology is solely to produce generalizations at the highest possible level of abstraction, preferably universal generalizations. As argued earlier, personality psychology needs to attend to at least four different kinds of objectives, ranging from general theory through the study of individual differences and specific classes of behavior to the study of individual persons. Although there is some transfer between these four levels, they are at least partially independent of each other. To the cry of, "How can you generalize from that idiographic study?," the equally appropriate response is, "How can you particularize from that group or population study?" Work on all four tasks is necessary, and the fact that inquiry at one level does not automatically answer questions at the other levels is not a telling criticism.

A second objection is that interpretations of individual cases are seen as too arbitrary or subjective. For example, "The events of most people's lives are sufficiently variegated and multifarious that virtually any theoretical template can be validated. The case study simply allows the investigator freedom to locate the facts lending support to his or her preformulated convictions" (Gergen, 1977, p. 142). Is interpretation of the single case little more than an arbitrary application of one's theoretical prejudices? It may be possible to interpret any life with any theory, but often only at the cost of distortion or selective presentation of the evidence. Any explanatory conjecture can be made, but not all of them stand up under rigorous cross-examination.

A third objection is that it is not only impractical, but literally impossible to conduct an idiographic study of every individual. If individuals are largely dissimilar, then "every sparrow would have to be separately identified, named and intuitively understood" (Murray, 1938, p. 715). If all individuals are unique, then it would be necessary to formulate "as many theories as there are persons in the universe" (Levy, 1970, p. 76). This criticism raises an important question about the costs and benefits of detailed studies of individuals. Granted that there are not sufficient resources for studying every individual in the universe, it is still entirely feasible to conduct detailed idiographic studies of individuals of particular interest to us, including historical figures such as Adolf Hitler, Sigmund Freud, and Virginia Woolf, particular clinical patients, and other individuals of interest. We do not have the time and money to study all individuals, but neither do we have the resources to test all possible theories. It is necessary to be selective, both in theoretical inquiries and in studies of specific individuals.

A fourth objection, and the final one to be discussed here, is that there is nothing wrong with the idiographic study of individuals, but it is not science. Levy (1970), for example, argues that the meaning of data about individual cases "can only be found within the context of laws that hold for all individuals. . . . It is not possible to go beyond this and remain within the confines of science" (p. 76).

The suggestion that science as a whole is not concerned with the study of particulars is clearly untenable, as this criterion would rule out significant portions of geology, astronomy and cosmology, and evolutionary biology. These sciences are concerned not solely with general principles and processes but also with topics, respectively, such as the structure and evolution of this particular earth, the structure and origins of our solar system, and the particular sequence of species leading to the evolution of humans. There is, in short, a whole set of "historical sciences"

(Gould, 1989) concerned with the study of particular historical processes as well as with theoretical generalizations. Personality psychology, in order to study persons and lives, must be (in part) a historical science as well as a nomothetic science.

A useful way of looking at methodological and epistemological problems in the study of individual lives is to consider the extent to which such research programs are "progressive" or not. What constitutes progress in our knowledge and understanding of an individual life? To the extent that progress occurs, what processes bring it about? And finally, how do advances in other areas of personality psychology relate to progress in the study of individual lives?

For example, what progress, if any, has there been in our psychological understanding of Adolf Hitler during the course of research on his life, from the Office of Strategic Services study in World War II (Langer, 1972), to Alan Bullock's classic biography in 1952, to Robert Waite's *The Psychopathic God: Adolf Hitler* (1977)? What progress, if any, has there been in our knowledge and understanding of Sigmund Freud, from an early biography by Wittels (1924), to Ernest Jones' standard three-volume biography (1953–1957), to more recent studies by Roazen (1975), Sulloway (1979), Gay (1988), and others? Finally, in the clinical realm, what advances, if any, have there been in our knowledge and understanding of Freud's classic case studies of Little Hans, the Wolf Man, the Rat Man, Dora, and others through decades of reanalysis and reinterpretation (e.g., Ellenberger, 1970; Kanzer & Glenn, 1980)?

A. Conceptualizing Progress in Biography

To respond to questions about whether certain sequences of life history studies are progressive or not requires a clarification and definition of the concept of progress. The literature on the concept of progress is surprisingly extensive, from studies of the history of the idea of progress, to analyses of progress in physics, biology, the social sciences, history, and other disciplines, to progress in technology and material benefits, to economic progress, to progress in morals, and, finally, to progress in human welfare as a whole (cf. Almond, Chodorow, & Pearce, 1982).

Underlying these many uses of the concept of progress, the idea may be defined most simply as change over time in a direction perceived as desirable or preferable. Thus, it involves a temporal or historical component and a valuative component. A third possible component of the idea of progress, which is sometimes but not necessarily implied, is that of progress as *inevitable*. Let me make clear that I am *not* claiming that a sequence of biographical studies is necessarily progressive. Some are, and some are not. Rather, the concept of progress is introduced as a way of addressing epistemological issues in the study of lives, as a way of comparing life history studies not to some absolute standard of truth, which can be impossibly difficult to specify, but rather of comparing a given study with prior studies in terms of a variety of specifiable criteria.

How should we look at progress in our knowledge and understanding of individual lives? It seems to me that progress in psychobiographical studies can be meaningfully assessed in terms of criteria such as (1) the comprehensiveness of the evidential base, (2) the insightfulness and persuasiveness of interpretation, and (3) the literary or aesthetic appeal of the narrative account. This discussion focuses on the first two of these criteria, the quality of evidence and of interpretation, while other works have focused on literary appeal and other criteria (Novarr, 1986). Advances in understanding can occur through a variety of processes, such as collecting additional evidence, developing more powerful background theory and research to draw on, and proposing and testing new interpretations.

The processes involved in advancing our knowledge and understanding of individual lives can, for the sake of simplicity, be divided into eight steps or components, as in Figure 2. This set of processes is related to the specific criteria I am proposing. Other criteria of progress, such as moral rectitude, metaphoric expressiveness, and political correctness, would suggest a somewhat different set of processes.

The components in Figure 2 have been numbered from 1 to 8 for purposes of identification, rather than to identify any rigidly fixed sequence of steps. The top left-hand box, Evidence, and Processes of Data Collection, includes activities such as finding additional letters or diaries, conducting further interviews, and finding additional archival records or physical evidence. In research on Hitler, for example, this would include material such as *Mein Kampf,* interviews with and documents by those who knew him, the discovery of his burned corpse, records of his personal physician, and the alleged discovery of previously unknown "Hitler Diaries." The second step is the Critical Examination of Evidence and Sources, including activities such as detecting forgeries or falsifications in the evidential base and learning how much weight to give to the testimony of different witnesses. In the case of Hitler research, dental records supported the claim that the partly

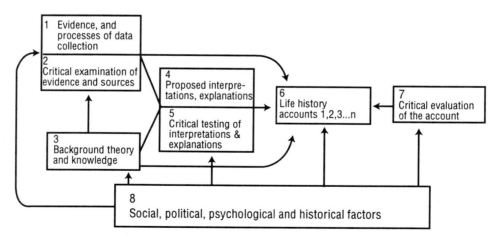

FIGURE 2 Advances in our knowledge and understanding of individual lives: a simplified model of component processes.

burned body found by Russian soldiers outside the Fuhrer's air raid shelter in Berlin was that of Hitler (Waite, 1977), while a study of the paper used in the alleged Hitler diaries revealed that it was produced after his death.

The third component is Background Theory and Knowledge, which is drawn upon in interpreting the individual case, and would include theories of personality development, an understanding of the relevant cultural and historical background, and knowledge of relevant medical conditions and biological processes. In particular, this background theory and knowledge would include advances in all other areas of personality, such as general theories of personality, research on individual and group differences, and studies of specific processes and classes of behavior. The fourth step is the generation of new interpretations and explanations of the individual case, while the fifth step is the critical evaluation and attempted falsification of proposed interpretations (cf. Runyan, 1981).

The sixth component is the production of a narrative account of the life, which incorporates a number of specific interpretations and explanations, organizes a substantial amount of data about the life, and draws on theoretical and background knowledge. The numbered subscripts indicate a whole sequence of accounts which might be produced about the same life, such as a biography of Hitler in 1944, one in 1952, and another in 1977. All of the preceding five processes used in constructing the account can be repeated in an iterative cycle.

The seventh step is the critical evaluation of the narrative account, as in the form of a book review for a biography or a case conference for a clinical presentation, considering factors such as the adequacy of the evidence, the appropriateness of the background theory, and the credibility of the proposed interpretations. The eighth and final component is Social, Political, Psychological, and Historical Factors which influence each of the other processes. They influence what data are collected and seen as relevant, and how critically they are scrutinized. These factors influence the kinds of background theory and knowledge which are drawn upon, influence the interpretations which are proposed and how critically they are evaluated, affect the shape and structure of the finished narrative account, and influence the critical reception that the finished work receives.

The impetus for a new psychobiographical study can come from developments in any one of the eight components in Figure 2, such as the discovery of new sources of evidence, advances in theoretical knowledge which make possible the interpretation of previously inexplicable events, or the critique and dismissal of earlier interpretations and the proposal of new ones.

IV. RELATIONSHIPS BETWEEN THE STUDY OF LIVES AND OTHER AREAS OF PERSONALITY PSYCHOLOGY

What relations are there between progress in the psychological analysis of individual lives and advances in other branches of personality psychology? What relations, if any, are there between progress in the study of individual lives and progress in general personality theory, research on individual and group differences, or research on specific processes and classes of behavior? In terms of Figure 1, this is equivalent to asking what connections there are between the study of individual persons in the fourth row with developments in the top three rows.

Studies of individual lives can have implications for inquiry at each of the other three levels. Methodology texts often state that the study of single cases can provide hypotheses, which then need to be tested with quantitative or experimental methods (as in the second and third rows). Or, general theories of personality can be influenced by their personal or subjective origins in the lives of individual personality theorists, as Stolorow and Atwood (1979) have argued is true in the work of Sigmund Freud, Carl Jung, Wilhelm Reich, and Otto Rank. Abraham Maslow has reported that his ideas about self-actualization came initially from reflections about the similarities of two of his mentors, Max Wertheimer and Ruth Benedict (Maslow, 1971). Rae Carlson (1988) has discussed how psychobiographical research can contribute to the development of general theories of personality.

There unquestionably are many influences of the study of individual lives on other lines of research in personality, but for the present discussion, I will focus on influences going in the other direction—the ways in which progress in the study of individual lives has been influenced by advances in other areas of personality psychology. Most simply, how is the course of research on individual lives influenced by advances in general theories of personality, by studies of individual and group differences, and/or by research on specific processes and classes of behavior?

In terms of Figure 2, which focuses on processes contributing to progress in the study of lives, all of these developments in personality theory and research would be channeled through the third component, Background Theory and Knowledge. This background theory and knowledge would include developments in all other areas of personality psychology, but is not restricted to advances in personality psychology, and also includes advances in other areas of psychology and contributions from disciplines such as history, sociology, anthropology, political science, and biology.

The contributions of other areas of personality psychology to the study of lives will be reviewed under four different headings: (1) influences of general personality theory upon the study of lives, including psychoanalytic, neoanalytic, and nonanalytic theories of personality; (2) influences of research on individual and group differences upon the study of lives, such as research on intelligence or categories of psychopathology; (3) influences of research on specific processes and classes of behavior, such as altruistic behavior; and (4) influences of all different kinds of personality theory and research as they are funneled into the study of a single life, such as that of Adolf Hitler.

First, what influences have there been from advances in general theories of personality upon psychobiography and the study of individual lives? The most extensive influence upon the study of individual lives is certainly from psychoanalysis, beginning with Freud and his Viennese followers, spreading through Europe and the United States, and taking another step forward with Erik Erikson's work in *Young Man Luther* (1958) and *Gandhi's Truth* (1969). Recent discussion and reviews of the influence of psychoanalytic theory upon biography and psychobiography are contained in Edel (1984), Mack (1971), and Moraitis and Pollock (1987).

Within psychoanalysis, the influence of different schools or traditions of psychoanalytic theory upon biography and psychobiography can be analyzed in more detail, such as moving from traditional Freudian drive theories to ego psychology, object relations theory, and self-psychology. Developments in ego psychology and object relations theory approaches to psychobiography are reviewed by Loewenberg (1988), who uses examples such as Richard Nixon and Adolf Hitler to illustrate how changing theoretical frameworks within psychoanalysis have led to revised interpretations of the same historical figures. In the area of self-psychology, Strozier (1985) covers applications of Kohutian self-psychology to biography and history, and Strozier and Offer (1985) examine a number of applications of self-psychology to political leaders such as Abraham Lincoln, Woodrow Wilson, Kaiser Wilhelm II, and Mahatma Gandhi. At a clinical level, the implications of changes in psychoanalytic theory for the reinterpretation of Freud's case studies of Dora, Little Hans, the Rat Man, the Schreber Case, and the Wolf Man are explored in a volume edited by Kanzer and Glenn (1980).

What, though, about the uses of personality theories other than psychoanalysis in psychobiography? In principle, any theory of personality could be drawn on in interpreting an individual life history, so psychoanalytic psychobiography could be supplemented with behavioral psychobiography, phenomenological-humanistic psychobiography, cognitive psychobiography, and so on. What, though, has actually been done in using these other theoretical frameworks in psychobiography?

Perhaps the most extensively developed behavioral interpretation of a life is in the three volumes of B. F. Skinner's autobiography (1976, 1979, 1983), in which he attempts to describe his own life in terms of changes in the external environment and their effect on his overt behavior, without reference to inner experiences or feelings. One rare attempt to apply social learning theory in a book-length psychobiography is a study of Elizabeth Cady Stanton in terms of Bandura's social learning theory (Griffith, 1984). In the clinical realm, a far greater number of individual cases have been interpreted in terms of behavioral or learning theory (e.g., Turkat, 1985; Ullmann & Krasner, 1965; Wolpe & Rachman, 1960).

Uses of phenomenological-humanistic personality theory may also occasionally be found, such as Carl Roger's reinterpretation of the case of Ellen West (1980), who suffered from anorexia nervosa and eventually committed suicide; a study of Clarence Darrow in terms of Charlotte Buhler's theory of stages of goal seeking (Horner, 1968); or Sartre's use of existential theory as well as psychoanalysis in his study of Flaubert (1981).

The uses of alternative theoretical perspectives in the study of lives are also indicated in a special issue of the *Journal of Personality* on "Psychobiography and Life Narratives" (McAdams & Ochberg, 1988b), which illustrates the application of Silvan Tomkins' script theory to the lives of Nathaniel Hawthorne and Eleanor Marx (Carlson, 1988) and to the analysis of personal documents and clinical material

(Alexander, 1988); the quantitative analysis of Eriksonian themes of identity, intimacy, and generativity in the writings of Vera Brittain (Stewart, Franz, & Layton, 1988); and a study of achievement affiliation, and power motives in Richard Nixon (Winter & Carlson, 1988). In spite of the growing number of applications of other personality theories in psychobiography, it still seems fair to say that far more psychobiographical studies have been influenced by some versions of psychodynamic theory than any other personality theory, or even all the others in combination. Elsewhere I have speculated on different possible explanations for the relative contributions of psychoanalytic and nonanalytic theory in psychobiography (Runyan, 1988a).

Looking at the second row of Figure 1, we may ask what developments in the study of individual and group differences have been used in advancing our understanding of individual lives? To mention just a few examples, let us start with the example of intelligence. Lewis Terman began trying to estimate the I.Q.'s of historical figures such as Francis Galton (Terman, 1917), and Terman's student Catherine Cox (1926) estimated the childhood I.Q.'s of 301 famous men and women in *The Early Mental Traits of Three Hundred Geniuses* (1926). For example, on I.Q. ratings for recorded behavior up to age 17, the estimate for John Stuart Mill was 190, for Goethe, 185, Pascal, 180, Voltaire, 170, David Hume, 155, Hegel, 150, Descartes, 150, Thomas Jefferson, 145, Napoleon, 135, and so on. Cox and Terman are explicit that these estimates are only for early *recorded* behavior, and may or may not accurately reflect the individual's actual I.Q. I am not trying to vouch for the adequacy of these analyses, but rather to indicate how advances in the study of individual differences, in this case, I.Q., were used in the study of particular historical figures. Terman points out how biographer's ignorance of age norms in the development of intelligence led them to misinterpret the behavior of their subjects. For example, Karl Pearson's biography of Francis Galton reports data on Galton's childhood performance and then says that it gives no significant indication of his future genius, where Terman assesses the same material and says it indicates a childhood I.Q. of near 200.

Staying at the level of individual differences, consider the implications of advances in psychodiagnostic categories for our understanding of individual lives. George III, King of England during the American Revolution and whose reign lasted from 1760 to 1820, suffered from a perplexing combination of physical and psychological disorders periodically throughout his later life, including symptoms such as delirium, excitement, sleeplessness, painful weakness of the arms and legs, visual and auditory disturbances, delusions, and agitated talking and hyperactivity. How was such a puzzling array of symptoms to be explained? To simplify, the history of different explanations of the king's disorders can be roughly divided into five stages: (1) contemporaneous explanations, which fell back on the theory of an imbalance between the four humours of black bile, yellow bile, phlegm, and choler; (2) classification according to 19th century descriptive psychiatry, in which he was diagnosed as having "ordinary acute mania"; (3) a psychodynamic explanation in 1941, in which his breakdowns were understood as breakdowns of his vulnerable defenses under pressure of stressful political and domestic events; (4) explanations in the 1960s in terms of the metabolic disease porphyria, which leads to physical and psychological disorders similar to those of George III; and (5) finally to criticisms of the porphyria hypothesis because the genetic evidence seems inconsistent with it, and a search for alternative explanations consistent with both George III's symptoms and with the genetic evidence. Details of these symptoms and the changing classifications and diagnostic assessments of the King's disorders are presented elsewhere (Runyan, 1988b), but the point for present purposes is to show how understanding of an individual case is dependent upon changing background knowledge in the form of available diagnostic systems and categories. As new diagnostic categories emerge, such as borderline disorders or narcissistic disorders, they are then freshly applied to a host of historical and clinical cases, such as Adolf Hitler, Thomas Wolfe, or Pablo Picasso.

Looking at the third row of Figure 1, how has research on specific processes and classes of behavior affected our knowledge and understanding of individual lives? What contributions to biographical and case study analyses have been made through research on such classes of behavior as specific psychiatric symptoms, sexual behavior, anti-Semitism, creativity, obedience to authority, bystander intervention, altruism, stress and coping, drug use, or suicide? To mention one example, Samuel and Pearl Oliner in *The Altruistic Personality: Rescuers of Jews in Nazi Europe* (1988) draw on the existing literature on altruism, prosocial behavior, moral reasoning, interpersonal attachment, and empathy in their study of more than 400 rescuers of Jews in Nazi-occupied Europe.

As a second example, consider that Woodrow Wilson did not learn his letters until age 9, and could not read until he was 11. Alexander George and Juliette George (1964) originally suggested that Wilson as a boy was filled with rage at his demanding and perfectionist father which he could not openly acknowledge or express, and that his failure to learn was motivated by unconscious resentment of his father. In response, Weinstein, Anderson, and Link (1978) argued that Wilson's delay in reading was not due to emotional difficulties, but to developmental dyslexia, which is caused by a delay in the establishment of dominance of one hemisphere, usually the left, for language.

In rebuttal, the Georges (1981–1982) drew on details of recent research on dyslexia. In particular, they argued that it is not established that the absence of cerebral dominance is responsible for dyslexia, that many specialists continue to believe that emotional factors are responsible for some reading disorders, and that details of Wilson's life—such as the amount of his reading, the neatness of his handwriting, and his excellent spelling—are all inconsistent with a diagnosis of developmental dyslexia. In this debate they draw on a specialized body of psychological theory and research on a particular class of behavior in order to critique an alternative explanation and to argue that the bulk of the evidence is consistent with their original interpretation. (This debate continued in subsequent years, with references cited in Link et al., 1986.)

A. Adolf Hitler

Thus far, I've indicated how advances in the areas of general theory, the study of individual differences, and research on specific processes and classes of behavior have been used in the study of individual lives. The array of uses of other areas of personality psychology in the study of lives can also be illustrated from the bottom up, as it were, by examining the course of research on a specific life and seeing how it has been affected by theory and research from different areas of personality psychology. The individual life can be used as a fulcrum or lens from which to view the range of uses of psychology. This array of uses of psychological theory and research will be illustrated with a psychobiographical study, *The Psychopathic God: Adolf Hitler* (1977) by Robert Waite.

At the level of general theory, Waite draws most heavily on psychoanalytic theory, with discussions of the anal stage in Hitler's development (pp. 148–149), of a "primal scene trauma" and its consequences (pp. 162–168), of Hitler's Oedipus complex (pp. 162–165), and of the operation of defense mechanisms such as displacement and projection in his anti-Semitism (p. 190). Waite also draws on the psychosocial theory of Erik Erikson in discussions of trust and mistrust in Hitler's childhood, with pervasive feelings of mistrust remaining consequential throughout his life (pp. 383–386), and with discussions of identity development and identity crises in Hitler's adolescence and early adulthood (pp. 184–205).

At the level of individual and group differences, research on a number of groups to which Hitler could be assigned were drawn upon in interpreting his life, such as borderline personalities, monorchids (males with one testicle), anal characters, and anti-Semites. For example, on the basis of Soviet autopsy reports on Hitler's partially burned body, Waite believes there is convincing evidence that Hitler's left testicle was missing. Hitler also had a wide variety of psychological characteristics which match those of studies of other patients with this characteristic, such as feelings of social inadequacy, concerns with bowel movements and feces, belief in themselves as special persons, and passive tendencies with a reaction formation against them in an insistence on hardness, toughness, and ruthlessness. Another study suggests that monorchid patients often have an intense concern with redesigning and reconstructing buildings, as if to quell anxieties about defects in their own bodies, which is consistent with Hitler's preoccupation with designing and redesigning elaborate architectural plans for Linz, Vienna, and Berlin (pp. 150–162).

Hitler's psychodiagnostic and medical classification has been a subject of extensive debate, and Waite reviews at least six different diagnostic possibilities, including Parkinson's disease with psychiatric side effects, medical poisoning (from an incompetent physician), rapidly progressive coronary arteriosclerosis, syphilis, damage to his left cerebral hemisphere, and borderline personality (pp. 349–359). Waite finds the last of these diagnoses most persuasive, as it best fits many (though not all) of Hitler's behavior patterns.

At the level of research on specific classes of behavior and experience, Waite draws on studies in areas such as anti-Semitism (pp. 359–373), survivor guilt (over the death of his brother) (pp. 171–172), sexual perversion, in that Waite argues that Hitler had women urinate or defecate on his head (pp. 237–243), masochistic or self-destructive behavior, which Waite argues was partially responsible for some of Hitler's disastrous military decisions such as invasion of the Soviet Union or declaring war on the United States (pp. 391–411), and finally suicide, in an attempt to understand Hitler's end (pp. 411–426).

This discussion is not an exhaustive analysis of Waite's use of psychology in interpreting Hitler, but does illustrate how our understanding of an individual life can be informed by theory and research at the three levels of general theories of personality, studies of individual and group differences, and research on specific processes and classes of behavior. An intriguing question for future inquiry is what additional advances in personality and other branches of psychology can or will be drawn upon in further illuminating Hitler's behavior, personality, and career.

V. THE STUDY OF LIVES AS A "SOFT SYNTHESIS" IN PSYCHOLOGY

A simple hard to soft dimension seems useful in thinking about the array of theoretical orientations, objectives, and research methods that constitute the field of personality psychology (see Fig. 3). The "hard" end of the continuum is concerned with quantitative measurement, experimental control, objectivity, and being scientific in a natural science sense, while the "soft" end of the continuum is concerned with subjective experience, meaning and interpretation, social-historical context, and being scientific in a human science tradition (see Fig. 3).

	"Hard"		"Soft"	
Traditions	Behaviorist Psychometric Cognitive Biological		Psychoanalytic Study of lives	Phenomenological- humanistic Culture & personality
Objectives	(1) Developing general theories of personality (2) Analyzing individual and group differences (3) Studying specific processes and classes of behavior			(4) Understanding lives in social-historical context
Methods, Disciplines	Experimental (laboratory, field, multi-variate, quasi-experimental)	Quantitative (psychometric, correlational, taxonomic, epidemiological, probabilistic)	Longitudinal (prospective, retrospective, sequential)	Interpretive (language, symbolization, intentionality, meaning) · Historical-Contextual (case study, narrative, particular context, randomness, complex sequences, psychobiographical, cross-cultural, transhistorical)

FIGURE 3   "Hard" and "soft" traditions, objectives, and methods in personality psychology.

With a hard to soft continuum on a horizontal axis, we can roughly place a number of personality psychology's theoretical traditions, objectives, and methods along this dimension. In terms of traditions or theoretical orientations, as shown in the top row of Figure 3, the behavioral, cognitive, psychometric, and biological traditions would be at the hard end of the continuum, while the psychoanalytic, study of lives, phenomenological-humanistic, and culture and personality traditions would be at the soft end. In the middle row, where the four major objectives of personality psychology discussed earlier are considered, the objective of studying specific processes and classes of behavior is at the hard end, understanding lives in their social-historical context is at the soft end, and developing general theories of personality and analyzing individual and group differences are in the middle. Methods of research are in the bottom row, with experimental and quantitative methods at the hard end, interpretive and historical-contextual methods at the soft end, and longitudinal methods in the middle.

There is a tendency for theoretical traditions, objectives, and research methods at the "hard" end of the continuum to go together. Behavioral and cognitive traditions are, for example, likely to be concerned with studying specific processes and classes of behavior, and to use primarily experimental and quantitative methods, rather than interpretive or historical methods. At the other end of the continuum, the "soft" traditions, objectives, and methods also tend to cluster together. For example, the psychoanalytic tradition is concerned primarily with developing a general theory of the mind and with understanding particular lives, and relies primarily on interpretive and historical or case study methods rather than quantitative or experimental methods.

This is, certainly, only an approximation, as theoretical traditions may pursue a variety of objectives and utilize a variety of research methods. Psychoanalysis, for example, may be tested with quantitative and experimental methods (Fisher & Greenberg, 1977), although it is more closely associated with clinical case study and interpretive methods. The point of the diagram is that the relative emphasis on different objectives and research methods is not randomly distributed across different theoretical traditions, but rather that there is a rough clustering into hard and soft traditions, objectives, and methods.

A. Toward a "Soft Synthesis" in Personality Psychology

In the history of psychology as a whole, one can identify roughly three stages in the way the field has been divided. The first stage was the division of psychology into major systems or schools, such as structuralism, functionalism, psychoanalysis, behaviorism, gestalt, and purposive or hormic psychology, up until roughly 1935 (cf. Heidbreder's classic *Seven Psychologies,* 1933; Hilgard, 1987). A second stage, from approximately 1935 to recent years, divided the discipline into the familiar "areas" of social, personality, developmental, clinical, experimental, physiological, and comparative psychology. A third period, which has emerged in recent years, is the integration of different areas of psychology with other disciplines into synthetic fields such as "cognitive science" and "neuroscience," as well as "sensory science" and behavior genetics.

Productive as these new syntheses may be, an important limitation is that they are restricted to the "hard" end of psychology and leave out a number of objectives and methods of the "soft" traditions such as psychoanalysis, humanistic psychology, the study of lives, and culture and personality. Their methods are typically experimental and quantitative, with relatively little attention given to the use of interpretive, case study, and historical-contextual methods. These hard syntheses in cognitive science and neuroscience raise an important set of questions, but they also leave unaddressed an important set of questions about the understanding of persons and lives, of inner subjective experience, of texts and their meanings, and of relations with the social-historical context as traditionally pursued in the soft end of psychology.

One intriguing possibility is that there might also be an emerging synthesis at the "soft" end of psychology around the study of lives in their social-historical context, a synthesis which could fruitfully integrate a number of common concerns of personality, social, developmental, and clinical psychology with those in adjoining social and historical sciences (Runyan, 1988a). At its best, such a synthesis might identify shared issues at the soft end of psychology, clarify research methods and criteria, provide fresh energy and optimism for "soft" psychology, and lead to integrative theoretical and empirical work cutting across separate areas.

One important component of this soft synthesis is that it emphasizes the overlap of psychology with the social sciences and humanities, in contrast to the hard syntheses, which emphasize overlaps with the biological sciences and computer science. Howard Gardner's (1985) extremely useful survey of the history of cognitive science emphasizes the overlap of cognitive psychology with artificial intelligence, linguistics, philosophy, anthropology, and neuroscience, but explicitly deemphasizes "the influence of affective factors or emotions, the contribution of historical and cultural factors, and the role of the background context in which particular actions or thoughts occur" (p. 6). It is just such neglected factors which may be central to a "soft synthesis" around the study of persons and lives.

In one of the two plenary addresses at the first annual convention of the American Psychological Society in 1989, George Miller said that he would give a young person starting out in psychology two pieces of advice: Learn all you can about biology, and learn all you can about computers. This may be responsible advice for the hard end of psychology, but not for the field as a whole, and certainly not for the soft end of psychology. The complementary advice for those going into the softer human science end of psychology might be, Learn all you can about the social sciences and humanities which overlap with psychology, and learn all you can about people and lives, including yourself. These are different pieces of advice, coming from different perspectives on the discipline. Together, they point toward a more adequate and comprehensive vision of the whole field of psychology.

Although there is a lot of recent work on the study of persons and lives (Alexander, 1990; Elms, 1994; Gardner, 1993; McAdams, 1990; McAdams & Ochberg, 1988a; Rabin, Zucker, Emmons, & Frank, 1990; Runyan, 1992, 1988a, 1988b), it may be too early to talk about this soft synthesis as something already constructed or completed. Rather, there are diverse lines of work in progress which might well be integrated into such a wider synthesis, or have only partially been integrated into such a synthesis.

My own current view is that a soft synthesis would include at least the following five components: (1) theory and conceptualization, (2) quantitative empirical research, (3) clinical and practical-applied issues, (4) subjectivity, and (5) historical-interpretive work, such as case studies and psychobiography.

Hard syntheses focus on the first two of these issues, the relationships between theory and research, and in more liberal versions on the relation to practical-applied concerns as well. A soft synthesis would include attention to all five components, with subjectivity and historical-interpretive work being of substantial importance.

This conceptualization of the internal structure of a soft synthesis raises questions about the relationships between all five of these components. Consider, for example, the relationships of subjectivity to the other elements. What are the relationships of subjectivity to theory development, as in the subjective origins of personality theory? What are the relations of subjectivity to clinical practice, as in the extensive recent literature on "countertransference" and the use of self in clinical work? What are the relations of subjectivity to historical-interpretive work, as in Erikson's (1975) discussion of the use of "disciplined subjectivity" in psychohistory? These are samples of the kinds of issues left out of the hard syntheses, but central for a newly developing soft synthesis.

Additional questions suggested by these five components include, What are the relative contributions of theory, research, clinical case experience, and subjective self-awareness to clinical practice? How are theory and research related to historical-interpretive work? To what extent is the value of a theory (such as psychoanalytic theory) determined by its relations to clinical practice, to quantitative-empirical work, to subjective self-understanding, and/or to historical-interpretive work? There is, in short, a whole set of important questions about the relationships between theory, research, applied work, subjectivity, and historical-interpretive work which can only be suggested here, but which have long preoccupied "soft" psychologists, are peripheral to most "hard" psychologists, and may be freshly illuminated with developments coming out of a soft synthesis between psychology and the human–social–historical sciences.

A soft synthesis would draw on a variety of methods, including hermeneutic-interpretive, case study, idiographic, psychobiographical, historical, and narrative methods (Bromley, 1986; Meehl, 1973; Polkinghorne, 1988; Runyan, 1982). The integrative synthesis around this set of problems and methods could also draw on developments in related fields such as philosophy of the social sciences, philosophy of mind and consciousness, principles of other historical sciences, psychohistory, and the philosophy of history (Campbell, 1988; Fiske & Shweder, 1986; Searle, 1983).

One form of this soft synthesis may well be around the study of lives in social-historical contexts. This, however, need not be the only soft synthesis. Just as there are a variety of syntheses at the hard end of psychology, such as cognitive science, neuroscience, and sensory science, so may there be several different syntheses emerging at the soft end of psychology.

At their best, such syntheses can raise new issues, apply novel methods, and have important practical applications, as well as casting fresh light on old problems and pointing out similarities and integrations between previously disparate and unconnected lines of work. Many have spoken in recent years about a renaissance or revitalization of personality psychology (cf. Cantor & Kihlström, 1987; Craik, 1986; Hogan, 1985; Maddi, 1984; Millon, 1984; Pervin, 1990; Tomkins, 1981). A synthesis around the study of lives in social-historical context can be an important contributor both to personality psychology and to the whole softer social–developmental–clinical side of psychology.

VI. CONCLUSION

To summarize, this chapter argued that the structure of personality psychology can usefully be seen as involving four central tasks or objectives, namely, developing general theories of personality, analyzing individual and group differences, studying specific classes of behavior, and developing a better understanding of individual persons. This conceptual framework has the virtue of raising intriguing questions, both theoretical and historical, about the possible and actual relationships between each of these four enterprises. I then briefly sketched the dynamics of "progress" in the study of lives. The next section explored relationships between the study of lives and other lines of work within personality psychology. Finally, I outlined a "hard" to "soft" array of theoretical orientations, objectives, and methods in personality psychology, and suggested the possibility of a soft synthesis around the study of persons and lives.

Advances in theory, in personality measurement, in the causal analysis of personality processes, and in the understanding of individual lives are all important objectives for personality psychology. The challenge is to help clarify relationships between the possibilities and the limitations of theoretical, psychometric, experimental, and life-historical forms of inquiry. Such an understanding of the relationships between these four enterprises can contribute to a better understanding of the structure and history of the field.

One way of viewing the history of personality psychology is in its changing emphases on these four different tracks of inquiry. When personality psychology crystallized as a field in the 1930s with the seminal books by Allport (1937) and Murray (1938), it could be seen as reacting against the sterile formalisms of academic psychophysics, and as an effort to integrate the rigor of academic methods with the understanding of persons and lives. In the turn away from the study of lives in the 1950s and 1960s, there was far greater emphasis on the "hard" traditions of measurement and experimentation, with a decline of interest in the "softer" issues of studying whole persons and in developing general theories of personality. With the current resurgence of interest in the study of persons and lives, there is a need to reexamine the relationships between the array of hard to soft traditions, objectives, and methods. Such reexamination can lead to a more coherent and broadly integrative vision of personality psychology and contribute to the intellectual and institutional revitalization of the field. While much work in recent years has focused on syntheses at the hard end of psychology, such as cognitive science and neuroscience, there are now exciting possibilities for a synthesis at the soft end of psychology around the study of lives in their social, cultural, and historical contexts.

References

Alexander, I. E. (1988). Personality, psychological assessment, and psychobiography. *Journal of Personality, 56*(1), 265–294.

Alexander, I. E. (1990). *Personology: Content and method in personality assessment and psychobiography.* Durham, NC: Duke University Press.

Allport, G. W. (1937). *Personality: A psychological interpretation.* New York: Holt.

Allport, G. W. (1942). *The use of personal documents in psychological science.* New York: Social Science Research Council.

Allport, G. W. (1962). The general and the unique in psychological science. *Journal of Personality, 30,* 405–422.

Allport, G. W. (1965). *Letters from Jenny.* New York: Harcourt, Brace & World.

Almond, G., Chodorow, M., & Pearce, R. (Eds.). (1982). *Progress and its discontents.* Berkeley: University of California Press.

Anderson, J. W. (1981a). The methodology of psychological biography. *Journal of Interdisciplinary History, 11,* 455–475.

Anderson, J. W. (1981b). Psychobiographical methodology: The case of William James. In L. Wheeler (Ed.), *Review of personality and social psychology* (Vol. 2, pp. 245–272). Beverly Hills, CA: Sage.

Anderson, J. W. (1988). Henry A. Murray's early career: A psychobiographical exploration. *Journal of Personality, 56*(1), 139–172.

Barron, F. (1969). *Creative person and creative process.* New York: Holt, Rinehart & Winston.

Bromley, D. B. (1986). *The case-study method in psychology and related disciplines.* Chichester, England: Wiley.

Bullock, A. (1952). *Hitler; A study in tyranny.* New York: Harper.

Campbell, D. T. (1988). *Methodology and epistemology for social science.* Chicago: University of Chicago Press.

Cantor, N., & Kihlström, J. F. (1987). *Personality and social intelligence.* Englewood Cliffs, NJ: Prentice-Hall.

Carlson, R. (1981). Studies in script theory: I. Adult analysis of a childhood nuclear scene. *Journal of Personality and Social Psychology, 40,* 501–510.

Carlson, R. (1988). Exemplary lives: The uses of psychobiography for theory development. *Journal of Personality, 56*(1), 105–138.

Cohler, B. J. (1988). The human studies and the life history: The *Social Service Review* Lecture. *Social Service Review, 62*(4), 552–575.

Cox, C. (1926). *The early mental traits of three hundred geniuses.* Stanford, CA: Stanford University Press.

Craik, K. H. (1986). Personality research methods: An historical perspective. *Journal of Personality, 54*(1), 18–51.

Cronbach, L. J. (1957). The two disciplines of scientific psychology. *American Psychologist, 12,* 671–684.

Cronbach, L. J. (1975). Beyond the two disciplines of scientific psychology. *American Psychologist, 30,* 116–127.

Dollard, J., Doob, L. W., Miller, N. E., Mowrer, O. H., & Sears, R. R. (1939). *Frustration and aggression.* New Haven, CT: Yale University Press.

Dooley, L. (1916). Psychoanalytic studies of genius. *American Journal of Psychology, 27,* 363–416.

Edel, L. (1984). *Writing lives: Principia biographica.* New York: Norton.

Ellenberger, H. F. (1970). *The discovery of the unconscious.* New York: Basic Books.

Elms, A. C. (1972). Allport, Freud, and the clean little boy. *Psychoanalytic Review, 59,* 627–632.

Elms, A. C. (1980). Freud, Irma, Martha: Sex and marriage in the "Dream of Irma's injection." *Psychoanalytic Review, 67,* 83–109.

Elms, A. C. (1981). Skinner's dark year and Walden Two. *American Psychologist, 36,* 470–479.

Elms, A. C. (1987). The personalities of Henry A. Murray. In R. Hogan & W. Jones (Eds.), *Perspectives in personality* (Vol. 2, pp. 1–14). Greenwich, CT: JAI Press.

Elms, A. C. (1988a). Freud as Leonardo: Why the first psychobiography went wrong. *Journal of Personality, 56*(1), 19–40.

Elms, A. C. (1988b, August). *The psychologist as biographer.* Henry A. Murray Award Lecture, American Psychological Association annual convention, Atlanta, GA.

Elms, A. C. (1994). *Uncovering lives: The uneasy alliance of biography and psychology.* New York: Oxford University Press.

Erikson, E. H. (1958). *Young man Luther: A study in psychoanalysis and history.* New York: Norton.

Erikson, E. H. (1969). *Gandhi's truth.* New York: Norton.

Erikson, E. H. (1975). *Life history and the historical moment.* New York: Norton.

Fisher, S., & Greenberg, R. P. (1977). *The scientific credibility of Freud's theories and therapy.* New York: Basic Books.

Fiske, D., & Shweder, R. (Eds.) (1986). *Metatheory in social science: Pluralisms and subjectivities.* Chicago: University of Chicago Press.

Freud, S. (1957). *Leonardo da Vinci and a memory of his childhood.* In J. Strachey (Ed. and Trans.), *The standard edition of the complete psychological works of Sigmund Freud* (Vol. 12, pp. 3–82). London: Hogarth Press. (Original work published 1910)

Freud, S. (1958). *The interpretation of dreams.* In J. Strachey (Ed. and Trans.), *The standard edition of the complete psychological works of Sigmund Freud* (Vols. 4–5, pp. 1–621). London: Hogarth Press. (Original work published 1900)

Gardner, H. (1985). *The mind's new science: A history of the cognitive revolution.* New York: Basic Books.

Gardner, H. (1993). *Creating minds: An anatomy of creativity seen through the lives of Freud, Einstein, Picasso, Stravinsky, Eliot, Graham, and Gandhi.* New York: Basic Books.

Gay, P. (1988). *Freud: A life for our time.* New York: Norton.

George, A. L., & George, J. (1964). *Woodrow Wilson and Colonel House: A personality study.* New York: Dover.

George, J. L., & George, A. L. (1981–1982). Woodrow Wilson and Colonel House: A reply to Weinstein, Anderson, and Link. *Political Science Quarterly, 96,* 641–665.

Gergen, K. J. (1977). Stability, change, and chance in understanding human development. In N. Datan & H. Reese (Eds.), *Life-span developmental psychology: Dialectical perspectives on experimental research.* New York: Academic Press.

Gilmore, W. J. (1984). *Psychohistorical inquiry: A comprehensive research bibliography.* New York: Garland.

Gould, S. J. (1989). *Wonderful life.* New York: Norton.

Griffith, E. (1984). *In her own right: The life of Elizabeth Cady Stanton.* New York: Oxford University Press.

Hall, C. S., & Lindzey, G. (1957). *Theories of personality.* New York: Wiley.

Hall, G. S. (1917). *Jesus, the Christ, in the light of psychology.* Garden City, NY: Doubleday.

Hartshorne, H., & May, M. A. (1928). *Studies in deceit.* New York: Macmillan.

Heidbreder, E. (1933). *Seven psychologies.* New York: Century.

Helson, R. (1984–1985). E. Nisbet's forty-first year: Her life, times and symbolizations of personality growth. *Imagination, Personality, and Cognition, 4,* 53–68.

Hilgard, E. (1987). *Psychology in America: A historical survey.* San Diego, CA: Harcourt Brace Jovanovich.

Hogan, R. W. (1985). Introduction. In R. Hogan & W. Jones (Eds.), *Perspectives in personality* (Vol. 1). Greenwich, CT: JAI Press.

Horner, A. (1968). The evolution of goals in the life of Clarence Darrow. In C. Buhler & F. Massarik (Eds.), *The course of human life.* New York: Springer.

Jones, E. (1953–1957). *The life and work of Sigmund Freud* (Vols. 1–3). New York: Basic Books.

Kanzer, M., & Glenn, J. (Eds.). (1980). *Freud and his patients.* New York: Aronson.

Kinsey, A., Pomeroy, W., & Martin, C. (1948). *Sexual behavior in the human male.* Philadelphia: Saunders.

Kinsey, A., Pomeroy, W., & Martin, C. (1953). *Sexual behavior in the human female.* Philadelphia: Saunders.

Langer, W. C. (1972). *The mind of Adolf Hitler.* New York: Basic Books.

Levy, L. (1970). *Conceptions of personality.* New York: Random House.

Liebert, R. M., & Spiegler, M. D. (1987). *Personality: Strategies and issues* (5th ed.). Chicago: Dorsey Press.

Link, A., et al. (Eds.). (1986). Introduction. In *The papers of Woodrow Wilson* (Vol. 54). Princeton, NJ: Princeton University Press.

Loewenberg, P. (1988). Psychoanalytic models of history: Freud and after. In W. M. Runyan (Ed.), *Psychology and historical interpretation* (pp. 126–156). New York: Oxford University Press.

Mack, J. E. (1971). Psychoanalysis and historical biography. *Journal of the American Psychoanalytic Association, 19,* 143–179.

MacKinnon, D. W. (1978). *In search of human effectiveness: Identifying and developing creativity.* Buffalo, NY: Creative Education Foundation.

Maddi, S. (1984). Personology for the 1980s. In R. Zucker, J. Aronoff, & A. Rabin (Eds.), *Personality and the prediction of behavior* (pp. 7–41), New York: Academic Press.

Maslow, A. (1971). *The farther reaches of human nature.* New York: Viking Press.

McAdams, D. P. (1985). Fantasy and reality in the death of Yukio Mishima. *Biography, 8,* 292–317.

McAdams, D. P. (1990). *The person: An introduction to personality psychology.* San Diego, CA: Harcourt Brace Jovanovich.

McAdams, D., & Ochberg, R. (Eds.). (1988a). *Psychobiography and life narratives.* Durham, NC: Duke University Press.

McAdams, D., & Ochberg, R. (Eds.). (1988b). Psychobiography and life narratives [Special issue]. *Journal of Personality, 56*(1).

McClelland, D. C., Atkinson, J. W., Clark, R. A., & Lowell, E. L. (1953). *The achievement motive.* New York: Appleton-Century-Crofts.

Meehl, P. E. (1973). Why I do not attend case conferences. In Meehl, P. E. (Ed.), *Psychodiagnosis: Selected papers.* Minneapolis: University of Minnesota Press.

Mendelsohn, G. A. (1985). *La Dame aux Camelias* and *La Traviata:* A study of dramatic transformations in the light of biography. In R. W. Hogan & W. Jones (Eds.), *Perspectives in personality* (Vol. 1). Greenwich, CT: JAI Press.

Millon, T. (1984). On the renaissance of personality assessment and personality theory. *Journal of Personality Assessment, 48,* 450–466.

Millon, T., & Klerman, G. (Eds.). (1986). *Contemporary directions in psychopathology.* New York: Guilford Press.

Mischel, W. (1966). Theory and research on the antecedents of self-imposed delay of reward. In B. A. Maher (Ed.), *Progress in experimental personality research* (Vol. 3, pp. 85–132). New York: Academic Press.

Mischel, W. (1968). *Personality and assessment.* New York: Wiley.

Mischel, W. (1981). *Introduction to personality* (3rd ed.). New York: Holt, Rinehart & Winston.

Monte, C. (1987). *Beneath the mask: An introduction to theories of personality.* (3rd ed.). New York: Holt, Rinehart & Winston.

Moraitis, G., & Pollock, G. H. (Eds.). (1987). *Psychoanalytic studies of biography.* New York: International Universities Press.

Murray, H. A., et al. (1938). *Explorations in personality.* New York: Oxford University Press.

Murray, H. A. (1981). *Endeavors in psychology: Selections from the personology of Henry A. Murray* (E. Shneidman, Ed.). Harper & Row.

Newton, P. M. (1984). Samuel Johnson's breakdown and recovery in middle age: A life span developmental approach to mental illness and its cure. *International Review of Psycho-Analysis, 11,* 93–118.

Novarr, D. (1986). *The lines of life: Theories of biography, 1880-1970.* West Lafayette, Ind.: Purdue University Press.

Oliner, S. P., & Oliner, P. M. (1988). *The altruistic personality: Rescuers of Jews in Nazi Europe.* New York: Free Press.

Pervin, L. A. (1980). *Personality: Theory, assessment, and research.* New York: Wiley.

Pervin, L. A. (Ed.). (1990). *Handbook of personality: Theory and research.* New York: Guilford Press.

Peterson, C. (1988). *Personality.* San Diego, CA: Harcourt Brace Jovanovich.

Phares, E. J. (1988). *Introduction to personality* (2nd ed.). Glenview, IL: Scott, Foresman.

Polkinghorne, D. (1988). *Narrative knowing and the human sciences.* Albany: State University of New York Press.

Prince, M. (1912, March 24). [Theodore] Roosevelt as analyzed by the new psychology. *New York Times,* pp. 1–2.

Prince, M. (1915). *The psychology of the Kaiser: A study of his sentiments and his obsession.* Boston: Badger.

Rabin, A. I., Zucker, R., Emmons, R., & Frank, S. (Eds.). (1990). *Studying persons and lives.* New York: Springer.

Roazen, P. (1975). *Freud and his followers.* New York: Knopf.

Rogers, C. R. (1980). Ellen West—and loneliness. In C. R. Rogers, *A way of being.* Boston: Houghton Mifflin.

Runyan, W. M. (1981). Why did Van Gogh cut off his ear? The problem of alternative explanations in psychobiography. *Journal of Personality and Social Psychology, 40,* 1070–1077.

Runyan, W. M. (1982). *Life histories and psychobiography: Explorations in theory and method.* New York: Oxford University Press.

Runyan, W. M. (1983). Idiographic goals and methods in the study of lives. *Journal of Personality, 51,* 413–437.

Runyan, W. M. (Ed.). (1988a). *Psychology and historical interpretation.* New York: Oxford University Press.

Runyan, W. M. (1988b). Progress in psychobiography. *Journal of Personality, 56*(1), 295–326.

Runyan, W. M. (1994). Coming to terms with the life, loves, and work of Henry A. Murray. *Contemporary Psychology, 39*(7), 701–704.

Sartre, J.-P. (1981). *The family idiot: Gustave Flaubert, 1821-1857* (Vol. 1) (C. Cosman, Trans.). Chicago: University of Chicago Press.

Searle, J. (1983). *Intentionality.* Cambridge, England: Cambridge University Press.

Skinner, B. F. (1976). *Particulars of my life.* New York: Knopf.

Skinner, B. F. (1979). *The shaping of a behaviorist.* New York: Knopf.

Skinner, B. F. (1983). *A matter of consequences.* New York: Knopf.

Spotts, J. V., & Shontz, F. C. (1980). *Cocaine users: A representative case approach.* New York: Free Press.

Staub, E. (1980). *Personality: Basic aspects and current research.* Englewood Cliffs, NJ: Prentice-Hall.

Stewart, A. J., Franz, C., & Layton, L. (1988). The changing self: Using personal documents to study lives. *Journal of Personality, 56*(1), 41–74.

Stolorow, R. D., & Atwood, G. E. (1979). *Faces in a cloud: Subjectivity in personality theory.* New York: Aronson.

Strozier, C. (Ed.). (1985). *Self-psychology and the humanities.* New York: Norton.

Strozier, C., & Offer, D. (Eds.). (1985). *The leader: Psychohistorical essays.* New York: Plenum Press.

Sulloway, F. J. (1979). *Freud, biologist of the mind: Beyond the psychoanalytic legend.* New York: Basic Books.

Terman, L. (1917). The intelligence quotient of Francis Galton in childhood. *American Journal of Psychology, 28,* 209–215.

Tomkins, S. S. (1981). The rise, fall and resurrection of the study of personality. *Journal of Mind and Behavior, 2,* 443–452.

Turkat, I. D. (Ed.). (1985). *Behavioral case formulation.* New York: Plenum Press.

Ullmann, L. P., & Krasner, L. I. (Eds.). (1965). *Case studies in behavior modification.* New York: Holt, Rinehart & Winston.

Waite, R. G. L. (1977). *The psychopathic god: Adolf Hitler.* New York: Basic Books.

Watson, J. B. (1913). Psychology as the behaviorist views it. *Psychological Review, 20,* 158–177.

Weinstein, E., Anderson, J., & Link, A. (1978). Woodrow Wilson's political personality: A reappraisal. *Political Science Quarterly, 93,* 585–598.

White, R. W. (1952). *Lives in progress.* New York: Holt, Rinehart & Winston.

White, R. W. (Ed.). (1963). *The study of lives.* New York: Atherton.

White, R. W. (1972). *The enterprise of living.* New York: Holt, Rinehart & Winston.

Wiggins, J. S., Renner, K. E., Clore, G. L., & Rose, R. J. (1976). *Principles of personality.* Reading, MA: Addison-Wesley.

Winter, D. G., & Carlson, L. (1988). Using motive scores in the psychobiographical study of an individual: The case of Richard Nixon. *Journal of Personality, 56*(1), 75–104.

Wittels, F. (1924). *Sigmund Freud: His personality, his teaching, and his school.* New York: Dodd, Mead.

Wolpe, J., & Rachman, S. (1960). Psychoanalytic "evidence": A critique based on Freud's case of Little Hans. *Journal of Nervous and Mental Disease, 131,* 135–148.

PART II

CONCEPTUAL AND MEASUREMENT ISSUES IN PERSONALITY

CHAPTER 3

UNITS OF ANALYSIS FOR THE DESCRIPTION AND EXPLANATION OF PERSONALITY

JOHN A. JOHNSON

PENNSYLVANIA STATE UNIVERSITY, DUBOIS CAMPUS

I. THE NEED FOR UNITS OF ANALYSIS

Every science has a nomenclature that describes and defines its domain of study. Nuclear physicists talk about subatomic particles; chemists analyze molecules and compounds; and evolutionary biologists ponder genes, populations, and species. In what sort of language do psychologists describe and explain personality?

The list of the units of analysis used by personality psychologists is wildly diverse: cognitive styles, complexes, current concerns, dispositions, folk concepts, goals, instincts, interests, motives, needs, personal projects, plans, personal constructs, strivings, sentiments, themas, types, and values are a few (cf. D. M. Buss & Cantor, 1989; Emmons, 1989, this volume, chap. 20). The length and complexity of this list suggest that our problem concerns organizing and simplifying our potpourri of conceptual units rather than choosing among them.

This chapter suggests that the apparent diversity of the proposed units of analysis masks a unity underlying them and that this unity is captured by the term *trait* (Allport, 1937). I begin by examining the meaning of *traits* and suggest that the trait notion is virtually required for a systematic understanding of personality. I then review criticisms of the trait concept and suggest that these criticisms are not always well founded.

Next I distinguish between phenotypic and genotypic traits, and discuss the implication of this distinction for the twin tasks of description versus explanation and for the validity of self-assessments versus observer assessments. This leads to the view that, in the process of assessment, the genotypic/phenotypic distinction disappears. Finally, I consider whether a special unit of analysis is necessary to describe the uniqueness of individuals, and whether type language might be as useful as trait language.

II. TRAITS AS UNITS OF ANALYSIS

A. The Meaning of the Trait Concept

Traits are consistent patterns of thoughts, feelings, or actions that distinguish people from one another. The reader should note three features of the foregoing definition. First, traits can refer to thoughts, feelings, *or* behavior. This point is often overlooked by psychologists who define personality only in terms of consistent behaviors. Second, trait ascription invariably involves comparisons between people. If I say that Jones is *obsessive-compulsive,* I mean that he seems to have more intrusive thoughts and guilt feelings and demonstrates more ritualistic behavior than people in general. Third, for traits to distinguish people from one another, they must display some distinctive *consistency.* If Jones's obsessesive experiences and compulsive activities diminish to the point that they are no more frequent than those of the general population, then they would no longer distinguish Jones from people in general.

Traits seem to be required for science of personality, because any science involves detecting and explaining consistent patterns (Hanson, 1958). Imagine trying to construct a science of chemistry if elements and compounds did not possess stable properties—if sodium chloride were only sometimes water soluable. If people had no stable properties (i.e., traits), they could not be studied scientifically.

B. The Situationist Challenge to the Trait Concept

Although a science of personality seems to depend on studying consistencies, the existence of traits has been questioned from World War I to the present (see Kenrick & Funder, 1988, for a review). It is primarily writers with a behaviorist orientation who doubt the existence of traits. They claim that behavior depends on social contexts and that consistencies are an artifact of a person being in similar situations (Ross, 1977). Stimulus–response behaviorism (Hendrick, 1977) seeks to identify stable S → R laws rather than stable properties of persons.

The claim that behavior depends on situational cues seems congruent with common sense. We behave differently at wedding receptions and funerals. We behave differently in the different roles we play, for example, as employee, spouse, or parent. These examples from everyday experience are consistent with the view that social situations determine our behavior. Behaviorists have confirmed this common sense observation countless times in their laboratories, where they show that people's behavior responds to experimental treatments or manipulations (A. H. Buss, 1989). As further evidence for the power of situations, trait critics cite Mischel's (1968) claim that personality test scores (which presumably reflect traits) seldom correlate higher than .30 with behavioral criteria.

C. Responses to the Situationist Challenge

Despite the intuitive appeal of the behaviorist argument, their demonstrations fail to disprove the existence of traits for five reasons.

1. Reliable Situational Influence Requires an Enduring Capacity to Be Influenced

First, if situations reliably control behavior, then people must have a capacity to respond to situational cues, that is, the trait of being responsive to situations. This point has been recognized even by the most vocal critics of traits (e.g., Ross, 1977, p. 176): "For instance, in accounting for Jack's purchase of a house the 'situational' explanation (i.e., 'because *it* was so secluded') implies a disposition on the part of this particular actor to favor seclusion."

2. Individuals Respond Differently to the Same Situation

Second, even in the most (allegedly) powerful situations, such as the Asch perceptual conformity paradigm, people's responses to the situation will differ as a function of personality (Barron, 1953). This point has also been acknowledged by trait critics (Ross & Nisbett, 1992).

3. Having a Trait Means Reacting Consistently to the Same Situation, Not Different Situations

Third, the fact that a person is inconsistent across *different* situations is completely irrelevant to the validity of the trait concept. This point is often overlooked even by trait defenders (e.g., Kenrick & Funder, 1988), who state that traits imply "*cross-situational* consistency." I regard the issue of cross-situational consistency as a red herring. Salt need not dissolve in benzene before we describe it as water soluable; likewise, persons need not exhibit identical behaviors in different environments before we can say they have traits. The trait concept implies consistent reactions to *similar* situations over time, not consistent reactions *across* different situations. Being characterized by a trait automatically implies the relevant type of situation; for example, *cooperative* means consistently complying *with reasonable requests* (Alston, 1975), not indiscriminately complying with others' wishes on every occasion.

4. Having a Trait Does Not Mean Your Reactions Are Absolutely Consistent

Fourth, for behavior to be consistent across time (temporal continuity) it need not be identical in *every* relevant situation. For example, a *lascivious* person takes advantage of opportunities for sex more often than the average person, but does not attempt to copulate with every person he or she meets (Johnson, 1993). This point is missed by those who criticize trait measures for not predicting behavior in a single experimental situation.[1] Proponents of traits never claimed that their measures could do this. Rather, trait measures predict trends in behavior over time (Epstein, 1983). A trait score is like a batting average. Knowing that a baseball player hits .300 does not allow you to predict what he or she will do in a particular at-bat, but does predict his or her performance over the course of a season.

5. *Behavioral Inconsistency Does Not Rule Out Inner Consistency*

Fifth, the lack of consistency in behavior over time does not rule out the existence of emotional or cognitive traits. An emotional trait, for example, may be rarely expressed because of conflicts with other emotional traits. A person might consistently desire to attend parties, but might do so infrequently due to a stronger consistent desire to work (Alston, 1975). Lack of opportunity can also prevent the expression of emotional and cognitive traits. A courageous person—that is, someone who could certainly overcome fear and act decisively in an emergency—may rarely be faced with emergencies in which he or she could actually be heroic. Cognitive personality traits (e.g., persistently attending to details) likewise might not be detected unless a person is given the opportunity to demonstrate the trait. Finally, Alston (1975) also points out that needs may be (like hunger) cyclical.

D. Phenotypic versus Genotypic Traits

Two forms of traits have been traditionally distinguished (Allport, 1937; MacKinnon, 1941): outer traits that can be directly observed (behavioral traits) and inner traits (emotional and cognitive traits) that must be inferred. Meehl (1956) borrowed from biology the terms *phenotypic* and *genotypic* to distinguish the two types of traits. Others (Weimer, 1974; Wiggins, this volume, chap. 4) use a linguistic metaphor. Behavioral traits are analagous to the surface structure of a sentence whose meaning is indeterminate, whereas inner traits represent the intention or deep structure that disambiguates (explains) the meaning of behavior.

Two common assumptions about the two types of traits are worth noting. The first concerns the view that outer traits are descriptions of behavior that need explanation, whereas inner traits are the causes or reasons that explain the outer traits (Alston, 1975; Johnson, 1990a; Wiggins & Trapnell, this volume, chap. 28). Second, observers are assumed to have privileged access to outer traits, and actors to inner traits. This access, in turn, is assumed to affect the validity of observer

---

[1] Trait measures can also fail to predict behavior because they lack reliability or validity (Block, 1977). When reliable, valid measures are used, Mischel's alleged .30 ceiling is easily broken (Hogan, DeSoto, & Solano, 1977).

ratings versus self-ratings of the two types of traits. Although both assumptions have merit, they are only partially correct, as I argue below.

E. Traits as Descriptions and as Explanations

To explain behavior in terms of traits—e.g., Joe hit Fred *because* Joe is aggressive—is sometimes criticized as description rather than a genuine explanation (Weimer, 1984). Trait critics often note the apparent circularity in statements such as "He acted aggressively because he is [behaviorally] aggressive" (Rholes, Newman, & Ruble, 1990, p. 371). However, to explain a *single* behavioral act as an exemplification of a behavioral trait is a valid account of an act (Wiggins, this volume, chap. 4)[2]. When I say that Joe hit Fred because Joe is an aggressive person, this implies that Joe's behavior is not unusual for him and therefore requires no further explanation.[3] Many nonscientists are satisfied with explanations such as "that's typical" or "that's his or her nature" (Young, 1975). People generally seek deeper explanations only for behaviors that are out of character or unusual.

Psychologists, on the other hand, also want to explain normal behavioral traits. One approach to this is to hypothesize inner emotional and cognitive traits that generate the behavioral traits. In many accounts, these inner traits form part of the basic level of theoretical explanation, as illustrated in the following (see Weimer, 1984):

behavioral act, "Joe hit Fred"	fact	explained nonexplainer
↑	↑	↑
behavioral trait, aggressiveness	law	explained explainer
↑	↑	↑
inner trait, aggressive feelings	theory	nonexplained explainer

In the Weimer (1984) model, "explained nonexplainers" are single events that require an explanation but themselves explain nothing. Isolated behavioral acts fit this category. "Explained explainers" are empirical regularities or laws used to explain single events, but require an explanation themselves. Common behavioral traits fall into this category. "Nonexplained explainers" are metatheoretical assumptions about nonverifiable, structural entities that explain empirical laws but are themselves beyond explanation. Unobservable, psychic structures represent a type of metatheoretical primitive.

The notion that emotional and cognitive traits underlie and explain behavioral traits is actually common sensical and "familiar to all of us since childhood" (Alston,

---

[2] Behavioral traits can also be invoked to help explain the reactions of an audience to the actor, that is, as part of a social-psychological explanation. For example, the poor morale and unproductivity of a team might be attributed to the ineffective behavioral traits of the leader.

[3] Alternatively, what I might really mean when I say, "Joe hit Fred because Joe is an aggressive person," is that Joe has hostile, aggressive urges or feelings. If this is the case, I am invoking "aggressive" as a motivational concept rather than a behavioral trait.

1975, p 24). An example from Johnson (1990a) illustrates this. Suppose that Mary, a therapist, consistently treats her clients in an empathic manner. She uses reflective listening to promote accurate understanding, appears attentive and interested in her clients' problems, and often reassures and supports them. The trait *empathic* aptly describes her counseling style. Why is Mary consistently empathic?

A common sense explanation would refer to Mary's desires (emotional traits) and beliefs (cognitive traits). Presumably, Mary wants to promote her clients' psychological well-being. There are many ways to say this: Mary *desires* their well-being; she *values* their well-being; she has established their well-being as a *goal.* The precise term is unimportant—what counts is that Mary is motivated to promote her clients' well-being. Being motivated to achieve goals involves emotional processes (see Averill, this volume, chap. 21). Promoting the well-being of her clients makes Mary feel good whereas failing to achieve this goal would make her feel bad.

Mary's motives, desires, or goals provide only half of the explanation, however. We also need to know about her beliefs concerning how she can achieve her goals. Mary believes that treating her clients empathically will have positive outcomes for them. In short, Mary behaves empathically because (a) she wants to promote the well-being of her clients, and (b) believes that behaving empathically will help her enhance their well-being.

Should this seem too simple, I might note that behavioral traits often serve several goals simultaneously. Mary's empathic behavior may satisfy not only her need to promote her clients' well-being, but also her need to be liked and admired by her clients. She might also believe that her empathic style will lead to a good performance evaluation and a larger paycheck.

Furthermore, some behavioral traits may be habits that once promoted goals but now are no longer useful. Or, if the depth psychologists are correct, behavioral traits may express unconscious desires. Depth psychologists also suggest that conflicting motives can become fused and lead to a compromise activity not clearly linked to any one goal. Ethologists talk about *displacement activities,* (e.g., eating, self-grooming) that serve to relieve tension when conflicting instincts arise. Thus, there is not always a simple one-to-one correspondence between behavioral traits and underlying motivational or cognitive traits.

Even if one could identify all of the relevant motives and beliefs underlying a behavioral trait, some would regard *this* explanation as incomplete. One might further inquire into the origin of the motives and beliefs. *Why* does Mary want to be a therapist rather than a truck driver? How did she conclude that Rogerian therapy is more effective than Freudian therapy? The answers to these questions can be found in personality development (e.g., Eder & Mangelsdorf, this volume, chap. 9) and in evolutionary psychology (e.g., D. Buss, this volume, chap. 13; A. Buss, this volume, chap. 14). Developmental and evolutionary explanations complement intentional explanations (Wakefield, 1989).

Some psychologists feel that it is insufficient to explain behavioral traits in terms of goals and beliefs for yet another reason: "Scientific" explanations should transcend common sense (McCrae, Costa, & Piedmont, 1993). Theoretical physics is often presented as a science that contradicts our common sense assumptions about the solidity of objects and the absolute nature of time and space. From this perspective, the most important concepts in personality psychology are not well represented in ordinary language. McCrae (1990) proposes *openness to experience* as an example of such a concept.

Hofstee, de Raad, and Goldberg (1992) warn us, however, about the dangers of stepping out of the area of common language: "There is nothing against this advice, as long as the pertinent outcomes do not have to be communicated in words" (p. 162). Cattell transcended ordinary language with terms such as Harria, Presemsia, Alaxia, and Protension; ultimately these terms had to be translated into common trait language to be useful to practitioners (IPAT Staff, 1979).

In summary, most psychologists regard "outer" (behavioral) traits as descriptions that need explanation, and they assume that "inner" (emotional and cognitive) traits generate and therefore explain outer traits. Behavioral traits or consistencies may be determined by the interaction of several emotional and cognitive traits. Some personality psychologists, in order to provide deeper explanations of inner traits, inquire into their genetic and physiological bases, developmental histories, and roots in the evolution of the human species. Whether a scientific conception of traits needs to go beyond ordinary trait language is a matter of current debate.

III. Issues in the Assessment of Traits

A. Genotypic and Phenotypic Traits from the Perspective of the Self and Others

Self-ratings of traits correlate substantially (rs in the .4–.6 range—see Johnson, 1994) with ratings of the same trait made by others. Nonetheless, in individual cases, self-ratings sometimes disagree with ratings by other persons. This raises an interesting issue: When self-ratings disagree with ratings by others, whom are we to believe? The chapters in this handbook by Funder and Colvin (chap. 24) and Robins and John (chap. 25) discuss this issue in some detail. This section addresses the accuracy of ratings of genotypic versus phenotypic traits made by the self and others.

1. Actors Can Directly Experience Their Own Inner Traits, but Observers Must Infer Others' Inner Traits

The outer/inner trait distinction is often assumed to affect the validity of personality assessment by self-ratings versus ratings by other persons. Self-assessment of genotypic traits is potentially more valid than other-assessment of these traits because people may directly experience their own inner traits whereas observers must infer them from verbal reports and nonverbal behavior. For example, anxious individuals should be aware of their anxiety level, whereas observers must infer their anxiety from signs such as a furrowed brow, sweaty palms, tremors, and hesitant speech style. Kenrick and Stringfield (1980) report that personality scores are more valid—

i.e., self-ratings correlate more highly with other ratings—for individuals who openly express their traits (see also Funder & Colvin, this volume, chap. 24). Funder and Dobroth (1987) found interjudge agreement to be higher for traits related to be highly visible.

2. Observers Can Directly Experience Others' Outer Traits, but Actors Must Infer Their Own Outer Traits

Individuals may have direct access to their inner traits, but they cannot directly observe their own behavior. This implies that external observers may provide a more valid assessment of a person's phenotypic traits. For example, people are typically poor judges of how charming they are, but this outer trait is obvious to an observer. Cooley's (1902) concept of the "looking glass self" suggests that our understanding of our own personality is determined by the feedback reflected from others around us, at least until we are able to take the perspective of others to imagine how we appear to them (Mead, 1934). Whether we listen to a real or an imagined audience, our knowledge of our outer traits is indirect and inferential.

3. Defensiveness Hinders Accurate Self-Assessment

Although the relationship between outer/inner traits and the validity of self- and other-assessment may seem intuitively compelling, it is incomplete. Individuals may be unaware, mistaken, or self-deceived about their inner traits (Averill, this volume, chap. 21; Paulhus & Reid, 1991; Paulhus, Fridhandler, & Hayes, this volume, chap. 22; Robins & John, this volume, chap. 25). Aspects of personality that are unknown to the individual but known to others are found in the "blind area" of the Johari window (named after Joe Luft and Harry Ingram; see Luft, 1966). The Johari window is illustrated in Figure 1. In the case of blind spots, observers provide more accurate assessments of inner personality than the person observed.

Individuals may also be reluctant to describe all their inner traits as they actually perceive them, preferring instead to describe traits that they would like others to believe they have. Paulhus and Reid (1991) call this process impression management. Inner traits that are not described to others are the "secret area" of the Johari window.

Known to Self   Unknown to Self

	Known to Self	Unknown to Self
Known to Others	Public Area	Blind Area
Unknown to Others	Secret Area	Unconscious Area

FIGURE 1   The Johari window.

The Johari window and Paulhus' research on social desirability responding suggest that self-reports of inner traits *may* be more accurate than observer assessments, but in the case of self-deception the converse is true. We may also have "secret areas" that we choose not to reveal.

4. Self-Observer Agreement Requires a Common Understanding of Language

Accurate knowledge of one's inner traits and a willingness to share this with others are still insufficient to ensure agreement between self-description and description of the self provided by others. Full agreement also depends on the actor and observer using the same semantic and pragmatic rules for communication. For example, a person rating himself or herself for *thoughtfulness* will provide an inappropriate rating if he or she believes *thoughtful* to mean *considerate* but the rater believes the term means *contemplative*. Misunderstandings of the meaning of trait terms occur more often than researchers may realize (Goldberg & Kilkowski, 1985).

When we assess personality with questionnaires rather than rating scales, we encounter pragmatic as well as semantic misunderstandings. Pragmatic rules are implicit social conventions about meaning that can vary across subcultures who share the same language. The impact of pragmatics on measurement validity is virtually unexplored, but I can cite two illustrations here.

First, Johnson (1997) notes that item 77 on the California Psychological Inventory (CPI; Gough, 1987), "When I get bored I like to stir up some excitement," is a phrase used by delinquents who relieve their boredom by doing something illegal. For this reason, Johnson (1997) interprets the item as reflecting (lack of) conscientiousness. McCrae et al. (1993) apparently prefered a more literal interpretation and they judged the item to reflect extraversion. We do not know how a typical respondent interprets this item.

We do know that people who focus on the narrow, literal meaning of words often miss the broader social implications of personality items and therefore respond inappropriately (Johnson, 1993). A punctual and conscientious person who answers "false" to the item, "I am never late to appointments," because he or she thinks never means literally *never* has missed the point of the item. Pragmatic rules—i.e., our social conventions of language use—allow punctual people to say, "I am never late," because we know this really means, "I am a conscientious person who is rarely late." Similarly, pragmatic rules suggest that an intellectual person should answer "true" to CPI item 152, "I read at least ten books a year," even if he or she reads only three books a year.

The point of these examples of pragmatic ambiguity is as follows. People might be perfectly aware of their actual dispositions to be delinquent, extraverted, conscientious, intellectual, and so forth, and also be quite willing to acknowledge these dispositions through the items discussed above. Nonetheless, their responses to these items will convey valid information only when the test taker and test constructor interpret the item response in the same way.

5. *Observer Ratings of Outer Traits Are Valid Almost by Definition*

Whereas observer ratings of another person's inner traits are only rarely more valid than self-ratings, observer ratings of outer traits are usually more accurate than self-ratings of outer traits. An exception might be a case where an observer is prejudiced against the person he or she is rating. But on the whole, outer traits are—almost by definition—whatever impressions an actor makes on observers. If an individual is perceived by others as a loudmouth, then by definition that person is a loudmouth. This implies that observer ratings constitute an "ultimate criterion" of sorts for validating self-reports of outer traits (Hofstee, 1994).

Outer traits are social constructions of reality (Berger & Luckmann, 1966). From a social constructivist perspective, the "actual" traits that are assigned to a person are whatever the majority of observers believe should be assigned. Hogan and Briggs (1986) refer to the social consensus as a person's *reputation.* A person's view of his/her own reputation may be as correct but not more correct than his/her reputation as constructed by the social group.

To summarize, self-ratings of one's inner traits tend to be more valid than observer ratings of those traits except in cases of blind areas (self-deception) or secret areas (impression management). Conversely, observer ratings of one's outer traits (reputation) are almost always more valid than self-ratings of outer traits. People must have highly developed perspective-taking skills to describe accurately the way they appear to others (Mills & Hogan, 1978).

The fact that individuals may not provide valid self-ratings in the blind and secret areas presents problems for those of us who wish to assess personality with questionnaires and self-rating scales. How does one address this problem?

One possible solution is to identify subtle items, that is, items with less-than-obvious psychological significance or implications. Different responses to subtle items covary empirically with individual differences along a trait dimension for reasons unknown to the test taker and sometimes even the test constructor. Subtle items can be found through brute, dust-bowl empiricism. Unfortunately, research has demonstrated that subtle items are almost invariably not valid (Johnson, 1993). Valid self-assessment of blind and secret areas remains a challenge for personality researchers who are attempting to build better mousetraps.

6. *Controversy Surrounds the Assessment of Unconscious Traits*

The Johari window contains one more pane we have not discussed: the unconscious area. Unconscious traits are the foundation of psychoanalytic theories, but are often ignored by mainstream personality psychologists working within the cognitive Zeitgeist (Hogan, 1979; Weinberger & McClelland, 1990). Some might argue that unconscious traits, because they are unseen by the self or others, are not amenable to scientific study. Others would counter that unconscious traits are like nuclear particles. We cannot see these particles, but they leave traces in cloud chambers and certainly have a palpable impact on us. Unconscious traits similarly cannot be directly observed, but leave traces of their activity and have an impact on us. The question is whether we can devise the equivalent of a cloud chamber or Geiger counter to assess unconscious traits.

Although clinicians often rely on their own intuition to access unconscious traits (Reik, 1948), some modern researchers claim that projective tests constitute a cloud chamber for the unconscious. Projective tests are simply stimuli (inkblots, photographs, sentence fragments) with open-ended response options. Rather than responding true or false, respondents can say or write as little or as much as they like. Their responses are then scored according to a set of rules to yield an evaluation of the respondent's level on various unconscious needs or motives.

An influential review paper by Entwistle (1972) cast serious doubts on the reliability and validity of projective tests. Undaunted, McClelland and his colleagues (McClelland, 1980; Weinberger & McClelland, 1990) marshalled further evidence for the reliability, validity, and utility of projective measures. McClelland also replaced the usual psychoanalytic framework for projective testing with an ethological framework. Summarizing research on projective measures in applied settings, Hogan (1991) concluded that these tests are about as valid as objective measures.

Scores on projective tests tend not to correlate with scores on objective tests measuring the same construct (Weinberger & McClelland, 1990). This finding led McClelland (1980) to assert that projective and objective tests measure two different kinds of traits. Specifically, he suggested that projective tests tap a more primitive, biologically based, affect-laden type of trait, whereas questionnaires assess a more cognitive, symbolic type of trait. The Weinberger and McClelland (1990) chapter reviews studies indicating that projective and objective measures predict different types of activities.

Is McClelland correct to argue that qualitatively different kinds of traits exist and that we need different kinds of measures to assess these types of traits? That is the question addressed next.

B. Trait Measurement through Questionnaires

1. Do Different Questionnaires Measure Different Kinds of Traits?

The Edwards Personal Preference Schedule (EPPS; Edwards, 1959) purports to measure Murray's needs, Gough's (1987) CPI allegedly assesses "folk concepts," the Guilford–Zimmerman Temperament Inventory (GZTS; Guilford, Zimmerman, & Guilford, 1976) obviously aims to measure temperaments, and the Myers–Briggs Type Indicator (MBTI; Myers & McCaulley, 1985) is supposed to capture the cognitive functions in Jung's psychological types. Do these four tests actually measure four different kinds of traits?

According to McCrae and Costa (1989; McCrae, 1989; McCrae et al., 1993; Piedmont, McCrae, & Costa, 1992) the answer to this question is clearly no. McCrae and Costa have demonstrated that the scales on these inventories assess the same five traits measured by their own NEO-PI (Costa & McCrae, 1992): Neuroticism, Extraversion, Openness to Experience, Agreeableness, and Conscientiousness. In fact, McCrae and Costa have ingeniously and systematically demonstrated that virtually every major inventory assesses some or all of the "Big Five" or Five-Factor Model (FFM) traits.

A look at actual items on these inventories also suggests that they are *not* measuring different kinds of traits. Consider the following items: "I like to plan and organize the details of any work that I have to undertake." "I always see to it that my work is carefully planned and organized." "You like work that requires considerable attention to details." "When you start a big project that is due in a week, do you (a) take time to list the separate things to be done and the order of doing them, or (b) plunge in?" "I like to follow a strict routine in my work." Can you tell which item measures a need, which measures a folk concept, and which measures a cognitive style?

All the items indicate a planful and serious-minded approach to work. But anyone unfamiliar with these inventories would likely be unable to tell that they came from the EPPS, CPI, GZTS, MBTI, and NEO-PI, respectively. The empirical and semantic overlap in the items across these instruments does not imply that needs, folk concepts, temperaments, and cognitive styles are identical *concepts*. Nonetheless, the *questionnaires* seem to be measuring similar, if not identical, constructs.[4] It the items reflect patterns of thoughts, feelings, or actions, one might as well use the generic term *trait* to describe what they measure.

I think it is pointless to worry about conceptual distinctions between trait constructs if they are measured in identical ways or if scores from different measures behave in similar ways (e.g., predict the same criteria equally well). Kilkowski (1975), for example, provides an interesting six-page analysis of the conceptual differences between Allport's traits and Murrays' needs. But he does not describe different methods for measuring traits and needs.

2. Do Questionnaires Measure Phenotypic or Genotypic Traits?

A closer look at the five items listed above shows that two refer to actual planful *behavior* and three refer to a *liking* for organization. Might it be important to distinguish phenotypic (outer behavioral) items from genotypic (inner cognitive or emotional) items? Angleitner, John, and Löhr (1986) and Werner and Pervin (1986) report that different inventories contain different proportions of phenotypic and genotypic items. They then assert that item characteristics may affect test validity,

---

[4] Emmons (this volume, chap. 20) also has hinted at the futility of trying to distinguish allegedly different goal constructs from each other. As he points out, the statements in Table 2 of his chapter representing four purportedly different goal constructs—current concerns, personal projects, life tasks, and personal strivings—are very similar.

but neither research team examined whether phenotypic or genotypic items were superior for predicting nontest criteria.

Johnson (1993a) examined the ability of phenotypic and genotypic items on the CPI to predict acquaintance ratings. He found that phenotypic items predicted extraversion ratings better than genotypic items. In domains other than extraversion, however, reference to outer or inner traits was not related to validity. I think genotypic versus phenotypic wording is unrelated to validity because genotypic tendencies normally find phenotypic expression. For example, people who want to get ahead eventually act in ambitious ways; conversely, people who act ambitiously normally have ambitious motives. Thus, to endorse the genotypic item, "I have a strong desire to be a success in the world," is tantamount to endorsing the phenotypic item, "I do whatever I can to get ahead" (and vice versa).

Because personality questionnaires simultaneously assess phenotypic and genotypic traits, I have found it useful to think about personality in terms of a trait construct that incorporates both levels of personality: *self-presentational style.* Self-presentations are any behaviors (including responses to questionnaire items) guided by inner traits that create impressions in others. I believe that all noncognitive questionnaires assess self-presentational styles (Johnson, 1981; Mills & Hogan, 1978). It does not matter whether the test is intended to measure moral reasoning (Johnson & Hogan, 1981a), vocational interests (Johnson & Hogan, 1981b), attitudes (Johnson, Hogan, Zonderman, Callens, & Rogolsky, 1981), or philosophical world views (Johnson, Germer, Efran, & Overton, 1988); responses to these various inventories create a distinctive impression on those who see the responses.

Self-presentation of traits that are already well known to everyone (the public area of the Johari window) is direct and straightforward (Wolfe, 1993). In the public area of personality one can take item responses at face value. If someone endorses the item, "I am rarely late for appointments," we can accept that this person is punctual. I agree with Wolfe (1993) that personality assessment via questionnaires proceeds in a straightforward fashion in most cases, even in contexts such as personnel selection (Hogan, 1991).

Nonetheless, self-presentation on questionnaires—like social behavior in everyday life—contains both conscious, intentional and unconscious, unintentional elements. This implies that we cannot *always* take item responses at their face value; ultimately we must determine, in an empirical fashion, what an item response means (Meehl, 1945). In particular, we cannot trust item content when blind, unconscious, or secret aspects of personality are being assessed.

Clearly, persons cannot disclose blind or unconscious traits by endorsing items whose content describes the trait. An overly critical person who is unaware that he or she is overly critical cannot validly respond to an item such as "I am overly critical." What is needed is an item that allows an observer to infer the trait. A more oblique item, such as "Spare the rod and spoil the child," might be endorsed by overly critical but unaware individuals. In everyday interactions, perceptive observers can make inferences about blind or unconscious areas from another person's slips of the tongue or body language; in questionnaires we depend upon nonobvious empirical correlates of personality items to reveal information beyond the manifest content of the item.[5]

During normal interaction we know that people do not always tell the truth. We may, therefore, watch for signs of dissembling such as laughing nervously, averting the eyes, and touching one's face. Questionnaire items do not give us the nonverbal cues to detect dissembling, but over the years researchers have developed various techniques for detecting intentional misrepresentation. Items on dissembling keys often contain "unlikely virtues" (see Gough, 1987; Tellegen, in press)—they describe behaviors that are socially desirable but unlikely to be literally true (e.g., "I have never told a lie"). Interpreting these dissembling scales is problematic, however, because people exaggerate their virtues in everyday life as well as on questionnaires, and unlikely virtue scales predict nontest behavior (Johnson, 1990b).

This section has argued that all personality *questionnaires* measure a trait I call self-presentational style. Do other assessment modes such as cognitive tests (Emmons, this volume, chap. 20) and projective tests also measure self-presentational style? I believe so. Although the format of cognitive tests differs from questionnaires, I believe that persons who endorse statements such as those found in Table 2 of Emmons's (this volume, chap. 20) chapter will create a distinctive impression on others. Whether scores from the measures of cognitive style and needs are empirically distinguishable from each other and from ordinary personality questionnaire scores remains to be seen.

I am less certain about projective tests. Gough (1948) long ago argued that responding to projective tests involves self-presentation. More recently, however, Weinberger and McClelland (1990) have argued that scores on projective tests are uncorrelated with scores on objective tests because responses to the two types of tests are generated from two different parts of the brain. I think it is important to link units of personality analysis to neurophysiology, but I also think much more data will be required to forge this link. Until then I will stand by my view that responses to all forms of personality assessment involve self-presentation.

IV. ALTERNATIVES TO TRAITS

A. Units for Capturing Uniqueness

Because each person is obviously unique, psychologists occasionally suggest that we should use special units of analysis designed to capture the uniqueness of individual personality. This position, called the *idiographic* approach, contrasts with the *nomothetic* view that we should compare individuals with a common set of units.

I believe that the idiographic–nomothetic issue concerns how detailed our descriptions are rather than what kind of units we use to describe personality.

---

[5] Sadly, however, the track record for subtle items is very poor (Johnson, 1993b). We simply have not been very successful at designing subtle but valid items.

Ordinary traits are perfectly capable of describing what is unique about us. Consider the definition of traits as patterns of consistent thoughts, feelings, or actions *that distinguish persons from one another.* Traits, *by definition,* describe how we differ from one another, and the sum of these differences defines our uniqueness.

I think the real objection of idiographic psychologists to nomothetic trait description is that a limited number of trait dimensions (e.g., the Big Five; see Section III.B.1) fail to capture the richness and complexity of a unique person. Indeed, the Big Five, even broken down into six facets each (Costa & McCrae, 1992), cannot describe *everything* about someone's personality. But to think that the Five-Factor Model or any other model of personality can completely describe a person is to misunderstand models in science (Holt 1962; Rosenblueth & Wiener, 1945). A useful model is, by definition, a simplification: it retains only the *important* features of the infinitely complex domain it represents (Eckhardt, 1979). The precise number of important traits is still a matter of debate, but we cannot expect any of our limited models to capture every detail about personality.

B. Types versus Traits

One final possible unit of analysis in the study of personality is the *type* construct. The notion of personality types is nearly as complex as personality traits, and I will not examine all of these complexities. Grant Dahlstrom (1972) has written a definitive monograph on the meaning of type. I also recommend articles by Gangestad and Snyder (1985, 1991) and by Paul Meehl (1992). Rather than reviewing these works, I will discuss two properties of types that are most often cited as distinguishing types from traits: their holistic character and their discrete character. To anticipate my conclusion, I believe that, in practice, the trait and type concepts are actually almost indistinguishable.

1. Are Types Holistic?

In previous writings, I have stressed the holistic nature of the type concept (Hogan & Johnson, 1981; Johnson & Ostendorf, 1993). I conceptualized types as constellations or patterns of traits that naturally co-occured in persons. My metaphor for a type was a chemical compound composed of simpler elements. Types, like compounds, possess *emergent* properties, that is, properties not found in the traits (elements) taken by themselves—e.g., hydrogen and oxygen do not resemble water. If types have emergent properties, then the holistic addage, "the whole is more than the sum of its parts," applies.

In an important paper, Mendelsohn, Weiss, and Feimer (1982; see also Weiss, Mendelsohn, & Feimer, 1982) provide a persuasive empirical and conceptual argument against the holistic conception of types. If their argument is correct, and it seems to be, properties of types can be derived from an understanding of the properties of the traits that make up the type, not from an emergent configuration of trait properties. For example, the type notion "extravert" can be broken down into the traits of gregariousness, impulsivity, and excitement-seeking, and all that is predictable about extraverts can be traced to these traits. And so on for all the other type concepts.

If type concepts are not holistic and we reconceptualize them as collections (rather than configurations) of traits, types become nearly synonymous with *broad traits*. Consider the "Big Five" traits assessed by Costa and McCrae's (1992) NEO-PI; each trait is decomposed into narrower facets. These facets can be further decomposed into more specific thoughts, feelings, and behaviors described by individual items. So perhaps my metaphor that contrasts types as compounds with traits as elements is misleading. It may be more accurate to say that types and traits vary on a continuum of breadth.

2. Are Types Discrete?

The second alleged difference between types and traits is that types are discrete or discontinuous, whereas traits exist along a continuum of values. This may be true at a conceptual level, but at the level of assessment and application, this distinction vanishes (Hofstee & de Raad, 1992). To apply typologies in a continuous manner, one need only describe a person's degree of resemblance (on as finely a graded a scale as one desires) to as many type constructs as one desires.

3. But Are Traits Continuous?

At a conceptual level, traits exist along a continuum of values. However, at the level of measurement, a person's score on a trait questionnaire does not necessarily indicate the degree or amount of the trait possessed. In the words of Meehl and Hathaway (1946), "simply counting how many responses . . . have been made seems to be very crude; . . . [our mathematical scaling procedures] should not mislead us into supposing that we are doing anything very close to what the physicist does when he cumulates centimeters" (p. 557).

In actuality, the number of keyed responses endorsed by a person yields a probability statement about whether the positive or negative pole of the trait concept applies to him or her. This point is most clearly seen in the case of scales constructed empirically by contrasting the responses of two criterion groups (e.g., schizophrenics versus normals). If one has a very high score, it becomes more probable that we should apply the (type!) label "schizophrenic." But a score at the midpoint does not necessarily mean that the person is moderately schizophrenic. This may be true, but technically an average score means that the probability of correctly labeling the person (as normal or schizophrenic) approaches zero. Average scores on scales constructed by rational means or internal consistency are also ambiguous. An average score on a rationally constructed scale of, say, sociability may indicate either (a) a moderate amount of sociability or (b) uncertainty about the applicability of the labels "unsociable" or "sociable" (see Baumeister & Tice, 1988).

In practice, personality test users often convert trait scores into type categories. And, contrary to popular belief, one can do this without losing much information.

Hofstee and de Raad (1992) explain:

> An optimistic estimate of the proportion of true trait variance of a personality scale, after subtraction of both unreliable and method variance, is 0.5, giving a standard error of measurement of 0.7. So, a standard score would have to be below −1.4 or over +1.4 to be significantly ($p = .05$) different from 0. To trichotomize a population into extraverts, introverts, and neither accordingly would be quite realistic in view of the large error of measurement. (p. 62)

Real-world decisions about persons are almost always binary (yes–no) or categorical (friend–foe). This means that trait scores are usually transformed into categorical terms. Consider a programmer's task of deciding whether a particular personality description should be triggered in a computer-generated personality report (Johnson, 1996). Either the score is high (or low) enough to print the narrative paragraph or it is not. Consider an employer hiring people on the basis of personality test scores. Either their scores are sufficiently auspicious to hire the person or they are not. The same situation occurs when counselors decide what careers to recommend or which therapies to administer to clients.

I conclude, then, that the trait concept, interpreted as a facet of a person's self-presentational style, serves as the best unit of analysis for personality research. In applied settings, however, the real world forces trait continua to be treated as discrete types.

ACKNOWLEDGMENTS

Part of this chapter was written while I was a visiting research fellow at Universität Bielefeld, supported by a fellowship from the Alexander von Humboldt-Stiftung. I express my gratitude to Alois Angleitner and Robert Wicklund for helping to arrange my stay and to the psychology department at Bielefeld and the von Humboldt-Stiftung for their support during that time. I also thank Robert Hogan and Jerry Wiggins for their feedback on an earlier draft of this chapter.

REFERENCES

Allport, G. W. (1937). *Personality: A psychological interpretation.* New York: Holt.

Alston, W. P. (1975). Traits, consistency, and conceptual alternatives for personality theory. *Journal for the Theory of Social Behaviour, 5,* 17–48.

Angleitner, A., John, O. P., & Löhr, F.-J. (1986). It's *what* you ask and *how* you ask it: An itemmetric analysis of personality questionnaires. In A. Angleitner & J. S. Wiggins (Eds.), *Personality assessment via questionnaires* (pp. 61–107). NY: Springer-Verlag.

Barron, F. (1953). Some personality correlates of independence of judgment. *Journal of Personality, 21,* 287–297.

Baumeister, R. F., & Tice, D. M. (1988). Metatraits. *Journal of Personality, 56,* 571–598.

Berger, P. L., & Luckmann, T. (1966). *The social construction of reality.* New York: Doubleday.

Block, J. (1977). Advancing the psychology of personality: Paradigmatic shift or improving the quality of research? In D. Magnusson & N. S. Endler (Eds.), *Personality at the crossroads* (pp. 37–63). Hillsdale, NJ: Erlbaum.

Buss, A. H. (1989). Personality as traits. *American Psychologist, 44,* 1378–1388.

Buss, D. M., & Cantor, N. (1989). Introduction. In D. M. Buss & N. Cantor (Eds.), *Personality psychology: Recent trends and emerging directions* (pp. 1–12). New York: Springer-Verlag.

Cooley, C. H. (1902). *Human nature and the social order.* New York: Scribner's.

Costa, P. T., Jr., & McCrae, R. R. (1992). *Revised NEO Personality Inventory (NEO PI-R^{TM}) and NEO Five-Factor Inventory (NEO-FFI) professional manual.* Odessa, FL: Psychological Assessment Resources.

Dahlstrom, W. G. (1972). *Personality systematics and the problem of types.* Morristown, NJ: General Learning Press.

Eckhardt, R. B. (1979). *The study of human evolution.* New York: McGraw-Hill.

Edwards, A. L. (1959). *Edwards Personal Preference Schedule manual.* New York: Psychological Corporation.

Emmons, R. A. (1989). Exploring the relations between motives and traits: The case of narcissism. In D. M. Buss & N. Cantor (Eds.), *Personality psychology: Recent trends and emerging directions* (pp. 32–44). New York: Springer-Verlag.

Entwistle, D. R. (1972). To dispel fantasies about fantasy-based measures of achievement motivation. *Psychological Bulletin, 77,* 377–391.

Epstein, S. (1983). Aggregation and beyond: Some basic issues on the production of behavior. *Journal of Personality, 51,* 360–392.

Funder, D. C., & Dobroth, K. M. (1987). Differences between traits: Properties associated with interjudge agreement. *Journal of Personality and Social Psychology, 52,* 409–418.

Gangestad, S., & Snyder, M. (1985). "To carve nature at its joints": On the existence of discrete classes in personality. *Psychological Review, 92,* 317–349.

Gangestad, S., & Snyder, M. (1991). Taxonomic analysis redux: Some statistical considerations for testing a latent class model. *Journal of Personality and Social Psychology, 61,* 141–146.

Goldberg, L. R., & Kilkowski, J. M. (1985). The prediction of semantic consistency in self-descriptions: Characteristics of persons and of terms that affect the consistency of response to synonym and antonym pairs. *Journal of Personality and Social Psychology, 48,* 82–98.

Gough, H. G. (1948). The frame of reference of the Thematic Apperception Test. *Journal of Clinical Psychology, 4,* 90–92.

Gough, H. G. (1987). *CPI administrator's guide.* Palo Alto, CA: Consulting Psychologists Press.

Guilford, J. S., Zimmerman, W. S., & Guilford, J. P. (1976). *The Guilford-Zimmerman Temperament Survey handbook: Twenty-five years of research and application.* San Diego, CA: EdITS.

Hanson, N. R. (1958). *Patterns of discovery.* Cambridge, England: Cambridge University Press.

Hendrick, C. (1977). Social psychology as an experimental science. In C. Hendrick (Ed.), *Perspectives on social psychology* (pp. 1–74). Hillsdale, NJ: Erlbaum.

Hofstee, W. K. B. (1994). Who should own the definition of personality? *European Journal of Personality, 8,* 149–162.

Hofstee, W. K. B., & de Raad, B. (1992). Personality structure through traits. In G.-V. Caprara & G. L. Van Heck (Eds.), *Modern personality psychology: Critical reviews and new directions* (pp. 56–72). New York: Harvester Wheatsheaf.

Hofstee, W. K. B., de Raad, B., & Goldberg, L. R. (1992). Integration of the big five and circumplex approaches to trait structure. *Journal of Personality and Social Psychology, 63,* 146–163.

Hogan, R. (1979, September). *Role theory as a depth psychology.* Paper presented at the 87th annual convention of the American Psychological Association, New York.

Hogan, R. (1991). Personality and personality measurement. In M. D. Dunnette & L. M. Hough (Eds.), *Handbook of industrial and organizational psychology* (2nd ed., Vol. 2, pp. 873–919). Palo Alto, CA: Consulting Psychologists Press.

Hogan, R., & Briggs, S. R. (1986). A socioanalytic interpretation of the public and private selves. In R. F. Baumeister (Ed.), *Public self and private self* (pp. 179–188). NY: Springer-Verlag.

Hogan, R., DeSoto, C. B., & Solano, C. (1977). Traits, tests, and personality research. *American Psychologist, 32,* 255–264.

Hogan, R., & Johnson, J. A. (1981, September). *The structure of personality.* Paper presented at the 89th annual convention of the American Psychological Association, Los Angeles.

Holt, R. R. (1962). Individuality and generalization in the psychology of personality. *Journal of Personality, 30,* 377–404.

IPAT Staff. (1979). *Admininstrator's manual for the 16PF.* Champaign, IL: Institute for Personality and Ability Testing.

Johnson, J. A. (1981). The "self-disclosure" and "self-presentation" views of item response dynamics and personality scale validity. *Journal of Personality and Social Psychology, 40,* 761–769.

Johnson, J. A. (1990a). Empathy as a personality disposition. In R. C. MacKay, J. R. Hughes, & E. J. Carver (Eds.), *Empathy in the helping relationship* (pp. 49–64). New York: Springer.

Johnson, J. A. (1990b, June). *Unlikely virtues provide multivariate substantive information about personality.* Paper presented at the 2nd annual meeting of the American Psychological Society, Dallas, TX.

Johnson, J. A. (1993a). *The impact of item characteristics on item and scale validity.* Manuscript submitted for publication.

Johnson, J. A. (1993b, August). *Sex roles do not lead to gender differences in personality.* Paper presented at the annual conference of the Human Behavior and Evolution Society, Binghamton, NY.

Johnson, J. A. (1994). *Interpreter's guide to the Bipolar Adjective Rating Scales (BARS).* Unpublished manuscript, Pennsylvania State University.

Johnson, J. A. (1996). *Computer narrative interpretations of individual profiles.* Manuscript submitted for publication.

Johnson, J. A. (1997). Seven social performance scales for the California Psychological Inventory. *Human Performance, 10,* 1–31.

Johnson, J. A., Germer, C. K., Efran, J. S., & Overton, W. F. (1988). Personality as the basis for theoretical predilections. *Journal of Personality and Social Psychology, 55,* 824–835.

Johnson, J. A., & Hogan, R. (1981a). Moral judgments and self-presentations. *Journal of Research in Personality, 15,* 57–63.

Johnson, J. A., & Hogan, R. (1981b). Vocational interests, personality, and effective police performance. *Personnel Psychology, 34,* 49–53.

Johnson, J. A., & Hogan, R., Zonderman, A. B., Callens, C., & Rogolsky, S. (1981). Moral judgment, personality, and attitudes toward authority. *Journal of Personality and Social Psychology, 40,* 370–373.

Johnson, J. A., & Ostendorf, F. (1993). Clarification of the five factor model with the Abridged Big Five-Dimensional Circumplex. *Journal of Personality and Social Psychology, 65,* 563–576.

Kenrick, D. T., & Funder, D. C. (1988). Profitting from controversy: Lessons from the person–situation debate. *American Psychologist, 43,* 23–34.

Kenrick, D. T., & Stringfield, D. O. (1980). Personality traits and the eye of the beholder: Crossing some traditional philosophical boundaries in the search for consistency in all of the people. *Psychological Review, 87,* 88–104.

Kilkowski, J. M. (1975). Traits, situations, and the logic of explanation in psychology: A selective review of the issues and evidence. *Oregon Research Institute Research Monograph 15*(3).

Luft, J. (1966). *Group processes: An introduction to group dynamics.* Palo Alto, CA: National Press.

MacKinnon, D. W. (1944). The structure of personality. In J. McV. Hunt (Ed.), *Personality and the behavior disorders* (pp. 3–48). New York: Plenum Press.

McClelland, D. C. (1980). Motive dispositions: The merits of operant versus respondent measures. In L. Wheeler (Ed.), *Review of personality and social psychology* (Vol. 1, pp. 11–41). Beverly Hills, CA: Sage.

McCrae, R. R. (1989). Why I advocate the five-factor model: Joint factor analyses of the NEO-PI with other instruments. In D. M. Buss & N. Cantor (Eds.), *Personality psychology: Recent trends and emerging directions* (pp. 237–245). New York: Springer-Verlag.

McCrae, R. R. (1990). Traits and trait names: How well is Openness represented in natural languages? *European Journal of Personality, 4,* 119–229.

McCrae, R. R., & Costa, P. T., Jr. (1989). Reinterpreting the Myers-Briggs Type Indicator from the perspective of the five-factor model of personality. *Journal of Personality, 57,* 17–40.

McCrae, R. R., Costa, P. T., Jr., & Piedmont, R. (1993). Folk concepts, natural language, and psychological constructs: The California Psychological Inventory and the five-factor model. *Journal of Personality, 61,* 1–26.

Mead, G. H. (1934). *Mind, self, and society.* Chicago: University of Chicago Press.

Meehl, P. E. (1945). The "dynamics" of structured personality tests. *Journal of Clinical Psychology, 1,* 296–303.

Meehl, P. E. (1956). Problems in the actuarial characterization of a person. In H. Feigl & M. Scriven (Eds.), *Minnesota studies in the philosophy of science: Vol. I. The foundations of science and the concepts of psychology and psychoanalysis* (pp. 205–222). Minneapolis: University of Minnesota Press.

Meehl, P. E. (1992). Factors and taxa, traits and types, differences of degree and differences in kind. *Journal of Personality, 60,* 117–174.

Meehl, P. E., & Hathaway, S. R. (1946). The K factor as a suppressor variable in the Minnesota Multiphasic Personality Inventory. *Journal of Applied Psychology, 30,* 525–564.

Mendelsohn, G. A., Weiss, D. S., & Feimer, N. R. (1982). Conceptual and empirical analysis of the typological implications of patterns of socialization and femininity. *Journal of Personality and Social Psychology, 42,* 1157–1170.

Mills, C., & Hogan, R. (1978). A role theoretical interpretation of personality scale item responses. *Journal of Personality, 46,* 778–785.

Mischel, W. (1968). *Personality and assessment.* New York: Wiley.

Myers, I. B., & McCaulley, M. H. (1985). *Manual: A guide to the development and use of the Myers-Briggs Type Indicator.* Palo Alto, CA: Consulting Psychologists Press.

Paulhus, D. L., & Reid, D. B. (1991). Enhancement and denial in socially desirable responding. *Journal of Personality and Social Psychology, 60,* 307–317.

Piedmont, R. L., McCrae, R. R., & Costa, P. T., Jr. (1992). An assesement of the Edwards Personal Preference Schedule from the perspective of the five-factor model. *Journal of Personality Assessment 58,* 67–78.

Reik, T. (1948). *Listening with the third ear: The inner experiences of a psychoanalyst.* New York: Farrar, Straus.

Rholes, W. S., Newman, L. S., & Ruble, D. N. (1990). Understanding self and other: Developmental and motivational aspects of perceiving persons in terms of invariant dispositions. In E. T. Higgins & R. M. Sorrentino (Eds.), *Handbook of motivation and cognition* (Vol. 2, pp. 369–407). New York: Guilford Press.

Rosenblueth, A., & Wiener, N. (1945). The role of models in science. *Philosophy of Science, 12,* 316–321.

Ross, L. (1977). The intuitive psychologist and his shortcomings: Distortions in the attribution process. In L. Berkowitz (Ed.), *Advances in experimental social psychology* (Vol. 10, pp. 174–221). New York: Academic Press.

Ross, L., & Nisbett, R. E. (1992). Perspectives on personality and social psychology: Books waiting to be written. *Psychological Inquiry, 3,* 99–102.

Tellegen, A. (in press). *Multidimensional Personality Questionnaire.* Minneapolis: University of Minnesota Press.

Wakefield, J. C. (1989). Levels of explanation in personality theory. In D. M. Buss & N. Cantor (Eds.), *Personality psychology: Recent trends and emerging directions* (pp. 333–346). New York: Springer-Verlag.

Weimer, W. B. (1974). Overview of a cognitive conspiracy: Reflections on the volume. In W. B. Weimer & D. S. Palermo (Eds.), *Cognition and the symbolic processes* (pp. 415–442). Englewood Cliffs, NJ: Erlbaum.

Weimer, W. B. (1984). Limitations of the dispositional analysis of behavior. In J. R. Royce & L. P. Mos (Eds.), *Annals of theoretical psychology* (Vol. 1, pp. 161–198). New York: Plenum Press.

Weinberger, J., & McClelland, D. C. (1990). Cognitive versus traditional motivational models: Irreconcilable or complementary? In E. T. Higgins & R. M. Sorrentino (Eds.), *Handbook of motivation and cognition* (Vol. 2, pp. 562–597). New York: Guilford Press.

Weiss, D. S., Mendelsohn, G. A., & Feimer, N. R. (1982). Reply to the comments of Block and Ozer. *Journal of Personality and Social Psychology, 42,* 1182–1189.

Werner, P. D., & Pervin, I. A. (1986). The content of personality inventory items. *Journal of Personality and Social Psychology, 51,* 622–628.

Wolfe, R. N. (1993). A commonsense approach to personality measurement. In K. H. Craik, R. Hogan, & R. N. Wolfe (Eds.), *Fifty years of personality psychology* (pp. 269–290). New York: Plenum Press.

Young, N. P. (1975). The psychology of explanation and the measurement of explanatory satisfaction (Doctoral dissertation, Pennsylvania State University). *Dissertation Abstracts International, 36,* 5775B–5776B.

CHAPTER 4

IN DEFENSE OF TRAITS[1]

JERRY S. WIGGINS
UNIVERSITY OF BRITISH COLUMBIA

In a recent review of the field generally designated "personality assessment," I rendered the optimistic albeit highly qualified opinion that visible signs of progress could be discerned in this still youthful science (Wiggins, 1973). Such a conclusion is considerably more sanguine than that reached a decade earlier by Vernon (1964), or more recently by Mischel (1968). My disagreement with Vernon involves little more than a tendency on my part to view glasses as half-full, rather than half-empty. My differences with Mischel are more profound. In a classic Rashomon-type example of individual differences in perception, Mischel and I observed the same events, but provided quite different narratives. This disagreement is all the more striking when it is realized that the two observers appear to share many of the same conceptual biases (e.g., the importance of generalizability, utility analysis, and explicit theoretical bases for assessment).

Different perspectives on fields as broad as personality assessment frequently arise from stylistic differences in taxonomic behaviors. Categories may be broad or narrow, concrete or overinclusive. In this respect, Vernon (1964) exhibited a preference for categories of broad width when he lumped together decision making, psychoanalytic theory, psychotherapy, descriptive psychiatry, and all things "clinical" within a single and particularly unwholesome bin (Wiggins, 1964). Mischel (1968) erred even more in the direction of overinclusion when he categorized such

---

[1] Invited address to the Ninth Annual Symposium on Recent Developments in the Use of the MMPI, held in Los Angeles on February 28, 1974. An earlier version of this paper was presented as a seminar at the Institute of Personality Assessment and Research in Berkeley on November 27, 1973.

diverse offenses against human nature as psychodynamic theory, factor analysis, and the medical model as all belonging to a monolithic "trait" conspiracy.

Quibbling over taxonomic niceties should generally be left to textbook writers and others who continue the scholastic tradition. But there is more at stake in the present instance. Conclusions stemming from Mischel's broadband view of the "trait construct" have had an extraordinary impact on our field. Behaviorally inclined clinicians appear to be celebrating a decisive victory, a blitzkrieg, so to speak, that defined and destroyed the enemy almost simultaneously. Psychodynamically oriented clinicians, long used to being "sold up the river," to use Holt's (1958) phrase, must now bear the added humiliation of having multivariate-trait psychologists as traveling companions.

Mischel's (1968) textbook, and his subsequent writings along similar lines (Mischel, 1969, 1971, 1973a, 1973b), have had a considerable impact on the field of personality in general, and personality assessment in particular. His views have not gone unchallenged, and there is a still-growing literature of criticisms directed at one or another facet of his arguments (Alker, 1972; Averill, 1973; Bowers, 1973; Craik, 1969; Wachtel, 1973a, 1973b; Wallach & Leggett, 1972). Yet Mischel's writings have tended to polarize his readership into a relatively homogeneous group of satisfied social behaviorists and social psychologists on the one hand, and a highly heterogeneous and most dissatisfied group of clinicians, psychometricians, and personality theorists on the other.

The reason that Mischel's writings have had such a diffuse effect is that his arguments themselves are diffuse and multipronged. At one level, he is challenging the field of personality as traditionally defined and the field of personality assessment as it has traditionally been implemented. At another level, he is extolling the virtues of social-behavioral conceptions, as opposed to psychodynamic and other nonbehavioral views. And at still another level, he is arguing for the utility of certain methods of behavior modification and control for both practical and theoretical purposes. When considered one at a time, these are each complex issues worthy of debate. However, when considered *in toto,* they appear as a shifting myriad of targets against which it is difficult, if not impossible, to take aim. For example, if one must assume that the recent triumphs of some clinicians in reducing or eliminating fears of snakes in their clients reflect unfavorably on the psychometric adequacy of multivariate personality inventories, then one is doomed to argue from a position of weakness and bewilderment.

To bring the issues into clearer focus, I would like to consider the trait concept: (1) as it is used, or could be used, in personality measurement and assessment, and (2) as it is used, or should be used, in a theory of personality. The two sets of considerations are not unrelated. The most modest attempts to quantify personal characteristics should be guided by explicit theoretical considerations; the grandest theories must eventually be assessed with reference to concrete measurement procedures. With this in mind, I will first attempt to discredit the growing philosophical skepticism that has been expressed regarding the existence of traits, and then suggest the place that trait measures may have within a theory of personality.

I. THEORIES AND VIEWPOINTS

For a number of reasons, it is convenient to consider (the field of) "personality" as the general psychology of *individual differences* (Wiggins, Renner, Clore, & Rose, 1971). In attempting to account for (the fact of) individual differences, a variety of viewpoints must be brought to bear on a common subject matter. At the least, it would seem that the methods and concepts of biological, experimental, social, and psychometric-trait approaches are necessary for providing a complete account of human differences. Pitting one approach against another can result in such fluid controversies as the ancient "heredity versus environment" issue or the recently revived "trait versus situation" debate.

When one approach to knowledge is compared with another, the game is not zero sum. Whether from genuine conviction or from the observance of good form, it is common to concede that *other* approaches have virtues as well as limitations, triumphs as well as failures. Nevertheless, while the biological, experimental, and social approaches have all recently had their days in the sun, the psychometric-trait approach has fallen upon extremely bad times. The possibility exists that the methods and distinctions of the trait approach have simply outlived their usefulness in comparison with recent advances in other viewpoints. I personally do not believe this to be the case. Instead, I believe that a widespread discontent with certain *theories* of personality has resulted in an attempted purge of concepts essential to the psychometric-trait *viewpoint* in personality study. The distinction between viewpoint and theory is critical here.

A viewpoint is an approach to the empirical study of personality that is based on assumptions concerning the importance of certain kinds of constructs and that advocates the use of certain methods of observation and measurement (Wiggins et al., 1971). The term "viewpoint" is used in place of "method" to emphasize that methods involve constructs and that they impose constraints upon observations. A theory is an extended construct system of broad range and scope that typically attempts an integration of constructs from several viewpoints.[2]

I believe it fair to say that the viewpoints of personality study are reasonably "established" in their own right, because they represent traditional and respectable areas of psychological investigation (biological psychology, experimental psychology, social psychology, and psychometrics). Theories of personality are, of course, another story. And it is important to note at the outset that although a theory of personality may achieve a certain prestige by emphasizing a particular viewpoint, the methods of the viewpoint cannot be substituted for the propositions of the theory. Bowers (1973) has made this point in reference to the misidentification of S-R theory with the experimental method:

---

[2] This distinction between viewpoint and theory is similar to Fiske's (1971) distinction between *mode* and *perspective*.

As it happens, the experimental method as generally employed is differentially sensitive to the impact of situational variables, and correspondingly insensitive to organismic variables. . . . However, the experimental method does not, so to speak, comment on this differential sensitivity; it is simply a procedure for acquiring a controlled observation. Thus, independent–dependent variable relationships are metaphysically neutral. This is not the case for their S-R counterparts, which do carry a great load of metaphysical freight. (p. 309)

The converse is also true. Just as a method cannot be used to justify a theory, a theory can be discredited without discrediting the method that it espouses. A discreditation of S-R theory is no reflection on the experimental method. However, I believe it to be the case that the psychometric-trait viewpoint has recently been judged guilty in virtue of its association with certain personality theories. The fact that trait-like or dispositional concepts are so ubiquitous in personality theory should not make one particular *interpretation* of traits subject to the criticisms of other interpretations. Traits are many things to many theorists, and it is precisely this conceptual plurality that has provided a composite straw man for those who have criticized trait measurement.

One of the chief concerns of the psychometric approach to personality study is the development of quantitative procedures for the measurement of human tendencies (pronenesses, proclivities, propensities, dispositions, inclinations) to act or not to act in certain ways on certain occasions. These tendencies are not "postulated," they are accepted from common sense as expressed in ordinary language usage. If persons are not more or less prone to behave in certain ways on certain occasions, then the psychometric approach is out of business at the outset, as are all approaches to personality study.

Because of its concern with human tendencies as expressed in ordinary language, a case could be made for the psychometric-trait viewpoint being propaedeutic to other approaches to personality study. However, as I hope to make clear later, the closeness of the psychometric-trait approach to the obvious subject matter of personality study need not imply, and in fact should not imply, that trait concepts will figure prominently in our eventual systematic accounts or explanations of that subject matter. It seems more likely that theoretical explanations of human tendencies will emerge from the social, experimental, and biological viewpoints.

In the material that follows, I hope to illuminate the nature of the trait concept by considering the ways in which trait terms are employed in everyday discourse. But to show that a consistent and meaningful account of traits is provided by ordinary language usage is not to show that a scientific account of traits is easily achieved. A number of additional steps are required, the first of which has to do with the specification of measurement procedures. However, although the current state of psychometrics may be primitive in comparison with measurement in the physical sciences, it is clear from reading Fiske's (1971) recent book that the primary obstacle to measuring the concepts of personality has been conceptual rather than mensurational. Within the field of personality, there appears to be greater agreement concerning how concepts should be measured (e.g., Fiske, 1971) than on what concepts should be measured (e.g., Levy, 1970). Thus, achievement of a working consensus on the nature of the trait concept would be a large first step toward a psychology of personality.

Most previous discussions of the trait concept in psychology have focused on traits as attributes of *persons*. Thus, the first task of psychometrics has been considered that of developing scales and inventories to measure the "tendencies" of persons to act in certain ways on certain occasions (e.g., Edwards, 1970). But this logically presupposes a clear conception of which particular actions are to be accounted for on what particular occasions. To say that a person is "aggressive" is to say that the person has behaved or is likely to behave "aggressively" on certain occasions. But what is an aggressive action? And how would we quantify the "aggressiveness" of an action?

I intend to distinguish among statements expressing: qualities of *actions* ("John pushed the boy aggressively"), (2) properties of *persons* ("John is aggressive"), and (3) aspects of future *occurrences* ("If frustrated, John is likely to behave aggressively"). I will argue that the first statement conveys an institutional fact; the second, a categorical summary of the general trend of a person's conduct to date; and the third, a hypothetical proposition that is inferred, but not deduced, from statements of the second type. In the specialized terminology of the psychometric-trait approach to personality, these distinctions correspond roughly to those sometimes made among "observation," "assessment," and "prediction."

II. TRAITS AS ATTRIBUTES OF BEHAVIOR

"John pushed the boy" describes an action or sequence of behavior. "John pushed the boy hard, repeatedly, and for a long time" qualifies the description in terms of qualities which may be thought of as attributes of the action, rather than of John, or of the observer. The observer is making judgments here (How hard is "hard"? How often is "repeatedly"? How long is "long"?), but the normative basis for such judgments can easily be made explicit. The important point is that the descriptive qualities tell how John pushed the boy, not why John pushed, nor why the observer described John's actions in these terms.

"John pushed the boy aggressively" qualifies the description of the action, but in a different way. Its meaning is not synonymous with the description yielded by the use of primary attributes (amplitude, frequency, duration). Nor can the quality of aggression be recorded by mechanical devices in the absence of a human observer. Nevertheless, the qualifier ("aggressively") should not automatically be relegated to the domain of emotive responses (evaluations) simply because an observer is involved. One can describe John pushing aggressively, affectionately, or playfully in a thoroughly dispassionate manner. That, of course, is what is meant by an "objective" observer.

The description of John's pushing as "aggressive" does not, in ordinary usage, refer to John's intentions. As Anscombe (1963) put it, "We do not add anything attaching to the action at the time it is done by describing it as intentional" (p. 28). The description "aggressively" tells how John pushed the boy, not why John pushed, nor whether the action was "voluntary" or "involuntary." The latter distinction typically arises in connection with actions that result in improprietous outcomes (Ryle, 1949, pp. 69–74). We may determine whether a person meant or intended to do something (wrong) by inquiring whether he was competent to do it right (and failed to do so) or by establishing whether or not external factors prevented him from performing properly. But it is the description of the present action as "aggressive" that establishes its character, and subsequent attempts to excuse or condemn John for taking that kind of action represent a distinctly different line of inquiry.

The characterization of John's pushing as "aggressive" does not refer to John's disposition to perform aggressive acts in this or other circumstances. The word "aggressively" modifies the verb (pushed) and not the subject (John). The sentence "Quite uncharacteristically John gave the boy an aggressive push" makes good sense and conveys both that the act was aggressive and that John is not. True, if John continues to shove people around, we might wish to revise our original appraisal of his aggressiveness. But the direction of inferences is from act to disposition and not the converse.

Could it be that the action under consideration is described as "aggressive" because of its relation to certain antecedent conditions? It is true, for example, that aggression may follow frustration and in that sense be "provoked." Thus, it might be the case that "aggressive" refers to a class of actions which are likely to follow actions or circumstances that are harmful, insulting, or frustrating to the actor. But the lawfulness of the implied R-R relation does not seem strong enough to enable us to avoid frequent miscategorizations. Provocations may be (and often are) met with a smile, ignored, or submitted to. More damaging to the "antecedent" account of aggression, however, is the fact that the term "aggressive" is applied to topographically dissimilar actions that follow submissive, generous, dominant, affectionate, or almost any conceivable kind of action. It is, of course, possible to distinguish "provoked" and "unprovoked" aggression. But such an inquiry into the reasons for an action does not illuminate the qualities that made that action "aggressive" in the first place.

If an action is not classified as "aggressive" on the basis of antecedent events, perhaps it is classified on the basis of consequent events or outcomes. Let us try: An act is described as "aggressive" if and only if it results in (is followed by) the harm, injury, discomfort, or ridicule of another. This basis for discriminating the attribute of aggressiveness has one clear advantage over the antecedent event account: topographically dissimilar actions (pushing, hitting, swearing) are encompassed by a single term, "aggressive," which connotes a common property. But the requirement that a specific outcome must occur is too strong. Not all aggressive actions result in harm or injury. If John takes a swing at the boy with a meat axe and misses, the action is still unambiguously "aggressive."

Thus far, I have argued that the sense of the attribute of "aggressiveness" is not to be found in: (1) primary qualities of the act, (2) evaluative responses of the observer, (3) intentions of the actor, (4) tendencies of the actor, (5) the conditions antecedent to the act, or (6) the immediate consequences of the act. What is left? Clearly, we have not exhausted all possibilities; but rather than pursue additional false leads, it seems appropriate to state what I believe is meant when a trait quality is attributed to an action: *the action belongs to a class of actions that are likely to lead to a particular outcome.*

The "outcomes" at issue here are *social* in nature. They may be characterized by such phrases as "being harmed, injured, discomforted, or ridiculed," "being praised, admired, revered, or lauded," and "being influenced, directed, persuaded, or restrained," considering the likely effects of aggressive, deferential, and dominant actions, respectively. But how do we know these things, and what is it that we know?

Searle (1969, pp. 50–53) has proposed a useful epistemological distinction between "brute facts" and "institutional facts." Brute facts are, roughly, those objects, relations, and primary qualities that lend themselves to direct observation and with which the natural sciences are concerned. In contrast, institutional facts do not stand on their own, but presuppose the existence of certain human institutions. These institutions are systems of constitutive rules of the form "X counts as Y in context C".

Consider the following institutional facts reported in a newspaper: "In the closing minutes of the game, pass interference was called in the Redskin's end zone and the Dolphins won by a score of 6 to 0." Clearly, the existence of the facts recorded in this statement presupposes the existence of the institution of football, an institution that furnishes the rules that impart a special meaning to the various brute facts of the game. One rule is of the following form:

"An action (pushing) that is likely to prevent a receiver from catching the ball (X) counts as interference (Y) in the context of the rules of football (C)."

Similarly, the statement "John pushed the boy aggressively" contains an institutional fact defined by the following:

"An action (pushing) that is likely to harm or injure another (X) counts as aggressive (Y) in the context of the rules for classifying the consequences of social actions (C)."

To designate trait qualities as institutional is not to imply that they are (merely) conventions instead of (actual) facts. Trait attributions are conventions about reporting facts.

As psychologists, we are perhaps less interested in the ontological status of institutional facts than we are in the origins and functions of the rules which, in ordinary usage, provide definitions of those facts. It seems likely that trait terms were coined to express the law-like relations that have been observed between certain kinds of human actions and particular classes of social outcomes. Given the variety and complexity of actions that may result in the same social outcome, it is not possible for single individual to learn, by direct experience, even a fragment of these regularities. Trait attributions convey the shared folk wisdom concerning actions and outcomes in an extraordinarily efficient manner. Because the truth of a trait attribution is not defined by a particular immediate outcome, the sense of the law-like relation conveyed is "probabilistic" rather than deterministic. Indeed, it would be a surprise—if not an embarrassment—if the laws of common sense psychology were stronger than those of scientific psychology.

One final point regarding traits as attributes of behavior: most psychologists like to think of actions that share a common attribute as constituting a "response class." On an observational level, we have defined trait attributes as response classes that have common environmental effects. Hence, our definition should be acceptable to groups as divergent as ordinary people, Skinnerians, and trait theorists. As we move from behavior observation to conceptualization, however, we find that these groups diverge in their views. Both Skinnerians and trait theorists impose additional requirements beyond the level of a single observation. In addition to requiring that members of a response class share the attribute of a common environmental effect, Skinnerians require that the actions enter into the same functional relationships with "controlling" stimulus conditions. The additional requirement imposed by trait theorists is that members of a response class exhibit significant covariation within a group of individuals. Ordinary people could be talked into either conceptualization since the level of discourse is that of psychological theory and not that of common sense. But agreement as to what trait attributes are on an observational level is not to be treated lightly. It suggests that we all know what trait attributes are, and that they "really" exist.

III. TRAITS AS ATTRIBUTES OF PERSONS

Having identified the conditions under which trait qualities are ascribed to behavior, the manner in which trait terms are used to describe persons should be fairly evident. To say, "John is aggressive," is to say that in certain circumstances, John has behaved, or is likely to behave, in a manner likely to result in harm, injury, or discomfort to others.

But which is it: "has behaved" or "is likely to behave"? The "is likely to behave" account is the classical argument of Gilbert Ryle, who maintained that traits are dispositions which function as law-like inference tickets. The "has behaved" account is a refutation of the classical argument which maintains that trait attributions are summarizing statements that do not commit the speaker to conditional predictions (Hampshire, 1953). The two views are sufficiently disparate to warrant separate consideration.

A. Traits as Causal Dispositions

Ryle (1949) maintained that trait attributions to persons function in the same manner as dispositional statements in physics. Thus, to say "John is aggressive" is akin to saying "The glass is brittle" or "The sugar is soluble." In this sense, all trait statements are hypothetical propositions that convey law-like relationships. The status of dispositional concepts, as applied to objects, is reasonably clear: "To be brittle is just to be bound or likely to fly into fragments in such and such conditions" (Ryle, 1949, p. 43). Thus, the statement "The glass is brittle" can be verified with reference to a bilateral reduction sentence (Carnap, 1936) of the following form:

If a case x (the glass) satisfies the test condition S (being struck with a stone), then x is an instance of C (brittle) if and only if x shows the response R (shatters).

According to the dispositional view, when we say that John is aggressive, we are asserting that *it is a good bet that in certain circumstances, John will behave aggressively*. But the form of the subjunctive conditional and the conditions for its verification are different, in several respects, from those involved in the meaning and verification of dispositional statements applied to physical objects:

1. The "good bet" (Ryle's words) indicates that the subjunctive conditional is probabilistic in form, rather than "if and only if." This is not damaging to the position since it could be argued that all predictions are probabilistic, or certainly all predictions of human behavior. There is, of course, the question of how good the bet has to be before we will make it, but that question is problematic for any account of the prediction of behavior.

2. The "in certain circumstances" clause embraces a much larger set of conditions than is the case with physical objects. Whereas brittleness is a single-tract disposition that can be defined in terms of a reduction sentence involving a single, sufficient occurrence (shattering), traits convey an indefinite series of hypothetical propositions. It is not clear which of the many possible circumstances should serve as the test condition for John's aggressiveness, nor is it clear whether disconfirmation of the hypothetical proposition in a specific instance could be discounted on the grounds that the wrong circumstance had been selected.

3. The criteria by which we could decide that John had "behaved aggressively" are not as evident as shattering in the case of brittleness. Ryle insists that all trait words are dispositional words, and thus makes no provision for actions which may be described as "aggressive actions" (Powell, 1959). In his view, actions may be described as exercises of John's aggressive disposition in the same way that speech acts may be described as exercises of John's knowledge of French. But just as there are no brittle occurrences, there are no aggressive actions. Although the concept of a physical disposition avoids circularity by specifying a manageable number of criterion responses, this is not so easily achieved with reference to the concept of a trait disposition.

B. Traits as Categorical Summaries

Hampshire (1953) contends that trait attributions do not involve hypothetical or quasi-hypothetical statements. Instead, trait attributions are summarizing statements that describe the general trend of a person's conduct to date. The claim of the dispositional statement is of the form, "So far, the word aggressive is the right word to summarize the general trend of John's conduct."

Hampshire's arguments rely on a distinction between statements expressing causal properties and categorical statements that merely summarize. For Ryle, statements about human dispositions are statements expressing causal properties that can be restated in terms of reduction sentences of the "if . . . then" form. For Hampshire, statements about human dispositions are summarizing statements that do not comment on causality. Such statements may also be applied to material objects:

> . . . one may often choose, or may be compelled by ignorance, to summarize the general character of some physical things, rather than to describe their behavior in terms of their physical constitution and of the laws which govern the behavior of objects so constituted. (Hampshire, 1952, p. 7)

Examples of such statements would be "It tends to rain in Vancouver" and "This river tends to overflow its banks."

Hampshire emphasizes three bases for distinguishing summarizing statements from causal statements: (1) Summarizing statements imply that manifestations of the disposition have occurred in the past; causal statements do not: sugar may be soluble without ever having dissolved. (2) Summarizing statements imply that a disposition manifests itself more or less continuously over some period of time; causal statements do not: "being electrically charged is a property which may be switched on and off" (p. 8). (3) The manifestations of dispositions described by summarizing statements are various and indeterminate (John's aggressiveness may be manifested in a multitude of behaviors). Manifestations of causal dispositions are specific and determinate (shattering and dissolving).

If, in ordinary usage, the statement "John is aggressive" conveys that *John has been observed to engage in topographically dissimilar aggressive actions over a period of time*, then the advantages of Hampshire's summarizing statement account over Ryle's causal statement account are evident. Therefore, it seems worthwhile to consider at least the more obvious objections that might be raised to the implications just stated.

That the manifestations of a trait are heterogeneous and indeterminate is already conceded in Ryle's account. But could we, or would we, describe John as aggressive on the basis of his repeatedly performing a single act in a given situation? The disposition to perform a single act in a single situation is ordinarily referred to as a habit rather than as a trait. In the case of aggressive behavior, such an action might even be referred to as a tic or mannerism.

Would it make sense to assert that John is aggressive if John had never been observed to perform an aggressive act? Brandt (1970) does not see such an assertion as a contradiction. He argues: If we knew a person had lived a sheltered life and had never been required to act courageously, we would not infer that the person *cannot* be courageous. Further, "there are conceivable psychological tests such that, given a certain result on these tests, we would say that the person is *probably* a courageous person" (p. 26). The fact that such an assertion is probabilistic "shows something, not about the meaning of courageous (or other trait-names of interest to us), but about our convictions on what is adequate evidence for trait-ascriptions" (p. 26).

It is readily conceded that if we never observed a person in a situation in which a manifestation of a trait would have been expected or likely, we cannot conclude that the person does *not* have the trait. Nor, of course, can we conclude that the person has the trait. We simply do not know. The "conceivable psychological tests" argument is more likely to appeal to philosophers than to those of us familiar with the grim realities of psychological testing. But to show that such probabilistic inferences might be made, in principle, is not to give an account of the ordinary usage of trait terms.

The major argument that Brandt (1970) puts forth to show that the summary view is "simply wrong" is based on the fact that trait inferences may be made on the basis of a *single* act:

> But how could we draw such an inference, with high confidence, from any amount of information about a single situation if trait-affirmations were assertions about the frequency of behavior in the past? (The present behavior is, of course, one case; but to say that a person is courageous is surely not to say merely that he has acted courageously once). (p. 26)

There are circumstances in which a trait inference may be drawn on the basis of a single action. At issue are the relations that may exist between the dispositional assertion (D), the single action just observed (A_1), and past actions that are heterogeneous manifestations of the trait (A_n). Table I outlines the assertions and negations that may be made under different sets of conditions. For simplicity, the single action just observed (A_1) is not considered a subset of past actions (A_n), although both are members of the larger set of all possible trait manifestations (A_t).

The first statement in Table I asserts that John is aggressive (D), that John pushed the boy aggressively on this occasion (A_1), and that other instances of John's

TABLE I

Possible Assertions about a Disposition (D), an
Action Just Observed (A_1), and Past Actions
That Are Manifestations of the Disposition (A_n)

1. Typical assertion	D & A_1 & A_n
2. Typical negation	$\overline{D}$ & $\overline{A_1}$ & $\overline{A_n}$[a]
3. Implausible	D & $\overline{A_1}$ & $\overline{A_n}$
4. Contrary disposition	$\overline{D}$ & A_1 & A_n
5. Special circumstances	D & $\overline{A_1}$ & A_n
6. Out of character	$\overline{D}$ & A_1 & $\overline{A_n}$
7. Change of character	$\overline{D}$ & $\overline{A_1}$ & A_n
8. Single occurrence	D & A_1 & $\overline{A_n}$

[a] Overbar denotes the opposite connotation; for example, $\overline{D}$ lacks the disposition under discussion.

aggressiveness have been observed in the past (A_n). The second statement asserts that none of these is true. The normalcy of both these statements is recognized by Brandt (1970, pp. 25–26). The third statement is considered by Brandt to be "not contradictory," but, on the evidence he offers, is labeled *implausible*. At best, one could argue that John is "potentially" aggressive, with all the attendant difficulties in disproving such an assertion.

In the fourth statement John is said not to be aggressive, even though he just pushed the boy, and even though he has acted aggressively in the past. Such a statement can be true when the speaker is able to cite a variety of incidents which serve as evidence of a *contrary disposition:* "the final and conclusive argument must be a balancing of one set of actual incidents against another set of actual incidents" (Hampshire, 1953, p. 6). In this example, it is assumed that accounts of John's loving, cooperative, and pacifistic behaviors in the past are weighed more heavily than accounts of his aggressive actions.

In the fifth statement John is said to be aggressive, in light of his past history of aggressive actions, even though he did not push the boy on this occasion. Such an apparent exception to trait attribution rules does not pose a problem for either the causal-dispositional or summary view. Ryle (1949) distinguishes tendencies from capacities: "tends to" implies "can" but is not implied by it (p. 131). Hampshire (1953) considers the possibility of an exception "part of the force of calling statements of disposition summarizing statements" (p. 7). But neither position provides an explanation of this apparent exception. If there is good reason to believe that John is aggressive (e.g., his past actions) and he does not push the boy aggressively, we could appeal to some *special circumstances* such that John "would have" pushed the boy aggressively were it not for those circumstances. However, in the case of desirable or socially sanctioned actions (not pushing), we are unlikely to seek "excuses," "justifications," "extenuations," and the like (Austin, 1957).

In Statement 6, John is said to be not aggressive, in light of the lack of aggressive incidents in his past, even though he pushed the boy on this occasion. Since the action in this case may be considered reprehensible (pushing), excuses or justifications are likely to be sought. Although special circumstances could be cited (e.g., extreme provocation), the best explanation (defense) would seem to be John's record. In light of the lack of aggressive actions in his past, it could be argued that John's pushing was an action *out of character*. This is not to infer, as have some moral philosophers, that character "causes" actions (Pitcher, 1961). Rather, it is to recognize the possibility of uncharacteristic actions in virtue of the argument that although D is dependent on A_n, A_1 is independent of D (Powell, 1959). That is, although our characterization of John as "aggressive" requires past incidents of aggressive actions, we may classify John's pushing the boy as "aggressive" independently of John's disposition to be or not to be aggressive. It is not clear how an aggressive action could be performed by a nonaggressive person within Ryle's account (Powell, 1959).

In Statement 7, John does not push the boy nor is he said to be aggressive, even though there are incidents of aggression in his past. When an aggressive person fails to perform an aggressive action, special circumstances may be invoked. But, as in the present case, when a person with a history of aggressive actions fails to behave aggressively and is called "not aggressive," the possibility of a *change of character* may be entertained. Although the "Contrary disposition" account would be more compelling, people do change, or at least we revise our opinions about them. However, this explanation cannot be invoked too often: "Character may change suddenly; but it must not change suddenly too often, or it ceases to be character" (Hampshire, 1953, p. 6).

The eighth statement is the one that Brandt considers damaging to the summary view. On the basis of a single action (pushing), and in the absence of previous aggressive actions, the disposition to be aggressive is attributed to John. Although such inferences may not be drawn "often," as Brandt puts it, they may, on some occasions, be drawn. The issue is whether or not the inference is consistent with the claim of a summarizing statement: "So far, the word aggressive is the right word to summarize the general trend of John's conduct."

Clearly, a dispositional inference could be in the form of a summarizing statement if the act in question (e.g., pushing) was the first and only action ever observed. But Brandt is concerned with the situation in which previous (and presumably extensive) observations were not occasions of trait manifestations. He appears to be arguing that John was (latently?) aggressive all this time, but that the disposition had not been previously brought into play. This might be analogous to a glass that has always been brittle, though never struck, and therefore never shattered.

If we were to unpack all, or some, of the hypothetical propositions implied in the statement that John is aggressive, we would have to conclude that the circumstances of the subjunctive conditionals (e.g., "If John is frustrated . . . ") had never before been satisfied. That one condition was satisfied on this recent occasion, and that John did perform an aggressive act (however that might be determined within the causal-dispositional framework), is apparently sufficient to justify a trait attribution, in Brandt's view. And such an attribution is indeed inconsistent with a summary view of dispositions since no hypothetical propositions are implied by that view, and since the attribution would not provide an accurate summary of conduct to date.

Uncontrived examples of the borderline case considered by Brandt do not immediately come to mind. The research of Megargee and his associates (Megargee, 1966; Megargee & Mendelsohn, 1962; Megargee & Menzies, 1971) may provide one such example. Briefly, Megargee has studied the histories and personality characteristics of prisoners who committed extremely assaultive crimes (e.g., murder), moderately assaultive crimes (e.g., battery), or nonassaultive crimes (e.g., robbery). Both case histories and psychological test data suggested that a substantial proportion of prisoners who committed extremely assaultive crimes were *less* aggressive, more controlled, and less likely to have committed previous offenses than other prisoners. Newspaper accounts of extremely assaultive crimes also tended to corroborate these findings: "In case after case the extremely assaultive offender proves to be a rather passive person with no previous history of aggression" (Megargee 1966, p. 2).

Both Megargee's research and newspaper accounts of such "puzzling," "sense-less," and "shocking" crimes are fascinating, or at least, extremely interesting. It is informative to ask why this is the case. Would an adherent of the causal-dispositional view answer, "It is amazing that these aggressive persons should have been so sheltered from circumstances that would provide occasions for the expression of their violence"? Perhaps. But newspaper readers, the psychologists who conducted this research, and adherents of the summary view would answer, "It is amazing that such heinous crimes could be committed by such *non*aggressive persons."

It is important to note that a "change of character" does not seem to have been involved since psychological testing and behavior observations made after incarceration still revealed a picture of a nonaggressive personality. Murder is, of course, an aggressive action. But murder can be committed by nonaggressive persons, at least according to the summary view.

To opt for the categorical-summary view over the causal-dispositional account is not to deny the importance of Ryle's original distinction between dispositions and tendencies on the one hand and episodes and occurrences on the other. When we say that John is aggressive, we are asserting that the general trend or disposition of his conduct, to date, has been to engage in a variety of aggressive actions over a period of time. John's "aggressiveness" is not something that occurs over and above, or under and below, his aggressive actions. It is not something that occurs for short or long periods of time, in a real world or in a transpatial world. Nor, and here is where we depart from Ryle, is John's aggressiveness the cause of, or reason for, his aggressive actions. In addition to appearing closer to ordinary usage, the categorical-summary account carries less metaphysical freight.

IV. TRAITS AS PREDICTORS OF BEHAVIOR

A. Prediction in Everyday Life

We can, and on occasion do, use our knowledge of persons' past actions as a basis for predicting their future behavior. But the extent to which such predictions are made in everyday social transactions has probably been exaggerated. According to George Kelly's (1955) model of The Human as Scientist, persons are almost continuously engaged in gathering data, erecting hypotheses, and subjecting hypotheses to test by prediction. Although this model has provided a heuristic metaphor for psychological research, it should not be interpreted literally. As Little (1972) has noted, to say that all persons are scientists (or predictors) smacks of *academico-mimesis:* "Everyone is just like me." Some individuals may spend significant portions of their lives predicting the future behavior of others, but others may be mainly concerned with reflecting on the past, or pondering the present.

The philosophical view of persons as in a constant state of readiness to unpack the conditional predictions entailed by their trait attributions seems equally academicomimetic. If you were to assert that John is aggressive, and I were to ask you what you *meant* by that, you would probably cite corroborative incidents of aggressive actions from John's past. It seems unlikely you would reply that you intended to convey the proposition that *if* John were in such and such a situation, *then* John would act in such and such a way. The equating of the meaning of a statement with the method of its verification is a philosophical language game, not an ordinary discourse game. If you and I were psychologists, we might conspire to contrive a situational test of John's aggressiveness, but ordinary people seldom engage in such practices. Nor would ordinary people be bound to agree that the original attribution was false if the experiment yielded negative findings.

B. Prediction in Personality Assessment

There may be unresolved questions concerning the extent to which persons engage in predictive behaviors in ordinary life, but there is little question that prediction is the major professional activity of the applied personality assessment psychologist (Wiggins, 1973). Since the principal charge leveled against the trait construct in recent times has been that of a lack of predictive utility (Mischel, 1968; Peterson, 1968), it is instructive to consider what kinds of behaviors, and in what circumstances, trait measures would be reasonably expected to predict.

Although there is still room for refinement of current psychometric trait measures, the relatively poor showing of such measures in predicting behavioral criteria may very well reflect inappropriateness of the criteria rather than shortcomings of the predictors. This line of reasoning has recently been pursued by Martin Fishbein and his associates (Fishbein, 1973; Fishbein & Ajzen, 1972, 1974) in the context of attitude–behavior relationships. Fishbein and Ajzen (1974) have demonstrated that whereas dispositional measures are relatively poor predictors of single acts, they are substantially related to criteria based on multiple acts in varied circumstances.

Jaccard (1974) has recently extended this line of reasoning to the evaluation of traditional trait measures. He assembled a set of multiple-act criterion measures of dominance that included behaviors likely to be performed by dominant persons in a variety of circumstances. His subjects were also administered Gough's (1957) CPI dominance scale, Jackson's (1967) PRF dominance scale, and a single, self-rated scale of dominant tendencies. The average correlations of the trait scales with individual dominant behaviors were barely .20 and were not statistically significant. In contrast, the correlations of the trait measures with the sum of the multiple acts were close to .60 and were highly significant. If we choose, as did Mischel (1968), to express the relation between trait and behaviors as a "personality coefficient" based on the average relation between a trait and single behaviors, then we are likely to obtain coefficients of disappointing size. But if we choose to express the relation as the correlation between a trait measure and a criterion of multiple acts in multiple situations, there is good reason to believe that the magnitude of validity coefficients will be similar to those found by Jaccard (1974). And such a choice would be consistent with a summary view of traits.

A psychometric measure of a trait should reflect the general trend of a person's conduct to date. In assessing a single individual, the trait measure should be based on items that provide a broad and representative sampling of relevant acts in multiple situations. Most prediction in personality assessment is nomothetic, however, and thus we must devise measures that also reflect the *relative* tendencies of persons to behave in certain ways on certain occasions. Fishbein's work in attitude measurement is also relevant here, since he has demonstrated the importance of several previously neglected item properties that should increase differentiation among persons. These include: (1) the probability of a trait given an act, $p(T \mid A)$, (2) the probability of a trait given the act is not performed, $p(T \mid \tilde{A})$, and the base rate of the act in the situation $p(A)$. The difference between the first two probabilities is a powerful index of item validity (Fishbein & Ajzen, 1974).

The predictive utility of a trait measure is a direct function of the ability of the measure to *postdict* the general trend of an individual's past behavior. Once this is realized, it becomes clear that attempts to assess underlying motives, latent tendencies, and the like are quite beside the point. Prediction from trait measures is based on the logic of the old adage that the best indication of what a person will do in the future is what that person has done in the past. When this is not the case, other measures may be called for, but they are not properly called trait measures.

V. TRAITS AS EXPLANATIONS OF BEHAVIOR

The summary view of traits that I have advanced thus far does not comment on the causal properties of traits or on the use of traits as explanations of behavior. It is true, of course, that a summary of a person's conduct to date does not provide an account or explanation of his or her conduct. At issue is whether ordinary trait attributions are *intended* to be explanations. Attribution theorists think they are so intended and they view trait attributions as "naive causal inferences" based for the most part on insufficient data (Heider, 1958; Jones & Nisbett, 1971; Kelley, 1967). But the subjects of attribution studies are *required* to provide "causal" explanations on the basis of insufficient data, leaving open the possibility that naiveté may be attributed more justly to those who design such experiments.

According to the summary view, trait attributions are made in just those circumstances in which the speaker is ignorant of the true causes of the behavior pattern at issue. It may be that such attributions are meant to "stand in" for explicit explanations (Harré & Secord, 1972, p. 270), but it seems farfetched to regard attributions of traits as proffered explanations of either a scientific or a prescientific sort. When I say that it tends to rain in Vancouver (or that Vancouver is rainy), I do not presume to be offering an explanation of that tendency, nor to have intimate knowledge of the nature of whatever meteorological forces may be operative. Were you to ask me *why* it rains in Vancouver, which is a quite different issue, you would expose my "naive inferences" based on my lack of knowledge of meteorology. When I say that John is aggressive (or tends to be aggressive), I would also not be so presumptuous as to think that I was providing anything resembling an explanation of John's acts in terms of a well-substantiated theory of human nature.

There are circumstances in which the ascription of a trait to a person serves as a partial explanation of that person's behavior. If you are not acquainted with John and if you ask me why John pushed the boy on a certain occasion, I might reply that John is aggressive. In effect, I am saying that such behavior is not unusual or unexpected for John, and such an "explanation" might serve as an answer to your question. However, if you and I both know John well, my telling you that John is aggressive does not answer your question. Were I to inform you that the boy had pushed John yesterday, you might very well feel that I had provided a satisfactory account of the incident (see Averill, 1973, p. 280). These two different "causal attributions" correspond, roughly, to the person versus situation dichotomy discussed by attribution theorists (e.g., Jones & Nisbett, 1971). But the first is simply a statement to the effect that the behavior is not unusual and the second is primarily a justification of that behavior. Neither statement specifies the efficient cause of the behavior in question.

Although laymen use trait terms to "stand in" for explanations, psychologists have used them as explanatory constructs. In moving from the level of ordinary language description to the level of theoretical explanation, virtually all "trait theorists" (Allport, 1937; Cattell, 1957; Eysenck, 1953; Guilford, 1959; Murray, 1938) consider traits to be causal entities rather than categorical summaries. Patterns of past conduct are *energized* and granted explanatory status as efficient causes of future behavior. To avoid charges of circularity of reasoning, trait theorists speak of traits as "hypothetical constructs," inferred from patterns of past conduct and used to predict future behavior. But hypothetical trait constructs often suffer from an intrinsic conceptual fuzziness that blurs distinctions between reasons and causes in the explanation of social behavior. Persons are seen as having certain dispositions in virtue of having certain hypothetical constructs, but these constructs are an ambiguous blend of institutional facts and efficient natural causes.

The tradition of using traits as causal explanations of behavior has a long history that stems from the early faculty psychologists to the present day. Behavior is explained by reference to generative mechanisms (traits, dispositions, needs, instincts, motives, etc.) which are structurally isomorphic with the behavior pattern requiring explanation. Thus a person behaves aggressively because he or she "has" an aggressive trait, need, or whatever that causes him or her to so behave. The behavior is described as phenotypic, manifest, or surface, while the trait is genotypic, latent, or source. The general pattern of the person's social behavior is mirrored in an underlying "structure" of personality traits.

This type of theorizing seems, to me, implausible. Recall, first of all, that the criteria for classifying behaviors as instances of a trait are institutional (social) in nature. These criteria would be expected to vary, not only cross culturally, but within cultural subgroups (what is "aggressive" behavior for one socioeconomic group may not be for another). Similarly, the situations or "occasions" on which these behaviors occur will be defined quite differently in different cultural settings. Hence, the subject of an efficient cause or of a physical basis for a set of institutional conventions must be approached with great caution. Institutional rules impart meaning to topographically dissimilar actions in varied circumstances. The existence of generative mechanisms which are structurally isomorphic with institutional rules seems most unlikely. It conjures up the image of a cultural homunculus within each of us.

The organization or "structure" of traits may well reside within a pattern of interrelated institutional rules, rather than within individuals. This strong form of the "biosocial" position is implicit in the writings of ethnomethodologists (e.g., Garfinkel, 1967; Goffman, 1959), and is quite explicit in the formulations of ethogenic personality theorists (e.g., Harré & Secord, 1972) who would locate "personas" in the shared perceptions of others and who reject substantive interpretations of traits.

Within the realm of personality assessment, one of the most highly "structured," replicable, and theoretically meaningful systems of behavioral classification has been found in the domain of interpersonal behavior (Wiggins, 1968, 1973). Here I refer to the work of Leary (1957) and his associates and its subsequent development and refinement by Lorr and McNair (1963), Stern (1970), and others. From both observational and self-report data, it is clear that the relation among the major categories of interpersonal behavior may be represented structurally as a two-dimensional circumplex of trait vectors. But what is reflected in that structure?

The traditional view of the interpersonal circumplex is that it reflects the organization of needs or traits *within* individuals. Descriptively this organization refers to summaries of past conduct; but theoretically, the organization is held to mirror the arrangement of internal needs, dynamisms, or whatever. I think it more plausible that the structure of interpersonal behavior mirrors a set of interrelated social rules for classifying behavior in terms of its likely interpersonal consequences. The remarkable structural convergences that have been found among diverse theoretical systems of interpersonal behavior (Foa, 1961) do not stem from the similarity of generative mechanisms postulated (needs, traits, dynamisms, etc.). Instead, the convergences reflect the common system of institutional rules that classifies interpersonal behavior measured by different techniques. Further, the promising typologies developed by Leary (1957) and Lorr, Bishop, and McNair (1965) for identifying central interpersonal dispositions (e.g., managerial-autocratic) are more properly viewed as institutionally defined roles than as internal generative mechanisms. Finally, the sequential patterns of interpersonal transactions that have been described by Leary and others (e.g., power provokes obedience) seem to represent normative rules of conduct rather than mechanistic chain reactions.

Once we have clearly separated what is to be explained (patterns of past conduct) from plausible explanatory constructs (generative mechanisms that cause persons to be rule-following agents), the enormity of the task of personality theory becomes evident. In our present state of ignorance of the nature of human nature, we have lapsed into the layman's tendency to allow trait terms to "stand in" for genuine explanations. As a consequence, we have neglected the promising leads of those trait theorists who have recognized, at least implicitly, the importance of a distinction between traits and generative mechanisms.

Cattell (1946) has, for many years, distinguished *surface traits* (ordinary language descriptions of person attributes) from *source traits* (underlying generative mechanisms responsible for behavior classified by ordinary language). Perhaps the conceptual significance of this distinction has been overlooked because: (1) despite the use of neologisms, "source" traits appear to represent familiar "surface" themes, (2) it does not seem intuitively obvious that source mechanisms can be detected by the multivariate analysis of ordinary language attributions, and (3) identified "source" patterns have been interpreted, rather casually, by reference to psychoanalytic mechanisms. But the *conceptual* distinction between surface traits and source mechanisms resembles, or is at least compatible with, Chomsky's (1965) distinction between the surface and deep structures of language, a model that may be especially useful in stimulating thought about the plausible origins of personality traits (Harré & Secord, 1972; Stagner, 1973).

ACKNOWLEDGMENTS

I am grateful to Kenneth H. Craik and Brian R. Little for their advice and encouragement.

REFERENCES

Alker, H. A. (1972). Is personality situationally specific or intrapsychically consistent? *Journal of Personality, 40,* 1–16.

Allport, G. W. (1937). *Personality: A psychological interpretation.* New York: Holt.

Anscombe, G. E. M. (1963). *Intention* (2nd ed.). Oxford, England: Basil Blackwell.

Austin, J. L. (1957). A plea for excuses. *Proceedings of the Aristotelian Society, 57,* 1–30.

Averill, J. R. (1973). The dis-position of psychological dispositions. *Journal of Experimental Research in Personality, 6,* 275–282.

Bowers, K. B. (1973). Situationism in psychology: An analysis and critique. *Psychological Review, 80,* 307–336.

Brandt, R. B. (1970). Traits of character: A conceptual analysis. *American Philosophical Quarterly, 7,* 23–37.

Carnap, R. (1936). Testability and meaning. *Philosophy of Science, 3,* 419–471.

Cattell, R. B. (1946). *The description and measurement of personality.* Yonkers-on-Hudson, NY: World Book.

Cattell, R. B. (1957). *Personality and motivation structure and measurement.* Yonkers-on-Hudson, NY: World Book.

Chomsky, N. (1965). *Aspects of the theory of syntax.* Cambridge, MA: MIT Press.

Craik, K. H. (1969). Personality unvanquished. *Contemporary Psychology, 14,* 147–148.

Edwards, A. L. (1970). *The measurement of personality traits by scales and inventories.* New York: Holt, Rinehart & Winston.

Eysenck, H. J. (1953). *The structure of human personality.* London: Methuen.

Fishbein, M. (1973). The prediction of behaviors from attitudinal variables. In C. D. Morteen & K. K. Sereno (Eds.), *Advances in communication research* (pp. 3–31). New York: Harper & Row.

Fishbein, M., & Ajzen, I. (1972). Attitudes and opinions. *Annual Review of Psychology, 23,* 487–544.

Fishbein, M., & Ajzen, I. (1974). Attitudes toward objects as predictors of single and multiple behavioral criteria. *Psychological Review, 81,* 59–74.

Fiske, D. W. (1971). *Measuring the concepts of personality.* Chicago: Aldine.

Foa, U. G. (1961). Convergences in the analysis of the structure of interpersonal behavior. *Psychological Review, 68,* 341–353.

Garfinkel, H. (1967). *Studies in ethnomethodology.* Englewood Cliffs, NJ: Prentice-Hall.

Goffman, E. (1959). *The presentation of self in everyday life.* New York: Doubleday Anchor Books.

Gough, H. G. (1957). *California Psychological Inventory Manual.* Palo Alto, CA: Consulting Psychologists Press.

Guilford, J. P. (1959). *Personality.* New York: McGraw-Hill.

Hampshire, S. (1953). Dispositions. *Analysis, 14,* 5–11.

Harré, R., & Secord, P. F. (1972). *The explanation of social behaviour.* Oxford, England: Basil Blackwell.

Heider, F. (1958). *The psychology of interpersonal relations.* New York: Wiley.

Holt, R. R. (1958). Clinical *and* statistical prediction: A reformulation and some new data. *Journal of Abnormal and Social Psychology, 56,* 1–12.

Jaccard, J. J. (1974). Predicting social behavior from personality traits. *Journal of Research in Personality, 7,* 358–367.

Jackson, D. N. (1967). *Personality Research Form Manual.* Goshen, NY: Research Psychologists Press.

Jones, E. E., & Nisbett, R. E. (1971). *The actor and the observer: Divergent perceptions of the causes of behavior.* New York: General Learning Corporation.

Kelley, H. H. (1967). Attribution theory in social psychology. *Nebraska Symposium on Motivation, 14,* 192–241.

Kelly, G. A. (1955). *The psychology of personal constructs* (Vols. 1 and 2). New York: Norton.

Leary, T. (1957). *Interpersonal diagnosis of personality.* New York: Ronald Press.

Levy, L. H. (1970). *Conceptions of personality: Theories and research.* New York: Random House.

Little, B. R. (1972). Psychological man as scientist, humanist and specialist. *Journal of Experimental Research in Personality, 6,* 95–118.

Lorr, M., Bishop, P. F., & McNair, D. M. (1965). Interpersonal types among psychiatric patients. *Journal of Abnormal Psychology, 70,* 468–472.

Lorr, M., & McNair, D. M. (1963). An interpersonal behavior circle. *Journal of Abnormal and Social Psychology, 67,* 68–75.

Megargee, E. I. (1966). Undercontrolled and overcontrolled personality types in extreme antisocial aggression. *Psychological Monographs, 80* (No. 3, Whole No. 611).

Megargee, E. I., & Mendelsohn, G. A. (1962). A cross-validation of twelve MMPI indices of hostility and control. *Journal of Abnormal and Social Psychology, 65,* 431–430.

Megargee, E. I., & Menzies, E. S. (1971). The assessment and dynamics of aggression. In P. McReynolds (Ed.), *Advances in psychological assessment* (Vol. 2, pp. 133–156). Palo Alto, CA: Science and Behavior Books.

Mischel, W. (1968). *Personality and assessment.* New York: Wiley.

Mischel, W. (1969). Continuity and change in personality. *American Psychologist, 24,* 1012–1018.

Mischel, W. (1971). *Introduction to personality.* New York: Holt, Rinehart & Winston.

Mischel, W. (1973a). On the empirical dilemmas of psychodynamic approaches: Issues and alternatives. *Journal of Abnormal Psychology, 82,* 335–344.

Mischel, W. (1973b). Toward a cognitive social learning reconceptualization of personality. *Psychological Review, 80,* 252–283.

Murray, H. A. (1938). *Explorations in personality.* New York: Oxford University Press.

Peterson, D. R. (1968). *The clinical study of social behavior.* New York: Appleton-Century-Crofts.

Pitcher, G. (1961). Necessitarianism. *Philosophical Quarterly, 11,* 201–212.

Powell, B. (1959). Uncharacteristic actions. *Mind, 68,* 492–509.

Ryle, G. (1949). *The concept of mind.* New York: Barnes & Noble.

Searle, J. R. (1969). *Speech acts: An essay in the philosophy of language.* Cambridge, England: Cambridge University Press.

Stagner, R. (1973, August). *Traits are relevant: Theoretical analysis and empirical evidence.* Paper presented at the annual meetings of the American Psychological Association in Montreal.

Stern, G. G. (1970). *People in context: Measuring person-environment congruence in education and industry.* New York: Wiley.

Vernon, P. E. (1964). *Personality assessment: A critical survey.* New York: Wiley.

Wachtel, P. L. (1973a). Psychodynamics, behavior therapy, and the implacable experimenter: An inquiry into the consistency of personality. *Journal of Abnormal Psychology, 82,* 324–334.

Wachtel, P. L. (1973b). On fact, hunch, and stereotype: A reply to Mischel. *Journal of Abnormal Psychology, 82,* 537–540.

Wallach, M. A., & Leggett, M. I. (1972). Testing the hypothesis that a person will be consistent: Stylistic consistency versus situational specificity in size of children's drawings. *Journal of Personality, 40,* 309–330.

Wiggins, J. S. (1964). A review of Vernon, P. E., Personality assessment: A critical survey. *Educational and Psychological Measurement, 24,* 983–985.

Wiggins, J. S. (1973). *Personality and prediction: Principles of personality assessment.* Reading, MA: Addison-Wesley.

Wiggins, J. S., Renner, K. E., Clore, G. L., & Rose, R. J. (1971). *The psychology of personality.* Reading, MA: Addison-Wesley.

CHAPTER 5

INDIVIDUALS AND THE DIFFERENCES BETWEEN THEM

JAMES T. LAMIELL
GEORGETOWN UNIVERSITY

Sechrest once observed that

> to too great an extent the field of personality has been dominated . . . by psychologists pursuing the ubiquitous but elusive, and maybe even chimerical, *differences between persons.* Paradoxically, these psychologists have operated more often than not from a theory that posits *not differences but universals.* Freud's developmental states, Adler's striving for superiority, Jung's animus-anima, Maslow's need hierarchy, and many other concepts were meant to apply *to everyone everywhere,* but psychologists became bogged down in studying differences in a way that has never been very productive.
>
> *(1976, p. 4, emphasis added)*

My own position on personality psychology's current state takes these remarks by Sechrest very seriously. *Contra* the view that has dominated the thinking of mainstream personality investigators for much of the greater part of the present century, I have been arguing that the assessment and study of individual *differences* is fundamentally and irremediably ill-suited to the task of advancing personality theory. As an alternative to what many have, for years, been pleased to believe qualifies as nomothetic inquiry, I have further argued that the overarching theoretical objectives of personality psychology would be better served by inquiry that proceeds "idiothetically" (Lamiell, 1981). However infelicitous that neologism may have been, what I have meant to suggest by it is an approach to the investigation of psychological phenomena which respects the *individuality* of those phenomena—the fact that every perception, emotion, cognition, and action is *someone's*—without compromising the search for truly general or nomothetic principles, that is, principles in terms of which one might understand the perceptions, emotions, cognition, actions, and so forth of *everyone* (Lamiell, 1987, 1990a, 1990b). "Idiothetic" inquiry *accommodates* individual differences without making those differences themselves the focus of inquiry.

Consistent with the editors' vision of the present volume as a handbook, my objective in this chapter is to trace the major lines of my argument as it has been developed to date. The reader interested in a more detailed exposition is referred to my *Psychology of Personality: An Epistemological Inquiry* (1987; see also Lamiell, 1990a).

I. WHY INDIVIDUAL DIFFERENCES RESEARCH CANNOT ADVANCE PERSONALITY THEORY

Actually, the case against individual differences research as a framework for the advancement of personality psychology's theoretical concerns is logically quite straightforward, and can be stated concisely as follows:

Thesis 1: Any theory of personality is a conceptual framework designed to provide explanations for and hence an understanding of *individual* behavior/psychological functioning.[1]

Thesis 2: Except under hypothetical conditions never realized in practice, the reliability and validity coefficients and other statistical indices generated by studies of individual differences variables (alone or in combination with "situational" or "treatment" variables; see Cronbach, 1957) *bear no legitimate interpretation of any kind whatsoever at the level of the individual.*

Conclusion: Knowledge of the sort yielded by individual differences research is fundamentally and irremediably ill-suited to the task of advancing theories of individual behavior/psychological functioning—however useful that same knowledge might be for other purposes—and the discipline of personality psychology is therefore in need of a viable alternative research paradigm.

To the best of my knowledge, no one has ever seriously questioned Murray's (1938) contention that, in the psychology of personality, "the objects of study are *individual organisms* and *not aggregates of organisms*" (p. 127, emphasis added). Thus, we may take Thesis 1 as one for which there is and has always been general agreement. But if this is so, and if Thesis 2 is also true, then the conclusion follows by force of logic, and the debate over whether investigators

---

[1] This is not to deny legitimate theoretical divergences concerning such matters as the sources of personality and the dynamics of its development. It is merely to point out that individual persons are the loci of personality functioning, whatever its presumed sources and dynamics. This is true, for example, even for theorists who would emphasize various facets of socialization in their theoretical conception of personality and its development (see, e.g., Harré, 1984; Hurrelmann, 1988).

should abandon traditional "nomothetic" inquiry in favor of a more apposite framework is over. This is only how things ought to be, since, as a matter of logical fact, Thesis 2 above *is* true. Alas, it is just this point with which apologists for conventional "nomothetic" inquiry cannot or will not reconcile themselves (see, e.g., Dar & Serlin, 1990; Ozer, 1990; cf. Lamiell, 1990b), and it is at least partly for this reason that the debate continues.

A. Knowledge about Individual Differences Variables Is Not Knowledge about Individuals

The difficulty here is vividly illustrated by the following example, which, though anecdotal, is not apocryphal: Several years ago I attended a lecture given by a senior and still very prominent personality investigator who, in the course of his comments, chided a peer for making generalizations about individuals on the basis of experimental treatment group means. The lecture then proceeded with a very enthusiastic report of numerous validity coefficients he had obtained in a longitudinal study of selected individual difference variables. I later asked the speaker if he was in any way troubled by the fact that the Pearson product—moment correlation coefficients by which he was placing such store as grounds for *his* generalizations about individuals were *themselves* group means. He replied, "Well, there are group means and then there are group means."

And so there are. Specifically, and with regard to the legitimacy of using group means as empirical grounds for generalizations about individuals, there are those around which the variances are zero, and then there are those around which the variances are not zero. The former will logically support at least some generalizations about individuals, and the latter will not. So too with the Pearson product—moment correlation coefficients that, in the (all too) appropriate words of Bem and Allen (1974), are "the sacred coin of the realm" in mainstream personality research: there are correlations which are perfect, and then there are correlations which are not perfect. The former will bear at least some interpretation at the level of the individual precisely because they are, in effect, group means around which the variances are zero. The latter, that is, correlations which are not perfect, will *not* bear *any* interpretation at the level of the individual precisely because they are, in effect, group means around which the variances are not zero.

The problem here is not that a statement about an individual based on a group mean around which the variance is nonzero, or on a Pearson r of which the absolute value is less than 1.00, is knowably false for all individuals. The problem is that such a statement is *not knowably true* for *any* individual, and this is because the statement is *certainly false* for *some* individuals—though we could not say which ones without investigating the matter case by case—and *possibly false* for *all* of the individuals. Within a discipline in which the overriding objective is to explain and understand the behavior/psychological functioning of individuals, it is difficult to imagine an epistemologically worse state of affairs. That the person after whom personality psychologists' most prized statistic has been named would have been untroubled by this state of affairs is properly seen not as a failure of discernment on the part of Karl Pearson (1857–1936) but instead as a reflection of the fact that *he was not interested in individuals:*

> It is almost impossible to study any type of life without being impressed by the small importance of the individual . . . Evolution must depend upon substantial changes in considerable numbers and its theory therefore belongs to that class of phenomena which statisticians have grown accustomed to refer to as mass phenomena.
>
> *(Pearson, 1901/1902, p. 3; quoted in Porter, 1986, p. 306)*

It is arguably one of the great ironies of late twentieth century psychology that Pearson's most visible legacy has become the linchpin of a paradigm widely fancied as appropriate for handling questions about—of all things—human *individuality!* But irony or not, since the problem identified above is a logical and not an empirical one, it is not going to vanish or wilt in the face of any findings of any empirical study. One either recognizes that knowledge about individual differences variables is neither equivalent to nor substitutable for knowledge about individuals or one violates logic. There are no other choices, even where there seem to be.

For example, many (perhaps most) contemporaries are pleased to believe that the traditional paradigm can be rescued from this critique by using group means or other aggregate statistics as the basis for *probabilistic* statements about individuals (see, e.g., Paunonen & Jackson, 1986a, pp. 471–473). Let us consider the matter from an epistemological standpoint.

Take a statement of the form, "The probability is p that Smith will do X." The question is, under what values of p could such a statement be empirically verified or falsified as a claim to knowledge about Smith?

Clearly, the values 1.0 and 0 will "work" here, because substituting either one of those values for p would amount to an assertion of certainty that Smith will (if $p = 1.0$) or will not (if $p = 0$) do X. As a claim to knowledge about Smith, either statement logically admits the possibility of disconfirmation in the face of evidence that Smith does or does not do X. Brief reflection will reveal, however, that the values 1.0 and 0 are the only values that will "work" in this context. Let $p = .9$, for example. As a claim to knowledge about Smith, how is the statement "The probability is .9 that Smith will do X" possibly to be empirically evaluated? If Smith in fact does X, is the statement to be considered verified or falsified, and in either case why? If Smith does X, is it not possible that the probability that he would have done so was 1.0 all along, and not .9? If so, then what is the truth value of the assertion that the probability was .9? Alternatively, if Smith does not do X, would this disconfirm the assertion that the probability was .9 that he would? If so, why? After all, the assertion made no claim to certainty about what Smith would do. And yet if not, why not? If Smith has in fact not done X, then perhaps the probability that he would do X was in fact 0 all along and not .9 at all. Again, when probabilistic statements about individuals are based on the results of individual differences research, how are such statements to be evaluated as claims to scientific knowledge about those individuals?

The answer, of course, is that they *are not* to be so evaluated. The reason is that they *cannot* be so evaluated, *and that is the problem.* When it is based on the findings of individual differences research, a statement such as "the probability is .9 that Smith will do X" simply means that given Smith and 99 other individuals identical to Smith with respect to the predictor variable(s), 90 will do X and 10 will not. Just which 90 will and which 10 will not is a question left untouched by the probability statement. This means that not only is the probability statement not really a claim—least of all a scientific one—to knowledge about Smith, it is not really a claim to knowledge about any one of the other 99 individuals either. It is quite literally a claim to knowledge about *no one,* and that is why it fails to get at anything consequential in the domain of personality theorizing.

Now some would point out, as did Paunonen and Jackson (1986b, p. 472, footnote 1), that a statement of the form "The probability is .9 that Smith will do X" might be based on evidence pertaining to Smith's behavior across many situations, where it has been observed that in 90% of those situations Smith has engaged in behavior X and in 10% of those situations he has not. Under these conditions, there is a sense in which the probability statement could be empirically verified or falsified as a claim to knowledge about Smith. But that is because all of the data from which the statement issues refer to observations *about Smith,* which means that we are no longer discussing individual differences research, either as the source of the statement or as the locus of its subsequent verification/falsification. In other words, to achieve this sort of knowledge about individuals one must step *outside* of the individual differences framework.

B. Individual Behavior Is Not Caused by and Cannot Be Explained in Terms of the Difference(s) between That Individual and Others

For all of the foregoing, many will cling to the intuitively appealing notion that the psychological differences between individuals are relevant to and must therefore somehow be incorporated into explanations for their respective actions. As compelling as this notion seems to be, it is found wanting on close inspection.

Let us say, for example, that among his other personality characteristics Smith is an extraverted individual, and that Jones is, among his other personality characteristics, an introverted individual. Thus, along the dimension of individual differences known as introversion–extraversion, Smith's status is E while Jones' status is I. Let us further suppose that as a direct result of his "E-ness," Smith's behavior is consistently chatty (C) at social gatherings, and that as a direct result of his "I-ness," Jones' behavior is consistently quiet (Q) in such settings.

Now from a theoretical standpoint, the concern in this little scenario would be to explain Smith's "C-ness" in terms of his "E-ness," and to explain Jones' "Q-ness" in terms of his "I-ness." In individual differences research, however, what an investigator is actually looking at on the psychological ("predictor variable") side is neither E nor I per se, but instead and quite literally at the difference between the two, [E − I]. Similarly, what the investigator is actually looking at on the behavioral ("criterion variable") side is neither C nor Q per se, but instead and quite literally at the difference between the two, [C − Q]. As a result, the focus in individual differences research is actually on the relationship between the two *differences,* and it is finally for this reason that, in such research, one's vision of the individual persons between whom differences are being studied becomes blurred.

The problem is this: How can the *difference between* the respective psychological constitutions of Smith and Jones possibly be said to influence, determine, or cause Smith's behavior *or* Jones' behavior? If one adheres to the logic of the traditional individual differences approach, one is eventually forced to concede that the *difference* between Smith's extravertedness (E) and Jones' introvertedness (I) exists psychologically *neither* for Smith *nor* for Jones. Presumably, what exists psychologically for Smith is simply his extravertedness (E)–and not the difference between his extravertedness and Jones' introvertedness, [E − I]. Similarly, what presumably exists psychologically for Jones is simply his introvertedness (I), and not the difference between his introvertedness and Smith's extravertedness, [E − I]. Hence, to try to explain Smith's and Jones' respective behaviors by reference to [E − I] is to ground each of the respective explanations in an entity which, though it might well be said to exist in some sense *for an onlooker* of Smith and Jones, cannot be said to exist for either Smith or Jones.

Of course, one might object at this point that the entity [E − I] could serve some sort of explanatory function if one sets as one's task explaining neither Smith's chattiness (C) nor Jones' quietude (Q) per se, but instead the difference between the two [C − Q]. The response to this objection is not merely to concede it but to underscore it as the point: the coherence that such individual differences research explanations can *in principle* ever offer requires that the discussion be limited to the *differences between* individuals, and that it never be permitted to lapse over into a discussion about *individuals.* What the "laws" embodying such "explanations" would "explain" is merely between-person variance in the criterion variable(s), and the "explanation" would be between-person variance in the predictor variable(s). Such "explanations" might well serve to advance purely demographic or actuarial agendas. They might even serve to advance theories of *data.* But they will never advance theories of *persons,* and this is troublesome because that happens to be what personality theories are.

No person's psychological constitution *is* between-person variance on the predictor-variable side of a regression equation, and no person's behavior *is* between-person variance on the criterion side of a regression equation. Indeed, as they have been conceptualized by the ersatz "nomotheticists" of our discipline, it is necessarily the case that *individual differences variables do not exist for individuals.* Hence, no discussion of individual differences variables can be a discussion of individuals. Moreover, would-be general laws, the terms of which are individual differences variables, cannot possibly be laws that explain individual behavior. Because such laws pertain to individual *differences,* and because individual differences do not exist for individuals, one is forced to conclude that such laws pertain, quite literally, to no one. Laws that pertain to no one cannot possibly be laws that pertain to everyone, and it is to the latter that any *nomothetic* personality psychology worthy of the name would aspire.

II. Some Issues in Need of Clarification

A. Relationship of the Present Argument to Allport's Views

Many readers will detect in what has been said thus far traces of the so-called "nomothetic versus idiographic" controversy which has dogged the field now for over 50 years. Following the German philosopher Wilhelm Windelband, Gordon Allport (1937) introduced the terms "idiographic" and "nomothetic" into the discourse of personality psychologists as a way of highlighting, among other things, the difference between the study of *persons* on the one hand and the study of *person variables,* that is, variables with respect to which persons have been differentiated, on the other. Allport noted, quite properly, that mainstream personality research was thoroughly dominated by studies of the latter sort—which in his view qualified as nomothetic—and he steadfastly insisted that a proper understanding of personalities would require that the knowledge yielded by such studies be supplemented by knowledge that could be obtained only through studies of the former sort, that is, studies of the sort he labeled idiographic. Given (a) the points of convergence between Allport's views and my own, and (b) the fact that shortly before his death in 1967 Allport quite explicitly "cried uncle and retired to his corner" (cf. Allport, 1966, p. 107), the reader might wonder what reason(s) I might have for presuming that some gain could be realized through yet another seance with Holt's (1962) "Teutonic ghost." Put briefly, my presumption in this regard stems from the conviction that, as forceful and incisive as Allport was in certain respects, he failed in several important ways to prosecute effectively and/or correctly the case against the established individual differences framework.

To begin with, I doubt that Allport aided his own cause by labeling the sort of inquiry he advocated "idiographic." For even if his usage of this term was consistent with Windelband's (1894/1904), the latter had coined the expression to refer to knowledge about unique, historically configured events or phenomena, had identified such knowledge as the goal of inquiry within the humanities (*die Geisteswissenschaften*), and had explicitly distinguished such knowledge from the sort of knowledge sought within the natural sciences (*die Naturwissenschaften*). At a time when mainstream academic psychologists were still quite sensitive about their credentials as scientists—on the natural science model, of course—Allport wittingly or otherwise invited the charge of "antiscientist," and it is one which his critics pressed swiftly (e.g., Skaggs, 1945) and sometimes harshly (e.g., Nunnally, 1967).[2]

But if Allport's use of the term "idiographic" was ill-advised, his use of the term "nomothetic" was simply *wrong* in the sense that it was not consistent with the meaning that Windelband had intended. For Windelband, the term *nomothetic* referred to knowledge that could be expressed in the form of *allgemeine Gesetze*— general laws. Any such law specifies *was immer ist*—what always is—in some specified empirical domain. It specifies, in other words, what obtains *in each and every recurrent instance* of the event or phenomenon it putatively governs, what is thus *common to all* of those recurrent instances, and it is precisely a law's alleged generality that is thrown into doubt by its failure to perform in this way.

The German expression for *general* is *allgemein,* a word which itself derives from the expression *allen gemein—common to all.* Without doubt, this is the meaning Windelband attached to the term "nomothetic." It is most unfortunate that this meaning was not preserved when Allport branded as "nomothetic" the kind of knowledge about personality produced by inquiry conducted within the traditional individual differences framework. We have already noted that such inquiry produces aggregate statistics that can be interpreted in a scientifically meaningful way *for no individual* (cf. Danziger, 1990). Such "laws" as can be formulated on the basis of such statistics, therefore, cannot possibly be regarded as laws found to hold recurrently for each of many persons, and for this reason cannot possibly be *nomothetic* laws *of personality* in the sense intended by Windelband (1894/1904).[3]

Nevertheless, Allport *called* the traditional individual differences approach to the study of personality "nomothetic," and in so doing only threw his intellectual adversaries into the proverbial briar patch. For given *Windelband's* conception of nomothetic knowledge as knowledge of the sort sought by and produced within the natural sciences psychology was trying to desperately to emulate, Allport's contemporaries could scarcely have wished for better than to be accused (sic) by a critic of pursuing their subject matter in a way that conformed to the methods and knowledge objectives of the natural sciences. Had Allport more fully appreciated the foregoing considerations (or more vigorously pursued their logical implications), he would never have labeled the traditional paradigm "nomothetic" to begin with, and the entire history of the nomothetic versus idiographic controversy might have

---

[2] Allport himself seems to have been sensitive to this charge, judging by his attempt in 1962 to substitute the term "morphogenic" (borrowed from the scientifically respectable discipline of biology) for the term "idiographic." It seems that by then, however, the damage had been done. The proposed terminological graft never took, and despite his efforts Allport never succeeded in altering the widespread perception of idiographic inquiry as antiscientific.

[3] That Windelband himself would have seen no contradiction whatsoever in speaking about nomothetic knowledge within the domain of personality is clear from other portions of the original text. Alas, but without doubt, the number of authors who have written on the nomothetic versus idiographic controversy exceeds greatly the number of those who have read Windelband's text or familiarized themselves with its actual contents (Windelband, 1894/1904; cf. Lamiell, 1992a).

taken a different (and rather more productive) course. But all speculation on this count aside, I personally do not see how the fact can any longer be ignored that what Allport *called* the "nomothetic" approach to the study of personality is not now and has never been anything of the sort under the meaning of the term *nomothetic* intended by Windelband.

B. The Need to Distinguish between Uniqueness and Individuality

In my view, Allport and others who have followed his thought have made yet a third strategic error of sufficient conceptual consequence to warrant separate discussion. The difficulty to which I allude here is nicely illustrated by the following passages, which appeared in a monograph published in 1955 within a section subtitled "The Dilemma of Uniqueness":

> If there is to be a science of personality at all it should do better than it has in the past with the feature of personality that is most outstanding—its manifest *uniqueness* of organization.
>
> *(p. 21, emphasis added)*

> Nor is it helpful to take refuge in the example of other sicences . . . (On the contrary . . .) we should refuse to carry over the indifference of other sciences to the problem of *individuality.*
>
> *(p. 22, emphasis added)*

What I would highlight in these passages is the ease with which Allport moves from the term "uniqueness" to the term "individuality," with no apparent inclination to draw any distinction between the two. Space permitting, countless other examples of this phenomenon could be cited, and not only from the writings of Allport.

By making such an issue of uniqueness as he argued his case against the adequacy of traditional "nomothetic" inquiry, I think that Allport succeeded—unfortunately—in creating the impression that, in his view, the inability of such inquiry to accommodate the possibility that in certain respects each person would be found to be like no other person was its critical flaw. But as confirmed "nomotheticists" have long well known, the individual differences paradigm is in fact *not* logically incapable of accommodating the phenomenon of uniqueness, at least in a certain sense of that term.

Historically, "nomotheticists" have been guided in their work by the notion that "the" human personality is structured by a finite number of underlying attributes in some amount of which every individual is endowed by nature and/or nurture. In accordance with this notion, it has been assumed that once the elements or components of the presumed generic structure have been isolated, the particular features of any one individual's personality will be comprehensively specifiable as that individual's measured coordinates or "location" within the structure (consider, for example, the recent work of McCrae & Costa, 1986, 1987; see also Angleitner, 1991; Asendorpt, 1995; McCrae & Costa, 1995).

Since it is logically possible that each measured individual would be found to take up a position occupied by no other measured individual within the multidimensional space, it is clear that, in this view, there is at least one sense in which uniqueness—and individuality if that just means uniqueness—is a phenomenon that can be accommodated by traditional "nomotheticism." Thus have many "nomotheticists" found license to proceed with business as usual without having to either concede the validity of Allport's assault on conventional practices or explicitly reject his thesis concerning individuality qua uniqueness.

Not altogether satisfied with this ploy, Allport's strategy was to point out that "nomotheticism's" accommodation of uniqueness would "work" only insofar as the putative elements or components of the presumed generic structure were known to be universally applicable, and only insofar as those elements or components could be specified comprehensively. If either or both of these conditions failed to obtain, an investigator would inevitably fail to capture Smith's uniqueness because (a) the investigator would characterize Smith in terms that did not apply to Smith, (b) the investigator would fail to characterize Smith in terms that did apply to Smith, or (c) both.

The mainstream response to this position has typically been that the issues raised are empirical matters best handled in accordance with the established principles of construct validation as set forth by Campbell and Fiske (1959; see also Cronbach & Meehl, 1955). The notion here has been that competently executed research focused on the reliability, convergent validity, and discriminant validity of various individual differences constructs would eventually reveal those attribute dimensions necessary and sufficient for identifying any given individual's personality characteristics (again, see the previously cited work by McCrae & Costa for current examples).

Now, for reasons already mentioned, investigations into the reliability, convergent validity, and discriminant validity of various measures of individual differences *cannot* logically resolve the aforementioned concerns of Allport, no matter how competently those investigations are executed, and no matter what findings they unearth. The questions Allport raised concerned the grounds on which it would be determined whether or not some putative personality attribute X could or could not be meaningfully applied to any given individual. The correlation coefficients in which evidence concerning reliability, convergent validity, and discriminant validity subsists simply beg such questions, because when they are less than $+/-1.00$—and they always are—they are uninterpretable for individuals. Thus, the traditional "nomothetic" response to Allport's concerns regarding the celebrated assumption of universal applicability (Bem & Allen, 1974) is inadequate at its very epistemological core—persistent and widespread beliefs to the contrary notwithstanding (see, e.g., Paunonen & Jackson, 1986a, 1986b; cf. Lamiell & Trierweiler, 1986)—and Allport need not have retreated one inch on this score.

But if I would criticize traditional "nomotheticists" for pretending to meet the challenges Allport mounted when in fact they never have done and never can do so, I would also criticize Allport himself for making such an issue of uniqueness in the first place.[4] To see why, let us grant for just a few moments, and solely for discursive purposes, the validity of McCrae and Costa's (1987) claim to have isolated five basic dimensions necessary and (for now at least) sufficient as terms in which to describe the major features of any given individual's personality. Let us now suppose that the requisite five measurements have been made of the person Smith.

Now if these five measurements serve their intended purpose at all, then they convey valid information about what is, rather than what is not, the case as regards Smith's personality. They do this in virtue of the fact that the intersection of the five measurements within the multidimensional space locates Smith at a particular point and not at any of the other possible points within that space. Ensembled, the measurements state that Smith is "here" and not "there" or anywhere else in the space. It is for statements of just this sort, that is, statements about what is, rather than what is not, the case as regards the personality of a specific individual, that I would propose we reserve the term *individuality*.[5]

But now with this putative knowledge about Smith's individuality at hand, in what research direction would we be led by concerning ourselves with the question of Smith's uniqueness? In the spirit of traditional "nomotheticism," for example, suppose that we wished to know whether the location occupied by Smith in the five-dimensional space proposed by McCrae and Costa is or is not also occupied by one or more other individuals.

It is important to see here that in posing this question a distinction between Smith's individuality on the one hand, and his uniqueness on the other, has already and necessarily been made, if only implicitly. For in order to determine if what is the case regarding Smith's personality is the case for Smith and no one else—i.e., is the case for Smith uniquely—one must first have at hand some knowledge of what is the case for Smith. Thus, knowledge about Smith's individuality—what is rather than what is not the case concerning Smith—is both distinct from the logically prior to any knowledge about Smith's uniqueness or lack thereof.

A second crucial observation to be made is that if knowledge about Smith's individuality is at hand, then some basis exists for pursuing questions concerning how Smith came to be as he is, what keeps him as he is, and what might change the way he is, and how answers to these questions might be used to explain why Smith currently acts as he does and, perhaps, to predict how he will act in certain future circumstances. Hence, given some initial knowledge about Smith's individuality, an investigator might well opt *not* to pursue the question of uniqueness at all, and to pursue instead questions of the sort that Leon Levy (1970, p. 29) identified as central to personality

---

[4] I should note here that on this score Allport's views were very much in line with those of Windelband, for whom the thought that he might *not* be unique was utterly abhorrent.

[5] This is not to say that I regard the traditional individual differences paradigm as well-suited to the formulation of such statements. Indeed, I do not. However, since this issue is tangential to our immediate concerns, I let it pass here.

psychology's overriding theoretical concerns. By the same token, if the question of uniqueness (which, it may be noted, is not to be found among those cited by Levy) is to be pursued, then the questions concerning personality dynamics (development, maintenance, change, etc.) must inevitably be held in abeyance.

Bearing the above in mind, let us now suppose with McCrae and Costa (1986), and in traditional "nomothetic" fashion, that the five attribute dimensions in terms of which Smith's individuality has been articulated can be meaningfully applied to all of the other individuals with reference to whom the question of Smith's uniqueness is to be settled. Of course, in granting this assumption we already finesse one of Allport's major concerns with respect to the dilemma of uniqueness (see above). But ignoring this fact for now, let us focus instead on the fact that even if the assumption is granted, another very serious problem immediately arises, namely, that of determining how many—and which—other individuals should be compared with Smith before concluding that he is or is not unique in the sense under discussion.

To say that someone is unique is to say that there is no one else just like him. But is the phrase "no one else" to mean, literally, not one other human being who has ever lived, is now living, or who will ever live? If so, then in taking up the question of Smith's uniqueness we have, to say the least, set a rather formidable task for ourselves. On the other hand, if this is not what the phrase "no one else" is to mean, then the question of what the phrase is to mean remains. Furthermore, any answer that we might offer to this question will demand a rationale, that is, an explanation for why the phrase "no one else" should be given any meaning other than its literal meaning as expressed above.

But just to be sporting, let us suppose that somehow all of these matters have been resolved: (1) that the population of individuals with reference to whom the question of Smith's uniqueness is to be settled has been specified in a conceptually defensible and practically workable way; (2) that the assumption that McCrae and Costa's five attribute dimensions can be applied meaningfully to every individual within that population has been justified *properly,* and (3) that measurements of each one of those individuals with respect to the five attribute dimensions are at long last available.[6]

Now let us suppose that, as it has turned out, none of the other n individuals within the investigated population has been found to occupy the same position in the multidimensional space where we had previously located Smith. At long last, empirical grounds would exist for claiming that, in at least one sense of the term, Smith is unique.

But now a new question arises: What do we know *about Smith's personality*

[6] Incidentally (and as if we were not in this up to our necks already), how long should we expect the data-gathering process to take? And if and when it is completed, should we expect to find Smith at just that location in the multidimensional space where we left him? Or might he have moved by then? And if by then he has moved, what, if any, problems would this create? As important and difficult as these questions are, it would be a shame to let them block our passage at this late stage of our discussion, so let us pretend that these questions, too, can be satisfactorily answered: that all of the needed measurements have been gathered within a reasonable length of time, and that Smith, God bless him, has stayed put at the precise coordinates within the multidimensional space where we had located him originally.

that we did not know before the question of his uniqueness was settled? Is he any *more* the person we originally found him to be by virtue of the subsequently established fact that there is no one else just like him? Surely, the answer to this question must be "no," for if it is "yes," then it follows that Smith is no longer the person he was, in which case the validity of the conclusion that he is unique is thrown back into doubt. Alternatively, suppose that our investigation has turned up indisputable evidence that there exists at least one other individual, Jones, whose personality is organized exactly like Smith's. The question is, is Smith any less the person we originally found him to be by virtue of the subsequently established fact that he is not unique in this regard? Once again, the answer to this question must be "no," for if it is "yes," then our original measurements of Smith no longer represent his individuality, in which case he really might be unique after all, and in any case can no longer be regarded as identical to Jones.

The lesson here is not difficult to see: whatever the fidelity of our original assertions concerning Smith's individuality, that fidelity can be neither compromised nor enhanced by the results of inquiry into Smith's uniqueness. Smith cannot be any more the person he is simply by virtue of our establishing (as if, somehow, we ever really could) that he is unique, and he cannot be any less the person he is even if it is discovered that he is not unique. Smith's individual personality—his individuality—is what it is whether he is unique or not. Moreover, the questions of genuine theoretical—and practical—consequence cited earlier concerning personality development, maintenance, and change remain whether in the important features of his personality Smith is, to paraphrase Murray and Kluckholm's (1953) much too celebrated observation, "like all other persons, like some other persons, or like no other persons."

What Allport called "the dilemma of uniqueness" should be laid permanently to rest. It is not only unproductive but actually counterproductive to continue to level against "nomotheticism" the charge that it fails to accommodate the possibility of individual uniqueness. In the first place, there is at least one logical sense in which the charge simply is not true, and committed "nomotheticists" will always be quick to reassert that fact (see, e.g., Jackson & Paunonen, 1988). In the second place, while there is also a sense in which the charge is true, it is also true that, when all is said and done, the point is moot. It is the fact of individuality, not the altogether separate and finally inconsequential matter of uniqueness, that undermines conventional "nomotheticism" as a framework for the advancement of personality psychology's pantheoretical agenda.[7]

[7] This is as good a place as any to point out that in calling for an approach to the study of personality that respects the *individuality* of psychological phenomena, one *need* not—and I *do* not—seek to promote a kind of individual*ism* in the traditional sense of that term (see in this regard the excellent article by Sampson, 1988). In this connection Alfred Adler's individual psychology comes immediately to mind as a very clear example of a view which is at once respectful of individuality but is anything but a celebration of what Sanford calls "self-contained individualism." Indeed, Adler's concept of *das Gemeinschaftsgefühl* is the very antithesis of such individualism, and is in fact much more in the spirit of what Sanford calls "ensembled individualism." Similarly, William Stern's *critical personalism* (Stern, 1906, 1917, 1918, 1924; cf. Lamiell, 1996, 1992b) offers a comprehensive framework for conceiving of the human person in a way that is mindful of individuality yet disdainful of individualism.

III. "IDIOTHETIC" INQUIRY AS AN ALTERNATIVE TO TRADITIONAL "NOMOTHETICISM"

Bem (1982) observed that, historically, the fatal problem with recommending something like what Allport thought of as idiographic (or morphogenic) inquiry has always been that "one is never quite sure what to do next" (p. 23). In view of this problem, and as my own views are clearly akin to Allport's—even though, as I have tried to make clear, they deviate from Allport's in several significant respects—I intend to focus in the remainder of this chapter on some basic principles of "idiothetic" inquiry which I believe can and should guide us as we move from the traditional individual differences paradigm toward a more adequate alternative. Following Rorer and Widiger's (1983) worthwhile recommendation, I will proceed by relating my views to a very sobering but insightful epistemological commentary offered sometime ago by Paul Meehl (1978).

A. Synopsis of Meehl's Views on the Slow Progress of "Soft" Psychology

The following passage nicely conveys Meehl's views concerning the notion that theoretical assertions in the so-called "soft" areas of psychology—among which he explicitly included personality psychology—can be corroborated adequately by means of conventional tests of statistical significance carried out against the null hypothesis, in accordance with the inferential principles set forth by the renowned Sir Ronald Fisher:

> I suggest to you that Sir Ronald has befuddled us, mesmerized us, and led us down the primrose path. I believe that the almost universal reliance on merely refuting the null hypothesis as the standard method for corroborating substantive theories in the soft areas is a terrible mistake, is basically unsound, poor scientific strategy, and one of the worst things that ever happened in the history of psychology.
>
> *(1978, p. 817)*

The major problem here, Meehl notes, is the fact that the null hypothesis is almost always false, and knowably so with virtual certainty a priori (see also on this point, Bakan, 1966). Population means are virtually never precisely equal, and population correlation coefficients are virtually never precisely zero. Consequently, a statistical relationship large enough to reach that magical $p < .05$, and thus to reject the null hypothesis, is virtually guaranteed regardless of the substantive merits of the theoretical proposition under putative test, provided only that one is able and willing to make a sufficient number of observations. Meehl quite properly concludes from this that much of what has historically passed for theory testing in "soft" psychology reduces to "meaningless substantive constructions on the properties of the statistical power function" (p. 823).

Adopting what might be termed a "neo-Popperian" philosophy of science, Meehl thus argues that, for all practical purposes, it is simply oxymoronic to speak of "risking" theoretical propositions against the possibility of failing to reject the null hypothesis. His conception of a more apposite approach is conveyed through the following example:

> If I tell you that Meehl's theory of climate predicts that it will rain sometime next April, and this turns out to be the case, you will not be much impressed with my "predictive success." Nor will you be impressed if I predict more rain in April than in May, even showing three asterisks (for $p < .001$) in my t-test table! If I predict from my theory that it will rain on 7 of the 30 days of April, and it rains on exactly 7, you might perk up your ears a bit, but still you would be inclined to think of this as a "lucky coincidence." But suppose that I specify which 7 days in April it will rain and ring the bell; then you will start getting seriously interested in Meehl's meteorological conjectures. Finally, if I tell you that on April 4th it will rain 1.7 inches (66 cm), and on April 9th 2.3 inches (90 cm) and so forth, and get seven of these correct within reasonable tolerance, you will begin to think that Meehl's theory must have a lot going for it. You may believe that Meehl's theory of the weather, like all theories, is, when taken literally, false, since probably all theories are false in the eyes of God, but you will at least say, to use Popper's language, that it is beginning to look as if Meehl's theory has considerable *verisimilitude,* that is, truth-likeness. . . . An unphilosophical chemist or astronomer or molecular biologist would say that this was just good sensible scientific practice, that a theory that makes precise predictions and correctly picks out narrow intervals or point values out of the range of experimental possibilities is a pretty strong theory.
>
> *(Meehl, 1978, pp. 817–818, emphasis and parentheses in original)*

With Meehl's thoughts in mind—and most especially those expressed in the last statement of the above quotation—let us now turn to a consideration of studies that I and various colleagues have been conducting over the past several years in the area of subjective personality judgments.

B. Studies in the Epistemology of Subjective Personality Judgments

First, a bit of background. If one digs beneath the reliability and validity coefficients (and, occasionally, other aggregate statistical indices) issuing from studies of individual differences to the conceptual core of the paradigm, one finds at bedrock an unwavering conviction that meaningful statements about the extent to which any given individual's personality is endowed with one or more underlying attributes (traits, predispositions, etc.) can be derived only by comparing that individual with others. In this view, our knowledge of who Smith is is necessarily and inextricably tied to our knowledge of who others are. Though manifest in a variety of ways, this conviction finds its most visible and formal expression in the logic of the normative measurement operations which have long been regarded as the *sine qua non* of scientifically negotiable statements about personality.[8]

Several years ago, however, I arrived (via studies focused on the so-called "illusory correlation" phenomenon; see Lamiell, 1980; Lamiell, Foss, & Cavenee, 1980; see also Shweder, 1975, 1980) at the hypothesis that, in formulating and expressing subjective judgments about their own and one another's personality characteristics, lay persons do *not* routinely rely on a normative reasoning process. Instead, I hypothesized, Smith relies on what I later came to appreciate as an essentially *dialectical* reasoning process by which his judgments of, say, Jones, are framed not by contrasting Jones with others, but by contrasting Jones with a conception of who Jones is not but might otherwise be, i.e., with a conception of the *negation* of Jones.

A question which often arises here is, would not Smith's conception of who Jones is not itself require prior knowledge (existing "now" as memory traces of previous experiences) of who others are? A "yes" answer here would, of course, imply that the judgments Smith makes of Jones (or, for that matter, of himself) are grounded in normative considerations after all. My answer, however, is "no." The thesis is that Smith's ability to conceive of who Jones is not but might otherwise be does not require prior knowledge of who others are. Indeed, the contention here is that were it not for the capacity to frame judgments dialectically, and hence independent of considerations about individual differences, it would be impossible for knowledge about individual differences to be framed. The claim here, in other words, is that it is dialectical reasoning that makes normative (and for that matter, ipsative) reasoning possible, and not the other way around. Nor, if this is true, could it be so only for the lay person. To the contrary, it would have to be true as well for personality investigators themselves, and elsewhere I have tried to explain both that and why this is the case (Lamiell, 1987, chap. 5). Suffice it for now to say that it is here where one finds the most important methodological implications of this line of inquiry for those investigators who are interested in trait measurement and in search of a viable technique (see Equation 2 in Lamiell, 1981, p. 282) with which to replace the heretofore favored normative operations.[9]

---

[8] To be sure, investigators have long recognized the possibilities offered by ipsative measurement. However, prevailing wisdom has always been that individual differences research, and hence inquiry grounded in the logic of normative measurement, is a logical precursor to any viable attempt to measure individuals ipsatively (see, e.g., Beck, 1953; Eysenck, 1954; Falk, 1956).

[9] Warning: those investigators who are merely looking for a better way to measure individual differences (as appears to be the case, for example, with Paunonen & Jackson, 1986a, 1986b; see also Asendorpf, 1988) will simply have to look elsewhere. The objective, in my view, is not to improve individual differences research but to abandon it. In this same vein, the notion should be resisted that my proposed methodological alternatives can properly be evaluated according to the psychometric criteria of the individual differences paradigm. The realization that those criteria are inadequate to the task(s) at hand is what gave rise to the proposed methodological alternatives in the first instance.

Given the hypothesis that lay persons reason dialectically rather than normatively in formulating subjective personality judgments, the challenge, à la Popper, was to devise a means of exposing that hypothesis to the risk of disconfirmation in empirical observations. To this end, several studies have to date been carried out (Lamiell & Durbeck, 1987; Lamiell, Foss, Larsen, & Hempel, 1983; Lamiell, Foss, Trierweiler, & Leffei, 1983).

In all of those studies, the subject's task was very simple: he or she was presented with a series of 30–40 activity protocols and told that each such protocol conveyed valid information about the extent to which one of his or her peers typically invests his or her time or effort in each of a number of activities. The subject was requested to consider the information displayed in each protocol, to form a judgment about the degree to which the indicated activity pattern reflected each of a number of underlying personality attributes (e.g., warm versus cold, sociable versus unsociable, industrious versus lazy), and then to express each judgment by marking a rating scale.

Now if in a task of this sort the subject's judgments are of a normative nature, then the actual ratings made of the targets by a particular subject should be well predicted by formal measurements of those same targets derived nonactuarially (Lamiell, Trierweiler, & Foss, 1983; cf. Conger, 1983; Woody, 1983) via the arithmetic proper to normative measurement operations. Alternatively, if the subject's reasoning process is not of a normative nature but is instead dialectical, and hence patterned after the logic of what Cattell (1944) once called *interactive* measurement, then measurements of the targets derived nonactuarially via the arithmetic proper to such measurement should better predict the subject's actual ratings of those targets.

Note carefully the approach that was taken here: on the basis of two competing and precisely articulated theoretical conceptions of the psychological process engaged by the experimental task, specific point predictions were derived nonactuarially for where a given subject's ratings of the targets would literally fall on a specified scale. The sensible thing to do at this point was not to fashion some sort of a null hypothesis test, and certainly not to set about analyzing individual differences in the subjects' perceptions of the targets (e.g., by engaging one or another of the various data analysis procedures discussed by Schneider, 1973). The sensible thing to do was to check, for each subject, the degree of correspondence between each of the two sets of predicted ratings and that subject's actual ratings. Using for this purpose the well-known index of profile dissimilarity devised by Cronbach and Gleser (1953), the findings obtained with one subject who participated in the study by Lamiell and Durbeck (1987) are displayed in Table I.

Focusing for the moment on the dissimilarity indices shown in the first row of Panel IV in the table, one can see that, for Target 1, the index resulting from a comparison of the subject's actual ratings to the interactively derived point predictions (.11) was lower (indicating less dissimilarity) than that resulting from a comparison of the subject's actual ratings to normatively derived point predictions (.55). The dialectical theoretical conception of the subjective judgment process thus showed greater verisimilitude in this instance, and it is important to see that *this* conclusion

TABLE I
Predicted Ratings, Actual Ratings, and Proportional Profile Dissimilarities (One Subject, 40 Targets)

Target	Panel I: Predictions from normative model (N) Attribute			Panel II: Predictions from interactive model (I) Attribute			Panel III: Actual Ratings (A) Attribute			Panel IV: Profile dissimilarities	
	1	2	3	1	2	3	1	2	3	N vs A	I vs A
1	17.32	0.00	10.39	12.01	7.14	12.54	10	8	13	.55	.11
2	8.65	19.81	.22	9.19	12.67	7.95	5	15	4	.27	.23
3	13.57	16.39	8.41	10.79	12.67	7.95	4	9	8	.53	.36
4	9.09	5.40	19.34	9.33	8.65	16.58	8	8	12	.38	.23
5	0.00	4.23	13.99	6.37	8.32	14.16	8	12	11	.57	.25
6	20.00	4.07	9.56	12.88	8.28	12.16	9	14	8	.69	.38
7	14.27	6.76	6.43	11.01	9.03	10.75	14	8	8	.09	.19
8	7.90	20.00	5.54	8.95	12.72	10.35	7	13	7	.32	.17
9	10.95	12.72	11.36	9.94	10.69	12.98	7	8	7	.34	.33
10	3.67	7.16	12.38	7.57	9.14	13.66	6	5	8	.24	.30
11	14.09	9.88	12.30	10.96	9.90	13.40	7	8	8	.40	.32
12	7.57	2.34	8.46	8.34	7.80	11.67	8	8	7	.27	.22
13	8.08	4.94	12.49	9.00	8.52	13.49	8	13	8	.43	.33
14	8.63	6.11	7.23	9.18	8.84	11.11	7	10	8	.21	.20
15	10.60	10.25	6.78	9.82	10.00	10.91	7	10	12	.31	.15
16	3.91	8.67	1.28	7.64	9.56	8.42	6	13	4	.22	.23
17	2.83	14.48	4.43	7.30	11.18	9.85	6	14	8	.21	.16
18	2.79	8.46	19.58	7.28	9.50	16.69	8	8	14	.35	.14
19	9.51	18.64	11.14	9.47	12.34	12.88	9	14	9	.24	.20
20	16.71	12.50	5.94	11.81	10.63	10.53	7	9	11	.57	.25
21	12.84	5.37	14.54	10.55	8.64	14.42	12	7	9	.28	.28
22	11.26	8.91	11.21	10.04	9.63	12.91	12	8	11	.06	.16
23	7.24	7.96	7.78	8.73	9.36	11.36	8	12	12	.28	.14
24	15.21	2.13	14.13	11.32	7.73	14.23	10	7	12	.37	.13
25	15.81	6.08	10.65	11.52	8.84	12.66	10	12	14	.43	.18
26	8.01	11.57	5.73	8.98	10.37	10.44	8	12	10	.22	.10
27	9.02	7.53	5.99	9.31	9.24	10.55	8	12	7	.22	.22
28	13.34	11.02	4.90	10.72	10.22	10.06	7	13	4	.28	.31
29	10.19	12.07	0.00	9.69	10.51	7.84	6	13	6	.31	.20
30	15.70	7.68	7.38	11.48	9.28	11.18	13	13	7	.26	.26
31	19.67	8.21	7.35	12.78	9.43	11.17	11	7	5	.40	.30
32	13.46	2.13	12.77	10.75	7.73	13.62	8	7	8	.41	.29
33	13.80	11.05	8.10	10.87	10.22	11.50	8	13	12	.34	.19
34	9.42	5.57	8.58	9.44	8.70	11.72	7	8	12	.23	.12
35	9.90	10.25	11.64	9.60	10.00	13.10	10	8	11	.12	.15
36	10.16	12.84	10.29	9.68	10.73	12.49	8	8	11	.26	.17
37	5.53	7.44	14.94	8.17	9.22	14.60	7	14	11	.35	.28
38	17.19	9.38	12.08	11.97	9.76	13.30	9	11	15	.41	.17
39	6.43	0.74	20.00	8.47	7.35	16.88	7	12	18	.45	.20
40	6.10	4.56	9.90	8.36	8.42	12.32	7	12	9	.36	.24

Means of the profile dissimilarity values	.33	.22
Standard deviations of the profile dissimilarity values	.13	.07
t value for differences between correlated means (N vs I)	5.71	($p < .01$)

Source: "Whence Cognitive Prototypes in Impression Formation? Some Empirical Evidence for Dialectical Reasoning as a Generative Process," by J. T. Lamiell and P. Durbeck, 1987, Journal of Mind and Behavior, 8, pp. 223–244. Reprinted with permission of publisher.

does not appeal to any p value, or to any inferential statistic of any sort. There is no null hypothesis here to reject or fail to reject.

Of course, a critic might object that the results just discussed represent those obtained in one instance only. And so they do. But by scanning the remainder of Panel IV in the table, one can see that point predictions based on the interactive (dialectical) model approximated actual ratings better than did point predictions based on the normative model in 31 instances, and failed to do so in only 9 instances. Here, the possibility for putting a test of the null hypothesis to good use does arise. For example, a t test comparing the two arrays of dissimilarity values might be carried out (see bottom of Table I). Alternatively, a simple chi-square analysis might be conducted, in which we would enter 31 tallies in one cell of the chi-square table to represent the 31 "hits" for the dialectical theory, and 9 tallies in another cell to represent the 9 "misses" for that theory. The distribution of "hits" versus "misses" thus obtained *for this individual subject* could in turn be tested for statistical significance against chance expectations, which in this example would be a distribution of 20 "hits" and 20 "misses."

For the record, the obtained value of chi-square in this instance equals 12.1, a value which, at one degree of freedom, would occur by chance alone much less often than 1 time in 100. It is vitally important to recognize, however, that in this context the statistical analysis did *not* serve as a test of the substantive theoretical proposition. It served instead as a means of determining whether or not tests of that theoretical proposition already accomplished by other and entirely independent means have confirmed or disconfirmed the proposition with a degree of regularity sufficient to regard it as empirically corroborated.

But now what of the objection that, for all of this, we have still considered but one subject? The argument, of course, is that scientific theories or theoretical propositions cannot stand or fall on results obtained with just one subject. And so they cannot. But suppose that I had at hand evidence (and I do; see Lamiell & Durbeck, 1987) that in the study from which the data displayed in Table I were obtained, which involved a total of 67 subjects (investigated individually, of course), there were 57 for whom the hypothesis that the subjective reasoning process is dialectical was confirmed, 10 for whom that hypothesis was not clearly confirmed, and none—not one—for whom the competing hypothesis (that the subjective reasoning process is normative) was confirmed instead. This distribution of "hits" and "misses" could likewise be submitted to a chi-square analysis, but to what end? The obtained ratio of "hits" to "misses" appears to be overwhelming for the simple and very good reason that it is, and any conventional statistical test at this point would be merely gratuitous.

C. Implications

One thing I certainly do not wish to suggest by the foregoing is that studies of subjective personality impressions should now take center stage in the activity of personality investigators. Those studies do serve, in my view, the worthy function of demonstrating that individuals *can* be characterized, in terms of their salient personality attributes, through the exercise of a reasoning process that is at once coherent and exceedingly systematic, but which at no point requires the comparison of one individual to another. With respect to the enterprise of trait measurement, the question raised by these findings is, If lay persons can proceed in the manner just described as they formulate and express their "subjective" impressions, then why could not personality investigators proceed in like fashion as they formulate and express their "objective" impressions, in the form of personality profiles? The answer is that they *could,* and in my view they *should.*

It is also to be hoped that the studies mentioned above will awaken at least some contemporaries to the theoretical possibilities that are opened up by taking seriously the concept of dialectical reasoning. The possibility suggests itself, for example, that the subjects of our inquiries reason in this fashion not only when they are engaging a fairly sterile experimental task involving personality ratings, but routinely, in the appraisal of the circumstances of their day-to-day lives (consider, for example, the dialectical themes that emerge in Frijda's [1988] discussion of the laws of emotion; see also Rychlak, 1981, 1988). In short, there is, potentially at least, a great deal more of genuine theoretical consequence here than might immediately meet the eye, and it is unlikely that those possibilities are going to be vigorously explored so long as the majority of investigators within the field are busy searching for—or celebrating the "discovery" of—personality psychology's answer to the periodic table of elements.

I believe, with Meehl, that if basic research in the psychology of personality is ever to prove successful in advancing personality theory, there is going to have to be a sharpening of hypotheses to the point that they enable one to make point predictions, or at least narrow interval predictions, from the range of experimental possibilities which are presented to the subjects. When one is positioned to do this, as we were in our studies of subjective personality judgments, tests of statistical significance are, as we have just seen, either obviated altogether or relegated to an epistemological role entirely different from—and decidedly more limited than—that which such tests have played heretofore.

The major advantages of this alternative approach vis-à-vis the objective of fashioning a genuinely (rather than merely pseudo-) nomothetic paradigm for basic personality research are not difficult to see. First of all, and as the studies mentioned above illustrate, it is possible to carry out theoretically relevant studies of individuals without either resorting to radical behaviorism or compromising methodological rigor. The "trick" here, if that is what it is, is to bring two or more divergent and well-articulated theoretical propositions to bear on the task of predicting what Smith will literally do in specified circumstances. Hypothesis testing is then a matter of investigating the correspondence between those divergent predictions and what Smith actually does. A test of this particular sort need engage no inferential statistics because it is not a test of a null hypothesis.

Second, since empirical research designed in this way neither involves nor invites any comparison between what Smith does and what others do, the investigation of each individual becomes a coherent study unto itself. This is just as it should be in a discipline that would advance our theoretical understanding of individuals.

Third, the foregoing logically compromises not at all the search for general or nomothetic principles. To the contrary, in a discipline where individuals are the entities over which generality is sought, the rigorous examination of theoretical propositions at the level of the individual is not only not antithetical to the quest for generality but is in fact logically central thereto. If reliance on conventional null hypothesis testing procedures is one of the worst things that has ever happened in the history of psychology, then another is surely the ascendance of the notion that genuinely nomothetic principles of personality could somehow be established without studying individuals.[10]

Fourth, nothing in the approach I am advocating requires one to reject the fact of individual differences. As mentioned in the introductory comments to this chapter, the crucial difference between "idiothetic" inquiry and the traditional paradigm is that while the former simply *accommodates* individual differences, the latter makes those differences the focus of investigation. For example, in the impression formation studies discussed previously the subjects most certainly did differ in their ratings of the targets, and no feature of the employed methodology rendered inadmissable the possibility (nay, the certainty) that such would be the case. Nor, however, was the study of those differences the point of the research. The point of the research was to empirically evaluate alternative theoretical conceptions of the reasoning process through which each individual subject arrived at his or her ratings, and there is simply no analysis of the differences between the ratings that could have shed light on that question (see Lamiell, 1987, chapter 6, for a further discussion of this point). Here and elsewhere I have discussed the problems which arise when individual differences are made the focus of investigation. I stand by the conviction that those problems are fatal to personality psychology's overriding scientific objectives, and that those same problems are irremediable within the traditional paradigm (cf. Dar & Serlin, 1990; Lamiell, 1990a, 1990b; Ozer, 1990).

Finally, I should not fail to acknowledge that as attempts to proceed along the lines I have sketched are put into practice, great challenges are bound to arise. It is, after all, one thing to generate theoretically based point predictions in studies of subjective personality judgments—even that was not so simple as it might now appear to have been—and quite another thing to generate comparable predictions in many of the other substantive areas in which personality investigators have legitimate and important concerns. At the very least, however, I hope to have provided the outlines of an ideal toward which I believe we should be

---

[10] It is interesting to note that, at its beginnings, experimental psychology was very much an "$N = 1$" affair in the domain of research methodology even at its objective was to discover *general* laws of human psychological functioning. The notion that one *either* seeks such knowledge *or* studies individuals but not both is a myth that developed later on (see Danziger, 1990).

striving. Knowing what one is trying to achieve can be very helpful, even if one cannot at a given point in time claim to have achieved it fully.

When all is said and done, perhaps the most pressing current problem with personality psychology is that, over the years, the majority of those who animate the field has gradually lost the ability to distinguish between the genuinely scientific business of formulating and testing theoretically derived propositions concerning the behavior/psychological functioning of individuals on the one hand and the merely actuarial business of accounting for variance in countless measures of individual differences in behavior/psychological functioning on the other. Or perhaps the ability to make this distinction remains, but the role of the actuary is simply preferred in much larger numbers. In any case, I for one am greatly disturbed by the witting or unwitting ascendance of the notion, evidence of which abounds in the literature, that our subjects are not so much beings to be understood, to the end of enlightening us not only about them but about ourselves, as they are objects to be wagered on (cf. Paunonen & Jackson, 1986a, pp. 471–472), like so many horses. "Idiothetic" inquiry is not about placing bets, with the objective of maximizing payoffs in the long run. It is not about regarding *persons* as *things* or as mere *matter* (see the above cited works by Stern). It is about the serious business of advancing theoretical conceptions of individual behavior–psychological functioning, toward the end of improving our understanding of ourselves and one another. I do not know for certain that the framework as I have sketched it up to now will get us where we want to go. I do know that the long-dominant individual differences paradigm will not. It is time to move on. The epistemological basis for doing so is at hand, even if an exquisitely detailed map of all of the territory is not.

REFERENCES

Allport, G. W. (1937). *Personality: A psychological interpretation.* New York: Holt, Rinehart & Winston.

Allport, G. W. (1955). *Becoming: Basic considerations for a psychology of personality.* New Haven, CT: Yale University Press.

Allport, G. W. (1962). The general and the unique in psychological science. *Journal of Personality, 30,* 405–422.

Allport, G. W. (1966). Traits revisited. *American Psychologist, 21,* 1–10.

Angleitner, A. (1991). Personality psychology: Trends and developments. *European Journal of Personality, 5,* 185–197.

Asendorpf, J. B. (1988). Individual response profiles in the behavioral assessment of personality. *European Journal of Personality, 2,* 155–167.

Asendorpf, J. B. (1995). Persönlichkeitspsychologie: Das empirische Studium der individuellen Besonderheit aus spezieller und differentieller Perspektive [Personality psychology: The empirical study of individuality from special and different perspective]. *Psychologische Rundschau, 46,* 235–247.

Bakan, D. (1966). The test of significance in psychological research. *Psychological Bulletin, 66,* 423–437.

Beck, S. J. (1953). The science of personality: Nomothetic or idiographic? *Psychological Review, 60,* 353–359.

Bem, D. J., & Allen, A. (1974). On predicting some of the people some of the time: The search for cross-situational consistencies in behavior. *Psychological Review, 81,* 506–520.

Bem, D. J. (1982). Toward a response style theory of persons in situations. In R. A. Dienstbier and M. M. Page (Eds.), *Nebraska Symposium on Motivation 1982: Personality—Current theory and research,* Volume 30, pp. 201–231. Lincoln: University of Nebraska Press.

Campbell, D. T., & Fiske, D. W. (1959). Convergent and discriminant validation by the multitrait-multimethod matrix. *Psychological Bulletin, 56,* 81–105.

Cattell, R. B. (1944). Psychological measurement: Normative, ipsative, interactive. *Psychological Review, 51,* 292–303.

Conger, A. J. (1983). Toward a further understanding of the intuitive personologist: Some critical evidence on the diabolical quality of subjective psychometrics. *Journal of Personality, 51,* 248–258.

Cronbach, L. J. (1957). The two disciplines of scientific psychology. *American Psychologist, 12,* 671–684.

Cronbach, L. J., & Gleser, G. (1953). Assessing similarity between profiles. *Psychological Bulletin, 50,* 456–473.

Cronbach, L. J., & Meehl, P. E. (1955). Construct validity in psychological tests. *Psychological Bulletin, 52,* 281–302.

Danziger, K. (1990). *Constructing the subject: Historical origins of psychological research.* New York: Cambridge University Press.

Dar, R., & Serlin, R. C. (1990). For whom the bell curve toils: Universality in individual differences research. In D. N. Robinson & L. P. Mos (Eds.), *Annals of theoretical psychology* (Vol. 6, pp. 193–199). New York: Plenum Press.

Eysenck, H. J. (1954). The science of personality: Nomothetic! *Psychological Review, 61,* 339–342.

Falk, J. (1956). Issues distinguishing idiographic from nomothetic approaches to personality theory. *Psychological Review, 63,* 53–62.

Frijda, N. H. (1988). The laws of emotion. *American Psychologist, 43,* 349–358.

Harré, R. (1984). *Personal being.* Cambridge, MA: Harvard University Press.

Holt, R. (1962). Individuality and generalization in the psychology of personality. *Journal of Personality, 30,* 377–404.

Hurrelmann, K. (1988). *Social structure and personality development.* New York: Cambridge University Press.

Jackson, D. N., & Paunonen, S. V. (1988, August). *The measurement of uniqueness in personality.* Paper presented at the 96th annual convention of the American Psychological Association, Atlanta, GA.

Lamiell, J. T. (1980). On the utility of looking in the "wrong" direction. *Journal of Personality, 48,* 82–88.

Lamiell, J. T. (1981). Toward an idiothetic psychology of personality. *American Psychologist, 36,* 276–289.

Lamiell, J. T. (1987). *The psychology of personality: An epistemological inquiry.* New York: Columbia University Press.

Lamiell, J. T. (1990a). Explanation in the psychology of personality. In D. N. Robinson & L. P. Mos (Eds.), *Annals of theoretical psychology* (Vol. 8, pp. 153–192). New York: Plenum.

Lamiell, J. T. (1990b). Let's be careful out there: Reply to commentaries. In D. N. Robinson & L. P. Mos (Eds.), *Annals of theoretical psychology* (Vol. 6, pp. 219–231). New York: Plenum.

Lamiell, J. T. (1992a, August). *What did Windelband mean by nomothetic?* Paper presented at the 100th annual convention of the American Psychological Association, Washington, DC.

Lamiell, J. T. (1992b, August). *William Stern, differential psychology and the problem of individuality.* Paper presented at the 100th annual convention of the American Psychological Association, Washington, DC.

Lamiell, J. T. (1996). William Stern: More than the I.Q. Guy. In G. A. Kimble, C. A. Boneau, & M. Wertheimer (Eds.), *Portraits of pioneers in psychology: Volume II* (pp. 72–85). Hillsdale, NJ: Erlbaum.

Lamiell, J. T., & Durbeck, P. (1987). Whence cognitive prototypes in impression formation? Some empirical evidence for dialectical reasoning as a generative process. *Journal of Mind and Behavior, 8,* 223–244.

Lamiell, J. T., Foss, M. A., & Cavenee, P. (1980). On the relationship between conceptual schemes and behavior reports: A closer look. *Journal of Personality, 48,* 54–73.

Lamiell, J. T., Foss, M. A., Larsen, R. J., & Hempel, A. (1983). Studies in intuitive personology from an idiothetic point of view: Implications for personality theory. *Journal of Personality, 51,* 438–467.

Lamiell, J. T., Foss, M. A., Trierweiler, S. J., & Leffel, G. M. (1983). Toward a further understanding of the intuitive personologist: Some preliminary evidence for the dialetical quality of subjective personality impressions. *Journal of Personality, 53,* 213–235.

Lamiell, J. T., & Trierweiler, S. J. (1986). Idiothetic inquiry and the challenge to conventional "nomotheticism." *Journal of Personality, 54,* 460–469.

Lamiell, J. T., Trierweiler, S. J., & Foss, M. A. (1983). Theoretical vs. actuarial analyses of personality ratings, and other rudimentary distinctions. *Journal of Personality, 51,* 259–274.

Levy, L. (1970). *Conceptions of personality: Theories and research.* New York: Random House.

McCrae, R. R., & Costa, P. T., Jr. (1986). Clinical assessment can benefit from recent advances in personality psychology [Comment]. *American Psychologist, 41,* 1001–1003.

McCrae, R. R., & Costa, P. T., Jr. (1987). Validation of the five-factor model of personality across instruments and observers. *Journal of Personality and Social Psychology, 52,* 81–90.

McCrae, R. R., & Costa, P. T., Jr. (1995). Trait explanations in personality psychology. *European Journal of Personality, 9,* 231–252.

Meehl, P. E. (1978). Theoretical risks and tabular asterisks: Sir Karl, Sir Ronald, and the slow progress of soft psychology. *Journal of Consulting and Clinical Psychology, 46,* 806–834.

Murray, H. A. (1938). *Explorations in personality.* London: Oxford University Press.

Murray, H. A., & Kluckholm, C. (1953). Outline of a conception of personality. In C. Kluckholm, H. A. Murray, & D. Schneider (Eds.), *Personality in nature, society, and culture* (2nd ed., pp. 3–52). New York: Knopf.

Nunnally, J. C. (1967). *Psychometric theory.* New York: McGraw-Hill.

Ozer, D. J. (1990). Individual differences and the explanation of behavior. In D. N. Robinson & L. P. Mos (Eds.), *Annals of theoretical psychology* (Vol. 6, pp. 201–209). New York: Plenum Press.

Paunonen, S. V., & Jackson, D. N. (1986a). Idiothetic inquiry and the toil of Sisyphus. *Journal of Personality, 54,* 470–477.

Paunonen, S. V., & Jackson, D. N. (1986b). Nomothetic and idiothetic measurement in personality. *Journal of Personality, 54,* 447–459.

Pearson, K. (1901–1902). Editorial. *Biometrika, 1,* 3.

Porter, T. M. (1986). *The rise of statistical thinking, 1820–1900.* Princeton, NJ: Princeton University Press.

Rorer, L. G., & Widiger, T. A. (1983). Personality structure and assessment. *Annual Review of Psychology, 34,* 431–463.

Rychlak, J. F. (1981). *A philosophy of science for personality theory* (2nd ed.) Malabar, FL: Krieger.

Rychlak, J. F. (1988). *The psychology of rigorous humanism* (2nd ed.). New York: New York University Press.

Sampson, E. E. (1988). The debate on individualism: Indigenous psychologies of the individual and their role in personal and societal functioning. *American Psychologist, 43,* 15–22.

Schneider, D. J. (1973). Implicit personality theory: A review. *Psychological Review, 79,* 294–309.

Sechrest, L. (1976). Personality. *Annual Review of Psychology, 27,* 1–27.

Shweder, R. A. (1975). How relevant is an individual differences theory of personality? *Journal of Personality, 43,* 455–484.

Shweder, R. A. (1980). Factors and fictions in person perception: A reply to Lamiell, Foss, and Cavenee. *Journal of Personality, 48,* 74–81.

Skaggs, E. B. (1945). Personalistic psychology as science. *Psychological Review, 52,* 234–238.

Stern, W. (1906). *Person und Sache: System der philosophischen Weltanschauung, Band I: Ableitung und Grundlehre* [*Person and thing: Systematic philosophical world view. Volume I: Philosophical foundations*]. Leipzig: Barth.

Stern, W. (1917). *Die Psychologie und der Personalismus* [*Psychology and personalism*]. Leipzig: Barth.

Stern, W. (1918). *Person und Sache: System der philosophischen Welftanschauung, Band II: Die menschliche Persönlichkeit* [*Person and thing: Systematic philosophical world view, Volume II: The human personality*]. Leipzig: Barth.

Stern, W. (1924). *Person und Sache: System des kritischen Personalismus, Band III: Wertphilosophie* [*Person and thing: System of critical personalism, Volume III: Philosophy of values*]. Leipzig: Barth.

Windelband, W. (1904). *Geschichte und Naturwissenschaft* (3rd unaltered ed.). Strassburg: Heitz. (Original work published 1894).

Woody, E. Z. (1983). The intuitive personologist revisited: A critique of dialectical person perception. *Journal of Personality, 51,* 236–258.

CHAPTER 6

PERSONALITY MEASUREMENT

RELIABILITY AND VALIDITY ISSUES

STEPHEN G. WEST
ARIZONA STATE UNIVERSITY

JOHN F. FINCH
TEXAS A&M UNIVERSITY

The present chapter introduces researchers to some of the classic work in personality measurement. We consider three fundamental issues in personality measurement: the nature of constructs, reliability, and validity. Throughout the chapter, our presentation will focus on techniques that hold promise of making future contributions to the enhancement of our basic, theoretical understanding of personality. Consequently, we will also generally favor approaches that begin with at least a rudimentary theory of the construct. No attempt will be made to address issues that arise solely in applied personality research. Our focus on fundamental issues also precludes consideration of more advanced statistical models for testing and structure of personality measures (see Ozer & Reise, 1994; West & Finch, 1996, for reviews).

I. THE NATURE OF PERSONALITY CONSTRUCTS: BASIC ISSUES

To appropriately interpret psychometric evidence, it is important to understand the "theory" of the construct being investigated (Ozer & Reise, 1994). Here, we will simply introduce several questions that should be addressed in the theory of the construct that are relevant to the psychometric issues addressed later in this chapter. More complete discussions of construct theory issues can be found in Cronbach and Meehl (1955), Loevinger (1957), Messick (1989), and Wiggins (1973).

1. What is the expected degree of relationship among items that constitute the measure of the construct? Researchers often assume that items should have an adequate degree of intercorrelation (high internal consistency). For the trait and ability measures typically utilized by personality researchers, this assumption is nearly always reasonable. According to this conception, each item should be influenced to a degree by the underlying trait construct, giving rise to a pattern of positive intercorrelations so long as all items are oriented (worded) in the same direction. For example, the Beck Depression Inventory (Beck, Ward, Mendelson, Mock, & Erbaugh, 1961) includes items assessing negative mood, sleep disturbance, and lack of energy, which are expected to be positively related.

Alternative conceptions exist that do not lead to expectations of positive relations among items, among which are the following examples: (a) The original conception of life events (Holmes & Rahe, 1967) treated life events such as death of a spouse and getting a mortgage as being virtually random occurrences; little if any relation among them would be expected (see Bollen & Lennox, 1991). The critical measure is the total amount of life stress associated with all of the life events that occur to each person in a specified time period. (b) Frederiksen and Ward (1978) proposed that the mean level of creativity on a series of intellectual tasks does not sharply differentiate highly creative from less creative people. Rather, it is the maximum level of creative work on the tasks (capability) that should be utilized. (c) Psychodynamic and motivational perspectives often assume a hydraulic model in which one mode of expression of a conflict or motive may be in competition with another mode. A measure of compulsive behaviors, for example, may find that items measuring avoidance of stepping on cracks in sidewalks and repetitive handwashing could even be negatively related.

2. What is the structure of the construct? Personality researchers typically (and often implicitly) assume that a single dimension underlies each construct. The dimension may be assumed to be bipolar as in a mood scale that is anchored by "high degree of positive mood" and "high degree of negative mood" as its two ends. Alternatively, dimensions may be unipolar as in a mood scale that is anchored by "negative mood not present" and "high degree of negative mood." More complex dimensional structures of single constructs may be also proposed, most commonly hierarchical structures. For example, Costa and McCrae (1992) have proposed that each of the Big Five dimensions of personality has an underlying hierarchical structure. For example, extraversion is composed of lower order dimensions (facets) of warmth, gregariousness, assertiveness, activity, excitement seeking, and positive emotions. Finally, conceptions have been proposed in which types or latent classes are believed to underlie the measures. Gender is a straightforward example: There are two discrete types (male, female). Latent class conceptualizations of other personality variables (e.g., self-monitoring) have also recently been proposed (Gangestad & Synder, 1985, 1991).

3. What is the stability of the construct? Researchers studying traits and abilities have typically assumed that their constructs were stable over time. However, other researchers have studied state variables (e.g., mood) that would be expected to vary from day to day. Still other researchers have taken developmental perspectives in which some constructs are expected to be stable only within a specified period of development.

4. What is the pattern of relationships of measures of the construct of interest with other measures of the same construct and with measures of other constructs? Cronbach and Meehl (1955) long ago proposed the model of a nomological net in which laws relate "(a) observable properties of quantities to each other; or (b) theoretical constructs to observables; or (c) different theoretical constructs to each other." (p. 290). Although only the rudiments of a nomological net may be specifiable for a new construct, the nomological net should become increasingly well specified as research proceeds. Specification of such a net provides a blueprint for testing the construct theory. At the same time, researchers should ideally identify other constructs that can be proposed as competing interpretations. For example, investigators studying assertiveness may need to clearly distinguish their construct and its measures from aggression.

These questions are introduced so that readers will recognize that evidence about internal consistency, structure, stability, and relations with other measures and other constructs must be evaluated in terms of the theory of the construct under investigation. High internal consistency and stability are typically desirable properties for traits; they are *not* desirable properties for measures of life stress in terms of the original Holmes and Rahe conception. Some conceptions of the structure of self-esteem propose a single general underlying dimension, whereas other conceptions emphasize several related dimensions. The more clearly the construct theory can specify answers to each of the above questions, the easier it is for researchers to collect evidence that provides straightforward tests of the theory.

II. RELIABILITY

A. Classical Test Theory Perspective

An important property of good measures is reliability. At its heart, reliability is a simple concept—it is an index of the reproducibility or dependability of measurements. Personality researchers have traditionally treated issues of reliability within the framework of classical test theory (Crocker & Algina, 1985; Gulliksen, 1950; Lord & Novick, 1968; Nunnally & Bernstein, 1993), which will be emphasized here. However, certain aspects of reliability and certain data structures that severely violate the assumptions of this framework, which we shortly describe, may best be treated using alternative approaches (see Feldt & Brennan, 1989, for a comprehensive overview).

Classical test theory begins by partitioning each observed measurement (X) into two components: "true score" (T) and measurement error (E). Each true score represents the mean of a very large number of measurements on a specific individual. In contrast, measurement error lumps together all of the transient influences that can affect test scores. Such influences are presumed to fluctuate randomly from measurement occasion to measurement occasion. Feldt and Brennan (1989; see also Stanley, 1971; Thorndike, 1951) have identified some of the potential general sources of these influences:

1. Subject-related characteristics (e.g., health, concentration, recent life events)
2. Characteristics of testing situation (e.g., noisiness of room)
3. Examiner characteristics (e.g., examiner race, idiosyncrasies or subjectivity in ratings or observations)
4. Characteristics of instruments (e.g., equipment problems, sampling of items)

Classical test theory begins with the notion of parallel forms of a test (or measure). Parallel forms implies that the different versions of the test have the same mean, variance, and distributional characteristics, and correlate equally with each other as well as with external criteria in large samples (see Lord & Novick, 1968). Under these assumptions, true score and measurement error can be treated as independent. This implies that the variance of the observed test scores will equal the sum of the variance of the true scores and the variance of the measurement error, $\sigma_X^2 = \sigma_T^2 + \sigma_E^2$. Reliability ($\rho_{XX}$) is then defined as the ratio of the variance of the true scores to the variance of the observed scores, $\rho_{XX} = \sigma_T^2 / \sigma_X^2$.

In practice, reliability is assessed in several different ways, each of which makes somewhat different assumptions; is prone to different biases; and has a different meaning. Two procedures, internal consistency and test–retest, are utilized most commonly in personality research.

1. *Internal consistency.* Questions about the degree of relationship among items that constitute a measure are typically addressed using an index of internal consistency. The internal consistency of a measure can be evaluated by dividing each subject's test into two halves according to a specified procedure (e.g., odd versus even numbered items) and then correlating the score on the two halves. Cronbach's (1951) coefficient α is the most commonly used of these measures and is equal to the mean of the correlations between all possible split halves of the test. An equivalent statistic for dichotomous items is provided by Kuder–Richardson's (1937) Formula 20. Coefficient α provides a good estimate of reliability in terms of the sampling of items from the content area, often the major source of measurement error (Nunnally & Bernstein, 1993), and normally provides a good estimate of the reliability of an alternate form of a test. However, coefficient α does not take into consideration fluctuations in the subjects, situation, examiner, or instruments that may occur *between* testing occasions. Feldt, Woodruff, and Salih

(1987) present statistical tests of coefficient α in one-sample and multiple-sample cases.

Coefficient α also increases with increasing test length. The value of coefficient α for a longer test can be estimated using the Spearman–Brown prophecy formula (see Crocker & Algina, 1986). The formula is

$$\rho_{pp} = \frac{k\rho_{XX}}{1 + (k - 1)\rho_{XX}},$$

where ρ_{pp} is the estimated internal consistency of the projected (long) test, k is the ratio of the length of the long to the short test, and ρ_{XX} is the reliability of the short test. For example, if an existing 10-item test has a coefficient $\alpha = .70$ and a 20-item test is proposed, the estimated internal consistency of the new test is .82. This estimate assumes that items for the projected long test would be sampled from the same content domain and have the same distributional properties as the existing 10 items. Consequently, coefficient α is often regarded as an estimate of reliability for a test of a specified length.[1]

2. *Test–retest.* Measures of test–retest reliability are typically used to address questions about the stability of personality constructs. In test–retest reliability, the Pearson correlation between subjects' scores on a measure at Time 1 and the scores of the same group of subjects on the same measure (identical items) at Time 2 is computed. This approach makes two strong assumptions: (a) subjects' levels on the ability or trait in question should not change between test administrations,[2] and (b) subjects should have no useful memory for the items that could affect their responses on the second administration. Since stability of traits and abilities tends to decrease over time (Conley, 1984), relatively short intervals between test and retest are normally recommended. However, very short test–retest intervals can easily lead to overestimates of the reliability of the test with respect to day-to-day influences because of implicit pressures on the respondent to give consistent responses (see McClelland, 1980).

It should be noted that these two forms of reliability focus on different questions. Internal consistency addresses the sampling of the items and within-test fluctuations in subject characteristics (e.g., changes in concentration) (Nunnally & Bernstein, 1993). Test–retest measures address day-to-day variations in subject characteristics, the testing situation, and the examiner. Given that a constant set of items is utilized, the adequacy of sampling of items is not addressed. Personality

---

[1] Technically, coefficient α assumes that tests are at least tau equivalent (Lord & Novick, 1968), meaning that the factor loading for each item is identical. Consequently, coefficient α will underestimate the internal consistency of tests composed of items with unequal factor loadings (see Bollen, 1989). At the same time, coefficient α does not address fluctuations between testing occasions which can reduce the reliability of a test.

[2] Pearson correlations are not influenced by shifts in mean level, only by shifts in the relative ranking of the subjects in z-score terms from Time 1 to Time 2. When mean shifts are theoretically also considered to be sources of error, the intraclass correlation coefficient is more appropriate.

researchers normally focus on trait and ability measures which should ideally be high on both types of reliability. However, as noted earlier in The Nature of Personality Constructs (Section I), other patterns may be reasonable for certain constructs. A measure of angry mood would be expected to have high internal consistency, but low test–retest reliability. A measure of daily life events that have occurred during the past week might be expected to have low internal consistency (e.g., school events and relationship events will tend to be minimally related) and low test–retest reliability of the events that occur during non-overlapping time periods. Nonetheless, short-term retrospective recall of the events of a previous week should exhibit high reliability when compared with the original reports (Sandler & Guenther, 1985). Thus, the nature of reliability evidence sought for a measure should depend on the theoretical conception of the measure (Ozer & Reise, 1994).

B. Generalizability Theory Perspective

Classical test theory lumps together all influences that may produce measurement error. Generalizability theory (Cronbach, Gleser, Nanda, & Rajaratnam, 1972; Shavelson & Webb, 1991; Wiggins, 1973) is a general alternative to classical test theory that yields more refined measures of reliability and accommodates a wider variety of data structures. The theory also serves as an important heuristic tool for thinking about issues of reliability and generalizability.

The application of generalizability theory begins by designing measurement studies in which facets that potentially influence the observed scores are deliberately varied. An observational study might collect measurements of aggressiveness on each child in the sample under each possible combination of the following facets: (a) observers, (b) days of the week, and (c) classroom topics (e.g., Math, English). Drawing on extensions of analysis of variance models (Cronbach et al., 1972; Lindquist, 1953), the variance attributable to each of the facets and their two-way and three-way interactions can be estimated. It may turn out that some of the facets account for a trivial percentage of the variance and can be neglected, whereas others are very important and must be considered in any study. Intraclass correlation coefficients (analogous to reliability coefficients) can be calculated that, for example, describe the relationship between the observation of one or more of the observers and a universe of similar observers. These coefficients are useful in planning subsequent studies. For example, if a follow-up study can collect data only three days per week or can only utilize two instead of four observers, the theory provides clear methods of estimating the level of expected reliability of the measurements under each measurement plan. Generalizability theory accommodates a wide variety of data structures that cannot be addressed in classical test theory without significant modification of the formulas. For example, the Attributional Style Questionnaire (Peterson et al., 1982) has subjects give three separate responses to each item, meaning that these responses are not independent. Generalizability theory permits straightforward calculation of appropriate reliability coefficients once the data collection design is known.

Generalizability theory has often been utilized by educational researchers, but only rarely by personality researchers in assessing the reliability of measures (see, e.g., Farrell, Mariotto, Conger, Curran, & Wallander, 1979). In part, this may reflect the discomfort that many psychologists appear to experience in mixing correlational and analysis of variance approaches (Cronbach, 1957). There are, in addition, appreciable difficulties in utilizing the approach. Among these are the complexities in understanding and specifying analysis of variance models with several random factors, the instability of the variance estimates with small sample sizes, and the possibility of obtaining negative estimates for some of the variance components (Jones & Appelbaum, 1989; Shavelson & Webb, 1991). Despite these difficulties, generalizability theory continues to hold considerable promise for researchers interested in carefully probing the dependability of their measures. In particular, the usefulness of generalizability theory has received special emphasis from researchers studying consensus and self–other agreement (Kenny, 1993).

C. Importance of Reliability

Researchers originally trained in experimental psychology or social psychology frequently underestimate the importance of reliability, often using one-item measures or measures of unknown reliability in their research. In a simple correlational study, if the true scores of two measures have a .5 correlation and the reliability of each measure is .6, the obtained correlation can be expected to be 0.3. This means that degree of relationship is underestimated and that a much larger sample size will be needed to detect the relationship between the two variables than would be the case if they were measured with perfect reliability. Unreliability of the delivery of the treatment or in measurement of the dependent variable in a randomized experiment also leads to underestimation of the magnitude of the treatment effect. In multiple regression analyses, the inclusion of one highly reliable predictor among a set of correlated predictor variables that are measured with less reliability can easily lead to overestimation of the importance of the more reliable predictor. In the analysis of multitrait–multimethod matrices to be discussed in a later section, differential reliability of the measures can lead to mistaken conclusions about convergent and discriminant validity. In short, unreliable measures have considerable potential to bias all results to which they contribute.

A perhaps less obvious example of this problem occurs when a single measure of behavior is collected and used as a "gold standard" criterion for a personality measure. For example, a self-report measure of aggressiveness might be correlated with the "gold standard" of the intensity of electric shocks ostensibly delivered to a confederate as punishment for mistakes. In such studies, no information is typically provided about the reliability of the behavioral measure of aggressiveness across days, across confederates, or across types of punishment (e.g., electric shock versus aversive noise). If the two measures do not show the expected degree of correlation, this lack of information makes it impossible to define whether the source of the problem is a failure of the construct theory or lack of dependability of the behavioral measure. Moskowitz and Schwarz (1982) and Gormly (1984) provide cogent examples of the use of different forms of aggregation to produce more reliable measures which then correlate with other measures of the same construct. Epstein (1983) and Rushton, Brainerd, and Pressley (1983) present more complete discussions of this issue.

III. VALIDITY

Once it is established that a measure has adequate reliability, the issue of validity arises. Closely following Messick (1989, p. 13), we define validity as the *degree* to which empirical evidence and theoretical rationales support the adequacy of interpretations based on test scores or other measures. This definition underscores the close relationship between construct theory and validity and highlights the field's increasing emphasis on construct validity (American Psychological Association, 1985; Angoff, 1988; Cronbach, 1989). Based on this definition, we next identify a few of the characteristics and complexities of validity.

1. Validity is a property of the *interpretation* of a measure, not of the measure itself. To illustrate, there is considerable body of evidence supporting the interpretation of scores on the Stanford–Binet test as a measure of intelligence in young children. There is a paucity of evidence supporting the interpretation of these scores as a measure of creativity in children and relatively weaker evidence supporting the interpretation of these scores as intelligence in adult college students.

2. Validity involves the interpretation of (a hypothesis about) the meaning of scores based on a measure. The better developed the theory of the hypothesized underlying construct and the specification of alternative underlying constructs, the easier it will be to collect clear empirical evidence for or against a particular interpretation of a test score.

3. The validity of an interpretation is always based on the current preponderance of evidence and is subject to change. New evidence may arise to challenge an existing interpretation or a new alternative account of the existing evidence may be proposed. The validity of an interpretation of a measure is never established; it is only currently supported to the degree warranted by the empirical evidence.

4. The validity of an interpretation has been difficult to present in the form of a convenient quantitative index. Perhaps because of this difficulty, researchers all too often report quantitative evidence of reliability (indices of internal consistency, test–retest correlations, or both), but fail to report evidence supporting the validity of their preferred interpretation of their measures. When validity evidence has been reported, researchers have traditionally relied on either a qualitative summary of the evidence provided by the body of available research or a listing of a selected string of correlations with other measures. At least for some validity questions, newer techniques including generalizability theory (Kane, 1982) and meta-analysis

(Hedges, 1988; Mabe & West, 1982; Schmidt, Hunter, Pearlman, & Hirsh, 1985) offer the promise of providing more comprehensive, quantitative estimates.

Readers wishing more in-depth discussions of validity, its historical evolution as a concept, and its philosophy of science underpinnings should refer to Angoff (1988), Cronbach (1989), and Messick (1989).

A. Forms of Validity Evidence

As with any hypothesis, a variety of different forms of evidence may be sought with which to probe the validity of the interpretation of the measure. Several commonly utilized forms of validity evidence are briefly presented next. The importance of each of the forms of evidence will vary depending on the nature of the validity question being addressed and the construct theory, issues we raised earlier in the chapter.

1. Content

Evidence about the validity of the content of a measure involves comparisons of the actual coverage of the items with the domain implied by the construct theory. This means that the clearest evidence about the adequacy of the content will be available when a well-specified theory specifies the domain and facets of the construct. Three potential problems with measures may arise. First, important facets of the construct may be underrepresented by having too few or no items. For example, Jackson, Ahmed, and Heapy (1976) originally proposed that six facets (competitiveness, concern for excellence, status with experts, status with peers, acquisitiveness, and achievement via independence) constitute need for achievement. In terms of Jackson et al.'s conception, a measure that did not include items on status with peers would underrepresent the construct of need for achievement. Second, a facet or even a small portion of a facet may be represented by a large number of items relative to other facets. Severe oversampling of items can increase the perceived importance of an aspect of the construct, turning what is in reality a minor dimension into an apparent major one (sometimes termed a "bloated specific factor"). Third, additional dimensions not specified by the construct theory may be reliably measured. For example, if most of the items of a measure of need for achievement were worded in a socially desirable manner or if several of the items measured fear of failure, then the measure could be contaminated by these construct-irrelevant dimensions.

The adequacy of the measure's coverage of the content of the construct is normally assessed in two ways. First, judges can review the items for completeness and evenness of coverage of the domain of the construct. Depending on the type of measure being developed, experts in the content area or representatives of the subject population or both may serve as judges. As a first step in providing evidence concerning the validity of the measure, the judges should reach consensus that adequate coverage of the domain of the construct has been achieved. Indeed, with a construct theory that clearly specifies the domain and the facets of the construct, item writers working independently should ideally be able to produce highly related (and in the limit, interchangeable) measures of the construct.

Second, psychometric investigations should indicate that the data are consistent with the structure hypothesized by the construct theory. For example, Snyder's (1974) self-monitoring scale, which was originally proposed to have a single underlying dimension (factor), was later found by Briggs, Cheek, and Buss (1980) to have three underlying dimensions. Jackson et al. (1976) found that data were not consistent with their hypothesis that need for achievement is a hierarchically organized construct with six distinct facets (second-order factor model). Failures to confirm the structure of the hypothesized construct typically indicate that the measure, the construct, or both need further revision. Data consistent with the hypothesized structure support the continued use of both the measure and the construct theory.

Given the importance that has historically been placed on measures having only one underlying factor (dimension) and the frequency with which one factor structures have been proposed, it is useful to examine the issue of single factoredness in greater detail. Several cases exist in the literature in which a one-dimensional structure was hypothesized, but was not initially subjected to a strong empirical test. Rotter's (1966) internal–external (I-E) locus of control scale and Snyder's (1974) self-monitoring (S-M) scale, to cite two examples, have been criticized in the literature on the grounds that several largely independent factors actually underlie the items (see, for example, Collins, 1974; Mirels, 1970, for I-E; Briggs & Cheek, 1988; Briggs et al., 1980, for S-M). In these cases, one underlying dimension of the measure can be responsible for correlations with one set of criterion variables, whereas another underlying dimension is responsible for correlations with a second set of criterion variables. Worse still, it is theoretically possible for the two dimensions to correlate in opposite directions with a set of criterion variables, producing an overall 0 relationship. Zuckerman and Gerbasi (1977) provide a nice illustration of some of these problems, showing that many of the ambiguities in a portion of the I-E literature could be clarified by consideration of the multifactor structure of the measure. Neuberg, Judice, and West (in press) show how greater empirical and conceptual clarity can be brought to the literature on need for closure (Webster & Kruglanski, 1994) through careful consideration of the two largely independent dimensions that underlie this measure. Unidimensional measures are clearly preferred unless a well-developed theory precisely details the relationships among the multiple dimensions (or classes) that compose the construct as well as their first-order and interactive relationships with external criteria. Masculinity–femininity scales provide an important illustration of how a construct originally conceived of as unidimensional (Constantinople, 1973) has been reconceptualized as being composed of two separate dimensions (Bem, 1974; Spence & Helmreich, 1978). Carver (1989), Hull, Lehn, and Tedlie (1991), Messick (1989), and Jackson and Paunonen (1985) present general discussions of some of these issues; Sternberg and Weil (1980) offer an empirical illustration of how well-developed theory can guide tests of the construct's hypothesized structure and its relationship with external criteria.

The desirability and ease of interpretation of unidimensional tests have long been recognized (e.g., Cronbach, 1951; Guilford, 1954; Loevinger, 1947, 1948; McNemar, 1946; see Walker, 1931, for an early mention). Numerous indices that purport to assess unidimensionality have been developed over the years (Hattie, 1985). Nonetheless, the index most commonly utilized by personality researchers for this purpose is an *inappropriate* one, Cronbach's (1951) coefficient α, which, as discussed previously is a measure of internal consistency. Typically in practice, if a scale has a coefficient α of about .70 or better for a reasonable length test, it is taken as an adequate measure of the underlying dimension. A unidimensional scale will necessarily produce a high coefficient α. Unfortunately, scales having multiple underlying factors can also easily produce high levels of coefficient α. For example, Green, Lissitz, and Mulaik (1977) have shown in a simulation that a 10-item test in which scores were produced by five underlying factors can produce values of coefficient α greater than .80! Consequently, we recommend that investigators utilize more sensitive techniques to detect departures from unidimensionality. These techniques include confirmatory factor analysis (Bollen, 1989) for ratings, and item response theory (Hambleton, Swaminathan, & Rogers, 1991) for dichotomous items (see Ozer & Reise, 1994; West & Finch, 1995, for overviews). Coefficient α should be restricted to its intended use as a measure of internal consistency in line with Cronbach's (1951) original recommendations.

2. External Criteria

A second source of validity evidence comes from the degree to which the measure can predict external criteria that are theoretically expected to be related to the construct being measured. Loevinger (1957) has in particular emphasized the importance of external criteria in validational efforts: "It seems reasonable to require that complete validation of any test include a demonstration of some non-zero relationship with a non-test variable" (p. 675). The criteria may occur simultaneously with the measurement of the construct or be expected to occur in the future. Potential criteria may come from a wide variety of different sources, such as behavioral samples in laboratory or naturalistic settings, ratings by knowledgeable informants or clinicians, biographical data, physiological data, and other self-report measures of the same construct. The usefulness of each potential criterion source will depend on the nature of the construct and the type of measure being validated (Moskowitz, 1986).

As a simple illustration of the validation of a construct against external criteria, a measure of extraversion might be expected to discriminate current members of social clubs from nonmembers. Or, it might be expected to predict the likelihood that an individual would initiate future conversations with strangers. Or, it might be expected to predict that individuals scoring as extroverts on the measure would be rated as being extraverted by their spouses and their employers. Such types of evidence support the preferred interpretation of the measure as extraversion.

However, it is possible that other theoretically distinguishable characteristics (e.g., anxiety) may also be assessed by the measure that also predict the external criteria. In such cases, the measure will better predict the criterion (e.g., membership in social clubs) to the extent it reflects all of the factors (e.g., high extraversion and low anxiety) that influence the external criterion. Extended validation efforts in which the measure successfully predicts different external criteria in several separate studies make a much more convincing case for the interpretation, particularly if a strong nomological network is developed linking the construct to a diverse set of predicted outcomes (Cronbach & Meehl, 1955). Yet, even such programs of validation still must be carefully scrutinized to determine whether other variables may form a common basis for group membership or the occurrence of the predicted behavior (Houts, Cook, & Shadish, 1986).

3. Experimental Manipulations

Experimental designs in which the subject's level on the construct is directly manipulated can also provide important validity information about measures of certain constructs. Measures of *state* variables such as negative mood should show significant change when subjects are exposed to an appropriate manipulation such as sad films or news stories. Predictions about *trait* variables such as depression are less clear and depend on the strength of the manipulation and the degree of overlap between the state and the trait constructs. Exposing subjects to a sad film is unlikely to result in significant changes on those facets of a measure of depression related to sleep disturbance and lack of energy. In contrast, psychotherapeutic interventions that are known to be effective should produce significant changes relative to an untreated control group on a new measure of depression.

B. Convergent and Discriminant Validation

Validation of a measure requires a twofold approach. First, as outlined in the previous sections, evidence bearing on predictions made by the construct theory needs to be collected. A measure of assertiveness might be validated through a variety of methods such as asking knowledgeable informants to rate each person on assertiveness, behavioral observations in a standard assertiveness test situation, or correlation with scores on another existing measure of assertiveness. This seeking of confirmatory evidence for the proposed interpretation of the measure has been termed *convergent validation*. Second, evidence is also needed showing that the measure under consideration differs from measures of other constructs. For example, it should be possible to empirically distinguish a new measure of assertiveness from existing measures of aggressiveness. This second approach, termed *discriminant validation*, helps to justify the proposal of a new construct.

Studies of convergent and discriminant validity need to be planned carefully as a number of biases can distort the results. Measures purporting to assess the same construct can be based on radically different definitions or theories of the construct. For example, correlations between different measures of self-esteem range from high (.6 to .8) to low negative ($-.2$) (Briggs & Cheek, 1986). Different types of measures may reflect the same or different facets of the construct. Co-worker, spouse, and peer informants may reach a relatively high level of agreement concerning a target person's degree of extraversion, whereas they may reach no agreement concerning the individual's recent stressful life events since each individual observes only one domain of the person's life. The degree of discriminant validity will reflect the diversity of the sample of construct measures that are included. For example, Backteman and Magnusson (1981) found that teacher ratings strongly discriminated between aggressiveness and timidity, but provided a much weaker differentiation between aggressiveness, motor disturbance (fidgeting), lack of concentration, and lack of school motivation. Ideally, discriminant validity studies should provide a strong test of the new measure: Measures of those specific constructs that represent the most plausible alternative interpretations of the new measure should always be included.

Convergent and discriminant validity studies are most typically conducted at the level of tests (measures), but can also be conducted at the item level. Indeed, Jackson (1971) has advocated a test construction procedure in which measures of two or more constructs are developed simultaneously, with item selection based on both convergent and discriminant evidence. Powerful statistical techniques based on confirmatory factor analysis have been developed that permit strong tests of convergent and discriminant validity at either the item or the test level (see Bollen, 1989; Finch & West, 1996).

C. Multitrait–Multimethod Matrix

Campbell and Fiske (1959; see also Marsh, 1989b) developed a stringent technique for probing the convergent and discriminant validity of measures. They argue that systematic variance in test responses may be divided into trait-related and method-related components. To the extent that two measures share the same method-related components, their intercorrelation will be inflated. For example, if self-report measures of sense of humor and driving ability both reflect individuals' tendencies to bias their reports in a positive direction, then the correlation obtained between these two measures would be seriously inflated.

To address this problem, Campbell and Fiske (1959) proposed the strategy of the multitrait–multimethod (MTMM) matrix. In this approach, several constructs (typically traits or abilities) are measured using multiple measurement techniques. For example, as part of a larger study by Gersten, Beals, West, and Sandler (1987), a large sample of children were assessed using three different methods (structured interviews with each child, child reports, and parent reports) to measure three different dimensions of symptoms (anxiety, depression, and conduct problems). In general, to the extent that different methods of measuring a single construct produce high correlations relative to those obtained using a single method of measuring different constructs, convergent and discriminant validity are demonstrated.

To illustrate the use of this technique more concretely, consider the three idealized examples shown in Table I, panels A, B, and C, which are based on hypothetical data. Three traits, neuroticism (N), extraversion (E), and openness to experience (O) are measured using two methods, self-reports (1) and spouse reports (2). We assume that all measures have equal reliabilities in examples IA and IB and introduce the complication of unequal reliabilities in example IC.

TABLE I
Illustration of Hypothetical Multitrait–Multimethod Matrices with Three Traits and Two Methods

Traits		Method 1[a]			Method 2[b]		
		N1	E1	O1	N2	E2	O2
A. Convergent and discriminant validity with minimal methods effects							
Method 1	N1 Neuroticism	(.9)					
Self-report	E1 Extraversion	*.4*	(.9)				
	O1 Openness	*.2*	*.2*	(.9)			
Method 2	N2 Neuroticism	**.6**	.2	.1	(.9)		
Spouse-report	E2 Extraversion	.2	**.6**	.1	*.4*	(.9)	
	O2 Openness	.1	.1	**.4**	*.2*	*.2*	(.9)
B. Strong methods effects							
Method 1	N1 Neuroticism	(.8)					
Self-report	E1 Extraversion	*.6*	(.8)				
	O1 Openness	*.5*	*.5*	(.8)			
Method 2	N2 Neuroticism	**.2**	.1	.0	(.8)		
Spouse-report	E2 Extraversion	.1	**.3**	.0	*.6*	(.8)	
	O2 Openness	.0	.0	**.2**	*.5*	*.5*	(.8)
C. Effects of unreliability and lack of discriminant validity (02)							
Method 1	N1	(.4)					
Self-report	E1 Extraversion	*.3*	(.9)				
	O1 Openness	*.1*	*.2*	(.9)			
Method 2	N2 Neuroticism	**.4**	.2	.1	(.9)		
Spouse-report	E2 Extraversion	.1	**.6**	.1	*.4*	(.9)	
	O2 Openness	.1	.1	**.4**	*.2*	*.5*	(.9)

Note: Reliabilities are printed on diagonal in parentheses. Validity coefficients are printed in boldface type. Correlations between different traits measured with the same method are printed in italics. Correlations between different traits measured with the different methods are printed in standard typeface.
[a] Self-report.
[b] Spouse report.

Following Campbell and Fiske (1959, pp. 82–83), four criteria are normally utilized in examining multitrait–multimethod matrices.

1. The correlations of different methods of measuring the same trait (convergent validity coefficients) should be statistically significant and large enough in magnitude to justify further consideration. For example, in Table IA the values of $r_{N1,N2}$ (.6), $r_{E1,E2}$ (.6), and $r_{O1,O2}$ (.4; values printed in bold) are all statistically significant and of reasonable magnitude.

2. Each of the convergent validity coefficients should be higher than the correlations of different methods of measuring different traits located in the corresponding column and row. For example, in Table IA, $r_{E1,E2}$ (.6) is larger than other values in the same column ($r_{E1,N2} = .2$; $r_{E1,O2} = .1$) and row ($r_{E2,N1} = .2$, $r_{E2,O1} = .1$). This should hold true for all analogous comparisons within the different-trait, different-method block of correlations that appears in standard print in Table IA.

3. Each of the convergent validity coefficients should be higher than the correlations of the same method of measuring different traits located in the corresponding column and row. For example, in Table IA, $r_{N1,N2} = .6$ is larger than the value of $r_{N1,E1}$ (.4) and $r_{N1,O1}$ (.2) in the same column and the values of $r_{N2,E2}$ (.4) and $r_{N2,O2}$ (.2) in the same row. (Some thought may be required to locate these latter two values in the triangular form in which MTMM matrices are typically presented.) This relationship should hold true for all analogous comparisons within the different-trait, same-method triangles that are printed in italics in Table IA.

Campbell and O'Connell (1982) have more recently noted that this third criterion may be overly stringent. Although sharing the same method may inflate correlations between different traits, the use of different methods to assess the same trait in the validity coefficients may produce nonshared variance that will tend to attenuate these correlations. Thus, *minor* failures to meet this criterion should be interpreted carefully rather than leading to an automatic conclusion of a lack of discriminant validity.

4. Finally, the same general pattern of relationships should hold for each of the triangles in the different-trait, different-method block (standard print) and the different-trait, same-method block (italics). Such a finding suggests that the correlations between the true scores for each of the traits are independent of the method of measurement.

Applying these criteria to Table IA, we see that they are all easily met. Hence, there is strong evidence for the convergent and discriminant validity of the three traits. In Table IB, we see an idealized example in which a strong method effect has been added to the MTMM matrix; this confounding leads to inflated correlations whenever two traits are measured by the same method and hence produces problems in meeting the third criterion. Thus, the E1–E2 correlation (.3) in Table IB is lower than the E1–N1 (.6), the E1–O1 (.5), the E2–N2 (.6), or the E2–O2 (.5) correlations. This result combined with the relatively small values of the validity coefficients suggests serious problems with the convergent and discriminant validity of the measures.

Finally, in Table IC two alterations have been introduced into the MTMM matrix relative to Table IA. First, the reliability of the self-report measure of neuroticism (.4) is very low and substantially attenuates all of the correlations in the N1 column. Second, a higher correlation between spouse reports of extraversion and openness ($r_{E2,O2} = .5$) is reported. Applying the four Campbell and Fiske criteria to Table IC, we see that criteria 1 and 2 are passed but criteria 3 and 4 are not. The validity correlation for neuroticism, $r_{N1,N2}$ (.4), does not exceed $r_{N2,E2}$ (.4). This is an artifact of the low reliability of N1 and would not be a problem if the correlation matrix were corrected for attenuation prior to analysis (Althauser & Heberlein, 1970; Jackson, 1969). On the other hand, the validity correlation for openness, $r_{O1,O2}$ (.4), is exceeded by $r_{O2,E2}$ (.5), which is not an artifact of differential reliability. Note also that the pattern of correlations in the Method 2–Method 2 different-trait triangle differs from the pattern of correlations in all of the other different-trait triangles. This pattern of results with respect to criteria 3 and 4 suggests that openness fails to exhibit discriminant validity with respect to spouse reports.

These examples clearly illustrate the utility of the Campbell–Fiske approach in probing issues of convergent and discriminant validity. However, the Campbell–Fiske approach has several limitations of which investigators should be aware in interpreting their results.

1. The Campbell–Fiske approach makes a strong assumption that the measures have equal reliabilities and no restriction of range. As we saw in our analysis of Table IC, these problems can lead to artifactual failures to satisfy the four criteria unless the correlation matrix is corrected for these sources of attenuation.

2. The cookbook nature of the Campbell–Fiske approach has unfortunately facilitated choices of methods and traits for inclusion in the MTMM on the basis of convenience rather than theory. Investigators need to use the construct theory of the traits as a guide in the choice of traits and methods to be included. Theoretically, which traits is it important to discriminate between?

3. The large number of nonindependent comparisons that are required for the statistical analysis of MTMM matrices leads to potential problems of quantifying and interpreting the results. Steiger (1980) and Meng, Rosenthal, and Rubin (1992) have proposed methods that may be adapted to the basic analysis of MTMM matrices. Confirmatory factor analysis approaches (Marsh & Grayson, 1995) provide direct tests of the fit of the data to MTMM models.

4. The Campbell–Fiske criteria assume that trait and method factors are uncorrelated, that trait and method factors do not interact, that method factors are uncorrelated, and that all traits are influenced equally by the method factors. These assumptions may be violated in some applications, making the results difficult to interpret. Again, confirmatory factor analysis approaches have begun to provide some methods of dealing with these violated assumptions.

Despite these limitations, the Campbell and Fiske (1959) criteria provide an excellent, though stringent, strategy for the study of MTMM matrices. As Messick (1989) notes, the Campbell–Fiske approach "is a tough (often humbling) heuristic device that forces the investigator to confront simultaneously both convergent and discriminant evidence, or the lack thereof" (p. 47). Indeed, Fiske and Campbell (1992) have recently lamented that psychologists have made but little progress in improving the convergent and discriminant validity of their measures during the past 35 years. Careful consideration of method effects can potentially lead to substantive interpretations that further inform our understanding of the trait constructs (Ozer, 1989). More sophisticated analytical techniques for MTMM matrices are currently being developed; however, the Campbell–Fiske criteria provide an important and informative baseline from which the results of such analyses can be more easily interpreted (Marsh, 1989a).

IV. CONCLUSION

Two underlying themes have emerged in this chapter that are appearing with increasing frequency in modern writings on measurement.

1. This chapter moves away from a cookbook approach and advocates strong theoretical guidance of all investigations. Even consideration of reliability should be guided by the construct theory. The definition, domain, and theoretical structure of the construct affect the sampling of items and even the types of measures that should be sought. The construct theory determines the types of criteria that should be sought in attempting to establish the validity of the measure.

2. This chapter also emphasizes the importance of identifying and testing alternative hypotheses about the interpretation of constructs. Houts et al. (1986) emphasize the importance of examining one's own work and even entire research literatures for the possibility of common biases that may contribute to the results. Probing research literatures for common assumptions, asking what aspects of the construct theory have *not* been tested, and listening carefully to one's critics are methods of identifying such biases. For example, nearly all of the research on the Big Five Personality Traits has involved self-reports or the reports of knowledgeable others rather than observational measures (Digman, 1990). Similarly, the stringent tests provided by the inclusion of the most serious contending interpretations of a construct in convergent and discriminant validity studies (ideally utilizing multitrait-multimethod matrices) offer promise in refining our understanding of these constructs. Tests of competing models of personality structure offer the strongest evidence for or against a hypothesized structure.

We believe that the increased emphasis on the theoretical bases of personality constructs advocated here will have a salutatory effect on personality measurement. A movement away from attempts to routinize approaches to measurement may help foster more careful planning and implementation of measurement designs.

Modern measurement techniques are reemphasizing the interdependence of theoretical, methodological, measurement, and statistical analysis choices.

ACKNOWLEDGMENTS

We thank Peter Bentler, Sanford Braver, William Chaplin, Clifford Clogg, William Graziano, Joseph Hepworth, Jay Hull, Douglas Jackson, John Johnson, Herbert Marsh, Robert McCrae, Hee-choon Shin, Jeffrey Tanaka, Howard Tennen, and Jenn-Yun Tein for their comments on an earlier version of this chapter. A major section that was originally part of earlier versions of this chapter is now included in another article (Finch & West, 1996). One of the authors (S. G. W.) was partially supported by National Institute of Mental Health Grant P50MH39246 during the writing of this chapter.

REFERENCES

Althauser, R. P., & Heberlein, T. A. (1970). Validity and the multitrait-multimethod matrix. In E. F. Borgotta & G. W. Bohrnstedt (Eds.), *Sociological methodology 1970* (pp. 151–169). San Francisco: Jossey-Bass.

American Psychological Association, American Educational Research Association, & National Council on Measurements Used in Education. (1985). *Standards for educational and psychological tests.* Washington, DC: American Psychological Association.

Angoff, W. H. (1988). Validity: An evolving concept. In H. Wainer & H. I. Braun (Eds.), *Test validity* (pp. 19–32). Hillsdale, NJ: Erlbaum.

Backteman, G., & Magnusson, D. (1981). Longitudinal stability of personality characteristics. *Journal of Personality, 49,* 148–160.

Beck, A. T., Ward, C. H., Mendelson, M., Mock, J., & Erbaugh, J. (1961). An inventory for measuring depression. *Archives of General Psychiatry, 4,* 561–571.

Bem, S. L. (1974). The measurement of psychological androgyny. *Journal of Consulting and Clinical Psychology, 42,* 155–162.

Bollen, K. A. (1989). *Structural equations with latent variables.* New York: Wiley (Interscience).

Bollen, K. A., & Lennox, R. (1991). Conventional wisdom on measurement: A structural equation perspective. *Psychological Bulletin, 110,* 305–314.

Briggs, S. R., & Cheek, J. M. (1986). The role of factor analysis in the development and evaluation of personality scales. *Journal of Personality, 54,* 106–149.

Briggs, S. R., & Cheek, J. M. (1988). On the nature of self-monitoring: Problems with assessment, problems with validity. *Journal of Personality and Social Psychology, 54,* 663–678.

Briggs, S. R., Cheek, J. M., & Buss, A. H. (1980). An analysis of the self-monitoring scale. *Journal of Personality and Social Psychology, 38,* 679–686.

Campbell, D. T., & Fiske, D. W. (1959). Convergent and discriminant validation by the multitrait-multimethod matrix. *Psychological Bulletin, 56,* 81–105.

Campbell, D. T., & O-Connell, E. J. (1982). Methods as diluting trait relationships rather than adding irrelevant systematic variance. In D. Brinberg & L. Kidder (Eds.), *Forms of validity in research* (pp. 93–111). San Francisco: Jossey-Bass.

Carver, C. S. (1989). How should multifaceted personality constructs be tested? Issues illustrated by self-monitoring, attributional style, and hardiness. *Journal of Personality and Social Psychology, 56,* 577–585.

Collins, B. E. (1974). Four components of the Rotter Internal-External Scale: Belief in a difficult world, a just world, a predictable world, and a politically responsible world. *Journal of Personality and Social Psychology, 29,* 381–391.

Conley, J. J. (1984). The hierarchy of consistency: A review and model of longitudinal findings on adult individual differences in intelligence, personality, and self-opinion. *Personality and Individual Differences, 5,* 11–25.

Constantinople, A. (1973). Masculinity-femininity: An exception to a famous dictum. *Psychological Bulletin, 80,* 389–407.

Costa, P. T., Jr., & McCrae, R. R. (1992). *Revised NEO Personality Inventory (NEO-PI-R) and NEO Five-Factor Inventory (NEO-FFI) professional manual.* Odessa, FL: Psychological Assessment Resources.

Crocker, L., & Algina, J. (1986). *Introduction to classical and modern test theory.* Fort Worth, TX: Harcourt Brace Jovanovich.

Cronbach, L. J. (1951). Coefficient alpha and the internal structure of tests. *Psychometrika, 16,* 297–334.

Cronbach, L. J. (1957). Beyond the two disciplines of scientific psychology. *American Psychologist, 30,* 116–127.

Cronbach, L. J. (1989). Construct validation after thirty years. In R. L. Linn (Ed.), *Intelligence: Measurement, theory, and public policy. Proceedings of a symposium in honor of Lloyd G. Humphries* (pp. 147–171). Urbana: University of Illinois Press.

Cronbach, L. J., Gleser, G. C., Nanda, H., & Rajaratnam, N. (1972). *The dependability of behavioral measurements: Theory of generalizability for scores and profiles.* New York: Wiley.

Cronbach, L. J., & Meehl, P. E. (1955). Construct validity in psychological tests. *Psychological Bulletin, 52,* 281–302.

Digman, J. M. (1990). Personality structure: Emergence of the five-factor model. *Annual Review of Psychology, 41,* 417–440.

Epstein, S. (1983). Aggregation and beyond: Some basic issues of the prediction of behavior. *Journal of Personality, 51,* 360–392.

Farrell, A. D., Mariotto, M. J., Conger, A. J., Curran, J. P., & Wallander, J. L. (1979). Self-ratings and judges' ratings of heterosexual social anxiety and skill: A generalizability study. *Journal of Consulting and Clinical Psychology, 47,* 164–175.

Feldt, L. S., & Brennan, R. L. (1989). Reliability. In R. L. Linn (Ed.), *Educational measurement* (3rd ed., pp. 105–146). New York: Macmillan.

Feldt, L. S., Woodruff, D. J., & Salih, F. A. (1987). Statistical inference for coefficient alpha. *Applied Psychological Measurement, 11,* 93–103.

Finch, J. F., West, S. G. (1996). *The investigation of personality structure: Statistical models.* Unpublished manuscript, Arizona State University, Department of Psychology, Tempe.

Fiske, D. W., & Campbell, D. T. (1992). Citations do not solve problems. *Psychological Bulletin, 112,* 393–395.

Frederiksen, N., & Ward, W. C. (1978). Measures for the study of creativity in scientific problem solving. *Applied Psychological Measurement, 2,* 1–24.

Gangestad, S. W., & Snyder, M. (1985). "To carve nature at its joints": On the existence of discrete classes in personality. *Psychological Review, 92,* 317–349.

Gangestad, S. W., & Snyder, M. (1991). Taxonomic analysis redux: Some statistical considerations for testing a latent class model. *Journal of Personality and Social Psychology, 61*, 141–146.

Gersten, J. C., Beals, J., West, S. G., & Sandler, I. (1987, March). *A measurement model of major constructs of child psychopathology.* Paper presented at the meeting of the Society for Research in Child Development, Baltimore, MD.

Gormly, J. (1984). Correspondence between personality trait ratings and behavioral events. *Journal of Personality, 52*, 220–232.

Green, S. B., Lissitz, R. W., & Mulaik, S. A. (1977). Limitations on coefficient alpha as an index of test unidimensionality. *Educational and Psychological Measurement, 37*, 827–838.

Guilford, J. P. (1954). *Psychometric methods* (2nd ed.). New York: McGraw-Hill.

Gulliksen, H. (1950). *Theory of mental tests.* New York: Wiley.

Hambleton, R. K., Swaminathan, H., & Rogers, H. J. (1991). *Fundamentals of item response theory.* Newbury Park, CA: Sage.

Hattie, J. (1985). Methodology review: Assessing unidimensionality of tests and items. *Applied Psychological Measurement, 9*, 139–164.

Hedges, L. V. (1988). The meta-analysis of test validity studies: Some new approaches. In H. Wainer & H. I. Braun (Eds.), *Test validity* (pp. 191–212). Hillsdale, NJ: Erlbaum.

Holmes, T. H., & Rahe, R. H. (1967). The social readjustment rating scale. *Journal of Psychosomatic Research, 14*, 213–218.

Houts, A. C., Cook, T. D., & Shadish, W. R., Jr. (1986). The person-situation debate: A critical multiplist perspective. *Journal of Personality, 54*, 52–105.

Hull, J. G., Lehn, D. A., & Tedlie, J. C. (1991). A general approach to testing multifaceted personality characteristics. *Journal of Personality and Social Psychology, 61*, 932–945.

Jackson, D. N. (1969). Multimethod factor analysis in the evaluation of convergent and discriminant validity. *Psychological Bulletin, 72*, 30–49.

Jackson, D. N. (1971). The dynamics of structured personality tests. *Psychological Review, 78*, 229–248.

Jackson, D. N., Ahmed, S. A., & Heapy, N. A. (1976). Is achievement a unitary construct? *Journal of Research in Personality, 10*, 1–21.

Jackson, D. N., & Paunonen, S. V. (1985). Construct validity and the predictability of behavior. *Journal of Personality and Social Psychology, 49*, 554–570.

Jones, L. V., & Appelbaum, M. I. (1989). Psychometric methods. *Annual Review of Psychology, 40*, 23–43.

Kane, M. T. (1982). A sampling model for validity. *Applied Psychological Measurement, 6*, 125–160.

Kenny, D. A. (1993). A coming of age for research on interpersonal perception. *Journal of Personality, 61*, 789–807.

Kuder, G. F., & Richardson, M. W. (1937). The theory of the estimation of test reliability. *Psychometrika, 2*, 151–160.

Lindquist, E. F. (1953). *Design and analysis of experiments in psychology and education.* Boston: Houghton-Mifflin.

Loevinger, J. (1947). A systematic approach to the construction and evaluation of tests of ability. *Psychological Monograph, 61*(No. 4, Whole No. 285).

Loevinger, J. (1948). The technique of homogeneous tests. *Psychological Bulletin, 45*, 507–529.

Loevinger, J. (1957). Objective tests as instruments of psychological theory. *Psychological Reports, 3*, 635–694.

Lord, F. M., & Novick, M. R. (1968). *Statistical theories of mental test scores.* Reading, MA: Addison-Wesley.

Mabe, P. A., III, & West, S. G. (1982). Validity of self-evaluations of ability: A review and meta-analysis. *Journal of Applied Psychology, 67,* 280–296.

Marsh, H. W. (1989a). Confirmatory factor analyses of multitrait-multimethod data: Many problems and a few solutions. *Applied Psychological Measurement, 13,* 335–361.

Marsh, H. W. (1989b). Multitrait-multimethod analyses. In J. P. Keeves (Ed.), *Educational research methodology, measurement and evaluation: An international handbook.* Oxford, England: Pergamon Press.

Marsh, H. W., & Grayson, D. (1995). Latent variable models of multitrait-multimethod data. In R. H. Hoyle (Ed.), *Structural equation modeling: Concepts, issues, and applications* (pp. 177–198). Thousand Oaks, CA: Sage.

McClelland, D. C. (1980). Motive dispositions: The merits of operant and respondent measures. *Review of Personality and Social Psychology, 1,* 10–41.

McNemar, Q. (1946). Opinion-attitude methodology. *Psychological Bulletin, 43,* 289–374.

Meng, X.-L., Rosenthal, R., & Rubin, D. B. (1992). Comparing correlated correlation coefficients. *Psychological Bulletin, 111,* 172–175.

Messick, S. (1989). Validity. In R. L. Linn (Ed.), *Educational measurement* (3rd ed., pp. 13–104). New York: Macmillan.

Mirels, H. L. (1970). Dimensions of internal versus external control. *Journal of Consulting and Clinical Psychology, 34,* 226–228.

Moskowitz, D. S. (1986). Comparison of self-reports, reports by knowledgeable informants, and behavioral observation data. *Journal of Personality, 54,* 294–317.

Moskowitz, D. S., & Schwarz, J. C. (1982). Validity comparison of behavior counts and ratings by knowledgeable informants. *Journal of Personality and Social Psychology, 43,* 518–528.

Neuberg, S. L. Judice, T. N., & West, S. G. (in press). What the need for closure scale measures and what it does not: Toward differentiating among related epistemic motives. *Journal of Personality and Social Psychology.*

Nunnally, J. C., & Bernstein, I. H. (1993). *Psychometric theory* (3rd ed.). New York: McGraw-Hill.

Ozer, D. J. (1989). Construct validity in personality assessment. In D. M. Buss & N. Cantor (Eds.), *Personality psychology: Recent trends and emerging directions* (pp. 224–234). New York: Springer-Verlag.

Ozer, D. J., & Reise, S. P. (1994). Personality assessment. *Annual Review of Psychology, 45,* 357–388.

Peterson, C., Semmel, A., von Baeyer, C., Abramson, L. Y., Metalsky, G. I., & Seligman, M. E. P. (1982). The Attributional Style Questionnaire. *Cognitive Therapy and Research, 6,* 287–299.

Rotter, J. B. (1966). Generalized expectancies for internal versus external control of reinforcement. *Psychological Monographs, 80*(1, Whole No. 609).

Rushton, J. P., Brainerd, C. J., & Pressley, M. (1983). Behavioral development and construct validity: The principle of aggregation. *Psychological Bulletin, 94,* 18–38.

Sandler, I. N., & Guenther, R. T. (1985). Assessment of life stress events. In P. Karoly (Ed.), *Measurement strategies in health psychology* (pp. 555–600). New York: Wiley (Interscience).

Schmidt, F. L., Hunter, J. E., Pearlman, K., & Hirsh, H. R. (1985). Forty questions about validity generalization and meta-analysis. *Personal Psychology, 38,* 697–798.

Shavelson, R. J., & Webb, N. M. (1991). *Generalizability theory: A primer.* Newbury Park, CA: Sage.

Snyder, M. (1974). Self-monitoring of expressive behavior. *Journal of Personality and Social Psychology, 30,* 526–537.

Spence, J. T., & Helmreich, R. L. (1978). *Masculinity and femininity: Their psychological dimensions, correlates, and antecedents.* Austin: University of Texas Press.

Stanley, J. C. (1971). Reliability. In R. L. Thorndike (Ed.), *Educational measurement* (2nd ed., pp. 356–442). Washington, DC: National Council on Measurement in Education.

Steiger, J. H. (1980). Tests for comparing elements of a correlation matrix. *Psychological Bulletin, 87,* 245–251.

Sternberg, R. J., & Weil, E. M. (1980). An aptitude-strategy interaction in linear syllogistic reasoning. *Journal of Educational Psychology, 72,* 226–234.

Thorndike, R. L. (1951). Reliability. In E. F. Lindquist (Ed.), *Educational measurement* (pp. 560–620). Washington, DC: American Council on Education.

Walker, D. A. (1931). Answer-pattern and score scatter in tests and examinations. *British Journal of Psychology, 22,* 73–86.

Webster, D. M., & Kruglanski, A. W. (1994). Individual differences in need for cognitive closure. *Journal of Personality and Social Psychology, 67,* 1049–1062.

Wiggins, J. S. (1973). *Personality and prediction; Principles of personality measurement.* Reading, MA: Addison-Wesley.

Zuckerman, M., Gerbasi, K. C. (1977). Belief in internal control or belief in a just world: The use and misuse of the I-E scale in prediction of attitudes and behavior. *Journal of Personality, 45,* 356–379.

CHAPTER 7

PERSONALITY INFLUENCES ON THE CHOICE OF SITUATIONS

WILLIAM ICKES
UNIVERSITY OF TEXAS AT ARLINGTON

MARK SNYDER
UNIVERSITY OF MINNESOTA

STELLA GARCIA
UNIVERSITY OF TEXAS AT SAN ANTONIO

Chip and Priscilla, a Yuppie couple from Chicago, have just moved to Dallas and are sampling some of the trendier nightspots on Lower Greenville Avenue. As they push through the swinging doors of what appears to be a quaint little Western saloon right out of the TV series *Gunsmoke*, they are confronted by six huge bikers from the motorcycle gang Los Diablos, who turn on their barstools to glare at them. The bikers have an average height of more than six feet, an average weight of more than 250 pounds, an average beard growth of more than six days, and an average of more than two tattoos and three missing teeth. The fumes they emit smell flammable. Two of them stare with contempt at Chip, and one leers evilly at Priscilla. "This doesn't look like our kind of place," Chip says to Priscilla, as they prepare to beat a hasty retreat.

Just as in this fictional example, real people in their everyday lives deliberately choose to enter some situations and to avoid others. The goal of this chapter is to review a rapidly growing body of data which suggests that these choices are determined, at least in part, by the degree to which people perceive certain situations as either "fitting" or failing to "fit" such aspects of their own personalities as their traits, their attitudes, and their self-conceptions. Because this chapter is intended primarily as a review of the available literature, the major theoretical perspectives that bear on this work are described only in their broadest outlines. For a more detailed discussion of these theoretical perspectives, the reader is referred to the original sources as well as to the theoretical integration by Snyder and Ickes (1985).

I. WHAT DOES "CHOOSING SITUATIONS" MEAN?

The idea that people actively choose to be in situations that best "fit" their personalities is hardly a novel concept. In fact, its relevance to the matter of behavioral consistency has long been recognized by personality theorists. For example, as early as 1937, G. W. Allport noted that individuals play an active role in seeking out environments that are congruent with their dispositions. Some decades later, Mischel (1969, 1977) and Block (1968) argued that personality may be a function of situational contingencies, and Magnusson (1981, 1988, 1990; see also Endler, 1988) asserted that an understanding of human behavior requires an understanding of the situations in which humans behave. Taking this argument full circle back to Allport (1937), Bowers (1973) stated that "people foster consistent social environments which then reciprocate by fostering behavioral consistency" (p. 329), and Bandura (1982) noted that by constructing their environments, individuals achieve some regularity in their behavior. Recently, Snyder and Ickes (1985) have proposed that "one's choices of the settings in which to live one's life . . . may reflect features of one's conceptions of self, one's characteristic dispositions, one's attitudes and values, and other attributes of personality" (p. 915). Similarly, Caspi, Bem, and Elder (1989) have argued that "a person's selection and creation of environments is one of the most individuating and pervasive expressions of his or her personality" (p. 377).

Common to most, if not all, of these statements is the assumption that, in the natural course of their lives, individuals can freely choose to be in certain situations and to avoid others. These preferred environments provide opportunities for personal dispositions to be manifested and reinforced. Once individuals are in their chosen situations, their words and actions are genuine reflections of their personalities, and the fact that they display these behaviors in settings they have specifically chosen ensures a substantial degree of consistency in their behavior.

The interest of personality psychologists in the relation between personality and situational choices is due, in no small measure, to their long-standing interest in understanding the processes that govern temporal stability and cross-situational consistency in behavior. As Snyder and Ickes (1985) have noted, personality psychologists were guided first by a *dispositional strategy* that viewed traits and other relatively stable and enduring dispositions as responsible for behavioral consistency.[1] Later, in part as a reaction to critiques of the trait approach, especially that of Mischel (1968), the statistical or *mechanistic* version of an *interactional strategy* emerged. This approach viewed behavior as the product of the interaction between the person and the situation. Such interactions were assumed to be unidirectional such that personal and situational variables could influence, but not be influenced by, individuals' behavior (Cantor & Kihlstrom, 1980; Magnusson & Endler, 1977; Snyder & Ickes, 1985).

The most recent phase of this endeavor has seen the emergence of a *dynamic interactional strategy* that views behavioral consistency as the product of the *reciprocal* causal relation between personality and environment. It is assumed that people have a tendency to choose to enter and participate in those situations that they perceive to be most conducive to the behavioral expression of their own traits and dispositions. Because these situations are typically the ones in which reinforcement of the expressed behaviors is most likely to occur, the choice of situations is an important cause of the temporal stability in individuals' behavior.

II. CONCEPTUAL AND METHODOLOGICAL ISSUES

If the notion that peoples' personalities influence their choice of situations is not a new idea, why have personality psychologists only recently begun to study this phenomenon? Argyle, Furnham, and Graham (1981) have proposed one answer to this question. They have noted that, whereas personality theorists have been fairly successful in making conceptual distinctions among person concepts (traits), they have not yet undertaken the analogous (but potentially more difficult) task of developing an appropriate taxonomy of situations. Similar calls for appropriate conceptual work have been made by Runyan (1978), Duke and Nowicki (1982), and Endler (1983).[2]

---

[1] Throughout this chapter, we intend a traditional usage of the terms *traits* and *dispositions,* defining them as relatively stable internal structures that guide, and therefore partially determine, behavioral acts. This usage is consistent with Allport's (1931, 1966) view of traits as "neurodynamic structures" whose reality can be presumed even if their precise forms and functions cannot yet be specified (see also Funder, 1991). Our use of the term *cross-situational consistency* is reserved for those topographically similar or dissimilar behaviors that appear to have the same general meaning across a wide range of situations to the actor who performs them, and can therefore be viewed as a patterned manifestation of an underlying trait or disposition (e.g., punctuality). Obviously, the term *cross-situational consistency* cannot be applied to cases in which the behaviors displayed in different situations have substantially different meanings for the actor, despite their topographical similarity (e.g., taking money from someone can variously be interpreted as "receiving one's wages," "getting a rebate," "taking a bribe," or "stealing").

[2] Given the conceptual difficulties involved, we do not propose to solve the problem of defining *situation* here. We will simply note that situations can be conceptualized as (a) multidimensional fields of action in which (b) behavior is to some degree constrained by environmental press, and which (c) can be viewed from any of a number of different perspectives that are available to a given perceiver. These perspectives, discussed as "the forms of social awareness" by Wegner and Giuliano (1982), include tacit and focal self-awareness, tacit and focal other awareness, and tacit and focal group awareness.

The lack of relevant conceptual work is not the only problem, however. Another, and possibly more serious, problem is that most researchers are still committed to the assumptions of mechanistic interactionism and the conventions of traditional empirical methods such as the laboratory experiment. As Snyder and Ickes (1985, pp. 914–915) have pointed out, the assumptions underlying the experimental method are, in at least two respects, inconsistent with those underlying a dynamic interactional approach wherein the individuals' choice of situations is both a cause and a consequence of the disposition-based stability in their behavior. The limitations imposed by this inconsistency are discussed below.

A. Limitations of the Experimental Approach

First, a key component for conducting a sound experiment is the direct experimental manipulation of independent variables which, in most psychological experiments, are aspects of the situation to which the subject is exposed. Great care is taken to ensure that the different levels of the independent (i.e., situational) variable are made sufficiently distinct from each other to guarantee effects on the behavior of the participants assigned to these different conditions. This, in fact, is the major strength of the experimental methodology: it provides maximal opportunities for researchers to witness the impact of situations on behavior. At the same time, however, controlling some aspects of the situation through manipulation of the independent variables tends to work against the goals of the personality researcher. Specifically, to the extent that the psychological "strength" of the experimental situation constrains the subjects' behavior in a way that minimizes individual differences, the very phenomena which personality theorists seek to observe and understand become increasingly less evident (Ickes, 1982; Snyder & Ickes, 1985).

Second, another essential component for conducting a sound experiment is the random assignment of participants to the different treatment conditions. This step is necessary to control for individual differences across conditions so that a more valid causal conclusion can be made about the impact of the independent variable on the dependent variable. Despite its methodological importance, however, randomly assigning participants to treatment conditions eliminates one major vehicle by which individuals' attributes are manifested. That is, by assigning participants to specific treatment conditions, the experimenter denies them the opportunity to choose whether or not to be exposed to the assigned condition instead of to one of the remaining conditions, of whose nature and even existence they are frequently kept unaware. Further, once they are in a treatment condition, they can exert minimal influence on the situation and can only react to the manipulated independent variable(s). Thus, the experimental procedure effectively and intentionally minimizes the extent to which behavior in the experimental situation is a reflection of the individual's attributes.

The manipulation of variables and the random assignment of subjects to treatment conditions are, of course, the essential and defining features of the experimental method. They are precisely the features that make this method so well suited to testing casual hypotheses about the effects of manipulated independent variables on measured dependent variables. However, in real world settings, people are not typically denied the freedom to be where they want to be, when to be there, and with whom to be there. In real world settings, people are most often found in situations of their own choosing. Viewed from this perspective, conventional experimental paradigms can be seen as highly unusual and constraining situations that eliminate the usual opportunities by which people choose to be in certain settings.

Practitioners of the situational strategy for studying personality differences are thus faced with an important dilemma (Snyder & Ickes, 1985). On the one hand, by experimentally controlling features of the situation and randomly assigning participants to the treatment conditions, investigators of the dynamic interactional approach are assured of attenuating, and possibly even eliminating, the personality processes that are presumably of greatest interest to them. On the other hand, because the same experimental procedures typically guarantee the internal validity of any findings obtained, researchers may be understandably reluctant to give them up.

B. Alternative Research Methods

The obvious challenge, then, is to identify and understand the consistencies in behavior that are expressed through the selection of situations without breaking the rules of conventional empirical investigation. Fortunately, through the efforts of a growing number of researchers, several novel methodologies have been developed to achieve this goal.

These methodologies all reflect the fundamental assumption of the dynamic interactional approach. As we have noted, dynamic interactionism is a reciprocal or transactional model which assumes that the situation is both a *cause* and a *consequence* of the person's behavior (Endler & Edwards, 1986). Given this assumption of bidirectional causality, it is possible either (a) to view some aspect of the situation as the independent (or predictor) variable and some aspect of the person as the dependent (or criterion) variable, or (b) to view some aspect of the person as the predictor variable and some aspect of the situation as the criterion variable. The first view is the traditional one embodied in most experimental research; the second view is one that is currently guiding much of the empirical research on how individuals' personalities affect their choice of situations.

The methodologies most consistent with the second view can be grouped into three broad categories: (1) studies of actual situational choices in the real world, (2) studies of actual situational choices in the laboratory, and (3) studies of hypothetical situational choices (e.g., in response to survey or questionnaire items). After reviewing some representative studies in each of these three categories, we will briefly note a number of other empirical methods that can be used by practitioners of the dynamic interactional strategy.

1. Studying Actual Situational Choices in the Real World

In research consistent with the view that personality traits constrain people's everyday choices of situations, Furnham (1981) studied how individuals' activity preferences vary as a function of their personality. He found that extraverts were more likely than introverts to report being in situations that invited competition, intimacy, and assertion. Similarly, Holland (1966, 1985) has shown (in research to be described later in this chapter) that people's occupational preferences are also determined to a significant degree by their personality.

In conceptually related research, the experience sampling method (Csikszentmihalyi & Figurski, 1982; Csikszentmihalyi & Kubey, 1981; Hormuth, 1986) or similar techniques (Wheeler, Reis, & Nezlek, 1983) have been used to study the naturally occurring selection of situations. For example, Emmons, Diener, and Larsen (1986) had people keep records of specific behaviors and moods in a number of situations they typically encountered in their own environments. One of their findings revealed that extraverts spent more time and felt more positive in situations that provided social, as opposed to solitary, recreation activities. In another study using the experience sampling method, Diener, Larsen, and Emmons (1984) found that people who had a high need for order chose to be in common or "typical" situations more often than in novel situations.

It should be noted that this approach can also be used to identify situations that individuals choose to *avoid*. For example, Furnham (1981) reported that neurotics tended to avoid situations that were high in social stimulation and provided opportunities for extended social interaction.

2. Studying Actual Situational Choices in the Laboratory

It is not necessary, however, to abandon laboratory procedures when conducting research of this type. For example, in a laboratory study of self-monitoring processes, Snyder and Gangestad (1982) found that high self-monitors preferred situations that provided them with precise and unambiguous specifications of the type of person called for in the setting to ones that provided them with a minimally defined character. In contrast, low self-monitors preferred situations that permitted them to act in accordance with their own dispositions.

Obviously, laboratory studies such as this are correlational rather than experimental, since the participants are free to choose the situation or "condition" they wish to enter rather than being randomly assigned to it. On the other hand, because the experimental convention of random assignment forces some participants to be in a situation that they would otherwise not choose to enter, all truly experimental situations can justifiably be described as "artificial" in the sense that they are determined by the experimenter instead of being chosen by the participants themselves (Diener et al., 1984; Wachtel, 1973).

3. Studying Hypothetical Situational Choices

As an alternative to presenting people with a choice between *actual* situations, some researchers have developed paper-and-pencil measures designed to assess variations in individuals' habitual choices of, or characteristic preferences for, *hypothetical* situations that are described in less immediate, more abstract terms.

Because the situational strategist is interested in people's choices of situations as a function of their attributes, a valid assessment device would be one that measures the strength of situational preferences. Although most existing scales were not designed to measure such preferences (cf. Furnham, 1981; L. A. Pervin, 1981), at least a few promising scales of this type have been developed. For example, Furnham (1982) has used the Social Situation Scale to study how situational preferences vary as a function of psychoticism and social desirability. Crozier (1979) and Wolpe and Lang (1964) have used the Fear Survey Schedules to assess the degree to which people would be anxious or fearful in various situations (e.g., situations involving criticism or negative evaluation). In other research, W. H. Jones, Russell, and Cutrona (1985) have used the Shyness Situations Measure to identify the type of situations in which the dispositionally shy are most likely to feel shy (e.g., eating in a restaurant or giving a speech).

4. Other Methods for Studying Situational Choices

Still another method for investigating the type of situations certain individuals choose is the template-matching technique proposed by D. J. Bem and Funder (1978; D. J. Bem, 1981). In one study applying this technique, Lord (1982) proposed that a person's behavior should be consistent across situations to the degree that there is similarity in the person's templates for the situations. Lord's (1982) study revealed that cross-situational consistency emerged when the perceived situational similarity was *idiographic* but not when it was *nomothetic* (i.e., consensual). These results not only demonstrated that the template-matching technique can be used to study individual differences in situation selection but provided further support for D. J. Bem and Allen's (1974) assertion that consistency in behavior is manifested at the idiographic level.

Finally, there are a number of other empirical methods that can be used by the situational strategist. The researcher can obtain the subjects' verbal or written expressions about their level of comfort in and preference for a particular situation (Mehrabian, 1978). The researcher can also obtain cognitive representations of chosen situations to determine if there are characteristic schemas that people hold for the settings they are likely to spend time in (Price, 1981). And, to complement these self-report techniques, the researcher can obtain behavioral measures of situational preference (e.g., degree of exploration, the physical movement of avoiding or approaching tasks/persons in the available settings, and the length of stay).

C. Some Unresolved Problems

Although all of the methods described above can profitably be employed by situational strategists, some final words of caution are in order. First, as D. J.

Bem and Allen (1974) have noted, the English language presents us with a rich vocabulary for describing *traits* but an impoverished vocabulary for describing *situations*. Asking people to identify their choices of situations or to indicate on a questionnaire their likelihood of entering a particular situation presumes that they can *semantically* distinguish one situation from another. Researchers must be aware of this linguistic obstacle and find ways to overcome it. Second, and in a related vein, individuals (a) may not have much experience in discriminating one situation from another, (b) may interpret descriptions of situations quite differently from the way the experimenter intends, (c) may view rating scales as not particularly relevant to their cognitive representations of situations, (d) may use a different frame of reference than that of the experimenter, (e) may view past situations as dissimilar to future situations, (f) may presume that they are responding to functionally equivalent situations when filling out a questionnaire, or (g) may view situations in fairly nonspecific and global terms (Argyle et al., 1981; Furnham, 1982; Furnham & Jaspars, 1983; Lord, 1982; Runyan, 1978). These considerations can pose formidable, though not insurmountable, challenges to the study of situational preferences.

III. ASSESSING THE DIMENSIONS OF SOCIAL SITUATIONS

Few dynamic interactionists would question the assertion that people choose to enter and spend time in situations that allow and/or enable them to behave in a manner that reflects features of their personalities. Inherent in such an assertion, however, is the assumption that individuals can assess the behavioral opportunities provided by a given setting. In other words, people are aware of and can identify features of the situation that are particularly conducive to the behavioral expression of their personal attributes. Considerable evidence is available to suggest that individuals can indeed assess the appropriateness of specific behaviors for specific situations, and that they can also assess the constraints that certain situations place on certain behaviors (e.g., Argyle et al., 1981; Cantor, Mischel, & Schwartz, 1982a,b; Glick, 1985; Price, 1974; Price & Bouffard, 1974; Smith-Lovin, 1979; Snyder & Gangestad, 1982). Armed with this type of knowledge about situations, people ought to be able to determine the specific setting(s) that will permit and promote the expression of their own personalities.

A number of theories have been proposed to specify the mechanisms that individuals use to aid them in choosing dispositionally relevant situations. For our present purposes, it is convenient to group these theories into three categories: (1) goal-based motivational theories (e.g., Argyle et al., 1981), (2) cognitive representational theories (e.g., Cantor et al., 1982a,b), and (3) the affect congruence model (Emmons, Diener, & Larsen, 1985). The reader should note, however, that there is a substantial degree of conceptual overlap among the three approaches, and that the assumptions and processes that are explicit in one approach may be implicit in the other two.

A. Goal-Based Motivational Theories

Some of the theories proposed to specify the mechanisms underlying situational choice are variants of the goal-based motivational theory, which is premised on the notion that situations consist of relatively well-defined goal structures (Argyle, 1980; Argyle et al., 1981; Cantor, Norem, & Langston, 1991; Emmons & Diener, 1986a; Emmons et al., 1986; Furnham, 1981). Goal structures refer to the opportunities provided by the situation that may aid people in accomplishing their goals. People with specific needs or objectives are presumably aware that such goal structures exist, and are therefore motivated to actively seek out the specific situations that they believe will best facilitate the attainment of their goals.

These goal-structure theories of situational choice have already received at least some empirical support. Gorta (1985), for example, presented subjects with verbal descriptions of situations and asked them the purposes that would lead them to be in each of those settings. She then described a set of particular goals to subjects, in each case asking them to respond by describing the situations they would most likely choose in order to achieve these specific objectives. The general finding of the study was that the specific goal that subjects had in mind highlighted particular aspects of the situation as important, which in turn affected their perception of the situation as well as their preference for entering it. Although Gorta did not specifically investigate personality factors that might affect situational choice, her methodology provides one possible way of testing how situational choices are guided and channeled by personal attributes.

In a study using the more compelling methodology of the time-sampling technique (e.g., Csikszentmihalyi & Figurski, 1982; Csikszentmihalyi & Kubey, 1981), Emmons and Diener (1986b) found the relation between an individual's objectives and the goal structure of the situation to be stronger in those cases in which the individual had the opportunity to choose the situation rather than having it imposed on him or her. Consistent with Gorta's (1985) findings, the results of Emmons and Diener's (1986a; see also 1986b) study indicate that the choice of situation is linked to the goal(s) a person wishes to achieve and to the goal structure of the social setting(s) which he or she chooses to enter.

B. Cognitive Representational Theories

Other theories of situational choice focus on the cognitive representations that people have formed regarding the features of different situations. Theorists and researchers in the cognitive social learning tradition assume that people schematically encode, store, and retrieve information about the specific aspects of a setting that are of particular interest to them (e.g., Cantor et al., 1982a; Lord, 1982; Mischel, 1977). Given this assumption, a number of investigators have tried to identify dimensions of social settings that contribute to the type of inferences people make regarding the behavior that can be expressed in particular social situations (Wish, 1975; Wish, Deutsch, & Kaplan, 1976; Wish & Kaplan, 1977).

For example, Wish et al. (1976) identified situational dimensions that people perceive as relevant to the conduct of certain kinds of social relationships. Specifically, they found that the dimension of cooperative/friendly versus competitive/hostile was a more salient aspect of the social situation for older than for younger subjects, for married than for single persons, and for politically right than for politically left individuals. With regard to another situational dimension, they found that inequality was important for subjects with unconventional religious beliefs whereas equality was identified as pertinent for Christians.

In many cases, the most salient feature of a given setting is the type of person most likely to be found in that setting. The findings of some studies (e.g., Cantor, 1980; Cantor & Mischel, 1979) suggest that individuals share prototypic images of the person most likely to be found in a given setting. When the participants in these studies were asked to describe the characteristics of the "ideal" person in a particular setting, the results revealed that regardless of the level of situational abstraction (e.g., superordinate categories such as "social" or "stressful" situations versus less abstract categories such as "party" or "interview"), there was a consensual person-for-a-situation prototype for each category.

Before leaving this topic, we should note that other advocates of the social learning approach place somewhat less emphasis on cognition and somewhat more emphasis on the notion that behavioral regularities are the conditioned (and conditional) products of situational reinforcements. An article by L. A. Pervin (1981) provides a useful discussion of this perspective.

C. The Affect Congruence Model

A final theory that attempts to account for the processes that individuals use to assess whether situations are conducive to the behavioral expression of their attributes is the affect congruence model proposed by Emmons et al. (1985). As they have noted, "affect experienced in the situation will partially determine future decisions to enter or avoid that situation . . . thus, to the extent that individuals experience affect which is compatible with their psychological predispositions, the probability of choosing that situation again in the future will be increased" (p. 695).

Studies reported by Emmons and his colleagues provide some preliminary support for this theory. For example, Emmons and Diener (1986b) found that positive affect (satisfaction) was associated with goal attainment in both chosen and imposed situations, whereas negative affect was marginally related to the nonattainment of goals in imposed situations only. In related studies, (a) extraverts reported experiencing more positive affect when studying in the library than when studying at home, (b) highly sociable persons reported feeling more positive when they were in chosen social recreational situations, and (c) neurotics tended to report negative affect in any situation they entered (Diener et al., 1984; Emmons & Diener, 1986a; Emmons et al., 1985, 1986).

D. Commonalities and Contrasts

In general, the theories we have just reviewed suggest that individuals attempt to identify and selectively enter those situations that encourage and reinforce the expression of their own particular attributes. A common assumption of these theories is that the more the person's disposition "fits" the situation, the better the outcome the person can expect to obtain. A second common assumption is that specific motives underlie people's choices of dispositionally congruent situations.

The theories differ, however, in the specific motives they posit. In the goal-based theories, for example, the person is presumably motivated to accomplish or attain a particular goal, such as satisfying the need for affiliation, esteem, or status. In the cognitive representational theories, the person is presumably motivated to understand dimensions of situations so that future choices of dispositionally relevant situations will be easier to make. Finally, in the affect congruence model, the person is presumably motivated to obtain some form of affective satisfaction as a consequence of having made an appropriate situational choice.

These differences in the assumed motives for situational choice imply corresponding differences in the individual's *perception* of the situations that he or she encounters. The goal-based theories emphasize the individual's perception of the opportunity structures for goal attainment available in different situations (e.g., Argyle et al., 1981). In contrast, the cognitive representational theories emphasize the individual's perception of those abstract features and dimensions that signal the potential congruence/incongruence between the situation and the individual's own disposition(s). Finally, the affect congruence model emphasizes the individual's perception of the anticipated positive or negative affect to be derived from entering and taking part in the situation.

IV. UNDERSTANDING INDIVIDUALS IN TERMS OF SITUATIONAL CHOICES

If people can assess situations according to the opportunities available for the behavioral expression of their dispositions, do they in fact systematically choose to enter and spend time in such opportune settings? Our review of the literature reveals that there are several categories of studies which document the influence of individual dispositions on situational choices:

1. The first and largest category includes studies that have investigated differences in situational choices as a function of specific personality traits such as sensation-seeking (e.g., Segal, 1973; Zuckerman, 1978), self-monitoring (e.g., Snyder & Gangestad, 1982; Snyder & Kendzierski, 1982), introversion/extraversion

(e.g., Eysenck, 1974; Furnham, 1981), and shyness (e.g., A. K. Watson & Cheek, 1986).

2. A second category includes studies documenting instances in which people choose to enter those specific settings that help them sustain existing self-concepts, for example, studies of self-esteem maintenance (Berglas & Jones, 1978; Tesser, 1988; Tesser & Moore, 1987) and self-verification (Swann, 1987; Swann & Read, 1981; Swann, Stein-Seroussi, & Giesler, 1992; Swann, Wentzlaff, & Krull, 1992).

3. A third category includes studies that document how situational choices can vary as a function of social attitudes (e.g., Kahle & Berman, 1979; Snyder & Kendzierski, 1982; Wilson & Nias, 1975).

4. A fourth category includes studies designed to investigate the settings within which people choose to conduct particular types of relationships (e.g., Argyle, 1980; Argyle & Furnham, 1982; Glick, 1985; Jellison & Ickes, 1974; Snyder, Gangestad, & Simpson, 1983; D. G. Winter, 1973).

5. A fifth category includes studies that examine the personal origins of choices of leisure situations (e.g., Bishop & Witt, 1970; Furnham, 1981), educational settings (e.g., Eddy & Sinnett, 1973; B. A. Pervin & Rubin, 1967; Stern, Stein, & Bloom, 1956), and occupational situations (e.g., Atkinson, 1958; Holland, 1985; Rosenberg, 1957; Vroom, 1964).

6. In addition to the various categories of studies that have demonstrated the choice of dispositionally congruent situations, there is a smaller category of studies that have explored people's responses to dispositionally *incongruent* situations. These studies reveal, as expected, that people typically choose to avoid dispositionally incongruent situations (e.g., Furnham, 1981). They also reveal, however, that in those cases in which people enter dispositionally incongruent situations, they often attempt to alter the situations to make them more congruent with their own personalities (e.g., Srull & Karabenick, 1975; D. Watson & Baumal, 1967). In a theoretical treatment of this issue, Snyder and Ickes (1985) have proposed some conditions in which people deliberately choose to enter dispositionally incongruent situations in order to effect desired changes in themselves, in the situation, or in other people.

7. Finally, to complement the relatively large category of studies that have examined the influence of dispositions on situational choice, there is a much smaller category of studies that have examined the reciprocal influence of situational choices and personality development. These studies suggest that the press of the different situations encountered throughout an individual's life can dramatically shape the behaviors that eventually become part of that individual's personality (e.g., Caspi, 1987; Caspi & Bem, 1990; Caspi et al., 1989; Caspi & Herbener, 1990; Caspi, Herbener, & Ozer, 1992; Ickes & Turner, 1983; Runyan, 1978).

In summary, there are several different lines of evidence for the proposition that people choose to enter and spend time in situations that promote the expression of their own trait-relevant behavior. A more detailed look at this evidence is provided in the following sections.

A. Characteristic Dispositions and Situational Choices

Many studies have investigated the relation between personality dispositions and situational preferences. In general, the results of these studies offer compelling evidence that people choose to enter and spend time in situations that will foster, promote, and encourage the behavioral manifestations of their own traits and dispositions.

For example, people with low arousal-seeking tendencies appear to prefer settings that are relatively low in complexity, and they are likely to avoid highly informative situations. People with high arousal-seeking tendencies, on the other hand, tend to seek out environments that are highly informative and relatively complex (Mehrabian, 1978; Mehrabian & Russell, 1973). According to the findings of several studies, individuals with an internal locus of control are more likely to choose test settings that require skill or ability than are individuals with an external locus of control (Kahle, 1980; Rotter, 1966; Srull & Karabenick, 1975; D. Watson & Baumal, 1967). In other research, extraverts have been found to seek out stimulating leisure situations (e.g., ones that involve physical pursuits) whereas introverts prefer more passive recreational situations (e.g., reading; Furnham, 1981).

Furnham (1982) has reported that psychotics choose to interact in spontaneous and volatile situations as opposed to more formal and stable ones. With regard to the dispositionally shy, A. K. Watson and Cheek (1986; see also Russell, Cutrona, & Jones, 1986) have found that novelty is perhaps the most salient factor eliciting shyness reactions in social settings (e.g., engaging in conversation with strangers). In another domain, Snyder and his colleagues have shown that low self-monitors are unwilling to enter into situations that are relatively incongruent with their personal beliefs and attitudes about certain issues, whereas high self-monitors may actively choose situations that cast them in different roles (Snyder, 1979; Snyder & Gangestad, 1982; Snyder & Kendzierski, 1982).

Other studies provide further evidence of the congruence between a person's situational choices and his or her characteristic dispositions. Machiavellians prefer face-to-face interactions, because encounters of this type enable them to optimally apply their tactics for exploiting others (Christie & Geis, 1970; Geis, 1978). In the context of therapy situations, field-dependent patients seem to be happiest in supportive therapies with well-defined structures, whereas field-independent patients prefer to play a more active role in the content and progress of their therapy (Karp, Kissin, & Hustmyer, 1970). Related research has shown that field-dependent individuals are more likely than field-independent individuals to rely on other people for useful information in otherwise ambiguous settings (Gates, 1971; Goodenough, 1978; Greene, 1973; Mausner & Graham, 1970; Nevill, 1974).

Research on high sensation-seekers has provided extensive evidence of their preference for situations that are novel and intensely arousing. For example, relative to low sensation-seekers, high sensation-seekers are more likely to volunteer for unusual experiments (e.g., drug studies) and to report having experienced a greater variety of sexual activities (Zuckerman, 1974, 1978). In studies conducted in business environments, extraverts with an internal locus of control have been shown to actively participate in the interior design of their offices (McElroy, Morrow, & Ackerman, 1983; Osborn, 1988). Finally, people with a high need for approval seem to value highly those situations that provide them with cues that help to guide and organize their behavior (Millham & Jacobson, 1978).

B. Self-Conceptions and Situational Choices

Research investigations have focused on other categories of dispositions in addition to traits. These studies provide evidence that people choose situations for the sake of congruency with these other classes of dispositions as well. A number of these studies have shown, for example, that people also actively choose to enter and spend time in settings that preserve, sustain, or maintain their conceptions of self.

The "self-handicapping" studies by E. E. Jones and Berglas (Berglas & Jones, 1978) provide evidence that people who are concerned about threats to their self-perceived competence will attempt to protect and to sustain their self-image by putting themselves in situations in which they can explain away their failures and take credit for their successes. On the other hand, if situations fail to protect and, instead, threaten their self-competent image, there is evidence that individuals will choose to leave these settings (Conolley, Gerard, & Kline, 1978).

In some situations, people strive to maintain or increase their self-evaluation by engaging in a comparison or a reflection process. According to Tesser and his colleagues (Tesser, 1984, 1985, 1988; Tesser & Campbell, 1980, 1982, 1983; Tesser & Moore, 1987; Tesser & Paulhus, 1983; Tesser & Smith, 1980), certain factors such as the relevance of another person's performance on a task, the perceived closeness of the other, and the other's actual performance determine the particular strategy one uses to preserve one's self-esteem. For example, in order to protect or regain their self-esteem, people may either increase their efforts on a task or distort the perception of their own performance relative to the performance of others (Tesser, Campbell, & Smith, 1984).

In other cases, people will seek to validate their self-concepts by using certain "congruency" (Backman, 1988; Secord & Backman, 1961, 1965) or "self-verification" (Swann, 1987; Swann, Stein-Seroussi, & Giesler, 1992) strategies when interacting with those whom they encounter in the situations they have selected. Both Secord and Backman's congruency theory and Swann's self-verification approach assert that people not only choose, but at times actively construct, certain features of their situations for the purpose of maintaining a stable self-image. For example, Swann and Read (1981, Study 1) found that people who saw themselves as likable spent more time reading an interaction partner's appraisal of them, particularly if the interaction partner viewed them as likable. In another study, Swann and Hill (1982) reported that self-conceived dominants who had been labeled as submissive by their interaction partners subsequently reacted with some vehemence toward their partners in order to reassert their dominant personalities.

Of course, not all people are highly motivated to use "congruency" or "self-verification" strategies to help ensure that their self-conception can be sustained in the face of situational pressures that might threaten it. As Snyder and his colleagues have repeatedly shown (for a review, see Snyder, 1987), some people are so sensitive and responsive to situational pressures that they strive for congruency by presenting themselves as being whatever kind of person the situation apparently demands. These high self-monitors seem to adopt different personalities to match the different situations they enter. In contrast, low self-monitors are more likely to selectively enter those situations that allow them to behave in a manner consistent with their typical self-conception (Snyder and Gangestad, 1982). For more detailed discussions of congruency theory and its relevance to the question of how situational choices vary as a function of personality, see Backman (1988) and Snyder and Ickes (1985, pp. 921–932).

C. Social Attitudes and Situational Choices

Another set of studies that examine people's situational choices have focused on the settings chosen for the specific purpose of behaviorally expressing one's attitudes. The underlying assumption is that people prefer to enter settings that provide them with opportunities to express and act upon their opinions and beliefs. For example, Kahle and Berman (1979) reported that people with favorable attitudes toward particular candidates for a political office actively seek out situations in which they will be exposed to messages favorable to their candidate. Similarly, low self-monitors have been found to gravitate toward settings that dispose them to behave in ways that will enhance the congruence between their attitudes and their behavior (Snyder & Kendzierski, 1982).

As another example, several studies have shown that authoritarians tend to choose not to accept any information that may change their attitude toward a particular object (Dillehay, 1978; Katz, 1960; Katz, McClintock, & Sarnoff, 1957). Other research suggests that extraverts, being more permissive than introverts in their attitudes about social behavior, choose to engage in behaviors that involve more risks, such as having sexual intercourse more frequently, in more different ways, and with more different partners (Wilson & Nias, 1975; see also Gangestad & Simpson, 1990). Extraverts are also more likely to break institutional rules and wind up in prison more often than introverts (Eysenck, 1971).

Other research indicates that smokers with an external locus of control tend to be more "chance oriented" than smokers with an internal locus of control. That is, believers in external control are more likely to continue such behavior despite warnings about the consequences of heavy smoking. In addition, they are more likely to be members of social fraternities and less likely to attend church than are nonsmokers or smokers with an internal locus of control (James, Woodruff, & Werner, 1965; Straits & Sechrest, 1963). In a similar vein, it has been reported that women with an external locus of control are less likely to practice effective birth control than are those with an internal locus of control (Lundy, 1972).

D. Social Relationships and Situational Choices

A number of empirical studies have begun to explore how situational choices can vary as a function of one's relationship with others. In fact, the types of relationship that exist between people can have a profound impact on their choice of situations (cf. Duck & Gilmore, 1981). For example, Argyle and Furnham (1982) found that type of relationship could be used to predict the type of situation chosen. Marital relationships had the most powerful influence on choice of situations, with domestic, informal, intimate, and recreational settings being chosen most frequently. Friend-ships exerted the next most powerful influence on situational choices, with less domestic and more task-oriented situations selected for these relationships. On the other hand, the situations chosen for interacting with disliked colleagues were relatively short in duration, infrequent, and formal (e.g., morning coffee, meetings).

Other studies have begun to address the question of how personality influences preferences for *both* situations *and* types of relationships. For example, Glick (1985) studied the conditions chosen by high and low self-monitors for initiating relation-ships. He found that low self-monitors chose potential dating partners on the basis of the partners' personality characteristics, whereas high self-monitors selected potential dating partners on the basis of their physical attractiveness. In addition, Glick's findings revealed some systematic differences in situational preferences for the particular type of partner chosen. Low self-monitors preferred to initiate the relationship with a partner who had desirable personality characteristics in a roman-tic situation; they avoided romantic situations if they were forced to interact with partners who had less-than-desirable characteristics. High self-monitors, by the same token, chose to interact with physically attractive partners in romantic settings and avoided such settings if the partner was physically unattractive. Further analysis revealed that romantic situations provide specific opportunities that can be strategi-cally employed to facilitate romantic relationships with one's preferred type of partner. For example, these situations involved less structured and longer interac-tions, took place at a different time of the day, and provided future opportunities to pursue the relationship.

In a similar study, Snyder et al. (1983) found systematic differences between high and low self-monitors in the type of partner chosen for leisure activities. High self-monitors chose leisure partners according to their particular skills (i.e., being a "specialist") in the activity domain, whereas low self-monitors preferred activity partners who were nonspecialists but whom they particularly liked. In terms of the preferred situations in which to conduct such relationships, high self-monitors preferred to interact with a specific partner for particular activities only. Low self-monitors, on the other hand, were less likely to differentiate their social worlds this way, and instead chose to spend time with well-liked partners regardless of the type of activity involved.

E. Choice of Leisure, Educational, and Occupational Settings

Finally, there is considerable evidence that people's dispositions can influence their choices of leisure activities, educational settings, and occupational situations.

1. Dispositional Influences on Choice of Leisure Situations

With regard to leisure activities, Furnham (1981) found that extraverts preferred a distinctively different pattern of recreational activities than did introverts. For example, extraverts preferred to engage in activities that were affiliative, stimulating, physical, and informal. Introverts, on the other hand, chose leisure activities that required a sense of order and planning. In a related study, Emmons et al. (1986) found that extraverts not only preferred social recreational settings but also reported more positive affect when they were in chosen social settings than in imposed nonsocial situations (e.g., reading). They also found that people with a high need for play experienced positive affect in chosen recreational situations and were less happy in imposed work settings.

2. Dispositional Influences on Choice of Educational Situations

With regard to educational settings, people with a strong power motivation are more likely to choose courses dealing with the application of direct and legitimate power (e.g., science, law, or politics; D. G. Winter, 1973; D. G. Winter & Stewart, 1978). Moreover, students with a high need for power are more often officers in university student organizations, dormitory counselors, student newspaper and radio workers, and members of faculty–student committees (D. G. Winter & Stewart, 1978). In a related vein, Stern et al. (1956) have reported that people with an authoritarian disposition disproportionately choose to enter military academies.

Other research suggests that extraverted, action-oriented students are particularly likely to spend time in those areas of the campus that encourage affiliation and social interaction (e.g., lobbies and parks; Eddy & Sinnett, 1973). And, as we have noted previously, field independents, who tend to value cognitive skills, prefer to enter and achieve success in academic and vocational areas, whereas field dependents, who do not particularly value such skills, prefer areas that deal with other people (Goodenough, 1978; Levy, 1969; Winter, Moore, Goodenough, & Cox, 1977).

3. Dispositional Influences on Choice of Occupational Situations

With regard to choices about occupational situations, people who believe it is important to be autonomous and independent on the job tend to select occupations that are characterized by relatively high levels of uncertainty and worker autonomy (Morse, 1975). In other examples, individuals high in people-orientation are particularly likely to choose such jobs as social work, medicine, and teaching; individuals with a high need for self-expression tend to prefer careers in architecture, journalism, and art; and individuals high in reward-orientation prefer to enter occupations that involve sales, finance, and management (Rosenberg, 1957). Finally, achievement-oriented people are especially likely to choose companies that emphasize individual advancement over those emphasizing power and status (Andrews, 1967).

In a recent book, Holland (1985) has proposed six personality types that are associated with distinctly different vocational interests. For instance, because the investigative type is task-oriented and prefers thinking rather than acting out problems, this individual is more likely to choose a scientific occupation (e.g., design engineer). In contrast, the social type can be found in human services jobs because of this individual's trait of sociability. Whereas the enterprising type is dominating and adventurous and is therefore well-suited to business or sales positions, the conventional type is conforming and conservative and tends to gravitate toward occupations such as bookkeeping. The realistic type favors tackling concrete instead of abstract problems and is therefore found in mechanical occupations. Finally, the artistic type is sensitive to emotions and expressions of individuality and is more likely to be a playwright or a commercial artist. The results of a number of studies are reviewed as being consistent with Holland's theory (e.g., Benninger & Walsh, 1980; Costa, McCrae, & Holland, 1984; Walsh, Horton, & Gaffey, 1977).

F. Reactions to Dispositionally Incongruent Situations

We have marshalled many empirical examples to illustrate the proposition that people are particularly likely to enter and to spend time in situations reflecting their self-conceptions, their attitudes, their personal tastes in leisure, educational, and occupational activities, and the types of relationships they have. We now consider the complementary issue of how people respond to dispositionally *incongruent* situations.

In general, reactions to dispositionally incongruent situations take one of three forms: (a) choosing deliberately *to avoid* dispositionally incongruent settings, (b) inadvertently entering such settings and then attempting *to cope* with the lack of congruity between the setting and one's own dispositions, and (c) choosing deliberately *to enter* such settings, to change either one's own dispositions or features of the setting itself.

1. Avoiding Incongruent Situations

First, and most obviously, people may choose *not* to enter and spend time in dispositionally incongruent settings. The act of deliberately *avoiding* certain settings and situations can at times be just as revealing and reflective of a person's dispositions and traits as the act of deliberately *entering* other settings and situations (cf. E. E. Jones & Davis, 1965; E. E. Jones & McGillis, 1976). For example, Furnham (1982) reported that people with high social desirability scores preferred to enter situations that are socially simple and informal but to avoid ones in which they could become the focus of attention. Research by Efran and Boylin (1967) suggests that they also tend to avoid situations that are highly evaluative or that call for some degree of assertiveness (e.g., group discussions).

For another example, people with an avoidant personality disorder are assumed to desire social contact but at the same time to fear rejection or humiliation. As a result, they choose not to expose themselves to social settings in which there is the potential for rejection and humiliation. If they are caught in such a setting, they act socially detached and withdrawn (Millon & Everly, 1985). Similarly, individuals diagnosed as having a schizoid personality disorder may be "in" a situation physically but avoid it psychologically by being unresponsive to the behavior of other people (e.g., by being interpersonally passive and bland; Millon & Everly, 1985). In educational settings, people high in trait anxiety tend to report a higher level of state anxiety about situations characterized by social and academic failure and, thus, tend to avoid such situations (Hodges & Felling, 1970). It has also been shown that neurotic extraverts are likely to withdraw from academic settings because of fear of failure whereas neurotic introverts are likely to withdraw for medical/psychiatric reasons (Eysenck, 1974; Wankowski, 1973). Lastly, Cox, Endler, Swinson, and Norton (1992) have noted that individuals with panic disorders typically avoid situations that are agoraphobic in nature (e.g., walking alone in busy streets).

2. Attempting to Cope with Incongruent Situations

Despite the foresight that people frequently display in their choice of situations, they may at times still find themselves in situations that are incongruent with their own dispositions. Some research evidence suggests that, when inadvertently confronted by such situations, people will react negatively to the situation and/or try to change some aspect(s) of the situation in order to make it more congruent with their own dispositions. Both of these processes were evident in a study of interracial interactions reported by Ickes (1984). In this study, whites whose disposition was either to seek out or to avoid interaction with blacks inadvertently found themselves in a situation that required them to wait for an indefinite period in the company of a black person. Relative to whites who preferred to seek out interaction with blacks, those who preferred to avoid interaction with blacks (a) reported heightened feelings of anxiety and concern about the interactions, and (b) tried to minimize their psychological involvement with their black partners by looking and smiling at them less.

3. Choosing Incongruent Situations

The last, and seemingly most paradoxical, reaction to dispositionally incongruent situations is to deliberately choose to enter and spend time in them. According to Snyder and Ickes (1985), this course of action may not actually be paradoxical at all. Instead, it may reflect people's desires to use the personality-shaping properties of such dispositionally incongruent settings either (a) to change themselves (e.g., to effect either a temporary or more permanent change in their own dispositions) or (b) to exert their influence so as to change the situation itself (e.g., convert a vacant lot into a playground) or to change the behavior of other people in the situation (e.g., convert gang members into a basketball team).

There is, unfortunately, a conspicuous dearth of empirical studies concerning these last ways of reacting to dispositionally incongruent situations. As a stimulus to the collection of relevant data, we have previously offered some theoretical speculations about the dynamics of these activities (Snyder & Ickes, 1985). Our intent was to explain, among other things, why we might find shy people in swinging singles' bars, snake phobics in reptile houses, paunchy sybarites in wilderness survival courses, and sinners in the front rows of church. We noted that, in all of these cases, the situations these people choose to enter are incongruent with their current dispositions and attributes at the time that they enter them. We proposed, however, that these same situations may be quite congruent with the dispositions and attributes these people would like to possess at some time in the future.

Our theoretical speculations also concerned the motives of the preacher in the house of ill repute, the temperance lady in the local tavern, the pacifist in the Pentagon, and the healthy individual caring for persons with AIDS (e.g., Omoto & Snyder, 1990). We proposed that a common motive for these individuals' behavior may be their desire to exert influence in and on the situation in order to change the setting itself or to change other people. People whose choice of incongruent situations is determined by this motive tend to cast themselves in the role of social reformer on a scale that may vary greatly in ambition and in degree of influence. Missionaries, proselytizers, social workers, reformers, revolutionaries, and radical activists provide relatively dramatic examples, but more mundane examples (e.g., the slum-reared gatecrasher of a high society social affair) can also be identified.

G. The Role of Choosing Situations in Personality Development

The reciprocal causal relationship between personality and situation obviously raises the important questions of (a) how personality traits assessed during childhood influence situational choices made in adolescence and adulthood, and (b) how situational influences at different points in the life cycle contribute to the development of personality. These questions have recently been addressed in research reported by Caspi, Elder, and Bem (e.g., Caspi, 1987; Caspi, et al., 1989, 1992; Caspi & Elder, 1988; Caspi, Elder, & Bem, 1987, 1988; Caspi & Herbener, 1990; Elder & Caspi, 1988; Elder, Caspi, & Burton, 1988).

These investigators have begun to document some of the processes that help promote life-course continuities in trait-relevant behavior. Using life records of particular individuals (L-data) to explore the effects of situational influences on personality across the life span, Caspi and his colleagues have compiled some impressive evidence for the stability and consistency in individuals' situational choices as a function of dispositions and traits. For example, they found that males who were dispositionally shy as children tended—as adolescents and later as adults—to be aloof, withdrawn, and lacking in social poise. These men were also found to experience greater marital instability and less occupational stability, and appeared to have more difficulty making transitions to adult roles than the other males in their cohort. Dispositionally shy females, on the other hand, were found to follow or choose, in later adult life, a traditional, conventional, or domestic lifestyle of marriage and family.

Other research in this tradition has further documented the reciprocal developmental influences of situational factors and personality traits. For example, Ickes and Turner (1983; cf. Ickes, 1983) found that college-age men who had the experience of being raised with one or more older sisters received more eye contact and greater liking from their female partners in an initial interaction than did men who had only younger sisters. Block, Block, and Keyes (1988) reported that young girls exposed early in life to a family environment that emphasized dependency, disorder, constant disappointment from parents, and less emphasis on propriety, convention, and religion, tended to develop personalities (e.g., dysphoric, distancing, distrustful, and defensive) that were consistent with the type of situations they subsequently chose to be in (e.g., drug use). And Elder and Caspi (1988) reported that males who were assessed to have an above average tendency for losing control before the Great Depression of the 1930s developed explosive personalities after being exposed to this particular situational (i.e., societal) stress. Behavioral manifestations of their explosive personalities were subsequently evident in their marital and family relationships.

Caspi and Elder (1988) have argued that the reciprocal relation between personality and situation is so strong and far reaching in its effects that unstable personalities can be reproduced across generations through the maintenance of particular situational conditions such as unstable family relationships, marital tension, and ineffective parenting. They reported that the styles of behavior expressed by grandparents can still be seen in the behavior patterns of the fourth generation of children.

V. CONCLUSION

It is practically a truism of contemporary psychology that behavior is a function of the person and of the situation. Beginning with Lewin's early assertion that "every psychological event depends upon the state of the person and at the same time on the environment, although their relative importance is different in different cases" (1936, p. 12), the task of defining the precise nature of the function that joins person and situation has been central to the theoretical and empirical missions of researchers in personality and social psychology.

Although many approaches have been taken to defining the "person by situation" function (for a review, see Snyder & Ickes, 1985), in this chapter we have chosen to focus on one approach to specify this function—the dynamic interactionist or "situational" strategy for the study of personality and social behavior. This approach concentrates on the reciprocal influences of individuals and situations, examining especially the active role that individuals play in choosing to enter and spend time in particular social situations, as well as the consequent opportunity that chosen situations gain for guiding and directing the behavior of those who have placed themselves therein.

That people actively gravitate toward some types of situations and deliberately avoid others, and that their choices of situations are reflections of features of their personal identities (including such dispositions as attitudes, traits, and conceptions of self), may constitute major sources of the regularities, stabilities, and consistencies in behavior that are typically regarded as the defining characteristics of personality. As evidence in support of these propositions, we have reviewed research findings from a variety of sources, including both laboratory and field studies of both actual and hypothetical behavior. This accumulated (and still rapidly growing) body of evidence is substantial, and it convincingly implicates a wide range of traits and dispositions, conceptions of self and identity, attitudes and beliefs, and other personal attributes in the processes of choosing situations. In addition, researchers have begun to explore some of the mechanisms by which people choose situations, in particular the dimensions along which situations are perceived, categorized, and ultimately responded to.

Although our chapter has concentrated on the choosing of situations, we wish to emphasize that such activities do not constitute the sum total of individuals' active structuring of the circumstances in which they operate. Space permitting, we could have surveyed the research literature indicating that, just as people choose their situations, they may also systematically choose their roles and their personal and social relationships. Moreover, they may make these choices in ways that allow them to take on roles and to participate in relationships that provide opportunities to act upon their attitudes, values, traits, dispositions, and conceptions of self. Space limitations have also prevented us from dealing with the related phenomenon of people's attempts to influence and modify situations (either ones that they have previously chosen to enter or ones in which they find themselves through no choice of their own) in ways that make these situations more supportive of their personalities and identities (see Snyder, 1981; Snyder & Ickes, 1985). Together, through their choices of and influence upon situations, roles, and relationships, people may construct social worlds that are conducive to their own personalities.

As much has been accomplished in demonstrating that people do actively choose their situations, in probing the determinants of these choices, and in specifying their consequences, even more remains to be done. As we have indicated, comparatively little is known about people's choices of discrepant situations, that is, those instances in which people actively place themselves in situations that tend to dispose behaviors that run counter to their own current personal attributes. Because hypotheses about the nature, antecedents, and consequences of these choices are readily generated, we anticipate that such processes will become productive areas of study for future research.

We also expect that the psychology of development will prove highly amenable to inquiries guided by dynamic interactionist considerations of choosing situations.

Theoretical analyses have pointed to the importance of considering people's choices of situations and the constraining influences these chosen situations have on the course of development, either through facilitating certain developmental trajectories or by closing the doors on alternative developmental courses (cf. Block, 1971; Gangestad & Snyder, 1985). Moreover, using archival data from the Berkeley Guidance Study, Caspi et al. (1989) have examined the ways in which behavior patterns can be sustained across the life course by, among other mechanisms, individuals' entry into environments that reinforce and sustain interactional styles and behavioral dispositions.

As this review has clearly demonstrated, the notion that individuals choose situations on the basis of their personality traits and other dispositions is a well-established fact. As the field of personality reckons with this fact, two important outcomes are guaranteed. The first outcome is that the field will inevitably gravitate toward a dynamic interactional approach to the study of personality—one in which situations both influence and are influenced by the personalities of the individuals who are found in them. The second outcome is that the developing interest in studying these dynamic, causally reciprocal influences will increasingly take personality researchers out of their laboratories and into the real world situations in which individuals live their lives.

ACKNOWLEDGMENT

Library research for the preparation of this chapter was supported by funds provided by the Department of Psychology, University of Texas at Arlington.

REFERENCES

Allport, G. W. (1931). What is a trait of personality? *Journal of Abnormal and Social Psychology, 25,* 368–372.

Allport, G. W. (1937). *Personality: A psychological intepretation.* New York: Holt, Rinehart & Wilson.

Allport, G. W. (1966). Traits revisited. *American Psychologist, 21,* 1–10.

Andrews, J. D. W. (1967). The achievement motive and advancement in two types of organizations. *Journal of Personality and Social Psychology, 6,* 163–168.

Argyle, M. (1980). The analysis of social situations. In M. Brenner (Ed.), *The structure of action.* New York: St. Martin's Press.

Argyle, M., & Furnham, A. (1982). The ecology of relationships: Choice of situations as a function of relationship. *British Journal of Social Psychology, 21,* 259–262.

Argyle, M., Furnham, A., & Graham, J. A. (1981). *Social situations.* New York: Cambridge University Press.

Atkinson, J. W. (Ed.). (1958). *Motives in fantasy, action, and society.* Princeton, NJ: Van Nostrand.

Backman, C. (1988). The self: A dialectical approach. In L. Berkowitz (Ed.), *Advances in experimental social psychology* (Vol. 21 San Diego, CA: Academic Press.

Bandura, A. (1982). The psychology of chance encounters and life paths. *American Psychologist, 37,* 747–755.

Bem, D. J. (1981). Assessing situations by assessing persons. In D. Magnusson (Ed.), *Toward a psychology of situations: An interactional perspective* (pp. 295–257). Hillsdale, NJ: Erlbaum.

Bem, D. J., & Allen, A. (1974). On predicting some of the people some of the time: The search for cross-situational consistency in behavior. *Psychological Review, 81,* 506–520.

Bem, D. J., & Funder, D. C. (1978). Predicting more of the people more of the time: Assessing the personality of situation. *Psychological Review, 85,* 485–501.

Benninger, W. B., & Walsh, W. B. (1980). Holland's theory and non-college-degree working men and women. *Journal of Vocational Behavior, 17,* 18–88.

Berglas, S., & Jones, E. E. (1978). Drug choice as an externalization strategy in response to noncontingent success. *Journal of Personality and Social Psychology, 36,* 405–417.

Bishop, D. W., & Witt, P. A. (1970). Sources of behavioral variance during leisure time. *Journal of Personality and Social Psychology, 16,* 352–360.

Block, J. (1968). Some reasons for the apparent inconsistencies of personality. *Psychological Bulletin, 70,* 210–212.

Block, J. (1971). *Lives through time.* Berkeley, CA: Bancroft.

Block, J., Block, J. H., & Keyes, S. (1988). Longitudinally foretelling drug usage in adolescence: Early childhood personality and environmental precursors. *Child Development, 59,* 336–355.

Bowers, K. (1973). Situationism in psychology: An analysis and a critique. *Psychological Review, 80,* 307–336.

Cantor, N. (1981). Perceptions of situations: Situation prototypes and person situation prototypes. In D. Magnusson (Ed.), *Toward a psychology of situations: An interactional perspective* (pp. 229–244). Hillsdale, NJ: Erlbaum.

Cantor, N., & Kihlstrom, J. F. (1980). Cognitive and social processes in personality: Implications for behavior therapy. In C. M. Franks & G. T. Wilson (Eds.), *Handbook of behavior therapy.* New York: Guilford Press.

Cantor, N., & Mischel, W. (1979). Prototypes in person perception. In L. Berkowitz (Ed.), *Advances in experimental social psychology* (Vol. 12 pp. 3–52). New York: Academic Press.

Cantor, N., Mischel, W., & Schwartz, J. (1982a). A prototype analysis of psychological situations. *Cognitive Psychology, 14,* 45–77.

Cantor, N., Mischel, W., & Schwartz, J. (1982b). Social knowledge: Structure, content, use, and abuse. In A. M. Isen & A. H. Hastorf (Eds.), *Cognitive social psychological,* (pp. 33–72). New York: Elsevier/North-Holland.

Cantor, N., Norem, J., & Langston, C. (1991). Life tasks and daily life experience. *Journal of Personality, 59,* 425–451.

Caspi, A. (1987). Personality in the life course. *Journal of Personality and Social Psychology, 53,* 1203–1213.

Caspi, A., & Bem, D. J. (1990). Personality continuity and change across the life course. In L. Pervin (Ed.), *Handbook of personality: Theory and research* (pp. 549–575). New York: Guilford Press.

Caspi, A., Bem, D. J., & Elder, G. H., Jr. (1989). Continuities and consequences of interactional styles across the life course. *Journal of Personality, 57,* 375–406.

Caspi, A., & Elder, G. H., Jr. (1988). Emergent family patterns: The intergenerational construction of problem behavior and relationships. In R. A. Hinde & J. Stevenson-

Hinde (Eds.), *Relationships within families: Mutual influences.* Oxford, England: Oxford University Press.

Caspi, A., Elder, G. H., Jr., & Bem, D. J. (1987). Moving against the world: Life-course patterns of explosive children. *Developmental Psychology, 23,* 308–313.

Caspi, A., Elder, G. H., Jr., & Bem, D. J. (1988). Moving away from the world: Life-course patterns of shy children. *Developmental Psychology, 24,* 824–831.

Caspi, A., & Herbener, E. S. (1990). Continuity and change: Assortative marriage and the consistency of personality in adulthood. *Journal of Personality and Social Psychology, 58,* 250–258.

Caspi, A., Herbener, E. S., & Ozer, D. J. (1992). Shared experiences and the similarity of personalities: A longitudinal study of married couples. *Journal of Personality and Social Psychology, 62,* 281–291.

Christie, R., & Geis, F. L. (Eds.). (1970). *Studies in Machiavellianism.* New York: Academic Press.

Conolley, E. S., Gerard, H. B., & Kline, T. (1978). Competitive behavior: A manifestation of motivation for ability comparison. *Journal of Experimental Social Psychology, 14,* 123–131.

Costa, P. J., McCrae, R. R., & Holland, J. L. (1984). Personality and vocational interests in an adult sample. *Journal of Applied Psychology, 42,* 390–400.

Cox, B., Endler, N. S., Swinson, R. P., & Norton, G. R. (1992). Situations and specific coping strategies associated with clinical and nonclinical panic attacks. *Behavior Research and Therapy, 30,* 67–69.

Crozier, W. R. (1979). Shyness as a dimension of personality. *British Journal of Social and Clinical Psychology, 18,* 121–128.

Csikszentmihalyi, M., & Figurski, T. J. (1982). Self-awareness and aversive experience in everyday life. *Journal of Personality, 50,* 15–28.

Csikszentmihalyi, M., & Kubey, R. (1981). Television and the rest of life: A systematic comparison of subjective experience. *Public Opinion Quarterly, 45,* 317–328.

Diener, E., Larsen, R. J., & Emmons, R. A. (1984). Person x situation interactions: Choice of situations and congruence response models. *Journal of Personality and Social Psychology, 47,* 580–592.

Dillehay, R. (1978). Authoritarianism. In H. London & J. E. Exner (Eds.), *Dimensions of personality* (pp. 85–127). New York: Wiley.

Duck, S., & Gilmour, R. (1981). *Personal relationships* (4 vols.). London: Academic Press.

Duke, M. P., & Nowicki, S., Jr. (1982). A social learning theory analysis of interactional theory concepts and a multidimensional model of human interaction constellations. In J. C. Anchin & D. J. Kiesler (Eds.), *Handbook of interpersonal psychotherapy.* New York: Pergamon Press.

Eddy, G., & Sinnett, E. (1973). Behavior setting utilization by emotionally disturbed college students. *Journal of Consulting and Clinical Psychology, 40,* 210–216.

Efran, J. S., & Boylin, E. R. (1967). Social desirability and willingness to participate in a group discussion. *Psychological Reports, 20,* 402.

Elder, G. H., Jr., & Caspi, A. (1992). Studying lives in a changing society: Sociological and personological explorations. In Robert A. Zucker, Albert I. Rabin, J. Aronoff & S. J. Frank (Eds.), *Personality structure in the life course: Essays on personality in the Murray tradition* (pp. 276–322). New York: Springer.

Elder, G. H., Jr., Caspi, A., & Burton, L. M. (1988). Adolescent traditions in development perspective: Sociological and historical insights In M. Gummas & W. A. Collins (Eds.), *Minnesota Symposia on Child Psychology* (Vol. 120, pp. 151–179). Hillsdale, NJ: Erlbaum.

Emmons, R. A., & Diener, E. (1986a). A goal-affect analysis of everyday situational choices. *Journal of Research in Personality, 20,* 309–326.

Emmons, R. A., & Diener, E. (1986b). Situation selection as a moderator of response consistency and stability. *Journal of Personality and Social Psychology, 51,* 1013–1019.

Emmons, R. A., Diener, E., & Larsen, R. J. (1985). Choice of situations and congruence models of interactionism. *Personality and Individual Differences, 6,* 693–702.

Emmons, R. A., Diener, E., & Larsen, R. J. (1986). Choice and avoidance of everyday situations and affect congruence: Two models of reciprocal interactionism. *Journal of Personality and Social Psychology, 51,* 815–826.

Endler, N. S. (1983). Interactionism: A personality model, but not yet a theory. In M. M. Page (Ed.), *Nebraska Symposium on Motivation* (pp. 155–200). Lincoln: University of Nebraska Press.

Endler, N. S. (1988). Interactionism revisited: "On the role of situations in personality research." In S. G. Cole & R. G. Demaree (Eds.), *Applications of interactional psychology: Essays in honor of Saul B. Sells* (pp. 179–188). Hillsdale, NJ: Erlbaum.

Endler, N. S., & Edwards, J. M. (1986). Interactionism in personality in the twentieth century. *Personality and Individual Differences, 7,* 379–384.

Eysenck, H. J. (1971). *Readings in extraversion-introversion: II. Fields of application.* London: Staples.

Eysenck, H. J. (1974). Personality and learning: The experimental approach. *Proceedings, Association of Educational Psychologists Conference.*

Funder, D. C. (1991). Global traits: A neo-Allportian approach to personality. *Psychological Science, 2,* 31–39.

Furnham, A. (1981). Personality and activity preference. *British Journal of Social Psychology, 20,* 57–68.

Furnham, A. (1982). Psychoticism, social desirability, and situation selection. *Personality and Individual Differences, 3,* 43–51.

Furnham, A., & Jaspars, J. (1983). The evidence for interactionism in psychology: A critical analysis of the situation-response inventories. *Personality and Individual Differences, 4,* 627–644.

Gangestad, S., & Simpson, J. (1990). Toward an evolutionary history of female sociosexual variation. *Journal of Personality, 58,* 69–96.

Gangestad, S., & Snyder, M. (1985). "To carve nature at its joints": On the existence of discrete classes of personality. *Psychological Review, 92,* 317–349.

Gates, D. W. (1971). Verbal conditioning, transfer and operant level "speech style" as functions of cognitive style (Doctoral dissertation, City University of New York). *Dissertation Abstracts International, 32,* 3634B.

Geis, F. L. (1978). Machiavellianism. In H. London & J. E. Exner, Jr. (Eds.), *Dimensions of personality,* (pp. 305–363). New York: Wiley.

Glick, P. (1985). Orientations toward relationships: Choosing a situation in which to begin a relationship. *Journal of Experimental Social Psychology, 21,* 544–562.

Goodenough, D. R. (1978). Field dependence. In H. London & J. E. Exner, Jr. (Eds.), *Dimensions of personality,* (pp. 165–216). New York: Wiley.

Gorta, A. (1985). Choosing situations for a purpose. *European Journal of Social Psychology, 15,* 17–35.

Greene, L. R. (1973). Effects of field independence, physical proximity and evaluative feedback on affective reactions and compliance in a dyadic interaction (Doctoral dissertation, Yale University). *Dissertation Abstracts International, 34,* 2284B–2285B.

Hodges, W. F., & Felling, J. P. (1970). Types of stressful situations and their relation to trait anxiety and sex. *Journal of Consulting and Clinical Psychology, 34,* 333–337.

Holland, J. L. (1966). *The psychology of vocational choice.* Waltham, MA: Blaisdell.

Holland, J. L. (1985). *Making vocational choices: A theory of vocational personality and work environments* (2nd ed.). Englewood Cliffs, NJ: Prentice Hall.

Hormuth, S. E. (1986). The sampling of experience *in situ. Journal of Personality, 54,* 262–293.

Ickes, W. (1982). A basic paradigm for the study of personality, roles, and social behavior. In W. Ickes & E. S. Knowles (Eds.), *Personality, roles, and social behavior* (pp. 305–341). New York: Springer-Verlag.

Ickes, W. (1983). Influences of past relationships on subsequent ones. In P. Paulus (Ed.), *Basic group processes* (pp. 315–337). New York: Springer-Verlag.

Ickes, W. (1984). Compositions in black and white: Determinants of interaction in interracial dyads. *Journal of Personality and Social Psychology, 47,* 330–341.

Ickes, W., & Turner, M. (1983). On the social advantages of having an older, opposite-sex sibling: Birth-order influences in mixed-sex dyads. *Journal of Personality and Social Psychology, 45,* 210–222.

James, W., Woodruff, A., & Werner, W. (1965). Effects of internal and external control upon changes in smoking behavior. *Journal of Consulting Psychology, 29,* 184–186.

Jellison, J. M., & Ickes, W. (1974). The power of the glance: Desire to see and be seen in cooperative and competitive situations. *Journal of Experimental Social Psychology, 10,* 444–450.

Jones, E. E., & Davis, K. E. (1965). From acts to dispositions: The attribution process in person perception. In L. Berkowitz (Ed.), *Advances in experimental social psychology* (Vol. 2, pp. 219–266). New York: Academic Press.

Jones, E. E., & McGillis, D. (1976). Correspondent inferences and the attribution cube: A comparative reappraisal. In J. H. Harvey, W. Ickes, & R. Kidd (Eds.), *New directions in attribution research* (Vol. 1, pp. 389–420). Hillsdale, NJ: Erlbaum.

Jones, W. H., Russell, D., & Cutrona, C. (1985). *A personality congruent analysis of situations.* Unpublished manuscript, University of Tulsa, Department of Psychology, Tulsa, OK.

Kahle, L. (1980). Stimulus condition self-selection by males in the interaction of locus of control and skill-chance situations. *Journal of Personality and Social Psychology, 38,* 50–56.

Kahle, L., & Berman, J. J. (1979). Attitudes cause behaviors: A cross-lagged panel analysis. *Journal of Personality and Social Psychology, 37,* 315–321.

Karp, S. A., Kissin, B., & Hustmyer, F. E. (1970). Field dependence as a predictor of alcoholic therapy dropouts. *Journal of Nervous and Mental Disease, 150,* 77–83.

Katz, D. (1960). The functional approach to the study of attitude. *Public Opinion Quarterly, 24,* 163–204.

Katz, D., McClintock, C., & Sarnoff, I. (1957). The measurement of ego defense as related to attitude change. *Journal of Personality, 25,* 465–474.

Levy, S. (1969). *Field independence-field dependence and occupational interests.* Unpublished master's thesis, Cornell University, Ithaca, NY.

Lewin, K. (1936). *A dynamic theory of personality.* New York: McGraw-Hill.

Lord, C. G. (1982). Predicting behavioral consistency from an individual's perception of situational similarities. *Journal of Personality and Social Psychology, 42,* 1076–1088.

Lundy, J. R. (1972). Some personality correlates of contraceptive use among unmarried female college students. *Journal of Psychology, 80,* 9–14.

Magnusson, D. (1981). Problems in environmental analyses—an introduction. In D. Magnusson (Ed.), *Toward a psychology of situations: An interactional perspective,* (pp. 3–7). Hillsdale, NJ: Erlbaum.

Magnusson, D. (1988). On the role of situations in personality research: An interactional perspective. In S. G. Cole & R. G. Demaree (Eds.), *Applications of interactional psychology: Essays in honor of Saul B. Sells* (pp. 155–178). Hillsdale, NJ: Erlbaum.

Magnusson, D. (1990). Personality development from an interactional perspective. In L. Pervin (Ed.), *Handbook of personality: Theory and research* (pp. 193–222). New York: Guilford Press.

Magnusson, D., & Endler, N. S. (1977). *Personality at the crossroads: Current issues in interactional psychology.* Hillsdale, NJ: Erlbaum.

Mausner, B., & Graham, J. (1970). Field dependence and prior reinforcement as determinants of social interaction in judgment. *Journal of Personality and Social Psychology, 16,* 486–493.

McElroy, J. C., Morrow, P. W., & Ackerman, R. J. (1983). Personality and interior office design: Exploring the accuracy of visitor attributions. *Journal of Applied Psychology, 68,* 541–544.

Mehrabian, A. (1978). Characteristic individual reactions to preferred and unpreferred environments. *Journal of Personality, 46,* 717–731.

Mehrabian, A., & Russell, J. (1973). A questionnaire measure of arousal seeking tendency. *Environment and Behavior, 5,* 315–333.

Milham, J., & Jacobson, L. (1978). The need for approval. In H. London & J. E. Exner (Eds.), *Dimensions of personality,* (pp. 365–390). New York: Wiley.

Millon, T., & Everly, G. S. (Eds.). (1985). *Personality and its disorders: A biosocial learning approach.* New York: Wiley.

Mischel, W. (1968). *Personality and assessment.* New York: Wiley.

Mischel, W. (1969). Continuity and change in personality. *American Psychologist, 24,* 1012–1018.

Mischel, W. (1977). The interaction of person and situation. In D. Magnusson & N. S. Endler (Eds.), *Personality at the crossroads: Current issues in interactional psychology,* (pp. 333–352). Hillsdale, NJ: Erlbaum.

Morse, J. (1975). Person-job congruence and individual adjustment and development. *Human Relations, 28,* 841–861.

Nevill, D. (1974). Experimental manipulation of dependency motivation and its effect on eye contact and measures of field dependency. *Journal of Personality and Social Psychology, 29,* 72–79.

Omoto, M., & Snyder, M. (1990). Basic research in action: Volunteerism and society's response to AIDS. *Personality and Social Psychology Bulletin, 16,* 152–165.

Osborn, D. R. (1988). Personality traits expressed: Interior design as behavior-setting plan. *Personality and Social Psychology, 14,* 368–373.

Pervin, L. A., & Rubin, D. B. (1967). Student dissatisfaction with college and the college dropout: A transactional approach. *Journal of Social Psychology, 72,* 285–295.

Pervin, L. A. (1981). The relation of situations to behavior. In D. Magnusson (Ed.), *Toward a psychology of situations: An interactional perspective,* (pp. 343–360). Hillsdale, NJ: Erlbaum.

Price, R. H. (1974). The taxonomic classification of behaviors and situations and the problem of behavior-environment congruence. *Human Relations, 27,* 567–585.

Price, R. H. (1981). Risky situations. In D. Magnusson (Ed.), *Toward a psychology of situations: An interactional perspective,* (pp. 103–112). Hillsdale, NJ: Erlbaum.

Price, R. H., & Bouffard, D. L. (1974). Behavioral appropriateness and situational constraint as dimensions of social behavior. *Journal of Personality and Social Psychology, 30,* 579–586.

Rosenberg, M. (1957). *Occupations and values.* Glencoe, IL: Free Press.

Rotter, J. B. (1966). Generalized expectancies for internal versus external control of reinforcement. *Psychological Monographs, 80*(Whole No. 609).

Runyan, M. W. (1978). The life course as a theoretical orientation: Sequences of person-situation interaction. *Journal of Personality, 46,* 569–593.

Russell, D., Cutrona, C. E., & Jones, W. H. (1986). A trait-situational analysis of shyness. In W. H. Jones, J. M. Cheek, & S. R. Briggs (Eds.), *Shyness: Perspectives on research and treatment.* New York: Plenum Press.

Secord, P., & Backman, C. (1961). Personality theory and the problem of stability and change in individual behavior: An interpersonal approach. *Psychological Review, 68,* 21–32.

Secord, P., & Backman, C. (1965). An interpersonal approach to personality. In B. Maher (Ed.), *Progress in experimental personality research* (Vol. 2, pp. 91–125). New York: Academic Press.

Segal, B. (1973). Sensation-seeking and anxiety: Assessment of response to specific stimulus situations. *Journal of Consulting and Clinical Psychology, 41,* 135–138.

Smith-Lovin, L. (1979). Behavior settings and impressions formed from social scenarios. *Social Psychological Quarterly, 42,* 31–43.

Snyder, M. (1979). Self-monitoring processes. In L. Berkowitz (Ed.), *Advances in experimental social psychology* (Vol. 12, pp. 85–128). New York: Academic Press.

Snyder, M. (1981). On the influence of individuals on situations. In N. Cantor & J. F. Kihlström (Eds.), *Personality, cognition, and social interaction,* (pp. 309–329). Hillsdale, NJ: Erlbaum.

Snyder, M. (1987). *Public appearances/private realities: The psychology of self-monitoring.* New York: Freeman.

Snyder, M., & Gangestad, S. (1982). Choosing social situations: Two investigations of self-monitoring processes. *Journal of Personality and Social Psychology, 43,* 123–135.

Snyder, M., Gangestad, S., & Simpson, J. A. (1983). Choosing friends as activity partners: The role of self-monitoring. *Journal of Personality and Social Psychology, 45,* 1061–1072.

Snyder, M., & Ickes, W. (1985). Personality and social behavior. In G. Lindzey & E. Aronson (Eds.), *The handbook of social psychology* (Vol. 2, pp. 883–947). New York: Random House.

Snyder, M., & Kendzierski, D. (1982). Choosing social situations: Investigating the origins of correspondence between attitudes and behavior. *Journal of Personality, 50,* 280–295.

Srull, T. K., & Karabenick, S. A. (1975). Effects of personality-situation locus of control congruence. *Journal of Personality and Social Psychology, 32,* 617–628.

Stern, G. G., Stein, M. I., & Bloom, B. S. (1956). *Methods in personality assessment of human behavior in complex social settings.* New York: Free Press.

Straits, B. C., & Sechrest, L. (1963). Further support of some findings about characteristics of smokers and non-smokers. *Journal of Consulting Psychology, 27,* 282.

Swann, W. (1987). Identity negotiation: Where two roads meet. *Journal of Personality and Social Psychology, 53,* 1038–1051.

Swann, W., & Hill, C. (1982). When our identities are mistaken: Reaffirming self-conceptions through social interaction. *Journal of Personality and Social Psychology, 43,* 59–66.

Swann, W., & Read, S. J. (1981). Self-verification processes: How we sustain our self-conceptions. *Journal of Experimental Social Psychology, 17,* 351–372.

Swann, W., Stein-Seroussi, A., & Giesler, R. B. (1992). Why people self-verify. *Journal of Personality and Social Psychology, 62,* 392–401.

Swann, W., Wentzlaff, R. M., & Krull, D. S. (1992). Allure of negative feedback: Self-verfication strivings among depressed persons. *Journal of Abnormal Psychology, 10,* 293–306.

Tesser, A. (1984). Self-evaluation maintenance processes: Implications for relationships and development. In J. Masters & K. Yarkin (Eds.), *Boundary areas of psychology: Social and development.* New York: Academic Press.

Tesser, A. (1985). Some effects of self-evaluation maintenance on cognition and action. In R. M. Sorrentino & E. T. Higgins (Eds.), *The handbook of motivation and cognition: Foundations of social behavior.* New York: Guilford Press.

Tesser, A. (1988). Toward a self-evaluation maintenance model of social behavior. In L. Berkowitz (Ed.), *Advances in experimental social psychology* (Vol. 21). New York: Academic Press.

Tesser, A., & Campbell, J. (1980). Self-definition: The impact of the relative performance and similarity of others. *Social Psychology Quarterly, 43,* 341–347.

Tesser, A., & Campbell, J. (1982). Self-evaluation maintenance and the perception of friends and strangers. *Journal of Personality, 59,* 261–279.

Tesser, A., & Campbell, J. (1983). Self-definition and self-evaluation maintenance. In J. Suls & A. Greenwald (Eds.), *Research on motivation in education: The classroom milieu.* New York: Academic Press.

Tesser, A., Campbell, J., & Smith, M. (1984). Friendship choice and performance: Self-evaluation maintenance in children. *Journal of Personality and Social Psychology, 46,* 561–574.

Tesser, A., & Moore, J. (1987). On the convergence of public and private aspect of self. In R. Baumeister (Ed.), *Public self and private self* (pp. 99–116). Berlin: Springer-Verlag.

Tesser, A., & Paulhus, D. (1983). The definition of self: Private and public self-evaluation management strategies. *Journal of Personality and Social Psychology, 44,* 672–682.

Tesser, A., & Smith, J. (1980). Some effects of friendship and task relevance on helping: You don't always help the one you like. *Journal of Experimental Social Psychology, 16,* 582–590.

Vroom, V. H. (1964). *Work and motivation.* New York: Wiley.

Wachtel, P. L. (1973). Psychodynamics, behavior therapy, and the implacable experimenter: An inquiry into the consistency of personality. *Journal of Abnormal Psychology, 82,* 324–334.

Walsh, W. B., Horton, J. A., & Gaffey, R. L. (1977). Holland's theory and college degreed working men and women. *Journal of Vocational Behavior, 10,* 180–186.

Wankowski, J. A. (1973). *Temperament, motivation, and academic achievement.* Birmingham, AL: University of Birmingham Educational Survey and Counselling Unit.

Watson, A. K., & Cheek, J. M. (1986). Shyness situations: Perspectives of a diverse sample of shy females. *Psychological Reports, 59,* 1040–1042.

Watson, D., & Baumal, E. (1967). Effects of locus of control and expectation of future control upon present performance. *Journal of Personality and Social Psychology, 6,* 212–215.

Wegner, D. M., & Giuliano, T. (1982). The forms of social awareness. In W. Ickes & E. S. Knowles (Eds.), *Personality, roles, and social behavior* (pp. 165–198). New York: Springer-Verlag.

Wheeler, L., Reis, H. T., & Nezlek, J. (1983). Loneliness, social interaction, and sex roles. *Journal of Personality and Social Psychology, 45,* 943–953.

Wilson, G. D., & Nias, D. K. B. (1975). Sexual types. *New Behavior, 2,* 330–332.

Winter, D. G. (1973). *The power motive.* New York: Free Press.

Winter, D. G., & Stewart, A. J. (1978). The power motive. In H. London & J. E. Exner (Eds.), *Dimensions of personality,* (pp. 391–447). New York: Wiley.

Winter, H. A., Moore, C. A., Goodenough, D. R., & Cox, P. (1977). Field-dependent and field-independent cognitive styles and their educational implications. *Review of Educational Research, 47,* 1–64.

Wish, M. (1975). Subjects' expectations about their own interpersonal communication: A multidimensional approach. *Personality and Social Psychological Bulletin, 1,* 11–20.

Wish, M., Deutsch, M., & Kaplan, S. J. (1976). Perceived dimensions of interpersonal relations. *Journal of Personality and Social Psychology, 33,* 409–420.

Wish, M., & Kaplan, S. (1977). Toward an implicit theory of interpersonal communication. *Sociometry, 40,* 234–246.

Wolpe, J., & Lang, P. J. (1964). A fear survey schedule for use in behavior therapy. *Behavior Research and Therapy, 2,* 27–30.

Zuckerman, M. (1974). The sensation seeking motive. In B. Maher (Ed.), *Progress in experimental personality research* (Vol. 7, pp. 79–148). New York: Academic Press.

Zuckerman, M. (1978). Sensation-seeking. In H. London & J. E. Exner, Jr. (Eds.), *Dimensions of personality,* (pp. 487–559). New York: Wiley.

PART III

DEVELOPMENTAL ISSUES

CHAPTER 8

STAGES OF PERSONALITY DEVELOPMENT

JANE LOEVINGER

WASHINGTON UNIVERSITY

One of the first and still greatest achievements of psychologists in the field of individual differences was Binet's breakthrough toward the measurement of intelligence. For Binet, in order to measure a child's intelligence, one held him or her up against the average adult as a standard, and determined how far he or she approached the adult in achievement. There have been many refinements, but intelligence is still measured by using the achieved adult status as the measure and standard.

Piaget broke with that tradition. For him, the child's mistakes, which did not seem to interest Binet, were just what was interesting. When the child achieved adult status, Piaget lost interest. By studying the child's mode of thought via the evolution of errors, Piaget discerned stages in the development of intelligence: sensorimotor, preoperational, concrete operational, and formal operational. Piaget's methods and point of view, his search for the sense in the child's nonsense, have influenced much of contemporary psychology.

I. MEASUREMENT OF PERSONALITY

Success in measuring intelligence, particularly in Binet-type tests, has led psychologists to believe that they can also measure personality by similar techniques. In this they have gone astray. Personality is not like intelligence in its formal properties, and the differences all favor the measurability of intelligence and the resistance of personality to any easy measurement.

The disanalogies between personality and abilities (to broaden the discussion beyond the controversial topic of "intelligence") are just those qualities that render intelligence and other abilities relatively measurable. In the first place, abilities tend to increase with age, monotonically during the ages when their measurement is most studied, that is, during youth and early adult life. In the second place, all abilities tend to be positively correlated. That is, abilities may be correlated positively or not at all, but one ability will rarely interfere with another one. Personality traits, on the other hand, may have any relation with one other: positive, negative, or curvilinear.

Personality traits often, perhaps typically, increase with time up to some point, and then tend to decrease. This curvilinear relation with age has as its consequence possible curvilinear relations with other personality traits. Two personality traits that are manifestations of the same underlying developmental continuum can have any correlation whatsoever, provided that they maximize at different stages (Loevinger, 1984). The ensuing complexities are great. Because the tools of the psychometrician are almost entirely based on linear hypotheses, psychometric or statistical solutions to the riddle of personality structure are quite ineffective, no matter how potent they are in the study of abilities.

To be sure, there have been a number of effective studies of personality using strictly psychometric approaches, and even some modest but real predictions of particular outcomes. But for the above reasons, there are also limitations, particularly when one is seeking the fundamental structure of personality rather than specific predictions.

II. PERSONALITY STAGES AND TYPES

A totally different approach to the structure of personality is based on the idea of personality stages and types. The idea that there are types of people and stages in the development of personality is as old as recorded history and older than any attempts at measurement. For example, stages can be found in the Bhagavad Vita and types of people in the Iliad. However, many of the older typologies have been discredited by modern psychology. For one thing, they were interpreted as arguing for a discontinuity between types. All the evidence lies in the other direction, favoring continuous variation.

For a type to be anything different from a trait, there must be some evidence that diverse, separable traits or aspects vary more or less together. Similarly, for stages, there must be various aspects that change more or less simultaneously. Synchronous development has come under criticism, even in relation to intelligence (Fischer, 1980); even Piaget (1972) does not hold to an extreme claim. Indeed, Piaget (1932) never asserted that there are stages in the moral domain, which is about as close as he came to personality.

For a type or stage theory to be plausible, there must be some logical or at least intelligible structure to the diverse elements constituting a type or stage. That is the feature that theorists have delighted in demonstrating. Their arguments, however, are mainly theoretical. Without empirical evidence, other psychologists are not easily convinced of the force of their arguments.

III. Kohlberg: Stages of Moral Judgment

In relation to personality, stage theories in recent years have been dominated by a neo-Piagetian school whose leader was Lawrence Kohlberg (1969). His theory of stages of development of moral judgment is well known. The distinctive feature of his theory is that knowledge of the highest or end state is used to define previous states, a feature borrowed from Piaget's theory of intelligence. That is not the same, however, as Binet's definition of intelligence in terms of percentage of adult status achieved. Kohlberg, like Piaget, allows for a more dialectical course of evolution. The logical endpoint is necessary as the guiding principle of stage order. Many investigators studying related variables have followed this aspect of the Kohlbergian neo-Piagetian methodology.

Kohlberg and many other developmental theorists have used story completion methods to study personality development. Typically they have used stories presenting a moral dilemma. The stage assigned to a subject depends not primarily on the solution chosen for the dilemma but rather on the structure of the subject's reasoning. This method has the advantage that the interviewer can press the subject to clarify his meaning when there is an ambiguous response. The disadvantage is that which attends all interview methods: it is time consuming and likely to be somewhat unreliable in both its administration and its scoring. When written forms of the interview are used, both the advantages and the disadvantages of the interview are foregone.

IV. A Stage-Type Theory: Ego Development

In studying ego development as a broad aspect (or collection of aspects) of personality, my colleagues and I have followed a different methodology. In the first place, I have argued that types represent the trace of stages (Loevinger, 1966). To that extent, I am following Binet in taking advantage of age changes as a partial criterion for personality development as a dimension of individual differences.

Taking stages as a major clue or criterion allows the use of age as a guiding principle; this has the merit that age can be measured almost without error, something that cannot be said for any general facet of personality. Thus the empirical approach begins by looking for average age changes. Then, by observing which changes occur together in some diverse sample, one has a clue as to what can reasonably be called personality types.

Types can, in turn, be used to refine our conception of stages. For, after all, many kinds of development occur simultaneously, and some art is required to discern what elements go together to define a stage. Height is not an element of ego development, even though both increase together in time. The two variables are separated logically, of course, and empirically by their lack of correlation within any age cohort taken by itself. Kohlberg and the neo-Piagetians also use age changes as their guide to stages, but they are less clear about studying individual differences with age held constant.

Although Kohlberg and his fellow neo-Piagetians have used age changes, they have taken logical coherence as their ultimate criterion for stage structures. The study of ego development, by contrast, has been built around an empirical, partly psychometric approach, seeking the common thread in stages and types. This common element defines ego development as something more than an age progression and something more than a one-dimensional trait of individual differences. The content of those stage types is best denoted by describing the stages.

To study ego development, our major instrument has been the Sentence Completion Test (SCT) (Loevinger & Wessler, 1970; Loevinger, Wessler, & Redmore, 1970). The SCT has proven to be well adapted to the task of refining the definition of the stages in accord with data from thousands of cases.

The theory of ego development has been criticized because it does not present each stage as a logically coherent whole, it does not prescribe higher stages as better, and it "confuses" structure with content (Broughton & Zahaykevich, 1977; Kohlberg, 1981). These criticisms are approximately correct, factually; the question is whether these are strengths or weaknesses of the method.

The root difference between the SCT method and the method of the neo-Piagetians is the reliance of the SCT method on masses of data. Because the definition of stages is derived from data, it cannot also be guaranteed to be strictly logical, any more than people are strictly logical. Stages are characterized in terms of both structure and content of the subjects' responses, because both vary with ego level, sometimes structure and sometimes content of thought supplying the best clue as to level. Methods have been evolved for parlaying responses of subjects at high levels to reveal the next higher level. But this too is empirical and does not give us license to declare that the highest level is the "best."

The psychological coherence of the resulting stage pictures is impressive and intuitively evident to most of those who have studied the material. This constitutes a kind of validation of the conception of ego development and of the SCT method.

The stages of moral development delineated by Kohlberg (Colby & Kohlberg, 1986) and the stages of ego development (Table I) are very similar at the lower stages; at the higher stages it is harder to draw exact parallels. The same comments hold for many other developmental stage theories propounded in recent years (Loevinger, 1976).

V. STAGES OF EGO DEVELOPMENT

The lowest stage or stages are inaccessible to those whose research is based on analysis of word usage and sentences. The foundations of ego development are lost

TABLE I
Some Characteristics of Levels of Ego Development

Level	Characteristics		
	Impulse control	Interpersonal mode	Conscious preoccupation
Impulsive	Impulsive	Egocentric, dependent	Bodily feelings
Self-protective	Opportunistic	Manipulative, wary	"Trouble," control
Conformist	Respect for rules	Cooperative, loyal	Appearances, behavior
Self-aware	Exceptions allowable	Helpful, self-aware	Feelings, problems, adjustment
Conscientious	Self-evaluated standards, self-critical	Intense, responsible	Motives, traits, achievements
Individualistic	Tolerant	Mutual	Individuality, development, roles
Autonomous	Coping with conflict	Interdependent	Self-fulfillment, psychological causation

Note: Adapted from Loevinger (1976, 1993c, & elsewhere).

in the mists of infancy. The earliest stage that can be measured is the Impulsive Stage. At this stage the small child has achieved awareness of self as a separate person. Impulses are a kind of verification of that separateness, but the child has at first no control of the impulses. The emotional range is narrow. In small children this stage is charming; when it persists into adolescence and adulthood, it is at best maladaptive and in some cases psychopathic.

At the next stage the child is aware of impulses as such, enough to exert some control in order to protect himself or herself and to secure at least immediate advantage. This is the Self-Protective Stage. One must almost use a different vocabulary in describing its manifestations in childhood and in adult life, though in principle the core is the same. In small children there is a natural dependence, egocentricity, and calculation of advantage for self. The small child's love of ritual is probably part of the early effort at self-control. In adolescents and adults one sees exploitation of other people, taking advantage, preoccupation with being taken advantage of, hostile humor, and related traits. W. C. Fields, or the characters he portrayed, is the perfect exemplar. The emotional range is limited and the conceptual range simple. Normally this stage is outgrown in childhood or adolescence. However, unlike the Impulsive Stage, a person who remains at the Self-Protective Stage can sometimes become a big success in adolescence and adult life.

The next stage is the Conformist Stage; probably no stage or type has been so often described as the Conformist. The Conformist has progressed to the point of identifying self with the group, however wide that group may be: family in childhood, and later peer group, school, and so on. Thinking tends to be in terms of stereotypes. The emotional range is limited to standard clichés and banalities—happy, sad, mad, glad, and so on—but it is wider than in previous stages.

The next level that has been thoroughly studied with the SCT is called the Self-Aware Stage. (Previously this was called a transitional level, Conscientious-Conformist, but it appears to be a stable position). This is perhaps the level that has been least often described previously, though it is the modal stage in late adolescence and adult life, at least in urban United States (Holt, 1980). The person at this level has gone beyond the simplified rules and admonitions of the Conformist to see that there are allowable contingencies and exceptions, described in conventional and broad terms. Although still basically a conformist, the person at this level is aware that he or she does not always live up to the group's professed standards. There is a wider emotional and cognitive range. There is greater awareness of self as separate from the group, sometimes leading to a characteristic loneliness or self-consciousness. That does not mean, however, that persons at this level are any less adjusted than those of other levels. Every stage has its own strengths and weaknesses (which is why it is erroneous to refer to this continuum as "ego strength," as is sometimes done).

At the next or Conscientious Stage, the person lives by his or her own ideals and standards, rather than merely seeking group approval. By this stage the person has acquired a richly differentiated inner life, with a wide vocabulary to express cognitively shaded emotions. Older adolescents and adults at earlier stages do not lack the vocabulary to understand such cognitively shaded emotions, but they are not as likely to use such terms spontaneously. By this stage, the person has long-term goals and ideals. The elements of a mature conscience are present; in fact, the person may be oppressively conscientious.

The level beyond the Conscientious Stage is termed the Individualistic Stage. At this level one begins to see an awareness of paradoxes and contradictions in life. Persons become aware of development as a process and of its place in their own life; they think in terms of psychological causation; they take a broad view of life as a whole.

At the Autonomous Stage there is a further development of the characteristics that appear at the Individualistic level. Where the Self-Protective person uses hostile humor, the Autonomous person will often display a kind of existential humor, seeing the irony in life situations. Rather than seeing situations in terms of diametrically opposite choices of good and bad, there is awareness of the multifaceted complexity of situations and life choices. Above all, there is respect for other persons and their need for autonomy, even people such as one's own children for whom one has some responsibility. To that extent there is a lessening of the overburdened conscience of persons at the Conscientious Stage. At the same time, there is a growing tendency to see one's own life in context of wider social concerns.

The theoretical highest stage, Integrated, is rarely seen in random samples from the general population. At this stage the characteristics of the Individualistic and Autonomous Stages are more fully developed. In addition, there is some capacity to integrate the vital concerns of one's own life with those of the wider society. A good characterization of this stage is Maslow's (1954) description of the Self-Actualizing person.

Assuming that the names of stages are merely markers on what is a continuous line of development—and there is no contrary evidence—one may ask how the lines between the stages are drawn. For ego development, the rule has been that when a new vocabulary is needed to describe the characteristics of the stage, a new stage has appeared. Because our stage descriptions are arrived at and perfected empirically, the descriptions are richest in the range where the most people are found, that is, at the level of the Conformist, the Self-Aware, and the Conscientious Stages. Paradoxically, the greatest interest is often in the earliest and the highest stages. The earliest stages are important because when they persist into adult life, they are maladaptive. The highest stages, despite their rarity, hold a fascination for many students in the field, perhaps because we all aspire to be such a person, or at least to see ourselves as such a person.

Nothing would be more deceptive than to define the lowest stages and the highest stages and encourage the inference that the path from very low to very high is a straight line progression. We do have some access to the lowest stages by observing youngsters and by observing some persons who have trouble making it in society. The highest stages are more problematic, in part because, in principle, people (presumably including psychologists) can understand stages already passed through much more clearly than stages still beyond their own attainment (Rest, Turiel, & Kohlberg, 1969). It is only a slight exaggeration to say that one cannot understand fully the stages beyond one's own.

Reviewing many expositions of stages of personality development (including moral development and related variables), I have the impression that every theorist projects onto his picture of the highest stage a kind of *apologia per vita sua*.

To address this problem rather than to perpetuate it, the study of ego development by means of the SCT has used data to bootstrap the theory into its highest region. Although Kohlberg and other theorists undoubtedly used data informally to construct their theories, they did not have a formal technique for utilizing data in the refinement of the stage types. That has been the distinctive contribution of the ego development research method (Loevinger, 1993b, 1993c).

VI. SOURCES OF ERROR

Although the stages are empirically grounded, that does not make them infallible descriptions of personality development, for many reasons. The obvious reason is that personality is much too complex to yield all its secrets to any single method. Indeed, many psychologists and psychoanalysts believe that only clinical and depth-psychological methods can yield important insights; our work, among others, proves otherwise.

The weakness of the method lies elsewhere, in confounding factors. The universe, including the universe of interpersonal relations, does not present itself to us as a set of orthogonal variables. In life ego development is intertwined with socioeconomic status, intelligence, and verbal ability. A relatively intelligent person of relatively high socioeconomic status with good verbal ability will probably have a higher level of ego development than a person less blessed in those respects. One can find enough exceptional individuals, either higher or lower than one would expect on the basis of such demographic variables, to guarantee that the concept of ego development is not dispensible because of those correlations in nature. But the correlations do pose a problem, because what appears empirically to be a sign of ego level may in fact be a sign of another associated variable, such as intelligence, social class, or verbal fluency. There is no way to guarantee otherwise. Because such correlations are to be expected on the basis of the long history of psychological testing, they can be interpreted as validation of the developmental continuum. To a hard-boiled psychometrician, however, they are not signs of the success of convergent validity so much as the failure of discriminative validity (Campbell & Fiske, 1959).

Granted that there are confounding variables that will always make the measurement of ego development subject to error, just as all other personality measurements are, there still is a substantive gain for psychological theory from this study, for no matter how long one stared at intelligence, social status, and verbosity data, one would never come up with the rich description of these stages of development of which only a small glimpse has been given here. This is the case for the study of ego development by the sentence completion method, particularly when viewed against psychometrically based criticism.

VII. STAGES VERSUS FACTORS

In recent years some proponents of trait theories have claimed the entire field of personality measurement as their purview, and, in particular, they have reduced personality to five factors: extraversion, agreeableness, conscientiousness, neuroticism, and a fifth factor called, among other things, openness or intellect (Goldberg, 1990; McCrae & Costa, 1990).

There are many differences between the views of personality taken by the factor theorists and those taken by stage theorists in general, and ego development theorists in particular (Westenberg & Block, 1993). For example, stage theories are based on tracing development, whereas development is largely ignored by factor–trait theorists. Developmental theories allow for dialectical growth, something hardly admissable in the linear logic of factor-traits.

One of the most striking differences is that the factor-trait called *conscientiousness* confounds characteristics of the Conformist and the Conscientious stages. Most adults studied by psychologists, for example, college students, fall within this range. A distinction like that between the Conformist and the Conscientious person is recognized by most stage theories. This difference, and the whole dimension of ego development to which it gives access, apparently is hidden from factor theory, at least in the current five-factor and related versions (Loevinger, 1993a).

Traditional psychometric methods, based on objectively scored paper-and-pencil (or computerized) tests, easily adaptable to factorial methods, will always play a large part in psychological approaches to personality. I do not claim that a consensus is emerging in favor of stage theories, nor do I predict that it ever will; nor do I wish it so. For, as Mill (1859) said, "He who knows only his own side of the case, knows little of that." Stage and type theories will remain a rich and indispensable source of insights into personality structure.

REFERENCES

Broughton, J., & Zahaykevich, M. (1977). Review of J. Loevinger's *Ego development: Conceptions and theories. Telos, 32,* 246–253.

Campbell, D. T., & Fiske, D. W. (1959). Convergent and discriminant validation by the multitrait-multimethod matrix. *Psychological Bulletin, 56,* 81–105.

Colby, A., & Kohlberg, L. (1986). *The measurement of moral judgment.* New York: Cambridge University Press.

Fischer, K. W. (1980). A theory of cognitive development: The control and construction of hierarchies of skills. *Psychological Review, 87,* 477–531.

Goldberg, L. R. (1990). An alternative "description of personality": The Big-Five factor structure. *Journal of Personality and Social Psychology, 59,* 1216–1229.

Holt, R. R. (1980). Loevinger's measure of ego development: Reliability and national norms for male and female short forms. *Journal of Personality and Social Psychology, 39,* 909–920.

Kohlberg, L. (1969). Stage and sequence: The cognitive-developmental approach to socialization. In D. A. Goslin (Ed.), *Handbook of socialization theory and research* (pp. 347–480). Chicago: Rand McNally.

Kohlberg, L. (1981). *The meaning and measurement of moral development.* Worcester, MA: Clark University Press.

Loevinger, J. (1966). The meaning and measurement of ego development. *American Psychologist, 21,* 195–206.

Loevinger, J. (1976). *Ego development: Conceptions and theories.* San Francisco: Jossey–Bass.

Loevinger, J. (1984). On the self and predicting behavior. In R. A. Zucker, J. Aronoff, & A. I. Rabin (Eds.), *Personality and the prediction of behavior* (pp. 347–480). Orlando, FL: Academic Press.

Loevinger, J. (1993a). Conformity and conscientiousness: One factor or two stages? In D. C. Funder, R. D. Parke, C. Tomlinson-Keasey, & K. Widaman (Eds.), *Studying lives through time: Personality and development* (pp. 189–205). Washington, DC: American Psychological Association.

Loevinger, J. (1993b). Ego development: Questions of method and theory. *Psychological Inquiry, 4,* 56–63.

Loevinger, J. (1993c). Measurement of personality: True or false. *Psychological Inquiry, 4,* 1–16.

Loevinger, J., & Wessler, R. (1970). *Measuring ego development. 1. Construction and use of a sentence completion test.* San Francisco: Jossey–Bass.

Loevinger, J., Wessler, R., & Redmore, C. D. (1970). *Measuring ego development. 2. Scoring manual for women and girls.* San Francisco: Jossey–Bass.

Maslow, A. H. (1954). *Motivation and personality.* New York: Harper & Row.

McCrae, R. R., & Costa, P. T., Jr. (1990). *Personality in adulthood.* New York: Guilford Press.

Mill, J. S. (1859). Of the liberty of thought and discussion. *On liberty* (Chap. 2).

Piaget, J. (1932). *The moral judgment of the child.* New York: Free Press.

Piaget, J. (1972). Intellectual evolution from adolescence to adulthood. *Human Development, 15,* 1–12.

Rest, J. R., Turiel, E., & Kohlberg, L. (1969). Level of moral judgment as a determinant of preference and comprehension of moral judgments made by others. *Journal of Personality, 37,* 225–252.

Westenberg, P. M., & Block, J. (1993). Ego development and individual differences in personality. *Journal of Personality and Social Psychology, 65.* 792–800.

CHAPTER 9

THE EMOTIONAL BASIS OF EARLY PERSONALITY DEVELOPMENT

IMPLICATIONS FOR THE EMERGENT SELF-CONCEPT

REBECCA A. EDER
ST. LOUIS CHILDREN'S HOSPITAL

SARAH C. MANGELSDORF
UNIVERSITY OF ILLINOIS, URBANA-CHAMPAIGN

I. THE EMOTIONAL BASIS OF EARLY PERSONALITY DEVELOPMENT

In recent years, personality psychologists have made a great deal of progress toward advancing our understanding of the structure of personality. For example, investigators have suggested that the structure of personality can be best described in terms of the so-called "Big Five" traits of openness, conscientiousness, extraversion, agreeableness, and neuroticism (see McCrae & Costa, 1985, 1987). Despite these advances in personality research, little is known about the emergence and developmental course of those traits described as characteristic of adult personality.

We believe that the common thread between early personality development and later adult personality lies in individual differences in emotionality. We propose that personality development in the first 8 years of life occurs in five basic steps in which the child progresses (1) from organized patterns of behaviors (probably due initially to innate temperament and early patterns of caregiving), (2) to a rudimentary nonverbal conception of emotional states, (3) to a rudimentary verbal conception of emotional states, (4) to a verbal conception of dispositions, and, finally, (5) to a full metatheory of self. We conceive of the first step as a precursor to personality and the latter four steps as personality development per se. Given the emergent self-concept's importance to personality and its relative neglect by previous researchers, the main focus of our chapter is on dispositional conceptions of self. Specifically, we will emphasize the child's early phenomenological experience, the ages in which important aspects of the self-concept develop, and those mechanisms that are involved in its development.

II. INFANT PERSONALITY DEVELOPMENT: FIRST SIGNS OF THE SELF-CONCEPT

In hypothesizing how individual differences in emotionality emerge, it is useful to examine the following influences: (1) the influence of the parent's personality on the developing child, (2) the parent's perceptions of the child, (3) the child's own behavior and characteristics or temperament, and (4) the attachment relationship between the child and the parent. It is clear that it is difficult to disentangle the independent effects of each of these influences. In our view they are mutually influential and interact to produce the child's phenomenological experience. For example, early individual differences in children's behavior may interact with parental beliefs, expectations, and values regarding these behaviors to further influence the child's sense of him- or herself as worthy or unworthy of love and affection.

In the following section, we will examine how these varied influences interact to influence the child's developing self-concept. We begin by discussing the relations between parental personality and temperament, parental personality and attachment, and infant temperament and attachment. Thereafter, we elaborate on our view that infant–caregiver attachment and infant temperament are both fundamental to the development of one's self-concept.

A. Association between Parental Personality and Childhood Temperament

A substantial number of researchers have noted a relation between parental personality and child temperament.[1] More specifically, parents who endorse negative

---

[1] One of the major problems confronting temperament researchers is the definition of temperament. For the purposes of this chapter we utilize McCall's definition. According to McCall, "temperament consists of relatively consistent, basic dispositions inherent in the person that underlie and modulate the expression of activity, reactivity, emotionality, and sociability" (McCall, in Goldsmith et al., 1987, p. 524). We utilize this integrative definition of temperament throughout this chapter. For more thorough reviews of these definitional issues, readers should refer to Bates (1987) and Goldsmith et al. (1987).

statements about themselves (particularly regarding anxiety, general negative affectivity, or depression) have been found to also rate their babies as having more negative temperamental traits (Bates, 1987; Daniels, Plomin, & Greenhalgh, 1984; Mangelsdorf, Gunnar, Kestenbaum, Lang, & Andreas, 1990; Vaughn, Bradley, Joffe, Seifer, & Barglow, 1987). Similarly, mothers who rate themselves as high on positive emotionality also tend to rate their babies as having high positive affect (Goldsmith, Losoya, Bradshaw, & Campos, 1994). Recently, Goldsmith and his colleagues (1994) suggested four reasons why parental personality might relate to child temperament: (1) parental personality may bias reports of child temperament, leading to artifactual associations between these two variables; (2) similarities may be due to genetic transmission of parental personality characteristics to their offspring; (3) parental personality is part of the developmental context for children's personality development; and (4) child temperament may influence parental personality. The first of these reasons is discussed in detail by Bates (1987). Based on a careful review of the literature, he concludes that "tendencies to endorse negative statements about oneself are correlated with tendencies to see more negative temperamental traits in one's baby . . . . However, while the effect has been replicated, it has not been any stronger overall, than the evidence that there are correlates of the perceptions in (objective) observations of infant behavior (Bates & Bayles, 1984)" (Bates, 1987, p. 1136).

The remaining reasons cited by Goldsmith et al. (1994) regarding the association between a particular child's temperament and his or her parent's personality are more or less straightforward. That is, an anxious parent may have passed this trait on to his or her child. Likewise, an anxious parent may be visibly anxious when interacting with his or her child and may communicate this anxiety, resulting in a more anxious child. Finally, an anxious fussy child may make parents feel more anxious about themselves and their parenting abilities. We believe that all of these explanations have merit, and all of them likely explain part of the observed correspondence between parent and child personality. Hence, there must be a bidirectional relation between maternal personality and child personality. A mother's personality, for example, can influence both her perception of and her behavior toward her child, and can also be influenced by her child's temperament.

B. Association between Parental Personality and Infant–Caregiver Attachment

According to Bowlby (1969/1982), all infants become "attached" to the people who care for them. He claims that humans have an innate need for social interaction that becomes focused on a specific figure over the course of the first year of life. This attachment to a specific figure (or figures) has evolutionary significance in that it has survival value for the species. If infants are attached to specific caregivers and seek to maintain proximity with them, they will be protected from predators.

However, these attachment relationships may vary in quality as a function of the type of caregiving that each infant receives.

Evidence suggesting that maternal personality is related to mother–infant attachment has been accrued by researchers using non-normative samples. For example, children of mothers diagnosed with affective disorders are more likely to be insecurely attached than children of normal parents (Gaensbauer, Harmon, Cytryn, & McKnew, 1984; Radke-Yarrow, Cummings, Kuczynski, & Chapman, 1985). Similarly, when parents are abusive or neglectful, their offspring are at much greater risk for insecure attachment (Crittenden, 1985; Egeland & Sroufe, 1981; Lyons-Ruth, Connell, Grunembaum, Botein, & Zoll, 1984; Schneider-Rosen, Braunwald, Carlson, & Cicchetti, 1985). Few relations, however, have been found between normal range variations in maternal personality and security of attachment. For example, using a large battery of measures, Egeland and Farber (1984) found that only two variables—maternal maturity and complexity of thinking—predicted security of attachment at 12 months. Similarly, Belsky and Isabella (1988) found that only two of a large battery of measures were correlated with attachment: (1) mothers of secure (B) babies scored higher on interpersonal affection than mothers of insecure (A and C) infants, and (2) mothers of avoidant (A) infants were found to display significantly poorer levels of ego strength than those of either secure (B) or resistant (C) infants. Weber, Levitt, and Clark (1986) used the Dimensions of Temperament Scale (DOTS) to measure maternal temperament and reported that mothers of group A infants scored significantly higher on intensity of reaction than mothers of either B or C babies. Mothers of C infants, however, did not differ from those of B infants on any of the DOTS dimensions.

The lack of strong relations between attachment classifications and normal range maternal personality differences may be partly due to the categorical nature of the infant attachment classifications. These classifications do not allow for substantial variability among children, particularly within the securely attached group.[2] Another reason may be that the relation between these variables is not direct, but is instead mediated by other variables (e.g., child temperament). This would also account for the conflicting evidence regarding the relation between child temperament and attachment classifications. We discuss this topic in the next section.

The categorical nature of the attachment coding system, the unbalanced distribution of subjects across the three categories of avoidant, resistant, and secure, and the differences in the distribution between samples from different Western countries greatly limit the nature of analyses performed using strange situation data. Hence, attachment researchers have recently attempted to assess the construct in a variety of other ways. For example, Waters and Deane (1985) developed a Q-Set for rating attachment behavior.

---

[2] The Q-sort method for assessing attachment (Waters, 1995; Waters & Deane, 1985) allows for more variability and should therefore remedy this problem.

C. Association between Temperament and Attachment

It has been argued that measures of attachment quality reflect characteristics of the *relationship* rather than characteristics of only one or the other member of the dyad (Ainsworth, Blehar, Waters, & Wall, 1978). Of course, one would imagine that extremely deviant characteristics of either the mother (as in the case of affective disorders) or the infant might dictate the course of the relationship. In this regard, several researchers have emphasized the crucial role played by infant temperament, and have proposed a number of ways in which temperament might influence the infant–caregiver relationship (see Goldsmith, Bradshaw & Riesser-Danner, 1986; Lamb, Thompson, Gardner, & Charnov, 1985).

The most extreme position is that of Kagan (1982), who claims that individual differences observed in the strange situation are probably due to endogenous differences in infants rather than to variations in the quality of caregiving as proposed by attachment theorists (e.g., Ainsworth et al., 1978). Another perspective on the relation between temperament and attachment is that individual differences among infants may make some babies more or less difficult to parent (Waters & Deane, 1982). For example, parents would have more difficulty in responding sensitively to a highly irritable or "difficult" baby and this would result in an insecure attachment relationship. There is some evidence that supports this perspective when behavioral evaluations of newborns (rather than parental reports) are used (Belsky & Isabella, 1988).

On the other hand, the very notion of "sensitive parenting" implies that the parent is attuned to the needs of the individual child, whatever these needs may be. Indeed, attachment theorists suggest that the truly sensitive parent should be able to overcome obstacles in parenting presented by infants of different temperaments (e.g., Ainsworth, 1983). This implies that the sensitive parent should be equally capable of being sensitive to all children.

We believe that the effects of infant temperament on infant–caregiver attachment are indirect and are mediated by such variables as maternal personality and social support. Parents will be differentially sensitive to particular temperamental characteristics in their infants. For example, some parents might be better able to tolerate irritable or "difficult" children than others, and this will determine whether a secure or insecure attachment relationship results. This third perspective can be discussed as a "goodness of fit" model. Such a perspective assumes that it is the *fit* between child temperamental characteristics and parental personality that determines relationship (e.g., attachment) outcomes. An implication of this perspective is that one would be unlikely, except perhaps in extreme cases, to find main effects of either infant characteristics or parental characteristics on attachment. However, it has been documented that in the case of extreme irritability (e.g., van den Boom, 1989) or prematurity (Mangelsdorf et al., 1996) in babies or maternal psychopathology (e.g., Radke-Yarrow, Cummings, Kucynski & Chapman, 1985), such main effects are noted. Such a model is consistent with attachment theory in that it takes into account the evidence that consistent and sensitive maternal behavior is associated with secure attachment relationships (e.g., Ainsworth et al., 1978; Belsky, Rovine, & Taylor, 1984; Egeland & Farber, 1984; Isabella, 1993; Isabella & Belsky, 1991). However, a goodness of fit model would suggest that we need to examine how infant and parent characteristics interact to predict secure versus insecure attachments.

In support of a goodness of fit model, Crockenberg (1981) reported that newborn irritable temperament is predictive of insecure attachment only in conjunction with low maternal social support. That is, her research did not reveal significant main effects of either temperament or social support. Instead, the *interaction* between these two variables predicted insecure attachment. Similarly, Mangelsdorf et al. (1990) found that security of attachment, as assessed at 13 months in Ainsworth's strange situation, could be predicted by an interaction between infants' proneness-to-distress temperament measured at 9 months in a standardized laboratory temperament assessment (Matheny & Wilson, 1981) and maternal personality. That is, mothers who scored high on the Constraint scale of Tellegen's (1982) Multidimensional Personality Questionnaire (MPQ) and who had high-scoring infants on proneness-to-distress at 9 months were also likely to have insecurely attached infants at 13 months. As in the Crockenberg (1981) study, there was no significant main effect of either temperament or maternal personality; rather, it was the interaction between the two that predicted insecure attachment. It is easy to imagine how the combination of a fearful and rigid mother (i.e., the profile of high scorers on MPQ Constraint) with an easily distressed infant could result in a less than optimal relationship.

Thus, the findings from these studies support a goodness of fit model. What remains to be examined, however, are the parameters of such a model. Are there certain infant characteristics such as irritability or proneness-to-distress that are more likely to lead to insecure attachment than others? Which parental characteristics are particularly important to attachment relationships? Future research must examine more thoroughly the particular variables that go into the "fit" between infant and parental characteristics.

Aspects of infant temperament have been found to be predictive of certain infant behaviors in the strange situation. For example, Vaughn, Lefever, Seifer, and Barglow (1989) found that mothers' ratings of infants' negative emotionality or "difficult temperament" were significantly related to the negative emotionality that these infants displayed during the separation episodes of the strange situation. It is also noteworthy, however, that temperament ratings alone did not predict negative emotionality during the reunion episodes with the caregiver, nor did they relate to overall attachment classifications (i.e., A, B, or C). Gunnar, Mangelsdorf, Larson, and Hertsgaard (1989) found that proneness-to-distress assessed at 9 months predicted proneness-to-distress in the strange situation at 13 months, but not overall attachment classifications. Hence, there is some stability in infants' behaviors across different contexts, but this consistency, in and of itself, cannot predict the quality of infant–caregiver attachment relationships. Rather, the attachment relationship emerges out of a complex interaction among a variety of factors, including (but not limited to) infant temperament, maternal personality, and maternal social support.

Thus far we have examined how maternal personality is related to infant temperament and infant–caregiver attachment. We have also examined whether infant temperament and infant–caregiver attachment constitute separate constructs and the extent to which these constructs are related. These previous topics are necessary for apprehending the emergent self-concept because, in our view, one's self-concept arises from the combination of one's attachment relationships, one's temperamental characteristics, and the reactions of influential figures (e.g., parents) to one's temperamental characteristics. In the following sections, we will explore the infant's phenomenological experience. Specifically, we will address the role of infant attachment and temperament in the emergent self-concept.

D. Theoretical Relation between Attachment and Infant Self-Concept

According to attachment theorists, attachment is an "affective bond" (Ainsworth, 1973; Sroufe, 1979). According to Sroufe and Waters (1977) this term is meant as a metaphorical description of the construct suggesting that there is an enduring, stable quality to the attachment relationship. This metaphor is important because the patterns of behavioral organization (or the affective bond) endure despite the finding that the discrete behaviors reflective of attachment in infancy (e.g., proximity seeking, contact maintaining, and separation protest) are likely to change or disappear over time. The emotional distress observed in young children during separations from their attachment figures makes it clear that the bond is an affective one. In this section we examine the relation between this affective bond and one's developing self-concept.

Attachment theorists propose that the self is an organization of attitudes, expectations, and feelings which are derived from the infant's interactions with his or her caregiver during the first year of life (Bowlby, 1973; Bretherton, 1991; Sroufe, 1990). Alternatively, one could conceive of the self as developing out of the affective bond called "attachment" (Bretherton, 1991; Sroufe, 1990). According to Bowlby (1973), infants come into the world prepared to engage in social relations and as a result of ongoing interactions, particularly with the primary caregiver, develop internal representations or "working models" of attachment figures and of themselves. These models help the young child to perceive, interpret, and predict events. For example, a central feature of the infant's working model of the world involves how the attachment figures are expected to respond to events. Thus, an internal working model of an attachment figure might be composed of a representation of that person as available to meet one's needs. Models of self and other, according to Bowlby, tend to be reciprocal or complementary. That is, a cold, rejecting parent will lead to a child simultaneously viewing the parent as unloving and him/herself as unlovable. A securely attached child is "likely to possess a representational model of him/herself as at least a potentially lovable and valuable person" (Bowlby,

1980, p. 242). Note that these internal models are essentially evaluative: propositions such as "my caregiver is good to me and can be trusted" coexist with notions such as "I am good."

The concept of internal working models is very helpful for imagining how the attachment relationship is experienced by the child, and how it affects the child's emerging self-concept. In support of this point, Cassidy (1988) found moderate relations between 6-year-olds' attachment classification and their responses on several self-concept measures. She concluded that her results support the "hypothesized presence of connections between quality of attachment to mother and child's representation of self" (p. 130).

One limitation with the concept of internal working models, however, is that it can account only for global evaluative self-concepts. That is, according to this view, children will develop a conception of themselves as either good or bad, depending on their attachment relationship. The notion of internal working models, therefore, may be helpful for understanding the acquisition of global self-concepts (e.g., self-esteem) and most certainly would aid in apprehending typical versus atypical self-concept development (e.g., Bretherton, 1991). However, it is not helpful for predicting the rather substantial variability evidenced in normal children's self-concepts by 3 years of age (Eder, 1990). How then might children develop these more differentiated conceptions of their world and their place in it? We suggest that an understanding of children's phenomenological experience of their own temperament is crucial to answering this question.

E. Theoretical Relation between Infant Temperament and Infant Self-Concept

Very little has been written about the influence of early temperament on the developing self-concept. However, we can speculate in much the same way as those who have written about the role of attachment on internal working models. One view of temperament is that it consists of individual differences in the expression of basic emotions such as fear, anger, and happiness (Campos, Barrett, Lamb, Goldsmith, & Stenberg, 1983). For example, some children have lower thresholds for responding to stressful events with fear than others. Such differences surely must result in differences in infants' phenomenological experience. That is, with increasing cognitive development, continuity in these early emotional experiences eventually becomes incorporated into a system of understanding about the world. For example, infants with low thresholds for fear may come to view the world as a dangerous place. In this way, temperament and self-concept are thought to be separate experiences that interact and contribute to early personality development (see also Goldsmith et al., 1987).

Parental perceptions of, and reactions to, early individual differences may influence the child's self-concept. Malatesta and Wilson (1988) suggest that the contingent response of parents to an infant's state (e.g., "You're feeling cranky today, aren't you?", p. 94) is a central factor in the development of self-awareness.

This explanation can account for children's understanding of basic emotional states such as anger, fear, and happiness, but it does not explain the acquisition of nonspecific affects (e.g., negative affectivity) that are also a part of one's self-concept (Watson & Clark, 1984). More general evaluations of the child's emotional states must also play a role in the child's developing self-concept. For example, a child who is perceived as "difficult" may well come to internalize notions of himself or herself as "difficult" or as "a failure." If this pattern continued into adulthood, such a child would score high on measures of negative emotionality.

Thomas and Chess (1977) suggest that "goodness of fit" between the infant's temperament and the environment is important in predicting child outcomes. Although they do not directly address the influence of an infant's temperament on his or her developing self-concept, it is clear that variations in parental personality might interact with infant temperament to affect the child's self-concept. We illustrate this point using activity level because it is thought to be a early emerging, heritable trait that is somewhat stable over time (Buss & Plomin, 1984). Imagine a very active infant. This child may develop very different self-conceptions depending on the environment in which he or she is raised. If this child is raised by parents who are also active, who appreciate the child's energetic approach to life, and who channel the child's energy into constructive activities, this child will develop a very different self-concept than if he or she is born into a family in which high energy levels are considered a shortcoming and the child is frequently reprimanded for his or her behavior. In the first case, the child might come to feel "I like to run fast," "I am good at sports," "I am competent," and "I am good." In the second instance, the child might eventually believe "I am a bother," "I get in trouble a lot," "I am naughty," and "I am bad." This example also illustrates the difficulty of predicting adult personality traits from infant temperament. In the first instance, activity level might result in an adult who scores high in achievement and well-being (i.e., one who would score high on measures of positive affect). In the second instance, activity level might result in an adult who is a low scorer on measures of constraint.

Although there is little consensus on the exact *number* of infant temperamental characteristics, there is agreement that temperament is reflected in early individual differences in behavioral tendencies along several different dimensions (e.g., activity level and emotionality). The findings of several different temperamental dimensions suggests that individual differences in infant temperament would result in children acquiring quite differentiated views of the world (e.g., it is dangerous versus safe, fun versus tedious). Parental reactions to infant characteristics must also become incorporated into the child's self-concept (e.g., "I am a sissy") and would result in still more differentiation.

In sum, whereas the working model derived from the attachment relationships leads the child to form a global view of themselves as good versus bad, early temperamental characteristics are speculated to contribute to one's system of understanding the world. Together, these processes should allow for the highly differentiated self-concepts that are observed in older children and adults. In the next section, we address the empirical evidence concerning the development of the self-concept in infancy.

F. When Does the Self-Concept Develop?

There is some debate concerning the age at which the infant can be said to possess a self-concept. The prevailing view, initially proposed by Freud (1950, 1955) and elaborated upon by other theorists (Mahler, 1967; Mahler, Pine & Bergman, 1975; Piaget, 1952; Sullivan, 1953), is that infants go through a period when self and other are undifferentiated and that the infant only gradually comes to see him/her self as distinct from others and the rest of the world. This sense of oneself as distinct is thought to be a prerequisite for the development of the self-concept.

Mahler et al. (1975) outlined a comprehensive developmental model of the phases the infant goes through in the development of the self. They proposed that during the first months of life children are in an undifferentiated phase during which they are in a state of symbiosis with their mothers. This phase is proposed to last until 7 or 8 months. Gradually, the infant emerges from this symbiotic state and in the next phase comes to achieve a sense of self through the processes of separation and individuation. Separation involves the capacity to recognize that other human beings are not part of oneself. Individuation entails developing a sense of identity as an autonomous person. In this view, the child gradually emerges from these processes (of which four subphases are proposed) with a self-concept identifiable sometime between 25 and 36 months. This self-concept integrates perception, memory, cognition, emotion, and other ego functions into a unitary personality.

Sroufe's (1979) view is similar to Mahler et al.'s (1975) in a number of ways. For example, he proposes that the self-concept emerges sometime between 18 and 36 months, although he believes that self-assertion is often exhibited earlier in the second year. In Sroufe's theory of socioemotional development the interdependence of affective and cognitive development is emphasized. It is not surprising, then, that he proposes that the emergence of the self-concept coincides with cognitive changes such as those described by Piaget in the sixth and final stage of sensorimotor thought, when the child is thought to achieve representational (i.e., symbolic) thought.

Lewis (1987) proposes that the self has two components that unfold with development: (1) the *existential* self, which is the experience of oneself as distinct from other persons and objects, and (2) the *categorical* self, which consists of the ways that we think about ourselves. These components are similar to those described by William James (1892) as the "I" and the "Me", respectively. In contrast to James, who believed that the "Me" (i.e., one's representation of oneself) could be studied by psychologists whereas the "I" (i.e., oneself experienced) should be left to philosophers, Lewis regards both the existential and the categorical selves as amenable to psychological inquiry. In line with the previous investigators, Lewis suggests that at about 18 months, infants are able to think categorically about themselves. In support of this suggestion, he reports that infants demonstrate self-recognition in a mirror by this age.[3] He claims that common early self-representational categories are gender, age, competence, and value (good or bad).

A strikingly different view is that of Stern (1985), who places the age at which infants have an organized sense of self much earlier than other investigators. Stern proposes that in order for the infant to have a sense of core self, he or she must possess self-agency, self-coherence, self-affectivity, and self-history. Self-agency involves controlling one's actions. Self-coherence entails having a sense of being a physical whole. Self-affectivity involves experiencing emotions that are attached to events concerning oneself. Finally, self-history involves having a sense of continuity with one's past. According to Stern, these four self-experiences constitute what he calls a sense of core self that forms between 2 and 6 months.

Some of the differences among previous researchers can be attributed to variations in definitions. Most researchers view the self-concept as a system of understanding represented in memory (e.g., Eder, 1988; Markus & Sentis, 1982), or what James called the "Me" and what Lewis calls the categorical self. Given that such a definition requires that infants have the cognitive ability necessary for representing information in memory, these researchers tend to place the emergence of the self-concept at approximately 18 months. In contrast, a minority of investigators have emphasized one's experience or sense of self (i.e., what James called the "I"). If a sense of self does not have to be represented and/or organized in memory, then it can be present very early on (perhaps even at birth).

What is the role of a sense of self versus a self-concept in early personality development? Stern suggests that affective experiences in the first 6 months of life are one of the "invariants" in the developing self. This sense of self is "prerepresentational," according to Emde (1983), in that it exists before children have the ability for abstract mental representation. That is, early affective experiences (e.g., fear) become linked by a common thread that comes to characterize a particular individual (e.g., fearful). In support of this view, very young infants have been found to be capable of expressing identifiable facial expressions of emotion. For example, the expressions for joy, interest, disgust, and physical distress have been identified in neonates (Izard, 1977). Others have also suggested that expressions of sadness and surprise were evident in neonates during a Brazelton exam (Field & Walden, 1982).

At present, however, there is some disagreement among investigators on the degree to which these early expressions reflect the infant's affective state. That is, some researchers claim that infants who express recognizable facial expressions of emotion also experience the corresponding emotional state. Proponents of this view, which is called "discrete emotions theory," suggest that very young infants, perhaps even neonates, experience several distinct affective states (see Izard & Malatesta, 1987). Others, however, claim that although early expressions may be precursors to later affective states, they do not necessarily signal the existence of

---

[3] Given that this research is not directly related to psychological self-conceptions, it it not discussed in this chapter. See Harter (1983) for a discussion of the role of self-recognition in the self-concept.

affective states comparable to those experienced by adults with similar expressions (e.g., Emde, Kligman, Reich, & Wade, 1978; Kagan, 1984; Sroufe, 1979). According to Sroufe, the differentiation of emotions from these precursors does not begin until after 3 months of age. These viewpoints are not yet reconcilable, although physiological correlates of emotional expressions may eventually clarify our understanding of infants' affective experiences.

Regardless of whether infants experience distinct emotional states, we believe that until affective states are organized and represented into a conceptual system, they cannot become integrated into the child's self-concept. We speculate on when this might occur in the next section. To anticipate, it is likely that because of constraints of cognitive development, this does not occur until after the first 6 months of life. To gain further insight into these issues, we review the research on the conceptual development of infants in the next section.

G. Conclusion: Infancy

In our opinion, a sense of oneself—as described by Stern (1985)—is one of the first phenomenological experiences of self, and as such is an important precursor to personality development. However, if these sense-of-self experiences are not integrated into a conceptual system, they do not contribute to children's understanding of their world and themselves. Stern also suggests that self-history or a sense of one's continuity over time is an important aspect of what he calls one's core self. We agree that memory is an important aspect of the self-concept, for how can we know who we are, unless we know who we were? Research on infant memory indicates that infants as young as 5 months can recognize a photograph of a face that they had seen a week earlier, and infants as young as 3 months of age reenact motor activities learned several days earlier (Rovee-Collier, 1987). However, little is known about the organization of infant memory. Some investigators, however, have argued that most studies of infant categoric knowledge do not clearly demonstrate that infants are capable of forming non-perceptually based categories (Markman & Callanan, 1984). Hence, although young infants are able to recognize familiar information, they may not be integrating information into a system of understanding (i.e., a concept) in the first 6 months of life. We are intrigued by how 2- to 6-month-old infants might possess a sense of their continuity over time without having developed the cognitive skills necessary for organizing previous autobiographical events in memory. We should emphasize that like Stern, we stress the importance of early affective experiences. Our view differs from Stern's only regarding *when* these experiences become integrated into the child's self-concept.

In sum, during infancy, early affective experiences form the basis for the child's developing self-concept. As soon as children can begin to represent and categorize their experiences (sometime after 6 months of age), they form a representation of their world and their place in it. This representation grows out of the interaction betweeen early temperamental characteristics, parental personality, and the infant–caregiver attachment relationship.

III. THE TRANSITION BETWEEN INFANCY AND CHILDHOOD: TODDLERS' SOCIAL UNDERSTANDING

An important development in the child's self-concept occurs during toddlerhood (i.e., 2 years of age) when children begin to label their internal states (e.g., thoughts, drives, and feelings). In several naturalistic studies children were observed to use words for their thoughts, desires (e.g., "want"), and drives (e.g., "hungry") by 2 years of age (Bretherton & Beeghly, 1982; Dunn, Bretherton, & Munn, 1987). Internal states are common to all persons and are therefore not idiosyncratic to particular individuals, whereas dispositions are frequent, enduring tendencies that can be used to characterize and differentiate specific persons. It is not surprising that the young child conceives of and talks about the more generally applicable internal states prior to articulating explicit dispositional concepts (see Wellman & Gelman, 1987, for an elaboration of this point).

Conceptions of the internal states of self and other seem to be acquired simultaneously (Bretherton & Beeghly, 1982), providing support for the notion that children jointly represent their social world and their place in it. Bretherton, Fritz, Zahn-Waxler, and Ridgeway (1986) believe that "the ability to think of one's own past or future is conceptually similar to the ability to attribute internal states to others" (Bretherton et al., 1986, p. 533). Hence, young children do have some self-awareness which they can articulate by 2 years of age, but do not yet conceive of themselves and their characteristics as enduring.

Stern (1985) makes the intriguing suggestion that the onset of language may make children's experience of themselves less direct than it was earlier. He speculates that the autobiography constructed by children during this period significantly alters their felt experiences. Theories of infantile amnesia suggest that in addition to being less direct, these experiences also become more memorable once they are encoded in language. For example, Schachtel (1947) proposed that the majority of one's earliest memories are for experiences that occurred after the first 3 years of life as a function of the onset of language and the continuity provided to verbally encoded events.

IV. PERSONALITY DEVELOPMENT IN EARLY CHILDHOOD

As in the area of infant temperament, a great deal of research has been devoted to understanding individual differences in personality among preschool and kindergarten children. Similar to the work on temperament, this research has primarily relied on the reports of other persons and/or behavioral observations. It may be divided into roughly three categories: research on control and/or inhibition, research on broader personality constructs (e.g., ego resiliency), and research on emotional expressiveness.

By 4 years of age, children demonstrate individual differences in the extent to which they are able to delay gratification. Moreover, individual differences are also apparent in the cognitive strategies that high versus low self-control children use to delay gratification (see Mischel, Shoda, & Rodriguez, 1989, for a review). Individual differences have also been uncovered in preschoolers' willingness to approach novel objects in unfamiliar contexts. Furthermore, these differences are related to a variety of different physiological measures of arousal (Kagan, Resnick, & Snidman, 1988). Although this research is very informative about individual differences in preschool children's *behavior,* it is not clear whether these differences in behavior correspond to differences in children's self-concept or phenomenological experience.

This information would be particularly informative for constructs such as inhibition that are thought to be related to adult personality traits. For example, Kagan et al. (1988) suggest that childhood inhibition is analogous to and possibly predictive of adult introversion/extraversion (p. 167). Hence, it would be of considerable interest to know whether children low on inhibition, for example, also view themselves as outgoing and talkative. Such information would lead to a fuller picture of personality development in these preschool years because it would clarify the emotional basis of constructs such as inhibition. One component that is crucial to introversion/extraversion in adulthood is one's energy level (see Watson & Clark, in this volume, for a discussion of the emotionality underlying extraversion). Kagan and his colleagues (1988), however, suggest that children high on inhibition feel fearful in unfamiliar social settings. In the absence of information about children's actual experience of unfamiliar social settings, we can only infer their experiences from observing their responses to these events. Having children's self-report would enable us to specify the emotion underlying these traits. For example, it would allow us to determine whether children rated as high in inhibition actually *feel* fear in social settings or some alternative emotion (e.g., lethargy).

The construct of ego resiliency developed by the Blocks (e.g., J. H. Block & Block, 1980) is a broad personality construct used to describe the degree to which individuals approach problems in a flexible manner. Children are identified as high or low on this dimension through the reports of others (e.g., teachers' Q-sorts). Raters are also asked to infer aspects of the children's self-concept through items such as "Appears to feel unworthy; thinks of self as 'bad.'" Children rated as securely attached are found to score higher on Q-sort indices of ego resiliency at ages 4 to 5 (Arend, Gove, & Sroufe, 1979). These results suggest that measures of ego resiliency may tap some aspects of children's ideas about themselves (i.e., their "internal working model"). Unfortunately, because self-report measures were not obtained from the child, this connection remains speculative and must be established in future research.

Individual differences have also been uncovered in children's expressive behaviors. These findings are particularly relevant to research which has defined infant temperament as essentially reflecting individual differences in emotional expressivity (e.g., Goldsmith & Campos, 1986). For example, children rated as having more expressive faces are also likely to have been rated as higher on extraversion by their teachers (Buck, 1977; Field & Walden, 1982). Hence, individual differences are apparent in the degree to which children spontaneously express emotions.

A recent study also revealed individual variability in the extent to which children are able to exert control over their expressive behaviors. In this study, 3- and 5-year-old children were rated by their teachers on a modified version of Snyder's (1974) self-monitoring scale (Eder & Jones, 1989). Children scoring in the top and bottom third of the measure were tested (in counterbalanced order) on their ability (1) to recognize standardized photographs of facial expressions of emotion (Ekman & Friesen, 1975), and (2) to produce six basic emotional expressions (e.g., happiness, sadness, anger). High scorers on the self-monitoring scale were significantly better at both recognizing and producing emotional expressions than low scorers. The usual developmental (i.e., age) differences found in recognition and production were not significant. However, self-monitoring interacted significantly with age such that high 3-year-olds, for example, were better at posing emotional expressions than low 5-year-olds, and high 5-year-olds were better than low adults. These results demonstrate that individual differences in the control of expressive behavior are apparent at an early age.

Of future interest is whether high self-monitoring children are generally more expressive than low self-monitoring children, or are simply better at controlling their expressive behaviors (thus making them less expressive in situations requiring display rules such as masking). Also of concern is the relation between spontaneous and controlled emotional expressiveness and felt emotions (i.e., one's feelings about oneself). If these two constructs are independent, they would be expected to show a different pattern of correlations with children's self-report. To speculate, children who are high in expressivity may feel more accepted by themselves and others and thus should demonstrate self-concepts that reflect these feelings (e.g., well-being). On the other hand, children who are able to control their expressive displays might feel especially comfortable in social settings, and their self-reports that demonstrate corresponding differences in sociability.

In sum, although there is substantial research on individual differences in preschool and kindergarten children's personality, the majority of this research has emphasized behavioral observations and/or the reports of other persons. This research is very informative for those aspects of personality that are noticed by other persons, but neglects children's own representation of their personalities. Indeed, this self-representation undergoes many important developments during the preschool years; these changes are discussed next.

A. Development of the Self-Concept in Preschool and Early School-Age Children

Several features characterize the majority of research on the self-concepts of preschool and kindergarten children. Note that each of these characteristics contrasts with the traditional research on children's personality development discussed previously. First, most researchers have focused on children's self-descriptions, rather than on behavioral or observer data. Second, these investigators have generally ignored emotions and have instead been concerned with the role of cognitive development in children's self-understanding. Third, investigators have tended to emphasize age (i.e., group) rather than individual differences.

In a frequently cited study, Keller, Ford, and Meacham (1978) categorized the responses of 3- to 5-year old children to open-ended and fill-in-the-blank questions (e.g., "I am a boy/girl who ————"). More than half of the responses referred to actions (e.g., "I am a boy who plays"). Hart and Damon (1986) interviewed children from 6 to 16 years using a variety of free-response questions such as "What are you like?" Responses were categorized according to four types of content (i.e., physical, active, social, and psychological) and for four possible developmental levels, with higher levels indicating increasing abstraction. Strong correlations between age and developmental level were found.

Using a slightly different approach, Bannister and Agnew (1976) examined the role of memory in young children's self-concepts. In their study, 5- to 9-year-olds' responses to questions about themselves were tape recorded. All situational cues about the identity of the children were eliminated and the answers were rerecorded in a single adult voice. When children were reinterviewed, 4 months later, they heard several answers to each question and were asked to identify their own previous answer. In addition, they were asked to provide reasons for their choices. In providing reasons for their responses, most of the youngest children simply said that they remembered their responses, whereas the majority of the oldest subjects indicated that they based their answers on their general likes and dislikes. Bannister and Agnew concluded that young children rely more on their specific memories for information about themselves, but older children are capable of using a more general theory of self. From findings such as those described above, early reviewers concluded that the structure of young children's self-concepts becomes more general with increasing age, and that the content of these self-concepts becomes more psychological with age (see especially Harter, 1983).

More recently, these conclusions have been reexamined in light of work from cognitive and language development. Specifically, if the self-concept is actually a concept, it should depend on a person's memory. Hence, age differences in young children's self-concepts should be similar to those found in memory studies. Given that the ability to retrieve general memories is already present by 3 years of age, whereas the ability to access specific memories emerges between 4 and 5 years of age (Hudson, 1986), a similar pattern should also be expected for children's self-concept.

Perhaps early investigators, in asking only one type of question, confounded structure and content in their studies. To examine this question, Eder and her colleagues asked 3- to 7-year-old children general and specific questions about their behaviors and internal states (Eder, 1989; Eder, Gerlach, & Perlmutter, 1987). General questions involved frequent and/or typical activities and were not located in one particular point in time. Specific requests were temporally located. Behavior questions concerned activities and involved action verbs; requests about internal states involved adjectives. The findings supported those from previous research on children's memory by revealing that general memories about oneself dominated the responses of the youngest children, whereas specific memories increased substantially from 3 to 6.

The old view that young children do not evidence any psychological self-understanding has also been disputed by recent investigators (Miller & Aloise, 1989). For example, Wellman and Gelman (1987) suggest that two distinct types of personological conceptions were confounded in earlier work, namely, conceptions of internal states and of dispositions. The distinction is important because the young child may possess an awareness of internal states prior to acquiring dispositional concepts. Indeed, as we indicated earlier, even 2-year-olds describe internal states of themselves and others in their conversations, suggesting that they already have a rudimentary understanding of internal states by this age (e.g., Bretherton & Beeghly, 1982). Sixty percent of the 3-year-olds in Eder's studies (Eder, 1989; Eder et al., 1987) responded to state questions with appropriate descriptions of their internal states and emotions. For example, in response to the question, "Tell me how you've usually been when you're scared," one $3\frac{1}{2}$-year-old girl said, "Usually frightened." Even when the children did not generate state terms, they used appropriate behaviors in their responses, for example, responding to the question, "Tell me how you usually have felt when you've been happy," with "smiling." Finally, even the youngest children seemed to understand the relation between emotions and other internal states (e.g., beliefs, attitudes). Thus, they often justified their responses by referring to a belief or attitude. For example, one $3\frac{1}{2}$-year-old boy stated, "I don't feel that good with grownups, 'cause I don't like grownups."

Most other research, however, indicates that full-blown dispositional conceptions do not emerge until 7 to 8 years (e.g., Ruble & Rholes, 1981; Shantz, 1983). This raises the question of what develops in children's self-understanding between 2 years (when they understand emotional states) and 7 years (when they understand dispositions). Research on adults' conceptions of states and traits reveal that two types of features are evident in their personological conceptions: situational features (e.g., cross-situational consistency) and temporal features (e.g., duration; see Chaplin, John, & Goldberg, 1988). Previous research has indicated that the situational aspects of dispositions are not present in young children's personological conceptions. For example, Rholes and Ruble (1984) reported that children do not regard dispositions as the tendency to behave consistently across situations until they are 7 or 8 years old. In contrast, children probably possess an awareness of the temporal aspects of dispositions by 3 years of age. That is, the general memories reported by young children in Eder's research (e.g., Eder, 1989) were representations of behaviors and/or internal states that were stable and enduring, indicating young children conceive of themselves and other persons as having characteristics that are enduring across time. These early general memories may form the basis for the more mature dispositional conceptions held by older children and adults.

Eder (1990) examined whether such general memories are organized into meaningful and consistent self-conceptions. She presented children, in a random order, with pairs of statements reflecting 10 of Tellegen's lower-order personality dimensions (e.g., Achievement, Alienation, Well-Being; see Tellegen, 1985). It was assumed that if children selected statements in a nonrandom fashion, then they must possess a corresponding organizing construct (i.e., a trait).

To examine this, a new method was developed for assessing young children's self-concepts. One hundred and eighty children between 3 and 8 years were presented with pairs of statements representing the low and high endpoints of Tellegen's dimensions by two puppets. For example, one puppet would state, "It's not fun to scare people," and the other would say, "It's fun to scare people," thus representing the high and low endpoints of aggression. Children were then asked to pick the statement that better described themselves.

Responses were factor analyzed with varimax rotation. A three-factor solution best described the responses for every age group, although the constructs differed for the different age groups. The factors that emerged for the 3-year-olds were labeled Self-Control, General Self-Acceptance, and Rejection. The factors that emerged for the 5-year-olds were Self-Control, Self-Acceptance via Achievement, and Self-Acceptance via Affiliation. Finally, those that were revealed for the 7-year-olds were Emotional Stability, Extraversion, and Determined Fearlessness. Separate higher-order factor scales were computed for each age group and these were found to be psychologically meaningful and to demonstrate good internal consistency in every age group (e.g., average alphas = .75, .78, and .78, for the 3-, 5-, and 7-year-olds, respectively).

These results indicate that by 3 years of age, children possess common underlying dispositional constructs for organizing information about themselves. Furthermore, by 7 years two of the constructs resemble in content and degree of complexity those that have been identified in adults. Specifically, the Emotional Stability factor corresponds to Eysenck's construct of Neuroticism (reversed) and to Tellegen's Negative Emotionality. The Extraversion factor is analogous to Eysenck's Extraversion/Intraversion and, to a lesser extent, Tellegen's Positive Emotionality.

1. New Approaches

Early research tended to neglect the content of young children's self-conceptions, focusing more on the particular categories that they used to describe themselves. Very little information was gleaned regarding the *nature* of these self-conceptions or of children's feelings about themselves. Unfortunately this provided a discontinuity between research with preschoolers and research on the evaluative aspects of the self (i.e., self-esteem) in infants and older children and adolescents.

Further, research on young children's self-conceptions largely focused on age differences in children's self-descriptions, whereas investigators of the self-concepts of older children and adults emphasize individual differences. For example, Harter (1982) demonstrated that by third grade, children differ from one another in perceived self-competence (i.e., the extent to which they view themselves as competent in a variety of different domains) and in their global self-worth (i.e., the degree to which they view themselves as worthwhile persons).

In spite of their importance, previous investigators have largely ignored individual differences in preschool and kindergarten children's self-concepts. We suggest several reasons for this: First, developmentalists tend to place more importance on age differences, believing that individual differences may ultimately reflect error. Second, the measures used to study individual differences in older children and adults (e.g., rating scales, adjective checklists) are not suitable for use with young children. Third, as we indicated previously, early research suggested that young children did not demonstrate psychological self-conceptions. If young children do not have any trait-like personological conceptions, then there is little reason to seek out individual differences in their self-understanding.

However, it is possible that conclusions derived from early studies underestimate the true level of children's self-understanding. Previous investigators used open-ended questions to study children's self-concepts. One limitation of this format is that it depends on the language production skills of the subject. Much research with preschool children shows that they comprehend more than they produce (e.g., Kuczaj & Maratsos, 1975). It is not surprising then that they perform better on language comprehension, rather than language production, tasks (see Kuczaj, 1986, for a review). This may be especially true for studies on the psychological aspects of the self-concept, because state and trait adjectives are relatively recent additions to young children's vocabularies (Ridgeway, Waters, & Kuczaj, 1985).

For these reasons, Eder (1990) utilized a comprehension task to test children's self-conceptions. She found that when children listened to pairs of statements presented in a random order and were asked to pick the one that best described themselves, even 3-year-olds made their selections in a nonrandom fashion. It was concluded that these children made use of underlying organizing constructs (e.g., traits) when evaluating information.

The presence of dispositional self-conceptions is a necessary, but not sufficient, condition for the existence of individual differences in self-report. Even if children conceive of themselves in terms of a construct, for example, "well-being," they might not differ significantly from one another in their self-view on that construct (e.g., they might all conceive of themselves as high in well-being). Hence, Eder also examined whether individual differences were evident in children's self-conceptions. Children's mean scores on both the dimensions and the higher-order factor scales were close to midpoint; moreover, the standard deviations revealed considerable variation, indicating their self-conceptions differed from child to child. Finally, these differences showed some stability over time. That is, $3\frac{1}{2}$-, $5\frac{1}{2}$-, and $7\frac{1}{2}$-year-old children's responses on every higher-order factor yielded statistically significant 1-month test–retest correlations. These stability coefficients averaged .47, .60, and .65 for the $3\frac{1}{2}$-, $5\frac{1}{2}$- and $7\frac{1}{2}$-year-olds, respectively.

We are not suggesting that 3-year-old children conceive of themselves as "High in Self-Acceptance" or even as "The type of person who feels accepted by others." Rather, it is likely that they are using an organizing principle which they are unable to articulate in much the same manner as they use implicit language rules (see Bretherton & Beeghly, 1982, for a similar point). These young children possess a working theory, but not a metatheory, about themselves.

What is the organizing principle behind children's statements? Perhaps children group together similar behaviors (e.g., that they go down slides headfirst and climb things that are high) and then simply remember these clusters of similar behaviors. Whereas this explanation may account for the consistency on some dimensions (especially lower-order ones such as Harm–Avoidance), children also combined quite dissimilar items such as "I climb things that are really high," "When I get angry, I hit people," and "I get upset a lot." A more compelling alternative explanation is that children selected statements based on their underlying emotionality. An examination of Table I provides one with a strong sense of the hedonic tone underlying the scales that were formed based on the factor analyses of children's responses. Hence, these self-concepts are reflective of how young children *feel* about themselves, rather than necessarily indicating how they behave. In sum, 2-year-olds are able to label emotional states and 3-year-olds demonstrate very differentiated dispositional self-conceptions on which they show stable and meaningful differences. These trait conceptions not only have characteristics similar to those observed in adults (e.g., they are internally consistent), but by 7 years, they begin to look strikingly similar to those dispositions that have been described in adult research.

V. PUTTING IT ALL TOGETHER: A MODEL OF PERSONALITY DEVELOPMENT

Traditional research on personality development has been subdivided into several distinct domains, with each domain developing and utilizing its own characteristic questions and methods. For example, temperament researchers have emphasized maternal and/or teacher reports to understand individual differences in biologically based constructs. In contrast, attachment researchers have mostly depended on observations of mother–child interactions in the strange situation to arrive at a child's attachment classification. Finally, early self-concept researchers have assessed children's own self-descriptions and emphasized age, rather than individual, differences.

We propose that these literatures have more in common than a superficial analysis would indicate. Specifically, each of these areas is essential for understanding the emotional basis of early personality, and thus they jointly provide a satisfactory answer to the question, "What is important in personality development?" In this final section, we use this theme to integrate the bodies of research that we have described previously.

Recent research on adult personality has consistently stressed the affective basis of personality dimensions; that is, responses on self-report are first and foremost indicative of how individuals feel about themselves, rather than how they behave, for example (J. Block, 1989; Lazarus, 1975; Tellegen, 1985; Watson & Clark,

TABLE I
Examples of Items on the Factor Scales

Low items	High items

3½-year-olds
Factor 1: Self-control

When I get angry, I feel like hitting someone.	When I get angry, I feel like being quiet.
I sometimes try to push in front of people on line.	I don't ever try to push in front of people on line.
I get mad a lot.	I get mad a little.
Sometimes I get in trouble for being bad.	I never get in trouble for being bad.

Factor 2: General self-acceptance

I like work that's not very hard.	I like hard work.
It's more fun to do things by myself than with other people.	It's more fun to do things with other people.
I'm not usually very happy.	I am usually happy.
Sometimes I feel like I just don't like myself.	I really like myself.

Factor 3: Rejection

I don't ever feel people want bad things to happen to me.	I sometimes feel people want bad things to happen to me.
When my friends visit they play with me and not my toys.	When my friends visit they play with my toys and not with me.
People don't usually say mean things to me.	People always say mean things to me.
I am the leader in "Follow the Leader."	Other people are the leader in "Follow the Leader."

5½-year-olds
Factor 1: Self-control

When I get angry, I feel like hitting someone.	When I get angry, I feel like being quiet.
I sometimes try to push in front of people on line.	I don't ever try to push in front of people on line.
I get mad a lot.	I get mad a little.
Sometimes I get in trouble for being bad.	I never get in trouble for being bad.

Factor 2: Self-acceptance via achievement

I like work that's not very hard.	I like hard work.
Other people pick the game to play.	I pick the game to play.
I don't like to have people look at me.	I like to have people look at me.
Sometimes, I just don't like myself.	I really like myself.

Factor: Self-acceptance via affiliation

People always say mean things to me.	People don't usually say mean things to me.
I don't have a best friend.	I have a best friend.
I'm happiest when I'm by myself.	I'm happiest when I'm around people.
I am not a good boy (girl).	I am a good boy (girl).

continues

TABLE I *continued*

Low items	High items

$7\frac{1}{2}$-year-olds
Factor 1: Emotional stability

Low items	High items
When I get angry, I feel like hitting someone.	When I get angry, I feel like being quiet.
I sometimes think no one cares what happens to me.	I know that people care what to me.
A lot of things make me upset.	It's hard for me to get upset.
Sometimes, I just don't like myself.	I really like myself.

Factor 2: Extraversion

Low items	High items
It's not fun to scare people.	Sometimes it's fun to scare people.
I'm happiest when I'm by myself.	I'm happiest when I'm around people.
I don't like to show things at "Show and Tell" at school.	I like to show things at "Show and Tell" at school.
I don't like to boss people around.	I like to boss people around.

Factor 3: Determined fearlessness

Low items	High items
When I'm scared, I run away.	When I'm scared, I stand up to what scares me.
When I see something scary on TV, I cover my face.	I like to look at scary things on TV.
It's not fun to ride in a fast car.	It's fun riding in a fast car.
I get scared a lot.	I never get scared.

1984). Indeed, self-reported distress is one criterion for diagnosing pathology in the DSM framework (American Psychiatric Association, 1980). How do individuals come to feel the way they do? How is it that someone comes to be high on Negative Emotionality? Recall that we anticipated this discussion by suggesting earlier that personality development occurs in five steps.

A. Step 1: Organized Patterns of Behavior

The first component in how humans feel about themselves is probably evidenced soon after birth. Neonates demonstrate substantial individual differences in their behaviors. Such "temperamental" differences, for example, in activity level, emotional expressiveness, and attention, are thought to be genetic in origin and are thought to be evidence that aspects of one's personality structure are present at birth. In our view, many of these temperamental differences are necessary antecedents of certain later personalities, but none are themselves sufficient. That is, the early structures will interact with future contents in important ways. Hence, one cannot predict what a person will be like as an adult from only knowing his or her infant temperament. This is because these differences act as constraints on potential individual differences in personality traits, rather than fully accounting for them. For example, infants who are very low on energy may never become extraverted adults. However, energetic infants may or may not become extraverts, depending on other experiences (e.g., their attachment relationship). Relatedly, the content may affect the original structure in fundamental ways. For example, children who develop high positive affect from their life experiences may show more energy than would be expected from their original temperament.

One approach (e.g., Goldsmith & Campos, 1986) has emphasized that these first individual differences are experienced by the infant in terms of basic emotional states (e.g., happiness, anger, fear). Whereas all children experience basic emotional states (e.g., Ekman & Friesen, 1975), they differ in the degree, frequency, and intensity with which these states are experienced (Izard, Hembree, & Huebner, 1987). We believe that, with increases in cognitive development, these initial temperamental differences can lead to differences in children's views and feelings about the world they inhabit. For example, infants who have a low threshold for fear may develop into individuals who view their world as a dangerous place.

Moreover, such temperamental differences also affect parents' reactions to their children. These reactions are further influenced by parental personality. For example, active infants may be perceived by parents as "energetic" or as "hyperactive," depending on the parents' personalities (or their own activity level). Recent research provides indirect support for this suggestion. Mothers who score high on Negative Emotionality on Tellegen's (in press) measure are likely to also rate their 3- and 5-year-old children as being Under-Socialized, perhaps demonstrating an intolerance of these mothers for the rather high activity level characteristic of most preschool and kindergarten children (Eder & Mahmood, 1989).

If complete random selection occurred, active children, for example, would have an equal likelihood of having parents who perceive them as energetic as with those that view them as hyperactive. However, recent findings suggest that there is a genetic relation between children's temperament and their parents' personalities (Goldsmith et al., 1994) that may constrain the actual combinations of parent and infant temperament that occur in the world.

Temperamental factors in children and parents probably also set a range of attachment relations. That is, secure attachments are less likely to occur for certain combinations of parental personality and child temperament. However, a wide margin of possible combinations can allow for attachment. For example, mothers who are intermediate in activity are in a better position to provide sensitive parenting to children who are either slightly more lethargic or more active than average than to children at either extreme. The margin of this range also depends on another personality variable, that is, parental flexibility, with flexible parents having a wider range of temperaments they can tolerate in order to be effective parents (Mangelsdorf et al., 1990).

B. Step 2: Nonverbal Conceptions

Whereas temperament may provide a child with a sense of his or her world (e.g., it is a dangerous place), attachment has been thought to provide children with a sense of themselves. The "working model" of self that attachment provides is exclusively self-evaluative (i.e., good/bad). Specifically, children who develop secure relationships with their caretaker are thought to develop working models of themselves as "worthy of love" (e.g., Bretherton, 1991). Conversely, those who develop insecure attachments have negative self-evaluations. Temperament, on the other hand, provides more differentiated views of the world. Together, these provide the initial emotional basis of the child's personality. By the second step (when children have the capacity to form nonverbal concepts), children begin to have a sense of the world and their place in it. Thus, a child who views the world as a dangerous place may also feel that he or she is worthy of the protection he or she demands and receives from his or her parents. We might view such a child as both cautious and content.

We want to stress that we do not consider infant temperament to be sufficient for accounting for adult personality traits. Rather, temperamental dispositions combine with the child's emotional experience to produce these traits. For example, the temperamental disposition of activity must combine with emotions such as positive affect and sociability to produce the adult trait of extraversion (see also Watson and Clark, this volume, chap. 29).

C. Step 3: Verbal Conceptions

The transition between these two steps occurs when the child develops some labels (either articulated or not) about his or her emotional states. This is thought to occur around 2 years of age (e.g., Bretherton & Beeghly, 1982). In addition to articulating felt emotions, 2-year-olds can pretend to be experiencing a state other than their own as illustrated in the following example (from Dunn, 1988, p. 21): ·

> C: Bibby on.
> M: You don't want your bibby on. You're not eating.
> C: Chocolate cake. Chocolate cake.
> M: You're not having any chocolate cake either.
> C: Why? (Whines) Tired.
> M: You're tired? Ooh!
> C: Chocolate cake.
> M: No chance.

D. Step 4: Dispositions

At this point (approximately 3 years of age), children use some underlying constructs to organize and evaluate information about themselves. Some of these constructs might reflect children's responses to the labels and/or reactions of others (e.g., parents). For example, children who are fearful and receive negative reactions might view themselves as babies or sissies. Children who were responded to more positively, on the other hand, might feel as self-righteous need for caution or care.

We speculate that as they acquire the ability to control their emotions (probably also at about 3 years; see Cole, 1985), children will begin to inhibit their expression of poorly received emotions. For example, children who receive disapproval for their fearful behavior might inhibit future expressions of fear. Children who generally receive negative reactions (e.g., abused and/or neglected children) might inhibit the expression of most emotions (see Camras et al., 1988), whereas others might only inhibit those that seemed especially offensive to their parents. These findings illustrate how the emotional basis of personality is also manifested in emotion expression (i.e., behavior).

Although children have the ability to label their emotions at this time, they do not have full metatheories of themselves. That is, that they can state that they get scared a lot (versus a little), hide from thunder and lightning (versus go look at it), and so forth. However, they are not able to state that they are high (or low) on fearfulness or Harm–Avoidance. Hence they employ an underlying construct to organize their feelings, but can articulate only specific feelings, not the construct itself. Furthermore, we believe that the construct they employ may actually be a view of the world (e.g., it is dangerous), and not a view of themselves per se. Alternatively, this view of self may be tied to their view of the world.

E. Step 5: Dispositional Conceptions

At approximately 7 or 8 years of age, children can articulate the constructs they use. They begin to describe themselves and others in terms of traits (e.g., honest) and use trait information to make judgments about past and future behavior (see Rholes & Ruble, 1984).

Stern (1985) suggests that children's construction of their experiences differs from the actual experiences. The implication is that the constructs evident during Step 5 are probably related to—but not isomorphic with—the earlier views held by the young child. For example, a child who scores high on constraint (and describes him/herself as "careful") may have felt as an infant (and still may actually feel) that the world is a dangerous place. Thus, the emotional basis of the self-concept is directly experienced but seldom directly stated.

It is probable that the emerging ability to articulate one's self-conception affects the way that the child construes new experiences. Epstein (1973) has suggested that an implication of having a self-theory is that one engages in theory confirmation. For example, once children conceive of themselves as "generous" they begin to remember specific examples of their generosity and tend to overlook cases in which they behaved ungenerously.

Some adult-like dimensions seem to be present in 7-year-olds. The dimensions of Emotional Stability and Extraversion have been revealed in children's responses by 7 years of age (Eder, 1990). The degree of continuity between these early emerging traits and similar adult structures must still be established. Nonetheless, it appears that personality development is at least partially completed by 7 years of age—as Freud originally concluded.

VI. CONCLUSION

Whereas previous accounts of early personality development typically stress those aspects of the child that are noticed by other persons, we were interested in understanding children's own phenomenological experience. Hence, we explored the emergence of dispositional self-conceptions in infancy and early childhood. Based on previous theoretical and empirical work, we suggested that these conceptions unfold from (1) organized patterns of behavior, (2) to nonverbal conceptions of emotional states, (3) to verbal conceptions of emotional states, (4) to verbal conceptions of dispositions, (5) to a metatheory of self similar to what is held by older children and adults. An appreciation of developmental changes in the structure of infants' and young children's self-concepts is informative of what children of a particular developmental period have *in common*. However, a full account of early personality development also requires an understanding of how the self-conceptions of same-aged children *differ* from child to child. We proposed that individual differences in the self-concept reflect differences in underlying emotionality and emerge as a result of a complex interaction of variables such as parental personality, parents' perceptions of the child, children's own behavior and/or temperament, and the infant–caregiver attachment relationship. We suspect that the emotionality inherent in one's self-concept provides a common core between early self-conceptions and those held later in life. Focusing on the emotional basis of personality should allow for a better correspondence between research on child and adult personality, eventually leading to a better understanding of the course of personality development. If this proves to be the case, then it will eventually be possible to predict the course of individual self-conceptions across the life span.

ACKNOWLEDGMENTS

We thank Lila Braine, Susan Crockenberg, Alan Elms, Bob Emmons, Eva Schepeler, and David Watson for their insightful comments on earlier versions of this paper. Nancy Kohn's help with references is also appreciated.

REFERENCES

Ainsworth, M. D. S. (1973). The development of infant–mother attachment. In B. M. Caldwell & H. N. Ricciuti (Eds.), *Review of child development research* (Vol. 3, pp. 1–94). Chicago: University of Chicago Press.

Ainsworth, M. D. S. (1983). Patterns of infant-mother attachment as related to maternal care. In D. Magnusson & V. Allen (Eds.), *Human development: An interactional perspective,* (pp. 35–55). New York: Academic Press.

Ainsworth, M. D. S., Blehar, M., Waters, E., & Wall, S. (1978). *Patterns of attachment: A psychological study of the strange situation.* Hillsdale, NJ: Erlbaum.

American Psychiatric Association. (1980). *Diagnostic and statistical manual of mental disorders* (3rd ed.). Washington, DC: Author.

Arend, R., Gove, F., & Sroufe, L. A. (1979). Continuity of individual adaptation from infancy to kindergarten: A predictive study of ego-resiliency and curiosity in preschoolers. *Child Development, 50,* 950–959.

Bannister, D., & Agnew, J. (1976). The child's construing of self. In J. Cole (Ed.), *Nebraska Symposium on Motivation* (pp. 100–125). Lincoln: University of Nebraska Press.

Bates, J. E. (1987). Temperament in infancy. In J. D. Osofsky (Ed.), *Handbook of infant development* (pp. 1101–1149). New York: Wiley.

Bates, J. E., & Bayles, K. (1984). Objective and subjective components in mothers' perception of their children from age 6 months to 3 years. *Merrill-Palmer Quarterly, 30*(2), 111–130.

Belsky, J., & Isabella, R. (1988). Maternal, infant, and social-contextual determinants of attachment security. In J. Belsky & T. Nezworski (Eds.), *Clinical implications of attachment,* (pp. 41–94). Hillsdale, NJ: Erlbaum.

Belsky, J., Rovine, M., & Taylor, D. (1984). The origins of individual differences in infant-mother attachment: Maternal and infant contributions. *Child Development, 55,* 718–728.

Block, J. (1989). Critique of the act frequency approach to personality. *Journal of Personality and Social Psychology, 56,* 234–245.

Block, J. H., & Block, J. (1980). The role of ego-control and ego-resiliency in the organization of behavior. In W. A. Collins (Ed.), *Minnesota Symposia on Child Psychology* (Vol. 13, pp. 39–101). Hillsdale, NJ: Erlbaum.

Bowlby, J. (1973). *Attachment and loss: Vol. 2 Separation.* New York: Basic Books.

Bowlby, J. (1980). *Attachment and loss: Vol. 3. Loss, sadness and depression.* New York: Basic Books.

Bowlby, J. (1982). *Attachment and loss: Vol. 1. Attachment* (2nd ed.). New York: Basic Books. (Original work published 1969).

Bretherton, I. (1991). Pouring new wine into old bottles: The social self as internal working model. In M. Gunnar & L. A. Sroufe (Eds.), *Minnesota Symposium of Child Psychology* (Vol. 23, pp. 1–41). Hillsdale, NJ: Erlbaum.

Bretherton, I., & Beeghly, M. (1982). Talking about internal states: The acquisition of an explicit theory of mind. *Development Psychology, 18,* 906–921.

Bretherton, I., Fritz, J., Zahn-Waxler, C., & Ridgeway, D. (1986). Learning to talk about emotions: A functionalist perspective. *Child Development, 55,* 529–548.

Buck, R. (1977). Nonverbal communication of affect in preschool children: Relationships with personality and skin conductance. *Journal of Personality and Social Psychology, 35,* 225–236.

Buss, A. H., & Plomin, R. (1984). *Temperament: Early developing personality traits.* Hillsdale, NJ: Erlbaum.

Campos, J. J., Barrett, K. C., Lamb, M. E., Goldsmith, H. H., & Stenberg, C. (1983). Socioemotional development. In P. H. Mussen (Series Ed.) & M. H. Haith & J. J. Campos (Vol. Eds.), *Handbook of child psychology: Vol. 2. Infancy and developmental psychobiology* (pp. 783–915) New York: Wiley.

Camras, L. A., Ribordy, S., Hill, J., Martino, S., Spaccarelli, S., & Stefani, R. (1988). Recognition and posing of emotional expressions by abused children and their mothers. *Developmental Psychology, 24,* 776–781.

Cassidy, J. (1988). Child-mother attachment and the self in six-year-olds. *Child Development, 59,* 121–134.

Chaplin, W. F., John, O. P., & Goldberg, L. R. (1988). Conceptions of states and traits: Dimensional attributes with ideals as prototypes. *Journal of Personality and Social Psychology, 54,* 541–557.

Cole, P. M. (1985). Display rules and the socialization of affective displays. In G. Zivin (Ed.), *The development of expressive behavior: Biology-environment interactions* (pp. 269–290). Orlando, FL: Academic Press.

Crittenden, P. M. (1985). Maltreated infants: Vulnerability and resilience. *Journal of Child Psychology and Psychiatry, 26,* 85–96.

Crockenberg, S. B. (1981). Infant irritability, mother responsiveness, and social support influences on the security of infant-mother attachment. *Child Development, 52,* 857–865.

Daniels, D., Plomin, R., & Greenhalgh, J. (1984). Correlates of difficult temperament in infants. *Child Development, 55,* 1184–1194.

Dunn, J. (1988). *The beginnings of social understanding.* Oxford, England: Basil Blackwell.

Dunn, J., Bretherton, I., & Munn, P. (1987). Conversations about feeling states between mothers and their young children. *Developmental Psychology, 23,* 132–139.

Eder, R. A. (1988). The self conceived in memory. *Early Child Development and Care, 40,* 25–51.

Eder, R. A. (1989). The emergent personologist: The structure and content of $3\frac{1}{2}$-, $5\frac{1}{2}$-, and $7\frac{1}{2}$-year-olds' concepts of themselves and other persons. *Child Development, 60,* 1218–1228.

Eder, R. A. (1990). Uncovering children's psychological selves: Individual and developmental differences. *Child Development, 61,* 849–863.

Eder, R. A., Gerlach, S. G., & Perlmutter, M. (1987). In search of children's selves: Development of the specific and general components of the self-concept. *Child Development, 58,* 1044–1050.

Eder, R. A., & Jones, M. (1989, April). *The early emergence of self-monitoring: Individual differences in the recognition and production of emotional expressions.* Paper presented at the biennial meeting of the Society for Research in Child Development, Kansas City, MO.

Eder, R. A., & Mahmood, N. (1989, July). *Mothers' self-perceptions, mothers' pereceptions of their children, children's self-perceptions.* Paper presented at the biennial meeting of the International Society for the Study of Behavioral Development, Jyvaskyla, Finland.

Egeland, B., & Farber, E. (1984). Infant-mother attachment: Factors related to its development over time. *Child Development, 55,* 753–771.

Egeland, B., & Sroufe, L. A. (1981). Attachment and early maltreatment. *Child Development, 52,* 44–52.

Ekman, P., & Friesen, W. (1975). *Unmasking the face.* Englewood Cliffs, NJ: Prentice Hall.

Emde, R. N. (1983). The prerepresentational self and its affective core. *Psychoanalytic Study of the Child, 38,* 165–192.

Emde, R. N., Kligman, D., Reich, J., & Wade, T. (1978). Emotional expressions in infancy: Initial studies of social signaling and an emergent model. In M. Lewis & L. Rosenblum (Eds.), *The development of affect* (pp. 125–148). New York: Plenum Press.

Epstein, S. (1973). The self-concept revisited. *American Psychologist, 28,* 404–416.

Field, T. M., & Walden, T. (1982). Perception and production of facial expressions in infancy and early childhood. In H. W. Reese & L. P. Lipsett (Eds.), *Advances in child development and behavior* (Vol. 16, pp. 169–211). New York: Academic Press.

Freud, S. (1950). Instincts and their vicissitudes. *Collected papers of Sigmund Freud.* London: Hogarth Press. (Original work published 1915)

Freud, S. (1955). Beyond the pleasure principle. *Collected papers of Sigmund Freud.* London: Hogarth Press. (Original work published 1920)

Gaensbauer, T. J., Harmon, R. J., Cytryn, L., & McKnew, D. H. (1984). Social and affective development in infants with a manic-depressive parent. *American Journal of Psychiatry, 141,* 223–229.

Goldsmith, H. H., Bradshaw, D., & Riesser-Danner, L. (1986). Temperament as a potential development influence on attachment. In J. V. Lerner & R. M. Lerner (Eds.), *Temperament and social interaction in infants and young children.* (New Directions in Child Development No. 31, pp. 5–34). San Francisco: Jossey-Bass.

Goldsmith, H. H., Buss, A. H., Plomin, R., Rothbart, M. K., Thomas, A., Chess, S., Hinde, R. A., & McCall, R. B. (1987). Roundtable: What is temperament? Four approaches. *Child Development, 58,* 505–529.

Goldsmith H. H., & Campos, J. J. (1986). Fundamental issues in the study of early temperament: The Denver twin temperament study. In M. E. Lamb, A. L. Brown, & B. Rogoff (Eds.), *Advances in developmental psychology* (Vol. 4, pp. 231–283). Hillsdale, NJ: Erlbaum.

Goldsmith, H. H., Losoya, S. H., Bradshaw, D. L., & Campos, J. J. (1994). Genetics of personality: A twin study of the five factor model and parental-offspring analyses. In C. Halverson, R. Martin, & G. Kohnstamm (Eds.). *The developing structure of temperament and personality from infancy to adulthood,* (pp. 241–265). Hillsdale, NJ: Erlbaum.

Gunnar, M. R., Mangelsdorf, S., Larson, M., & Hertsgaard, L. (1989). Attachment, temperament, and adrenocortical, activity in infancy: A study of psychoendocrine regulation. *Developmental Psychology, 25,* 355–363.

Hart, D., & Damon, W. (1986). Developmental trends in self-understanding. *Social Cognition, 4,* 388–407.

Harter, S. (1982). The perceived competence scale for children. *Child Development, 53,* 87–97.

Harter, S. (1983). Developmental perspectives on the self-system. In P. H. Mussen (Series Ed.), & E. M. Hetherington (Vol. Ed.), *Handbook of child psychology: Vol. 4. Socialization, personality, social development* (pp. 275–385). New York: Wiley.

Hudson, J. A. (1986). Memories are made of this: General event knowledge and the development of autobiographical memory. In K. Nelson (Ed.), *Event knowledge: Structure and function in development* (pp. 97–118). Hillsdale, NJ: Erlbaum.

Isabella, R. (1993). Origins of attachment: Maternal interactive behavior across the first year. *Child Development, 64,* 605–621.

Isabella, R., & Belsky, J. (1991). International synchrony and the origins of infant-mother attachment: A replication study. *Child Development, 62,* 373–384.

Izard, C. E. (1977). *Human emotion.* New York: Basic Books.

Izard, C. E., Hembree, E. A., & Huebner, R. R. (1987). Infants' emotion expressions to acute pain: Developmental change and stability of individual differences. *Developmental Psychology, 23,* 105–113.

Izard, C. E., & Malatesta, C. Z. (1987). Perspectives on emotional development I: Differential emotions theory of early emotional development. In J. Osofsky (Ed.), *Handbook of infant development* (2nd ed., pp. 494–554). New York: Wiley.

James, W. (1892). *The principles of psychology.* New York: Holt.

Kagan, J. (1982). *Psychological research on the human infant: An evaluative summary*. New York: W. T. Grant Foundation.

Kagan, J. (1984). *The nature of the child*. New York: Basic Books.

Kagan, J., Resnick, J. S., & Snidman, N. (1988). Biological basis of childhood shyness. *Science, 240*, 167–171.

Keller, A., Ford, L. M., & Meacham, J. A. (1978). Dimensions of self-concept in preschool children. *Developmental Psychology, 14*, 483–489.

Kuczaj, S. A., II. (1986). Thoughts on the intentional basis of early object word extension: Evidence from comprehension and production. In S. A. Kuczaj, II & M. D. Barrett (Eds.), *The development of word meaning: Progress in cognitive development research* (pp. 99–120). New York: Springer-Verlag.

Kuczaj, S. A., II, & Maratsos, M. P. (1975). What children *can* say before they *will*. *Merrill-Palmer Quarterly, 21*, 89–111.

Lamb, M. E., Thompson, R. A., Gardner, W., & Charnov, E. L. (1985). *Infant-mother attachment*. Hillsdale, NJ: Erlbaum.

Lazarus, R. S. (1975). The self-regulation of emotion. In L. Levi (Ed.), *Emotions—Their parameters and measurements* (pp. 47–67). New York: Raven Press.

Lewis, M. (1987). Social development in infancy and early childhood. In J. Osofsky (Ed.), *Handbook of infant development* (pp. 419–493). New York: Wiley.

Lyons-Ruth, K., Connell, D., Grunembaum, H., Botein, S., & Zoll, D. (1984). Maternal family history, maternal caretaking, and infant attachment in multiproblem families. *Preventive Psychiatry, 2*, 403–425.

Mahler, M. (1967). On human symbiosis and the vicissitudes of individuation. *Journal of the American Psychoanalytic Association, 15*, 740–763.

Mahler, M., Pine, F., & Bergman, A. (1975). *The psychological birth of the infant*. New York: Basic Books.

Malatesta, C. Z., & Wilson, A. (1988). Emotion cognition interaction in personality development: A decrete emotions functionalist analysis. *British Journal of Social Psychology, 27*, 91–112.

Mangelsdorf, S., Gunnar, M., Kestenbaum, R., Lang, S., & Andreas, D. (1990). Infant proneness-to-distress temperament, maternal personality, and mother-infant attachment: Associations and goodness of fit. *Child Development, 61*, 820–831.

Mangelsdorf, S., Plunkett, J., Dedrick, C., Berlin, M., Meisels, S., & McHale, J. (1996). Attachment security in extremely-low-birth weight infants. *Developmental Psychology, 32*, 914–920.

Markman, E. M., & Callanan, M. A. (1984). An analysis of hierarchical classification. In R. J. Sternberg (Ed.), *Advances in the psychology of human intelligence* (pp. 325–365). Hillsdale, NJ: Erlbaum.

Markus, H., & Sentis, K. (1982). The self in social information processing. In J. Suls (Ed.), *Psychological perspectives on the self* (Vol. 1, pp. 41–70). Hillsdale, NJ: Erlbaum.

Matheny, A. P., & Wilson, R. S. (1981). Development tasks and rating scales for laboratory assessment of infant temperament. *JSAS Catalog of Selected Documents in Psychology, 11*(MS. No. 2367).

McCrae, R. R., & Costa, P. T., Jr. (1985). Updating Norman's "adequate taxonomy": Intelligence and personality dimensions in natural language and in questionnaires. *Journal of Personality and Social Psychology, 49*, 710–721.

McCrae, R. R., & Costa, P. T., Jr. (1987). Validation of a five-factor model of personality across instruments and observers. *Journal of Personality and Social Psychology, 52*, 81–90.

Miller, P. H., & Aloise, P. A. (1989). Young children's understanding of the psychological causes of behavior: A review. *Child Development, 60,* 257–285.

Mischel, W., Shoda, Y., & Rodriguez, M. L. (1989). Delay of gratification in children. *Science, 244,* 933–937.

Piaget, J. (1952). *The origins of intelligence in children.* New York: Rutledge & Kegan Paul.

Radke-Yarrow, M., Cummings, E. M., Kuczynsky, L., & Chapman, M. (1985). Patterns of attachment in two- and three-year-olds in normal families and families with parental depression. *Child Development, 56,* 884–893.

Rholes, W. S., & Ruble, D. N. (1984). Children's understanding of dispositional characteristics of others. *Child Development, 55,* 550–560.

Ridgeway, D., Waters, E., & Kuczaj, S. A., II. (1985). Acquisition of emotion-descriptive language: Receptive and productive vocabulary norms for ages 18 months to 6 years. *Developmental Psychology, 21,* 901–908.

Rovee-Collier, C. (1987). Learning and memory in infancy. In J. Osofsky (Ed.), *Handbook of infant development* (pp. 98–148). New York: Wiley.

Ruble, D. N., & Rholes, W. S. (1981). The development of children's perceptions and attributions about their social world. In J. H. Harvey, W. Ickes, & R. F. Kidd (Eds.), *New directions in attribution research* (Vol. 3, pp. 3–36). Hillsdale, NJ: Erlbaum.

Schachtel, E. G. (1947). On memory and childhood amnesia. *Psychiatry, 10,* 1–26.

Schneider-Rosen, K., Braunwald, K. G., Carlson, V., & Cicchetti, D. (1985). Current perspectives in attachment theory: Illustration from the study of maltreated infants. *Monographs of the Society for Research in Child Development, 50,* 194–210.

Shantz, C. V. (1983). Social cognition. In P. H. Mussen (Series Ed.) & J. H. Flavell & E. M. Markman (Vol. Eds.), *Handbook of child psychology: Vol. 3. Cognitive development* (pp. 495–555). New York: Wiley.

Snyder, M. (1974). The self-monitoring of expression behavior. *Journal of Personality and Social Psychology, 30,* 526–537.

Sroufe, L. A. (1979). Socioemotional development. In J. Osofsky (Ed.), *Handbook of infant development* (pp. 462–516). New York: Wiley.

Sroufe, L. A. (1990). An organizational perspective on the self. In D. Cicchetti & M. Beeghly (Eds.), *The self in transition: Infancy to childhood,* (pp. 281–307). Chicago: University of Chicago Press.

Sroufe, L. A., & Waters, E. (1977). Attachment as an organizational construct. *Child Development, 48,* 1184–1199.

Stern, D. N. (1985). *The interpersonal world of the infant: A view from psychoanalysis and developmental psychology.* New York: Basic Books.

Sullivan, H. S. (1953). *The interpersonal theory of psychiatry.* New York: Norton.

Tellegen, A. (1985). Structures of mood and personality and their relevance to assessing anxiety, with an emphasis on self-report. In A. H. Tuma & J. D. Maser (Eds.), *Anxiety and the anxiety disorders* (pp. 681–706). Hillsdale, NJ: Erlbaum.

Tellegen, A. (1982). *Manual for the Multidimensional Personality Questionnaire.* Unpublished manuscript. University of Minnesota.

Thomas, A., & Chess, S. (1977). *Temperament and development.* New York: Brunner/Mazel.

van den Boom, D. C. (1989). Neonatal irritability and the development of attachment. In G. A. Kohnstamm, J. E. Bates, & M. K. Rothbart (Eds.), *Temperament in childhood* (pp. 299–318). Chichester, England: Wiley.

Vaughn, B. E., Bradley, C. F., Joffe, L. S., Seifer, R., & Barglow, P. (1987). Maternal characteristics measured prenatally are predictive of ratings of temperamental "difficulty" on the Carey Infant Temperament Questionnaire. *Developmental Psychology, 23,* 152–161.

Vaughn, B. E., Lefever, G. B., Seifer, R., & Barglow, P. (1989). Attachment behavior, attachment security, and temperament during infancy. *Child Development, 60,* 728–737.

Waters, E. (1995). The attachment Q-set. In E. Waters, B. E. Vaughn, G., Posada, & K. Kondo-Ikemura. Caregiving, cultural, and cognitive perspectives on secure-base behavior and working models: New growing points of attachment research. *Monographs of the Society for Research in Child Development, 60*(2–3), 234–246.

Waters, E., & Deane, D. (1982). Infant-mother attachment: Theories, models, recent data, and some tasks for comparative developmental analysis. In L. W. Hoffman, R. A. Gandelman, & H. R. Schifman (Eds.), *Parenting: Its causes and consequences* (pp. 19–54). Hillsdale, NJ: Erlbaum.

Waters, E., & Deane, K. E. (1985). Defining and assessing individual differences in attachment relationships: Q-methodology and the organization of behavior in infancy and early childhood. *Monographs of the Society for Research in Child Development, 50,* 41–65.

Watson, D., & Clark, L. A. (1984). Negative affectivity: The disposition to experience aversive emotional states. *Psychological Bulletin, 96,* 465–490.

Weber, R. A., Levitt, M. J., & Clark, M. C. (1986). Individual variation in attachment security and strange situation behavior: The role of maternal and infant temperament. *Child Development, 57,* 56–65.

Wellman, H. M., & Gelman, S. A. (1987). Children's understanding of the nonobvious. In R. J. Sternberg (Ed.), *Advances in the psychology of human intelligence* (Vol. 4, pp. 99–135). Hillsdale, NJ: Erlbaum.

CHAPTER 10

FAMILY INFLUENCES ON PERSONALITY DEVELOPMENT

CHARLES F. HALVERSON, JR.
UNIVERSITY OF GEORGIA

KAREN S. WAMPLER
TEXAS TECH UNIVERSITY

I. INTRODUCTION

This essay is mostly about missing data. As we began the review of the voluminous literature on parent–child relationships and their effects on personality development, it became apparent to us that there is yet another emerging crisis in the study of personality. In the past decade, there has been an increasing awareness that the data on personality development in the family context are seriously incomplete and problematic. This state of affairs exists because nearly all studies of the influence of the family on personality development have used a model that assumed that the influences of family characteristics could adequately be assessed by using mostly one-time assessments of some aspect of the family that focused on one parent— usually the mother—and one child in each family.

And indeed, over the past 75 or 80 years we have amassed an enormous data base documenting how parents' child-rearing styles influence the child. Certainly the main-effect, single-child, single-parent models assessed in many studies have shown relations between parenting styles and children's temperament and personality. Beginning with the early studies (e.g., Baldwin, Kalhorn, & Breese, 1949; Baumrind, 1967, 1971, 1983; Kagan & Moss, 1962; Sears, Maccoby, & Levin, 1957; Sears,

Rau, & Alpert, 1965; Yarrow, Campbell, & Burton, 1968), we have indications of family influences on children.

For example, Baldwin's analyses of the Fels Study showed democratic parenting to be associated with assertiveness, vigor, high activity level, and sociability. In contrast, controlling parenting was associated with obedience, fearfulness, and withdrawal (Baldwin, 1949). Baumrind's classic study (e.g., 1967) found that authoritarian, controlling parents had children who were dependent and not particularly sociable. In contrast, authoritative parents (rational, loving, firm parents) had independent and socially competent children.

Countless studies have subsequently replicated in one form or another these general main-effect findings. Parenting has been studied in terms of control, warmth, involvement, and various combinations of the three. Consistent, high levels of parental control have been associated with children who are not aggressive and generally well controlled (J. H. Block & Block, 1979; Patterson & Bank, 1989), and who show high levels of sociability and initiative. Low levels of control (permissiveness) have been associated with the opposite poles of the above dimensions (e.g., aggression, impulsivity, high activity level; see Maccoby & Martin, 1983; B. Martin, 1987; Rollins & Thomas, 1979, for excellent summaries of this traditional literature). Similarly, warmth and affection in families—particularly mothers—are associated with attachment security, compliance, altruism, and a range of prosocial behaviors indicative of competence, including agreeableness and self-esteem (see, for example, Ainsworth, Blehar, Waters, & Wall, 1978; Bretherton, 1985; Graziano & Eisenberg, this volume, chap. 30; Radke-Yarrow & Zahn-Waxler, 1984, 1986).

II. THREE CRISES FOR PERSONALITY DEVELOPMENT RESEARCH

A. Direction of Effects

The *first* real crisis that influenced the socialization literature could be called the bidirectional watershed. In 1968 R. Q. Bell published his now classic review of the literature demonstrating the plausibility of child effects on parents. Since that time, it has become nearly pro forma to refer to correlational data obtained in socialization studies as supporting interpretations of either child effects on parents or vice versa (see R. Q. Bell & Harper, 1977; Harper, 1989). The crisis was that it was no longer clear who might be responsible for children's personality development. Maybe, just maybe, parent–child correlations reflected the action of constitutional characteristics of the child on parenting and not the other way around.

B. Transactional Models

The *second* crisis that further complicated the picture of the family influence on personality development was the elaboration of the transactional model of development (A. Sameroff & Chandler, 1975). In Sameroff's original formulation of the model, the child and the caretaking environment were conceptualized as always in a state of mutual feedback; infant characteristics modified parental practices, which in turn modified infant behavior that then further modified parental behavior. From this point of view, the partners in an intimate relationship over time could never be characterized without examining the reciprocal causality of one or the other over time. Investigators need to examine the shifting covariances between adults and offspring over time, paying close attention to the mechanisms underlying such covariance (see Wachs, 1992, especially chapters 7 and 8, for an excellent discussion of these issues). Since the original formulation, there has been a veritable flood of theoretical and empirical articles from this transactional perspective (see, for example, Belsky, 1981, 1984; Belsky, Rovine, & Fish, 1989; Lerner, 1989; Lerner & Spanier, 1978; R. P. Martin, 1983, A. J. Sameroff & Seifer, 1983; Wachs, 1983; Werner, Bierman, & French, 1971; Werner & Smith, 1977, 1982). These theorists propose that neither the family context, nor the child, nor the physical environment can be viewed as the sole significant determinant of any specific adaptive outcome.

A. Sameroff and Chandler (1975) elegantly pointed out that when development is considered prospectively rather than retrospectively, there is a considerable lessening of the main effect of children *or* parents on development. In fact it is not possible to trace many simple main-effect characteristics that reside either in the organism or in the child-rearing environment (usually thought of as the parents).

These authors proposed a *continuum of caretaking causality.* At one end, the parental environment is sufficient to compensate for almost any developmental deviation so that it would not result in later behavioral or intellectual difficulties. On the other end of the continuum, the parenting environment lacks the resources to deal with even minor deviations from that which is normal in the child, thus providing an environment that serves to maintain maladaptive behavior over time. The authors identified three socialization models: (a) *the single-factor model* that focuses on either constitutional or environmental determinants of development (e.g., the main-effects model, either parents or children), (b) the *interactional model,* where child factors combine additively with parental characteristics so that child characteristics would be augmented or reduced by better or worse parenting environments, and (c) *the transactional model* in which development is proposed to result from the continual interplay between a changing organism and a changing family environment. Not only is it no longer clear who affects whom, but it is also not clear whether stability or change resides in organisms, environments, or some complex interplay between the two.

C. Within-Family Effects

The *third* crisis in socialization research on personality development is of relatively recent origin and is, in our opinion, the most far-reaching in its implications. Nearly all of the studies of family and parental influences on the personality of the child are based on only one child per family. Whether they focus on the mother (as most have), on the father (a recent innovation), or on the family as a unit (an even more recent innovation), the relationship is typically described for only one child per family. There has been almost no consideration of sibling and parent similarities and differences in terms of personalities and relationships *within* the same families. It is important to remember that we have long made generalizations about the effects of children and parents on each other (generic children and parents at that), as if these relations hold *within* families when data have been derived from *between*-family analyses. For example, the oft-found relation of parental punitiveness and child aggression is interpreted as holding for parent–child relations in general, a main effect as it were, for all children in families; if one had a punitive, authoritarian parent, the outcome was likely to be aggressive children (presumably *all* the children in the family!).

About 10 years ago, the developmental behavior genetics researchers began to question the logic of this argument based on their research with twins and adoptees (Plomin, DeFries, & Loehlin, 1977; Scarr & McCartney, 1983; Scarr, Webber, Weinberg, & Wittig, 1981). In an early study of twin data (Loehlin & Nichols, 1976), the startling conclusion was that there appeared to be no common family variance that led to sibling similarity in personality. From the data investigators concluded that about 50% of the variance in child personality was genetic; the rest due to apparently "nonshared" environmental variance. In a scholarly review of the existing data on twins, adoptees, and siblings, Plomin and Daniels (1987) concluded that children in the same family do not resemble each other very much in personality development. In contrast, identical twins, even those raised apart, were similar and had similar developmental spurts and lags (see Matheney, 1989).[1]

It is this "discovery" that environmental factors are experienced differently by siblings growing up in the same families that is one of the major findings in the behavior genetic research. Siblings resemble each other to a degree, presumably because of shared DNA, not shared experiences. The behavior geneticists designate this category of environmental influence as "E_1", "specific," or, more generally, "nonshared." This index of "nonshared" environment comes from data that compare sibling differences in personality to similarities, particularly in studies of MZ twins raised together and apart when compared to siblings raised in biological and adoptive families. The first notice of the nonshared environment came from Loehlin and Nichols' classic study of personality in high school twins (1976). They concluded that environment was important for determining personality—about half the variance—but it was environment where twin pairs were *not* correlated. Environmental effects, instead of being uniform within the family, were random and not predictable (see also Dunn & Plomin, 1991; Rowe, 1990). If there are main effects of parenting and family variables on personality development (as documented in the large literature on parental control, love, protectiveness, sensitivity, etc.), then why don't children in the same family resemble each other more than they do? Plomin and

---

[1] But see McCartney, Harris, and Bernieri (1990) who show some adult diminution of identical twin similarities over age in those twinships raised apart compared to those raised in close contact.

Daniels (1987) also summarized data from four recent adoption studies that show that the average adoptive parent–child personality correlations average about .05. The sibling correlations in such families are for the most part below .20 on personality measures (see also Scarr et al., 1981). Although it is obvious that at *some* level, siblings share the same family environment, it is also obvious that important characteristics of that environment are largely nonshared for personality development.

A corollary to the "nonshared" issue must be noted here as it also has profound effects on traditional socialization research. In addition to discovering the importance of environment in child measures, the behavior geneticists have recently documented the importance of genetically mediated effects on most of our traditional measures of "environment" (see Loehlin, 1992; Plomin & Bergeman, 1991, for extended discussions). A number of studies have shown that our environmental measures are themselves in part measures with a genetic influence. If our measures are really proxies for individual differences in parents, raters, and others who populate family environments, then genetic architecture can passively create correlations between our predictor measures of family characteristics and our outcome measures of child behavior. There may be some cause for pessimism here. Studies of biological parents and their offspring may also be confounded even at the level of supposedly "independent", "environmental" assessments. Taken along with the devastating critiques of self-report measures as valid indicators of both parenting techniques and family functioning (Holden & Edwards, 1989; Wampler & Halverson, 1993), the issue of genetic confounding of our measures must be carefully examined in future research on family predictors of personality development.

We asserted at the beginning of this chapter that this essay was mostly about missing data. Given the perspectives of child effects, transactionism, and low within-family concordances on personality dimensions, most of the literature appears to be only weakly applicable to discovering what it is in families that may contribute to personality development.[2] In fact, most of the relations obtained in the socialization literature on parental impact on child functioning may have really been mostly documenting the *child* main effects on parents.

A study not often cited in the socialization literature—but should be cited as one of the paradigmatic studies in socialization—is a model socialization experiment done by Freedman (1958). Freedman was influenced by the work of Scott and Fuller (1965) who showed that there were considerable temperamental differences among four purebred breeds of dogs, beagles, basenjis, wire-haired fox terriers, and Shetland sheep dogs. As every owner of dogs know, dogs come in a remarkably wide range of temperamental propensities. Freedman examined the interaction between "inborn" temperamental characteristics and a classic parenting environment: whether the "parent" was strict or permissive.

---

[2] A recent article has offered some interesting speculations on which parent–child systems may be most susceptible to stability, change, and mutual influence (Cairns et al., 1990).

Dogs from each breed were socialized daily from the 3rd week of life through the 8th week. Dogs from each breed were assigned to either a permissive–indulged or strict rearing regimen. The permissive–indulged regimen was one where the dogs were never punished, and there was much encouragement of play and aggression via rough and tumble interactions with the human "parent." In the strict regimen, there was much emphasis on teaching to sit, stay, come, and so on (basically, the classic obedience training characterized by many dog schools).

After 5 weeks of this regimen, a classic resistance-to-temptation paradigm was employed to test the effects of the parenting regimen. The dogs were all hungry and were all placed in front of a bowl of meat, and for 3 min the caretaker prevented the animal from eating by swatting the rump of the dog with a rolled newspaper and shouting "No!" every time the dog approached the food. The handler then left the room and the experimenter recorded the elapsed time before the dog ate the meat. This test situation was repeated for 8 days. What is so elegant about this model is that it examined breed (temperament) by rearing strategy interactions for an important developmental outcome—the ability to resist temptation. Obviously, dogs who were not able to inhibit their impulse to eat in such a test would immediately eat the food. If parenting had a main effect, then the disciplined dogs would not eat, whereas the indulged dogs would. If there were no important breed differences, then we could attribute any systematic differences to the rearing environment. The results were indeed curious. The Shetland sheep dogs never ate the food under either regimen. In contrast, all the basenjis ate the food right away—it did not matter whether they were raised in a permissive or a strict environment.

There was an interaction between breed and the rearing environment for terriers and beagles: it was, however, the reverse from what we would predict from human parenting theory. The indulged terriers and beagles took much longer to eat the food than the disciplined terriers and beagles. The importance of this study is that it underscores a fairly obvious point: If the researchers had studied only terriers and beagles they would have found that the socialization environment interactively determined self-control (even if backward from theory). If, however, they had studied Shetlands or basenjis, they would have determined that socialization was ineffective.[3]

D. Metaphors from Biology

This study serves to illustrate two metaphors that are useful when discussing human socialization studies, *reaction range* and *canalization,* both concepts introduced by

---

[3] Crawford and Anderson (1989) provide further examples from animal research. They propose that the behavior genetic models emphasizing heritability coefficients may miss many gene-by-environment interactions that operate at the "breed" level and hence have zero heritabilities. For example, Sackett, Ruppenthal, Farenbruch, Holm, and Greenough (1981) found that rearing different breeds of monkeys in social isolation had differential effects by breed, with some breeds being relatively unaffected (see also Hinde & Stevenson-Hinde, 1973, for more examples).

Waddington (1957, 1962). Although neither of these concepts can be measured directly in human socialization studies, they serve to point to important possibilities in the research literature. The first of these, *reaction range,* refers to the fact that heredity is not rigidly related in any way to behavior, but instead establishes a range of possible responses to different environments. In the dog example, the socialization environments provided were within the reaction range for terriers and beagles, but were ineffective with the other two breeds. Closely related is the concept of *canalization,* which refers to the fact that some genotypes will be more difficult to deflect from a maturational pattern of growth than others. Some individuals are difficult to deflect from a pattern while others are relatively easy. Within individuals some traits are relatively easy to deflect while others will turn out to be relatively difficult (see Cairns, Gariepy, & Hood, 1990, for a different view).

E. Studies from the Parent–Child Domain

For the parent–child area, we use an example from our own research (Halverson & Martin, 1981). One way to begin to assess the relative contributions of the parent and the child to the developing relationship is by having data on parents *before* and *after* they have children and data on infants before the possible effects of socialization have had much cumulative impact (see also Belsky et al., 1989; Cowan, Cowan, Heming, & Miller, 1991). We need to replace retrospective socialization accounts with actual event sequences over time (see as an example Jack Block's excellent study of the stability and change in personality from childhood to adulthood; J. Block, 1971).

For this analysis we used data from the Bethesda Longitudinal Study (see, for example, Jacobs & Moss, 1976; Yang, Zweig, Douthitt, & Federman, 1976). The sample included only those mothers and children with complete data at five points in time—newlywed, pregnancy (3rd trimester), birth, postpartum (3 months), and preschool (3 years). The analysis involved all five time periods and included 28 boys, 28 girls, and their mothers. To study reciprocal parent–infant influences, we devised a measure of maternal competence for the five time periods based on seven adjectives in a cluster score: calm, confident, organized, and thrifty, and—negatively weighted—dependent, selfish, and temperamental.

We divided the mothers into stable and unstable groups, and we used an iterative procedure that maximized the correlations between periods for one group while minimizing the correlations between periods for the other. All correlations in the unstable group were nonsignificant and differed statistically ($ps<.001$) from the stable group's significant coefficients (average $r = .62$).

Data on the children were derived factor analytically at each period. Specifically, the behavioral measures indicating high-magnitude behavior at each period were subjected to separate principle components factor analyses, and the first principle component in each of these three analyses was chosen and represented an activity/irritability dimension at each period.

Our initial prediction was that mothers with stable attitudes (both high and low) would form stable relationships with their infants and, therefore, the infants would show stability of their behavior. The activity–irritability behavior in infants in terms of mothers with stable attitudes did not fulfill our expectations. Indeed, the correlations among the three periods were all essentially zero. In contrast, for mothers unstable in competency, we found that infants of these mothers were highly stable over time (average $r = .54$). Further, activity–irritability at 3 months predicted maternal adequacy when the child was 3 years old. As 3-month irritability increased, maternal competence at 3 years decreased ($r[28] = -.65, p < .001$). No comparable correlation was obtained for stable mothers and infants ($r[28] = .06$). In addition, the contemporaneous correlation between child and maternal scores at the 3-year period was highly significant ($r[28] = -.71, p < .001$), with increases in activity–irritability again associated with decreases in maternal competence. No comparable correlations were obtained between child data and maternal data for the stable group.

Considering the findings for both stable and unstable groups, there was a strong *infant* effect on mothers who were predisposed to having unstable feelings of competency. Infants who showed strong continuities over time had mothers who showed discontinuities over time. It appears possible that these infants' temperamental characteristics were influential in contributing to maternal instability in the area of competency as evidenced by the negative correlations between infant and maternal data over time. On the other hand, for stable mothers, it may have been their stability of competency that disposed them to be relatively immune to the influences of infant temperamental characteristics.

When we divided our stable and unstable samples into mothers who had boys or girls, we found that instability in mothers was primarily in the male sample. To explore this sex difference further, we analyzed the mean levels of maternal competency over the four periods as a function of having either a boy or a girl child. A maternal competence (stable, unstable) by sex of child (male, female) by stage (marriage, pregnancy, postpartum, 3-year) repeated measures analysis of variance revealed a significant three-way interaction among stability of maternal competence, sex, and stage.

Mothers who had unstable attitudes during pregnancy and *had a boy* showed significant declines in competency for both the postpartum and the 3-year periods. The other three groups were not significantly different from each other at any period. These data are consistent with our other findings in that it was the less-competent mothers with irritable and fussy males who found that child-rearing may have been as difficult as they expected. In contrast, if mothers entered into pregnancy or childbirth with stable feelings of competency, they were able to cope well with having an active/irritable male child. A most interesting finding was that those mothers who tended to have unstable feelings of competency but who had a female child may have discovered child-rearing was not so bad after all (since their scores did not decline over time).

Our results also show that when mothers are stable across the four time periods. infants show no stability of activity/irritability. In contrast, when mothers are unstable, high stability of infant functioning was obtained. We interpret these results as implicating a strong *parent effect on infants* when maternal behavior was stable. In contrast, a strong *child effect on mothers* was implied when mothers were unstable. Specifically, stable children seem to affect maternal instability whereas stable mothers seem to affect child instability.

The points to be emphasized are (a) that we must characterize both the child *and* the family environment as *differentially* canalized and susceptible to direction of effects, and (b) that the main direction of effect (from child to family or family to child) will depend on important characteristics of both parenting and child systems. Two others examples from our research emphasize this point further.

F. Congenital Contributors to Interactions

Clearly, there is a need to examine both child and family effects in any study. There is also a requirement to identify and measure child and family characteristics independently of each other in order to examine reciprocal effects. As we have seen earlier in this paper, this is very hard (impossible?) to accomplish when children and parents share genes that relate (confound) "environments" and outcomes. One solution is the twin and/or adoption study. Another would be to use biological families but look for a possible *early* environmental contributor to personality that would make children within families different from each other very early on. If we could locate a nongenetic but congenital contributor to individual differences, we could examine "how the twig is bent" within families of biologically related individuals, searching for both "child-driven" and "family driven" effects over time.

In our past research, we have investigated a congenital contributor to the expression of sociability and impulsivity as related to activity level (R. Q. Bell & Waldrop, 1982; Halverson & Victor, 1976; Halverson & Waldrop, 1973; Waldrop, Bell, & Goering, 1976; Waldrop, Bell, McLaughlin, & Halverson, 1978; Waldrop & Halverson, 1971; Waldrop, Pedersen, & Bell, 1968). These characteristics of impulsivity and sociability have often been part of the formulations of child temperament and personality (A. H. Buss, 1988; A. R. Buss & Plomin, 1975; 1984; Eysenck, 1970).

1. Child Minor Physical Anomalies

The congenital contributor to these behaviors is indexed by the number of minor physical anomalies present at birth. There are 18 anomalies that can be assessed at any age and consist of minor growth abnormalities of the head, hands, and feet. The 18 anomalies are best known for their occurrence in Down's Syndrome but individual anomalies are present in the general population with an average of 2 to 4 anomalies per person (range 0–18). These minor developmental deviations most likely result from either some form of genetic transmission or from some event occurring in embryogenesis that mimics genetic transmission (Quinn, Renfield,

Burg, & Rapoport, 1977; Rapoport, Quinn, & Lamprecht, 1974; Waldrop & Halverson, 1971). The speculation is that the anomalies are the sequelae of events occurring in the first trimester of pregnancy that also affect the physiology, structure, or biochemistry of the central nervous system that can later lead to problems of either under- or overcontrol. Stability from birth to 7 years is high ($r = .87$; Waldrop & Halverson, 1971).

The importance of the anomaly index in predicting impulsive, aggressive behavior in boys aged 2 to 12 years has been established in many studies (R. Q. Bell & Waldrop, 1982; Burg, Hart, Quinn, & Rapoport, 1978; Firestone, Peters, Riviere, & Knights, 1978; Halverson, 1989b; Halverson & Victor, 1976; Quinn et al., 1977; Rapoport et al., 1974; von Hilsheimer & Kurko, 1979; Waldrop et al., 1968, 1978; Waldrop & Halverson, 1971). Longitudinal data have indicated that the incidence of anomalies at birth predicts, at 3 years of age, the behavioral triad of impulsivity, short attention span, and high activity for males (Waldrop et al., 1978) and withdrawn and low activity behavior for girls (R. Q. Bell & Waldrop, 1982; Halverson, 1989a; Waldrop et al., 1976). All of this past research points to a strong main effect for the anomaly variable.

We have speculated that the anomalies arise from mild teratogenic agents in pregnancy (e.g., viruses, high blood pressure, stress) that tend to slow development at a time when there is the differential exposure to circulating androgens necessary for sex differentiation, with males being exposed to the male hormones and females lacking such exposure. We suspect that there must be interactions between pregnancy stress agents and male hormone in the first trimester which produces this dimorphic response as indexed later by high- and low-magnitude behaviors.

2. Study 1: Anomaly–Environment Interactions

The anomaly index was done at birth, at 3 months, and at 3 years of age in the Bethesda study. Anomalies of the head include circumference out of normal range, low-set or malformed ears, epicanthal folds, hyperteliorism, high steepled palate, and furrowed tongue. Anomalies of the hand include single transverse creases, short fifth finger, and clinodactyly of the fifth finger. Anomalies of the feet include wide spacing between first and second toes, partial syndactyly of the second and third toes, and third toe longer than second (see Halverson & Shetterley, 1989, for scoring details). For the present analysis we used the 3-year index because of missing data at the earlier periods, although it should be noted that for a subsample of 23 boys (Waldrop et al., 1978), the index was stable from birth to 3 years ($r = .86$) and had good interrater reliability ($r = .87$). Children were divided at the median based on the larger sample of 199 into high- and low-anomaly children (scores ranged from 0 to 14, *median* = 4.2). Since there was a sex difference in the anomaly score (boys had more), there were unequal subsets of high- and low-anomaly boys and girls.

Research participants were drawn from a larger longitudinal sample of 199 three-year-old children and their parents. In turn, the parents were a subsample of a larger cohort of parents who were participants in the Bethesda Longitudinal Study.

Data were collected at five points in time: 3 months of marriage, during the first pregnancy, at the birth of the child, 3 months postpartum, and when the child was 3 years of age. For the present analysis, we focus on 131 children (69 boys, 62 girls) with complete data at the marriage and preschool periods. As part of an extensive test battery at 3 months of marriage, each spouse responded to an extensive questionnaire on their marital relationship. Through cluster and factor analysis based on much larger samples of around 2,000 couples, one prominent factor emerged that described *couple complaints* (for example, see Ryder, Kafka, & Olson, 1971). Based on 45 items for each spouse, a factor score was computed for each couple. The factor score was reliable and cross-validated across several subsamples of the larger sample. The score summarized complaints that each spouse had in the area of recreation, affection, friends, sexual satisfaction, money, housekeeping, and communication. For the present analysis, couples were split at the median (based on the number of couples in the longitudinal sample, $N = 199$) into high-complaint couples or low-complaint couples at 3 months of marriage.

At 3 years of age, children attended a 4-week mixed-sex nursery school. Comprehensive assessments of their behavior were done by a team of three observers and a male and female teacher who observed and rated each child's behavior daily in three behavior settings—indoor free play, rest time, and outdoor free play.

Analysis focused on behaviors that were reliable as well as stable across time and setting. Data were summarized and condensed by factor analysis of 27 items including time-sampled observations of play and social behavior, ratings of child behavior by the teachers, and codings of behavior in experimental settings designed to assess problem-solving ability and competence. Two varimax rotated factors emerged from the analysis: impulsivity and sociability.

Data were cast into a 2 (complaints at early marriage—high, low) by 2 (males, females) × 2 (anomalies—high, low) design for each of the two dependent variables, impulsivity and sociability. Since Ns were small and unequal from cell to cell, data were analyzed with planned comparisons for each dependent variable.

For impulsivity, there was an additive effect of anomalies and marital complaints on the expression of impulsive behavior for males. High-anomaly males with high-complaint parents were significantly more impulsive than any of the other groups, whereas the low-anomaly boys with low-complaint parents were less impulsive than any of the other groups. When one factor was present, either anomalies or complaints, boys were moderately impulsive and not different from each other. There were significant main effects for both anomalies and complaints. For girls, the data indicate that neither anomalies nor complaints moderated the expression of impulsivity (or better, the lack of expression of impulsivity). Girls were uniformly low and differed significantly from all boys except those who were low on both anomalies and complaints.

For *sociability,* the effect of newlywed complaints on 3-year-old children's sociability was moderated by whether children were high or low anomaly. For both boys and girls, complaints affected low-anomaly children. In boys, the least sociable children were the low-anomaly boys with high-complaint parents, but for girls the combination of low anomalies and low complaints led to the most sociable group of girls. Between the sexes, low-anomaly, high-complaint boys were significantly less social than the same subgroup of girls, yet there was a trend for the low-anomaly/low-complaint girls to be more sociable than their male counterparts. The main effect for anomalies was marginally significant for boys ($p = .06$) and girls ($p = .10$). The main effect for complaints was significant for boys and borderline for girls ($p = .10$).

We can see how a child congenital variable and a family variable together contribute to improve our predictions of personality development. While there were main effects on child behavior for both child anomalies and newlywed complaints, we can see how in some cases the constitutional variable of a child moderated the impact of a preexisting family characteristic. For the present sample, high-anomaly children were less affected by variation in family complaints than were low-anomaly children. For the low-anomaly children, the predominant influence in this limited data set was family complaints. Further, as expected, the gender of the child also influenced the nature of the problem behavior when it occurred, with boys exhibiting more externalizing behaviors, and girls more internalizing behaviors. Because of the different behavioral styles associated with gender, it is important to measure more than one outcome variable. For example, impulsivity for girls was not a very important variable—in fact, most of the low-scoring children on this dimension were girls and there was a large sex difference for the total sample ($t[127] = 4.07$, $p < .001$). If we had used only impulsivity, we would have concluded that there was a clear additive effect of constitution and families for boys, but nothing for girls. With sociability as the dependent variable, however, we observed both the congenital and the family variables having a differential impact on boys and girls. We have completed analyses in a new longitudinal sample of young children and families that generally replicate the above findings (Halverson & Wampler, 1993).

Other results in the literature support the above transaction findings. Matheney (1986) found stability in temperament between 12 and 24 months, especially when mothers were involved and expressive. Further *changes* in sociability (increases) over that same time period were associated with the same maternal personality characteristics. Engfer (1986) found in a sample of German mothers that infants increased in difficulty more from 4 to 18 months when the parents were under stress than when they were not under stress. Belsky (1984; Belsky et al., 1989) found similar results.

There are characteristics of the child responsible in part for continuity, but maternal and family variables probably play a role as well. Patterson and Bank (1989) proposed that the transactional system involves family characteristics, marital relationships, depression, and so forth that may at times "overshadow" the impact of an aggressive child on the parent–child relationships. Further, they tested and found considerable support for the *parallel continuities hypothesis*—that child antisocial behavior was stable over a 2-year interval when there was concomitant stability in the parenting system. We continue to see new studies of development from the transactional perspectives that followed Belsky's (1984) important theorizing about the determinants of parenting by using constructs that encompass more than one causal mechanism at more than one level in describing the child-rearing environment.

G. The Family as a Unit

One factor many researchers do not include in their models is some conceptualization of the family as a unit and its impact on child behavior and personality. Interest in this linkage has gained prominence with the family therapy movement where theorists view the functioning of the family as a whole as the primary locus of health or pathology in children (see Gurman & Kniskern, 1981, and Minuchin, 1988, for recent summaries of theoretical and treatment approaches within the family therapy tradition).

Even though the family therapy approach has gained acceptance, the assumptions underlying this approach to the treatment of problems in children have not been tested systematically. Some evidence for the impact of family characteristics on child characteristics can be construed from positive results of outcome studies of family treatment (Gurman & Kniskern, 1981; Olson, Russell, & Sprenkle, 1989). More direct evidence is available from studies comparing families with a disturbed child with control families (Alexander, 1973; L. G. Bell & Bell, 1992; Doane, 1978; Ferreira, 1963; Fischer, 1980; Garbarino, Sebes, & Schellenbach, 1984; Jacob, 1975; Lewis, Beavers, Gossett & Phillips, 1976; Lewis, Rodnick, Michael, & Goldstein, 1981; Minuchin, Rosman, & Baker, 1978; Mishler & Waxler, 1968; Riskin & Faunce, 1972; Shepperson, 1982; Van der Veen & Novak, 1974; Westley & Epstein, 1969; Wynne, Jones, & Al-Khayyal, 1982). Almost all of this research has focused on adolescents in treatment. See Minuchin et al. (1978) for research with younger school-age children and L. G. Bell and Bell (1982), Lewis et al. (1976), and Westley and Epstein (1969) for nonclinical studies.

Characteristics that have been found to differentiate between families of competent, well-socialized, and problem-free adolescents and multiple-problem adolescents include positive affect (e.g., warmth, support, cohension), appropriate control (e.g., no parent–child coalition, parents in charge of family), clear communication (e.g., low communication deviance, high agreement, low negative affective style), and problem-solving ability (e.g., flexibility, low conflict).

H. The Marital Relationship

Most family therapists view the parents' marriage as the primary dysfunctional subsystem in relation to negative child characteristics like aggression, impulsivity, and poor ego control; that is to say, this relation is seen both as a direct effect of parental disagreement about child-rearing and as an indirect effect of parents who avoid problems in their marriage by focusing on problems in their child. Most of the research on the effects of the marital relationship on children has been done by child behavior therapists who recognized that more than parental skill deficits produced behavior problems in children (Cole & Morrow, 1976; Patterson, 1976; Patterson & Bank, 1989). Comparisons of clinic and nonclinic groups of children and adolescents have produced consistent evidence that parents of children with negative personality traits also experience higher levels of marital distress (Fischer, 1980; Forehand, Griest, Wells, & McMahon, 1982; Griest, Forehand, Wells, & McMahon, 1980; Johnson & Lobitz, 1974; Oltmanns, Broderick, & O'Leary, 1977; Porter & O'Leary, 1980; Schwarz & Getter, 1980; Westley & Epstein, 1969).

While many investigators are moving toward using multilevel transactional models in studying family–child linkages, much of it still remains ambiguous as to direction of effects issues. Many researchers do not include individual differences measures of children like temperament or personality. Some use retrospective reports or reports from only one parent, thus confounding developmental, family, and child factors inherent in single-method approaches. Those studies in which the impact of child temperament is appropriately examined rather consistently find evidence for a child effect (Hetherington, Stanley-Hagan, & Anderson, 1989; Lambert, 1988; Powers, Hauser, Kilner, 1989). Elder makes a convincing case for the impact of child temperament on later relationships, particularly marital and parent–child relationships (Caspi & Elder, 1988; Elder, Caspi, & Downey, 1986; Liker & Elder, 1983). Even research based on a strong assumption of a predominant direction of effect from the family to the child tends to produce evidence of a child effect. For example, in a series of research studies, Patterson (1982; Patterson & Bank, 1989; Patterson & Dishion, 1988) has produced evidence of a strong relation between parenting practices and negative child characteristics like aggression and noncompliance. Yet, he also finds that parents are less adept at parenting the child with negative characteristics than they are at parenting more normal siblings, thus suggesting a child effect. Patterson (1982) has also found that decreasing the child's antisocial behavior leads to decreases in the mother's depression.

Our point here is not to reiterate simply the importance of child effects. Rather, we believe that much research is still guided by a unidirectional model of the family influencing the child and that when adequate measures of child and parent are included, evidence for child effects is often more compelling than that for family effects. What we are saying is that the magnitude of the effects of children on parents may be greater than the magnitude of effects of parents on children. We propose that investigators consider the magnitude of effects issue seriously, since it represents a new direction in the conceptualization of the role of parenting in the family.

These general points were considerably elaborated upon by Sandra Scarr (1992) in her presidential address to the Society for Research in Child Development. Her thesis was that child-rearing environments within the normal species range were sufficient for normal development but did *not* produce individual differences in personality. Those arise from differences in genetics after the normal developmental process were present. "Normal" in this context applies to a great variety of parenting environments that are sufficient for unremarkable outcomes. When we see differences in parental treatment, they may be due mostly to parental *reactions* to different children's personalities—a point we have been making throughout this chapter. This view has elicited much concern among socialization researchers (see Baumrind, 1983; Jackson, 1993; Scarr, 1993). These researchers have been marshalling evidence against the position that being reared in one family or another makes little or no difference in the development of personality (see also Hoffman, 1991). Clearly, the responses to the crises we have been writing about here are beginning to appear.

We have proposed that children also are active self-socializers (C. L. Martin & Halverson, 1981, 1983). Young children begin early to appraise their roles vis-à-vis others and learn and practice behaviors considered appropriate (e.g., for boys or girls, for persons like me). This activity may occur independently of parenting practices and is similar to the notions of active gene–environment correlations where children either create or pick niches from available environments (Scarr & McCartney, 1983; see the following sections).

I. New Models

We summarize here models we have recently tested in our new longitudinal study of family influences on child development (The Georgia Longitudinal Study; Halverson & Wampler, 1993; Wampler, Halverson, & Deal, 1996).

1. Study 2: The Georgia Longitudinal Study

Briefly, our major main-effect model involved seven latent variables derived for 94 families seen in the first two waves of our longitudinal data set (the Georgia Longitudinal Study). Six of the constructs were derived from our first wave and were formed into a model to predict, first, child outcome in Year 2, and then in a second model, family function in Year 2.

We predicted that child outcome in Year 2, operationalized as child externalizing behavior (active, impulsive, difficult conduct), would be predicted *first* by a direct path from child minor physical anomalies (MPAs). This prediction was based on our earlier work (summarized previously) where MPAs have been consistently positively related to aggressive, impulsive, high active behavior. In addition to the direct path to child behavior, we predicted that MPAs would have an indirect effect on child externalizing through their effects on both the constructs of marital quality and competent parenting. For the first time, we also employed parental MPAs in our model, predicting that parental MPAs would have direct effects on three family subsystems, marital quality, individual parent stress, and family cohesion. The effects of parent MPAs on child aggressive, impulsive, externalizing behavior could be mediated by paths from marital quality, to parenting, to child outcome, and by a path from parent stress, to family cohesion, to child outcome. We predicted these paths in the expectation that MPAs would be related in adults to parental personality, most likely some aspect of negative emotionality, anxiety, and the tendency to become angry or easily upset.

The second model employed the same latent variables but the focus was instead on *family cohesion* in Year 2 as the outcome. We chose family cohesion to represent competent family functioning; our interest was in how aggressive, impulsive, externalizing child behavior would have an impact on family cohesion. We predicted again that child MPAs would directly relate to their externalizing behavior and that parental MPAs would have a direct impact on parent stress and marital quality, which would, in turn, relate to family cohesion.

Using a multimeasure (self-report and observation) definition of our constructs (see Halverson & Wampler, 1993, for details) we found that for preschool boys and their families, externalizing was mainly related to the congenital variable, MPAs. It was not predicted by parenting or family measures. For girls, MPAs were not related to externalizing behavior but were instead predicted by parenting quality (i.e., self-ratings of competent behavior, observations of parenting skill): the more competent the parent, the less externalizing. Using child externalizing as a predictor of family cohesion, we found, for boys, a moderate effect of externalizing on cohesion, as well as on marital quality and parental stress—having difficult boys had an impact on all the family systems. For girls, there was no effect of externalizing on family cohesion.

2. The Revised Model

For expository purposes, we propose a match—mismatch model (or goodness of fit; Lerner, 1989; Thomas & Chess, 1977) between families and children in order to examine the relative importance of aspects of the family environment that moderate the direction of influence between parents and children. The model predicts that certain temperamental or personality characteristics of children associated with minor physical anomalies (e.g., impulsivity, aggression) will describe "difficult" children. The goodness of fit model predicts that when difficult children are reared by problem families (those with limited resources, stress, etc.) both families and children will function less well over time; the predominant direction of effects will be from child (high MPA) to family (vulnerable to child effects). This could be termed the "child-driven" model. When these same difficult children are reared by competent, cohesive, effective parents, children will, over time, become less problematic and the families will continue to be competent over time. The direction of effect in this case would be from family to child (the "family-driven" model). Rather than an effect of one or the other, our model focuses on the question, under what conditions is change predominantly child-driven and when is it predominantly family-driven?

From our revised transactional perspective, different child and adult domains may be relatively important at different points in time. For example, during infancy, the baby's personality may be the least important factor in predicting marital relationships in a competent, peer-oriented couple, while during later childhood the child's increasingly difficult personality may assume an expanding role in the adjustment of the spouses to each other.

In this transactional context we need to refer to yet another useful metaphor from the behavior genetics literature, that of the genotype—environment correlation (Plomin et al., 1977; Scarr & McCartney, 1983). These authors have elegantly discussed how, within biological families, parents' child-rearing and child characteristics are correlated. By far the majority are positively correlated (e.g., active children with active parents) while some may be negatively correlated. Functionally, this concept is the same as the goodness of fit notion adapted from the temperament literature. The really interesting proposal about gene by environment correlations is the proposal that some environments and children passively resemble each other, while in others the child *evokes* similarities in the environment (e.g., sociable children elicit sociable responses in others in many family forms), and at other times the child (usually older children, adolescents, and adults) pick niches that are congruent with their personalities (see Caspi & Herbener, 1990, for an adult example). From our research, and the model of influence we propose, the first two concepts, the passive and evocative correlations, need some qualifying. Some characteristics will be influential and others will not, depending on how vulnerable (or buffered) the parenting system is to child effects. Further, congenital effects (i.e., nongenetic) may lower or even turn positive gene–environment correlations into negative ones where parents will pressure children to change, possibly magnifying contrasts with siblings.

While the research we have reviewed here (including our own) goes some way toward acknowledging direction-of-effects issues by focusing on transactional processes and moderators of who will effect whom when, most studies are still, unfortunately, silent on the issue of family effects that are shared or not by siblings in the same family. As we reviewed earlier, most family effects on personality must be of the unshared type (Plomin & Daniels, 1987); siblings do not resemble each other to any great degree on personality measures. There are several possible responses to this very real dilemma. One possibility is that personality traits are simply not very responsive to what parents do: shaping, instruction, punishing, monitoring, discussion, or whatever. It is possible they are pretty much "given" in the biological template and that most of the correspondences we track are either child effects on parents (idiosyncratic to each sibling within families) or shared passive genotype–environment correlations between children and parents.

Another response is that the big differences among siblings in the same family may be due to unsystematic, idiosyncratic life events within each family. If, however, we were to entertain seriously this rather forbidding prospect, we would probably not do research on this issue—we would be left with essentially case studies of life histories to account for each highly idiographic life course.

In a recent study involving a sample of Swedish twins and adoptees, Plomin, McClearn, Pedersen, Nesselroade, and Bergman (1988) found that using the Family Environment Scale (FES; Moos & Moos, 1984) to obtain adult twin adoptee retrospective ratings of their child and family environments produced puzzling results. Analyses revealed strong genetic influences on 9 of the 10 subscales of the FES (for example, MZ twins raised apart were in substantial agreement about the similarity of their early environments in *different* homes, while siblings in the same homes did not agree; (see also Pedersen, Plomin, McClearn, & Frieberg, 1988; Rowe, 1981, 1983). This approach seems limited at best. Family members do not report differential treatment in very refined ways. We are not very confident from data in our study and others that children or parents accurately track what may be very subtle transactional processes.

In our study, we used Block's Q-set items to measure parenting for two children in each of our families and are faced with little discrimination on parents' reports of practices. Parents told us that they treat all their children the same (i.e., they have global, trait-like self-perceptions). In contrast, children focus on differences between how each is treated. From their vantage point, everything is differential and state-like. We are not convinced, however, that young siblings of different ages know that a parent is reacting differentially to personality–temperament differences in the sibling pair. Our present failure to describe the relevant constructs responsible for these sibling variations within families is due in part to the poverty of our attempts to develop decent measurement models (see Wampler & Halverson, 1993). Given our current data base, it is not possible even to begin to document any one kind of systematic nonshared environmental effects directly. We suspect that direct observation combined with multisituation constructs is the initial step in identifying nonshared environmental influences.

We propose a strategy that may facilitate the search. Recall that the correlations between siblings is low (or even zero in some cases). What can be done is to select for sibling similarity and dissimilarities. With a zero correlation, one can form four equal-size groups from median splits of the variable: both siblings high on trait, both low, one high and one low, and vice versa. One can study, for example, the differences between families in those families who have siblings who are very similar on sociability and those who have siblings who are very different. If there are common family environments discriminating similar and different siblings, we can begin to document the main important nonshared contributors to differences and similarities across families.

Most of the *nonshared* environment at this time is also *nonvisible,* arrived at by default subtractions in heritability equations (Wachs, 1983). We need hypotheses about what the important processes might be. For example, Chess (1987) proposed that "poor" parenting might serve to increase differences between siblings. Parents with limited or coercive styles that are not adaptable to differences in the children may produce even *larger* differences between siblings than those that show sensitive, flexible parenting. In fact, it seems likely that such sensitive, flexible parenting may serve to increase sibling *similarities,* not differences, particularly when effective parents expend considerable effort on some valued outcome. We may not have measured or even conceptualized well those things that parents do that enhance their ability to influence even the most intractable, "canalized" children (or siblings) who start life with very different predispositions.

Our discussion of the transactional perspective on personality development goes beyond the outlines of similar models in the literature (e.g., Belsky, 1984) in that some specification of the variables moderating the direction and magnitude of effects between domains over time has been attempted. We feel strongly that it is not particularly helpful to state that the child and the rearing environment are actively changing each other (Belsky, 1984; Plomin et al., 1977; A. J. Sameroff, & Seifer, 1983; Scarr & Grajek, 1981). For example, Belsky's model does not really specify how domains jointly and separately contribute to either family or child development. Our model is more than a metamodel serving to explicate domains of potential relevance. What is needed is the difficult theorizing and empirical work of the specification of *when* and for *what group* of families *child* characteristics would predominantly "drive" the parenting system, or *when* and for *what group* of families the *parenting* system would "drive" behavior change in the child. Some characteristics take on importance only when considered in the light of other dimensions of the contextual systems.

When the theoretical delineation of the "individual differences" of *contexts or domains* is afforded the same importance as individual differences in *persons,* we will move closer to conceptualizing the complexity of relationship development. The difficult tasks for future research are specifying the details of not one "transactional model" but a series of such models that hold for certain families at certain times across development. Further, such models need to account not only for variance between families but for differential socialization of parents and children within families. Such studies will need to be multicontext longitudinal studies of multichildren families with a wide range of functioning, including clinical, at-risk, and healthy groups. Samples of families will need to be large and representative so regression analyses can be cross-validated and strong external validation ensured. The task we have outlined is a major one—the determination of the direction and the amount of variance that can be attributed to contexts controlling development of children and families. And it has only just begun.

By way of summary, we suggest several guidelines to such a transactional–ecological approach:

1. The nature of family and child adaptations should always be considered jointly. The adaptations are complex and multiply determined. The adaptations range from genetic and constitutional expression in children and parents to development histories and the personalities of parents and children, to the nature of the interpersonal relationship within the family, to the social world outside the family.

2. Close attention must be paid to the shifting hierarchial nature of the contextual inputs to functional outcomes (adaptations). Theory must be developed and tested regarding the particular structures of these hierarchial models *across time* and subgroups of families. This process will require an interdisciplinary approach, using the theoretical insights of child developmentalists, marriage and family researchers, pediatricians, school personnel, and so forth. It is particularly important to assess the contributors to long-term stability from childhood into adulthood. Few studies deal with the thorny conceptual problems of an early, relatively global personality developing into adult varieties of the "Big Five" personality dimensions

(see A. H. Buss, 1988; A. H. Buss & Finn, 1987). In fact, we have puzzled over the almost complete *lack* of any research on personality traits and structure beyond the differences described under the rubric of temperament. If we must describe children, one possible set of dimensions might be the Big Five (John, 1990). In our work (Halverson, Kohnstamm, & Martin, 1994; Havill, Allen, Halverson, & Kohnstamm, 1994) we have began to develop measurement instruments for children based on the Big Five typology in order to begin to trace the continuities to these same constructs in adulthood. The findings emerging are promising and we anticipate the elaboration of the measurement of dimensions like Agreeableness, Conscientiousness, and Openness to Experience in children and how personality structure may be moderated by family contexts and vice versa. Until now, this area is an *empty set* in the developmental area (see Halverson et al., 1994, for the research agenda around these issues). Many interesting possibilities for linking adult and child personality research are opened by having a common or overlapping set of traits to trace over time.

3. Only through the representative sampling of varieties of cultural contexts in which families and children live can these models be elaborated and tested (Lancaster, Altmann, Rossi, & Sherrod, 1987). Individual differences and contextual differences must be coordinated in such models.

4. Emphasis must be placed on differential socialization within families where different models may hold for different children in the family at the same time or overtime (Scarr & Grajek, 1981).[4]

ACKNOWLEDGMENTS

The writing of this chapter was supported by NIMH Grants MH39899 and MH50302. The Bethesda Longitudinal Study was supported by the NIMH Intramural Program. The authors express their appreciation to William Graziano, Robert Hogan, John Johnson, Roy Martin, Hilary Rose, and James Walters for comments on earlier versions of this chapter.

REFERENCES

Ainsworth, M. D. S., Blehar, M. C., Waters, E., & Walls, S. (1978). *Patterns of attachment.* Hillsdale, NJ: Erlbaum.

Alexander, J. F. (1973). Defensive and supportive communications in normal and deviant families. *Journal of Clinical and Consulting Psychology, 40,* 223–331.

Baldwin, A. L. (1949). The effect of home environment on nursery school behavior. *Child Development, 20,* 49–62.

---

[4] While beyond the scope of this paper, we must consider family relationships across the lifespan. We have focused on young children, but adult children have parents and these relationships have not been much studied as factors in maintaining or changing adult personality (Caspi & Herbener, 1990; Hagestad, 1990).

Baldwin, A. L., Kalhorn, J., & Breese, F. H. (1949). The appraisal of parent behavior. *Psychological Monographs, 63*(Whole No. 299).

Baumrind, D. (1967). Child care practices anteceding three patterns of preschool behavior. *Genetic Psychology Monographs, 75,* 43–88.

Baumrind, D. (1971). Current patterns of parental authority. *Developmental Psychology Monographs, 4*(No. 1, Part 2).

Baumrind, D. (1983). Rejoinder to Lewis' reinterpretation of parental firm control effects: Are authoritative families really harmonious? *Psychological Bulletin, 94,* 132–142.

Bell, L. G., & Bell, D. C. (1982). Family climate and the role of the female adolescent: Determinants of adolescent functioning. *Family Relations, 31,* 519–527.

Bell, R. Q. (1968). A reinterpretation of the direction of effects in studies of socialization. *Psychological Review, 75,* 81–95.

Bell, R. Q., & Harper, L. V. (1977). *Child effects on adults.* Hillsdale, NJ: Erlbaum.

Bell, R. Q., & Waldrop, M. F. (1982). Temperament and minor physical anomalies. *Ciba Foundation Symposium, 89,* 206–220.

Belsky, J. (1981). Early human experience: A family perspective. *Developmental Psychology, 17,* 3–23.

Belsky, J. (1984). The determinants of parenting: A process model. *Child Development, 55,* 83–96.

Belsky, J., Rovine, M., & Fish, M. (1989). The developing family system. In M. R. Gunnar & E. Thelen (Eds.), *Minnesota Symposia on Child Psychology* (Vol. 22, pp. 119–166). Hillsdale, NJ: Erlbaum.

Block, J. (1971). *Lives through time.* Berkeley, CA: Bancroft.

Block, J. H., & Block, J. (1979). The role of ego control and ego resiliency in the organization of behavior. In W. A. Collins (Ed.), *Minnesota Symposia on Child Psychology* (Vol. 13, pp. 39–101). Hillsdale, NJ: Erlbaum.

Bretherton, I. (1985). Attachment theory: Retrospect and prospect. *Society for Research in Child Development,* No. 209, *50*(1–2), 3–35.

Burg, C., Hart, D., Quinn, P., & Rapoport, J. (1978). Newborn minor physical anomalies and the prediction of infant behavior. *Journal of Austism and Childhood Schizophrenia, 8,* 427–429.

Buss, A. H. (1988). *Personality: Evolutionary heritage and human distinctiveness.* Hillsdale, NJ: Erlbaum.

Buss, A. H., & Finn, S. E. (1987). Classification of personality traits. *Journal of Personality and Social Psychology, 52,* 432–444.

Buss, A. R., & Plomin, R. (1975). *A temperament theory of personality development.* New York: Wiley (Interscience).

Buss, A. R., & Plomin, R. (1984). *Temperament: Early developing personality traits.* Hillsdale, NJ: Erlbaum.

Cairns, R. B., Gariepy, J., & Hood, K. E. (1990). Development, microevolution, and social behavior, *Psychological Review, 97,* 49–65.

Caspi, A., & Elder, G. H. (1988). Emergent family patterns: The intergenerational construction of problem behavior and relationships. In R. A. Hinde & J. Stevenson-Hinde (Eds.), *Relationships with families: Mutual influences* (pp. 218–240). Oxford, England: Oxford University Press.

Caspi, A., & Herbener, E. S. (1990). Continuity and change: Assortative marriage and the consistency of personality in adulthood. *Journal of Personality and Social Psychology,* 1990, *58,* 250–258.

Chess, S. (1987). Let us consider the roles of temperament and fortuitous events. *Brain and Behavior Sciences, 10,* 21–22.

Cole, C., & Morrow, W. R. (1976). Refractory parent behavior in behavior modification training groups. *Psychotherapy, 13,* 162–169.

Cowan, C. P., Cowan, P. A., Heming, G., & Miller, N. B. (1991). Becoming a family: Marriage, parenting and child development. In P. A. Cowan & E. M. Hetherington (Eds.), *Family transitions* (pp. 126–141). Hillsdale, NJ: Erlbaum.

Crawford, C. B., & Anderson, J. L. (1989). Sociobiology: An environmentalist discipline? *American Psychologist, 44,* 1449–1459.

Doane, J. A. (1978). Family interaction and communication deviance in normal and disturbed families: A review of research. *Family Process, 17,* 357–376.

Dunn, J., & Plomin, R. (1991). Why are siblings so different? The significance of differences in sibling experiences within the family. *Family Process, 30,* 271–284.

Elder, G. H., Jr., Caspi, A., & Downey, G. (1986). Problem behavior and family relationships: Life course and intergenerational themes. In A. B. Sorensen, F. E. Weinert, & L. R. Sherrod (Eds.). *Human development and the life course: Multidisciplinary perspectives* (pp. 293–340). Hillsdale, NJ: Erlbaum.

Engfer, A. (1986). Antecedents of behavior problems in infancy. In. A. Kohnstamm (Ed.), *Temperament discussed* (pp. 98–112). Berwyn, PA: Swets North America.

Eysenck, H. J. (1970). *The structure of human personality* (Rev. ed.). London: Methuen.

Ferreira, A. (1963). Decision making in normal and pathologic families. *Archives of General Psychiatry, 8,* 68–73.

Firestone, P., Peters, B., Riviere, M., & Knights, R. M. (1978). Minor physical anomalies in hyperactive, retarded, and normal children and their families. *Journal of Child Psychology and Psychiatry, 19,* 155–160.

Fischer, J. L. (1980). Reciprocity, agreement, and family style in family systems with a disturbed and nondisturbed adolescent. *Journal of Youth and Adolescence, 9,* 391–406.

Forehand, R., Griest, D. L., Wells, K. C., & McMahon, R. J. (1982). Side effects of parent counseling on marital satisfaction. *Journal of Counseling Psychology, 29,* 104–107.

Freedman, D. G. (1958). Constitutional and environmental interactions in rearing four breeds of dogs. *Science, 127,* 585–586.

Garbarino, J., Sebes, J., & Schellenbach, C. (1984). Families at risk for destructive parent-child relations in adolescence. *Child Development, 55,* 174–183.

Griest, D. L., Forehand, R., Wells, K. C., & McMahon, R. J. (1980). An examination of differences between nonclinic and behavior-problem-clinic-referred children and their mothers. *Journal of Abnormal Psychology, 89,* 497–501.

Gurman, A. S., & Kniskern, D. P. (1981). Family therapy outcome research: Knowns and unknowns. In A. S. Gurman & D. P. Kniskern (Eds.), *Handbook of family therapy* (pp. 742–775). New York: Brunner/Mazel.

Hagestad, G. O. (1990). Social perspectives on the life course. In R. Binstock & L. George (Eds.), *Handbook of aging and the social processes* (pp. 35–61). San Diego, CA: Academic Press.

Halverson, C. F. (1989a). *Activity level: Measurement issues and implications for personality structure in children.* Unpublished manuscript.

Halverson, C. F. (1989b). *Minor physical anomalies and sex differences in behavior.* Unpublished manuscript.

Halverson, C. F., Kohnstamm, G. A., & Martin, R. P. (1994). *The developing structure of temperament and personality from infancy to adulthood.* Hillsdale, NJ: Erlbaum.

Halverson, C. F., & Martin, C. L. (1981, April). *Parent-child stability over time.* Paper presented at the meeting of the Society for Research in Child Development, Boston.

Halverson, C. F., & Shetterly, K. (1989). *Revised manual for minor physical anomalies.* Unpublished manuscript.

Halverson, C. F., & Victor, J. B. (1976). Minor physical anomalies and problem behavior in elementary school children. *Child Development, 47,* 281–285.

Halverson, C. F., & Waldrop, M. F. (1973). The relations of mechanically recorded activity level to varieties of preschool behavior. *Child Development, 44,* 678–681.

Halverson, C. F., & Wampler, K. S. (1993). The mutual influence of child externalizing behavior and family functioning: The impact of a mild congenital risk factor. In R. E. Cole & D. Reiss (Eds.), *How do families cope with chronic illness?* (pp. 120–147). Hillsdale, NJ: Erlbaum.

Harper, L. V. (1989). *The nurture of human behavior.* Norwood, NJ: Ablex.

Havill, V., Allen, K., Halverson, C. F., Kohnstamm, G. A. (1994). Parents use a Big 5 categories in their natural language description of children. In C. F. Halverson, G. A. Kohnstamm, & R. P. Martin (Eds.), *The developing structure of temperament and personality from infancy to adulthood* (pp. 371–386). Hillsdale, NJ: Erlbaum.

Hetherington, E. M., Stanley-Hagan, M., & Anderson, E. R. (1989). Marital transitions: A child's perspective. *American Psychologist, 44,* 303–312.

Hinde, R., & Stevenson-Hinde, J. (1973). *Constraints on learning.* New York: Academic Press.

Hoffman, L. W. (1991). The influence of the family environment on personality. *Psychological Bulletin, 110,* 187–203.

Holden, G. W., & Edwards, L. A. (1989). Parental attitudes toward childrearing: Instruments, issues and implications. *Psychological Bulletin, 106,* 29–58.

Jackson, J. F. (1993). Human behavioral genetics, Scarr's theory, and her views on interventions: A critical review and commentary on their implications for African American children. *Child Development, 64,* 1318–1332.

Jacob, T. (1975). Family interaction in disturbed and normal families: A methodological and substantive review. *Psychological Bulletin, 82,* 33–65.

Jacobs, B. S., & Moss, H. A. (1976). Birth order and sex of sibling as determinants of mother-infant interaction. *Child Development, 47,* 315–322.

John, O. P. (1990). The "Big Five" factor taxonomy: Dimensions of personality in the natural language and in questionnaires. In L. A. Pervin (Ed.), *Handbook of personality: Theory and research* (pp. 66–100). New York: Guilford Press.

Johnson, S. M., & Lobitz, G. K. (1974). The personal and marital adjustment of parents as related to observed child deviance and parenting behaviors. *Journal of Abnormal Child Psychology, 2,* 193–207.

Kagan, J., & Moss, H. (1962). *Birth to maturity.* New York: Wiley.

Lambert, N. M. (1988). Adolescent outcomes for hyperactive children. *American Psychologist, 43,* 786–799.

Lancaster, J. B., Altmann, J., Rossi, A. S., & Sherrod, L. R. (1987). *Parenting across the lifespan.* New York: de Gruyter.

Lerner, R. M. (1989). Individual development and the family system: A life-span perspective. In K. Kreppner & R. M. Lerner (Eds.), *Family systems and life-span development* (pp. 15–32). Hillsdale, NJ: Erlbaum.

Lerner, R. M., & Spanier, G. B. (1978). *Child influences on marital and family interaction: A lifespan perspective.* New York: Academic Press.

Lewis, J. M., Beavers, W. R., Gossett, J. T., & Phillips, V. A. (1976). *No single thread: Psychological health in family systems.* New York: Brunner/Mazel.

Lewis, J. M., Rodnick, E. H., Michael, J., & Goldstein, P. (1981). Intrafamilial interactive behavior, parental communication deviance, and risk for schizophrenia. *Journal of Abnormal Psychology, 90,* 448–457.

Liker, J. K., & Elder, G. H., Jr. (1983). Economic hardship and marital relations in the 1930s. *American Sociological Review, 48,* 343–359.

Loehlin, J. C. (1992). *Genes and environment in personality development.* Newbury Park, CA: Sage.

Loehlin, J. C., & Nichols, R. C. (1976). *Heredity, environment, and personality.* Austin: University of Texas Press.

Maccoby, E. E., & Martin, J. A. (1983). Socialization in the context of the family: Parent-child interaction. In P. H. Mussen (Series Ed.) & E. M. Hetherington (Vol. Ed.), *Handbook of child psychology: Vol. 4. Socialization, personality and social development* (pp. 1–102). New York: Wiley.

Martin, B. (1987). Developmental perspectives on family theory and psychopathology. In T. Jacob (Ed.), *Family interaction and psychopathology: Theory, methods and findings* (pp. 163–202). New York: Plenum Press.

Martin, C. L., & Halverson, C. F. (1981). A schematic processing model of sex typing and stereotyping in children. *Child Development, 52,* 1119–1134.

Martin, C. L., & Halverson, C. F. (1983). The effects of sex typing schemas on young children's memories. *Child Development, 54,* 563–574.

Martin, R. P. (1983). Temperament: A review of research with implications for the school psychologist. *School Psychology Review, 12,* 266–273.

Matheny, A. P. (1986). Stability and change of infant temperament: Contributions from infant, mother, and family environment. In G. Kohnstamm (Ed.), *Temperament discussed* (pp. 81–97). Berwyn, PA: Swets North America.

Matheney, A. P. (1989). Children's behavioral inhibition over age and across situations: Genetic similarity for a trait during change. *Journal of Personality, 57,* 215–235.

McCartney, K., Harris, M. J., & Bernieri, F. (1990). Growing up and growing apart: A developmental meta-analysis of twin studies. *Psychological Bulletin, 107,* 226–237.

Minuchin, P. (1988). Relationships within the family: A systems perspective on development. In R. A. Hinde & J. Stevenson-Hinde (Eds.), *Relationships within families: Mutual influences* (pp. 7–27). Oxford England: Oxford University Press.

Minuchin, S., Rosman, B. L., & Baker, L. (1978). *Psychosomatic families.* Cambridge, MA: Harvard University Press.

Mishler, E., & Waxler, N. (1986). *Interaction in families: An experimental study of family processes and schizophrenia.* New York: Wiley.

Moos, R. H., & Moos, B. S. (1984). *Family environment scale manual* (Rev. ed.). Palo Alto, CA: Consulting Psychologists Press.

Olson, D. H., Russell, C. S., & Sprenkle, D. H. (1980). Marital and family therapy with children. *Journal of Marriage and Family Therapy, 42,* 973–995.

Oltmanns, T. F., Broderick, J. E., & O'Leary, K. D. (1977). Marital adjustment and the efficacy of behavior therapy with children. *Journal of Consulting and Clinical Psychology, 45,* 724–729.

Patterson, G. R. (1976). The aggressive child: Victim and architect of a coercive system. In L. A. Hamerlynk, L. C. Hardy, & E. J. Mash (Eds.), *Behavioral modification and families: I. Theory and research* (pp. 189–216). New York: Brunner/Mazel.

Patterson, G. R. (1982). *A social learning approach to family intervention: II. Coercive family processes.* Eugene, OR: Castalia.

Patterson, G. R., & Bank, L. (1989). Some amplifying mechanisms for pathologic processes in families. In M. R. Gunnar & E. Thelen (Eds.), *Systems and development: The Minnesota Symposium on Child Psychology* (Vol. 22, pp. 167–209). Hillsdale, NJ: Erlbaum.

Patterson, G. R., & Dishion, T. J. (1988). Multilevel family process models: Traits, interactions, and relationships. In R. A. Hinde & J. Stevenson-Hinde (Eds.), *Relationships within families: Mutual influences* (pp. 283–310). Oxford, England: Oxford University Press.

Pedersen, N. L., Plomin, R., McClearn, G. E., & Frieberg, L. (1988). Neuroticism, extraversion, and related traits in adult twins reared apart and reared together. **55,** 950–957.

Plomin, R., & Bergeman, C. S. (1991). The nature of nurture: Genetic influences on environmental measures. *Behavioral and Brain Sciences, 14,* 373–427.

Plomin, R., & Daniels, D. (1987). Why are children in the same family so different from one another? *Behavioral and Brain Sciences, 10,* 1–60.

Plomin, R., DeFries, J. C., & Loehlin, J. C. (1977). Genotype-environment interaction and correlation in the analysis of human behavior. *Psychological Bulletin, 84,* 309–322.

Plomin, R., McClearn, G. E., Pedersen, N. L., Nesselroade, J. R., & Bergeman, C. S. (1988). Genetic influence on childhood family environment perceived retrospectively from the last half of the life span. *Development Psychology, 24,* 738–745.

Porter, B., & O'Leary, K. D. (1980). Marital discord and childhood behavior problems. *Journal of Abnormal Child Psychology, 8,* 289–295.

Powers, S. I., Hauser, S. T., & Kilner, L. A. (1989). Adolescent mental health. *American Psychologist, 44,* 200–208.

Quinn, P., Renfield, M., Burg, C., & Rapoport, J. (1977). Minor physical anomalies: A newborn screening and a one-year follow-up. *Journal of Child Psychiatry, 16,* 662–669.

Radke-Yarrow, M., & Zahn-Waxler, C. (1984). Roots, motives, and patterns in children's prosocial behavior. In E. Staub, D. Bar-Tal, J. Karglowski, & J. Reykowski (Eds.), *Development and maintenance of prosocial behavior: International perspectives* (pp. 81–99). New York: Plenum Press.

Radke-Yarrow, M., & Zahn-Waxler, C. (1986). The role of familial prosocial behavior: Research findings and questions. In D. Olweus, J. Block, & M. Radke-Yarrow (Eds.) *Development of antisocial and prosocial behavior* (pp. 207–233). Orlando, FL: Academic Press.

Rapoport, J. L., Quinn, P. O., Lamprecht, F. (1974). Minor physical anomalies and plasma dopamine B-hydroxylase activity in hyperactive boys. *American Journal of Psychiatry, 131,* 387–390.

Riskin, J., & Faunce, E. (1972). An evaluative review of family interaction research. *Family Process, 11,* 365–456.

Rollins, B. C., & Thomas, D. L. (1979). Parental support, power, and control techniques in the socialization of children. In W. R. Burr, R. Hill, F. I. Nye, & I. L. Reiss (Eds.), *Contemporary theories about the family: research-based theories* (Vol. 1, pp. 317–364). New York: Free Press.

Rowe, D. C. (1981). Environmental and genetic influences on dimensions of perceived parenting: A twin study. *Developmental Psychology, 17,* 203–208.

Rowe, D. C. (1983). A biometrical analysis of perceptions of family environment: A study of twin and singleton sibling kinships. *Child Development, 54,* 416–423.

Rowe, D. C. (1990). As the twig is bent? The myth of child rearing influences on personality development. *Journal of Counseling and Development, 68,* 606–611.

Ryder, R. G., Kafka, J. S., & Olson, D. H. (1971). Separating and joining influences in courtship and early marriage. *American Journal of Orthopsychiatry, 41,* 450–464.

Sackett, G., Ruppenthal, G., Farenbruch, C., Holm, R., & Greenough, W. (1981). Social isolation rearing effects in monkeys vary with genotype. *Developmental Psychology, 17,* 313–318.

Sameroff, A. J. & Chandler, M. J. (1975). Reproductive risk and the continuum of caretaking casualty. In F. D. Horowitz, E. M. Hetherington, S. Scarr, & G. M. Siegel (Eds.), *Review of child development research* (Vol. 4, pp. 187–244). Chicago: University of Chicago Press.

Sameroff, A. J., & Seifer, R. (1983). Familial risk and child competence. *Child Development, 54,* 1254–1268.

Scarr, S. (1992). Developmental theories for the 1990s: Development and individual differences. *Child Development, 63,* 1–9.

Scarr, S. (1993). Biological and cultural diversity: The legacy of Darwin for development. *Child Development, 63,* 1333–1353.

Scarr, S., & Grajek, S. (1981). Similarities and differences among siblings. In M. Lamb & B. Sutton-Smith (Eds.), *Sibling relationships* (pp. 357–381). Hillsdale, NJ: Erlbaum.

Scarr, S., & McCartney, K. (1983). How people make their own environments: A theory of genotype-environment effects. *Child Development, 54,* 424–435.

Scarr, S., Webber, P. L., Weinberg, R. A., & Wittig, M. A. (1981). Personality resemblance among adolescents and their parents in biologially related and adoptive families. *Journal of Personality and Social Psychology, 40,* 885–898.

Schwarz, J. C., & Getter, H. (1980). Parental conflict and dominance in late adolescent maladjustment: A triple interaction model. *Journal of Abnormal Psychology, 89,* 573–580.

Scott, J. P., & Fuller, J. L. (1965). *Genetics and the social behavior of the dog.* Chicago: University of Chicago Press.

Sears, R. R., Maccoby, E. E., & Levin, H. (1957). *Patterns of childrearing.* Evanston, IL: Row, Peterson.

Sears, R. R., Rau, L., & Alpert, R. (1965). *Identification and childrearing.* Stanford, CA: Stanford University Press.

Shepperson, V. L. (1982). Differences in assertion and aggression between normal and neurotic family triads. *Journal of Personality Assessment, 46,* 409–414.

Thomas, A., & Chess, S. (1977). *Temperament and development.* New York: Brunner/Mazel.

Van der Veen, F., & Novak, A. L. (1974). The family concept of the disturbed child: A replication study. *American Journal of Orthopsychiatry, 44,* 763–773.

von Hilsheimer, G., & Kurko, V. (1979). Minor physical anomalies in exceptional children. *Journal of Learning Disabilities, 12,* 462–469.

Wachs, T. D. (1983). The use and abuse of environment in behavior genetic research. *Child Development, 54,* 396–407.

Wachs, T. D. (1992). *The nature of nurture.* Newbury Park, CA: Sage.

Waddington, C. H. (1957). *The strategy of the genes.* London: Allen & Unwin.

Waddington, C. H. (1962). *New patterns in genetics and development.* New York: Columbia University Press.

Waldrop, M. F., Bell, R. Q., & Goering, J. D. (1976). Minor physical anomalies and inhibited behavior in elementary school girls. *Journal of Child Psychology and Psychiatry, 17,* 113–122.

Waldrop, M. F., Bell, R. Q., McLaughlin, B., & Halverson, C. F. (1978). Newborn minor physical anomalies predict short attention span, peer aggression and impulsivity at age 3. *Science, 199,* 563–564.

Waldrop, M. F., & Halverson, C. F. (1971). Minor physical anomalies and hyperactive behavior in young children. In J. Helmuth (Ed.), *The exceptional infant* (Vol. 2, pp. 343–380). New York: Brunner/Mazel.

Waldrop, M. F., Pedersen, F. A., & Bell, R. Q. (1968). Minor physical anomalies and behavior in preschool children. *Child Development, 39,* 391–400.

Wampler, K. S., & Halverson, C. F. (1993). Quantitative measurement in family research. In P. N. Boss, W. Doherty, R. Larossa, W. Schumm, & S. Steinmetz (Eds.), *Sourcebook of family theories and methods: A contextual approach* (pp. 181–194). New York: Plenum Press.

Wampler, K. S., Halverson, C. F., & Deal, J. E. (1996). Risk and resiliency in nonclinical young children: The Georgia Longitudinal Study. In M. Hetherington & E. Blechman (Eds.), *Stress, coping and resiliency in children and the family* (pp. 135–153). Hillsdale, NJ: Erlbaum.

Werner, E. E., Bierman, J., & French, F. (1971). *The children of Kauai.* Honolulu: University of Hawaii Press.

Werner, E. E., & Smith, R. S. (1977). *Kauai's children come of age.* Honolulu: University of Hawaii Press.

Werner, E. E., & Smith, R. S. (1982). *Vulnerable but invincible.* New York: McGraw-Hill.

Westley, W. A., & Epstein, N. B. (1969). *The silent majority.* San Francisco: Jossey-Bass.

Wynne, L. C., Jones, J. E., & Al-Khayyal, M. (1982). Healthy family patterns: Observations in families "at risk" for psychopathology. In F. Wash (Ed.), *Normal family processes* (pp. 142–167). New York: Guilford Press.

Yang, R. K., Zweig, A. R., Douthitt, T. C., & Federman, E. J. (1976). Successive relationship between maternal attitudes during pregnancy, analgesic medication during labor and delivery and newborn behavior. *Developmental Psychology, 12,* 6–15.

Yarow, M. R., Campbell, J. D., & Burton, R. V. (1968). *Childrearing: An inquiry into research and methods.* San Francisco: Jossey-Bass.

CHAPTER 11

LONGITUDINAL STABILITY OF ADULT PERSONALITY

PAUL T. COSTA, JR., AND ROBERT R. MCCRAE
GERONTOLOGY RESEARCH CENTER, NATIONAL INSTITUTE ON AGING, NATIONAL
INSTITUTES OF HEALTH, BALTIMORE, MARYLAND

Borgatta and Lambert's 1968 handbook on personality included chapters on childhood and adolescent development and reviewed volumes of research conducted on college students, but said almost nothing about personality in adults over age 30. Gerontologists and life span developmentalists (e.g., Block, 1971; Siegler, George, & Okun, 1979) studied personality and aging, but the relevance of their findings for the field of personality was not widely appreciated. In the past decade, however, the striking evidence of stability in adult personality traits has commanded more attention. Personality researchers and theorists are beginning to understand that the period of adulthood cannot be ignored, just as gerontologists have come to recognize that personality is central to the study of aging (McCrae & Costa, 1990). This chapter reviews empirical evidence on the stability of personality and outlines some of the implications of stability for personality psychology.

I. THE DEFINITION AND ASSESSMENT OF PERSONALITY

An examination of stability or change in personality presupposes a definition of personality and a method or methods of assessing it. In principle, one could examine changes in personal constructs, instinctual impulses, cognitive styles, life structures, ego levels, or Jungian functions. In practice, most research has been conducted on *traits,* dimensions of individual differences in tendencies to show consistent patterns of thoughts, feelings, and actions.

This is not as serious a limitation as it might first appear, because traits are not the static, superficial, or artifactual entities they are sometimes depicted as being. As dispositions, traits are dynamic, in some respects equivalent to motives and needs (Costa & McCrae, 1988b); they are also inherently interactive, leading to the selection of situations and the evocation of actions in others (Buss, 1992). Far from being superficial, traits are among the central determinants of the life course (Conley, 1985b) and the sense of identity (McCrae & Costa, 1988), and traits familiar from questionnaires and from English language adjectives are closely related to such theoretical constructs as Jungian attitudes and functions (McCrae & Costa, 1989b) and personality disorders (Wiggins & Pincus, 1989). And traits are certainly not artifacts of person perception, as D'Andrade (1965) once argued. There is now ample evidence from both observational studies (Moskowitz, 1988; Small, Zeldin, & Savin-Williams, 1983) and cross-observer rating studies (Funder & Colvin, 1988; McCrae & Costa, 1989a) to confirm the objective reality of personality traits.

It is sometimes objected that trait measures should not be used to study personality change, because traits are, by definition, enduring dispositions. This is a specious argument. Traits must persist across situations and over a period of days or weeks; otherwise, we would not be able to distinguish them from transient states. But there is no requirement that trait levels must remain stable over years or decades. Similarly, the fact that trait measures must demonstrate short-term retest reliability does not ensure that they will show long-term stability. A reliable measure can show either stability or change; an unreliable measure would not be able to show either.

Perhaps more than in any other approach to personality, trait theories have been tied to measures. While this has allowed rigorous empirical tests of the hypotheses of trait theorists, it has also meant that critiques of trait measures have clouded the reputation of traits as constructs. It is doubtless true that many published scales were poorly developed and validated, but as Block (1977) has argued, the value of trait theory must be judged from the best exemplars of scale construction, not the worst. Studies using instruments like the Personality Research Form (PRF; Jackson, 1984), the Interpersonal Adjective Scales (Wiggins, 1979), and the Eysenck Personality Inventory (EPI; Eysenck & Eysenck, 1964) have demonstrated their value in hundreds of applications.

In recent years, two major concerns about trait measures have been largely resolved: Social desirability is not a serious contaminant of self-reports, and self-reports can be consensually validated by observer ratings. Although researchers and test constructors have been preoccupied by the specter of social desirability since the 1950s, a solid body of evidence has demonstrated that individual differences in the tendency to endorse favorable items are weak in comparison with individual differences in substantive traits (Block, 1965; Dicken, 1963; McCrae & Costa, 1983; McCrae et al., 1989). Similarly, skepticism about agreement between self-reports and ratings (Fiske, 1978) has been answered by a number of studies which confirm that when knowledgeable raters use reliable instruments, substantial correlations (in the range of .4 to .6) can be seen among raters and between self-reports and observer ratings (Funder & Colvin, 1988; McCrae & Costa, 1989a; Woodruffe, 1985). These findings should bolster confidence in trait-based research on personality and aging.

Until recently, one of the major drawbacks of the trait approach was the sheer number of trait measures and constructs. Thousands of words, hundreds of published scales, and dozens of traits systems competed for the researcher's or reviewer's attention. How could one make any generalization about the influence of age on personality traits when there appear to be an unlimited number of traits?

Although it was widely understood that a few major dimensions pervaded most of these traits, there was little agreement on what those dimensions were. In 1968, Wiggins concluded that Neuroticism and Extraversion (in some form and under some label) were well established; in the 1980s a growing consensus (Borkenau, 1988; Digman & Inouye, 1986; Goldberg, 1982; McCrae & Costa, 1987) recognized the need to add the dimensions of Openness, Agreeableness, and Conscientiousness to complete what Norman (1963) called "an adequate taxonomy of personality."

The five-factor model provides a common basis for classifying natural language trait terms, scales from a wide variety of personality inventories, and the items of the California Q-Set (Block, 1961; McCrae, Costa, & Busch, 1986). It can therefore be used as a framework for integrating research on aging and personality. Because it is comprehensive, conclusions about the five domains of Neuroticism, Extraversion, Openness, Agreeableness, and Conscientiousness can confidently be treated as conclusions about the full range of personality traits.

II. STABILITY OF MEAN LEVELS

The first of two major questions about personality stability or change concerns normative shifts in the mean levels of personality. Do individuals mature and grow in wisdom as they age, or do they lose their youthful exuberance and become depressed? Are old people better characterized as *mellowed* or *cranky?* Are there stages or cycles of development, bringing predictable periods of crisis? Hypotheses might be based on either common stereotypes or on focused theories of aging (e.g., Erikson, 1950; Levinson, Darrow, Klein, Levinson, & McKee, 1978), but in fact most research has been exploratory, seeking to document age differences or changes in various periods of adulthood.

Research on aging faces two formidable problems rarely encountered in other branches of psychology. First, the independent variable, maturation, cannot be manipulated; in consequence, only quasi-experimental designs can be used, and these face well-known threats to their validity (Schaie, 1977). Second, aging is a process which requires decades to unfold; researchers who wish to study changes (instead of simple age differences) must study the life span in segments, or build upon the work of earlier researchers.

A. Cross-Sectional Studies

The most convenient way to estimate age changes is by studying age differences in a cross-sectional design, and most research on age and personality has adopted this strategy. Neugarten's 1977 review of these studies suggested that there were very few consistent results, although there appeared to be evidence that older men and women scored lower on measures of Extraversion. Since then, a number of large-scale studies have been published which included cross-sectional analyses (usually as part of a multiage-group longitudinal design). Douglas and Arenberg (1978) examined age differences on the Guilford–Zimmerman Temperament Survey (GZTS; Guilford, Zimmerman, & Guilford, 1976) in two samples of men aged 17 to 98 (Ns = 605, 310). Siegler et al. (1979) used the Sixteen Personality Factor Questionnaire (16PF; Cattell, Eber, & Tatsuoka, 1970) in a study of 331 men and women aged 54 to 70. Costa and McCrae (1988a, 1988b) correlated age with Murray's needs as measured by the PRF in a sample of 296 men and women aged 24 to 81, and with the five factors of personality as measured by the NEO Personality Inventory (NEO-PI; Costa & McCrae, 1985b, 1989a) in a different sample of 983 men and women aged 21 to 96.

These studies can be compared if the scales are classified in terms of the five-factor model. Most of the Neuroticism (e.g., 16PF Q4, Tension) and Conscientiousness (e.g., PRF Order) scales showed no age differences. Extraversion appeared to decline, as seen in lower scores for older subjects on GZTS General Activity and Ascendance, PRF Dominance, Exhibition, and Play, and NEO-PI Extraversion. Older subjects also scored lower on PRF needs for Change and Sentience and on NEO-PI Openness, suggesting a decline in Openness; however, there were cross-sectional increases in PRF need for Understanding, another measure of Openness. Finally, Agreeableness appeared to be higher for older subjects, as seen in positive correlations between age and GZTS Friendliness, PRF Abasement, and NEO-PI Agreeableness, and a negative correlation between age and PRF Aggression.

One problem with all of these studies is the possibility of sampling bias. Early cross-sectional studies compared college students with nursing home residents and inappropriately concluded that older people were much lower in intelligence, mental health, and morale. The studies cited above avoided such obvious confounds, but it is not clear how representative they were of the entire population. However, a recent follow-up study of a national sample of noninstitutionalized civilians (Cornoni-Huntley et al., 1983) can claim to be representative. Short scales measuring Neuroticism, Extraversion, and Openness were administered to over 10,000 men and women aged 32 to 88. As Figure 1 shows, plots of personality scores by age group showed little association; correlations with age ranged from −.12 for Neuroticism to −.19 for Openness (Costa et al., 1986). Note that this pattern held for women as well as for men, and for blacks as well as for whites.

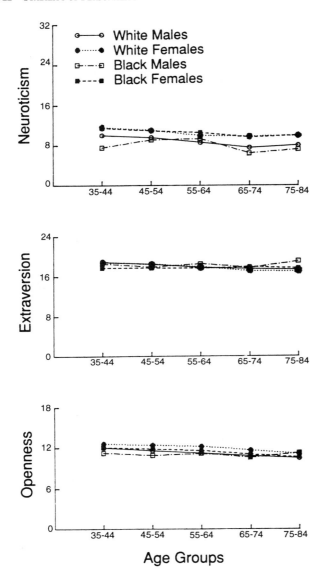

FIGURE 1 Mean levels of Neuroticism, Extraversion, and Openness to Experience for 10-year age groups of white men, black men, white women, and black women, aged 35 to 84 years (from Costa et al., 1986).

Taken together, these cross-sectional studies suggest that older subjects are less extraverted and open and more agreeable than younger subjects. However, two qualifications are in order. First, the magnitude of the associations is uniformly small, especially considering the exceptionally wide age range and the near-perfect reliability of measures of age. Less than 10% of the variance of any of the personality scales considered here is accounted for by age. Second, as cross-sectional studies, these findings are ambiguous as indicators of maturation. In particular, cross-sectional studies confound generational differences with maturational changes. We do not know whether the oldest subjects in Figure 1 are lower in Openness because age leads to constriction and conservativism, or because individuals born in the first decades of this century were brought up to be more closed to experience than were subsequent generations.

B. Longitudinal and Sequential Studies

The most common approach to deconfounding age and birth cohort is by conducting a longitudinal study in which the same individuals are measured at two or more times. In these repeated measures designs, subjects are matched on date of birth, as well as on education, gender, and many other features; the longitudinal design is therefore quite powerful in detecting changes. Yet Siegler et al. (1979) found only one longitudinal change over the 8-year period of their study: Intelligence scores increased slightly, perhaps due to repeated practice on the same items. Douglas and Arenberg (1978) reported declines over 7 years in General Activity, Friendliness, Thoughtfulness, Personal Relations, and Masculinity, but concluded that only the changes in General Activity and Masculinity were likely to be true maturational changes. It was unlikely, for example, that the observed decline in Friendliness was age related, because cross-sectional analyses had shown that older people were more friendly than younger. In a 6-year study of NEO-PI scales, Costa and McCrae (1988a) found a significant decline in Neuroticism but no change in Extraversion or Openness. Three-year longitudinal analyses of Agreeableness and Conscientiousness scales suggested a decline in both these variables.

These longitudinal findings show no consistent picture of personality change, nor do they replicate the trends found in cross-sectional studies. Neuroticism as measured by the NEO-PI showed a small decline, but closely related scales in the 16PF and GZTS did not. Of the several scales related to Extraversion, only one, General Activity, showed longitudinal change. None of the Openness scales (NEO-PI Openness; 16PF Tender-Mindedness, Imaginativeness, and Liberal Thinking; and GZTS Thoughtfulness) declined. NEO-PI Agreeableness scores declined, in contradiction to cross-sectional findings of increased Agreeableness in older subjects. Scales measuring Conscientiousness showed little or no change. These results strongly suggest that the small cross-sectional differences reported earlier were due to generational differences, not maturation.

Longitudinal studies are also subject to confounding influences. Readministration of the test may itself affect scores, and changes between one administration and the next may reflect social and historical change during the period, rather than any universal maturational shift. Alternative analytic designs have been devised to tease out these confounds, although they are themselves subject to other confounds. It is impossible to remove all confounding, because time, date, and age are mathematically dependent. However, by interpreting results from a variety of designs, reasonable inferences can be made about maturational effects (Costa & McCrae, 1982). When information from cross- and time-sequential analyses is added to the cross-sectional and longitudinal results, it reinforces the conclusion that there is little change during most of adulthood in the mean levels of personality traits (Costa & McCrae, 1988a; McCrae & Costa, 1990). A case could be made for declines in activity level, but these probably reflect physical aging rather than psychological aging, and in any case, even these changes are small. Some 80-year-olds are more active than many 30-year-olds.

C. Implications of Mean Level Stability

Null findings rarely excite attention, and yet the pervasive lack of evidence for maturational change in personality is extraordinarily important. It flatly contradicts age stereotypes that portray older men and women as hypochondriacal, socially withdrawn, rigid in attitudes, irritable, and egocentric. These traits are no more (or less) common in older groups than in younger. Disease, cognitive and sensory impairment, and societal neglect may mimic these traits and may help explain the stereotypes, but healthy individuals do not show normative changes on these personality dimensions simply as a result of growing old.

These findings should force a reconsideration of some forms of personality theory. They provide no evidence for the discrete stages of adult development which a number of theories depict (Erikson, 1950; Gould, 1978; Levinson et al., 1978)—a failure that is also seen in more focused investigations of the midlife crisis (Costa & McCrae, 1980b; Farrell & Rosenberg, 1981). Perhaps these theories should be recast as developmental progressions in life structures or current concerns; they do not seem to reflect changes in mood, social interaction, desire for novelty, nurturance, or achievement strivings, because all these are stable across adulthood.

Social psychologists sometimes construe personality in terms of social roles and argue that role changes necessarily entail changes in personality (Veroff, 1983). Such theories might predict declines in nurturance in empty-nest women or declines in achievement striving in retired men; these predictions would be wrong. Roles clearly change with age, but roles are not personality and apparently do not have much influence on it. Indeed, it is more likely that personality traits affect the roles we choose to play and the ways in which we interpret both chosen and assigned roles (McCrae & Costa, 1990).

III. STABILITY OF INDIVIDUAL DIFFERENCES

The fact that mean levels of most personality variables show little or no change with age does not necessarily imply that individuals do not change. Mean level stability could be observed even if all the individuals in the sample had undergone dramatic changes in the level of all personality variables—as long as the increases of some subjects were balanced by decreases of others. The second major question about stability thus concerns the maintenance of rank order in individual differences. This form of stability is usually measured as a stability coefficient, a retest correlation based on readministration of a measure after a period of years. Note that longitudinal studies that follow the same individuals over time are required for research on stability in individual differences; there are no cross-sectional short-cuts.

A. Retest Stability in Self-Reports

Aside from the early studies of Strong (1951) on vocational interests and Kelly (1955) on personality from college ages to middle adulthood, virtually all the evidence on this question comes from studies published in the past 20 years. Table I summarizes studies using self-report methods. Across instruments, sexes, initial ages, and retest intervals, there is consistent evidence of substantial stability, with median correlations ranging from .34 to .77. A careful examination of this table suggests that the magnitude of the stability coefficient depends more on the instrument than on initial age or retest interval. Instruments like the MMPI, which is better regarded as a measure of psychopathology than an inventory of normal personality, and the Edwards Personal Preference Schedule (EPPS; Edwards, 1959), which introduces distortion through a forced-choice format (Radcliffe, 1965), show relatively low stability; standard personality questionnaires such as the California Psychological Inventory (CPI; Gough, 1987), GZTS, and NEO-PI, show much higher values.

There is some evidence that retest correlations are lower for subjects initially under age 30. Finn's (1986) comparison of young and middle-aged adults on MMPI factor scales over a 30-year interval showed substantially higher stability for the older subjects, and Block (1977) found higher stability on CPI scales for his over-30 subjects than Helson and Moane (1987) reported for their under-30 subjects (although in this case initial age is confounded with retest interval). Siegler et al. (1990) concluded that about half the variance in true scores for personality scales is stable between college and middle age.

B. Artifact and Attenuation in Estimates of Stability

The data in Table I are all taken from self-report instruments, and it might be hypothesized that artifacts of that method are responsible for the apparent stability. Individuals may wish to present a consistent image of themselves, recall how they answered previously, and duplicate their earlier answers. This argument is hardly plausible for long retest intervals, and one study that empirically examined it provided no support. Woodruff (1983) asked middle-aged men and women to recall how they had answered the California Test of Personality 25 years earlier when they had been in college; she also asked them to complete the test as it described them now. Subjects' recollections were poor; in fact, original scores were more

TABLE I
Stability Coefficients for Recent Longitudinal Studies Using Self-Report Instruments

Study	Instrument	N	Sex	Initial age	Retest interval	Correlations Range	Correlations Median
Block (1977)	CPI	219	M, F	31–38	10		.71
Costa and McCrae (1978)	16PF	139	M	25–82	10	.24–.64	.50
Siegler et al. (1979)	16PF	331	M, F	45–70	2		.50
Leon et al. (1979)	MMPI	71	M	45–54	13	.07–.82	.50
				58–67	17	.03–.76	.52
				45–54	30	.28–.74	.40
Costa et al. (1980)	GZTS	60	M	20–44	12	.61–.85	.72
		87	M	45–59	12	.64–.85	.75
		32	M	60–76	12	.59–.87	.73
Mortimer et al. (1982)	Self-concept	368	M	Seniors	10	.51–.63	.55
Conley (1985a)	KLS factors	378	M, F	18–35	20	.34–.57	.46
Howard and Bray[a]	EPPS	266	M	Young managers	20	.31–.54	.42
	GAMIN	264	M		20	.45–.61	.57
Stevens and Truss (1985)	EPPS	85	M, F	College students	12	−.05–.58	.34
		92	M, F		20	−.01–.79	.44
Finn (1986)	MMPI factors	96	M	17–25	30	−.14–.58	.35
		78	M	43–53	30	.10–.88	.56
Helson and Moane (1987)	CPI	81	F	21	22	.21–.58	.37
				27	16	.40–.70	.51
	ACL	78	F	27	16	.49–.72	.61
Costa and McCrae (1988a)	NEO-PI	234	M	25–84	6	.60–.87	.74
		164	F	25–84	6	.58–.85	.73
Costa and McCrae (1992a)	GZTS	140	F	23–82	7	.65–.84	.73
Costa and McCrae (1992b)	GZTS	133	M	30–67	24	.61–.71	.65
Helson and Wink (1992)	CPI	101	F	43	9		.73
	ACL	96	F	43	9		.73
Costa et al. (in press)	CQS scales	273	M, F	17–83	6	.66–.83	.77

Note. CPI, California Psychological Inventory; 16PF, Sixteen Personality Factor Questionnaire; MMPI, Minnesota Multiphasic Personality Inventory; GZTS, Guilford–Zimmerman Temperament Survey; KLS, Kelly Longitudinal Study; EPPS, Edwards Personal Preference Schedule; GAMIN, Guilford/Martin Inventory of Factors; ACL, Adjective Check List: NEO-PI, NEO Personality Inventory; CQS, California Q-Set. Adapted in part from Costa and McCrae (1989b).
[a] Howard and D. W. Bray, personal communication, May 10, 1985.

strongly correlated with current scores than with recalled previous scores. Memory does not seem to inflate stability estimates.

A second hypothesis concerns response sets: To the extent that personality scores are determined by acquiescence, social desirability, or other response sets or styles, the stability of personality may reflect stability of these artifacts. However, when Costa, McCrae, and Arenberg (1983) partialled out the effects of acquiescence, extreme responding, naysaying, and falsification from 6-year stability coefficients in the GZTS, they found no appreciable decrease in stability. These data, again, suggest that the stability seen in Table I reflects substantive continuity of personality.

It is sometimes argued that even retest coefficients of .70 account for only half the variance in test scores and can be interpreted to mean that there is as much change as stability in individual differences. These arguments overlook the fact that personality tests are fallible indicators of personality traits. True stability is always underestimated because of short-term unreliability. Costa, McCrae, and Arenberg (1980) reported estimated 12-year stability coefficients on the GZTS of .80 to 1.00, and Costa and McCrae (1988a) found that Neuroticism, Extraversion, and Openness scales all showed stability coefficients of .90 or above when corrected for unreliability.

An alternative procedure for estimating true score stability utilizes an external criterion. When spouse ratings of Neuroticism, Extraversion, and Openness scales from the NEO-PI gathered in 1980 were correlated with concurrent self-reports on the same scales, the median cross-observer convergent correlation was .48. When the same ratings were correlated with self-reports obtained 6 years later, the median correlation was .47 (Costa & McCrae, 1988a). Clearly, the passage of 6 years had little effect on the cross-observer validity of the spouse ratings, suggesting little change in true personality. Mathematically, the ratio of the cross-lagged correlation to the concurrent correlation estimates the stability of the true score. In this study, the median estimated 6-year stability coefficient was therefore .98.

C. Stability in Personality Ratings

Although response biases and memory do not appear to inflate stability estimates, it can be argued that self-reports merely reflect the individual's self-image, and that these data speak only to the stability of the self-image. Rosenberg (1979) claimed that "people who have developed self-pictures early in life frequently continue to hold to these self-views long after the actual self has changed radically" (p. 58). If so, stability coefficients may reflect only a crystallized self-concept.

Personality ratings made by external observers provide a way to test this hypothesis. Studies of observer ratings on the California Q-Set (CQS; Block, 1961, 1971) provided early evidence of longitudinal consistency in personality. Block and his colleagues assessed men and women in junior high school, senior high school, and when subjects were in their 30s. Different panels of judges rated the individuals at different time periods. Correlations between senior high school and adulthood for 90 CQS items ranged from −.11 to .61; the median correlation was .26; and 61% of the correlations were statistically significant. These correlations are, of course, much lower than those seen in Table I, but that is understandable: They are based on single items instead of scales, confound changes due to aging with differences between the two panels of judges, and trace personality from adolescence, when it is not yet fully formed, into adulthood.

More direct evidence is provided by a 6-year study of spouse ratings of Neuroticism, Extraversion, and Openness to Experience in a sample of 167 men and women in the BLSA (Costa & McCrae, 1988a). Ranging from .62 to .83 for men and from .63 to .86 for women, these correlations were very similar to those found in studies of self-reports. A study of peer ratings for all five major dimensions of personality over a 7-year interval showed retest correlations ranging from .63 to .84 (Costa & McCrae, 1992b).

Because unreliability affects observer ratings just as it does self-reports, there is again reason to suppose that these coefficients underestimate true stability of personality. Because they are based on observer ratings, it is also clear that the high levels of stability are not artifacts of a crystallized self-concept.

IV. ADULT DEVELOPMENT: CHANGE IN THE 20s

The findings of stability during most of the adult period do not necessitate a return to the view that developmental psychology ends with the 18th birthday. Although Block demonstrated some continuity from high school into middle adulthood, the coefficients are not as high as those found between periods of adulthood, and several recent studies have suggested that personality development continues into college and beyond. Haan, Millsap, and Hartka (1986) argued from their findings that personality is not fully formed until it is shaped by the adult responsibilities of work and marriage. Helson and Moane (1987) studied women between ages 21 and 27 and 27 and 43 and noted that stronger correlations were found for the latter interval than for the former, despite the longer period of time covered. They concluded that "age 27 seems to have been at or near a watershed" (p. 179). Recent research thus seems to confirm the speculation of William James (1890) that character is set at about age 30.

Relatively low retest correlations imply greater variability of individual differences over time. There is also evidence for systematic mean level changes during this period. Mortimer, Finch, and Kumka (1982) used self-concept scales in a 10-year follow-up study of college seniors. They found increases in psychological well-being and competence, and decreases in sociability and unconventionality. Bachman, O'Malley, and Johnston (1978) also reported increases in self-esteem in late adolescence, and Jessor (1983) reported an increase in conventionality. In terms of the five-factor model, these findings suggest decreases in Neuroticism (increased well-being and self-esteem), Extraversion (sociability), and Openness (unconventionality), and an increase in Conscientiousness (competence). A comparison of student and adult norms on the NEO-PI provides cross-sectional confirmation of these age changes: College students score higher in Neuroticism, Extraversion, and Openness, and lower in Agreeableness and Conscientiousness, than do adults (Costa & McCrae, 1989a). Data from the Revised NEO-PI continue to support these generalizations (Costa & McCrae, 1994b).

These trends do not appear to be limited to college students. Navy recruits in the age range from 17 to 21 show a very similar profile to college students, although the men are more closed to values than college men, and the women are higher in excitement seeking than college women (J. Holland, personal communication, February 15, 1989). In both college students and Navy recruits, the most conspicious age difference is seen for Excitement Seeking, which is a full standard deviation above the mean of normative adult samples. Zuckerman (1979) has reported similar age trends for his measure of Sensation Seeking. Adults over the age of 30, regardless of educational background, appear to be less emotional and more settled and socialized than are individuals in their 20s. The effects of this change can be seen in the well-known decline in delinquency during the decade of the 20s, and historian Michael Rouche (1985/1987) even suggested that the violence, intemperance, and rowdiness that characterized the Franks in the early Middle Ages might be attributable in part to such age differences in personality: "A society with more than 60% of the population under age twenty-five could not avoid being youthful and energetic, no matter how often death struck" (p. 460).

V. ALTERNATIVE APPROACHES TO STABILITY OR CHANGE

A. Alternative Statistical Approaches

Most theory and research on personality in adulthood focuses on stability or change in mean levels or rank ordering, but some alternative statistical approaches have been advocated. A few studies have reported comparisons of factor structures in different age groups (e.g., Costa & McCrae, 1976, 1980b; McCrae, Costa, & Arenberg, 1980; Monge, 1975). Changes in factor structure would suggest changes in the relations among variables, perhaps reflecting qualitative changes in the organization of personality. Such changes would, of course, complicate and qualify the interpretation of mean level changes and stability coefficients. However, evidence to date points to the constancy of structure across age groups. In particular, the five-factor model of personality appears to apply equally well to school children (Digman & Inouye, 1986), college students (Norman, 1963), and adults from the full age range (McCrae & Costa, 1987).

Gerontologists sometimes assert that variability increases with age (e.g., Fozard, Thomas, & Waugh, 1976); apparently this is true for some cognitive and physiological variables. Personality variables, however, do not seem to show such increases. We tested equality of variances for subjects over and under the age of 60 who completed the NEO-PI in 1986 (Costa & McCrae, 1988a). Younger men showed significantly larger variance in NEO-PI Openness and Agreeableness scores than did older subjects (Fs [207, 293] = 1.41 and 1.38, respectively, $p < .05$), whereas younger women showed significantly larger variance than older women in Conscientiousness (F[268, 211] = 1.36, $p < .05$). Neither sex showed age differences in the variance of Neuroticism or Extraversion scores. Even the significant differences seen here are quite small in magnitude; there is apparently little change in variance across the adult age span.

Some writers have called for an examination of ipsative changes among personality variables over time (e.g., Mortimer et al., 1982). Such analyses would seek to find increases in the relative salience of personality characteristics. Bray and Howard (1983) examined age-related changes in a longitudinal study of AT&T managers who had taken the EPPS; the ipsative format of this instrument dictates that it can only assess the strength of motives relative to one another. Bray and Howard reported relative increases in the needs for Achievement and Autonomy and relative decreases in needs for Deference, Affiliation, and Intraception. Stevens and Truss (1985) also examined the EPPS over 12- and 20-year intervals, and interpreted the results to show maturational increases in Achievement, Autonomy, and Dominance, and decreases in Affiliation and Abasement for both sexes. Because both these studies began with subjects in their 20s, the results may reflect the same personality changes reviewed in Section IV. However, when Murray's (1938) needs were measured by a normative instrument, Jackson's PRF, in a sample ranging in age from 22 to 90 (Costa & McCrae, 1988a) none of these age relations was replicated cross sectionally.

The California Q-Set is also an ipsative measure of personality, and Q-correlation across its 100 items on two occasions gives an estimate of the stability of rank order of personality attributes within an individual. Corrected for interrater unreliability, Block (1971) showed mean Q-correlations of .54 for women and .56 for men from senior high school to their mid-30s. Costa, McCrae, and Siegler (in press) reported Q-correlations based on self-reports ranging from .12 to .86 over a 6-year interval; the median Q-correlations were .72 for women and .71 for men. Both studies suggest that the relative salience of personality characteristics is stable, particularly after adolescence.

B. Stability or Change in Other Personality Variables

We have focused on studies of trait measures from self-reports or ratings because most aging research has employed these instruments and because they have shown themselves to be reliable and valid. However, it is of some interest to note that most studies using other theoretical perspectives and measurement approaches have also generally failed to find substantial age effects. A two-year longitudinal study of the perceptual variables measured by the Holtzman Inkblot Technique showed no evidence of maturational effects (Costa & McCrae, 1986a). Sentence completion measures of ego development have shown stability in adulthood (McCrae & Costa, 1980; Vaillant & McCullough, 1987), and although Vaillant (1977) has reported maturation of defenses between college age and early adulthood, most studies of ways of coping in adults have found that a wide variety of coping strategies are used equally by adults of all ages (Lazarus & DeLongis, 1983; McCrae, 1982).

It is, of course, possible to demonstrate age effects if instruments are tailored to reflect social or psychological characteristics that do change in adulthood. For example, there are regular changes in the proportion of individuals who consider themselves middle-aged versus old or elderly (Bultena & Powers, 1978). Age identification, however, seems to be a relatively minor issue for most adults, and is rarely mentioned as part of the spontaneous self-concept (McCrae & Costa, 1988).

C. Subjective Personality Change

The idea that personality is fundamentally stable in adulthood is counterintuitive to some people, who may perceive a great deal of change in their own personalities. It has also been challenged by proponents of a phenomenological approach to the study of life span development (Ryff & Heincke, 1983), who are concerned with subjective conceptions of stability and change. A recent study by Krueger and Heckhausen (1993) asked young, middle-aged, and older adults to describe the developmental course of traits from each of the five personality domains. For all age groups and all domains, respondents predicted increases in desirable traits (e.g., *energetic, good-natured, purposeful, realistic, intelligent*) up to age 60, with modest declines thereafter. Their subjective impressions of personality change corresponded to Bühler's (1935) famous "curve of life," but were inconsistent with objective data: When the three age groups were asked to rate themselves on the traits, there were no age differences.

Krueger and Heckhausen (1993) argued that these data may be interpreted in two ways, either as evidence that subjective age changes are unfounded stereotypes, or—more provocatively—as a demonstration of the insensitivity of self-report personality measures to real age changes. In particular, they suggest that individuals may rate themselves *relative to others their own age,* effectively eliminating any main effects for age in both cross-sectional and longitudinal comparisons. If valid, this objection would undermine much of the psychometric research on personality and aging reviewed in this chapter.

But there are powerful reasons to believe that it is not valid. First, the data show telltale signs of stereotyping. Subjects appear to be much more sensitive to the desirability of the traits than to their specific content; their responses appear to reflect an evaluation of aging rather than an accurate understanding of it. Second, this theory would make it difficult to explain the age differences that are occasionally observed, such as the increase in conscientiousness after adolescence and the decline in activity among older individuals: Why are these differences not eliminated by the same process of implicit age adjustment? Third, the theory does not explain why age is singled out by respondents as the basis for comparison instead of, for example, race, social status, or gender. The fact that gender differences are routinely reported shows that self-report measures are sensitive to sex differences, although a priori one might expect that people would use gender as often as age as a basis of social comparison. Fourth, McFarland, Ross, and Giltrow (1992) explicitly tested this theory by asking older subjects to explain the basis of their self-ratings. In response to an open-ended question, none of the subjects mentioned comparison with age peers, and only 28% endorsed that option when it was one of two forced choices. McFarland et al. concluded that "subjects do not appear to evaluate their current status by comparing themselves with same-age peers" (p. 844).

A few longitudinal studies have contrasted subjective and objective changes. Woodruff and Birren (1972) compared personality scores from the California Test of Personality taken in college with actual and recalled scores from an administration 25 years later. They found that objective changes in personality were small, but subjective changes were large. Most individuals "thought that their adolescent level of adjustment was much lower than it actually had been" (p. 257). Krueger and Heckhausen (1993) pointed out that that study, too, could be explained by a changing basis of comparison at the two time points, but a later analysis of the data casts considerable doubt on the accuracy of subjective perceptions of change: Woodruff (1983) showed that recalled scores were poorly correlated with initial scores. Subjective age adjustments would affect mean levels but not retest correlations, so these data are best interpreted as evidence of the fallibility of memory and the need for objective longitudinal measures of personality.

When we asked subjects who completed the NEO-PI in 1986 if they had "changed a good deal," "changed a little," or "stayed pretty much the same" in personality since 1980, 51% reported that they had stayed the same, and 35% said they had changed only a little (Costa & McCrae, 1989b). A substantial minority, 14%, felt that they had changed substantially. However, when 6-year retest correlations were examined for these three subgroups separately, the median values ranged from .79 to .82, and repeated measures analyses showed little evidence of mean level changes. It appears that most people perceive stability in their personalities, and the few who do not are contradicted by objective evidence.

VI. Some Implications of Personality Stability

In the course of adult life individuals accumulate a lifetime of experience. They age biologically and face acute and chronic diseases. They pass through a variety of social roles, from novice parents and workers to grandparents, widows, and retirees. They share with others the impact of great social and cultural changes, and face their own personal history of triumphs and tragedies. Yet all these events and experiences have little or no impact on basic personality traits. This fact should be the basis for a new perspective: Personality is not a product of the life course, an outcome or dependent variable, but a robust and resilient set of dispositions within the individual that themselves help shape the life course. People are not mere pawns of the environment, but active agents who steadfastly pursue their own style of being throughout life.

A. Implications for Society and the Individual

Gerontologists interested in social planning have been concerned with normative personality change as a basis for policy. If people tended to withdraw and disengage from society with age, as Cumming and Henry (1961) proposed, then society should leave them alone. If social activity is better for morale (Maddox, 1963), then society should develop community centers and provide transportation and opportunities for socializing. Clearly, our review supports neither of these hypotheses: We find little evidence for normative changes of any kind. If we wish to serve the psychological needs of older citizens, we should offer them a range of options as wide as the range of individual differences in personality. For the lifelong open introvert, a bookmobile may be more appropriate than a social center.

For the individual, stability in personality is a source of identity and continuity, and is a basis for future planning. We must be able to anticipate our needs, interests, and attitudes if we wish to plan intelligently for career or family or retirement. Ideally, we should also be able to forecast how the significant others in our lives will behave and respond in years to come, and the stability of personality traits allows such predictions. Sadly, marriage counselors must often confront the problems that arise when one spouse assumes that he or she will be able to change the other.

The stability of personality poses a challenge for psychotherapy (Costa & McCrae, 1986b). The fact that most people do not change as a result of aging and the experience it typically brings does not mean that people cannot change, given the right therapeutic conditions. But it does suggest that people who are dissatisfied with their personality should seek help, because spontaneous improvement is unlikely. It also means that expectations for therapy may need to be modified. Perhaps we will come to see high Neuroticism or low Conscientiousness as conditions that people must learn to live with, rather than as diseases that can be cured. In that case, psychotherapy might well be viewed as an attempt to teach social skills and ways of coping that help the individual compensate for and adapt to basic personality dispositions.

B. Implications for Personality Research and Theory

Most research on the topic of personality and aging has asked what we have come to believe is the wrong question: How does personality change as a result of maturation or the formative experiences of the life course? Evidence on the stability of personality suggests a very different question: How do stable personality dispositions shape the life course and affect adjustment at all ages?

An example of this new perspective is found in research on psychological well-being. Instead of viewing happiness or unhappiness as a response to life events and circumstances, or to stages of development that yield a crisis at midlife and depression in old age, we have come to see happiness as the expression of enduring dispositions (Costa & McCrae, 1980a; Emmons & Diener, 1985; Watson & Clark, 1984). Individuals high in Neuroticism are prone to experience dysphoric affect, whereas those who are high in Extraversion are temperamentally high-spirited. Love and work also contribute to happiness, particularly for those high in Agreeableness and Conscientiousness (McCrae & Costa, 1991). Because personality dispositions endure, morale, well-being, and life satisfaction can be predicted 10 to 20 years in advance, and we can reinterpret the "mid-life crisis" as the form dysphoria takes during middle age in individuals chronically high in Neuroticism (Costa & McCrae, 1980a, 1984).

High levels of stability are generally assumed by researchers in psychosomatic medicine who attempt to link disease outcomes with psychological dispositions (e.g., Williams et al., 1980). It is far more plausible to suggest that a lifetime of hostility may predispose to coronary disease than to imagine that a transient phase of hostility in young adulthood will have lasting physiological consequences. However, the recent demonstrations of continued personality development up to age 30 suggest that psychosomatic researchers may want to begin their longitudinal studies after that age rather than in college, as has commonly been done (Siegler et al., 1990).

Longitudinal studies were essential for establishing the stability of personality; given the evidence for stability, they become useful in other ways (Costa & McCrae, 1992a). One particularly valuable feature of longitudinal research is the ability to accumulate data on a single sample. Every psychological variable is best evaluated in terms of its relation to other variables, but there is a practical limit to the number of questionnaires that subjects can be asked to complete at a single session. Over the course of decades, however, periodic assessments can yield increasingly rich archives of data (e.g., Eichorn, Clausen, Haan, Honzik, & Mussen, 1981). If the subjects were over age 30 when the data were collected, the assessments may for many purposes be considered concurrent (Costa & McCrae, 1985a).

Finally, the remarkable robustness of personality traits has clear implications for personality theory (Costa & McCrae, 1994a). Many different theories, from evolutionary to psychoanalytic, are consistent with the data on personality stability, but many others are not. Behaviorist, social learning, and social role theories in particular—theories that emphasize the shaping forces of the environment—cannot easily account for dispositions that endure over long periods of time and proportionately varied circumstances. This does not, of course, mean that the processes of learning or of enacting roles are not important in determining behavior. They do not, however, appear to affect the basic tendencies of the individual. Personality theories of the future will need to consider how processes of learning and adaptation allow individuals to cope with changing life circumstances while preserving their inner dispositions.

References

Bachman, J. G., O'Malley, P. M., & Johnston, J. (1978). *Adolescence to adulthood: Change and stability in the lives of young men.* Ann Arbor, MI: Institute for Social Research.

Block, J. (1961). *The Q-sort method in personality assessment and psychiatric research.* Springfield, IL: Charles C. Thomas.

Block, J. (1965). *The challenge of response sets.* New York: Appleton-Century-Crofts.

Block, J. (1971). *Lives through time.* Berkeley, CA: Bancroft Books.

Block, J. (1977). Advancing the psychology of personality: Paradigmatic shift or improving the quality of research? In D. Magnusson & N. S. Endler (Eds.), *Personality at the crossroads: Current issues in interactional psychology* (pp. 37–64). Hillsdale, NJ: Erlbaum.

Borgatta, E. F., & Lambert, W. W. (Eds.). (1968). *Handbook of personality theory and research.* Chicago: Rand McNally.

Borkenau, P. (1988). The multiple classification of acts and the Big Five factors of personality. *Journal of Research in Personality, 22,* 337–352.

Bray, D. W., & Howard, A. (1983). The AT&T longitudinal studies of managers. In K. W. Schaie (Ed.), *Longitudinal studies of adult psychological development* (pp. 266–312). New York: Guilford Press.

Bühler, C. (1935). The curve of life as studies in biographies. *Journal of Applied Psychology, 19,* 405–409.

Bultena, G. L., & Powers, E. A. (1978). Denial of aging: Age identification and reference group orientations. *Journal of Gerontology, 33,* 748–754.

Buss, D. M. (1992). Manipulation in close relationships: Five personality factors in interactional context. *Journal of Personality, 60,* 477–499.

Cattell, R. B., Eber, H. W., & Tatsuoka, M. M. (1970). *The handbook for the Sixteen Personality Factor Questionnaire.* Champaign, IL: Institute for Personality and Ability Testing.

Conley, J. J. (1985a). Longitudinal stability of personality traits: A multitrait-multimethod-multioccasion analysis. *Journal of Personality and Social Psychology, 49,* 1266–1282.

Conley, J. J. (1985b). A personality theory of adulthood and aging. In R. Hogan & W. H. Jones (Eds.), *Perspectives in personality* (Vol. 1, pp. 81–115). Greenwich, CT: JAI Press.

Cornoni-Huntley, J., Barbano, H. E., Brody, J. A., Cohen, B., Feldman, J. J., Kleinman, J. C., & Madans, J. (1983). National Health and Nutrition Examination I—Epidemiologic Followup Survey. *Public Health Reports, 98,* 245–251.

Costa, P. T., Jr., & McCrae, R. R. (1976). Age differences in personality structure: A cluster analytic approach. *Journal of Gerontology, 31,* 564–570.

Costa, P. T., Jr., & McCrae, R. R. (1978). Objective personality assessment. In M. Storandt, I. C. Siegler, & M. F. Elias (Eds.), *The clinical psychology of aging* (pp. 119–143). New York: Plenum Press.

Costa, P. T., Jr., & McCrae, R. R. (1980a). Influence of extraversion and neuroticism on subjective well-being: Happy and unhappy people. *Journal of Personality and Social Psychology, 38,* 668–678.

Costa, P. T., Jr., & McCrae, R. R. (1980b). Still stable after all these years: Personality as a key to some issues in adulthood and old age. In P. B. Baltes & O. G. Brim, Jr. (Eds.), *Life span development and behavior* (Vol. 3, pp. 65–102). New York: Academic Press.

Costa, P. T., Jr., & McCrae, R. R. (1982). An approach to the attribution of age, period, and cohort effects. *Psychological Bulletin, 92,* 238–250.

Costa, P. T., Jr., & McCrae, R. R. (1984). Personality as a lifelong determinant of well-being. In G. Malatesta & C. Izard (Eds.), *Affective processes in adult development and aging* (pp. 141–157). Beverly Hills, CA: Sage.

Costa, P. T., Jr., & McCrae, R. R. (1985a). Concurrent validation after 20 years: Implications of personality stability for its assessment. In J. N. Butcher & C. D. Spielberger (Eds.), *Advances in personality assessment* (Vol. 4, pp. 31–54). Hillsdale, NJ: Erlbaum.

Costa, P. T., Jr., & McCrae, R. R. (1985b). *The NEO Personality Inventory manual.* Odessa, FL: Psychological Assessment Resources.

Costa, P. T., Jr., & McCrae, R. R. (1986a). Age, personality, and the Holtzman Inkblot Technique. *International Journal of Aging and Human Development, 23,* 115–125.

Costa, P. T., Jr., & McCrae, R. R. (1986b). Personality stability and its implications for clinical psychology. *Clinical Psychology Review, 6,* 407–423.

Costa, P. T., Jr., & McCrae, R. R. (1988a). Personality in adulthood: A six-year longitudinal study of self-reports and spouse ratings on the NEO Personality Inventory. *Journal of Personality and Social Psychology, 54,* 853–863.

Costa, P. T., Jr., & McCrae, R. R. (1988b). From catalog to classification: Murray's needs and the five-factor model. *Journal of Personality and Social Psychology, 55,* 258–265.

Costa, P. T., Jr., & McCrae, R. R. (1989a). *The NEO-PI/NEO-FFI manual supplement.* Odessa, FL: Psychological Assessment Resources.

Costa, P. T., Jr., & McCrae, R. R. (1989b). Personality continuity and the changes of adult life. In M. Storandt & G. VandenBos (Eds.), *The adult years: Continuity and change* (pp. 45–77). Washington, DC: American Psychological Association.

Costa, P. T., Jr., & McCrae, R. R. (1992a). Multiple uses for longitudinal personality data. *European Journal of Personality, 6,* 85–102.

Costa, P. T., Jr., & McCrae, R. R. (1992b). Trait psychology comes of age. In T. B. Sonderegger (Ed.), *Nebraska Symposium on Motivation: Psychology and aging* (pp. 169–204). Lincoln: University of Nebraska Press.

Costa, P. T., Jr., & McCrae, R. R. (1994a). "Set like plaster"? Evidence for the stability of adult personality. In T. Heatherton & J. Weinberger (Eds.), *Can Personality Change?* (pp. 21–40). Washington, D.C.: American Psychological Association.

Costa, P. T., Jr., & McCrae, R. R. (1994b). Stability and change in personality from adolescence through adulthood. In C. F. Halverson, G. A. Kohnstamm, & R. P. Martin (Eds.), *The developing structure of temperament and personality from infancy to adulthood* (pp. 139–150). Hillsdale, NJ: Erlbaum.

Costa, P. T., Jr., McCrae, R. R., & Arenberg, D. (1980). Enduring dispositions in adult males. *Journal of Personality and Social Psychology, 38,* 793–800.

Costa, P. T., Jr., McCrae, R. R., & Arenberg, D. (1983). Recent longitudinal research on personality and aging. In K. W. Schaie (Ed.), *Longitudinal studies of adult psychological development* (pp. 222–265). New York: Guilford Press.

Costa, P. T., Jr., McCrae, R. R., & Siegler, I. C. (in press). Continuity and change over the adult life cycle: Personality and personality disorders. In C. R. Cloninger (Eds.), *Personality and psychopathology.* Washington, DC: American Psychiatric Press.

Costa, P. T., Jr., McCrae, R. R., Zonderman, A. B., Barbano, H. E., Lebowitz, B., & Larson, D. M. (1986). Cross-sectional studies of personality in a national sample: 2. Stability in neuroticism, extraversion, and openness. *Psychology and Aging, 1,* 144–149.

Cumming, E., & Henry, W. (1961). *Growing old.* New York: Basic Books.

D'Andrade, R. B. (1965). Trait psychology and componential analysis. *American Anthropologist, 67,* 215–228.

Dicken, C. (1963). Good impression, social desirability, and acquiescence as suppressor variables. *Educational and Psychological Measurement, 23,* 699–720.

Digman, J. M., & Inouye, J. (1986). Further specification of the five robust factors of personality. *Journal of Personality and Social Psychology, 50,* 116–123.

Douglas, K., & Arenberg, D. (1978). Age changes, cohort differences, and cultural changes on the Guilford-Zimmerman Temperament Survey. *Journal of Gerontology, 33,* 737–747.

Edwards, A. L. (1959). *Edwards Personal Preference Schedule manual.* New York: The Psychological Corporation.

Eichorn, D. H., Clausen, J. A., Haan, N., Honzik, M. P., & Mussen, P. H. (Eds.), (1981). *Present and past in middle life.* New York: Academic Press.

Emmons, R. A., & Diener, E. (1985). Personality correlates of subjective well-being. *Personality and Social Psychology Bulletin, 11,* 89–97.

Erikson, E. H. (1950). *Childhood and society.* New York: Norton.

Eysenck, H. J., & Eysenck, S. B. G. (1964). *Manual of the Eysenck Personality Inventory.* London: University Press.

Farrell, M. P., & Rosenberg, S. D. (1981). *Men at midlife.* Boston: Auburn House.

Finn, S. E. (1986). Stability of personality self-ratings over 30 years: Evidence for an age/cohort interaction. *Journal of Personality and Social Psychology, 50,* 813–818.

Fiske, D. W. (1978). *Strategies of personality research.* San Francisco: Jossey-Bass.

Fozard, J. L., Thomas, J. C., & Waugh, N. C. (1976). Effects of age and frequency of stimulus repetitions on two-choice reaction times. *Journal of Gerontology, 31,* 556–563.

Funder, D. C., & Colvin, C. R. (1988). Friends and strangers: Acquaintanceship, agreement, and the accuracy of personality judgment. *Journal of Personality and Social Psychology, 55,* 149–158.

Goldberg, L. R. (1982). From ace to zombie: Some explorations in the language of personality. In C. D. Spielberger & J. N. Butcher (Eds.), *Advances in personality assessment* (Vol. 1, pp. 203–234). Hillsdale, NJ: Erlbaum.

Gough, H. G. (1987). *California Psychological Inventory administrator's guide.* Palo Alto, CA: Consulting Psychologists Press.

Gould, R. L. (1978). *Transformations.* New York: Simon & Schuster.

Guilford, J. S., Zimmerman, W. S., & Guilford, J. P. (1976). *The Guilford-Zimmerman Temperament Survey Handbook: Twenty-five years of research and application.* San Diego, CA: EdITS.

Haan, N., Millsap, R., & Hartka, E. (1986). As time goes by: Change and stability in personality over fifty years. *Psychology and Aging, 1,* 220–232.

Helson, R., & Moane, G. (1987). Personality change in women from college to midlife. *Journal of Personality and Social Psychology, 53,* 176–186.

Helson, R., & Wink, P. (1992). Personality change in women from the early 40s to the early 50s. *Psychology and Aging, 7,* 46–55.

Jackson, D. N. (1984). *Personality Research Form manual* (3rd ed.), Port Huron, MI: Research Psychologists Press.

James, W. (1890). *Principles of psychology.* New York: Henry Holt.

Jessor, R. (1983). The stability of change: Psychosocial development from adolescence to young adulthood. In D. Magnusson & V. L. Allen (Eds.), *Human development: An interactional perspective* (pp. 321–341). New York: Academic Press.

Kelly, E. L. (1955). Consistency of the adult personality. *American Psychologist, 10,* 659–681.

Krueger, J., & Heckhausen, J. (1993). Personality development across the adult life span: Subjective conceptions vs cross-sectional contrasts. *Journal of Gerontology: Psychological Sciences, 48,* P100–P108.

Lazarus, R. S., & DeLongis, A. (1983). Psychological stress and coping in aging. *American Psychologist, 38,* 245–254.

Leon, G. R., Gillum, B., Gillum, R., & Gouze, M. (1979). Personality stability and change over a 30 year period—middle age to old age. *Journal of Consulting and Clinical Psychology, 47,* 517–524.

Levinson, D. J., Darrow, C. N., Klein, E. B., Levinson, M. L., & McKee, B. (1978). *The seasons of a man's life.* New York: Knopf.

Maddox, G. L. (1963). Activity and morale: A longitudinal study of selected elderly subjects. *Social Forces, 42*, 195–204.

McCrae, R. R. (1982). Age differences in the use of coping mechanisms. *Journal of Gerontology, 37*, 454–460.

McCrae, R. R., & Costa, P. T., Jr. (1980). Openness to experience and ego level in Loevinger's sentence completion test: Dispositional contributions to developmental models of personality. *Journal of Personality and Social Psychology, 39*, 1179–1190.

McCrae, R. R., & Costa, P. T., Jr. (1983). Social desirability scales: More substance than style. *Journal of Consulting and Clinical Psychology, 51*, 882–888.

McCrae, R. R., & Costa, P. T., Jr. (1987). Validation of the five-factor model of personality across instruments and observers. *Journal of Personality and Social Psychology, 52*, 81–90.

McCrae, R. R., & Costa, P. T., Jr. (1988). Age, personality, and the spontaneous self-concept. *Journal of Gerontology: Social Sciences, 43*, S177–S185.

McCrae, R. R., & Costa, P. T., Jr. (1989a). Different points of view: Self-reports and ratings in the assessment of personality. In J. P. Forgas & M. J. Innes (Eds.), *Recent advances in social psychology: An international perspective* (pp. 429–439). Amsterdam: Elsevier.

McCrae, R. R., & Costa, P. T., Jr. (1989b). Reinterpreting the Myers-Briggs Type Indicator from the perspective of the five-factor model of personality. *Journal of Personality, 57*, 17–40.

McCrae, R. R., & Costa, P. T., Jr. (1990). *Personality in adulthood.* New York: Guilford Press.

McCrae, R. R., & Costa, P. T., Jr. (1991). Adding *Liebe und Arbeit:* The full five-factor model and well-being. *Personality and Social Psychology Bulletin, 17*, 227–232.

McCrae, R. R., Costa, P. T., Jr., & Arenberg, D. (1980). Constancy of adult personality structure in adult males: Longitudinal, cross-sectional and times of measurement analyses. *Journal of Gerontology, 35*, 877–883.

McCrae, R. R., Costa, P. T., Jr., & Busch, C. M. (1986). Evaluating comprehensiveness in personality systems: The California Q-Set and the five-factor model. *Journal of Personality, 54*, 430–446.

McCrae, R. R., Costa, P. T., Jr., Dahlstrom, W. G., Barefoot, J. C., Siegler, I. C., & Williams, R. B., Jr. (1989). A caution on the use of the MMPI K-correction in research on psychosomatic medicine. *Psychosomatic Medicine, 51*, 58–65.

McFarland, C., Ross, M., & Giltrow, M. (1992). Biased recollections in older adults: The role of implicit theories of aging. *Journal of Personality and Social Psychology, 62*, 837–850.

Monge, R. H. (1975). Structure of the self-concept from adolescence through old age. *Experimental Aging Research, 1*, 281–291.

Mortimer, J. T., Finch, M. D., & Kumka, D. (1982). Persistence and change in development: The multidimensional self-concept. In P. B. Baltes & O. G. Brim, Jr. (Eds.), *Life-span development and behavior* (Vol. 4, pp. 264–315). New York: Academic Press.

Moskowitz, D. S. (1988). Cross-situational generality in the laboratory: Dominance and friendliness. *Journal of Personality and Social Psychology, 54*, 829–839.

Murray, H. A. (1938). *Explorations in personality.* New York: Oxford University Press.

Neugarten, B. L. (1977). Personality and aging. In J. E. Birren & K. W. Schaie (Eds.), *Handbook of the psychology of aging* (1st ed., pp. 626–649). New York: Van Nostrand-Reinhold.

Norman, W. T. (1963). Toward an adequate taxonomy of personality attributes: Replicated factor structure in peer nomination personality ratings. *Journal of Abnormal and Social Psychology, 66*, 574–583.

Radcliffe, J. A. (1965). [Review of *Edwards Personal Preference Schedule*]. In O. K. Buros (Ed.), *The sixth mental measurements yearbook* (pp. 195–200). Highland Park, NJ: Gryphon Press.

Rosenberg, M. (1979). *Conceiving the self.* New York: Basic Books.

Rouche, M. (1987). The early Middle Ages in the West. In P. Veyne (Ed.), *A history of private life: I. From pagan Rome to Byzantium* (A. Goldhammer, Trans., pp. 411–549). Cambridge, MA: Harvard University Press. (Original work published 1985).

Ryff, C. D., & Heincke, S. G. (1983). Subjective organization of personality in adulthood and aging. *Journal of Personality and Social Psychology, 44,* 807–816.

Schaie, K. W. (1977). Quasi-experimental research designs in the psychology of aging. In J. E. Birren & K. W. Schaie (Eds.), *Handbook of the psychology of aging* (1st ed., pp. 39–69). New York: Van Nostrand-Reinhold.

Siegler, I. C., George, L. K., & Okun, M. A. (1979). Cross-sequential analysis of adult personality. *Developmental Psychology, 15,* 350–351.

Siegler, I. C., Zonderman, A. B., Barefoot, J. C., Williams, R. B., Jr., Costa, P. T., Jr., & McCrae, R. R. (1990). Predicting personality in adulthood from college MMPI scores: Implications for follow-up studies in psychosomatic medicine. *Psychosomatic Medicine, 52,* 644–652.

Small, S. A., Zeldin, R. S., & Savin-Williams, R. C. (1983). In search of personality traits: A multimethod analysis of naturally occurring prosocial and dominance behavior. *Journal of Personality, 51,* 1–16.

Stevens, D. P., & Truss, C. V. (1985). Stability and change in adult personality over 12 and 20 years. *Developmental Psychology, 21,* 568–584.

Strong, E. K., Jr. (1951). Permanence of interest scores over 22 years. *Journal of Applied Psychology, 35,* 89–91.

Vaillant, G. E. (1977). *Adaptation to life.* Boston: Little, Brown.

Vaillant, G. E., & McCullough, L. (1987). The Washington University Sentence Completion Test compared with other measures of adult ego development. *American Journal of Psychiatry, 144,* 1189–1194.

Veroff, J. (1983). Contextual determinants of personality. *Personality and Social Psychology Bulletin, 9,* 331–343.

Watson, D., & Clark, L. A. (1984). Negative affectivity: The disposition to experience aversive emotional states. *Psychological Bulletin, 96,* 465–490.

Wiggins, J. S. (1968). Personality structure. *Annual Review of Psychology, 19,* 293–350.

Wiggins, J. S. (1979). A psychological taxonomy of trait-descriptive terms: The interpersonal domain. *Journal of Personality and Social Psychology, 37,* 395–412.

Wiggins, J. S., & Pincus, A. L. (1989). Conceptions of personality disorders and dimensions of personality. *Psychological Assessment: A Journal of Consulting and Clinical Psychology, 1,* 305–316.

Williams, R., Haney, T., Lee, K., Kong, Y., Blumenthal, J., & Wahlen, R. (1980). Type A behavior, hostility and coronary heart disease. *Psychosomatic Medicine, 42,* 539–549.

Woodruff, D. S. (1983). The role of memory in personality continuity: A 25 year follow-up. *Experimental Aging Research, 9,* 31–34.

Woodruff, D. S., & Birren, J. E. (1972). Age changes and cohort differences in personality. *Developmental Psychology, 6,* 252–259.

Woodruffe, C. (1985). Consensual validation of personality traits: Additional evidence and individual differences. *Journal of Personality and Social Psychology, 48,* 1240–1252.

Zuckerman, M. (1979). *Sensation seeking: Beyond the optimal level of arousal.* Hillsdale, NJ: Erlbaum.

═══ CHAPTER 12 ═══

IS THERE ADULT DEVELOPMENT DISTINCTIVE TO WOMEN?

RAVENNA HELSON, JENNIFER PALS, AND MARJORIE SOLOMON
INSTITUTE OF PERSONALITY AND SOCIAL RESEARCH,
UNIVERSITY OF CALIFORNIA, BERKELEY

Adult development usually refers to positive personality change after late adolescence, such as increased competence, perspective, maturity, and understanding (Vaillant, 1977; White, 1966). It may be conceptualized as taking place in the process of meeting the psychosocial needs of identity, intimacy, generativity, and integrity (Erikson, 1963), or through developmental tasks such as rearing children or assuming responsibilities in work (Havighurst, 1948). It can refer to the actualization of one's individual potential (Bühler, 1971; Jung, 1931/1960). Some would take adult development to be evidenced in the sequence of events that make a life story, or perhaps in the differentiation and coherence of one's life story (McAdams, 1993). Though attention tends to be focused on change in the positive direction, change may also be retrogressive (Baltes, 1987). Gains in self-control, for example, may be made at the cost of a loss in spontaneity.

There is disagreement about whether features of adult development can be demonstrated in most people or in some people in some circumstances, or whether patterns of variation are so great and depend on so many factors as to render the construct of adult development of doubtful scientific use. The disagreement depends in part on diverse conceptualizations of what development consists of, on the way personality and personality change are to be measured, and on difficulties inherent in making comparisons across cultures or historical periods (Helson, 1993a; Helson &

Stewart, 1994). Whether there is adult development is a version of the question of the meaning of life and the extent to which we can control our destinies. People are interested in such questions, but they are not easy to answer.

To ask whether there is adult development distinctive to women involves all of the above issues along with considerations of what is special about women. Gender differences seem very small in some contexts and very large in others (J. H. Block, 1976; Eagley, 1995; Maccoby & Jacklin, 1974), and policies to either minimize or maximize these differences have perplexing consequences (Hare-Mustin & Marecek, 1990). For example, emphasizing differences between men and women is often said to justify and perpetuate inequalities. However, minimizing gender differences may support the failure of society to take into account women's special needs, such as those associated with childbirth. Research designs present numerous dilemmas and agendas. If one compares women with men, one neglects aspects of development unique to women or of special interest to women. If one studies women alone, one leaves unclear the extent of difference between men and women. If one studies middle class white women, results cannot safely be attributed to women in general (Yoder & Kahn, 1993). Research agendas are not neutral. If one emphasizes biological differences, there is the implication of universality and enduringness. If one emphasizes how social institutions subjugate women, there is the implication that any picture one gets of women's adult development is incomplete or distorted. If one shows how sex differences are construed differently from one cultural group, society, or period of history to another, it would appear that women's adult development must be studied in context.

The purpose of this chapter is not to conclude that there is or is not a pattern of adult development distinctive among women, but to explore this very large question. Whether there are general features in the way women change over the course of adulthood cannot be decided on the basis of any single investigation. Although cross-sectional studies (in which individuals of different ages are studied at the same time) may sometimes be useful, what appears to be an age difference in such studies may actually be attributable to differences in cohort experience. (A cohort consists of people born about the same time who experience the same historical events at the same stage of life.) One needs longitudinal studies (that is, studies of the same individuals followed over time), conducted in a variety of historical and cultural contexts.

Not only is no one study sufficient to show whether there is adult development distinctive to women, but also it seems likely that no one point of view is sufficient. Theoretical perspectives are like searchlights that clarify certain areas but throw others into obscurity. Therefore, we will discuss several theoretical approaches and use them all.

The organization of this chapter is as follows: first we state several assumptions about the question of women's adult development. Then we consider four theoretical approaches to it, present two hypotheses or guiding ideas, and, after a brief review of social history affecting women since the 1920s, we evaluate evidence for the hypotheses in studies of American women born at various periods of the century.

I. SOME ORGANIZING ASSUMPTIONS

Knowing how different people are, and the great variety of conditions under which they live, is it reasonable to expect that their adult development could show important common features? Tooby and Cosmides (1990) make the case that human nature, which they define as a species-typical collection of complex psychological adaptations, is the same across races, ethnic groups, and classes (because of the evolutionary genetics of sexual recombination), but that males and females do constitute different "morphs." They believe that a complex coordination between the physiological and psychological systems of males and females has evolved to support sexual reproduction (see also Buss, 1989).

Our assumption in this chapter is that biological differences as socially interpreted and elaborated and as experienced by individuals produce lives with content that is substantially different for men and women. There are universal differences in the early socialization of male and female offspring (Chodorow, 1978). In most cultures there is a gender-based division of labor. Women have almost always occupied a subordinate position in society: they have been directed by men, possessed less income or property, and held fewer positions of high status. Women's sexual attractiveness to men and their childbearing function have always played key roles in the social construction of women's lives.

A second assumption is that the lives of men and women are more different in some cultures and in some periods of history than in others, and that they are never entirely different. In the United States in the 1950s, many men went to work in the city while their wives maintained their suburban homes. Today both men and women do paid work. Even when gender differences are pronounced, however, men and women share experiences that give an important shape to adult development: both women and men see their children mature and their parents die.

A third assumption is that there are not only main themes but also main variations in women's life stories (Lott, 1987). For example, there are usually women who follow the pattern expected of them in their society along with others whose attitudes and values are more like those of men. There are women who emphasize mothering, those who emphasize the role of intimate companion, and those who emphasize work and career. Other variations may be related to culture, class, cohort, or psychological pattern.

In sum, it is reasonable to look for general features in women's adult development as long as one realizes the complexity of the search.

II. SOME IDEAS AND THEORIES ABOUT WOMEN'S ADULT DEVELOPMENT

Ideas about women's adult development may be grouped for the purposes of this chapter into four categories: functionalist, relational, conflict, and normative. Each category includes a mixture of theories and what are more properly considered as interpretive frameworks or perspectives.

A. Functionalist Perspectives

Functionalists interpret personality differences between men and women at different stages of life as manifesting and as having the function of supporting the biological or social system out of which they are said to have arisen. For example, Buss (1989) showed that across many cultures young women valued ambition and industriousness in a mate more than young men did, whereas young men valued physical attractiveness in a mate more than young women did. He interpreted these differences in terms of evolutionary selection pressures which led to different reproductive strategies in males and females.

Similar gender differences might be given an alternative functionalist interpretation in terms of the division of labor in society between instrumental and affective tasks (Parsons & Bales, 1955). Perhaps it is found that young women are more interested in finding a marital partner than young men, who are more interested in vocational goals; or perhaps young women are less planful and more adaptable than young men. These differences may be construed as serving the function of preparing for adult roles: for example, not having plans of their own, women can adapt more easily to the husband's way of life.

Erikson (1963, 1968) characterizes the developmental task of adolescence and the transition into adulthood as the formation of identity, with the resulting capacity to give fidelity to work, values, and other people. His treatment of differences between males and females in the development of identity is functionalist in that it assumes the importance of biology in determining gender roles. In discussing the development of identity in young men, or in a general way, he emphasizes vocational choice. For a young woman, he says, identity formation involves the recognition of her "inner space" (reproductive capacity) and its integration into other aspects of her self. The choice of a husband, he says, is both the expression of a young woman's identity and an important determinant of it. Thus, he links the process of identity formation in a young woman to anatomy, potential for parenting, and partner.

The functionalist theory with the broadest life-span reach on the topic of sex differences is that of Gutmann (1987). The personalities of young adults show a gender specialization, he says, that is conducive to the propagation of the species. Young men accentuate personality characteristics appropriate for earning a living and protecting the family, and young women accentuate characteristics appropriate for helping the husband and caring for children. In adapting to young adult roles, each sex has to suppress characteristics construed as typical of the other; but in the second half of life, men and women each begin to relax this suppression and show more of the characteristics that had been attributed to the other.

B. Women's Development in Relationships

A second framework may be considered to have affiliations with object relations theory, the major modern development within psychoanalysis. A central idea is that the self in all human beings develops from early childhood throughout life in the context of important relationships. The influence of relationships is particularly evident in women, because men tend to resist what they construe as dependence and emphasize autonomy (Jordan, Kaplan, Miller, Stiver, & Surrey, 1991).

Whereas Erikson considers intimacy a developmental task that requires a previous development of identity, relational theorists maintain that issues of identity and intimacy are inextricably linked in female development, if not in the development of both males and females (Franz & White, 1985). Josselson (1987) describes women's lives as unfolding in the context of organizing relationships that she calls "anchors." While each woman constructs her own sense of personal identity, the anchoring process by which this sense of self-definition comes about demonstrates the relational dimension of development characteristic of women. In Josselson's study, women successful in careers had anchoring relationships with mentors.

Gilligan (1982) emphasized relational issues in her three-stage model for women's moral growth. Initially there is a focus on caring for the self to ensure survival. The next phase is one in which the woman develops a connection between self and others that is articulated by the concept of responsibility. The notion of responsible care is confused with self-sacrifice, so that women at this stage have limited awareness of their own needs and agency. The transition to the third stage is preceded by a recognition of the "illogic of the inequality between the other and the self" (p. 74). Responsible care then becomes a self-chosen value which takes into account both the possibilities and the limitations of one's actions in the lives of others as well as one's responsibility for self-development.

Feminists who hold the relational perspective believe that women's interest in others and their gift for sharing and mutuality are downgraded and misinterpreted as dependence and triviality by a patriarchal society (Gilligan, 1982; Jordan et al., 1991; Miller, 1976). These theorists say that Erikson (1963), Kohlberg (1973), and Levinson (1978) wrongly assume the central importance of autonomy in their accounts of development. Women may appear inferior by these male standards, but should be assessed in terms of their own.

C. Conflict Perspectives

Conflict theorists, of whom Karl Marx is the best known example, study processes maintaining the distribution of power in society and the consequences of this distribution. Most feminists hold a conflict perspective. Without disputing the existence of the differences between men and women described by functionalists and relationalists, those with a conflict perspective attribute the origin of these differences to the subordinate position of women in society. For example, if women are more adaptable than men, they would say that it is because society makes women dependent on men.

"What peculiarly signalizes the situation of woman," wrote Simone de Beauvoir (1953) more than 40 years ago, "is that she—a free and autonomous being like all human creatures—nevertheless finds herself living in a world where men compel her to assume the status of the Other" (p. xxviii). She analyzed how this situation affected young women, married women, aging women, and women in special categories, such as lesbians, independent women, and prostitutes. "The first twenty years of [a] woman's life are extraordinarily rich. . . . [But] at twenty or thereabouts mistress of a home, bound permanently to a man, a child in her arms, she stands with her life virtually finished forever" (p. 451). Of old women she said, "Old women take pride in their independence; they begin at last to view the world through their own eyes . . . [but] the highest form of liberty available to the woman parasite is stoical defiance or skeptical irony. At no time in her life does she succeed in being at once effective and independent" (p. 561).

Women's lives in the West have changed a great deal since Beauvoir wrote *The Second Sex.* However, American feminists of the 1970s continued to provide evidence that women's subordinate status caused them pain and restricted their development. Bernard (1972) wrote on the inequities of "his and her" marriage, and Bart (1971) described depression in "empty-nest" women whose whole adult lives had consisted of mothering their children.

Contemporary feminists, among other holders of the conflict perspective, often hold a constructivist position, according to which we do not discover reality but actively construct the meanings that shape our experience (K. J. Gergen, 1985; Hare-Mustin & Marecek, 1990). They argue that power elites assert their authority through control over these meanings. For example, the idea that the menopause is devastating for women is attributed to patriarchal bias in functionalist constructions, which reduce women to their biological roles and disregard the fact that most women do not want to continue having children (Barnett & Baruch, 1978; Datan, 1986).

Some feminists work toward new constructions of women's lives (M. M. Gergen, 1990; Heilbrun, 1988), including constructions that bring to light the influence on women of subordinate status and the resourcefulness of individual women despite low power (Franz & Stewart, 1994; Stewart, 1994).

D. Normative Perspectives

The normative perspective is concerned with how adult development takes place under the structuring influence of social norms. Neugarten (1977) described the timing norms or "social clock" that regulates the age-appropriateness of various endeavors for men and women, in part through feelings of anxiety or self-esteem that one experiences in recurrent appraisals of how well one is doing for one's age.

Helson, Mitchell, and Moane (1984) developed the concept of "social clock projects" related to the major commitments of adult life: family and work. They illustrated the idea in a sample of college women who grew up in an era (the late 1950s) when they were expected to marry in their early 20s. Most women started out on the "feminine social clock" pattern of marriage, child-rearing, and homemaking, but some followed the "masculine occupational clock." Some women with a feminine social clock project were "late" in finding a husband or becoming a mother; others experienced the disruption of their project through divorce. Personality characteristics influenced the path a woman followed, and in turn her experience in the different phases of her project (becoming a mother, for example) influenced subsequent personality change. According to Helson et al., historical periods vary in the structure and strictness of timing norms about the age at which various advances in social clock projects should be accomplished, how different the projects assigned to men and women are, and how projects evolve or are combined over time. In their view, adult development is related to the social clock projects available and to individual differences in the ability to make commitments and to change with different phases of the project or with changing times.

Social clock projects are influenced not only by norms but also by the occurrence and timing of major social events or changes in social climate. Stewart and Healy (1989) believe that events that occur in late adolescence or early in young adulthood have the biggest influence on the formation of identity, because at this time the individual is uncommitted and looking for guidelines. Duncan and Agronick (1995) found that women who had recently graduated from college during the height of the women's movement were more likely at midlife to report this event as having been a major influence on their lives than women who were older (and already committed to wife–mother roles) when the women's movement was at its height.

III. WOMEN'S LIVES FROM THE 1920s TO THE 1990s

Before turning to our hypotheses and to empirical studies of women's adult development, let us review briefly some social history affecting American women since World War I. The 1920s brought strong cultural ferment that included a break with Victorian conceptions of gender roles. However, both the Great Depression of the 1930s, when the male role of provider was threatened (Elder, 1974), and then World War II, when the male role of soldier and protector needed support, reinforced the traditional notions. The psychosocial effects of the Depression and World War II seem to have fed an exaggerated cult of women's domestic role in the late 1940s and 1950s. Even though women had in fact participated heavily in the labor force during World War II, they were "helping out." Their place was at home. During this time they married at a younger age, had more children, and dropped in educational level. Thus, the conception of gender roles remained unusually firm and distinct for three decades (Skolnick, 1991). Then a complex of long-term and newly arising factors led to dramatic changes in gender roles in the 1960s and 1970s. These factors included increased longevity and overpopulation, leading to changes in attitudes toward birth control, a reduction in birth rate, and an elongated stretch of "child-free" time for women; the need for women as service workers in the expanding postwar economy, and beginning in the early 1970s the need for two wage-earners in a family to combat inflation; the changing structure of the family, including a rising divorce rate; increasing levels of graduate and professional education among women; and the women's movement (Bianchi & Spain, 1986; Chafe, 1972; Giele, 1993; Skolnick, 1991).

Figure 1 shows replies from a questionnaire returned by more than 700 alumni of a west coast women's college. The question was, When you were in college, how long did you expect to do paid work? It is apparent that women who attended college in different decades from the 1920s to the 1970s had very different life expectations.

Central to this chapter is the fact that several longitudinal studies cover these eras of rapid change, and if it is possible to compare their information we may be able to obtain much of value on the generality of adult development in women.

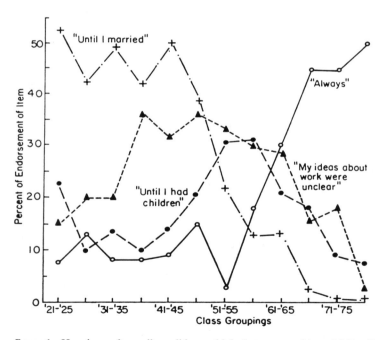

FIGURE 1   How long after college did you think that you would work? Replies from 700 Mills College alumni of 12 age groups. Figure is from R. Helson, T. Elliott, and J. Leigh, "Adolescent Personality and Women's Work Patterns," in *Adolescence and Work* (p. 266), by D. Stern and D. Eichorn (Eds.), 1989, Hillsdale, NJ: Erlbaum. Copyright 1989 by Lawrence Erlbaum Associates, Inc.

IV. SOME POSSIBLE GENERAL FEATURES OF WOMEN'S ADULT DEVELOPMENT

What shall we look for from these studies? We have chosen two hypotheses, both derived from functionalist ideas, because the functionalist perspective has a longer history and a more central place in the field of psychology than the relational, conflict, and normative perspectives. However, we will draw upon all four perspectives in evaluating the evidence for or against these hypotheses. The evidence comes from four longitudinal studies and one cross-sectional study, each representing a different cohort.

The first hypothesis is that in late adolescence women are primarily interested in marriage and family and do not have strong vocational goals. This is a functionalist hypothesis because of its supposition that young women prepare themselves for the biological and social roles of mothering. When data are available from both men and women, young men are expected to emphasize vocational goals over marriage. The strength of a goal may be manifested by its frequency of mention in response to a question about goals, its being given a high priority, or a demonstration that it predicted subsequent behavior.

The second hypothesis tests Gutmann's conception (1987, see section II.B) of a biosocial parental imperative that relaxes with age. Young adult women are expected to show nurturance and suppression of their own assertiveness as part of a division of labor conducive to child-rearing, but to increase in independence and planfulness in later life. Men are expected to show independence and planfulness in the period of early parenting but to become less achievement oriented and more concerned with relationships in later life.

To evaluate these hypotheses we will examine longitudinal studies in which the average participant was about 25 years old in the middle of the Great Depression (the Terman Study), in the era following World War II (IHD studies), or in the early 1960s (Mills Study), and then turn to samples of younger males and females who have been followed over shorter time spans or in preadolescence and adolescence alone.

V. RELATIONAL AND VOCATIONAL GOALS OF YOUNG WOMEN

A. The Terman Study

The Terman sample consisted of men and women first identified as having high IQs as school children (see the Appendix for details). Both men and women were highly educated for the times, but it is particularly impressive that 67% of the women graduated from college and 24% completed graduate degrees (usually M.A.'s) during the 1930s, when less than 8% of the California population was graduating from college (Tomlinson-Keasey & Keasey, 1993).

Most Terman women were between the ages of 23 and 27 in 1936. At this time the sample was asked, "Have you definitely chosen your life work?" and "Describe your ultimate goals as fully as you can at this time." Nearly all of the men answered the question about goals with the name of one occupation, but many of the women gave at least two responses. Of codable replies from 290 women who had participated in both 1936 and 1972, half mentioned homemaking and 61% mentioned occupational goals (Holahan, 1994). This rather surprising amount of work orientation may be attributable to the fact that they were adolescents in the 1920s, when there was questioning of prevailing gender roles, combined with the fact that they had been identified as gifted and were highly educated. Also, during the Depression, women often needed to bring in income, though they were subject to the prejudice that women who worked were taking jobs away from men and were expected to give up their jobs when they married.

"The careers of women are often determined by extraneous circumstances rather than by training, talent, or vocational interest" (Terman & Oden, 1959, p. 144). It is true that 88% of the women married, and that from then on they generally derived their identity from their husbands and their social status from his achievements (Tomlinson-Keasey & Keasey, 1993). Being single or divorced or being married with no children was highly related to employment, and Terman and Oden (see above) saw these features of life style as "extraneous factors" rather than as expressions of the women's own desires. Nevertheless, the Terman women were not entirely husband oriented and malleable: there was a significant relation between plans for homemaking or career during young adulthood and the predominant life pattern as described by the women many years later (Holahan, 1994). Though the largest categories of paid employment for these gifted, college-educated women were office worker and school teacher, about 60% of the women in 1972 (average age 61) classified themselves as career or income workers and 40% as homemakers.

In sum, as young adults the Terman women were interested in marriage and expected to accommodate the needs of the husband and family. However, many also expressed occupational interests, and despite family priorities, those who did tended eventually to go on to stable work patterns.

B. The IHD Studies

Women in the IHD samples (see the Appendix for details) were studied as high school students in the late 1930s or early 1940s, a time of strongly differentiated gender roles. IHD investigators agree that the women were socialized to want a traditional gender role (Stroud, 1981) and that they were programmed for marriage (Clausen, 1993). They were not given the encouragement that their brothers received to go to college, and if they worked, they did not expect to stay in the job. According to Clausen (1993), young women gave more thought than young men to the kind of person they wanted to marry.

In a study of planful competence in adolescents, Clausen (1993) measured competence as the sum of three components: dependability, intellectual investment, and self-confidence. In males the three components were correlated and predicted vocational success and much else in their lives. For female adolescents competence was a much less powerful variable. It predicted status of husband and number of children, but little else. For females, the component of self-confidence was strongly related to physical attractiveness, and it predicted both marital satisfaction and life satisfaction more strongly than the total competence score.

According to Stroud's study (1981) of college-educated women in the more advantaged of the two IHD samples, there was little evidence for career motivation among these women as adolescents. "The distinctive characteristics of adolescent girls who became work-committed women was their exclusion from . . . traditional pathways. . . . Viewed as the least attractive physically and the least sex-typed in feminine style and behavior, they were self-conscious, basically anxious, self-defensive, and had bodily concern" (p. 373). Only much later did these women come to differ from their peers in intellectual orientation and assertiveness.

These findings from studies of samples in the IHD studies corroborate the functionalist conception that late adolescent women are primarily interested in a good marriage and that physical attractiveness is an important resource in attaining this goal. Traits conducive to vocational success (planful competence) were, as hypothesized, more important in young men than in young women.

C. The Mills Study

After World War II and throughout the 1950s there was much emphasis on early marriage and a big family. The Mills women were studied first as college seniors in 1958 or 1960 (see the Appendix for details). The world was changing, but 88% of the Mills women had plans or hopes to marry, and 75% of them wanted to have 3 or more children (Helson, 1993b). (They actually had an average of 2.2 children, as compared with 3.4 for the IHD women.)

Some 20% had long-term career aspirations, and many more had qualified or contingent career interests. Though planning was difficult, they expected to work until they had children, after their children were older, if their husbands were cooperative, or as long as family interests were not adversely affected (Helson, 1993b).

As might be expected, women with traditional life plans were clearest in their goals. A personality index of the characteristics of purposiveness, independence, and ambition (labeled agency) at age 21 did not predict work status at age 27, when most women were having or expecting children, but it did predict work status at age 43 (Roberts, 1994). Physical attractiveness in college (rated from yearbook pictures) was not so powerful an advantage in this sample as in the IHD sample: beautiful women married earlier but were also more likely to divorce (Kaner, 1994).

In the early adult years, the marriage and family orientation of the Mills women fit fairly well the functionalist framework. However, the women did not lack the capacity to develop vocational goals; rather, the nature of the "feminine social clock project" they expected to carry out, especially the idea that their lives would be shaped by the man they married, precluded differentiated planning and attached only marginal relevance to their college-age vocational goals. Over the next 15 years the women completed the most intensive phase of child-rearing and the social world changed considerably, providing opportunities for the expression of vocational goals.

D. Illinois Valedictorian Project

As detailed in the Appendix, this study began with high achievers, more than half of them women, from the graduating classes of Illinois high schools in 1981. The sample was followed through the next decade (Arnold, 1993). Although there were no gender differences in high school, the intellectual self-esteem of the women dropped sharply by the sophomore year of college. It rose somewhat by senior year, but remained significantly lower than that of the men. A persistent theme among the young women was concern about combining a career and family. As seniors in college, their professional expectations tended to be vaguer that those of the men in the sample.

    This vagueness, found also in the Mills women, can be interpreted in several ways. Arnold argues that the realization of early promise is more difficult and complex for women than for men, at least in part because they lack "tacit knowledge," defined as career-related understanding that is rarely verbalized and not explicitly taught. Women, Arnold says, are constrained in the development of their career identity by their lack of support from models and their inability to see themselves in high-level career settings. She gives two case studies. One of them describes a young woman with many self-doubts and uncertainties who became highly successful in her profession through excellent support and role modeling. The other describes a young woman who had not developed a career identity. In Arnold's view, at least one factor was that she had not found sufficient support.

    The Valedictorian study gives evidence that despite radical changes in opportunities for women and in attitudes toward their career achievement, young women continued to suffer uncertainty about investment in careers.

E. Identity Formation in High School Males and Females

Archer (1985) studied the process of identity formation in a sample of 6th, 8th, 10th, and 12th graders in order to test the idea that many adolescent women engage in a "pseudoexploration" of occupational identity in order to fill time until marriage. She interviewed male and female students to assess their identity development overall and in relevant domains including occupational choice and career–family priorities. For each domain, the state of identity formation was assessed as a function of two major dimensions of self-definition, the exploration of possibilities and the commitment to a self-defining choice (Marcia, 1980).

    In the domain of occupational choice, Archer found no gender differences in the process of identity formation. In the domain of career–family priorities, however, girls were more likely than boys to demonstrate evidence for both exploration and commitment. Among the 12th graders, girls were more likely than boys to anticipate conflict between occupational and family roles, and of those who anticipated conflict, girls were more than three times more likely than boys to express concern about the resolution of this conflict. Finally, 12th-grade girls were more likely than boys to be in a state of active exploration with regard to the overall sense of personal identity.

These findings suggest that contemporary young women actively explore future occupational possibilities to the same degree as young men, but that their career exploration is more complex and ultimately more difficult to resolve because of their greater concern and questioning about having both family and career. Furthermore, this conflict appears to be central to their sense of identity, particularly in the later teenage years. Archer concludes: "Exploration for these girls is genuine; it is not pseudoexploration. This is in the face of a society that offers little support to these girls about to be torn between two greatly valued goals in their lives" (p. 311). These were high school students. We have already seen from the Illinois Valedictorian Study (Arnold, 1993) how the identity exploration of capable young women becomes more confused as the realities of adult life draw near.

F. Summary and Discussion

All studies show that most late adolescent women have considerable interest in marriage and family. In the older studies family and career were considered separate tracks, so that serious investment in one tended to preclude the other. Nevertheless, a high proportion of Terman women (61%) were interested in vocational goals. Most IHD women, representatives of the most conservative cohort, confined their ambitions to the roles of wife and mother. From the Mills sample to the most recent samples, many young women hoped to combine family and work. However, their vocational planning was found to be more diffuse and contingent than that of young men. This diffuseness may be functional for a sex-based division of labor, in that the young woman's willingness to relinquish or compromise vocational goals facilitated male careers, marriage, and the rearing of children.

From the conflict point of view, however, our findings show that women have been disadvantaged by lack of opportunities in the work world, and they continue to be handicapped by difficulties in developing clear goals. Aspiring to and actively working toward a clear career goal allows one to incorporate these future role expectations into the current self-concept (Heise, 1990; Markus & Nurius, 1986). Thus, self-esteem suffers when one lacks self-enhancing goals. This may be the reason that the Terman women had a persisting lack of confidence and guilt that they had not lived up to their potential (Tomlinson-Keasey, 1990). In the studies of the younger women, both Arnold and Archer took a conflict perspective in attributing the women's unclear life plans to lack of social support and an unfair share of responsibility.

Though young women's persistent concern for marriage and family may be counted as support for the functionalist perspective, it may also be construed as an indication of their relational nature. Holders of the relational point of view would call attention to the social value of this concern and question its construction in terms of deficiencies—"lack" of planfulness or the "failure" of women to undertake and persevere in demanding careers.

From the normative point of view, the demonstration of differences in career interest in different cohorts indicates the importance of the social world for women's motivational structure. The fact that the IHD sample showed more exclusive orientation toward marriage and family than the Terman and Mills women is consistent with the idea that people born in the 1920s grew up in a world structured by a sequence of conditions—depression, war, affluence, and stability—that produced and maintained particularly specialized gender roles (Skolnick, 1991).

VI. GENDER-RELATED PERSONALITY CHANGE

Now we consider the second hypothesis, that men and women change in personality as they assume and relinquish the responsibilities of parenting, or more generally, as they develop from young adulthood to later adulthood. In this section we will review findings only from the three longitudinal studies that cover the entire period from young adulthood to later life.

A. The Terman Study

The Terman Study has very few personality measures. However, there is information about interests and values of the men and women in the sample. Comparing a Terman subsample of college-educated men and women, Holahan (1984b) found that the men emphasized work values more than the women at both 30 and 70, but men's occupational concerns decreased more than women's by age 70, so that the gap narrowed considerably. Even more striking was the change in endorsement of home and family as life goals: in 1940 (age 30) only 7% of the men mentioned home and family as a life goal, in comparison with 64% of the women. In 1981 (age 70), 40% of the men and 47% of the women mentioned home and family as their life goal. The change in values of Terman men had begun before age 70: at age 62 Terman men derived even more satisfaction from their family life than from their occupational involvements (Sears, 1978).

In a study of longitudinal and cohort factors in marital attitudes, Holahan (1984a) showed that a college-educated sample of Terman men expressed more agreement at age 70 than at age 30 with items such as "The husband and wife should express their love in words." Women were more inclined than men to agree with this item, but they had not changed significantly from ages 30 to 70. Recruiting a younger sample of 30-year-old men and women, she found that the younger cohort of men agreed significantly more with this item than the Terman men had at age 30, and did not differ from the younger women or from the Terman women. (The young men and women were less satisfied with their marriages, however, than the Terman men and women had been at the same age [see also Tomlinson-Keasey & Blurton, 1992]. Whether the younger men and women were freer in being critical, had higher standards for relationship, or were attesting to frustrations in modern marriage is not clear.) One concludes that the change in attitude on the part of the Terman men may be due in part to greater affiliativeness with age but that it may be due also to a change in social climate with a particular influence on men.

B. IHD Studies

Haan, Millsap, and Hartka (1986) conducted a study of personality change in men and women that combined the Oakland (OG) and Berkeley (BG) samples (see the Appendix). The combination of these two samples is not ideal for our purposes, because they differ in age by about 7 years. Nevertheless, we shall assume that the participants at age 30 (BG) and 37 (OG) were more actively engaged in parenting than at ages 40 (BG) and 47 (OG), and more so still than at ages 53 and 61. From ages 30 and 37 to ages 40 and 47, men and women both changed in the same directions, but only for women were the changes significant: women increased on Q-sort factors labeled self-confidence, cognitive commitment, outgoingness, and warmth. From ages 40 and 47 to ages 53 and 61 women decreased in assertiveness (a scale with connotations of undercontrol and hostility) and both men and women increased in warmth.

These findings are most consistent with an idea that has not been mentioned because it is not gender specific: that middle-aged adults show superior cognitive and executive abilities and relational skills (Neugarten, 1977; Stevens-Long, 1990). In addition, support for the Gutmann hypothesis may be found in the fact that only the women increased significantly in self-confidence, outgoingness, and cognitive commitment, and that the men increased significantly in warmth (though the women did also). Though the women's decline on assertiveness between the middle and the late periods may be taken as contrary to the Gutmann hypothesis, it may indicate that their self-assertion was sufficiently secure to reduce rebellious undercontrol and hostility. The Haan et al. study is valuable, but it was not intended to test the Gutmann hypothesis, and the evidence from it for this purpose remains fuzzy.

C. The Mills Study

Comparing the Mills women and their male partners at the early parental and postparental periods, Wink and Helson (1993) found that the husbands described themselves on the Adjective Check List (ACL) (Gough & Heilbrun, 1983) as less affiliative and as more competent and independent than their wives at the earlier time but not at the second. Looking at change in those couples who were the same individuals at both times of testing, they found that the men did not decline in competence, independence, and self-confidence but the women showed sharp increases. Husbands increased significantly in affiliation, whereas wives did not.

Overall, the findings were in the direction predicted by Gutmann. However, women without children changed in the same ways as women with children, so that literal parenting did not explain the findings. Furthermore, data available from a subsample of the parents of the Mills women did not give the same results. The parents had filled out the ACL only once but at the same postparental ages as their daughters and sons-in-law. Even at age 52, the mothers scored lower on competence and independence than their husbands. Very few of the mothers did paid work, and they had received less education than their spouses and daughters.

D. Summary and Discussion

The three longitudinal studies that we have examined used different kinds of measures and covered different age spans and periods of history. Nevertheless, all show some support for the idea that gender differences in interests and personality decrease with age. The fact that Mills women with and without children changed in the same ways indicates that literal parenting was not the critical factor. However, from a functionalist perspective, a broad biosocial explanation (perhaps in terms of shifting hormonal balances) is not ruled out.

From the relational point of view, evidence that women become more independent and assertive with age is consistent with Gilligan's idea that it is a moral advance for women to develop the ability to take care of themselves as well as others. Increased affiliativeness in men is similarly consistent with the idea that it is desirable for men to develop communal skills and integrate them into their agentic orientation (Bakan, 1966).

From the conflict point of view, an increase in independence and assertiveness in women from young to later adulthood can be interpreted as a result of the greater social control of women during their years of sexual attractiveness, fertility, and active mothering. When this control lessens, women may have more autonomy, at least if they have prospects for interpersonal power. In both the United States and Kenya, middle-aged women showed more power motivation than younger women when participants had high social status, but among women of low social status the middle-aged and young adult women did not differ (Todd, Friedman, & Kariuki, 1990). Researchers with a conflict perspective point out that the clearest evidence for increases in independence and assertiveness in women come from samples in which opportunities for women increased between their young adulthood and late middle age. Thus, the Vaillants (1990) report the appearance of late-life accomplishments among creative Terman women that they attribute to increased opportunities for women by the 1970s and 1980s. In the Mills Study, women who remained in the traditional role of nonworking wife and mother did not increase significantly in independence and assertiveness between ages 21 and 43 as other women did (Helson & Picano, 1990).

The importance of social opportunity for women's increases in independence and self-confidence would also be emphasized by exponents of the normative point of view. The fact that the mothers of the Mills women did not seem to have shown the change that their daughters did seems to indicate that social resources and expectations moderate any biosocial factor (Gutmann, 1987) that may be involved. Holahan's study of marital attitudes points out the danger of attributing universality to changes that are attributable to social climate or cohort experience.

VII. Overview and Implications

Traditional science sets up a competitive relation among theories: the strongest wins. The conflict point of view often attacks traditional science as narrow and biased. The relational view advocates connection over competition. In bringing together multiple frameworks for a larger understanding of the complexities of adult development, we have tried to achieve a research strategy that maintains respect for scientific procedures while asserting the value of recognizing and "connecting" a variety of perspectives.

A second distinctive feature of this chapter is its use of longitudinal studies. Several major longitudinal studies began in the 1920s as a promising new approach to child development. Seventy years later we see that there are studies of lives over several generations, and by comparing them we hope to address previously inaccessible questions about social and historical influences on personality development. It is not easy to make these comparisons, however. Different studies provide different kinds of information. Participants have been studied at different ages and differed in background and resources. If the comparative study of longitudinal findings becomes recognized as a valuable endeavor, researchers can build on measures they have in common across studies to address particular questions (Helson, Stewart, & Ostrove, 1995) and develop techniques to increase and improve the knowledge obtained (Helson, 1993a). For example, with particular questions in mind, researchers can recruit new samples comparable (in intelligence, for example) to the older ones, using some of the same questions or instruments (Holahan, 1984a; Mitchell & Helson, 1990; Tomlinson-Keasey & Blurton, 1992).

Has our attempt to study complex questions with a new strategy and longitudinal data from several generations of men and women been successful? Within the limits of our study, we believe that we have presented information instructive for evaluating our two hypotheses. According to the first, young women were said to be primarily interested in marriage and family and to lack clear vocational goals. The evidence examined shows that from the oldest to the most recent samples, young women did give higher priority to marriage and family than young men. Only in the IHD samples did young women show almost exclusive interest in marriage and family, but in the other samples vocational goals tended to be unstable or unclear. Thus, there seems to be considerable support for this hypothesis.

From the normative perspective, however, the large differences among the studies reviewed give ample evidence that changing social norms and expectations affected the planning of young women. From the conflict perspective, women are not by nature less able than men to set vocational goals, but the web of life circumstances associated with their subordinate status as helpers has made the process difficult. Even in the younger samples the complexity of the responsibility of planning for both family and career and insufficient social support for women's pursuit of careers contribute to ambivalent or tentative vocational plans. From the relational perspective, the importance of long-range vocational goals for most men and women has been overestimated by achievement-oriented academics. Women are experts at contingency planning, reconciliation of conflicting interests, and taking advantage of opportunities when they arise. The processes of "connecting," to work issues as well as to people, need to be studied and supported in adult development.

The second hypothesis was that men and women's personalities change between young adulthood and later life, in part because of a biosocial parental imperative that relaxes over time, so that each sex shifts in the direction of interests or characteristics associated with the other. This is a very broad hypothesis, and it is not surprising that the research literature shows conflicting findings, depending in part on the age span tested, characteristics of the sample, and effects of cohort and social climate that vary with the personality measures used (Bengston, Reedy, & Gordon, 1985; Parker & Aldwin, in press).

In all three longitudinal studies that we examined, however, the findings showed at least part of the hypothesized pattern. From youth to old age, Terman men became less interested in occupation and more interested in family, and Terman women changed in the opposite direction. IHD women became more confident and intellectually invested as they moved from early to late adulthood; IHD men did not. Husbands of Mills women were more competent and independent and less affiliative than their wives in young adulthood, but not by their 50s.

Though there was considerable support for the hypothesized pattern, the findings were sometimes mixed or uneven. For example, both the IHD and the Mills studies found more change for women than for men, and the hypothesis was supported by data from the Mills women and their partners, but not from their parents, so that cohort influences would seem to be involved. Longitudinal findings are not yet reported from a cohort in which there was not a distinct gender-related division of labor in young adulthood. Thus, the functionalist perspective has vitality, up to the present, but other perspectives pose important questions and alternative explanations for the findings, as reviewed in Section VI.D.

Each new generation wants to know the story of its own adult development. At the same time, many people find comfort and meaning in images that convey a common human wisdom, or a common feminine wisdom. Because many factors, interacting in numerous ways, shape the course of gendered lives, no life plot is inevitable, but cultural patterns recur. The answer to the question of an adult development distinctive to women may be imagined as a complex structure of more or less common patterns, forever interpretable from different vantage points. The attempt to trace out this structure will teach us much about the factors that shape our lives and prepare us for finding out whether young people under modern conditions of life are moving it in a new direction.

VIII. APPENDIX

A. The Terman Study

When the Terman Study began, participants (672 girls and 856 boys) were California school children with a minimum IQ of 135. Most were born between 1907 and 1915. Information was obtained from parents and teachers as well as from the children themselves. Questionnaires were sent to participants 10 times over their adult years and covered academic, family, and employment histories, reports of leisure interests, and at some ages a few personality trait ratings. There were also measures of marital satisfaction. Some representative publications on the Terman sample in adulthood are those of Holahan and Sears (1995); Sears (1978), Terman and Oden (1959), Tomlinson-Keasey and Keasey (1993), and Vaillant and Vaillant (1990).

B. IHD Studies

The two main longitudinal studies conducted at the Institute of Human Development (IHD) at the University of California, Berkeley, included males and females born in the early 1920s in Oakland (Oakland Growth Study) and in the late 1920s in Berkeley (Berkeley Guidance Study). The samples were intended to be representative of the community, though there was some bias toward the middle class. The participants were studied in childhood or adolescence and as adults in 1958–1959, 1969–1970, and 1982, when members of the Berkeley group were about 30, 41, and 53, and members of the Oakland group about 37, 48, and 61. In 1982, 233 men and women from the combined studies were interviewed. Studies of adult development in the IHD samples depend particularly on demographics, interviews, and measures derived from the California Q-Sort (J. Block, 1978), a set of 100 statements about personality that the rater uses to describe an individual by assigning them to one of nine categories according to their salience in his or her personality. Four books on the IHD samples are by J. Block (1971), Clausen (1993), Eichorn, Clausen, Haan, Honzik, and Mussen (1981), and Elder (1974).

C. The Mills Study

The Mills College Longitudinal Study began in the late 1950s, recruiting 140 women from the senior classes of 1958 and 1960. Participants were followed up by mail at ages 26–27, 43, and 52 (1963–1964, 1981, 1989). At all times of testing the study included personality inventories, demographic data, and ratings and open-ended questions about various areas of life. The California Psychological Inventory was administered at each testing, and the Adjective Check List was obtained from both the women and their partners at two ages. The California Q-Sort is available at age 43. Representative articles are those by Helson, Mitchell, and Moane (1984), Mitchell and Helson (1990), Wink and Helson (1993), and York and John (1992).

D. The Illinois Valedictorian Study

This study began with 46 women and 35 men who were top achievers in Illinois high schools in 1981. Participants were interviewed five to six times over their college years and in the 10th year of the study, 1990–1991. Questionnaire data, including a measure of intellectual self-esteem, were collected on four occasions, and measures of gender roles, achievement motivation, and work plans were obtained in 1985. The study was begun by Terry Denny and is described by Arnold (1993, 1996).

ACKNOWLEDGMENT

The writing of this chapter was supported by a grant from the National Institute of Health (MH 43948).

REFERENCES

Archer, S. L. (1985). Career and/or family: The identity process for adolescent girls. *Youth & Society, 16,* 289–314.

Arnold, K. D. (1993). Academically talented women in the 1980s: The Illinois valedictorian project. In K. D. Hulbert & D. T. Schuster (Eds.), *Women's lives through time: Educated American women of the twentieth century* (pp. 393–414). San Francisco: Jossey-Bass.

Arnold, K. D. (1996). *Lives of promise: What becomes of high school valedictorians.* San Francisco: Jossey-Bass.

Bakan, D. (1966). *The duality of human existence.* Boston: Beacon Press.

Baltes, P. B. (1987). Theoretical propositions of life-span developmental psychology: On the dynamics between growth and decline. *Developmental Psychology, 23,* 611–626.

Barnett, R. C., & Baruch, G. K. (1978). Women in the middle years: A critique of research and theory. *Psychology of Women Quarterly, 3,* 187–198.

Bart, P. (1971). Depression in middle-aged women. In V. Gornick & B. K. Moran (Eds.), *Women in sexist society* (pp. 163–186). New York: Basic Books.

Beauvoir, Simone de. (1953) *The second sex.* New York: Knopf.

Bengston, V. L., Reedy, M. N., & Gordon, C. (1985). Aging and self-conceptions: Personality processes and social contexts. In J. E. Birren & K. W. Schaie (Eds.), *Handbook of the psychology of aging* (pp. 544–593). New York: Van Nostrand-Reinhold.

Bernard, J. (1972). *The future of marriage.* New York: World-Time.

Bianchi, S. M., & Spain, D. (1986). *American women in transition.* New York: Russell Sage Foundation.

Block, J. (1971). *Lives through time.* Berkeley, CA: Bancroft.

Block, J. (1978). *The Q-sort method in personality assessment and psychiatric research.* Palo Alto, CA: Consulting Psychologists Press.

Block, J. H. (1976). Debatable conclusions about sex differences. *Contemporary Psychology, 22,* 517–522.

Bühler, C. (1971). Basic theoretical concepts of humanistic psychology. *American Psychologist, 26,* 378–386.

Buss, D. M. (1989). Sex differences in human mate preferences: Evolutionary hypothesis tested in 37 cultures. *Behavioral and Brain Sciences, 12,* 1–49.

Chafe, W. H. (1972). *The American woman: Her changing social, economic, and political roles, 1920–1970.* New York: Oxford University Press.

Chodorow, N. (1978). *The reproduction of mothering.* Berkeley: University of California Press.

Clausen, J. A. (1993). *American lives: Looking back at children of the great depression.* New York: Free Press.

Datan, N. (1986). Corpses, lepers, and menstruating women: Tradition, transition, and the sociology of knowledge. *Sex Roles, 14,* 693–703.

Duncan, L. E., & Agronick, G. S. (1995). The intersection of life stage and social events: Personality and life outcomes. *Journal of Personality and Social Psychology 69,* 558–568.

Eagley, A. H. (1995). The science and politics of comparing women and men. *American Psychologist, 50,* 145–158.

Eichorn, D. H., Clausen, J. A., Haan, N., Honzik, M. P., & Mussen, P. (Eds.). (1981). *Present and past in middle life.* San Diego, CA: Academic Press.

Elder, G. H., Jr. (1974). *Children of the great depression.* Chicago: University of Chicago Press.

Erikson, E. (1963). *Childhood and society* (2nd ed.). New York: Norton.

Erikson, E. (1968). *Identity: Youth and crisis.* New York: Norton.

Franz, C. E., & Stewart, A. J. (Eds.). (1994). *Women creating lives.* Boulder, CO: Westview Press.

Franz, C. E., & White, K. M. (1985). Individuation and attachment in personality development: Extending Erikson's theory. *Journal of Personality, 53,* 136–168.

Gergen, K. J. (1985). The social constructionist movement in modern psychology. *American Psychologist, 40,* 266–275.

Gergen, M. M. (1990). Finished at 40: Women's development within the patriarchy. *Psychology of Women Quarterly, 14,* 471–493.

Giele, J. Z. (1993). Women's role change and adaptation, 1920–1990. In K. D. Hulbert & D. T. Schuster (Eds.), *Women's lives through time* (pp. 32–60). San Francisco: Jossey-Bass.

Gilligan, C. (1982). *In a different voice: Psychological theory and women's development.* Cambridge, MA: Harvard University Press.

Gough, H. G., & Heilbrun, A. B., Jr. (1983). *Manual for the Adjective Check List.* Palo Alto, CA: Consulting Psychologists Press.

Gutmann, D. L. (1987). *Reclaimed powers: Toward a new psychology of men and women in later life.* New York: Basic Books.

Haan, N., Millsap, R., & Hartka, E. (1986). As time goes by: Change and stability in personality over fifty years. *Psychology and Aging, 1,* 220–232.

Hare-Mustin, R. T., & Marecek, J. (1990). Gender and the meaning of difference: Postmodernism and psychology. In R. T. Hare-Mustin & J. Marecek (Eds.), *Making a difference:*

Psychology and the construction of gender (pp. 22–64). New Haven, CT: Yale University Press.

Havighurst, R. J. (1948). *Developmental tasks and education.* New York: David McKay.

Heilbrun, C. G. (1988). *Writing a woman's life.* New York: Ballantine.

Heise, D. R. (1990). Careers, career trajectories, and the self. In J. Rodin, C. Schooler, & K. W. Schaie (Eds.), *Self-directedness: Cause and effects throughout the life course* (pp. 59–84). Hillsdale, NJ: Erlbaum.

Helson, R. (1993a). Comparing longitudinal samples: Towards a paradigm of tension between stability and change. In D. C. Funder, R. D. Parke, C. Tomlinson-Keasey, & K. Widaman (Eds.), *Studying lives through time* (pp. 93–119). Washington, DC: American Psychological Association.

Helson, R. (1993b). The Mills classes of 1958 and 1960: College in the fifties, young adulthood in the sixties. In K. D. Hulbert & D. T. Schuster (Eds.), *Women's lives through time* (pp. 190–210). San Francisco: Jossey-Bass.

Helson, R., Mitchell, V., & Moane, G. (1984). Personality and patterns of adherence and non-adherence to the social clock. *Journal of Personality and Social Psychology, 46,* 1079–1096.

Helson, R., & Picano, J. (1990). Is the traditional role bad for women? *Journal of Personality and Social Psychology, 59,* 311–320.

Helson, R., & Stewart, A. J. (1994). Personality change in adulthood. In T. Heatherton & J. Weinberger (Eds.), *Can personality change?* (pp. 201–225). Washington, DC: American Psychological Association.

Helson, R., Stewart, A. J., & Ostrove, J. (1995). Identity in three cohorts of midlife women. *Journal of Personality and Social Psychology 69,* 544–557.

Holahan, C. K. (1984a). Marital attitudes over 40 years: A longitudinal and cohort analysis. *Journal of Gerontology, 39,* 49–57.

Holahan, C. K. (1984b). The relationship between life goals at thirty and perceptions of goal attainment and life satisfaction at seventy for gifted men and women. *International Journal of Aging and Human Development, 20,* 21–31.

Holahan, C. K. (1994). Women's goal orientations across the life cycle: Findings from the Terman study of the gifted. In B. F. Turner & L. E. Troll (Eds.), *Women growing older* (pp. 35–67). Newbury Park, CA.: Sage.

Holahan, C. K., & Sears, R. R. (1995). *The gifted group in later maturity.* Stanford, CA: Stanford University Press.

Jordan, J. V., Kaplan, A. G., Miller, J. B., Stiver, I. P., & Surrey, J. L. (1991). *Women's growth in connection.* New York: Guilford Press.

Josselson, R. (1987). *Finding herself: Pathways to identity development in women.* San Francisco: Jossey-Bass.

Jung, C. G. (1960). The stages of life. In H. Reed, M. Fordham, & G. Adler (Eds.), *Collected works* (Vol. 8, pp. 387–403). Princeton, NJ: Princeton University Press. (Original work published 1931)

Kaner, A. (1994). *Physical attractiveness and women's lives: Findings from a longitudinal study.* Unpublished doctoral dissertation, University of California, Berkeley.

Kohlberg, L. (1973). Continuities in childhood and adult moral development revisited. In P. B. Baltes & K. W. Schaie (Eds.), *Lifespan developmental psychology* (pp. 179–204). New York: Academic Press.

Levinson, D., with Darrow, C. N., Klein, E. B., Levinson, M. H., & McKee, B. (1978). *The seasons of a man's life.* New York: Knopf.

Lott, B. (1987). *Women's lives: Themes and variations.* Belmont, CA: Brooks/Cole.

Maccoby, E. E. (1990). Gender and relationships: A developmental account. *American Psychologist, 45,* 513–520.

Maccoby, E. E., & Jacklin, C. N. (1974). *The psychology of sex differences.* Stanford, CA: Stanford University Press.

Marcia, J. E. (1980). Identity in adolescence. In J. Adelson (Ed.), *Handbook of adolescent psychology* (pp. 159–187). New York: Wiley.

Markus, H., & Nurius, P. (1986). Possible selves. *American Psychologist, 41,* 954–969.

McAdams, D. P. (1993). *The stories we live by: Personal myths and the making of the self.* New York: Morrow.

Miller, J. B. (1976). *Toward a new psychology of women.* Boston: Beacon Press.

Mitchell, V., & Helson, R. (1990). Women's prime of life: Is it the fifties? *Psychology of Women Quarterly, 14,* 451–470.

Neugarten, B. L. (1977). Personality and aging. In J. E. Birren & K. W. Schaie (Eds.), *Handbook of the psychology of aging* (pp. 626–649). New York: Van Nostrand-Reinhold.

Parker, R., & Aldwin, C. M. (in press). Does sex-role identity change in adulthood? Differentiating age, cohort, and period effects. In M. E. Lachman & J. B. James (Eds.), *Multiple paths of midlife development.* Chicago: University of Chicago Press.

Parsons, T., & Bales, R. F. (1955). *Family, socialization and interaction process.* Glencoe, IL: Free Press.

Roberts, B. W. (1994). *The reciprocal relation between personality and work experiences from college to midlife.* Unpublished doctoral dissertation, University of California, Berkeley.

Sears, R. R. (1978). Sources of life satisfaction of the Terman gifted men. *American Psychologist, 32,* 119–128.

Skolnick, A. (1991). *Embattled paradise: The American family in an age of uncertainty.* New York: Basic Books.

Stevens-Long, J. (1990). Adult development: Theories past and future. In R. A. Nemiroff & C. A. Colarusso (Eds.), *New dimensions in adult development* (pp. 125–165). New York: Basic Books.

Stewart, A. J. (1994). Toward a feminist strategy for studying women's lives. In C. Franz & A. J. Stewart (Eds.), *Women creating lives: Identities, resilience, resistance* (pp. 11–35). Boulder, CO: Westview Press.

Stewart, A. J., & Healy, J. M., Jr. (1989). Linking individual development and social changes. *American Psychologist, 44,* 30–42.

Stroud, J. G. (1981). Women's careers: Work, family, and personality. In D. H. Eichorn, J. A. Clausen, N. Haan, M. P. Honzik, & P. Mussen (Eds.), *Present and past in middle life* (pp. 353–389). New York: Academic Press.

Terman, L. M., & Oden, M. H. (1959). *Genetic studies of genius: Vol. 5. The gifted group at mid-life.* Stanford, CA: Stanford University Press.

Todd, J. Friedman, A. & Kariuki P. W. (1990). Women growing stronger with age: The effect of status in the United States and Kenya. *Psychology of Women Quarterly, 14,* 567–578.

Tomlinson-Keasey, C. (1990). The working lives of Terman's gifted women. In H. Y Grossman & N. L. Chester (Eds.), *The experience and meaning of work in women's lives* (pp. 213–239). Hillsdale, NJ: Erlbaum.

Tomlinson-Keasey, C., & Blurton, E. U. (1992). Gifted women's lives: Aspirations, achievements, and personal adjustment. In J. S. Carlson (Ed.), *Advances in cognition and educational practice: A research annual* (Vol. 1, pp. 151–179). Greenwich, CT: JAI Press.

Tomlinson-Keasey, C., & Keasey, C. B. (1993). Graduating from college in the 1930s: The Terman genetic studies of genius. In K. D. Hulbert & D. T. Schuster (Eds.), *Women's lives through time* (pp. 63–92). San Francisco: Jossey-Bass.

Tooby, J., & Cosmides, L. (1990). On the universality of human nature: The role of genetics and adaptation. *Journal of Personality, 58,* 17–67.

Vaillant, G. E. (1977). *Adaptation to life.* Boston: Little-Brown.

Vaillant, G. E., & Vaillant, C. O. (1990). Determinants and consequences of creativity in a cohort of gifted women. *Psychology of Women Quarterly, 14,* 607–616.

White, R. W. (1966). *Lives in progress* (2nd ed.). New York: Holt, Rinehart, & Winston.

Wink, P., & Helson, R. (1993). Personality change in women and their partners. *Journal of Personality and Social Psychology, 65,* 597–605.

Yoder, J. D., & Kahn, A. S. (1993). Working toward an inclusive psychology of women. *American Psychologist, 48,* 846–850.

York, K. L., & John, O. P. (1992). The four faces of Eve: A typological analysis of women's personality at midlife. *Journal of Personality and Social Psychology, 63,* 494–508.

PART IV

BIOLOGICAL DETERMINANTS OF PERSONALITY

CHAPTER 13

EVOLUTIONARY FOUNDATIONS OF PERSONALITY

DAVID M. BUSS
UNIVERSITY OF TEXAS, AUSTIN

In the mid-1990s, after several hundred years of scientific scrutiny, only one scientific theory remains viable to account for all major characteristics of organic life, past and present—the theory of evolution by natural selection (Darwin, 1859). Only two competing "theories" have received even marginal scientific attention—creationism (all forms of life created by a supreme being) and seeding theory (life planted on earth by extraterrestrial beings). The problems with creationism and seeding theory are (1) that multiple seedings or creations over time and space are required to account for the paleontological data, and (2) these theories are heuristically bankrupt—they lead to no important domains of inquiry and to no testable predictions (Daly & Wilson, 1988).

To remain as the sole scientific theory proposed to account for the major characteristics of all living forms surely qualifies evolutionary theory as a "great" theory (Alexander, 1979). Indeed, it serves as the major metatheory in the biological sciences. Although many details of the theory are vigorously debated (e.g., unit of selection, conceptualization of adaptation), the essentials of evolutionary theory are now paradigmatic and largely undisputed.

It seems reasonable, therefore, to adopt an initial premise that millions of years of evolution might have left some mark on human psychology. Humans are part of the organic world, and there is no reason to assume that we are somehow exempt from the laws of organic life that govern all other living forms. Precisely what the consequences of this premise are for psychology, however, remains stridently debated by a few and largely ignored by many.

Part of the problem is that it has not been immediately obvious what the implications of adopting this premise are. Consider a noncontroversial example—the larynx (Symons, 1987). The larynx rises when we swallow, thus preventing food from getting into our lungs. One can grant that the larynx exists because it evolved over time by natural selection, that it solved (and continues to solve) the adaptive problem of getting food down the right passage, and that those who had no larynx or an inefficient larynx were more likely to have choked to death in our evolutionary past, and therefore experienced lower reproductive success than did those with an efficiently functioning larynx.

In this presumably noncontroversial example, it is not clear that the theory of evolution by natural selection has added materially to, or is even necessary for, our understanding of the larynx. Human intuition has picked out the "prevent choking" function, and studies of the proximate workings of the larynx can proceed perfectly adequately without being informed by explicit evolutionary considerations.

In the domain of psychology, where basic mechanisms that might have evolved are difficult to identify or even point to among the flux of human behavior, it has remained even less clear what role evolutionary theory should or could serve. Psychologists, like anatomists, can proceed with their research agendas to some extent ignoring the evolutionary forces that led to the origins of our psychological mechanisms.

I argue in this chapter, however, that it is a mistake to do so—that anchoring personality psychology in evolutionary biology is essential and unavoidable. The problem is precisely how this can be done. The purpose of this chapter is to outline some of the promising directions for doing so, and to point out the problems and pitfalls that have stymied previous attempts.

I. EVOLUTION: FACT, PATH, THEORY, AND HYPOTHESIS

Much confusion centers around the use of the term "evolution." Ruse (1986) distinguished among three different uses—evolution as fact, as path, and as theory. I will add to these the use of evolution to refer to specific evolutionary hypotheses.

A. Evolution as Fact

Evolution as fact refers to the natural unfolding or change of organisms down through the generations from earlier forms. Evolution in this sense, referring to change over time, was known to occur long before Darwin. The lines of evidence supporting the fact of evolution include *biogeography* (geographical distribution of organisms), *comparative anatomy* (the study of the relations between the forms of organisms, for example, isomorphism between the bones and arms of humans and the forelegs of horses, the wings of birds, and the paws of mole), *embryology* (the study of early forms of organisms and their development; the embryos of humans and those of dogs, for example, are indistinguishable due to common evolutionary origins), and *paleontology* (the study of the fossil record).

The only conclusion that can be drawn from these multiple sources of data is that evolution in the sense of change in organic structure over time, although almost entirely unobservable directly, is a fact.

B. Path of Evolution

A second meaning of "evolution" refers to the specific series of changes that led to a current form—the evolutionary phylogeny, trajectory, or descent of a given species. The fossil record tells us much about the path of evolution. We know, for example, that the path of evolution is not one uninterrupted drive from past to present, that it involves multiple branchings rather than a continuous ladder, and that evolutionary dead ends are far more common than successes—most species that have evolved, 90% by some estimates, are extinct.

We know from this record that life on earth emerged roughly 3,500 million years ago. It evolved beyond simple cells 500 million years ago. Mammals, of which we are one, emerged 200 million years ago. Dinosaurs reached their demise 60 million years ago. Primates made their first appearance on earth 55 million years ago, roughly 5 million years after the dinosaur extinction. Human beings came on the scene roughly 2–4 million years ago. And Neanderthal became extinct about 35,000 years ago, strangely coincidental with the emergence of Cro Magnan, our current form. Although many details of the path of human evolution remain unknown, we do have the rough outlines of the specific evolutionary trajectory that can be traced from our mammalian and primate ancestors to our current modern forms.

It is from the path of evolution, and in particular an examination of our own primate line, that a previous generation of psychologists attempted to glean insight into human functioning. There is some value to gauging trends in evolution through comparisons with other mammals and other primates (cf. A. Buss, this volume, chap. 14). It is now generally recognized, however, that this form of "referential modeling" (selecting this or that primate species for comparative analysis) is highly problematic, can be seriously misleading, and lacks the generativity typically associated with a good theory (Tooby & DeVore, 1987).

C. Theory of Evolution

The theory of evolution, Darwin's contribution to the understanding of change in organic form, refers to *natural selection,* the mechanism or process by which change takes place. If variations in the organic world leading to greater survival and reproduction recur frequently enough over generations, the cumulative effect will be evolutionary.

Darwin did not simply want to account for the evolution of organisms, he wanted to explain *why* they are the way they are. This implies a central role of *adaptation* in his theory. We have fingers, hands, feet, eyes, keeness of sight, and fleetness of foot because those who had these mechanisms were better able to survive and reproduce than those lacking these mechanisms, or whose mechanisms were different.

Although natural selection is referred to as the *theory* of evolution, it has received overwhelming empirical support. It has been observed in laboratory experiments and in the wild in thousands of instances. Indeed, new species have been evolved "artificially" through applying the principles of selection in the laboratory. In its essential forms, no one doubts that evolution occurs principally by natural selection, and that human beings, as part of natural organic life, have also evolved by natural selection. In this sense, we are all Darwinians (Symons, 1987). What is in doubt is the veracity of specific evolutionary hypotheses advanced about human behavior.

D. Specific Evolutionary Hypotheses

Specific evolutionary hypotheses refer to propositions about the function of a particular mechanism, structure, or feature of human behavior. One hypothesis, for example, is that male sexual jealousy evolved to ensure paternity in putative offspring by preventing encroachment by competing males. Males throughout our evolutionary past whose behavior reflected a mechanism of sexual jealousy experienced greater reproductive success than did males who were indifferent to the sexual contact that their mates had with other males. In this instance, considerable evidence has accrued to support this hypothesis (Buss, Larsen, Westen, & Semmelroth, 1992; Daly, Wilson, & Weghorst, 1982).

Another hypothesis is that males have evolved a mechanism to detect when females are ovulating. The ability to detect when women ovulate would enable a man to focus mating efforts (generally a costly enterprise) more effectively, not bothering to attempt copulations with those females for whom conception at that moment is unlikely. In this case, the empirical data do not support the hypothesis—there is no evidence that human males can detect when females are ovulating (Symons, 1987).

Several crucial points can be made about specific evolutionary hypotheses. First, it is important to evaluate each one separately. There is no such thing as "the" evolutionary hypothesis about a given phenomenon. Indeed, for any given feature or attribute, there are likely to be several different competing evolutionary hypotheses (cf. Buss, 1990a, 1990b; Rancour-Laferiere, 1985).

Second, evolutionary hypotheses should be subjected to the same empirical scrutiny as other scientific hypotheses. They have no special or elevated status by virtue of their being evolutionary.

Third, specific evolutionary hypotheses differ in precision and testability. Gould and Lewontin (1979), for example, have marshaled the argument that many specific evolutionary hypotheses are "just so" stories, fictional speculations that are imprecise and incapable of being subjected to the rigors of empirical scrutiny. There is some merit in their accusation. Many specific evolutionary hypotheses have indeed been sloppy, imprecise, and empirically vacuous. Perusing any recent copy of a journal in personality and social psychology, however, suggests that those with an evolutionary perspective do not have a monopoly on sloppy, imprecise, and ungrounded hypotheses. Indeed, in any scientific discipline, hypotheses vary in their precision, theoretical anchoring, and testability. The key point is that useful evolutionary hypotheses are those that are specified sufficiently precisely so that they can receive the same scientific scrutiny and be subjected to rigorous evidentiary standards (see, e.g., Bailey, Gaulin, Agyei, & Gladue, in press; Buss et al., 1992; Cosmides, 1989; Daly & Wilson, 1988; Gangestad and Simpson, 1990; Graziano & Eisenberg, this volume, Chapter 30; Kenrick, Groth, Trost, & Sadalla, 1993; Singh, 1993).

II. BASICS OF EVOLUTIONARY PSYCHOLOGY

This section outlines the basics of current evolutionary psychology (Buss, 1991, in press; Cosmides & Tooby, 1987, 1989; Daly & Wilson, 1988; Symons, 1987, 1992; Tooby & Cosmides, 1990a, 1990b, 1992). This provides a foundation for the analysis of issues of central concern to the field of personality psychology.

A. Humans as Evolved Problem Solvers

Humans, like other organisms, can be viewed as organized structures that exist in their present form because of a long history of natural selection, operating over millions of years. Each one of us owes our existence to a long and unbroken line of ancestors who successfully solved problems posed by survival and reproduction in our evolutionary past. Therefore, human structures, as well as human psychological mechanisms, *at some fundamental level of description,* can be analyzed in terms of the problems they solve.

But "survival" and "reproduction" are broad categories, each subsuming a large and complex array of subproblems. To the extent that the evolutionary psychologist can identify the nature of the *specific* problems that humans have evolved to solve, she or he has some advantage over the nonevolutionary psychologist in discovering the nature of human nature.

Darwin identified many of the major survival problems, subsumed by what he called "the hostile forces of nature." These include food shortages, climate, weather, diseases, parasites, predators, and natural hazards such as cliffs. But survival, from an evolutionary perspective, is only a start. Natural selection operates on survival only insofar as survival is necessary for reproduction. Thus, a second major class of problems consists of reproductive problems.

At the broadest level, reproduction problems that must be solved are: (1) *successful intrasexual competition,* beating out members of your own sex to obtain desirable mates of the opposite sex; (2) *mate selection,* choosing from among the pool of potential mates those with the greatest value to one's reproductive success; (3) *conception,* engaging in the necessary social and sexual behaviors to fertilize, or to become fertilized; (4) *mate retention,* preventing the encroachment of intrasexual poachers as well as preventing one's mate from defecting (this problem must often be solved in order to actualize the promise of reproductive effort); (5) *parental investment,* engaging in the necessary set of behaviors to ensure the survival and reproductive success of one's offspring; and (6) *extraparental nepotistic investment,* incurring costs to self that benefit nondescendant genetic relatives.

Each of these six problems, of course, is extremely broad and subsumes a host of subproblems. Successful intrasexual competition, for example, might require acquisition of resources required by a potential mate, appeasing, or not alienating, relatives and friends of the potential mate, or (c) successfully courting the potential mate, while simultaneously rendering intrasexual competitors less attractive to the potential mate (e.g., derogating competitors). A psychologist able to understand these problems that humans face in our environment of evolutionary adaptedness (EEA) is in a position to identify and explore the psychological (cognitive, emotional, behavioral) solutions that have evolved to solve them.

B. Other Humans Are the Most Important Source of Adaptive Problems and Adaptive Solutions

Although traditional images of evolution evoke "nature red in tooth and claw" and "survival of the fittest," sheer physical survival may not have been the most important adaptive problem governing *human* evolutionary history. There appears to be growing consensus that the most important problems were posed by members of our own species. In other words, we are our own hostile force of nature.

Findings that point to this conclusion come from the prevalence of group warfare (e.g., Alexander, 1987), the evolution of language and nonverbal signs for manipulating others (Dawkins & Krebs, 1978; Pinker, 1994; Pinker & Bloom, 1990), the intense sociality of humans (Alexander, 1979), the extreme degree of reciprocal altruism among humans (Trivers, 1971), the extreme degree of parental investment among humans (Trivers, 1972), the degree of sexual dimorphism among humans, suggesting the importance of intrasexual competition (Short, 1979), the extensive and prolonged mating rituals among humans (Daly & Wilson, 1983), the existence of domain-specific psychological mechanisms governing social exchange (Cosmides, 1989), and the intensity of human effort devoted to status, reputation, and hierarchy (Hogan, 1983). These suggest that the most important problems that humans have had to face in our EEA for survival and reproduction have been social problems.

Within each social adaptive problem lies dozens of subproblems. Forming a successful dyadic alliance, for example, may require *identifying* key resources possessed by potential friends, *assessing* which individuals possess these resources, *modeling* the values of those individuals, *gauging* potential sources of strategic interference, *initiating* sequential and incremental chains of reciprocity, and *detecting* signs of "cheating" or nonreciprocity (see Cosmides & Tooby, 1989). All of these subproblems require solutions for the formation of a successful friendship.

Humans are probably unique in the duration and complexity of social relationships that they form. Humans sometimes form lifelong mating relationships, develop friendships that last for decades, and maintain contact with their brothers, sisters, and other relatives over great expanses of time and distance. Because social adaptive problems were so crucial for human survival and reproduction, many of the most important features of our evolved psychological mechanisms will necessarily be social in nature. Social adaptive problems have been so important over human evolutionary history that many of the dedicated psychological mechanisms currently studied by cognitive, personality, and developmental psychologists, in addition to those studied by social psychologists, are inherently social.

C. Psychological Mechanisms as Evolved Strategies for Solving Problems

A third essential feature of current evolutionary thought is the increasingly apparent necessity to understand fundamental psychological mechanisms as evolved solutions to specific evolutionary problems (e.g., Barkow, 1989; Buss, 1989a; Cosmides & Tooby, 1987, 1989; Shepard, 1987; Symons, 1987). Cosmides (1989), for example, has developed a computational theory of the psychological mechanisms that must have evolved in order for humans to solve problems associated with social exchange. Organisms engaging in social exchange must have a psychological mechanism that permits the detection of cheaters—those who accept the benefit of a social exchange without paying the reciprocal cost. In a series of experiments, Cosmides (1989) has demonstrated that humans do indeed have such a mechanism, and that the mechanism is domain-specific in the sense that it operates particularly on problems structured as social exchanges.

Buss (1989a), to take another example, has studied preferences as evolved psychological mechanisms that solved certain problems associated with mate choice. Because human males and females differ somewhat in the nature of the reproductive problems they must solve, psychological mechanisms surrounding reproduction are expected to be somewhat sexually dimorphic (Symons, 1987). Sexually dimorphic mate preference mechanisms for age, physical appearance, and external resources have been documented across 37 cultures located in 33 countries on six continents and five islands (Buss, 1989a).

Attempts to elucidate the nature of these psychological mechanisms is just beginning. Undoubtedly, existing research in social, cognitive, personality, clinical, and developmental psychology will be invaluable when examined from an evolutionary perspective. Even given this incipient and somewhat inchoate stage in evolutionary psychology, several important features of evolved psychological mechanisms seem apparent.

D. Many Psychological Mechanisms Will Be Domain Specific

Consider the human body. Although an integrated whole, the body can to some useful degree be studied as a set of interrelated parts, each serving specific functions or solving specific problems. We have sweat mechanisms that solve the problem of overheating, shivering mechanisms that solve the problem of extreme temperature drop, a larynx that solves the problem of preventing chocking, a liver that solves the problem of filtering impurities, rods that solve the problem of night vision, and a retina that solves the problem of depth perception. Because the problems that require solutions are radically different from one another, there is no reason to assume that a mechanism that evolved to solve one problem will be effective for solving a different problem. To paraphrase von Neumann, when you are trying to maximize n functions, when n is equal to or greater than 2, you have to be very, very lucky. My sweat glands will not solve the problem of getting my food down the right passage, nor will my larynx solve the problem of accurate visual perception. Different problems require different solutions. In this sense, a psychologist with an evolutionary perspective expects that evolved solutions are likely to be domain-specific.

By analogy to the human body, the number of social problems posed by successful reproduction is also large. The psychological mechanisms needed to engage in successful social exchange (e.g., detect-cheater algorithm) are likely to be radically different from the preference mechanisms needed to choose a valuable mate. There is no reason to assume that psychological solutions to either of these problems will be directly applicable to the psychological mechanisms that might have evolved to solve problems of parental investment (e.g., empathy, nurturance, parental feeling) or those needed to retain a mate and fend off poachers (e.g., sexual jealousy). In this sense, an evolutionary perspective leads psychologists to suspect that many psychological mechanisms will be domain-specific.

This view is at odds with the traditional assumption made in behaviorism that organisms possess only one or a few general learning processes that operate in the same manner across content domains and across species. But it is consonant with many of the major empirical advances that point to the existence of a large number of motives (Herrnstein, 1977), the content-specificity of fears and phobias (Seligman & Hagar, 1972), and the great specificity of learning (e.g., Rozin & Schull, 1988). Indeed, without domain-specific psychological mechanisms, humans could not achieve the great flexibility in behavior that is observed (Cosmides & Tooby, 1989).

E. Behavioral Flexibility Derives from Complex and Dedicated Psychological Mechanisms

The earlier evolutionary psychological views of James, McDougall, and even Lorenz and Tinbergen postulate instincts (or fixed action patterns) that connote rigidity and intractability in their manifestation. Similarly, early sociobiological views that genes hold culture (and presumably behavior) on a leash connote automaton-like inflexibility of human behavior. Few things are more obvious, however, than the extreme flexibility, discriminativeness, and context-dependency of human action (Cantor & Kihlström, 1987).

But what psychological mechanisms could produce extreme behavioral flexibility? Although some implicit thinking in psychology assumes that simple, amorphous psychological structures must underlie flexibility, current evolutionary thought stresses precisely the opposite:

> Extreme behavioral plasticity implies extreme mental complexity and stability; that is, an elaborate human nature. Behavioral plasticity for its own sake would be worse than useless, random variation suicide. During the course of evolutionary history the more plastic hominid behavior became the more complex the neural machinery must have become to channel this plasticity into adaptive action.
>
> *(Symons, 1987, p. 127)*

A carpenter's flexibility comes not from having a single domain-general "all purpose tool" that is used to cut, saw, screw, twist, wrench, plane, balance, and hammer, but rather from having many, more specialized tools, each designed to perform a particular function. It is the numerousness and specificity of the tools in the entire tool kit that give the carpenter great flexibility, not a highly "plastic" single tool.

F. The Importance of Identifying the Classes of Acts to Which Psychological Mechanisms Correspond

A somewhat more controversial feature of current evolutionary thought is an emphasis not just on psychological mechanisms, but also on the classes of acts to which they correspond, and without which they cannot be understood. Consider the psychological mechanism of "male sexual jealousy." The most well-supported evolutionary hypothesis is that this mechanism evolved in men to increase confidence in paternity (maternity never being in doubt) (Buss, 1988b; Buss et al., 1992; Daly & Wilson, 1983; Daly et al., 1982).

Men in human evolutionary history who were indifferent to the sexual contact that their mates had with other men presumably experienced lower reproductive success than did males who tended toward a jealous rage whenever they detected cues to potential pair-bond defection or the presence of potential intrasexual poachers. Such a mechanism could not possibly evolve unless it produced behavior or action by the male that functioned to prevent pair-bond defection, interfere with poaching males, and thus increase the probability of paternity. The psychological mechanism of jealousy cannot be understood without identifying this class of "jealous acts." Mechanisms can evolve only if they produce behavior that carries certain consequences.

Symons (1992) argues that "Darwin's theory of natural selection sheds light on human affairs only to the extent that it sheds light on phenotypic design, and design is usually manifested at the psychological rather than behavioral level." I would argue that Symons' dichotomy between psychological and behavioral web is too strongly drawn. It is not just that psychological mechanisms such as jealousy cannot be understood without identifying the corresponding class of jealous acts, the class of acts is part of the scientific description of the nature of that mechanism.

Most single acts are ambiguous with respect to intention, motive, function, or design. Furthermore, single acts are invariably manifestations of several psychological mechanisms. Consider the following acts: He called her at unexpected times to see who she was with; He did not take her to the party where other males would be present; He threatened to break up if she ever cheated on him; He made her feel guilty about talking to other men; He stared coldly at the guy who was looking at her. Each act considered alone is a product of several different psychological mechanisms. One involves concealing a mate from competitors, another involves an empathic understanding of the emotional states of the partner and how those states can be manipulated (e.g., guilt induction), and still another involves knowledge about the effects of "cold stares" on an intrasexual competitor.

What all of these acts have in common, however, is that they were all presumably produced in part by the operation of a "sexual jealousy" mechanism. Jealousy is the common denominator of this class. The nature and function of jealousy is illuminated by considering these acts *as a class* rather than individually or in isolation. This class of acts constitutes the behavioral strategy component of the psychological mechanism of male sexual jealousy.

Seen in this light, psychological mechanisms cannot be understood without identifying the class of acts that composes the evolutionary *raison d'etre* of the mechanism. The acts are part of the mechanism—part of the phenotypic design that must be understood. There can be no science of evolutionary psychology divorced from classes of acts to which the psychological mechanisms correspond.

Evolutionary thought in psychology has evolved dramatically over the past century. The most compelling shifts involve a change from a view of humans as possessing a rigid set of instincts or fixed action patterns that are genetically determined and that invariably, intractably manifest themselves in behavior to a new view: humans are strategic problem solvers, whose evolved psychological mechanisms are at least somewhat domain-specific and whose behavioral products are highly dependent on eliciting context.

G. Specific Evolutionary Models

Modern evolutionary psychology clearly recognizes that evolutionary theory is a theory about the *origins* of human nature, but *not* a theory of that nature itself (Cosmides & Tooby, 1989). As Symons says, "That Darwin's theory of adaptation constitutes the only scientifically tenable account of the origin and maintenance of organic design does not imply that this theory constitutes a Royal Road to the detection of design" (Symons, 1989, p. 136). Thus, a clear limitation is a predictive limitation. Evolutionary theory provides some broad guidelines about what is unlikely to have evolved (e.g., adaptations that favor other species), but within those broad constraints, it cannot specify what must have or will have evolved. There is no substitute for developing *specific evolutionary models* of narrower sets of phenomena (e.g., a paternity confidence hypothesis of sexual jealousy, an evolution-based theory of social exchange) and testing predictions based on these more circumscribed models. In this sense, current evolutionary psychology is consonant with existing practice within psychology, the elucidation of domain-specific psychological phenomena.

The difficulties of cleaving psychological phenomena into functionally significant units beset all of psychology. A focus on function simply makes explicit a treacherously difficult task that has been largely bypassed in 20th century psychology—a nonarbitrary description of basic psychological mechanisms.

III. FOUNDATIONAL IMPLICATIONS FOR PERSONALITY PSYCHOLOGY

This section draws out the most important implications for formulating the evolutionary foundations of personality. These include a specification of the core of human nature—the major directional tendencies toward which humans are motivated—and identifying important individual differences, clarifying the concepts of adaptation and adjustment, and reframing the debate over personality consistency and behavioral specificity.

A. Directional Tendencies of Human Action: Motives, Goals, and Desires

Identifying the major motives of humans has occupied personality psychologists since Freud postulated the "sex instinct" as the central energizing force behind human action. All major theories of personality contain assumptions, implicit or explicit, about what these major directional tendencies are. Maslow posited self-actualization, Adler the striving for superiority, and Sullivan the negotiation of interpersonal relations.

A conception of major motives, desires, or directional tendencies must form the core of any major theory of personality. They specify what energizes the organism, what causes us to do something rather than nothing, and toward what goals human behavior is directed. Although individuals clearly differ in the particulars of the major motives, all personality theories specify a core of species-typical motives around which individuals differ.

Modern evolutionary theory specifies three broad classes of such directional tendencies: *survival, reproduction,* and *genetic investment.* Each of these broad classes, in turn, may be partitioned into several important subclasses. Survival problems, for example, can be partitioned into striving to combat the "hostile forces of nature." Reproductive problems include selecting, attracting, and retaining a mate. Investment problems include deciding how to socialize children and which genetic relatives to channel resources toward.

It is not by chance that preindustrial human groups devote a large portion of their time to hunting and gathering; that individuals who sneeze or display signs of ringworm are actively shunned; that we shiver, sweat, cover up, or strip down in response to extremes of weather; that infants refuse to crawl over a "visual cliff"; and that snakes, spiders, darkness, and strangers are vigorously avoided. Individuals who failed to be motivated in these directions tended to become no one's ancestors.

In sum, an evolutionary psychologist expects that human action will be directed, in part, toward solving the problems associated with survival, growth, and maintaining organismic integrity (Buss, 1986). But what is the conceptual status of these directional tendencies? Contrary to accounts implicit and explicit in sociobiology, *there is no reason to expect that humans will have domain-general motives at the level of abstraction of fitness maximization.*

Evolutionary theory is a theory about the *origins* of human nature, but is *not* itself a theory of that human nature. Many sociobiologists have conflated these, and much conceptual confusion has resulted. To propose that humans have as motives "survival" or "reproduction" or "fitness maximization" would be like programming a computer chess strategy with the single instruction "win." A chess program with such a global instruction would have no possible means of winning—it would not have the slightest clue about what moves to make in response to this or that array of pieces. Computer chess programs instead contain many thousands of highly detailed, context-specific, if–then statements. It is only through this detailed design that the program can solve the many problems that are correlated with, and sometimes necessary for, winning.

Similarly, natural selection could not produce an organism with global motives like "survive," simply because the organism would have no way of knowing how to behave when confronted with extreme cold, putrid meat, a thousand-foot cliff, or a poisonous snake. Instead, millions of years of natural selection have produced highly detailed, context-specific adaptations that solve specific problems that are associated with survival.

Although maintaining and enhancing organismic integrity, at an abstract level, describes one central directional tendency of human nature, the goals, motives, preferences, fears, and desires that constitute part of human nature are considerably more specific. It is in the details of the specific survival problems that we can identify the end states toward which human action is directed. Human nature, therefore, in part consists of the specific survival-related directional tendencies (problems that must be solved to survive) *combined with* the species-typical solutions or adaptations that have evolved in humans to accomplish these ends.

Survival motives, however, may not be the most central to personality psychologists. More important, perhaps, are those directional tendencies that involve social interaction. Group living confers reproductive advantage on those so doing to the extent that reproductively relevant resources are concentrated within groups. The fact that all known human groups are intensely social provides *prima-facie* justification for attempting to identify precisely what those resources are.

Although the survival advantages of group living, in the forms of protection (e.g., through coalitional aggression and defense) and food provisions (e.g., through hunting), are fairly clear, the advantages for solving *mating problems* require close attention. Humans who successfully mated in our evolutionary past are our ancestors; those who failed to mate are no one's ancestors.

Although reproduction provides a broad directional tendency toward which human action is directed, the "problem" at this level of abstraction is too broad to constitute a motive of human nature. Like survival, successful reproduction requires the solution of a number of more specific problems. Three of the most important mating problems are: (1) successful intrasexual competition (Buss, 1988a), (2) successful mate selection (Buss, 1989a), and (3) successful mate retention (Buss, 1988b; Flinn, 1988).

Although group living confers on members a concentrated pool of potential mates, it also imposes a field of intrasexual competitors. Since mates differ tremendously in reproductively relevant ways, competition will be intense for those mates who are most desirable. Success at intrasexual competition constitutes a major directional tendency for human action.

But even this "problem" contains numerous subproblems. Successful intrasexual competition often will involve (a) besting members of one's own sex in status, rank, prowess, or resources, and (b) competing to embody those characteristics that members of the opposite sex desire. Thus evolutionary theory leads to the expectation that a central directional tendency of humans will be to accomplish these tasks.

Given successful intrasexual competition, a second major problem of mating is selecting a reproductively valuable mate. This problem differs in substance for human males and females. Although male and female mate preferences are highly similar for many characteristics (e.g., both sexes worldwide appear to value kindness, intelligence, stability, and dependability in potential mates), they differ in the nature of the problems that must be solved by the act of mate selection.

For males more than for females, reproductive success is limited by ability to mate with fertile mates. Female fertility, however, is an internal characteristic that cannot be directly observed. Age and hence physical appearance correlates of age appear to provide the most powerful probabilistic cues to fertility. The hypothesis that males prefer youth and value physical appearance in potential mates more than do females has been confirmed in 37 cultures worldwide (Buss, 1989a).

Females face a different reproductive constraint. Relative to humans males, the reproductive potential of human females is low and the variance in number of offspring is low. Trivers' (1972) theory of parental investment and sexual selection predicts that under certain ecological and mating conditions, females will select mates in part based on the external resources that a male can provide for her and her offspring. This is especially true where resources can be defended and accrued, where males are inclined to invest these resources in mating effort, and where males differ substantially in their ability and willingness to provide resources.

The general hypothesis that women value resources, as well as cues to resource acquisition (e.g., ambition, industry), more than do men has been verified in 37 cultures (Buss, 1989a). In sum, although men and women are both faced with the problem of mate selection, the directional tendencies of men and women are expected to differ because the nature of the problems that must be solved differs.

A mate gained must be retained. This is true in contexts where long-term mating bonds are formed, and where reproductive success is impaired by loss or defection of a mate. Thus, a third directional tendency subsumed by mating is mate retention.

In a study of mate retention tactics (Buss, 1988b), I found a tremendous diversity of acts and tactics devoted to mate retention. These ranged from *vigilance* (e.g., He called her at unexpected times to see who she would be with; She had her friends check up on him; He snooped through her personal belongings; At the party, she did not let him out of her sight) to *violence* (e.g., He hit the guy who made a pass at her; She picked a fight with the woman who was interested in her mate; He vandalized the property of the guy who had made a pass at her). Human mating effort is directed not simply toward competing for initial access to mates and choosing among available alternatives—substantial effort appears to be directed toward retaining mates who have been acquired.

In sum, evolutionary theory provides a powerful heuristic for identifying the ends toward which human action is directed. As such, it yields a model for the "core" of personality that is anchored not in arbitrary speculations, but rather in the biological process that governs all known forms of organic life—evolution by natural selection.

B. Identifying Important Individual Differences

Personality psychologists have long been concerned with identifying the most important ways in which individuals differ. From among the thousands of dimensions of difference, which ones should galvanize the attention of personality theorists and researchers? As Goldberg (1972) succinctly phrased the question: Why measure *that* trait? Rationales for designating some individual differences as particularly important have come from folk psychology (Gough, 1968), factor analysis (Cattell, 1946), lexical analysis (Norman, 1963), and the act frequency approach (Buss & Craik, 1985), to name a few. An important alternative rationale resides in evolutionary criteria for importance (Buss, 1984).

Individual differences that are closely linked with components of natural selection, sexual selection, and life-history reproductive strategies are crucial using an evolutionary rationale for designating importance. Kenrick, Sadalla, Groth, and Trost (1990), for example, demonstrate that personality characteristics such as dominance, friendliness, and emotional stability are intimately linked with sexual selection in that they are central to mate choice (cf. Buss, 1989a). The possibility that these individual differences have previously been, and may currently be, linked with evolution by selection grants them special importance from an evolutionary perspective, when contrasted with those individual differences not so linked.

One could argue that personality psychologists have long studied the dimensions of dominance, friendliness, and emotional stability, and do not need an evolutionary perspective for pointing them out. This argument is correct as far as it goes—indeed, these three dimensions are part of nearly every taxonomy in personality psychology (e.g., Goldberg, 1981; McCrae & Costa, 1989; Wiggins, 1979). But what an evolutionary perspective does, in this case, is provide a further rationale for why these dimensions are so important. In this sense, it adds a useful supplement to existing taxonomic efforts by anchoring dimensions in criteria of evolutionary importance.

Another example, however, suggests that an evolutionary perspective can *call attention to important individual differences that were previously ignored,* thought to be unimportant, or not subsumed within current taxonomic efforts. A good example of this comes from the work of Gangestad and Simpson (1990). Using an evolutionary perspective, they argued theoretically and found empirically that individuals differ substantially in what they call "sociosexuality." At one end of this dimension are individuals who are "restricted" in sociosexuality—they require more time, attachment, and commitment prior to entering a sexual relationship. At the other end are those who are "unrestricted" in sociosexuality—they require less time, attachment, and commitment prior to sexual intercourse.

These ends of the sociosexual dimension represent alternative strategies that individuals use to pursue reproductive success. Those who are restricted tend to provide and obtain from their mates high levels of parental investment in their children. Those who are unrestricted, in the case of men, tend to obtain a larger number of matings with less parental investment devoted to any particular offspring. Unrestricted women, in contrast, tend to obtain temporary mates who are highly attractive to women. This presumably enables them to pass on to their offspring genes that will lead to offspring who themselves will be highly attractive to the opposite sex. Thus, reproductive success is achieved by two different strategies, suggesting an important dimension of individual difference that is not currently part of traditional taxonomies of individual differences.

C. Environmentally Induced Strategic Individual Differences

Evolutionary psychology provides a powerful set of conceptual tools for understanding the origins of individual differences. The construction workers who are laboring on the building next door have thick calluses on their hands. My academic colleagues down the hall do not. These individual differences in callous thickness are highly stable over time. At one level of analysis, the variance can be traced solely to variance in the reliably recurring experiences of the two groups. At another level of analysis, the existence of the species-typical callous-producing mechanism is a central and necessary element in the causal explanation of observed individual differences. *Just as men and women differ in the adaptive problems they confront, different individuals within each sex face different adaptive problems over time.* Some manifest individual differences are the strategic products of species-typical mechanisms responding to recurrently different adaptive problems across individuals.

In this callous example, the individual differences in skin friction experiences are in some sense "environmental." If any academic colleagues were to trade places with the construction workers, then the manifest individual differences would reverse. Nonetheless, we cannot rule out the genotype–environment correlation processes proposed by Plomin, DeFries, and Loehlin (1977) and Scarr and McCartney (1983). Some individuals, because of heritable skills, interests, or proclivities may preferentially select academic work or construction work as occupations. These selections, in turn, may create repeated exposure to friction-free versus friction-prevalent environments, which then differentially activate the species-typical callous-producing mechanism.

There are three central points: (1) stable manifest individual differences can be caused by differences in the recurrent adaptive problems to which different individuals are exposed; (2) the complex species-typical mechanisms are necessary and central ingredients in the causal explanation of individual differences, because without them the observed individual differences could not occur; and (3) the manifest individual differences are strategic outcomes of recurrently different input into species-typical mechanisms.

There are undoubtedly many recurrent environmental individual differences of precisely this sort. First-born children probably face recurrently different adaptive problems compared with second-born children. These apparently trigger in first-born children greater identification with the status quo, the parents, and the established power structure. This tendency may be responsible for the fact that first-borns typically oppose revolutionary scientific theories (Sulloway, 1996). Later-borns, who confront a niche already filled by an older sibling, tend to rebel more against established traditions, which may lead them to a greater identification with revolutionary scientific theories (Sulloway, 1996).

Individuals who grow up in environments where resources are unpredictable, such as among Hungarian Gypsies, may adopt a more impulsive personality style, and even mating style, where it would be adaptively foolish to delay gratification (Bereczkei, 1993). In contrast, those growing up in environments where resources and future prospects are more predictable may adopt a personality strategy involving greater delay of gratification, including sexual gratification. The resulting individual differences represent strategic solutions to the different adaptive problems encountered. Recurrently different environmental input into species-typical mechanisms can produce stable strategically patterned individual differences.

D. Heritably Induced Strategic Individual Differences

Recurrently different input into species-typical psychological mechanisms, of course, may come from heritable individual differences, whatever their ultimate origin (i.e., whether they originated from selection for alternative genetically based strategies, frequency-dependent selection, genetic noise, pathogen-driven selection for genetic uniqueness, or assortative mating). Individuals with an ectomorphic body type, for example, confront different adaptive problems than those who are mesomorphic.

Ectomorphs may risk being at the receiving end of greater aggression than their more muscular peers, an adaptive problem that typically must be solved by means other than physical aggression. Genetic differences, in other words, pose different adaptive problems for different individuals.

In addition to facing different adaptive problems, some individuals experience *greater success* at pursuing certain strategies rather than others. "Selection operates through the achievement of adaptive goal states, and any feature of the world—either of the environment, *or of one's own individual characteristics*—that influences the achievement of the relevant goal state may be assessed by an adaptively designed system" (Tooby & Cosmides, 1990b, p. 59, emphasis added). Individuals who are mesomorphic, for example, typically will experience far greater success at enacting an aggressive strategy than individuals who are ectomorphic. Tooby and Cosmides (1990b) call this phenomenon "reactive heritability."

Consider individual differences in physical attractiveness. There is evidence that physically attractive men are more successful at pursuing a "short-term" mating strategy involving many sexual partners (Gangestad & Simpson, 1990). Physically attractive women are better able to pursue a long-term strategy of seeking and actually obtaining higher-status, higher-income marriage partners (Taylor & Glenn, 1976). Heritable differences in physical attractiveness affect the success of pursuing different mating strategies. The *manifest* strategy differences are in some sense "heritable," but only indirectly and reactively. Relative physical attractiveness functions as "input" into species-typical or sex-typical psychological mechanisms, which then canalize the strategies of different individuals in different directions.

Heritable dimensions of individuals—such as differences in body type, keenness of vision, oratory skills, physical attractiveness, and spatial ability—provide important input into species-typical mechanisms. These individually different inputs tell the organism about the adaptive problem it is facing and the strategic solutions likely to be successful. The resulting product consists of *strategic individual differences* that are stable over time. The observed strategic differences are *correlated* with genetic variance, but cannot be understood apart from the central role played by our species-typical psychological mechanisms that were "designed" to receive input, both environmentally and heritably based, about the adaptive problems confronted and the strategic solutions likely to be successful.

E. The Five-Factor Model—Personality and the Adaptive Landscape

One need not believe that there are *only* five important personality dimensions (see, e.g., de Raad & Hoskens, 1990; Tellegen, 1985) to reach the conclusion that the five discovered so repeatedly—(1) Surgency (dominance, power, extraversion versus submissiveness, weakness, and introversion), (2) Agreeableness (cooperative and trustworthy versus aggressive and suspicious), (3) Conscientiousness (industrious, responsible versus lazy and irresponsible), (4) Emotional Stability (secure and stable versus insecure and anxious), and (5) Intellect–Openness (intelligent, perspicacious, and creative versus stupid, boarish, and unimaginative)—must surely be included in some form within any major personality taxonomy. Descriptive work documents the robustness of these factors, but does not elucidate *why* they are so frequently found.

From an evolutionary perspective, there are three ways to approach this crucial question. The first, discussed above, is that these individual differences may represent strategic differences, based on either heritable or environmental differences. Second, they may signify mere "noise" in the system—variations that were neutral with respect to natural and sexual selection. The third approach, entirely compatible with the first, is that these five dimensions of individual differences *summarize the most important features of the social landscape* that humans have had to adapt to (Buss, 1989b). From this second perspective, "to know others is an adaptive necessity" (Symons, 1979, p. 310).

The core of the "personality as adaptive landscape" view is that perceiving, attending to, and acting upon differences in others has been (and likely still is) crucial for solving adaptive problems. The first piece of evidence in favor of this view is that trait terms are inherently evaluative. Peabody (1985) found that less than 3% of trait terms were evaluatively neutral, the remaining 97% having definite evaluative (as well as descriptive) aspects (see also Hofstee, 1990). Hogan (1983) argues that trait terms reflect observer evaluations of others as potential contributors to, or exploiters of, the group's resources. For example, the Intellect of others (Factor 5) must be evaluated so that a person knows whom to go to for advice. Conscientiousness (Factor 3) must be evaluated to know who to trust with tasks. Borkenau argues that a selective advantage would accrue to those persons who have the ability to perceive and act upon these major individual differences in others. Graziano and Eisenberg (this volume, chap. 30) place Agreeableness (Factor 2) in evolutionary perspective. They argue that coordinated group action is best accomplished when individuals are willing to cooperate and conform to group norms, and suspend their individual concerns for the good of the group (see also Wiggins, 1991, for a similar account).

Humans are an intensely group-living species. Groups afford protection from predators, protection from other groups of aggressive males, the possibility of cooperative hunting of large game, and a population of potential mates. But groups also carry costs. With group living comes an intensification of competition, risks of communicable diseases, and aggression from other group members. Other humans can cripple our survival and reproductive success. Other humans are our primary sources of strategic interference. Other humans are our primary "hostile force of nature" (Alexander, 1987). In a phrase, other humans define our primary adaptive landscape, and are capable of facilitating or interfering with our reproductive strategies (see also Byrne & Whiten, 1988).

I have argued that personality traits summarize the most important features of that adaptive landscape (Buss, 1989b). They provide a source of information for answering important life questions: Who is high or low in the social hierarchy? Who is likely to rise in the future? Who will make a good member of my coalition? Who possesses the resources that I need? With whom should I share my resources? Who will share their resources with me? Whom can I depend on when in need? With whom should I mate? Who should I befriend? Who might do me harm? Who can I trust? Who can I go to for sage advice? The hypothesis is that people have evolved psychological mechanisms sensitive to individual differences in others that are relevant to answering these critical adaptive questions.

Two of the most important features of human groups are: (1) they are intensely *hierarchical,* with important reproductive resources closely linked with position in the hierarchy (e.g., Hogan, 1983; Lopreato, 1984), and (2) they are characterized by elevated forms of *cooperation* and *reciprocal alliance formation* (Axelrod, 1984; Cosmides & Tooby, 1989; Trivers, 1971). The importance of hierarchy suggests that location of others in the hierarchy, as well as proclivities to ascend in the hierarchy, are extremely important features of the human adaptive landscape. The prevalence of reciprocal alliance formation suggests that a second critical feature of the human adaptive landscape is the differential proclivity of others to ''cooperate'' or to ''defect'' (see Jones, Couch, & Scott, this volume, chap. 19).

The persistent emergence of Surgency (dominance–submissiveness) and Agreeableness (cooperative–aggressive) as the *two major axes* in interpersonal taxonomies (e.g., Wiggins, 1979) and as the *first two factors* in personality-descriptive taxonomies (McCrae & Costa, 1989; Trapnell & Wiggins, 1990) represents the adaptive significance to all humans of discerning in others their hierarchical position and proclivity and their willingness to form reciprocal alliances (Buss, 1989b). In human evolutionary history, those individuals who were able to accurately discern and act upon these individual differences likely enjoyed a considerable reproductive advantage over those who were oblivious to these consequential individual differences. Evidence from studies of competition and mating support specific predictions from an evolutionary analysis of these features of the human adaptive landscape. For example, kindness (Factor 2), dependability (3) emotional stability (4) and intelligence (5) are among the most valued characteristics in potential mates (Buss et al., 1990).

Historically, evolutionary approaches have ignored individual differences. The recent work shows that models can gain increased sophistication and precision by incorporating an analysis of individual differences. The integration of basic psychological mechanisms with evolved strategic individual differences may provide the most compelling theoretical bridge to close the current chasm between the branches of psychology that deal with typical human mechanisms and those that focus on individual differences.

F. An Evolutionary Psychological Metatheory of Sex Differences

Evolutionary psychology, in addition to shedding light on individual differences *within* sex, also provides a unique metatheory for understanding differences *between* the sexes: Men and women are expected to differ in their underlying psychology only in the delimited domains where they have faced recurrently different adaptive problems. In domains where the sexes have faced the same adaptive problems, no sex differences are expected. Alternative theories of sex differences typically cannot specify *in advance* the domains in which sex differences will be found, in which direction they will be found, and why they will be found in these domains and directions.

Men and women historically have faced many adaptive problems that are highly similar. Both sexes needed to maintain body temperature, so both sexes have sweat glands and shivering mechanisms. Repeated friction to certain areas of the skin was a "hostile force of nature" to both sexes in ancestral environments, so men and women have evolved callous-producing mechanisms. Both sexes needed to solve the adaptive problem of identifying a good cooperator for strategic confluence when seeking a long-term mate, and this may be one reason why both sexes value "kindness" in a partner so highly across all cultures whose partner preferences have been studied (Buss, 1989a).

In several domains, however, the sexes have faced different adaptive problems. For 99% of human evolutionary history men faced the adaptive problem of hunting and women of gathering, possible selective reasons for men's greater upper body strength and spatial rotation ability and for women's greater spatial location memory ability (Silverman & Eals, 1992). Internal female fertilization and gestation created the adaptive problem of uncertainty of parenthood for men, but not for women. Cryptic ovulation created the adaptive problem for men of knowing when a woman was ovulating—a possible causal force in the origins of sexual activity through the entire cycle and the emergence of long-term committed mating bonds between a man and a woman (Alexander & Noonan, 1979). The dual male mating strategy of seeking both short-term sexual partners and long-term marriage partners created an adaptive problem for women of having to discern whether particular men saw them as temporary sex partners or as potential spouses (Buss & Schmitt, 1993). Sex differences in mate preferences (Buss, 1989a), courting strategies (Buss, 1988a; Tooke & Camire, 1991), jealousy (Buss et al., 1992), mate guarding tactics (Buss, 1988b; Flinn, 1988), sexual fantasies (Ellis & Symons, 1990), and sexual desires (Buss, 1994) correspond remarkably well to these sex-linked adaptive problems. Evolutionary psychology offers the promise of providing a coherent theory of strategic sexual differences as well as strategic sexual similarities.

G. Anchoring Conceptions of Adaptation and Adjustment

Concepts such as adaptation and adjustment have been central to nearly all frameworks of personality. As typically used, these concepts signify an ability to deal effectively with the varied demands of everyday living. The related dimensions of neuroticism (Eysenck, 1981), and emotional instability (Norman, 1963), which imply ineffective negotiation of life's tasks, are central to nearly every taxonomic system of personality. These concepts represent a particular manner of coping, typically one with high levels of subjective distress, intrapsychic discomfort, large fluctuations of mood or affect, and a relative inability to terminate negative subjective states.

The concept of adaptation is also central to evolutionary biology, although it is defined somewhat differently. Adaptations in evolutionary biology refer to evolved solutions to problems posed by the complex tasks of survival and reproduction. Not all features of behavior or morphology are considered to be adaptations, and the evidential standards that must be met for considering something an adaptation are complex and often difficult to meet (Williams, 1966). Nonetheless, the effectiveness with which reproductive problems are solved provides a biologically anchored meaning of "adjustment."

Draper and Belsky (1990) articulate an intriguing evolutionary theory of alternative reproductive strategies based on the *environments* that humans encounter in early childhood. They propose that in environments and cultures where fathers are present during early childhood, the reproductive strategy tends to involve delayed puberty, delayed onset of sexual activity, stability of adult pair-bonds, and a set of concomitant personality characteristics that facilitate this strategy such as low self-monitoring and high cooperativeness. In environments and cultures where fathers tend to be relatively absent, an alternative personality constellation and reproductive strategy is followed, one involving early onset of puberty and sexual activity, instability of adult pair-bonds, low parental investment, high self-monitoring, and high aggressiveness.

What is intriguing about this theory is that it posits that *both* strategies are part of our species-typical repertoire—we all have the capacity to follow either strategy. But which one we do follow depends on the *environment* that we encounter while growing up. Draper and Belsky emphasize that it is possible to rear children successfully under both regimes, and that neither strategy is inherently superior or inferior to the other—they are both "adaptive" in the environmental contexts in which they occur. This implies that conceptual clarity might be achieved from anchoring definitions of "adjustment" and "adaptation" in the effectiveness with which reproductive problems are solved in particular environments. The definition of adjustment would shift from the *content* of the strategy (i.e., it is not necessarily maladjusted to be impulsive or aggressive) to the *success* of the strategy in a specific environment.

In sum, evolutionary thinking has implications for how personality psychologists might conceptualize adaptation and adjustment. It suggests that the equation of maladjustment with strategies that might appear distasteful or repugnant (e.g., those that are aggressive, impulsive, or wanton) is inappropriate. These strategies may be functional in the particular environments in which they occur (e.g., where resources are unstable or unpredictable). The effectiveness with which survival and reproductive problems are solved is one biological criterion by which the concepts of "adapted" and "adjusted" can be anchored.

H. Implications for Personality Stability and Change

This framework provides a coherent theoretical rationale for *when* we will observe personality stability and change, and, perhaps even more importantly, an answer to *why* some aspects of personality remain stable while others change. Stability is expected at several levels. First, many of our evolved species-typical mechanisms will remain stable over time, even if they remain unactivated. All humans, including cloistered academics, retain their callous-producing mechanisms, even if they rarely encounter the repeated skin friction necessary for their activation. This is stability in the species-typical sense.

Second, stability in the individual differences sense can be produced by stable environmental recurrences in exposure to adaptive problems—stability in manifest individual differences. Just as differences in callous thickness between academics and construction workers are stable over time, so differences experiencing hostility from others may be stable over time (Dodge & Coie, 1987). Differences in expressions of jealousy, to use another example, may be stable over time due to being married to a spouse who displays frequent cues to infidelity. Stable differences in the adaptive problems to which one is exposed, of course, may be created by properties of individual actors, either heritably or environmentally based. The recurrent barrage of sexual "come-ons" experienced by physically attractive women, for example, may be an adaptive problem that stems from heritable differences in physiognomy. The key point is that stability of *manifest* personality is determined in part by the recurrences in the adaptive problems to which individuals are exposed.

A third source of stability stems from the retention of successful or well-practiced problem solving strategies. Some strategies rely on the exploitation of certain personal qualities. Those with many resources, for example, can retain their mates with lavish gifts that are inaccessible to the less endowed. Those lacking positive inducements of any kind may be forced to resort to self-abasing tactics, such as subordinating oneself to the goals of one's mate, or cost-imposing tactics, such as threats and violence (Wilson & Daly, 1992). Well-practiced strategies are generally more effective than less-well-practiced ones, and so some stability occurs through the retention of well-practiced effective strategies. This account is similar to the fascinating theory recently proposed by Caspi and Moffitt (in press) that suggests that individual differences manifest themselves most strongly in times of transition, in part because individuals deploy strategies to deal with those transitions that have worked for them in the past, can be enacted quickly, and cost little energy, presumably because they have been well practiced.

This framework simultaneously provides a metatheoretical account of when and why we will observe change. First, change in underlying mechanisms may occur over ontogeny with species-typical shifts in adaptive problems. The most obvious example is puberty. Women develop enlarged breasts and their reproductive apparatus becomes functional to solve adaptive problems that were irrelevant during childhood. Predictable *psychological* shifts undoubtedly accompany these changes, such as increased interest in the opposite sex, a honing of one's mate preferences, increased attention to one's physical appearance, and the onset of vivid sexual and romantic fantasies.

Second, change can occur as a result of developmental shunting of individuals down one path versus another. Those growing up in father-absent households, for example, may be shunted into a more promiscuous short-term mating strategy, whereas those growing up with an investing father may be shunted into a more monogamous long-term mating strategy (Belsky, Steinberg, & Draper, 1991). Presumably, individuals have psychological mechanisms that determine whether securing a long-term investing mate is likely, or whether the individual would do better to extract a variety of different resources from different shorter-term mates.

Third, change in *manifest* behavior can occur as result of change in the adaptive problems to which one is exposed. Just as shifting from a friction-prevalent occupation to a friction-free one causes change in one's manifest callouses, so a shift from a low-Conscientious to a high-Conscientious mate may cause a change in manifest jealousy. More transient shifts in the adaptive problems to which one is exposed may produce more transient shifts in manifest behavior.

The fourth source of change occurs when an old strategy for solving an adaptive problem is eliminated, or a new strategy is acquired or activated. Crying as a tactic for getting one's way becomes less effective as one moves from childhood to adulthood, prompting its diminution with development. Gaining a job promotion may permit the use of resource-bestowal as a strategy for attracting and retaining mates, a strategy that was previously inaccessible. New strategies are added and old strategies are jettisoned, in part based on changes in the assets one can exploit and on shifts in effectiveness with changing circumstances.

Thus, personality stability and personality change can both be understood within a single integrative conceptual framework. This framework provides a metatheoretical account of *why* we expect stability and change and *under what conditions* we expect stability and change. Perhaps through this integrative framework for examining stability and change, we can start bridging the traditions that historically have isolated the study of individual differences from the study of human nature.

IV. CONCLUSIONS

The evolutionary conception of personality proposed here starts with the premise that personality cannot be properly understood without articulating the problems that humans have had to solve over thousands of generations of human history—problems that are ultimately related to survival and reproduction. Personality, from this perspective, consists centrally of the *psychological mechanisms* and *behavioral strategies* that humans have evolved for solving these problems. Because the problems that must be solved are numerous and complex, the psychological mechanisms and strategies that have evolved are likely to be many and, at least in part, domain-specific.

This view differs from previous "evolutionary" approaches to personality that attempt to trace "traits" in humans by comparing them with other primate species such as chimpanzees or baboons. These early approaches fail because: (1) all species, including humans, are unique in some respects, (2) selection of particular species for comparative analysis is often misleading (Tooby & DeVore, 1987), and

(3) they ignore the core of Darwinian theory—the evolution of *adaptation* by natural selection. Adaptation must be central to evolutionary personality psychology, and the adaptations of greatest interest to personality psychologists occur in the form of psychological mechanisms and behavioral strategies.

Evolutionary psychology permits personality psychology to escape from the endless anchorless speculations about what the *basic* directional tendencies of human nature are. Since evolution by natural selection is the *principle guiding force* responsible for the creation of all known structures of organic life, there is no reason to believe that humans have been exempt from this process. This suggests that the numerous reproductive problems that humans have had to solve (e.g., competition for mates, selection of mates, ensuring paternity in children, rearing children in particular ways, aiding genetic relatives, forming reciprocal alliances, negotiating social hierarchies) must be the core directional tendencies toward which human action is directed.

In addition to specifying the core directional tendencies, an evolutionary perspective clarifies several confusing debates that have dominated the field for the past 20 years. Evolutionary psychology provides sound criteria for identifying important individual differences, and leads researchers to dimensions previously not considered; anchors the concepts of adaptation and adjustment in ways that escape the previous arbitrary and value-laden definitions; and provides a powerful framework for resolving the debate over personality consistency and behavioral specificity.

In a curious way, an evolutionary perspective also brings together two segments of the field that have been separated for decades—the segment that focuses on grand theories of personality and the segment that focuses on understanding individual differences. Personality psychology historically is that branch of psychology that is in principle the broadest and most integrative of all the subfields of psychology. An evolutionary perspective provides the framework within which its breadth and integration can be achieved.

ACKNOWLEDGMENT

This chapter was supported in part by a fellowship from the Center for Advanced Study in the Behavioral Sciences and by NIMH Grant MH-44206. The author thanks Leda Cosmides, Martin Daly, Don Symons, John Tooby, and Margo Wilson for illuminating discussions of the issues in this chapter.

REFERENCES

Alexander, R. D. (1979). *Darwinism and human affairs.* Seattle: University of Washington Press.
Alexander, R. D. (1987). *The biology of moral systems.* New York: de Gruyter.

Alexander, R. D., & Noonan, K. M. (1979). Concealment of ovulation, parental care, and human social evolution. In N. A. Chagnon & W. Irons (Eds.), *Evolutionary biology and human social behavior: An anthropological perspective* (pp. 402–435). North Scituate, MA: Duxbury Press.

Axelrod, R. (1984). *The evolution of cooperation.* New York: Basic Books.

Bailey, J. M., Gaulin, S., Agyei, Y., & Gladue, B. A. (1994). Effects of gender and sexual orientation on evolutionarily relevant aspects of human mating psychology. *Journal of Personality and Social Psychology, 66,* 1074–1080.

Barkow, J. (1989). *Darwin, sex, and status.* Toronto: University of Toronto Press.

Belsky, J., Steinberg, L., & Draper, P. (1991). Childhood experience, interpersonal development, and reproductive strategy: An evolutionary theory of socialization. *Child Development, 62,* 647–670.

Bereczkei, T. (1993). r-selected reproductive strategies among Hungarian Gypsies: A preliminary analysis. *Ethology and Sociobiology, 14,* 71–88.

Brown, D. E. (1991). *Human universals.* Philadelphia: Temple University Press.

Buss, A. H. (in press, this volume). An evolutionary perspective on personality traits. In Hogan et al. (eds.), *Handbook of Personality Psychology.* New York: Academic Press.

Buss, D. M. (1984). Toward a psychology of person-environment (PE) correlation: The role of spouse selection. *Journal of Personality and Social Psychology, 47,* 361–377.

Buss, D. M. (1986). Can social science be anchored in evolutionary biology? *Revue Europeene des Sciences Sociales, 24,* 41–50.

Buss, D. M. (1988a). The evolution of human intrasexual competition: Tactics of mate attraction. *Journal of Personality and Social Psychology, 54,* 661–628.

Buss, D. M. (1988b). From vigilance to violence: Tactics of mate retention. *Ethology and Sociobiology, 9,* 291–317.

Buss, D. M. (1989a). Sex differences in human mate preferences: Evolutionary hypotheses tested in 37 cultures. *Behavioral and Brain Sciences, 12,* 1–49.

Buss, D. M. (1989b, June 26–30). *A theory of strategic trait usage: Personality and the adaptive landscape.* Paper presented at the Invited Workshop on Personality Language, University of Groningen, The Netherlands.

Buss, D. M. (1990a). Evolutionary social psychology: Prospects and pitfalls. *Motivation and Emotion, 14,* 265–286.

Buss, D. M. (1990b). Toward a biologically informed psychology of personality. *Journal of Personality, 58,* 1–16.

Buss, D. M. (1991). Evolutionary personality psychology. *Annual Review of Psychology* (pp. 459–491). Palo Alto, CA: Annual Reviews, Inc.

Buss, D. M. (1994). *The evolution of desire: Strategies of human mating.* New York: Basic Books.

Buss, D. M. (1995). Evolutionary psychology: A new paradigm for psychological science. *Psychological Inquiry, 6,* 1–300.

Buss, D. M., Abbott, M., Angleitner, A., Asherian, A., Biaggio, A. (plus 45 additional authors). (1990). International preferences in selecting mates: A study of 37 societies. *Journal of Cross-Cultural Psychology, 21,* 5–47.

Buss, D. M., & Craik, K. H. (1985). Why *not* measure that trait? Alternative criteria for identifying important dispositions. *Journal of Personality and Social Psychology, 48,* 934–946.

Buss, D. M., Larsen, R., Westen, D., & Semmelroth, J. (1992). Sex differences in jealousy: Evolution, physiology, and psychology. *Psychological Science, 3,* 251–255.

Buss, D. M., & Schmitt, D. P. (1993). Sexual Strategies Theory: A contextual evolutionary analysis of human mating. *Psychological Review, 100,* 204–232.

Byrne, R., & Whiten, A. (Eds.). (1988). *Machiavellian intelligence.* Oxford: Clarendon Press.

Cantor, N., & Kihlström, J. (1987). *Social intelligence.* New York: Academic Press.

Caspi, A., & Moffitt, T. (in press). *Psychological Inquiry.*

Cattell, R. B. (1946). *Description and measurement of personality.* Yonkers-on-Hudson, NY: World Book.

Cosmides, L. (1989). The logic of social exchange: Has natural selection shaped how humans reason? *Cognition, 31,* 187–276.

Cosmides, L., & Tooby, J. (1987). From evolution to behavior: Evolutionary psychology as the missing link. In J. Dupré (Ed.), *The latest on the best: Essays on evolution and optimality.* Cambridge, MA: MIT Press.

Cosmides, L., & Tooby, J. (1989). Evolutionary psychology and the generation of culture. Part II: Case study: A computational theory of social exchange. *Ethology and Sociobiology, 10,* 51–98.

Daly, M., & Wilson, M. (1983). *Sex, evolution, and behavior.* Boston: Willard Grant Press.

Daly, M., & Wilson, M. (1988). *Homicide.* New York: de Gruyter.

Daly, M., Wilson, M., & Weghorst, S. J. (1982). Male sexual jealousy. *Ethology and Sociobiology, 3,* 11–27.

Darwin, C. (1859). *On the origin of the species by means of natural selection, or, Preservation of favoured races in the struggle for life.* London: Murray.

Dawkins, R., & Krebs, J. R. (1978). Animal signals: information or manipulation. In J. R. Krebs & N. B. Davies (Eds.), *Behavioral ecology: An evolutionary approach* (pp. 282–309). Oxford: Blackwell.

de Raad, B., & Hoskens, M. (1990). Personality descriptive nouns. *European Journal of Personality, 4,* 131–146.

Dodge, K. A., & Coie, J. D. (1987). Social-information-processing factors in reactive and proactive aggression in children's peer groups. *Journal of Personality and Social Psychology, 53,* 1146–1158.

Draper, P., & Belsky, J. (1990). Personality development in evolutionary perspective. *Journal of Personality, 58,* 141–163.

Ellis, B. J., & Symons, D. (1990). Sex differences in sexual fantasy: An evolutionary psychological approach. *Journal of Sex Research, 27,* 527–556.

Eysenck, H. J. (1981). *A model for personality.* Berlin: Springer-Verlag.

Flinn, M. (1988). Mate guarding in a Caribbean village. *Ethology and Sociobiology, 9,* 1–28.

Gangestad, S. W., & Simpson, J. A. (1990). Toward an evolutionary history of female sociosexual variation. *Journal of Personality, 58,* 69–96.

Goldberg, L. R. (1972). Some recent trends in personality assessment. *Journal of Personality Assessment, 36,* 547–560.

Goldberg, L. R. (1981). Language and individual differences: The search for universals in personality lexicons. In L. Wheeler (Ed.), *Review of personality and social psychology* (pp. 141–165). Beverly Hills, CA: Sage.

Gough, H. G. (1968). An interpreter's syllabus for the California Psychological Inventory. In P. McReynolds (Ed.), *Advances in psychological assessment* (Vol. 1, pp. 55–79). Palo Alto, CA: Science & Behavior Books.

Gould, S. J., & Lewontin, R. C. (1979). The spandrels of San Marco and the Panglossian paradigm: A critique of the adaptationist programme. *Proceedings of the Royal Society of London, Series B, 205,* 581–598.

Herrnstein, R. (1977). The evolution of behaviorism. *American Psychologist, 32,* 593–603.

Hofstee, W. K. B. (1990). The use of everyday personality language for scientific purposes. *European Journal of Personality, 4,* 77–88.

Hogan, R. (1983). A socioanalytic theory of personality. In M. M. Page (Ed.), *Nebraska Symposium on Motivation.* Lincoln: University of Nebraska Press.

Kenrick, D. T., Groth, G. E., Trost, M. R., & Sadalla, E. K. (1993). Integrating evolutionary and social exchange perspectives on relationships: Effects of gender, self-appraisal, and involvement on level of mate selection. *Journal of Personality and Social Psychology, 64,* 951–969.

Kenrick, D. T., Sadalla, E. K., Groth, G., & Trost, M. R. (1990). Evolution, traits, and the stages of human courtship: Qualifying the parental investment model. *Journal of Personality, 58,* 97–116.

Lopreato, J. (1984). *Human nature and biocultural evolution.* Boston: Allen & Unwin.

McCrae, R. R., & Costa, P. (1989). The structure of interpersonal traits: Wiggins circumplex and the five-factor model. *Journal of Personality and Social Psychology, 56,* 586–595.

Norman, W. T. (1963). Toward an adequate taxonomy of personality attributes: Replicated factor structure in peer nomination personality ratings. *Journal of Abnormal and Social Psychology, 66,* 574–583.

Peabody, D. (1985). *National Characteristics.* Cambridge, England: Cambridge University Press.

Pinker, S. (1994). *The language instinct.* New York: Wm. Morrow.

Pinker, S., & Bloom, P. (1990). Natural language and natural selection. *Behavioral and Brain Sciences, 13,* 707–784.

Plomin, R., DeFries, J. C., & Loehlin, J. C. (1977). Genotype-environment interaction and correlation in the analysis of human behavior. *Psychological Bulletin, 84,* 309–322.

Rozin, P., & Schull, J. (1988). The adaptive-evolutionary point of view in experimental psychology. In R. C. Atkinson, R. J. Herrnstein, G. Lindzey, & R. D. Luce (Eds.), *Steven's handbook of experimental psychology.* New York: Wiley.

Ruse, M. (1986). *Taking Darwin seriously: A naturalistic approach to philosophy.* Oxford: Blackwell.

Scarr, S., & McCartney, K. (1983). How people make their own environments: A theory of genotype → environment effects. *Child Development, 54,* 424–435.

Seligman, M. E. P., & Hagar, J. L. (Eds.) (1972). *Biological boundaries of learning.* New York: Appleton-Century-Crofts.

Shepard, R. N. (1987). Toward a universal law of generalization for psychological science. *Science, 237,* 1317–1323.

Short, R. V. (1979). Sexual selection and its component parts, somatic and gentical selection, as illustrated by man and great apes. *Advances in the Study of Behavior, 9,* 131–158.

Silverman, I., & Eals, M. (1992). Sex differences in spatial abilities: Evolutionary theory and data. In J. Barkow, L. Cosmides, & J. Tooby (Eds.), *The adapted mind* (pp. 533–549). New York: Oxford University Press.

Singh, D. (1993). Adaptive significance of waist-to-hip ratio (WHR) and female attractiveness. *Journal of Personality and Social Psychology, 65,* 293–307.

Sulloway, F. (1996). *Born to rebel: Radical thinking in science and social thought.* Cambridge, MA: MIT Press.

Symons, D. (1979). *The evolution of human sexuality.* New York: Oxford University Press.

Symons, D. (1987). If we're all Darwinians, what's the fuss about? In C. Crawford, M. Smith, & D. Krebs (Eds.), *Sociobiology and psychology: Ideas, issues, and applications* (pp. 121–146). Hillsdale, NJ: Erlbaum.

Symons, D. (1989). A critique of Darwinian anthropology. *Ethology and Sociobiology, 10,* 131–144.

Symons, D. (1992). On the use and misuse of Darwinism in the study of human behavior. In J. Barkow, L. Cosmides, & J. Tooby (Eds.), *The adapted mind* (pp. 137–159). New York: Oxford University Press.

Taylor, P. A., & Glenn, N. D. (1976). The utility of education and attractiveness for females' status attainment through marriage. *American Sociological Review, 41,* 484–498.

Tellegen, A. (1985). Structures of mood and personality and their relevance to assessing anxiety, with an emphasis on self-report. In A. H. Tuma & J. D. Maser (Eds.), *Anxiety and the anxiety disorders.* Hillsdale, NJ: Erlbaum.

Tooby, J., & Cosmides, L. (1990a). The past explains the present: Emotional adaptations and the structure of ancestral environments. *Ethology and Sociobiology, 11,* 375–424.

Tooby, J., & Cosmides, L. (1990b). On the universality of human nature and the uniqueness of the individual: The role of genetics and adaptation. *Journal of Personality, 58,* 17–68.

Tooby, J., & Cosmides, L. (1992). Psychological foundations of culture. In J. Barkow, L. Cosmides, & J. Tooby (Eds.), *The adapted mind* (pp. 19–136). New York: Oxford University Press.

Tooby, J., & DeVore, I. (1987). The reconstruction of hominid behavioral evolution through strategic modeling. In W. G. Kinzey (Ed.), *The evolution of human behavior: Primate models* (pp. 183–237). New York: State University of New York Press.

Tooke, W., & Camire, L. (1991). Patterns of deception in intersexual and intrasexual mating strategies. *Ethology and Sociobiology, 12,* 345–364.

Trapnell, P. D., & Wiggins, J. S. (1990). Extension of the Interpersonal Adjective Scales to include the Big Five dimensions of personality (IASR-B5). *Journal of Personality and Social Psychology, 59,* 781–790.

Trivers, R. (1971). The evolution of reciprocal altruism. *Quarterly Review of Biology, 46,* 35–57.

Trivers, R. (1972). Parental investment and sexual selection. In B. Campbell (Ed.), *Sexual selection and the descent of man: 1871–1971* (pp. 136–179). Chicago: Aldine.

Wiggins, J. S. (1979). A psychological taxonomy of trait descriptive terms: The interpersonal domain. *Journal of Personality and Social Psychology, 37,* 395–412.

Wiggins, J. S. (1991). Agency and communion as conceptual coordinates for the understanding and measurement of interpersonal behavior. In W. Grove & D. Cicchetti (Eds.), *Thinking clearly about psychology* (Vol. 2). Minneapolis, MN: University of Minnesota Press.

Williams, G. C. (1966). *Adaptation and natural selection: A critique of some current evolutionary thought.* Princeton, NJ: Princeton University Press.

Wilson, M., & Daly, M. (1992). The man who mistook his wife for a chattel. In J. Barkow, L. Cosmides, & J. Tooby (Eds.), *The adapted mind* (pp. 289–322). New York: Oxford University Press.

CHAPTER 14

EVOLUTIONARY PERSPECTIVES ON PERSONALITY TRAITS

ARNOLD H. BUSS

UNIVERSITY OF TEXAS

Three evolutionary perspectives may help us to understand human personality traits. The first emphasizes similarities between humans and the animals with whom we share an *evolutionary heritage* in behavior, personality, and adaptations related to personality traits. Like the sociobiological approach, this perspective focuses on similarities between our species and others, but it differs in two ways. First, the similarities are limited to mammals and primates. Second, the focus is mainly on behavior and personality traits, not on principles involving the propagation of genes.

The second perspective is broader: *evolutionary trends* in the line that led to our species. An example is the waning of instinct as a determinant of behavior. Thus in lower mammals, stimuli often serve as releasers of an entire program of innate behavior, whereas in our species, stimuli typically serve as conditioned stimuli, cues for instrumental behavior, or information to be cognitively processed.

Like other species, we differ anatomically and psychologically from all other species, and we posses personality traits unique to us. We study them, and not the other way around. Clearly, a third perspective is needed, one that examines how we are *distinctively human.*

The chapter is organized around these perspectives, which are discussed in sequence. I cite literature on mammalian, primate, and human behavior and personality, but also attempt a conceptual integration of this knowledge.

I. THE COMMON HERITAGE

The animals closest to us in evolutionary terms are the primates. Primates have of course been shaped by evolutionary processes and therefore share behavior with other mammals and with highly social mammals, but some features are distinctively primate. In what follows, imagine that we are nothing more than primates, especially the great apes, and even more specifically, the species closest to us, chimpanzees.

A. Primates as Mammals

Like other mammals, primates follow a daily rhythm of *activity,* which descends to a low ebb at night during sleep and reaches various peaks during the day, usually before feeding. During the day there are also intense bursts of energy in aggression, escape, sexual behavior, or just frisky play. Within any particular species, there are marked individual differences in the level of energy expenditure, which are well known to owners of pets and have been reported in chimpanzees by de Waal (1982).

Many mammals range over a territory, sniffing and searching for any changes that might occur. The tendency to *explore* is especially strong in the line from which primates evolved. Their curiosity can lead to contact with unfamiliar animals of their own species and members of other species. Then they are wary and less mobile. Thus when the chimpanzees at Gombe first saw Jane Goodall, they retreated and kept their distance, though her behavior objectively posed no threat (Goodall, 1986). Exploratory behavior temporarily diminished but slowly returned to its previous level. Only after many months of her continued presence were they able to overcome their shyness and allow her to approach closely and occasionally interact with them.

Such timidity may be one component of a more general tendency to be *fearful.* When a young primate is exposed to excessive social novelty, temporary abandonment, or threat, it reacts by howling, shrieking, clutching, and kicking. Puppies and kittens tend to wail and whine. Despite species differences among mammals in the expressive display of fear, there is a common set of reactions triggered by activation of the sympathetic nervous system: increased rate of breathing, higher blood pressure, and shunting of blood from the digestive system to the skeletal muscles—all preparations for flight.

Primates share with other mammals a behavioral repertoire of *aggressive* responses. The fighting of cats and dogs is well known, against both their own kind and members of other species. Earlier field studies of chimpanzees found them to be gentle and peaceful, but later research has revealed clear patterns of aggression (Goodall, 1986).

B. Primates as Sociable Mammals

Primates are part of a group of mammals that are highly sociable, some of the best examples being elephants, dolphins, and dogs. They prefer to associate with one another and become upset when cut off from companionship. Dogs mourn for their masters, and chimpanzees become depressed by the absence of their companions (H. F. Harlow & Harlow, 1962). After social isolation, reunion elicits not just relief but also elation. Dogs greet comrades by nuzzling and licking each other; primates seem to enjoy grooming others and being groomed.

All mammalian mothers form an attachment bond with their newborn offspring. In less sociable mammals, this bond wanes and gradually disappears as the offspring become capable of self-help. But primates and other highly social mammals form *enduring bonds of attachment,* which may continue throughout life. Adult primates, especially the great apes, show affection to friends by grooming, hugging, patting, or even kissing. When such attachment is observed among humans, we call it deep friendship or love.

Primate infants may become accustomed to being the sole focus of the mother's affection and refuse to share this affection with others. When the mother gives birth to the next child, the older sibling may become intensely *jealous.* Jealousy is not limited to the young, however, and is a potential consequence of any close bond of affection. Pet dogs have been known to display jealousy when another pet is introduced into the household or after the birth of a child.

C. Two Kinds of Emotions

I group jealousy, love, elation, and grief under the heading of *relationship emotions.* They are absent in nonsocial mammals (cougars, leopards) and occur in weak form among moderately social mammals such as the common cat. It is clear that love is part of attachment and that jealousy can arise when exclusive love is demanded. The origins of elation and grief were mentioned earlier. Grief occurs when a social animal is isolated from an attached other, and joy is elicited by acceptance and affection from others. The primordial reaction of a social animal to separation from its fellows is melancholy, just as the primordial reaction to being reunited is elation.

Three other emotions—fear, rage, and sexual arousal—are grouped under the heading of *arousal emotions.* All three involve a massive reaction of the sympathetic division of the autonomic nervous system. Fear and rage are part of the preparation of the body for fight or flight (Cannon, 1927). The physiological reactions in sexual arousal are more complex, but in the late stages of sex at least, there is the same kind of bodily arousal as in fear and anger (Masters & Johnson, 1966).

In the relationship emotions, however, there is little or no autonomic arousal. Consider the affection of friends or the love of a mother for her children. These are physiologically placid emotions, though the feelings may be experienced as intense.[1] Similarly, there is no autonomic arousal in grief or depression, and there may even be a lowered arousal. There may be autonomic arousal in jealousy but only when there is a strong anger component. Subtract the anger component from jealousy, and autonomic arousal is absent.

Given that the arousal emotions occur in all mammals and the relationship emotions occur in all highly social mammals, they are likely to be adaptive. The arousal emotions can be seen as aiding survival. Fear and rage are part of bodily preparation for the massive muscular exertion of fight or flight in the face of possible injury or death. Sexual arousal enhances the sexual motivation required for the continuity of the genes. Thus the arousal emotions are crucial in survival of the genetic material (sex) or in survival of the individual (fear and rage).

It is doubtful whether the relationship emotions play a similar direct role in survival. If they have an indirect adaptive function, it may be to facilitate group cohesiveness and cooperation. The joy of being accepted and welcomed by others in the group reinforces the tendency to affiliate with them. The grief of isolation from others is sufficiently aversive to motivate affiliative behavior, which ends the melancholy. And an individual's depression spurs others to offer the help that might lift the individual's mood. Thus the emotions of love, joy, and grief may serve to enhance sociality, which is known to be adaptive (Wilson, 1975). Jealousy may be merely a nonadaptive consequence of love in children. However, in adults jealousy is often the result of a demand for exclusiveness is a relationship. Women require exclusivity of love, and men of sex (see David Buss, this volume, chap. 13).

In brief, when emotions are examined from an evolutionary perspective, two different kinds can be discerned. They differ in arousal, prevalence among mammals, and adaptive functions (see Table I).

The potential for aggressive behavior may be one reason that affiliative animals tend to have a social organization that minimizes aggression, usually one based on *dominance*. Larger, stronger animals use aggression or threats to achieve superior status over smaller, weaker members of the group. Being dominant usually means having better access to food, to attention from others, and often to females. Domi-

---

[1] The assertion that elation involves no autonomic arousal may contradict personal experience. I suggest three reasons why we should not rely on such experience. First, it confuses the feeling of being on top of the world with physiological arousal. Second, a joyful person may dance or leap in the air or otherwise have sufficient muscular exertion to elevate heart rate and breathing rate. Subtract the muscular exertion, and there is no particular physiological arousal in elation. Third, what is the base rate against which autonomic arousal should be compared? If we compare the physiological state that accompanies joy with that accompanying complete quiescence or NREM sleep, joy might be regarded as a mild state of arousal. But quiescence is an inappropriate baseline condition. Instead, we should use the physiological arousal that occurs in such nonemotional states as problem-solving (Lacey, 1956) or the orienting reflex to novel stimuli (Lynn, 1966). When elation, unaccompanied by exercise, is compared with the nonemotional state of attention (to one's own thoughts or to external stimuli), it is clear that elation has none of the physiological arousal of fear, rage, or sexual arousal.

TABLE I
Arousal and Relationship Emotions

	Arousal	Relationship
Emotions	Fear, rage, sex	Love, jealousy, joy, grief
Autonomic arousal	High	Low
Reaction	To threat or a sexual stimulus	To acceptance or rejection
Adaptive function	Survival of individual/genes	Group cohesion
Occurrence	In all mammals	In very social mammals

nant primates tend to be groomed by subordinate ones. And those who associate with a dominant animal, either as companions or as sex partners, may share some of the ascendant animal's status.

The concepts of dominance and status seem necessary to account for the social organization of primates and other highly social mammals. Dominance refers to the animal's position in the group that derives mainly from its own strength and ferocity, but also from cleverness and guile. Status refers to the position and privileges of the animal, which derive not only from dominance but also from age (older animals have higher status), reproductive status (ovulating females have higher status), and even genealogy (rank of the mother). Genealogy is more important for females, whereas dominance through fighting is more important for males.

D. Distinctively Primate Features

The primate behavioral tendencies relevant to personality represent extensions of features seen in lower mammals. The mammalian tendency to explore contains an element of curiosity, but primates are even more curious. And primates, especially the great apes, are distinctive in displaying *cognitive curiosity*. In the laboratory, they will work to receive stimulation (Butler, 1957). Chimpanzees are known to solve puzzles and other problems in the absence of any extrinsic reward, just to satisfy an insatiable curiosity. There is an anecdote about an experimenter who used banana slices to reward a chimpanzee for solving problems. The animal was not hungry and just lined up the banana slices as he solved the problems, but eventually the experimenter's supply was exhausted. He continued to present puzzles and was astonished to receive a banana slice after each puzzle was solved. The chimpanzee obviously was rewarding the experimenter with banana slices and continued to do so until the experimenter regained all of them. More generally, the curiosity of primates, especially chimpanzees, extends beyond the seeking of tangible rewards to an intrinsic interest in solving problems and seeking novel stimuli.

Their curiosity is abetted by a capacity for *manipulation* that is far beyond that of other mammals. Chimpanzees have been taught such fine motor acts as striking a match, lighting a cigarette, and wielding a paint brush. Given their manipulative ability, primates' curiosity often takes the form of poking, prying, squeezing, and generally handling objects in the environment. And like any young human child left unsupervised in a home, they open every unlocked cabinet, closet, and drawer, strewing the contents around the room.

Primates are exceedingly *imitative*. A Japanese's macaque monkey discovered that sweet potatoes tasted better when she washed off the dirt in water. Later, she ventured to cast wheat on shallow ocean water, where the clinging sand sank to the bottom and the wheat could easily be scooped up and eaten. The cleaning of potatoes and wheat quickly spread throughout the troop until virtually all the monkeys in the troop had adopted it.

The childhood of primate young is longer than that of most mammalian young, especially in relation to the life span of the species. This extended childhood may be necessary, for young primates have much to learn. In the potato-washing incident, the novel behavior was adopted first by younger monkeys and only later by their elders, a reminder that the young tend to be the most imitative, perhaps because they have so much to learn. This incident also suggests that primates are especially educable, and the longer childhood provides ample opportunity to learn the ways of their group.

The variety of primate behavioral features are summarized in Table II. The underlying assumption is that in the line that led to our species there is a progression from mammals to social mammals to primates. Species higher in this progression retain features seen in species lower in the progression but have added behavioral tendencies. Thus primates possess features seen in mammals and social mammals, as well as specific to primates.

1. Development

The focus here is on developmental issues that affect personality traits. In primates, only two developmental eras are necessary: infancy and the juvenile period.

a. Infancy. Like all mammalian infants, newborn primates are completely helpless and would perish without adult assistance. The mother supplies food, protection, and love. Infants respond to this maternal care, and a close bond of affection develops.

TABLE II
Evolution and Behavior/Traits

Mammals	Social mammals	Primates
Activity	Sociability	Manipulativeness
Exploration	Enduring attachment	Cognitive curiosity
Fear	Jealousy	Close imitation
Aggression	Dominance	Greater educability

The period of attachment in primates has been divided into three phases (H. F. Harlow, Harlow, & Hansen, 1963). At first the mother is solicitous and completely accepting of the infant, and she is a haven of safety and nurturance. The infant's feeling of security depends in large part on the mother. If she is sufficiently protective and available, the infant will be secure enough to venture out in the wider environment. Primate infants appear to be motivated by two opposing tendencies: the need to seek novelty and stimulation versus the need for security and protection (Mason, 1970). An insecure infant remains close to the mother, too scared to explore the environment. A secure infant tends to be low in fear and can venture away from the mother so long as she is in sight.

In the second phase of attachment, the mother withdraws affection, diminishing attention to the infant, and starts to punish the infant. The latter may react with withdrawal, anger, resistance, or negativism. These first signs of independence are typically met by even more irritability and punishment by the mother.

In the third phase, the mother is often occupied with the birth of the next offspring and therefore is even more rejecting of her older child. The presence of this new infant is likely to elicit jealously and temper tantrums by the displaced sibling. If the mother can spare some attention and affection for her older sibling, the latter's jealousy and annoyance should gradually wane.

The events of the attachment period may be expected to affect personality traits. The mother's behavior should be regarded as only one determinant, albeit an important one, of her youngster's personality. If she is not sufficiently protective and a haven of security, her infant may become fearful and inhibited. If she fails to provide enough attention and social stimulation, her infant may become withdrawn and less sociable. And if she cannot share at least some affect with her older offspring after the birth of a new one, the older one may become intensely jealous. In brief, the events of attachment are assumed to affect the personality traits of fearfulness, impulsivity (the opposite of inhibition), sociability, and the anger component of aggressiveness (jealousy).

b. Juvenile Period. Like mammalian young, juvenile primates love to play. They especially prefer rough-and-tumble play fighting, chasing one another, and follow-the-leader. While their muscles and coordination are developing, so are bonds of friendship and alliance. Now peers and unrelated animals can substitute for the mother in offering attention and social stimulation.

Gender affects the social bonds that develop. Females tend to stay closer to their mothers and are intensely interested in infants. While still in the juvenile period, they start to practice mothering or attempts to do so with available infants. After becoming mothers, they form the nucleus of a group that includes their own offspring and other mothers and their offspring. Thus the sociability of females is enhanced by close interpersonal relationships.

Male juveniles tend to separate more from their mothers and are less interested in infants. The social bonds established by males during play are more important, especially the bonds of friendship needed for alliances (Goodall, 1986).

The other side of friendship in social interaction is *power relationships.* Dominance is ordinarily achieved through aggression. It starts with the mock aggression of juvenile play, and often becomes real as males struggle for ascendance. Size and strength are crucial. Larger, stronger males tend to win fights and become dominant. Smaller, weaker males tend to lose fights and become submissive. Some males, however, tend to be ferocious, overcoming physical liabilities with sheer determination to win fights, and others assume leadership through guile. But size and strength usually win. Thus older males tend to dominate juveniles, and males tend to dominate females.

Gradually, a dominance hierarchy develops, and each primate knows his or her place. Enduring status in the hierarchy diminishes aggression, except for instances when older primates become weaker and younger ones attain adult size and strength. Clearly, the outcome of power struggles is a major determinant of the traits of aggressiveness and dominance.

2. Primate Personality Traits

Recall that in this examination of the common heritage, humans are being regarded as just primates. Issues relevant to personality traits have been discussed on the assumption that a particular set of traits is common to primates, especially the great apes and our species. The seven traits listed below have already been mentioned in previous sections. They may be divided into two groups.

The first involves *activation,* which is defined as involving various kinds of arousal (here defined broadly):

1. *Activity,* the total energy output as observed in rate of movements and their vigor
2. *Fearfulness,* wariness, running away, cowering, and the concomitant physiological arousal
3. *Impulsivity,* acting suddenly and on the spur of the moment; the opposite is the tendency to inhibit behavior

The second set of personality traits are all social:

4. *Sociability,* preferring being with others (though primates are a highly social group, there are still individual differences in sociability within each species)
5. *Nurturance,* helping others, especially those who need help, even at a cost to the helper (altruism)
6. *Aggressiveness,* attacking or threatening others
7. *Dominance,* seeking and maintaining superior status over others versus the opposite pole, submissiveness

Though all four traits are in the realm of social behavior, they differ markedly. The first two can be characterized as prosocial in that they involve seeking the presence of others (sociability) or helping them (nurturance). The second two involve conflict (aggressiveness) or a struggle for power (dominance). As a means of attaining superior status, aggression is closely linked to dominance. However, it is possible to be irritable and strike at others without seeking power, just as it is possible to attain superior status vicariously (through association with a dominant individual), by trickery, or even by leadership ability. Thus it is worthwhile to distinguish between aggression and dominance, though the two are closely linked in primates.

Keen observers of primate behavior have described individual differences in six of the seven traits just described, the two most prominent observers being Goodall (1986) in the wild and de Waal (1982) in a more restricted environment. Concerning activity, de Waal (1982) described two extreme chimpanzees. One moved slowly, became fatigued easily, and generally was lethargic. The other was "the moving force behind all developments. His boundless energy and boisterous, provocative behavior has had the effect of a catalyst" (p. 70). No one would be surprised to see such extremes among domestic pets, and marked differences in activity have been systematically recorded in domestic cats (Feaver, Mendl, & Bateson, 1986).

Individual differences in fearfulness have repeatedly been documented. Goodall (1986) described a chimpanzee male who went to pieces in tense social situations, rushing to others for reassurance or clutching his own genitals. De Waal (1982) observed a female chimpanzee who was always the first to raise the alarm and who became so scared that she shook or vomited.

The personality trait of sociability is also manifest in chimpanzees: "Luis is much more sociable than Yeroen. He has an open and friendly character and sets great store by company" (de Waal, 1982, p. 63). And cats vary considerably in gregariousness with each other and with humans (Feaver et al., 1986).

Individual differences in nurturance have been largely ignored by observers of animal behavior, but Goodall (1986) reported sharp differences among mothers in whether they shared nuts their offspring could not obtain. Some were completely selfish, whereas others shared the food with even their 6-year-old offspring.

Concerning aggression and dominance, individual differences in these behaviors have been the focus of many observers. No one seriously questions the existence of these traits in primates.

In addition to observations of individual primates, there have also been systematic studies of monkeys, complete with factor analyses. Chamove, Eysenck, and Harlow (1972) coded the behavior of rhesus monkeys and came up with three factors: fear, hostility (aggressiveness), and affiliativeness (sociability). A 4-year study by Stevenson-Hinde, Stillwell-Barnes, and Zung (1980) yielded three bipolar dimensions: fearful, tense, and subordinate versus aggressive, effective, and confident; slow and equable versus active and excitable; and solitary versus sociable.

These studies of monkeys have provided evidence for six of the seven primate traits. The only one missing is impulsiveness, though there is a hint of it in the term *excitable*. Notice that impulsivity is also missing from the earlier descriptions of the behavior of individual animals. Most observers of animal behavior tend to ignore personality traits, and the handful who do observe individual differences may not have attended to behaviors indicating impulsiveness. I predict that when observers search for evidence of impulsiveness in primates, they will find it. Meanwhile, its status as a primate trait must be considered as tentative.

II. EVOLUTIONARY TRENDS

Our common heritage includes features we share with mammals, highly social mammals, and primates (see Table II). The evolutionary sequence just mentioned implies evolutionary trends in the features that affect behavior and personality. These trends may be divided into those that occurred during mammalian evolution in the line that led to primates and those that occurred during primate evolution in the line that led to our species.

A. Mammals to Primates

Anatomical adaptations are important throughout the animal kingdom, but they are especially important among lower mammals. Thus some animals have claws which are anatomically specialized for gripping and ripping. But other animals, primates especially, have hands, which are open up a wide range of *behavioral* adaptations.

Though some mammals give birth to a *single offspring,* many have litters. All primates give birth to a single offspring, which means that the mother–infant bond is closer to that individual. This affectional tie is strengthened by the *longer childhood* of primates in relation to total life span, another trend in mammalian evolution. A long childhood offers youngsters more time to learn the ways of their group and their species.

Linked to the stretching out of childhood is a corresponding waning of innate behavioral tendencies, a shift from *instinct to learning.* Primates have fewer instincts, and they tend to be more generalized and diffuse than the innate tendencies of lower mammals. And as might be expected, the relationship between hormones and behavior is weaker in primates than in lower mammals.

Innate tendencies are crucial for animals that mature quickly (and therefore have little time to learn). But primates care for their young for years, which diminishes the need for having innate tendencies immediately and automatically available for the contingencies of everyday life. For lower mammals the gap between adaptive needs and behavior that satisfies these needs is filled largely by instinct. For primates, especially the great apes, it is filled largely by learning.

As learning became a more prominent mechanism during mammalian evolution, the role of stimuli changed. No longer mainly releasers of innate behavioral programs, stimuli came to serve as *cues* providing information about how to act rather than simply triggering acts. And learning became more complex in a variety of ways: delays, detours, and chaining of responses. Greater complexity of learning required a *larger brain,* and during mammalian evolution the brain/body ratio increased markedly. A larger, better brain continued the cycle by making possible

TABLE III
Evolutionary Trends: Mammals to Primates

From	To
Anatomical adaptations	Behavioral adaptations
Shorter childhood	Longer childhood
Instincts, releasers	Learning, cues
Conditioning	Cognitive learning
Small brain	Large brain
Less individuality	More individuality

even higher forms of learning: learning to learn, learning sets, and matching-to-sample (H. F. Harlow, 1949). Such advanced kinds of learning were, essentially, *cognitive learning*.

The manipulative ability of primates is the result of another evolutionary trend: the freeing of the hands to hold, carry, or grasp objects. This ability combined with a larger, better brain, which delivered at least primitive cognition, could then lead to tool use. The use of tools, thereby extending what can be done only with the limbs, is the most conspicuous example of a behavioral adaptation, in contrast to an anatomical adaptation that uses only the body. These evolutionary trends are summarized in Table III.

As the right-hand column of this table suggests, primates (especially the great apes) are similar to humans in behavioral adaptations. More than lower mammals, the lives of primates are shaped by their everyday experiences, which differ from one animal to the next. Having fewer innate tendencies, a longer childhood, and a greater range of life experiences, primates are more likely than lower mammals to be different from one another in behavior. Thus the inevitable outcome of these evolutionary trends is greater individuality, as reflected in the seven personality traits that humans share with primates.

III. DISTINCTIVELY HUMAN TENDENCIES

Most of these evolutionary trends continued during the evolution of humans: the predominance of behavioral adaptations, a longer childhood, more advanced cognitions, a larger and more complete brain, and greater individuality. These trends, especially the psychological adaptation of a high level of cognitive ability, produced a species distinct from all others. Let me offer an example of how a small change, working over time, can produce a qualitative difference. Consider two 5-year-old boys, one of whom learns to read and the other who does not. At first there will be little difference in their cognitions. But within a few years the nonreader will have to drop out of school, or if he remains, he will learn little there. He will be shut out of the world of the written word, and his intellectual growth will be stunted. The reader will be exposed to a wide array of information not available to nonreaders, and he will proceed normally into advanced cognitions. The small quantitative difference of early childhood will inevitably widen into a gulf large enough for an observer to infer qualitative differences in cognitive ability and information. Similarly, we were set on a path which diverged from that of other primates so that now the difference between us and them is sufficiently large to yield psychological tendencies unique to our species.

A. Tools

Primates move about mainly on four limbs, which means that the hands are only partially free for manipulation. The freeing of the hands was completed with the evolution of bipedalism in our species. The human hand offers a paradoxical example of an anatomical and behavioral adaptation. It is a fairly typical primate hand, the only difference being an opposable thumb, which means the human hand is anatomically unspecialized. But when we consider the potential uses of the hand, especially when a tool is placed in it, we can see that it is essentially a behavioral adaptation.

The occasional use of tools by primates was inevitable once they possessed the requisite manipulative ability and a brain capable of integrating a task with a means of performing the task. But two points need to be made. First, primates use tools only occasionally; they do not need tools and can get along well without them. We use tools most of the time; we need tools and cannot survive without them.

Second, after we marvel at the inventiveness of chimpanzees who fashion sticks to poke into termite mounds or use leaves as sponges, we must bear in mind that these devices are so primitive that they barely qualify as tools. Though the great apes possess rudimentary imagery and planning ability, these two cognitive processes are far advanced in our species. When such cognitions are harnessed to the superior brain–hand connections of our species, we can produce sophisticated tools that multiply our native capabilities: engines to multiply the power of muscles, telescopes and radar to amplify the senses, and computers to enhance our cognitions.

B. Childhood

The second trend that continued was the elongation of the period of childhood, which occupies a portion of our life cycle larger than that of any other species. This extension of childhood has given rise to the concept of *neoteny:* the persistence of infantile or juvenile characteristics into adulthood. The concept may be appreciated when a more advanced species is compared with a less advanced species. In the less advanced species, most childish features disappear in adulthood, and adults look and act entirely different from the young. In more advanced species, childish features are retained. An infant chimpanzee, for instance, has these human-like features: a small, flat face; a relatively large brain and brain case; small teeth; thin nails; and sparse body hair. It more closely resembles a human than does an adult chimpanzee. As Gould (1977) has written, "this associated complex of characters— neoteny, large brains . . . , slow development, small litters, intense parental care, large body size— must have suggested a look in the mirror" (p. 351). He is more specific about the sequence of events:

> I assume that major human adaptations acted synergistically throughout their gradual development. The interacting system of delayed development–upright posture–large brain is such a complex: delayed development has produced a large brain by prolonging fetal growth rates and has supplied a set of cranial proportions adapted to upright posture. Upright posture freed the hand for tool use and set selection pressures for an expanded brain. (p. 339)

Two psychological examples of neoteny may be seen in our species. Mammalian and primate young are extremely playful but their playfulness declines with maturity. We are playful throughout life. Primate young are intensely curious. We remain curious all our days.

C. Cognitions

The evolutionary trend toward greater cognitive capability started during mammalian evolution and continued during the evolution of humans, and it is cognitive capability that most clearly distinguishes us from primates and all other animals. Thus we can originate complex and abstract concepts, examples of which are revealed in science, religion, and the arts. Our imagery enables us to envision worlds that do not exist, for we alone are capable of conceptions such as heaven and hell, ghosts, and black holes. We are as curious as any animal but go beyond curiosity to the search for understanding, so that we seek causes and make attributions.

Adult humans can leave behind the egocentricity of children and animals to view the world from perspectives other than our own. Thus an adult may adopt a child's perspective, a hunter the perspective of his prey, and a teacher the perspective of a learner. Chimpanzees are capable of learning sign language (Gardner & Gardner, 1969), but it is impoverished compared to human adults' language. When teaching is connected to language, we can render knowledge cumulative by passing it on to future generations. And we make rules; primates and other mammals play, but we are the only species to have games, which are distinguished from other play by the presence of (arbitrary) rules.

Our social cognitions are unique. We make social comparisons; for example, by engaging in downward comparison of others less fortunate in order to make ourselves feel better. We derive considerable pleasure from the achievements of those close to us, vicariously sharing the joy of their successes. And our personal cognitions are unique, for example, repression and projection as mechanisms of defense against anxiety.

D. Self

Advanced cognitions also establish a potential for self-consciousness, which may occur in rudimentary form in the great apes but is fully developed only in humans.

This statement requires elaboration, for research has established that primates display behavior that can be interpreted as awareness of self, for example, recognition of self in a mirror. When a chimpanzee has a red dot surreptitiously placed on its head and looks in a mirror, it tries to touch the marked area on its head (Gallup, 1970). This finding and related results have led Gallup (1977) to conclude that "the extent that self recognition implies a rudimentary concept of self, these data show that contrary to popular opinion and preconceived ideas, man may not have a monopoly on the self-concept. Man may not be evolution's only experiment in self-awareness" (p. 333). As to the question of why self-recognition is restricted to the great apes and humans, Gallup (1977) suggests that "the monkey's inability to recognize himself may be due to the absence of a sufficiently well-integrated self-concept" (p. 334). Notice the conceptual leap from recognition of self in a mirror to a well-integrated self-concept.

Adult humans are capable of mirror-image recognition, which is absent in infants and develops slowly during the second year of life as part of more general trends in cognitive development. By the age of 2 years most infants possess this capacity (Amsterdam, 1972; Schulman & Kaplowitz, 1977). Does this mean that children of 2 years have a self-concept and the same kind of self-awareness as older children and adults? There are five cognitive attributes present in older children that are absent in 2-year-olds, which suggests that the answer is no.

The first is *self-esteem*. The basis for later self-esteem may be laid down in 2-year-olds, but children of this age do not show behavior that allows us to infer the general self-evaluation called self-esteem. This diffuse feeling of self-worth develops gradually and can be measured perhaps by the age of 4 years. Nor are infants clearly aware of the difference between their private feelings and public behavior. It is still too early for the sense of *covertness* and an awareness that private thoughts and feelings cannot be observed. Infants and primates lack the sense of covertness that can be inferred in children of 4 years.

Infants are still egocentric and do not know that others view the world from different perspectives. Even children of several years of age are limited in social perspective-taking. In one study children were asked to select gifts for their parents, teacher, brother, sister, and self (Flavell, 1968). Most 3-year-olds selected the same gifts for others as for themselves. Some 4-year-olds selected gifts appropriate for others, half the 5-year-olds did, and all the 6-year-olds did. Social perspective-taking evidently emerges during the fifth year of life. Linked to perspective-taking is the ability to view oneself as a social object. Such *public self-awareness,* as seen in the reaction of embarrassment, does not occur until the fifth year of life (Buss, Iscoe, & Buss, 1979).

The last facet of the advanced self to develop is *identity*. It may be a personal identity, the sense of being different from everyone else in appearance, behavior, character, or personal history, or it may be social identity, knowing oneself to be a member of a nation, religion, race, vocation, or any other group that offers a sense of belonging to something larger than oneself. And most of us have a sense of continuity, identifying ourselves as the same person across decades of time or across diverse social roles.

Thus five aspects of the self are absent in 2-year-old human children: self-esteem, a sense of covertness, perspective-taking, public self-awareness, and identity. These may be regarded as evidence for an advanced or cognitive self, which is conspicuously absent in human infants and the great apes. They do appear to have a primitive, sensory self—an awareness of where the body ends and not-me begins, and mirror-image recognition (Buss, 1980). But they lack the advanced cognitive self that is implicit in constructs such as self-concept, self-esteem, self-consciousness, and identity, constructs easily applied to older human children and adults.

E. Socialization

Advanced cognitions also affect the way we train our offspring to function in the world. Primates are capable of primitive social roles based on gender and dominance, but human roles are more complex. Every society defines masculine and feminine roles, and has complicated rules involving status; when property is involved, social classes based on ownership are sure to follow. And every society develops religion and a code of morality.

On the basis of a survey of literature, Dubin and Dubin (1963) found that these minimal goals were common to most cultures:

1. Control of elimination and of grabbing of food
2. Control of thumb sucking and masturbation
3. Learning how and what can be touched
4. Learning how to relate to others, including control of aggression

Another survey, this one of the files on 50 different countries, revealed that starting in the 5- to 7-year period, children are inculcated in the traditions, beliefs, and values of their society (Rogoff, Sellers, Perrotta, Fox, & White, 1975). They must adhere to the rules and prepare for adulthood by practicing roles they will assume later in life. Boys and girls tend to be separated and trained for divergent sex roles.

F. Human Distinctiveness

These singular human tendencies are summarized in Table IV. It is not much of a stretch to conclude that superior cognitive ability is the engine of all the attributes in the table. This ability has set us on a path different from all other animals, culminating in two revolutions in tools: substituting machines for muscle and substituting machines (computers) for some of our cognitive functions.

Our advanced intelligence rests on the continuation of two evolutionary trends mentioned earlier. The first is the trend toward a larger brain in relation to body size. The ratio of brain to body size, already large in primates, continued to increase,

Table IV
Distinctively Human Tendencies

Tools	Sophisticated and necessary
Cognitions	Abstract concepts; search for understanding; sociocentric perspective; advanced language; rules
Self	Self-esteem; sense of covertness; public self-awareness; identity
Socialization	Kinship; advanced social rules; culture; religion; morality

ours being four times that of primates (Jerison, 1976). The second trend was an increase in cerebral cortex and frontal lobes, anatomical adaptations that underlie our advanced cognitions.

These evolutionary traits have strongly shaped human personality. A longer childhood, strong socialization pressure, true social roles, and a variety of work and social contexts combine to widen the environments in which humans exist. Advanced cognitions and language extend the human response repertoire. These distinctively human features have produced two effects. First, the traits shared with primates have been elaborated in ways to be described shortly. Second, there are uniquely human personality traits.

G. Elaborated Primate Traits

In humans *activity* continued to consist of tempo and vigor of response, but now it also manifested in the rate and loudness of speech. And the complexity of human environments has added contexts in which the expenditure of energy may be seen. Thus physical activity occurs in a variety of sports and types of exercise. The current fitness fad may appeal to those high in activity but not those at the other end ("When I have the urge to exercise, I lie down until it passes"). Many factory and farm jobs require considerable vigor, and the assembly line demands a speedy rate of response. Just living in a city like New York may require a fast pace of responding.

The major addition to *fear* is cognitions. As far as we know, we are the only species that worries. The down side of our ability to imagine the future is a fear of dying. We can teach great apes to use sign language, but would they then be subject to existential anxiety? The range of possible apprehensions has been opened up in the modern world: fear of flying, fear of a nuclear attack, and fear of contracting AIDS, to name just a few. And our advanced cognitions have probably contributed to two problems of adjustment unique to our species: panic and agoraphobia.

The trait of *impulsivity* has been strongly affected by socialization practices. All societies require some inhibition of behavior, and some push hard for delay of gratification. As a result, the trait dimension of impulsivity has been extended at the inhibition end. Impulsivity has also been elaborated by the human propensity for planning and by the need to make decisions, which means that the trait is much more complex in our species.

For those who are *sociable* there is an added human outlet of formal groups of people: work, sports, clubs, politics, or organized spectator activities. The low end of sociability is extended by the possibility of privacy, which is available to humans but not to primates. But because humans may become isolated, the issue of loneliness now becomes important, especially for those high in sociability.

To the trait of *nurturance* is added the imagery that allows us to put ourselves in the place of another person (empathy), which facilitates nurturant behavior (Davis, 1983). Socialization practices strongly push the helping of others. More than any other animal, we are likely to save women and children first and to render aid to the old and infirm. Furthermore, there are charitable organizations, religious orders, and occupations that by their nature enhance nurturance tendencies or provide an outlet for them (e.g., medicine, nursing, and child care).

Aggressiveness is expanded by the availability of language. We are the only species to curse, derogate, maliciously tease, verbally threaten, and spread nasty gossip. The combination of advanced cognitions and language enables us to make negative attributions to others, engage in prejudice, and generally to hate others. Our advanced tools also allow us to inflict greater harm on others.

The trait of *dominance* is elaborated in several ways. The presence of organized competition in our species allows an individual to attain dominance by means of success sin competition—politics, for example. Closely allied to competitiveness are the traits of achievement (McClelland, Atkinson, Clark, & Lowell, 1953), power (Winter, 1973), and Machiavellianism (Christie & Geis, 1970), all of which are linked to dominance. More than any other species, humans can attain dominance by means of nonaggressive leadership through personality traits (charisma) or qualities the group seeks in a leader.

At the opposite end of the dominance dimension, submissiveness is also elaborated. Submissive humans have the outlet of deference not just to a leader but to generalized authority: the trait of authoritarianism (Adorno, Frenkel-Brunswik, Levinson, & Sanford, 1950).

In brief, evolutionary trends in the line that led to our species have resulted in the elaboration of primate personality traits. Specifically, three human features are important here. Cognitions and tools have added to our response repertoire, socialization has emphasized one or another end of trait dimensions, and a broader range of environments has opened up possibilities for personality traits that are not present in other species.

How important are these seven traits in personality research and theory? In one form or another they are listed in virtually all classifications of personality (see Buss & Finn, 1987). Eysenck's (1970) superfactor of *extraversion* consists mainly of sociability and impulsivity, though activity also appears as a minor aspect. His *neuroticism* appears to be mainly fearfulness. The four social traits have been emphasized in one way or another in circumplex models of interpersonal behavior. To cite just one example, Kiesler (1983) uses two axes: dominant versus submissive and sociable versus aggressive.

H. Uniquely Human Traits

1. Self

As the only species with advanced, cognitive self-consciousness, humans are unique in possessing traits that concern the reactions to or awareness of oneself (Fenigstein, Scheier, & Buss, 1975). *Private self-consciousness* refers to a focus on the nonobservable aspects of oneself, as may be seen in a typical item: "I'm generally attentive to my inner feelings." *Public self-consciousness* involves oneself as a social object and being concerned with appearance or behavior that can be observed by others: "I'm self-conscious about the way I look." *Body self-consciousness* involves a focus on internal bodily sensations: "I can often feel my heart beating" (Miller, Murphy, & Buss, 1981).

Social anxiety, which is related to acute public self-consciousness as well as to fear, has been assessed as a global trait (Fenigstein et al., 1975). But two component traits have been isolated. One is speech anxiety: "I always avoid speaking in public if possible" (Slivken & Buss, 1984). The other trait is shyness, which also appears to be a combination of fear and public self-consciousness (with correlations of .50 and .26, respectively; Cheek & Buss, 1981).

Self-esteem is well known and apparently such a generalized, pervasive trait that all measures of it intercorrelate. Finally, humans are capable of putting on an act to please other people, behavior that has been called *self-presentation.* The best self-report measure is called ability to modify self-presentation: "I have the ability to control how I come across to people, depending on the impression I want to give them" (Lennox & Wolfe, 1984).

2. Other Cognitive Traits

Humans make attributions, but there are individual differences in the kind of attributions made and the extent to which people make them. The most prominent attributional trait is *locus of control* (Rotter, 1960), which consists of several components (Collins, 1974). A more recent trait, called *general causality orientation* (Deci & Ryan, 1985), involves whether people seek autonomy or control or whether they feel controlled.

Individual differences in imagery are tapped by two related traits. *Absorption* is the tendency to have intense subjective experiences: "If I wish, I can imagine (or daydream) some things so vividly that they hold my attention as a good movie or story does" (Tellegen & Atkinson, 1974). *Openness to experience* consists of being interested in novelty, the arts, and, especially, one's fantasies and feelings (McCrae & Costa, 1983).

There are also several cognitive styles which deal with the way information is processed (see Goldstein & Blackman, 1978, for a review). The best known trait is *field dependence–independence,* also known as *psychological differentiation* (Witkin, Dyk, Faterson, Goodenough, & Karp, 1962).

IV. THREE PERSPECTIVES

The first perspective deals with the animal heritage of human personality. It starts with this question: What if we are regarded as nothing but primates? If so, we can examine personality relevant features that primates share with other animals. Thus primates have arousal and relationship emotions and a long childhood, and they tend to be cognitively curious, manipulative, and especially educable. We can examine the events of infancy, especially attachment, and the long juvenile period and see how they affect personality. The focus on our primate heritage culminates with a list of seven personality traits present in primates and humans.

The second perspective alerts us to evolutionary trends in the line that led to our species. There are the broad trends of mammalian evolution toward behavioral adaptations, longer childhood, learning, and the beginning of cognitions. A crucial trend concerns the innate, species-wide behavioral tendencies called instincts. Instincts wane as a determinant of behavior and so do hormones. Instinctive behavior persists in humans, but instinct is often overridden by learning. Hormones can affect human behavior—the sexual motivation of women, for instance. But unlike other mammalian females, women do not come into heat, and their sexual behavior is determined less by hormonal changes than by socialization, learning, and cognition. These biological determinants still affect our behavior but much less so than in other animals.

There are also narrower trends that occurred in the evolution of humans from ancestral primates such as advanced cognitions, which led to tool use and its many consequences, especially true socialization. Infants do not possess the advanced cognitions they will later have, and of course they have not been exposed to significant socialization. It follows that with respect to personality, human infants should be regarded as nothing more than primates. The only personality traits seen in infants are some of those we share with primates.

These trends lead directly to the third perspective: humans as distinctly different. There are novel personality traits in humans not seen in other species: self-related traits and cognitive traits. These uniquely human traits differ in two ways from the traits we share with primates. First, they derive from our advanced cognitions and socialization practices. Second, all the primate traits are known to be inherited in humans (see Buss, 1988, for a review), but the inheritance of the uniquely human traits has yet to be established.

The evolutionary perspective also shows how the traits humans share with primates become more elaborate in our species. We have a wider range of response options, especially those of cognitive nature. Thus humans have a larger repertoire of aggressive and dominant behavior, which means that these traits are more differentiated in our species. And we live in a wider range of social environments: work, home, school, and play. Consequently, an active child might be energetic at home or on the playground but relatively still in the classroom. As this example illustrates, the traits we share with primates are likely to show less consistency in humans.

A final comment concerns the practices of those who study personality. The seven traits we share with primates have been the focus of interest by personality psychologists for many decades. As mentioned earlier, these traits are found in virtually all classifications of personality traits. In contrast, the uniquely human traits, with the exception of self-esteem, have received less attention. And these distinctly human traits tend to be omitted from most classifications of personality. Why have the seven traits we share with primates been examined more? Perhaps they are more observable. Or perhaps these traits are regarded as more important because, as derivatives of our evolutionary past, they are more closely linked to adaptive needs in the line that led to our species.

REFERENCES

Adorno, T. W., Frenkel-Brunswik, E., Levinson, D. J., & Sanford, R. N. (1950). *The authoritarian personality.* New York: Praeger.

Amsterdam, B. (1972). Mirror self-image reactions before the age of two. *Developmental Psychology, 5,* 297–305.

Buss, A. H. (1980). *Self-consciousness and social anxiety.* San Francisco: Freeman.

Buss, A. H. (1988). *Personality: Evolutionary heritage and human distinctiveness.* Hillsdale, NJ: Erlbaum.

Buss, A. H., & Finn, S. E. (1987). Classification of personality traits. *Journal of Personality and Social Psychology, 52,* 432–444.

Buss, A. H., Iscoe, I., & Buss, E. (1979). The development of embarrassment. *Journal of Psychology, 103,* 227–230.

Butler, R. A. (1957). The effect of deprivation of visual incentives on visual exploration in monkeys. *Journal of Comparative and Physiological Psychology, 50,* 177–179.

Cannon, W. B. (1927). *Bodily changes in pain, hunger, fear and rage.* New York: Appleton.

Chamove, A. S., Eysenck, H. J., & Harlow, H. F. (1972). Personality in monkeys: Factor analyses of rhesus social: Behavior. *Quarterly Journal of Experimental Psychology, 24,* 496–504.

Cheek, J. M., & Buss, A. H. (1981). Shyness and sociability. *Journal of Personality and Social Psychology, 41,* 330–339.

Christie, R., & Geis, F. L. (Eds.). (1970). *Studies in Machiavellianism.* New York: Academic Press.

Collins, B. E. (1974). Four components of the Rotter Internal-External scale: Belief in a difficult world, a just world, a predictable world, and a politically responsive world. *Journal of Personality and Social Psychology, 29,* 381–391.

Davis, H. (1983). Measuring individual differences in empathy: Evidence for a multidimensional approach. *Journal of Personality and Social Psychology, 44,* 113–136.

Deci, E. L., & Ryan, R. M. (1985). *Intrinsic motivation and self-determination in human behavior.* New York: Plenum Press.

de Waal, F. (1982). *Chimpanzee politics.* New York: Harper & Row.

Dubin, E. R., & Dubin, R. (1963). The authority inception period in socialization. *Child Development, 34,* 885–898.

Eysenck, H. J. (1970). *The structure of human personality* (Rev. ed.). London: Methuen.

Feaver, J., Mendl, M., & Bateson, P. (1986). A method for rating individual distinctiveness in cats. *Animal Behaviour, 34,* 1016–1025.

Fenigstein, A., Scheier, M. F., & Buss, A. H. (1975). Public and private self-consciousness: Assessment and theory. *Journal of Consulting and Clinical Psychology, 42,* 523–527.

Flavell, J. (1968). *The development of role-taking and communication skills in children.* New York: Wiley.

Gallup, G. G., Jr. (1970). Chimpanzee: Self-recognition. *Science, 167,* 86–87.

Gallup, G. G., Jr. (1977). Self-recognition in primates: A comparative approach to bi-directional properties of consciousness. *American Psychologist, 32,* 329–338.

Gardner, R. A., & Gardner, B. T. (1969). Teaching sign language to a chimpanzee. *Science, 165,* 664–672.

Goldstein, K. M., & Blackman, S. (1978). *Cognitive style.* New York: Wiley (Interscience).

Goodall, J. (1986). *The chimpanzees of Gombe.* Cambridge, MA: Harvard University Press.

Gould, S. J. (1977). *Ontogeny and phylogeny.* Cambridge, MA: Harvard University Press.

Harlow, H. F. (1949). The formation of learning sets. *Psychological Review, 56,* 51–65.

Harlow, H. F., & Harlow, M. K. (1962). Social deprivation in monkeys. *Scientific American, 207*(5), 136–146.

Harlow, H. F., Harlow, M. K., & Hansen, E. W. (1963). The maternal affectional system of monkeys. In H. L. Rheingold (Ed.), *Maternal behavior in mammals* (pp. 254–281). New York: Wiley.

Jerison, H. (1976). Paleoneurology and the evolution of mind. *Scientific American, 234,* 90–101.

Kiesler, D. J. (1983). The 1982 interpersonal circle: A taxonomy for complementarily in human transactions. *Psychological Review, 90,* 185–214.

Lacey, J. I. (1956). The evaluation of autonomic responses: Toward a general solution. *Annals of the New York Academy of Sciences, 67,* 123–163.

Lennox, R. D., & Wolfe, R. N. (1984). Revision of the Self-Monitoring Scale. *Journal of Personality and Social Psychology, 46,* 1349–1364.

Lynn, R. (1966). *Attention, arousal and the orientation reaction.* Oxford, England; Pergamon Press.

Mason, W. A. (1970). Motivational factors in psychosocial development. In U. J. Arnold & M. M. Page (Eds), *Nebraska Symposium on Motivation* (pp. 335–364). Lincoln: University of Nebraska Press.

Masters, W. H., & Johnson, V. E. (1966). *Human sexual response.* Boston: Little, Brown.

McClelland, S. C., Atkinson, J. W., Clark, R. A., & Lowell, E. L. (1953). *The achievement motive.* Englewood Cliffs, NJ: Prentice-Hall.

McCrae, R. R., & Costa, P. T., Jr. (1983). Joint factors in self-reports and ratings: Neuroticism, extraversion, and openness to experience. *Personality and Individual Differences, 4,* 245–255.

Miller, L. C., Murphy, R., & Buss, A. H. (1981). Consciousness of body: Private and public. *Journal of Personality and Social Psychology, 41,* 397–406.

Rogoff, B., Sellers, J., Perrotta, S., Fox, N., & White, S. (1975). Age of assignment of roles and responsibilities in children. *Human Development, 18,* 353–369.

Rotter, J. B. (1960). Generalized expectancies for internal versus external control of reinforcement. *Psychological Monographs, 80*(Serial No. 609).

Schulman, A. H., & Kaplowitz, L. (1977). Mirror-image response during the first two years of life. *Developmental Psychology, 10,* 133–142.

Slivken, K. E., & Buss, A. H. (1984). Misattributions and speech anxiety. *Journal of Personality and Social Psychology, 47,* 396–402.

Stevenson-Hinde, J., Stillwell-Barnes, R., & Zung, M. (1980). Subjective assessment of rhesus monkeys over four successive years. *Primates, 21,* 66–82.

Tellegen, A., & Atkinson, G. (1974). Openness to absorbing and self-altering experiences ("absorption"), a trait related to hypnotic susceptibility. *Journal of Abnormal Psychology, 43,* 111–122.

Wilson, E. O. (1975). *Sociobiology.* Cambridge, MA: Harvard University Press.

Winter, D. G. (1973). *The power motive.* New York: Free Press.

Witkin, H. A., Dyk, R. B., Faterson, H. F., Goodenough, D. R., & Karp, S. A. (1962). *Psychological differentiation.* New York: Wiley.

CHAPTER 15

GENETICS, TEMPERAMENT, AND PERSONALITY

DAVID C. ROWE
UNIVERSITY OF ARIZONA

One founder of the theory of evolution, Charles Darwin, theorized that emotions and their accompanying facial expressions had a natural origin. In his book *The Expressions of Emotions in Man and Animals* (1872/1965), of the emotions of joy and pleasure, he observed that "with all the races of man the expression of good spirit appears to be the same, and is easily recognized" (p. 211). He further analyzed the specific facial features involved: ". . . when in good spirits . . . the eyes sparkle, with the skin a little wrinkled round and under them, and the mouth a little drawn back at the corners" (p. 16). Darwin queried "missionaries and protectors" of native peoples around the world about the facial expressions showing emotions. The descriptions they returned matched his own observations of western Europeans. From the expression of emotion's universality in all races, its early appearance in infancy, and its similarity in many species (including primates and dogs), Darwin decided that the emotions were biologically inherited. According to his description of the young woman pictured in Figure 1, she was tearing up a photograph of a despised lover. Who would mistake her disdain for the feelings of fear, joy, or surprise?

In cross-cultural field studies, Eibl-Eibesfeldt (1975) collected evidence on the universality of emotional expression more objective than Darwin's. He toured diverse, nonwestern societies with a special camera, one fitted with a false forward looking lens and a hidden, side viewing one. From the latter lens, he took motion pictures of people who were unaware of the camera's eye. As had Darwin, Eibl-Eibesfeldt concluded that emotions and their accompanying facial expressions were

FIGURE 1   A woman showing disdain from Darwin's *The Expressions of Emotions in Man and Animals.*

human universals based upon biological instincts. For instance, in all human groups, a flirting girl made similar facial gestures: first a smile at her partner and a brief lift of the eyebrows, and then a turning away from the person of her affection. She may cover her face with a hand and may laugh or smile in embarrassment. Thus everywhere people can communicate in universal "language" of emotional expression.

This chapter examines the genetic bases of temperament and personality. Undoubtedly, our ability to infer subtle emotions from facial appearance, to use facial expressions to deceive others, and to use them to conform to social norms is more elaborate than in other animal species. Nonetheless, it is good to consider the above evidence on the biological bases of emotion because in western Europe and the United States a cultural belief that all human behavior is mainly shaped by culture and experience prevails.

This chapter first discusses methods used in the field of behavior genetics for the estimation of genetic and environmental components of personality variation (Plomin, 1990). Second, it surveys evidence of genetic variation in temperamental and personality traits. The third section of the chapter considers several special topics, namely, shared environmental influence on personality variation, genetic variation in environmental measures, and a theory of personality development.

I. Separating Nature and Nurture

The idea of separating nature and nurture is sometimes greeted with deep skepticism by the lay-public and by social scientists alike. The social critics of behavior genetic results may ask, "How can a scientist separate nature and nurture, when people need both genes (in the DNA from parents) and an environment in which to develop physically and psychologically?"

These concerns are understandable, but they are also misdirected. Although always a part of behavioral development, genetic and environmental influences are separable as components of trait variation. In the context of trait variation, nature can be clearly more influential than nurture, and vice versa. For instance, in spoken accents, variation may depend on the environmental factor of geographic locale, whereas in physical height or weight, variation may depend on which genes were inherited from one's parents. That is, as established by research, most physical traits possess a strong genetic component in their variation. In this regard, the reader may consider the striking physical resemblance of identical (also called monozygotic, MZ) twins, whether they were reared apart or together (Bouchard, Lykken, McGue, Segal, & Tellegen, 1990). What degree of genetic influence exists in behavioral trait variation is thus a scientific question, to be settled through careful empirical studies of individual differences.

A. Heritability

The heritability coefficient is a numerical estimator of the genetic component of trait variation. The equation that gives its mathematical definition is

$$\text{heritability} = h^2 = \frac{\text{Genetic variation in a trait}}{\text{Phenotypic variation in a trait}},$$

where "phenotypic" is the measured trait variation across individuals and "genetic variation" is that part attributable to the substitution of genes for one another. If all variation in a trait were attributable to genetic variation, then the heritability coefficient would be 1.0, or 100%. At the other extreme, when it takes a value near zero, gene substitutions would lack effects upon trait variation (e.g., as possibly illustrated by speech accents).

A true example corresponding to the former case—nearly 100% heritability—is a genetic disease named Huntington's chorea. This disease is caused by a single gene mutation that is dominantly inherited. When only one copy of the defective gene is received, all affected people (who live long enough) will die of progressive neuronal degeneration. When two normal genes are inherited, no one will die of the disease. Of course, except for such devastating single-gene diseases, human traits typically lack heritabilities near 1.0. Bouchard et al.'s (1990) study of separated MZ twins allows the estimation of heritabilities of several physical and psychological traits. Consider these heritabilities ordered from highest to lowest: fingerprint ridge count, .97; intellectual ability (IQ), .69; systolic blood pressure,

.64; heart rate, .49; California Psychological Inventory Traits, .48; and Jackson Vocational Interests, .43.[1] Except for fingerprint ridge counts (i.e., a quantitative measure of the fingerprint), no heritability coefficient approached 1.0.

Estimates of heritability can take one of two meanings. The first meaning is *narrow-sense* heritability. It represents genetic effects transmissible in families. A parent–child correlation on a trait is calculated as one-half the narrow-sense heritability (e.g., if the former were .30, then the parent–child trait correlation would be .15). The narrow-sense heritability has one limitation, however; it fails to account for possible interactions among genes, which may be located separately in the DNA. *Epistasis* is the interaction of genes on different chromosomes, whereas *dominance* is an interaction of genes at a single genetic locus.

Broad-sense heritability removes this deficiency; it is used to estimate all genetic variation contributing to trait variation, including both types of gene–gene interactions. An analogy may aid the reader's understanding (Lykken, McGue, Tellegen, & Bouchard, 1992). Suppose that we regard parents as giving their children cards from separate decks. If the father gives a daughter a 10 and a 9, whereas her mother gives her a 7, a 5, and a Queen, then the girl has the cards with which to construct an unexciting poker hand—the high card would be a Queen. But suppose now that the father gives his daughter an Ace and a King, whereas her mother provides a Queen, a Jack, and a 10. With these cards, the daughter would have the makings of an extraordinary poker hand—a royal flush. Specific combinations of genes may thus construct rare and extreme traits (ones that would not be transmissible from parent to child, because, except very rarely, this *combination* of genes would fail to reoccur). Lykken et al. named traits in which the gene–gene interaction component is large "emergenic" traits. They observed that combinations of rare genes (i.e., "cards") might produce a child who achieves the status of "a Ramanujan [a mathematical genius], a new Olympic record—or a True Crime miniseries for television" (p. 1575).

Although in behavior genetic studies the meaning of h^2 is not always identified, the reader should be aware that estimates derived from *the twin study research design*—either MZ twins raised apart or MZ and fraternal (also called dizygotic, DZ) twins compared—would be heritabilities in the broad sense. Because MZ twins share (as they originate biologically from one fertilized egg cell) the exact

[1] Because of sampling variation, heritability estimates are inexact. Falconer's (1981) formula for the standard error of the correlation coefficient is $[(1 - r^2)^2/(N \text{ pairs} - 1)]^{0.5}$. The standard errors were fingerprint ridge count, .01; systolic blood pressure, .08; heart rate, .11; WAIS full scale IQ, .08; California Psychological Inventory, .13; and Jackson Vocational Interest Survey, .12. Because of sampling variation and different selections of local genotypes (i.e., peoples' genetic compositions) and local environmental conditions, heritability coefficients may thus vary from one study to another. This variation, however, does not mean that heritability coefficients are nongeneralizable from one population to another. Once sampling variation has been excluded, heritability coefficients may be generalizable across social class contexts and other environmental clines—the degree of generalizability is an empirical issue that can be addressed with behavior genetic research designs (Rowe & Waldman, 1993).

same combination of genes, their trait resemblance contains all genetic variation, that which can be attributed to the main effect of genes, as well as that which can be attributed to the gene–gene interactions. Often, heritabilities from twin studies are greater than those estimated from other research designs, and epistatic effects may be part of this.

B. Environmental Variation

As heritabilities for most personality traits have been found to be less than 1.0, and often they were considerably less than this limit, environmental variation must also contribute to trait variation among individuals. In behavior genetic research designs, this environmental variation is also subject to an analytic decomposition. The two main subcomponents of environmental variation are called the *nonshared* and *shared* components.

By definition, nonshared environmental variation refers to all environmental effects acting uniquely on individuals and *not* contributing to psychological resemblance among family members (e.g., the alikeness of brother and sister). To calculate this component properly, measurement error variation must be removed from the environmental component of variation. Nonshared environmental effects can make genetically matched MZ twins dissimilar in behavior.

The shared component of variation refers, by definition, to environmental effects correlated across family members and which operate to make them psychologically alike. For instance, social class level is correlated across siblings and may make them alike in a psychological outcome (e.g., risk-taking).

In summary, trait variation can be separated into three main variance components: (1) heredity, (2) shared environment, and (3) nonshared environment. The strength of each component, as a proportion of total trait variation, is represented by a proportion that can take any value between 0 and 1. The heritability coefficient is symbolized as h^2, the shared environment component as c^2, and the nonshared environment component as e^2 or u^2 (the latter being used to distinguish it from measurement error, which is also sometimes symbolized as e^2).

C. Behavior Genetic Research Designs

All classic behavior genetic research designs were first used in the late 19th or early 20th centuries. They may involve the comparison of adoptive children with their biological or adoptive parents, the comparison of MZ twins raised apart, or the comparison of MZ and DZ twins.

1. Adoption Studies

In the adoption research design, trait variation is apportioned through the comparison of children raised apart from their biological parents. Adoptive children are placed in adoptive families that are often different in social circumstances from those of their biological parents. Hence, a type of "experiment" is created in which the genetic similarity of parent and child is eliminated. The adoptive parents raise children who have a genetic constitution that is different from theirs in an environment that is different from that which they would have received had their biological parents not decided on adoption. The correlation coefficient is used to express family members' psychological resemblance. In the adoptive study, one-half the genetic effect is realized in the trait correlation of the adoptive child and biological parent. *One-half* the genetic effect is expressed because first degree relatives (e.g., siblings or parents–children) can be expected to possess only one-half their (polymorphic[2]) genes. The full genetic effect (h^2) may be calculated as twice the correlation coefficient of adoptive child and biological parent.

In an adoptive study, the family environmental effect is realized in the trait correlation of adoptive parent and adoptive child. Because these family members do not share genes (except by chance), their psychological similarity can be inferred to arise from exposure to common environmental influences.

2. MZ Twins Raised Apart

The study of MZ twins raised apart is a special type of adoption design. The research design falls into the adoption design category because at least one twin would be raised by adoptive parents. In the ideal separated twin design, the MZ twins would be separated and, by simple chance, assigned for adoption. Of course, real adoptions can only approximate the requirements of the ideal design. For instance, one MZ twin may remain with his biological parents, whereas the other is adopted; or both may be raised by different parents who are related by blood to the twins' biological parents; or, approaching an ideal design, each twin may be raised by separate adoptive parents, who lack any connection to the twins' biological parents. The two most recent studies of twins raised apart were the Minnesota Study of Twins Reared Apart (Bouchard et al., 1990) and the Swedish Adoption/Twin Study of Aging (Pedersen, Plomin, McClearn, & Friberg, 1988). The latter study included about 350 pairs of twins raised apart, and so was larger than the entire world's previous samples of separated twins.

3. The Comparison of MZ and DZ Twins

Another research design is that comparing MZ and DZ twins. MZ twins share exactly the same genes. Expressed as a correlation coefficient, their genetic similarity would be $r = 1.0$. In contrast, as any first degree relative DZ twins share only 1/2 their genes (on average), yielding a genetic correlation of $r = .50$. Heritability is estimable from this research design by a simple calculation,

$$h^2 = 2(r_{MZ} - r_{DZ}),$$

where h^2 is the heritability, r_{MZ} is trait correlation in identical twin pairs, and r_{DZ} is that in fraternal twin pairs.

---

[2] Polymorphic genes are variable. For instance, the genes for eye color are polymorphic because different forms of these genes yield different eye pigment colors.

Among several assumptions, this twin design requires the assumption of *equal treatments* (relevant to a particular trait) for MZ and DZ twins. Clearly, if MZ twins were treated more alike than DZ twins, and this treatment were to *affect a particular trait,* then the attribution of MZ twins' greater resemblance to genetic variation may be flawed. Although the assumption of equal treatments may be false for some traits, for a majority of behavioral traits it has received considerable support (Loehlin & Nichols, 1976). The main reason that the assumption has been safe was not that the treatment of MZ and DZ twins was exactly alike in all cases. Rather, it survived because many environmental treatments (contrary to widespread cultural beliefs) failed to influence the personality traits that the treatments were expected to influence.

One particular concern about equal twin treatment deserves consideration. Many critics of twin studies (Lewontin, Rose, & Kamin, 1984) suppose that MZ twins would be especially alike in behavior because they physically look alike. This criticism of the twin research design, though, is unconvincing. The association of physical, facial features with personality traits is generally weak ($r < .25$) or nonexistent. Given low facial appearance–personality trait correlations, appearance alone cannot induce much of a personality correlation across twin pairs (the reader should note also that MZ twins are not *exactly* alike in their physiques or facial appearances).

4. Model-Fitting Approaches

In model-fitting research designs, studies can be extended to cover any combination of family types. That is, they can be done with many combinations of relatives (e.g., step-siblings, half-siblings, adoptees, and families of MZ twin aunts or uncles). In model-fitting designs, equations are first written to express the correlational data from the different family types in terms of the variance components described above. The equations are then solved mathematically for them.

An example should help to clarify these ideas for the reader. Adoptive siblings from successive placements in a home would be biologically unrelated to one another. Similarly, a biological child and an adoptive child raised in the same family would be biologically unrelated because their biological parents would be different. In both family structures, because the siblings have different biological parents, their hereditary constitution would be dissimilar (i.e., uncorrelated). As the siblings' trait similarity must arise entirely from common exposures to environmental experiences, the equation

$$r_{\text{URT}} = c^2$$

would hold, where r_{URT} is the trait correlation in biologically unrelated children reared together and c^2 is the shared environmental effect.

Now suppose that this correlation is combined with one from MZ twins raised together. The latter's trait resemblance can be attributed potentially to a combination of shared environmental and hereditary influences. Because MZ twins also possess exactly the same genetic constitution, as mentioned above, the equation

$$r_{\text{MZT}} = h^2 + c^2$$

follows, where r_{MZT} is the trait correlation in MZ twins raised together.

Using these equations together, one can solve for the variance components, h^2 and c^2. For example, if the MZ twin correlation were .53, whereas that in adoptive siblings was .17, then $c^2 = .17$ and $h^2 = .36$. Of course, this example would become more complex if more traits or family types were added. The general point is that model-fitting gives a flexible analysis of kinship data, one that allows these data to be fit and theoretical assumptions to be evaluated simultaneously. In this regard then, the classical research designs of MZ twins raised apart, MZ and DZ twins compared, and adoptive families are but important special cases of a more general method of handling kinship data.

II. GENETIC VARIATION IN TEMPERAMENTAL AND PERSONALITY TRAITS

A. The Heritability of Childhood Temperament

Temperament is the first expression of personality in the very young. As Darwin observed, infants reveal many rudiments of a complex emotional life:

> We may see children, only two or three years old, and even those born blind, blushing from shame; and the naked scalp of a very young infant reddens from passion. Infants scream from pain directly after birth, and all their features then assume the same form as during subsequent years. (p. 351)

Modern temperament theorists also focus on infancy, on that first appearance of individual differences in personality (Goldsmith et al., 1987). Theorists have differed in their particular definitions of temperament and in their assessment of the main temperamental traits. As shown in Table I, Goldsmith chose temperamental catego-

TABLE I
Trait Categories in Different Models of Temperament

Darwin	Goldsmith	Buss & Plomin	Rothbart	Thomas & Chess
Low spirits	Sadness		Distress	Predominant mood
High spirits	Joy, pleasure	Sociability	Smiling	Intensity of mood
Hatred & anger	Anger	Anger		Approach/withdrawal
Disdain, disgust	Disgust			Adaptability
Surprise, fear	Fear	Fear	Fear	Sensory threshold
Shame, shyness				Distractibility
	Interest		Orienting	Persistence/attention
	Activity	Activity	Activity	Activity
			Soothability	Rhythmicity

Note. Trait categories from Goldsmith et al. (1987).

ries on the basis of basic emotions. His categories overlap considerably with Darwin's. Buss and Plomin (1984), on the other hand, identified just three broad temperaments: emotionality (which can be subdivided into general arousal, fear, and anger), activity, and sociability. Activity level refers to total motoric activity—the amount of movement, such as pacing and running. Sociability refers to the preference for social interactions with others, as opposed to being alone. Rothbart's (1981) temperamental categories included Buss and Plomin's activity and several others with an emotional flavor such as Darwin's and Goldsmith's. One of Rothbart's temperaments referred to a more cognitive, attentional aspect of behavior, that is, duration of orienting. Finally, Thomas and Chess (1977) defined nine categories of temperament. They shared with the other theorists a category of activity. Approach/withdrawal may be related to both emotionality and sociability; it did not appear as a separate factor in a joint factor analysis of Thomas and Chess's and Buss and Plomin's temperament items (Rowe & Plomin, 1977). They also added two categories with a possible basis in cognition (i.e., distractibility, persistence/attention span). Although these proposed categories of temperament were different among research groups, some agreement also exists among the temperamental traits proposed. Together, they adequately span the variety of individual differences in infancy that first drew Darwin's attention.

In light of twin and adoption studies, evidence has accumulated that basic temperaments are heritable. Buss and Plomin (1984) extensively explored the heritability of four temperaments: the three listed in Table I and impulsivity. Because the evidence of impulsivity's heritability was poor, they decided it was not a temperamental trait by their (somewhat restrictive) criteria that a temperament must be heritable.

Table II presents heritabilities for sociability, activity, and emotionality on the basis of twin data that Buss and Plomin pooled over studies. These correlations were computed in three ways: (1) as the r_{MZ} itself, (2) as twice the difference of $r_{MZ} - r_{DZ}$, and (3) as twice the r_{DZ}. The first estimate, of course, assumes an absence of family (shared) environmental influences on temperament. The second

Table II
Heritability Estimate from EAS Questionnaire

	Broad sense		Narrow sense
	h^2 Method 1	h^2 Method 2	h^2 Method 3
Activity	.62	1.50	< 0
Sociability	.53	1.12	< 0
Emotionality	.63	1.02	.24

Note. Method 1 is the MZ twin correlation; Method 2, 2 ($r_{MZ} - r_{DZ}$); Method 3, $2r_{DZ}$. Data given in Buss and Plomin (1984, Table 9.2, p. 122). $N = 228$ MZ twin pairs and 172 DZ twin pairs.

estimate—that of the classical MZ versus DZ twin comparison—assumes "equal" twin environments *relevant* to the temperamental traits. Like the first, the last estimate assumes an absence of family (shared) rearing influences. As noted above, because the DZ twins share only half their genes (on average), their trait correlation must be doubled to estimate heritability.

As shown in Table II, these heritability estimates appear to conflict with one another. The r_{MZ} twin estimate was the most reasonable one—across the three traits, a mean of 51% of variation was attributable to genetic variation. Both the classical twin and the r_{DZ}-based estimates, however, were nonsensical, which was an outcome of small DZ twin trait correlations. The former estimates were nearly 1.0; the latter were 0 or less than 1 (but a variance component can never take a value less than 0.00 because variances are always positive numbers).

Why were the DZ twin correlations so small? Buss and Plomin suggested one possible reason for it: the data on twins' temperament depended almost entirely on parental ratings of behavior. If parents tend to contrast their fraternal twins with one another and so accentuate their differences, then this rating bias would make them appear more dissimilar in temperament than they really were. This rating artifact could create zero, or even a negative, DZ twin correlation on the temperamental traits, yielding the unreasonable heritabilities (i.e., Methods 2 and 3 above).

Data from twin studies using objective measures permit an evaluation of Buss and Plomin's contrast effect conjecture. Consider the trait of *activity*. As shown in Table II, parents rate the DZ twins as no more alike in activity than randomly paired children—the r_{DZ} was about 0. Activity is clearly a temperamental trait for which an observational alternative to parental ratings exists—mechanically recording the twins' bodily movements on an instrument that records them. In a study of twin infants (mean age = 8 months; Saudino & Eaton, 1991), actometers were attached to 78 MZ twins (in 39 pairs) and to 42 same-sex DZ twins. The activity data were collected over a 2-day period. The twin correlations for composite actometer activity were $r_{MZ} = .76$ and $r_{DZ} = .56$. Heritability estimates by the three methods above are .76, .40, and 1.08, respectively. The high estimate from doubling the DZ twin correlation (1.08) may reflect an influence of shared environment on infants' activity level. From the MZ versus DZ twin comparison, this estimate of shared environmental variation would be .36.[3] Adjusting the DZ correlation for this effect results in a more consistent heritability estimate on the basis of Method 3 (i.e., doubling the adjusted DZ twin correlation; $h^2 = .40$). None of the heritability estimates is precise, of course, because of the small number of twin pairs. Nonetheless, a tendency towards 0 or negative DZ twin correlations was clearly absent in these *objective* measurements of activity.

---

[3] Shared environmental variation (c^2) was estimated as $2r_{DZ} - r_{MZ}$. For further details of the basis of this derivation, see Rowe (1994). Because the twins could play together, shared environment here may be the result of the twins influencing one another.

Another study leads to similar conclusions for other temperamental traits (Emde et al., 1992). As shown in Table III, for parental ratings of temperament the heritability estimate as derived from the DZ twin correlation alone was always inconsistent with the other estimates. In contrast, estimates from the observational measures varied widely, but except for task orientation, were never inconsistent (i.e., 0 or less than 0 whereas other estimates were positive). The one exception, task orientation, yielded a greater DZ (.22) than MZ twin (.15) correlation. Hence, the comparison of MZ with DZ twins suggested that this observed trait was not heritable (one of the few such nonheritable traits among 23 traits examined by Emde et al.). In summary, these data strongly suggest that contrast rating effects led to inconsistent heritability estimates when parental ratings were used for inhibition, shyness, and activity.[4]

Moreover, the narrow-sense heritability as estimated from the DZ twin correlations was substantial for temperamental traits. Averaged over inhibition, shyness,

Table III

Heritabilities Based on Observational versus Parental Report Measures of Infant Temperament

	Broad-sense		Narrow sense
	h^2 Method 1	h^2 Method 2	h^2 Method 3
	Laboratory observational measures		
Inhibition	.57	.62	.52
Shyness	.70	.50	.90
Activity	.42	.58	.26
Task orientation*	.15	< 0	.44
	Parental ratings on the CCTI		
Emotionality	.35	.74	.04
Shyness	.38	.82	< 0
Sociability	.35	.64	.06
Activity	.50	1.50	< 0
Attention/ persistence	.38	.84	< 0

Note. CCTI, Colorado Childhood Temperament Inventory (Rowe & Plomin, 1977). Data were from Emde et al. (1992).

* $r_{DZ} > r_{MZ}$

[4] In Emde et al. (1992), another parental rating scale did not produce low DZ twin correlations for the traits of negative and positive emotionality. As not all parental ratings produce contrast effects, more research is needed comparing rating formats and the semantic globality versus specificity of rating items.

and activity, the mean h^2 was .56. The broad-sense heritabilities (i.e., with MZ twins) averaged over the same three traits were .57 and .56, respectively. Because the narrow- and broad-sense heritabilities were close in magnitude, I believe that effects of gene–gene interactions on temperament variation were minor (at least for these temperaments). Although this brief review has neglected many excellent studies of the inheritance of temperament (see Goldsmith, 1983), the omitted studies mainly reinforce the conclusion stated here: one-third to one-half of individual differences in temperamental traits can be attributed to genetic variation among children.

B. The Heritability of Personality in Adulthood

The domain of adult personality is characterized by an extensive behavior genetic literature. Studies have been done using a great variety of self-report questionnaires. As different theories of personality propose somewhat different sets of adult traits, and also use different self-report scales, the domain of adult personality would seem confusing. Fortunately, personality theorists have reached a consensus that at least five independent personality factors exist (i.e., the "Big Five," John, 1990). Many personality traits, although given different names than one of the Big Five trait factors, may be actually synonymous with one of them or represent a combination of several of them. The Big Five trait factors are listed in Table IV, along with adjectives representative of them. The table uses the factor names popularized by Norman (1963), except that the first trait factor was named *extraversion* instead of Norman's *surgency*.

Loehlin (1992) reanalyzed data on the Big Five factors from studies around the world that used behavior genetic research designs. He fit a variety of behavior

TABLE IV
The "Big Five" Trait Dimensions

I Extraversion	II Agreeableness	III Conscientiousness	IV Emotional stability	V Culture
Talkative	Sympathetic	Organized	Tense	Wide interests
Active	Appreciative	Planful	Nervous	Intelligent
Outgoing	Soft-hearted	Responsible	Worrying	Insightful
Dominant	Generous	Dependable	Fearful	Sophisticated
Enthusiastic	Helpful	Precise	Self-pitying	Clever
Retiring	Hard-hearted	Slipshod		Unintelligent
Withdrawn	Quarrelsome	Irresponsible		Shallow
Silent	Unfriendly	Frivolous		Simple
Shy	Cold	Disorderly		Narrow interests
Reserved	Fault-finding	Careless		Commonplace

Note. Adapted from Loehlin (1992), with permission. Copyright 1992 by Sage Publications.

genetic models to kinship correlations for Big Five factors, seeking the most parsimonious and theoretically convincing explanation for variation in each one. His results led to a remarkable finding that fairly simple models can give an account of personality variation.

One behavior genetic model worked for the world's adoption data on *extraversion*. Loehlin's model postulated just two sources of trait variation: heredity and nonshared environment. On the basis of the best statistical fit, the heritability of extraversion was .35, and the nonshared environmental contribution was .65. The shared environmental part of variation was set to zero ($c^2 = .00$). The reason for eliminating the latter was that a model without this parameter fit statistically nearly as well one with it. The "loss" of the shared environment was therefore not costly in terms of the model's explanatory power.

Table V presents actual extraversion correlations and those model-fitted to them. In the case of biologically unrelated family members, the model-fitted correlation was 0. In the case of biologically related family members, it was .18. The latter value is one-half the model-estimated heritability of extraversion ($h^2 = .36$). These two model-fitted correlations matched the obtained correlations closely enough that the model was accepted statistically. Note that under this model's assumptions, *all* family resemblance for personality was merely attributable to shared genes. That is, once the genetic similarity was removed (i.e., via adoptive family relationships), family members were no more alike in personality than persons reared in *different* families.

Data from additional family types on the Big Five personality factors, however, required more complex models than the heredity–nonshared environment one. Loehlin found that two models gave equally good descriptions of the personality variation in the Big Five. One model required the variance components of (1) transmissible heredity, (2) a special shared environment in MZ twins, (3) shared environment, and (4) nonshared environment. The other model had the same

TABLE V
Obtained and Model-Fitted Correlations on Extraversion

Family relationship	r observed	N (pairs)	r fitted
Mother and biological child	.12	621	.18
Father and biological child	.21	547	.18
Mother and adoptive child	−.01	571	.00
Father and adoptive child	.03	522	.00
Biologically related siblings	.20	570	.18
Biologically unrelated siblings	−.07	258	.00

Note. N (pairs), total number of pairs across three studies. Correlations weighted average correlations from Loehlin's (1992) Table 2.4, p. 32.

variance components, except that one for gene–gene interactions replaced that of special MZ twin environments.

Table VI shows the parameter estimates for this second theoretical model. Over the Big Five trait factors, the mean narrow-sense heritability was .30, whereas the mean broad-sense was .42. In contrast, the mean estimate of shared environmental effects was relatively small in magnitude ($c^2 = .08$). The remainder of trait variation, of course, would be due to nonshared environmental effects ($e^2 = .50$). About 40% of this nonshared variation would be attributable to measurement error, and the remainder to the lasting consequences of experiences uniquely changing each person. In Loehlin's second model—the one allowing for a special MZ twin environment rather than emergenic gene action—the variance component estimate for shared environment was also small (mean $c^2 = .05$, not shown in Table VI). In summary, the heritability and shared environmentability of the major Big Five factors suggest that first degree relatives will correlate only about .15–.20 on them, and shared genes, not shared experiences, mainly determine the familial resemblance of "blood" relatives.

III. FURTHER TOPICS OF INTEREST

A. The Absence of Shared Rearing Effects

A widespread cultural belief in western European countries and in the United States is that variation in parenting styles will create variations in children's personality traits. The behavior genetic findings reviewed above generally refute this cultural belief. For example, none of Loehlin's adoption models required a parameter representing an environmental effect of parental behavior on the development of children's traits. Moreover, as noted above, the variance component of environments shared by siblings was always small, from 2 to 11% of trait variation in Table VI. The consensus currently held by behavior geneticists is that family environments in the normal range may lack influence on personality development (Rowe, 1994;

TABLE VI
Estimates of Variance Components in "Big Five" Personality Traits

Big Five trait factor	Narrow-sense heritability h^2	Gene–gene interactions i^2	Shared environment c^2
I. Extraversion	.32	.17	.02
II. Agreeableness	.24	.11	.11
III. Conscientiousness	.22	.16	.07
IV. Emotional stability	.27	.14	.07
V. Culture/openness	.43	.02	.06
Mean	.30	.12	.08

Note. Adapted from Loehlin (1992, Table 3.2, p. 67).

Scarr, 1992, 1993). In other words, although different parents treat children in different ways—for instance, showing affection demonstrably, covertly, or not at all—except for extremes (i.e., child abuse or neglect), these parental treatments would be equivalent to one another in their effects on child development.

The assertion of the essential *equivalence* of family environments, which to many observers of families appear very different, has provoked heated controversy among social scientists (see Baumrind, 1993; Jackson, 1993; Scarr, 1993). The reason for the controversy is easy to comprehend. The shared environment relates most directly to the relative malleability of traits in response to family social influences. A shared environment of strong effects means that a trait would be highly malleable, in the sense that if children were "swapped" from one family rearing circumstance to another their trait scores would greatly change. A small shared component means the opposite, that in range of family environments studied, all of them would be roughly equivalent in their effects on children's traits. If changing rearing circumstances has little consequence, then moving children from one family environment to another will not change them. The reader should note that the shared environment is more relevant to the social malleability of traits than is heritability. In her 1991 presidential address to the *Society for Research in Child Development,* Scarr (1992) explained these implications of behavior genetic results for personality malleability:

> The flip side of this message is that it is not easy to intervene deliberately in children's lives to change their development, unless their environments are outside the normal species range. . . . for children whose development is on a predictable but undesirable trajectory and whose parents are providing a supportive environment, interventions have only temporary and limited effects. . . . Should we be surprised? Feeding a well-nourished but short child more and more will not give him the stature of a basketball player. Feeding a below-average intellect more and more information will not make her brilliant. Exposing a shy child to socially demanding events will not make him feel less shy. The child with a below-average intellect and the shy child may gain some specific skills and helpful knowledge of how to behave in specific situations, but their enduring intellectual and personality characteristics will not be fundamentally changed. (pp. 16–17)

Further details on the issue of rearing effects can be found in an exchange of views among Sandra Scarr (1993) and her two critics who adopt strong environmentalist positions, Baumrind (1993) and Jackson (1993).

B. Genetic Variation in Environmental Measures

Social scientists may regard measures of environmental influences as independent of genetic ones in the DNA. This view may ignore a major characteristic of environmental measures widely used in child development research: that they summarize the behavior of individuals. For instance, consider the measure "number of books in the home," which has been related to children's IQ variation. For young children, parents must decide which books to purchase and how many; hence, "books in the home" may indirectly assess heritable personality traits such as general intelligence (IQ) and the Big Five factor trait of *culture*. In a review article on genetic variation in environmental measures, Plomin and Bergeman (1991) observed, "Environments have no DNA and can show no genetic influence. *Measures* of the environment . . . may be perfused with characteristics of individuals, however . . . [they] can show genetic influence" (p. 374, italics in original).

Plomin and Bergeman's review documents that genetic variation occurs in a variety of environmental measures. Social economic status (SES) is often assessed by the measures of "years of education," incomes, or occupational prestige. Although parental SES is associated with children's current "environments," these measures also distill in themselves the behavior of a parent over many years, who either had the traits leading to educational and occupational success or who lacked them. Summarizing behavior genetic studies of SES, Plomin and Bergeman concluded that its heritability was about .40. Hence, SES cannot be regarded as capturing purely environmental variation.

Therefore, contrary to most interpretations of social class, a correlation of an SES measure with a personality trait outcome is *not* proof of environmental influence. Common genes may make parent and child alike for *different* traits, so that the effects of genes can be mistaken for environmental ones when statistical data are interpreted. For example, in parents the genes may be expressed as differences in SES; in their children, they may be expressed as another trait, for instance, general intelligence (IQ). Perhaps social science editors should adopt the policy that both genetic and environmental alternatives be posed when an SES–child personality statistical relationship is found. Such hypotheses can be investigated in behavior genetic studies that include measures of social class (Rowe & Waldman, 1993).

Genetic variation also can be found in measures of parenting styles. In my twin studies of adolescent twins' reports of parental behavior, I have found evidence for genetic variation in measures of parental affection/warmth, but not in those of parental control (Rowe, 1981, 1983). Plomin and his colleagues took the reverse approach. Genetic variation in parenting styles of adult twins (who had families) was investigated. In the Swedish Adoption Twin Study of Aging (Plomin McClearn, Pedersen, Nesselrode, & Bergeman, 1989), adult twins reported on their general home environments on the Family Environments Scale questionnaire. Twin pair correlation coefficients were then computed for four types of pairs: MZ twins raised apart, MZ twins raised together, DZ twins raised apart, and DZ twins raised together. In the different groups, the number of twin pairs ranged from 50 to 129. As shown in Table VII several scales produced statistically significant heritabilities: expressiveness, culture, organization, and control. Across the nine home environment scales, the average heritability was .25. About *one-quarter* of variation in home environment is thus attributable to genetic variation.

Other environmental measures reviewed by Plomin and Bergeman (1991) also revealed a genetic component. Television viewing (total hours) yielded a heritability of .44. Controllable life events had a heritability of .43, and uncontrollable

TABLE VII
Heritability Estimates for Home Environment
Scales

Home environment scale	Broad-sense heritability h_2
Cohesion	.19
Expressiveness	.27*
Conflict	.25
Achievement	.12
Culture	.40*
Active	.21
Organization	.26*
Control	.26*
Mean	.25

Note. Adapted from Plomin and Bergeman (1991, p. 376).
*$p < .05$.

life events, .18. Perceived adequacy of social support had a heritability of .30. Adolescents' choice of different peer groups (e.g., delinquent or nondelinquent) was also heritable. It is no exaggeration to say that genetic variation suffuses measures of the environment. Social scientists should be encouraged to consider this genetic variation whenever interpreting "effects" of environmental measures. Furthermore, whether genetic variation in measures of "environment" represents gene effects shared with known personality traits (i.e., the Big Five), or whether it is really something unique and outside the domain of most personality traits, should be investigated (Chipuer, Plomin, Pedersen, McClearn, & Nesselroade 1993).

C. A Theory of Personality Development

To advance social science knowledge, the findings in this chapter must be placed into a general theory of personality development. Behavior genetics *is* part of a general theory of personality development that requires an integration of behavior genetics with other psychological subdisciplines. This theory attributes trait variation to variation in the biology of the human nervous and endocrine systems. An analytic layer between the genes and measured traits is being investigated through a whole range of new brain imaging systems. Hypotheses about physiological bases of personality variation are currently becoming more refined (see Geen, this volume, chap. 16). Behavior genetics also explains the intergenerational transmission of traits: in the absence of strong biological selection and given large population sizes (certainly true of humans), genetic variation in one generation will be reliably transmitted to the next. Both within-population variation in personality, and some population mean differences (Kagan, Arcus, & Snidman, 1993), may thus possess a basis in genetic variation.

Despite scientific progress, many interesting and unresolved questions remain to complete a general theory of personality. Some fundamental questions are, Why do family environments have so little effect on personality development? What maintains genetic variability in personality over many generations? Is genetic variation related to human adaptive traits, or is it merely genetic "junk"? How does environmental transmission occur? Can the specific environmental causes of "nonshared" environmental variation be found?

With regard to the first question posed above, behavior genetics gives the metaphor of "niche picking" (Scarr & McCartney, 1983). Just as a nonhuman animal "niche picks" by finding a local environment most suited to its adaptive strengths, so may people find the local social environments most suited to their heritable traits, which would tend to reinforce them and would allow their full expression. Moreover, as do other animals, people may also *change* local environments to suit themselves. Hence, only when environmental opportunities have been severely constrained would a child fail to develop heritable personality traits to nearly their inherent potentials.

The questions asked in this chapter should occupy the next generation of social scientists concerned with trait variation. The field has come a long way since Darwin's rudimentary concepts of genetic and environmental transmission. His incorrect Lamarckian view that traits may be inherited merely because they are exercised has been abandoned in the 20th century. Yet many puzzles about temperament and personality remain to be solved. As Darwin wrote, "the language of the emotions, as it has sometimes been called, is certainly of importance for the welfare of mankind. To understand, as far possible, the source or origin of the various expressions which may be hourly seen on the faces of men around us . . . ought to possess much interest for us" (p. 366).

REFERENCES

Baumrind, D. (1993). The average expectable environment is not good enough: A response to Scarr. *Child Development, 64,* 1299–1317.

Bouchard, T. J., Jr., Lykken, D. T., McGue, M., Segal, N. L., & Tellegen, A. (1990). Sources of human psychological differences: The Minnesota study of twins reared apart. *Science, 250,* 223–228.

Buss, A. H., & Plomin, R. (1984). *Temperament: Early developing personality traits.* Hillsdale, NJ: Erlbaum.

Chipuer, H. M., Plomin, R., Pedersen, N. L., McClearn, G. E., & Nesselroade, J. R. (1993). Genetic influence on family environment: The role of personality. *Developmental Psychology, 29,* 110–118.

Darwin, C. (1872/1965). *The expression of the emotions in man and animals.* Chicago & London: University of Chicago Press.

Eibl-Eibesfeldt, I. (1975). *Ethology: The science of behavior*. New York: Holt, Rinehart & Winston.

Emde, R. N., Plomin, R., Robinson, J., Corley, R., DeFries, J., Fulker, D. W., Reznick, J. S., Campos, J., Kagan, J., & Zahn-Waxler, C. (1992). Temperament, emotion, and cognition at fourteen months: The MacArthur longitudinal twin study. *Child Development, 63,* 1437–1455.

Falconer, D. S. (1981). *Introduction to quantitative genetics* (2nd ed.). New York: Longman.

Goldsmith, H. H. (1983). Genetic influences on personality from infancy to adulthood. *Child Development, 54,* 331–355.

Goldsmith, H. H., Buss, A. H., Plomin, R., Rothbart, M. K., Thomas, A., Chess, S., Hinde, R. A., & McCall, R. B. (1987). Roundtable: What is temperament? Four approaches. *Child Development, 58,* 505–529.

Jackson, J. F. (1993). Human behavioral genetics, Scarr's theory, and her views on interventions: A critical review and commentary on their implications for African American children. *Child Development, 64,* 1318–1332.

John, O. P. (1990). The "Big Five" factor taxonomy: Dimensions of personality in the natural languages and in questionnaires. In L. A. Pervin (Ed.), *Handbook of personality: Theory and research* (pp. 83–100). Lisse, The Netherlands: Swets & Zeitlinger.

Kagan, J., Arcus, D., & Snidman, N. (1993). The idea of temperament: Where do we go from here? In R. Plomin & G. E. McClearn (Eds.), *Nature, nurture, and psychology* (pp. 197–210). Washington, DC: American Psychological Association.

Lewontin, R. C., Rose, S., & Kamin, L. (1984). *Biology, ideology, and human nature: Not in our genes*. New York: Pantheon Books.

Loehlin, J. C. (1992). *Genes and environment in personality development*. Newbury Park, CA: Sage.

Loehlin, J. C., & Nichols, R. C. (1976). *Heredity, environment, & personality: A study of 850 sets of twins*. Austin & London: University of Texas Press.

Lykken, D. T., McGue, M., Tellegen, A., & Bouchard, T. J., Jr. (1992). Emergenesis: Genetic traits that may not run in families. *American Psychologist, 47,* 1565–1577.

Norman, W. T. (1963). Toward an adequate taxonomy of personality attributes: Replicated factor structure in peer nomination personality ratings. *Journal of Abnormal and Social Psychology, 66,* 574–583.

Pedersen, N. L., Plomin, R., McClearn, G. E., & Friberg, L. (1988). Neuroticism, extraversion, and related traits in adult twins reared apart and reared together. *Journal of Personality and Social Psychology, 55,* 950–957.

Plomin, R. (1990). *Nature and nurture: An introduction to human behavioral genetics*. Pacific Grove, CA: Brooks/Cole.

Plomin, R. & Bergeman, C. S. (1991). The nature of nurture: Genetic influence on "environmental" measures. *Behavioral and Brain Sciences, 14,* 373–386.

Plomin, R., McClearn, G. E., Pedersen, N. L., Nesselroade, J. R., & Bergeman, C. S. (1989). Genetic influence on adults' ratings of their current environment. *Journal of Marriage and the Family, 51,* 791–803.

Rothbart, M. K. (1981). Measurement of temperament in infancy. *Child Development, 52,* 569–578.

Rowe, D. C. (1981). Environmental and genetic influences on dimensions of perceived parenting: A twin study. *Developmental Psychology, 17,* 203–208.

Rowe, D. C. (1983). A biometrical analysis of perceptions of family environment: A study of twin and singleton sibling kinships. *Child Development, 54,* 416–423.

Rowe, D. C. (1994). *The limits of family influence: Genes, experience, and behavior.* New York: Guilford Press.

Rowe, D. C., & Plomin, R. (1977). Temperament in early childhood. *Journal of Personality Assessment, 41,* 150–156.

Rowe, D. C., & Waldman, I. D. (1993). The question "How?" reconsidered. In R. Plomin & G. E. McClearn (Eds.), *Nature, Nurture, & Psychology* (pp. 355–373). Washington, DC: American Psychological Association.

Saudino, K. J., & Eaton, W. O. (1991). Infant temperament and genetics: An objective twin study of motor activity level. *Child Development, 62,* 1167–1174.

Scarr, S. (1992). Developmental theories for the 1990s: Development and individual differences. *Child Development, 63,* 1–19.

Scarr, S. (1993). Biological and cultural diversity: The legacy of Darwin for development. *Child Development, 64,* 1333–1353.

Scarr, S., & McCartney, K. (1983). How people make their own environments: A theory of genotype → environment effects. *Child Development, 54,* 424–435.

Thomas, A., & Chess, S. (1977). *Temperament and development and behavior disorders in children.* New York: New York University Press.

CHAPTER 16

PSYCHOPHYSIOLOGICAL APPROACHES TO PERSONALITY

RUSSELL G. GEEN
UNIVERSITY OF MISSOURI

I. INTRODUCTION

Theories based on biological processes are among the oldest approaches to explaining human personality. The Roman physician Galen of Pergamon (A.D. 130–200) expanded the theory of the four humors of the body, an idea originating in the writings of Hippocrates and Empedocles, to stipulate the existence of four temperaments. In some ways the theory of Galen anticipated modern temperamental theories of personality (H. J. Eysenck, 1981; Stelmack & Stalikas, 1991). The humoral theory dominated Western medicine and provided the principal explanations for somatic processes and dysfunctions, until the 17th century; it was eventually replaced in the 18th century by theories that attributed these processes to the properties and functions of the nerves (Drinka, 1984). "Nervousness" thereafter became the preferred explanation for the etiology of such disorders as hysteria, hypochondria, and melancholia (e.g., Jackson, 1986; Veith, 1965). One observation made during this period seems particularly relevant to the hypothesized link between personality and psychophysiology: patients' reports of irritability or variations in mood were often accompanied by reports of somatic complaints and symptoms (Fahrenberg, 1992). Such a correlation was attributed to underlying individual differences in nervousness; translated into more modern terminology, the observation might be that a state of autonomic activation is often accompanied by negative affectivity.

The study of biological factors in personality was facilitated by the emergence of psychophysiology in the 19th century. Clinical interest in newly developed electrotherapies led to early studies by Vigoroux and Feré in which the electrodermal response was measured in samples of hysteric and nonhysteric patients (Neumann & Blanton, 1970). These studies probably represent the first attempts at what we today call the psychophysiological approach to personality.

In the writings on humoral and neurological theories of individual differences we see a prefiguration of the essential elements of modern approaches to the biological bases of personality. The major assumptions of this approach have been summarized by Gale (1987). A few of these assumptions may be noted:

1. Accounts of human behavior can be considered adequate only if they include individual variations.

2. Biological factors, which are transmitted genetically, account for much of this individual variation.

3. These biological factors are manifested in a number of complex ways in the neuroanatomy, biochemistry, and neurophysiology of the individual. These systems interact with each other in many ways and are represented in the person's experience, behavior, and psychophysiology.

4. Individual variations develop within a psychoevolutionary context. They have adaptive significance for the species and are therefore observed across not only the range of human cultures, but also in other species that have developed under the same evolutionary pressures.

5. Living systems are characterized by transmission, storage, allocation, and discharge of energy. The construct of arousal has heuristic value in describing biological links to personality, even though its explanatory status is debatable.

6. Living systems are not passive receptors of environmental or biologically engendered influences. They use feedback from the environment and from the consequences of their own actions to adapt and maintain a stable equilibrium. The relation of individual difference variables to biological disposition is therefore not simple and reactive, but transactive and complex.

We will return to some of these points, and to some of their implications for evaluating research findings, in subsequent sections of this chapter. For now, however, we will concentrate on item 5, because it leads to a consideration of a major viewpoint in the study of the biological bases of personality: the *arousability hypothesis*.

II. THEORIES OF AROUSABILITY

A. Eysenck's Theory

The modern era of interest in the biological approach to personality began with the pioneering work of H. J. Eysenck in the late 1940s. Eysenck's original theory of personality structure, which was based on factor analysis of a number of existing psychometric instruments, stipulated two factors: a general activity factor labeled Extraversion–Introversion (E-I) and an emotionality factor designated Neuroticism (N). From the beginning, H. J. Eysenck (1947) sought to locate the bases for these factors in underlying biological processes. At first the basis for E-I was thought to lie in the Pavlovian constructs of excitation and inhibition, with introverts showing a general tendency toward excitation and extraverts an overall tendency toward inhibition. This explanation relied on a metaphoric model of brain physiology derived mainly from Pavlov which did not link E-I to any specific anatomical or physiological processes.

The study of the psychophysiological basis of personality took a major step forward in 1967 with the publication of H. J. Eysenck's *The Biological Basis of Personality.* In this book Eysenck described a revised version of the theory, along with a review of studies designed to test the new approach both behaviorally and physiologically. The revised theory located both E-I and N in specific cortical and subcortical centers of the brain. Central to the theory was the construct of *general arousal,* a diffuse energization of the body's major response systems correlated with observable physiological activity (e.g., electrodermal conductance, cortical activation, cardiovascular activity). Following an approach taken by general arousal theorists in the 1950s (e.g., Lindsley, 1957), Eysenck considered general arousal to represent nonspecific activity in the ascending reticular activating system (ARAS). Extraverts were described as people with relatively high thresholds for ARAS activation, with the result that they are relatively less aroused than introverts in response to given levels of stimulation. The ARAS is activated by both external stimuli and ascending and descending pathways to the limbic system. Thus general arousal can be the result of either external stimulation or emotional activity arising within the person. The revised theory described Neuroticism in terms of individual differences in the activity of the limbic system, manifested in emotional arousal in response to stressful or threatening situations. Given the neural connections between the limbic system and the ARAS, a moderate positive correlation between E-I and N has often been reported. Finally, H. J. Eysenck (1967) related E-I to behavior by invoking the concept of an optimal level of arousal, another idea popular in the 1950s and 1960s: extraverts were described as engaging in highly arousing activities and expressing preference for complex and exciting stimuli in order to elevate their arousal levels to some desired intermediate range.

The number of empirical investigations stimulated by Eysenck's theory over the 45 years since its original publication is literally in the thousands. To a large extent the theory's popularity is due to several notable strengths. It is built on a solid theoretical base. It involves rigorously developed and validated psychometric assessment. It generates predictions of not only psychophysiological differences along the E-I and N dimensions, but also experiential and behavioral differences that are related to the psychophysiological differences, and to each other, in theoretically relevant ways.

B. Gray's Theory

Gray (1972, 1981) proposed a modification of Eysenck's theory of E-I that attributes the individual differences to underlying activity in both the ARAS and the medial septal area, the hippocampus, and the orbital frontal cortex. The revised theory follows from the observation that small injections of sodium amobarbital in rats leads to behavior that has been characterized as similar to that of human extraverts: impulsive, relatively uninhibited, and generally not susceptible to threats of punishment (Gray, 1972). Similar "extravert-like" behavior has been observed in animals that have undergone lesions in the septal area or the orbital frontal cortex. The upshot of such findings is that Gray proposes a septal–hippocampal–frontal cortex system in which the biological basis of introversion and extraversion is to be found.

In a later version of the theory (e.g., Gray, 1981), two antagonistic control centers in the central nervous system are postulated: a behavioral activation system (BAS) and a behavioral inhibition system (BIS), the latter of which was described in the 1972 paper cited above. Whereas the BIS controls passive avoidance, the BAS controls active avoidance and is set in motion by signals of reward or nonpunishment. Active avoidance, therefore, is not motivated by fear or anxiety, which are associated with the BIS, but rather by incentive motivation. As has already been noted, Gray (1972) proposes that the physiological basis for introversion is a high level of activity in the neural centers that constitute the BIS. Introverts, therefore, are especially susceptible to stimuli that signal punishment or frustrative nonreward. Extraverts, on the other hand, are more sensitive to signals of reward or nonpunishment.

C. Related Constructs

1. Sensation-Seeking

One conclusion that came out of research on the effects of sensory deprivation that was conducted in the 1950s and 1960s is that people differ from one another in the extent to which they seek out exciting events in their surroundings (Zuckerman, 1969). The individual difference variable associated with these behaviors was labeled sensation-seeking (SS) (Zuckerman, 1971). Zuckerman (1984, 1990) assumes a biological basis for sensation-seeking and argues that the trait has a psychoevolutionary basis. The theory of SS therefore generates predictions about both behavior and physiological activity. Zuckerman once proposed that sensation-seeking is related to the quest for an optimal level of stimulation, a view that suggested a commonality between that trait and extraversion. That view is no longer held, as will be noted in a subsequent section of this review.

2. Impulsiveness and Augmenting/Reducing

The traits of extraversion–introversion and sensation-seeking both involve to some degree individual differences in impulsive behavior. H. J. Eysenck (1967) considered impulsiveness to be one of the two main characteristics of the extraverted personality and Zuckerman found tendencies toward disinhibition to be an element in sensation-seeking. Some investigators have concluded that the individual differences in arousability attributed to extraversion–introversion are indicators of differences in impulsivity (Revelle, Humphreys, Simon, & Gilliland, 1980; Schalling & Åsberg, 1985).

The concept of augmenting/reducing was introduced by Petrie (1967) on the basis of studies of the degree to which subjects overestimate or underestimate the intensity of a stimulus following prolonged stimulus bombardment. Using a methodology involving tactile stimulation to the hand, Petrie found that some people—designated "reducers"—tend to underestimate stimulus intensity under such conditions whereas other ("augmenters") tend to overestimate. Augmenting/reducing, though assessed peripherally, was assumed to reflect underlying differences in the central nervous system. Subsequent studies (e.g., Sales, 1971) showed that augmenters tend to behave much as introverts and that reducers show many of the same characteristics as extraverts (cf. H. J. Eysenck & Eysenck, 1985). More recently, the augmenting/reducing dimension has been operationally defined in terms of individual differences in evoked responses at the level of the cerebral cortex (Buchsbaum & Silverman, 1968), and has been shown to be related to both sensation-seeking and impulsivity. Research pertaining to this conclusion is reviewed in a later section.

3. Strength of the Nervous System

Certain similarities have been observed between Eysenck's dimension of extraversion–introversion and the concept, first described by Pavlov, of *strength of the nervous system* (Gray, 1964; Strelau, 1987). This term refers to the strength of excitatory processes generated in the central nervous system by increasing levels of stimulation. Pavlov taught that excitation in the central nervous system is directly related to stimulus intensity over moderate to high stimulus intensity levels, but that as stimulus intensity is increased beyond these levels, the point is eventually reached at which the nervous system exceeds its working capacity and goes into a state of inhibition. Beyond that level, increasing stimulus intensity evokes progressively *less* excitation. The level of stimulus intensity at which excitation gives way to inhibition is called the *threshold of transmarginal inhibition.*

Psychologists working in the Pavlovian tradition have used several experimental procedures to classify subjects according to the intensity of stimuli needed to bring about transmarginal inhibition (Strelau, 1983). Those in whom transmarginal inhibition is induced by a relatively less intense stimulus are classified as having "weak" nervous systems; those who require relatively more intense stimulation are designated "strong." Strelau (1987) has observed that persons in the former category appear to respond to stimulation in the same way as introverts, augmenters, low sensation-seekers, and low impulsives, whereas those of the latter category resemble extraverts, reducers, high sensation-seekers, and high impulsives. Strelau (1983) has added his own variable of high versus low *reactivity* to this list, with high reactives showing the properties of the weak nervous system.

III. CRITICISM OF THE AROUSABILITY HYPOTHESIS

Although the concept of general arousal continues to be used among psychologists and to retain a certain heuristic value in theory construction, it has been largely rejected by psychophysiologists at least since 1967, when Lacey published a widely cited critique. The core of Lacey's (1967) argument was that indicators of activity in the various physiological systems of the body (e.g., cortical, motor, autonomic) are at best weakly intercorrelated, and that activity in these systems and behavioral activation are likewise not tightly coupled. In addition, certain indicators of physiological activity show increases in the same situations that evoke decreases in other measures, a phenomenon that Lacey called *directional fractionation.* Finally, individuals manifest a high degree of *autonomic response specificity:* the profile of autonomic responding for a given person tends to be relatively stable across time and situations but often to be different from the profiles of other people undergoing the same experiences.

Problems such as these suggest that the arousability hypothesis cannot be tested adequately in limited studies that involve only a few psychophysiological variables or situations. Larger investigations that involve behavioral and subjective measurement along with psychophysiological indicators, and which include a wide array of situational manipulations, are necessary (Fahrenberg, 1992). The results of studies of this type offer no support for the notion of general arousability.

A growing number of psychophysiologists have proposed that if arousal is to be a useful construct, it will be in the context of a multiple-systems approach. For example, Myrtek (1984), while finding no evidence for a second-order construct of autonomic lability, found evidence of individual reactivity in a number of primary systems (e.g., heart rate, blood pressure, respiration volume). The key to the role played by energy transfer in the living system may lie in the complex ways in which these various systems interact with each other. In effect, such an emphasis would call for change in the basic underlying model that has been used to conceptualize arousal—from a simple mechanistic one that Venables (1984) has called the "foot-on-the-accelerator" view to one based more on the principles of cybernetics and control mechanisms. The several somatic systems that are characterized by individual differences in activation interact in such a way that some may activate, and some inhibit, other systems.

Actually, such a control model has been implicit in discussions of human action for some time. Venables (1984) has pointed out, for example, that John Hughlings Jackson wrote on the hierarchical levels of brain organization more than a century ago, and that he emphasized that "what happened at any one level was determined by interaction between levels" (Venables, 1984, p. 138). More recently, Claridge (1967) has developed a sophisticated model of arousal organized around two hypothetical systems. One, the *tonic arousal system,* maintains the person's gross level of activation in response to stimulus inputs. The other, the *arousal modulating system,* has two regulatory functions. One is to control the level of activity in the tonic system; the other is to integrate the input to both systems through either facilitation or inhibition of stimulation. The systems work together to maintain a balance or steady state of activation, even when antecedent stimulus conditions vary. A study by Birchall and Claridge (1979) indicates a possible modulating mechanism involving augmenting/reducing of the cortical evoked response and the hypothesized tonic arousal system. They found that subjects who manifested relatively high levels of skin conductance tended to be reducers as the intensity of incoming stimulation increased, whereas those low in skin conductance level tended to be augmenters. If, as Birchall and Claridge reason, skin conductance level is a reflection of a hypothetical arousal system, this finding suggests that the augmenting/reducing function serves to dampen or sharpen the amount of stimulation that the person receives from the environment.

IV. PSYCHOPHYSIOLOGICAL STUDY OF PERSONALITY

In spite of the criticisms noted in the preceding section, the arousability hypothesis has generated a large amount of research on personality. Multimodal investigations involving the role of personality in the complex interactions among systems are relatively rare. It must be recognized at the outset that the study of activity in the central and autonomic nervous systems among human subjects rests on indirect evidence. In general, arousal and emotionality have been inferred from three types of data: verbal reports of experience (e.g., Endler, Edwards, & Vitelli, 1989; Thayer, 1970); observation of behavior that is linked to underlying brain processes on theoretical grounds (e.g., Gray, 1964; Strelau, 1983); and the measurement of psychophysiological indicators. This review will be focused on the last of these three (for earlier reviews, see Stelmack, 1981, 1990; Stelmack & Geen, 1992).

A. Extraversion–Introversion

If introverts are more arousable than extraverts because of differential thresholds of reactivity in the ARAS, we might expect that the clearest evidence of E-I differences would be found in electrocortical measures. The majority of studies on extraversion and arousal have involved the use of such measures. Overall, whereas some of the findings support Eysenck's theory, the results have been mixed and complex, reflecting the possible operation of several situational moderator variables.

1. Electroencephalograph (EEG)

The EEG depicts a complex waveform consisting of several frequencies. The most commonly studied bandwidth is the alpha wave (7.5 to 13.5 Hz), with frequency and amplitude as the main dependent measures. In general, an alpha wave showing large amplitude and low frequency is associated with relatively low cortical arousal. Low-amplitude, high-frequency activity is taken as an indicator of high arousal. If E-I differences are linked to cortical arousal, introverts should show higher basal or resting levels of low-amplitude, high-frequency activity than extraverts. Extravert–introvert differences in EEG activity have been the subject of several reviews (e.g., Gale, 1981, 1983, 1987). In each of these reviews, Gale has shown that much of the research on the problem has been flawed by weak methodologies and lack of theoretical sophistication and that replicability across studies is uncommon because critical situational variables have not been controlled. However, even studies based on sounder methods fail to offer much support for the notion of higher basal levels of cortical arousal in introverts (e.g., Golding & Richards, 1985; Matthews & Amelang, 1993).

2. Evoked Responses (ER)

a. Cortical Evoked Response. Somewhat stronger evidence of E-I differences is found in studies of evoked responses (ER). The average evoked cortical potential is a momentary change in brain wave activity that occurs in response to brief presentations of a stimulus or during cognitive processing. It presents a complex waveform consisting of successive positive and negative peaks. ERs are superimposed on the EEG pattern and are extracted from EEG records by a technique of averaging over a large number of such responses. In general, earlier peaks in the waveform of the ER are most likely determined by physical characteristics of the eliciting stimulus and later peaks (later than 300 ms after the onset of the stimulus) reflect attentional and endogenous cognitive processes (Hillyard & Hansen, 1986). Several variables influence ERs, among them stimulus intensity, rate of presentation, and overall arousal levels. It follows from the latter that extraverts and introverts should show different levels of amplitude over various segments of the ER waveform.

Stimulus frequency was found to interact with E-I to influence the amplitude of the N_1P_2 component (the section of the waveform evoked approximately 90–250 ms after the stimulus) in a study by Stelmack, Achorn, and Michaud (1977). When a tone of low frequency (500 Hz) was used, the N_1P_2 amplitude in introverts was greater than that of extraverts, but no E-I differences were found when a tone of higher (8000 Hz) frequency was used. This finding could have reflected E-I differences in sensitivity to the low-frequency tone, but it could also be explained in terms of heightened attention on the part of introverts or more rapid habituation to the tone on the part of extraverts. To test these possibilities, Stelmack and Achorn-Michaud (1985) presented subjects with 500-Hz tones under instructions either to attend to the tones or to ignore them. Introverts displayed a larger N_1P_2 amplitude than extraverts in response to the first tone in a series of four in both the attend and the ignore conditions, ruling out the possibility that differential attention caused the personality difference. In addition, Stelmack and Achorn-Michaud found that whether the tones were presented in a repetitious way that fostered habituation or in a way that retarded habituation, E-I differences were not affected. Thus the greater N_1P_2 amplitude of introverts seems to be linked to their greater sensitivity to low-frequency stimuli.

The results of a study by Bartussek, Diedrich, Naumann, and Collet (1993) addresses another facet of differences between introverts and extraverts within the context of research on the ER. This study was based on Gray's (1981) revision of Eysenck's theory, according to which introverts are more reactive to signals of punishment than extraverts, whereas extraverts are more susceptible to signals of rewards than introverts. Subjects were required to guess which of two tones varying in frequency (800 or 1600 Hz) would be delivered on each trial. The occurrence of the tone then indicated whether the guess had been correct or incorrect. Each correct guess was followed by a monetary reward and each incorrect guess by a loss of money. Analysis of the P_2 wave (relative to the baseline amplitude) showed that extraverts manifested greater amplitude than introverts in response to tones that signaled a correct guess and subsequent reward, and that introverts showed a greater amplitude than extraverts when the tone indicated that the guess had been incorrect. Similar E-I differences in ER amplitude were found in the N_2 wave and in a later segment designated P_3 (details follow). However, in each of the latter, E-I differences were moderated by other variables in the experiment. Nevertheless, the data for the P_2 component support Gray's extension of Eysenck's approach.

E-I differences have also been found in later components of the cortical ER wave. The P_3 is a late positive spike (approximately 300 ms after the stimulus) that is evident during tasks in which target events must be detected or in which the event serves a feedback signal to the subject. Amplitude of the P_3 is a function of several variables, among which are the importance of the stimulus event, the information-processing demands (whether or not more than one stimulus must be processed simultaneously), and the novelty or unexpectedness of the event. P_3 amplitude therefore reflects the allocation of limited attentional resources to the task. Because introverts have been shown to manifest better performance in monotonous signal-detection tasks (e.g., Gange, Geen, & Harkins, 1979), and because sustained attention appears to be related to higher levels of arousability (e.g., Matthews, Davies, & Holley, 1990), introverts should show greater P_3 amplitudes than extraverts.

Subjects in a study by Daruna, Karrer, and Rosen (1985) took part in a lengthy and monotonous task of guessing which of two tones would occur on each trial. As expected, introverts showed higher P_3 amplitudes than extraverts, leading the authors to conclude that introverts allocated more attention to the task. Similar findings come from a study by Ditraglia and Polich (1991). Using a methodology similar to that of Daruna et al., these investigators presented the tone pairs in two separate blocks separated by approximately 2 min. Although they found no overall E-I differences in P_3 amplitude, they found an E-I difference by blocks interaction: extraverts showed a decline in P_3 amplitude across blocks whereas introverts did not. This finding suggests that E-I differences may be due to a progressive decrement in attention to the stimuli among extraverts.

b. Brainstem Auditory Evoked Response.   Another evoked response has been measured at the level of the brainstem. This brainstem auditory evoked response (BAER) consists of a series of seven positive waves within the first 10 ms of a brief auditory stimulus (e.g., a click). Like the cortical evoked response, it is detected through averaging over a large number of trials. The seven waves are evaluated in terms of both their absolute latency (i.e., the elapsed time from the stimulus to the peak of the wave) and their interpeak latencies (i.e., the time that elapses from one wave peak to another). These are preferred to measures of amplitude because of the relative unreliability of the latter. It is widely believed that Waves I and II reflect mainly activity in the auditory nerve; that Waves III, IV, and V indicate activity in centers within the brainstem; and that Waves VI and VII may reflect the beginning of activity within the cortex.

The evidence relating E-I differences to the BAER is mixed. In an early study, Andress and Church (1981) found that introverts showed shorter Wave I–V interpeak latencies than extraverts in response to relatively loud (80 dB) clicks but not to clicks of lower intensity. In another early study, Campbell, Baribeau-Brown, and Braun (1981) found no E-I differences in BAER activity. Stelmack and Wilson (1982) found that introverts displayed shorter Wave V latencies than extraverts in response to tone pips of 2000- and 4000-Hz frequencies, but that extraverts revealed shorter latencies when a 500-Hz pip was used. Of greater importance was Stelmack and Wilson's finding of significant positive correlation between extraversion and Wave I latencies when clicks of either 75, 80, or 85 dB intensity were presented. This finding showed that introverts manifested shorter Wave I latencies than extraverts. Inasmuch as Wave I activity reflects activity at the level of the auditory nerve, this finding suggests greater peripheral sensitivity of introverts without having a bearing on the hypothesized E-I difference in central arousal. In a more recent investigation, Stelmack, Campbell, and Bell (1993) tested for E-I differences in BAER activity during presentation of clicks in the 80- to 90-dB range, and, although some suggestion of shorter latencies in introverts was found, none of the differences reached the .05 level of statistical significance.

One study has shown relatively strong support for a hypothesis relating E-I to the BAER. Bullock and Gilliland (1993) delivered clicks at an intensity 80 dB above subject's auditory threshold and found that Wave V latency was shorter in introverts than in extraverts. In addition, introverts had shorter Wave I–III and Wave I–V interpeak latencies than extraverts. Bullock and Gilliland also administered caffeine, in either a high or a moderate dosage, to two groups of their subjects while running the third in a placebo condition. They found that the subjects who had received caffeine in either the moderate or the large dose group manifested faster Wave I–III and Wave I–V latencies than those given the placebo. The effects of caffeine, a known source of arousal, therefore showed the same pattern of interpeak latencies as individual differences in E-I. This convergence of effects from different operations strengthens the argument that E-I differences are related to arousability.

3. Audiomotor Reflex

The audiomotor reflex (AMR) is a phasic startle reaction elicited by sudden visual, auditory, cutaneous, or electrical stimulation. It involves a number of synaptic connections in the brainstem and subsequent effector processes, one of the latter being activation of the facial nerve and, through it, of the *orbicularis oculi* muscle. As the intensity of the eliciting stimulus is increased, the amplitude and probability of the AMR increase, and AMR latency decreases. Britt and Blumenthal (1991) have shown that individual differences in E-I moderate the stimulus intensity effect. Introverts showed a clear discrimination in the latency of eyeblink AMRs to auditory stimuli of 60 and 85 dB, with the latter evoking the shortest latency reaction. Extraverts showed no shorter latencies with the more intense stimulus than with the less intense one. Differences between extraverts and introverts in the amplitude of the auditory AMR has been shown by Ljubin and Ljubin (1990), who found that introverts manifested a greater response amplitude than extraverts to a stimulus of 100 dB intensity.

4. Electrodermal Activity

A large body of evidence indicates that extraversion interacts with levels of environmental stimulation to influence electrodermal conductance (e.g., Smith, 1983). The significance of skin conductance activity for personality in general, or for Eysenck's theory of E-I in particular, has not been spelled out in detail, but there is some evidence that sweat gland activity is initiated in situations involving aversive motivation. The relationship, moreover, appears to be linear: as the aversiveness of stimulation increases, electrodermal activity increases also (Fowles, 1983). In addition, increased skin conductance has long been recognized as a component of the orienting response to less intense stimulation (Sokolov, 1963). Thus, skin conductance activity is part of a broadly conceived "arousal" response in both defensive and orienting behavior. We might expect, therefore, that the differential arousability of extraverts and introverts should include an electrodermal component.

The study of the role played by E-I involves systematic manipulation of environmental conditions to elicit varying degrees of electrodermal activation and observation of E-I differences within that setting. Three methods of manipulating arousal have been reported. The first involves administration of stimuli of varying intensities (e.g., Fowles, Roberts, & Nagel, 1977; Geen, 1984; Smith, Wilson, & Davidson, 1984). The effect of such treatments is to increase arousal monotonically. The second consists of giving subjects a stimulant drug such as caffeine (e.g., Smith, Rypma, & Wilson, 1981; Smith, Wilson, & Jones, 1983). It is assumed that the arousing effect of caffeine summates with that of the eliciting stimulus. The third method differs from the other two in that instead of increasing stimulation above a baseline level it reduces stimulation below that level. This method consists of giving the subject a preliminary signal before the stimulus for the electrodermal response (Smith et al., 1984; Smith, Rockwell-Tischer, & Davidson, 1986). By removing uncertainty regarding the onset of the stimulus, the signal should reduce arousal. Most of the studies discussed below involve the use of one or more of these three methods of arousal manipulation.

Geen (1984) studied differences in electrodermal activity among extraverts and introverts who were either allowed to choose the intensity of stimuli they received (ostensibly as a background stimulus) or were assigned stimuli by the experimenter. Some persons of each personality classification were assigned a stimulus equal in intensity to that chosen by a yoked person of the other type. The dependent variable was the number of specific skin conductance responses occurring during a 4-min period just before and during the first trial of a learning task. Extraverts selected noise of a higher intensity than introverts. Extraverts and introverts who had chosen background stimulus levels were equally aroused in response to their respective chosen stimuli, as were extraverts and introverts who had been assigned stimuli at those levels. Introverts who were given noise at an intensity chosen by extraverts were more aroused than all other groups, and extraverts assigned noise at introverts' chosen level of intensity were the least aroused. Thus both introverts and extraverts choose, when possible, a level of stimulation that evokes an optimal level of arousal, and that level of arousal is approximately the same for both groups.

5. Cardiovascular Activity

A small number of studies have addressed the question of whether introverts and extraverts differ in cardiovascular activity. The results are mixed and inconclusive. Although they found evidence of E-I differences in skin conductance and vasomotor activity, Stelmack, Bourgeois, Chien, and Pickard (1979) found no comparable differences in heart rate. However, Gange et al (1979) observed higher heart rates in introverts than in extraverts in all conditions of an experiment on visual vigilance, including one in which no task was performed. These investigators found no E-I differences in heart rate during a baseline rest period. Their findings may therefore indicate that E-I differences reflect to some extent a reaction on subjects' part to any sort of experimental procedures.

To understand the role played by E-I in cardiovascular activity, however, it is necessary first to consider the functional significance of heart rate change. Two viewpoints on this are represented in the E-I literature. Orlebeke and Feij (1979) have taken the position that phasic cardiac acceleration is a component of the defensive response whereas phasic deceleration is a component of the orienting response (Graham, 1979). A similar argument is found in the intake–rejection hypothesis of Lacey (cf. Jennings, 1986): cardiac acceleration is prompted by conditions of threat or overstimulation that generate a reaction of shutting out environmental stimulation, whereas deceleration is evoked by conditions that call for attention and taking in stimulation. If we assume that introverts, relative to extraverts, tend to be stimulus-reducers who seek low levels of stimulation, it follows that introverts are more likely than extraverts to respond to high-intensity stimuli with the cardiac acceleration indicative of defense. On the other hand, and for the same reasons, extraverts should be more likely to show cardiac deceleration (i.e., orienting and taking in stimulation) than introverts when less intense stimuli are presented. In partial support of this hypothesis, Orlebeke and Feij (1979) found that introverts responded to a 60-dB, 1000-Hz tone with greater heart rate acceleration than extraverts. Also tending to support the theory is the finding by Harvey and Hirschman (1980) that introverts responded to highly aversive photographs (of persons who had died violent deaths) with greater immediate heart rate increases than extraverts, who showed no increase.

A study by Richards and Eves (1991) also supports the hypothesis of greater defensive cardiac increase in introverts. In their study, subjects were classified as "accelerators" or "nonaccelerators" on the basis of whether they showed large accelerative changes or tended to show deceleration in response to a tone of 110 dB intensity for 1 s. Accelerators, who showed the defensive acceleration most clearly, were found to have lower scores than nonaccelerators on a measure of extraversion (i.e., accelerators tended to be introverts) and to score higher in neuroticism.

B. Sensation-Seeking

The Sensation-Seeking Scale (Zuckerman, Eysenck, & Eysenck, 1978) operationally defines tendencies to seek and engage in activities that provide excitement and risk. In addition to giving a total score for sensation-seeking, the instrument has four subscales that yield scores for (1) thrill and adventure seeking (TAS), (2) experience-seeking, (3) disinhibition (Dis), and (4) susceptibility to boredom. The subscales that have been most commonly associated with physiological activity have been TAS and Dis. The TAS scale measures liking for risky and arousing physical activities and the Dis scale assesses the quest for excitement through such actions as social drinking, sexual activity, and a general lowering of social constraints on behavior.

1. The Psychophysiology of Sensation-Seeking

a. The Optimal Arousal Hypothesis.   The relation of sensation-seeking to standard psychophysiological measures is not clear. At first glance, SS would appear to have much in common with extraversion–introversion as defined by Eysenck, so that the person who is high in SS could be thought of as one who is characteristically underaroused and who seeks stimulation in order to attain an optimal level. This person would be comparable to the typical extravert. At one time Zuckerman (1969) took this position, but he has subsequently abandoned it largely because of drug studies that failed to support the theory. In a critical experiment, Carroll, Zuckerman, and Vogel (1982) administered a placebo, a stimulant, or a depressant to subjects who were either high or low in SS, and then assessed both mood and efficiency of performance. It was expected that high sensation-seekers would feel happiest and perform best after having received a stimulant because the drug would move arousal in the direction of the optimal level. For the same reason, low sensation-seekers were expected to feel happiest and perform best after having received a depressant. However, the results of the experiment showed that both high- and low- sensation-seekers felt and performed best after receiving a stimulant.

In addition, evidence from experiments using psychophysiological measures does not show a tendency for people high in SS to be underaroused. Although the findings involving electrodermal, cardiac, and cortical measures are complex and inconsistent, they suggest that people who are high in SS reveal an overall pattern of responsiveness similar to the orienting response, whereas those who are low in SS tend under the same conditions to manifest a pattern similar to the defensive or startle response.

b. *Electrodermal Activity.* In an early study, Neary and Zuckerman (1976) presented subjects with a simple visual stimulus for each of 10 trials, after which they ran 10 trials with a different stimulus. Male subjects who were high in SS emitted a greater number of skin conductance responses than low sensation-seekers on the first presentation of each stimulus but not on subsequent presentations of either. Neither basal skin conductance level nor rate of habituation was affected by SS differences. The effect of SS was therefore a short-lived reactivity to a novel stimulus that habituated rapidly. Similar results have been reported by others. Feij, Orlebeke, Gazendam, and Van Zuilen (1985) found a positive correlation between SS and skin conductance amplitude on the first of three presentations of a tone, but not on two succeeding trials; they found a similar correlation for the TAS subscale. Differences in phasic conductance responses to novel stimuli as a function of scores on the Dis subscale have been reported by Robinson and Zahn (1983).

However, not all studies have reported clearcut effects of SS on electrodermal activity. Ridgeway and Hare (1981) reported no difference between high and low sensation-seekers in the number of skin conductance responses elicited by a tone. Stelmack, Plouffe, and Falkenberg (1983) found that high sensation-seekers showed greater electrodermal reactivity than persons low in SS when meaningful words were used as stimuli, but weaker reactivity when meaningful pictures were used. This finding indicates that the nature of the stimulus may have an influence on the relationship of SS to skin conductance, and that failure to consider this influence could lead to inconclusive or conflicting results.

It should also be noted that in many of the studies reviewed here the effects of SS were limited to male subjects. In contrast, a study involving skin conductance and heart rate measurement by Zahn, Schooler, and Murphy (1986) showed evidence of a stronger relationship between these variables and SS among women than among men. Age may be another moderator variable of some importance. Plouffe and Stelmack (1986) found that a sample of young women showed a negative correlation between skin conductance level and SS whereas a sample of elderly women did not.

c. *Cardiovascular Activity.* Studies of electrodermal activity therefore suggest a positive association between strength of the orienting response to novel or interesting stimuli and either the total SS score or scores on one of the subscales of the trait. However, this conclusion is arguable because skin conductance is also part of the defensive and startle responses. To discover whether SS is related to orienting or to one of these other reactions we must analyze studies in which heart rate is the dependent variable. As we have noted, heart rate decelerates during orienting and accelerates in the defensive response.

As is the case with skin conductance, basal levels of heart rate are not related to SS (e.g., Ridgeway & Hare, 1981) whereas reactivity to stimuli reveals an SS effect. Ridgeway and Hare (1981) found that subjects who were high in SS showed heart rate deceleration on the first trial of a series of 60-dB tones, as did subjects who scored high on the Dis subscale. Subjects who were low in either sensation-seeking or disinhibition manifested a short latency acceleration on the first trial, followed by rapid habituation. Similar results were reported by Orlebeke and Feij (1979) and by Feij et al. (1985).

d. Evoked Potentials.   The magnitude of change from the positive peak of the cortical evoked potential occurring approximately 100 ms after the stimulus (the P_1 component) to the following negative peak occurring approximately 40 ms later (the N_1) forms the basis for the variable of augmenting–reducing (Buchsbaum & Silverman, 1968). In general P_1–N_1 amplitude increases as the intensity of the stimulus is increased. However, some people show this progressive increment only across low to moderate stimulus intensities. When stimulus intensities become more intense, these subjects show a progressive decline in P_1N_1 amplitude as stimulus intensity is increased. Other subjects show a continuing direct relationship between stimulus intensity and P_1N_1 amplitude even in response to highly intense stimuli. Persons in the first of these two groups are reducers and those in the second are augmenters. Thus, the augmenter–reducer (A-R) variable is based on the slope of the function relating P_1N_1 amplitude to stimulus intensity.

Beginning with a study by Zuckerman, Murtaugh, and Siegel (1974), several studies have shown A-R to be related to SS and its components. Zuckerman et al. (1974) found that subjects scoring above the median on the Dis scale showed augmenting in response to the brightest of a series of light flashes whereas those below the median showed reducing in response to the most intense flashes. These effects were replicated by Zuckerman, Simons, and Como (1988), but only on the first of two successive series of stimuli, suggesting that the relation between Dis and A-R may have dropped out because of habituation on the second set. Evidence of a positive correlation between augmenting for the P_1N_1 component and high scores on the Dis scale has also been reported by Blenner (1993).

2. The Biology of Sensation-Seeking

a. Monoamine Oxidase.   Sensation-seeking has been studied in relation to levels of monoamine oxidase (MAO) in the blood. MAO is an enzyme that is present in the mitochondria of neurons in the central nervous system as well as other parts of the body. Especially high concentrations are found in the limbic system, where MAO presumably plays a part in mediating various appetitive and emotional behaviors. Its function is to degrade the central monoaminergic transmitters such as norepinephrine and dopamine. For that reason it is supposed that MAO regulates the action of these central transmitters. Direct assessment of brain

MAO in living humans is not possible in the context of normal research. However, the level of MAO in the platelets of the blood correlates positively with the level in the brain. Platelet MAO levels therefore serve as indicators of the enzyme that can be studied in connection with other variables.

A few studies have tested the relation between the various sensation-seeking scales and platelet MAO, with mixed results. Neither Ballenger et al. (1983) nor Calhoon-La Grange, Jones, Reyes, and Ott (1993) found a relationship between MAO activity and sensation-seeking. However, Murphy et al. (1977) found significant correlations between MAO and three measures of SS (Total SS, Disinhibition, and Boredom Susceptibility). Whereas the findings of Murphy et al. held for male subjects only, Schooler, Zahn, Murphy, and Buchsbaum (1978) found a negative correlation between SS and platelet MAO levels among both men and women. The meaning of these correlations is somewhat obscured, however, by data reported by Schalling, Åsberg, Edman, and Oreland (1987) indicating that the relationship of scores on the overall SS scale to MAO levels is not linear. Subjects in this study who were characterized by moderate MAO levels were equal in SS to those low in MAO and higher in SS than those with high MAO levels. All of the subjects in this study were males. Possibly the link between MAO and SS is moderated by sex-related hormones. In this connection, it should be noted that a positive correlation between scores on the Dis scale and male sex hormones in male subjects has been reported (Daitzman & Zuckerman, 1980).

b. Central Catecholamines. A negative relationship between MAO levels and sensation-seeking would suggest that the biological substrate of the trait may lie in the activity of biogenic amines in the brain, such as norepinephrine and dopamine. If MAO depletes these neurotransmitters, then levels of MAO should be negatively correlated with central catecholamine activity, implying a positive relationship between sensation-seeking and the latter.

As has been noted earlier, Zuckerman (1983) abandoned his earlier theory of sensation-seeking, which had been based on the assumption that high sensation-seekers are motivated by a need to increase reticulocortical arousal to an optimal level. In subsequent formulations, Zuckerman has emphasized the importance of reward centers in the limbic system and the mediating role played by central neurotransmitters. Genetic inheritance determines the level of these central catecholamines, which in turn affect the activity of the limbic system. Zuckerman (1979) articulated a viewpoint formulated by Stein (1983), according to which neural circuits in which dopamine is the transmitting agent are the pathways for incentive motivation and norepinephrine circuits govern expectancies of positive reinforcement. High levels of dopamine should therefore initiate activity and exploratory behavior whereas high levels of norepinephrine should establish expectations of positive outcomes from situations or contacts with other people. Both of these outcomes are integral elements in sensation-seeking. In addition, through collaterals to the cortex, the active limbic centers initiate alertness and sensitivity to novel stimuli, which are manifested in the orienting response and augmentation of the evoked potential. The behavior of the sensation-seeker is therefore an expression of biologically determined incentives and not a response to a deficit in arousal as the original theory implied.

As is the case with the study of MAO, direct assessment of central neurotransmitters is difficult. However, the action of these substances is accompanied by the formation of metabolites, the concentrations of which vary positively with the activity of the transmitters. One metabolite of norepinephrine is 3-methoxy-4-hydroxyphenylglycol (MHPG). This substance, extracted from urine, is generally assumed to be derived from brain norepinephrine and therefore to reflect the action of the latter. Given the several assumptions made here, it should follow that sensation-seeking is positively correlated with levels of urinary MHPG. Such a correlation was reported by Buchsbaum, Muscettola, and Goodwin (1981), although the number of subjects in that study was small. Studies by Ballenger et al. (1983) and Thieme and Feij (1986) found no relation between sensation-seeking and MHPG activity.

Relatively few findings have been reported on the relation of sensation-seeking to biogenic amine activity. One study has, however, been influential in a revision of Zuckerman's theoretical model. In that study, Ballenger et al. (1983) analyzed levels of norepinephrine in the cerebrospinal fluid of male and female subjects and found that these levels varied negatively with sensation-seeking. A similar negative correlation was found between sensation-seeking and levels of dopamine-β-hydroxylase (DBH), an enzyme involved in the production of norepinephrine (cf. Umberkoman-Wiita, Vogel, & Wiita, 1981). These correlations are, of course, opposite in direction to what the model had predicted. Zuckerman (1984) has therefore proposed that high sensation-seekers may require high levels of activity and risk in order either to compensate for low levels of norepinephrine and DBH or to stimulate an optimal level of norepinephrine release. This is an optimal-level theory, but one grounded in central processes other than those mediated by the reticular activating system. Matters are somewhat complicated, however, by the finding in two more recent studies (Calhoon, 1988, 1991) of a positive correlation between DBH activity and sensation-seeking in selected samples of subjects (e.g., those over 30 years of age). This correlation is consistent with the earlier model described above, but not with Zuckerman's (1983) revision. The negative correlation between sensation-seeking and norepinephrine activity may also reflect the action of tyramine, which is known to release norepinephrine from its storage centers and thereby to bring about its depletion in neuronal tissue. Thieme and Feij (1986) found evidence of higher levels of urinary tyramine in high versus low sensation-seekers.

3. Conclusions

Zuckerman's model of the biological basis of sensation-seeking is a good example of an approach that brings together psychometric, behavioral, and biological findings in the service of an evolving theory. For that reason it offers the best explanation for the physiological side of this important personality trait. Future findings may lead to further refinements of the model. For example, there is some evidence that levels of endogenous opioid peptides, or endorphins, are correlated with sensation-seeking (Johansson, Almay, von Knorring, Terenius, & Astrom, 1979). In addition, Pivik, Stelmack, and Bylsma (1988) have found that the disinhibition component of sensation-seeking is negatively related to excitability of the spinal motoneurons; that is, high disinhibitors show evidence of less excitability than low disinhibitors. Extraverts in the Pivik et al. study also showed less excitability than introverts. These investigators argue that sensation-seeking is motivated not by a need for stimulation, but by a low level of motor excitability. This proposition must obviously be incorporated into future explanations of sensation-seeking.

C. Impulsivity

1. Components of Impulsivity

Assessment of impulsivity has been hindered by a lack of consensus on what the trait comprises (e.g., S. B. G. Eysenck & Eysenck, 1977), but some attempts have been made at defining its various components. One is the Barratt Impulsiveness Scale (Barratt, 1987), which measures three subtraits: (1) motor impulsiveness (e.g., acting rashly and without thought), (2) cognitive impulsiveness (e.g., rapid decision-making), and (3) nonplanning impulsiveness (i.e., concentration on the present more than on the future). Using this scale, Barratt, Pritchard, Faulk, and Brandt (1987) conducted a study in which subjects were stimulated with bright and dim flashes of light. Evoked responses were assessed at 13 sites on the scalp. Barratt and his associates found that each of the three components of impulsivity correlated significantly with augmenting of the N_1 component at most of the recording locations. A subsequent study by Carillo-de-la-Peña and Barratt (1993) reaffirmed the importance of N_1 augmenting as a discriminator of individual differences in impulsiveness. This measure revealed a consistent positive correlation with scores on all three impulsiveness subscales and with the total score at two of five recording sites on the scalp. No other component of the evoked response was related to impulsiveness.

2. Impulsiveness and Monotony Avoidance

In a program of research spanning two decades, Schalling and her colleagues have found several psychophysiological correlates of impulsivity. Early work associated impulsivity with the trait of Solidity as measured by the Marke–Nyman Temperament Schedule (Schalling, 1977). A high level of this trait is comparable to a low level of impulsivity. Research reviewed by Schalling (1976, 1977, 1978) found relationships between this trait and cortical activity, heart rate, and skin conductance. Much of this research dealt with impulsivity as a component of psychopathy, however, and is therefore beyond the scope of this review.

More recently, Schalling and her associates have developed two scales related to impulsiveness as part of the Karolinska Scales of Personality (KSP): Impulsiveness (I) and Monotony Avoidance (MA). The first assesses tendencies to act without forethought, to make hasty decisions, and to live in a carefree manner. The second measures the desire for novelty and change and an intolerance for the usual and the predictable. The MA scale correlates positively with the total SS scale, as well as with experience-seeking, disinhibition, and boredom susceptibility.

Some evidence links the I and MA scales to platelet MAO levels. In general, monotony avoidance and MAO levels are negatively related. Perris et al. (1980) found such a negative correlation in a sample of male and female hospitalized depressives, but no correlation between MAO and impulsivity. Schalling et al. (1987) obtained similar results with an all-male sample of university students. A study by af Klinteberg, Schalling, Edman, Oreland, and Åsberg (1987) found MAO negatively correlated with MA among high-school-aged boys but not among girls. However, in both sexes those subjects who were high in MAO levels were less impulsive (i.e., low in I) than were those low in MAO. Thus, for girls low impulsiveness was associated with high MAO levels whereas for boys both low I and low MA were associated with high MAO. Schalling, Edman, Åsberg, and Oreland (1988) found that I correlated negatively with MAO in a sample of male university students whereas MA was not related to MAO levels.

D. Neuroticism and Anxiety

In general, studies designed to test a link between psychophysiological processes and H. J. Eysenck's (1967) construct of neuroticism have not yielded impressive or consistent effects (e.g., Stelmack, 1981). The same is true for the study of trait anxiety as assessed by other means. Navateur and Freixa i Baque (1987) concluded from their extensive review of the literature that previous studies did not reveal a consistent relationship between anxiety and electrodermal activity. In their own study, Navateur and Freixa i Baque (1987) found that highly trait anxious subjects showed lower skin conductance levels, lower conductance amplitudes, and fewer spontaneous conductance responses than their less trait anxious counterparts in response to both neutral and stressful pictures. These results are inconsistent with what would be predicted from a simple arousal theory of anxiety, and could be explained post hoc by the authors only tentatively. A recent study by Britt and Blumenthal (1992) suggests a new direction in which studies on the psychophysiology of anxiety may go by showing that whereas low state anxious subjects manifested a more rapid periorbital startle response to an 85-dB tone than to a less intense (60-dB) tone, subjects high in state anxiety responded with equal latency to both tones. This finding suggests that high anxiety may be associated with relative motoneural insensitivity.

The study of the psychophysiology of anxiety requires some careful attention to certain details that have not always been observed in the past. One is the nature of the eliciting stimulus. Whereas weak or trivial laboratory stimuli cannot be expected to elicit the sort of somatic reaction associated with high levels of anxiety, ethical considerations set a limit on what can be done under such conditions. Another is the state–trait distinction made originally by Spielberger (1972): individual differences in trait anxiety will be related to psychophysiological differences only to the extent that they interact with situational conditions to produce state anxiety. The intensity of the eliciting situation noted above is obviously important in effecting this process. In addition, Spielberger has proposed that the level of trait anxiety influences the range of conditions that evoke state anxiety, with highly trait anxious people showing anxious states in a greater number of situations than their less trait anxious counterparts. This "range hypothesis" of trait anxiety has not been studied systematically.

Another matter to keep in mind is the nature of anxiety in normal life. Fahrenberg (1992) has called for increasing use of *in vivo* studies of persons who suffer from such anxiety-related disorders as panic attacks and agoraphobia in the hope that a "bottom-up" inductive approach may yield some generalizations that will ultimately lead to the construction of better scientific theories of anxiety. Finally, we must keep in mind the fact that humans deal with anxiety with a number of coping and defensive strategies that may reflect personality influences. Some recent developments suggest that individual differences in coping styles and in personal beliefs in the ability to deal with problems may be correlated with specific patterns of psychophysiological activity (e.g., Bandura, Cioffi, Taylor, & Brouillard, 1988; Miller & Mangan, 1983). These intervening processes may interact with anxiety level to influence the overall somatic response pattern elicited by threatening or stressful situations. Further research along these lines would be in the spirit of the multimodal approach discussed earlier in this review.

V. SUMMARY

The modern period in the study of personality and psychophysiology began with the hypothesis of individual differences in arousability. In his pioneering theory, Eysenck proposed two systems governing these differences: one, centered in the reticular activating system, formed the basis for introversion–extraversion; the other, centered in the limbic system, formed the basis for neuroticism and anxiety. Later theorists offered revisions of this model, extended it, and developed other constructs similar to it. The arousability hypothesis, in one form or another, has informed most of the research on personality and psychophysiology published to date. Some of that research has been reviewed in this chapter.

Many of the studies designed to test the arousability hypothesis have shown that psychometrically assessed personality variables are correlated with activity in the physiological systems of the body. Nevertheless, the arousability hypothesis has been criticized on several grounds: the results of the research are mixed and sometimes contradictory; the relationship of personality to physiological functioning is more complex than a simple general arousal model would suggest; studies that have been carried out to test the model have often been simplistic and badly designed ones that yield little more than simple correlations; and the idea of generalized arousal itself is no longer widely accepted. These are all legitimate criticisms, but in themselves they do not vitiate the study of personality through its connections with psychophysiology. This approach to personality remains an exciting and challenging option that can yield important insights into the nature of individual differences.

Several leading psychophysiologists are now calling for a thorough examination of the problems that have beset the area in the past and for a rigorous appraisal of steps that must be taken for the study of personality and psychophysiology to move on to the next plateau. The suggestions made by these observers should be followed by any student of personality wishing to enter this specialized field, and by senior researchers in personality who may wish to add psychophysiology to their armamentarium of methods. Typical of the points raised are those of Gale and Edwards (1986), whose main ideas are summarized next as a conclusion to this review.

First, the study of personality and psychophysiology must be based on rigorous theories of behavior. Both the personality and the physiological variables must be grounded in well-defined theoretical constructs connected to each other by an explicit syntax. The constructs must also be linked through operational definitions to observable and objective conditions that form the basis for testable hypotheses. In other words, research on personality and psychophysiology should manifest the characteristics of good theory-driven scientific research. The best research that has been reported to date—the work of investigators like Eysenck, Zuckerman, Stelmack, Schalling, and Barratt—shows these characteristics. This work should be the norm for all subsequent studies.

Second, statements about personality must be based on good psychometric measures. This means that scales used to assess traits must have high levels of reliability and construct validity. In addition, personality measures must, whenever possible, be used for the purposes for which they have been devised; scales that have been developed for one purpose should be used for other purposes only with caution and with realization of their possible shortcomings. Attention must also be paid to the extent to which the chosen personality variables converge on other such variables, and whether the ones chosen are only subsets of larger and more inclusive ones.

Third, psychophysiological assessment must be thorough enough to allow adequate tests of hypotheses. This requires measurement of several body systems (e.g., cardiac, muscular, electrodermal) as well as measurement of several aspects of one system (e.g., skin conductance, skin potential, and specific conductance responses within the electrodermal system). Some aspects of a given system may correlate with personality measures more highly than others. Attempts should also be made to use similar measures across studies within a research program and across laboratories. The study of personality and psychophysiology to date has shown a relatively low level of replication of findings; this has been due in large part to the lack of comparability of methods used in various programs.

Fourth, attention must be shifted from the quest for simple correlations between personality and psychophysiological variables that has characterized most of the work to date to a search for the processes that underlie the correlations. As has been noted in this chapter, some recent approaches call for the analysis of activation within specific somatic systems and for the study of ways in which these systems interact with each other. An important part of a process view of psychophysiological functioning is recognition that the person is not a passive recipient of stimuli from the environment. It has already been noted that among the determinants of reactions to the environment are the person's efforts to adapt to, and to cope with, stimuli (Gale, 1987). The general model of personality and psychophysiology that is emerging from this new viewpoint is one involving the several physiological components arranged in a larger control system. This model points to a need for large, multiprocess and multimodal studies.

The study of personality through its connections with physiological processes rests on a solid basis of previous research and theory, and it still presents a unique challenge today for those who wish to conduct careful theory-driven research on complex processes. The efforts needed to produce the next generation of findings will be great, but so will the ultimate reward.

REFERENCES

af Klinteberg, B., Schalling, D., Edman, G., Oreland, L., & Åsberg, M. (1987). Personality correlates of platelet monoamine oxidase (MAO) activity in female and male subjects. *Neuropsychobiology, 18,* 89–96.

Andress, D. L., & Church, M. W. (1981). Differences in brainstem auditory evoked responses between introverts and extraverts as a function of stimulus intensity. *Psychophysiology, 18,* 156–157.

Ballenger, J. C., Post, R. M., Jimerson, D. C., Lake, C. R., Murphy, D. L., Zuckerman, M., & Cronin, C. (1983). Biochemical correlates of personality traits in normals: An exploratory study. *Personality and Individual Differences, 4,* 615–625.

Bandura, A., Cioffi, D., Taylor, C. B., & Brouillard, M. E. (1988). Perceived self-efficacy in coping with cognitive stressors and opioid activation. *Journal of Personality and Social Psychology, 55,* 479–488.

Barratt, E. S.. (1987). Impulsiveness and anxiety: Information processing and electroencephalograph topography. *Journal of Research in Personality, 21,* 453–463.

Barratt, E. S., Pritchard, W. S., Faulk, D. M., & Brandt, M. E. (1987). The relationship between impulsiveness subtraits, trait anxiety, and visual N100 augmenting/reducing: A topographic analysis. *Personality and Individual Differences, 8,* 43–51.

Bartussek, D., Diedrich, O., Naumann, E., & Collet, W. (1993). Introversion-extraversion and event-related potential (ERP): A test of J. A. Gray's theory. *Personality and Individual Differences, 14,* 565–574.

Birchall, P. M. A., & Claridge, G. S. (1979). Augmenting-reducing of the visual evoked potential as a function of changes in skin conductance level. *Psychophysiology, 16,* 482–490.

Blenner, J. L. (1993). Visual evoked potential stimulus intensity modulation and sensation seeking in thrill seekers. *Personality and Individual Differences, 14,* 455–463.

Britt, T. W., & Blumenthal, T. D. (1991). Motoneuronal insensitivity in extraverts as revealed by the startle response paradigm. *Personality and Individual Differences, 12,* 387–393.

Britt, T. W., & Blumenthal, T. D. (1992). The effects of anxiety on motoric expression of the startle response. *Personality and Individual Differences, 13,* 91–97.

Buchsbaum, M. S., Muscettola, G., & Goodwin, F. K. (1981). Urinary MHPG, stress response, personality factors and somatosensory evoked potentials in normal subjects and patients with affective disorders. *Neuropsychobiology, 7,* 212–224.

Buchsbaum, M. S., & Silverman, J. (1968). Stimulus intensity control and the evoked cortical response. *Psychosomatic Medicine, 30,* 12–22.

Bullock, W. A., & Gilliland, K. (1993). Eysenck's arousal theory of Introversion–Extraversion: A converging measures investigation. *Journal of Personality and Social Psychology, 64,* 113–123.

Calhoon, L. L. (1988). Explorations into the biochemistry of sensation seeking. *Personality and Individual Differences, 6,* 941–949.

Calhoon, L. L. (1991). Sensation seeking, exercise, and dopamine beta hydroxylase. *Personality and Individual Differences, 9,* 903–907.

Calhoon-La Grange, L. L. Jones, T. D., Reyes, E., & Ott, S. (1993). Monoamine oxidase levels in females: Relationships to sensation seeking, alcohol misuse, physical fitness, and menstrual cycle. *Personality and Individual Differences, 14,* 439–446.

Campbell, K. B., Baribeau-Brown, J., & Braun, C. (1981) Neuroanatomical and physiological foundations of extraversion. *Psychophysiology, 18,* 263–267.

Carrillo-de-la-Peña, M. T., & Barratt, E. S. (1993). Impulsivity and ERP augmenting/reducing. *Personality and Individual Differences, 15,* 25–32.

Carroll, E. N., Zuckerman, M., & Vogel, W. H. (1982). A test of the optimal level of arousal theory of sensation seeking. *Journal of Personality and Social Psychology, 42,* 572–575.

Claridge, G. S. (1967). *Personality and arousal.* London: Pergamon Press.

Daitzman, J., & Zuckerman, M. (1980). Disinhibitory sensation seeking personality and gonadal hormones. *Personality and Individual Differences, 1,* 103–110.

Daruna, J. H., Karrer, R., & Rosen, A. J. (1985). Introversion, attention and the late positive component of event-related potentials. *Biological Psychology, 20,* 249–259.

Ditraglia, G. M., & Polich. J. (1991). P300 and introverted/extraverted personality types. *Psychophysiology, 28,* 177–184.

Drinka, G. F., (1984). *The birth of neurosis.* New York: Simon & Schuster.

Endler, N. S., Edwards, J. M., & Vitelli, R. (1989). *Endler multidimensional anxiety scales: Manual.* Los Angeles: Western Psychological Services.

Eysenck, H. J., (1947). *The dynamics of anxiety and hysteria.* London: Routledge & Kegan Paul.

Eysenck, H. J. (1967). *The biological basis of personality.* Springfield, IL: Charles C. Thomas.

Eysenck, H. J. (1981). General features of the model. In H. J. Eysenck (Ed.), *A model of personality* (pp. 1–37). New York: Springer-Verlag.

Eysenck, H. J., & Eysenck, M. W. (1985). *Personality and individual differences: A natural science approach.* New York: Plenum Press.

Eysenck, S. B. G., & Eysenck, H. J. (1977). The place of impulsiveness in a dimensional system of personality description. *British Journal of Psychology, 16,* 57–68.

Fahrenberg, J. (1992). Psychophysiology of neuroticism and anxiety. In A. Gale & M. W. Eysenck (Eds.), *Handbook of individual differences: Biological perspectives* (pp. 179–226). Chichester, England: Wiley.

Feij, J. A., Orlebeke, J. F., Gazendam, A., & van Zuilen, R. W. (1985). Sensation-seeking: Measurement and psychophysiological correlates. In J. Strelau, F. H. Farley, &

A. Gale (Eds.) *The biological bases of personality and behavior* (Vol. 1, pp. 195–210). New York: McGraw-Hill.

Fowles, D. C. (1983). Motivational effects on heart rate and electrodermal activity: Implications for research on personality and psychopathology. *Journal of Research in Personality, 17,* 48–71.

Fowles, D. C., Roberts, R., & Nagel, K. (1977). The influence of introversion/extraversion on the skin conductance response to stress and stimulus intensity. *Journal of Research in Personality, 11,* 129–146.

Gale, A. (1981). EEG studies of extraversion-introversion: What's the next step? In R. Lynn (Ed.), *Dimensions of personality: Papers in honour of H. J. Eysenck* (pp. 181–207). Oxford, England: Pergamon Press.

Gale, A. (1983). Electroencephalographic studies of extraversion-introversion: A case study in the psychophysiology of individual differences. *Personality and Individual Differences, 4,* 371–380.

Gale, A. (1987). Arousal, control, energetics and values—An attempt at review and reappraisal. In J. Strelau & H. J. Eysenck (Eds.), *Personality dimensions and arousal* (pp. 287–316). New York: Plenum Press.

Gale, A., & Edwards, J. A. (1986). Individual differences. In M. G. H. Coles, E. Donchin, & S. W. Porges, (Eds.), *Psychophysiology: Systems, processes, and applications* (pp. 431–507). New York: Guilford Press.

Gange, J. J., Geen, R. G., & Harkins, S. G. (1979). Autonomic differences between extraverts and introverts during vigilance. *Psychophysiology, 16,* 392–397.

Geen, R. G. (1984). Preferred stimulation levels in introverts and extraverts: Effects on arousal and performance. *Journal of Personality and Social Psychology, 46,* 1303–1312.

Golding, J. F., & Richards, M. (1985). EEG spectral analysis, visual evoked potential and photic driving correlates of personality and memory. *Personality and Individual Differences, 6,* 67–76.

Graham, F. K. (1979). Distinguishing among orienting, defense, and startle reflexes. In H. D. Kimmel, E. H. van Olst, & J. F. Orlebeke (Eds.), *The orienting reflex in humans* (pp. 137–167). Hillsdale, NJ: Erlbaum.

Gray, J. R. (1964). *Pavlov's typology.* London: Pergamon Press.

Gray, J. R. (1972). The psychophysiological nature of introversion-extraversion: A modification of Eysenck's theory. In V. D. Nebylitsyn & J. A. Gray (Eds.), *Biological bases of individual behavior* (pp. 182–205). New York: Academic Press.

Gray, J. R. (1981). A critique of Eysenck's theory of personality. In H. J. Eysenck (Ed.), *A model for personality* (pp. 246–276). Berlin: Springer.

Haier, R. J., Robison, D. L., Braden, W., & Williams, D. (1984). Evoked potential augmenting-reducing and personality differences. *Personality and Individual Differences, 5,* 293–301.

Harvey, F., & Hirschman, R. (1980). The influence of extraversion and neuroticism on heart rate responses to aversive visual stimuli. *Personality and Individual Differences, 1,* 97–100.

Hillyard, S. A., & Hansen, J. C. (1986). Attention: Electrophysiological approaches. In M. G. H. Coles, E. Donchin, & S. W. Porges (Eds.), *Psychophysiology: Systems, processes, and applications* (pp. 227–243). New York: Guilford Press.

Jackson, S. (1986). *Melancholia and depression.* New Haven, CT: Yale University Press.

Jennings, J. R. (1986). Bodily changes during attending. In M. G. H. Coles, E. Donchin, & S. W. Porges (Eds.), *Psychophysiology: Systems, processes and applications* (pp. 268–289). New York: Guilford Press.

Johansson, F., Almay, B. G. L., von Knorring, L., Terenius, L., & Astrom, M. (1979). Personality traits in chronic pain patients related to endorphin levels in cerebrospinal fluid. *Psychiatry Research, 1,* 231–239.

Lacey, J. I. (1967). Somatic response patterning and stress: Some revisions of activation theory. In M. H. Appley & R. Trumbull (Eds.), *Psychological Stress: Issues in research* (pp. 14–37). New York: Appleton-Century-Crofts.

Lindsley, D. B. (1957). Psychophysiology and motivation. In M. R. Jones (Ed.), *Nebraska Symposium on Motivation* (Vol. 5, pp. 44–105). Lincoln: University of Nebraska Press.

Ljubin, T., & Ljubin, C. (1990). Extraversion and audiomotor reflex. *Personality and Individual Differences, 11,* 977–984.

Lukas, J. H. (1987). Visual evoked potential augmenting-reducing and personality: The vertex augmenter is a sensation seeker. *Personality and Individual Differences, 8,* 385–395.

Lukas, J. H., & Mullins, L. F. (1983). Auditory augmenting-reducing and sensation seeking. *Psychophysiology, 20,* 457.

Lukas, J. H., & Mullins, L. F. (1985). Auditory augmenters are sensation seekers and perform better under high work loads. *Psychophysiology, 22,* 580–581.

Matthews, G., & Amelang, M. (1993). Extraversion, arousal theory and performance: A study of individual differences in the EEG. *Personality and Individual Differences, 14,* 347–363.

Matthews, G., Davies, D. R., & Holley, P. J. (1990). Extraversion, arousal, and visual sustained attention: The role of resource availability. *Personality and Individual Differences, 11,* 1159–1173.

Miller, S. M., & Mangan, C. E. (1983). The interacting effects of information and coping style in adapting to gynecologic stress: Should the doctor tell it all? *Journal of Personality and Social Psychology, 45,* 223–236.

Mullins, L. F., & Lukas, J. H. (1984). Auditory augmenters are sensation seekers if they attend the stimuli. *Psychophysiology, 21,* 589.

Murphy, D. L., Belmaker, R. H., Buchsbaum, M. S., Martin, N. F., Ciaranello, K., & Wyatt, R. J. (1977). Biogenic amine related enzymes and personality variations in normals. *Psychological Medicine, 7,* 149–157.

Myrtek, M. (1984). *Constitutional psychophysiology: Research in review.* Orlando, FL: Academic Press.

Navateur, J., & Freixa i Baque, E. (1987). Individual differences in electrodermal activity as a function of subjects' anxiety. *Personality and Individual Differences, 8,* 615–626.

Neary, R. S., & Zuckerman, M. (1976). Sensation seeking, trait and state anxiety, and the electrodermal orienting reflex. *Psychophysiology, 13,* 205–211.

Neumann, E., & Blanton, R. (1970). The early history of electrodermal research. *Psychophysiology, 6,* 453–475.

Orlebeke, J. F., & Feij, J. A. (1979). The orienting reflex as a personality correlate. In H. D. Kimmel, E. H. van Olst, & J. F. Orlebeke (Eds.), *The orienting reflex in humans* (pp. 567–585). Hillsdale, NJ: Erlbaum.

Perris, C., Jacobsson, L., von Knorring, L., Oreland, L., Perris, H., & Ross, S. I. (1980). Enzymes related to biogenic amine metabolism and personality characteristics in depressed patients. *Acta Psychiatrica Scandinavica, 61,* 477–484.

Petrie, A. (1967). *Individuality in pain and suffering.* Chicago: University of Chicago Press.

Pivik, R. T., Stelmack, R. M., & Bylsma, F. W. (1988). Personality and individual differences in spinal motoneuronal excitability. *Psychophysiology, 25,* 16–24.

Plouffe, L., & Stelmack, R. M. (1986). Sensation-seeking and the electroidermal orienting response in young and elderly females. *Personality and Individual Differences, 7,* 119–120.

Revelle, W. Humphreys, M. S., Simon, L., & Gilliland, K. (1980). The interactive effect of personality, time of day, and caffeine: A test of the arousal model. *Journal of Experimental Psychology: General, 109,* 1–31.

Richards, M., & Eves, F. F. (1991). Personality, temperament and the cardiac defense response. *Personality and Individual Differences, 12,* 999–1007.

Ridgeway, D., & Hare, R. D. (1981). Sensation seeking and psychophysiological responses to auditory stimulation. *Psychophysiology, 18,* 613–618.

Robinson, T. N., Jr., & Zahn, T. P. (1983). Sensation seeking, state anxiety, and cardiac and EDR orienting reactions. *Psychophysiology, 20,* 465.

Sales, S. M. (1971). Need for stimulation as a factor in social behavior. *Journal of Personality and Social Psychology, 19,* 124–134.

Schalling, D. (1976). Anxiety, pain, and coping. In I. G. Sarason & C. D. Spielberger (Eds.), *Stress and anxiety* (Vol. 3, pp. 49–71). Washington, DC: Hemisphere.

Schalling, D. (1977). The trait-situation interaction and the physiological correlates of behavior. In D. Magnusson & N. Endler (Eds.), *Personality at the crossroads* (pp. 129–141). Hillsdale, NJ: Erlbaum.

Schalling, D. (1978). Psychopathy-related personality variables and the psychophysiology of socialization. IN R. D. Hare & D. Schalling (Eds.), *Psychopathic behavior: Approaches to research* (pp. 85-106). Chichester, England: Wiley.

Schalling, D., & Åsberg, M. (1985). Biological and psychological correlates of impulsiveness and monotony avoidance. In J. Strelau, F. H. Farley, & A. Gale (Eds.), *The biological bases of personality and behavior: Vol. 1. Theories, measurement techniques, and development* (pp. 181–194). Washington, DC: Hemisphere.

Schalling, D., Åsberg, M., Edman, G., & Oreland, L. (1987). Markers for vulnerability to psychopathology: Temperament traits associated with platelet MAO activity. *Acta Psychiatrica Scandinavica, 76,* 172–182.

Schalling, D., Edman, G., Åsberg, M., & Oreland. L. (1988). Platelet MAO activity associated with impulsivity and aggressivity. *Personality and Individual Differences, 9,* 597–605.

Schooler, C., Zahn, T. P., Murphy, D. L., & Buchsbaum, M. S. (1978). Psychological correlates of monoamine oxidase in normals. *Journal of Nervous and Mental disease, 166,* 177–186.

Smith, B. D. (1983). Extraversion and electrodermal activity: Arousabilty and the inverted-U. *Personality and Individual Differences, 4,* 411–419.

Smith, B. D., Rockwell-Tischer, S., & Davidson, R. (1986) Extraversion and arousal: Effects of attentional conditions on electrodermal activity. *Personality and Individual Differences, 7,* 293–303.

Smith, B. D., Rypma, C. B., & Wilson, R. J. (1981). Dishabituation and spontaneous recovery of the electrodermal orienting response: Effects of extraversion, impulsivity, sociability, and caffeine. *Journal of Research in Personality, 15,* 233–240.

Smith, B. D., Wilson, R. J., & Davidson, R. (1984). Electrodermal activity and extraversion: Caffeine, preparatory signal and stimulus intensity effects. *Personality and Individual Differences, 5,* 59–65.

Smith, B. D., Wilson, R. J., & Jones, B. E. (1983). Extraversion and multiple levels of caffeine-induced arousal: Effects on overhabituation and dishabituation. *Psychophysiology, 20,* 29–34.

Sokolov, E. N. (1963). *Perception and the conditioned reflex.* New York: Pergamon Press.

Spielberger, C. D. (1972). Anxiety as an emotional state. In C. D. Spielberger (Ed.), *Anxiety: Current trends in theory and research* (Vol. 1 pp. 23–49). New York: Academic Press.

Stein, L. (1983). The chemistry of positive reinforcement. In M. Zuckerman (Ed.), *Biological bases of sensation, seeking, implusivity, and anxiety* (pp. 151–175). Hillsdale, NJ: Erlbaum.

Stelmack, R. M. (1981). The psychophysiology of extraversion and neuroticism. In H. J. Eysenck (Ed.), *A model for personality* (pp. 38–64). New York: Springer-Verlag.

Stelmack, R. M. (1990). Biological bases of extraversion: Psychophysiological evidence. *Journal of Personality, 58,* 293–311.

Stelmack, R. M., & Michaud, Achorn, A. (1985) Extraversion, attention, and the habituation of the auditory evoked response. *Journal of Research in Personality, 19,* 416–428.

Stelmack, R. M., Achorn, E., & Michaud, A. (1977). Extraversion and individual differences in auditory evoked response. *Psychophysiology, 14,* 368–374.

Stelmack, R. M., Bourgeois, R., Chien, J. Y. C., & Pickard, C. (1979). Extraversion and the OR habituation rate to visual stimuli. *Journal of Research in Personality, 13,* 49–58.

Stelmack, R. M., Campbell, K. B., & Bell, I. (1993) Extraversion and brainstem auditory evoked potentials during sleep and wakefulness. *Personality and Individual Differences, 14,* 447–453.

Stelmack, R. M., & Geen, R. G. (1992). The psychophysiology of extraversion. In A. Gale & M. W. Eysenck (Eds.), *Handbook of individual differences: Biological perspectives* (pp. 227–254). Chichester, England: Wiley.

Stelmack, R. M., Plouffe, L., & Falkenberg, W. (1983). Extraversion sensation seeking and electrodermal response: Probing a paradox. *Personality and Individual Differences, 4,* 607–614.

Stelmack, R. M., & Stalikas, A. (1991). Galen and the humor theory of temperament. *Personality and Individual Differences, 12,* 255–263.

Stelmack, R. M., & Wilson, K. G. (1982). Extraversion and the effects of frequency and intensity on the auditory brainstem evoked response. *Personality and Individual Differences, 3,* 373–380.

Stenberg, G., Rosen, I., & Risberg, J. (1988). Personality and augmenting/reducing in visual and auditory evoked potentials. *Personality and Individual Differences, 9,* 571–579.

Strelau, J. (1983). *Temperament, personality, activity.* New York: Academic Press.

Strelau, J. (1987). Personality dimensions based on arousal theories: Search for integration. In J. Strelau & H. J. Eysenck (Eds.), *Personality dimensions and arousal* (pp. 269–286). New York: Plenum Press.

Thayer, R. E. (1970). Activation states as assessed by verbal reports and four psychophysiological variables. *Psychophysiology, 7,* 86–94.

Thieme, R. E., & Feij, J. A. (1986). Tyramine, a new clue to disinhibition and sensation seeking? *Personality and Individual Differences, 7,* 349–354.

Umberkoman-Wiita, B., Vogel, W. H., & Wiita, P. J. (1981). Some biochemical and behavioral (sensation seeking) correlates in healthy adults. *Research Communications in Psychology, Psychiatry, and Behavior, 6,* 303–316.

Veith, I. (1965). *Hysteria: The history of a disease.* Chicago: University of Chicago Press.

Venables, P. H. (1984). Arousal: An examination of its status as a concept. In M. G. H. Coles, J. R. Jennings, & J. A. Stern (Eds.), *Psychophysiological perspectives: Festschrift for Beatrice and John Lacey* (pp. 134–142). New York: Van Nostrand-Reinhold.

von Knorring, L. (1981). Visual evoked responses and platelet monoamine oxidase in patients suffering from alcoholism. In H. Begleiter (Ed.), *The biological effects of alcohol* (pp. 270–291). New York: Plenum Press.

Zahn, T. P., Schooler, C., & Murphy, D. L. (1986). Autonomic correlates of sensation seeking and monoamine oxidase activity: Using confirmatory factor analysis on psychophysiological data. *Psychophysiology, 23,* 521–531.

Zuckerman, M. (1969). Theoretical formulations. In J. P. Zubek (Ed.), *Sensory deprivation: Fifteen years of research* (pp. 407–432). New York: Appleton-Century-Crofts.

Zuckerman, M. (1971). Dimensions of sensation seeking. *Journal of Consulting and Clinical Psychology, 36,* 45–52.

Zuckerman, M. (1979). *Sensation seeking: Beyond the optimal level of arousal.* Hillsdale, NJ: Erlbaum.

Zuckerman, M. (1983). A biological theory of sensation seeking. In M. Zuckerman (Ed.), *Biological bases of sensation seeking, impulsivity, and anxiety* (pp. 37–76). Hillsdale, NJ: Erlbaum.

Zuckerman, M. (1984). Sensation seeking: A comparative approach to a human trait. *Behavior and Brain Sciences, 7,* 413–471.

Zuckerman, M. (1990). The psychophysiology of sensation seeking. *Journal of Personality, 58,* 313–345.

Zuckerman, M., Eysenck, S. B. G., & Eysenck, H. J. (1978). Sensation seeking in England and America: Cross-cultural, age, and sex comparisons. *Journal of Consulting and Clinical Psychology, 46,* 139–149.

Zuckerman, M. Murtaugh, T. T., & Siegel, J. (1974). Sensation seeking and cortical augmenting-reducing. *Psychophysiology, 11,* 535–542.

Zuckerman, M., Simons, R. F., & Como, P. G. (1988). Sensation seeking and stimulusintensity as modulators of cortical, cardiovascular, and electrodermal response: A cross-modality study. *Personality and Individual Differences, 9,* 361–372.

Part V

Social Determinants of Personality

CHAPTER 17

PERSONALITY AND SOCIAL STRUCTURE

SOCIAL PSYCHOLOGICAL CONTRIBUTIONS

THOMAS F. PETTIGREW

THE UNIVERSITY OF CALIFORNIA, SANTA CRUZ

I. INTRODUCTION

"How can the individual," asked Gordon Allport (1968, p. 9), "be both a cause and a consequence of society?" This is a fundamental question for social psychology—indeed, for all social sciences and personality psychology as well. It opens questions of the complex causal linkages between personality and various levels of social structure (Elder, 1973). Once social structure is defined as relatively persistent social patterning, these questions become essential for placing personality considerations in their needed social context.

A. A Basic Area of Social Science

Virtually all major social theorists have fashioned concepts and developed hypotheses for explaining the linkages between personality and social structure. Many of these broad efforts have centered on the presumed negative effects on individuals of the decline of traditionalism and the rise of modern institutions. Hence, the decline of religious institutions and political stability for Emile Durkheim (1951) was the cause of personal isolation and depression, while for Gustave Le Bon (1897) it allowed the ugly, irrational side of humanity to burst forth in the crowd. For Karl Marx (1964), the new technology and property relations led to worker alienation from their work, their colleagues, and even themselves. For Max Weber (1968), the growth of bureaucracy threatened dehumanizing and depersonalizing outcomes. Even the triumph of equality, for Alexis de Tocqueville (1945), could lead to envy and resentment. And for Sigmund Freud (1930), modern life deepened the conflict between an individual's impulses and their repression.

It remained for the social psychologist and philosopher Georg Simmel (1955) to see any good in the momentous structural changes taking place around these 19th and early 20th century theorists. He noted that the social differentiation that characterized modern institutions made it possible for individuals to develop "a web of affiliations" in nonascriptive groups. This "web," argued Simmel, ran the risk of role conflict, even social marginality, in its newly differentiated and cross-cutting social relationships. But it also made possible the individualization of personality and the recognition of uniqueness. Observe the *mediated* form of Simmel's theory: altered macro-structure leads first to cross-cutting group memberships and face-to-face interactions that in turn cause individuation. This mediated argument, we shall note later, remains the principal form of personality and social structure theories in social psychology.

B. Twentieth Century Development of the Area

Personality and social structure constitute an interdisciplinary field par excellence; political scientists, anthropologists, sociologists, and psychiatrists as well as psychologists have all contributed. As outlined by House (1981), it formally emerged as a specialty between the world wars, using gross molar conceptions of both personality and social structure. Broad Freudian notions prevailed, and whole societies were considered as homogeneous entities. Margaret Mead's (1935) influential and controversial work, *Sex and Temperament in Three Primitive Societies,* typifies this period. During World War II, American specialists attempted to contribute to the war effort by advancing sweepingly expansive analyses of the Japanese, Russians, and Germans. The extremely holistic and crude nature of these analyses is illustrated by Gorer's (1943) contentions about Japanese national character. Their character structure was capsuled as anal-compulsive and attributed to early and severe toilet training in childhood. The most lasting thesis of these national character studies was the analysis of authoritarianism as applied to Nazi Germany (Adorno, Frenkel-Brunswik, Levinson, & Sanford, 1950).

Psychoanalytic theory inspired the most prevalent model of this work. Societal maintenance systems were held to shape particular child-rearing practices that in turn shaped the personalities of the society's members. This mediated model is best seen in the work of Kardiner (1945) and later Whiting and Child (1953). But tests of the model typically failed to measure the key components directly. In addition, an unrealistic homogeneity of both a society's practices and its personalities was assumed. So cross-national probability surveys were introduced by Cantril (1965),

Almond and Verba (1965), and others to establish national differences more firmly. Yet survey data alone could not explain the differences uncovered.

The past generation has witnessed a shift to more viable, if more modest, approaches (House, 1981). Both theory and research in the field have become less holistic in their conceptions of both personality and society. Freudian concepts of personality are less utilized, and increased attention is now given to intrasocietal as well as intersocietal differences. Explanations also center now more on structural than cultural factors. Moreover, while interest in the area waned during the 1970s, the 1980s witnessed a revival—as evinced by such seminal papers as those by House (1981), Ryff (1987), and Smelser and Smelser (1981).

C. The Potential Social Psychological Contribution

Within this new, more specified approach, social psychology is better able to partici-pate in the field. But, as Ryff (1987) makes clear, experimental social psychologists have not as yet exploited this enhanced potential. Figure 1 outlines in broad strokes where the discipline is best equipped to make its distinctive contribution to this necessarily interdisciplinary enterprise. Four causal routes are possible between the

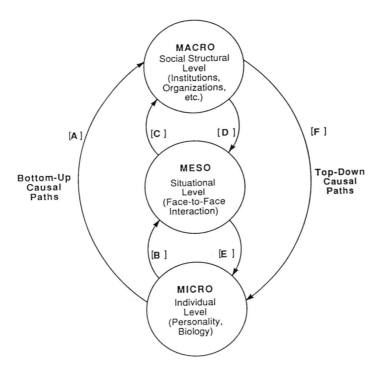

FIGURE 1   Six causal paths.

personality and larger structural levels of analysis. Paths A, B, and C are "bottom-up" routes where influence is assumed to flow upward from personality changes to social structural changes. Path A is a direct path; personality factors in this route shape structural alterations without the mediation of meso-level, situational factors. Paths B and C provide the same causal route except that the personality influence is first mediated by situational factors before indirectly shaping structural changes. Paths D, E, and F are "top-down" routes where influence is assumed to flow downward from initial social structural changes to personality changes. Paths D and E assume that this downward flow of influence is first mediated by situational factors; Path F allows direct structure-to-personality effects. This chapter will provide specific empirical illustrations of each of these four causal paths between personality and social structure.

Like other social sciences, social psychology has the potential to contribute to the understanding of all four potential paths. But its distinctive expertise is found in Paths B and E, the bottom-up and top-down links between personality and face-to-face situations. Note, for example, the overwhelming proportion of studies working exclusively at the Path B and E levels in the December 1987 issue of *The Journal of Personality and Social Psychology* devoted entirely to "integrating personality and social psychology." The field, then, is best at uncovering how the two-way influences between personality and social structure are mediated at the meso-situational level of analysis.

But not all, or even most of, social psychology is engaged in this process. Only one branch of the discipline, the survey-oriented contextualists (Pettigrew, 1980), have concerned themselves with the field of personality and social structure. Indeed, only the contextualists, found largely in sociology departments in the United States, have continued to concern themselves with personality questions of any type. Herein lies an apparent paradox, one we must consider to understand the limits of social psychological contributions to the study of personality in recent years.

II. AN APPARENT PARADOX

The apparent paradox involves the way the two social psychologies, sociological and psychological, treat the study of personality. Many social psychologists in sociology, the macro social science that studies social structure, have over the past generation taken the study and concept of personality far more seriously than social psychologists in psychology, the micro social science that studies individuals.

There are many indications of this paradoxical situation. Consider the differential attention provided personality in the two handbooks of the social psychological discipline. The Rosenberg and Turner (1981) volume, *Social Psychology: Sociological Perspectives,* contains 21 chapters, 10 of which involve personality concepts, data, and theory. Three chapters dwell on socialization processes; 1 concerns identity formation and another the self-concept; and no fewer than 5 deal directly with personality and society. By contrast, the third edition of Lindzey and Aronson's

(1985) *Handbook of Social Psychology* devotes only 3 of its 30 chapters to largely personality concerns—1 on altruism and aggression, another on adult socialization, and a 3rd on personality and social behavior. An updated version of the classic chapter in the first and second *Handbook* editions on national character by Inkeles and Levinson (1954, 1968) was omitted from the third edition in 1985.

Further evidence for the neglect of personality in psychological social psychology is provided by the protests some years ago in Division 8 of the American Psychological Association (APA) among personality psychologists that their interests were not fairly represented. One response to these objections took the form of altering the basic format of *The Journal of Personality and Social Psychology,* with a separate section for "personality processes and individual differences."

The fact that personality and social psychology have long been joined together in the same major APA division and journals heightens the paradox. Personality considerations have historically played a large role in the development of psychological social psychology. By contrast, there is a far less strong tradition in sociological social psychology. Indeed, social psychologists in sociology are often suspect for their micro-level interests (DiRenzo, 1977). Thus, in the Rosenberg and Turner (1981) volume, several writers felt it necessary to defend their focus on personality as relevant to the larger discipline of sociology. In his excellent chapter on the self-concept, for example, Rosenberg (1981, p. 593) begins by allowing that the concept "may appear to be peculiarly ill-suited as a subject for sociological concern."

A. So Why the Paradox?

Three interrelated factors explain this apparent paradox, and these factors are important for understanding the study of personality and social structure within contextual social psychology. First, social psychologists in the sociological mold have different—though not conflicting—aims from their psychological colleagues. Second, there has been over the past generation a general trend throughout psychology toward situationalism. And, finally, sociological social psychology has been shielded from these psychological influences. Let us consider each of these factors further.

1. Different Theoretical Aims

Social psychology serves as both the most macro-focused subdiscipline of psychology and the most micro-focused subdiscipline of sociology. As such, social psychologists on the two sides of the disciplinary divide often have somewhat different, though complementary, theoretical aims. Social psychologists in psychology are concerned heavily with the links between the individual and the situational levels of analysis (Paths B and E in Fig. 1). Consistent with their interest in broader social structure, sociological social psychologists are sometimes also concerned with the links to such larger social structures as institutions (Paths A, C, D, and F in Fig. 1).

Experimental social psychology broke from Kurt Lewin's fascination with human motivation and has increasingly been swept up with the cognitive revolution throughout psychology. Many of the most notable advances in the discipline in recent decades have come in the subfield of social cognition. This motivation-to-cognition shift is important for understanding the paradox under discussion. A focus on motivation lends itself to personality considerations; the theory and work of my teacher, Gordon Allport, offer evidence of this close connection. As the longtime editor of the old *Journal of Abnormal and Social Psychology,* he was both a personality and a social psychologist. Allport experienced no role conflict in this dual role, given his emphasis on both motivation and individual uniqueness.

But the increasing focus on cognition in recent decades has weakened this connection between the two fields that compose Division 8. Cognitive variables have substituted for personality variables as micro indicators for much experimental social psychological work over the past generation. Jones (1985) notes further that attention to the fundamental attribution error (Ross, 1977) acted to erode further interest in approaches that assigned weight to internal dispositions. This marked shift from motivation and personality concerns to cognition was made even more pronounced by the lack of interest in individual differences in cognition. Cognitive variables and processes have generally been assumed (but rarely empirically demonstrated) to operate universally.

Given their theoretical aims, many sociologists are less prone to make such easy assumptions of universality. Social psychologists in the personality and social structure tradition often wish to see how different types of people are attracted to particular institutions (a Paths A and B-C self-selection problem), and how different institutions alter individuals (a Paths D-E and F institutional-shaping problem). Some cognitive variables are of interest for these issues. But cognitive variables cannot fully substitute for personality variables in such personality-structure work.

2. *General Psychological Trend toward Situationalism*

The move from motivational to cognitive concerns in experimental social psychology was furthered by other trends within psychology as a whole, especially personality psychology. McGuire (1985) holds that there have been 25- to 30-year swings of the pendulum between the personal and the situational poles of theoretical emphasis. And Snyder and Ickes (1985) detect a returning interest in personal consistency. But the sharp decline in experimental social psychology's interest in personality in the 1960s coincided with the rise of an extreme situationalism. Mischel's (1968) influential book, *Personality and Assessment,* marks the high point of this latest return to the Hartshorne and May (1928) emphasis on the situation. The most memorable and cited part of Mischel's critique was his contention on the limits of personality predictions of behavior across situations: the magic correlation coefficient of .30, just 9% of the variance, became part of psychological—but not sociological—lore.

The differential influence of Mischel's arguments can be traced in the citations to his 1968 book and related articles. In the Rosenberg and Turner (1981) volume on sociological social psychology, only two references to this work are made; in the Lindzey and Aronson (1985) *Handbook* published 4 years later, a dozen such references are made. There is an irony here, perhaps. Jones (1985) asserts that it is the Lewinians who have most focused on situations, while it is the non-Lewinians who have taken Lewin's famous B = f (P,E) equation more seriously. In any event, the rise of situationalism in personality psychology itself in the late 1960s proved influential because the overwhelming power of situations to shape unexpected behavior had already become an empirical preoccupation of psychological social psychology. From Asch's (1956) famous conformity study and Milgram's (1974) obedience studies to Zimbardo's (1970) prison simulation and Tajfel's (1970) "minimum situation," much of the exciting empirical work in the field provided powerful support for a situational framework that did not require, beyond cognitive variables, attention to the Person component to Lewin's formulation. Even the scant attention that has been paid to individual differences in psychological social psychology has generally been within this situational perspective. Hence, a leading personality measure in experimental studies of the 1970s was Rotter's (1966) external–internal locus of control variable—a measure that fits easily within a largely situational framework.

3. The Shielding of Contextual Social Psychology from These Psychological Influences

If these influences converged to lessen social psychology's interest in personality within psychology, why did they not also cause a similar decline in social psychology within sociology? There are both theoretical and empirical answers to this question. But, first, several distinctions must be made among sociology's various branches of social psychology. Symbolic interactionists have traditionally distrusted stable personal attributes in their emphasis on specifically situated and emerging definitions and meanings (Blumer, 1969). Likewise, the ethnomethodologists have little use for dispositional concepts. They focus on how people make sense of their social environment; in doing so, they are inspired in part by modern linguistic theory and often employ conversational analysis in their empirical work (Handel, 1982). Unfortunately, symbolic interactionists and ethnomethodologists rarely read the psychological literature, and vice versa. For these two branches, then, the paradox under discussion does not exist. They have never systematically used personality variables, and they arrived at their own versions of situationalism largely independent of psychological influence.

The sociological group of interest is the "contextual social psychologists"—so named because of their special concern for the social context of social psychological phenomena. They are thoroughly familiar with the psychological literature, edit *The Social Psychology Quarterly,* and compose most of the membership of the Social Psychology Section of the American Sociological Association (Pettigrew, 1980). They often use survey and other field methods in an attempt to balance external and internal validity concerns. Less mobilized than symbolic interactionists and ethnomethodologists, this largest group of sociological social psychologists have traditionally employed and continue to employ personality variables. And both the theory and the methods of contextual social psychologists acted to shield them from the recent situationalist influences in psychology.

a. Theoretical Shielding.   Social psychologists in psychology use personality measures as both independent and dependent variables. But the theoretical interests of contextual social psychologists in sociology lead to a virtually exclusive use of personality variables as dependent measures of the effects of social structure (DiRenzo, 1977; Elder, 1973; but see exceptions in Part IV of Smelser & Smelser, 1963). For this purpose, the attacks on personality variables as predictors were irrelevant. More generally, sociological theory, with its emphasis on the power of social structure, had long served to immunize sociologists against the fundamental attribution error that operated among extreme dispositionalists in psychology. Thus, the Asch, Milgram, Zimbardo, and Tajfel experimental demonstrations did not seem nearly so surprising, dramatic, and "nonobvious" to social psychologists in sociology as they did to those in psychology. Contextual social psychologists had long before gravitated to a person–situation–structure interactionist position closer to the Lewinian formulation left behind by many Lewinians. This position shielded them from the rampant situationalism these publicized studies triggered in psychology.

This point highlights the difference in familiarity with social structure between social psychologists in the two fields. Accustomed to dealing with social structure, contextual social psychologists in sociology have seen no reason to deemphasize personality just because strong effects of situations are demonstrated. By contrast, experimental social psychologists have little training in social structure, and, after a third of a century of famous situational experiments, the branch has yet to formulate a taxonomy of situations or to specify a consistent means of measuring and comparing situations.

b. Empirical Shielding.   While some sociological social psychologists conduct experiments, most researchers in the contextual tradition use a variety of field methods—particularly surveys. This work often requires regression and other techniques quite different from the standard analyses of variance designs routinely used in experimental social psychology. This fact has meant that contextualists have benefited from the advances in empirical techniques and statistical treatments that have characterized sociology generally in recent years. This statistical upgrading was made more rapid by sociology's adaptations of econometric techniques—for all their problems, still by far the most sophisticated in social science. While the sociologists were upgrading along econometric lines, psychological social psychologists were not keeping pace.

This differential statistical sophistication is part of the answer to the paradox under discussion. Mischel's magic coefficient of .30 as the presumed predictive limit of personality variables, which impressed many psychologists, had no impact on sociologists more skilled with regression analyses and accustomed to similar coefficients from such crudely measured variables as social class. The role of error in both independent and dependent variables, the need for aggregated measures, and similar considerations were more widely appreciated in sociology. To be sure, Epstein (1979) and others countered the Mischel arguments with these points in psychology, but it took a decade for these correctives to appear.

B. The Foci of Contextual Social Psychology

While psychological social psychologists have focused less in recent decades on personality, they have focused more on the specification of interactional processes. It is precisely these processes that are needed to explain the causal linkages between the various levels of analyses. Indeed, numerous commentators agree that the general failure to specify linkage processes is the glaring weakness of the personality and social structure realm (DiRenzo, 1977; Elder, 1973; Ryff, 1987). To make our discussion concrete, let us review illustrations of the various paths and some of the linkage processes that have been advanced to explain the shaping of social structure by personality.

III. PERSONALITY SHAPES SOCIAL STRUCTURE

Sweepingly global "great man" theories of history have put in disrepute the contention that an individual can make a major difference in society. Had Napoleon not lived, goes the counter, who is to say that the *zeitgeist* would not have produced a similar charismatic French leader with little change on history? At this gross level of abstraction, of course, such arguments are of little value. Yet it has been demonstrated that personality *does* shape social structure once the measures at both levels and the hypothesized effect have been more narrowly specified. Indeed, laboratory research even supports a narrowed version of "great man" theory when placed in the specific context of small task-oriented groups (Borgatta, Bales, & Couch, 1954).

We have already noted that, following from Figure 1, two principal "bottom-up" causal paths are possible. One involves the direct effects of Path A—unmediated alterations of social structure by personality factors. The other involves mediated effects, Paths B and C of Figure 1, where personality first alters situations that in turn shape larger social structures. Consider examples of each of these bottom-up causal paths between personality and social structure.

A. Direct Effects (Causal Path A)

Max Weber's (1930) theory of the rise of capitalism constitutes the classic Path A linkage between personality and social structure. In his *Protestant Ethic and the Spirit of Capitalism,* Weber countered Marx by holding that such micro phenomena as beliefs, motives, and values could independently shape macro structure. With 17th century Hollanders particularly in mind, he explained why ascetic Protestant sects often met with economic success even though they viewed wealth as dangerous for the soul. He argued that the Protestant ethic, epitomized in the anxiety-arousing Calvinist doctrine of predestination, explained the riddle. A self-denying, frugal, and work-oriented routine in busy preparation for final judgment led to accumulated wealth. Weber also held that social structure shapes personality in a reciprocal cycle, and he understood that the Protestant ethic's influence on capitalism was mediated by family, work, and other face-to-face, meso-level situations. Yet his famous theory remains the prototype of a Path A causal theory involving personality and social structure.

Building on Weber's thesis, David McClelland (1955, 1961) posited that the association between the Protestant ethic and capitalism was mediated by the achievement motive. Fostered by child-training practices consistent with the Protestant ethic, the need for achievement, he maintained, is both challenged and satisfied by entrepreneurial activity that characterizes capitalism in its early stages. Both high-need achievers and entrepreneurs are independent-minded, relatively autonomous, and strivers for success. The only situational mediation McClelland specifies is that such people seek out situations in which they can feel personally responsible for clearly measurable results of their efforts (Atkinson & Hoselitz, 1958). Carrying his analysis to the macro level, McClelland (1961) attempted to show that the achievement motive played a significant part in the rapid economic growth of the West. He emphasized cross-national and longitudinal relationships between levels of achievement and a variety of measures of technological growth.

Psychohistorical studies, from biographies of such famous figures as Luther and Gandhi (Erikson, 1958, 1969) to analyses of such broad social phenomena as racism (Kovel, 1970), offer additional examples of such sweepingly broad, Path A theories. But increasingly research and theory in this vein are more delimited in scope and more differentiated in prediction. For example, Gluckstern and Packard (1977) studied change in a prison. In viewing the personalities of change agents, they noted that different styles acquired greater salience at different times in the process of organizational change. Such results suggest the interactive nature of personality and social structural relationships, a major point to which we shall return.

B. Mediated Effects (Causal Paths B and C)

We have noted that social psychology makes its distinctive contribution by explaining the links between the individual and the situational levels of analysis—both Path B and Path E (Pettigrew, 1988). In doing so, the discipline provides distinctive variables and explanations together with a general situational perspective largely missing from the analyses of other social sciences. These distinctive variables and explanations usually involve subjective interpretations of the social environment. Hence, for the Path B approach, the field conceptualizes personality as individual susceptibilities to respond differentially to particular situations. These individual difference variables, then, lend themselves to links with the situational level. Thus, Rotter's (1966) internal–external locus of control is one of the most used individual measures in social psychological research.

Applied social psychology's remedies for problems using this bottom-up direction usually take the form of special training—for the critically ill, the lonely, the shy, the elderly, burnouts, rape victims, and those facing major surgery and other serious life events—to reconceptualize their situation. Often self-imposed, maladaptive dispositional attributions are converted to situational attributions when appropriate. These remedies resemble superficially typical therapeutic attempts to change internal qualities of individuals. But actually these remedies are directed primarily at changing the behavior of individuals in problematic situations. Ultimately, most social psychological remedies try to alter the nature of human interaction in situations.

Both personality and social psychologists have produced literally hundreds of Path B studies over the years. This most popular of bottom-up paths demonstrates how personality makes a significant difference at the situational level. Much of the work of this genre following World War II was conducted in the small group research tradition, the most important of which came from Freed Bales and his colleagues. In time, this work led to the most developed, data-based model that exists of the complex interaction of personality and task group structure (Bales, 1970). This interactive model encompasses linkages of both Paths B and E of Figure 1 by combining group roles with personality traits in a three-dimensional value space. On the basis of personality measures alone, for example, the model generates predictions concerning likely coalitions and behavior in the task-oriented group.

Other early work showed how a single disruptive person (a schoolroom deviant, an alcoholic, a mental patient) could radically alter the operation of a family or classroom (Gnagey, 1960; Jackson, 1956; Yarrow, Clausen, & Robbins, 1955). More recently, following the cognitive revolution, such individual factors as causal attributions are shown to affect situational perception and interaction. Such studies predominate in the December 1987 issue of *The Journal of Personality and Social Psychology* dedicated to "integrating" the two psychologies, even though as we have noted this substitution of cognitive for personality factors is a principal way experimental social psychology has neglected personality considerations in recent decades. However, in one of the collection's papers, an individual's gender role orientation and level of moral reasoning are shown to relate to the influence exerted by the subject on a group decision-making task (McGraw & Bloomfield, 1987).

But Path C studies from the meso situation to the macro structural level are understandably rare in psychology. This missing link results in an incomplete understanding of the mediated, bottom-up causal path from personality via situations to institutions. The necessity of interdisciplinary cooperation is underscored, for Path C examples are commonplace in sociology and organizational research. Often these studies involve negotiation over the nature of social roles and the informal operations of the social structure. Hence, informal communication and exchange processes at the situational level can create continual modifications in the structure of highly bureaucratized governmental agencies (Blau, 1955). Such negotiation can even occur in "total institutions." Sykes (1958) demonstrated how prisoners, working collectively at the situational level, managed to alter the structure of a maximum security prison. Especially unpopular formal rules went unenforced, and prisoners gained considerable authority over their own lives within the constraints of neither escaping nor rebelling. The mismatching of personality with roles and social structure is not always correctible, of course, and the individual alienation and stress that results from such mismatching constitute "top-down" effects.

IV. SOCIAL STRUCTURE SHAPES PERSONALITY

The most hypothesized and studied links between personality and social structure involve the top-down causal links. Instead of being the initial causal agent, personality factors are now the dependent variables. We have noted that two general paths are possible—the direct, unmediated route (Path F of Figure 1) and the mediated route (Paths D and E) through which structural changes shape personality by first altering the face-to-face human interaction in situations.

A. Direct Effects (Causal Path F)

Mediated causal theories are to be preferred, because their linkage processes between levels are generally far better specified. Direct effect theories, whether Path A or F, generally signal a failure to demonstrate how the causal sequence carries through the face-to-face interaction stage—though this is not to deny the possibility of true direct effects that go unmediated at the situational level. In recognition of this fact, the overwhelming proportion of top-down theories in social science generally, and social psychology in particular, are mediated, Paths D and E contentions.

Why should this trend toward more situational specification be more evident than for bottom-up theories? Two interrelated speculations suggest themselves. First, the fundamental attribution bias—the tendency to magnify the causal power of individuals—operates for social scientists as well as others. Indeed, psychologists may be even more prone to the bias than most human beings. Second, there has been considerably less awareness of and attention to "the compositional fallacy" than to the corresponding "ecological fallacy." The compositional fallacy occurs when the dynamics of groups and collectivities are simply extrapolated from the aggregate of tendencies of individual persons composing the group. Such extrapolation, often seen at its worst when social problems are viewed as mere cumulated extensions of individual tendencies, leads to error because it denies the operation of distinctive group-level processes. In reverse, the ecological fallacy occurs when individual characteristics are simply extrapolated from aggregated data. Psychologists and bottom-up theorists seldom discuss the compositional error. But there is in sociology an extended literature on the ecological fallacy (e.g., Robinson, 1950), and most top-down theorists are keenly aware of it. A major means of avoiding the ecological error is to specify the linkage processes through a mediated model.

At any rate, direct Path F examples are hard to find in the social science literature. Perhaps, for illustrative purposes, two famous studies in political science come closest. Almond and Verba (1965) studied five democratic nations with varying "political cultures." They used survey methods to ascertain each nation's political attitudes; then they compared these data with each nation's political institutions. The most relevant of their contentions concerns their structural explanations for the wide attitudinal differences across the five populations that remain even after such variables as education are controlled. For example, British respondents evinced considerable confidence in both their administrative and their political-legislative officials; Germans particular confidence in administrative officials; Americans in legislative officials; and Italians and Mexicans in neither. Almond and Verba accounted for these aggregated individual differences in terms of the contrasting structural histories across the countries. Thus, Germany had witnessed the establishment of an early and stable bureaucracy, but late and unstable political development. The United States had much the reverse history, with a late developing civil service but an early foundation of its political structure. The United Kingdom was seen as having experienced early development of both institutions, while Italy and Mexico had suffered late development of both.

The work of Gurr (1970) on the important role of relative deprivation in revolution across 119 nations affords a second example of Path F theorizing. Using a popular social psychological concept (Pettigrew, 1978; Walker & Pettigrew, 1984), Gurr assumes in his measurement of relative deprivation an unmediated development of this motivational condition of individuals from particular structural conditions. Hence, he directly infers the relative deprivation of individuals from such aggregated measures as the proportion of the population excluded from valued positions and the increase in migrants to the cities. Then Gurr shows a positive, Path A relation between "relative deprivation" and political unrest. In truth, then, this is a pseudo-demonstration of a personality and structure relationship. By committing the ecological fallacy, Gurr's research operations actually check on relationships between structural variables and simply assumes that relative deprivation is the psychological connection underlying these relationships.

For present purposes, the striking feature of these two studies is their unmediated character. Just how did the differentially rooted administrative and political structures across the five countries shape individual attitudes? Were they reflected in different socialization patterns concerning politics? In different mobilization at the face-to-face level? Or, in Gurr's work, just how does exclusion from valued positions and migration to the city produce relative deprivation? In other words, how did the meso level of situations—the principal level of social psychology—transform the structural differences across nations into attitudinal and motivational differences? Without such mediation, the linkage processes involved remain unspecified, and the theory left open to numerous plausible alternative explanations.

B. Mediated Effects (Causal Paths D and E)

Social psychology's distinctive situational focus causes it to prefer manipulable situational variables (Pettigrew, 1988). This focus is a great advantage when applications are made to practical problems, because it is far easier and more ethical to alter situations than to alter people. For the Path E, top-down approach, the discipline searches for characteristics of situations that shape and elicit specific behavior from individuals. Aronson's jigsaw cooperative learning design for classroom offers a superb example (Aronson, Blaney, Stephan, Sikes, & Snapp, 1978). When pressed for advice in solving practical problems, the field differs from psychology's bottom-up remedies by typically advancing top-down, situation-to-individual recommendations: change the situation (increase choice, cease labeling, allow more participation, etc.) and individual improvements are predicted (improved morale, less sense of being stigmatized, greater involvement, etc.).

   Often the linkage processes invoked to explain these Path E relationships involve role playing or family expectations. Hence, in his famous study of industrial plant foremen and stewards, Lieberman (1950) demonstrated how attitude changes followed role changes. Newly appointed foremen soon became more procompany in their views, while newly appointed stewards soon became more prounion. Within 3 years, the two groups had established almost "diametrically opposed sets of attitudinal positions." And for those foremen and stewards who returned to the production line as regular workers, there was a tendency to revert to earlier held attitudes. The classic example of family process linkage is provided by the "double-bind" theory of the family origins of schizophrenia, in which children find themselves caught in the midst of conflicting parental expectations (Bateson, Jackson, Haley, & Weakland, 1956).

   But, unlike the case with bottom-up causal theories, mediated, Paths D and E, top-down work is plentiful in the contextual social psychology literature. Many of the best exemplars focus on the individual effects of social stratification. The longitudinal research of Sewell and Hauser (1975), for instance, demonstrated the powerful influence of socioeconomic status on educational aspirations and attainments. Mediated through such situational contexts as neighborhoods and schools, the strong effects of social class remain even after measured ability and gender are controlled.

   Three major contextual social psychological projects over the past generation have played a dominant role in defining top-down analyses of structural and cultural shaping of personality. The first of these involve Melvin Kohn and his colleagues. In a notable series of interrelated studies, he has attempted to specify class and personality linkages. He emphasizes the importance of occupational demands mediated by family socialization patterns for shaping self-direction versus conformity. First, Kohn (1969; Pearlin & Kohn, 1966) showed that in both the United States and Italy middle-class parents more often stressed intent and self-direction while lower- and working-class parents more often stressed obedience to external authority.

Next, in studies with Carmi Schooler (Kohn & Schooler, 1969, 1973), self-direction values were shown to be positively associated with occupational position. Those in higher-status positions valued self-direction the most; this trend reflected, Kohn and Schooler (1969) argued, their greater opportunities to exercise occupational self-direction—to use initiative, thought, and independent judgment in their work. Likewise, those in lower-status positions, who largely had to obey others, valued obedience to authority. Hence, the demands of the workplace generalized to the home and the preferred parental means of socializing children. Kohn thus provides an answer to the broad question, How does the social stratification inherent in the structural differentiation of the labor market translate into differential values? The class and value relationship derives, he maintains, from class-associated—particularly occupational—conditions of life: "It is chiefly by shaping the everyday realities people must face that social structure exerts its psychological impact" (Kohn, 1977, p. xlviii).

The second famous project utilizing causal Paths D and E extends this analysis of occupational effects both conceptually and cross-nationally. Alex Inkeles (1960, 1969, 1978; Inkeles & Smith, 1974) argues that industrialization leads to similar forms of social organization across six culturally divergent societies. These "modern" organizations shape face-to-face situations that in time produce similar patterns of "modern" beliefs, perceptions, values, and even thought.

Note that this is strictly a social *structural* theory—not to be confused with such cultural ideas as "the culture of poverty" (Lewis, 1961). That is, both Kohn and Inkeles emphasize the importance of the *patterning* rather then the *content* of modern society. Kerckhoff (1976) contrasts the two types of explanation in terms of *allocation* (indirect transmission through structural constraints and imperatives plus selection criteria) versus *socialization* (direct transmission of learned skills, motives, attitudes, etc.). In our terms, allocation theses lend themselves to top-down analyses, while socialization theses assume bottom-up and top-down forms, though in practice the two approaches are not fully separable—indeed, they are complementary. But the distinction is important for considering the full social context of personality.

Inkeles (1960, 1969, 1978; Inkeles & Smith, 1974) surveyed 6,000 industrial and agricultural male workers in six developing countries—Israel, Argentina, Chile, India, Nigeria, and what is now Bangladesh. Of special interest is his careful specification of the independent variables (the structural positioning of the workers) and the dependent variable (the "individual modernity" personality syndrome). Proving considerably more important than national cultures were the structural components considered together: education, factory experience, mass media exposure, urban residence, possession of consumer goods, and age. A syndrome was predicted across these six nations that deserves attention from personality psychologists. Its seven components are: (1) openness to new experience; (2) assertion of independence from traditional figures to an allegiance to modern leaders; (3) belief in scientific efficacy rather than fatalism; (4) ambitious occupational and educational goals for one's self and children;

(5) concern for punctuality and planning; (6) interest and participation in local politics; and (7) interest in national and international news.

The third of the defining research projects in this area is Morris Rosenberg's (1965, 1979, 1981) ground-breaking work on self-esteem. Not only has this work produced the most useful measure of this elusive phenomenon, but it neatly illustrates the application of directly testable social psychological linkage processes. Rosenberg and Pearlin (1978) considered in detail a finding that both the Kohn and the Inkeles projects had repeatedly uncovered—a strong positive relationship among adults between social class and self-esteem. But this relationship is weak among adolescents and disappears among younger children. Why? These investigators used this finding as an instructive means of formulating and testing four different process possibilities for this structure-to-personality linkage (see also Demo & Savin-Williams, 1983).

(1) Social comparison process. Adults meet a far wider class range of persons than children, and perceive class differences more than children. Moreover, adult perception of class differences accounts for a significant part of the class and self-esteem relationship.

(2) Reflected appraisal process. Likewise, since we see ourselves in part as others see us, the wider class contacts of adults may also shape self-esteem through how others react to us.

(3) Self-perception process. In the manner advanced by Bem (1972), we partly form our self-image by observing our own behavior as others observe it. Rosenberg and Perlin (1978) note that the class standing of children is ascribed while that of adults is more likely to be achieved. Hence, adults are more likely to make inferences concerning their self-worth from their social class standing.

(4) Psychological centrality processes. The more centrally important social class dimensions are, the more they should influence self-esteem. Indeed, for adults who most value money, the income and self-esteem association is strongest. In addition, children often either deny or are confused about their social class position; thus, it is not likely to be central for them.

Another facet of top-down analyses involves historical events. Social change is, of course, just as inevitable and relentless as personal change, so dynamic treatment of social structure becomes essential. But when historical events are involved, macro-level causes are often difficult to untangle. Three overlapping possibilities arise: generation, life-cycle, and cohort effects. For example, the Smelsers (1981) point out how all three interpretations can account for the finding that a young cohort changed its political attitudes extensively over an 8-year period toward those of the parental generation (Jennings & Niemi, 1975). Was this because their youthful rebelliousness receded (a generation effect), because of their passage from adolescence to young adulthood (a life-cycle effect), and/or because of their special experience with a particular historical event or situation (a cohort effect)? Longitudinal data are obviously necessary, but even then the decomposition can be difficult.

Elder's (1974) study of the effects of the Great Depression presents a model for a Paths D and E, cohort study using historical events as the macro causes. From longitudinal data on 167 families followed from 1932 to 1964, Elder looked at the effects of unemployment and economic deprivation on family structure and interaction at the meso-situational level and personality at the micro level. The Depression led to economic loss that generated severe social strains and altered family life through changes in marital relations, parent–child relations, and the division of labor. Traditional attitudes about gender roles were reinforced, for example, by the need for girls to take disproportionately more responsibility for home duties and for boys to earn outside income. Taking early jobs for the boys meant "an accelerated movement toward the adult world." At the personality level, these changes led to a lasting enhanced need for stability and security among this cohort of children. These effects were greater for those families whose income loss during the Depression was especially profound.

V. PERSONALITY AND SOCIAL STRUCTURE SHAPE TOGETHER

For heuristic purposes, we have discussed the causal paths of multilevel analyses as if only simple main effects applied. In reality, of course, social causation is far more complex. Indeed, multilevel additive, multiplicative, and interactive effects provide many of the most intriguing and theoretically suggestive findings in the personality and social structure domain.

Consider Parker and Kleiner's (1964) penetrating study of the mental health of blacks in Philadelphia. They found that social mobility, either upward or downward, when combined with high levels of personal goal striving was associated with both mental illness and either ambivalent or weak racial identity. Similarly, Cohn (1978) has shown that unemployment, when combined with a strong sense of internal locus of control, can lead to severe dissatisfaction with oneself.

Such mutual shaping underscores once again the fundamental tenet of social psychology: ". . . if men define situations as real, they are real in their consequences" (Thomas & Thomas, 1928, p. 567). Culture and social structure impinge on individuals through their subjective interpretation. A major social psychological contribution to this area is its insistence that the linkages between personality and social structure must involve processes that include the individual's perceptions of the social environment.

VI. ADVANTAGES OF THE PERSONALITY AND SOCIAL STRUCTURE PERSPECTIVE

Ryff (1987) provides a succinct discussion of five interrelated advantages of the personality and social structure perspective for personality and social psychology. First, neither personality nor social psychology has probed deeply into the generalization of its theories, findings, or assumptions. Is it really part of the human condition, for example, for peoples everywhere to operate with a "just-world hypothesis"? Or is this just an assumption of Westerners? The personality and social structure perspective provides a theoretical and empirical entry into such questions.

Likewise, the influence of normative culture can be approached through this tradition. What do subjects bring to the personality inventory or the laboratory? Ryff (1987) points out, for instance, that the fundamental attribution bias may not be as "fundamental" as we think in cultures, such as India's, where individuals are viewed more holistically as part of their social context.

A third advantage concerns broad description as opposed to process explanation. The study of personality and social structure has focused on description—with such outstanding exceptions as the Rosenberg and Pearlin (1978) work discussed previously. By contrast, both personality and social psychology have stressed process. Here, argues Ryff (1987) convincingly, the fields can mutually enrich each other. Attribution and self-discrepancy theories, for example, both focus on process. But what is the prevalence and distribution in the general population of particular attributional styles and discrepancy types?

A fourth advantage to be gained by exploiting the personality and social structure perspective has been emphasized throughout this discussion. Only a multilevel approach can provide an explicit specification of the social context for personality. And such a context is essential for utilizing the fifth advantage. Since persons, situations, and societies are all changing continuously, we need broad, multilevel models to attempt to capture the dynamics of change. Rather than regard such efforts as virtually hopeless (e.g., Gergen, 1973), the personality and social structure perspective provides a promising approach for coming to grips with this challenge.

REFERENCES

Adorno, T., Frenkel-Brunswik, E., Levinson, D. J., & Sanford, R. N. (1950). *The authoritarian personality.* New York: Harper.

Allport, G. W. (1968). The historical background of modern social psychology. In G. Lindzey & E. Aronson (Eds.), *The handbook of social psychology* (Vol. 1, pp. 1–80). New York: Random House.

Almond, G. A., & Verba, S. (1965). *The civic culture.* Boston: Little, Brown.

Aronson, E., Blaney, N., Stephan, C., Sikes, J., & Snapp, M. (1978). *The jigsaw classroom.* Beverly Hills, CA: Sage.

Asch, S. (1956). Studies of independence and conformity: A minority of one against a unanimous majority. *Psychological monographs, 70*(9, Whole No. 416).

Atkinson, J. W., & Hoselitz, B. F. (1958). Entrepreneurship and personality. *Explorations in Entrepreneurial History, 10,* 107–112.

Bales, R. F. (1970). *Personality and interpersonal behavior.* New York: Holt, Rinehart & Winston.

Bateson, G., Jackson, D. D., Haley, J., & Weakland, J. (1956). Toward a theory of schizophrenia. *Behavioral Science, 1,* 251–264.

Bem, D. J. (1972). Self-perception theory. In L. Berkowitz (Ed.), *Advances in experimental social psychology* (Vol. 6, pp. 1–62). New York: Academic Press.

Blau, P. (1955). *The dynamics of bureaucracy.* Chicago: University of Chicago Press.

Blumer, H. (1969). *Symbolic interactionism: Perspective and method.* Englewood Cliffs, NJ: Prentice-Hall.

Borgatta, E. F., Bales, R. F., & Couch, A. S. (1954). Some findings relevant to the great man theory of leadership. *American Sociological Review, 19,* 755–759.

Cantril, H. (1965). *The pattern of human concerns.* New Brunswick, NJ: Rutgers University Press.

Cohn, R. M. (1978). The effect of employment status change on self-attitudes. *Social Psychology, 41,* 81–93.

Demo, D. H., & Savin-Williams, R. C. (1983). Early adolescent self-esteem as a function of social class: Rosenberg and Pearlin revisited. *American journal of Sociology, 88,* 763–774.

DiRenzo, G. J. (1977). Socialization, personality, and social systems. *Annual Review of Sociology, 3,* 261–95.

Durkheim, E. (1951). *Suicide* (J. A. Spaulding & G. Simpson, Trans.). New York: Free Press.

Elder, G. (1973). On linking social structure and personality. *American Behavioral Science, 16,* 785–800.

Elder, G. (1974). *Children of the great depression.* Chicago: University of Chicago Press.

Epstein, S. (1979). The stability of behavior: I. On predicting most of the people much of the time. *Journal of Personality and Social Psychology, 37,* 1097–1126.

Erikson, E. H. (1958). *Young man Luther.* New York: Norton.

Erikson, E. H. (1969). *Gandhi's truth.* New York: Norton.

Freud, S. (1930). *Civilization and its discontents.* New York: Macmillan.

Gergen, K. (1973). Social psychology as history. *Journal of Personality and Social Psychology, 26,* 309–320.

Gluckstern, N. B., & Packard, R. W. (1977). The internal-external change agent team: Bringing change to a "closed institution." *Journal of Applied Behavioral Science, 13,* 41–52.

Gnagey, W. J. (1960). Effects on classmates of a deviant student's power and response to a teacher-exerted control technique. *Journal of Educational Psychology, 51,* 1–8.

Gorer, G. (1943). Themes in Japanese culture. *Annals of the New York Academy of Sciences, 5,* 106–124.

Gurr, T. R. (1970). *Why men rebel.* Princeton, NJ: Princeton University Press.

Handel, W. (1982). *Ethnomethodology: How people make sense.* Englewood Cliffs, NJ: Prentice-Hall.

Hartshorne, H., & May, M. A. (1928). *Studies in the nature of character.* New York: Macmillan.

House, J. S. (1982). Social structure and personality. In M. Rosenberg & R. Turner (Eds.), *Social psychology: Sociological perspectives* (pp. 525–561). New York: Basic Books.

Inkeles, A. (1960). Industrial man: The relations of status to experience, perception, and value. *American Journal of Sociology, 66,* 1–31.

Inkeles, A. (1969). Making men modern. On the causes and consequences of individual change in six developing countries. *American Journal of Sociology, 75,* 208–225.

Inkeles, A. (1978). National differences in individual modernity. *Comparative Studies in Sociology, 1,* 47–72.

Inkeles, A., & Levinson, D. (1954). National character: The study of modal personality and social systems. In G. Lindzey (Ed.), *Handbook of social psychology* (Vol. 2, pp. 975–1020). Cambridge, MA: Addison-Wesley.

Inkeles, A., & Levinson, D. (1968). National character: The study of modal personality and sociocultural systems. In G. Lindzey & E. Aronson (Eds.), *Handbook of social psychology* (Vol. 4, pp. 418–506). Reading, MA: Addison-Wesley.

Inkeles, A., & Smith, D. (1974). *Becoming modern: Individual change in six developing countries.* Cambridge, MA: Harvard University Press.

Jackson, J. K. (1956). The adjustment of the family to alcoholism. *Marriage and Family Living, 18,* 361–369.

Jennings, M., & Niemi, R. (1975). Continuity and change in political orientations: A longitudinal study of two generations. *American Political Science Review, 60,* 1316–1335.

Jones, E. E. (1985). Major developments in social psychology during the past five decades. In G. Lindzey & E. Aronson (Eds.), *Handbook of social psychology* (Vol. 1, pp. 47–108). New York: Random House.

Kardiner, A. (1945). *The psychological frontiers of society.* New York: Columbia University Press.

Kerckhoff, A. C. (1976). The status attainment process: Socialization or allocation? *Social Forces, 55,* 368–381.

Kohn, M. L. (1969). *Class and conformity: A study in values.* Homewood, IL: Dorsey.

Kohn, M. L. (Ed.) (1977). Reassessment, 1977. In *Class and conformity* (2nd ed.). Chicago: University of Chicago Press.

Kohn, M. L., & Schooler, C. (1969). Class, occupation and orientation. *American Sociological Review, 34,* 659–678.

Kohn, M. L., & Schooler, C. (1973). Occupational experience and psychological funtioning: An assessment of reciprocal effects. *American Sociological Review, 38,* 97–118.

Kovel, J. (1970). *White racism: A psychohistory.* New York: Pantheon.

Le Bon, G. (1897). *The crowd.* London: Unwin.

Lewis, O. (1961). *The children of Sanchez.* New York: Random House.

Lieberman, S. (1950). The effects of changes in roles on the attitudes of role occupants. *Human Relations, 9,* 385–403.

Lindzey, G., & Aronson, E. (Eds.). (1985). *Handbook of social psychology* (Vols. 1 and 2). New York: Random House.

Marx, K. (1964). Economic and philosophical manuscripts. In T. B. Bottomore (Ed. 2nd Trans.), *Early writings* (pp. 63–219). New York: McGraw-Hill.

McClelland, D. C. (Ed.). (1955). *Studies in motivation.* New York: Appleton-Century-Crofts.

McClelland, D. C. (1961). *The achieving society.* Princeton, NJ: Van Nostrand.

McGraw, K. M., & Bloomfield, J. (1987). Social influence on group moral decisions: The interactive effects of moral reasoning and sex role orientation. *Journal of Personality and Social Psychology, 53,* 1080–1087.

Mcguire, W. J. (1985). Attitudes and attitude change. In G. Lindzey & E. Aronson (Eds.), *Handbook of social psychology* (Vol. 2, pp. 233–346). New York: Random House.

Mead, M. (1935). *Sex and temperament in three primitive societies.* New York: Morrow.

Milgram, S. (1974). *Obedience to authority: An experimental view.* New York: Harper & Row.

Mischel, W. (1968). *Personality and assessment.* New York: Wiley.

Parker, S., & Kleiner, R. J. (1964). *Mental illness in the urban Negro community.* New York: Free Press.

Pearlin, L. I., & Kohn, M. L. (1966). Social class, occupation and parental values. *American Sociological Review, 31,* 466–479.

Pettigrew, T. F. (1978). Three issues in ethnicity: Boundaries, deprivations, and perceptions. In J. M. Yinger & S. J. Cutler (Eds.), *Major social issues: A multi-disciplinary view* (pp. 25–49). New York: Free Press.

Pettigrew, T. F. (1980). Social psychology's potential contributions to an understanding of poverty. In V. T. Covello (Ed.), *Poverty and public policy: An evaluation of social science research* (pp. 189–233). Boston: Hall.

Pettigrew, T. F. (1988). Influencing policy with social psychology. *Journal of Social Issues, 44*(2), 205–219.

Robinson, W. S. (1950). Ecological correlations and the behavior of individuals. *American Sociological Review, 15,* 351–357.

Rosenberg, M. (1965). *Society and the adolescent self-image.* Princeton, NJ: Princeton University Press.

Rosenberg, M. (1979). *Conceiving the self.* New York: Basic Books.

Rosenberg, M. (1981). Self-concept: Social product and social force. In M. Rosenberg & R. Turner (Eds.), *Social psychology: Sociological perspectives* (pp. 591–624). New York: Basic Books.

Rosenberg, M., & Pearlin, L. I. (1978). Social class and self-esteem among children and adults. *American Journal of Sociology, 84,* 53–77.

Rosenberg, M., & Turner, R. (Eds.) (1981). *Social psychology: Sociological perspectives.* New York: Basic Books.

Ross, L. (1977). The intuitive psychologist and his short-comings. In L. Berkowitz (Ed.), *Advances in experimental social psychology* (Vol. 10, pp. 173–220). New York: Academic Press.

Rotter, J. (1966). Generalized expectancies for internal vs. external control of reinforcement. *Psychological Monographs, 80*(1, Whole No. 609).

Ryff, C. D. (1987). The place of personality and social structure research in social psychology. *Journal of Personality and Social Psychology, 53,* 1192–1202.

Sewell, W. H., & Hauser, R. M. (1975). *Education, Occupation, and Earnings: Achievement in the Early Career.* New York: Academic Press.

Simmel, G. (1955). *Conflict and the web of group affiliations* (K. H. Wolff & R. Bendix, Trans.). New York: Free Press.

Smelser, N. J., & Smelser, W. T. (Eds.). (1963). *Personality and social systems.* New York: Wiley.

Smelser, N. J., & Smelser, W. T. (1981). Group movements, sociocultural change, and personality. In M. Rosenberg & R. Turner (Eds.), *Social psychology: Sociological perspectives* (pp. 625–652). New York: Basic Books.

Snyder, M., & Ickes, W. (1985). Personality and social behavior. In G. Lindzey & E. Aronson (Eds.), *Handbook of social psychology* (Vol. 2, pp. 883–948). New York: Random House.

Sykes, G. (1958). *The society of captives.* Princeton, NJ: Princeton University Press.

Tajfel, H. (1970). Experiments in intergroup discrimination. *Scientific American, 223*(5), 96–102.

Thomas, W. I., & Thomas, D. S. (1928). *The child in America.* New York: Knopf.

Tocqueville, A. de (1945). [1840] *Democracy in America* (Vols. 1 and 2). New York: Vintage.

Walker, I., & Pettigrew, T. F. (1984). Relative deprivation theory: An overview and conceptual critique. *British Journal of Social Psychology, 23,* 301–310.

Weber, M. (1930). *The Protestant ethic and the spirit of capitalism* (T. Parsons, Trans.). New York: Scribner.

Weber, M. (1968). *Economy and society: An outline of interpretive sociology.* (G. Roth & C. Wittich, Trans.). Berkeley: University of California Press.

Whiting, J. W. M., & Child, T. L. (1953). *Child training and personality: A cross-cultural study.* New Haven, CT: Yale University Press.

Yarrow, M. R., Clausen, J. A., & Robbins, P. R. (1955). The social meaning of mental illness. *Journal of Social Issues, 11*(4), 33–48.

Zimbardo, P. (1970). The human choice: Individuation, reason, and order versus deindividuation, impulse, and chaos. In W. J. Arnold & D. Levine (Eds.), *Nebraska Symposium on Motivation* (Vol. 17, pp. 237–307). Lincoln: University of Nebraska Press.

CHAPTER 18

CROSS-CULTURAL PERSPECTIVES ON PERSONALITY

HARRY C. TRIANDIS

UNIVERSITY OF ILLINOIS AT CHAMPAIGN-URBANA

The subfield of culture and personality is the oldest of cross-cultural psychology. Bruner (1974) assessed it as a "magnificent failure," based on the observation that cultural antecedents of personality attributes change meaning depending on the context in which they occur. Klineberg (1980) chastised those who wrote about "national character" without taking seriously Linton's (1945) distinction between *universals,* which apply to all adult members of a society; *specialties,* found in certain roles (e.g., priest, warrior, male); *alternatives,* behaviors among which one can choose; and *variants,* found only in certain relatively rare individuals.

Many writers (e.g., Klineberg, 1954; Mead, 1953) prescribed how culture and personality studies should be done, but almost no one has followed these prescriptions, because they are too demanding. Klineberg, for instance, suggested that it was necessary to first study the general pattern of a culture and determine the distribution of key charactersitics of the population based on a multimethod approach (experiments, biographies, opinion surveys, tests, etc). We may have an approximation of this approach if we synthesize studies done in Japan (Hayashi, 1992; Stoetzel, 1955), but there are no other examples of this very expensive strategy.

Jahoda (1980) criticized many attempts in this area (e.g., Berry, 1976; Cole, 1975; LeVine, 1973) because they did not provide clear definitions and operationalizations of culture. He saw little chance to develop this field without a proper definition of culture. He urged the development of a theory of culture that is tailor-made for psychologically oriented cross-cultural work. Triandis (1994) has provided such a theory, but it has yet to be evaluated in the literature.

Inkeles and Levinson (1969) examined national character by using the construct of a "modal personality." The operationalization of this construct is also very demanding, since any society is likely to be multimodal and the determination of the distributions of traits in a culture is likely to be very expensive.

Tapp (1981) has provided a review of the major reviews of the field, such as the work of Kluckhohn and Murray (1948), Inkeles and Levinson (1954, 1969), Hsu (1972), Kaplan (1961), Child (1968), and DeVos and Hippler (1969), but found little convergence in methodology or findings.

Draguns (1979, 1990) has suggested that the strategy should consist of an examination of dimensions of personality across cultures. This is the strategy that will be described in this chapter.

The chapter will discuss (a) dimensions of cultural variation, (b) dimensions of social behavior, and (c) dimensions of personality variation, and suggest how the three sets of dimensions can be placed into an integrated theoretical framework. But first, some preliminary major differences of opinion among specialists in this field must be considered, and some methodological issues must be mentioned.

I. PRELIMINARY CONSIDERATIONS

A. Do Personality Dimensions Maintain More or Less the Same Meaning across Cultures or Do They Change Their Meaning in Every Cultural Context?

This is an important difference of opinion that cannot be ignored. Anthropologists (e.g., Shweder & LeVine, 1984; Stigler, Shweder, & Herdt, 1990), with their interest in seeing the world the way "the natives" see it (Malinowski, 1944), take the view that the construct of personality changes meaning in each cultural context. Behavior is a consequence of the specific meaning that the situation has for each individual, this meaning is culturally determined, and thus a "cultural psychology" (Shweder & Sullivan, 1990) requires the examination of the "semiotic subject" that does not have traits, mental states, or psychological processes that are independent of culture.

This is the "relativist" position (Berry, Poortinga, Segall, & Dasen, 1992). It contrasts with the "absolutist" position that assumes that traits and psychological processes are universal and unaffected by culture. An example of that position is the work of Eysenck and Eysenck (1983), who measure traits across the world with relatively little concern about the equivalence of what they measure. Critics (Bijnen, Van der Net, & Poortinga, 1986) have argued that this work is indefensible.

Cross-cultural psychologists (e.g., Berry et al., 1992; Pepitone & Triandis, 1987) take an intermediate position, rejecting both relativism and absolutism. First, they distinguish emic and etic elements of any construct. The emic are culture specific; the etic are universal. For example, the trait "self-reliance" has some common meaning across cultures. What is common in these meanings across cultures is etic. But self-reliance has somewhat different goals in collectivist cultures (e.g., traditional) than in individualistic cultures (e.g., the West). In collectivist cultures it often takes the form "I am self-reliant so I will not burden my group." In individualist cultures it takes the form "I am self-reliant so I can have fun and do my own thing." Clearly, the meaning is different across cultures; thus our task is to measure both the etic and the emic aspects of the construct.

Culture-free measurement is very difficult, but cross-cultural psychologists have developed methodological strategies that they believe can deal with the influence of culture. Specifically, they emphasize separate construct validations in each culture, emic measurement of etic constructs, multimethod measurement, and the control of rival hypotheses (see Triandis, 1992, 1994, for details).

If the building blocks of personality are trait descriptions, we need to recognize that such descriptions depend on categorization, that is, treating discriminably different entities as the same. While all cultures use categories (Triandis, 1964), the entities that are grouped and considered "the same" for the purpose of categorization are not the same. For example, "yellow" does not include the identical chips from the Munzel charts in every culture. We need methods that will take that fact into account. Such methods have been available for some time (e.g., Triandis, Davis, & Takezawa, 1965), but are time-consuming, and hence unpopular.

B. Is the Variance of Traits Similar across Cultures?

If we measure an important trait in culture A that has essentially no variance in culture B, it would be very difficult to compare the two cultures, beyond saying that culture B does not seem to have the trait. Ethnocentrism is an important aspect of the human condition (Triandis, 1994), because we all start life by knowing only our own culture, and even when we learn about other cultures we tend to incorporate the new information into the framework that our own culture has created. Other cultures "make sense" only in relation to our own. Thus, in this situation we are likely to use the following logic: "The trait is important in my culture. I do not detect it in that other culture. It must be that my measurements are inadequate. Therefore, it is a universal trait, that is poorly measured in culture B." But is it really a universal trait?

This issue becomes salient in discussions of cultures where behavior follows a script so that one cannot see many individual differences. Geertz (1983), for instance, paints such a picture of social behavior in Bali. While this position is probably extreme, since actors in our theaters who follow a script still show some variations in behavior, and even insects are genetically extremely variable (Jeanne, 1988) it is a view that cannot be ignored. A related issue is that the within-culture variance may be much larger than the between-cultures variance (Minturn & Lambert, 1964), in which case the association of culture with personality becomes extremely hazardous.

C. Are the Correlations among Traits the Same or Different across Cultures?

This issue links with the viewpoint that we ought to develop "indigenous psychologies" (Heelas & Lock, 1981; Kim & Berry, 1993). One can visualize a table in which each psychological phenomenon has a row, and each culture a column (Kim & Berry, 1993, p. 279). As we synthesize the information on each row, the common elements are the etics of the phenomenon. What is different in each cell of that row from the etics of the phenomenon provides the emics of the phenomenon. As we synthesize each column we identify the indigenous theory of personality that summarizes how the various phenomena occur in one culture. For example, particular correlations among variables may have unique values in one culture. Finally, as we integrate across both rows and columns we arrive at a universal psychology, of which the indigenous psychologies are special cases. The important thing to remember here is that current psychology is one of the indigenous psychologies—the one from the West.

D. Rival Hypotheses

It is easy to assume that a difference that has been observed between two or more cultures is in fact due to "culture." Before making such an assumption one must check rival hypotheses. A mundane one is that people have reacted to the measurements differently. This is why multimethod measurement is so important. Only if different kinds of measurements detect the same difference, and we have controlled for response sets (Hui & Triandis, 1989; Triandis, 1972), can we be reasonably sure that we have detected a difference.

It is also possible that the difference is due to some demographic attribute that happens to be correlated with culture, such as differences in social class, age, sex, religion, occupation, education, and so forth. Social class is especially important. Researchers have often assumed that differences in prejudice were due to race or that differences in child-rearing patterns were due to nationality, when in fact they were differences due to social class (W. E. Lambert, 1992; W. E. Lambert, Hamers, & Frasure-Smith, 1979; Triandis & Triandis, 1960, 1962). Only after checks have been made that Linton's "specialties" do not explain the obtained differences can we be relatively sure that we have observed a cultural difference.

We turn now to an examination of different kinds of cultural, behavioral, and personality variations.

II. DIMENSIONS OF CULTURAL VARIATION

A psychological, metaphorical definition of "culture" is that it is to society what memory is to individuals (Kluckhohn, 1954). It includes what "has worked" in the past and can be identified by examining the extent to which psychological processes, such as beliefs, attitudes, and values, are shared and transmitted from one generation to the next. Historical analysis is also likely to show that the shared patterns were adaptive at some point in the history of the society.

This definition, however, is too abstract. One way to make it more useful is to consider "cultural syndromes"—shared sets of beliefs, attitudes, norms, values, and behavior organized around a central theme and found among speakers of one language, in one time period, and in one geographic region.

In specific geographic/language regions one can observe shared human-made attributes, such as tools, laws, norms, values, perspectives, information processing strategies, and other elements of subjective culture. Subjective culture (Triandis, 1972) is a cultural group's characteristic way of perceiving the human-made part of the environment. It consists of the categories used to cut the pie of experience, the associations among these categories, the norms of social behavior, the roles, and the values of the cultural group. Language, of course, is intimately linked to subjective culture.

Each of the elements of subjective culture can be measured and tested to determine if the within-culture variance is smaller than the between-cultures variance, in which case it is useful to use that element in the description of the specific culture. Such studies, ideally, should use half a dozen widely dispersed cultures to estimate the between cultures variance.

The elements of subjective culture are not randomly distributed. On the contrary, they are organized around central themes of great importance to the culture. It is these organizations of elements of subjective culture that we call "cultural syndromes."

In any culture there are diverse, often contradictory elements of subjective culture and cultural syndromes that can be sampled by any individual. Sampling can reflect both genetic predispositions and experiential factors. People place themselves in situations where they can obtain the most rewards (e.g., resources), consistent with their biologically determined needs and learned situation–behavior sequences. Behaviors with rewarding consequences increase in frequency.

Culture then can be conceptualized as providing a "tool kit" of habits, skills, styles, perspectives, norms, roles, and values out of which each individual can *construct* a potentially unique strategy for action. This strategy will depend on the way the situation is perceived by the individual.

More generally, culture can be conceived in numerous ways: (a) as a set of schedules of reinforcement (Skinner, 1981), (b) as knowing the "rules of the game" (Goodenough, 1981), (c) as a system of symbols through which people experience and express meaning (Keesing, 1981), and (d) as a strategy for adapting to an environment. People can potentially construct an infinitely large set of idiosyncratic patterns of action. However, since people share features of the ecology in which they live, some of these strategies of action are similar. For example, one can identify *cultural scripts,* that is, patterns of social interaction that are characteristic of a particular cultural group (Triandis, Marin, Lisansky, & Betancourt, 1984).

Thus the way to proceed in this area is to identify particular features of the ecology that result in particular cultural scripts and syndromes, and show how these features are likely to increase the frequency of specific behaviors. The implications of this perspective are clear: There is no one-to-one correspondence between culture and personality. There are only probabilistic links, where the cultural syndrome increases the probability that it will be sampled, and behaviors consistent with it might be observed among significant segments of the population of a society.

We will discuss three interrelated cultural syndromes: *complexity, tightness,* and *individualism–collectivism. Complexity* contrasts the modern, industrial, affluent cultures with the simpler cultures, such as the hunters and gatherers, or the residents of a monastery.

Tightness (Pelto, 1968) contrasts cultures where norms are imposed very tightly, allowing very little deviation from "proper" behavior, with cultures that allow considerable deviation from norms. Triandis (1994) has suggested that tight cultures are more homogeneous (in order to impose a norm, members of the culture must agree on what is proper behavior) and are likely to have a high population density (it is more functional to have norms when there is high density; in low-density environments such as in the open frontier, the desert, or the Arctic, loose imposition of norms is widely accepted). It is also likely that people who have interdependent jobs will insist that others behave as expected, and thus be "tight."

Individualism is a cultural syndrome whose elements are organized around autonomous individuals, and is maximal in environments that are complex and loose. *Collectivism* is a syndrome in which the elements are organized around one or more collectives and is maximal in environments that are simple and tight.

In collectivist cultures people define themselves as members of collectives; when there is a conflict between the goals of the collective and the individual the goals of the collective are considered "obviously" as the ones that have priority. In individualism, on the other hand, the goals of the individual have priority in such cases (Triandis, 1990, 1994).

Research (Hofstede, 1980; Triandis, 1990; Triandis et al., 1986; Triandis, Bontempo, Villareal, Asai, & Lucca, 1988; Triandis, McCusker, & Hui, 1990) suggests that collectivism is especially high in traditional societies and in East Asia, and is high in most of the cultures of Africa, Asia, Latin America, and the Pacific Islands. Individualism is especially high in North America north of the Rio Grande, in North and West Europe, and Australia-New Zealand. Moderate levels of individualism can be found in the remaining parts of Europe, but collectivism can be found in parts of Eastern Europe and in Souther Italy and rural Greece. In addition to ecological–environmental factors, a number of other factors are likely to affect collectivism–individualism: gender, age, education, affluence, and so forth.

These syndromes are related to personality. Cultural complexity corresponds to cognitive complexity; cultural tightness corresponds to conscientiousness and intolerance for ambiguity, as well as to the use of narrow categories in thinking about events; individualism corresponds to idiocentrism.

Consider the cultural and cognitive complexity correspondence. Cognitive complexity can be measured in a number of different ways (Witkin & Berry, 1975). Specifically, field-independent people, placed on a tilted chair, who are asked to adjust lines so that they are parallel to the sides of the room, are not influenced by the tilted chair as much as people who are field-dependent; that is, their judgments are relatively independent of the frame (the tilted chair). Thus they are more complex. Similarly, field-independent people can pick out a figure in a complex pattern quickly and reliably, while people who are field-dependent have trouble doing this task (Witkin & Berry, 1975). Field-independent people are good when making spatial judgments, so they can be good mechanics, architects, and so forth. Field-dependent people are interpersonally sensitive, so they are good at occupations requiring good human relationships.

The field-dependent cognitive style is more likely to emerge in agricultural societies (Berry, 1976), where people have to learn to cooperate and to obey authorities that organize the work (e.g., digging ditches for irrigation). For that reason child rearing emphasizes obedience. The field-dependent style characterizes people who pay a lot of attention to the context of conversations, that is, the frame, and for that reason they can intuitively figure out what other people are feeling.

Similarly Kohn (1969, 1987) found that the upper classes in modern societies value self-reliance, creativity, and independence, while the lower classes value obedience, reliability, and conformity. It is clear that it is functional for a person to be creative in upper-class occupations and conforming in lower-class occupations. Similarly, it is functional to be obedient when a society needs to perform many coordinated tasks, but it is functional to be creative when working alone or doing intellectual tasks of the kind rewarded in an information society.

In sum, while there is too little research on this point to be sure, it is likely that corresponding to cultural complexity there is a *personality* dimension of cognitive complexity. Cognitively complex individuals tend to use many dimensions for the judging of events, they make finer discriminations along these dimensions, and they integrate the dimensions into meaningful conceptual wholes (Harvey, Hunt, & Schroeder, 1961). However, within cultures there is likely to be much variation on this personality type, so we do not expect particular cultures as a whole to be high or low on this dimension.

I know of no reliable research linking cultural tightness to *conscientiousness,* though observations of tight cultures suggest that there may be such a link. Corresponding to tightness is also *low tolerance for ambiguity* (Budner, 1962; Draguns, 1990). High tolerance for ambiguity corresponds to looseness.

A related personality variable is narrow versus wide categorization. Detweiler (1980) has found that narrow categorizers (Pettigrew, 1959) adjust to other cultures with greater difficulty than do wide categorizers. A test item such as that used in Figure 1 can measure this attribute. The more check marks on the 24 figures of this item the wider is the category width used by the individual. People from tight cultures have more difficulty adjusting to other cultures, since they insist that the behavior of other people should be just as they expect it. High tolerance for ambigu-

Suppose this figure is a ZUPF.

Place a check in all the figures below that you consider to be ZUPFS.

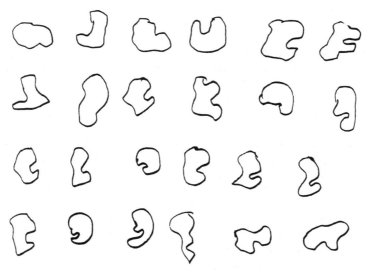

Figure 1   Example of the kind of item used in a test of category width.

ity is a great advantage in cross-cultural adaptation, and the avoidance of culture shock.

Corresponding to individualism is the personality pattern called idiocentrism. Corresponding to collectivism is the personality pattern called allocentrism (Triandis et al., 1985). Idiocentrics see themselves as independent of groups. Allocentrics see themselves as parts of groups. When personal goals and group goals are in conflict, idiocentrics are likely to direct their energies toward personal goals, and allocentrics toward group goals. Allocentrics feel interdependent with others (Markus & Kitayama, 1991), emphasize relationships, and behave according to their duty. Idiocentrics feel independent of others, emphasize personal attributes, and behave so as to maximize pleasure. Numerous hypotheses on these patterns have been proposed (Triandis, 1990, 1994) and some have been tested (Triandis et al., 1986; Triandis, Bontempo et al., 1988; Triandis, McCusker, & Hui, 1990).

Attitudes, norms, and values among allocentrics reflect interdependence, including ingroup security, obedience, duty, ingroup harmony, concern for virtuous action as defined by the ingroup, and persistence to achieve ingroup goals (Triandis, Bontempo, Leung, & Hui, 1990). Attitudes, norms, and values among idiocentrics reflect independence, emotional detachment from ingroups, pleasure, achievement, competition, freedom to do own thing, autonomy, fair exchange, concern for "the truth," and action consistent with principles.

The greatest calamity for allocentrics is to be excluded or rejected from the group; the greatest calamity for idiocentrics is to become dependent on the group.

Allocentrics have few ingroups, but very close relationships with them. Idiocentrics have many ingroups and loose, emotionally noninvolving relationships with them. Ingroups are perceived as more homogeneous than outgroups by allocentrics and more heterogeneous than outgroups by idiocentrics. Conflict with outgroups is expected by allocentrics, and accepted but not desired by idiocentrics. Allocentrics prefer social behaviors that are submerged in large groups (where individual behavior is unnoticed), while idiocentrics prefer social behaviors on a one-on-one basis (the cocktail party is a Western invention). For example, Korean skiers are more likely to ski in groups, and American skiers to ski alone (Brandt, 1974).

The most important relationships for allocentrics are vertical (e.g., mother–son), and for idiocentrics horizontal (e.g., spouse–spouse). Even horizontal relationships are "converted" into vertical relationships in collectivist cultures (e.g., in India, the friend who is one day older is supposed to receive more respect from the "younger" friend than the other way around), and vertical relationships are converted into horizontal relationships in individualistic cultures (e.g., the student calling the professor by a first name). Allocentrics are comfortable with asymmetric status relationships, while idiocentrics are uncomfortable.

The evidence concerning the relevance of this syndrome for cognition, emotion, and motivation was very well reviewed by Markus and Kitayama (1991). The relevance of this syndrome for social behavior in situations where collectivists interact with individualists has been presented by Triandis, Brislin, and Hui (1988).

Child-rearing patterns can be conceptualized as differing along the two important dimensions (Adampoulos & Bontempo, 1984) shown in Figure 2: Acceptance versus Rejection and Dependence versus Independence. High and low values on each dimension result in four kinds of child-rearing patterns. Collectivists are especially concerned with conformity to ingroup norms, so they generally

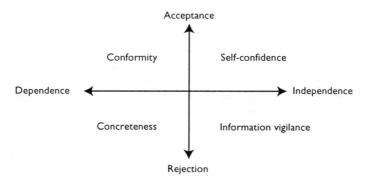

FIGURE 2   Socialization patterns and behavioral outcomes (Adamopoulos & Bontempo, 1984).

use acceptance and foster dependence. Individualists are especially concerned with self-reliance and self-confidence, so they generally use acceptance and foster independence.

Collectivism and individualism may be distinguished into vertical and horizontal types, thus obtaining a 2 by 2 typology. This typology can be linked to Fiske's (1990, 1992) definition of four etic patterns of social behavior that acquire an emic character in each culture. Fiske's four patterns are:

1. Communal sharing (CS), where if one belongs to a group one is entitled to a share of most resources of that group. It is the pattern of behavior most frequently found in families around the world.

2. Authority ranking (AR), where status determines how resources are to be distributed. Those with most status get a disproportional share of the group's resources. Inequality is expected. Rank has its privileges.

3. Equality matching (EM), where each person is entitled to an equal share of whatever is to be distributed. If one person goes through the door first, then the other must go through the door first next time, and so on.

4. Market pricing (MP), where each person obtains resources in proportion to own contributions. The more you give the more you get. If you invest a lot your interest is high.

Vertical collectivism (CV) corresponds to CS and AR, and horizontal collectivism (HC) to CS and EM. Vertical individualism (VI) corresponds to MP and AR, and horizontal individualism (HI) to MP and EM. Triandis (1995) argues that all four types can be found in all cultures, but will have distinct distributions. For example, one culture may be 80% VC, 10% HC, 3% VI, and 7% HI, while another might be 5% VC, 15% HC, 45% VI, and 35% HI. If we take the modal pattern into account, we may call a culture by that pattern, but this will be an obvious oversimplication. In any case, he has reviewed ethnographic and other work suggesting that vertical collectivism is widely found in India and many traditional societies. Horizontal collectivism is frequently found in the Israeli kibbutz. Vertical individualism is widely found in the United States, France, and many of the Central European countries. Horizontal individualism is modal in Scandinavia and Australia.

There is much within-culture variation on idiocentrism–allocentrism. There are idiocentrics in collectivist cultures (e.g., many graduate students who return from the United States to their collectivist cultures have trouble adjusting to their home cultures because they have become idiocentrics in the United States). Similarly, there are allocentrics in individualist cultures (they may join communes, gangs, social movements, religious sects).

Triandis et al. (1985) found that U.S. allocentrics report receiving more social support and feel less loneliness than U.S. idiocentrics. This relationship was replicated in Puerto Rico (Triandis, Bontempo et al., 1988), suggesting that there may be a general tendency for allocentrics to receive more social support than idiocentrics.

A. Are There Additional Cultural Syndromes?

There are probably more cultural syndromes that we do not know of as yet, and a lot more research is needed in this area. Hofstede (1991) describes what seems to be a cultural syndrome characteristic of the East (Orient) as opposed to the West (Europe). Using data about Chinese values (Chinese Culture Connection, 1987), he argues that there is a unique Chinese viewpoint that emphasizes the importance of *virtue,* in contrast to a Western viewpoint that emphasizes the importance of *truth.* This can be seen most clearly in the philosophic positions of Confucius and the Eastern religions of Hinduism, Buddhism, Shintoism, and Taoism versus the views of the three monotheistic religions—Judaism, Christianity, and Islam. The Eastern ideologies emphasize the importance of virtuous action and the need for carrying out the prescribed rituals. The monotheistic religions emphasize the importance of "belief." For the East what you do is more important than what you believe; for the West what you believe is more important than what you do.

I am not sure that this is an additional syndrome. It is based on empirical measurements, but such measurements often produce "echoes" in factor analyses. It is as if you are looking at an elephant from different directions, and each direction produces something that looks different when in fact it is the same elephant. As more research is done, we may be able to sort out whether virtue–truth is really different from collectivism–individualism. In the mean time, the contrast between virtue and truth is intriguing and useful for viewing the differences between East and West.

B. The Self and Cultural Syndromes

The self consists of all statements made by a person, overtly or covertly, that include the words "I," "me," "mine," and "myself." That is a large universe of statements. People in any culture sample such statements in ways that maximize their well-being. How the self is sampled can influence the social behaviors that are most probable. For example, sampling the "I am a member of my group" statement will increase the probability of paying attention to group norms.

It is useful to distinguish three kinds of "self" statements: *private* (e.g., "I am kind"), *public* (e.g., "Most people think I am kind"), and *collective* (e.g., "My co-workers think I am kind"). We can identify separate domains, within our memory structure, that contain the private, public, and collective elements (Trafimow, Triandis, & Goto, 1991). People in different kinds of cultures have more or less differentiated private, public, and collective selves. When one of these selves is highly differentiated, that is, has many elements, it is more likely to be sampled by people in that culture. Thus, Triandis (1989) has argued that people in complex cultures tend to sample more frequently the public and the private self and less frequently the collective self. The more individualistic the culture the more frequent is the sampling of the private self and the less frequent the sampling of the collective self. Collectivism, external threat, competition with outgroups, and common fate increase the sampling of the collective self. Tightness also results in sampling of the collective self.

Cheek (1989) and his associates have developed a scale that measures personal, social, and collective identity. Subjects are asked to rate on a five-point scale (from "Not important to my sense of who I am" to "Extremely important to my sense of who I am") a set of statements. Personal identity is reflected by emphasis on the importance of "My dreams and imagination," "My thoughts and ideas," and so forth. Social identity requires emphasis on items such as "The things I own, my possessions" and "My sex, being male or female." Collective identity is reflected by endorsement of "My religion," "My race or ethnic background," and so forth. Very good alphas have been obtained for personal and social identity and further work on collective identity is in progress. Susceptibility to shame and public self-consciousness were found related to social identity, and susceptibility to guilt and private self-consciousness were related to personal identity. High personal identity seems to buffer subjects against threats to social esteem.

The sampling of the collective self, which is more probable in simple and tight cultures, has important implications. Such sampling increases the salience of the collective elements of subjective culture, such as norms, roles, and values. The patterns of social behavior associated with collectivism; for example, the great differentiation of ingroups and outgroups, can be seen to be the consequences of such sampling. A similar argument made about the other cultural syndromes; for example, in complex and loose cultures there will be greater sampling of the private self, resulting in more sampling by individuals of their affect toward the behavior (is this going to be fun?) and their perceptions of the utility of the behavior for them (what will I get out of this?).

III. DIMENSIONS OF SOCIAL BEHAVIOR

Triandis (1978) has argued that every social behavior can be described as a point in a four-dimensional mathematical space defined by the dimensions *association* (positive, supportive behavior) versus *dissociation* (avoidance or aggression, negative behavior); *superordination* (domination, taking the initiative) versus *subordination* (conformity, reacting to initiative taken by other); *formality* (following a script provided by the norms of the culture) versus *intimacy* (spontaneous, disclosing behavior); and *overt* (visible muscle movements) versus *covert* (fantasies, nonobservable behavior).

Lonner's (1980) review of cross-cultural universals strongly supported the universality of the first two dimensions. These also correspond to dimensions discussed by Leary, Hogan, and others.

The third and fourth dimensions have not yet been established as universals, though they are plausible etics. If the Geertz (1973) description of Bali is correct, most behavior in that culture is formal; hence there would not be a "dimension" of intimacy–formality in that culture, but it surely can be seen in other cultures.

Furthermore, I find it difficult to believe that Balinese behavior is *equally* formal in all situations. Thus, I suspect that, after careful study, this dimension will be found in all cultures.

The lack of studies of overt versus covert (fantasies) behavior is understandable, since covert behavior is difficult to study.

A. Relation between Cultural Syndromes and Social Behavior

In our previous discussion we presented many specific points about the way the cultural syndromes are related to social behavior. While such details are very useful, we also need to link the cultural syndromes to the association–dissociation, superordination–subordination, intimacy–formality, and overt–covert description of social behavior in order to link the cultural syndromes to the dimensions of personality we discuss later.

Collectivism is characterized by higher rates of association with the ingroup and of dissociation with the outgroup than is individualism; also, collectivism involves greater emphasis on the subordination–superordination dimension of social behavior than is found in individualism. Finally, in collectivist cultures more behavior is formal and covert than in individualist cultures. This is because norms are more important than attitudes, and conformity to the collective can be oppressive and thus individuals escape in fantasy life.

B. Dimensions of Personality Variation

Hogan (1983) has shown that most dimensions of personality are various combinations of the two social behavior dimensions mentioned above: association–dissociation and superordination–subordination.

We can broaden this perspective by arguing that the quality of social behavior can be determined by examining the frequencies of associative–dissociative, superordinate–subordinate, and intimate–formal behaviors for different kinds of actors (e.g., gender, status, culture, age) responding to different kinds of targets (e.g., gender, status, culture, age) in settings that involve particular configurations of goal interdependence (e.g., competition, cooperation).

Hogan's (1983) socioanalytic theory of personality is based on the first two dimensions of social behavior discussed above. He has reviewed many studies that can be placed in a framework of high–low sociability (associative behavior) and high–low conformity (subordinate behavior). The classic dimensions of personality isolated via inventories can be seen as mixtures of these basic dimensions. For example, adjustment, extroversion, and other dimensions are related to associative–subordinate behaviors, while neuroticism is linked to superordinate–dissociative behaviors, anxiety is linked to subordinate–dissociative behaviors, and originality to associative–superordinate behaviors.

The mistake of some psychologists has been to try to account for *one* behavior of a particular individual in a specific setting. The use of traits to predict behavior has not been fruitful (Nisbett, 1980) when used in such a simple form. But indexes based on many behaviors have been much more successful (Epstein, 1979, 1980). Most promising is the use of dimensions, the expectation being that the higher an individual is on a dimension, the higher the probability that the individual's behavior will be summarized by that dimension.

What kinds of indexes and dimensions should we look for? One direction that seems promising was suggested by Goldberg (1981), who reviewed all typologies of personality and asked the question, what typology is most likely to be universal? He suggests that the so-called "Big Five" (Norman, 1969) *may* be universal. The five dimensions are:

1. Surgency: talkative, sociable, adventurous, open
2. Agreeableness: good natured, cooperative, mild
3. Conscientiousness: responsible, scrupulous, persevering
4. Emotionally stable: calm, composed, poised
5. Cultured: intellectual, artistic, imaginative, polished

He believes that there are some questions all humans are likely to ask:

(1) Is X *active and dominant* or passive and submissive (Can I bully X or will X try to bully me)? (2) Is X *agreeable* (warm and pleasant) or disagreeable (cold and distant)? (3) Can I count on X (Is X *responsible* and *conscientious* or undependable and negligent)? (4) Is X *crazy* (unpredictable) or sane (stable)? (5) Is X *smart* or dumb (How easy will it be for me to teach X)? Are these universal questions?

(Goldberg, 1981, p. 161)

We cannot be sure, but the argument seems plausible. There is some empirical support for Goldberg's speculation from a study of Yang and Bond (1990). These authors started from a pool of Chinese personality descriptors and then asked Chinese subjects to rate several targets on these descriptors. They extracted five dimensions of personality and found reasonable correlations between the Chinese indigenous dimensions and the Big Five.

Table I presents the Chinese indigenous factors. Table II shows the correlations between the Chinese factors and the Big Five. This table shows that the Chinese dimension of Social Orientation is related to the Big Five dimension of Agreeableness; Competence to both Emotional Stability and Culture; Expressiveness to Extroversion; Self-Control to Agreeableness also; and Optimism to Emotional Stability. If one takes into account the unreliability of measurements, the correlations are not bad, but they are certainly not good.

The one Big Five factor that did not emerge among the Chinese is Conscientiousness. It is only mildly related to three of the five Chinese factors. My speculation is that this is so because Chinese culture is very high in emphasizing "virtuous" (Hofstede, 1991), "reliable" behavior; people are socialized to be conscientious to

TABLE I
Most Salient Variables and Their Average Varimax Loadings on the Five Factors

Salient variable	Average loading	Salient variable	Average loading
	Social Orientation–Self-Centeredness		
Honest	.61	Untruthful	−.53
Good and gentle	.57	Selfish	−.50
Loyal	.55	Opportunistic	−.49
Cordial	.55	Sly	−.49
Kind	.54	Greedy	−.47
Friendly	.48	Naughty	−.47
Frank	.48	Ruthless	−.45
Morally clean	.47	Merciless	−.44
Responsible	.45	Hostile	−.44
Gracious	.43	Harsh	−.44
	Competence–Impotence		
Determined	.46	Dependent	−.49
Resolute and firm	.46	Fearful	−.48
Capable	.46	Timid	−.48
Tactful	.46	Childish	−.43
Brave	.44	Foolish	−.41
Smart	.43	Dull	−.40
Rational	.43	Shallow	−.39
Independent	.42	Vulgar	−.36
Wise	.42	Shy	−.35
Quick and sharp	.41	Self-disdainful	−.34
	Expressiveness–Conservatism		
Vivacious	.56	Old-fashioned	−.46
Passionate	.47	Conservative	−.46
Straightforward	.43	Rigid	−.45
Humorous	.43	Solemn	−.43
Talkative	.43	Awkward	−.41
Mischievous	.41	Introverted	−.41
Optimistic	.39	Stubborn	−.35
Broad-minded	.38	Indifferent	−.35
Gracious	.37		
Generous	.36		
	Self-Control–Impulsiveness		
Quiet and refined	.42	Impulsive	−.55
Cultured	.41	Irritable	−.53
Modest	.40	Frivolous	−.42
Upright and correct	.38	Bad-tempered	−.42
Self-possessed	.37	Headstrong	−.39
Steady	.36	Stubborn	−.38
Objective	.35	Opinionated	−.37
		Extreme	−.37

(*continues*)

TABLE I *continued*

Salient variable	Average loading	Salient variable	Average loading
		Optimism–Neuroticism	
Optimistic	.47	Moody	−.67
Pleasant	.38	Worrying	−.64
Self-confident	.34	Pessimistic	−.55
		Anxious	−.50
		Sensitive	−.42
		Self-pitying	−.38

Note. Data are derived from the 150 adjective scales for the six target persons (i.e., father, mother, teacher, neighbor, friend, and self). After Yan and Bond (1990).

such an extent that individual differences on this variable do not stand out. If everyone in a culture is high on a particular attribute, there is no point for people in that culture to notice that attribute. That observation is important, because it tells us that some etic dimensions may not be important in some cultures, and some emic dimensions that indigenous cultures generate may not be known to us. I argued earlier that Association–Dissociation and Superordination–Subordination are etic dimensions. Another important etic dimension is frequency of interaction (Chapple, 1970). For example, Native Americans and people who live in the Arctic do not consider it necessary to talk unless they have something to say. In the United States we tend to think that silence implies hostility, so we make small talk even when we have nothing important to communicate.

The Big Five are related to these three dimensions of social behavior. First, frequency of interaction is clearly related to Surgency/Extroversion. In our discussion of cultural syndromes we suggested greater Surgency in individualistic cultures

TABLE II

Average Correlations between the Emic and the Imposed Etic Factors

Imposed etic factor	Emic factors				
	S-S	C-I	E-C	S-I	O-N
Extraversion	.21 (.12–.46)	.09 (.00–.14)	.51 (.46–.59)	.01 (−.07–.15)	.16 (.09–.25)
Agreeableness	66 (.41–.77)	.29 (.13–.37)	.30 (.12–.44)	.56 (.40–.66)	.14 (.09–.21)
Conscientiousness	.28 (−.08–.48)	.31 (.06–.53)	−.09 (−.32–.07)	.29 (.13–.40)	.01 (−.13–.11)
Emotional Stability	.35 (.27–.40)	.55 (.36–.68)	.36 (.32–.41)	.43 (.34–.52)	.44 (.40–.48)
Culture	.29 (.16–.47)	.50 (.40–.62)	.37 (.22–.53)	.28 (.07–.39)	.11 (.05–.20)

Note. Data derived from the six target persons (i.e., father, mother, teacher, neighbor, friend, and self). S-S, Social Orientation–Self-Centeredness; C-I, Competence–Impotence; E-C, Expressiveness–Conservatism; S-I, Self-Control–Impulsiveness; O-N, Optimism–Neuroticism. After Yang and Bond (1990).

than collectivist cultures, especially when new groups are present. Associative behaviors are clearly related to Agreeableness. We can expect more Agreeableness among collectivists interacting with ingroup members than among individualists, especially since they have important long-term relationships with ingroup members.

Second, if Hogan is correct in linking Associative–Subordination to Adjustment and Dissociative–Subordination to Anxiety, we might argue that Associative–Subordination (Adjustment) corresponds to Conscientiousness and Dissociative–Subordination (Anxiety) corresponds to Emotional Instability. This would suggest that Associative–Superordination (calm, composed) is Emotional Stability, and Dissociative–Superordination reflects the opposite of Adjustment—aggression, attack. Again, we might expect more Emotional Stability and less Aggression within the ingroup among collectivists than individualists, and the opposite pattern for relationships with outgroups.

That leaves only the Culture dimension unaccounted for, but that may well be a fourth universal dimension, since it reflects intelligence. Granted, intelligence is defined somewhat differently in each culture. Nevertheless, it has common elements across cultures. Even those who define an intelligent person as one "who is slow and correct and knows what the elders expect" would agree that one needs to be able to learn what the elders expect, and would agree with Goldberg's question, Is X smart? The Big Five personality dimension labeled Culture, then, can be etic if we allow it to have drastically different content in each culture; for example, familiarity with Beethoven in the West and Indian classical music in India. There is no reason to expect that the cultural syndromes will be related to it.

Now if the Big Five are the way to study personality, we need to ask, how can we study personality across cultures? And, what theoretical framework do we use to link culture and personality?

First, let us consider some of the ways we can study the Big Five across cultures. In specific geographic/language regions we can

1. Ask individuals to observe themselves and rate themselves on scales such as those that reflect the Big Five.
2. Ask them to observe their own group's behavior and rate it on the same scales, which would provide their *autostereotypes* (see Triandis & Vassiliou, 1967).
3. Ask them to observe and rate other groups, which will provide their *heterostereotypes* (see Triandis, 1971).

Convergence among these three ratings, that is, extraction of common elements among these data sets, would indicate a good deal about the attributes of the group being rated.

We could, of course, do the same study for each of the nations we wish to understand. Specifically, if Americans (i) rate themselves ("I tend to be") on the scales of the Big Five and (ii) rate the stimulus "Americans tend to be" on the same scales, and if (iii) we collect data from 10 diverse countries who supply "Americans tend to be" ratings on the same scales, it is likely that some common elements would emerge. It seems reasonable to assume that the *common* elements are indicative of the attributes of Americans.

This view is supported by Fischer and Trier's study (1962) on the attributes of French and German Swiss. There was considerable overlap of auto- and hetero-stereotypes. Similarly, a study of Hispanic and non-Hispanic auto- and heterostereotypes (Triandis et al., 1984) showed convergence. The addition of self-ratings would make it even more likely that the common elements of the three data sets are reliable and valid.

While stereotypes have limited validity, they are not entirely invalid. For example, the stereotypes Bangladeshis had about the *piousness* of members of different Bangladeshi tribes were found to be valid (Schuman, 1966) when compared with observations of the frequency of praying. However, note that in the case of Muslims, prayers can be readily observed. Most stereotypes reflect traits that are not reliably observed. Nevertheless, when there is agreement across several sources of data, the chances are that something reliable and valid has been identified.

In addition, we can observe, ask questions, and set up experiments to check for the consistency between stereotypes and actual behavior. Feldman (1968), for example, checked the stereotype of how "honest" taxi drivers were in three foreign cities by asking 50 taxis in each city to take him between randomly determined points and checking whether the taxis took him the long or the direct way.

Another source of data is ethnographic. We define a valid stereotype as a *sociotype.* If the ethnographers have done a good job, they have provided sociotypes. W. W. Lambert (1984) suggested that it would be fruitful to triangulate across different methods of study. In short, one can examine the convergence among *sociotypes* (obtained from ethnographies), *autostereotypes,* and *heterostereotypes.* When there is convergence there is likely to be validity. Hampson (1982) has argued that there are similarities in the structures of self-reports, reports by others, and reports by personality scientists. It may well be the case that such similarities also exist across sociotypes, autostereotypes, and heterostereotypes.

Suppose that we did find evidence that ethnographies and auto- and heterostereotypes converge. How would we assemble the information into a meaningful whole? The framework that is presented next suggests how this may be done.

IV. A FRAMEWORK FOR STUDIES OF CULTURE AND PERSONALITY

Figure 3 presents a framework for studies of culture and personality which expands and modifies the frameworks proposed by John and Beatrice Whiting (Whiting & Whiting, 1975) and Robert LeVine (1973). The basic elements of the framework are ecology (e.g., there is fish that can be eaten), environments (i.e., schedules of reinforcement associated with specific behavior settings), history (e.g., wars), maintenance system (e.g., hunting, fishing, agriculture, industry), the interindividual system (e.g., socialization practices), innate behaviors (e.g., tropisms, need arousal), learned behaviors (e.g., conformity), and the projective system (e.g., myths, reli-

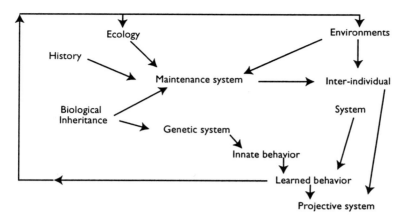

FIGURE 3   A framework for the study of culture and personality. Some definitions follow: *ecology,* climate, flora, fauna, terrain, resources; *environment,* factory, school, church, and other behavior settings; *history,* migrations, wars, revolutions, inventions, transfer of ideas; *maintenance system,* subsistence patterns, means of production, settlement patterns, social structure, division of labor, subjective culture; *interindividual system,* child-rearing patterns, interaction rates, attributions about the other person's behavior; *innate behaviors,* tropisms, need arousal, levels of activity; *learned behaviors,* skills, performances, conflict resolution styles, value priorities; *projective system,* religion, magic, rituals, ceremonies, art, games, play, crime, suicide.

gion). Personality refers to all the individual differences reflected in innate and learned behavior, as well as behaviors within the projective system.

Thus, personality is the sum of innate and learned behaviors, plus the behaviors that are part of the projective system. It reflects the million years of biological and cultural evolution (Boyd & Richerson, 1985), the socialization experiences, and the influence of recent and historical events (the mass media, wars, etc.). Culture is the sum of the maintenance system, the environments, and the interindividual system. This framework shows that culture and personality are interrelated, but in a very loose way.

Numerous examples can be provided of the links summarized in this framework. Euler, Gumerman, Karlstrom, Dean, and Hevly (1979) showed that cultural and demographic changes on the Colorado plateaus coincided with environmental fluctuations that can be defined precisely by geoclimatic indicators. Triandis (1972) discussed the emergence of Greek subjective culture as a result, in part, of the low communication among geographic regions that was created by an ecology of mountains and islands. Environments have been shown to modify the maintenance system and to be good predictors of social behavior (Whiting & Edwards, 1988).

Extreme poverty (an attribute of the ecology) can modify interindividual behavior, such as the degree of a mother's attachment to an infant; extremely poor women feel emotionally distant from their babies and do not take care of them (Scheper-Hughes, 1985).

Maintenance systems are linked to interindividual systems. For example, when many females are available to take care of children, children are indulged more. Simple societies assign more chores to children, mothers receive more help, and children interact more with infants (Whiting & Whiting, 1975).

As discussed previously, aspects of the ecology, such as the isolation of a group of humans from other humans, can result in high agreement about how to raise children, an aspect of the interindividual system, and this leads to tightness (an aspect of culture) and to conformity, a learned behavior.

Some measures of conformity are especially interesting. In most cultures the right hand is considered "the correct" one, and people hold the norm that people should use their right hand to carry out important behaviors. If this norm did not exist, because of variations in genetic make-up, about 12% of the population would be left-handed. Tightness can be measured by the percentage of the population that is not left-handed. The lower the percentage of the population that is left-handed, the greater the tightness.

Dawson (1974) has used several tests of handedness—for example, which hand was used to deal cards, unscrew a jar, manage chopsticks, sweep, thread a needle, write, strike a match, throw a ball, use a hammer, toothbrush, racket, and so forth. He found rates of left-handedness in hunting and fishing societies of around 10% (Australian Aboriginal males, 10.7%, females, 10.3%; Chinese boat people males, 5.4%, females, 12.9%; Eskimo males 12.5%, females, 10.3%). Western samples had rates around 6%. In agricultural societies, where conformity is high, the rates were around 1% (e.g., African Congo males .8%, females, 0%; Temne of Africa males, 3.8%, females, 0%, University of Hong Kong Chinese men, 2.7%, women, 0%). Extremely low levels of left-handedness have also been reported from other societies that are very strict in their child rearing, e.g., Nigeria, 0.28%, reported by Bakare (1974).

In sum, it appears that, if left alone, samples of humans have a tendency to use the left hand about 12% of the time. Western samples are between this level and zero, while the more conforming agricultural samples, that typically use severe methods of socialization, are close to 0% in left-handedness.

The interindividual system results in differences in behavior. For example, drunkenness is found more commonly in cultures that limit the indulgence of dependence in infancy, emphasize demands for achievement in childhood, and limit dependent behavior in adulthood (Bacon, 1973). Many individualistic cultures limit dependence, because they believe that children should become independent of their parents as soon as feasible. They pay the price in higher rates of alcoholism than collectivist cultures.

Rohner (1986) has reported studies linking parental acceptance–rejection to the child's behavior. Rejected children are more likely to be dependent, hostile, and aggressive, or passive aggressive, anxious, and emotionally unstable, and to have low self-esteem and a negative world view (distrust others). Numerous findings supportive of this link can be found also in Munroe, Munroe, and Whiting (1981).

The projective system has also been studied in terms of child-rearing patterns. For example, cultures where supernatural beings are perceived to be malevolent have been found to use socialization patterns characterized by rejection (Rohner, 1986, p. 158). Similarly, in cultures where the gods were malevolent, child-rearing patterns were found to be very strict and severe punishment was common (W. W. Lambert, Triandis, & Wolf, 1959).

This study found also a relationship between children being beaten by nurturing agents (usually the parents) and properties of the supernaturals in several nonliterate societies. The relationship indicates that in cultures where children are frequently beaten, supernaturals are perceived to be aggressive.

Figure 3 shows that there is considerable distance between the interindividual system, which includes child-rearing patterns, and the projective system, which includes the kinds of supernaturals found in a culture. The theory behind Figure 3 has a logical structure: the more distant the constructs, the weaker will be the relationships. In short, finding a relationship between the interindividual system and the projective system is very supportive of the theory.

Finally, the theory assumes that there are feedback loops, such as behavior changing ecology. Examples include the greenhouse effect and changes in the ozone layer. Obviously, behavior also creates history and new genetic forms, and changes the kinds of environments in which people behave, but those relations are not shown in Figure 3 for simplicity's sake.

Of course, the few studies that interrelate the theory's elements do not as yet validate the theory. It is only a beginning. Much more research will be needed before we can discuss it with confidence.

V. SUMMARY

The intuition that culture is related to personality is not supported by empirical research because there is too much variation in personality within cultures. However, if we know the cultural syndromes of the people whose behavior we wish to predict, we can make accurate probabilistic behavioral predictions. Though we cannot say whether *this* person will act in this or that way, we can say that in that culture, on the average, people are more likely to act in this or that way. When that information is combined with information about personality (How is this person likely to see this social situation? What are the person's habitual ways of behaving?) there is a good chance that behavior can be predicted.

REFERENCES

Adamopoulos, J., & Bontempo, R. (1984). A note on the relationship between socialization practice and artistic preference. *Cross-Cultural Psychology Bulletin, 18,* 4–7.

Adorno, T. W., Frenkel-Bruswik, E., Levinson, D. J., & Sanford, R. N. (1950). *The authoritarian personality*. New York: Harper & Row.

Bacon, M. K. (1973). Cross-cultural studies in drinking. In P. G. Bourne & R. Fox (Eds.), *Alcoholism: progress in research and treatment* (pp. 171–194). New York: Academic Press.

Bakare, C. (1974). The development of laterality and right-left discrimination in Nigerian children. In J. L. M., Dawson & W. J. Lonner (Eds.), *Readings in cross-cultural psychology* (pp. 150–166). Hong Kong: University of Hong Kong Press.

Berry, J. W. (1976). *Human ecology and cognitive style*. Beverly Hills, CA: Sage.

Berry, J. W., Poortinga, Y., Segall, M., & Dasen, P. (1992). *Cross-cultural psychology*. New York: Cambridge University Press.

Bijnen, E. J., Van der Net, Z. J., & Poortinga, Y. H. (1986). On cross-cultural comparative studies with the Eysenck Personality Questionnaire. *Journal of Cross-Cultural Psychology, 17,* 3–16.

Boyd, R., & Richerson, P. J. (1985). *Culture and the evolutionary process*. Chicago: University of Chicago Press.

Brandt, V. S. (1974). Skiing cross-culturally. *Current Anthropology, 15,* 64–66.

Bruner, J. (1974). Concluding comments and summary of conference. In J. L. M. Dawson & W. J. Lonner (Eds.), *Readings in cross-cultural psychology* (pp. 381–391). Hong Kong: University of Hong Kong Press.

Budner, S. (1962). Intolerance of ambiguity as a personality variable. *Journal of Personality, 30,* 29–50.

Chapple, E. D. (1970). *Culture and biological man*. New York: Holt, Rinehart & Winston.

Cheek, J. M. (1989). Identity orientations and self-interpretation. In D. M. Buss & N. Cantor (Eds.) *Personality psychology: Recent trends and emerging directions* (pp. 275–285). New York: Springer.

Child, I. (1968). Personality in culture. In E. F. Borgatta & W. W. Lambert (Eds.), *Handbook of personality theory and research* (pp. 82–148). Chicago, Rand McNally.

Chinese Culture Connection. (1987). Chinese values and the search for culture-free dimensions of culture. *Journal of Cross Cultural Psychology, 18,* 143–164.

Cole, M. (1975). An ethnographic psychology of cognition. In R. D. Brislin, S. Bochner, & W. Lonner (Eds.), *Cross-cultural perspectives on learning* (pp. 157–176). New York: Wiley.

Dawson, J. (1974). Ecology, cultural pressures toward conformity and left-handedness: A bio-social psychological approach. In J. L. M. Dawson & W. J. Lonner (Eds.), *Readings in cross-cultural psychology* (pp. 124–149). Hong Kong: University of Hong Kong Press.

Detweiler, R. (1980). The categorization of the actions of people from another culture: A conceptual analysis and behavioral outcome. *International Journal of Intercultural Relations, 4,* 275–293.

DeVos, G., & Hippler, A. A. (1969). Cultural psychology: Comparative studies of human behavior. In G. Lindzey & E. Aronson (Eds.), *The handbook of social psychology*. Reading, MA: Addison-Wesley.

Draguns, J. G. (1979). Culture and personality. In A. J. Marsella, R. G. Tharp, & T. J. Ciborowski (Eds.), *Perspectives on cross-cultural psychology* (pp. 179–208). New York: Academic Press.

Draguns, J. (1990). Normal and abnormal behavior in cross-cultural perspective: Specifying the nature of their relationship. In J. Berman (Ed.), *Nebraska Symposium on Motivation, 1989* (pp. 235–278). Lincoln: University of Nebraska Press.

Epstein, S. (1979). The stability of behavior. I. On predicting most of the people much of the time. *Journal of Personality and Social Psychology, 37,* 1097–1126.

Epstein, S. (1980). The stability of behavior. II. Implications for psychological research. *American Psychologist, 35,* 790–806.

Euler, R. C., Gumerman, G. J., Karlstrom, T. N., Dean, J. S., & Hevly, R. H. (1979). The Colorado plateaus: Cultural dynamics and paleoenvironment. *Science, 205,* 1089–1101.

Eysenck, H. J., & Eysenck, S. B. G. (1983). Recent advances in the cross cultural study of personality. In J. N. Butcher & C. D. Spielberger (Eds.), *Advances in personality assessment* (Vol. 2, pp. 41–69). Hillsdale, NJ: Erlbaum.

Feldman, R. E. (1968). Response to compatriot and foreigner who seek assistance. *Journal of Personality and Social Psychology, 10,* 202–214.

Fischer, H., & Trier, U. P. (1962). *Das Verhaeltnis zwischen Deutschschweizer und Westschweizer: Eine sozialpsychologische Untersuchung.* Bern: Hans Huber.

Fiske, A. P. (1990). *Structures of social life: The four elementary forms of human relations.* New York: Free Press.

Fiske, A. P. (1992). The four elementary forms of sociality: Framework for a unified theory of social relations. *Psychological Review, 99,* 689–723.

Geertz, C. (1973). *The interpretation of cultures.* New York: Basic Books.

Geertz, C. (1983). *Local knowledge: Further essays in interpretive anthropology.* New York: Basic Books.

Goldberg, L. (1981). Language and individual differences. The search for universal in personality lexicons. In L. Wheeler (Ed.), *Review of personality and social psychology* (pp. 141–161). Beverly Hills, CA: Sage.

Goodenough, W. H. (1981). *Culture, language, and society* (2nd ed.). Menlo Park, CA: Benjamin/Cummings.

Hampson, S. (1982). *The construction of personality: An introduction.* London: Routledge & Kegan Paul.

Harvey, O. J., Hunt, D. E., & Schroeder, H. M. (1961). *Conceptual systems and personality organization.* New York: Wiley.

Hayashi, C. (1992). Belief systems and the Japanese way of thinking. In H. Motoaki, J. Misumi, & B. Wilpert (Eds.), *Proceedings of the 22nd International Congress of Applied Psychology* (pp. 3–34). Hove, England: Erlbaum.

Heelas, P., & Lock, A. (1981). *Indigenous psychologies: The anthropology of the self.* London: Academic Press.

Hofstede, G. (1980). *Culture's consequences.* Beverly Hills, CA: Sage.

Hofstede, G. (1980). *Cultures and organizations.* London: McGraw-Hill.

Hogan, R. (1983). A socioanalytic theory of personality. In *Nebraska Symposium on Motivation, 1982* (pp. 55–89). Lincoln: University of Nebraska Press.

Hsu, F. L. K. (Ed.). (1972). *Psychological anthropology: Approaches to culture and personality.* Cambridge, MA: Schenkman.

Hui, C. C. H., & Triandis, H. C. (1989). Effects of culture and response format on extreme response style. *Journal of Cross Cultural Psychology, 20,* 296–309.

Inkeles, A., & Levinson, D. J. (1954). National character: The study of model personality and sociocultural systems. In G. Lindzey (Ed.), *Handbook of social psychology* (pp. 975–1020). Reading, MA: Addison-Wesley.

Inkeles, A., & Levinson, D. J. (1969). National character: The study of model personality and sociocultural systems. In G. Lindzey & E. Aronson (Eds.), *Handbook of social psychology* (pp. 418–506). Reading, MA: Addison-Wesley.

Jahoda, G. (1980). Theoretical and systematic approaches in cross-cultural psychology. In H. C. Triandis & W. W. Lambert (Eds.), *Handbook of cross-cultural psychology* (pp. 69–141). Boston: Allyn & Bacon.

Jeanne, R. L. (Ed.). (1988). *Interindividual behavioral variability in social insects.* Boulder, CO: Westview Press.

Kaplan, B. (Ed.). (1961). *Studying personality cross-culturally.* Evanston, IL: Row, Peterson.

Keesing, R. M. (1981). Theories of culture. In R. W. Casson (Ed.), *Language, culture, and cognition: Anthropological prespectives* (pp. 42–66). New York: Macmillan.

Kim, U., & Berry, J. W. (1993). *Indigenous psychologies: Research and experience in cultural context.* Newbury Park, CA: Sage.

Klineberg, O. (1954). *Social psychology.* New York: Holt.

Klineberg, O. (1980). Historical perspective: Cross-cultural psychology before 1960. In H. C. Triandis & W. W. Lambert (Eds.), *Handbook of cross-cultural psychology* (Vol. 1, pp. 31–68). Boston: Allyn & Bacon.

Kluckhohn, C. (1954). Culture and behavior. In G. Lindzey (Ed.), *Handbook of social psychology* (Vol. 2, pp. 921–976). Cambridge, MA: Addison-Wesley.

Kluckhohn, C., & Murray, H. (Eds.). (1948). *Personality and nature society and culture.* New York: Knopf.

Kohn, M. L. (1969). Class and conformity. Homewood, IL: Dorsey.

Kohn, M. L. (1987, August). Cross-national research as an analytic strategy. Presidential Address to the Annual Meeting of the American Sociological Association, in Chicago.

Lambert, W. E. (1992). Challenging established views on social issues: The power and limitations of research. *American Psychologist, 47,* 533–542.

Lambert, W. E., Hamers, J., & Frasure-Smith, N. (1979). *Child rearing values.* New York: Praeger.

Lambert, W. W. (1984, Fall). Some brief reflections of the construction of culture. *Society for Cross-Cultural Research Newsletter,* p. 9.

Lambert, W. W., Triandis, L. M., & Wolf, M. (1959). Some correlates of beliefs in the malevolence and benevolence of supernatural beings: A cross-cultural study. *Journal of Abnormal and Social Psychology, 58,* 162–169.

LeVine, R. A. (1973). *Culture, behavior, and personality.* Chicago, IL: Aldine.

Linton, R. (1945). *The cultural background of personality.* New York: Appleton-Century-Crofts.

Lonner, W. (1980). The search for psychological universals. In H. C. Triandis & W. W. Lambert (Eds.), *Handbook of cross-cultural psychology* (Vol. 1, pp. 143–204). Boston: Allyn & Bacon.

Malinowski, G. (1944). *A scientific theory of culture.* Chapel Hill: University of North Carolina Press.

Markus, H., & Kitayama, S. (1991). Culture and self: Implications for cognition, emotion and motivation. *Psychological Review, 98,* 224–253.

Mead, M. (1953). National character. In A. L. Kroeber (Ed.), *Anthropology today* (pp. 642–667). Chicago: University of Chicago Press.

Minturn, L., & Lambert, W. W. (1964). *Mothers of six cultures.* New York: Wiley.

Munroe, R. H., Munroe, R. L., & Whiting, B. B. (1981). *Handbook of cross-cultural human development.* New York: Garland.

Nisbett, R. E. (1980). The trait construct in lay and professional psychology. In L. Festinger (Ed.), *Retrospections on social psychology* (pp. 109–130). New York: Oxford University Press.

Norman, W. T. (1969). "To see ourselves as others see us!" Relations among self-perceptions, peer perceptions, and expected peer-perceptions of personality attributes. *Multivariate Behavioral Research, 4,* 417–443.

Pelto, P. J. (1968, April). The difference between "tight" and "loose" societies. *Transaction,* pp. 37–40.

Pepitone, A., & Triandis, H. C. (1987). On the universality of social psychological theories. *Journal of Cross-Cultural Psychology, 18,* 471–498.

Pettigrew, T. (1959). The measurement of correlates of category width as a cognitive variable. *Journal of Personality, 26,* 532–544.

Rohner, R. P. (1986). *The warmth dimensions: Foundations of parental acceptance-rejection theory.* Newbury Park, CA: Sage.

Rokeach, M. (1960). *The open and closed mind.* New York: Basic Books.

Scheper-Hughes, N. (1985). Culture, scarcity, and maternal thinking: Maternal detachment and infant survival in a Brazilian shantytown. *Ethos, 13,* 291–317.

Schuman, H. (1966). Social change and the validity of regional stereotypes in East Pakistan. *Sociometry, 29,* 426–440.

Shweder, R. A., & Bourne, E. J. (1982). Does the concept of person vary cross-culturally? In A. J. Marsella & G. M. White (Eds.), *Cultural conceptions of mental health and therapy* (pp. 97–137). London: Reidel.

Shweder, R. A., & LeVine, R. (1984). *Culture theory.* Chicago: University of Chicago Press.

Shweder, R. A., & Sullivan, M. A. (1990). The semiotic subject of cultural psychology. In L. A. Pervin (Ed.) *Handbook of personality theory and research* (pp. 399–416). New York: Guilford Press.

Skinner, B. F. (1981). Selection by consequences. *Science, 213,* 501–504.

Stigler, J. W., Shweder, R. A., & Herdt, G. (Eds.). (1990). *Cultural psychology: Essays on comparative human development.* New York: Cambridge University Press.

Stoetzel, J. (1955). *Without the crysanthemum and the sword: A study of attitudes of youth in post-war Japan.* London: Heinemann.

Tapp, J. L. (1981). Studying personality development. In H. C. Triandis & A. Heron (Eds.), *Handbook of cross-cultural psychology* (Vol. 4, pp. 343–424). Boston: Allyn & Bacon.

Trafimow, D., Triandis, H. C., & Goto, S. (1991). Some tests of the distinction between the private and the collective self. *Journal of Personality and Social Psychology, 60,* 649–655.

Triandis, H. C. (1964). Cultural influences upon cognitive processes. In L. Berkowitz (Ed.), *Advances in experimental social psychology* (Vol. 1, pp. 1–48). New York: Academic Press.

Triandis, H. C. (1971). *Attitudes and attitude change.* New York: Wiley.

Triandis, H. C. (1972). *The analysis of subjective culture.* New York: Wiley.

Triandis, H. C. (1978). Some universals of social behavior. *Personality and Social Psychology Bulletin, 4,* 1–16.

Triandis, H. C. (1989). Self and social behavior in differing cultural contexts. *Psychological Review, 96,* 269–289.

Triandis, H. C. (1990). Cross-cultural studies of individualism and collectivism. In J. Berman (Ed.), *Nebraska Symposium on Motivation, 1989* (pp. 41–133). Lincoln: University of Nebraska Press.

Triandis, H. C. (1992). Cross-cultural research in social psychology. In D. Granberg & G. Sarup (Eds.), *Social judgment and intergroup relations: Essays in honor of Muzafer Sherif* (pp. 229–244). New York: Springer-Verlag.

Triandis, H. C. (1994). *Culture and social behavior.* New York: McGraw-Hill.

Triandis, H. C. (1995). *Individualism and collectivism.* Boulder, CO: Westview Press.

Triandis, H. C., Bontempo, R., Betancourt, H., Bond, M., Leung, K., Brenes, A., Georgas, J., Hui, C. H., Marin, G., Setiadi, B., Sinha, J. B. P., Verma, J., Spangenberg, J., Touzard, H., & de Montmollin, G. (1986). The measurement of etic aspects of individualism and collectivism across cultures. *Australian Journal of Psychology, 38,* 257–267.

Triandis, H. C., Bontempo, R., Leung, K., & Hui, C. H. (1990). A method for determining cultural, demographic, and personal constructs. *Journal of Cross-Cultural Psychology, 21,* 302–318.

Triandis, H. C., Bontempo, R., Villareal, M. J., Asai, M., & Lucca, N. (1988). Individualism and collectivism: Cross-cultural perspectives on self-ingroup relationships. *Journal of Personality and Social Psychology, 54,* 323–338.

Triandis, H. C., Brislin, R., & Hui, C. H. (1988). Cross-cultural training across the individualism-collectivism divide. *International Journal of Intercultural Relations, 12,* 269–289.

Triandis, H. C., Davis, E. E., & Takezawa, S. (1965). Some determinants of social distance among Americans, German, and Japanese students. *Journal of Personality and Social Psychology, 2,* 540–551.

Triandis, H. C., Leung, K., Villareal, M., & Clack, F. L. (1985). Allocentric versus idiocentric tendencies: Convergent and discriminant validation. *Journal of Research in Personality, 19,* 395–415.

Triandis, H. C., Lisansky, J., Setiadi, B., Chang, B., Marin, G., & Betancourt, H. (1982). Stereotyping among Hispanics and Anglos: The uniformity, intensity, direction, and quality of auto- and heterosterotypes. *Journal of Cross-Cultural Psychology, 13,* 409–426.

Triandis, H. C., Marin, G., Lisansky, J., & Betancourt, H. (1984). *Simpatia* as a cultural script of Hispanics. *Journal of Personality and Social Psychology, 47,* 1363–1375.

Triandis, H. C., McCusker, C., & Hui, C. H. (1990). Multimethod probes of individualism and collectivism. *Journal of Personality and Social Psychology, 59,* 1006–1020.

Triandis, H. C., & Triandis, L. M. (1960). Race, social class, religion, and nationality as determinants of social distance. *Journal of Abnormal and Social Psychology, 61,* 110–118.

Triandis, H. C., & Triandis, L. M. (1962). A cross-cultural study of social distance. *Psychological Monographs, 76.* (No. 21, Whole No. 540).

Triandis, H. C., & Vassiliou, V. (1967). Frequency of contact and stereotyping. *Journal of Personality and Social Psychology, 7,* 316–328.

Triandis, H. C., Vassiliou, V., & Nassiakou, M. (1968). Three cross-cultural studies of subjective culture. *Journal of Personality and Social Psychology, Monograph Supplement, 8*(4), 1–42.

Whiting, B. B., & Edwards, C. P. (1988). *Children of different worlds.* Cambridge, MA: Harvard University Press.

Whiting, B. B., & Whiting, J. W. M. (1975). *Children of six cultures—a psycho-cultural analysis.* Cambridge, MA: Harvard University Press.

Witking, H., & Berry, J. W. (1975). Psychological differentiation on cross-cultural perspective. *Journal of Cross-Cultural Psychology, 6,* 4–87.

Yang, K. S., & Bond, M. H. (1990). Exploring implicit personality theories with indigenous or imported constructs: The Chinese case. *Journal of Personality and Social Psychology, 58,* 1087–1095.

═══ CHAPTER 19 ═══

TRUST AND BETRAYAL

THE PSYCHOLOGY OF GETTING ALONG AND GETTING AHEAD

WARREN H. JONES
UNIVERSITY OF TENNESSEE

LAURIE COUCH
FORT HAYS STATE UNIVERSITY

SUSAN SCOTT
UNIVERSITY OF TULSA

An interesting problem emerges in considering the role of personality in the context of social life. On the one hand, various personality factors clearly contribute to one's acceptance by peers, which in turn is associated with happiness, health, and adjustment. Furthermore, it is reasonable to suppose that the ability to "get along" with others has been a key feature in the evolution of human personality; specifically, the propensity for "banding together" (i.e., group formation and group living) was the key to human evolution and the survival of human beings as a species, as well as in the development of culture. Thus, individual differences in such themes as trust, friendliness, kindness, and sincerity were likely selected in human evolution because such propensities better ensured individual survival to reproduce through the mechanisms of group acceptance and popularity. On the other hand, individual human beings inevitably compete with one another for scarce natural and social resources, not only between groups, but between individuals within groups. All human groups are stratified according to status and power, and having status and power are also closely linked to health, survival, and the quality of mate selection. These factors not only contribute to individual happiness and well-being, but also influence the likelihood of individual survival for reproduction and must have been selected by evolutionary forces. Herein lies the problem. There is a fundamental and unavoidable tension between behaviors which promote "getting along" and those associated with "getting ahead." Whereas being accepted by others is facilitated by trust, friendliness, and sharing, status and power often depend on ambition, competitiveness, and cunning. Thus, they involve different behaviors and dispositions, and furthermore, success in one domain is likely to result in failure in the other. For example, popularity may be acquired at the price of foregoing status, whereas status often creates jealousy and envy in others.

Our chapter emphasizes the tension between trust—what many consider the *sine qua non* of the personality factors necessary for mature and mutually satisfying relationships—and violations of trust or what we will call betrayals. We begin with a review of our approach to personality including our assumptions about the nature of human nature and individual differences. Next, we present definitions of trust found in the literature and present conceptual distinctions we believe will facilitate subsequent research and theory in this area. We then examine research on trust in some detail, including generalized trust (e.g., global trust in human nature) and particularly relational trust, that is, trust of specific relational partners. Also, we present extant theoretical perspectives on relational trust including developmental approaches, a component model, and the appraisal model. We then turn our attention to research on violations of trust—what we call betrayal experiences—in which we highlight our own recent program of research. We conclude with a brief overview and discussion of the implications of the trust–betrayal dialectic for understanding the nexus between personality and social life.

I. PSYCHOLOGY OF PERSONALITY

Traditional theories of personality (e.g., psychoanalysis) were designed to explain the origins of neurosis. In general, these theories are not very helpful in trying to understand trust and betrayal for three reasons: (a) they have little to say about positive striving or moral character (one could even argue that traditional theories tend to stigmatize successful people); (b) they emphasize overt and individualized psychopathology without regard for the subtle and nonneurotic ways in which people undermine themselves and others; and (c) they are hostile to the influence of society, suggesting that people who are normally socialized into the values and norms of a culture are, at the same time, deeply neurotic. By contrast, our perspective on personality, socioanalytic theory (Hogan, 1976, 1983; Hogan, Jones, & Cheek, 1985), assumes that the purpose of personality theory is to explain social action and that the important differences among people concern differences in social acumen and the initiative to pursue the overarching goals of status and acceptance. From the socioanalytic perspective, neurosis and other psychopathologies are not the products of oversocialization; rather, they reflect an inability to get along with others and to get ahead in social life and are important primarily for these reasons.

A. Personality Dynamics

On the basis of our evolutionary history (i.e., as group-living, culture-dependent animals concerned with maximizing individual and group fitness), it is reasonable to assume that, at a deep, organic level, we all need status and social acceptance in our social groups. Status and acceptance enhance the chances of individual reproductive success or fitness; fitness, defined in these terms, is the ultimate agenda in biology and evolutionary theory. Status and acceptance (both of which promote fitness) cannot be demanded; they must be negotiated, and the principal vehicle for these negotiations is individual identities. In order to take part in the larger social process, we must have roles to play in society, and those roles are defined by our social identities (i.e., individual differences in personality). Much of what people do in everyday life, therefore, is to assert, defend, reinforce, or modify their identity claims in response to the reactions of others. Identity negotiation is not a lighthearted exercise; it is always serious and sometimes it is a matter of life and death.

   Identity negotiations are carried out through strategic self-presentation. Identities are idealized self-images; these self-images are like templates that constrain, direct, and guide social behavior in an often unconscious attempt to control the manner in which others perceive us. Obviously there are extensive individual differences in every aspect of this process. Some people are tactless bumpkins who rarely concern themselves with how others perceive and evaluate them. Other people are neurotically obsessed with social evaluation (cf. Hogan et al., 1985). Most of us are somewhere in between these two poles. Moreover, this process of strategic self-presentation is largely unconscious, and necessarily so. Self-conscious self-presentation leads to awkward, stilted, and unconvincing social performances.

B. Social Reputation

Personality must be defined from the perspective of both the actor and the observer. Status and social acceptance depend on how observers evaluate the performances of actors. These evaluations are summarized and communicated in a social system in terms of individual reputations. Reputations are consequential, they are highly correlated with each person's status and social acceptance, and to a large extent they predict quality of life and reproductive success.

   The deep structure of reputations turns out to be relatively simple and stable. Research evidence since the 1960s has steadily supported the notion that reputation is encoded in three to seven broad categories (cf. Digman & Takemoto-Chock, 1981). In what is sometimes called the "Big Five" theory, observers' descriptions of actors are found to reflect judgments about the following characteristics of actors: (1) intellectual capacities, (2) emotional stability, (3) dependability, (4) assertiveness, and (5) likability. We can now speak with some confidence about the structure of personality from an external or observer's perspective, and this structure is the basis for individual reputations.

Our perspective on personality, then, may be briefly summarized as follows: People need status and social acceptance from the members of their social groups. They negotiate for these commodities using self-presentations which are constrained and guided by individual differences in social identity. The results of their negotiations are recorded in terms of their reputations, and these reputations can be profiled in terms of five relatively independent categories of social evaluation.

II. THE PSYCHOLOGY OF TRUST

A. Definition and Conceptualization

Several observers have suggested that trust is critical to human existence and vital to the effective functioning of all levels of human systems: individuals, dyads, groups, organizations, and nations (Rotenberg, 1991; Rotter, 1967; Stack, 1978). For example, Scott (1980) suggested that trust is an essential ingredient in the process of organizational effectiveness. Several researchers have found that high-trust groups perform better on certain tasks than low-trust groups, and, in fact, it has been argued that trust lies at the heart of group processes (Golembiewski & McConkie, 1975). Dyads are also clearly influenced by each member's trust of the other. Research on dyadic trust suggests that a person's trust in another strongly influences the other's trust in that person. Several authors (e.g., Erikson, 1950; Rotter, 1967; Wrightsman, 1974) have suggested that trust is the essential basis for the development of any personal relationship. Also, it has been suggested that the development of trust is an important component in adjustment and a "healthy personality." For example, Schill, Toves, and Ramanaiah (1980) reported that individuals low in trust tend to have higher stress scores and report more emotional and physical distress than persons scoring high in trust. In short, trust is a ubiquitous concept permeating the interface between people and their social environments.

Several definitions of trust have been proposed. Erikson (1963) offered a general theory of trust as a stage in the development of personality. In this view, the first crisis of development concerns whether or not to trust the primary caregiver. According to the theory, every person must learn to trust at least one other person to care for them, or fail to survive. The "initial trust" described by Erikson is presumably imperative for all other aspects of personality development because it initiates subsequent social growth. Deutsch (1958) believed that the concept of trust is vital to the understanding of social life and personality development as well. Specifically, Deutsch explained the importance of risk-taking behaviors associated with trust and argued that trust and trustworthiness are very strongly related; specifically, the object of trust will likely have some bearing on the amount of trust placed in him or her by an individual. He also proposed that trust would be dependent on the perceived power of the object (i.e., the other person) to cause desired events, the relationship between the individual and the object, the influence of communication, third party influences, and the individual's level of self-esteem.

Similarly, Rotter (1967) developed the concept of interpersonal trust as an expectancy of a person or group regarding the likelihood that a promise will be kept. This particular conceptualization (and the scale he developed for its measurement) has enjoyed widespread usage in the literature, including, for example, investigations of the dynamics of interpersonal trust, client–therapist trust, trust in work/team situations (including game playing), the development of trust in children, and political or public trust. Many of these studies used Rotter's definition in a slightly different sense to mean expectancies about the trustworthiness of people in general (Stack, 1978; Wrightsman, 1974).

Some authors have suggested the utility of distinguishing among different types of trust. For example, Driscoll (1978) suggested dividing trust into two further categories: a general attitudinal/affective component and a specific situational/cognitive component. Stack (1978) further proposed five determinants of situational trust: communication, risk, credibility of promises, social evaluation, and generalized trust. Each of these determinants is viewed in terms of past, present, and future events so as to ascertain the likelihood that trust will emerge. Risk is perhaps the most prevalent of these determinants in the literature on trust. Trusting another person involves a certain amount of vulnerability for the trusting individual. The individual must be willing to accept this risk in order to experience intimacy (Rempel, Holmes, & Zanna, 1985). Information about the degree of vulnerability an individual will be placed in can be obtained through communication and experience. When one accepts a vulnerable position and experiences a negative outcome, one will be less likely to risk trusting the same partner in the future, and perhaps other people as well.

We concur regarding the utility of drawing conceptual distinctions in this area and would elaborate on the distinctions among these concepts. First, it is important to distinguish between, on the one hand, the trust of an observer in a social actor (or all social actors) and, on the other hand, the trustworthiness of the actor. This distinction is similar to the two definitions of personality as internal structures and processes versus social reputation.

Second, distinctions may be drawn on the basis of the scope or target of trust, for which we propose two levels. Most broadly, trust is often described (cf. Wrightsman, 1974) as a generalized expectancy that other people in general are reliable and honest. This is what Erikson, Deutsch, Wrightsman, and most of the earlier scholars have meant by the concept of trust. We refer to this as *generalized trust*—its opposite is misanthropy or paranoia—and would argue that it is also what Rotter meant by his concept of interpersonal trust. Within generalized trust, one may imagine trust of others or people in general, without regard to their specific behaviors (i.e., trustworthiness) or their personal characteristics. Although such a concept is explicit in the work of earlier scholars, we suspect that this is primarily relevant in some hypothetical and/

or philosophical sense, but less so in everyday experience. If not, dark alleys would be more densely populated than they appear to be, and there would be no need for social anxiety. We suspect that experientially, generalized trust is circumscribed by social identity; that is, one trusts people in general so long as they are in some way similar to oneself, for example, like-minded or belong to the same group, nationality, or race. At the very least we require that others abide by the same expectations for social interchange—creatures from outer space, the insane, foreigners, deviants, and other "outsiders" are not necessarily malevolent in their intentions, but cannot always be relied upon to play by the rules. Although rarely acknowledged in the literature, we suspect that this is really what has been meant by generalized trust. In any case, generalized trust is important because it accounts for the expectations people carry with them into their social experiences.

By contrast, what we call *relational trust* refers to the trust one has for a specific person or groups of people. In a sense relational trust derives from one's participation in specific relationships and interpersonal exchanges (e.g., marriage, friendships, boss–subordinate relationships, work colleagues, family relationships, neighbors), and yet it does not reduce to the trustworthiness of one's relational partners. Instead, relational trust refers to the motivation and ability to permit oneself to become vulnerable to others through the development of the relationship itself. We have argued elsewhere (cf. W. H. Jones & Burdette, in press) that although necessary for psychological well-being, involvement in personal relationships contains two principal psychological risks—rejection and betrayal. Thus, relational trust requires risking being betrayed by one's relational partners.

B. Generalized Trust

According to the literature, one's level of generalized trust is determined by his or her general expectations of the social motives of others or the nature of the world (i.e., one's philosophy of life). If a person expects others to behave honorably and without malice (i.e., is trusting of others across many situations), he or she is said to be high in generalized trust. This trust implies a confidence and assurance in one's fellow human beings. Conversely, if a person is not very trusting or is typically distrustful of others he or she would be considered low in generalized trust.

Some level of generalized trust appears to be necessary for a normal and satisfying life. Although especially high levels of trust could possibly be seen as gullibility, it has been demonstrated in many studies that people with high trust are no more gullible than people who score low on trust (Rotter, 1967, 1980). Research suggests that high trust participants interpret cues from their interpersonal environment as well as low trust participants do in order to determine if trust is appropriate in a given situation. But when there are no cues on which to base that decision, the high trusters, because of their general expectations of the actions of people in the world, may be fooled by trusting individuals who are not worthy of that trust. However, the person low in trust may be fooled also by not trusting the honest individual.

Research indicates that most people trust individuals whom they perceive as trustworthy and that the level of generalized trust is correlated with one's own trustworthiness (Rotter, 1971). The more trusting an individual is, the less likely it is that he or she will lie or cheat (Rotter, 1971, 1980). Studies also have shown that generalized trust is inversely related to alienation (Rotter, 1971), socioeconomic status (Rotter, 1971), and communication of information (MacDonald, Kessel, & Fuller, 1972). Almost without exception, the literature appears to favor the person higher in trust. Studies have found that people high in trust are seen by others and see themselves as happier, more ethical, more attractive to the other sex, and more desirable as a close friend (Rotter, 1980). Other studies seem to support the idea that people high in trust are better adjusted individuals (Schill et al., 1980).

C. Relational Trust

The literature on trust in close relationships is a fairly new one. But, trust as a relational variable is not a new idea. Much of the research concerning self-disclosure indicates a strong relationship between that construct and relational trust. For example, trust is considered a central component of self-disclosure (Broder, 1987), and the two constructs are positively correlated (e.g., Steel, 1991). Trust has also been strongly tied to relationship satisfaction (Canary & Spitzberg, 1989; D. C. Jones, 1991; Larzelere & Huston, 1980), conflict and its resolution in relationships (Canary & Cupach, 1988; Canary & Spitzberg, 1989; Collins & Read, 1990; Ponzetti & Cate, 1986; Simpson, 1990), attachment (Simpson, 1990), love (Larzelere & Huston, 1980; Rempel et al., 1985), and commitment (Becker, 1987; Fichman & Levinthal, 1991; Larzelere & Huston, 1980).

Three main approaches to the study of relational trust have emerged. Each supposes that trust is a critical element in close relationships, but each addresses very different aspects of this process. The contributions to the literature discussing these approaches have been proposed primarily by John Holmes and John Rempel. The first approach includes a number of theories about the development of trust through stages of a relationship. Another is a component model of trust. The last to be discussed is a model of the effects of trust on previously established relationships.

1. Developmental Approaches to Relational Trust

The developmental approach to trust has been described in conjunction with intimate relationships. During the early stages of romantic love, trust may be overshadowed by love itself. Instead of facing the potential pain of rejection, one denies that trust is an issue. Larzelere and Huston (1980) found that trust does tend to be strongly related to feelings of love at this early stage of relationship development, and Dion and Dion (1976) reported that love and a sense of trust emerged together during an initial unstable infatuation period in romantic relationships. Trust will only become salient if feelings of asymmetric attachment emerge; that is, feelings of uncertainty may arise that are not satisfied. For example, when an individual begins to feel that the partner in a relationship is losing interest, mistrust regarding the partner's actions or verbalizations ensues.

Subsequently, as relationships develop, the risk of becoming increasingly dependent on the partner becomes more salient. This is characteristic of the evaluative stage. Three theoretical perspectives explain the role of trust at this point. The first claims that love and trust are likely to promote one another in a circular fashion (Holmes, 1991). If trust is not established, a satisfying relationship cannot result. An alternative theory holds that trust can be described as a reduction of uncertainty (Kelley & Thibaut, 1978). Once the basic issues of the relationship have been resolved, questions arise as to the future. According to this view, a partner's behaviors indicate a pattern which will likely continue. If the partner behaves predictably and dependably during the initial stage, the more likely it is that an individual will trust that partner. The third theoretical perspective emphasizes reciprocal attachment. Each partner must provide the other with a confidence that their feelings will be reciprocated at every stage in the relationship in order for trust to develop. In the development of romantic relationships, the risk of rejection is obvious. But, if the partner reciprocates the individual's feelings and his or her actions seem to demonstrate an adequate level of commitment, this exchange reduces uncertainty and risk by ensuring equality in risk and in involvement in the relationship (Holmes, 1991; Holmes & Rempel, 1989).

Once the relationship is more-or-less established, new issues arise. Conflicts may occur as each person begins to see his or her partner in a new and different light. Attempts to negotiate differences and/or compromises are carried out during this accommodation stage. This is seen as a time when a couple engages in diagnostic processes which "test" the level of trust (Holmes, 1991). Because relationships at this point of development are often characterized by frequent and heated conflict—risking the end of the relationship—actions on the part of the partner which show empathy or sensitivity to one's personal needs are seen as more significant and act to pull the couple closer. Security in this stage comes from the feelings of control over one's "fate" which are brought about through intimacy.

One study in particular (Larzelere & Huston, 1980) produced results supportive of the developmental model of trust. Trust and love were strongly correlated, as were trust and intimacy of self-disclosure, particularly for longer married couples. Furthermore, trust was reciprocated more than either love or level of intimacy, and trust varied with the level of commitment to the relationship.

2. A Component Model of Relational Trust

Rempel et al. (1985) proposed a component theory of relational trust. This model is based on four assumptions: (1) trust is seen to derive from past experience and develop along with the relationship; (2) in order to be trusted the partner must be seen as trustworthy (e.g., reliable, dependable, and concerned with providing expected rewards); (3) trust involves accepting the risk of relying on a partner's word through intimate disclosure and by sacrificing present rewards for future gains; and (4) trust is interpreted as confidence in the partner's caring.

Three components of trust, predictability, dependability, and faith, are described. Predictability—the most concrete and specific component—simply refers to an expectation of the occurrence of specific behavioral patterns of the partner. If the partner conforms to this expectancy, the individual is able to move from concerns about the stability of his or her partner to more pressing matters of trust. Predictability is influenced by many factors, including the amount of experience in the relationship, consistency of recurrent behaviors, and stability of the social environment (Rempel et al., 1985). This stage is the most basic and probably accounts for most of the trust early in a relationship.

As relationships develop, trust shifts from specific actions to a focus on the other person in general. This component is known as the partner's dependability, the second component of relational trust. Dependability is closely related to predictability because a partner's predictability is a meaningful basis of information from which to draw dispositional attributions. For example, if a partner behaves in a stable manner and in doing so is responsive to the individual's needs, one may attribute dependability to that partner. These dispositional attributions can be transformed into what an individual views as his or her partner's trustworthiness. This component also marks the necessary presence of risk as a factor in an individual's decision to trust another.

The first two components of trust, predictability and dependability, involve attention to the past. But, the issue of trust also concerns the future. After all, the true "test" of trust comes when new situations arise, for which relevant experience and/or knowledge may be unavailable. This requires faith, the third component of trust. Faith is considered the most important component of trust. It may be the inherent quality in an individual that allows him or her to accept the unknown future and deal with it gracefully. Faith goes beyond an emphasis on dispositional attributions, but is possibly related to both predictability and dependability in that the past is an important basis for generalizing to future situations. However, predictability and dependability reflect the partner whereas faith is a quality of the individual who does the trusting, and may also be related to personality factors, such as self-esteem and personal security.

Rempel et al. (1985) presented empirical support for their component model of trust. Among a sample of romantically involved couples, women followed the predicted hierarchical pattern discussed in the model, but among men each component appeared to function independently of the others. The results also indicated that individuals tend to project their own motives onto their partners. Love was strongly related to the faith component of trust, moderately related to the dependability component, and weakly correlated with predictability. The correlations were stronger for women than men. Love was also strongly related to reports of partners having intrinsic motivations and instrumental motivations, but much less so for those who saw their partner's motivations as extrinsic. Women were more likely to feel love strongly when their partner was viewed as having instrumental motivations. This, along with gender differences, was interpreted as evidence that women are more concerned than men about the basics of interpersonal behavior and appear to have a more integrated view of trust. Faith and intrinsic motivations were strongly related, but instrumental and extrinsic motivations generated no significant correlations. Predictability was related to instrumental and extrinsic motivations, and dependability was related to instrumental motives.

3. The Appraisal Model

A more recent addition to the literature is the appraisal model formulated by Holmes and Rempel (1989) and Holmes (1991) which focuses on the consequences of trust in established relationships. High, medium, and low trusters are seen to assess their relational interactions differently and thus "color" their interpretation of events. Trusting persons tend to evaluate the course of events in a relationship over a more extended period of time (Holmes, 1991). High trusting individuals do not judge single events as having much weight in determining the outcome or quality of a relationship. Positive events are viewed as confirming the trust that has been given, and single negative events are not seen as a threat to the relationship.

Individuals uncertain about trusting (those with more moderate levels of trust) display a very different pattern. Because they are motivated to reduce uncertainty, these individuals actively assess their partner's motives and levels of responsiveness in most interactions. Moderate trusters are hopeful that their assessments will yield positive results and allow them to trust their partner, but their expectations are limited by their fear of vulnerability (Holmes, 1991). Positive behaviors are readily viewed as relevant to greater matters of loving or caring. Negative behaviors are also perceived as very important, relating to the overall appraisal of the relationship. Risk is greatest at this level of trust because a single negative event has heightened implications for the continuation of the relationship.

Low-trust couples may have had negative experiences which caused a lack of trust in the first place. This deficiency in trust usually implies that a breach of security has transpired. It is important to note, however, that little research has been done to establish the factors that contribute to the deterioration of trust (Holmes & Rempel, 1989), so researchers have been left only to speculate as to any connections between betrayal and low trust. Low-trust partners are likely to approach their relationship with a relatively closed mind, which is very similar to the strategy of high-trust couples. They react as if they have concluded that their partner is not concerned about them or the relationship (Holmes, 1991). They are suspicious of positive behaviors and proceed cautiously. On the other hand, negative behaviors are likely to reinforce the lack of trust that previously exists (Holmes & Rempel, 1989).

D. Summary of Trust Research

Research and theorizing on the phenomenon of trust suggest four general conclusions. First, some minimal level of generalized trust appears to be necessary for "normal" social life and possibly for the development of specific relationships as well. Second, research evidence overwhelmingly supports the contention that higher levels of both generalized and relational trust are associated with enhanced functioning of individuals and groups at least under optimal conditions (e.g., when others behave honorably); higher trust is related to better communication, greater satisfaction with various relationships, higher levels of performance, and so forth. Third, relational trust appears related to and is possibly necessary for many of the basic mechanisms of relationship development (e.g., communication and self-disclosure), although there is some evidence that relational trust may be limited by dispositional characteristics of the observer, as well as by both the similarity and the trustworthiness of the actor. Fourth, although their relative merits are difficult to assess at present, recent conceptualizations of relational trust afford numerous testable hypotheses regarding the role of trust in the development and dissolution of relationships.

One particular issue unresolved in the understanding of trust is what happens to the relationship when trust is violated, in other words, when relational circumstances are less than optimal. In our view, most of the literature on trust clearly implies that violations of relational trust reduce the level of generalized trust of the victim and place the relationship in question in jeopardy. Although this pattern may be common, we believe an evolutionary–social perspective suggests that such a model is overly simplistic for several reasons including the conflict between status and acceptance which makes at least some degree of betrayal more-or-less inevitable. Also, our assumptions regarding the importance of status and acceptance and negotiated identities suggest that a victim's interpersonal options are constrained by complex social and psychological processes which may inhibit leaving every relationship in which one's partner behaves dishonorably. In any case, the literature on trust has not focused extensively on violations of trust per se, and thus this is the topic to which we will now turn.

III. THE PSYCHOLOGY OF BETRAYAL

As noted at the outset, although apparently necessary for health and well-being, it is also evident that the pursuit of close personal relationships engenders certain interpersonal risks. We believe there are two basic risks, rejection and betrayal. Not all interpersonal approaches are welcomed and this is part of what makes social encounters with strangers and certain interpersonal overtures (e.g., asking for a date) anxiety arousing (e.g., Russell, Cutrona, & Jones, 1985). We find it useful to draw a distinction between rejection—referring to rebuffs of various social overtures early in or prior to the development of interdependence and the negotiated identity of being a pair (e.g., a couple or two friends) which characterize relationships—and betrayal. We conceptualize betrayal as any violation of trust and allegiance as well as other forms of intrigue, treachery, and harm-doing in the context of established and ongoing relationships.

As painful as rejection may be, we suspect that betrayal is potentially much worse because of its likely psychological consequences. For example, similar to rejection, betrayal is likely to have direct emotional (e.g., anger and depression) and other psychological implications. However, to the extent that one has invested one's identity and sense of self in one's relationship with the instigator of the betrayal, there may also be profound indirect consequences.

In one sense, the literature on betrayal is extensive. However, previous research tends to be scattered across distinct literatures on such topics as deception, adultery, abuse, and other forms of malevolence (cf. Lawson, 1988; Metts, 1989; Miller, Mongeau, & Sleight, 1986). By contrast, in our approach to studying betrayal we have sought to subsume various types of betrayal as well as betrayals among varying populations and types of relationships in order to discern communalities in the determinants, concomitants, and consequences of these experiences. Finally, in research described later (Carver & Jones, 1992; Hansson, Jones, & Fletcher, 1990; W. H. Jones, 1988; W. H. Jones & Burdette, in press; W. H. Jones, Cohn, & Miller, 1991) we have operationalized betrayal in three different ways: (a) descriptions of specific betrayal incidents which we call betrayal narratives; (b) individual differences in the tendency to betray; and (c) betrayal as a dimension of the social network.

A. Betrayal Narratives

One approach to understanding the betrayal of trust has been to ask people to describe and answer general, but direct, questions about their experiences with betrayal. Accordingly, we have asked samples of college students and others to describe their most significant experience of having betrayed a relational partner and their most significant experience of having been betrayed by a significant other. For both instances, participants were then asked to indicate their relationship to the other person (e.g., friend, spouse, parent, sibling), the presumed motives underlying the betrayal incident, when the event took place, and the consequences of the incident, if any, for the relationship in question. For descriptions of having betrayed another, respondents were also asked whether or not the other person (i.e., the victim) was aware of what the respondent had done to betray them. Subsequently, these descriptions and answers were thematically categorized and compared on the basis of gender, perspective (i.e., whether the respondent was the victim or the perpetrator of the betrayal), and other relevant variables.

1. Types of Relationships

Results suggested that the types of relationships described varied as a function of the age of respondents. For example, among adults, spouses were most frequently cited as both victims and instigators of betrayals, but same-sex friends, parents, one's children, and work-related relationships (e.g., colleagues, bosses, subordinates) were also frequently cited. College students more frequently cited dating partners, friends, and parents, whereas children and adolescents frequently described betrayals involving siblings, friends, and parents. Interestingly, psychiatric patients almost exclusively cited parents as victims and instigators of betrayal episodes. In any case, it is clear from data involving multiple samples that the betrayal incidents described almost always involve a significant relationship in the life of the individual describing the betrayal.

2. Type of Betrayal

But what is it that people do or have done to them that constitute significant betrayals of trust? Again, the specifics of betrayal incidents vary somewhat with age and life circumstances. For example, married adults most often cited extramarital affairs as instances of significant betrayals, whereas students more often described instances of jilting or being jilted by one's boy- or girlfriend. Other common types of betrayal which appeared in various samples included telling lies, betraying confidences, inadequate emotional support and attention, acts of disloyalty, excessive criticism, and ignoring and avoiding. Less common but obviously more dramatic instances of betrayal cited by respondents included abandonment, giving a child up for adoption, physical and sexual abuse, and incest.

3. Motives for Betrayal

Not surprisingly, the motives that respondents gave for their betrayals and those of others depend, almost exclusively, on the perspective of the respondent describing the betrayal. By perspective we mean whether one is the victim or the instigator of the betrayal. When describing their own betrayals of significant others, a majority of respondents attributed their own motives to intentional and internal, but unstable, causes, thereby reducing their own culpability. For example, instigators of betrayal incidents often cited temporary emotional and cognitive stages (e.g., anger, depression, a desire for excitement) and physiological/psychological conditions (e.g., being intoxicated) as extenuating reasons for their actions. By contrast, descriptions of having been betrayed most often involved explanations of intentionality, internality, and stability as illustrated by references to the instigator's "mean streak," "inherent weaknesses," or "lack of principles." Others are therefore seen as both responsible for their actions of betrayal and likely to betray again.

4. Relationship Change

Narrative responses to questions regarding how betrayal affects relationships were classified as one of three categories of change: termination/worse (i.e., the relationship ended, or if it continued it was characterized as less satisfying and intimate), no change (i.e., some initial distrust, followed by a return to what the relationship had been previously, or no effects of betrayal); and improvement (i.e., the relationship was described as better following the betrayal than before). Again, analyses clearly indicated that perceived change in the relationship varied as a function of perspective. When describing their betrayals of others, approximately half of the respondents admitted that the relationship had ended or was worse than before, whereas the remaining half claimed that it had remained the same or even improved. By contrast, when describing instances in which they were the victims of betrayals, respondents overwhelmingly (>90% of the cases) indicated that the relationship had been terminated or was worse as a result, and these contrasting patterns emerged in studies involving differing samples of participants of varying ages and life circumstances.

5. *Other Issues*

Several additional issues were examined in these studies. For example, we found that both men and women reported that men were more likely to be instigators of betrayal in these narrative accounts, and that the accounts of betrayals by others against the respondent involved more "serious" violations of trust than did those detailing the respondents' betrayals of significant others in their lives. We also found that betrayals of others were more recent events, whereas the narratives of having been betrayed were, on average, alleged to have taken place significantly earlier in the lives of respondents. Similarly, most of these events were described as having taken place during adolescence or early adulthood, and this held even among elderly participants.

Two additional findings are of note. First, instances for which a respondent described two betrayals involving the same type of event (e.g., the respondent and his or her spouse both having an extramarital affair) or the same person (e.g., as a victim in one account and the instigator in the other) were not associated with greater insight or forgiveness. Instead, respondents tended to diminish their own culpability by citing extenuating circumstances while also holding relational partners morally responsible for their transgressions. Second, there was a gender difference regarding the role of victim awareness in betrayals of others. For men, relationships in which the partner was aware of the respondent's betrayal were described as having ended or changed for the worse, whereas when the partner was not aware the relationship was seen as improving or remaining the same. By contrast, among women there was no relationship between partner awareness and relationship change.

B. Individual Differences in Betrayal

In a second series of studies we developed a brief, self-report measure of the tendency to betray called the Interpersonal Betrayal Scale (IBS). Items referred to commonplace instances of betraying others as illustrated by the following: "lying to a family member," "making a promise to a friend or family member with no intention of keeping it." Respondents were instructed to respond to each item by indicating the frequency with which they had engaged in the behavior described.

1. *Biographical Correlates of Betrayal*

Analyses of responses to the IBS suggested important biographical correlates of self-reported betrayal. Specifically, IBS scores were found to be inversely correlated with age, level of education, and length of marriage. Married persons scored significantly lower on the IBS than did divorced persons, and IBS scores were found to be related to indications of personal and interpersonal problems (e.g., scores were higher for psychiatric patients, delinquents, and alcoholics). On the other hand, IBS scores have not varied as a function of gender in our research thus far.

2. *Psychological and Interpersonal Correlates*

As would be expected, scores on the IBS were found to be significantly related to personality measures of guilt, resentment, suspicion, and personality disorder dimensions such as borderline, paranoid, antisocial, and passive-aggressive personality dimensions. Conversely, IBS scores were inversely related to such personality dimensions as self-control, well-being, responsibility, tolerance, intellectual efficiency, psychological mindedness, and communality. Finally, both self-descriptions and ratings by significant others suggested that betrayers are best described as solitary, aloof, exploitive, gossipy, jealous, suspicious, envious, and cynical.

Not surprisingly, IBS scores were also found to be related to variables assessing relational and interpersonal functioning. For example, scores on the IBS were found to be directly related to the number of marital problems reported as well as the tendency to blame one's spouse for problems (Monroe, 1990). IBS scores were also significantly and directly correlated with loneliness and inversely related to satisfaction with the family with whom one was raised. Finally, individuals scoring high on the IBS have been found to report less social support (i.e., comfort and companionship from members of one's social network) and to have fewer voluntary relational partners (e.g., friends).

C. Betrayal and the Social Network

In our final approach to operationalizing betrayal, we have modified the Social Network List (cf. W. H. Jones & Moore, 1987) to include identification of persons betrayed by the respondent as well as persons who have betrayed the respondent. Our version of the Social Network List instructs participants to identify persons who are important to the respondent and with whom the respondent has at least occasional face-to-face contact. In addition, participants are asked to indicate the age, gender, type of relationship (e.g., spouse, friend, brother, or work colleague) and length of acquaintance with each person listed, as well as to rate various interpersonal dimensions for each (e.g., satisfaction with the relationship, reciprocity, jealousy, love, disagreements).

Results suggested that almost half the participants indicated that they have betrayed at least one current member of their social network, and a comparable number of respondents indicated that they have been betrayed by a member of their social network. On average, roughly 20% of network members are identified as being either victims or instigators of betrayal. In addition, these results suggest that betrayals are most likely to involve one's closest relationships: spouses, family, and close friends.

Furthermore, identification of a network member as having betrayed the respondent was associated with significantly lower scores on positive dimensions describing network members (e.g., satisfaction, reciprocity, love, dependability, can turn to for help) and higher scores on negative descriptive dimensions (e.g., regret, disagreements, jealousy). Also, IBS scores were significantly related to the proportion of the network identified as victims and instigators of betrayals.

D. Summary of Betrayal Research

Our research on violations of trust may be summarized as suggesting the following four basic conclusions: First, betrayal is fairly commonplace and most likely to occur in one's most important relationships. Second, betrayal is associated with stable biographic and personality based individual differences, with the exception of gender, for which our data are inconsistent across differing measures of betrayal. Third, the consequences and meaning of betrayal seem to vary as a function of one's perspective as either the victim or the instigator. Fourth, although clearly associated with negative perceptions and attributions, violations of trust do not always result in the termination of a relationship. It is important to note also that although a few findings appear to depend on the characteristics of the sample under investigation, most of these results have been replicated across samples varying in age and other life circumstances.

IV. CONCLUSION

The integration of research on trust and betrayal affords a unique opportunity to view the complex and dialectical nature of getting along and getting ahead in human groups and hence the complexity of understanding the role of personality in social life. Research and theorizing about trust suggest that (1) trust is a necessary precursor to group living and the development of specific relationships, and (2) higher levels of trust are associated not only with greater likeability—as would be expected—but greater adjustment and happiness as well. On the other hand, the very process of trusting specific people increases the likelihood of being betrayed and apparently does so dramatically, and the persons most likely to do so are one's closest friends and relations.

That most people continue to trust and take other interpersonal risks in view of both the likelihood and the potential damage of being betrayed by one's partners is the surprising phenomenon here and suggests a fundamental and primitive need for human involvements and companionship. Recognizing that much of what people do in their interpersonal lives represents efforts to balance interpersonal risks and rewards or to balance getting along and getting ahead raises an interesting issue about moral development, and this is the point with which we would like to close. Far from the detached, intellectualized, and philosophical abstractions (e.g., moral judgments) portrayed by some researchers, viewed from the perspective of trust and betrayal, issues of morality are immediate, messy, practical, and decidedly interpersonal. Indeed, the central questions regarding moral development here might be stated as follows: (1) how do people proceed to trust specific others given the realistic possibility that they could be betrayed? and (2) how do some people continue to trust and engage others in relationships even after they have been betrayed by them?

REFERENCES

Becker, C. S. (1987). Friendship between women: A phenomenological study of best friends. *Journal of Phenomenological Psychology, 18,* 59–72.

Broder, S. N. (1987). Helping students with self-disclosure. *School Counselor, 34,* 182–187.

Canary, D. J., & Cupach, W. R. (1988). Relational and episodic characteristics associated with conflict tactics. *Journal of Social and Personal Relationships, 5,* 305–325.

Canary, D. J., & Spitzberg, B. H. (1989). A model of the perceived competence of conflict strategies. *Human Communication Research, 15,* 630–649.

Carver, M. D., & Jones, W. H. (1992). The Family Satisfaction Scale. *Social Behavior and Personality, 20,* 71–84.

Collins, N. L., & Read, S. J. (1990). Adult attachment, working models, and relationship quality in dating couples. *Journal of Personality and Social Psychology, 58,* 644–663.

Deutsch, M. (1958). Trust and suspicion. *Conflict Resolution, 2,* 265–279.

Digman, J. M., & Takemoto-Chock, N. R. (1981). Factors in the natural language of personality: Re-analysis, comparison, and interpretation of six major studies. *Multivariate Behavioral Research, 16,* 149–170.

Dion, K. L., & Dion, K. K. (1976). Correlates of romantic love. *Journal of Consulting and Clinical Psychology, 41,* 51–56.

Driscoll, J. W. (1978). Trust and participation in organizational decision making as predictors of satisfaction. *Academy of Management Journal, 21,* 44–56.

Erikson, E. H. (1950). *Childhood and society.* New York: Norton.

Erikson, E. H. (1963). *Childhood and society* (2nd ed.). New York: Norton.

Fichman, M., & Levinthal, D. A. (1991). Honeymoons and the liability of adolescence: A new perspective on duration dependence in social and organizational relationships. *Academy of Management Review, 16,* 442–468.

Golembiewski, R. T., & McConkie, M. (1975). The centrality of interpersonal trust in group processes. In C. L. Cooper (Ed.), *Theories of group process* (pp. 131–185). London: Wiley.

Hansson, R. O., Jones, W. H., & Fletcher, W. L. (1990). Troubled relationships in later life: Implications for support. *Journal of Social and Personal Relationships, 7,* 451–463.

Hogan, R. (1976). Egoism, altruism, and culture. *American Psychologist, 31,* 363–366.

Hogan, R. (1983). A socioanalytic theory of personality. In M. M. Page (Ed.), *Nebraska Symposium on Motivation: Personality—Current theory and research* (pp. 55–90). Lincoln: University of Nebraska Press.

Hogan, R., Jones, W. H., & Cheek, J. M. (1985). Socioanalytic theory: An alternative to armadillo psychology. In B. Schlenker (Ed.), *Self and identity: Presentation of self in social life.* New York: McGraw-Hill.

Holmes, J. G. (1991). Trust and the appraisal process in close relationships. In W. H. Jones & D. Perlman (Eds.), *Advances in personal relationships* (pp. 57–106). London: Jessica Kingsley Publishers.

Holmes, J. G., & Rempel, J. K. (1989). Trust in close relationships. In C. Hendrick (Ed.), *Close relationships* (pp. 187–220). Newbury Park, CA: Sage.

Jones, D. C. (1991). Friendship satisfaction and gender: An examination of sex differences in contributors to friendship satisfaction. *Journal of Social and Personal Relationships, 8,* 167–185.

Jones, W. H. (1988, July). *Psychological and interpersonal issues in betrayal and treachery.* Paper presented at the Fourth International Conference on Personal Relationships, Vancouver, British Columbia, Canada.

Jones, W. H., & Burdette, M. P. (in press). Betrayal in close personal relationships. In A. Weber & J. H. Harvey (Eds.), *Perspectives on close relationships* (pp. 243–262). New York: Allyn & Bacon.

Jones, W. H., Cohn, M. G., & Miller, C. E. (1991). Betrayal among children and adults. In K. J. Rotenberg (Ed.), *Children's interpersonal trust: Sensitivity to lying, deception, and promise violations* (pp. 118–134). New York: Springer-Verlag.

Jones, W. H., & Moore, T. L. (1987). Loneliness and social support. *Journal of Social Behavior and Personality, 2,* 145–156.

Kelley, H. H., & Thibaut, J. W. (1978). *Interpersonal relations: A theory of interdependence.* New York: Wiley.

Larzelere, R. E., & Huston, T. L. (1980). The dyadic trust scale: Toward understanding interpersonal trust in close relationships. *Journal of Marriage and the Family, 42,* 595–604.

Lawson, A. (1988). *Adultery.* New York: Basic Books.

MacDonald, A. P., Kessel, V. S., & Fuller, J. B. (1972). Self-disclosure and two kinds of trust. *Psychological Reports, 30,* 143–148.

Metts, S. (1989). An exploratory investigation of deception in close relationships. *Journal of Social and Personal Relationships, 6,* 159–179.

Miller, G. R., Mongeau, P. A., & Sleight, C. (1986). Fudging with friends and lying to lovers: Deceptive communication in personal relationships. *Journal of Social and Personal Relationships, 3,* 495–512.

Monroe, P. (1990). *A study of marital problems, marital satisfaction, and commitment.* Unpublished doctoral dissertation, University of Tulsa, Tulsa, OK.

Ponzetti, J. J., & Cate, R. M. (1986). The developmental course of conflict in the marital dissolution process. *Journal of Divorce, 10,* 1–15.

Rempel, J. K., Holmes, J. G., & Zanna, M. P. (1985). Trust in close relationships. *Journal of Personality and Social Psychology, 49,* 95–112.

Rotenberg, K. J. (Ed.). (1991). *Children's interpersonal trust.* New York: Springer-Verlag.

Rotter, J. B. (1967). A new scale for the measurement of interpersonal trust. *Journal of Personality, 35,* 651–665.

Rotter, J. B. (1971). Interpersonal trust, trustworthiness, and gullibility. *American Psychologist, 35,* 1–7.

Rotter, J. B. (1980). Interpersonal trust, trustworthiness, and gullibility. *American Psychologist, 35,* 651–665.

Russell, D., Cutrona, C. E., & Jones, W. H. (1985). A trait-situational analysis of shyness. In W. H. Jones, J. M. Cheek, & S. R. Briggs (Eds.), *Shyness: Perspectives on research and treatment* (pp. 239–249). New York: Plenum Press.

Schill, T., Toves, C., & Ramanaiah, N. (1980). Interpersonal trust and coping with stress. *Psychological Reports, 47,* 1192.

Scott, D. (1980). The causal relationship between trust and the assessed value of management by objectives. *Journal of Management, 6,* 157–175.

Simpson, J. A. (1990). Influence of attachment styles on romantic relationships. *Journal of Personality and Social Psychology, 59,* 971–980.

Stack, L. (1978). Trust. In H. London & J. E. Exner (Eds.), *Dimensions of personality* (pp. 561–599). New York: Wiley.

Steel, J. L. (1991). Interpersonal correlates of trust and self-disclosure. *Psychological Reports, 68,* 1319–1320.

Wrightsman, L. S. (1974). *Assumptions about human nature: A social-psychological approach.* Monterey, CA: Brooks/Cole.

PART VI

DYNAMIC PERSONALITY PROCESSES

CHAPTER 20

MOTIVES AND LIFE GOALS

ROBERT A. EMMONS
UNIVERSITY OF CALIFORNIA, DAVIS

Motivation has always been seen as central to personality psychology, although interest in motivational concepts has waxed and waned over the past 50 years. McAdams (this volume, Chap. 1) includes concern with motivation and dynamics as one of the three distinguishing features of the field. Hogan (1986) argues forcefully that motivational concepts are the "explanatory concepts par excellence in personality psychology" (p. 50). Historically, concepts such as instinct, need, and drive carried the burden of motivational theorizing. As Pervin (1983) and Cofer (1981) noted though, the demise of drive theory in the late 1950s tended to result in a diminution of interest in motivational concepts in general. In contrast, today theorists and researchers are more willing to invoke motivational concepts into their descriptive and explanatory models. Terms such as tasks, goals, concerns, projects, strivings, and motives are part of the everyday motivational parlance. I have argued elsewhere (Emmons, 1993) that the recent revitalization of the field of personality (see also McAdams, this volume, chap. 1, and Runyan, 1990) has been due in large part to a resurgence of interest in motivational concepts. The application of the motive concept in predicting important life outcomes in domains outside of the laboratory and the heightened interest in studying behavior as it unfolds over time in natural contexts and in life transitions are two of the factors responsible for the long awaited return of motivation to the field of personality.

This chapter begins with a brief review of the literature on motive dispositions, as it represents how the concept of motivation has been traditionally handled within personality psychology. The review will of necessity be selective—new and innovative directions will be emphasized. Metatheoretical perspectives on goal-directed behavior will be reviewed next. An analysis of the construct of goals in personality psychology will then be considered, and both nomothetic and idiographic perspectives will be covered. One of the most important trends has been the recent movement toward the "personalization" of motivation. Thus, of particular focus will be idiographic approaches to personal goals. Since it would appear that this is where the action will be in the future, the time is right for a critical review of this literature. Psychometric and methodological considerations will be highlighted. After briefly considering the relationship between goals and personality traits, the chapter concludes with recommendations for future directions.

I. THE MOTIVE DISPOSITION APPROACH

Motivation in personality psychology has been traditionally conceived of in terms of stable individual differences in the strength of motive dispositions. A motive disposition refers to a class or cluster of affectively tinged goals (McClelland, 1985). Motives energize, direct, and select behavior. Considerable literatures have developed around what may be called the Big Three motives: Achievement, Affiliation/ Intimacy, and Power. These motives are assessed via content analysis of brief imaginative stories produced in response to pictures similar to those used in the Thematic Apperception Test (TAT). Although battles over the psychometric properties of this measure have been waged, there exists now a greater awareness of the factors affecting the reliability and validity of scores derived in this manner (Spangler, 1992).

Achievement motivation can be defined as a recurrent preference or readiness in thought and behavior for experiences of attaining excellence—of competing with a standard of excellence (McClelland, 1985). Affiliation motivation can be defined as a recurrent preference in thought and behavior for experiences of establishing, maintaining, and restoring a positive affective relationship (Atkinson, Heyns, & Veroff, 1954). Intimacy motivation can be defined as a recurrent preference in thought and behavior for experiences of warm, close, and communicative interactions with others. The preference is for interpersonal exchange as an end in itself rather than a means to another end (McAdams, 1980). Intimacy-oriented individuals are concerned with establishing and maintaining close interpersonal relationships and report positive emotions in the presence of others (McAdams & Constantian, 1983). Power motivation can be defined as a recurrent preference in thought and behavior for experiences of feeling strong and having impact on others. Among other correlates, power-oriented individuals are concerned with attaining status and prestige, choose as friends persons low in power motivation, and are highly promiscuous in heterosexual relationships (Winter & Stewart, 1978). As has been argued (Winter, 1991), these are not the only important human motives, but they do include many of the most important human goals and concerns.

Several scholarly reviews of the motive literature have recently appeared (Jemmott, 1987; McAdams, 1994; McClelland, 1985; Smith, 1992; Stewart & Chester, 1982; Winter, 1996). The edited volume by Smith (1992) is an especially impressive collection and includes the scoring systems for the major motive systems as well as psychosocial orientations and cognitive styles. Therefore, a comprehensive review of this voluminous literature will not be attempted here. Instead, three recent trends will be discussed: (1) the role of social motives in physical health and disease; (2) contextual factors and motive dispositions; and (3) the measurement of motives in personal documents. Emphasis is placed on these three topics as they are typically ignored in textbooks on personality (Emmons, 1989a), yet represent three directions being pursued in this literature with great applicational promise.

A. Motive Dispositions and Physical Health

The effect of the needs for affiliation/intimacy and power on physical health has been studied extensively by David McClelland and his associates (see Jemmott, 1987, for a review). The available evidence points to power motivation as having a deleterious effect on health (especially when combined with power stressors) whereas affiliation/intimacy motivation has a buffering effect. However, it is not the individual effect of these motives that is critical but rather their joint influence as expressed in various motive patterns. Two of these patterns have been identified: the Inhibited Power Motive Syndrome (IPMS) and the Relaxed Affiliative Syndrome (RAS).

The IPMS is characterized by a stronger need for power than need for affiliation/intimacy, and a high degree of self-restraint, or activity inhibition. Activity inhibition is measured by the frequency of negations (use of the word ''not'' or its contracted form) in TAT protocols. This syndrome, then, characterizes individuals who are high in the need for power but are inhibited in expressing it. This syndrome has been linked with high blood pressure, high degree of self-reported physical illnesses, and lower levels of immunocompetence as measured by secretory immunoglobulin A (S-IgA; Jemmott, 1987). The release of stress hormones, cortisol and epinephrine, due to chronic sympathetic activity is the likely culprit responsible for these effects. It is important to note that need for power is not in itself related to sympathetic activation and subsequent disease but only when it is blocked by internal inhibition or external stressors (see also Fodor, 1984). The relationship between IPMS and immune system functioning has not been limited to S-IgA; this motive pattern has also been related to natural killer cell activity. This is important in that S-IgA as a measure of immunocompetence is controversial (Stone, Cox, Valdimarsdottir, & Neale, 1987). In addition, manipulations designed to increase power motivation in the laboratory (viewing a war film) resulted in diminished immunocompetence in individuals characterized by IPMS (McClelland & Kirschnit, 1988). Independent investigations (Fontana, Rosenberg, Marcus, & Kerns, 1987) also report that IPMS is associated with systolic blood pressure reactivity. In contrast to the deleterious effects of power motivation, affiliation/intimacy motivation seems to have a salubrious effect on health. RAS is defined as having a higher need for affiliation/intimacy than need for power, combined with low activity inhibition. Several studies report that RAS is associated with better health, across a variety of outcomes. RAS has been linked with lower blood pressure, reporting fewer illnesses, and better immunologic functioning (Jemmott, 1987). Manipulations designed to increase affiliation/intimacy (viewing a film of Mother Teresa of Calcutta) resulted in an increase of S-IgA (McClelland & Kirschnit, 1988). More recent research, however, suggests a more complicated relationship between these social motives and health. McClelland (1989) suggested the need for a more fine-grained analysis of power and affiliation/intimacy motivation. Certain types of affiliation and power motivation, labeled affiliative trust and agentic power, are associated with better health, whereas cynical trust and stressed power motivation, respectively, have disruptive health effects.

B. Measuring Motives in Personal Documents

Research on motive dispositions is sometimes limited due to its reliance on the picture-story exercise for assessing motives. There are many purposes for which it would be desirable to have an estimate of motive strength in individuals for whom it is impossible to administer the TAT, for instance, deceased historical figures. Winter (1991) has developed a method of assessing motives in "running text" which allows researchers to code speeches, interviews, and other personal documents and biographical materials for the motive dispositions. In short, it can be applied to any written text or written transcripts of spoken material that are at least in part imaginative.

Measuring motives "at a distance" has been most widely applied in the realm of political psychology. In particular, Winter (Donley & Winter, 1970; Winter, 1987, 1988; Winter & Stewart, 1978) has applied the scoring system to the inaugural addresses of U.S. Presidents with the purpose of predicting outcomes in office, such as greatness ratings, assassination attempts, and entry into war. Motive scores obtained in this way can also be used in psychobiographical studies, as Winter has demonstrated in his analyses of John Kennedy (Winter, 1991) and Richard Nixon (Winter & Carlson, 1988). In another interesting application, Winter (1987) showed that congruence between presidential and societal motive profiles predicted presidential appeal, defined in terms of electrol success.

A complete overview of the integrated running text scoring system, its psychometric properties, and a review of studies that have employed it can be found in Winter (1991). Winter marshals a good deal of evidence for the validity of the integrated running text scoring system.

C. Studying Motivation in Context

A third emerging theme in the study of motivation is what might be termed as "contextual" perspective. A contextual perspective emphasizing social-historical and social structural factors has been emerging in developmental, personality, and social psychology (Bolger, 1988; Caspi, 1987; Ryff, 1987). A contextual perspective applied to motivation implies that motivational processes cannot be understood without taking into account a variety of contexts within which a person is embedded.

Motivational theorists have long recognized the importance of contextual or situational factors. Murray's (1938) theory of personality emphasized not only personality needs but the environmental press relevant to those needs. A leading spokesperson for the contextual approach to motivation has been Joseph Veroff. Veroff (1983, 1986; Veroff & Smith, 1985) has advocated the necessity of taking into account the influence of historical, cultural, developmental, organizational, and interpersonal contexts in understanding patterns of constancy and change in social motives. Veroff (1983) provided a contextual interpretation of achievement and affiliation motives and persuasively demonstrated how the meaning of a motive may vary depending upon the five contexts. Veroff and Feld (1970) examined the ways in which the three social motives interacted with three important social roles (marriage, parenting, and work) within a dynamic, contextual framework. In such a framework, not only do motives affect the perceptions of these roles, but the roles themselves shape the nature and expression of the motives. Veroff's work points to the importance of addressing how motivational content and processes are influenced by a variety of contextual factors. Ryff (1987) provides a pointed example of how cultural values in Japan and the United States influence child-rearing practices, which in turn lead to personality differences in such characteristics as autonomy versus interdependence.

A quite different contextual approach to motivation is represented in McAdams' (1985b, 1990, 1993) theory of identity as a life story. Identity, that which binds together past, present, and future, lends coherence, unity, and purpose of personality and allows adaptation to changing contexts. One's identity is organized around imagoes—idealized and personified images of the self. Imagoes are the central elements of a person's identity and represent instantiations of two fundamental thematic lines in people's lives: agency (power/mastery/separation) and communion (intimacy/surrender/union). Imagoes are broad, superordinate constructs which encompass interpersonal styles, values and beliefs, and personal needs and motives (McAdams, 1985a). McAdams is most concerned with the historical context; the life story model of identity provides a framework for conceptualizing the development and history of the person from birth to death.

II. METATHEORETICAL PERSPECTIVES ON GOALS

Several metatheoretical perspectives offer a framework within which to interpret goal-directed action. This review will focus on three of them: control theory, living systems framework, and action theory. The basic ideas of each of these will be presented.

A. Control Theory

One of the most simple yet potentially powerful models for representing goals and goal-directed behavior is control theory (Carver & Scheier, 1981, 1982; Hyland, 1987, 1988; Powers, 1973, 1978). According to control theory, behavior is seen as a discrepancy reduction process operating in terms of a negative feedback loop, where individuals act to minimize the discrepancy between their present condition and a desired standard or goal. There are five components in standard control-theory models. Goals or standards are checked against feedback received by a sensor; a comparator compares the feedback with the standard, outputting the result to a decision mechanism which activates an effector system to operate on the environment to further reduce the discrepancy. From the standpoint of this chapter, goals and feedback are the crucial components: feedback is information that provides individuals with a basis for decisions about changing either the course of their behavior or the goals themselves.

Control theory has been criticized on two main grounds. One charge is that it ignores the role of emotion. Carver and Scheier (1990) have attempted to eradicate this charge by addressing the role of emotion within control theory. A second criticism is that control theories are mechanistic. Powers (1978) argues that this belief is mistaken as control theory can account for dynamic, flexible aspects of behavior. This second criticism has served as an impetus for the development of the living systems framework, which is discussed next.

B. Living Systems Framework

Several recent formulations have proposed system-theoretic conceptions of personality in which goals play a major role. For instance, Powell, Royce, and Voorhees (1982) depict personality as a complex hierarchical information processing system (CHIPS) with goal directedness as a major component. Perhaps the most impressive of these efforts is the living systems framework (LSF; D. H. Ford, 1987; D. H. Ford & Ford, 1987). Central to this formulation is the idea that people are active organisms who intentionally set and strive for goals. There is a strong emphasis on goal directedness at all levels of organization. Goals organize and direct the activity of the system. Much of their theory can be viewed as a formalization and elaboration of control-theory ideas. A classical control system (mechanistic) model is transformed into a living system by adding self-organizing and self-constructing functions. The functioning of a control system involves five interrelated and interdependent processes: directive, information collection, regulatory, control, and action. The system is self-regulating in that the activity of the system is part of the input controlling the functioning of the system.

Of greatest relevance for a chapter on goals is what is labeled the directive function: the personal goals and aspirations of the individual. The directive function includes the formulation, revision, and elaboration of goals. Goals in the LSF are defined as cognitive representations of desired and undesired conditions. Subordinate to the directive function are the control (planning and problem solving) and regulatory (progress monitoring) functions. The volume by D. H. Ford and Ford (1987) illustrates the utility of the LSF in designing research and in professional application. The potential scope of the framework is broad—problems in social competence, emotion development, prosocial behavior, and clinical and counseling psychology are just a few of the domains in which the LSF can lead to greater understanding.

C. Action Theory

Action theory, an information-processing approach to motivation and goals, has been gathering momentum (Frese & Sabini, 1985; Halisch & Kuhl, 1987; Semmer & Frese, 1985; Heckhausen, 1991; Kuhl & Beckman, 1985). Action theory was developed largely in Germany and treats goal-directed action as the unit of analysis. Action is contrasted with behavior, the latter not being goal directed. The major task of action theory is to fill the gap between the cognitive representation of desired states and the execution of acts designed to achieve the desired states. In order to close this gap, at least four questions need to be answered to the agenda set forth by Kuhl & Beckman (1985): (1) How do cognitive structures arouse motivational states? (2) How does one understand the processes underlying temporal changes in these motivational states? (3) What are the mechanisms that mediate the formation and enactment of intentions? (4) What are the mechanisms that mediate the final execution of a sequence of behaviors?

Kuhl (1985a) proposed that action versus state orientation is an important determinant of action control. A person is action oriented when his or her attention is focused on some aspect of the present state, some aspect of a future state, the discrepancy between the two, and at least one action alternative that can reduce the discrepancy. State orientation exists when one of the four elements is missing, for example, when a person dwells on the current state without reference to the future or fails to develop action alternatives that could reduce the discrepancy. This distinction is important in that it is a primary reason for the lack of enactment of an intention. A high degree of action orientation directs and controls cognitive processes the facilitate the enactment of the intention. State orientation impedes performance since it involves repetitive and dysfunctional focusing on fixed aspects of the situation.

Frese and Sabini (1985) provide multiple applications of action theory, with counterpoint commentaries provided by researchers outside the paradigm. Industrial/organizational, educational, and clinical and counseling applications of action theory are presented.

Critics of action theory (Klinger, 1985; Warren, 1987) contend that it is lost in thought: it is overly rational, and the role of dynamic and affective processes are minimized. Thus, it is unlikely to ever address motivational processes such as goal conflict, since in an expectancy–value framework, it will be a rare case that competing goals will have equal arithmetic valences; thus there will be no conflict. Another criticism is that research emanating from the paradigm has focused nearly exclusively on trivial laboratory behavior. Lastly, action theory is concerned nearly exclusively with process, and has been silent with regard to motivational content. Kuhl (1985b) has attempted to answer these criticisms.

III. GOAL APPROACHES OF PERSONALITY

A. Nomothetic Approaches to Goals

Early efforts into the inquiry of a phenomena are often taxonomic in nature. Therefore, it is not surprising that one objective of the research using normatively constructed goal lists has been in constructing a taxonomy of human goals. Several empirically derived taxonomies reflecting content categories into which goals are organized have recently been uncovered. Much of this work is summarized in Novacek and Lazarus (1990) and M. E. Ford (1992). The general procedure in this research is to present subjects with a standardized list of goals and have subjects rate these goals on a preselected dimension, typically importance or relevance. Intercorrelations of these ratings are then subjected to factor or cluster analysis to derive basic groupings. Often these goals are based on prior lists generated by a sample possessing similar characteristics to the sample doing the rating, but in at least one case "goals are generated intuitively by the senior author without explicit recourse to prior classifications" (Wicker, 1984, p. 288). Table I shows the goal categories that have emerged in a number of different investigations. There seems to be evidence of five general factors, which have been labeled (1) Enjoyment, (2) Self-Assertion, (3) Esteem, (4) Interpersonal, and (5) Avoidance of Negative Affect. The fact that these clusters reemerge in several studies points to possibly an uncovering of a basic motivational structure. These categories will need to be replicated in cross-cultural samples before such a claim can be made, however. It is encouraging, though, that these factors are similar to the "basic motives" postulated by several theories of motivation, including those of Maslow (1970) and Hogan (1983).

B. Idiographic Goal Approaches

Nomothetic approaches such as those just noted are appealing because of their amenability to comparison, both across individuals and studies. After all, the logic of taxonomy building requires normalization across individuals. However, a number of other investigators have argued quite forcefully that any attempt to understand an individual's goal system in terms of a consensually defined a priori list of goals is likely to be highly misleading and restrictive, since individuals strive for goals in highly individualized ways. Thus, there has been an increasing trend recently toward the adoption of more circumscribed, idiographic units to account for human motivation. Without a doubt, the most important development in motivational approaches to personality has been the recent trend toward the personalization of motivation. The constructs of "current concern" (Klinger, 1975), "personal project" (Little, 1983), "life task" (Cantor, Brower, & Korn, 1985), and "personal striving" (Emmons, 1986) have been proposed as idiographic goal-directed units for personality psychology. An overview of each of the four major constructs is considered next.

TABLE I
Summary of Studies Reporting Common Goal Clusters

Study		Factors			
	Enjoyment	Self-Assertion	Esteem	Interpersonal	Avoidance of Negative Affect
Pervin (1983)	Relaxation/Fun	Aggression/Power	Self-Esteem	Affection/Support	Anxiety/Threat Reduction
Emmons and Diener (1986)	Hedonistic	Self-Achievement		Interpersonal	
Novacek and Lazarus (1990)	Sensation-Seeking	Achievement/Power	Personal Growth	Affiliation	Stress Avoidance
Wicker (1984)	Exploration/Play	Competitive Ambition	Individual Striving*	Interpersonal Concern	Harmony Seeking*
Buhler (1964)	Need Satisfactions	Creative Expansion	Upholding of Internal Order	Need Satisfaction	Self-Limiting Adaptation
M. E. Ford and Nichols (1987)	Affective	Task	Cognitive	Social Relationships	Subjective Organization

* Second-order factor.

C. Four Major Constructs

1. Current Concerns

Klinger (1975, 1977, 1987) has argued that experience is organized around the pursuit of incentives, and that these pursuits are represented by a "current concern." A current concern is a hypothetical motivational state in between two points in time: the commitment to a goal and either the consumation of the goal or the disengagement from it. This hypothetical state guides a person's ongoing thoughts, emotional reactions, and behavior during the time it is active. Klinger developed the notion of a "current concern" out of dissatisfaction with the failure of the motive dispositions to predict spontaneous thought content. However, there is no assumption about the representation of the concern in consciousness, and it is assumed that for the majority of the time, the concern is not reflected in on-line cognitive processing. People simultaneously possess a number of current concerns, as there is a different concern for each goal a person is committed to. The range of potential concerns is diverse, as each individual possesses an idiographic set which frequently changes. Examples of current concerns are going on a trip, keeping a dentist appointment, losing weight, and maintaining a love relationship. Other examples of current concerns along with examples of the other personal goal constructs are shown in Table II. Concerns may be defined narrowly or broadly, and may last anywhere from a few seconds to a life time. The primary purpose of the current-concern construct has been as a carrier for motivational influences on thought processes. Klinger, Barta, and Maxeiner (1981) found that the degree to which current concerns are valued, committed to, and threatened predicted the frequency with which these concerns are thought about. According to Klinger, thoughts are triggered by environmental cues that are related to current concerns, and it is the emotional properties of concerns that affect the processing of these cues. Other research has shown that words related to current concerns surreptitiously presented on the left side of a computer screen interfered with a lexical decision-making task (Young, 1988), indicating the automatic quality with which concern-related cues affect cognition. Klinger (1989a) reviews research showing that concern relatedness and emotional arousingness of a word predict its recall. These findings are taken as evidence that current concerns influence cognitive processing because the concern state predisposes the individual to react with emotional arousal to cues associated with the concern.

While initially serving as a link between motivation and cognition, the current-concern framework has also proven useful in applied contexts. The concept has been extended into the realms of depression (Ruehlman & Wolchik, 1988), alcoholism (Klinger & Cox, 1986), and work satisfaction (Roberson, 1989).

2. Personal Projects

A similar though independently developed concept is the personal project (Little, 1983, 1987, 1989; Palys & Little, 1983). Rooted in Murray's (1951) concept of a serial program, personal projects are "an interrelated sequence of actions intended

Table II
Examples of Personal Goals

Current concerns	Personal projects
Eating lunch	Putting out the cat
Going camping next weekend	Coping with cancer
Finishing the writing of a book	Sailing the Atlantic
Getting the garden planted	Making a dress
Gaining a promotion	Learn how to ski
Eating dinner tonight	Graduate from University
Taking a skiing vacation	Get Tom to stop biting his nails
Maintaining a marital relationship	Not losing my job
Buying a fly swatter	Becoming more responsive to Pierre
Getting closer to God	Revenging my father's death

Life tasks	Personal strivings
Maturing beyond my high school mentality	Make attractive women notice me
Finding a girlfriend	Do as many nice things for people as I can
Establishing future goals	Get to know new people
Getting good grades	Maintain an above average beauty
Planning for the future	Force men to be intimate in relationships
Developing an identity	Have as much fun as possible
Being productive at work	Avoid being dependent on my boyfriend
Making friends	Make it appear that I am intelligent
Being on one's own away from family	Avoid arguments when possible
Managing time	Make life easier for my parents

to achieve a personal goal" (Palys & Little, 1983, p. 1223). They have also been defined as "extended sets of personally relevant action" (Little, 1989, p. 15). Personal projects are things that people think about, plan for, carry out, and sometimes, but not always, complete (Little, 1983). Everyday activity is organized around these personal projects. Examples of personal projects are "going to the prom with Brad," "finding a part-time job," and "shopping for the holidays" (Little, 1983). The concept was developed and promoted by Little as an interactional unit linking the individual to his or her sociocultural context. Little (1987) stresses three types of contexts that are necessary for understanding action: the intentional context, in which the purposes underlying the projects are discerned; the systemic context, the relation of projects to each other within a project system; and the ecological context, the environmental and historical milieu in which the action takes place.

Interestingly, the term "personal project" was first used by Nuttin (1957) to describe "fundamental dynamic orientations" of personality and were defined as "personal tasks to be accomplished" (p. 194). These projects, according to Nuttin, represent the personalized version of needs and account for the unity of personality functioning. The personal project concept has been applied in studies of subjective well-being. For instance, Palys and Little (1983) found that individuals who were involved in short-term important projects that were highly enjoyable and moderately difficult were more satisfied with their lives than individuals who possessed projects that were longer range in scope and from which they derived little immediate enjoyment. Ruehlman and Wolchik (1988) reported that interpersonal support and hindrance in personal project pursuit were related to well-being and distress, respectively, and that hindrance was also related to low well-being.

3. Life Tasks

Cantor and her colleagues (Cantor, 1990; Cantor et al., 1985; Cantor & Kihlström, 1987, 1989; Cantor & Langston, 1989; Cantor, Norem, Niedenthal, Langston, & Brower, 1987) recently developed the concept of life tasks, defined as "problems that people are currently working on (Cantor & Kihlström, 1987, p. 4) and "the set of tasks that the person sees himself or herself working on and devoting energy to solving during a specified period of life" (Cantor et al., 1987, p. 1179). These life tasks, consensual in nature, organize and give meaning to a person's everyday activities, and are especially salient during life transitions, such as marriage or graduation from college. The life task concept emerged within Cantor and Kihlström's social-cognitive approach to personality, an approach emphasizing discriminativeness and flexibility in human action. It was originally developed in order to explore how people use social intelligence in dealing with tasks posed by life transitions. Examples of life tasks include "succeeding academically," "making friends," and "being on my own" (Cantor et al., 1987).

Research on life tasks has been aimed at demonstrating how the cognitive basis (social intelligence) of personality in the problem-solving strategies chosen by the individual in approaching his or her life tasks. Two of these strategies have been identified: defensive pessimism in dealing with academic life tasks (Norem, Illingworth, & Shaun, 1993 and social constraint in dealing with social life tasks (Cantor & Langston, 1989). Other research (Zirkel & Cantor, 1990) demonstrated how individual differences in the construal of the life task of "achieving independence" impacted on activity choices, affective experience, and perceived stress.

4. Personal Strivings

The concept of personal strivings (Emmons, 1986, 1989c, 1996; Emmons & King, 1988, 1989) was developed in order to describe the recurring, characteristic goal-striving behavior of individuals. Personal strivings are rooted in Floyd Allport's (1937) concept of "teleonomic trends." Personal strivings are idiographically coherent patterns of goal strivings and represent what an individual is typically trying to do. Each individual can be characterized by a unique set of these "trying to do" tendencies. For example, a person may be "trying to appear attractive to the opposite sex," "trying to be a good listeners to his or her friends," and "trying to be better than others." Personal strivings can be thought of as superordinate abstracting qualities, or motivational organizing principles that render a cluster of goals functionally equivalent for an individual. In this sense, a striving is similar to the definition of a motive disposition given earlier. However, the critical differences lies in the idiographic nature of the personal striving. A personal striving is a unifying construct—it unites what may be phenotypically different goals or actions around a common quality or theme. Thus, a striving can be achieved in a variety of ways and satisfied via any one of a number of concrete goals. The personal striving concept has been primarily employed to account for individual differences in psychological and physical well-being. For example, Emmons and King (1988) found that conflict within and between strivings was associated with psychological distress and physical illness, both concurrently as well as prospectively. Another line of research (Emmons & King, 1989) has investigated the relationship between personal striving differentiation or complexity and affective reactivity. Reactive individuals (those experiencing intense and variable moods) were found to possess a highly differentiated (more unrelated strivings) striving system. Emmons (1996) presents a thorough review of the literature on personal strivings and subjective well-being.

C. Distinguishing between the Personal Goal Units

Before turning to the assessment of these personal goal units, it is useful to discuss similarities and differences among them. In the framework of control theory, all can be viewed as reference values, discrepancies from which initiate and organize action. Each construct involves a somewhat different representation of goals: goals as concerns, goals as projects, goals as tasks, and goals as strivings. Each construct is both idiographic and nomothetic. Individuals possess a personalized list of these goals, yet the goals can be appraised on common dimensions (discussed later) that permit nomothetic comparisons and generalizations, thus avoiding the formlessness of strictly idiographic approaches.

Klinger (1989b) has taken the initial step in highlighting the differences between these constructs (see also Cantor & Zirkel, 1990, for a comprehensive analysis of cognitive units of personality). Current concerns refer to hypothetical underlying states and thus connote a continuing dispositional state. Personal projects refer not to hypothetical states but to a set of related acts over time—the observable behavior that presumably corresponds to a concern. They are not what the person has, but rather what the person does. Life tasks focus on nontrivial problems that the individual wishes to solve. These tasks are rooted in developmental stages and could be viewed as a subset of concerns or projects that are made salient by life transitions. Read and Miller (1989) point out that life tasks capture the organizations of goals and strategies that are organized around specific periods and contexts in people's lives, and are less suited for describing individual differences more generally. A personal striving, defined as a class of goals that is characteristic for a particular person, describes enduring and recurring personality characteristics. Unlike current concerns and life tasks, the personal striving approach was not developed as a reaction against the motive disposition approach, and in fact is quite compatible with it (Emmons, 1989b).

Hyland's (1988) analysis of reference criteria within control theory is useful in helping further distinguish between these constructs. Life tasks represent end-state reference criteria. An end state is a completed piece of work with a definite termination point. Once one has graduated from college, it need not be negotiated again. Concerns and projects may also serve as end-state reference criteria, though they need not be limited to these. Personal strivings are more likely to represent doing or being reference criteria: a recurring and enduring concern with a class of goals rather than the attainment of a particular end state. They are not normally terminated by successful or unsuccessful experiences. For example, a person who is trying to "see the best in difficult situations" is not likely to be content with a single accomplishment of this striving and from then on adopt a pessimistic orientation of situations.

Personal projects or life tasks can be initiated by noting a discrepancy between a current state of affairs and a desired outcome. For example, a person's ideal self, to be slim and athletic, can be a reference value, and a project of "lose 20 pounds" may be initiated in the service of it. While such distinctions between the units are possible in principle, in reality the boundaries between them are often obscured. Many if not most of the examples shown in Table II could be switched around without doing much damage to the construct. Part of the difficulty lies in the ambiguously defined category breadth and time frame of the respective constructs.

Breadth of the construct (narrow and concrete versus broad and abstract) is important in that it defines the range of outcomes that are acceptable as goal attainments. For example, "trying to get to know others better" may be satisfied by a wider range of outcomes from "getting Sue to go to the dance." The majority of the goal units are not explicit with reference to category width. Life tasks may vary in scope, from "becoming a good person" to "getting good grades" (Cantor & Langston, 1989). According to Little (1987), projects can be defined at a micro-behavioral and a macro-intentional level (e.g., "go to church on Sunday" versus "explore my religious convictions"). Projects, tasks, and concerns can all vary between these extremes. Strivings, on the other hand, possess greater category breadth, as they are postulated to occupy a higher level in the hierarchy of motivational control (Emmons, 1989c).

D. Assessing Personal Goals

1. Generating Goals

The assessment of personal goals begins with having respondents freely generate a list of their concerns, tasks, projects, or strivings. In this initial step, the definition of the construct is given, usually with examples, and subjects write down as many goals as they can within a specified time period, ranging from 10 min (projects) to a few days (strivings). Klinger's (1987) interview questionnaire (IntQ) requires subjects to list their current concerns in 14 major life areas (friends, employment, family, and so forth). Some of the categories are further subdivided and are accompanied by illustrative concerns.

In personal projects analysis, subjects are told their personal projects are activities and concerns that people have and are provided with examples, such as "complete my English essay" and "getting more outdoor exercise" (Little, 1983). They are instructed to list all of their personal projects that they are engaged in or are thinking about at the time, and are told that these projects should represent everyday activities and concerns and not necessarily major life projects.

The life task methodology requires subjects to list their current life tasks, defined as things they felt they were working on in their lives. More specifically, respondents in one study were asked to focus on "the areas to which you have been and expect to be directing your energies" (Cantor et al., 1985, p. 326). They are then told to categorize the tasks into one of six normative life task categories: three academic and three interpersonal.

In the case of personal strivings, individuals are given the definition of a personal striving as "the things that you typically or characteristically are trying to do in your everyday behavior." They are then provided with several examples, such as "trying to persuade others one is right" and "trying to help others in need of help." It is stressed that these strivings are phrased in terms of what the person is "trying" to do, regardless of whether the person is actually successful. They are also instructed that the strivings may be either positive or negative, and that the striving must refer to a repeating, recurring goal, not to a one-time concern.

2. Personal Goal Dimensions

Following elicitation of the personal goals, respondents are asked to rate each goal on several dimensions. The dimensions used in any one study are derived from a number of sources. An analysis of the motivational literature typically results in the inclusion of such key goal attributes as value, expectancy for success, instrumentality, and commitment. Other dimensions are included because of their presumed relevance to the particular study. While current concerns, personal projects, life tasks, and personal strivings are idiographic, they are also nomothetic. That is, the specific list of concerns, projects, and tasks is unique to each individual. Yet these concerns, projects, and tasks can be compared along such nomothetic dimensions as value, expectancy for success, complexity, and difficulty, and in this sense comparisons across individuals can be made. In addition, it is these nomothetic properties which tie these concepts to cognition, emotion, and action. With these common properties, general statements tying goals to affective, cognitive, and behavioral outcomes can be made which are likely to transcend the idiographic content of these units. The dimensions that have been used are shown in Table III. There are none listed for life tasks since these duplicate those used in personal projects analysis. Several investigators have examined the factorial structure of these dimensions. A summary of these findings is presented in Table IV. In general, three to five dimensions emerge. Although the labels and loading variables vary somewhat from study to study, the most robust dimensions appear to embody (1) the degree of commit-

TABLE III
Goal Dimensions

Current concern	Personal project	Personal goal	Personal striving
Commitment	Importance	Importance	Commitment
Positivity	Challenge	Positivity	Value
Loss	Difficulty	Probability	Probability
Negativity	Negative impact	Difficulty	Difficulty
Instrumentality	Positive impact	Activity	Effort
Probability of success	Visibility to others	Self-efficacy	Confidence
Confidence in probability	Progress	Attribution	Causal attribution
Nearness in time	Challenge	Clarity	Clarity of means
Time available	Enjoyment	Opportunity	Environmental opportunity
Causal attribution	Absorption	Progress	Past attainment
Sense of drain	Time adequacy	Challenge/threat	Satisfaction with progress
	Initiation	Steps	Social desirability
	Stress	Investment	Importance
	Control		Ambivalence
	Value congruency		Probability of success if no action
	Self-identity		Impact

ment/investment in the goal, (2) the degree to which the goal is perceived as stressful/challenging, and (3) the anticipated outcome/reward of the goal.

3. Goal Instrumentality Matrix

A number of investigators have pointed to the possibility of assessing the degree of inter-goal conflict within the person's goal system. This can be accomplished by constructing for each person a matrix in which both the rows and columns list the person's goals. Respondents are asked to rate the degree of conflict/instrumentality between each pair of goals, until the entire matrix is filled out. Each goal is in effect rated twice, in terms of the effect that it has on other goals and the effect that other goals have on it. While asymmetrical affects are potentially possible, in reality the effects are nearly symmetrical, with correlations between conflict generated and conflict received typically close to .8 (Emmons & King, 1988). For the matrix as a whole, the average amount of conflict or instrumentality in the person's goal system is determined and is used as a variable in between-subject analyses.

E. Psychometric Properties

The personal goal approaches differ in the degree to which they have been concerned with formal psychometric considerations such as reliability and validity. Klinger (1987; Klinger et al., 1981) makes a compelling case for why traditional reliability estimates are only partially appropriate for both the content and the dimensions of personal goals. Somewhat different criteria need to be developed than is typical for traditional measures of personality (i.e., trait inventories). As Klinger (1987)

TABLE IV
Goal Dimension Factors

Factors (personal projects)[a]		
Mastery	Strain	Self-involvement
Progress	Difficulty	Value
Time	Stress	Self-identity
Absorption	Challenge	Initiation
Outcome	Negative	Control
Enjoyment	Impact	Outcome

Factors (life tasks)[b]		
Anxiety/Absorption	Personal Responsibility	Rewardingness
Challenge	Initiative	Enjoyment
Absorption	Control	Progress
Time spent	Progress	Absorption
Stress		
Difficulty		
Importance		

Factors (life tasks)[c]		
Importance/Absorption	Stressfulness	Reward/Control
Time spent	Stress	Progress
Absorption	Difficulty	Control
Importance	Challenge	Initiative
Challenge		Enjoyment
Other's view		

Factors (personal strivings)[d]			
Degree/Intensity	Success	Ease	Desirability
Value	Progress	Environmental opportunity	Internality
Importance	Probability	Success probability if no action	Desirability
Commitment	Attainment	Difficulty(−)	Clarity
Attainment	Confidence	Effort(−)	Ambivalence(−)
Effort	Ambivalence(−)		
Probability			

[a] Ruehlman and Wolchik, 1988.
[b] Cantor and Langston, 1989, Wave 1.
[c] Same as b, Wave 3.
[d] Emmons, 1986.

and Nesselroade (1987), argue, lack of stability (a psychological process) need not imply lack of reliability (a psychometric situation). Internal consistency estimates are not wholly appropriate either. Since there is no assumption of homogeneity of goal content, there is no reason to expect high internal consistencies. Although such values have been computed for various goal dimensions and have been shown to be high (Emmons & King, 1989), the meaning of these is not clear-cut.

While acknowledging these difficulties, some efforts have been made at estimating reliabilities of these measures. Both the stability of the goals themselves and the goal dimensions have been examined. Emmons (1986) computed both 3- and 6-month stability coefficients for the 18 striving assessment dimensions. The stabilities of the individual scales ranged from .58 to .91 for the 1-month interval (with a mean of .73) and from .47 to .70 for the 3-month period (with a mean of .60). Social desirability and importance were the most stable, while effort and impact were the least stable. Klinger and Cox (1986) administered the IntQ to 42 alcoholic inpatients upon intake and 1 month later. The test–retest correlations of 8 concerned dimensions ranged from .07 to .77, with a mean of .30. Cantor and Langston (1989) administered the meaning dimensions a year and a half apart in order to assess change in task appraisals, but unfortunately do not present correlations between the dimensions over this time period.

The stability of the goals themselves has also been investigated. In a sample of 40 undergraduates, after 1 year 82% of personal strivings listed at Time 1 were still present (with minor wording changes; Emmons, 1989c). After 18 months, 45% were still present, and a 3-year follow-up yielded a stability of just over 50%. Thus, there is evidence that strivings reflect enduring concerns in people's lives. Many of the 50% that were no longer present were associated with a particular life context (college environment) that was no longer part of the person's life.

F. Goal Equivalence Classes

The personal goal units, are, by definition, idiographic. Indeed, the respective proponents of each approach have argued that therein lies their advantage. For certain research purposes, however, a more abstract level of analysis is desirable. The categories that have been used for the different units along with percentages of goals falling within each category are shown in Table V. Categorizing goals in this manner permits comparison of the frequency of goals in terms of gender, age, and other social structural variables (Ryff, 1987). The ability to categorize personal goals will enable researchers to traverse the territory between idiographic and nomothetic levels of analysis.

G. Goal Properties: Conflict and Complexity

Among all of the goal attributes previously discussed, perhaps none is more important than conflict. This was aptly expressed by Powers (1973), who contended that "conflict represents the most serious kind of malfunction of the brain short of

TABLE V
Personal Goal Categories

Current concerns	%	Personal projects	%	Personal strivings	%	Personal goals	%
Pastimes/Travel	20	Interpersonal	14	Positive	85	Work/school	20
Family	15	Academic	13	Negative	15	Social Life	19
Job/finances	11	Recreational	12	Interpersonal	57	Leisure	18
Education	10	Finance/legal	7	Intrapersonal	43	Family Life	15
Religion/politics	10	Health/body	6	Achievement	18	Material/ environment	14
Love/sex	8	Cultural/aesthetic	6	Affiliation/intimacy	31	Personal growth	8
Friends	8	Sports	5	Power	12	Other/general	6
Physical health	7	Estate	5	Personal/Growth	24		
Miscellaneous	6	Intrapersonal	5	Self-presentation	12		
Emotional health	4	Family	4	Self-sufficiency	7		
		Drinking/drugs	4				
		Occupational	4				
		Boyfriend/girlfriend	3				
		Hobbies	2				
		Reading	2				
		Sex	2				
		Vacations/trips	2				
		Spiritual	1				

physical damage" (p. 253). Similarly, Pervin (1985) concluded his Annual Review chapter by stating that "I am struck by the power of conflicting motivations in my patients and the absence of such phenomena in the literature" (p. 105). Theorists and researchers beginning with Freud have stressed the necessity of avoiding inner conflict by maintaining consistency and harmony among aspects of the self and the psychologically injurious consequences of failing to do so. Goal conflict and motivational conflict more generally have had a long history. It has been of central concern in psychodynamic (Freud 1927; Horney, 1945), behavioral (Lewin, 1935; Miller, 1959), and cognitive formulations (Lecky, 1945). Until recently, however, little progress had been made in understanding the dynamics of nonpathological forms of conflict. Fortunately, there has been some movement in this area as of late, and a comprehensive review of this literature can be found in Emmons, King, and Sheldon (1993).

Wilensky (1983) discusses the various types of conflict that can occur between goals, at both an intrapersonal and an interpersonal level. At the intrapersonal level, goals may be negatively related to each other (the pursuit of one interferes with the pursuit of another). At the interpersonal level, the goals of two or more individuals may either compete or be in accordance. Wilensky's thorough analysis includes a discussion of the various classes of reasons why goals can come into conflict, and offers suggestions as to how such conflicts might be resolved. Peterson (1989) has also explored interpersonal goal conflict in the context of dyadic relationships.

Traditionally, conflict has been associated with tension, vacillation, uncertainty, and confusion (Miller, 1959) as well as anxiety, depression, hostility, delusions, and hallucinations (Powers, 1973). There is supporting empirical evidence. Palys and Little (1983) found that conflict between personal projects was associated with low life satisfaction, and Emmons and King (1988) reported that conflict between and within personal strivings was related to measures of psychological distress. The pathological effects of conflict have not been limited to the psychological domain either. As mentioned earlier, chronic motivational conflict in the form of the inhibited power motive syndrome is predictive of high blood pressure, lowered immunocompetence levels, and increased risk of coronary heart disease. Emmons and King (1988) found that conflict between personal strivings is associated with a variety of physical symptoms as well as in an increase in health center visits. These authors also found that individuals tended to dwell on conflicting strivings but to inhibit acting on them. In action theory terminology, it might be said that these individuals have adopted a state orientation. Pennebaker's (1985, 1989) inhibition model of psychosomatic illness has been used to explain why conflict results in physical illness. Personal striving conflict may be particularly debilitating, since it reflects conflicts at higher levels in the motivational hierarchy (Powers, 1973).

So although there has been a scattering of work since Pervin's charge, there is still much work remaining to be done before we fully understand (1) the types of motivational conflicts that people suffer from; (2) the effects of such conflicts on cognition, emotion, behavior, and psychosomatic disease; and (3) how such conflicts may be resolved. On the positive side, it does appear that people are aware of and are able to report conflicts between their goals (as well as ambivalence over a goal) and that such conflict has measurable consequences. The development of alternative measures of goal conflict, in addition to the conflict matrix, should be a priority. It is possible that ratings on it are susceptible to a host of contaminating influences, such as mood at the time it is filled out. Longitudinal studies on the long-term effects of conflict are also needed, as it has been suggested that conflict may be adaptive in the long run (Brim & Kagan, 1980; Emmons et al., 1993).

Another goal attribute that has begun to receive some attention is goal complexity. Complexity is a structural attribute of goal systems and consists of two components: differentiation and integration. Differentiation refers to the degree of interdependence (low differentiation) and independence (high differentiation) among the elements (goals) in the system. Interdependent goals are goals that affect, in an instrumental or conflicting way, other goals within a person's goal system. Greater similarity among one's goals is indicative of simplicity, whereas greater differentiation is a sign of complexity in the system. Integration refers to the number of linkages between the goals. Complexity also refers to the number of different plans, or means–end connections, that are associated with each goal. Complex goals in this sense are goals that can be successfully achieved in a variety of different ways. Note that this meaning of complexity refers to individual goals whereas the previous use of complexity referred to the goal system as a complete unit. A similar concept is that of plan reflectivity (Cantor et al., 1987), defined in terms of richness of plan elaboration for achieving life tasks.

The differentiation component of self-complexity has been examined in an intriguing series of studies by Linville (1982, 1985). She has demonstrated that the complexity of self-representation in terms of traits or social roles is inversely related to the extremity and variability of affective experience. Emmons and King (1989) attempted to expand the notion of differentiation to also encompass goal differentiation, as Linville's work has been limited to the trait and social role domains. They found, in contrast to Linville, that goal differentiation was related to greater levels of emotional reactivity. The results were interpreted as supporting an arousal-regulation theory of affect intensity (Larsen & Diener, 1987). Similarly, Donahue, Robins, Roberts, and John (1993) found that self-concept differentiation was predictive of psychological distress. They suggested that differentiation reflects pathological fragmentation rather than flexibility within the self. Clearly, more research is needed in order to settle these contradictory results.

IV. Conclusions and Future Directions

In a review such as this, it is the norm to apologize for omitting certain topics. This will be no exception. Topics that would have been covered were it not for space considerations include script theory (Tomkins, 1987), the dynamics of action (Atkinson & Birch, 1970), self-determination theory (Deci & Ryan, 1985), and the theory of relational dynamics (Nuttin, 1984). Fortunately, there are a number of excellent sources on these approaches that the interested reader can consult.

A natural candidate for future directions will be the exploration of the linkages between motive dispositions and personal goals. These two literatures have tended to go their separate ways. This is not totally surprising, in that some of the personal goal approaches were developed as a reaction against the perceived shortcomings in the motive dispositional approach. Yet motives refer to goals and goal-directed action, and goals represent the personalization of motives in individual lives. A decomposition of the motives into their constituent goals may be a necessary task for settling persistent controversies in the motive literature, such as sex differences (Stewart & Chester, 1982) and the difference between affiliation and intimacy motivation (McAdams, 1980).

McClelland and his associates (McClelland, Koestner, & Weinberger, 1989) have distinguished two forms of motivation. One is an affectively/biologically based system, termed "implicit motives," and the other is a cognitively/experientially based system, termed "self-attributed motives," or "explicit motives." These correspond to the social motive and idiographic goal approaches described earlier. These two systems are believed to develop independently, to operate independently of each other, and to predict different classes of behavior. The degree to which they are independent, however, is disputable. Emmons and McAdams (1991) found significant relations between personal strivings (a form of self-attributed motives) and motive dispositions as assessed by a picture-story exercise (implicit motives). King (1995) rerported significant correlations among explicit measures of the same motive, yet relative independence between explicit and implicit measures of the same motive. Future research should aim to identify conditions under which measures of implicit and explicit motives converge or fail to converge. Future work should also include multiple units (both explicit and implicit measures) as predictors of relevant outcomes. McClelland (1981), Veroff and Smith (1985), and Biernat (1989) have demonstrated the virtues of combining motives with other units such as values and traits in achieving greater predictive accuracy. Attention should also be directed toward the development of alternative means of assessing implicit and explicit motives, in addition to the picture-story exercise and free-response listing procedures described earlier in this chapter. Emmons and King (1992) provide an integrative review of the relation of thematic measures of motivation to other cognitive and affective constructs, such as schemas, scripts, and relational patterns.

The personal goal units can and should be applied in the psychobiographical study of individuals. Although the units claim to be idiographic, the whole person is missing from these approaches. Since a major task in most psychobiographical endeavors is to extract recurrent goal themes, the application of the personal goal units would seem to be a natural step to take. There may be advantages to framing these recurrent themes in terms of personal goals. Since careful attention has been paid to the assessment of these units, it may make it easier to uncover recurrent themes in the form of these goals in personal documents and other archival material.

Perhaps the most significant conclusion that can be drawn from a review of the motivational literature is that substantial progress is being made in narrowing the gap between social-cognitive and traditional personological approaches to motivation. The goals concept appears to be highly desirable, given its hierarchical structure; the flexibility, discriminativeness, and coherence that the concept implies; and its amenability to measurement and individual differences. We may now be in a position to answer G. W. Allport's (1968) query, "What units should we employ?"

REFERENCES

Allport, F. (1937). Teleonomic description in the study of personality. *Character and Personality, 5,* 202–214.

Allport, G. W. (1968). What units should we employ? In. G. Lindzey (Eds.), *Assessment of human motives* (pp. 239–260). New York: Grove Press.

Atkinson, J. W., & Birch, D. (1970). *The dynamics of action.* New York: Wiley.

Atkinson, J. W., Heyns, R. W., & Veroff, J. (1954). The effect of experimental arousal of the affiliation motive on thematic apperception. *Journal of Abnormal and Social Psychology, 49,* 405–410.

Biernat, M. (1989). Motives and values to achieve: Different constructs with different effects. *Journal of Personality, 57,* 69–96.

Bolger, N. (Ed.). (1988). *Persons in context: Developmental processes.* Hillsdale, NJ: Erlbaum.

Brim, O., & Kagan, J. (1980). Constancy and change: A view of the issues. In O. Brim & J. Kagan (Eds.), *Constancy and change in human development* (pp. 1–26). Cambridge, MA: Harvard University Press.

Buhler, C. M. (1964). *The course of human life.* New York: Springer.

Cantor, N. (1990). From thought to behavior: "Having" and "doing" in the study of personality and cognition. *American Psychologist, 45,* 735–750.

Cantor, N., Brower, A., & Korn, H. (1985). Cognitive bases of personality in a life transition. In E. E. Roskam (Ed.), *Measurement and personality assessment* (pp. 323–331). New York: Elsevier.

Cantor, N., & Kihlström, J. F. (1987). *Personality and social intelligence.* Englewood Cliffs, NJ: Prentice-Hall.

Cantor, N., & Kihlström, J. F. (1989). Social intelligence and cognitive assessments of personality. In R. S. Wyer, Jr. & T. K. Srull (Eds.), *Advances in social cognition* (Vol. 2, pp. 1–59). Hillsdale, NJ: Erlbaum.

Cantor, N., & Langston, C. A. (1989). Ups and downs of life tasks in a life transition. In L. A. Pervin (Ed.), *Goal concepts in personality and social psychology* (pp. 87–126). Hillsdale, NJ: Erlbaum.

Cantor, N., Norem, J., Niedenthal, P., Langston, C., & Brower, A. (1987). Life tasks, self-concept ideals, and cognitive strategies in a life transition. *Journal of Personality and Social Psychology, 53,* 1178–1191.

Cantor, N., & Zirkel, S. (1990). Personality, cognition, and purposive behavior. In L. A. Pervin (Ed.), *Handbook of personality* (pp. 135–164). New York: Guilford Press.

Carver, C. S., & Scheier, M. F. (1981). *Attention and self-regulation: A control theory approach to human behavior.* New York: Springer-Verlag.

Carver, C. S., & Scheier, M. F. (1982). Control theory: A useful conceptual framework for personality-social, clinical, and health psychology. *Psychological Bulletin, 92,* 111–135.

Carver, C. S., & Scheier, M. F. (1990). Origins and functions of positive and negative affect: A control-process view. *Psychological Review, 97,* 19–35.

Caspi, A. (1987). Personality in the life course. *Journal of Personality and Social Psychology, 53,* 1203–1213.

Cofer, C. N. (1981). The history of the concept of motivation. *Journal of the History of the Behavioral Sciences, 17,* 48–53.

Deci, E., & Ryan, R. M. (1985). *Self-determination theory.* New York: Plenum Press.

Donahue, E. M., Robins, R. W., Roberts, B. W., & John, O. P. (1993). The divided self: Concurrent and longitudinal effects of psychological adjustment and social roles on self-concept differentiation. *Journal of Personality and Social Psychology, 64,* 834–846.

Deci, E., & Ryan, R. M. (1985). *Self-determination theory.* New York: Plenum Press.

Donley, R. E., & Winter, D. G. (1970). Measuring the motives of public officials at a distance: An exploratory study of American presidents. *Behavioral Science, 15,* 227–236.

Emmons, R. A. (1986). Personal strivings: An approach to personality and subjective well-being. *Journal of Personality and Social Psychology, 51,* 1058–1068.

Emmons, R. A. (1989a). The big three, the big four, or the big five? *Contemporary Psychology, 34,* 644–646.

Emmons, R. A. (1989b). Exploring the relations between traits and motives: The case of narcissism. In D. M. Buss & N. Cantor (Eds.), *Personality psychology: Recent trends and emerging issues* (pp. 32–44). New York: Springer-Verlag.

Emmons, R. A. (1989c). The personal striving approach to personality. In L. A. Pervin (Ed.), *Goal concepts in personality and social psychology* (pp. 87–126). Hillsdale, NJ: Erlbaum.

Emmons, R. A. (1993). *Current status of the motive concept.* In K. Craik, R. Hogan, & R. Wolfe (Eds.), *Fifty years of personality psychology* (pp. 187–196). New York: Plenum Press.

Emmons, R. A. (1996). Striving and feeling: Personal goals and subjective well-being. In P. M. Gollwitzer & J. A. Bargh (Eds.), *The psychology of action-linking cognition and motivation to behavior* (pp. 313–337). New York: Guilford Publications, Inc.

Emmons, R. A., & Diener, E. (1986). A goal-affect analysis of situational choice and avoidance. *Journal of Research in Personality, 20,* 309–326.

Emmons, R. A., & King, L. A. (1988). Conflict among personal strivings: Immediate and long-term implications for psychological and physical well-being. *Journal of Personality and Social Psychology, 54,* 1040–1048.

Emmons, R. A., & King, L. A. (1989). Personal striving differentiation and affective reactivity. *Journal of Personality and Social Psychology, 56,* 478–484.

Emmons, R. A., & King, L. A. (1992). Thematic analysis, experience sampling, and personal goals. In C. Smith (Ed.), *Motivation and personality: Handbook of thematic content analysis* (pp. 73–86). New York: Cambridge University Press.

Emmons, R. A., King, L. A., & Sheldon, K. (1993). Goal conflict and the self-regulation of action. In D. M. Wegner & J. W. Pennebaker (Eds.), *Handbook of mental control* (pp. 528–551). Englewood Cliffs, NJ: Prentice-Hall.

Emmons, R. A., & McAdams, D. P. (1991). Personal strivings and motive dispositions: Exploring the links. *Personality and Social Psychology Bulletin, 17,* 648–654.

Foder, E. M. (1984). The power motive and reactivity to power stresses. *Journal of Personality and Social Psychology, 47,* 853–859.

Fontana, A. F., Rosenberg, R. L., Marcus, J. L., & Kerns, R. D. (1987). Type A behavior pattern, inhibited power motivation, and activity inhibition. *Journal of Personality and Social Psychology, 52,* 177–183.

Ford, D. H. (1987). *Humans as self-constructing living systems.* Hillsdale, NJ: Erlbaum.

Ford, D. H., & Ford, M. E. (1987). Humans as self-constructing living systems: An overview. In M. E. Ford & D. H. Ford (Eds.), *Humans as self-constructing living systems: Putting the framework to work* (pp. 1–46). Hillsdale, NJ: Erlbaum.

Ford, M. E. (1992). *Motivating humans: Goals, emotions, and personal agency beliefs.* Newbury Park, CA: Sage.

Ford, M. E., & Nichols, C. W. (1987). A taxonomy of human goals and some possible applications. In M. E. Ford & D. H. Ford (Eds.), *Humans as self-constructing living systems: Putting the framework to work* (pp. 289–311). Hillsdale, NJ: Erlbaum.

Frese, M. & Sabini, J. (Eds.). (1985). *Goal directed behavior: The concept of action in psychology.* Hillsdale, NJ: Erlbaum.

Freud, S. (1927). *The ego and the id.* London: Institute for Psychoanalysis and Hogarth Press.

Halisch, F., & Kuhl, J. (Eds.). (1987). *Motivation, intention, and volition.* Berlin: Springer-Verlag.

Heckhausen, H. (1991). *Motivation and action.* Berlin: Springer-Verlag.

Hogan, R. (1983). A socioanalytic theory of personality. In M. M. Page (Ed.), *Nebraska Symposium on Motivation* (pp. 55–90). Lincoln: University of Nebraska Press.

Hogan, R. (1986). What every student should know about personality psychology. In V. P. Makosky (Ed.), *The G. Stanley Hall Lecture series* (Vol. 6, pp. 43–64). Washington, DC: American Psychological Association.

Horney, K. (1945). *Our inner conflicts.* New York: Norton.

Hyland, M. E. (1987). Control theory interpretation of psychological mechanisms of depression: Comparison and integration of several theories. *Psychological Bulletin, 102,* 109–121.

Hyland, M. E. (1988). Motivational control theory: An integrative framework. *Journal of Personality and Social Psychology, 55,* 642–651.

Jemmott, J. B. (1987). Social motives and susceptibility to disease: Stalking individual differences in health risks. *Journal of Personality, 55,* 267–298.

King, L. A. (1995). Wishes, motives, goals, and personal memories: Relations of measures of human motivation. *Journal of Personality, 63,* 985–1007.

Klinger, E. (1975). Consequences of commitment to and disengagement from incentives. *Psychological Review, 82,* 223–231.

Klinger, E. (1977). *Meaning and void: Inner experience and the incentives in people's lives.* Minneapolis: University of Minnesota Press.

Klinger, E. (1985). Missing links in action theory. In M. Frese & J. Sabini (Eds.), *Goal directed behavior: The concept of action in psychology* (pp. 311–319). Hillsdale, NJ: Erlbaum.

Klinger, E. (1987). The interview questionnaire technique: Reliability and validity of a mixed idiographic-nomothetic measure of motivation. In J. N. Butcher & C. D. Spielberger (Eds.), *Advances in personality assessment* (Vol. 6, pp. 31–48). Hillsdale, NJ: Erlbaum.

Klinger, E. (1989a). Emotional mediation of motivational influences on cognitive processes. In F. Halisch & J. van den Bercken (Eds.), *International perspectives on achievement and task motivation* (pp. 317–326). Nisse, Netherlands: Swets & Zeitlinger.

Klinger, E. (1989b). Goal orientation as psychological linchpin: A commentary on Cantor and Kihlström's "Social intelligence and cognitive assessments of personality. In R. S. Wyer, Jr. & T. K. Srull (Eds.), *Advances in social cognition* (Vol. 2, pp. 123–130). Hillsdale, NJ: Erlbaum.

Klinger, E., Barta, S. G., & Maxeiner, M. E. (1981). Current concerns: Assessing therapeutically relevant motivation. In P. C. Kendall & S. Hollon (Eds.), *Assessment strategies for cognitive-behavioral interventions* (pp. 161–195). New York: Academic Press.

Klinger, E., & Cox, W. M. (1986). Motivational predictors of alcoholics responses to inpatient treatment. *Advances in Alcohol and Substance Abuse, 6,* 35–44.

Kuhl, J. (1985a). Volitional mediators of cognition-behavior consistency: Self-regulatory processes and action versus state orientation. In J. Kuhl & J. Beckmann (Eds.), *Action control: From cognition to behavior* (pp. 101–128). Berlin: Springer-Verlag.

Kuhl, J. (1985b). From cognition to behavior: Perspectives for future research on action control. In J. Kuhl & J. Beckmann (Eds.), *Action control: From cognition to behavior* (pp. 267–275). Berlin: Springer-Verlag.

Kuhl, J., & Beckman, J. (Eds.). (1985). *Action control: From cognition to behavior.* Berlin: Springer-Verlag.

Larsen, R. J., & Diener, E. (1987). Affect intensity as an individual difference characteristic: A review. *Journal of Research in Personality, 21,* 1–39.

Lecky, P. (1945). *Self-consistency: A theory of personality.* New York: Island Press.

Lewin, K. (1935). *A dynamic theory of personality.* New York: McGraw-Hill.

Linville, P. W. (1982). Affective consequences of complexity regarding the self and others. In M. S. Clark & S. T. Fiske (Eds.), *Affect and cognition* (pp. 79–109). Hillsdale, NJ: Erlbaum.

Linville, P. W. (1985). Self-complexity and affective extremity: Don't put all of your eggs in one basket. *Social Cognition, 3,* 94–120.

Little, B. R. (1983). Personal projects: A rationale and method for investigation. *Environment and Behavior, 15,* 273–309.

Little, B. R. (1987). Personal projects and fuzzy selves: Aspects of self-identity in adolescence. In T. Honess & K. Yardley (Eds.), *Self and identity: Perspectives across the life-span* (pp. 230–245). London: Routledge & Kegan Paul.

Little, B. R. (1989). Personal projects analysis: Trivial pursuits, magnificent obsessions, and the search for coherence. In D. M. Buss & N. Cantor (Eds.), *Personality psychology: Recent trends and emerging issues* (pp. 15–31). New York: Springer-Verlag.

Maslow, A. H. (1970). *Motivation and personality* (2nd ed.). New York: Harper & Row.

McAdams, D. P. (1980). A thematic coding system for the intimacy motive. *Journal of Research in Personality, 14,* 413–432.

McAdams, D. P. (1985a). The "imago": A key narrative component of identity. In P. Shaver (Ed.), *Review of personality and social psychology* (Vol. 6, pp. 115–141). Beverly Hills, CA: Sage.

McAdams, D. P. (1985b). *Power, intimacy, and the life story: Personological inquiries into identity.* Homewood, IL: Dorsey Press.

McAdams, D. P. (1990). Unity and purpose in human lives: The emergence of identity as a life story. In A. I. Rabin, R. A. Zucker, R. A. Emmons, & S. Frank (Eds.), *Studying persons and lives* (pp. 148–200). New York: Springer.

McAdams, D. P. (1993). *The stories we live by: Personal myths and the making of the self.* New York: W. Morrow.

McAdams, D. P. (1994). *The person: An introduction to personality psychology* (2nd Edition). Forth Worth, TX: Harcourt Brace.

McAdams, D. P., & Constantian, C. A. (1983). Intimacy and affiliation motive in daily living. An experience-sampling analysis. *Journal of Personality and Social Psychology, 45,* 851–861.

McClelland, D. C. (1980). Motive dispositions: The merits of operant versus respondent measures. In L. Wheeler (Ed.), *Review of personality and social psychology* (Vol. 1, pp. 11–41). Beverly Hills, CA: Sage.

McClelland, D. C. (1981). Is personality consistent? In A. I. Rabin, R. Zucker, & J. Aronoff (Eds.), *Further explorations in personality* (pp. 87–113). New York: Wiley.

McClelland, D. C. (1985). *Human motivation.* Glenview, IL: Scott, Foresman.

McClelland, D. C. (1989). Motivational factors in health and disease. *American Psychologist, 44,* 675–683.

McClelland, D. C., & Kirschnit, C. (1988). The effect of motivational arousal through films on salivary immunoglobulin A. *Psychology and Health, 2,* 31–52.

McClelland, D. C., Koestner, R., & Weinberger, J. (1989). How do self-attributed and implicit motives differ? *Psychological Review, 96,* 690–702.

Miller, N. E. (1959). Liberalization of basic S-R concepts: Extensions to conflict behavior, motivation, and social learning. In S. Koch (Ed.), *A study of psychology as a science* (Vol. 2, pp. 196–292). New York: McGraw-Hill.

Murray, H. A. (1938). *Explorations in personality.* New York: Oxford University Press.

Murray, H. A. (1951). Some basic psychological assumptions and conceptions. *Dialectica, 5,* 266–292.

Nesselroade, J. R. (1987). Some implications of the trait-state distinction for the study of development across the life span: The case of personality. In P. B. Baltes, D. L. Featherman, & R. M. Lerner (Eds.), *Life-span development and behavior* (Vol. 8). New York: Academic Press.

Norem, J. K., Illingworth, K., & Shaun, S. (1993). Strategy-dependent effects of reflecting on self and tasks: Some implications of optimism and defensive pessimism. *Journal of Personality & Social Psychology, 65,* 822–835.

Novacek, J., & Lazarus, R. (1990). The structure and measurement of personal commitments. *Journal of Personality, 58,* 693–715.

Nuttin, J. (1957). Personality dynamics. In H. P. David & H. von Bracken (Eds.), *Perspectives in personality theory* (pp. 183–196). New York: Basic Books.

Nuttin, J. (1984). *Motivation, planning, and action.* Hillsdale, NJ: Erlbaum.

Palys, T. S., & Little, B. R. (1983). Perceived life satisfaction and the organization of personal project systems. *Journal of Personality and Social Psychology, 44,* 1221–1230.

Pennebaker, J. W. (1985). Traumatic experience and psychosomatic disease: Exploring the roles of behavioral inhibition, obsession, and confiding. *Canadian Psychology, 26,* 82–95.

Pennebaker, J. W. (1989). Confession, inhibition, and disease. In L. Berkowitz (Ed.), *Advances in experimental social psychology* (Vol. 22, pp. 211–244). New York: Academic Press.

Pervin, L. A. (1983). The stasis and flow of behavior: Toward a theory of goals. In M. M. Page (Ed.), *Nebraska Symposium on Motivation* (pp. 1–53). Lincoln: University of Nebraska Press.

Pervin, L. A. (1985). Personality: Current controversies, issues, and directions. *Annual Review of Psychology, 36,* 83–114.

Peterson, D. R. (1989). Interpersonal goal conflict. In L. A. Pervin (Ed.), *Goal concepts in personality and social psychology* (pp. 327–361). Hillsdale, NJ: Erlbaum.

Powell, A., Royce, J. R., & Voorhes, B. (1982). Personality as a complex information-processing system. *Behavioral Science, 27,* 338–376.

Powers, W. T. (1973). *Behavior: The control of perception.* Chicago: Aldine.

Powers, W. T. (1978). Quantitative analysis of purposive systems: Some spadework at the foundations of scientific psychology. *Psychological Review, 85,* 417–435.

Roberson, L. (1989). Development and validation of the Work Concerns Inventory: A measure of employee work goals. *Organizational Behavior and Human Decision Processes, 44,* 345–367.

Ruehlman, L. S., & Wolchik, S. A. (1988). Personal goals and interpersonal support and hindrance as factors in psychological distress and well-being. *Journal of Personality and Social Psychology, 55,* 293–301.

Runyan, W. M. (1990). Studying individual lives and the structure of personality psychology. In A. I. Rabin, R. A. Zucker, R. A. Emmons, & S. Frank (Eds.), *Studying persons and lives* (pp. 10–40). New York: Springer.

Ryff, C. D. (1987). The place of personality and social structure research in social psychology. *Journal of Personality and Social Psychology, 53,* 1192–1202.

Semmer, N., & Frese, M. (1985). Action theory in clinical psychology. In M. Frese & J. Sabini (Eds.), *Goal directed behavior: The concept of action in psychology* (pp. 296–310). Hillsdale, NJ: Erlbaum.

Smith, C. P. (Ed.). (1992). *Motivation and personality: Handbook of thematic content analysis.* New York: Cambridge University Press.

Spangler, W. D. (1992). Validity of questionnaire and TAT measures of need for achievement: Two meta-analyses. *Psychological Bulletin, 112,* 140–154.

Stewart, A. J., & Chester, N. L. (1982). Sex differences in human social motives. In A. Stewart (Ed.), *Motivation and society* (pp. 172–218). San Francisco: Jossey-Bass.

Stone, A. A., Cox, D. S., Valdimarsdottir, H., & Neale, J. M. (1987). Secretory IgA as a measure of immunocompetence. *Journal of Human Stress, 13,* 136–140.

Tomkins, S. S. (1987). Script theory. In J. Aronoff, A. I. Rabin, & R. A. Zucker (Eds.), *The emergence of personality* (pp. 147–216). New York: Springer.

Veroff, J. (1983). Contextual determinants of personality. *Personality and social Psychology Bulletin, 9,* 331–343.

Veroff, J. (1986). Contextual factors in the normal personality. In R. L. Rosnow & M. Georgoudi (Eds.), *Contextualism and understanding in behavioral sciences* (pp. 147–167). New York: Praeger.

Veroff, J., & Feld, S. (1970). *Marriage and work in America.* New York: Van Nostrand-Reinhold.

Veroff, J., & Smith, D. A. (1985). Motives and values over the adult years. *Advances in Motivation and Achievement, 4,* 1–53.

Warren, W. H. (1987). "Behavior" versus "action." *Contemporary Psychology, 32,* 120–121.

Wicker, F. W. (1984). Categorical goal hierarchies and the classification of human motives. *Journal of Personality, 52,* 285–305.

Wilensky, R. (1983). *Planning and understanding: A computational approach to human reasoning.* Reading, MA: Addison-Wesley.

Winter, D. G. (1987). Leader appeal, leader performance, and the motive profile of leaders and followers: A study of American presidents and elections. *Journal of Personality and Social Psychology, 52,* 196–202.

Winter, D. G. (1991). Measuring personality at a distance: Development and validation of an integrated system for scoring motives in running text. In A. J. Stewart, J. M. Healy, Jr., & D. J. Ozer (Eds.), *Perspectives in personality: Approaches to understanding lives* (Vol. 3, pp. 59–89). London: Jessica Kingsley Publishers.

Winter, D. G. (1996). *Personality: Analysis and interpretation of lives.* New York: McGraw-Hill.

Winter, D. G., & Carlson, L. (1988). Using motive scores in the psychobiographical study of an individual: The case of Richard Nixon. *Journal of Personality, 56,* 75–102.

Winter, D. G., & Stewart, A. J. (1978). The power motive. In H. London & J. E. Exner, Jr. (Eds.), *Dimensions of personality* (pp. 391–448). New York: Wiley.

Young, J. (1988). *The role of selective attention in the attitude-behavior relationship.* Doctoral dissertation, University of Minnesota, Minneapolis.

Zirkel, S., & Cantor, N. (1990). Personal construal of life tasks: Those who struggle for independence. *Journal of Personality and Social Psychology, 58,* 172–185.

CHAPTER 21

THE EMOTIONS

AN INTEGRATIVE APPROACH

JAMES R. AVERILL

UNIVERSITY OF MASSACHUSETTS, AMHERST

I. INTRODUCTION

If you want to know what people are like, ask about their loves and hates, hopes and fears, joys and sorrows, and the myriad of other emotions that lend meaning to their lives. But what is an emotion?

II. THE DOMAIN OF EMOTION

We all know what an emotion is—until we are asked to give a definition. Then we seem to be at a loss for words. Or are we? Roughly 550 to 600 words (nouns, verbs, adjectives, and adverbs) in the English language have a rather clear-cut emotional connotation (Averill, 1975; Johnson-Laird & Oatley, 1989; Storm & Storm, 1987). Some languages have a larger vocabulary to describe emotions than does English; others have a much smaller vocabulary (Russell, 1991). For example, Lutz (1982) found no general term equivalent to "emotion" among the Ifaluk, a people of Micronesia, and only 58 words that she considered unambiguously emotional in connotation ("about our insides"). But simply counting words is of little interest. What do the words signify? And more generally, what is the relation between language and emotion?

A. The Meaning of Emotional Concepts

The class of emotions is held together by what Wittgenstein (1953) called "family resemblances." To illustrate, consider an actual family, the Smiths. Most members of the Smith family have big ears, but not everyone; most have hazel eyes, but not everyone; and most have stocky builds, but not everyone. No single member of the family need have all these characteristic features (big ears, hazel eyes, and a stocky build), yet the family forms a recognizable unit.

Although opinions vary (cf. Wierzbicka, 1992), emotions, too, form a recognizable unit based on family resemblances (Fehr & Russell, 1984; Shaver, Schwartz, Kirson, & O'Connor, 1987). And like the big ears, hazel eyes, and stocky build of the Smith family, three features are prototypic of emotions, namely, passivity, intentionality, and subjectivity.

1. Passivity

For most of Western history, from the ancient Greeks to about the middle of the 18th century, what we now refer to as emotions were called passions. The term "passion" and its cognate "passivity" stem from the Greek *pathe* via the Latin *pati, passiones.* The root meaning of these terms is to suffer or undergo change, particularly for the worse.

Although it is no longer common to speak of emotions as passions, the connotation of passivity (of being "overcome") is implicit in emotional concepts. We "fall" in love, are "gripped" by anger, "can't help" but hope, and so forth. Because emotional concepts connote passivity, emotions themselves have often been likened to reflexes and simple sensory experiences, which are also beyond personal control. As will be discussed below, however, people typically have more control over their emotions than the connotation of passivity would suggest.

2. Intentionality

Intentionality is another of those terms (like passion) that has a long history in psychological thought, but that can be easily misunderstood if interpreted in its ordinary, everyday meaning. Emotions are intentional in the sense that they are *about* something. People cannot simply be angry, they must be angry *at* something, afraid *of* something, hopeful *for* something, and so forth. That "something" is the intentional object of the emotion, the result of an evaluative judgment or appraisal (Solomon, 1993).

Intentionality helps distinguish emotions from reflexes, which presume no cognitive intermediary. Intentionality also renders suspect any theory that attempts to reduce emotional phenomena to simple sensory experiences, such as the James–Lange theory. Sensations, whether of a toothache or of bodily arousal, are not about anything; they do not point beyond themselves in the way that emotions do. Intentionality does not, however, distinguish emotions from rational judgments, which also are about something.

3. Subjectivity

In everyday discourse, it is common to speak of emotions as subjective and of rational judgments as objective. These terms (subjective and objective) are ambiguous, and hence the contrast between them is easily misunderstood. On one interpretation, emotions are subjective in the sense of being biased, whereas factual judgments are impartial (dispassionate). However, not all emotional judgments are misguided, and presumably rational judgments can be, and often are, self-serving and ill-founded. Hence, this contrast is not informative of the distinction between emotional and rational judgments.

At the most fundamental level, subjectivity refers to the *relation* of the object to the subject of experience. For example, if on a rainy day I see a rainbow, the rainbow is the *object* of my experience; I am the *subject*, the one who sees. Other persons could presumably see the same rainbow, but not exactly the way I do. When the unique contributions of individual observers are subtracted, what remains is an "objective" description of the rainbow as, for example, might be found in a book on optics. When the emphasis is on the seer rather than on the seen, as in an artist's rendition of a rainbow, the description is "subjective." Emotions are subjective in this sense; that is, they are an attribute of the subjective ("inner") pole of experience, rather than of the external object in and of itself. In many instances, this relation can itself be objectively assessed, for what is beautiful or ugly, beneficial or harmful, is not simply a matter of individual judgment. Society and, more indirectly, biology stipulate the kinds of relations that subserve the various emotions.

B. The Organization of Emotions

We have now established some of the (admittedly fuzzy) boundary conditions for distinguishing emotional from nonemotional phenomena, namely, passivity, intentionality, and subjectivity. We have yet to map the internal structure of the emotional domain—how emotions are organized with respect to one another. Two general approaches have been taken to this issue: categorical and dimensional.

1. Categorical Approaches

A categorical approach, as its name implies, assumes that emotions can be grouped into relatively homogeneous categories, and that these categories are systematically related to one another, typically in a hierarchical fashion. A zoological taxonomy is a familiar example of a categorical approach to classification. A number of taxonomies of emotion have been proposed, based primarily on theoretical considerations (e.g., de Rivera, 1977; Mees, 1991; Ortony, Clore, & Collins, 1988). We will consider in detail one empirically derived taxonomy, since it comes closest to our folk classification of emotion.

Storm and Storm (1987) investigated the semantic relations among 590 emotional terms. Four highly educated English speakers served as expert judges. Through a process of repeated classification, discussion, and reclassification, they were able to organize 525 of the words into a taxonomic tree, as illustrated in Figure 1.

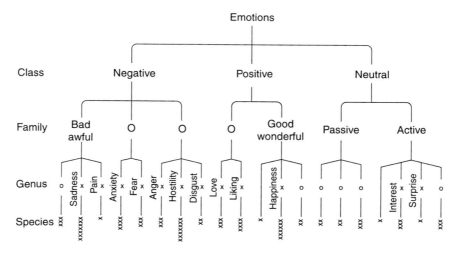

FIGURE 1 A taxonomic tree depicting the hierarchical organization of 525 emotional terms. Only categories at the generic level and above are named in the figure. An x represents a group of 1 to 20 closely related terms; an o represents a covert category (i.e., a category that has no name in English). Based on data from Storm and Storm (1987).

Four levels of the taxonomic tree are distinguished in Figure 1. For ease of reference, these levels are labeled (from top to bottom) roughly in the manner of a zoological taxonomy, namely, "class," "family," "genus," and "species." At the highest level of classification, three broad classes are distinguished, consisting of negative, positive, and neutral terms. At the next level, seven families of emotional concepts are identified, although only four of these (bad/awful, good/wonderful, passive and active) are named in ordinary language. These seven families subsume 20 genera of emotional concepts (sadness, pain, anxiety, fear, etc.), which in turn encompass 61 species. Each species could be further subdivided into smaller units (varieties), but these are not identified in Figure 1.[1]

---

[1] The taxonomy presented in Figure 1 is based on class inclusion; that is, emotions (or emotional concepts) lower in the hierarchy are presumed to be varieties of emotions higher in the hierarchy. Taxonomies can also be based on part–whole relations, as in anatomical schemes. The heart, for example, is part of, not a variety of, the cardiovascular system. Similarly, in some respects anger may be considered a part of jealousy, rather than jealousy being a subvariety of anger, as in Figure 1. Still other relations (e.g., cause–effect, similarity) are possible and sometimes used in both folk and scientific classifications; in the case of emotions, for example, jealousy may be linked to anger as a contributing cause, or because both may result in similar behavior (e.g., aggression). To the extent that the emotions are related to one another on bases other than class inclusion, Figure 1 gives a misleading picture. Perhaps most importantly, superordinate-subordinate relations may be reversed, depending on the context. For example, in one context jealousy may be considered subordinate to anger, and vice versa in another context (cf. Storm, Storm, & Jones, 1996). In spite of these considerable qualifications, Figure 1 does illustrate important points about our folk classification of emotion, and it will be referred to frequently in subsequent discussion (for a similar taxonomy, see Shaver et al., 1987).

Not all categories indicated in Figure 1, particularly at the higher levels of generality, are explicitly recognized in the English language. This is common in folk taxonomies (Berlin, Breedlove, & Raven, 1968). The unnamed or "covert" categories are indicated by an "O" in Figure 1; named categories are indicated by an "X." Actually, X represents not a single name, but a group (from 1 to 20) of closely related terms. The names actually listed in Figure 1 are those considered most representative of their respective groups.

Storm and Storm (1987) emphasize that theirs is a taxonomy of emotional words and concepts, not of emotions per se. This raises the question: What is the relation between language and emotion? Three general answers have been offered to this question.

(a) Emotions—at least certain fundamental or basic emotions—are biologically based and hence independent of language. That is, the language of emotion reflects preexisting divisions "in nature" (cf. Johnson-Laird & Oatley, 1989).

(b) Emotions are not divisible into discrete units; whatever distinctions are made in language reflect cultural exigencies, not anything fundamental about emotions per se. People in all cultures experience the full range of possible emotions, although they may conceptualize those experiences differently (cf. subsequent section on dimensional approaches).

(c) All people are initially capable of experiencing the full range of emotions; however, culture—as reflected in language—enables certain possibilities to be realized, while it closes off other possibilities. Without special training (acculturation), people in one culture can no more experience the emotions of another culture than they can understand the language of another culture.

Some variation of alternative (c) seems most consistent with current evidence and is the one adopted in this chapter. To adumbrate briefly, human beings have an evolutionary history, and the importance of our biological heritage cannot be denied. But societies also have a history of adaptations that are passed from one generation to the next. These social adaptations interact with biological potentials to form the various emotions actually observed in a culture. Language serves as a catalyst for that interaction. Thus, although emotional terms are not to be identified with emotions per se, neither are they simply labels arbitrarily pinned on independently existing entities [alternative (a)].

2. Dimensional Approaches

Some theorists maintain that emotions do not form discrete categories, but shade imperceptibly into one another [cf. alternative (b) mentioned above]. Theorists of this persuasion believe that the emotions can be mapped onto an "affective space" defined by two or more dimensions. A variety of statistical techniques (e.g., factor analysis, multidimensional scaling) have been used to identify the relevant dimensions, and the data analyzed have included facial expressions, self-reported affect, and emotional concepts. The results of many such studies can be summarized briefly (for details, see Larsen & Diener, 1992). Two bipolar dimensions are repeatedly observed—evaluation (negative–positive) and activation (aroused–unaroused). Often, a third and even fourth dimension have been found, but such additional dimensions typically account for a small proportion of the variance, and their nature tends to vary from one study to another.

Figure 2 illustrates the approximate location of 24 emotion terms within the affective space defined by the evaluation and activation dimensions. Research by Russell (1983) suggests that the two-dimensional space is consistent across a variety of language groups, including Chinese, Japanese, Gujarati, and Croatian.

In spite of the apparent universality of the evaluation and activation dimensions, disagreements remain. For example, Watson and Tellegen (1985) argue for a 45° rotation of the axes, as indicated by the dashed lines in Figure 2. Such a rotation changes the meaning of one dimension to *positive aroused affect* versus *negative unaroused affect* (e.g., excited versus bored), and of the other dimension to *negative aroused affect* versus *positive unaroused affect* (e.g., alarmed versus serene). Moreover, Haslam (1996) has presented data indicating that emotional concepts are not continuously distributed throughout the affective space, as a pure

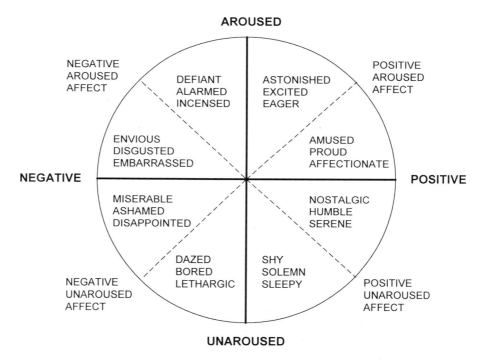

FIGURE 2 Organization of 24 emotional terms in a two-dimensional affective space. The horizontal dimension represents evaluation (negative versus positive affect), and the vertical dimension activation (unaroused versus aroused affect). The dashed lines represent a 45° rotation of the axes, as suggested by Watson and Tellegen (1985). The placement of terms may vary depending on context; the placement shown is based on data from Averill (1975) and Russell (1980).

dimensional approach would suggest, but form meaningful clusters within the space. As human beings, we tend to categorize events, and the emotions are no exception. But leaving such complications aside, we want to ask more generally, What is the value of a dimensional approach as opposed to a categorical approach?

The evaluation (negative–positive) and activation (aroused–unaroused) dimensions have been central to a number of theories of emotion, either by themselves (e.g., the *pleasure–arousal theory* of Reisenzein, 1994) or as elements in more inclusive theories (e.g., Mandler, 1984; Schachter, 1971). The basis of these dimensions therefore needs an explanation in terms of cognitive and/or underlying physiological mechanisms. Nevertheless, it is unlikely that a dimensional approach can provide an adequate framework for the analysis of emotion. An analogy will illustrate the problem. Animals can be arranged along dimensions, for example, large–small and ferocious–tame. Such dimensions (size, ferocity) are of both theoretical and practical importance; they cannot, however, substitute for a taxonomy of animals based on species, genera, and so forth. Similarly, a dimensional approach to the classification of emotions, although valuable for some purposes, is no substitute for a categorical approach.

III. A FRAMEWORK FOR THE ANALYSIS OF EMOTION

Any area of inquiry must start with some assumptions about the appropriate units of analysis. In the study of emotion, three main possibilities exist, each with somewhat different theoretical implications: (a) emotional syndromes, (b) emotional states, and (c) emotional reactions. To introduce the differences among these units, consider the following emotional terms:

A	B	C
Anger	Angry	Attacking
Fear	Afraid	Running
Grief	Sorrowful	Weeping
Love	Lustful	Kissing

The terms in column A are all abstract nouns. They refer to emotional *syndromes*. A syndrome is a theoretical entity; it exists "out there," so to speak, but only as an abstraction or explanatory device. To borrow an analogy from Plutchik (1980), when used to refer to syndromes, emotional concepts are analogous to the concept of an atom in chemistry. Whether atoms actually exist in the manner conceptualized (e.g., with a nucleus of protons and neutrons orbited by electrons) is a moot question. Atoms are inferences we make to explain chemical reactions. Similarly, emotional syndromes are inferences we make to explain the reactions of people.

Now consider the terms in column B. They are all adjectives that describe the emotional *state* of the individual. An emotional state is a temporary (episodic) disposition on the part of an individual to respond in a manner consistent with a corresponding emotional syndrome. Dispositional variables are quite common in the physical sciences, although they have often been viewed with skepticism by psychologists. Combustibility is a dispositional variable. A combustible material is liable to burst into flames if an appropriate stimulus is applied. Similarly, a person in an angry state is liable to "explode" if appropriately "triggered." Dispositional properties may be enduring characteristics of a material (as in the case of combustibility) or they may be transitory (as in the "attractiveness" of a reversible magnet). As psychological dispositions, emotional states are transitory; other psychological dispositions (e.g., temperamental traits) are more enduring.

The terms in column C refer to emotional *reactions;* that is, the actual responses an individual might make when in an emotional state. It is important to note that no single response, or type of response, is necessary or sufficient for the attribution of emotion. For example, a person who is in an angry state may act in a variety of different ways (e.g., physically or verbally attacking the instigator, plotting revenge, talking the incident over with a neutral party, withdrawing affection), all more-or-less consistent with our concept of anger as a syndrome.

To conflate emotional syndromes, states, and reactions is to commit what Ryle (1949) has called a "category mistake"; that is, to interpret a variable belonging to one logical category as though it belonged to another. Ryle uses the example of a young boy watching a parade to illustrate a category mistake. After observing the marchers, bands, and so forth, the boy wonders, "Where is the parade?" His mistake is to assume that the parade belongs to the same logical category as the constituents that make up the parade.

A particularly common category mistake is to identify emotional syndromes with specific reactions (e.g., physiological arousal, facial expressions, or subjective experience). Such an identification can be grossly misleading if it is assumed (as it often is) that what is true of the reaction is also true of the syndrome; for example, because some emotional reactions, such as facial expressions, last only a few seconds, the emotions themselves (i.e., as syndromes) must be correspondingly brief. Returning to Ryle's example of the young boy and the parade, one might just as well assume that because some marchers pass quickly by, the parade itself must pass quickly.

In addition to the three variables just described (emotional syndromes, states, and reactions), several other types of variables figure prominently in the study of emotion. One of these is the personality *trait.* Whereas emotional states are short-term dispositions to respond, traits are relatively long-enduring predispositions. For example, a generally imperturbable individual might be in an anxious state due to unusual circumstances, whereas another (trait-anxious) individual might be prone to frequent bouts of anxiety even in relatively benign circumstances. Many emotional concepts (like anxiety) can refer to either state or trait variables, a fact that has been the source of considerable confusion in the study of emotion (Spielberger, 1966).

Casting our conceptual net even more widely, it is not uncommon to find emotions linked with *biological systems* of behavior, or what used to be called instincts. McDougall (1936), for example, argued that anger is experienced when the aggressive instinct is aroused, that fear is experienced when the avoidance instinct is aroused, and so forth. Even though the notion of instinct has gone out of vogue, the idea that emotions—particularly "basic" emotions—are aspects of our biological heritage is a very common assumption among contemporary psychologists (cf. Ekman, 1984; Izard, 1991; Plutchik, 1980).

A resort to biology is one way to account for the experience of passivity, of being overcome, during emotion. But biology is not the only source of "instinctive" behavior. As Fox (1971) has pointed out, if a species were to lose its dependency on biological systems (as human beings largely have), then a certain class of cultural behavior would have to become like instincts. Such social instincts—or what we call *social systems* of behavior—would be largely unconscious and automatic, so as not to require undue deliberation for their operation, and they would be common to large segments of a society. They would also be, we might add, as passionately felt as any biological instinct.

A. Levels of Organization

We have now outlined six kinds of variables that have played important roles in psychological theories of emotion: reactions, states, syndromes, traits, and biological and social systems of behavior. Figure 3 organizes these variables into a general framework for the analysis of emotion. In explaining this figure, it is helpful to begin at the top (Level I) and work down.

1. Level I

Both historically and logically, the origins of behavior lie in the individual's *biological and social potentials*. The sum of a person's biological potentials is his or her genotype, i.e., the genetic endowment drawn (through the parents) from the gene pool of the species. The aspect of the genotype most relevant to emotions is that responsible for biological systems of behavior, as discussed above. Biological systems are manifested in responses that contribute to the survival of the species. Examples include aspects of reproductive behavior, various forms of aggression, and attachment.

In a manner analogous to biological potentials, we may speak of social potentials or, more specifically, of social systems of behavior—institutionalized patterns of response that help ensure the survival of a society. Whereas biological systems are encoded in the gene pool of the species, social systems are encoded in the symbols, artifacts, and customs of society. During socialization, the individual is endowed with the potential for relevant behaviors, a sociotype drawn from the total repertoire of behaviors available to members of the society.

2. Level II

Biological and social potentials interact to form, at the next lower level of organization, a person's *fundamental capacities* or psychological predispositions. This is the first level of organization that can be measured directly. It represents the "source

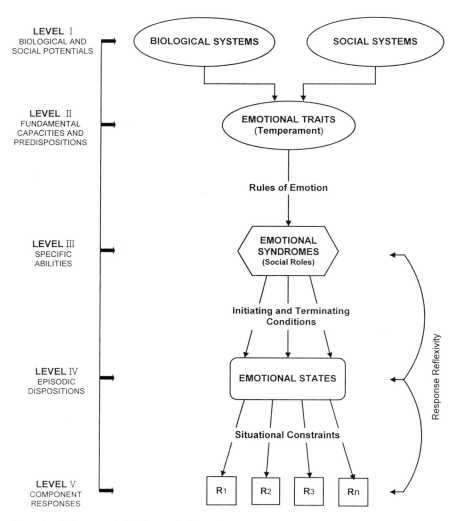

FIGURE 3   A framework for the analysis of emotional behavior.

traits" of personality theory, such as the "Big Five" discussed by Wiggins and Trapnell in Chapter 5 of this volume. We would also include within this category such traits as emotional intelligence, defined as the capacity to monitor one's own and others' emotions accurately and to respond adaptively (Mayer & Salovey, 1995; Salovey, Hsee, & Mayer, 1992), and emotional creativity, defined as the capacity to originate novel yet effective emotional syndromes (Averill, 1994a; Averill & Thomas-Knowles, 1991).

3. Level III

A distinction must be made between a *capacity* to respond (Level II), on the one hand, and the *ability* to respond (Level III), on the other. To illustrate, consider a person who has the biological potential for fine pitch discrimination, motor coordination, and whatever other biological endowment might be necessary to play a musical instrument. Assume also, that this person has been raised in a social environment in which music plays an important role (thus offering a strong social potential). Such a person would likely possess the capacity to be a good musician. However, before the person would have the ability to be a classical violinist, say, or a jazz pianist, he or she would have to acquire the rules and skills relevant to that musical genre. In other words, abilities are rule-constituted, and capacities are not, or at least not in the same sense.

As will be explained more fully further on, emotional syndromes can best be conceptualized at the level of specific abilities (from a psychological standpoint) or in terms of social roles (from a sociological standpoint).

4. Level IV

Given the ability to engage in a particular emotional syndrome (e.g., anger), appropriate initiating conditions will result in the activation of an emotional state. As already described, an emotional state is not a specific kind of response. Rather, it is a relatively short-term, *episodic disposition* to respond in any of a variety of ways consistent with the rules and expectations that help constitute an emotional syndrome.

5. Level V

The most concrete level of organization comprises the *component responses* that a person might exhibit when in an emotional state, depending upon constraints imposed by the situation. Shortly, we will discuss in detail some of the issues raised by different kinds of response (e.g., physiological change and instrumental acts).

B. Relations among Levels

One source of confusion among various kinds of variables is the fact that, in practice, levels of organization can be bypassed. This is indicated by the interconnected arrows at the left of Figure 3. For example, in certain circumstances, the activation of biological potentials (Level I) can directly elicit component responses (Level V), short-circuiting fundamental capacities (traits), specific abilities (syndromes), and episodic dispositions (states).

Similar considerations apply to social potentials and component responses. The salesperson is expected to smile and be friendly, the bereaved is expected to mourn, and the drill sergeant is expected to be belligerent, regardless of their emotional state at the moment (Hochschild, 1983). Because short-circuiting is common, it is easy to overlook logical differences among variables at different levels of organization, thus facilitating the kind of category mistakes described earlier.

One implication of the above considerations is that component responses are not inherently emotional, but attain that quality only when interpreted (experienced) as part of an emotional syndrome. Put differently, human emotional responses are reflexively related to the higher-order meanings that help constitute emotional syndromes. This is indicated in Figure 3 by the bidirectional curved arrows connecting component responses (Level V) to emotional states (Level IV) and syndromes (Level III). The issue of reflexivity is perhaps most problematic or controversial with reference to conscious experience. As here conceived, emotional feelings are one kind of component response, the nature of which is examined in more detail shortly.

IV. COMPONENT RESPONSES

Six broad categories of emotional responses can be distinguished: cognitive appraisals, physiological change, expressive reactions, instrumental acts, verbal behavior, and feelings. Each raises important empirical and theoretical issues. After introducing a particular kind of response (e.g., cognitive appraisals), several frequently asked questions regarding its function and significance are addressed.

A. Cognitive Appraisals

A sharp distinction is often made between stimuli and responses. The distinction is, however, misleading. Before an emotional response can occur, the stimulus must be appraised for its relevance to the individual (cf. the criteria of intentionality and subjectivity discussed earlier). The appraisal is itself a kind of response, an imposition of meaning on events. A more formal way of stating this fact is to say that appraisal produces the intentional object of an emotion. The nature of the appraised object is thus an appropriate starting point for further analysis.

1. What Is the Appraised Object of an Emotion?

Most emotional objects involve three aspects—the instigation, target, and objective. The eliciting condition (as appraised by the person) is the instigation; the person or thing at whom the emotion is directed is the target; and the goal of the emotion is the objective. For example, if Mary is angry at her friend Bill for insulting her and wants to "get even," the object of her anger consists of the perceived insult (the instigation), her friend Bill (the target), and getting even (the objective). Not all emotions emphasize all three aspects of an object equally. More than most emotions, love emphasizes the uniqueness of the target, and hence is not fungible, that is, easily transferrable from one person to another as circumstances change. Other emotions emphasize both the instigation and the objective, but leave the target relatively free to vary depending on the circumstances. Thus, abstracting from any specific target, we can say that the object of anger is revenge for wrongdoing and the object of fear is escape from danger. Still other emotions focus almost exclusively on the instigation, leaving both the target and the objective unspecified. Joy and grief are good examples.

2. Is Appraisal Necessary for the Activation of an Emotional State?

It is often assumed that the appraised object is the cause of an emotional state. However, as Dewey (1895) emphasized a century ago, the way a person appraises a situation is part of, not antecedent to, the emotion. For example, to perceive a bear as frightening is already to be in a fearful state. Some contemporary theorists go so far as to argue that emotions are in principle a kind of appraisal or evaluative judgment: fear *is* the judgment that we are in danger; anger *is* the judgment that we have been wronged; sadness *is* the judgment that we have been diminished through loss; and so forth (Sartre, 1948; Solomon, 1993).

3. If Not the Appraised Object, What Activates an Emotional State?

There are many potential links in the chain of events leading to an emotional state, from the primarily physical to the primarily cognitive (Izard, 1993). Under the influence of drugs or hormonal imbalances, an emotional state can sometimes be activated with little or no cognitive intervention (e.g., postpartum depression). Similarly, as will be discussed in more detail shortly, proprioceptive feedback from bodily responses can facilitate the occurrence of emotion. Motivational factors unrelated to the emotional episode can also play a role in how a situation is appraised. Love provides a familiar example: The target of one's affection is an idealization, partly based on reality and partly a projection of one's own needs and desires. Finally, at the risk of emphasizing the obvious, appraisal is not an all-or-none affair; a variety of cognitive steps, not all of which are emotional in and of themselves, are typically involved in the initiation of an emotional state (Scherer, 1984).

Once an appraisal is made, it can—like any other kind of response—stimulate further activity, including reappraisals. When a reappraisal unrealistically short circuits the emotional state for self-protective reasons, we may speak of cognitive defense mechanisms (Lazarus, 1991).

4. Is Each Emotion Associated with a Different Object?

With the possible exceptions of "free-floating" anxiety, depression, and mystic-like experiences, each emotion is associated with a distinct object (instigation, target, and/or objective). One of the main tasks of theorists is to identify the cognitions that help constitute the appraised objects of emotions. For example, is the instigation beneficial or harmful? What is the probability of its occurrence? When did—or might—the instigation occur (past, present, future), or is its occurrence indeterminate (ongoing)? With regard to the target, who or what initiated the instigation (oneself, another person, or chance events)? If the target is a person, is he or she responsible (deserving of reward or punishment)? With regard to the objective, what possibilities for action does the situation afford (approach, withdrawal, attack, etc.)? In various combinations, answers to questions such as these help account for the objects of most commonly experienced emotions (Frijda, 1986; Lazarus, 1991; Ortony et al., 1988; Roseman, Antoniou, & Jose, 1996; Smith & Ellsworth, 1985; Weiner, 1985).

B. Peripheral Physiological Change

Emotions, as the saying goes, are "gut" reactions. This metaphorical way of characterizing the emotions has a long history, dating back to the ancient Greeks. Its most famous modern formulation is that by William James (1890), who proposed "that *bodily changes follow directly the perception of the exciting fact, and that our feeling of the same changes as they occur* IS *the emotion*" (p. 449). Although James meant his formulation to include bodily changes of all kinds (including facial expressions, instrumental acts, and even central neural activity), most subsequent research and speculation has focused on the role of visceral activity during emotion (for a review, see Cacioppo, Klein, Bernston, & Hatfield, 1993). We may call this focus the "strong" version of James's thesis; it implies that different emotions are associated with different patterns of visceral activity, and that people are able to discriminate among those patterns in conscious experience. A somewhat weaker version of James's thesis asserts only that visceral arousal contributes an undifferentiated *quale* or feeling tone to experience, but that the differentiation among emotions reflects the way a person interprets the situation (e.g., Schachter, 1971).

1. Is Each Emotion Associated with a Different Pattern of Physiological Activity?

The answer to this question is a qualified yes. It requires no sensitive instrumentation and sophisticated statistical techniques to recognize that the visceral changes that accompany sexual arousal, say, are in important respects different than those that accompany fear, and that still other reactions are common during grief. However, before we become too sanguine about identifying different emotions with different patterns of physiological activity, several important qualifications must be kept in mind.

First, distinctions such as those just noted (e.g., among sexual arousal, fear, and grief) are between broad categories of emotions, that is, among emotions defined at the genus or even family levels depicted in Figure 1. Emotions defined at such global levels are probably associated with different biological potentials (systems of behavior; see Figure 3). For example, sexual arousal is related to reproductive behavior; fear to avoidance of danger; grief to the breaking of attachment bonds; and so forth. As explained earlier, what is true at one (global) level in a hierarchy need not be true at another (more specific) level. With regard to the issue at hand, there is little evidence for differential physiological patterning among *specific* emotions within a broad category (e.g., between anger and jealousy). Among specific emotions differentiation is based primarily on the appraised object (instigation/target/objective) of the emotion.

Second, physiological reactions (e.g., an increase in cardiac output) occur to support possible overt behavior, whether or not a response is actually made. Since the behavior associated with any given emotion can vary greatly depending on the person and the situation, so too will physiological reactions. To take an obvious example, the person who faints in fear is undergoing different physiological changes than the person who flees; and the angry person who writes a nasty letter to the editor is in a different physiological state than a person engaged in physical combat.

2. How Sensitive Are People to Physiological Changes when They Do Occur?

People are not very sensitive to these changes. Self-reports of ongoing physiological responses are typically poorly correlated with actual physiological activity (Reed, Harver, & Katkin, 1990). The viscera are not particularly sensitive structures and, as noted in response to the previous question, only gross distinctions are observed between broad classes of emotions when actual physiological responses are measured. This presents a paradox: People do *report* differential patterns of physiological arousal when asked to describe their emotional experiences. To what do those reports refer?

It is possible that self-reports of physiological activity during emotion reflect cultural stereotypes (e.g., a person "turns red" when angry and gets "cold feet" when fearful). However, considerable cross-cultural consistency has also been observed in self-reported physiological responses (Wallbott & Scherer, 1988). This would seem to obviate an explanation in terms of cultural stereotypes. Again, however, it should be noted that research on this issue has focused on emotions defined at a very high level of generality, or in terms of broad affective dimensions (e.g., evaluation and activation). It is possible that people are able to discriminate and report physiological differences between global categories and dimensions of emotion, especially if they focus on very intense episodes. It is also possible, as Rimé, Philippot, and Cisamolo (1990) suggest, that there is symbolic overlap between some emotional and physiological constructs. For example, feelings of joy may become associated with certain physiological processes, not because of any actual commonalities in underlying processes, but because both presumably give rise to "warm" feelings.

3. Is Physiological Change Necessary for Emotion?

Physiological change is not necessary for emotion. This answer might seem unduly conclusive, since most contemporary theories regard physiological change (differentiated or not) as a necessary condition for emotion (e.g., Mandler, 1984; Schachter, 1971). But before we accept uncritically the notion that physiological arousal is necessary for emotion, two facts should be noted: First, the *belief* that one is aroused, or the meaning of the arousal for the individual, may be more important in determining the experience of emotion than is the actual state of arousal (Reisenzein, 1983; Valins, 1967); second, noticeable physiological change is a prominent feature primarily of short-term, relatively intense emotional episodes (e.g., sudden fright as opposed to longer lasting but still episodic fear), and of some emotional syndromes but not others (e.g., fear as opposed to hope; Averill, Catlin, & Chon, 1990).

Why, then, has physiological change become so closely identified with emotional responses? As alluded to in response to the previous question, psychological phenomena may become associated with physiological responses on the basis of shared symbolic meaning rather than on any empirically demonstrated functional relationship. Once such an association is made, it can be extremely tenacious, as the history of theories of emotion amply illustrates (Averill, 1974, 1990b).

C. Expressive Reactions

Ever since Darwin's pioneering work on *The Expression of Emotion in Man and Animals* (1872/1965), expressive reactions—especially facial expressions—have played a central and often controversial role in the study of emotion (Ekman, 1994; Fridlund, 1994; Russell, 1995). Darwin proposed that some expressive reactions are innate and universal within the human species, and, moreover, that such reactions are associated with specific emotions. These are actually two separate hypotheses, although they are often treated as one. For example, according to Izard and Saxton (1988), "the best available criteria for the presence of a particular discrete emotion are the muscle movements or changes in appearance that characterize its innate, universal facial expression" (p. 631). The discrete, "fundamental" emotions that can be so characterized are presumably joy, surprise, sadness, anger, disgust, and fear. Izard and Saxton (1988) go on to note that "the evidence for the innateness and universality of the expression of the fundamental emotions is sufficiently robust to consider Darwin's hypothesis as an established axiom of behavioral science" (pp. 651–652).

Any hypothesis in the behavioral sciences that merits the status of an axiom obviously deserves close scrutiny. Therefore, we will break Darwin's hypothesis into its two components and evaluate each part separately. We will then consider the moderating effect that facial expression may have on a person's own experience of emotion.

1. Are Some Expressive Reactions Innate and Universal?

Research by Eibl-Eibesfeldt (1970), Ekman (1982), and Izard (1991), among others, strongly suggests that some facial expressions can be evoked by similar situations (e.g., danger, separation) across diverse cultures, and even in children who, because they were born blind and deaf, have had no chance to learn the expressions from others. Moreover, homologous expression can be observed in other primate species (Redican, 1982). The issue, then, is less the existence of innate facial expressions, but the meaning and significance of such expressions.

2. Are Innate Facial Expressions Associated with Specific Emotions?

Innate facial expressions are only indirectly associated with specific emotions. The issue here is similar to that with respect to the relation between physiological response patterns and specific emotions. The demonstration that some facial expressions are innate and universal suggests the existence of certain biological systems of behavior, for example, toward aggression, flight, attachment, and the like. These are the biological potentials represented at Level I of Figure 3. As already discussed, there is no direct connection between biological potentials and specific emotional syndromes. An example may serve to reinforce this point. A good deal of evidence suggests that aggressive tendencies are universal in the human species, and that such tendencies are manifested in facial displays and distinct patterns of physiological arousal, as well as in direct aggression. However, there is little evidence to suggest that anger *as a specific emotional syndrome* is always—or even usually—associated with aggressive tendencies; moreover, aggressive tendencies may enter into a wide variety of emotional and nonemotional syndromes other than anger, such as envy, jealousy, and sadism (Averill, 1982).

3. Can Facial Expressions Alter the Experience of Emotion?

Facial expressions can modify the experience of emotion, but only to a modest degree. William James (1890), it may be recalled, proposed that proprioceptive feedback from bodily changes accounts for the experience of emotion. James included feedback from the face among the relevant bodily changes, but most early speculation focused on the viscera as the primary source of emotional experience. For reasons reviewed earlier, however, peripheral physiological arousal is inadequate to provide the fine discriminations that we experience among emotions. Some theorists (e.g., Izard, 1991; Tomkins, 1981) have therefore looked to the face as a possible source of emotional experience. The skin and muscles of the face are richly innervated and capable of very fine nuances. It is thus not unreasonable to assume that the face might provide the kind of proprioceptive feedback presumed by James.

A meta-analysis of 16 studies designed to test the facial-feedback hypothesis suggests that only about 12% of the variance in self-reported emotional experience can be accounted for in terms of experimentally manipulated variations in facial expression (Matsumoto, 1987). Moreover, current data do not allow any conclusions regarding the specificity of the effect, that is, whether an angry expression results in angry feelings, a fearful expression in a fearful feelings, and so forth. About the best that can be said is that facial expressions can have a modest biasing effect on a person's mood, for example, along the negative-positive axis depicted in Figure 2 (Izard & Saxton, 1988; Leventhal & Tomarken, 1986). And even that minor effect need not be due to proprioceptive feedback from the facial musculature (for possible alternative mechanisms, see Laird & Bresler, 1992; Zajonc, Murphy, & Inglehart, 1989).

D. Instrumental Acts

In the psychological literature it is common to distinguish emotional from instrumental responses. For example, the two-factor theory of avoidance learning assumes that fear (an emotional response) motivates avoidance (an instrumental response). Similarly, anger presumably motivates aggression, love motivates courtship, and so forth. This is another variation on the distinction between passions and actions. In passion, we are moved "in spite of ourselves"; in action, we move "on purpose." When a distinction becomes embedded in ordinary language, as this one has, it acquires the aura of common sense, and when imported into scientific discourse, it may be accepted uncritically. That is a mistake.

1. Are Instrumental Acts Less Indicative of Emotion Than Physiological or Expressive Reactions?

If anything, instrumental responses are more, not less, important for the identification of emotional states and syndromes than are physiological or expressive reactions. This follows, in part, from our earlier discussion of the appraised object of an emotion. One aspect of the appraised object is the goal or *objective* of the response. Anger, for example, is not just a state of physiological arousal or a facial grimace occasioned by some appraised wrong; it also involves a desire to correct the wrong. To illustrate the same point in a somewhat different way, consider that a person may weep from sadness, anger, joy, or chopping onions. How do we infer which emotion is being experienced? In large part, by what the person does (or does not do) in order to change the situation.

E. Verbal Behavior

Two aspects of verbal behavior can be distinguished, what is said (the content of speech) and how it is said (e.g., loudness, tone, timing). The latter (expressive) aspect has received most attention from emotion theorists (Pittam & Scherer, 1993). On a broad conceptual level, however, the expressive aspects of speech involve many of the same advantages and limitations as facial expressions and physiological reactions, which we have already considered in some detail. In this section, therefore, we will focus on the instrumental aspect of verbal behavior, that is, on what is said rather than on how it is said.

Psychologists tend to distrust self-reports of emotion, and with good reason. It is easier to disguise our emotions with words than with any other kind of response. However, the distrust of verbal behavior by psychologists is not based simply on the fact that people can, and sometimes do, dissimulate. It is also based on the implicit (and, we believe, mistaken) assumption that the words we use to express emotional concepts are only labels that get attached, sometimes correctly and sometimes incorrectly, to preexisting states of affairs—the emotions per se.

1. Do Emotions Exist Independent of the Way They Are Conceptualized?

Emotions do not exist independent of their conceptualization. In order to explain this answer, we must return briefly to an issue discussed earlier, namely, the relation between language and emotion. At the risk of oversimplification, it can be said that the meaning of a word is based on a network of ideas and propositions—a kind of "implicit theory" (Murphy & Medin, 1985). For example, the meaning of the word "atom" presupposes a (scientific) theory of matter. In a similar manner, the meaning of the word "anger" presupposes a (folk) theory of emotion. But there is also an important dissimilarity between "atom" and "anger." Physical objects such as atoms do not change in any fundamental way as a function of how they are conceived. The same is not true of psychological phenomena. In the human sciences, the mere act of naming can change the phenomenon named.

Put differently, emotional concepts are not simply descriptive, they are also prescriptive. The network of ideas and propositions that lend meaning to our everyday emotional concepts also help constitute and regulate the behavior denoted by those concepts. Of course, once the meaning of a word has been acquired, verbal responses can be divorced from the remainder of a person's behavior and used to conceal as well as to reveal.

2. Are There Emotions for Which We Have No Words?

Not all concepts find expression in words. We have already noted this fact in connection with the emotional taxonomy presented in Figure 1. It will be recalled that "covert categories" are quite common in folk taxonomies (Berlin et al., 1968). Over time, as individuals and cultures develop, new concepts may emerge for which there are no names. Arieti (1976) has called such emerging cognitions "endocepts," to distinguish them from well-formed concepts. Endocepts are particularly important during the early stages of development, whether during childhood, or later during adulthood when a person is grappling with new ideas and experiences. When a person says, "I know how I feel, but I cannot put it into words," he or she is trying to express an emotional endocept. Much poetry, music, and painting can also be viewed as attempts to put into words and other symbolic forms emerging emotional experiences.

3. Do Preverbal Infants and Animals Experience Emotion?

Only in an extended sense do preverbal infants and animals experience emotion. At birth, the infant's emotional repertoire is limited primarily to the expression of biological potentials (Level I, Figure 3); socialization and individual experience have had little opportunity to exert their influence. It follows that infants cannot experience emotional syndromes which depend, in part, on social norms and rules. The fussing of an infant is literally a far cry from the anger of an adult. Similar considerations apply to animals. It would be fatuous to deny a continuity between humans and animals in the emotional as in the intellectual domain. This does not mean, however, that animals experience the same emotions as humans, for example, that the "anger" of a dog on having its bone removed is the same as the anger of a human on being robbed of a prized possession. Emotional continuity, whether ontogenetic or phylogenetic, does not entail sameness (Averill, 1984).

F. Feelings

We return now to the issue of feelings (the conscious awareness of being in an emotional state), which we introduced earlier in connection with the reflexivity of emotional responses. The terms "feeling" and "emotion" are often used interchangeably. To say, "I feel angry," means much the same as to say, "I am angry." This has led some theorists to assume that emotions are *really* feelings, or at least that feelings are essential features of emotions (cf. Oatley & Johnson-Laird, 1987; Ortony et al., 1988). Within the present framework, feelings are component responses; they are no more essential to an emotional state than are other kinds of response (e.g., physiological change). But that being granted, it is nevertheless true that feelings are an important component of most emotional states.

1. What Are Emotional Feelings Feelings Of?

Emotional feelings are not based on any one source. For example, the way we appraise a situation determines, to a large extent, the way we feel. This fact was particularly emphasized by Jung (1921/1971), who defined feelings as a kind of evaluative judgment. Thinking, according to Jung, tells us what a thing is (e.g., that stars are generated by hydrogen fusion); feeling tells us what a thing is good for in an evaluative sense (e.g., that stars are like diamonds in the sky). Feedback from peripheral physiological arousal and facial expressions also adds a certain quality to the experience of emotion, as discussed in response to earlier questions. Instrumental acts, whether actual or only desired, make an additional contribution to the way we feel. Is escape possible? Should I fight to overcome the potential harm? Or is there nothing I can do? Depending on how these questions are answered, a person may feel fear, anger, or depression.

In short, cognitive appraisals, physiological and expressive reactions, and instrumental acts all may contribute to emotional feelings. But an emotional feeling is not simply a by-product of other responses; it is a response in its own right. Sarbin (1986) has pointed out that when people are asked how they feel, they typically tell a story, a self-narrative. For example, when asked how she feels, the Olympic champion may respond with a few uninformative exclamations, such as "It's incredible," or "It's a wonderful feeling," and then launch into a story about the rigors of training, the role of fellow athletes, family support, the meaning of the contest, future plans, and so forth.

2. Can People Be Mistaken about Their Own Emotional Feelings?

As discussed earlier, emotional feelings are reflexive (i.e., involve an interpretation of one's own experience). It follows that people can always be mistaken about the way they feel. Such mistakes are commonplace in clinical practice. The person who is angry, jealous, envious, afraid, in love, and so forth, is sometimes the last and not the first to recognize the fact. Less common but theoretically more interesting are occasions when a person feels emotional without being in an emotional state. For example, the ebullience of a person in a hypomanic state may be taken, not as a sign of happiness, but of depression.

In some respects, "feeling" an emotion can be compared to "hearing" voices. No matter how vivid and realistic a voice might seem, it will not be considered real unless there is some adequate stimulus to account for its occurrence. Similar considerations apply to emotional experience. Feelings for which there are not adequate instigations are liable to be dismissed as illusory, false, or inauthentic (Averill, 1994b; Morgan & Averill, 1992). No less than other forms of behavior, feelings can deceive. In fact, if we want to deceive others, it is best first to deceive ourselves through our feelings.

V. EMOTIONAL STATES

We turn now from component responses (Level V, Figure 3) to emotional states (Level IV, Figure 3). As already described, an emotional state is an episodic disposition to respond in a manner consistent with an emotional syndrome (Level III, Figure 3). That, however, does not say a great deal. Dispositions must be explained in terms of underlying mechanisms, as when combustibility (a dispositional property) is explained in terms of molecular structure.

When it comes to the mechanisms that underlie emotional states, the temptation appears strong to postulate distinct processes (e.g., an "emotion system" and a "cognitive system") to correspond to the distinction between passions and actions. The bias of the present chapter is to resist that temptation. An analogy may help clarify the basis for this resistance. Diseases have traditionally been conceived of as passions of the body, things that the body "suffers." At one time it was common to postulate special processes to account for diseased states (including, for example, witchcraft and possession by the devil). However, most diseases can be explained in terms of normal physiological reactions to abnormal conditions (e.g., the presence of pathogens, injury, genetic mutations). There are no special "disease processes" or "laws of disease" in physiology. Similarly, it is most parsimonious to assume that emotional states can be accounted for in the way ordinary psychological processes are organized to meet unusual circumstances.

We need not rely on analogy to make a case against the "special process" view of emotional states. From a cognitive perspective, the emotions involve all those processes (e.g., attention, perception, memory, concept formation, language, and problem solving) that enter into nonemotional behavior. True, some forms of cognition may be more common during emotional than during more deliberate, "rational" states (Epstein, 1994), but that does not make such processes inherently emotional. Similar observations may be made with reference to the central neural mechanisms that mediate emotions. Many of the same brain circuits that are involved in emotional processes are also involved in "higher-order" thought processes (Davidson, 1994). At most, one might distinguish neural circuits that have some specificity for biological systems of behavior (e.g., aggression, attachment, sexual arousal) and for such broad dimensions of behavior as evaluation (negative–positive) and activation (aroused–unaroused). However, for reasons already discussed, biological systems and affective dimensions cannot be equated with specific emotions.

In short, an adequate discussion of the mechanisms that mediate emotional states would encompass nearly all of psychology. We must leave the matter at that.

VI. EMOTIONAL SYNDROMES

Fortunately, we need not wait for an adequate understanding of the mechanisms that mediate emotional states before we attempt to understand the principles by which emotional syndromes are organized. In this respect, we may draw an analogy between emotions and language. The psychological and physiological mechanisms that enable a person to speak are poorly understood. However, that does not prevent us from trying to understand the way a particular language is organized—English, say, as opposed to Chinese. Languages are organized according to rules—the rules of grammer. Emotional syndromes are also organized according to rules—the rules of emotion.

A. Emotional Rules

Three aspects of rules may be distinguished: constitutive, regulative, and procedural. For ease of discussion, it is easier to speak, not of aspects, but of different types of rules, depending on which aspect predominates.

To illustrate the difference among constitutive, regulative, and procedural rules, consider a game such as chess. Some rules (e.g., with regard to the nature of the pieces and way they may be moved) help *constitute* the game as a game of chess, as opposed, say, to a game of checkers. Other rules (e.g., limiting the time between moves) help to *regulate* how the game is played on any given occasion. Still other rules, called *procedural,* help determine strategy—how well the game is played.

Like the game of chess, an emotional syndrome is also constituted and regulated by rules, and its successful enactment requires skills based on procedural rules. The nature of the various rules is best illustrated by what happens when they are broken or misapplied. Take anger. If a constitutive rule of anger is broken, the response may be interpreted as a manifestation of some other condition (a neurotic syndrome, perhaps); it will not be considered true anger. If a regulative rule is violated, the response may be accepted as anger, but it will be considered inappropriate or delinquent. Finally, if a procedural rule is broken, the failing will be treated more a matter of ineptitude than inappropriateness. The individual is, in a sense, an emotional klutz.

The acquisition of appropriate procedural rules is a common goal in psychotherapy (e.g., skills training). All emotion theorists also recognize the importance of regulative rules in determining the way emotions are displayed, particularly across cultures (Ekman, 1982). The role of constitutive rules has been less frequently recognized. Change a constitutive rule, and the nature of the emotional syndrome itself changes, not just its display or enactment. If the change is for the worse, we speak of emotional disorders (Averill, 1988); if it is for the better, of emotional creativity (Averill & Nunley, 1992; Averill & Thomas-Knowles, 1991).

B. Emotional Roles

The rules of emotion help to establish a corresponding set of emotional roles; these roles are the various emotional syndromes that we recognize in ordinary language. An emotional role, like any other social role, can be analyzed in terms of privileges, restrictions, obligations, and entrance requirements. In the following discussion we will use as examples the roles of anger, romantic love, and grief, the details of which can be found elsewhere (Averill, 1982, 1985; Averill & Nunley, 1993, respectively).

1. Privileges

Emotional roles (syndromes) allow a person to engage in behavior that would be discouraged in ordinary circumstances. The specific behavior allowed or "excused" varies depending on the emotion. For example, when angry a person can literally get away with murder (i.e., have a crime of homicide mitigated from murder to manslaughter—a "crime of passion"). When in love, a person may engage in sexual behavior that otherwise might be viewed as socially inappropriate. And when grieving, a person is exempted from obligations related to work and entertainment, at least for a period of time.

2. Restrictions

There are limits to what a person can do when emotional and "get away with it." Emotional responses should be appropriate to the situation: They should not be too mild or too strong, too short or too prolonged, or too idiosyncratic. For example, a plea of anger will not be accepted in a court of law if the crime is committed in too cruel or unusual a manner. Similarly, lovers are expected to be discrete and honorable in their affairs. And, in the case of grief, if a bereaved wife begins dating too soon after the death of her husband, the genuineness of her grief may be cast into doubt.

3. Obligations

Whereas there are some things a person cannot do while emotional (restrictions), there are other things that must be done (obligations). An angry person, for example, is expected to take action to correct the wrong, or else the sincerity of his anger, or even his character, will be questioned. The same is even more evident in the case of love, which carries a commitment to the well-being of the loved one. Among the examples we have been using, it might seem that grief is an exception. It is, however, the exception that proves the rule. In all societies the bereaved are expected to perform certain mourning practices. These obligations can be neglected only at considerable risk; the individual who fails to comply with societal expectations following bereavement is often subject to severe sanction.

4. Entry Requirements

Most, though not all, social roles have entry requirements; that is, they can be occupied only by persons of a certain age, sex, training, and/or social position. No matter how skillfully enacted, something more is required to distinguish between merely "playing a role" and actually being "in the role." That "something more" is not simply sincerity or subjective involvement. A delusional schizophrenic might skillfully play the role of a judge, say, following all the relevant rules, and he might sincerely believe that he is a judge. Yet, he would not be a judge. Authentic role enactment requires social recognition and legitimacy. The same is true of emotional roles. (Recall from our earlier discussion that a person can *feel* emotional without *being* in an emotional state.)

The entry requirements for anger are vague but nevertheless discernable. For example, persons higher in authority (e.g., parents) are afforded more right to become angry than are persons lower in authority (e.g., children), and similarly with certain occupations (e.g., a drill sergeant as opposed to a minister). The entry requirements for love are more explicit. Below a certain age, a person is not "allowed" to fall in love, and if sexual infatuation should lead to sexual behavior, statutory rape may be charged. Grief, too, has its entry requirements. In many traditional societies the way grief is to be experienced may be stipulated according to the age or sex of the bereaved, as well as to the nature of the relationship of the bereaved to the decreased—spouse, parent, child, cousin, and so forth.

In addition to the above features (privileges, restrictions, obligations, and entry requirements), emotional roles can be distinguished from other social roles (such as that of judge, ballet dancer, or father) in that emotional roles are transitory or transitional. That is, emotional roles are for short-term occupancy only; they afford a means of transition from one state of affairs to another, when more "normal" modes of responding are not sufficient (Averill, 1990a; Oatley, 1992).

VII. EMOTIONAL POTENTIALS AND CAPACITIES

Emotional roles emphasize the "objective" nature of emotional syndromes. That is, unlike emotional states and component responses, emotional syndromes (roles) exist independent of the experiencing individual. A definition of emotional syndromes as social roles also emphasizes the importance of society in determining emotional behavior; it does not, however, ignore biology. Most social roles presume relevant biological as well as social potentials (see Level I, Figure 3). The role of judge, for example, presumes a degree of native intelligence; the role of ballet dancer, musical talent and motor dexterity; and the role of father, certain sexual characteristics. The same is no less true of emotional roles.

The emotional reactions of infancy (fussing, cooing, withdrawal, etc.) are primarily biological. It could not be otherwise. But almost immediately, socialization begins to occur through the mediation of parents and other caregivers. The temperamental traits (Level II, Figure 3) that eventually emerge from this interaction of genetic endowment and environmental influence typically have heritability coefficients of around $.50 \pm .10$, depending on the population studied. And, as explained earlier, temperamental traits are still only predispositions to emotion. Before an individual is able to enter into an emotional role, and hence to experience and express a specific emotion, the rules and beliefs that help constitute that emotion must be internalized. A person who has internalized the relevant rules and who is adroit in their application may be said to be emotionally intelligent (Mayer & Salovey, 1995; Salovey et al., 1992). But internalization is not a static, once-and-for-all affair. Rules can be changed, a fact that makes possible emotional creativity on both the individual and the social levels (Averill & Nunley, 1992; Averill & Thomas-Knowles, 1991).

VIII. CONCLUDING OBSERVATIONS

The emotions play a central role in most theories of personality. Yet, personality psychologists have shown a remarkable tolerance for ambiguity with regard to the nature of emotions per se. More often than not, emotional concepts have been used in a global, undifferentiated fashion, or else in a manner unique to each theory. The anxiety of the psychoanalyst, for example, is different from the anxiety of the existentialist, and both are different from the anxiety of the behaviorist. A fuller appreciation of the variety, organization, and principles of emotion is necessary for the advancement and possible integration of personality theory.

REFERENCES

Arieti, S. (1976). *Creativity: The magic synthesis.* New York: Basic Books.

Averill, J. R. (1974). An analysis of psychophysiological symbolism and its influence on theories of emotion. *Journal for the Theory of Social Behavior, 4,* 147–190.

Averill, J. R. (1975). A semantic atlas of emotional concepts. *JSAS Catalog of Selected Documents in Psychology, 5,* 330. (Ms. No. 1103)

Averill, J. R. (1982). *Anger and aggression: An essay on emotion.* New York: Springer-Verlag.

Averill, J. R. (1984). The acquisition of emotions during adulthood. In C. Z. Malatesta & C. Izard (Eds.), *Affective processes in adult development* (pp. 23–43). Beverly Hills, CA: Sage.

Averill, J. R. (1985). The social construction of emotion: With special reference to love. In K. Gergen & K. Davis (Eds.), *The social construction of the person* (pp. 90–109). New York: Springer-Verlag.

Averill, J. R. (1988). Disorders of emotion. *Journal of Social and Clinical Psychology, 6,* 247–268.

Averill, J. R. (1990a). Emotions as episodic dispositions, cognitive schemas, and transitory social roles: Steps toward an integrated theory of emotion. In D. Ozer, J. M. Healy, & A. J. Stewart (Eds.), *Perspectives in personality* (Vol. 3a, pp. 139–167). London: Jessica Kingsley Publishers.

Averill, J. R. (1990b). Inner feelings, works of the flesh, the beast within, diseases of the mind, driving force, and putting on a show: Six metaphors of emotion and their theoretical extensions. In D. E. Leary (Ed.), *Metaphors in the history of psychology* (pp. 104–132). New York: Cambridge University Press.

Averill, J. R. (1994a, July). *Emotional Creativity Inventory: Scale construction and validation.* Paper presented at the meetings of the International Society for Research on Emotion, Cambridge, England.

Averill, J. R. (1994b). I feel, therefore I am—I think. In P. Ekman & R. J. Davidson (Eds.), *The nature of emotion: Fundamental questions* (pp. 379–385). New York: Oxford University Press.

Averill, J. R., Catlin, G., & Chon, K. K. (1990). *Rules of hope.* New York: Springer-Verlag.

Averill, J. R., & Nunley, E. P. (1992). *Voyages of the heart: Living an emotionally creative life.* New York: Free Press.

Averill, J. R., & Nunley, E. P. (1993). Grief as an emotion and as a disease. In M. S. Stroebe, W. Stroebe, & R. O. Hansson (Eds.), *Handbook of bereavement* (pp. 77–90). New York: Cambridge University Press.

Averill, J. R., & Thomas-Knowles, C. (1991). Emotional creativity. In K. T. Strongman (Ed.), *International review of studies on emotion* (Vol. 1, pp. 269–299). London: Wiley.

Berlin, B., Breedlove, D., & Raven, P. (1968). Covert categories and folk taxonomies. *American Anthropologist, 70,* 290–299.

Cacioppo, J. T., Klein, D. J., Bernstom, G. G., & Hatfield, E. (1993). The psychophysiology of emotion. In M. Lewis & J. Haviland (Eds.), *Handbook of emotions* (pp. 119–142). New York: Guilford Press.

Darwin, C. (1965). *The expression of the emotions in man and animals.* Chicago: University of Chicago Press. (Original work published 1872)

Davidson, R. J. (1994). Complexities in the search from emotion-specific physiology. In P. Ekman & R. J. Davidson (Eds.), *The nature of emotion: Fundamental questions* (pp. 237–242). New York: Oxford University Press.

de Rivera, J. (1977). *A structural theory of the emotions.* New York: International Universities Press.

Dewey, J. (1895). The theory of emotion. II: The significance of emotions. *Psychological Review, 2,* 13–32.

Eibl-Eibesfeldt, I. (1970). *Ethology: The biology of behavior* (E. Klinghammer, Trans.). New York: Holt, Rinehart & Winston.

Ekman, P. (Ed.). (1982). *Emotion in the human face* (2nd ed.). Cambridge, England: Cambridge University Press.

Ekman, P. (1984). Expression and the nature of emotion. In K. Scherer & P. Ekman (Eds.), *Approaches to emotion* (pp. 319–343). Hillsdale, NJ: Erlbaum.

Ekman, P. (1994). Strong evidence for universals in facial expressions: A reply to Russell's mistaken critique. *Psychological Bulletin, 115,* 268–287.

Epstein, S. (1994). Integration of the cognitive and the psychodynamic unconscious. *American Psychologist, 49,* 709–724.

Fehr, B., & Russell, J. A. (1984). Concept of emotion viewed from a prototype perspective. *Journal of Experimental Psychology: General, 113,* 464–486.

Fox, R. (1971). The cultural animal. In J. F. Eisenberg & W. S. Dillon (Eds.), *Man and beast: Comparative social behavior* (pp. 273–296). Washington, DC: Smithsonian Institution Press.

Fridlund, A. J. (1994). *Human facial expression: An evolutionary view.* San Diego, CA: Academic Press.

Frijda, N. H. (1986). *The emotions.* Cambridge, England: Cambridge University Press.

Haslam, N. (1996). The discreteness of emotion concepts: Categorical structure in the affective circumplex. *Personality and Social Psychology Bulletin, 21,* 1012–1019.

Hochschild, A. R. (1983). *The managed heart.* Berkeley: University of California Press.

Izard, C. E. (1991). *The psychology of emotions.* New York: Plenum Press.

Izard, C. E. (1993). Four systems for emotion activation: Cognitive and noncognitive processes. *Psychological Review, 100,* 68–90.

Izard, C. E., & Saxton, P. M. (1988). Emotions. In R. C. Atkinson, R. J. Herrnstein, G. Lindzey, and R. D. Luce (Eds.), *Handbook of experimental psychology* (2nd ed., Vol. 1, pp. 627–676). New York: Wiley.

James, W. (1890). *The principles of psychology* (2 vols). New York: Henry Holt.

Johnson-Laird, P. N., & Oatley, K. (1989). The language of emotions: An analysis of a semantic field. *Cognition and Emotion, 3,* 81–123.

Jung, C. G. (1971). *Psychological types: Collected works* (Vol. 6). Princeton, NJ: Princeton University Press. (Original work published 1921)

Laird, J. D., & Bresler, C. (1992). The process of emotional experience: A self-perception theory. In M. S. Clark (Ed.), *Review of personality and social psychology* (Vol. 13, pp. 213–234). Newbury Park, CA: Sage.

Larsen, R. J., & Diener, E. (1992). Promises and problems with the circumplex model of emotion. In M. S. Clark (Ed.), *Review of personality and social psychology* (Vol. 13, pp. 25–59). Newbury Park, CA: Sage.

Lazarus, R. S. (1991). *Emotion and adaptation.* New York: Oxford University Press.

Leventhal, H., & Tomarken, A. J. (1986). Emotion: Today's problems. *Annual Review of Psychology, 37,* 565–610.

Lutz, C. (1982). The domain of emotion words on Ifaluk. *American Ethnologist, 9,* 113–128.

Mandler, G. (1984). *Mind and body: Psychology of emotion and stress.* New York: Norton.

Matsumoto, D. (1987). The role of facial response in the experience of emotion: More methodological problems and a meta-analysis. *Journal of Personality and Social Psychology, 52,* 769–774.

Mayer, J. D., & Salovey, P. (1995). Emotional intelligence and the construction and regulation of feelings. *Applied & Preventive Psychology, 4,* 197–208.

McDougall, W. (1936). *An introduction to social psychology* (23rd ed.). London: Methuen.

Mees, U. (1991). *Die Struktur der Emotionen.* Göttingen: Hogrefe.

Morgan, C., & Averill, J. R. (1992). True feelings, the self, and authenticity: A psychosocial perspective. In D. Franks & V. Gecas (Eds.), *Social perspectives in emotions* (Vol. 1, pp. 95–123). Greenwich, CT: JAI Press.

Murphy, G. L., & Medin, D. L. (1985). The role of theories in conceptual coherence. *Psychological Review, 92,* 289–316.

Oatley, K. (1992). *Best laid schemes: The psychology of emotions.* Cambridge, England: Cambridge University Press.

Oatley, K., & Johnson-Laird, P. N. (1987). Towards a cognitive theory of emotions. *Cognition and Emotion, 1,* 29–50.

Ortony, A., Clore, G. L., & Collins, A. (1988). The *cognitive structures of emotions.* Cambridge, England: Cambridge University Press.

Pittam, J., & Scherer, K. R. (1993). Vocal expression and communication of emotion. In M. Lewis & J. Haviland (Eds.), *Handbook of emotions* (pp. 185–197). New York: Guilford Press.

Plutchik, R. (1980). *Emotion: A psychoevolutionary synthesis.* New York: Harper & Row.

Redican, W. K. (1982). An evolutionary perspective on human facial displays. In P. Ekman (Ed.), *Emotion in the human face* (2nd ed., pp. 212–280). Cambridge, England: Cambridge University Press.

Reed, S. D., Harver, A., & Katkin, E. S. (1990). Interoception. In J. T. Cacioppo & L. G. Tassinary (Eds.), *Principles of psychophysiology: Physical, social, and inferential elements* (pp. 253–294). New York: Cambridge University Press.

Reisenzein, R. (1983). The Schachter theory of emotion: Two decades later. *Psychological Bulletin, 94,* 239–264.

Reisenzein, R. (1994). Pleasure-arousal theory and the intensity of emotions. *Journal of Personality and Social Psychology, 67,* 525–539.

Rimé, B., Philippot, P., & Cisamolo, D. (1990). Social schemata of peripheral changes in emotion. *Journal of Personality and Social Psychology, 59,* 38–49.

Roseman, I. J., Antoniou, A. A., & Jose, P. E. (1996). Appraisal determinants of emotions: Constructing a more accurate and comprehensive theory. *Cognition and Emotion, 10,* 241–277.

Russell, J. A. (1980). A circumplex model of affect. *Journal of Personality and Social Psychology, 39,* 1161–1178.

Russell, J. A. (1983). Pancultural aspects of the human conceptual organization of emotions. *Journal of Personality and Social Psychology, 45,* 1281–1288.

Russell, J. A. (1991). Culture and the categorization of emotions. *Psychological Bulletin, 110,* 426–450.

Russell, J. A. (1995). Facial expressions of emotion: What lies beyond minimal universality? *Psychological Bulletin, 118,* 379–391.

Ryle, G. (1949). *The concept of mind.* London: Hutchinson.

Salovey, P., Hsee, C. K., & Mayer, J. D. (1992). Emotional Intelligence and the self-regulation of affect. In D. M. Wegner & J. W. Pennebaker (Eds.), *Handbook of mental control* (pp. 258–277). Englewood Cliffs, NJ: Prentice-Hall.

Sarbin, T. R. (1986). Emotion and act: Roles and rhetoric. In R. Harré (Ed.), *The social construction of emotions* (pp. 83–97). Oxford, England: Basil Blackwell.

Sartre, J. P. (1948). *The emotions: Outline of a theory* (B. Frechtman, Trans.). New York: Philosophical Library.

Schachter, S. (1971). *Emotion, obesity, and crime.* New York: Academic Press.

Scherer, K. R. (1984). On the nature and function of emotion: A component process approach. In K. R. Scherer & P. Ekman (Eds.), *Approaches to emotion* (pp. 293–317). Hillsdale, NJ: Erlbaum.

Shaver, P., Schwartz, J., Kirson, D., & O'Connor, C. (1987). Emotion knowledge: Further exploration of a prototype approach. *Journal of Personality and Social Psychology, 52,* 1061–1086.

Smith, C. A., & Ellsworth, P. C. (1985). Patterns of cognitive appraisal in emotion. *Journal of Personality and Social Psychology, 48,* 813–838.

Solomon, R. C. (1993). *The passions: Emotions and the meaning of life* (Rev ed.). Indianapolis, IN: Hackett.

Spielberger, C. D. (1966). Theory and research on anxiety. In C. D. Spielberger (Ed.), *Anxiety and behavior* (pp. 3–20). New York: Academic Press.

Storm, C., & Storm, T. (1987). A taxonomic study of the vocabulary of emotions. *Journal of Personality and Social Psychology, 53,* 805–816.

Storm, C., Storm, T., & Jones, C. (1996). Aspects of meaning in words related to happiness. *Cognition and Emotion, 10,* 279–302.

Tomkins, S. S. (1981). The role of facial response in the experience of emotion: A reply to Tourangeau and Ellsworth. *Journal of Personality and Social Psychology, 40,* 355–357.

Valins, S. (1967). Emotionality and information concerning internal reactions. *Journal of Personality and Social Psychology, 6,* 458–463.

Wallbott, H. G., & Scherer, K. R. (1988). How universal and specific is emotional experience? Evidence from 27 countries on five continents. In K. R. Scherer (Ed.), *Facets of emotion* (pp. 31–56). Hillsdale, NJ: Erlbaum.

Watson, D., & Tellegen, A. (1985). Toward a consensual structure of mood. *Psychological Bulletin, 98,* 219–235.

Weiner, B. (1985). An attributional theory of achievement motivation and emotion. *Psychological Review, 92,* 548–573.

Wierzbicka, A. (1992). Defining emotion concepts. *Cognitive Science, 16,* 539–581.

Wittgenstein, L. (1953). *Philosophical investigations.* Oxford, England: Basil Blackwell & Mott.

Zajonc, R. B., Murphy, S. T., & Inglehart, M. (1989). Feeling and facial efference: Implications of the vascular theory of emotion. *Psychological Review, 96,* 395–416.

CHAPTER 22

PSYCHOLOGICAL DEFENSE
CONTEMPORARY THEORY AND RESEARCH

DELROY L. PAULHUS
UNIVERSITY OF BRITISH COLUMBIA

BRAM FRIDHANDLER
UNIVERSITY OF CALIFORNIA, SAN FRANCISCO

SEAN HAYES
PEPPERDINE UNIVERSITY

With some trepidation, we tackle the monumental task of reviewing the contemporary literature on psychological defense. The task is particularly daunting because (a) the literature is vast and scattered, (b) the empirical basis of the topics varies dramatically, and (c) many psychologists remain skeptical of the very notion of defense, often because of a general distrust of things psychoanalytic. For these reasons, we have given priority to claims with empirical support and to work conducted since the last handbook chapter on this topic (Eriksen & Pierce, 1968).

In its broadest sense, *psychological defense* refers to the process of regulating painful emotions such as anxiety, depression, and loss of self-esteem. *Defense mechanisms* are usually defined more narrowly as mental processes that operate unconsciously to reduce some painful emotion. In the classical sense, the latter have been further restricted to threats aroused by the individual's thoughts and wishes, particularly psychological conflict over issues of sex and aggression.

Our decision to address the larger topic of psychological defense is less a virtue than a necessity given that the term "defense mechanism" has been used so widely and liberally as to cover virtually all forms of psychological defense. For example, some influential theorists have argued for the inclusion of *conscious* mechanisms. Others have called for an expansion to cases where external realities (e.g., physical danger) are the source of threat.

In contrast to relaxing the traditional definition, some theorists have proposed further restrictions. Some, for example, favor restricting defense mechanisms to operations with maladaptive outcomes. Others have responded that the effectiveness of a defense cannot be determined prior to its use or independent of the context. Still others argue that certain defenses are a priori adaptive. Another proposed restriction requires intentionality of reducing distress as a necessary condition. This restriction is rejected, in turn, by theorists with a mechanistic, information-processing view of defense. Unfortunately, we cannot offer a solution to this lack of definitional consensus. Instead, we will refer to the broad topic of this paper as psychological defense while reminding the reader at times of the stricter classical definition of defense mechanisms.

We have organized the literature into digestible chunks by grouping together all the authors who share a conceptual framwork (e.g., Vaillant, Bond, Perry, Cooper). We cannot hope to do justice to each writer's work. At best, we can hope to provide a theoretical overview of each approach, a sampling of relevant research, and references to any reviews. The chapter will culminate with an attempt to link the common theoretical strands.

I. Contemporary Psychoanalysis

Although the concept of a defense mechanism originated with Sigmund Freud, his daughter Anna Freud (1936) was particularly influential in establishing the processes and distinctiveness of various defenses. Modern psychoanalytic writers have continued to dissect the concept of defense (S. H. Cooper, 1989; Gero, 1951; Schafer, 1968, 1976; Wallerstein, 1983). Only a handful, however, have had a significant impact on the psychoanalytic view of defense. One of these is Otto Kernberg (1976, 1984), who was strongly influenced in this regard by the "object relations" theory of Melanie Klein. Kernberg has defined a new diagnostic category, the "borderline personality organization," which differs from normal and neurotic organizations by virtue of its dependence on a particular variety of defense, namely, "splitting" and related defenses. These defenses, he argues, operate not by limiting awareness of offending wishes or ideas but by "dissociating them in consciousness." In other words, people with such personality organizations do experience their unacceptable or intolerable thoughts and feelings, unlike people with a neurotic organization who repress these mental contents. The essence of defensive activity in the "borderline" personality is recalling the tumultuous experiences almost as they had befallen someone else, blaming them on "bad" aspects of self or on irredeemably "bad" others, neither of which are felt to have substantial connections with the "good" self and others.

Renewed interest in psychoanalytic defense has led, somewhat ironically, to the rehabilitation of Freud's competitor, Pierre Janet (e.g., Bowers & Meichenbaum, 1984; C. Perry & Laurence, 1984). Janet saw defense as a constriction of consciousness rather than a shunting to the unconscious. A failure to integrate certain experiences within the personality was said to induce detached psychological automatisms. Although considerably less elaborate, Janet's view of defense provides a conception that is eminently compatible with modern information-processing theories.

Note, in conclusion, that many psychoanalysts eschew the notion of discrete defense mechanisms operating for limited periods of duration. Instead, they argue that defense is ubiquitous and pervasive: virtually every mental act involves a trade-off of anxiety and awareness. Some analysts go further to argue against any standard set of "defense mechanisms"; instead, any mental process or capacity can be used toward defensive ends (Brenner, 1982).

This view plays down the idea that some individuals are more defensive than others: instead, individuals differ in their *style* of defense. Indeed, this defensive style is so broad ranging that it represents a fundamental component of character. In recent times, this view has been well articulated by David Shapiro (1965, 1981).

Given space limitations, we cannot elaborate on these issues; we can only refer the reader to some key volumes. For discussion of other defenses and more elaborate discussions of theoretical issues, we recommend S. H. Cooper (1989), Erdelyi (1985, 1990), Sjoback (1973), and Wallerstein (1983). We also recommend Kline (1972) and Fisher and Greenberg (1977) for more extensive treatment and reviews of early research on defenses.

II. REPRESSION

In many ways, repression represents the flagship in the psychoanalytic fleet of defense mechanisms. Freud considered it so central that he labeled it the cornerstone of psychoanalysis. Subsequent analysts viewed repression as, if not a cornerstone, at least the prototype of defense mechanisms because it incorporated such central elements as emotional conflict, unconscious motivation, signal anxiety, and long-term unaccounted-for distress.

Here, our simple working definition of repression is the shunting of distressing emotions into the unconscious. Although inaccessible, the repressed emotion can create chronic distress.

In their handbook chapter on psychological defense, Eriksen and Pierce (1968) provided a thorough review of the early research. Those studies sought to show that memories associated with threat or distress were more difficult to recall. The studies that did show such effects, however, were later interpreted as interference effects due to stress, not repression. A particularly scathing review by Holmes (1974) virtually brought a halt to this era of research.

Recently, however, the topic of repression has attracted renewed attention under the label "repressed memories." Unfortunately, the documentation of this phenomenon consists primarily of unsystematic reports by therapists. The critiques leveled by experimental psychologists (e.g., Loftus, 1993) have centered around two pieces of evidence. First, laboratory research demonstrates unequivocally that emotional events are better recalled than nonemotional events. Second, when untrue suggestions are implanted in experimental subjects, they may be recalled with a certainty equal to that of true memories. Not surprisingly, many observers concluded that so-called "repressed memories" were, in fact, false memories implanted in the minds of their clients by certain "true believer" therapists (Ofshe & Watters, 1994).

In support of the scattered reports by therapists, however, are some recent prospective studies. For example, Williams (1994) interviewed 129 women with previously documented histories of sexual victimization in childhood. A large proportion of the women (38%) did not recall the abuse that had been reported 17 years earlier.

The problem with such studies for our purposes, is that they only address the question of whether these events can be forgotten, not whether they are *repressed*. To substantiate the latter, it must be shown that the memories can be recovered, thereby demonstrating that they were present in some form all along. Note that the harmful effects of child sexual abuse are not at issue; the issue is whether those children who forget the trauma are still distressed because a repressed conflict remains to fester. Until such studies are forthcoming, this topic will surely remain controversial.

III. DENIAL

Although overlapping with other defenses, denial refers primarily to defense against painful aspects of external reality (e.g., Goldberger, 1983). It is usually considered a primitive defense, both in the sense of developing early and in the sense of crudeness and simplicity (A. Freud, 1936). Nonetheless, detailed analysis by Breznitz (1983) and Spence (1983) has distinguished seven kinds of denial varying in subtlety and stage of analysis.

Recent theoretical treatments include several dealing with the denial of death (Becker, 1973; Kubler-Ross, 1969; Lifton, 1968; see also terror management in the next paragraph). Other comprehensive theoretical treatments of denial include those by Moore and Rubinfine (1969), Sjoback (1973), and Dorpat (1985).

Empirical treatments include those by Breznitz (1983) and Spence (1983). The most comprehensive experimental treatment is that by Greenberg, Pyszczynski, and Solomon (1986) on what they term "terror management (TM)." Based on the ideas of Ernest Becker (1973), the theme is that awareness of one's mortality creates the potential for overwhelming terror. This pervasive force is said to mold cultural beliefs to provide philosophies or religions that preclude the terror. In general these beliefs require (a) a means whereby individuals can escape their fate, for example, "If I behave morally, I will have everlasting life," and (b) a sense that one is satisfying the requirements for escape, that is, being a good person. The latter involves preserving one's self-esteem. In short, maintaining high self-esteem preserves one's death-exempt status thereby precluding the terror of certain death.

The authors have conducted a series of experiments to validate TM theory (Greenberg, 1986; Rosenblatt, Greenberg, Solomon, Pyszczynski, & Lyon, 1989). One robust finding is that exposing subjects to symbols of death increases their tendency to affirm cultural beliefs. The theory was also supported by Paulhus and Levitt (1987), who found that distracting subjects with death-related words increased their tendency to claim socially desirable traits. An extension of TM theory appeared recently (Pyszczynski et al., in press).

IV. SELF-DECEPTION

The term *self-deception* has been used in at least three distinguishable ways. In one usage, self-deception is a distinct form of defense in which the individual shows moral weakness in disavowing some unpleasant truth (e.g., Eagle, 1988; Fingarette, 1969; Sarbin, 1988). In another usage, self-deception is not a type of defense, but a state of affairs inherent in defense mechanisms: it is a motivated unawareness of one of two conflicting representations of the same target (Paulhus, 1988; Sackeim & Gur, 1978). Finally, self-deception is also used as a generic term to cover misperceptions about oneself (e.g., Gilbert & Cooper, 1985; Goleman, 1986).

Although often claimed to be paradoxical (Gergen, 1985; Sartre, 1943/1956), the notion of self-deception has commanded increased attention in recent years. This interest may be traced to a few seminal works. In philosophy, the first full-fledged treatise was published in 1969 by Herbert Fingarette. In sociobiology, a commentary by Trivers (1976) was followed quickly by more thorough treatments by Lockard (1978) and Alexander (1979).

In psychology, earlier empirical work by Frenkel-Brunswik (1939) and Murphy (1975) preceded the first rigorous experiment by Gur and Sackeim (1979). Increasing confidence in the scientific merit of this enterprise is evidenced by the recent spate of empirical reports on the subject (e.g., Gur & Sackeim, 1979; Jamner & Schwartz, 1987; Monts, Zurcher, & Nydegger, 1977; Paulhus, 1984; Quattrone & Tversky, 1984; Sackeim & Gur, 1978, 1979). Finally, books with "self-deception" in the title have begun to appear (Goleman, 1986; Lockard & Paulhus, 1988; Martin, 1985; Murphy, 1975; Sloan, 1987).

In the most general sense of false self-beliefs, the concept of self-deception has been applied in human ethology as well as social, clinical, and personality psychology. In ethology, for example, evidence for the adaptive value of limited self-knowledge in lower organisms implies an evolutionary basis for human self-deception (Alexander, 1979; D. T. Campbell, 1983; Lockard, 1978; Trivers, 1985). In social psychology, too, self-deception has sometimes been defined as a lack of awareness of internal psychological processes (e.g., Wilson, 1985).

Increasingly, self-deception is being applied more selectively in the sense of motivated unawareness. Among social psychologists, an increasing interest in motivated biases and distortions has legitimized the study of formerly taboo concepts such as self-deception (e.g., Gilbert & Cooper, 1985; Krebs, Denton, & Higgins, 1988; Snyder, 1985). Information-processing theories have also been brought to bear on self-deception (Greenwald, 1988; Paulhus & Suedfeld, 1988; Sackeim, 1988). In clinical psychology and psychiatry, the concept of self-deception has been widely applied (Dorpat, 1985; Eagle, 1988; Sackeim, 1983; Schafer, 1976).

The term, self-deception, has also been applied to a series of personality measures. Sackeim and Gur (1978) originally developed self-report measures of both self- and other deception. The former, labeled the Self-Deception Questionnaire, comprised accusations about threatening but common beliefs and feelings (e.g., "Have you ever worried that you might be a homosexual?"). Respondents giving a high number of extreme denials are scored as self-deceptive. These two scales were refined and validated to form Paulhus's (1984) Balanced Inventory of Desirable Responding (BIDR). In the most recent version of the BIDR, self-deception has been partitioned into enhancement and denial (Paulhus & Reid, 1991). Research using the BIDR has confirmed that the first component of social desirability variance found in self-reports is best interpreted as self-deceptive enhancement (e.g., Paulhus, 1984, 1986, 1991).

Many of the writings on this topic share a common theme—that self-deception is a normal and generally positive force in human behavior. The claimed benefits vary from perpetuating the genetic structure of the individual, to improving the individual's ability to deceive others, to minimizing interference with self-preserving behaviors, and to contributing to the psychological health, stability, and performance of the individual as well as society as a whole (Lockard & Paulhus, 1988).

V. TRAIT AND TYPE APPROACHES

The tendency to use defenses is often considered to be a continuous individual difference variable within the normal range of personality.[1] This concept underlies such measures as the Marlowe–Crowne scale (for a review, see Crowne, 1979), the MMPI K-scale (for a review, see Paulhus, 1991), and the Self-Deception Questionnaire (reviewed above).

A select few warrant special attention here because they have a psychoanalytic flavor in combination with a high level of empirical scrutiny. Normal individuals are measured on a single trait or type (combination of traits) and studied intensively.

A. Byrne

Although not fully consistent with the psychoanalytic meaning of repression, Byrne (1961) used the term *repressive style* to describe the trait-like tendency to defend

[1] In the realm of questionnaire research, such general tendencies are often called response styles (for a review, see Paulhus, 1991).

against threats. To measure this style, Byrne developed the widely used Repression–Sensitization (R-S) scale. Items on this scale reflect a clear theoretical assumption: Individuals reporting no anxiety must have a repressive cognitive style, that is, a tendency to minimize the existence or potency of threats, whereas those reporting excess distress must have a sensitizing cognitive style. Thus Byrne postulated a bipolar trait wherein both poles represent defensive styles and the midpoint represents good adjustment. After examining the accumulated evidence, however, Bell and Byrne (1978) concluded that pathology could be present in any of these three groups.

Originally a conceptually driven 156-item scale (Byrne, 1961), the final R-S was winnowed down to a 127-item version using part–whole correlations (Byrne, Barry, & Nelson, 1963). The ensuing flood of published research using the scale suggests a widespread acceptance of the notion of individual differences in defensiveness (see review by Bell & Byrne, 1978).

Among the most cited studies using the R-S scale is that conducted by M. S. Schwartz, Krupp, and Byrne (1971). They followed up the medical status of 50,000 patients who had completed the R-S scale. One striking finding was that repressors suffered primarily from organic problems whereas sensitizers suffered from psychological problems.

Nonetheless, a number of the later approaches to defense (discussed below) begin with a criticism of Byrne's approach. One major target was Byrne's theoretical assumption that defenses are trait-like, that is, cross-situational and inflexible (e.g., Haan, 1965; Lazarus & Folkman, 1984). The major criticism of the R-S scale itself has been its conceptual similarity and embarrassingly high correlation with measures of anxiety (Gleser & Ihilevich, 1969; Golin, Herron, & Lakota, & Reineck, 1967). The resulting paradox was that the same subjects diagnosed as repressors on the R-S were diagnosed as truly low-anxious (i.e., well-adjusted) on standard anxiety scales.

B. Weinberger and Schwartz

Weinberger and Schwartz and their colleagues have tackled the problematic confounding of the R-S scale with anxiety measures. Beginning with D. A. Weinberger, Schwartz, and Davidson (1979), they explained that measures based on self-reported distress were incapable of distinguishing repressors from the truly low-anxious. The problem is that some subjects (truly low-anxious) *accurately* report low anxiety; others (repressors) *defensively* disavow their anxiety.

Instead, following Boor and Schill (1967), Weinberger and associates developed a typology measure of repressive style and supported its validity with both experimental and correlational studies (for a review, see D. A. Weinberger, 1990). Repressors were one of four groups identified by crossing a self-report measure of trait anxiety (e.g., the Taylor Manifest Anxiety Scale) with a measure of defensiveness, the Marlowe–Crowne Social Desirability Scale (Crowne & Marlowe, 1964). Among low-defensives, both high- and low-anxious subjects are taken at their word. The low anxiety scores of subjects scoring high on defensiveness (repressors), however, are assumed to result from their avoidance of distressing knowledge about themselves, including knowledge of their levels of anxiety. The fourth group—high-defensive/high-anxious—are rare and, therefore, ignored (see Davis, 1990, p. 391).

New data as well as reinterpretation of previous studies have supported the validity of the typology index of repressive style. For example, D. A. Weinberger et al. (1979) found repressors to be higher than low-anxious subjects on six behavioral and physiological measures of anxiety, despite the fact that the repressors scored lower on the self-report anxiety measure. Asendorpf and Scherer (1983) replicated and extended these findings. Newton and Contrada (1992) also replicated the same verbal-autonomic response dissociation for repressors but only in a public-evaluation situation.

Other behaviors of repressors indicating a fundamental sensitivity to negative affect include avoidance of negative implications of new information, greater performance impairments under stress, and less empathy (reported in D. A. Weinberger, 1990). Weinberger offers several possible explanations for this pattern, including selective attention, altered construal of environmental and somatic cues, and attributional biases. Although D. A. Weinberger (1990) emphasized repressors' performance impairments under stress, their tendency to avoid processing sources of negative affect might actually benefit performance in certain tasks (Bonanno, Davis, Singer, & Schwartz, 1991).

Further exploring the repressor's character, Davis (1987, 1990; Davis & Schwartz, 1987) found that repressors not only lack awareness of their current emotional states, but also have difficulty gaining access to emotional memories.[2] A series of studies has suggested that repressors have a comparable range of emotional memories but are less able to access them, particularly when the memories involve anger, fear, and self-consciousness (Davis, 1990). Less elaborate processing of emotional experiences and disruptions in "indexing" of emotional memories were proposed as explanations. In the search for consequences, G. E. Schwartz (1990) found evidence that the repressive style impairs physical health and he offers a "psychobiological" model of repressive style. Under some circumstances (e.g., conjugal bereavement), however, repressive style has actually proved beneficial for physical health (Bonanno, Keltner, Holen, & Horowitz, 1995).

A nagging psychometric problem with the typological model is the confounding created by scoring only three groups of a conceptual 2×2 table. As a result, main effects may be responsible for some findings attributed to the interaction of anxiety and defensiveness scores (e.g., Warrenburg et al., 1989). Therefore,

---

[2] This finding is consistent with Bonanno and Singer's (1990) conclusion from a literature review that repressive style is associated with a preoccupation with relatedness and intimacy.

rather than a typology based on arbitrary cutoff points, we recommend a multiple-regression approach for future research.[3]

Note that this emerging picture of the "repressor" construct appears to differ in two important respects from the traditional definition of repression. First, repression has traditionally been defined as avoiding awareness of impulses or other mental contents, rather than avoidance of awareness of emotions as in the present paradigm. Second, as D. A. Weinberger (1990) notes, repressive personality style has traditionally been strongly associated with "hysterical" personality traits, which are in sharp contrast with the dour, phlegmatic, excessively rational subjects in the present studies. For these reasons and others, some critics have questioned the appropriateness of the label "repressor" for such individuals (Holmes & McCaul, 1989; Vaillant, 1992).

A related typology was recently suggested by Shedler, Mayman, and Manis (1993). Instead of being crossed with a defensiveness scale, however, the adjustment self-report is crossed with adjustment ratings by clinical judges. Thus the group high in self-reported and low in clinician-reported adjustment is assumed to be defensively denying their maladjustment. Results from a series of studies confirmed that, compared to the truly adjusted group, the defensive subjects showed more defensive word associations and higher levels of physiological responsivity to stress.

Clearly, the strong suit of trait and typology measures is their ease of administration and scoring—qualities that facilitate research. Their current status, for better or for worse, is exemplified in a recent study by Turvey and Salovey (1994): They found that extant measures, despite different origins and rationales, all converged empirically on one underlying factor of trait defensiveness. Nonetheless, they remain difficult to untangle from measures of anxiety (p. 288).

VI. HAAN AND COLLEAGUES

The work of Norma Haan has had the single strongest influence on contemporary work—on both defense mechanisms and coping. Beginning with a model similar to that of Kroeber (1963), Haan (1963, 1965, 1977) defined ego actions as processes that accommodate, assimilate, and maintain organization under conflict. The processes themselves are not tied to any specific psychoanalytic content (sexual or aggressive impulses). Nor are the ego functions inherently conscious or unconscious; their operation is best described as preconscious—available to discovery, but not persistently within awareness.

---

[3] This problem seems to be resolved within the more recent typology; rather than dividing subjects on defensiveness using the Marlowe–Crowne scale, they are divided on restraint, using a new self-report measure. Thus repressors are now defined as high restraint/low distress (D. A. Weinberger & Schwartz, 1990).

Hann and Kroeber reasoned that a taxonomy of ego actions should not be restricted to defenses involving maladaptive distortion of truth and reality, as previous work had. Instead, they proposed two independent, parallel modes of expression—coping and defense. Coping reflects purposeful, adaptive, conscious, flexible, and present-oriented behavior choices that adhere to reality and logic and are morally superior (Haan, 1985, 1986). Defenses are compelled, maladaptive, rigid, distorted, and past-oriented behaviors that distort reality. If either of these modes fail, then fragmentation may be invoked. The latter is characterized by irrationally expressed psychopathological symptoms such as ritualistic and automatic behavior, and involves clear violations of reality. Haan (1977) summarizes this triad by stating, "A person will cope if he can, defend if he must and fragment if he is forced to do so" (p. 79).

Within each of these modes of expression, the taxonomy was further subdivided into 10 generic subcategories of ego processes. For conceptual convenience, the 10 generic processes are clustered into those which are primarily cognitive, affective regulating, reflexive-introspective, and attention focusing. The choice of process and its mode of expression are dependent upon the situational demands and/ or a series of life situations that predispose the individual to idiosyncratic strategies.

Haan (1965) developed a Q-sort interview technique composed of 60 items, 3 for each of 20 coping and defense ego processes. The scales can be used by clinicians to assess a client's defensive profile. Haan (1965) also developed self-report versions of the ego-process scales by administering the MMPI and CPI scales. She could then identify for each scale those items which differentiated the subjects who were rated by clinicians as highly defensive from those who were not. Although used in more than 30 studies, neither the interview or the self-report versions were ever cross validated (Morrissey, 1977).

In response to criticisms of the original scales, Joffe and Naditch developed improved versions of the ego process scales (J-N; Joffe & Naditch, 1977). The authors selected those items from the CPI and the MMPI which predicted clinicians ratings of the 20 coping and defense processes outlined by the model. Those items which correlated the highest with the criterion ego ratings were then cross validated.

Factor analyses of the defense and coping mechanisms (Haan, 1963; Joffe & Naditch, 1977) indicate that the items can be categorized into Controlled Coping, Expressive Coping, Structured Defense, and Primitive Defense scores. The Haan scale and the J-N have shown some convergent validity with the Defense Mechanisms Inventory (Gleser & Ihilevich, 1969; Vickers & Hervig, 1981). There is also evidence for the predictive validity of the J-N in families coping with seriously ill children (Kupst & Schulman, 1981; Kupst et al., 1984), and as an antecedent to seeking psychotherapy (Gurwitz, 1981).

Use of defenses, as measured by the J-N, has been shown to be positively related to Speed and Impatience subscores of Type A behavior, whereas use of coping mechanisms was positively related to Job Involvement (Vickers, Hervig, Rahe, & Rosenman, 1981). Internal locus of control is associated with the use of coping, and external locus correlated with defenses (Vickers, Conway, & Haight,

1983). Haan (1985, 1986) investigated the relations between the Haan and J-N scales and moral development. She concluded that coping strategies facilitate, while defensiveness hinders, mature moral behavior.

In sum, Haan's coping–defense–fragmentation triad represents an expansion and elaboration of the theretofore narrow focus of defense mechanisms. In addition, the associated ego-process scales represent the first comprehensive battery designed to tap defenses.[4]

VII. Vaillant and Colleagues

George Vaillant continues to be a leader in the naturalistic study of defenses from a psychodynamic point of view (e.g., Vaillant, 1971, 1976, 1992; Vaillant, Bond, & Vaillant, 1986). His empirical work has been based primarily on three longitudinal samples from which copious data were available. His position has been that psychological defenses become clear only over long spans of time as the individual "adapts to life." Vaillant (1971) has used the term "defensive style" to refer to enduring tendencies to employ either specific mechanisms or, more often, mechanisms of a particular level of "maturity." He has taken a developmental view of defenses, describing their degree of adaptiveness and adherence to reality in terms of maturity (Vaillant, 1971) and seeking evidence that such maturity correlates with chronological age and with various measures of mental health.

Vaillant's methods, although always empirical in a broad sense, have a novelistic aspect, particularly in his early work (Vaillant, 1971). His approach relies, to a greater degree than most psychological research, on his own impressions of subjects. This has led to rich description and lucid theory, but has to some extent undermined his argument that individuals' defensive styles can be objectively identified. Nevertheless, he has demonstrated robust and theoretically important associations between maturity of defensive style and several measures of successful adaptation.

Vaillant's use of varied biographical and evaluative materials gathered longitudinally over the course of decades has permitted a direct assessment of defenses in significant life contexts. It is also possible through this method to distinguish enduring defenses from ones that recede once a particular circumstance has passed. Valliant codes defenses by first condensing life history materials into vignettes that demonstrate a subject's techniques of managing life problems and then grouping these vignettes according to which defense they seem to represent. A pair of raters then categorizes each group of vignettes within Vaillant's theoretical hierarchy of 18 defenses, ranging from psychotic to mature (Vaillant, 1971). The raters also code the prominence of each defense in the subject's overall style.

This coding procedure does not permit an assessment of the degree to which reliable ratings can be made directly from the life historical materials, because all ratings are mediated by Vaillant's own categorization of the materials. (See

---

[4] Recently, another Q-sort approach to defenses has appeared (Davidson & MacGregor, 1996).

McCullough, 1992, for a more stringent test of reliability using the same materials and defenses). Nonetheless, raters agreed in 70% of cases on the exact label assigned to a cluster. Interrater reliability of ratings of defense prominence ranged widely, from −.01 to .95. Reliability was consistently high (.72–.84), however, for the more critical dimension of defensive maturity (Vaillant, 1976).

Defensive maturity was found to correlate with adjustment and mental health, both cross sectionally and prospectively (Vaillant, 1992). Nevertheless, maturity of defense constitutes an independent dimension (Vaillant et al., 1986). There is some evidence that the use of mature styles increases over the course of adult development (Vaillant, 1976). Specific evidence for a causal role of defensive maturity in adult adjustment is provided by the moderating influence of childhood environment: defense maturity made a difference in adult adjustment primarily for subjects with bleak childhood environments (Vaillant et al., 1986). A related pattern has been found for social class. Correlations with Bond's Defense Style Questionnaire (DSQ) have provided some validation of the ratings of individual defenses. The DSQ is a self-report instrument in which subjects are queried about response styles related to defense (Bond, Gardner, Christian, & Sigal, 1983).

In his influential book, Vaillant (1992) reviewed theory and research in the psychoanalytic and psychiatric approach to the study of defense mechanisms. He summarized the history of these concepts in Freud's work, advocated a renewed emphasis on defenses in diagnosis and treatment planning, and surveyed several prominent nomenclatures (of which his own has been the most influential). Contributed chapters by other authors presented current research. Vaillant reviewed data from his three longitudinal samples and concluded that gender, SES, and culture do not significantly affect defensive style; however, the validity of this conclusion is limited by limitations in the method of rating defenses, as discussed previously. Finally, Vaillant presented a revised version of Haan's Q-sort as a new method of obtaining objective and statistically convenient ratings of defensive style from life historical or interview data. Reliability and validity do not yet appear adequate. (However, see Hart and Chmiel [1992] for a successful application of Vaillant's Q-sort.)

Perry, a former student of Vaillant, has, together with Cooper, studied the relation of defenses to psychiatric diagnosis and other aspects of functioning (J. C. Perry & Cooper, 1989, 1992). These authors developed the Defense Mechanisms Rating Scales (DMRS), which differ from Vaillant's in using videotaped interviews instead of extensive longitudinal materials and in providing more rigorous assessment of interrater reliability. Significant associations have been found between classes of defenses and psychological symptoms, both subjectively and objectively evaluated. Level of functioning has also shown significant associations with the defense classes (J. C. Perry & Cooper, 1989, 1992). However, associations with diagnosis have not been demonstrated in all of their studies (e.g., Bloch, Shear, Markowitz, Leon, & Perry, 1993).

Led by Perry, a group including Vaillant, Horowitz, Fridhandler, Cooper, and Bond contributed the Defensive Functioning Scale to the latest official psychiatric diagnostic system, the DSM—IV (American Psychiatric Association, 1994, pp. 751–757). This scale—drawn mainly from Vaillant's and Perry's systems with elements of Horowitz's—is a proposed additional "axis" of diagnosis. (The DSM—IV defines a diagnostic axis as a "domain of information that may help the clinician plan treatment and predict outcome [p. 25]"; currently, a full diagnosis requires assessment on five axes.) The Defensive Functioning Scale consists of 31 defined defenses, grouped into seven "levels" according to their mode of action and their degree of adaptiveness or maturity. As part of the diagnostic evaluation, the patient's most prominent current defenses and overall defensive level are rated. These ratings are based on the clinician's observations and his or her interpretation of the patient's history; that is, no interview protocol or operationalized rating procedure are included in the scale at this time. Although currently an optional part of diagnosis, and though its field reliability and validity are unknown, this scale represents the first officially sanctioned rating of defenses in psychiatric diagnosis and as such may ultimately have a significant impact on mental health diagnosis and treatment.

VIII. HOROWITZ AND COLLEAGUES

Mardi Horowitz and his colleagues (Horowitz, 1986; Horowitz, Markman, Stinson, Fridhandler, & Ghannam, 1990; Horowitz & Stinson, 1995) have advanced a theoretical model of defense that originated in a psychodynamic framework but gradually incorporated principles of cognitive psychology. The fundamental assumption in this model is that there exists an unconsciously operating system of "control processes" that govern what is represented in conscious awareness and determine what form this awareness takes. Following the structure of Haan's (1977) theory, several processes are posited, any one of which may have adaptive, maladaptive, or "dysregulatory" outcomes depending on the context in which it is employed.

The traditional psychoanalytic defenses are retained—29 are specifically cited (Horowitz, 1988)—but are not considered to be fundamental processes. Instead, following the distinction made by Wallerstein (1983), the traditional defenses are regarded as outcomes of more basic cognitive processes (Horowitz et al., 1990). For example, the psychoanalytic mechanism "undoing" is thought to be accomplished through the process of "sequencing ideas through switching concepts," that is, rapidly shifting one's beliefs or point of view (Horowitz, 1988, p. 202). The traditional psychoanalytic assumptions that defense or "control" operates unconsciously for the purpose of keeping conflictual material out of awareness are retained.

In addition to this synthesis of cognitive psychology with psychoanalytic approaches, Horowitz's view of defense is distinguished by the assertion that defense can be accomplished through activation of certain person schemas (Horowitz, 1988; Horowitz et al., 1990). In this view, individuals have multiple images of self and others, as well as multiple images of typical interactions, termed "role relationship models." One method of defense is to change the image or schema that is currently active, which in turn controls those specific aspects of self and other that are currently perceived. Aspects of this theory were drawn from the object-relations perspective, which is increasingly influential in psychoanalysis (Kernberg, 1976).

This approach originated in the study of psychological coping strategies following traumatic stress (Horowitz, 1986). Observing a regular pattern of "intrusions" and "omissions" in consciousness following trauma, Horowitz concluded that unconscious control processes must be present. Examination of videotaped psychotherapies of individuals with unresolved posttraumatic reactions revealed that therapists helped these persons to modify certain control operations, and the controls identified in this way became the basis for the developing taxonomy. Three levels of regulation were specified: regulation of mental set, regulation of person schemas, and, at the most fine-grained level, regulation of conscious representations and sequencing (Horowitz, 1988). Although the system is primarily theoretical, it is being applied in the intensive study of single subjects (Horowitz et al., 1994).

IX. ERDELYI AND COLLEAGUES

Erdelyi has offered the most sustained and detailed cognitive treatment of defense. He has proposed a broad theoretical framework subsuming the major experimental literatures on defense, namely, perceptual defense (Erdelyi, 1974) and repression effects on memory (Erdelyi & Goldberg, 1979). He argues (Erdelyi, 1985) that laboratory evidence demonstrates that "there can be selective information rejection from awareness" (p. 259), although it has not been experimentally established that this capacity is in *fact* used toward defensive ends. He has claimed further that defensive bias influences the entire sequence of information processing and that there is no reason to believe that a single mechanism is responsible for all this defensive activity. For example, perceptual defense may involve processes ranging from ocular fixation to selectivity in transfer from raw storage (e.g., iconic storage) into short-term memory.

In his more recent work (Erdelyi, 1990), he has proposed a mechanism for repression that he argues is fully consistent with Sigmund Freud's views, particularly his earlier ones. Erdelyi argues that "repression" refers to purposefully *not thinking* of a target memory (or thinking of something else), which results in the target being overtaken by "oblivescence" (or, more simply, forgetting), resulting in amnesia. He cites evidence that there are two contrary tendencies in memory, reminiscence and oblivescence/forgetting. Thinking about a memory—"rehearsing the remembered and searching for the inaccessible" (1990, p. 4)—promotes the former, and if pursued in a sustained way results in hypermnesia or greater accessibility of the memory. "Not thinking" yields the opposite results, namely, amnesia. This amnesia is not necessarily permanent, however; it is often reversible by thinking of the target memory. In other words, due to the properties of human memory, deliberate "not thinking" over time is sufficient to remove a memory from awareness. This process is potentially reversible, in keeping with therapist reports of recovery of repressed memories.

Erdelyi (1990) cites experimental findings to support this view. He compares classic findings on forgetting over time with one of his own studies (Erdelyi &

Kleinbard, 1978) showing *increasing* memory over time. This difference, he suggests, is due to thinking versus "not thinking." He also cites clinical findings with neurological amnesics that *declarative* facts may be forgotten while related *procedural* aspects of memory remain. This is consistent with Freud's contention that repressed childhood events are not remembered but are "repeated," in the form of actions and emotions.

Although psychoanalytic writers and many others (cf. Heilbrun & Pepe, 1985) have generally assumed that people are unaware of their defensive activity, Erdelyi asserts that there is nothing about repression that must be unconscious. In addition, he argues that repression need not be defensive at all. In this definition, repression is simply not thinking in order to produce amnesia, a process that may serve defensive or nondefensive ends.

Although Erdelyi focuses on repression, he offers a framework for understanding other defenses as well. This framework is based on Bartlett's view of memory as a *reconstructive* process. Such reconstructions might well be subject to defensive bias. Erdelyi (1990) provides an example of such bias. A 9-year-old girl was asked to read a brief story and then was asked to reproduce it on several successive occasions. In her early recall efforts, most of the frightening aspects of the story were absent. Such case studies, along with a few experimental studies, form the basis of Erdelyi's well-articulated theory of defense.

X. IHILEVICH AND GLESER

Goldine Gleser and David Ihilevich (1969; Ihilevich & Gleser, 1986) have developed a theory of responses to conflict and an instrument to assess them—the Defense Mechanisms Inventory (DMI). The authors proposed a two-tiered classification system to describe possible responses to threat. At the first level, they distinguished between problem-solving efforts that are directed at changing oneself and those efforts aimed at changing the surrounding context. Second, they classified all possible responses as problem-solving, coping, or defense strategies, although they admitted that they were unclear as to how these three levels interact.

Utilization of any of the three modes of response to conflict is assumed to reduce anxiety and enhance self-esteem. Problem-solving strategies (changing oneself, changing the environment) have a direct impact upon the threat. Coping strategies (assertiveness, trust, stoicism, responsibility, and hope) have an influence on the individual's mood or motivation expended upon the threat, not upon the threat itself, and are based in trust and reality. Defenses (aggression, projection, intellectualization, intrapunitive, and repressive actions) actually remove the problem from awareness or distort it, thus falsifying reality and offering an illusion of control.

Coping and defensive strategies arise only when problem-solving strategies are ineffective or inappropriate. In addition, the appropriateness and the adaptiveness of the choice of response are dependent upon the context and the individual's characteristic style.

The DMI (Ihilevich & Gleser, 1986) was designed to assess five categories of response to threat: Projection (PRO), Principalization (PRN), Turning Against Object (TAO), Turning Against Self (TAS), and Reversal (REV). Subjects respond to the 10 scenarios by selecting their most and least likely reactions, in terms of their actual behavior, affect, thoughts, and fantasy behavior. To date, the scale is the most extensively utilized self-report measure of defense mechanisms in research (Cramer, 1988; Vickers & Hervig, 1981; see Ihilevich & Gleser, 1986, for a comprehensive review). Generally, the DMI has found to have high retest and interitem reliability, but there are some problems with the conceptual status of TAO as a defense and weak validity for the PRN scale (Cramer, 1988). Concurrent validity has been shown between the DMI and the MMPI defensive scales, the Byrne Repression–Sensitization scale, Haan's Q-sort Technique, Joffe and Naditch's Ego Process scale, Schutz's Coping Operations Preference Enquiry, the Blacky Defense Preference Inquiry, and the denial subscale of the Marlowe–Crowne Social Desirability scale.

It has been suggested that the interrelationships among the five scales indicate that the DMI represents a single continuum. For example, males score higher on PRO and TAO, and TAO has been related to masculine orientation. Females score higher on TAS, which is related to feminine orientation. Assertive individuals endorsed PRN, whereas nonassertives endorsed TAO and TAS. As such, the DMI has been conceptualized as a continuum with acting-out defenses at one end and inwardly focused defenses at the other (Cramer, 1988; Juni & Yanishefsky, 1983). It has also been argued that this continuum represents an expression of aggression (TAO and PRO) at one pole, and an inhibition of aggression (REV and PRN) at the other. Clinical validity of the DMI was provided by the findings that TAO and PRO are higher in psychiatric patients, and TAS is higher in suicidal patients. Finally, the DMI scales have been linked to a promising new system of interpersonal defenses (Woike, Aronoff, Stollak, & Loraas, 1994).

XI. PERCEPT-GENETIC APPROACH

Over a period of four decades, a group of psychologists centered at Lund University in Sweden have advocated a dynamic-constructivist view of personality called *percept genesis* (PG). The theory concerns how perceptions evolve, how they are interlinked with behavior, and how they form the individual's conception of external reality. For a recent collection of studies, see Hentshel, Smith, and Draguns (1986).

Percept genesis was derived from the microgenesis work of the 1920s (e.g., Sander, 1928/1961), which presumed that unattended processes preceded conscious perception. In effect, the perception of external reality is an outcome of internal processes prone to subjective influences. Microgenesis assumes that the immediacy of percepts is in fact an illusion arising from the perceiver's focus on correct recognition of the stimulus. Analysis of the preparatory phase through repetition of brief presentations can reveal the processes leading up to recognition. PG theorists emphasize that these processes are highly influenced by the individual's personality and experiences. Thus, percepts are deeply rooted in the perceiver's developmental history.

The PG model further suggests that perception recapitulates ontogeny; that is, perception reflects the sequence of life experiences. One cannot examine a section of the process without reference to earlier stages. "PG sees the perceptual act as a process moving from the subjective prestages to the final intersubjective meaning of the stimulus" (Smith & Westerlundh, 1980, p. 109).

Tachistoscopic methods form the basis for a number of PG tests designed to measure defenses. Two of the most widely cited tests are the Defense Mechanisms Test (DMT; Kragh, 1960) and the Meta-Contrast Technique (MCT; Kragh & Smith, 1970; Smith & Henriksson, 1956). These methods entail an examination of a subject's changing interpretations of a hero stimulus—a focally central person. Initially below perceptual threshold, the exposure time is gradually increased until the subject reaches a stable identification of the hero stimulus. Next, a threatening stimulus (e.g., a monstrous figure sneaking up) is gradually introduced to provoke anxiety. Various defensive reactions are evaluated by analyzing the subject's changing interpretations of the hero and threatening stimuli, and/or the temporal delay to correct recognition of the stimuli. Subjects often show defensive interpretations of the stimulus before the threat has been accurately identified.

Using an array of associated methodologies, the PG researchers have provided evidence for their distinctive patterns of defenses during different perceptual stages and different life stages, and in different forms of psychopathology. In Sweden, the DMT is in standard use by the military for pilot selection. The tests have also been utilized to predict soldier and attack-diver abilities, and to distinguish decorated veterans from nondecorated veterans. These techniques are also regularly applied in clinical research. One finding was that repression is the central defense mechanism in hysterics, and isolation the central strategy for compulsives. (For a review of research, see Smith & Westerlundh, 1980).

Although research with PG methodologies appears to be widespread in Scandinavian nations and growing in other European countries (e.g., Cline, 1987; C. Cooper, 1988; Hentschel & Kiessling, 1990), for some reason it is still minimal in North America.

XII. PLUTCHIK AND COLLEAGUES

Plutchik and colleagues view defenses as more accessible and changeable than the strictly unconscious process assumed by other theoreticians (Plutchik and Kellerman, 1980). On the basis of Plutchik's (1962; Schaefer & Plutchik, 1966) theoretical and empirical work on emotions, the defenses are said to vary in their degree of similarity to each other, show a circular configuration, and lie on a continuum of most to least primitive. The 8 basic defenses are said to derive from 8 basic emotions within an evolutionary framework.

The authors identified 16 defense processes from psychiatric and psychoanalytic literature, and assembled them in The Life Style Index. On the basis of the responses of several normal samples, extreme and ambiguous items were eliminated, and only those items that differentiated the highest scorers from the lowest scorers were retained. Clinicians' matchings of the items to the defense mechanisms provided further refinement. A comprehensive review of findings with the scale is listed in Conte and Plutchik (1995).

Clinical validity was supported by the finding that schizophrenics scored significantly higher than college students on all scales. High-self-esteem individuals score lower on regression, compensation, projection, and intellectualization, and highly anxious individuals showed a reverse pattern plus low scores on denial. Rim (1987, 1989) showed subject gender and age to be moderating factors to Plutchik's scales, and found that Extraversion was positively correlated with minimization, mapping, and reversal, but was negatively correlated with blame, whereas neuroticism was positively related to minimization and suppression.

In short, the construct validity of this set of defenses is supported in that: (1) psychiatric patients use defenses more than do normals, and (2) among normals, those who use defenses tend to have lower self-esteem. Most recently, Plutchik and colleagues have extended the model to a parallel set of eight coping variables (Plutchik & Conte, 1989).

XIII. STRESS AND COPING

Although it is difficult to draw a clear line between the literature on coping and that on defense, coping concepts place more emphasis on (a) active, conscious efforts at managing, (b) process rather than trait measurement, and (c) variability across situations. The major predecessors of current work are Haan (1963), Moos (1974), and Pearlin and Schooler (1978).

In recent years, the most active program of theory and research on coping has been that of the Berkeley Stress and Coping Project, summarized in Lazarus and Folkman (1984). The approach postulates three distinguishable stages as critical mediators of stressful person–environment relations and their immediate and long-range outcomes: primary appraisal, secondary appraisal, and coping. Through primary appraisal, the person evaluates whether he or she has anything at stake in the encounter. Secondary appraisal involves evaluating what, if anything, can be done. Finally, coping is defined as the constantly changing cognitive and behavioral efforts to manage demands that exceed the person's resources (Lazarus & Folkman, 1984). An individual may use any one of a wide variety of coping responses, depending on the situation and recent events, as well as individual coping style.

Several standardized measurement instruments arose from this research program, including the Hassles and Uplifts scale (DeLongis, Coyne, Dakof, Folkman, & Lazarus, 1982) and the Ways of Coping scale (WOC; Folkman & Lazarus, 1985).

The WOC is perhaps the best-known and most widely utilized research tool. The respondent is asked to think of a recent stressful event or is supplied with a specific example. The subject then responds by checking the applicable responses from a list composed of a broad range of cognitive strategies ("I tried to forget the whole thing") and behavioral strategies ("I got professional help") that people use to manage internal or external demands in stressful encounters. The original WOC (Folkman & Lazarus, 1980) contained 68 items in a yes/no format indicating whether the respondent had or had not used each strategy. In the revised version containing 67 items (Lazarus & Folkman, 1984), the response format was changed from yes/ no to a four-point Likert scale (0, does not apply or not used; 1, used somewhat; 2, used quite a bit; 3, used a great deal). Early factor analyses of the WOC indicated two general factors: problem-focused and emotion-focused strategies (Lazarus & Folkman, 1984). More recent factor analyses have indicated eight factors: confrontive coping, distancing, self-controlling, seeking social support, accepting responsibility, escape–avoidance, planful problem solving, and positive reappraisal (Folkman, Lazarus, Dunkel-Shetter, DeLongis, & Gruen, 1986). McCrae and Costa (1986) have shown that, by changing the referent from a specific situation to "what you generally do," the WOC becomes a trait measure, linking different strategies to each of the Big Five dimensions of personality.

Studies by the Lazarus group tend to emphasize changes in strategies across situation. In a typical study, stress and coping among students were examined at three stages of a university examination (Folkman & Lazarus, 1985). Hopefulness, eagerness, worry, and fear were most common during preparation period whereas happiness, relief, disgust, and disappointment were more common after grades had been announced. During the intermediate stage, after the exam but before grades had been announced, high levels of all the above emotions were reported.

DeLongis and O'Brien (1990) have extended the model to incorporate an interpersonal factor. And the model has stimulated research by other groups. At least two other instruments have been developed that expand on the WOC scale (Carver, Scheier, & Weintraub, 1989; McCrae, 1984). Other researchers have focused on the processes underlying coping. For example, the notion of affect regulation has provided a homeostatic, hydraulic model for the process of coping with stress (e.g., G. E. Schwartz, 1977). Finally, Carver and Scheier (1981) have developed the most comprehensive process model, labeled attention/self-regulation theory.

Several independent programs of research on coping warrant brief mention here. Seymour Epstein has postulated a construct of "constructive" thinking that links all adaptive coping responses to a single global factor (Epstein & Meier, 1989). Suzanne Kobasa proposed the construct of "hardiness" to capture the psychological factors that minimize the physical health effects in those groups (e.g., executives) particularly subject to prolonged stress (Kobasa, Maddi, & Kahn, 1982). Finally, the Plutchik and Conte (1989) coping constructs were derived from Plutchik's evolutionary theory of emotion.

XIV. INFORMATION-PROCESSING APPROACHES

In tune with the cognitive revolution, Erdelyi (1974) called for an information-processing approach to studying defenses. Issues of consciousness, repression, and threat became issues of attention, memory, and filtering. Since then a number of theoretical pieces have been couched in such information-processing terms (Grzegolowska, 1976; Hamilton, 1983; G. E. Schwartz, 1977). Indeed, the impact of cognitive psychology may be seen in most modern analyses of defense either in terms of theory (e.g., Horowitz) or in terms of method (e.g., percept-genetic). Before we return to these broad theories, we will consider some smaller domains that have been subject to particular scrutiny.

A. Individual Differences

Heilbrun's recent work is a good example of the direct application of cognitive psychology to the measurement of defenses. In Heilbrun and Pepe (1985), for example, defenses are assessed by examining the cognitive processing of self-descriptions under various motivational conditions. Discrepancies between various conditions provide measures of projection, repression, rationalization, and denial. The authors concluded that unconscious utilization of projection and rationalization was related to successful control of stress, whereas unconscious repression was related to excessive stress. The conscious use of denial was related to a low level of stress.

B. Attention and Defense

The dynamics of defense can be studied by examining the interplay between selective attention and attentional breakdowns known as "intrusions," that is, the partial interference of threatening thoughts in some ongoing thought process. Sophisticated cognitive methodology and analyses (e.g., signal detection) are necessary to capture such phenomena. Spence (1983), for example, showed the indirect effects on speech patterns of weakly defended beliefs. Nielsen and Sarason (1981) examined disruptive effects of sexual and achievement-related distractors on a dichotic shadowing task. Bonanno and Wexler (1992) also found selective perception effects as a function of stimulus affective valence. Finally, Blum and his colleagues used hypnotic inductions to condition affect to arbitrary words (e.g., Blum, 1986; Blum & Barbour, 1979): the disruptive effects faded over time as selective inattention gradually developed.

Wegner's recent research (1989) has suggested that intrusions actually result from attempts to suppress unwanted thoughts. Subjects instructed to avoid a particular thought (e.g., white bears) were later reported to have more intrusions of such thoughts than a group of subjects actually instructed to think about white bears.

Finally, Paulhus and his colleagues have demonstrated a link between disruption and defense (Paulhus, Graf, & Van Selst, 1989). For example, Paulhus and Levitt (1987) found that, in the presence of threatening distractors, subjects showed a temporary increase in the positivity of self-descriptions. This sequence provides an automatic mechanism for defending the individual under stress (Paulhus, 1993). As a whole, this body of research points to a dynamic attentional substrate for psychological defense.

C. Subliminal Impact

Many cognitive psychologists have also come to accept the validity of subliminal perception, albeit in a form somewhat different from early models (Bargh, 1984; Dixon, 1981; Marcel, 1983; Zajonc, 1980). The work of Silverman and his colleagues (e.g., Silverman, 1983) on the Subliminal Psychodynamic Activation (SPA) of unconscious fantasies warrants some acknowledgement in a review of defense mechanisms literature. Some 100 articles and doctoral dissertations support the hypothesis and the efficacy of the methodology 4 to 1 (for reviews, see Hardaway, 1990; Silverman, 1983; J. Weinberger & Silverman, 1990). This extensive body of literature is well cited and has influenced the work of others, particularly the recent percept-genesis theoreticians (discussed later).

However, defenses per se, and research on individual differences, have not been the focus of the SPA investigations. Potentially, SPA could be used to stimulate defense in the laboratory (Geisler, 1986). However, the theoretical and empirical foundations of SPA have recently been the subject of trenchant critiques (for reviews, see Balay & Shevrin, 1988; Brody, 1988; for reply, see J. Weinberger, 1989).

D. Psychophysiology of Defense

The influence of cognitive psychology has also prompted wider use of psychophysiological measurements (e.g., Epstein & Clarke, 1970; Shevrin, 1988). For example, skin response has been used to indicate repression (e.g., Hare, 1966; D. A. Weinberger et al., 1979). Repression-prone individuals have also shown increased evoked potentials for unacknowledged threats (Shevrin, Smith, & Fritzler, 1970). Finally, Assor, Aronoff, and Messe (1986) studied the role of defensiveness in impression formation using physiological arousal as a dependent measure. In the study of defense, as in the study of psychopathology as a whole, a dual rationale for studying psychophysiological responses is that they are commonly seen as an indicator of psychological damage (Davidson, 1993) as well as defensive activity (Gerin et al., 1995).

XV. SOCIAL PSYCHOLOGY

For many years, the topics of defense and the unconscious were virtually taboo in social psychology.[5] This rejection peaked with the advent of attribution theory,

---

[5] At the same time, it seemed that certain core concepts, for example, cognitive dissonance, were simply euphemisms for the study of defense mechanisms.

where the tendency was to explain all mental processes in terms of "cold cognition," that is, cognition devoid of affect (e.g., Greenwald, 1980; Nisbett & Ross, 1979). Although traditional terminology is still eschewed, the 1980s and 1990s have seen an active interest in the elements of defense—motivation, the unconscious, and even the possible benefits of bias. Indeed, recent reviews of social cognition now accept the importance of these elements (e.g., Fiske & Taylor, 1991; Showers & Cantor, 1985).

In social psychology, the concept of a motivation has emphasized maintaining or enhancing self-esteem rather than warding off anxiety. Typically, threats to self-esteem are induced by fabricating academic and social failures (in contrast to psychoanalytic threats) that may be studied in the laboratory. In the revised theory of cognitive dissonance (Aronson, 1969), for example, a threat to self-esteem is considered necessary for dissonance reduction. The most comprehensive of these motivational models is Tesser's (1986) theory of self-esteem maintenance: Four factors (maintenance, relative performance, importance of the domain, and closeness of the comparison other) interact to determine threat to self-esteem and, therefore, subsequent behavior (Tesser & Campbell, 1982).

Greenwald's (1980) seminal article extended the notion of defense to cognitive conservation. Indeed, a sustained program of research by Swann has that defense of self-esteem is less important than shown defense of identity (e.g., Swann, 1992). Baumeister (1993) went further to cite the motivation to escape the self to explain a wide range of defensive phenomena. C. R. Snyder's elaboration of "excuse-making" (e.g., Snyder & Higgins, 1988) also broadened the range of defensive processes to include protection of self-image and sense of control.

The evidence for "depressive realism" (Mischel, 1979) has also encouraged social psychologists to consider possible positive consequences of inflated self-perceptions (e.g., Kruglanski, 1989). This view is best represented in the influential review by Taylor and Brown (1988). They lay out the benefits of positive illusions for mental health. They also distinguish these beneficial positive illusions from traditional defenses, which they view as maladaptive. The Taylor and Brown review was followed by up an entire issue of the Journal of Social and Clinical Psychology titled "Self-Illusion: When Are They Adaptive? (Snyder, 1989). Colvin and Block (1994) countered with data suggesting that self-enhancement illusions are fundamentally detrimental.

Over time, the term "defense" has gradually crept into a variety of social-psychological terms such as "defensive attribution," "defensive self-presentation," and "defensive pessimism" (Norem & Cantor, 1986). At least one active topic has retained the traditional term—projection (e.g., J. D. Campbell, 1986; Holmes, 1981; Paulhus & Reynolds, 1995) while distinguishing between attribution and defensive forms (Sherwood, 1980).

In sum, it appears that social psychologists have begun to address virtually the full gamut of psychoanalytic defenses, albeit with different labels. Many would argue that this delay was necessary because, only now, with improved laboratory technology and with less pressure from a dominant psychoanalytic community, can such phenomena be studied effectively.

XVI. DEVELOPMENTAL ANALYSES

A number of developmental psychologists (Chandler, Paget, & Koch, 1978; Cramer, 1983; Feldman & Custrini, 1988) have proposed that defenses can be conceptualized along a developmental continuum, according to their complexity and degree of maturity. Following Piaget's stage model of cognitive development, and based on the belief that defensive strategies vary in their complexity, these writers have argued that (a) the various defenses appear at different stages and (b) there are identifiable stages of development for each specific defense.

For example, denial occurs early in childhood and is linked to an infant's lack of muscular ability to remove itself from anxiety-arousing situations. Sleep is thus a common behavioral manifestation. Later, a child physically acts to exclude noxious stimuli (hands over eyes), and finally uses language to deny the existence of danger. More advanced defensive strategies, such as projection, emerge later in childhood, tied again to physical and cognitive developments. Intellectualization, asceticism, and identification appear still later, typically, in adolescence. Vestiges of all mechanisms can and do exist into adulthood, but a preponderance of the later-developing defenses is presumed to exist in the healthy adult.

There is some consensus about how the more advanced defenses emerge. Feldman and Custrini (1988) argue that as children mature, they gain an increased ability to perceive when others are being deceptive, and should better understand their own self-deceptive activities, such as when they utilize denial. Thus, a broader range of more effective defensive strategies is required to better deceive oneself and ward off anxiety. A child is forced to abandon an earlier, simpler defense in the light of an increasing awareness of its operation: a conscious defense is an ineffective defense (Cramer, 1983, 1991). Thus, it must be replaced with a more complex strategy that remains out of awareness, and therefore is effective.

Chandler et al. (1978) found evidence to support this developmental sequence. Preoperational children are incapable of comprehending any defensive strategy. At a slightly older age, concrete operational children are capable of inverse (repression, denial) and later reciprocal (displacement, reaction formation, rationalization) defenses. Finally, formal operational children can employ all types, including the most complex defenses, projection and introjection, which deal with statements about statements and second-order propositions. Cramer (1991) has confirmed a developmental sequencing of denial, projection, and identification. Feldman, Jenkins, and Popoola (1979) indirectly validated these findings in a study on the development of self-deception techniques in children.

For comprehensive treatments of defenses in children and adolescents, the reader is referred to recent books by Cramer (1991) and Smith and Danielsson (1982).

XVII. RELATIONS AMONG THEORETICAL TAXONOMIES

A number of the theoretical systems noted above include taxonomies of defense—some even describe the structural relations among them. Unfortunately, these taxonomies differ dramatically both in terminology and in organization. We note four common criteria for categorizing defensive processes: (a) their cognitive complexity and level of development (Chandler et al., 1978; Cramer, 1983), (b) their internal–external orientation (Gleser & Ihilevich, 1969; Ihilevich & Gleser, 1986), (c) their maturity–immaturity (Haan, 1956, 1969, 1977; Vaillant, 1971), and (d) their level of conscious awareness (Haan, 1977; Lazarus & Folkman, 1984; Vaillant et al., 1986).

However, there is less diversity than meets the eye. A closer examination reveals that these taxonomies have some fundamental similarities. By pointing out the similarities in their organizational principles, we may help reconcile apparently diverse systems.

For example, the Lazarus, Epstein, and DMI models involve a distinction between problem-focused responses (those altering the troubling transaction) and emotion-focused responses (those directed at affect regulation). This dichotomy, to some extent, parallels that between attentional and avoidance strategies (Suls & Fletcher, 1985; Taylor, 1990). Miller's (1989) distinction between monitoring and blunting has a similar flavor. Such theorists suggest that avoidant or emotion-focused strategies are superior in managing short-term or uncontrollable stress whereas attentional or problem-focused strategies may be more effective for long-term or controllable stressors (Lazarus, 1986; Suls & Fletcher, 1985; Taylor & Clark, 1986).

Another growing theme distinguishes defensive from enhancement processes: one form minimizes negative information about the self, and the other form promotes positive information (e.g., Sackeim, 1983). Some writers have argued further that, ultimately, a good offense can have defensive value, that is, it can buffer the individual from subsequent threats. Examples of enhancement processes include Taylor and Brown's (1988) positive illusions and Paulhus and Reid's (1991) self-deceptive enhancement. Although those writers see offensive and defensive processes as independent, Baumeister, Tice, and Hutton (1989) argue that they represent default strategies of high-versus low-self-esteem individuals.

Using another common organizing principle, Cramer and the DMI theorists argue that certain defenses are internally oriented (for example, turning against self) while others can be placed on an externally oriented pole (projection). Thus, in empirical work (e.g., Ihilevich & Gleser, 1986) attempts are made to relate defensive styles to field articulation and locus of control. Starting with Cohen (1964), a similar distinction has guided the articulation of the defensive styles of those with high self-esteem (defensives) and low self-esteem (projectives).

Another useful organizing principle is a hierarchy of maturity: Haan's coping–defense–fragmentation trio closely parallel Vaillant's four-tiered mature–immature/neurotic–psychotic defenses. Semrad, Grinspoon, and Fienberg (1973) also proposed a classification system of ontogenetic maturity. Similarly, the 29 defenses outlined by Horowitz (1988), the 28 described by J. C. Perry and Cooper (1989), and the 12 of Hauser (Jacobson et al., 1992) can be ordered along this mature–immature continuum. By contrast, Ihilevich and Gleser's DMI mechanisms all fall at the same level of the hierarchy, namely, the neurotic/immature level.

One can also order the defensive processes in terms of the degree of consciousness involved. The mature (Vaillant) or coping (Haan, Plutchik) processes (e.g., sublimation, suppression, humor) and some of the higher level neurotic defenses (e.g., intellectualization, isolation) are assumed to be more conscious than the lower-level psychotic or fragmented mechanisms (e.g., delusional projection). As with Haan's coping processes, those tapped by the Ways of Coping scale are held to be conscious. Thus, for example, Haan's or Vaillant's suppression resembles the WOC's self-control. However, when they become automatized and no longer require attentional resources, they lose status as coping processes (Lazarus & Folkman, 1984, p. 131). Plutchik and Conte (1989) are the most explicit in explaining how, as a defense becomes more conscious, it develops into a parallel coping process that is far more adaptive.

Note that some recent theorists have challenged the traditional requirement that defenses be fully unconscious (A. Freud, 1936). They emphasize instead the flexible interplay of all defenses with coping (Erdelyi, 1990; Plutchik & Kellerman, 1980).

It is instructive that three of these dimensions—mature–immature, conscious–unconscious, and primitive–complex—are assumed to be closely connected: That is, to the extent that defense is conscious and complex, it tends to be viewed as mature. Thus a central theme runs through these ostensibly different theoretical orderings. Unfortunately, this theme is burdened with evaluative and moral implications. Moreover, despite accumulating evidence to the contrary, the hierarchy is often assumed to correspond to increasing adaptiveness.

After conducting this review, we cannot accept the claim for a single dimension of adaptiveness for defenses. There are too many reasonable yet incommensurate criteria for adaptiveness: short-term distress, long-term distress, task performance, reproductive success, social adjustment, and so forth. In our view, the adaptiveness of defenses can be evaluated only *locally*—that is, only after specifying a precise criterion as well as a precise point in time.[6]

XVIII. CONCLUSION

Apropos the topic of psychological defense, this chapter required the balancing of two conflicting goals. We hoped to demonstrate the diversity of current theories and operationalizations of psychological defense. At the same time, we hoped to

---

[6] Kruglanski (1989) makes a similar point about evaluating accuracy in general.

integrate the literature. We suspect that we have been more successful at the former goal than the latter.[7]

There are already a number of useful integrative schemes currently available (e.g., S. H. Cooper, 1989; Horowitz et al., 1990; Conte & Plutchik, 1995; Vaillant, 1992). None of these taxonomies, however, can subsume all the literature reviewed here until there is more consensus on the terminology for various defenses. Even some theoretical models remain fatally incommensurate with others.

Nonetheless, all psychologists interested in psychological defense must agree that the current lack of consensus is a far cry better than the peremptory dismissal of the very notion of defense heard only a few years ago.

ACKNOWLEDGMENTS

Work on this chapter was supported by the Social Science and Humanities Research Council of Canada as well as the John D. and Catherine T. MacArthur Foundation.

REFERENCES

American Psychiatric Association (1994). *Diagnostic and Statistical Manual: (4th Edition).* Washington, DC: American Psychiatric Association.

Alexander, R. D. (1979). *Darwinism and human affairs.* Seattle: University of Washington Press.

Aronson, E. (1969). Cognitive dissonance: A current perspective. In L. Berkowitz (Ed.), *Advances in experimental social psychology* (Vol. 4, pp. 1–34). New York: Academic Press.

Asendorpf, J. B., & Scherer, K. R. (1983). The discrepant repressor: Differentiation between low anxiety, high anxiety, and repression of anxiety by autonomic-facial-verbal patterns of behavior. *Journal of Personality and Social Psychology, 45,* 1334–1346.

Assor, A., Aronoff, J., & Messe, L. A. (1986). An experimental test of defensive processes in impression formation. *Journal of Personality and Social Psychology, 50,* 644–650.

Balay, J., & Shevrin, H. (1988). The subliminal psychodynamic activation method: A critical review. *American Psychologist, 43,* 161–174.

Bargh, J. A. (1984). Automatic and conscious processing. In R. S. Wyer & T. K. Srull (Eds.), *Handbook of social cognition* (Vol. 3, pp. 1–43). Hillsdale, NJ: Erlbaum.

Baumester, R. F. (1993). *Escape from self.* New York: Guilford Press.

Baumeister, R. F., Tice, D. M., & Hutton, D. G. (1989). Self-presentational motivations and personality differences in self-esteem. *Journal of Personality, 57,* 547–579.

[7] Holmes (1974, 1981; Holmes & McCaul, 1989) deserves particular mention as a critic of the evidence for defense mechanisms. He continues to argue that no convincing evidence for the existence of these defenses has ever been produced. His reviews appear to have been highly influential; as he notes himself (Holmes & McCaul, 1989), the volume of laboratory work on repression declined drastically after his 1974 review. Equally careful reviewers (S. H. Cooper, 1992; Erdelyi, 1985), however, have drawn much more favorable conclusions from the same literature.

Becker, E. (1973). *The denial of death.* New York: Free Press.

Bell, P. A., & Byrne, D. (1978). Repression-sensitization. In H. London & J. E. Exner (Eds.), *Dimensions of personality* (pp. 449–485). New York: Wiley.

Bloch, A. L., Shear, M. K., Markowitz, J. C., Leon, A. C., & Perry, J. C. (1993). An empirical study of defense mechanisms in dysthymia. *American Journal of Psychiatry, 150,* 1194–1198.

Blum, G. S. (1986). *A computer model for unconscious interactions of affect potentials and cognitive processes* (Tech. Rep. No. 8611). Santa Barbara: University of California.

Blum, G. S., & Barbour, J. S. (1979). Selective inattention to anxiety-linked stimuli. *Journal of Experimental Psychology: General, 108,* 182–224.

Bonanno, G. A., Keltner, D., Holen, A., & Horowitz, M. J. (1995). When avoiding unpleasant emotions might not be such a bad thing: Verbal-autonomic response dissociation and midlife conjugal bereavement. *Journal of Personality & Social Psychology, 69,* 975–989.

Bonanno, G. A., Davis, P. J., Singer, J. L., & Schwartz, G. E. (1991). The repressor personality and avoidant information processing: A dichotic listening study. *Journal of Research in Personality, 25,* 386–401.

Bonanno, G. A., & Singer, J. L. (1990). Repressive personality style: Theoretical and methodological implications for health and psychology. In J. L. Singer (Ed.), Repression and dissociation: Implications for personality, psychopathology and health (pp. 435–470). Chicago: U Chicago Press.

Bonanno, G. A., & Wexler, B. E. (1992). The selective perception and recognition of single words from competing dichotic stimulus pairs. *Consciousness and Cognition, 1,* 241–264.

Bond, M., Gardner, S. T., Christian, J., & Sigal, J. J. (1983). Empirical study of self-rated defense styles. *Archives of General Psychiatry, 40,* 333–338.

Boor, M., & Schill, T. (1967). Digit symbol performance of subjects varying in anxiety and defensiveness. *Journal of Consulting Psychology, 31,* 600–603.

Bowers, K. S., & Meichenbaum, D. (Eds.). (1984). *The unconscious reconsidered.* New York: Wiley.

Brenner, C. (1982). *The mind in conflict.* New York: International University.

Breznitz, S. (Ed.). (1983). *The denial of stress.* New York: International University Press.

Brody, N. (1988). *Personality: In search of individuality.* San Diego: Academic Press.

Byrne, D. (1961). The repression-sensitization scale: Rationale, reliability, and validity. *Journal of Personality, 29,* 334–349.

Byrne, D., Barry, J., & Nelson, D. (1963). Relation of the revised Repression-Sensitization scale to measures of self-description. *Psychological Reports, 13,* 323–334.

Campbell, D. T. (1983). The two distinct routes beyond kin selection to ultrasociality: Implications for the humanities and social sciences. In D. Bridgeman (Ed.), *The nature of prosocial development: Theories and strategies* (pp. 38–58). New York: Academic Press.

Campbell, D. T. (1986). Similarity and uniqueness: The effects of attribute type, relevance, and individual differences in self-esteem and depression. *Journal of Personality and Social Psychology, 50,* 281–294.

Carver, C. S., & Scheier, M. F. (1981). *Attention and self-regulation: A control-theory approach to human behavior.* New York: Springer.

Carver, C. S., Scheier, M. F., & Weintraub, J. K. (1989). Assessing coping strategies: A theoretically based approach. *Journal of Personality and Social Psychology, 56,* 267–283.

Chandler, M. J., Paget, K. F., & Koch, D. A. (1978). The child's demystification of psychological defense mechanisms: A structural and developmental analysis. *Developmental Psychology, 14,* 197–205.

Cline, P. (1987). The scientific status of the DMT. *British Journal of Medical Psychology, 60,* 53–59.

Cohen, A. R. (1964). *Attitude change and social influence.* New York: Basic Books.

Colvin, C. R., & Block, J. (1994). Do positive illusions foster mental health? An examination of the Taylor and Brown formulation. *Psychological Bulletin, 116,* 3–20.

Conte, H. R., & Plutchik, R. (Eds.) (1995). *Ego defenses: Theory and measurement.* New York: Wiley.

Cooper, C. (1988). Predicting susceptibility to short-term stress with the Defence Mechanism Test. *Work and Stress, 2,* 49–58.

Cooper, S. H. (1989). Recent contributions to the theory of defense mechanisms: A comparative view. *Journal of the American Psychoanalytic Association, 37,* 865–891.

Cooper, S. H. (1992). The empirical study of defensive processes: A review. In J. W. Barron, M. N. Eagle, & D. L. Wolitzky (Eds.), *Interface of psychoanalysis and psychology* (pp. 327–346). Washington, DC: APA Press.

Cramer, P. (1983). Children's use of defense mechanisms in reaction to displeasure caused by others. *Journal of Personality, 51,* 79–94.

Cramer, P. (1988). The Defense Mechanism Inventory: A review of research and discussion of the scales. *Journal of Personality Assessment, 52,* 142–164.

Cramer, P. (1991). *The development of defense mechanisms: Theory, research, and assessment.* New York: Springer-Verlag.

Crowne, D. P. (1979). *The experimental study of personality.* Hillsdale, NJ: Erlbaum.

Crowne, D. P., & Marlowe, D. A. (1964). *The approval motive.* New York: Wiley.

Davidson, K. (1993). Suppression and repression in discrepant self-other ratings: Relations with thought control and cardiovascular reactivity. *Journal of Personality, 61,* 669–691.

Davidson, K., & MacGregor, M. W. (1996). Reliability of an idiographic Q-sort measure of defense mechanisms. *Journal of Personality Assessment, 66,* 624–639.

Davis, P. J. (1987). Repression and the inaccessibility of affective memories. *Journal of Personality and Social Psychology, 53,* 585–593.

Davis, P. J. (1990). Repression and the inaccessibility of affective memories. In J. L. Singer (Ed.), *Repression and dissociation: Implications for personality theory, psychopathology, and health* (pp. 387–404). Chicago: University of Chicago Press.

Davis, P. J., & Schwartz, G. E. (1987). Repression and the inaccessibility of affective memories. *Journal of Personality and Social Psychology, 52,* 155–162.

DeLongis, A., Coyne, J. C., Dakof, G., Folkman, S., & Lazarus, R. S. (1982). Relationship of daily hassles, uplifts, and major life events to health status. *Health Psychology, 1,* 119–136.

DeLongis, A., & O'Brien, T. (1990). An interpersonal framework for stress and coping: An application to the families of Alzheimer's patients. In M. A. P. Stephens, J. H. Crowther, S. E. Hobfoll, & D. L. Tennenbaum (Eds.), *Stress and coping in later-life families.* New York: Hemisphere Publishing.

Dixon, N. (1981). *Preconscious processing.* New York: Wiley.

Dorpat, T. L. (1985). The cognitive arrest hypothesis of denial. *International Journal of Psychoanalysis, 64,* 47–58.

Eagle, M. (1988). Psychoanalysis and self-deception. In J. S. Lockard & D. L. Paulhus (Eds.), *Self-deception: An adaptive mechanism?* (pp. 78–98). Englewood Cliffs, NJ: Prentice-Hall.

Epstein, S., & Clarke, S. (1970). Heart-rate and skin conductance during experimentally-induced anxiety: Effects of anticipated intensity of noxious stimulation and experience. *Journal of Experimental Psychology, 84,* 105–112.

Epstein, S., & Meier, P. (1989). Constructive thinking: A broad coping variable with specific components. *Journal of Personality and Social Psychology, 57,* 332–350.

Erdelyi, M. H. (1974). A new look at the new look: Perceptual defense and vigilance. *Psychological Review, 81,* 1–25.

Erdelyi, M. H. (1985). *Psychoanalysis: Freud's cognitive psychology.* New York: Freeman.

Erdelyi, M. H. (1990). Repression, reconstruction, and defense: History and integration of psychoanalytic and experimental frameworks. In J. L. Singer (Ed.), *Repression and dissociation: Defense mechanisms and personality styles: Current theory and research* (pp. 1–31). Chicago: University of Chicago Press.

Erdelyi, M. H., & Goldberg, G. (1979). Let's not sweep repression under the rug: Toward a cognitive psychology of repression. In J. F. Kihlstrom & F. J. Evans (Eds.), *Functional disorders of memory* (pp. 355–402). Hillsdale, NJ: Erlbaum.

Erdelyi, M. H., & Kleinbard, J. (1978). Has Ebbinghaus decayed with time? The growth of recall (hypermnesia) over days. *Journal of Experimental Psychology: Human Learning and Memory, 4,* 275–289.

Eriksen, C. W., & Pierce, J. (1968). Defense mechanisms. In E. F. Borgatta & W. W. Lambert (Eds.), *Handbook of personality theory and research* (pp. 1007–1040). Chicago: Rand McNally.

Feldman, R. S., & Custrini, R. J. (1988). Learning to lie and self-deceive: Children's nonverbal communication of deception. In J. S. Lockard & D. L. Paulhus (Eds.), *Self-deception: An adaptive mechanism?* (pp. 40–53). Englewood Cliffs, NJ: Prentice-Hall.

Feldman, R. S., Jenkins, L., & Popoola, L. (1979). Detection of deception in adults and children via facial expressions. *Child Development, 50,* 350–355.

Fingarette, H. (1969). *Self-deception.* New York: Humanities Press.

Fisher, S., & Greenberg, R. (1977). *The scientific credibility of Freud's theories and therapy.* New York: Basic Books.

Fiske, S. T., & Taylor, S. E. (1991). *Social cognition.* New York: McGraw-Hill.

Folkman, S., & Lazarus, R. S. (1980). An analysis of coping in a middle-aged community sample. *Journal of Health and Social Behavior, 21,* 219–239.

Folkman, S., & Lazarus, R. S. (1985). If it changes, it must be a process: Study of emotion and coping during three stages of a college examination. *Journal of Personality and Social Psychology, 48,* 150–170.

Folkman, S., Lazarus, R. S., Dunkel-Shetter, C., DeLongis, A., & Gruen, R. J. (1986). Dynamics of a stressful encounter: Cognitive appraisal, coping, and encounter outcomes. *Journal of Personality and Social Psychology, 50,* 992–1003.

Frenkel-Brunswik, E. (1939). Mechanisms of self-deception. *Journal of Social Psychology, 10,* 409–420.

Freud, A. (1936). *The ego and the mechanisms of defense.* New York: International Universities Press.

Geisler, C. (1986). The use of subliminal psychodynamic activation in the study of repression. *Journal of Personality and Social Psychology, 51,* 844–851.

Gergen, K. J. (1985). The ethnopsychology of self-deception. In M. W. Martin (Ed.), *Self-deception and self-understanding* (pp. 228–243). Lawrence: University Press of Kansas.

Gerin, W., Litt, M. D., Deich, J., & Pickering, T. G. (1995). Self-efficacy as a moderator of perceived control effects on cardiovascular reactivity: Is enhanced control always beneficial? *Psychosomatic Medicine, 57,* 390–397.

Gero, G. (1951). The concept of defense. *Psychoanalytic Quarterly, 20,* 565–578.

Gilbert, D. T., & Cooper, J. (1985). Social psychological strategies of self-deception. In M. W. Martin (Ed.), *Self-deception and self-understanding* (pp. 75–94). Lawrence: University Press of Kansas.

Gleser, G. C., & Ihilevich, D. (1969). An objective instrument for measuring defense mechanisms. *Journal of Consulting and Clinical Psychology, 33,* 51–60.

Goldberger, L. (1983). The concept and mechanisms of denial: As selective overview. In S. Breznitz (Ed.), *The denial of stress* (pp. 83–101). New York: International Universities Press.

Goleman, D. (1986). *Vital lies, simple truths: The psychology of self-deception.* New York: Simon & Schuster.

Golin, S., Herron, E. W., Lakota, R., & Reineck, L. (1967). Factor analytic study of the Manifest Anxiety, Extraversion, and Repression-Sensitization scales. *Journal of Consulting Psychology, 31,* 564–569.

Greenberg, J., Pyszczynski, T., & Solomon, S. (1986). The cause and consequences of a need for self-esteem: A terror management theory. In R. F. Baumeister (Ed.), *Public self and private self* (pp. 189–212). New York: Springer-Verlag.

Greenwald, A. G. (1980). The authoritarian ego: Fabrication and revision of personal history. *American Psychologist, 33,* 603–618.

Greenwald, A. G. (1988). Self-knowledge and self-deception. In J. S. Lockard & D. L. Paulhus (Eds.), *Self-deception: An adaptive mechanism?* (pp. 113–131). Englewood Cliffs, NJ: Prentice-Hall.

Grzegolowska, H. J. (1976). An activation theory approach to defense mechanisms. *Polish Psychological Bulletin, 7,* 225–233.

Gur, R. C., & Sackeim, H. A. (1979). Self-deception: A concept in search of a phenomenon. *Journal of Personality and Social Psychology, 37,* 147–169.

Gurwitz, P. M. (1981). Paths to psychotherapy in the middle years: A longitudinal study. *Social Science and Medicine, 15E,* 67–76.

Haan, N. (1963). Proposed model of ego functioning: Coping and defense mechanisms in relationship to I.Q. change. *Psychological Monographs, 77,* 1–23.

Haan, N. (1965). Coping and defense mechanisms related to personality inventories. *Journal of Consulting Psychology, 29,* 373–378.

Haan, N. (1969). A tripartite model of ego functioning values and clinical and research applications. *Journal of Nervous and Mental Disease, 148,* 14–30.

Haan, N. (1977). *Coping and defending.* New York: Academic Press.

Haan, N. (1985). Processes of moral development: Cognitive or social disequilibrium? *Developmental Psychology, 21,* 996–1006.

Haan, N. (1986). Systematic variability in the quality of moral action, as defined in two formulations. *Journal of Personality and Social Psychology, 50,* 1271–1284.

Hamilton, V. (1983). *The cognitive structures and processes of human motivation and personality.* New York: Wiley.

Hardaway, R. A. (1990). Subliminally activated symbiotic fantasies: Facts and artifacts. *Psychological Bulletin, 107,* 177–195.

Hare, R. D. (1966). Denial of threat and emotional response to impending painful stimulation. *Journal of Consulting Psychology, 30,* 359–361.

Hart, D., & Chmiel, S. (1992). Influence of defense mechanisms on moral judgment development—a longitudinal study. *Developmental Psychology, 28,* 722–730.

Heilbrun, A. B., Jr., & Pepe, V. (1985). Awareness of cognitive defences and stress management. *British Journal of Medical Psychology, 58,* 9–17.

Hentschel, U., & Kiessling, M. (1990). Are defense mechanisms valid predictors of performance on cognitive tasks? In G. I. van Heck, S. E. Hampson, J. Reykowski, & J. Zakrzewski (Eds.), *Personality psychology in Europe* (Vol. 3, pp. 203–223). Lisse, Amsterdam: Swets & Zeitlinger.

Hentschel, U., Smith, G., & Draguns, J. G. (Eds.). (1986). *The roots of perception: Individual differences in information processing within and beyond awareness.* New York: North-Holland.

Holmes, D. S. (1974). Investigations of repression: Differential recall of material experimentally or naturally associated with ego threat. *Psychological Bulletin, 81,* 632–653.

Holmes, D. S. (1981). Existence of classical projection and the stress-reducing function of attributive projection: A reply to Sherwood. *Psychological Bulletin, 90,* 460–466.

Holmes, D. S., & McCaul, K. D. (1989). Laboratory research on defense mechanisms. In R. W. J. Neufeld (Ed.), *Advances in the investigation of psychological stress* (pp. 161–192). New York: Wiley.

Horowitz, M. J. (1986). *Stress response syndromes* (2nd ed.). Northvale, NJ: Jason Aronson.

Horowitz, M. J. (1988). *Introduction to psychodynamics.* New York: Basic Books.

Horowitz, M. J., Markman, H. C., Stinson, C., Fridhandler, B. M., & Ghannam, J. H. (1990). A classification theory of defense. In J. L. Singer (Ed.), *Repression and dissociation: Implications for personality, psychopathology and health* (pp. 61–84). Chicago: University of Chicago Press.

Horowitz, M. J., Milbrath, C., Jordan, D., Stinson, C., Redington, D., Ewart, M., Fridhandler, B., Reidbord, S., & Hartley, D. (1994). Expressive and defensive behavior during discourse on unresolved topics. *Journal of Personality, 62,* 527–563.

Horowitz, M. J., & Stinson, C. H. (1995). Defense as aspects of person schemas and control processes. In R. Plutchik & H. Conte (Eds.), *Ego defenses: Theory and measurement* (pp. 79–97). New York: Wiley.

Ihilevich, D., & Gleser, G. C. (1986). *Defense mechanisms: Their classification, correlates, and measurement with the Defense Mechanisms Inventory.* Owosso, MI: DMI Associates.

Jacobson, A. M., Beardslee, W., Hauser, S. T., Noam, G., Powers, S. I., & Gelfand, E. (1992). Ego defense mechanisms manual. In G. E. Vaillant (Ed.), *Ego mechanisms of defense: A guide for clinicians and researchers* (pp. 261–278). Washington, DC: American Psychiatric Press.

Jamner, L. D., & Schwartz, G. E. (1987). Self-deception predicts self-report and endurance of pain. *Psychosomatic Medicine, 48,* 211–223.

Joffe, P., & Naditch, M. P. (1977). Paper and pencil measures of coping and defense processes. In N. Haan (Ed.), *Coping and defending: Processes of self-environment organization* (pp. 280–297). New York: Academic Press.

Juni, S., & Yanishefsky, D. S. (1983). Defensive style: State or trait? *Journal of Personality Assessment, 47,* 536–538.

Kernberg, O. F. (1976). *Object relations theory and clinical psychoanalysis.* New York: Jason Aronson.

Kernberg, O. F. (1984). *Severe personality disorders: Psychotherapeutic strategies.* New Haven, CT: Yale University Press.

Kline, P. (1972). *Fact and fantasy in Freudian theory.* London: Methuen.

Kobasa, S. C., Maddi, S. R., & Kahn, S. (1982). Hardiness and health: A prospective study. *Journal of Personality and Social Psychology, 42,* 168–177.

Kragh, U. (1960). The Defense Mechanism Test: A new method for diagnosis and personnel selection. *Journal of Applied Psychology, 44,* 303–309.

Kragh, U., & Smith, G. J. W. (Eds.). (1970). *Percept-genetic analysis.* Lund: Gleerups.

Krebs, D., Denton, K., & Higgins, N. C. (1988). On the evolution of self-knowledge. In K. MacDonald (Ed.), *Sociobiological perspectives on human development* (pp. 105–139). New York: Springer-Verlag.

Kroeber, T. C. (1963). The coping functions of the ego mechanisms. In R. White (Ed.), *The study of lives* (pp. 179–198). New York: Atherton.

Kruglanski, A. W. (1989). The psychology of being "right": The problem of accuracy in social perception and cognition. *Psychological Bulletin, 106,* 395–405.

Kubler-Ross, E. (1969). *On death and dying.* London: Macmillan.

Kupst, M. J., & Schulman, J. L. (1981). The CPI subscales as predictors of parental coping with childhood leukemia. *Journal of Clinical Psychology, 37,* 386–388.

Kupst, M. J., Schulman, J. L., Maurer, H., Honig, G., Morgan, E., & Fochtman, D. (1984). Coping with pediatric leukemia: A two-year follow-up. *Journal of Pediatric Psychology, 9,* 149–163.

Lazarus, R. S. (1986). The costs and benefits of denial. In S. Breznitz (Ed.), *Denial of stress* (pp. 1–30). New York: International Universities Press.

Lazarus, R. S., & Folkman, S. (1984). *Stress, appraisal, and coping.* New York: Springer.

Lifton, R. (1968). *Death in life: Survivors of Hiroshima.* New York: Random House.

Lockard, J. S. (1978). On the adaptive significance of self-deception. *Human Ethology Newsletter, 21,* 4–7.

Lockard, J. S., & Paulhus, D. L. (Eds.). (1988). *Self-deception: An adaptive mechanism?* Englewood Cliffs, NJ: Prentice-Hall.

Loftus, E. F. (1993). The reality of repressed memories. *American Psychologist, 48,* 518–537.

Marcel, A. J. (1983). Conscious and unconscious perception: Experiments on visual masking and word recognition. *Cognitive Psychology, 15,* 197–237.

Martin, M. W. (Ed). (1985). *Self-deception and self-understanding.* Lawrence: University Press of Kansas.

McCrae, R. R. (1984). Situational determinants of coping responses: Loss, threat, and challenge. *Journal of Personality and Social Psychology, 46,* 919–928.

McCrae, R. R., & Costa, P. T. (1986). Personality, coping, and coping effectiveness in an adult sample. *Journal of Personality, 54,* 385–405.

McCullough, L. (1992). Toward reliability in identifying ego defenses: Clinical techniques. In G. E. Vaillant (Ed.), *Ego mechanisms of defense: A guide for clinicians and researchers* (pp. 171–179). Washington DC: American Psychiatric Press.

Miller, S. M. (1989). Cognitive informational styles in the process of coping with threat and frustration. *Advances in Behavioral Research and Therapy, 11,* 223–234.

Mischel, W. (1979). On the interface of cognition and personality: Beyond the person-situation debate. *American Psychologist, 34,* 740–754.

Monts, J. K., Zurcher, L. A., & Nydegger, R. V. (1977). Interpersonal self-deception and personality correlates. *Journal of Social Psychology, 103,* 91–99.

Moore, B. E., & Rubinfine, D. L. (1969). *The mechanism of denial* (Monograph Series). New York: International Universities Press, Kris Study Group of the New York Psychoanalytic Institute.

Moos, R. H. (1974). Psychological techniques in the assessment of adaptive behavior. In G. V. Coelho, D. A. Hamburg, & J. E. Adams (Eds.), *Coping and adaptation* (pp. 101–111). New York: Basic Books.

Morrissey, R. F. (1977). The Haan model of ego functioning: An assessment of empirical research. In N. Haan (Ed.), *Coping and defending: Processes of self-environment organization* (pp. 250–279). New York: Academic Press.

Murphy, G. (1975). *Outgrowing self-deception.* New York: Basic Books.

Newton, T. L., & Contrada, R. J. (1992). Repressive coping and the verbal-autonomic response dissociation: The influence of social context. *Journal of Personality and Social Psychology, 62,* 159–167.

Nielsen, S. L., & Sarason, I. G. (1981). Emotion, personality and selective attention. *Journal of Personality and Social Psychology, 41,* 945–960.

Nisbett, R., & Ross, L. (1979). *Human inference: Strategies and shortcomings of social judgment.* Englewood Cliffs, NJ: Prentice-Hall.

Norem, J. K., & Cantor, N. (1986). Defensive pessimism: Harnessing anxiety as a motivation. *Journal of Personality and Social Psychology, 51,* 1208–1217.

Ofshe, R., & Watters, E. (1994). *Making monsters: False memories, psychotherapy, and sexual hysteria.* New York: Charles Scribner's Sons.

Paulhus, D. L. (1984). Two-component models of socially desirable responding. *Journal of Personality and Social Psychology, 46,* 598–609.

Paulhus, D. L. (1986). Self-deception and impression managment in test responses. In A. Angleitner & J. S. Wiggins (Eds.), *Personality assessment via questionnaire* (pp. 143–165). New York: Springer-Verlag.

Paulhus, D. L. (1988). Self-deception: Where do we stand? In J. S. Lockard & D. L. Paulhus (Eds.), *Self-deception: An adaptive mechanism?* (pp. 251–255). Englewood Cliffs, NJ: Prentice-Hall.

Paulhus, D. L. (1991). Measurement and control of response bias. In J. P. Robinson, P. R. Shaver, & L. S. Wrightsman (Eds.), *Measures of personality and social psychological attitudes* (pp. 17–59). San Diego, CA: Academic Press.

Paulhus, D. L. (1993). Bypassing the will: The automatization of affirmations. In D. M. Wegner & J. W. Pennebaker (Eds.), *Handbook of mental control* (pp. 573–587). Englewood Cliffs, NJ: Prentice-Hall.

Paulhus, D. L., Graf, P., & Van Selst, M. (1989). Attentional load increases the positivity of self-presentation. *Social Cognition, 7,* 389–400.

Paulhus, D. L., & Levitt, K. (1987). Desirable responding triggered by affect: Automatic egotism? *Journal of Personality and Social Psychology, 52,* 245–259.

Paulhus, D. L., & Reid, D. (1991). Attribution and denial in socially desirable responding. *Journal of Personality and Social Psychology, 60,* 307–317.

Paulhus, D. L., & Reynolds, S. (1995). Enhancing validity and agreement in personality impression: Putting the person back into person perception. *Journal of Personality and Social Psychology, 69,* 1233–1242.

Paulhus, D. L., & Suedfeld, P. (1988). A dynamic complexity model of self-deception. In J. S. Lockard & D. L. Paulhus (Eds.), *Self-deception: An adaptive mechanism?* (pp. 132–145). Englewood Cliffs, NJ: Prentice-Hall.

Pearlin, L. I., & Schooler, C. (1978). The structure of coping. *Journal of Health and Social Behavior, 19,* 2–21.

Perry, C., & Laurence, J. R. (1984). Mental processing outside of awareness: The contributions of Freud and Janet. In K. S. Bowers & D. Meichenbaum (Eds.), *The unconscious reconsidered* (pp. 9–48). New York: Wiley.

Perry, J. C., & Cooper, S. H. (1989). An empirical study of defense mechanisms: I. Clinical interview and life vignette ratings. *Archives of General Psychiatry, 46,* 444–452.

Perry, J. C., & Cooper, S. H. (1992). What do cross-sectional measures of defense mechanisms predict? In G. E. Vaillant (Ed.), *Ego mechanisms of defense: A guide for clinicians and researchers* (pp. 195–216). Washington, DC: American Psychiatric Press.

Plutchik, R., & Conte, H. R. (1989). Measuring emotions and their derivatives: Personality traits, ego defenses, and coping styles. In S. Wetzler & M. M. Katz (Eds.), *Contemporary approaches to psychological assessment: Clinical and experimental psychiatry* (Vol. 1, pp. 239–269). New York: Brunner/Mazel.

Plutchik, R., & Kellerman, H. (1980). *Emotion: Theory, research, and experience.* New York: Academic Press.

Pyszczynski, T., Greenberg, J., & Solomon, S. (in press). Why do we need what we need? A Terror Management perspective on the roots of human social motivation. *Psychological Inquiry.*

Quattrone, G. A., & Tversky, A. (1984). Causal versus diagnostic contingencies: On self-deception and the voter's illusion. *Journal of Personality and Social Psychology, 46,* 236–248.

Rim, Y. (1987). A comparative study of two taxonomies of coping styles, personality and sex. *Personality and Individual Differences, 8,* 521–526.

Rim, Y. (1989). Coping styles and use of means of influence in marriage. *Personality and Individual Differences, 10,* 87–91.

Rosenblatt, A., Greenberg, J., Solomon, S., Pyszczynski, T., & Lyon, D. (1989). Evidence for Terror Management Theory I: The effects of mortality salience on reactions to those who violate or uphold cultural values. *Journal of Personality and Social Psychology, 57,* 681–690.

Sackeim, H. A. (1983). Self-deception, self-esteem, and depression: The adaptive value of lying to oneself. In J. Masling (Ed.), *Empirical studies of psychoanalytic theories* (pp. 101–157). Hillsdale, NJ: Erlbaum.

Sackeim, H. A. (1988). Self-deception: A synthesis. In J. S. Lockard & D. L. Paulhus (Eds.), *Self-deception: An adaptive mechanism?* (pp. 146–165). Englewood Cliffs, NJ: Prentice-Hall.

Sackeim, H. A., & Gur, R. C. (1978). Self-deception, other-deception and consciousness. In G. E. Schwartz & D. Shapiro (Eds.), *Consciousness and self-regulation: Advances in research* (Vol. 2, pp. 139–197). New York: Plenum Press.

Sackeim, H. A., & Gur, R. C. (1979). Self-deception, other-deception, and self-reported psychopathology. *Journal of Consulting and Clinical Psychology, 47,* 213–215.

Sander, F. (1928). Experimentelle Ergebnisse der Gestaltpsychologie. In *Bericht uber den 10. Kongress fur experimentelle Psychologie.* (Reprinted *Ganzheitspsychologie,* by C. F. Sander & H. Volkelt, Eds., 1961, Munchen: Beck)

Sarbin, T. R. (1988). Self-deception in the claims of hypnosis-subjects. In J. S. Lockard & D. L. Paulhus (Eds.), *Self-deception: An adaptive mechanism?* (pp. 199–112). Englewood Cliffs, NJ: Prentice-Hall.

Sartre, J.-P. (1956). *Being and nothingness* (H. Barnes, Trans.). New York: Washington Square Press. (Original work published 1943)

Schaefer, E. S., & Plutchik, R. (1966). Interrelationships of emotions, traits, and diagnostic constructs. *Psychological Reports, 18,* 399–410.

Schafer, R. (1968). Mechanisms of defense. *International Journal of Psychoanalysis, 49,* 49–62.

Schafer, R. (1976). *A new language for psychoanalysis.* New Haven, CT: Yale University Press.

Schwartz, G. E. (1977). Psychosomatic disorders and biofeedback: A psychobiological model of disregulation. In J. D. Maser & M. E. P. Seligman (Eds.), *Psychopathology: Experimental models* (pp. 49–60). San Francisco: Freeman.

Schwartz, G. E. (1990). Psychobiology of repression and health: A systems perspective. In J. L. Singer (Ed.), *Repression and dissociation: Defense mechanisms and personality styles: Current theory and research* (pp. 405–434). Chicago: University of Chicago Press.

Schwartz, M. S., Krupp, N. E., & Byrne, D. (1971). Repression-sensitization and medical diagnosis. *Journal of Abnormal Psychology, 78,* 286–291.

Semrad, E. V., Grinspoon, L., & Fienberg, S. E. (1973). Development of an ego profile scale. *Archives of General Psychiatry, 28,* 70–77.

Shapiro, D. (1965). *Neurotic styles.* New York: Basic Books.

Shapiro, D. (1981). *Autonomy and rigid character.* New York: Basic Books.

Shedler, J., Mayman, M., & Manis, M. (1993). The illusion of mental health. *American Psychologist, 48,* 1117–1131.

Sherwood, G. G. (1980). Self-serving biases in person perception: A re-examination of projection as a mechanism for defense. *Psychological Bulletin, 90,* 445–459.

Shevrin, H. (1988). Unconscious conflict: A convergent psychodynamic and electrophysiological approach. In M. J. Horowitz (Ed.), *Psychodynamics and cognition* (pp. 117–167). Chicago: University of Chicago Press.

Shevrin, H., Smith, W. H., & Fritzler, D. (1970). Subliminally stimulated brain and verbal responses of twins differing in repressiveness. *Journal of Abnormal Psychology, 76,* 39–46.

Showers, C., & Cantor, N. (1985). Social cognition: A look at motivated strategies. *Annual Review of Psychology, 36,* 275–305.

Silverman, L. H. (1983). The subliminal psychodynamic activation method: Overview and comprehensive listing of studies. In J. Masling (Ed.), *Empirical studies of psychoanalytic theories* (pp. 41–61). Englewood Cliffs, NJ: Erlbaum.

Sjoback, H. (1973). *The psychoanalytic theory of defensive processes.* New York: Wiley.

Sloan, T. S. (1987). *Deciding: Self-deception in life choices.* London: Methuen.

Smith, G. J. W. (1984). Stabilization and automization of perceptual activity over time. In W. D. Frohlich, G. Smith, J. G. Draguns, & U. Hentschel (Eds.), *Psychological processes in cognition and personality* (pp. 135–142). Washington, DC: Hemisphere.

Smith, G. J. W., & Danielsson, A. (1982). *Anxiety and defense strategies in childhood and adolescence.* New York: International Universities Press.

Smith, G. J. W., & Henriksson, M. (1956). The effect on an established percept of a perceptual process beyond awareness. *Acta Psychologica, 11,* 346–355.

Smith, G. J. W. & Westerlundh, B. (1980). Perceptgenesis: A process perspective on perception-personality. In L. Wheeler (Ed.), *Review of personality and social psychology* (pp. 94–124). London: Sage.

Snyder, C. R. (1985). Collaborative companions: The relationship of self-deception and excuse-making. In M. W. Martin (Ed.), *Self-deception and self-understanding* (pp. 35–51). Lawrence: University Press of Kansas.

Snyder, C. R. (Ed.). (1989). Self-illusions: When are they adaptive? (Special issue). *Journal of Social and Clinical Psychology, 8,* 1–221.

Snyder, C. R., & Higgins, R. L. (1988). Excuses: Their effective role in the negotiation of reality. *Psychological Bulletin, 104,* 23–35.

Spence, D. P. (1983). The paradox of denial. In S. Breznitz (Ed.), *The denial of stress* (pp. 103–124). New York: International Universities Press.

Suls, J., & Fletcher, B. (1985). The relative efficacy of avoidant and nonavoidant coping strategies: A meta analysis. *Health Psychology, 4*(3), 249–288.

Swann, W. B. (1992). Seeking truth: Finding despair: Some unhappy consequences of a negative self-concept. *Current Directions in Psychological Science, 1,* 15–18.

Taylor, S. E. (1990). Health psychology: The science and the field. *American Psychogist, 45,* 40–50.

Taylor, S. E., & Brown, J. (1988). Illusion and well-being: A social psychological perspective on mental health. *Psychological Bulletin, 103,* 193–210.

Taylor, S. E., & Clark, L. F. (1986). Does information improve adjustment to noxious events? In M. J. Saks & L. Saks (Eds.), *Advances in applied social psychology* (Vol. 3, pp. 1–28). Hillsdale, NJ: Erlbaum.

Tesser, A. (1986). Some effects of self-evaluation maintenance on cognition and action. In R. M. Sorrentino & E. T. Higgins (Eds.), *The handbook of motivation and cognition: Foundations of social behavior* (pp. 435–464). New York: Guilford Press.

Tesser, A., & Campbell, J. D. (1982). Self-evaluation maintenance and the perception of friends and strangers. *Journal of Personality, 50,* 261–279.

Trivers, R. L. (1976). Foreward. In R. Dawkins, *The selfish gene.* New York: Oxford University Press.

Trivers, R. L. (1985). *Social evolution.* Menlo Park, CA: Benjamin/Cummings.

Turvey, C., & Salovey, P. (1994). Measures of repression: Converging on the same construct? *Imagination, Cognition & Personality, 13,* 279–289.

Vaillant, G. E. (1971). Theoretical hierarchy of adaptive ego mechanisms: A 30-year follow-up of 30 men selected for psychological health. *Archives of General Psychiatry, 24,* 107–118.

Vaillant, G. E. (1976). Natural history of male psychological health: The relation of choice of ego mechanisms of defense to adult adjustment. *Archives of General Psychiatry, 33,* 535–545.

Vaillant, G. E. (1992). *Ego mechanisms of defense: A guide for clinicians and researchers.* Washington, DC: American Psychiatric Press.

Vaillant, G. E., Bond, M., & Vaillant, C. O. (1986). An empirically validated hierarchy of defense mechanisms. *Archives of General Psychiatry, 43,* 786–794.

Vickers, R. R., Jr., Conway, T. L., & Haight, M. A. (1983). Association between Levenson's Dimensions of Locus of Control and measures of coping and defense mechanisms. *Psychological Reports, 52,* 323–333.

Vickers, R. R., Jr., & Hervig, L. K. (1981). Comparisons of three psychological defense mechanism questionnaires. *Journal of Personality Assessment, 45,* 630–638.

Vickers, R. R., Jr., Hervig, L. K., Rahe, R. H., & Rosenman, R. H. (1981). Type A behavior and coping and defense. *Psychosomatic Medicine, 43,* 381–396.

Wallerstein, R. (1983). Defenses, defense mechanisms, and the structure of the mind. *Journal of the American Psychoanalytic Association, Supplement, 31,* 201–225.

Warrenburg, S., Levine, J., Schwartz, G. E., Fontana, A. F., Kerns, R. D., Delaney, R., & Mattson, R. (1989). Defensive coping and blood pressure reactivity in medical patients. *Journal of Behavioral Medicine, 12,* 407–424.

Wegner, D. M. (1989). *White bears and other unwanted thoughts.* New York: Viking Press.

Weinberger, D. A. (1990). The construct validity of the repressive style. In J. L. Singer (Ed.), *Repression and dissociation: Implications for personality theory, psychopathology, and health* (pp. 337–386). Chicago: University of Chicago Press.

Weinberger, D. A., & Schwartz, G. E. (1990). Distress and restraint as superordinate dimensions of self-reported adjustment: A typological perspective. *Journal of Personality, 58,* 381–417.

Weinberger, D. A., Schwartz, G. E., & Davidson, R. J. (1979). Low-anxious high-anxious, and repressive coping styles: Psychometric patterns and behavioral and physiological responses to stress. *Journal of Abnormal Psychology, 88,* 369–380.

Weinberger, J. (1989). Response to Balay & Shevrin: Constructive critique or misguided attack? *American Psychologist, 44,* 1417–1419.

Weinberger, J., & Silverman, L. H. (1990). Testability and empirical verification of psychoanalytic dynamic propositions through subliminal psychodynamic activation. *Psychoanalytic Psychology, 7,* 299–339.

Williams, L. M. (1994). Recall of childhood trauma: A prospective study of women's memories of child sexual abuse. *Journal of Consulting & Clinical Psychology, 62,* 1167–1176.

Wilson, T. D. (1985). Self-deception without repression: Limits on access to mental states: In M. W. Martin (Ed.), *Self-deception and self-understanding* (pp. 95–116). Lawrence: University Press of Kansas.

Woike, B. A., Aronoff, J., Stollak, G. E., & Loraas, J. A. (1994). Links between intrapsychic and interpersonal defenses in dyadic interaction. *Journal of Research in Personality, 28,* 101–113.

Zajonc, R. B. (1980). Feeling and thinking: Preferences need no inferences. *American Psychologist, 35,* 151–175.

══ CHAPTER 23 ══

INTERNAL INHIBITIONS AND CONTROLS

EDWIN I. MEGARGEE
THE FLORIDA STATE UNIVERSITY

I. INTRODUCTION

If you turn back to the Table of Contents and review the topics covered in this *Handbook,* you will see that most personality theorists are interested in what people do and why they do it. This chapter is different. We are going to be discussing what people do *not* do and why they do *not* do it. Our focus will be on the internal inhibitions, controls, and restraints that cause people to refrain from behaviors that they consider to be wrong or inadvisable.

Most personality theorists concentrate on what I shall call the "positive" causes of behavior: the traits, habits, motives, and attitudes that lead an artist to create, that drive a "Type A" person to be competitive, or that cause a neurotic individual to become anxious. However, as Robert Frost pointed out in the "The Road Not Taken" (Untermeyer, 1955, p. 54), any decision to perform one act also involves the decision, conscious or unconscious, not to do something else. To understand how an automobile functions, we must study the steering and brakes as well as the engine and power train. To understand human behavior, we must examine controls and inhibitions as well as motives and drives.

As with the brakes and steering on our automobiles, we generally do not think much about inhibitions and controls until they fail. My interest in inhibition was born of necessity: I have spend most of my professional career studying antisocial behavior and violence. In contrast with most of my fellow contributors to this *Handbook,* the walls surrounding my research laboratories have often been topped with barbed wire rather than ivy, and featured gun towers instead of bell towers. Although I could go home at night, my subjects had to stay behind because society had decided that they required stringent *external* controls because they lacked adequate *internal* inhibitions and restraints. Naturally, in this setting I developed an interest in controls, and internal inhibitions are a major construct in my theoretical framework for the study of aggressive behavior.

In this chapter, internal inhibitions and controls will be discussed from a broad perspective, emphasizing concepts and theories from a range of disciplines. The views offered will be my own and should be regarded as hypotheses to stimulate thought and discussion rather than as "revealed truth." In the course of this discussion, we shall address the following topics:

1. Problems in defining what we mean by internal controls or inhibitions, semantically and operationally
2. Philosophical issues and interdisciplinary perspectives
3. How inhibitions and controls are acquired or enhanced
4. How inhibitions and controls are diminished, lost, or overcome
5. Methodological problems in doing empirical research on controls
6. Implications for research, theory, and practice

II. Definitional Issues: What Do We Mean by Internal Controls?

One of our first problems is the fact that internal controls and inhibitions are difficult to define. This is because they are "negative" constructs that must be defined by exclusion. Moreover, since inhibitions are linked to values which vary from person to person, society to society, and period to period, the specific behaviors that are inhibited will also differ. Let us examine each of these problems.

A. Defining a Negative Construct

Most personality constructs are adduced to explain why people engage in certain behaviors. Terms such as "leadership," "anxiety," and "achievement" all connote constellations of attributes and observable behaviors. These can be used to construct operational definitions of these constructs or to identify people who exemplify these traits. However, "inhibitions," "taboos," "internal constraints," "superego," and all other such terms in the thesaurus are used to explain why certain behaviors do *not* occur. It is obviously much easier to construct an operational definition of observable rather than suppressed behaviors.

B. Variability of Values

This problem is compounded by the fact that specific behaviors that are inhibited vary as a function of each person's values. Since values differ from one individual, social subgroup, or culture to the next, it is difficult to stipulate the behavioral omissions that suggest taboos are operating. At a fast food restaurant, you may observe a number of patrons choose the salad bar instead of a hamburger. Are they normally opposed to eating meat, or do they simply prefer vegetables? This leads us to the most difficult aspect of defining inhibitions, the need to rule out alternative explanations for failures to act.

C. Definition by Exclusion

Before we can conclude that someone's failure to perform some act results from internal prohibitions, we must exclude all the other reasons why that person might refrain from that act. Here are a few alternatives that must be ruled out:

1. Lack of Motivation

If an individual lacks the appropriate motivation, drive, incentive, or desire to perform the act in question, then his or her failure to respond cannot be attributed to inhibitions. This means researchers must establish that an appropriate drive state exists before they can conclude that a failure to perform some act results from inhibitions.

2. Inability to Perform

It may be that the response in question is not in the person's repertoire or that some external constraint prevents the person from engaging in the behavior in question. A recent film depicted a high school computer hacker who broke into his school's computer system and changed all his F's to A's. This film may have inspired thousands of students to emulate his behavior, but most were unable to do so because they lacked his technical expertise and/or his access to a computer.

3. Anticipation of a Negative Outcome

People will also refrain from behavior if it is not likely to be successful or if bad things are likely to happen to them as a result. Arthur Bremer stalked President Nixon but never shot at him because he was unable to penetrate the Secret Service screen (Institute of Medicine, 1984). His lack of internal inhibitions was amply demonstrated when he shot Governor George Wallace instead.

People will also refrain from behavior that is likely to result in unpleasant consequences. If several large and apparently vicious dogs raid my backyard barbecue and start eating the steaks, I will not attempt to retrieve my property from their slavering jaws. I can replace a Delmonico easier than my hand.

4. Response Competition

At any given moment, there may be a number of different responses competing which are mutually incompatible. You are presently reading this book. You are probably not solving the *New York Times* crossword puzzle, making love to your sweetheart, or mowing the lawn. The fact that you are reading this book does not imply that you have any internal inhibitions against engaging in any of these other behaviors. It simply means that at this point in the history of the world, for whatever reason, you have chosen to read this book.

To recapitulate the problems associated with excluding other explanations, a person's failure to perform some act that we would have expected them to perform at that time and place implies internal constraints or inhibitions only if we can be sure that (a) the appropriate motivational state was present, (b) the person was capable of performing the response, (c) the external situation did not indicate the response would fail or result in a negative outcome, and (d) we can be reasonably sure that the person did not simply prefer to do something else.

D. Other Problems

The difficulties listed thus far should surely give pause to those who would attempt to formulate a thoroughly satisfactory operational definition of internal inhibitions. However, there are other problems as well.

So far, we have been discussing occasions when some expected behavior failed to occur. Can we at least infer that internal constraints were absent if the behavior did take place? No. There may have been internal inhibitions that were simply inadequate in the face of strong temptation. It is no accident that, unlike any other item on the menu, many restaurants put the high-calorie desserts on a cart which is wheeled directly to the patron's table to maximize the temptation.

Another problem is that inhibitions and taboos can vary as a function of the time, the place, the object, and the specific act. It is all right for a football player to tackle an opposing player during a game Saturday but he should refrain from decking the President of the University at the prayer breakfast Sunday.

Internal constraints must also be differentiated from other similar constructs. One is repression. Might not our inhibitions be so strong that the forbidden drive is blocked from awareness? I may think the reason that I never purchased the controversial novel *Satanic Verses* in 1989 is because I had no (conscious) interest in reading that book. A psychoanalyst might argue that my apparent lack of interest actually stemmed from an unconscious need not to offend the late Ayatollah Khomeini, an obvious father figure, because I had not yet completely resolved my Oedipal conflict. Such unconscious conflicts will be beyond the scope of this chapter. Suffice it to say that any repressions that influence behavior will simply make life that much more difficult for researchers and theorists.

III. PHILOSOPHICAL ISSUES

As we have noted, internal controls and constraints are closely associated with values. As a result, people from a variety of disciplines have discussed them from a number of different perspectives. Indeed, many of the issues and concerns were raised centuries before the first psychologist drew breath.

Why such interest in this particular aspect of personality? Many people assume that internal controls and constraints necessarily involve ethical or moral prohibitions against performing acts that are disapproved of by society. Thus "internal constraints" are viewed as being synonymous with "conscience" or "morality," and the theoretical and empirical issues raised by psychologists are regarded as simply one more attempt to explore the age-old dilemma of good versus evil.

Actually, these concepts are not congruent. As the trials of the Nazi war criminals at Nuremberg demonstrated, some people have well-developed value systems that are at odds with the moral codes espoused by the larger society. Nevertheless, there is considerable overlap, and much of the thinking and research that have been done on such topics as moral development, social conformity, social deviance, psychopathy, cultural relativism, and, yes, good versus evil, are relevant to the issues we will be discussing.

Your theoretical perspective on the origin of internal controls is probably influenced by your basic view of human nature. Reduced to its essence, the basic philosophical question is whether people are fundamentally good or evil.

Those who maintain the people are basically good blame a corrupt society for human misery and evil. This is the allegory of the Garden of Eden before the snake intruded. One of the foremost proponents of this philosophy was Jean Jacques Rousseau (1712–1788), who wrote in *Emile* (1762), "Everything is good when it leaves the hands of the Creator; everything degenerates in the hands of man" (Beck, 1980, p. 264). This viewpoint underlies nondirective and humanistic approaches to psychotherapy that view the therapeutic task as removing acquired impediments to self-actualization and growth.

Diametrically opposed to this philosophy is the belief that people are basically evil and that left to their own devices they will exploit and prey upon one another. This is the Doctrine of Original Sin following the Fall. Thomas Hobbes (1588–1679) was one of the major advocates of this position. Whereas Rousseau, whose favorite book was *Robinson Crusoe,* extolled the virtues of people in a state of nature, Hobbes, in *Leviathan* (1651), described a state of nature as "No arts; no letters; no society; and, which is worst of all, continual fear and danger of violent death; and the life of man, solitary, poor, nasty, brutish, and short" (Beck, 1980, p. 264). Latter-day proponents of this view include Freud and his followers who maintained that a major goal of child rearing is to civilize and control the primitive id impulses and needs that are present from birth; i.e., to develop the ego.

A third view, developed somewhat more recently, holds that people have no innate good or bad tendencies, but instead are products of their environments. John Locke (1632–1704) used the analogy of a blank slate or *tabula rasa* to convey the notion that experience determines our character. More recently behaviorists and social learning theorists such as B. F. Skinner and Albert Bandura have espoused this view.

Theorists who believe in the innate goodness of humankind have no need to account for the development of values or controls. Their basic position is that the human animal comes equipped with these attributes. Instead, their theoretical task is to account for evil and explain what went wrong.

The people who adopt the latter two positions, namely, that people are born without innate controls, must explain how we acquire inhibitions. Obviously, one's academic discipline will influence one's theory. Religions often cite some form of redemption. Anthropology focuses on the transmission of culture, and sociology on the conflict of group values and loyalties. Psychiatry tends to seek signs of psychopathology, and psychology investigates individual personality characteristics. We shall examine some of these views, but we should remain aware of the fact that cutting across disciplines, these three basic philosophical perspectives influence the positions theorists adopt.

In the next section, we shall examine some of the hypotheses that have been advanced to explain how internal controls and inhibitions originate, and how they are overcome.

IV. ORIGINS OF INTERNAL INHIBITIONS

As we noted in Section II, there are all sorts of reasons why people may refrain from behaving in certain ways. Appropriate or adequate motivation may be lacking, the response may be outside their repertoire or beyond their capabilities, or external sanctions may be imposed. These factors, as important as they are in predicting behavior, are outside the purview of this section.

In this section we will focus on *internal* inhibitions and controls that deter us from behaviors that we would otherwise perform. As we shall see, these taboos are variable. Some inhibitions are general, while some are quite specific. Some are lasting, and some are temporary. The common denominator is that we are referring to internal impediments rather than external constraints.

A. Physiological Mechanisms

Given the fact that we are biological organisms, it is obvious that all our behavior has a physiological basis. What we do, say, or think depends on our neurons, hormones, organs, and tissues.

Nevertheless, partly because of the difficulties involved in doing physiological research on humans and partly because of an American bias in favor of environmental explanations, most theorists traditionally paid only lip service to the physiological bases for personality functioning.

This situation is changing. With the recent technological advances in our ability to study the basic genetic material and to conduct nonintrusive investigations of the central nervous system, we have come to recognize the role of physiological and hereditary factors in major mental disorders previously thought to have a purely functional basis. Concomitant with these clinical advances is a greater appreciation of the importance of physiological factors in normal personality functioning as well.

In a broad sense, there are many physical reasons why a person may refrain from doing something. Diabetes and circulatory problems can cause male sexual impotence, a broken leg will interfere with ski jumping, and acute nausea will sap one's motivation to do just about anything except retch and hope for an early demise. Ultimately, we all stop behaving because we die. However, these physical inhibitions are not what we mean by "internal controls," even though they may be very important in predicting behavior.

Physiological research on internal inhibitory mechanisms is still relatively primitive. We have already noted the difficulty of defining internal controls operationally. This problem is compounded by the limited range of physiological experiments we can ethically perform with humans. Even though animal studies permit greater precision, many will question their relevance. In this section we shall touch on possible hereditary influences and the central nervous system substrate for internal controls.

1. Genetic Mechanisms

Unfortunately, *homo sapiens* is a notoriously difficult species for behavioral geneticists to investigate given our propensity for assortative mating, our low reproduction rate, our long maturation period, and our hopelessly heterogeneous gene pools. Consequently relatively little is known about the genetic bases of personality functioning in general and restraints in particular. In this section, most of our speculations are based on inferences from other areas of research.

a. Research on Criminals. The first empirical research relevant to possible genetic determinants of internal controls and inhibitions was performed by scientists whose primary interest was in people who apparently lacked adequate controls, namely, convicted criminals. In the 19th century, Cesare Lombroso (1835–1909) hypothesized that criminals' savage behavior suggests that they are "atavistic reversals" or throwbacks to a more primitive stage of human evolution. Such atavism, Lombroso maintained, would be manifested by physical signs or "stigmata," such as low sloping foreheads. In the 20th century extensive studies were carried out by Goring (1913) and Hooton (1939) to test Lombroso's hypothesis, but sampling and methodological flaws rendered their results inconclusive (Rosenquist & Megargee, 1969).

Somewhat more convincing are studies showing a higher rate of concordance for criminality among monozygotic than dizygotic twins (Christiansen, 1977), and higher rates of criminality among adoptive children whose biological parents were criminals than among those whose biological parents were noncriminals, irrespective of the criminality of the adoptive parents (Mednick, Gabrielle, & Hutchings, 1984; Mednick & Volavka, 1980). However, any research using convicted criminals is only tangentially related to the question of the heritability of internal controls.

b. Heritability of Personality Factors. Using factor analysis, some personality researchers have suggested that five or six fundamental dimensions underlie our perceptions and descriptions of one another (Hogan, 1986). One of these dimensions, "conscientiousness," bears a passing resemblance to our concept of internal controls. According to Hogan, "conscientiousness contrasts people who are dependable and conforming with those who are undependable and nonconforming" (1986, p. 58).

Using personality test scores as operational definitions of these dimensions, researchers such as Bouchard (1984) and Loehlin and Nichols (1976) have compared the scores of monozygotic and dizygotic twins to estimate the heritability of these traits and concluded that about half the variance can be attributed to genetic factors.

    c. The Evolutionary Perspective.   Some scientists have suggested that inner controls are innate because they have selective value for the survival of the species. In his paper on "Moral Conduct and Character," Robert Hogan "assumes that morality is a natural phenomenon, an adaptive response to evolutionary pressure, and that an understanding of moral behavior is relative to our knowledge of man's biological and social nature" (1973, p. 218).

This evolutionary perspective has not only been used to explain general ethical tendencies, but also to account for specific taboos such as those against incest or homicide. Noting the near universality of the incest taboo, Gardner Lindzey (1967), in his presidential address to the American Psychological Association, theorized that it must be genetically based.

Lindzey noted that the literature on interpersonal attractiveness showed that people, like most creatures, are most attracted to one another on the basis of similarity, familiarity, and proximity. Without an incest taboo, these tendencies would ordinarily lead to a high level of inbreeding, for it is the members of one's immediate family who best fit these specifications. Since inbreeding would be deleterious for the species, Lindzey (1967, p. 1056) argued that "the biological necessity of outbreeding led to the evolution of a set of prohibitions against this powerful tendency . . . "

The noted ethologist Konrad Lorenz (1963/1966) maintained that inhibitions against aggressive behavior also have a genetic basis. In the normal course of evolution, animals that had the physical capacity to kill other members of their own species evolved inhibitions against the use of their deadly weapons when combating one another. Rattlesnakes, for example, fight by wrestling one another and never use their fangs because the venom would be lethal.

Because our ancestors were less ferocious, such inhibitions had little selective value, so modern humans did not inherit strong inhibitions against homicide. However, once we invented weapons and passed this knowledge down from generation to generation, we rapidly became a lethal species as the quick growth of technology outstripped the slow course of evolution. This imbalance, according to Lorenz, accounts for our high homicide rates.

    d. Selective Breeding.   Another line of evidence comes from selective breeding of animals. Although animal husbandrymen have been more interested in breeding aggressive strains of fighting bulls, cocks, dogs, and fish, it is well documented that animals can also be bred for docility and tractability.

The monks at the Hospice of St. Bernard recognized that the large dogs they were breeding to assist travelers lost in the snowy mountain passes would be of little help if they had the feisty temperament of a terrier or the aggressiveness of a pit bull. Hence they deliberately selected the gentlest animals as well as those with the most stamina, endurance, and intelligence (S. E. Megargee, 1942, 1954). Of course, it is questionable whether a dog's high threshold for aggressive behavior is equivalent to a person's internal controls, or whether being gentle and docile is conceptually equivalent to being controlled or inhibited.

e. Evidence on Genetic Mechanisms.   Thus it can be seen that there is no definitive evidence for the inheritance of generalized sets of values or specific inhibitions such as the incest taboo. Given the ethical constraints governing genetic research with humans, as well as the technical difficulties, it is unlikely that any definitive studies will be forthcoming in the foreseeable future. Nevertheless, despite the bias toward environmental explanations of internal controls, there is enough suggestive evidence to allow us to entertain genetic hypotheses.

2. Central Nervous System

The best evidence for a neurological substrate for internal inhibitions stems from clinical studies showing that various types of CNS impairment can lead to impulsivity and diminished ethical constraints. Beyond this broad observation, our knowledge of specific inhibitory mechanisms in the human brain is rather vague.

Specific centers have been identified that act to inhibit very basic forms of behavior such as eating and drinking. Photographs of immense rats that have gorged themselves into obesity after removal of the hypothalamic centers that signal satiety are a standard feature of introductory psychology texts, and scientists have "turned off" aggressive behavior in some animals by electrically stimulating areas of the brain believed to inhibit aggression (Johnson, 1972; Mark & Ervin, 1970). These central nervous system mechanisms are of primary importance to clinicians attempting to diagnose the possible causes of impulsive or poorly controlled behavior.

When we turn to a consideration of the neurological basis of higher ethical principles, much less is understood. It seems definite that the cortex is involved, and research on the development of moral and ethical sensitivity makes it clear that a certain level of cortical development is required for children to make "mature" ethical choices. Again, this is most relevant for examining those cases in which there has been a breakdown in ethical behavior. As we shall see, toxic substances or diseases that interfere with the cortex can have the effect of diminishing one's internal inhibitions.

3. Other Physiological Factors

Although their exogenous origin makes them outside the purview of "internal inhibitions" in the usual sense, it should be noted that drugs can be used to reduce undesirable behavior patterns. Some act to reduce drive strength, as in the appetite suppressants used by dieters or the so-called "chemical castration" sometimes advocated for sex offenders. Others strengthen a person's ability to inhibit undesirable behavior, that is, behavior that is contrary to the individual's own code of values. A recurrent problem in clinical settings are patients who are able to control their behavior while on medication in an inpatient setting but who discontinue their medication and act out after discharge.

B. Psychological Sources of Inhibitions

According to Rouseau (1758), "The first of all laws is to respect the law," but whence cometh this respect for law and order? Developmental psychologists such as Jean Piaget (1932), Lawrence Kohlberg (1981), and Robert Selman (1980) have charted distinct patterns and stages in children's comprehension and understanding of moral issues. Do these stages in moral development stem from maturation or from the growth of the child's cognitive abilities from a concrete, simplistic understanding to a more abstract and complex appreciation of the world?

Those who, like Rousseau, believe in the innate goodness of humankind do not have to explain how most children become socialized to their particular culture's values. For them, the unfolding of nature's plan is a sufficient explanation. Their task is to explain how society interferes with this normal process.

However, those who agree with Locke that we are born essentially unformed and are shaped by experience, or who subscribe to Hobbes' view that we are inherently selfish and amoral, must explain how it is that most of us are more or less civilized by the time we reach adulthood. To account for this process, theorists must answer two basic questions: (1) How do we learn the rules of our particular society? (2) Why is it that we obey them? We shall discuss these questions from the viewpoints of behaviorism, cognitive social learning theory, and psychoanalysis.

1. Socialization: Learning the Rules of the Culture

Somehow in the course of development, everyone acquires a sense of values, a moral code that specifies what we should and should not do. Broadly speaking, they learn behavior can be divided into "latitudes of acceptance" and "latitudes of rejection" (E. I. Megargee, 1973).

The behaviors included in these latitudes vary from one society to the next. Most Americans repudiate the practice of killing people who have different religious beliefs, but have no compunctions about the custom of butchering cattle for food. In India, however, Hindus who would be aghast at the thought of killing a cow slaughtered thousands of Muslims in the early 1950s (Luckenbill & Sanders, 1977).

In any given society, the latitudes of acceptance and rejection can change over time. In America, for example, homosexual relationships between consenting adults have become more accepted, while dueling, which was once *de riguer* in certain situations, is now rejected.

Not only do developing children learn the broad latitudes of accepted and rejected behavior in their cultures and subcultures, but with increasing years and sophistication they come to understand the subtleties within these latitudes. In the latitude of acceptance, certain behaviors are *prescribed,* but others are actually *preferred,* while in the latitudes of rejection, some behaviors are *proscribed* but others are *permitted* (E. I. Megargee, 1973). These distinctions, too, vary from place to place and change over time. In recent years, political dissent has shifted from being proscribed to permitted in the USSR while the opposite trend has taken place in China.

At the outset, children's behavior is guided and controlled by their caretakers, but in time, whether it is the Code of Hammurabi, the Ten Commandments, or the Analects of Confucius, children learn what is regarded as right and wrong in their culture. How does this come about?

a. Conditioning via Punishment. With regard to learning the basic "do's and don'ts" of the culture, there is broad general agreement that a system of rewards for approved behavior and punishments for "bad" behavior are necessary. Theorists disagree regarding whether these contingencies alone are a sufficient explanation.

Reinforcement or "rewards" are used to promote and encourage appropriate behavior and to foster positive role models. Punishments, on the other hand, are used to discourage disapproved behavior. Since we are focusing on inhibitions and restraints, we will concentrate on punishment.

It is, quite literally, a proverbial belief that punishment induces internal inhibitions: according to the Book of Proverbs (13:24), "He that spareth his rod hateth his son; but he that loveth him chasteneth him betimes," while a Chinese proverb states, "Beat your child once a day. If you don't know why, he does" (Tripp, 1970, p. 759).

Many, perhaps most, psychologists agree that punishment can foster internal inhibitions. Discussing how we develop inhibitions against aggression, for example, Dollard, Doob, Miller, Mowrer, and Sears (1939, p. 33) wrote, "The basic variable that determines the degree to which any specific act of aggression will be inhibited appears to be anticipation of punishment. . . . [T]he principle derives from the law of effect; those acts cease to occur which, in the past, have been followed by punishment." To this they added that injury to a love object also constitutes punishment and that anticipation of failure is equivalent to anticipation of punishment (Dollard et al., 1939, p. 34).

There is considerable popular support for these "common sense" notions. Since the days of Jeremy Bentham (1748–1832), modern penology has been based on the theory that properly administered punishment deters crime; "specific deterrence" means that once we have been punished we are less likely to repeat our transgressions, while "general deterrence" refers to inhibitions fostered in others who may observe our penalty.

There is no doubt that the immediate prospect of punishment can *suppress* behavior; witness how many cars reduce speed at the sight of a flashing blue light.

But the rapidity with which they resume speeding once they are out of sight of the police suggests that no lasting inhibitions, as we have defined them, were fostered.

Numerous studies attest to the fact that for punishment to be an effective deterrent it must be swift, sure, and sufficiently strong to outweigh the pleasures derived from the sanctioned act (Wilson & Herrnstein, 1985). In totalitarian countries, a mere accusation may result in immediate execution, a policy which one would suppose would be very effective in suppressing unwanted behavior. However, we should recall that in World War II, the French mounted an extremely effective underground resistance against the German Occupation forces despite the fact that the Gestapo and SS killed tens of thousands of French civilians in reprisal.

In the United States, many advocate increasing the severity of punishment to reduce crime. As long as less than 2% of the crimes committed result in imprisonment, and sentences are typically imposed months or years after the offense, simply increasing sentences will have little impact.

But what of the developing child? How well does the conditioned anticipation of punishment account for socialization? Behaviorists, particular the so-called "radical behaviorists," concentrate on finding fundamental laws governing the relationship between observable events such as stimuli and responses, laws that apply to all organisms and which should not depend on intervening variables or hypothetical constructs such as "traits" or "cognitions" (Skinner, 1971). Since punishment accounts for avoidance behavior in rats and pigeons as well as people, it is tempting to use it, coupled with rewards for appropriate behavior, as a sufficient explanation for human ethical judgment.

How adequate is this explanation? Let us return to Dollard et al.'s (1939) example of aggressive behavior. Over the years, I have developed and refined a theoretical framework for the analysis of aggressive behavior in which I balance the factors favoring an aggressive response against those that oppose it (E. I. Megargee, 1982, 1993). If the factors opposing it are stronger, then that response is blocked, but if the motivating factors are stronger, then that response is possible.

The motivating factors include anger ("intrinsic instigation") and the fact that aggression may be a means to some end ("extrinsic instigation"). (As Al Capone once noted, "You can get much farther with a kind word and a gun than you can with a kind word alone" [Peter, 1977, p. 141].) In addition, I include habit strength, which comes from having been rewarded for aggressive behavior in the past. Balanced against the elements which increase the likelihood of an aggressive response are those that inhibit aggression, both internal (conscience) and external (the presence of parent or a policeman).

Dollard et al. (1939) argued that punishment for aggressive behavior creates anxiety about performing forbidden acts that foster internal inhibitions. As we have noted, as long as punishment is swift and certain it can be effective, but few parents are all-knowing or ever-present. Sometimes the child's misbehavior may be punished, but other times not. In the absence of punishment, aggression will be rewarded, so gradually its habit strength increases. Moreover, since it was learned via partial reinforcement, the aggressive behavior will be very resistant to extinction.

The most likely outcome is a discrimination will be learned rather than a moral absolute; for example, only hit your sibling when your mother is not looking. From this standpoint, it seems unlikely that externally imposed rewards and punishments are sufficient to account for our elaborate rules regulating the expression of aggression, much less our overall moral codes.

 b. Social Learning. Unlike radical behaviorists, social learning theorists are willing to treat people as being different from other animals (Feshbach & Weiner, 1986). While not denying the importance of direct rewards and punishments, Bandura (1969, p. 118) argued that "virtually all learning phenomena resulting from direct experience can occur on a vicarious basis through observation of other persons' behaviors and its consequences to them." In kindergarten, if the first child to throw a spitball was severely disciplined, the rest of his classmates quickly learned to inhibit this behavior—at least when the teacher was looking.

 Even modeling and observational learning do not account for the broad range of rules and prohibitions that we acquire. *Cognitive* social learning theory goes beyond personal experience and observation and emphasizes the importance of stating the rules and stipulating the behaviors that will be rewarded or punished (Feshbach & Weiner, 1986). Moreover, cognitive social learning theorists stipulate that the child is not dependent on externally imposed rewards and punishments. Once they have incorporated values, they can and do reward themselves when they behave appropriately (Bandura, 1977) or feel badly when they do wrong or fail to live up to expectations (Feshbach & Weiner, 1986, p. 149f). This leads us to our next question: Why is it that people adopt these value systems and try to live by them?

2. Acquiring Controls and Introjecting Values

Given the fact that it is impossible to have an external reinforcer watching our every move, it is essential that we develop internal systems of control. But why is it that people come to reward themselves for doing well ("self-efficacy" in Bandura's [1977] terminology), or punish themselves for doing wrong ("guilt" in the jargon of both clergymen and psychologists).

 This question has intrigued theologians and philosophers for centuries. Some religions maintain that some form of direct intervention by the deity is responsible for people developing consciences. Philosophers such as Thomas Hobbes, David Hume, John Locke, and Jean Rousseau developed the theory of the "social contract" in which people agreed to trade the individual freedoms they enjoyed under anarchy for the security of an organized and lawful society.

 Psychologists tend to ascribe the development of values and morality to events that take place within the family in early childhood which make children want to please their parents. However, their specific explanations differ.

 a. Behaviorist Explanations. Behaviorists in the Watsonian tradition attributed children's identification with their parents to classical conditioning. While the infant is suckling, the mother's presence becomes associated with the reduction of hunger and with all sorts of pleasurable sensations. Through conditioning, she becomes a "secondary reinforcer" whose presence and approval are sought in their own right. To gain this reinforcement, the child learns to please her and live up to her expectations, and, presumably to a lesser extent, those of the father. Even when the children have grown to adulthood and become parents themselves, they may still evaluate their behavior according to whether it measures up to their mothers' values.

b. Social Learning Theory. Social learning theorists go beyond simple operant conditioning to explain the acquisition of complex behavior patterns (Bandura, 1977; Mischel & Mischel, 1976). They make a distinction between the acquisition and the performance of behavior.

Many habits are first acquired by imitating models. Modeling requires a relationship between the child and the figure being imitated, although that relationship may exist only in the mind of the imitator. Teachers, peers, television characters, athletes, and literary or religious figures may serve as examples, but in early childhood, the parents are usually the primary models. Through imitation, very complex patterns of behavior can be rapidly acquired, and no direct reinforcement is regarded as necessary (Feshbach & Weiner, 1986, p. 147). This contrasts with the slow shaping of behavior through direct rewards and punishments that behavior theory says is required.

As we have noted, social learning is facilitated by verbal processes, explicit rules, and explanations of contingencies. Once a behavior pattern is acquired and the child performs it, it must be reinforced if it is to be maintained. The agents of acculturation, who may or may not be the original models, must reward the behavior pattern, or the child must find it intrinsically satisfying and enjoyable (Feshbach & Weiner, 1986).

The social learning explanation is better at explaining how we learn "positive" behaviors than it is at accounting for inhibitions and restraints. It is easier to imitate something that is done than something that is not. Still, there are forceful models for inhibitions and controls; Martin Luther King became an international hero and exemplar for thousands by advocating and exemplifying self-control and nonviolence in the face of the most extreme provocation.

c. Psychoanalytic theory. Psychoanalytic theory preceded social learning theory by a half century, so Freud and his followers did not have the advantage of drawing on as rich a base of empirical research. Indeed, most of their observations were made on men and women who had been raised in Europe during the sexually repressed Victorian period and who were seeking treatment for serious neuroses. Many manifested serious sexual conflicts dating back to early childhood. Today, it seems likely that many had been abused.

As clinicians treating patients, Freud and other psychoanalysts felt no need to confine their theories to externally observable behavior. Instead their primary focus was on intrapsychic events as inferred from the verbal reports of their patients during treatment. From this rather skewed sample, Freud formulated a comprehensive theory of personality that has shown amazing vitality over the decades.

More than other approaches, psychoanalytic theory recognizes that stressful approach/avoidance conflicts are necessarily involved in moral and ethical decisions, clashes between what we want to do and what we should do, or, in analytic jargon, between the demands of the id, which is concerned only with hedonism and operates according to the pleasure principle, and "the strict super-ego, which lays down definite standards for . . . conduct and, which, if those standards are not obeyed, punishes it with tense feelings of inferiority and of guilt" (Freud, 1933/1965, p. 78).

According to Freud's formulation of the structure of personality, an aspect not typically included in other approaches, this rivalry is mediated by the ego, which operates according to the reality principle. As Freud wrote, "The poor ego . . . serves three severe masters and does what it can to bring their claims and demands into harmony with one another. These claims are always divergent and often seem incompatible. No wonder the ego fails so often in its task. Its three tyrannical masters are the external world, the super-ego, and the id" (1933/1965, p. 77).

At age three or four, during the "phallic stage" of development, when children are focused on their genitals as a source of excitement and stimulation, they develop a yearning for an exclusive relationship with their opposite sex parent and are consumed with jealousy of the same sex parent who demands so much of the other parent's time and attention. These feelings are frightening in their intensity and in their implications.

During the "Oedipal conflict," a boy fears his presumably omnipotent father will discover the son's incestuous yearning for his mother and castrate him to take revenge and prevent their union. This fear is no doubt exacerbated by the sight of little girls, whose external organs indicate that something of this nature must have taken place (Munroe, 1955). Repressing his desire for the mother, the boy identifies with his father, vicariously obtaining satisfaction by striving to be like him in every possible way. This includes introjecting his values, thereby creating the super-ego (Munroe, 1955).

Girls undergoing the "Electra complex" likewise repress their desire for the father and come to identify with the mother. This explains why boys and girls develop gender-specific values. Since girls had nothing to fear from castration, Freud asserted that identification and super-ego formation are never quite complete in women, a notion which Helen Bee (1985, p. 326) castigates as "totally unsupported by later research . . . "

This introjection of values does not take place in a vacuum. As Freud wrote, in a passage that could easily have been written by a contemporary social learning theorist, "The child is brought up to a knowledge of his social duties by a system of loving rewards and punishments, he is taught that his security in life depends on his parents (and afterwards other people) loving him and on their being able to believe that he loves them" (1933/1965, p. 164).

Quite apart from his hypotheses regarding the structure of personality, Freud is one of the few personality theorists who specifically acknowledged the important role religion can play in human behavior in general and in fostering and maintaining internal inhibitions in particular. Although he himself maintained that "religion is an illusion" (Beck, 1980, p. 679), Freud noted that people transfer their familial relations and values "unaltered into their religion. Their parents' prohibitions and demands persists within them as a moral conscience. With the help of this same system of rewards and punishments, God rules the world of men" (1933/1965, p. 164).

Unlike Freud, contemporary American psychology virtually ignores the influence of religion on behavior. Surveying the indices of the 19 current introductory psychology texts that happen to be on my shelves, I found only 2 had any entry for "religion"; one mentioned religion as a coping response on one page and the other discussed religious conversions. Not one mentioned religion as a factor influencing values or ethical decision making. Nevertheless, for many people religious beliefs and practices play an important role in fostering ethical behavior, and a religious conversion or loss of faith can greatly alter a person's values.

3. Some Factors Influencing the Development of Inhibitions

Although theorists disagree on how we become socialized and learn to control our behavior, there is general agreement in psychology and other disciplines on the environmental conditions that are most apt to foster a stable sense of values and the ability to regulate one's behavior in accordance with those values.

A warm nurturing environment in which the children form a close bond of affection and respect with their caregivers combined with fair, consistent discipline is most conducive to developing internal controls. The more the agents of socialization, first the parents, and later the neighborhood, the church, and the school, share and enforce a strong common set of values, and the more they live up to and consistently exemplify these principles in their everyday lives, the more likely it is that the children will incorporate them (Hogan, 1973; Hogan, Johnson, & Emler, 1978; W. McCord & J. McCord, 1959; Wilson & Herrnstein, 1985).

On the other hand, as we shall see, parental absence and disharmony, inconsistency, rejection, abuse, and poor role models are associated with problems in developing values and controlling behavior (S. Glueck & E. Glueck, 1950; W. McCord & J. McCord, 1959; E. I. Megargee, Parker, & Levine, 1971; Miller, 1958; Nye, 1958; Rosenquist & Megargee, 1969; Wilson & Herrnstein, 1985).

4. Other Sources of Inhibitions

In this section we have been concentrating on how we develop the sorts of internal inhibitions that fit our definition. To gain proper perspective, it should be noted that some of the factors that were excluded from this strict definition nevertheless serve an inhibitory function.

One is the prospect of bad things happening as a result of some action. A person who has no moral scruples against some illegal act such as insider trading might be deterred by the prospect of a prison term (Wilson & Herrnstein, 1985). Similarly, as Dollard et al. (1939) noted, the person may decide not to act if it seemed likely that the scheme would fail in its objective or that the act might bring pain or disgrace to loved ones.

These latter considerations involve calculating the risk or the odds that something bad will happen. As we have noted, the certainty of punishment has long been a major factor in deterrence theory. Recently Don and Steve Gottfredson have been developing the parallel notion of "stakes," arguing that the amount one has to lose in terms of reputation, property, and other considerations should also be included in the equation.

Recapping the psychological explanations for the development of internal controls and inhibitions, it is evident that there are many theories and much relevant information, but few definitive data. It is possible to describe the conditions favorable to and the stages of moral development, but the specific mechanisms are largely a matter for conjecture. Interestingly enough, many hypotheses about the "psychological" factors that foster the development of values were based on observations of people who were conspicuous for their lack of controls or restraint. We will turn now to a discussion of factors that inhibit the development of values and inhibitions and which may be used to diminish or overcome those ethical principles that have been acquired.

V. OVERCOMING INHIBITIONS

Sometimes preschool children take time off from the important developmental tasks of learning values and resolving their Oedipal conflicts to build towers with wooden blocks or to construct castles of sand. Doing so they may learn another of life's lessons—it is much easier to tear down a structure than it is to build it. So, too, with ethical codes.

Human nature is such that we are much more interested in moral lapses than moral triumphs. Examine the offerings in your television viewing guide or the titles in the VCR rental store. How many deal with the lives of saints and how many with sinners? Before you blame the low taste of the "mass audience," conduct a similar survey on your bookshelf and see what *you* selected.

If the titles dealing with human failings prevail, do not be distressed. It has always been thus. While you are surveying your bookshelf, take down the Old Testament and turn to the second and third chapters of *Genesis*. You will find that only 3 verses are used to describe Adam and Eve's life together in the Garden of Eden, but 24 verses are devoted to their temptation and fall from grace.

Social scientists are no exception; we are more likely to deal with the Cain's of this world than the Abel's. Anthropologists are especially interested in those members of the tribe that somehow fail to share its cultural values, sociologists have an entire subarea devoted to the study of "social deviance," and criminology is a discipline unto itself. The number of psychologist who deal with abnormal or deviant behavior vastly exceeds the number who focus on healthy functioning.

As we noted above, many of our theories about the origins of inhibitions stemmed from studies of people whose behavior is characterized by a lack of restraints. In general, the factors that are associated with a failure to develop adequate controls are the obverse of those conducive to positive socialization. Unfortunately it appears there are many more ways to diminish or overcome inhibitions than there are to foster them.

A. Physiological Mechanisms

As we noted earlier, all behavior is physiologically mediated. Thus whether we regard internal prohibitions and controls as resulting from the unfolding of an innate genetic pattern or as resulting from conditioning or learning, physiological factors must have an impact.

1. Genetic Mechanisms

In the previous section, we noted that personality researchers have obtained data that are consistent with the hypothesis that individual differences in controls and restraints are at least partially determined by heredity. Authorities differ regarding the mechanisms. Eysenck (1964, 1981) maintained that these genetic differences are mediated through actual differences in brain physiology, whereas Buss and Plomin (1984) suggested what is inherited are temperamental differences that predispose people toward being more or less restrained (Hogan, 1986).

If Eysenck's view is correct, then we might infer that factors which influence the central nervous system, as described further on, might overcome the innate pattern. On the other hand, if it is predispositions that are innate, then experiential factors become more important in determining whether or not these predispositions are realized.

2. Central Nervous System

Internal controls as we have defined them depend on the proper functioning of the brain. In order to make an ethical decision, I must first examine a proposed course of action and decide whether to classify it as "right" or "wrong" according to my unique set of values; if it is "wrong," then I must decide whether or not I will succumb to the temptation anyway. Recall the existential crisis of the dieter confronted by the chocolate mousse.

Except for specific inhibitory centers in the hypothalamus that govern consummatory behavior and, possibly, certain types of aggressive behavior, moral constraints and inhibitions seem to be cortical functions. It is, of course, the cerebral cortex that is the most recently evolved area of the human brain and the area associated with what we regard as "higher" functioning.

As we shall soon see, all sorts of things can go wrong with the central nervous system in general and the cortex in particular. The specific effects vary with the nature and the location of the damage, but a safe rule of thumb is that while brain damage may impair internal inhibitions, it virtually never augments them. Indeed, impulsive behavior and diminished ethical sensitivity are often among the first behavioral symptoms of cortical malfunctioning.

a. Traumas, Tumors, and Vascular Disorders.   Although it is encased in the skull, the brain is subject to injury from exogenous causes such as blows to the head or gunshot wounds. From within, cerebral vascular infarctions, aneurysms, arteriovenous malformations, and tumors can all create lesions.

Diffuse generalized cortical damage can be associated with a general lessening of ethical sensitivity, increased irritability, impulsive behavior, and impaired judgment. The effects of more focal lesions, such as those caused by tumors, wounds, and strokes, depend on the area that is damaged. Temporal lobe tumors and hypothalamic lesions are sometimes associated with aggressive acting out.

b. Disease and Infection.   A number of diseases can diminish cortical functioning. These include disorders which apparently have a genetic basis, such as Alzheimer's disease, Pick's disease, and the senile psychoses, as well as infectious diseases such as encephalitis and syphilis. Memory loss is the primary characteristics of the former group, but with both the innate and the infectious disorders, cortical impairment can be accompanied by a loss of ethical sensitivity and moral constraints. This may stem in part from cognitive impairment, since knowing the difference between right and wrong is a cognitive function. But it also seems clear that there is a reduced capacity to control one's behavior.

c. Chemical Substances.   Earlier, we noted that certain psychotropic medications may be prescribed to assist neuropsychiatric patients in controlling their behavior. Such substances can be remarkably effective; without them the widespread deinstitutionalization of the mentally ill would not have been possible. However, when these medications are withdrawn, the ability of these patients to control their behavior may decrease.

Other drugs, most notably alcohol, act to diminish inhibitions. Indeed, this is one reason they are so widely used. As Ogden Nash wrote, "Candy is dandy, but liquor is quicker."

3. Endocrinological System

The hormones secreted by the endocrinological system can have powerful effects on behavior. When the sympathetic portion of the autonomic nervous system is aroused, adrenalin is released and the body is prepared for action. The effect is similar to bringing a military unit to a full state of combat readiness, with weapons loaded and locked, safeties off, and senses alert for the first sign of enemy action. Given such a state of activation, people are prepared to respond instantaneously, and the influence of internal inhibitions is minimized.

Hormones secreted by the gonads play an important role in stimulating sexual desire or libido, especially in males. The Middle Eastern potentates who had eunuchs guard their harems may not have been endocrinologists, but they understood the effects of castration. Younger readers are probably well aware of how sexual arousal can overcome moral prohibitions; older readers can probably remember.

Testosterone also stimulates aggressive behavior and dominance in a variety of species. Along with thyroxine and progesterone, excessive testosterone can cause irritability. The autonomic nervous system and the endocrinological system are complexly intertwined with environmental and personality factors; the point to remember is that these factors are among those that can mitigate internal inhibitions against various forms of behavior.

4. Other Physiological Factors

A number of other physiological factors have been associated with diminished inhibitions. Some have speculated that psychopathy, which is characterized by a severely underdeveloped set of inhibitions, may have a physiological basis. Eysenck (1964) speculated that psychopaths have an innate deficit in their ability to be conditioned or to learn from their mistakes so that punishment is relatively ineffective. J. McCord and W. McCord (1964) speculated that brain damage, possibly to the hypothalamus, in combination with parental rejection might be responsible. Quay (1965, p. 181) suggested that perhaps "basal reactivity to stimulation is lowered so that more sensory input is needed to produce efficient and subjectively pleasurable cortical functioning." Because of this presumably innate deficit, the psychopath is driven to seeking additional sensory stimulation.

We should also note that physical illness can reduce external inhibitions. A person who has a terminal illness may feel that he or she has "nothing to lose" and engage in behavior that they would not otherwise have allowed themselves. This does not necessarily mean that they will do something antisocial or reprehensible. For example, one hardworking individual who had never allowed himself to take a vacation put work aside and went on a cruise when he learned he was suffering from an untreatable life-threatening illness.

B. Psychological Factors

Turning from the many physical factors than can diminish inhibitions, we will find that there is an even more varied array of "psychological" mechanisms. Before anthropologists, sociologists, psychiatrists, or theologians take umbrage, let me hasten to stipulate that the term "psychological" is being used in its broadest sense to mean "nonphysiological." As we shall see, theorists from a variety of disciplines have contributed a heterogeneous array of explanations.

Surveying these notions, it appears that by and large theorists have been addressing two distinct issues. The first is why some people in every society appear to have values that differ from that society's norms. The second is more concerned with determining why so many of us do not live up to our respective codes of values. We shall discuss each issue in turn.

1. Problems in Value Development

Almost everybody who has a reasonably adequate central nervous system develops some code of values. Whether or not this code is adequate is, in the truest sense of the word, a value judgment. Nevertheless, in virtually every society throughout history there have been some individuals whose values were deemed inadequate by their fellow citizens. How can this come about?

a. Deficient Values.   In general, the factors associated with defective value development are the obverse of those conducive to good socialization. The most serious deficiencies are likely to be observed in children reared in situations which prevented basic bonding, the resolution of the first developmental crisis described by Erik Erikson (1950) as "trust vs. mistrust." This might occur, for example, in children growing up under conditions of extreme deprivation such as the famine-ravaged areas of the Sahara or the war-torn sections of Lebanon. Children raised in totally impersonal institutions or in homes characterized by severe rejection and abuse might also be included, but probably to a somewhat lesser extent.

Studying the development of juvenile delinquency some years ago, Sheldon and Eleanor Glueck (1950) noted that a lack of cohesiveness and nurturance in the parental home was associated with delinquency, a finding that has oft been repeated in a variety of cultures (W. McCord & J. McCord, 1959; Rosenquist & Megargee, 1969; Wilson & Herrnstein, 1985). Coupled with this was inappropriate discipline; that is, discipline that is either lax or excessive, inconsistent or unfair. Obviously, if chastisement or punishment helps condition values, erratic schedules of negative reinforcement will interfere with such learning.

At a later age, familial situations that interfere with the process of identification and introjection are detrimental to value formation. In broken homes, the process of identification might be subverted by parental absence or by the efforts of one parent to diminish the other in the child's estimation (Bee, 1985, p. 332f).

Writing from a psychoanalytic perspective, Adelaide Johnson (1949) noted that some apparently well-socialized parents might obtain unconscious gratification from their children's acting out. In a family the writer was seeing in therapy, the father, who was overtly outraged over his son's auto thefts, was noted to whisper, "Gee that took real guts," when his son described the high-speed police chase that had ensued. Of course the father vehemently denied his *sotto voce* remark. Such dual messages, according to Johnson (1949), lead to what she termed "superego lacunae."

Previously we noted that value development is abetted by growing up in a milieu in which all the agents of socialization work together to foster a consistent set of values. Obviously, a situation in which this is not the case, in which the child is exposed to differing values or in which adults say one thing and do another, is less conducive to good moral development. These conditions may well yield values that differ from those prescribed by the larger society. We shall now turn to a discussion of such deviance.

b. Deviant Values. We often think of people who engage in socially reprehensible behavior as being immoral or amoral. The problem, however, may not be inadequate values but values that differ from those of the society at large or from the laws of that society. Sociologists interested in deviance have been especially interested in this phenomenon and have proposed a number of ways that it might come about.

Within a heterogeneous country like the United States, we will find many subgroups and subcultures with somewhat differing views of what constitutes acceptable and unacceptable behavior. It is not surprising that cultural conflict was one of the first explanations offered for deviant values (Sellin, 1938). While these subcultural gaps were most evident in the United States when immigration was at its peak, mass means of communication appear to have lessened the disparities somewhat (Rosenquist & Megargee, 1969; Velez-Diaz & Megargee, 1971). In Israel, however, some scholars have attributed deviant behavior to cultural conflicts between European and Sephardic immigrants (Shoham, 1962).

A number of sociologists have pointed to "anomie" or normlessness as a factor in producing deviant values. Robert Merton (1938, 1957) noted that the Horatio Alger myth requires that everyone, no matter what his or her prospects, should strive for status and material success. However, we are also supposed to be honest and upright. Many people may have to choose between these conflicting values, because, given their circumstances and abilities, there is no realistic way for them to do both. As Cloward and Ohlin (1960, p. 86) described it, "Faced with limitations on legitimate avenues of access of these goals, and unable to revise their aspirations downward, they experience intense frustration; the exploration of nonconformist alternatives may be the result."

This "differential opportunity" or "strain" theory dovetails neatly with Earnest Sutherland's (1939) "differential association" theory which emphasizes the influence of deviant role models. In an urban ghetto, the role models for success are rarely people who made it from the streets to the corporate boardrooms; instead it is the pimps and pushers with their gold chains and expensive cars who are conspicuous. If, during this period of exploring "nonconformist alternatives," youths are recruited by a gang (Salisbury, 1959) or have the opportunity to serve as runners for neighborhood crack dealers, they may be inducted into a very lucrative life of crime while still very young and become socialized with street values which are antithetical to the moral codes of the larger society.

Deviant subcultures are not only found in the streets and ghettos; they also exist at the upper end of the financial and political ladder (Clinard & Quinney, 1973; Vold, 1958; Vold & Bernard, 1986). Faced with a strain between ethical and legal restrictions and a get-rich-quick mentality, some Wall Street brokers recently adopted a deviant set of values and made money the truly old fashioned way—they stole it.

A strain between ends and means can occur in the political arena as well. Of those convicted of wrongdoing in connection with the Watergate break-in and the Iran–Contra affair, both G. Gordon Liddy and Oliver North appeared to have strong, well-developed, but deviant value systems which dictated that they should engage in illegal behavior to accomplish goals that they felt were more important than abiding by the law.

Although other theorists have also discussed deviant subcultures and culture conflict, let us turn to the interactionist or labeling perspective as an explanation for the development of deviant values. Becker (1964), Garfinkel (1956), Lemert (1967), and other interactionists maintained that society creates social deviance by formulating rules and applying sanctions to people who break them, thereby labeling them as deviants.

According to Garfinkel (1956), one consequence of a "degradation ceremony" such as suspension from school, a criminal conviction, or a commitment to a mental hospital is that the stigmatized individual may accept the label and adopt deviant values consistent with this new identity. Thus a person who is regarded as being "immoral," "crazy," or "bad" in some respect may start associating with other people who are similarly labeled and emulating their behavior. Of course this convinces the labelers of the correctness of their initial appraisal, and additional stigmatization may be applied that solidifies the deviant self-concept.

Although early childhood is when our basic values are formed, people continue to learn and to develop throughout their lives. Circumstances and reinforcement schedules may change, so the values we learned as a child may not equip us for the challenges we face as adults. A youthful idealist may find that the Golden Rule does not work well in the competitive world of business and that Charles Dickens was nearer to the mark when he wrote, "Do other men for they would do you. That is the true business precept" (Beck, 1980, p. 547). Military training is designed in part to help personnel overcome the taboo against killing other humans. Psychotherapy may be required to help adults overcome strong sexual inhibitions ingrained into them as children.

2. *Overcoming Controls*

It is virtually impossible for you to reach adulthood without having acquired a code of values. It may not agree with everyone else's code of values, and it may not even agree with *anyone* else's code, but it is yours and you will usually try, with greater or lesser success, to abide by it. Whether you succeed depends on your ability to control your behavior.

Internal controls operate only when we are tempted to do something that is contrary to our code of values. If there was no temptation, there would be no need for restraint.

Scruples get us involved in internal conflicts. These conflicts can be stressful and occasionally anxiety provoking. They also have the unfortunate effect of either preventing us from doing things we would like to do, like eating the chocolate mousse when we are dieting, or making us feel guilty if we do succumb. Given these circumstances, it is not surprising that most of us have devised ingenious ways of overcoming our moral inhibitions.

a. Rationalization. Rationalization can be used to justify acts and thereby circumvent the injunctions against them. Rationalizations are especially effective in situations in which the moral boundaries are fuzzy.

As we have noted, we must first categorize an act as belonging to that class of acts we regard as "wrong" before moral prohibitions come into play. In the current policy debates over capital punishment and abortion, all the participants agree that murder is wrong. The problem is that some classify executions and/or abortions as murder and others do not.

Rationalization can be used to convince us that an act that appears to be wrong actually is not. This makes it permissible. For example, most politicians probably would agree that it is wrong for public officials to accept bribes. But some legislators might reason that if they have already decided to vote for a piece of legislation it does no harm to accept a contribution from a contractor who will benefit from the project. Indeed, the official might reason that turning down the contribution would be tantamount to denying contractors their rights to participate in the political process. Why, it might even be contrary to the First Amendment!

One common form of rationalization is to concede the general principle, but to classify the present case as an exception to the general rule. The key word "but" is a good sign of this sort of rationalization: "I know she said 'no,' *but* she really didn't mean it"; "Sure, dealing drugs is bad, *but* if I don't sell them, someone else will and they might sell my customers bad stuff." As the old country preacher stated, "A lot of sinners slide into Hell on their 'buts.' "

b. Value Conflict. When two or more values conflict, they tend to neutralize one another (Sykes & Matza, 1957). If the values are not deeply held or evenly balanced, this does not pose a great conflict. Indeed we may be able to use this conflict to allow us to do what we want without feeling guilty. (After all, if the forbidden behavior was not fun, we would not be tempted in the first place.)

People can also use value conflicts to manipulate others into abandoning their scruples. Thus, a dieter who might refrain from ordering a piece of cake at a restaurant may acquiesce at a wedding if the bride and groom insist that they will be offended by a refusal. Maintaining their friendship seems more important than avoiding calories. Of course, the more one wants to do the forbidden act, the more effective value conflicts are in overcoming scruples.

The basic issue in many values conflicts is whether the end justifies the means. Politicians may feel that they need to get elected for the good of the country, even if it requires negative campaigning. The principles in the Iran–Contra affair felt that maintaining the security of their convert operation justified lying to Congress.

Hogan's (1970, 1973) theory of moral behavior postulates an ethical continuum from considerations of "personal conscience" to "social responsibility" that can dictate different solutions to certain ethical dilemmas such as whether one should do something one regards as personally wrong to benefit the overall social group. Such a moral dilemma is at the heart of Shakespeare's tragedy *Julius Caesar* in which the cunning Cassius used Brutus' patriotism to turn him against Caesar. After the assassination, an agonized Brutus attributed his participation to value conflict, explaining, "Not that I loved Caesar less, but that I loved Rome more" (III,ii,22). As Antony noted, "Brutus is an honorable man; So are they all, all honorable men" (III,ii,88).

When the competing values involve deeply held convictions, we are placed in a double approach–avoidance conflict, the type that creates the most stress and anxiety. Sometimes such conflict is resolved by attempting a compromise. Suppose that a young man's buddies ask his help in robbing a store. Which is worse, disloyalty or stealing? He may offer to help by being the lookout or driving the get-away car but not actually going into the store.

c. Suspension of Individual Values.   In the wake of World War II, a number of social psychologists began investigating how the Holocaust could occur. Studies by Asch (1956) on conformity and Milgram (1974) on obedience to authority showed that people will often suspend their individual values and instead let others dictate their behavior, even when they feel it is wrong. Similarly, studies of bystander intervention by Darley and Latane (1968) demonstrated that people who would be inclined to assist someone in distress refrain from doing so when there are other people present who are not helping.

Suspension of individual values is particularly strong in a group setting. Studies of group decision making have demonstrated that the decisions made by groups are apt to be riskier or more extreme than the decisions made by the individual participants. Janis' (1972) research on the phenomenon he dubbed "groupthink" following the Bay of Pigs invasion showed that, to maintain a consensus, a group of people will agree with decisions that they individually think are incorrect and/ or morally wrong.

Anonymity assists in this deindividuation. One of the first major steps in curbing the power of the Ku Klux Klan in the South was the passage of laws forbidding people to wear masks in public. From Kent, Ohio, to Beijing, China, it is easier to open fire on unarmed students if you are an anonymous soldier who is "following orders" rather than an individual dressed in civilian clothes acting on your own.

d. Dehumanization of the Victim.   The more empathy we have for someone, the more difficult it is for us to hurt or injure them, physically or emotionally. Our appreciation of that person's humanity serves to activate our internal inhibitions against doing wrong to our fellows.

By the same token, anything that dehumanizes a potential victim makes it easier for us to suspend these values. Oddly, it seems less reprehensible for someone to give an order that may result in the deaths of thousands of strangers in a far away land than it is for that person to strangle a single individual. Some kidnapped hostages have reported that their captors kept them in tents or covered their heads with bags to prevent the development of human ties that might inhibit the captors from killing their victims.

Racial, religious, social class, and gender differences increase the emotional distance between people and decrease their inhibitions against harming one another. The ordinary German was better able to tolerate the Holocaust as long as it was happening to the Jews, the Gypsies, and the mentally defective, just as the ordinary American was less concerned about AIDS when it appeared to be a disease confined to homosexuals and drug addicts. In preparation for combat, it is a standard tactic to tell the troops how different and reprehensible the enemy forces are in order to diminish inhibitions that might hinder their effectiveness.

e. Psychopathology.   Functional as well as organic mental disorders can also decrease inhibitions and controls. Daniel M'Naghten's inhibitions against shooting Sir Robert Peel were overcome by his paranoid delusion that Peel was persecuting him. Actually M'Naghten shot the wrong man, but his belief that he was acting in self-defense led to his acquittal and the formation of the M'Naghten test of legal sanity in 1843.

Other disorders can also lead to a diminution of inhibitions. A profoundly depressed person may feel there is nothing to live for so that ordinary inhibitions are ineffective. Extreme guilt may lead to self-punitive or suicidal behavior that would otherwise be inhibited. In a psychogenic fugue or multiple personality, a person may act out various repressed behavior patterns without being aware of doing so.

Although certain disorders can lead to diminished controls, it would be an error to equate mental disorders with uncontrolled and possibly dangerous behavior. A catatonic stupor, for example, is perhaps the ultimate in inhibited behavior.

VI. Methodological Problems

In the preceding pages we reviewed a diverse broad array of theories regarding the origins of internal inhibitions and how such inhibitions may be overcome. As scientists, most psychologists would prefer to test divergent theories empirically. Unfortunately, a number of conceptual, ethical, and methodological problems make it difficult to conduct definitive experiments on controls and inhibitions.

A. Acquisition of Values

Testing differing theories on the acquisition of values presents us with our most difficult challenge. Children obviously cannot be randomly assigned to various patterns of child rearing to test the effects of various disciplinary practices or to different families to determine the effects of single-parent homes. Although some animal experiments, such as Harlow's (1971) studies of monkeys reared by wire mesh surrogate mothers, are relevant to issues in child development, by and large infrahuman subjects are not suitable for research on the development of values.

In the absence of experimentation, we have to resort to correlational methods, naturalistic observations, and "experiments of nature." Since such studies are inevitably confounded, we must adopt a variety of strategies and use many different subject populations in the hope that the variables that confound one study will be absent in the next. Since values are culture specific, cross cultural research is vitally important. Gradually over time, a core of reliable associations should emerge.

As indicated earlier, there is general agreement that a warm, stable family setting is most conducive to developing values and controls, at least in our culture. Oddly enough, much of this consensus has come about through research on people who appear to have deficient values and/or inadequate controls, namely, juvenile delinquents and adult criminals. When examined more closely, even these studies show some cultural specificity. Comparing the family patterns associated with delinquency in three different cultures, Rosenquist and E. I. Megargee (1969) noted differences in the effects of the father–son relationship in Mexican, Mexican-American, and Anglo-American families.

More research is needed on the antecedents of positive socialization in a variety of cultures. While longitudinal research is desirable, other approaches can also be used. By identifying people differing in socialization, we can test hypotheses about their upbringing and antecedents. For example, we found that middle class college students who differed in socialization, as measured by the Socialization scale of the California Psychological Inventory (Gough, 1969), came, as predicted, from families that differed significantly in stability and cohesiveness (E. I. Megargee et al., 1971). But would the stability of the nuclear family be as important in a culture that relied on communal child rearing? This is an empirical question that needs to be answered before we overgeneralize from our own society.

One of the bright spots in the area of acquisition of values has been the research on moral development by psychologists such as Piaget, Selman, and Kohlberg. Their studies have shown that children in Western countries progress through a series of distinct stages in their moral judgments.

Are these stages universal or specific to Western culture? One test of moral judgment (Kohlberg, 1981) creates hypothetical ethical dilemmas by juxtaposing carefully chosen antithetical values. In one oft-cited example, the respondent is asked to decide whether "Heinz" was right or wrong when he stole an exorbitantly priced medicine he could not afford to purchase in order to save his dying wife. Western children "progress" from answering that Heinz was wrong because he broke the law to responding that human values supersede property values or laws. But is this sequence culturally universal? What would be found in a country such as North Korea in which positive socialization consisted of unquestioning obedience to the state and loyalty to the late Marshall Kim Il Sung, known and revered as the "Great Leader"?

As we noted, the physiological foundations for socialization and restraints remain largely unexplored. Perhaps the paradigms devised by developmental psychologists could be used to investigate the role of the central nervous system by applying them to people with various types of CNS impairment or developmental disabilities.

Comparative anthropological and ethnographic studies including data on child-rearing patterns and values can be used to help test the generality of our observations. Social histories and treatises on child rearing from various eras and cultures also provide a useful perspective on our ethnocentric assumptions. Fortunately data collection is easy and inexpensive, involving only a trip to the library, with, perhaps, a stop at the Anthropology Department for a quick consult. Aries and Duby's histories of private life in ancient Rome, Byzantium, and medieval Europe (1987–1988) and Benedict's (1934) and Mead's (1961, 1975) anthropological observations are good starting points.

As we have noted, studies of people with apparently deficient socialization have suggested that certain patterns of living and early life experiences are crucial to moral development. These hypotheses can be partly tested by prospective studies in which people who do and do not have these deficits are identified, *predictions are made,* and then the subjects are followed up over time to determine whether the predicted patterns emerge. This approach, which is much more powerful than the more common retrospective design, can be used to explore the sequelae of such factors as parental absence due to death or dissension, of being exposed at an early age to differing sets of values and mores, and even the long-term effects of severe deprivation and abuse.

B. Exercising Control or Restraint

It is considerably easier to conduct empirical studies, especially experiments, on when and whether people choose to behave according to their values than it is on how their values developed. Indeed, researchers in a variety of allied areas have already accumulated a number of relevant empirical findings even though they were primarily interested in studying different phenomena. As we have noted, social psychologists interested in conformity, obedience to authority, group decision making, and bystander intervention have contributed considerable information on those situations in which people do and do not behave in accordance with their values. Similarly, clinical psychologists studying the effects of alcohol on aggression and other social behaviors have provided us with relevant findings and, perhaps more important, research designs that can be used to study directly the effects of alcohol and other substances on controls and restraints.

Still, there are numerous problems. First and foremost is the problem we cited at the beginning of this chapter, namely, the fact that inhibitions and controls are negative concepts that must be defined by exclusion. How can one be certain that inhibitions prevented certain expected behaviors from occurring? Researchers may have to induce the appropriate motivational state at the outset of the experiment, include a manipulation check to make sure the procedure was effective, and go through a variety of contortions to make sure that various alternative explanations for restrained behavior are eliminated.

Fortunately, these sorts of dilemmas typically involve approach–avoidance conflicts and there may be verbal utterances and other indications of the existential struggles that are taking place. ("Oh, it looks so good but I really shouldn't. Are you positive that the Black Forest tort doesn't have any calories?") Similarly, long response latencies, vacillation, and signs of anxiety or guilt may help the observer to infer that inhibitions or constraints are operating.

Problems in studying controls and restraints are compounded by the fact that many taboos are very specific with respect to situations and targets. The classic research by Hartshorne and May (1928), for example, found that children cheat in some situations but not in others. A man that would never dream of hitting his mother might beat his wife, but only in private after he has been drinking. Hogan's (1970, 1973) research indicates that, in addition to socialization, we must also consider empathy, autonomy, and whether a person is guided more by his or her personal conscience or a sense of social responsibility.

A potentially fruitful area for research is on the situational factors that influence whether or not we act on our inhibitions and controls. In a series of studies, the present writer and his colleagues have investigated the situational factors that determine whether people high in Dominance, as assessed by the CPI Dominance scale, actually assume leadership (E. I. Megargee & Carbonell, 1988). A similar paradigm could be utilized to study the circumstances in which people with varying levels of socialization or self-control inhibit their behavior or succumb to temptation. Is the presence of others conducive or detrimental to self-control? Are we better behaved in the presence of some people than we are with others? What are the effects of prosocial or antisocial models?

Field research on actual examples of people exercising constraint or control because of value judgments they have made is a largely unexplored but potentially important source of data. Once again, an allied research area, in this case behavioral medicine, could be a valuable source of data and designs. The literature on compliance, dieting, and smoking cessation involves exercising restraints and self-control in real life situations with important contingencies involved.

In order for ethical values to come into play, it is necessary that a particular behavior be classified as "right" or "wrong." As we have noted, psychologists interested in moral development have constructed a number of hypothetical dilemmas to investigate moral reasoning.

These studies of artificial situations could be supplemented by research on "real life" ethical dilemmas. For many young men in the 1960s, participation in the Vietnam war presented such a crisis; for young women in the 1990s, abortion can be a similar issue (Gilligan, 1977). These problems often involve agonizing personal decisions and taking public stands. From a research standpoint, the particular issue and its resolution are not as important as the process by which the person decided whether or not the choice was congruent with his or her particular code of values, and the subsequent problems encountered in living with the decision. Research with people who have had to grapple with such dilemmas and their consequences could help us determine the generality of findings based on hypothetical situations.

C. Building for the Future

Psychological research on internal inhibitions and constraints and their influence on behavior is still in its infancy. Although we have several theories and a number of assumptions regarding the origins and operations of internal controls, relatively little has been established with certainty.

For various reasons, personality researchers have not been eager to study controls and inhibitions. Those studies that have been done have often involved people who failed to develop what others regarded as adequate or appropriate values or who failed to live up to them and behaved in an antisocial fashion. It is, perhaps, significant that the editors of this *Handbook* recruited a psychologist whose research has focused on criminal behavior and violence to write this chapter.

Of course, compared with other disciplines, we psychologists are new to the study of internal inhibitions and restraints. The first stages in any scientific inquiry are to review the literature, make preliminary observations, and form hypotheses. One of the primary theses of this chapter is that psychologists interested in studying internal inhibitions and controls should cast off our disciplinary blinders and consider the observations, speculations, and theories of anthropologists, criminologists, sociologists, ethicists, philosophers, and theologians—even playwrights and poets—in short, of all the scholars who have struggled with these issues over the years.

Controls involve behaving according to one's values, and individual values differ from culture to culture and from era to era. Therefore another thesis has been that observations and investigations of the origin and application of ethical values in our society must be replicated in other cultures, and that our studies in the present should be enriched by a consideration of how people behaved in the past.

A third thesis has been that a great deal of research relevant to these issues has been conducted by psychologists who were primarily interested in other questions. Among the areas cited were social psychology, behavioral medicine, and physiological psychology. A number of important observations and hypotheses can be derived by reviewing the literature in these areas to ascertain their relevance to controls and restraints.

Finally, no one would dream of formulating a theory of aesthetics supported only by observations of people who are color blind or tone deaf. Yet much, perhaps most, of our observations and theories about inhibitions and controls have been based on investigations of people who are poorly socialized or impulsive. In the future we should investigate people with positive as well as negative value systems and well functioning as well as deficient systems of controls.

ACKNOWLEDGMENT

Preparation of this chapter was supported in part by Grant No. 88-IJ-CX-0006 from the National Institute of Justice to Edwin I. Megargee and Joyce L. Carbonell.

REFERENCES

Aries, P., & Duby, G. (Eds.). (1987–1988). *A history of private life* (A. Goldhammer, Trans.) (Vols. 1 & 2). Cambridge, MA: Belknap Press of Harvard University Press.

Asch, S. E. (1956). Studies of independence and conformity: A minority of one against a unanimous majority, *Psychological Monographs, 70,* (Whole No. 416).

Bandura, A. (1969). *Principles of behavior modification.* New York: Holt.

Bandura, A. (1977). Self-efficacy: Toward a unifying theory of behavioral change. *Psychological Review, 84,* 191–215.

Beck, E. M. (1980). *Bartlett's familiar quotations* (15th ed.). Boston: Little, Brown.

Becker, H. S. (1964). *The other side: Perspectives on deviance.* New York: Free Press.

Bee, H. (1985). *The developing child.* New York: Harper & Row.

Benedict, R. (1934). *Patterns of culture.* Boston: Houghton-Mifflin.

Bouchard, T. J., Jr. (1984). Twins reared together and apart: What they tell us about human diversity. In S. W. Fox (Ed.), *Individuality and determinism* (pp. 147–184). New York: Plenum Press.

Buss, A. H., & Plomin, R. (1984). *Temperament: Early developing personality traits.* Hillsdale, NJ: Erlbaum.

Christiansen, K. O. (1977). A preliminary study of criminality among twins. In S. A. Mednick & K. O. Christiansen (Eds.), *Biosocial bases of criminal behavior* (pp. 89–108). New York: Wiley.

Clinard, M. B., & Quinney, R. (1973). *Criminal behavior systems: A typology* (2nd ed). New York: Holt, Rinehart & Winston.

Cloward, R. A., & Ohlin, L. E. (1960). *Delinquency and opportunity: A theory of delinquent gangs.* Glencoe, IL: Free Press.

Darley, J. M., & Latané, B. (1968). Bystander intervention in emergencies: Diffusion of responsibility. *Journal of Personality and Social Psychology, 8,* 377–383.

Dollard, J., Doob, L. W., Miller, N. E., Mowrer, O. H., & Sears, R. R. (1939). *Frustration and aggression.* New Haven, CT: Yale University Press.

Erikson, E. H. (1950). *Childhood and society.* New York: Norton.

Eysenck, H. J. (1964). *Crime and personality.* Boston: Houghton-Mifflin.

Eysenck, H. J. (1981). *A model for personality.* New York: Springer-Verlag.

Feshbach, S., & Weiner, B. (1986). *Personality* (2nd ed.). Lexington, MA: D. C. Heath.

Freud, S. (1965). *New introductory lectures on psychoanalysis* (J. Strachey, Trans.). New York: Norton. (Original work published 1933)

Garfinkel, H. (1956). Conditions of successful degradation ceremonies. *American Journal of Sociology, 61,* 420–424.

Gilligan, C. (1977). In a different voice: Women's conception of the self and morality. *Harvard Educational Review, 47,* 481–517.

Glueck, S., & Glueck, E. (1950). *Unraveling juvenile delinquency.* New York: Commonwealth Fund.

Goring, C. (1913). *The English convict: A statistical study.* London: His Majesty's Stationery Office.

Gough, H. G. (1969). *Manual for the California Psychological Inventory.* Palo Alto, CA: Consulting Psychologists Press.

Harlow, H. (1971). *Learning to love.* San Francisco: Albion.

Hartshorne, H., & May, M. A. (1928). *Studies in the nature of character: Vol. 1. Studies in deceit.* New York: Macmillan.

Hogan, R. (1970). A dimension of moral judgment. *Journal of Consulting and Clinical Psychology, 35,* 205–212.

Hogan, R. (1973). Moral conduct and moral character: A psychological perspective. *Psychological Bulletin, 79,* 217–232.

Hogan, R. (1986). What every student should know about personality psychology. In V. P. Makosby (Ed.), *The G. Stanley Hall lecture series* (Vol. 6, pp. 43–64). Washington, DC: American Psychological Association.

Hogan, R., Johnson, J. A., & Emler, N. P. (1978). A socioanalytic theory of moral development. *New Directions for Child Development, 2,* 1–18.

Hooton, E. A. (1939). *The American criminal, an anthropological study: Vol. 1. The native white criminal of native parentage.* Cambridge, MA: Harvard University Press.

Institute of Medicine Committee on Research and Training Issues Related to the Mission of the Secret Service. (1984). *Research and training for the Secret Service: Behavioral science and mental health perspectives.* Washington, DC: National Academy Press.

Janis, I. L. (1972). *Victims of groupthink.* Boston: Houghton-Mifflin.

Johnson, A. (1949). Sanctions for super-ego lacunae of adolescence. In K. Eissler (Ed.), *Searchlights on delinquency* (pp. 225–245). New York: International Universities Press.

Johnson, R. (1972). *Aggression in man and animals.* Philadelphia: Saunders.

Kohlberg, L. (1981). *Essays on moral development.* New York: Harper & Row.

Lemert, E. M. (1967). *Human deviance, social problems, and social control.* Englewood Cliffs, NJ: Prentice-Hall.

Lindzey, G. (1967). Some remarks concerning incest, the incest taboo, and psychoanalytic theory. *American Psychologist, 22,* 1051–1059.

Loehlin, J. C., & Nichols, R. C. (1976). *Heredity, environment and personality.* Austin: University of Texas Press.

Lorenz, K. (1966). *On aggression* (M. Latzke, Trans.). New York: Bantam Books. (Original work published 1963)

Luckenbill, D. F., & Sanders, W. B. (1977). Criminal violence. In E. Sagarin & F. Montanino (Eds.), *Deviants: Voluntary actors in a hostile world.* Morristown, NJ: General Learning Press.

Mark, V. H., & Ervin, S. R. (1970). *Violence and the brain.* New York: Harper & Row.

McCord, J., & McCord, W. (1964). *The psychopath: An essay on the criminal mind.* New York: Van Nostrand-Reinhold.

McCord, W., & McCord, J. (1959). *Origins of crime: A new evaluation of the Cambridge-Somerville study.* New York: Columbia University Press.

Mead, M. (1961). *Coming of age in Samoa: A psychological study of primitive youth for Western Civilization.* New York: W. Morrow.

Mead, M. (1975). *Growing up in New Guinea: A comparative study of primitive education.* New York: W. Morrow.

Mednick, S. A., Gabrielle, W. F., Jr., & Hutchings, B. (1984). Genetic influences in criminal convictions: Evidence from an adoption cohort. *Science, 224,* 891–894.

Mednick, S. A., & Volavka, J. (1980). Biology and crime. In N. Morris & M. Tonry (Eds.), *Crime and justice: An annual review of research* (Vol. 2, pp. 85–158). Chicago: University of Chicago Press.

Megargee, E. I. (1973). The heuristic value of the concept of "social deviance" for psychologists. *Representative Research in Social Psychology, 4,* 67–81.

Megargee, E. I. (1982). Psychological correlates and determinants of criminal violence. In M. Wolfgang & N. Weiner (Eds.), *Criminal violence* (pp. 81–170). Beverly Hills, CA: Sage.

Megargee, E. I. (1993). Aggression and violence. In H. E. Adams & P. B. Sutker (Eds.), *Comprehensive handbook of psychopathology* (2nd Ed., pp. 617–644). New York: Plenum Press.

Megargee, E. I., & Carbonell, J. C. (1988). Evaluating leadership with the CPI. In C. D. Spielberger & J. N. Butcher (Eds.), *Advances in personality assessment* (Vol. 7, pp. 203–219). Hillsdale, NJ: Erlbaum.

Megargee, E. I., Parker, G. V. C., & Levine, R. V. (1971). The relationship of familial and social factors to socialization in middle class college students. *Journal of Abnormal Psychology, 77,* 76–89.

Megargee, S. E., Jr. (1942). *Dogs.* New York: Harper & Brothers.

Megargee, S. E., Jr. (1954). *The dog dictionary.* New York: World.

Merton, R. (1938). Social structure and anomie. *American Sociological Review, 3,* 672–682.

Merton, R. (1957). *Social theory and social structure.* Glencoe, IL: Free Press.

Milgram, S. (1974). *Obedience to authority.* New York: Harper.

Miller, W. B. (1958). Lower class culture as a generating milieu of gang delinquency. *Journal of Social Issues, 14*(3), 5–19.

Mischel, W., & Mischel, H. N. (1976). A cognitive social learning approach to morality and self-regulation. In T. Lickona (Ed.), *Moral development and behavior. Theory, research and social issues.* New York: Holt.

Munroe, R. L. (1955). *Schools of psychoanalytic thought.* New York: Dryden Press.

Nye, F. I. (1958). *Family relationships and delinquent behavior.* New York: Wiley.

Peter, L. J. (1977). *Peter's quotations: Ideas for our time.* New York: W. Morrow.

Piaget, J. (1932). *The moral judgment of the child.* New York: Macmillan.

Quay, H. C. (1965). Psychopathic personality as pathological sensation seeking. *American Journal of Psychiatry, 122,* 180–183.

Rosenquist, C. M., & Megargee, E. I. (1969). *Delinquents in three cultures.* Austin: University of Texas Press.

Salisbury, H. E. (1959). *The shook-up generation.* New York: Harper & Row.

Sellin, T. (1938). *Culture conflict and crime.* New York: Social Science Research Council.

Selman, R. (1980). *The growth of interpersonal understanding.* New York: Academic Press.

Shoham, S. (1962). The application of the "culture conflict" hypothesis to the criminality of immigrants in Israel. *Journal of Criminal Law, Criminology, and Police Science, 53,* 207–214.

Skinner, B. F. (1971). *Beyond freedom and dignity.* New York: Knopf.

Sutherland, E. H. (1939). *Principles of criminology* (3rd ed.). New York: Lippincott.

Sykes, G., & Matza, D. (1957). Techniques of neutralization: A theory of delinquency. *American Sociological Review, 22,* 664–670.

Tripp, A. H. (1970). *International thesaurus of quotations.* New York: Thomas Y. Crowell.

Untermeyer, L. (1955). *Modern American and modern British poetry.* New York: Harcourt, Brace.

Velez-Diaz, A., & Megargee, E. I. (1971). An investigation of differences in value judgments between youthful offenders and nonoffenders in Puerto Rico. *Journal of Criminal Law, Criminology and Police Science, 61,* 549–553.

Vold, G. (1958). *Theoretical criminology.* New York: Oxford University Press.

Vold, G., & Bernard, T. (1986). *Theoretical criminology* (3rd ed.). New York: Oxford University Press.

Wilson, J. Q., & Herrnstein, R. J. (1985). *Crime and human nature.* New York: Simon & Schuster.

PART VII

PERSONALITY AND THE SELF

CHAPTER 24

CONGRUENCE OF OTHERS' AND SELF-JUDGMENTS OF PERSONALITY

DAVID C. FUNDER

UNIVERSITY OF CALIFORNIA, RIVERSIDE

C. RANDALL COLVIN

NORTHEASTERN UNIVERSITY

I. THE QUESTION OF SELF–OTHER AGREEMENT

A. Two Reasons for Being Interested in the Question

Do other people view you the same way you view yourself? Most people find this to be an interesting question, for two basic reasons. First, the self that a person presents to others, and the way that self is perceived by others, importantly influences how those others treat him or her and how the person views him- or herself. Someone viewed as *incompetent* will not be given a job, and someone viewed as *dishonest* will not be lent money, but someone viewed as *warm* will have many friends; the amount of self-esteem the individual develops may depend upon the degree to which he or she accepts each of these characterizations. Moreover, whether one is viewed positively or negatively, it is probably strategically useful to have an accurate idea of how one is regarded by the others in one's social world.

HANDBOOK OF PERSONALITY PSYCHOLOGY   617

Second, the opinions of others are a useful source of information about what a person might really be like. This may be a subtle point but it is an important one. If you want or need to know whether you have musical talent, it makes sense to consult an expert musician who has had a chance to observe you perform musically. If you want to know whether you have athletic talent, it makes sense to consult an expert coach who has seen you perform athletically. If you want to know what kind of personality you have, the situation is even simpler. Many individuals have seen you perform interpersonally, and everybody is an "expert."

B. Sociological and Psychological Perspectives on the Question

Empirical research on self–other congruence can be classified according to its relevance to one or the other of the two reasons just mentioned for finding such congruence important. Most research can be placed along a continuum which we will label as ranging from "sociological" through "social psychological" to "personality" perspectives. Sociological approaches to self–other congruence emphasize the social construction and consequences of the self-image, whereas psychological perspectives are more likely to attend to the possibility that self and others' views might actually characterize what a person is like.

From the sociological perspective, the self does not exist outside of the minds of those who behold it; it is little more than an arbitrary social construct. This perspective yields theorizing about the "looking-glass self" and symbolic interactionism (Blumer, 1937; Mead, 1934; Shrauger & Schoeneman, 1979; Stryker & Gottlieb, 1981), which focuses upon the self-image that arises out of ongoing social interaction between a person and his or her social world. Empirical research on self–other congruence emphasizes how the perceptions others have of us, and the assessments we make of others' perceptions of us, affect what we think of ourselves (Shrauger & Schoeneman, 1979). Such research regards emergent social consensus and the processes by which it comes about to the phenomena of interest, and pays little attention to what, if anything, might be correctly sayable about the person who is judged. In fact, in the view of this tradition, questions about accuracy are not really meaningful. Some writers even complain about how "language usage and convenience make it almost impossible to avoid writing as though the self were being conceived as a concrete entity" (Stryker & Gottlieb, 1981, p. 453)—which, in sociological theorizing, is generally regarded as a grave mistake.

Some theorizing within social psychology shares part of the outlook of the sociological approach. Modern-day "constructivists," exemplified by Kruglanski (1989, who sometimes also uses the term "phenomenal"), emphasize how reality and perceptions of reality are not easily separated, if they are separable at all. Therefore, this perspective also avoids regarding the self as a "concrete entity." As Funder and West (1993) note, the constructivist viewpoint focuses on the way judgments are made and how judgments of the "same" stimulus can vary according to point of view, while eschewing evaluation of any particular judgment as inaccurate.

This focus on the process of judgment is a general attribute of other social psychological approaches to self–other congruence. For example, Swann's (1984) work on identity negotiation investigates the tension between self verification, where a target strives to confirm his or her self-concept, and behavioral confirmation, where a target is led to behave in ways that confirm to the expectations and desires of others. Here we find some—a little—concern with how the targets of judgment actually behave (as opposed to the sociological and constructivist approaches noted previously, which manifest *no* such concern), and with the extent to which their behavior is accurately characterized by self and others' personality descriptions (albeit mostly as a result of self-fulfilling prophecies and the like).

Standing in strong contrast to all of the approaches considered so far is that of personality psychology. This approach is based on the assumption that individuals manifest differences in social behavior that may reflect actual differences in their personalities (Funder, 1995). Investigators who share this perspective regard the personality of the individual who is judged to be the phenomenon of central importance and are interested in the task of personality assessment. One possible method of assessment, frequently used, is simply to ask a person and his or her acquaintances for a description of the individual's personality. Congruence between self and others' judgments of personality then becomes a matter of convergent validity, judgments that agree with each other being presumed to be more accurate than judgments that do not agree (e.g., Cheek, 1982; Funder, 1980a; Funder & Colvin, 1988; Funder & Dobroth, 1987; Funder, Kolar, & Blackman, 1995; McCrae, 1982). Personality, from this perspective, is regarded as a relatively stable and coherent structure residing with the person, and in that sense *is* viewed as a "concrete entity." This structure is not directly visible, but is (partially) revealed through social behavior and can, in turn, be (imperfectly) inferred by the other people in an individual's social world.

C. Two Ways to Ask the Question

Examination of self–other congruence requires, of course, that the self and his or her acquaintances be asked for personality descriptions. The precise way this question is asked reveals much about the interests of the investigator, and has important consequences for interpreting the answers that will be obtained.

One way is to ask the target's acquaintances to describe, not the personality of the target, but how the target perceives or will describe his or her own personality. From about the 1930s to the early 1960s, this was the traditional method for research on accuracy. Bender and Hastorf (1950), in a typical early study, asked target students to provide self-descriptions on three measures: one of behavior in social situations, another on dominance, and another on emphatic ability. Another group of students, who were acquaintances of the targets, then completed the same three measures *as they thought the targets had answered them*. For two of the three measures, significant agreement was found between targets' and acquaintances' responses. Early researchers regarded this sort of ability to predict targets' self-judgments as an indicator of the acquaintances' degree of social sensitivity or empathy (e.g., Gage & Cronbach, 1955; Taft, 1966).

When accuracy research began to reappear during the middle 1980s, for some reason the opposite approach became common: Investigators asked the target to describe, not his or her own personality, but rather how the target believed he or she would be described by others. It is not clear why this change occurred, but notice how it constitutes a subtle shift in focus from a concern with what other people are like, to a concern with how one appears to others. Such a shift seems consistent with what some commentators have seen as an increasingly "narcissistic" cultural tone to the 1980s as opposed to the 1950s (e.g, Fine, 1986).

An advantage of these two approaches, one old and one new, is that both are designed to neatly finesse the whole issue of accuracy. They do this by giving accuracy an operational definition which is not quite the same as its everyday meaning, but which has the advantage of being directly measurable. In the older research, assessment of a subject's accuracy at predicting what somebody else would say about himself or herself seemed to be a straightfoward matter. Similarly, the newer studies can measure quite directly the degree to which a subject correctly predicts the descriptions provided by his or her acquaintances. Both methodologies are appropriate, and indeed necessary, if one is interested in the ontogeny of the self from a sociological viewpoint (Shrauger & Schoeneman, 1979). Even from a psychological viewpoint, these methodologies are appropriate and unproblematic if an investigator wants to understand no more than how well people can predict each others' questionnaire responses (and, more charitably, assuming generalizability, how well they understand each others' perceptions).

The use of operational definitions to finesse a conceptual issue never comes without cost, however (cf. Bronfenbrenner, Harding, & Gallwey, 1958; Cronbach, 1955). In this case, the cost is that no information is gathered relevant to the ordinary meaning of accuracy. That is, there is no indication whatsoever as to whether the descriptions provided by the self or the acquaintances actually correctly characterize anybody. This is because, in both methodologies, *one member of the self–other dyad is not asked to describe a person*. In the older research the acquaintance, and in the newer research the target, is merely asked to describe *judgments* provided by the other dyad member.

The other way to ask the descriptive question is simpler and, for a personality psychologist, more informative. It is to ask the target simply, "what are you like?", and to ask his or her acquaintance the parallel question, "what is this person like?" (e.g., Funder & Dobroth, 1987; Park & Judd, 1989). Self–other congruence in this context at least indicates how well two people agree about the target's actual personality, and assessing judgmental agreement in this manner is the only procedure that takes the question of accuracy in personality judgment seriously.[1]

D. Two Ways to Analyze Answers to the Question

However an investigator decides to ask the descriptive question, self–other agreement can be assessed in two fundamentally different ways. One involves the analysis of mean differences; the other involves the analysis of correlations. The first kind of analysis compares the mean placement of each descriptive item between others' and self-descriptions. For instance, do people give themselves higher ratings, on average, on desirable attributes than their acquaintances do? The second kind of analysis computes correlations between others' and self-judgments, either holistically or one item at a time. For instance, do people who give themselves relatively high ratings on sociability (compared to other subjects) tend to receive relatively high sociability ratings from their acquaintances?

As was noted long ago by Conrad (1932) and more recently by Funder (1980a), these two analyses and these two kinds of question are utterly orthogonal. It is entirely possible and plausible to find good agreement on ratings of a trait using one method and to find poor agreement on ratings of the same trait, among the same subjects, using the other method. A large mean difference could just as well be associated with either a high or a low correlation—so could a small mean difference.

When one fails to recognize that the two analyses are orthogonal, subsequent interpretations can be misleading. One such failure occurred in the often-cited review of self–other agreement by Shrauger and Schoeneman (1979). Their review, which reported finding no consistent self–other agreement, combined the results of both mean differences and correlational analyses (see their Table 2). When the results they report are discriminated according to the method of analysis, a different picture emerges. From among the studies we could discriminate on the basis of their Table 2, in 2 out of 12 samples self–other mean differences seemed to indicate a lack of agreement (significant self–other differences), whereas in 26 out of 45 samples self–other correlations indicated the presence of agreement (significant correlations). Clearly, if this review had recognized the distinct nature of the two analyses, its evaluation of research on self–other agreement might well have been different.

It is important to keep in mind, therefore, that the term "agreement" can have two entirely different and independent meanings. In what follows, we will consider each meaning separately.

---

[1] There is no reason why the accuracy question needs to be the central concern of everybody who investigates self–other agreement; as already noted, social psychologists and sociologists often have different and perfectly legitimate questions in mind. Our assumption is, however, that the accuracy question is the one of central concern to personality psychologists of the sort who might read a handbook like this one.

II. ANALYSES OF ABSOLUTE (MEAN) AGREEMENT

Psychologists investigating absolute or mean differences between others' and self-perceptions have focused on three issues: self-enhancement biases, the actor–observer effect, and the difference between internal and external personality traits.

A. Self-Enhancement Biases

Probably the most obvious place to look for differences between others' and self-descriptions of personality is in the area of self-enhancement or "self-serving" biases (e.g., Brown, 1986; Kunda, 1987; Miller & Ross, 1975). It certainly seems reasonable and consistent with everyday experience to expect that people will describe themselves in more laudatory terms than they will be described by others. However, most of the work on self-enhancement does not test this expectation directly. As Colvin and Block (1994) have argued, the assessment of self-enhancement requires a comparison of one's self-perception of personality against a valid external criterion. Because very little research actually includes any such criterion, many studies that supposedly address "self-enhancement" are open to a variety of alternative explanations.

A second area of research on self-enhancement focuses on causal attributions. The usual hypothesis tested by this research is that people take more causal responsibility for their successes than for their failures, relative to the attributions offered by outside observers. However, a review by Miller and Ross (1975) concluded that there is surprisingly little evidence in support of this hypothesis, at least in what these authors called its "most general form" (p. 213). While they concluded that the evidence shows people engage in self-enhancing attributions under conditions of success, they found little evidence of a self-enhancement bias under conditions of failure. Still, as Kunda (1987) has pointed out, research in a variety of domains seems to show with regularity, if not perfect consistency, that people engage in self-enhancement in perception (Erdelyi, 1974), memory (Greenwald & Pratkanis, 1984), attribution of responsibility (Lerner, 1980; Tetlock & Levi, 1982), and social comparison (Taylor, 1983).

The results of the studies just cited would seem to imply that, in the end, people should manifest more positive opinions of themselves than others will have of them, but none of these studies tests this prediction directly. The prediction was tested by Funder (1980a), who found no indication that self-descriptions were more favorable than descriptions provided by acquaintances. However, we can offer some previously unreported data that reexamine this issue within a much larger sample (approximately four times as large). One hundred fifty-seven undergraduates described their own personalities using the California Q-sort (Block, 1961/1978), as modified for nonprofessional use by Bem and Funder (1978). These same undergraduates were also described by two close acquaintances, and the two descriptions were averaged (for more procedural details, see Funder & Dobroth, 1987). The

TABLE I
Self-Placement Higher Than Acquaintance Placement

Q-sort item	Self-ratings	Acquaintance ratings	t (156)	p-level
46. Engages in personal fantasy and daydreams	5.90	5.06	5.70	.001
3. Wide range of interests	6.70	6.01	5.08	
16. Introspective	6.62	5.82	4.79	
60. Insight into own motives and behavior	6.41	5.62	4.76	
17. Is sympathetic or considerate	6.64	6.04	4.34	
66. Enjoys aesthetic impressions	6.57	5.93	4.12	
35. Has warmth; compassionate	7.20	6.57	4.05	
90. Concerned with philosophical problems	6.08	5.48	3.78	
29. Is sought for advice	5.75	5.19	3.73	
47. Readiness to feel guilt	4.93	4.43	3.15	.01
79. Has persistent preoccupying thoughts	5.94	5.45	2.88	
58. Enjoys sensuous experiences	6.69	6.26	2.79	
64. Perceptive to interpersonal cues	5.90	5.45	2.66	
39. Thinks and associates ideas in unusual ways	5.45	5.02	2.59	.05
19. Seeks reassurance	5.65	5.28	2.56	
71. High aspiration level	6.76	6.37	2.49	
89. Compares self to others	5.66	5.28	2.47	
95. Gives advice	5.34	5.02	2.26	
10. Anxiety and tension produce bodily symptoms	4.55	4.21	2.15	
83. Able to see to the heart of important problems	5.68	5.41	2.10	
24. "Objective," rational	5.83	5.50	2.05	

Note. p-values are two-tailed.

items placed higher in the self-ratings are shown in Table I; those items placed higher by the acquaintances are shown in Table II.[2,3]

What would traditionally be labelled a self-enhancement bias does seem evident in these tables. Acquaintances' ratings are higher than self-ratings, on average, on items such as "expresses hostility" and "dissatisfied" and "self-pitying." Self-ratings are higher on items such as "has warmth" and "is perceptive." This self-enhancement tendency can be demonstrated over the entire set of 100 items: Ratings of the favorability of each of the 100 items were correlated with each of the self–acquaintance mean difference scores; the resultant r was .37 ($p < .001$), a direct measure of the general tendency of targets to rate themselves higher on favorable traits than their acquaintances did.

This r might have been even higher but for a contrary effect. As will be discussed below, subjects seem to give themselves higher ratings than do acquain-

---

[2] All probability levels reported in this chapter are two-tailed values.

[3] The data in these tables have not been previously reported; studies from the same dataset by Funder and Dobroth (1987) and Funder and Colvin (1988) examine correlational agreement rather than mean differences.

TABLE II
Acquaintance Placement Higher Than Self-Placement

Q-sort item	Self-ratings	Acquaintance ratings	t (156)	p-level
100. Does not vary roles	3.53	4.40	−4.85	.001
36. Is subtly negativistic	2.87	3.43	−3.68	
94. Expresses hostility	3.34	3.92	−3.62	
45. Has brittle ego-defense system	3.32	3.81	−3.38	
88. Personally charming	5.45	5.91	−3.37	
52. Assertive	5.35	5.82	−3.04	.01
76. Projects own feelings and motivations onto others	4.10	4.60	−3.04	
7. Favors conservative values	4.11	4.62	−3.01	
86. Denies unpleasant thoughts and conflicts	3.52	3.96	−2.68	
9. Uncomfortable with uncertainty	4.36	4.76	−2.67	
57. Interesting, arresting person	5.92	6.25	−2.61	
99. Self-dramatizing	3.66	4.06	−2.60	
4. Talkative individual	5.52	5.89	−2.52	.05
59. Concerned with functioning of own body	5.24	5.59	−2.36	
49. Distrustful of people	3.32	3.66	−2.30	
97. Emotionally bland	2.99	3.38	−2.29	
21. Arouses nurturant feelings	4.04	4.42	−2.26	
14. Genuinely submissive	2.75	3.11	−2.13	
75. Internally consistent personality	5.02	5.39	−2.09	
61. Creates and exploits dependency in people	2.78	3.09	−2.04	
78. Self-pitying	2.70	3.00	−2.02	
74. Satisfied with self	4.55	4.86	−2.00	

Note. All p-values are two-tailed.

tances on traits that are relatively internal, or not outwardly observable, whereas acquaintances give subjects higher ratings on observable traits than do the subjects themselves (the r between observability and self–acquaintance mean differences is −.25, $p < .05$). Within the 100 items of the Q-set, observability and favorability are positively related ($r = .32$, $p < .01$); items like "thinks in unusual ways" or "has persistent preoccupying thoughts" are rated rather unfavorably and are also quite internal, whereas traits like "talkative" and "assertive" are both more favorable and more external or observable. (At present, it is not completely clear whether this relation holds generally across the trait domain or is specific to the 100 items in the Q-set we use.)

To disentangle the conjoined but opposing effects of favorability and observability, we computed partial correlations. Across the 100 items, the correlation between favorability and self–acquaintance mean differences, with observability partialled, is $r = .49$ ($p < .001$). (The correlation between observability and self–acquaintance mean differences, with favorability partialled, is $r = −.42$ [$p < .001$].) This finding seems to provide convincing evidence that people will, indeed, provide more favorable self-descriptions than other people will provide of them, separate from the influence of trait observability.

The "other people" in the results just cited were close acquaintances and, in most cases, close friends (the request we had made to our subjects was to help us recruit "the two people, among those on campus and available, who know you the best"). As was reported by Funder and Colvin (1988), each subject was also rated by judges who had seen them only on a 5-min videotape which showed him or her interacting spontaneously with another subject. The comparison between these "strangers' " judgments and self-judgments is dramatic. The self-descriptions were much more favorable; across the 100 traits, the correlation between self–stranger mean differences and favorability was $r = .66$ ($p < .001$). Interestingly, the comparison between the close acquaintances' ratings and the strangers' ratings yielded nearly the same finding; the correlation between acquaintance–stranger mean differences and favorability was $r = .60$ ($p < .001$); acquaintances described the targets much more favorably than did strangers, to nearly the same extent as the self.

These findings lead to two conclusions. First, the self-enhancement effect is much stronger when comparing self-ratings to ratings by strangers than when the comparison is to ratings by close acquaintances. This is only to be expected; it is reasonable to suppose that people are generally viewed positively by their close friends and acquaintances.

The second conclusion may be more interesting and important: The "self"-enhancement bias may be poorly named, because the effect seems similarly strong whether the comparison is between self-ratings and strangers' ratings, or between acquaintances' ratings and strangers' ratings. A major controversy in this area has been the question of whether self-enhancement effects are motivational or cognitive (Kunda, 1987; Miller & Ross, 1975). The present findings imply that if the mechanism that produces self–other mean differences is motivational, it is a motivational mechanism of an unusual sort. The motivation to enhance the self, if there is such a thing, seems to be experienced to a nearly equal degree by one's close acquaintances. Are we motivated to think well of our acquaintances (cf. (Cialdini & Richardson, 1980; Tesser & Campbell, 1982), or is something else going on?

The data currently available are not sufficient to answer this question. But we would like to offer an unusual speculation. Perhaps the self-enhancement "bias" is not a bias at all—not motivational, and not cognitive, either. This mild heresy can yield a parsimonious explanation if one assumes, reasonably we think, that positive attributes generally are *correct* characterizations of the subjects in most research (and certainly in our own), all of whom have, after all, passed the prescreening of college admissions committees. The subjects are in the best position to know these favorable facts about themselves, close acquaintances are in nearly as good a position, and the poor strangers, reduced in our research to basing judgments on 5-min observations of rather stilted, uncomfortable interactions, are simply not in an equally good position to see the truth. Indeed, if the strangers try to make appropriately regressive judgments, and guess the (unselected) population mean, their ratings will be both less positive and less accurate than the ratings provided by the student targets and their acquaintances. (The same line of reasoning can be extended to the interpretation of many findings concerning interpretations for success and failure. For the vast majority of college student subjects—who are generally successful people or they would not be in the subject pool—personal attributions for success and situational attributions for failure are probably *correct* in nearly all except artificial, experimental situations.)

B. The Actor–Observer Effect

Another mean difference between others' and self-judgments of personality, the "actor–observer" effect, was popularized by Jones and Nisbett (1987/1971; see Watson, 1982, for a later review). The effect is that people ordinarily offer explanations for their behavior that are relatively situational, whereas observers are more likely to explain behavior in more dispositional terms. Although this effect is not uniformly found (Monson & Snyder, 1977; Robins, Spronca, & Mendelsohn, 1996), the basic mechanism when it is found seems to involve point of view. Several studies have shown that observing a behavior from the point of view of the person who performs it leads to situational attributions relative to observing it from an outside perspective. Storms (1973) manipulated perspective via camera placement; Regan and Totten (1975) manipulated perspective through instructions to subjects to "empathize" with the target person; Funder (1980b) examined perspective as a function of the observers' levels of dispositional empathy; and Krones and Funder (1989) manipulated observational perspective as a function of time—viewing one-self in the past or future seems to cause one's attributions to become similar to those of an outside observer (and, hence, more dispositional). As Hirschberg (1978) noted, at the moment of action "people are interested in deciding what to do" (p. 58), not analyzing how their traits affect what they do. Only later, if ever, can actors take an external, more objective view and see how other people might have behaved differently in the same situation, and therefore how their own traits affected how they acted themselves.

As was discussed by Monson and Snyder (1977) and by Funder (1982), the dispositional–situational "dichotomy" is not a true dichotomy anyway. To say that someone gave money *because* he is generous (a disposition) implies that the giving situation was voluntary and not at gunpoint; to say that someone gave money *because* she was asked by a Girl Scout (a situation) implies that the subject is the sort of person who responds generously to such a request. These kinds of attributions implicitly recognize the contribution of both dispositional and situational influences to the determination of behavior. When the situational response is rare, one may legitimately suspect a dispositional inference, whereas if it is common, one might put more emphasis on the situation, but overall the difference is in emphasis more than content (see Funder, 1982, and Ross, 1977, for discussions of this point).

Nonetheless, the strong tradition within attribution theory is almost uniformly to assume dispositional attributions to be wrong, and situational attributions to be right (Funder, 1982; Nisbett, 1980; see als Miller & Porter, 1980; Moore, Sherrod,

Liu, & Underwood, 1979). Within this literature, the tendency to make dispositional attributions is often referred to as the "fundamental attribution error" (Ross, 1977).

Remarkably, this practice persists even though attribution research has identified many errors that produce attributions that are unduly *situational,* not dispositional. One example is the false consensus bias (Ross, Greene, & House, 1977). This effect leads people to see their behavior as more common in the population than it really is. Because such a tendency tends to yield (false) beliefs that one's own behavior is simply "what anybody would do" in the same situation, it yields attributions that are more situational and less dispositional than they normatively should be.

Situational attributions are neither always correct nor immune to error, therefore, and in general the actor–observer effect should not be regarded as a matter of accuracy (Funder, 1982). However, there may be some exceptions even to this general rule. For example, consider a behavior that is part of a chronic, maladaptive pattern. If the individual who performs it sees such a behavior as situationally caused, he or she can reasonably be considered to be wrong. An example was provided by McKay, O'Farrell, Maisto, Connors, and Funder (1989), who showed that previously hospitalized, long-term alcoholics tended to explain the causes of recent drinking relapses in terms of immediate situational influences (a stressful day at the office, a car breakdown). Their wives, however, were more likely to see the drinking as produced by the alcoholism. Given that most individuals do not respond to bad days at the office with lengthy drinking bouts, and that these particular individuals had been diagnosed and treated for alcoholism over a long period, it is hard not to conclude that in this example the alcoholics' situational attributions were incorrect, and the wives' dispositional attributions were correct.

On the other side of the actor–observer divide, there is at least one aspect of behavior that actors are in an exceptionally good position to witness. Nobody including personality psychologists would deny that people vary their behavior according to the person they are interacting with, and actors are in a better position to see this variation than is any single interaction partner (Swann, 1984). This effect is reflected in the Q-sort data reported above. Self-ratings of the item "Does not vary roles; relates to everyone in the same way" receives a lower rating in self-descriptions than in descriptions by either acquaintances or strangers (the means, respectively, are 3.53, 4.40, and 5.15; p for both self–other differences $<$ .001).

C. Internal versus External Traits

The third category of mean differences between others' and self-judgments of personality has received considerably less attention than the first two. Funder (1980a) classified the 100 items of the California Q-set along a dimension of "outward observability," on which items such as "talkative" or "charming" rated high, and items like "fantasizes and daydreams" or "ruminates and worries" rated low. It seems obvious that traits of the latter kind are more observable by the people who possess them than by acquaintances, because fantasizing, worrying, and other internal activities are only accessible to acquaintances to the extent that the persons who perform them let others in on the secret. It might be less obvious that the opposite comment could be made about more observable traits: attributes such as talkativeness, attractiveness, and charm may be more observable to other people than to the actor himself or herself. A particularly good example might be "is personally charming." We are all immune to our own charm; if you believe yourself to be charming, it is presumably not because you have charmed yourself, but rather because other people have responded to you in such a way that you conclude you must be charming. Our own access to this kind of external trait is almost as indirect as is the access of an acquaintance to our internal traits.

This line of reasoning leads to the prediction that people should give higher ratings to themselves on internal traits than do their acquaintances, whereas acquaintances will tend to give higher ratings to people on external traits than the individuals award themselves. This prediction was confirmed in the study by Funder (1980a) and replicated in our more recent data. Funder (1980a) reported that the correlation, across 100 Q-items, between the difference between acquaintances' and self-ratings on the one hand, and the outward observability of each item on the other, was .44. In our more recent data this correlation was .25 ($p < .05$), but when the counteracting influence of favorability (discussed above) was partialled, this correlation rose to $r = .42$ ($p < .001$).

These findings seem to indicate a fundamental difference in the way we look at our own personality, relative to how it is viewed by others. From our own perspective, our internal, private experiences and mental activities seem a more important and salient part of what we are than they seem to acquaintances who must view these attributes from the outside. But conversely, certain attributes of our personality that we project outward in our social behavior, such as talkativeness, assertiveness, and charm, are more visible and perhaps even more important to our acquaintances than they are to ourselves. Like the dispositional–situational "dichotomy," the difference here seems better characterized not as one of accuracy, but of point of view.

III. CORRELATIONAL ANALYSES OF AGREEMENT

The second way to assess self–other congruence in personality judgments is to calculate the correlation between the two sets of judgments. This correlation can be computed on personality profiles or on individual variables or items. The first method assesses the similarity between the complete set of personality judgments made by the self and the set of judgments made by an acquaintance (e.g., Andersen, 1984; Kenny & LaVoie, 1984). The X variables in the correlation are all the self-judgments of a particular individual, and the Y variables are all the judgments of that individual provided by a peer. This is "profile" agreement, and is calculated for one target–judge pair at a time. The second method examines congruence one variable at a time. Instead of comparing whole profiles, this method correlates acquaintances' and self-judgments on a single variable (e.g., Funder, 1980a; Funder & Colvin, 1988; Funder & Dobroth, 1987). The X variables in this analysis are the self-judgments of all the subjects in the sample on this one variable. The Y variables are the corresponding judgments on this variable offered by the subjects' acquaintances. The profile and variable or item methods each have advantages and disadvantages, as we shall see (see Bernieri, Zuckerman, Koestner, & Rosenthal, 1994, for a comparative analysis).

A. Methodological Issues: "Cronbach's Complaint"

The study of self–other congruence was a thriving subarea of social psychology from the 1930s into the early 1950s (see Taft, 1955, for a review). Work in this area was brought up short, however, by the methodological critique published by Cronbach (1955; Gage & Cronbach, 1955; foreshadowed by Hastorf & Bender, 1952). Cronbach demonstrated how the profile similarity scores that were calculated in nearly all studies might be contaminated to an unknown but probably large degree by extraneous influences including "stereotypic accuracy," "elevation," and "differential elevation." The dramatic effect of Cronbach's critique was to render nearly all research on self–other congruence to that date seemingly uninterpretable. The even more dramatic response of researchers on accuracy was to cease work on the topic, abruptly and nearly completely (Funder, 1987; Schneider, Hastorf, & Ellsworth, 1979). "Accuracy" had gotten a bad name.

There was no real reason why this had to happen. The artifacts Cronbach identified applied only to measures of profile similarity, and were not particularly difficult to obviate, in principle, in any case (Wiggins, 1973). It is hard to understand, 35 years later, why the general reaction of the scientific community to Cronbach's article was one that could be described only as panic. One factor might have been the style in which this influential critique was written. The article was highly critical and even slightly sarcastic, but also rather murky and hard to follow in many spots. Moreover, many of its analyses were presented in a highly (and perhaps needlessly) mathematized manner, including numerous equations utilizing unconventional notation. The result, apparently, was that many readers were as much intimidated as informed.

The substance of Cronbach's complaint was that profile similarity scores were typically influenced by several factors aside from the judge's ability to accurately discriminate properties of the target. Two of these, elevation and differential elevation, referred to the effect of shared response styles between judge and target; if the subject and his or her acquaintance happened to use the scale in a similar manner, their similarity scores would be artifactually increased; if they used the scale in a different manner, their similarity would be artificially lessened. Another Cronbachian confound was stereotype accuracy: The similarity of a judge's rating of a subject to the subject's self-rating can be influenced to an important degree by the extent to which the judge's rating resembles the average self-rating of all targets. In other words, a judge can usually earn a fair amount of accuracy, in terms of profile similarity, just by guessing the mean for every rating, and ignoring the individual target of judgment altogether.[4]

Given due care, these artifacts are not difficult to eliminate. Those involving elevation can be removed by using forced-choice rating techniques (e.g., a Q-sort) that constrain the ratings of all judges to have the same mean and variance across items. The matter of stereotypic accuracy is somewhat more complex, but can be approached by at least three different ways, depending on what the investigator regards as the focus of interest.

1. The Social Relations Model

An important contribution to the study of self–other congruence is the "social relations model" introduced by Kenny and LaVoie (1984; Kenny, 1994). The purpose of this analytic model is to account explicitly for every identifiable source of variance in others' and self-ratings. This purpose requires a complete, randomized "round robin" design in which all targets are judged by all raters. The data are then entered into a model based closely on the analysis of variance, which yields proportions of variance accounted for by the judge, the target, and their interaction.

The main advantage of this approach is its sophistication and thoroughness. Everything that can be pinned down is pinned down, and Cronbachian components of variance are not eliminated but rather are separately estimated. The model has yielded some interesting insights into, for example, the degree to which people can predict the way they will be rated by individual judges, as opposed to judges in general (DePaulo, Kenny, Hoover, Webb, & Oliver, 1987), and the degree to which valid "target variance" can be found even within ratings provided after only minimal acquaintance (Kenny, Albright, & Malloy, 1988).

Still, this technique has several disadvantages. First, use of the model imposes serious procedural burdens. Because all targets must be evaluated by all judges, it is difficult to do studies in which targets are judged by individuals who know them well (in fact, we are aware of no such studies to date).

Second, the results of an analysis with this model do not yield measures of agreement, such as correlation coefficients, that are easily communicated. Like item analyses, the method does not yield individual accuracy scores for either targets or judges. The model seems to do a better job at comparing the relative proportions of variance accounted for by various sources under specific circumstances than at reflecting simply how much congruence there is between ratings.

Finally, even the relative proportions that are found may not be straightforwardly interpretable. Analyses employing the social relations model have sometimes yielded conclusions such as "in four . . . studies there is at least twice as much partner variance as actor variance" (Kenny & LaVoie, 1984, p. 154). While such

---

[4] It is possible, and reasonable, to regard stereotype accuracy as being not an artifact at all, but an important component of valid judgment (Jackson, 1982). Specifically, it can be viewed as composing the component of accuracy that stems from a judge's knowledge of people in general.

statements are indeed accurate in the context of the numbers obtained by particular studies, one lesson we should have learned from the person–situation controversy is that it can be highly hazardous to move directly from the *statistical* apportionment of variance in a particular study to the *conceptual* apportionment of variance in general (Golding, 1975; similar problems bedevil behavioral genetics, Hirsch, 1986). For instance, the amount of variance contributed by any source is critically influenced by its range.[5] A social relations study that uses targets who are relatively similar to each other will find less target variance than a study that uses targets who are relatively different from each other—the same goes for judges and "partner variance."[6] And the most complex interaction term in the analysis always includes an error component that cannot be separated.

2. Profile Partial Correlations

The second method for assessing self–other congruence is relatively simple and yields an accuracy score for each target–acquaintance pair. It is simply to calculate a partial correlation between each set of acquaintance's and self-judgments, across items, correcting for both the average self-description and the average acquaintance's description (if what is of interest is the (sheer phenomenon of congruence), calculating a semipartial correlation correcting for the average self-judgment (if what is of interest is the ability of the judge to discriminate among how different targets describe themselves), or a semipartial correlation correcting for average acquaintance's judgment (if what is of interest is the ability of the target to discriminate how he or she is viewed differently from other targets). In our experience, the average self-judgment and average acquaintance judgment are highly correlated, so as a practical matter it matters little exactly which kind of partial correlation one elects to compute. This procedure yields a congruence score for every self–other pair. The score can be correlated with properties of the target or acquaintance that are regarded as potential moderators of congruence, or the mean congruence scores can be compared between experimental conditions in studies that manipulate something believed to affect congruence.

3. Item-Level Analysis

This last technique is, on the one hand, a method for obviating the influences of stereotype accuracy, and, on the other hand, an approach for studying the differences

---

[5] To their credit, Kenny and LaVoie (1984) explicitly acknowledged this limitation (p. 174); see also Kenny, 1994.

[6] To express this point with more precision: Even in a fully crossed design (every subject serves as a judge and as a target of all other subjects), actor variance will be restricted to the extent the sample of subjects is homogeneous with respect to the properties that are judged: partner variance will be restricted to the extent the sample of subjects is homogeneous with respect to properties that affect how one makes judgments. Very little is known about how these two kinds of properties might differ from each other, but they are not the same, and it is probably not safe to assume that they are equally variable in a given subject sample. Yet, this assumption is fundamental to some interpretations of results from the social relations model.

between traits. The most simple method for dealing with the influence of stereotype accuracy is to correlate item ratings instead of individual profiles. When a correlation is computed between acquaintances' and self-ratings on a single item, as previously described, the result is a number completely immune to enhancement by stereotype agreement. In fact, if all subjects in the sample simply guess the mean "stereotype," then this correlation will approach 0 (technically, it would be undefined). In general, any tendency by the raters to give the same, stereotypic ratings to all targets will severely attenuate, not enhance, item correlations. The disadvantage of this method is that it does not yield an accuracy score for each individual, nor for each judge. That fact makes cumbersome any attempt to investigate properties of the target or judge that might tend to enhance self–other agreement.

However, disadvantage in one case is turned to advantage in another. This method of analysis has been used extensively by Funder (1980a), Funder and Colvin (1988), and Funder and Dobroth (1987) to investigate the differences between items that lead to better and worse self–other agreement. In all three studies, for example, it was found using this analysis that more observable traits yield higher self–other agreement. In addition to being a useful method for studying differences between items, it also benefits from simplicity of use and ease of communication.

B. Substantive Issues

1. Does Self–Other Congruence Exist?

This basic question continues to arise occasionally. In an often-cited review, Shrauger and Schoeneman (1979) concluded that "there is no consistent agreement between people's self-perceptions and how they are actually viewed by others" (p. 549), a conclusion also reached by Bourne (1977) and by Kammann, Smith, Martin, and McQueen (1984). As mentioned earlier, Shraugher and Schoeneman failed to distinguish between the two fundamentally different kinds of agreement considered in this chapter. Moreover, their review failed to cite several studies that did find an important degree of congruence (e.g., Fiske & Cox, 1960; Hase & Goldberg, 1967; Norman, 1969; Norman & Goldberg, 1966; Scott & Johnson, 1972), and many others have appeared since (e.g., Andersen, 1984; Bem & Allen, 1974; Bernieri et al., 1994; Bledsoe & Wiggins, 1973; Borkenau & Liebler, 1993b; Cheek, 1982; Conley, 1985; Edwards & Klockars, 1981; Funder, 1980a; Funder & Colvin, 1988; Funder & Dobroth, 1987; Goldberg, Norman, & Schwartz, 1980; Gormly, 1984; Kenrick & Stringfield, 1980; Marsh, Barnes, & Schwartz, 1980; Gormly, 1984; Kenrick & Stringfield, 1980; Marsh, Barnes, & Hocevar, 1985; McCrae, 1982; Monson, Tanke, & Lund, 1980; Moskowitz, 1990; Park & Judd, 1989; Paunonen, 1989; Paunonen & Jackson, 1985; Watson, 1989; Woodruffe, 1985). It appears that self–other congruence in personality ratings is in fact a fairly robust phenomenon. The only times it is not found appear to be when overly strong self-presentational pressures are present, unreliable rating scales are used, or the judges and their targets have not had a chance to become acquainted with each other (Funder, 1980a, 1987).

2. What Moderates Self–Other Congruence?

If we can accept that a substantial degree of self–other congruence in personality judgments is a fairly typical finding, the next and more constructive question becomes, what kinds of variables make the degree of congruence larger and smaller? At the present time, we organize potential moderators of self–other agreement (and more generally, potential moderators of judgmental accuracy) into four categories, which we call good judge, good target, good trait, and good information.

a. Good Judge.

This is perhaps the most obvious moderator one might want to examine, and historically it has received the most attention: Is there such a thing as a good judge of personality, and, if so, what are the properties of the good judge? In an excellent review of the research to that time, Bronfenbrenner et al. (1958) concluded that the extant data did "not permit an unequivocal answer to these questions." The situation is not much different today, in part because research of the sort that could have addressed this question died out almost completely, if temporarily, from the late 1950s until quite recently.

Because the general reaction to Cronbach's article was for investigators to abandon the field rather than to improve their methodology, the question still has yet to receive the attention that it deserves, given its importance. More than three decades after Bronfenbrenner's review, it still seems premature to close the book on the good judge of personality. In fact, a recent study found reliable individual differences in judgmental ability that related to ratings of judges' concern about interpersonal relationships (Vogt & Colvin, 1996). This promising start suggests it may be a good time to take a second look at the good judge of personality.

Whatever the ultimate fate of the search for the generalized good judge might be, more recent research does suggest that certain judges might be particularly good at judging certain traits. A particularly interesting study is one by Park and Judd (1989), which found that judges for whom a certain trait term is "chronically accessible," that is, who use the trait often and spontaneously, tend to yield judgments of that trait that agreed highly with the target's own self-judgments. For instance, a judge who often uses the dimension "intelligent/conscientious" to characterize people also tends to rate this dimension in a way similar to the way targets rate themselves.

It is interesting to combine these results with those by Lewicki (1983, 1984), who has found what he calls "self-image bias" which leads people to evaluate others using those trait terms they believe to be most desirable in themselves. The conclusion would seem to be that people will judge those traits they see as desirable in themselves more accurately in others, because, according to Lewicki, they become what Park and Judd would call chronically accessible traits (see also Bargh & Pratto, 1986; Higgins, King, & Mavin, 1982). Research in this area seems still to be in its early stages, but does seem sufficient to make plausible the idea that different people have particular abilities to judge different traits more accurately. The possibilities for further investigation seem promising, indeed. One possibility that deserves investigation is that, if "chronicity" and resultant accuracy are a result of experience, then some kind of training might be possible to simulate this experience and improve the accuracy of judgment for at least one trait at a time.

    b. Good Target. A second possible moderator of self–other congruence is something that could be called "judgability": perhaps some individuals are easier to judge than are others. A prominent investigation into this possibility was the study by Bem and Allen (1974). These investigators simply asked their subjects, "how consistent are you?" on the traits of friendliness and conscientiousness, and found that self–other agreement on ratings of these traits (as well as other correlations between judges, between behaviors, and between judgments and behaviors) was higher within the self-identified consistent group than in the inconsistent group.

    Does this finding replicate? Chaplin and Goldberg (1985) reported an exhaustive attempt at replication that failed to find that self-rated consistency moderated self–other agreement. But Bem and Allen's basic result has been replicated in several other studies, including Campbell (1985), Cheek (1982), Kenrick and Stringfield (1980), and even Mischel and Peake (1982). Zuckerman et al. (1988) performed a meta-analysis of several studies in this area and concluded that the aggregate result was what they considered a small, but still significant, effect: there did seem to be a positive relationship between self-reported consistency and self–peer agreement.

    Later investigations by Zuckerman and his colleagues have tried to pin down the basis of this effect. Zuckerman, Bernieri, Koestner, and Rosenthal (1989) investigated three potential moderators of self–peer agreement: self-reported trait relevance, consistency of behavior, and observability of behavior. All three of these variables (when they were rated through a ranking procedure) were found to have significant moderator effects. (And, the observability finding is consistent with several studies considered, further on, under the heading Good Trait. In futher research, Zuckerman, Miyake, Koestner, Baldwin, and Osborne (1991) found that individuals who see themselves as particularly unusual on a given trait dimension tend to yield the best self–other agreement in ratings of that dimension.

    Cheek (1982) examined several personality variables as possible moderators of self–other congruence. The most promising results he reported were for the "acting ability" subscale of Self-Monitoring. Subjects earning high scores on this scale were described with better self–other agreement on each of four different personality traits. Cheek interprets this finding as a reflection of acting ability as a social skill: "If social skill leads to successful communication of one's self-image . . . then those who are socially skilled should have stronger agreements between self-ratings and peer ratings than those who are not so skilled" (p. 1265).

    Closely related to Cheek's notion of acting ability is the concept of "self-disclosure." Jourard (1971) suggests that self-disclosure is the process by which a person reveals his or her "thoughts, feelings, hopes and reactions to the past" (p. 5) to another person. Jourard (1971) has conducted empirical studies that indicate that there are individual differences in the amount that people disclose and the type of information that is disclosed. A more recent study by Koestner, Bernieri, and Zuckerman (1989) demonstrates that those traits which a person reports to be similar between his or her public versus private self also tend to be judged with better agreement between the self and his or her acquaintances.

In a very unusual study, Davidson (1993) presented evidence that self–other *disagreement* may occur when individuals engage in repression or suppression. In the former case, people will avoid particular thoughts and feelings but still express them through observable behaviors. Consistent with this idea, Colvin (1993a) argued that individuals who manifest a discrepancy between their private inner self and public outer self will be relatively difficult to judge, as manifested in lower self–other agreement. In the latter case, suppressors will avoid particular thoughts and feelings as well as their behavioral expression, although they may still respond to these "forbidden" ideas on a physiological level. The resulting lack of self-knowledge can be expected to produce discrepancies between the views of personality by the self and by others (Cheek, 1982; Colvin, 1993a).

Colvin's research is an attempt to integrate the literature on "judgability" (1993a, 1993b). In his first study, Colvin employed a multioperational, person-centered approach that demonstrated reliable individual differences in self–other agreement about entire personalities, rather than just specific traits. Individuals found to be most judgable, in this sense, were independently characterized as relatively extraverted, agreeable, emotionally stable, and conscientious. More generally, judgability was related to good psychological adjustment (Colvin, 1993a).

A further study showed that individual differences in judgability were stable from age 18 to age 23 (Colvin, 1993b). More important was the finding that adolescent ego-resiliency (a cocept closely akin to psychological adjustment) predicted judgability during young adulthood ($r = .54$ and $.45$ for men and women, respectively). This result is further evidence that individuals who are well adjusted are more likely to provide descriptions of their own personalities that agree well with the consensus of ratings by their friends and acquaintances.

c. Good Trait.   A third potential moderator of self–other congruence is the nature of the trait being evaluated: Are some traits judged with better agreement than others? Here, at least, the answer appears to be relatively simple yes.

Research about what might be a good trait in this sense goes back at least to a study by Estes (1938). Subjects attempted to judge the personalities of stimulus persons viewed in a brief movie film, and their accuracy was evaluated through comparison with judgments rendered of these persons by a panel of clinical judges. Estes found that, for example, inhibition–impulsion was judged more accurately than objectivity–projectivity. But no clear, overall pattern of results emerged, and it was also unclear whether the same traits were easiest to judge from the film would also be the easiest to judge in real life.

More recent research has been more informative and somewhat more consistent. Borgatta (1964), John and Robins (1993, 1994), Norman and Goldberg (1966), Hase and Goldberg (1967), McCrae (1982), Funder and Dobroth (1987), and Watson (1989) all showed that traits relevant to extraversion tended to manifest higher self–other congruence. Funder and Dobroth calculated agreement correlations between self-ratings and ratings by close acquaintances on each of the 100 items of the California Set (Block 1961/1978). They then correlated these 100 correlations with factor loadings of the 100 traits (as determined by McCrae, Costa, & Busch, 1986). The result is an indication of the kind of trait that yields the best agreement. By this method, self–acquaintance agreement was found to correlate $r = .29$ with extraversion, and $r = -.53$ with neuroticism (which is itself correlated $r = -.32$ with extraversion). Heath, Neale, Kessler, Eaves, and Kendler (1992) also found that extraversion yielded better self–other agreement than did neuroticism.

The trait property of subjective visibility has a quite general influence. For instance, the same traits that yield better self–acquaintance agreement also tend to yield better agreement among acquaintances (according to Funder & Colvin, 1988, $r = .57$, $p < .001$), and so it is not surprising that agreement among acquaintances correlates with subjective visibility with $r = .43$ ($p < .001$). Findings consistent with these have been reported by John and Robins (1993) and by Watson and Clark (1991). Moreover, Funder and Colvin asked each acquaintance to view a brief (5 min) videotape of a subject they did not know, and try to complete a Q-sort of that "stranger." A surprising amount of agreement was found between self-ratings and these strangers' ratings even in such impoverished circumstances (cf. Albright et al., 1988; Watson, 1989; see next section). More germane to the present point was the finding that self–stranger agreement correlated with subjective visibility with $r = .40$ ($p < .001$), and agreement between strangers correlated with subjective visibility with $r = .42$ ($p < .001$). The effect of subjective visibility on interjudge agreement seems powerful, robust, and general.[7]

This effect has philosophical implications, as well. If personality traits were no more than arbitrary social constructs, as implied by the sociological perspective discussed at the beginning of this chapter, then there would be no reason to expect some of them to be more observable than others. One can "construct" a trait like "fantasizes and daydreams" as readily as one can construct a trait like "is talkative." But, as Clark and Paivio (1989) point out, if different raters can agree better about more observable phenomena than they can about less observable phenomena, this finding implies that something is actually out there for these different raters to observe! The findings of higher interjudge agreement on more observable traits can therefore be added to the steadily accumulating evidence that personality traits are real properties of people (Funder, 1991; Kenrick & Funder, 1988).

---

[7] A possibility that must be borne in mind is that less visible traits also manifest less variance, and that therefore the lesser congruence on such traits might be an artifact of restricted range. In response to a suggestion by Lewis Goldberg, we computed the correlation between item variance and "visibility," which yielded $r = .52$, and the correlation between item variance and self–acquaintance agreement, which yielded $r = .49$. However, the partial correlation between visibility and agreement, controlling for variance, was still significant ($r = .39$). These results yield two conclusions. First, less visible traits are less variable, and yield lower agreement partially for that reason. But second, the effect of variance is not all there is to visibility. Judges seem not only to vary their ratings *less* when the items are less visible, they also seem to vary their ratings *less accurately*.

A different sort of "good trait" has been proposed by Gangestad, Simpson, DiGeronimo, and Biek (1992). From a functionalist perspective, these investigators propose that traits that are important for survival and reproduction would become more judgable as a result of evolutionary processes. They found that the trait of "sociosexuality," the tendency to be willing to engage in sexual relations in the absence of a personal relationship, was judged with better agreement than (in order) social potency, social closeness, and stress reaction. Their finding that social potency yielded better agreement than stress reaction is completely consistent with the work summarized above showing that extraversion yields better agreement than neuroticism. The finding about sociosexuality adds a new and interesting wrinkle.

   d. Good Information.   A final possible moderator of self–other congruence is the amount or kind of information upon which the peers' judgment is based.
   One conclusion that has emerged from recent research is that even a quite small amount of information can lead to judgments that appear to have a surprising amount of validity (see Ambady & Rosenthal, 1992, for a meta-analysis of this finding). Research on this topic has frequently employed the unfortunate term "zero acquaintance" to describe the relationship between target and judge. The term is misleading because in none of these studies is acquaintance in fact "zero," which we presume could only mean that no information about the target of judgment was available whatsoever. Each in fact provides the judge with minimal but real—and apparently useful—information. The judge may have observed the target only briefly in person, on a videotape, or in a photograph, and may have heard a voice recording or watched a brief behavioral episode. In any case, the conclusion that emerges from this research is that surprisingly valid ratings can emerge from minimal observation—but certainly *not* "zero acquaintance."
   Four studies are of particular interest. Each investigated self–other agreement in personality judgments among subjects who had little or no acquaintance with each other. Albright et al. (1988) examined ratings by subjects who sat in a small group together, but had not been given a chance to talk. These subjects were asked to describe each other's personality on each of five traits. Despite this minimal acquaintance, Albright et al. reported "a significant proportion of the variance [in ratings] was due to the stimulus target" (p. 387). Funder and Colvin (1988) looked at agreement between self-ratings on the Q-sort and judgments provided by observers who had viewed the subjects for only 5 min by watching a videotape. They found that 24 out of the 100 self–other agreement correlations were significant at the nominal .05 level, or nearly five times as many as would be expected by chance.
   In more recent research, Watson (1989) found that subjects in small groups who had heard each other speak their names, but nothing else, nonetheless manifested significant self–other agreement correlations for the traits of Extraversion, Conscientiousness, and (when the ratings of several peers were averaged) Agreeableness. Borkenau and Liebler (1993a) report that minimal observation was sufficient to yield significant self–other agreement on the traits of extraversion and conscientiousness, but not neuroticism, openness, or agreeableness.

It might not surprise the reader to learn that we believe one of the better-controlled studies of the effect of acquaintanceship on interjudge agreement may have been the one by Funder and Colvin (1988). In this study, as was mentioned earlier, targets were judged by two close acquaintances and by two strangers (acquaintances of other targets) who viewed them only on a brief videotape. The advantage of this design was that the acquaintanceship variable was manipulated experimentally; the targets and informants were the same under both the acquainted and the unacquainted conditions, and all that varied was the pairing between judges and targets. As was already mentioned, the self and strangers' Q-sort ratings agreed more strongly than might have been expected. But Funder and Colvin also found that more acquaintanceship led to better agreement: across all 100 items, the mean self-acquaintance $r = .27$ ($p < .01$), whereas the mean self–stranger $r = .05$ (ns). These means are significantly different, but statistics are hardly necessary because self–acquaintance agreement was higher than self–stranger agreement on each and every one of the 100 Q-sort items (but see Colvin & Funder, 1991, for a boundary condition for this effect).

Another well-controlled study, by Stinson and Ickes (1992), generalized the conclusion by Funder and Colvin. Stinson and Ickes found that friends agreed better than did strangers when trying to judge a person's thoughts and feelings. Even when the similarity between the target and the judge was statistically controlled, friends still demonstrated an advantage. Stinson and Ickes concluded that friends are more accurate in their inferences about their partner's thoughts and feelings as a result of their accumulated base of behavioral knowledge, which they use for prediction. Watson and Clark (1991) extended the acquaintanceship effect in a different direction, finding that well-acquainted peers agreed better than did relative strangers about each others' specifically emotional traits. Funder et al. (1995) examined, and ruled out, a couple of possible artifactual explanations for the effect of acquaintanceship on self–other and interjudge agreement. These included interjudge communication and assumed similarity. They concluded the most parsimonious explanation for the increase in judgmental agreement with acquaintanceship is also the most obvious one: that as you know somebody longer, the person becomes better known.

e. Moderators of Self–Other Agreement: General Comment. In an important and thought-provoking essay, Chaplin (1991) commented that the "blind" search for moderators of agreement is likely to produce only weak results that fail to replicate. However, moderator variables firmly grounded in theory are another story. When there are good, theoretical reasons to believe that a given construct will moderate the relationship between two other constructs, the operationalization of the moderator will be more similar to the "construct validity" approach (Cronbach & Meehl, 1955) than the currently more common "moderator of the week" approach. In the latter approach, researchers gather measurements of a moderator variable that might be interesting, and might be reliably measured, and give it a shot. In the former approach, much more attention will be given to the selection and measurement of relevant, reliable, and valid measures. Such additional effort is more likely to yield positive results. Theoretically derived moderators, as they begin to be hypothesized and then found, will be those that are most likely to replicate across studies and prove to be important (Funder, 1995).

IV. CONCEPTUAL ISSUES

A. Self–Other Agreement: Why Is It Important?

The issue of self–other congruence in personality judgments has generated a considerable amount of research over the years, and the pace of research has accelerated recently. Investigators seem to regard this issue as important for one of two reasons, and do subtly but importantly different kinds of research as a result.

The first reason to regard self–other agreement as important is as an end in itself (e.g., DePaulo et al., 1987; Kenny & LaVoie, 1984; Swann, 1984). The emphasis here is on how judgmental congruence is an intrinsically important feature of the social world. For instance, your ability to predict what others think of you could have some obvious strategic value in social interaction and negotiation. This is a perfectly plausible reason to regard self–other congruence as important, but research that follows this approach sometimes seems unfortunately reluctant to acknowledge personality as a real construct that could actually be judged accurately or inaccurately, as opposed to merely agreed or disagreed about (cf. Cook, 1984; Stryker & Gottlieb, 1981). This leads to a neglect of the possibility of gathering *other* data, independent of others' and self-judgments, that might help determine judgmental validity (Funder, 1995).

The other reason to regard self–other congruence as important is as a possible indicator of judgmental accuracy. But one must be careful; two equally serious kinds of mistake are often made about the connection between agreement and accuracy. The first is to regard the two terms of synonymous. More than a few articles in the literature include accuracy in their title but only agreement in their methods. Agreement is merely one possible and fallible indicator of accuracy; it deserves a place in the array of converging methodologies for assessing judgmental accuracy, but agreement is not accuracy itself. The second kind of mistake is just as bad—regarding agreement as totally irrelevant to accuracy. Researchers who enjoy investigating judgmental errors, for instance, typically regard whatever judgmental agreement exists as evidence only that illusions can be shared (Ross, 1977).

B. The Relation between Agreement and Accuracy

To regard agreement as irrelevant to accuracy is not a tenable position on either philosophical or empirical grounds. Logically, the relationship between agreement and accuracy is real although asymmetric: two judgments that agree may not be accurate, but two judgments that do not agree cannot both be accurate. In relation to the accuracy issue, therefore, the investigation of interjudge agreement is technically a matter of testing the null hypothesis. If agreement is found, accuracy cannot be implied. But if agreement is not found, then inaccuracy (of at least one judge) must be implied. Therefore, investigations of interjudge agreement serve to put at risk the hypothesis that judgments are accurate. Agreement is regularly found, as summarized in this chapter, and so the accuracy hypothesis has in this sense repeatedly survived potential disconfirmation. Many other well-established hypotheses in the psychological literature are supported, indirectly, in exactly the same way.

Still, the logical connection between agreement and accuracy remains less than airtight. Two judges can agree for the wrong reasons. It is reassuring, therefore, that a survey of the empirical data in this area also supports the existence of a connection. A fair amount of research leads to the following conclusion: Everything we can think of that, it seems, *should* improve judgmental accuracy, in fact *does* improve interjudge agreement. Some evidence has already been reviewed. Traits that seem, on common-sense grounds, to be more visible, in fact are judged with better agreement, no matter whose judgments are being compared (Funder & Colvin, 1988). Knowing a person better, or at least longer, seems like something that would improve accuracy. It is something that improves agreement.

C. Next Steps: Beyond Agreement

There seem to be good grounds for including the study of self–other (and other–other) agreement as part of the study of judgmental accuracy. But as accuracy research begins to enjoy its recent renewal and second childhood, it will need to branch out. Accuracy research should begin to include other criteria, including, most critically, the prediction of behavior (Funder, 1993, 1995).

This endeavor will not be easy. Too much research already has consisted of measuring some almost randomly chosen but convenient behavior in a sample of subjects, failing to find correlations between this behavior and some personality judgment, and concluding the judgment to be faulty. To be done properly, research in this area will have to be as careful establishing the reliability and construct validity of the behavioral measures as psychometricians traditionally have been in selecting their questionnaire items (Jackson & Paunonen, 1985). It is harder to measure behaviors than to ask questions though; the necessary research will be difficult and is, to date, almost untried.

The basic problem with using the ability to predict behavior as a criterion for judgmental accuracy is, ironically, the opposite problem from that entailed by using agreement as a criterion. The problem with agreement is that two judges that agree still might not be accurate. The problem with behavioral predictability is that a judgment that fails to predict a particular behavior still might be correct: maybe the wrong behavior was measured, or the right behavior was measured, but with such low reliability that prediction became impossible for that reason alone.

The use of behavioral prediction as a criterion for accuracy, promising as it seems, will be no panacea. Accuracy is a lot like construct validity (Cronbach &

Meehl, 1955); it may be exactly the same thing. You can never assess it directly, or prove it with one or even with several experiments. You can only accumulate evidence, try to use judgment, and gradually become convinced that it exists. The most convincing evidence consists of convergences between data of very different sorts, gathered through diverse and independent methods. Behavioral prediction is an excellent criterion for accuracy, but it is imperfect. In order to assess the accuracy of judgments of personality, we will always want to know, first, whether the judgments agree with each other.

ACKNOWLEDGMENTS

Preparation of this chapter and the original research it reports were supported by NIMH Grant R01-MH42427 to D.C.F. We are grateful to Oliver P. John and Robert R. McCrae for helpful comments on an earlier draft.

REFERENCES

Albright, L., Kenny, D. A., & Malloy, T. E. (1988). Consensus in personality judgments at zero acquaintance. *Journal of Personality and Social Psychology, 55,* 387–395.

Ambady, N., & Rosenthal, R. (1992). Thin slices of expressive behavior as predictors of interpersonal consequences: A meta-analysis. *Psychological Bulletin, 111,* 256–274.

Andersen, S. M. (1984). Self-knowledge and social inference: II. The diagnosticity of cognitive/affective and behavioral data. *Journal of Personality and Social Psychology, 46,* 294–307.

Bargh, J. A., & Pratto, F. (1986). Individual construct accessibility and perceptual selection. *Journal of Experimental Social Psychology, 22,* 293–311.

Bem, D. J., & Allen, A. (1974). On predicting some of the people some of the time: The search for cross-situational consistencies in behavior. *Psychological Review, 81,* 506–520.

Bem, D. J., & Funder, D. C. (1978). Predicting more of the people more of the time: Assessing the personality of situations. *Psychological Review, 85,* 485–501.

Bender, I. E., & Hastorf, A. H. (1950). The perception of persons: Forecasting another person's responses on three personality scales. *Journal of Abnormal and Social Psychology, 45,* 556–561.

Bernieri, F. J., Zuckerman, M., Koestner, R., & Rosenthal, R. (1994). Measuring person perception accuracy: Another look at self-other agreement. *Personality and Social Psychology Bulletin, 4,* 367–378.

Bledsoe, J. C., & Wiggins, R. G. (1973). Congruence of adolescents' self-concepts and parents' perceptions of adolescents' self-concepts. *Journal of Psychology, 83,* 131–136.

Block, J. (1978). *The Q-sort method in personality assessment and psychiatric research.* Palo Alto, CA: Consulting Psychologists Press. (Original work published 1961)

Blumer, H. (1937). Social psychology. In E. P. Schmidt (Ed.), *Man and society.* New York: Prentice-Hall.

Borgatta, E. F. (1964). The structure of personality characteristics. *Behavioral Science, 9,* 8–17.

Borkenau, P., & Liebler, A. (1992). Trait inferences: Sources of validity at zero acquaintance. *Journal of Personality and Social Psychology, 62,* 645–657.

Borkenau, P., & Liebler, A. (1993a). Consensus and self-other agreement for trait inferences from minimal information. *Journal of Personality, 61,* 477–496.

Borkenau, P., & Liebler, A. (1993b). Convergence of stranger ratings of personality and intelligence with self-ratings, partner ratings, and measured intelligence. *Journal of Personality and Social Psychology, 65,* 546–553.

Bourne, E. (1977). Can we describe an individual's personality? Agreement on stereotype versus individual attributes. *Journal of Personality and Social Psychology, 35,* 863–872.

Bronfenbrenner, U., Harding, J., & Gallwey, M. (1958). The measurement of skill in social perception. In D. McClelland (Ed.), *Talent and society: New perspectives in the identification of talent.* New York: Van Nostrand.

Brown, J. D. (1986). Evaluations of self and others: Self-enhancement biases in social judgments. *Social Cognition, 4,* 353–376.

Campbell, J. B. (1985, April). *Cross-situational consistency of personality attributes.* Paper presented at the annual meetings of the Eastern Psychological Association, Boston.

Chaplin, W. F. (1991). The next generation of moderator research in personality psychology. *Journal of Personality, 59,* 143–178.

Chaplin, W. F., & Goldberg, L. R. (1985). A failure to replicate the Bem and Allen study of individual differences in cross-situational consistency. *Journal of Personality and Social Psychology, 47,* 1074–1090.

Chaplin, W. F., & Panter, A. T. (1993). Shared meaning and the convergence among observers' personality descriptions. *Journal of Personality, 61,* 553–585.

Cheek, J. M. (1982). Aggregation, moderator variables, and the validity of personality tests: A peer rating study. *Journal of Personality and Social Psychology, 43,* 1254–1269.

Cialdini, R. B., & Richardson, K. D. (1980). Two indirect tactics of image management: Basking and blasting. *Journal of Personality and Social Psychology, 39,* 406–415.

Clark, J. M., & Paivio, A. (1989). Observational and theoretical terms in psychology: A cognitive perspective on scientific language. *American Psychologist, 44,* 500–512.

Colvin, C. R. (1993a). Judgable people: Personality, behavior, and competing explanations. *Journal of Personality and Social Psychology, 64,* 861–873.

Colvin, C. R. (1993b). Childhood antecedents of young-adult judgability. *Journal of Personality, 61,* 611–635.

Colvin, C. R., & Block, J. (1994). Do positive illusions foster mental health? An examination of the Taylor and Brown formulation. *Psychological Bulletin, 116,* 3–20.

Colvin, C. R., & Funder, D. C. (1991). Predicting personality and behavior: A boundary on the acquaintanceship effect. *Journal of Personality and Social Psychology, 60,* 884–894.

Conley, J. J. (1985). Longitudinal stability of personality traits: A multitrait-multimethod-multioccasion analysis. *Journal of Personality and Social Psychology, 49,* 1266–1282.

Conrad, H. S. (1932). The validity of personality ratings of preschool children. *Journal of Educational Psychology, 23,* 671–680.

Cook, M. (1984). *Issues in person perception.* London: Methuen.

Cronbach, L. J. (1955). Processes affecting scores on "understanding of others" and "assumed similarity." *Psychological Bulletin, 52,* 177–193.

Cronbach, L. J., & Meehl, P. E. (1955). Construct validity in psychological tests. *Psychological Bulletin, 52,* 177–193.

Davidson, K. W. (1993). Suppression and repression in discrepant self-other ratings: Relations with thought control and cardiovascular reactivity. *Journal of Personality, 61,* 669–691.

DePaulo, B. M., Kenny, D. A., Hoover, C. W., Webb, W., & Oliver, P. V. (1987). Accuracy of person perception: Do people know what kinds of impressions they convey? *Journal of Personality and Social Psychology, 52*, 303–315.

Donahue, E. M., Robins, R. W., Roberts, B. W., & John, O. P. (1993). The divided self: Concurrent and longitudinal effects of psychological adjustment and social roles on self-concept differentiation. *Journal of Personality and Social Psychology, 64*, 834–846.

Edwards, A. L., & Klockars, A. J. (1981). Significant others and self-evaluation: Relationships between perceived and actual evaluations. *Journal of Personality and Social Psychology, 7*, 244–251.

Erdelyi, M. H. (1974). A new look at the new look: Perceptual defense and vigilance. *Psychological Review, 81*, 1–25.

Estes, S. G. (1938). Judging personality from expressive behavior. *Journal of Abnormal and Social Psychology, 33*, 217–236.

Fine, R. (1986). *Narcissism, the self and society.* New York: Columbia University Press.

Fiske, D. W., & Cox, J. A., Jr. (1960). The consistency of ratings by peers. *Journal of Applied Psychology, 44*, 11–17.

Funder, D. C. (1980a). On seeing ourselves as others see us: Self-other agreement and discrepancy in personality ratings. *Journal of Personality, 48*, 473–493.

Funder, D. C. (1980b). The "trait" of ascribing traits: Individual differences in the tendency to trait ascription: *Journal of Research in Personality, 14*, 376–385.

Funder, D. C. (1982). On the accuracy of dispositional vs. situational attributions. *Social Cognition, 1*, 205–222.

Funder, D. C. (1987). Errors and mistakes: Evaluating the accuracy of social judgment. *Psychological Bulletin, 101*, 75–90.

Funder, D. C. (1989). Accuracy in personality judgment and the dancing bear. In D. M. Buss & N. Cantor (Eds.), *Personality psychology: Recent trends and emerging directions* (pp. 210–223). New York: Springer-Verlag.

Funder, D. C. (1991). Global traits: A Neo-Allportian approach to personality. *Psychological Science, 2*, 31–39.

Funder, D. C. (1993). Judgments as data for personality and developmental psychology. In D. Funder, R. Parke, C. Tomlinson-Keasey, & K. Widaman (Eds.), *Studying lives through time: Approaches to personality and development* (pp. 121–146). Washington, DC: American Psychological Association.

Funder, D. C. (1995). On the accuracy of personality judgment: A realistic approach. *Psychological Review, 102*, 652–670.

Funder, D. C., & Colvin, C. R. (1988). Friends and strangers: Acquaintanceship, agreement, and the accuracy of personality judgment. *Journal of Personality and Social Psychology, 55*, 149–158.

Funder, D. C., & Dobroth, K. M. (1987). Differences between traits: Properties associated with interjudge agreement. *Journal of Personality and Social Psychology, 52*, 409–418.

Funder, D. C., Kolar, D. C., & Blackman, M. C. (1995). Agreement among judges of personality: Interpersonal relations, similarity, and acquaintanceship. *Journal of Personality and Social Psychology, 69*, 656–672.

Funder, D. C., & West, S. G. (1993). Consensus, self-other agreement, and accuracy in personality judgment: An introduction. *Journal of Personality, 61*, 457–476.

Gage, N. L., & Cronbach, L. J. (1955). Conceptual and methodological problems in interpersonal perception. *Psychological Review, 62*, 411–422.

Gangestad, S. W., Simpson, J. A., DiGeronimo, K., & Biek, M. (1992). Differential accuracy in person perception across traits: Examination of a functional hypothesis. *Journal of Personality and Social Psychology, 62,* 688–698.

Goldberg, L. R., Norman, W. T., & Schwartz, E. (1980). The comparative validity of questionnaire data (16PF scales) and objective test data (O-A battery) in predicting five peer-rating criteria. *Applied Psychological Measurement, 4,* 183–194.

Golding, S. L. (1975). Flies in the ointment: Methodological problems in the analysis of the percentage of variance due to person and situations. *Psychological Bulletin, 82,* 278–288.

Gormly, J. (1984). Correspondence between personality trait ratings and behaviorial events. *Journal of Personality, 52,* 220–232.

Greenwald, A. G., & Pratkanis, A. R. (1984). The self. In R. S. Wyer & T. K. Srull (Eds.), *Handbook of social cognition* (pp. 129–178). Hillsdale, NJ: Erlbaum.

Hase, H. D., & Goldberg, L. R. (1967). Comparative validity of different strategies of constructing personality inventory scales. *Psychological Bulletin, 67,* 231–248.

Hastorf, A. H., & Bender, I. E. (1952). A caution respecting the measurement of empathic ability. *Journal of Abnormal and Social Psychology, 47,* 574–576.

Heath, A. C., Neale, M. C., Kessler, R. C., Eaves, L. J., & Kendler, K. S. (1992). Evidence for genetic influences on personality from self-reports and informant ratings. *Journal of Personality and Social Psychology, 63,* 85–96.

Higgins, E. T., King, G. A., & Mavin, G. H. (1982). Individual construct accessibility and subjective impressions and recall. *Journal of Personality and Social Psychology, 43,* 35–47.

Hirsch, J. (1986). Behavior-genetic analysis. In J. Medioni & G. Vaysse (Eds.), *Readings from the 19th international ethological conference: Genetic approaches to behavior* (pp. 129–138). Toulouse, France: Privat Publisher.

Hirschberg, N. (1978). A correct treatment of traits. In H. London (Ed.), *Personality: A new look at metatheories* (pp. 45–68). Washington, DC: Hemisphere.

Ickes, W. (1993). Empathic accuracy. *Journal of Personality, 61,* 587–610.

Jackson, D. N. (1982). Some preconditions for valid person perception. In M. P. Zanna, E. T. Higgins, & C. P. Herman (Eds.), *Consistency in social behavior: The Ontario Symposium* (Vol. 2). Hillsdale, NJ: Erlbaum.

Jackson, D. N., Neill, J. A., & Bevan, A. R. (1973). An evaluation of forced-choice and true-false item formats in personality assessment. *Journal of Research in Personality, 7,* 21–30.

Jackson, D. N., & Paunonen, S. V. (1985). Construct validity and the prediction of behavior. *Journal of Personality and Social Psychology, 49,* 554–570.

John, O. P. (1986). How shall a trait be called: A feature analysis of altruism. In A. Angleitner, A. Furnham, & G. van Heck (Eds.), *Personality psychology in Europe: Current trends and controversies* (pp. 117–140). Berwyn, PA: Swets North America.

John, O. P., & Robins, R. W. (1993). Determinants of interjudge agreement on personality traits: The Big Five domains, observability, evaluativeness, and the unique perspective of the self. *Journal of Personality, 61,* 521–531.

John, O. P. & Robins, R. W. (1994). Accuracy and bias in self-perception: Individual differences in self-enhancement and narcissisim. *Journal of Personality and Social Psychology, 66,* 206–219.

Jones, E. E., & Nisbett, R. E. (1987). The actor and observer: Divergent perceptions of the causes of behavior. In E. E. Jones, D. Kanouse, H. H. Kelley, R. E. Nisbett, S. Valins, &

B. Weiner (Eds.), *Attribution: Perceiving the causes of behavior* (pp. 79–94). Hillsdale, NJ: Erlbaum. (Originally published 1971).

Jourard, S. M. (1971). *The transparent self.* New York: Van Nostrand.

Kamman, R., Smith, R., Martin, C., & McQueen, M. (1984). Low accuracy in judgments of others' psychological well-being as seen from a phenomenological perspective. *Journal of Personality, 52,* 107–123.

Kenny, D. A. (1994). *Interpersonal perception: A social relations analysis.* New York: Guilford.

Kenny, D. A., & LaVoie, L. (1984). The social relations model. In L. Berkowitz (Ed.), *Advances in experimental social psychology* (Vol. 18, pp. 141–179). New York: Academic Press.

Kenrick, D. T., & Funder, D. C. (1988). Profiting from controversy: Lessons from the person-situation debate. *American Psychologist, 43,* 23–34.

Kenrick, D. T., & Stringfield, D. O. (1980). Personality traits and the eye of the beholder: Crossing some traditional philosophical boundaries in the search for consistency in all of the people. *Psychological Review, 87,* 88–104.

Koestner, R., Bernieri, F., & Zuckerman, M. (1989). Trait-specific versus person-specific moderators of cross-situational consistency. *Journal of Personality, 57,* 1–16.

Krones, J. M., & Funder, D. C. (1989). *The effect of perspective on attributions over time.* Unpublished manuscript, University of Illinois, Urbana.

Kruglarski, A. W. (1989). The psychology of being "right": The problem of accuracy in social perception and cognition. *Psychological Bulletin, 106,* 395–409.

Kunda, Z. (1987). Motivated inference: Self-serving generation and evaluation of causal theories. *Journal of Personality and Social Psychology, 53,* 636–647.

Lepper, M. R., Greene, D., & Nisbett, R. E. (1973). Undermining children's intrinsic interest with extrinsic rewards: A test of the "overjustification" hypothesis. *Journal of Personality and Social Psychology, 28,* 129–137.

Lerner, M. J. (1980). *The belief in a just world: A fundamental delusion.* New York: Plenum Press.

Lewicki, P. (1983). Self-image bias in person perception. *Journal of Personality and Social Psychology, 45,* 384–393.

Lewicki, P. (1984). Self-schema and social information processing. *Journal of Personality and Social Psychology, 47,* 1177–1190.

Marsh, H. W., Barnes, J., & Hocevar, D. (1985). Self-other agreement on multidimensional self-concept ratings: Factor analysis and multitrait-multimethod analysis. *Journal of Personality and Social Psychology, 49,* 1360–1377.

McCrae, R. R. (1982). Consensual validation of personality traits: Evidence from self-reports and ratings. *Journal of Personality and Social Psychology, 43,* 293–303.

McCrae, R. R., Costa, P. T., Jr., & Busch, C. M. (1986). Evaluating comprehensiveness in personality systems: The California Q-set and the five factor model. *Journal of Personality, 54,* 430–446.

McKay, J. R., O'Farrell, T. J., Maisto, S. A., Connors, G. J., & Funder, D. C. (1989). Biases in relapse attributions made by alchoholics and their wives. *Addictive Behaviors, 14,* 513–522.

Mead, G. H. (1934). *Mind, self and society.* Chicago: University of Chicago Press.

Miller, D. T., & Porter, C. A. (1980). Effects of temporal perspective on the attribution process. *Journal of Personality and Social Psychology, 39,* 532–541.

Miller, D. T., & Ross, M. (1975). Self-serving biases in the attribution of causality: Fact or fiction? *Psychological Bulletin, 82,* 213–225.

Mischel, W., & Peake, P. K. (1982). Beyond déja vu in the search for cross-situational consistency. *Psychological Review, 89,* 730–755.

Monson, T. C., & Snyder, M. (1977). Actors, observers, and the attribution process: Toward a reconceptualization. *Journal of Experimental Social Psychology, 13,* 89–111.

Monson, T. C., Tanke, E. D., & Lund, J. (1980). Determinants of social perception in a naturalistic setting. *Journal of Research in Personality, 14,* 104–120.

Moore, B. S., Sherrod, D. R., Liu, T. J., & Underwood, B. (1979). The dispositional shift in attribution over time. *Journal of Experimental Social Psychology, 15,* 553–569.

Moskowitz, D. S. (1990). Convergence of self-reports and independent observers: Dominance and friendliness. *Journal of Personality and Social Psychology, 58,* 1096–1106.

Nisbett, R. E. (1980). The trait construct in lay and professional psychology. In L. Festinger (Ed.), *Retrospections on social psychology* (pp. 109–130). New York: Oxford University Press.

Nisbett, R. E., Caputo, C., Legant, P., & Marecek, J. (1973). Behavior as seen by the actor and as seen by the observer. *Journal of Personality and Social Psychology, 27,* 154–165.

Nisbett, R. E., & Ross, L. (1980). *Human inference: Strategies and shortcomings of social judgment.* New York: Prentice-Hall.

Norman, W. T. (1969). "To see oursels as ithers see us!": Relations among self-perceptions, peer-perceptions, and expected peer-perceptions of personality attributes. *Multivariate Behavior Research, 4,* 417–433.

Norman, W. T., & Goldberg, L. R. (1966). Raters, ratees, and randomness in personality structure. *Journal of Personality and Social Psychology, 4,* 681–691.

Park, B., & Judd, C. M. (1989). Agreement on initial impressions: Differences due to perceivers, trait dimensions, and target behaviors. *Journal of Personality and Social Psychology, 56,* 493–505.

Paunonen, S. V. (1989). Consensus in personality judgments: Moderating effects of target-rater acquaintanceship and behavior observability. *Journal of Personality and Social Psychology, 56,* 823–833.

Paunonen, S. V., & Jackson, D. N. (1985). Idiographic measurement strategies for personality and prediction: Some unredeemed promissory notes. *Psychological Review, 92,* 486–511.

Regan, D. T., & Totten, J. (1975). Empathy and attribution: Turning observers into actors. *Journal of Personality and Social Psychology, 32,* 850–856.

Robins, R. W., Spranca, M. D., & Mendelsohn, G. A. (1996). The actor-observer effect revisited: Effects of individual differences and repeated social interactions on actor and observer attributions. *Journal of Personality and Social Psychology, 71,* 375–389.

Ross, L. (1977). The intuitive psychologist and his shortcomings. In L. Berkowitz (Ed.), *Advances in experimental social psychology* (Vol. 10, pp. 174–214). New York: Academic Press.

Ross, L., Greene, D., & House, P. (1977). The false consensus phenomenon: An attributional bias in self-perception and social perception processes. *Journal of Personality and Social Psychology, 34,* 485–494.

Schneider, D. J., Hastorf, A. H., & Ellsworth, P. C. (1979). *Person perception* (2nd ed.). Reading, MA: Addison-Wesley.

Scott, W. A., & Johnson, R. C. (1972). Comparative validities of direct and indirect personality tests. *Journal of Consulting and Clinical Psychology, 38,* 301–318.

Shrauger, J. S., & Schoeneman, T. J. (1979). Symbolic interactionist view of self-concept: Through the looking glass darkly. *Psychological Bulletin, 86,* 549–573.

Stinson, L., & Ickes, W. (1992). Empathic accuracy in the interactions of male friends versus male strangers. *Journal of Personality and Social Psychology, 62,* 787–797.

Storms, M. D. (1973). Videotape and the attribution process: Reversing actors' and observers' points of view. *Journal of Personality and Social Psychology, 27,* 165–175.

Stryker, S., & Gottlieb, A. (1981). Attribution theory and symbolic interactionism: A comparison. In J. H. Harvey, W. Ickes, & R. F. Kidd (Eds.), *New directions in attribution research* (Vol. 3). Hillsdale, NJ: Erlbaum.

Swann, W. B., Jr. (1984). Quest for accuracy in person perception: A matter of pragmatics. *Psychological Review, 91,* 457–477.

Taft, R. (1955). The ability to judge people. *Psychological Bulletin, 52,* 1–23.

Taft, R. (1966). Accuracy of empathic judgments of acquaintances and strangers. *Journal of Personality and Social Psychology, 3,* 600–604.

Taylor, S. E. (1983). Adjustment to threatening events: A theory of cognitive adaptation. *American Psychologist, 38,* 1161–1173.

Tesser, A., & Campbell, J. (1982). Self-evaluation maintenance and the perception of friends and strangers. *Journal of Personality, 50,* 261–279.

Tetlock, P. E., & Levi, A. (1982). Attribution bias: On the inconclusiveness of the cognition-motivation debate. *Journal of Experimental Social Psychology, 18,* 68–88.

Watson, D. (1982). The actor and the observer: How are their perceptions of causality divergent? *Psychological Bulletin, 92,* 682–700.

Watson, D. (1989). Strangers' ratings of the five robust personality factors: Evidence of a surprising convergence with self-report. *Journal of Personality and Social Psychology, 57,* 120–128.

Watson, D., & Clark, L. A. (1991). Self versus peer ratings of specific emotional traits: Evidence of convergent and discriminant validity. *Journal of Personality and Social Psychology, 60,* 927–940.

Wiggins, J. S. (1973). *Personality and prediction: Principles of personality assessment.* Reading, MA: Addison-Wesley.

Woodruffe, C. (1985). Consensual validation of personality traits: Additional evidence and individual differences. *Journal of Personality and Social Psychology, 48,* 1240–1252.

Vogt, D., & Colvin, C. R. (1996, August). *Individual differences in judgmental ability.* Paper presented at the Annual Meetings of the American Psychological Association, Toronto.

Zuckerman, M., Bernieri, F., Koestner, R., & Rosenthal, R. (1989). To predict some of the people some of the time: In search of moderators. *Journal of Personality and Social Psychology, 57,* 279–293.

Zuckerman, M., Koestner, R., DeBoy, T., Garcia, T., Maresca, B. C., & Sartoris, J. M. (1988). To predict some of the people some of the time: A reexamination of the moderator variable approach in personality theory. *Journal of Personality and Social Psychology, 54,* 1006–1019.

Zuckerman, M., Miyake, K., Koestner, R., Baldwin, C. H., & Osborne, J. W. (1991). Uniqueness as a moderator of self-peer agreement. *Personality and Social Psychology Bulletin, 17,* 385–391.

CHAPTER 25

THE QUEST FOR SELF-INSIGHT

THEORY AND RESEARCH ON ACCURACY AND BIAS IN SELF-PERCEPTION

RICHARD W. ROBINS
UNIVERSITY OF CALIFORNIA, DAVIS

OLIVER P. JOHN
UNIVERSITY OF CALIFORNIA, BERKELEY

I. INTRODUCTION

The quest for self-insight has been a pervasive concern for over 25 centuries. In the 7th century B.C., when the citizens of ancient Greece sought advice from the oracle at Delphi they were greeted with the salutation, "know thyself." The influence of this maxim on Western thought is generally attributed to Socrates, who questioned why people should pry into the heavens while they are still ignorant of their own selves. "The unexamined life is not worth living," Socrates told his disciples, for through self-knowledge lies the path to truth, virtue, and happiness.

The ancient Greek mandate to "know thyself" foreshadowed a perennial problem: What is self-insight and how does one acquire it? Since the early days of psychology, researchers interested in self-insight have explored a number of intriguing questions: How well do people know themselves? Which psychological processes promote accurate self-perception and which promote distortion? How can true self-knowledge be distinguished from self-deception and hubris? What criteria can be used to evaluate the veracity of a person's self-views?

This chapter provides a review and integration of current theory and research on self-perception accuracy in personality and social psychology.[1] We address two broad conceptual issues in the study of self-perception accuracy: (a) What is accuracy and how should it be measured? and (b) What psychological processes are involved in self-perception? To organize our review and analysis of the literature, we discuss two conceptual frameworks. The first defines the various criteria researchers have used to measure accuracy and classifies them into six broad categories: *operational, social consensus, functional/pragmatic, normative models, information processing, and internal consistency* (Robins & John, 1996a). The second framework characterizes the self-perception process from four different theoretical perspectives and uses a metaphor to capture the essence of each perspective: *the Scientist, the Consistency Seeker, the Politician,* and *the Egoist.* In the final section, we illustrate the heuristic value of these metaphors by applying them to our own research on self-enhancement bias. In this section, we also discuss the implications of accurate self-perception for mental health. Is self-insight worth pursuing, as Socrates suggested, or are people better off maintaining positive illusions about themselves (cf. Taylor & Brown, 1988)?

II. WHAT IS ACCURACY AND HOW SHOULD IT BE MEASURED?

A. The Criterion Problem

How do we know whether a person has self-insight? At first, the answer seems deceptively simple: Individuals have self-insight if they perceive themselves accurately. To study self-insight, then, one need only compare a person's view of him- or herself with what that person is truly like. And therein lies the problem. We do not know the true nature of the person. That is, there are no absolute, perfectly objective measures of a person's traits, capabilities, motives, and so on. Thus, although we can tell how tall people are by measuring their height with a ruler or how heavy they are by weighing them on a scale, we cannot tell how neurotic people are in an equally objective manner. For most attributes of interest to psychologists, we have only indirect measures (e.g., a questionnaire scale of neuroticism) from which the constructs of interest must be inferred. Thus, we are left with a conundrum: How can we study self-insight in the absence of an absolute standard for reality?

---

[1] In this chapter, we define the term accuracy broadly to include both validity and bias. Validity is typically defined by the correspondence (e.g., correlation) between self-perceptions and a criterion, whereas bias is typically defined in terms of directional deviations (e.g., positive or negative) from a criterion. These two measures are statistically independent; for example, self-perceptions could be more positive than a criterion but still be highly correlated with that criterion.

B. Defining Accuracy: Three Perspectives

Unfortunately, the criterion problem has no simple solution. Instead, researchers have conceptualized accuracy in ways that make it amenable to empirical inquiry. To provide an overview of these various conceptualizations, we summarize three perspectives below (see also Fiske, 1993; Hastie & Rasinski, 1988; Judd & Park, 1993; Jussim, 1993; Swann, 1984).

Kruglanski (1989) differentiated three notions of judgmental accuracy: consensus, correspondence, and pragmatic utility. The first, *consensus*, implies that a judgment is accurate if it agrees with judgments by others. The problem, however, is that human judgments are fallible and subject to bias. The *correspondence* notion of accuracy refers to the relation between a subject's judgment and a criterion for reality. For example, self-ratings of personality can be said to be accurate if they correspond with ratings by knowledgeable informants. The major problem, according to Kruglanski (1989), is identifying an appropriate criterion: "criteria for accurate judgments are not invariably self-evident. Often they need to be justified by complex argument or indirect evidence . . . . [T]he accuracy of any given criterion . . . is perennially open to criticism . . . [and] accuracy standards are themselves judgments contingent on argument and evidence" (p. 396). Kruglanski suggested that it is especially important for subjects and experimenters to agree about the appropriateness of the criterion. Kruglanski's third notion of accuracy involves considerations of *pragmatic utility*—the adaptive or functional value of the judgment. From this perspective, a judgment is accurate if it is useful to the individual, that is, if it is related to successful task accomplishment, goal attainment, and other desirable outcomes. Accuracy, then, should be assessed on the basis of outcomes that have adaptive significance for the individual.

Kenny (1991, 1994) focused on the use of observer judgments in research on accuracy and consensus (i.e., interjudge agreement) (Robins & John, 1996b). Noting that the human observer is "the most valued 'instrument' used by psychologists" (p. 156), Kenny provided a formal definition of accuracy formulated in terms of observer judgments: "the average judgment made by all possible observers of all possible target behaviors" (p. 159). This definition, intended as a theoretical ideal (like a true score), carries three basic assumptions derived from psychometric theory. First, averaging judgments across observers helps cancel out random errors in individual judgments. Second, the use of "all possible observers" eliminates systematic bias due to a particular sampling of observers. Third, the observation of all possible behaviors ensures that all relevant information is available to the judges. To Kenny, then, the truth about a person can be found at the intersection of judgments by all observers of all behaviors exhibited by the person.

Funder (e.g., 1987, 1990, 1993) has written extensively on accuracy issues, particularly in the context of personality judgments. He has argued that "the study of accuracy in judgment is exactly the same thing as measurement validity, where the measurements being validated are interpersonal judgments'' (Funder, 1990, p. 208). From this perspective, a personality judgment is accurate if it agrees with judgments by others and predicts behaviors relevant to the trait being judged. Although Funder did not equate interjudge agreement with accuracy, he pointed out that judgments that agree with each other are more likely to be accurate than judgments that do not agree. That is, consensus is a necessary but not sufficient condition for accuracy. Funder also emphasized the importance of studying accuracy in real-world contexts, noting that a judgment deemed an error in the laboratory may be accurate, or at least adaptive, in a person's everyday life. In this context, Funder contrasted two broad categories of judgment research, the accuracy paradigm and the error paradigm. Accuracy is usually gauged in real-world contexts by comparing subjects' judgments to an external criterion. Errors, in contrast, are usually gauged in experimental contexts by comparing subjects' judgments to criteria derived from a normative model that prescribes how the judgments should be made (e.g., Bayes' theorem).

C. Measuring Accuracy: Six Categories of Accuracy Criteria

The writings of Kruglanski, Kenny, and Funder point to the myriad ways accuracy has been conceptualized and assessed. However, each of these accounts is incomplete and the field has needed a comprehensive framework that would organize the various criteria used in empirical research. To this end, we recently reviewed the research literature and proposed a framework consisting of six distinct categories of accuracy criteria: *operational, social consensus, functional/pragmatic, normative models, information processing (cue use),* and *internal consistency* (see Robins & John, 1996a, for a more extensive discussion; 1996b). The six categories are conceptually based, rather than being based on the specific method or data source used. That is, the categories reflect different definitions of accuracy and classify criteria according to the assumptions that justify their use as standards for accuracy. Although we have described the framework in terms of self-perception accuracy, the categories apply equally well to research on social perception. We next review each category and provide examples.

Operational (or reality) criteria are difficult to find in the domain of personality. Nonetheless, some personality characteristics can be assessed in much the same way as height or weight. For example, talkativeness can be defined as the amount a person talks. Therefore, the number of words spoken in a conversation may be interpreted as a direct operational criterion for self-ratings of talkativeness. In this example, there is a direct correspondence between the *definition* of the construct being rated (talkativeness) and the *interpretation* of the criterion measure (number of words spoken). Another example of a direct criterion for reality comes from research on self-perceptions of test performance where a subject's actual test performance provides an operational criterion (e.g., Beyer, 1990). A third example comes from research on the accuracy of people's expectations about the future. We have used an actual outcome (course grades) as a criterion for students' expectations about what grade they will receive in the course (Robins, 1996). We found that about half of the students expected to attain higher grades in the beginning of the semester than they actually received, about one-quarter of the students expected lower grades than they received, and about one-quarter were accurate, receiving exactly the grades they expected. Finally, in studies of self-ratings of personality, the absence of a clear operational criterion has led some researchers to ask questions for which a direct criterion *is* available. For example, research on "reflected appraisals" examines people's beliefs about how they are seen by others (for a review, see Kenny, 1994). In this context, there is an obvious and conceptually defensible operational criterion, namely, how the individual is actually seen by others. However, this research cannot replace research on the accuracy of self-perceptions, which addresses a different question: Do people's views of themselves correspond with what they are truely like?

The use of *social consensus* criteria reflects the folk belief that self-insight means seeing oneself as others see one. In fact, judgments by others (e.g., friends, spouses, psychologists) are widely used to evaluate the validity of self-reports of personality (e.g., Cheek, 1982; Funder & Colvin, this volume, Chap. 24; John & Robins, 1993; McCrae & Costa, 1990). McCrae (1982) referred to this use of social consensus criteria as the principle of consensual validation, which is based on the assumption that aggregating measurements (e.g., across judges) cancels out random error associated with any single measurement (or individual judge). In other words, in the consensus lies the truth (Hofstee, 1994). Like all criteria, consensual judgments should not be used unthinkingly. However, when judgments are properly aggregated and a case is made for their validity, social consensus criteria can play a central role in accuracy research.

According to *functional* (or *pragmatic*) criteria, a judgment can be considered accurate if it helps an individual adapt in the real world. From this perspective, the accuracy of a belief should be evaluated according to how well it serves the goals of the perceiver, rather than by its correspondence with some absolute reality (Baron, 1988; Gibson, 1979; Swann, 1984). For example, a functionalist might argue that the accuracy of self-perceptions of height should be gauged by our success in predicting whether or not we can walk through a doorway without bumping our heads rather than by using a ruler. If a direct measure of adaptiveness is not available, researchers can use a proxy known to predict an adaptive outcome. For example, in our own research (John & Robins, 1994), we have argued that observer assessments of performance in a managerial simulation task provide a functional criterion for self-assessments of performance because they predict long-term career success.

Criteria derived from *normative models* are commonly used to evaluate the quality of human judgment (e.g., Einhorn & Hogarth, 1981; Nisbett & Ross, 1980). The basic assumption underlying this research is that statistical and probability models prescribe the optimal judgment against which human judgment can be compared. Discrepancies between judgments and the prescriptions of the model can therefore be interpreted as bias. Explicit normative models such as Bayes' theorem are rarely used in the self-perception literature (for an exception, see Krueger & Zeiger, 1993). Self-perception researchers typically rely on normative models that are left implicit. For example, several studies have shown that people's self-ratings are more positive than their ratings of a hypothetical "average other" (e.g., Brown, 1986). This finding has been widely interpreted as evidence of self-enhancement bias because, according to these researchers (e.g., Brown, 1991; Taylor & Brown, 1988), it is logically impossible for the majority of people to be better than average. The implicit model underlying this interpretation is the arithmetic notion that the average of the individual self-ratings should equal the rating of the average other. There are a number of reasons why one might question the appropriateness of this model. Most important, it is *not* logically impossible for more than 50% of a group of people to be above average: the majority of individuals can be above the arithmetic mean when the characteristic being rated is negatively skewed (rather than normally distributed). Thus, almost everyone can be above average when a small percentage of individuals are substantially below average. As this example illustrates, it is often difficult to interpret a lack of correspondence with a normative model, and a case must be made for the appropriateness of the model as an accuracy criterion.

Interest in *information-processing (cue use)* criteria was spurred by Brunswik's (1956) lens model, which provides a powerful framework for studying the appropriateness or optimality of people's use of informational cues. The lens model describes the relations among the attributes of a stimulus object (e.g., a person), cues in the environment (e.g., information about the person), and the judgment made by a perceiver (the self in the case of self-perception). Self-perception researchers have examined cue use by providing subjects with experimentally manipulated feedback about themselves. In a typical study, subjects are randomly provided with either positive or negative feedback about their performance in a task (e.g., Baumgardner, Kaufman, & Levy, 1989; Shrauger, 1975). In general, this research suggests that subjects operate in a self-serving manner when they process cues provided by the experimenter; that is, they tend to downplay the validity of negative feedback and inflate the validity of positive feedback. Although such experimental research has provided insights into the processes involved in the formation of self-perception biases, we know little about the actual cues people use to form an evaluation of themselves in realistic settings. For example, when college students appraise their academic competence relative to other students, to what extent do they base their judgments on success and failure experiences in school, on performance on standardized tests (e.g., SAT), on feedback from teachers, or on information they have about how other students perceive them? In addition to studying how people use cues, future research should study the link between cue use and self-perception accuracy. Although it seems reasonable to assume that accurate judgments are more likely to result from the use of valid cues than from the use of invalid cues, there is no necessary link between the process used to form a judgment and the accuracy of the resulting judgment.

Studies employing *internal consistency* criteria examine whether individuals' self-perceptions are consistent with their other beliefs about themselves. If a person sees him- or herself in an inconsistent manner (e.g., as both generally talkative and generally quiet), it seems unlikely that both beliefs are accurate. In a study of trait attributions, Borkenau and Ostendorf (1989) examined two types of consistency: descriptive (ascribing two traits that have the same descriptive meaning) and evaluative (ascribing two traits that are both evaluatively positive or evaluatively negative). They found that individuals often described themselves using two favorable traits even when the traits were descriptively inconsistent (e.g., generous and thrifty), but rarely described themselves using two descriptively consistent traits that were evaluatively inconsistent (e.g., thrifty and stingy). The internal consistency of the self-concept has also been conceptualized as the degree to which a person sees him- or herself as having similar personality characteristics in different social roles. Donahue, Robins, Roberts, and John (1993) found that most people had self-views that were fairly consistent across social roles; moreover, people who had consistent self-views across roles were better adjusted psychologically than were those who had a "divided" or "fragmented" self. Note, however, that although an inconsistent self-concept may suggest a conflict in a person's self-views, these inconsistent views may accurately reflect variability in a person's behavior across different roles. Thus, conclusions about accuracy based on internal consistency standards can be problematic.

D. Conclusions and Recommendations

Based on our review of the criteria used in accuracy research, we have made several recommendations (see Robins & John, 1996). First, accuracy researchers should be explicit about which of the six types of accuracy criteria they have chosen and thus clarify the conceptualization of accuracy entailed by that choice. Second, researchers need to make an argument for why the criterion is appropriate. For example, social consensus is a better criterion for physical attractiveness than for subjective well-being. Much confusion could be avoided if researchers would always present conceptual and empirical arguments for the cogency of their accuracy claims. Third, the criterion must be measured properly. For example, ratings of physical attractiveness made by blind people would not provide a good measure of the social consensus. Fourth, given the limitations of any one accuracy criterion, researchers should use multiple criteria to assess accuracy. For example, in our own research we have used several criteria to examine the accuracy of self-evaluations of performance in a group discussion task (John & Robins, 1994; Robins & John, 1997). The convergence of findings across all three criteria provides more powerful evidence about the accuracy (or inaccuracy) of self-perceptions than any single criterion. Fifth, assertions about accuracy should be criterion specific (e.g., "We found that self-perceptions were biased when compared to the prescriptions of our normative model"). Divergence from one type of accuracy criterion may not have the same psychological implications as divergence from another type. Clearly, lack of correspondence with a social consensus criterion may not imply the same psychological processes as lack of correspondence with the prescriptions of a normative model. Thus, an important next step in research on self-perception accuracy is to examine convergences across the types of accuracy criteria described here and to identify the psychological implications of deviating from each type of criterion.

III. SELF-PERCEPTION PROCESSES: FOUR METAPHORS OF THE SELF-PERCEIVER

Thus far we have discussed how accuracy has been conceptualized and assessed, and reviewed a conceptual framework that organizes the various accuracy criteria used in self-perception research. We now turn to the process of self-perception and ask: How do people form beliefs about themselves? In answering this question, we explore the psychological roots of self-insight and attempt to understand how inaccurate beliefs about the self are formed and maintained.

Researchers have approached the question of how people form beliefs about themselves from many perspectives. There are, in fact, hundreds of models and theories of the self-perception process. One reason why the literature on the self is so complex is the lack of an overarching and integrative framework. We believe some order can be found by organizing the various models in terms of several broad rubrics, each representing a coherent theoretical perspective captured by a unique metaphor of the person. Each metaphor embodies a set of assumptions about the role of motivation, information processing, and affect in the self-perception process.

We propose four metaphors as central to understanding the psychology of the self-perceiver: the Scientist, the Consistency Seeker, the Politician, and the Egoist. In some ways people act like Scientists, seeking out information about themselves in a dispassionate search for truth; in some ways people are Consistency Seekers, striving to confirm their preexisting self-views with little regard for reality; in some ways people behave like Politicians, striving to present themselves in ways that create the most favorable impressions on others; and in some ways people act like Egoists, narcissistically distorting information to enhance their self-worth. Our formulation of these metaphors and their application to the self-perceiver was inspired by existing models of human judgment. The Scientist and the Consistency Seeker are commonly used metaphors in the social cognition literature (Fiske & Taylor, 1991, pp. 9–12; Nisbett & Ross, 1980, chap. 1). The Politician was suggested by Tetlock (1992) as a general metaphor for research on judgment and choice. The Egoist metaphor derives from the large body of studies characterizing the self-perception process as ego driven (e.g., Greenwald, 1980; John & Robins, 1994; Taylor & Brown, 1988).[2]

The four metaphors provide broad rubrics that summarize the basic processes governing self-perception. They are *not* intended as four discrete syndromes or types of individuals. Rather, each metaphor provides a different lens through which the self-perceiver can be viewed, and each highlights a unique set of processes. Together, the four metaphors provide a framework for organizing the various self-processes that have been postulated to underlie self-perception biases. Although this framework, like most categorization systems, may blur distinctions among the theories and models categorized within each metaphor, we believe that the heuristic value of the framework outweighs the costs associated with broad categories.

Figure 1 summarizes the metaphors and illustrates how they can be differentiated in terms of: (a) the central *motive* driving self-perception; (b) how *information* about the self is *processed*; (c) the role of *affect* in the self-perception process; and (d) the *individual differences* constructs relevant to each metaphor.

A. The Scientist

> Every man is, in his own particular way, a scientist [whose] ultimate aim is to predict and control.
>
> *(Kelly, 1995, p. 5)*

The basic assumption guiding the Scientist metaphor is that individuals are driven to understand themselves and the world. This metaphor has its roots in George Kelly's personal construct theory and in the early attribution theories of Fritz Heider and Harold Kelley. George Kelly (1995) argued that just as the scientist develops empirically based theories, the layperson uses facts and observations to develop "personal constructs," or theories about the self and the world. Like scientific theories, these constructs allow people to interpret and predict behavior. Heider (1958) also noted the similarity between the goals of the scientist—to understand, predict, and control—and the goals of the layperson. Building on

---

[2] Obviously, other metaphors exist in the literature. The Intuitive Psychologist (Heider, 1958; Nisbett & Ross, 1980) is essentially a variant of the Scientist metaphor. The Cognitive Miser metaphor is another variant of the Scientist metaphor which focuses on the shortcomings of the person as scientist (Fiske & Taylor, 1991). The Computer metaphor (e.g., Greenwald & Pratkanis, 1984), which likens mental processes to the workings of a computer, also resembles the Scientist metaphor in that both focus on informational processes and deemphasize the importance of affect. The Lawyer metaphor was used initially to characterize attributions of responsibility (Fincham & Jaspers, 1980), but more recently has been used in a way that resembles the Consistency Seeker metaphor—to emphasize that people reason toward predetermined, specific conclusions (Baumeister & Newman, 1994). Finally, the Economist metaphor emphasizes that people are utility maximizers; that is, they act in ways that advance their own self-interest. However, this idea is not unique to the Economist metaphor as virtually all the other metaphors assume that individuals attempt to maximize their personal utility, but each metaphor specifies a different type of utility or motive.

The Scientist

Motive: Accuracy

Information-processing: Data driven -- objective evaluation of information about the self

Affect: Irrelevant -- dispassionate search for truth about the self

Individual differences: Private self-consciousness, need for cognition, attributional style

The Politician

Motive: Popularity

Information-processing: Audience driven -- biased by concern with impression made on others; self-perceptions as self-presentations

Affect: Affective state depends on whether the impressions others have of oneself are positive or negative

Individual differences: Need for approval, self-monitoring, Machiavellianism

The Consistency Seeker

Motive: Consistency

Information-processing: Theory driven -- biased by motivation to confirm internal representation of self

Affect: Affective state depends on whether self-perceptions are consistent or inconsistent with prior self-views

Individual differences: Self-concept stability, self-concept clarity

The Egoist

Motive: Self-enhancement

Information-processing: Ego driven -- biased by motivation to protect and enhance self-worth through positively distorted self-evaluation

Affect: Affective state depends on whether self-perceptions are positive or negative

Individual differences: Narcissism, self-esteem

FIGURE 1   Four metaphors of the self-perceiver

Heider's theory, Harold Kelley (1967) drew a parallel between the methods used in science and those used in everyday life. Kelley proposed that laypeople make causal inferences about themselves and the world in the same way as scientists, and formulated a model of the attribution process based on this assumption.

Several theories of the self also incorporate the notion that people act, at least in part, like scientists. In his social comparison theory, Festinger (1954) postulated a universal motive to acquire accurate self-knowledge: "There is a motivation in the human organism to hold *correct* opinions, beliefs, and ideas . . . and to know *precisely* what his abilities enable him to do in this world" (p. 194); in the absence of objective standards, people attempt to acquire an accurate appraisal of their abilities by comparing themselves to others. According to Bem (1972), individuals gain self-knowledge by observing their own behavior in much the same way as would an observer: Just as the empirically oriented scientist observes the world and draws conclusions, we observe ourselves, note the behaviors we exhibit, and form impressions accordingly. Thus, Bem's self-perception theory did not focus on the possibility that the process of perceiving oneself may be threatening and may therefore differ from the process of perceiving others (see John & Robins, 1993). Trope (1979) argued that people have a need for accuracy and found evidence that people prefer to engage in tasks that provide them with valid information about their abilities. Finally, Baumeister and Newman (1994) explicitly draw on ideas from the Scientist metaphor to understand the self-regulation of inferential processes.

In summary, the Scientist metaphor (a) focuses on the motivation to acquire accurate self-knowledge, (b) emphasizes perceptual and informational processes and highlights people's inferential strategies and shortcomings, and (c) deemphasizes affective processes, assuming that people's beliefs about themselves are largely immune to the influence of emotion. In short, the Scientist metaphor suggests that people are data driven and engage in a dispassionate search for accurate self-knowledge.

What are the implications of the Scientist metaphor for the accuracy of self-perception? The Scientist metaphor implies that, like the idealized scientist, people form opinions about themselves based on the available data, with no regard for how favorable the information is and with no regard for whether the information is consistent with their previous beliefs about themselves. Thus, beliefs about the self *should* be accurate, and their degree of correspondence with reality is constrained only by the individual's perceptual and informational limitations. Nisbett and Ross (1980) epitomize this position, although they argue that people are not particularly good at being scientists:

> We proceed from the working hypothesis that inferential and judgmental errors arise primarily from nonmotivational—perceptual and cognitive—sources. Such errors, we contend, are almost inevitable products of human information-processing strategies . . . .[M]any phenomena generally regarded as motivational (for example, self-serving perceptions and attributions, ethnocentric beliefs, and many types of human conflict), can be understood better as products of relatively

passionless information-processing errors than of deep-seated motivational forces.

(p. 12)

In the personality literature, the Scientist perspective is represented by McCrae and Costa's (e.g., 1990) interpretation of self-reports of personality as primarily reflecting underlying personality traits, rather than motivated self-presentations or response styles.

What about individual differences? We all know people who are aptly described by the Scientist metaphor and other people who are not. Although the metaphors do not refer to types of people, individuals may vary in the degree to which each metaphor characterizes them. Which individual-difference measures can be linked to the Scientist metaphor? Although there is no single personality construct that focuses on the need to "know thyself," measures of individual differences in attention and information processing (e.g., private self-consciousness, need for cognition, attributional style) should be relevant to the Scientist metaphor. For example, private self-consciousness (Buss, 1980) reflects the tendency to attend to and become aware of internal thoughts, motives, and feelings; the scale includes items such as "I'm always trying to figure myself out" and "I'm constantly examining my motives." A number of studies have shown that individuals high in private self-consciousness provide more accurate self-reports (e.g., Cheek, 1982). Thus, the Scientist metaphor should be particularly appropriate for characterizing the self-perception processes of privately self-conscious individuals, but less appropriate for those low in private self-consciousness.

Another individual-difference variable that might seem relevant to the Scientist metaphor is depression. Some researchers have argued that depressed individuals have more realistic self-views (e.g., Alloy & Abramson, 1988; Lewinsohn, Mischel, Chaplin, & Barton, 1980). We do not believe the self-perception processes of depressed individuals conform to the Scientist metaphor for two reasons. First, some research suggests that depressives have unrealistically negative, rather than accurate, self-perceptions (for critiques of the "depressive realism" literature, see Ackerman & DeRubeis, 1991; Colvin & Block, 1994; John & Robins, 1994). Second, even if depressives do perceive themselves accurately, it is unlikely that this occurs through the dispassionate search for accurate information captured by the Scientist metaphor. Thus, "depressive realism" illustrates the need to distinguish between the process of self-perception and the accuracy of the outcome. The Scientist metaphor describes a particular set of processes through which people form self-perceptions; it does not claim that the outcome of these processes will be necessarily accurate.

B. The Consistency Seeker

Stable self-conceptions act like the rudder of a ship, bolstering people's confidence in their ability to navigate through the sometimes murky seas of everyday social life.

(Swann, Pelham, & Krull, 1989, p. 783)

The Consistency Seeker metaphor assumes that individuals strive to see them-selves in a consistent manner. Its origins can be traced to self-consistency theory (e.g., Lecky, 1945), balance theory (e.g., Heider, 1958), and cognitive dissonance theory (e.g., Festinger, 1957). In these theories, consistency has two meanings. First, people strive to maintain consistency among their beliefs. Second, people strive to confirm their preexisting beliefs and maintain them across time and situations. All consistency theories share the view that the subjective experience of inconsistency produces an aversive state, and that people are therefore motivated to reduce or prevent inconsistency. Consistency also serves an interpersonal function, ensuring that people will honor the identities they negotiated in previous social interactions and act similarly over time.

Swann's (e.g., 1990) theory of self-verification builds on these earlier consis-tency theories and applies the notion of consistency directly to people's beliefs about themselves. He characterizes the person as an "architect of social reality," striving to bring reality into harmony with the self. In an extensive research program, Swann and his colleagues have amassed considerable evidence that people actively seek out and create contexts in which their self-views will be confirmed, even when their self-views are negative. For example, people with negative self-views prefer interacting with individuals who have a negative impression of them to interacting with those who have a favorable impression. Another way in which people verify their self-conceptions is through cognitive distortions (e.g., selective attention) that allow people to see more self-confirmatory evidence than actually exists. Research in the social cognition literature, for example, suggests that when people process information about themselves they are biased by their existing self-conceptions and expectations (Higgins & Bargh, 1987; Markus & Wurf, 1987). In summary, the Consistency-Seeker strives to maintain a consistent set of self-views by seeking out self-congruent information and by distorting incongruent information to create an illusion of consistency; when these mechanisms fail and the perceived reality is not in harmony with the self-view, the person experiences negative affect.

With regard to the accuracy of self-perception, consistency theories assume that preexisting self-conceptions anchor and drive perceptions of self. Thus, informa-tion that is inconsistent with current self-views, including valid information, may be distorted or simply avoided. In a sense, prior beliefs about the self provide a framework for processing new information and thus form a Procrustean bed for the acquisition of new beliefs about the self. Thus, the Consistency Seeker metaphor is particularly appropriate for generating hypotheses in research evaluating the accuracy of self-perceptions against information-processing criteria. For example, research on schematic processing suggests that people may fail to attend to valid information if it is incongruent with their self-schemas. Similarly, research on auto-biographical memories suggests that people selectively remember life events that are consistent with how they see themselves currently; that is, they reconstruct their past to fit their current self-views (Ross, 1989).

Are there individual differences in the tendency to act like the Consistency Seeker? In other words, do some people have a stronger need to confirm and maintain their preexisting self-conceptions than others? Rosenberg's (1979) Stability of Self Scale was designed to measure individual differences in the tendency to see oneself as the same person over time and across situations, and includes items such as "Do you ever find that on one day you have one opinion of yourself and on another day you have a different opinion?" More recently, Campbell (1990; Campbell & Lavallee, 1993) developed the construct of self-concept clarity, which she defines as the extent to which "self-beliefs are clearly and confidently defined, temporally stable, and internally consistent" (Campbell, Chew, & Scratchley, 1991, p. 475). Campbell (1990) found that individuals high in self-clarity showed more congruence between their self-concepts and their subsequent perceptions of their behavior in specific situations. Finally, Beyer and Bowden (in press) found a sex difference in consistency seeking; compared to men, women based their self-evaluations of task performance more on their initial (low) expectations than on their actual performance, contributing to a self-diminishment bias. Thus, the Consistency Seeker metaphor seems particularly appropriate for characterizing some self-perception processes of women and those of individuals high in self-concept stability and clarity.

C. The Politician

> The image of myself which I try to create in my own mind . . . is different from the image which I try to create in the minds of others in order that they may love me.
>
> *(W. H. Auden in Snyder, 1987)*

The view of the person as a political animal traces its historical roots to Aristotle and Machiavelli. In its contemporary form, the Politician metaphor represents a fusion of ideas from symbolic interactionism, role theory, and impression management theory, as well as more recent elaborations of these theories (e.g., Hogan, 1983; Schlenker, 1980; Snyder, 1987; Tetlock, 1992). These theories emphasize the reciprocal nature of social interaction; the person is both a product of the social context and a creator of social reality. Social reality is constructed and negotiated through interactions with others. In these interactions, people's behaviors represent public performances that "present images of the self for the social world to see and evaluate" (Schlenker, 1985. p. 21). The primary goals of these self-presentations are to *get along* (i.e., gain approval from others) and to *get ahead* (i.e., attain social status and power) (Hogan, Jones, & Cheek, 1985). Thus, in the social as well as the political arena. people attempt to influence and manipulate how they are seen by others. Just as politicians strive to gain the approval of their constituencies to become elected or remain in office, people attempt to make favorable impressions on others in order to gain approval and status.

Building on these ideas, Tetlock (1992) argued that the demands people face in their everyday life are similar to those faced by politicians. Like politicians, people are accountable to different audiences (or constituencies), which place multiple and often conflicting demands and expectations on them. The primary goal of the person-as-politician is to "maintain the positive regard of important constituencies to whom he or she feels accountable" (Tetlock, 1992, p. 332).

How are these ideas related to the self-perception process? A core assumption of symbolic interactionism, as well as of other theories subsumed by the Politician metaphor, is that the self-concept is defined, constructed, and negotiated through interactions with others. Self-presentations influence the self-concept in two fundamental ways. First, people are influenced by how others perceive and respond to their social behavior; that is, the impressions of others serve as a "looking glass," reflecting back an image of ourselves. Second, to some extent people "believe" the roles they play during their self-presentations and thus incorporate these beliefs into their self-concepts (e.g., Schlenker, Dlugolecki, & Doherty, 1994). More generally, there is a reciprocal relation between self-presentations and self-conceptions: the self-concept is shaped by attempts to gain acceptance and status through social interactions, and in turn, people's self-presentations are guided by their self-conceptions. In summary, the central assumptions driving the Politician metaphor are that individuals (a) are motivated by a concern with the impression they make on others, (b) alter their self-presentations to achieve status and approval from others, and (c) experience negative affect when they fail to gain approval.

How does a concern with others' impressions affect the accuracy of self-perception? At the most general level, many theories adopting the perspective of the Politician metaphor assume that people have no core self or personality; like an onion, when the layers of social roles and public presentations are peeled away, nothing remains. Thus, the person is viewed solely as a product of the social context, as nothing but a constantly shifting self-presentation. From this perspective, the accuracy question is misguided.

Another perspective is to assume that personality exists, but that self-reports should not be taken as a direct indication of an individual's personality because they may be distorted by self-presentational goals (e.g., Johnson, 1981; Mills & Hogan, 1978). That is, when people respond to questions on a personality questionnaire they do not report how they see themselves but how they would like to be seen, just as the consummate politician does not present personally held opinions to others but rather adopts whatever opinions are most popular. According to this view, people engage in impression management when they complete a questionnaire just as they engage in impression management when they interact with others.

If self-reports are analogous to self-presentations, then their validity should be influenced by whether they are obtained in a public or private context. Self-reports should be more indicative of a person's true self-views in a private context, where the expectations and demands of others are less salient and the impetus to engage in impression managment is consequently weaker. This is akin to asking politicians about their views during an interview on national television as compared to "off the record" in the privacy of their homes; the answers one would get in these two contexts are likely to be quite different. Of course, one could argue that a politician is never truly off the record, just as psychologists have argued that even private self-reports reflect self-presentations to real or imagined audiences (including presentations to oneself).

The Politician metaphor also suggests that manipulating a person's accountability to others will influence the accuracy of their self-reports. Although the effects of accountability on self-perception have not been examined directly, we do know that individuals are less prone to certain judgmental errors (e.g., overconfidence) when they are accountable to others, in part because accountability promotes a self-critical process that improves judgment in some contexts (Tetlock, 1992). For example, Tetlock and Kim (1987) found that subjects who thought that they would have to justify their judgments to others were more accurate at predicting how others would respond to personality questionnaires and also had more realistic levels of confidence in their judgments. In addition, Lerner, Spranca, and Tetlock (1994) found that people's behaviors were more consistent with their self-reported attitudes when they were accountable to others.

Similar research designs could be employed to examine the effect of accountability on the accuracy of self-perception. For example, it would be interesting to study whether people evaluate themselves more accurately when they think they will have to justify their self-evaluations to others. In this case (i.e., when *publicly* accountable to others), the person must weigh the potential benefits making a favorable impression on others against the potential costs of public exposure as a fraud or imposter. As Schlenker and Leary (1982) point out, "self-presentation involves maintaining a delicate balance among self-enhancement, accuracy, and humility" (p. 89).

In terms of the interpersonal processes that may hinder accurate self-perception, the Politician metaphor suggests that people will seek out "friendly" audiences who see them as they would like to be seen, regardless of reality. Conversely, people will avoid "hostile" audiences that provide feedback counter to their self-presentational goals, or suppress or distort the feedback if they cannot avoid such audiences. More generally, people attempt to negotiate with others an identity that suits their interpersonal and personal goals. For example, consider an individual who thinks that her boss values competitiveness but her spouse does not: she may attempt to get her boss to see her as competitive and her spouse to see her as cooperative.

There are a number of personality scales that should be relevant to the processes described by the Politician metaphor. Some of these scales directly measure the tendency to manipulate others to achieve desired goals (e.g., Machiavellianism), whereas others measure individual differences in concern with and sensitivity to the impressions of others (e.g., impression management, need for approval, public self-consciousness, self-monitoring; for reviews, see Paulhus, 1990; Snyder, 1987). Probably the best known measure is Snyder's (e.g., 1987) Self-Monitoring Scale, which includes items such as "In order to get along and be liked, I tend to be what people expect me to be rather than anything else." The high self-monitor, according to Snyder (1987), is a person who "is particularly sensitive to cues to the situational appropriateness of his or her social behavior, and who uses these cues as guidelines for monitoring . . . his or her expressive behavior and self-presentations" (p. 14). Thus, with regard to their motivation, information-processing orientation, and affective responses, high self-monitors should be particularly well characterized by the Politician metaphor.

D. The Egoist

> Normal human thought is marked not by accuracy but by positive self-enhancing illusions.
>
> *(Taylor, 1989, p. 7)*

The basic premise of the Egoist metaphor is that people want to like themselves and will adopt cognitive and interpersonal strategies to create and maintain a positive self-image. This perspective is reflected in many personality and self-concept theories (e.g., Allport, 1937; Epstein, 1990; Greenwald, 1980; James, 1890; Kohut, 1971; Rogers, 1959; Rosenberg, 1979). In fact, virtually every self-theory posits some variant of the motive to protect and enhance self-worth (Wells & Marwell, 1976). Allport (1937) referred to the defense of the ego as "nature's eldest law," and believed that ego enhancement is a fundamental human motive tied to the need for survival. Kohut (1971) argued that three motivational systems drive the person: ambitions, ideals, and the need for self-esteem. Greenwald (1980) referred to the "totalitarian ego" to convey the idea that self-perceptions are driven by egocentrism; that is, the self reconstructs personal history to fit self-worth needs. Finally, the self theories of Epstein (1990), Rosenberg (1979), and many others include self-enhancement as a basic motive.

Many contemporary models of self-perception have been infused with ideas from the Egoist metaphor. Researchers building on Festinger's social comparison theory have found that people use social comparisons to bolster their self-views; for example, people often compare themselves to less fortunate others so that they will seem better in comparison (e.g., Wills, 1991). Similarly, the self-worth motive is central to Tesser's (1988) self-evaluation maintenance model, which is based on social comparison theory. Cognitive dissonance research has also been reconceptualized in terms of self-esteem motivation; Greenwald and Ronis (1978) noted that dissonance theory has become "focused on cognitive changes occurring in the service of ego defense, or self-esteem maintenance, rather than in the interest of preserving psychological consistency" (pp. 54–55). Steele (1993) has reinterpreted and extended findings in the dissonance literature on the basis of his self-affirmation theory. In the attribution literature, researchers have moved beyond perceptual and informational accounts of self–other differences to explore motivational accounts (cf. Tetlock & Levi, 1982). More generally, there has been a shift away from conceptualizing self-perception in purely cognitive-informational terms toward the view of self-perception as driven by multiple motivations, including the need for self-worth.

Riding on the crest of self-based accounts of social phenomena, a large body of research emerged in the 1980s aimed specifically at documenting positivity biases in self-perception in a wide range of contexts, including self-conceptions of personality attributes, self-attributions of success and failure, perceptions of control, responses to feedback, and beliefs about the likelihood of future events. In a review of this literature, Taylor and Brown (1988) argued that self-perceptions exhibit pervasive and enduring positive distortions, presumably stemming from the basic motive toward self-enhancement (see also Lockard & Paulhus, 1988). Recent research in the Egoist tradition has explored the psychological bases of these biases, including the role of cognitive and affective processes and situational factors such as ego involvement. In summary, the Egoist (a) is motivated toward self-enhancement, (b) distorts information about the self to protect and enhance self-worth, and (c) regulates affect by protecting self-worth; that is negative self-views are avoided because they produce negative affect.

In the personality assessment literature, the Egoist metaphor is most noticeable in research on socially desirable responding. Paulhus (1984) distinguished between two kinds of socially desirable responding—impression management and self-deceptive positivity. Whereas impression management (the conscious manipulation of one's self-reports to make a favorable impression on others) falls within the domain of the Politician metaphor, self-deceptive positivity reflects honestly held but unrealistically positive self-views, and therefore falls within the domain of the Egoist metaphor. Egoists truly believe that they are exceptional people who are superior to others.

With regard to individual differences, the most theoretically relevant construct is narcissism. According to the DSM-IV criteria, the defining characteristics of the *Narcissistic Personality* include a grandiose sense of self-importance, a tendency to exaggerate accomplishments and talents, and an expectation to be noticed as "special" even without appropriate achievement. All clinical accounts of narcissism (e.g., Freud, 1914/1953; Kohut, 1971; Millon, 1990) concur that narcissistic individuals hold unrealistically exaggerated beliefs about their abilities and achievements. In support of these accounts, research suggests that narcissistic individuals respond to threats to their self-worth by perceiving themselves more positively than is justified (Gabriel, Critelli, & Ee, 1994; John & Robins, 1994; Robins & John, 1997) and by denigrating others (Morf & Rhodewalt, 1993).

The effects of another individual-difference variable, self-esteem, have been examined in numerous studies of self-enhancement biases. Compared with low self-esteem individuals, high self-esteem individuals are more likely to describe themselves more positively than they describe the "average other" (Brown, 1986), more likely to engage in compensatory self-enhancement following negative feedback (e.g., Baumeister, 1982), more likely to believe their abilities are unusual and their failings are common (e.g., Campbell, 1986), and more likely to derogate sources of negative feedback (e.g., Baumgardner et al., 1989). Thus, the Egoist metaphor seems to capture the self-processes of individuals high in narcissism and in self-esteem.

IV. AN APPLICATION OF THE FOUR METAPHORS TO SELF-ENHANCEMENT BIAS

At this point, one may wonder which metaphor offers the best characterization of the psychology of the self-perceiver. We feel that this question is misguided because each metaphor emphasizes a different aspect of the self-perception process. Like the fable of the blind men and the elephant, each metaphor by itself reveals only a part of the picture, but together they provide a more complete account. Thus, new insights may be gained when findings in the self-perception literature are interpreted from each of the four perspectives. Below we use the four metaphors to generate complementary accounts of one kind of self-perception bias that we have studied in our own research, namely, unrealistically positive self-perceptions.

In several studies, we have measured self-enhancement bias in a group discussion task in which subjects compete for a fixed amount of money that must be allocated consensually by the group (see John & Robins, 1994; Robins & John, 1997). After the group discussion is completed, subjects evaluate their performance relative to the other group members. To assess the accuracy of these self-evaluations, we compare them with performance evaluations made by the other group members and by a group of psychologists who observe the task but do not enter into the discussion (i.e., two social consensus criteria). Thus, self-insight is defined as knowing one's place relative to the other group members (just as in ancient Greece self-insight implied knowing one's place in life—above the animals but beneath the Gods). We find that, on average, subjects evaluate themselves more positively than they are evaluated by either their peers or the psychologists. This general self-enhancement bias is one of three positive illusions discussed by Taylor and Brown (1988).

How can the metaphors help us understand the mechanisms and motives that underlie self-enhancement bias? Below we discuss our research within the theoretical framework provided by the four metaphors and describe hypotheses generated by each metaphor.

A. The Scientist Metaphor: Perceptual and Informational Limitations

The Scientist metaphor assumes that people strive to acquire accurate self-knowledge and emphasizes the role of perceptual and informational processes in self-perception. Therefore, when self-perception biases are apparent, perceptual and informational mechanisms are invoked to explain the findings. For example, the self-enhancement bias in our research could be due to the different visual perspective of self and others. Visual perspective may be important because it can influence the information that is available and salient to a judge (Storms, 1973). When people are given the opportunity to observe their behavior from the same perspective as others see them, they may be better able to see their own shortcomings and thus be less inclined to self-enhance. In effect, reversing visual perspective could change the information available to the self, influence what is perceptually salient, and as a result make reality less ambiguous and more constraining.

To test this hypothesis, we examined the effects of visual perspective (manipulated via videotape) on self-enhancement bias (Robins & John, 1997). Subjects evaluated their performance in a group discussion task from two visual perspectives: (a) the "normal" perspective experienced by the self and (b) a "self-focused" perspective in which subjects watched themselves on videotape from the perspective of an external observer. Visual perspective did not affect the degree of self-enhancement bias; on average, subjects overestimated their performance to the same extent regardless of their visual perspective. Apparently, even when we *view* ourselves from the visual perspective of others, we still *see* ourselves from the emotional perspective of the self.

B. The Consistency Seeker: Confirming Prior Beliefs about the Self

The Consistency Seeker metaphor raises the possibility that in our experiment individuals were striving to confirm their prior beliefs about themselves. It is possible, for example, that when subjects evaluate their performance in a group discussion task they are biased by their more general beliefs about their effectiveness in group discussions. In a study currently under way, we tested this hypothesis by measuring subjects' beliefs about how well they typically perform in group discussions several weeks prior to the experiment. Subjects who reported that they are typically very effective tended to rate their performance in the group discussion more positively than was justified. Conversely, subjects reporting relatively poor typical performance rated their performance more negatively than justified. Thus, subjects based their self-evaluations, in part, on how they expected they would perform rather than on how they actually performed. This finding is consistent with the idea that the motive to maintain consistency contributes to self-perception biases.[3]

C. The Politician: Managing Public Impressions

The Politician metaphor raises the possibility that unrealistically positive self-evaluations reflect self-presentations aimed at gaining the approval of others, rather than privately believed distortions about the self. However, in most research on self-

---

[3] Although subjects' self-evaluations failed to conform with the social consensus criteria we used to assess accuracy, one might argue that subjects were appropriately weighting prior probabilities (i.e., their previous performance) when evaluating their current performance, and were therefore acting in accordance with Bayes' theorem. Thus, this might be a case in which subjects were inaccurate relative to one kind of criterion (social consensus) but accurate relative to another (the prescriptions of a normative model).

enhancement biases, including our own, self-evaluations are obtained in an anonymous context with no explicit accountability demands. Nonetheless, we can speculate about the effects of manipulating private versus public context and accountability. In our research, subjects knew they would not need to justify their self-evaluations to others. Consequently, the subjects may have felt free to self-enhance without fear of appearing conceited and boastful. If we had manipulated accountability (e.g., by telling subjects they would have to discuss their evaluations with the other group members), the Politician metaphor would predict a decrease in self-enhancement bias. In some public contexts, however, individuals may be more inclined to self-enhance; for example, professors discussing their research in the departmental hallways may exaggerate the quality of their research when the department chair joins the conversation. Another way to link the Politician metaphor to self-enhancement bias is to examine whether individual-difference measures related to impression management predict individual differences in the degree of self-enhancement bias. To test this possibility, we correlated several social desirability scales with self-enhancement bias and found weak and nonsignificant relations (John & Robins, 1992). Apparently, individuals who are more inclined to manage their impressions are *not* more likely to show self-enhancement bias in the private context of our research.

D. The Egoist: Narcissistic Self-Aggrandizement

The Egoist metaphor provides the most direct and compelling account of the self-enhancement effect—individuals want to like themselves and will attempt to do so regardless of reality. In our research, performing poorly is threatening to the subjects' (MBA students) self-image as successful future managers, which may lead them to distort reality to convince themselves that they are as capable as they would like to be. This account explains the general self-enhancement effect. However, it does not explain the substantial individual differences in self-enhancement that we have found in several samples. We find that only about 35% of the subjects show a clear self-enhancement bias whereas about 50% are relatively accurate and about 15% actually show self-diminishment bias (John & Robins, 1994).[4]

How can we account for the fact that some individuals self-enhance whereas others do not? Narcissism theories provide an individual-differences framework for research on self-enhancement bias. According to these theories, narcissistic individuals hold unrealistically positive beliefs about their abilities and achieve-

[4] This finding contrasts with Taylor and Brown's (1994a) claim that the percentage of subjects who show self-enhancement bias is typically "above 95%" (p. 973). This apparent inconsistency is a good example of the confusion that arises when researchers do not specify the criterion they use to justify their accuracy claim. The Taylor and Brown claim is based on a normative-model criterion (i.e., the discrepancy between expectations for the self and expectations for the "average other" should equal zero) whereas our accuracy claim is based on an expert-based social consensus criterion. Apparently, by their criterion virtually everyone self-enhances whereas by our criterion less than half do so.

ments. Thus, we predicted that individual differences in self-enhancement bias would be a function of narcissism. In support of this hypothesis, we found that both self-report and observer measures of narcissism predicted who would show the most pronounced self-enhancement bias in our experimental task (John & Robins, 1994). Our findings are summarized in Figure 2. Note that narcissists and nonnarcissists did not differ in actual performance, as defined by our accuracy criterion (judgments by 11 psychologists trained to evaluate performance in this task). However, they differed considerably in their self-evaluations: narcissists overestimated their performance relative to the criterion whereas nonnarcissists underestimated slightly. Thus, although narcissists did not actually perform better than nonnarcissists, they *believed* they performed substantially better (almost a full standard deviation). This finding replicated when we assessed accuracy using a second social consensus criterion (peer evaluations) and an operational criterion (an objectively assessed task outcome) (Robins & John, 1997).

What processes and mechanisms underlie the link between narcissism and self-enhancement bias? Our findings are consistent with the assumption that narcissists are more defensive than other individuals because their sense of self-importance and superior competence is inflated and thus more easily threatened (e.g., Westen, 1990). Thus, when they do not perform well in an ego-involving context, narcissistic

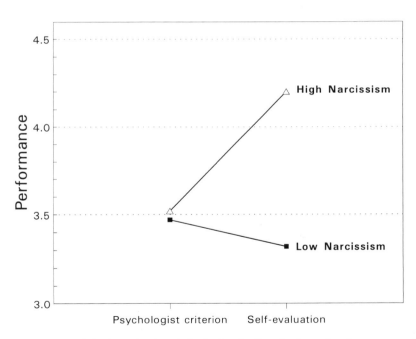

FIGURE 2 Psychologist evaluations (criterion) and self-evaluations of performance as a function of narcissism. (These analyses are based on data from John & Robins, 1994.)

individuals are particularly motivated to bolster their self-image by positively distort-ing their self-perceptions. Indeed, a reanalysis of our data (John & Robins, 1994) shows that the narcissism effect is even stronger for those subjects who did not perform well (as defined by the psychologist criterion); the correlation between narcissism and self-enhancement was .62 among the worst performers, compared to performers, respectively. This pattern indicates that poor performance (and therefore greater ego threat) accentuates the difference in self-enhancement bias between subjects high and low in narcissism.

A similar accentuation effect was found when we manipulated self-focused attention via videotape (Robins & John, 1997). Watching their performance on videotape further increased the disparity between the self-evaluations of narcissistic and nonnarcissistic individuals. Specifically, narcissists evaluated themselves even more positively whereas nonnarcissists saw themselves in a less positive light. Self-focused attention, like poor performance, is particularly threatening because self-evaluative processes are triggered, heightening awareness of the discrepancy be-tween reality and the inflated internal standards of the narcissists. Apparently, the self-focused condition further activated narcissists' self-esteem protective mecha-nisms, leading to even more inflated self-evaluations.

E. Implications of Self-Enhancement Bias for Mental Health

The link between narcissism and self-enhancement bias is relevant to an important issue currently debated in the literature: What are the implications of self-enhance-ment bias for mental health (Colvin & Block, 1994; Shedler, Mayman, & Manis, 1993; Taylor & Brown, 1988, 1994)? Narcissistic characteristics are generally considered to be indicative of psychological problems, and, at extreme levels, constitute a personal-ity disorder. Thus, our narcissism findings suggest that unrealistically positive self-views (as compared against both social consensus and operational criteria) reflect maladjustment. This view is consistent with those of Freud, Jahoda, and many clinical psychologists, who assumed that self-insight (i.e., the absence of either positively or negatively biased self-perceptions) is an essential aspect of mental health. As Allport (1937) noted, "Not infrequently insight is exalted to the highest place among the virtues, or therapeutically is regarded as a panacea for all mental ills" (p. 221). This traditional view has recently been challenged by Taylor and Brown (1988, 1994 Brown, 1993), who have argued that "positive illusions" about the self promote and maintain mental health. Our narcissism findings appear to contradict the Taylor and Brown thesis. Still, they do not provide direct counterevi-dence because one could argue that narcissism theories are wrong and narcissism is in fact adaptive.

To provide a more direct test, we examined whether self-enhancement bias is associated with maladjustment, as our narcissism findings suggest, or with better adjustment, as Taylor and Brown (1988) have suggested. Using data available for the subjects in the John and Robins (1994) study, we examined whether subjects who showed self-enhancement bias were better or worse adjusted than subjects

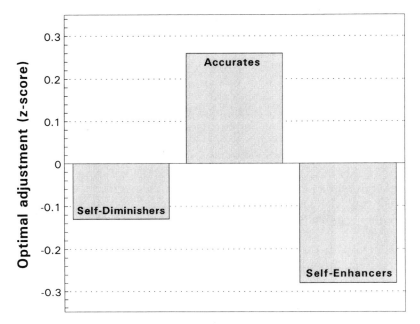

FIGURE 3 Optimal adjustment as a function of self-perception bias: Self-enhancers are not well adjusted according to psychologists. (These analyses are based on data from John & Robins, 1994.)

who were relatively accurate or showed a self-diminishment bias. The 102 subjects were divided into three groups: self-enhancers, who substantially overestimated their performance in the group discussion; accurates, who were relatively accurate in their self-evaluations; and self-diminishers, who substantially underestimated their performance. To assess adjustment, we used Block's (1961/1978) index of "optimal psychological adjustment," which is computed from Q-sort personality descriptions. In our study, five psychologists provided Q-sort personality descriptions of each subject; these psychologists observed the subjects in a wide range of activities over the course of a weekend-long assessment program and had ample opportunity to evaluate adjustment.[5]

Figure 3 shows the level of psychological adjustments for the self-enhancers, accurates, and self-diminishers. A one-way ANOVA showed that the three groups differed significantly in adjustment: $F(2, 99) = 3.1, p < .05$. Contrary to Taylor and Brown's (1988) prediction, the self-enhancers were the *least* well-adjusted of the three groups and differed significantly from the accurates, $t(99) = 2.4, p < .05$. This finding bolsters our interpretation of the narcissim effect: positive illusions (relative

---

[5] We used the peer criterion to index self-enhancement bias, thus ensuring that the bias measure was independent of the psychologists' ratings of adjustment.

to a social consensus criterion) are not necessarily associated with adjustment, and they may even be maladaptive. The two findings together (self-enhancement bias is associated with both maladjustment and narcissism) suggest that the maladjustment of self-enhancers is narcissistic in character, rather than taking the form of overt anxiety or low self-esteem. This interpretation receives further support from a recent longitudinal study which found that self-enhancement bias was associated with a generally narcissistic pattern of Q-sort correlates (Colvin, Block, & Funder, 1995).

Our findings, although replicated in an independent study, are nonetheless insufficient to warrant the conclusion that self-enhancement bias is necessarily maladaptive. This issue is complicated and more complex hypotheses need to be considered. Rather than pitting the two opposing claims against each other, future research should turn toward the question of when self-enhancement is adaptive, and when it is maladaptive. For example, does it have short-term benefits but long-term negative consequences? Is it adaptive in some contexts (e.g., when one has no control over the outcome), but maladaptive in others? Is there an optimal margin of illusion (Baumeister, 1989)—is a small bias beneficial but a large one harmful? Finally, so far we have studied self-enhancement bias relative to two types of criteria (social consensus and operational); whether or not self-enhancement relative to other types of criteria is maladaptive awaits empirical test. In conclusion, the important question of how self-insight and adjustment are related requires further examination to evaluate these various possibilities.

V. CONCLUSION

The ancient Greek mandate to "know thyself" inspired an enduring interest in the issue of self-insight. Our review and analysis of current theory and research reveals many complex issues with which researchers must grapple. The scientific study of self-perception accuracy requires an understanding of the person at three levels: as object (e.g., what is the true nature of the person?), as perceiver (e.g., how do people form self-perceptions?), and as researcher (e.g., how can we determine whether a self-perception is accurate?). At each level, philosophical, conceptual, and methodological issues must be considered. In this chapter, we have discussed these issues in the context of two conceptual frameworks, one that organizes the various criteria researchers use to assess the accuracy of self-perception, and another that organizes the different theoretical accounts of the self-perception process. We hope that these frameworks will stimulate and guide future research on self-insight and its causes and consequences.

ACKNOWLEDGMENTS

This chapter is based, in part, on the doctoral dissertation of R.W.R. Preparation of this chapter was supported by a National Science Foundation Graduate Fellowship and a Chancellor's Dissertation Fellowship from the University of California to R.W.R. and National Institute of Mental Health Grant MH49255 to O.P.J. We thank Sylvia Beyer, William Chaplin, Jonathan Cheek, Kenneth Craik, David Funder, Samuel Gosling, Ravenna Helson, Robert Hogan, William Ickes, John Johnson, Joachim Krueger, Gerald Mendelsohn, Jennifer Pals, Delroy Paulhus, Gerard Saucier, and William Swann for their comments on an earlier version.

References

Ackerman, R., & DeRubeis, R. J. (1991). Is depressive realism real? *Clinical Psychology Review, 11,* 565–584.

Alloy, L. B., & Abramson, L. Y. (1988). Depressive realism: Four theoretical perspectives. In L. B. Alloy (Ed.), *Cognitive processes in depression* (pp. 223–265). New York: Guilford Press.

Allport, G. W. (1937). *Personality: A psychological interpretation.* New York: Holt.

Baron, R. M. (1988). An ecological framework for establishing a dual-mode theory of social knowing. In D. Bar-Tal & A. W. Kruglanski (Eds.), *The social psychology of knowledge* (pp. 48–82). New York: Cambridge University Press.

Baumeister, R. F. (1982). A self-presentational view of social phenomena. *Psychological Bulletin, 91,* 3–26.

Baumeister, R. F. (1989). The optimal margin of illusion. *Journal of Social and Clinical Psychology, 8,* 176–189.

Baumeister, R. F., & Newman, L. S. (1994). Self-regulation of cognitive inference and decision processes. *Personality and Social Psychology Bulletin, 20,* 3–19.

Baumgardner, A. H., Kaufman, C. M., & Levy, P. (1989). Regulating affect interpersonally: When low self-esteem leads to greater enhancement. *Journal of Personality and Social Psychology, 56,* 907–921.

Bem, D. J. (1972). Self-perception theory. In L. Berkowitz (Ed.), *Advances in experimental social psychology* (Vol. 6, pp. 1–62). New York: Academic Press.

Beyer, S. (1990). Gender differences in the accuracy of self-evaluations of performance. *Journal of Personality and Social Psychology, 59,* 960–970.

Beyer, S., & Bowden, E. M. (in press). Gender differences in self-perceptions: Convergent evidence from three measures of accuracy and bias. *Personality and Social Psychology Bulletin.*

Block, J. (1978). *The Q-sort method in personality assessment and psychiatric research.* Palo Alto, CA: Consulting Psychologists Press. (Original work published 1961).

Borkenau, P., & Ostendorf, F. (1989). Descriptive consistency and social desirability in self- and peer reports. *European Journal of Personality, 3,* 31–45.

Brown, J. D. (1986). Evaluations of self and others: Self-enhancement biases in social judgments. *Social Cognition, 4,* 353–376.

Brown, J. D. (1991). Accuracy and bias in self-knowledge. In C. R. Snyder & D. F. Forsyth (Eds.), *Handbook of social and clinical psychology: The health perspective* (pp. 158–178). New York: Pergamon Press.

Brown, J. D. (1993). Coping with stress: The beneficial role of positive illusions. In A. P. Turnbull et al. (Eds.). *Cognitive coping, families, and disability* (pp. 123–137). Baltimore: Paul H. Brookes.

Brunswik, E. (1956). *Perception and the representative design of psychological experiments* (2nd ed.). Berkeley: University of California Press.

Buss, A. H. (1980). *Self-consciousness and social anxiety*. San Francisco: Freeman.

Campbell, J. D. (1986). Similarity and uniqueness: The effects of attribute type, relevance, and individual differences in self-esteem and depression. *Journal of Personality and Social Psychology, 50,* 281–294.

Campbell, J. D. (1990). Self-esteem and clarity of the self-concept. *Journal of Personality and Social Psychology, 59,* 538–549.

Campbell, J. D., & Lavallee, L. F. (1993). Who am I? The role of self-concept confusion in understanding the behavior of people with low self-esteem. In R. F. Baumeister (Ed.), *Self-esteem: The puzzle of low self-regard* (pp. 3–20). New York: Plenum Press.

Campbell, J. D., Chew, B., & Scratchley, L. S. (1991). Cognitive and emotional reactions to daily events: The effects of self-esteem and self-complexity. *Journal of Personality, 59,* 473–505.

Cheek, J. M. (1982). Aggregation, moderator variables, and the validity of personality tests: A peer rating study. *Journal of Personality and Social Psychology, 43,* 1254–1269.

Colvin, C. R., & Block, J. (1994). Do positive illusions foster mental health? An examination of the Taylor and Brown formulation. *Psychological Bulletin, 116,* 3–20.

Colvin, C. R., Block, J., & Funder, D. C. (1995). Overly positive self-evaluations and personality: Negative implications for mental health. *Journal of Personality and Social Psychology, 68,* 1152–1162.

Donahue, E. M., Robins, R. W., Roberts, B. W., & John, O. P. (1993). The divided self: Concurrent and longitudinal effects of psychological adjustment and social roles on self-concept differentiation. *Journal of Personality and Social Psychology, 64,* 834–846.

Einhorn, H. J., & Hogarth, R. M. (1981). Behavioral decision theory: Processes of judgment and choice. *Annual Review of Psychology, 32,* 53–88.

Epstein, S. (1990). Cognitive experiential self-theory. In L. A. Pervin (Ed.), *Handbook of personality: Theory and research* (pp. 165–192). New York: Guilford Press.

Festinger, L. (1954). Motivation leading to social behavior. In M. R. Jones (Ed.), *Nebraska Symposium on Motivation* (Vol. 2, pp. 191–218). Lincoln: University of Nebraska Press.

Festinger, L. (1957). *A theory of cognitive dissonance*. Palo Alto, CA: Stanford University Press.

Fincham, F. D., & Jaspers, J. M. (1980). Attribution of responsibility: From man the scientist to man the lawyer. In L. Berkowitz (Ed.), *Advances in experimental social psychology* (Vol. 13, pp. 81–137). New York: Academic Press.

Fiske, S. (1993). Social cognition and social perception. *Annual Review of Psychology, 44,* 155–194.

Fiske, S. T., & Taylor, S. E. (1991). *Social cognition* (2nd ed.). Reading, MA: Addison-Wesley.

Freud, S. (1953). On narcissism: An introduction. In J. Strachey (Ed.), *The standard edition of the complete psychological works* (Vol. 14, pp. 69–102). London: Hogarth Press, (Original work published 1914).

Funder, D. C. (1987). Errors and mistakes: Evaluating the accuracy of social judgment. *Psychological Bulletin, 101,* 75–90.

Funder, D. C. (1990). Process versus content in the study of judgmental accuracy. *Psychological Inquiry, 1,* 207–209.

Funder, D. C. (1993). Judgments as data for personality and developmental psychology: Error versus accuracy. In D. C. Funder, R. D. Parke, C. Tomlinson-Keasey, & K.

Widaman (Eds.), *Studying lives through time: Personality and development* (pp. 121–146). Washington, DC: American Psychological Association.

Gabriel, M. T., Critelli, J. W., & Ee, J. S. (1994). Narcissistic illusions in self-evaluations of intelligence and attractiveness. *Journal of Personality, 62,* 143–155.

Gibson, J. J. (1979). *The ecological approach to visual perception.* Boston: Houghton-Mifflin.

Greenwald, A. G. (1980). The totalitarian ego: Fabrication and revision of personal history. *American Psychologist, 35,* 603–618.

Greenwald, A. G., & Pratkanis, A. R. (1984). The self. In R. S. Wyer & T. K. Srull (Eds.), *Handbook of social cognition* (Vol. 3, pp. 129–178). Hillsdale, NJ: Erlbaum.

Greenwald, A. G., & Ronis, D. L. (1978). Twenty years of cognitive dissonance: Case study of the evolution of a theory. *Psychological Review, 85,* 53–57.

Hastie, R., & Rasinski, K. A. (1988). The concept of accuracy in social judgment. In D. Bar-Tal & A. W. Kruglanski (Eds.), *The social psychology of knowledge* (pp. 193–208). New York: Cambridge University Press.

Heider, F. (1958). *The psychology of interpersonal relations.* New York: Wiley.

Higgins, E. T., & Bargh, J. A. (1987). Social cognition and social perception. *Annual Review of Psychology, 38,* 369–425.

Hofstee, W. K. B. (1994). Who should own the definition of personality? *European Journal of Personality, 8,* 149–162.

Hogan, R. (1983). A socioanalytic theory of personality. In M. Page (Ed.), *Nebraska Symposium on Motivation* (pp. 55–89). Lincoln: University of Nebraska Press.

Hogan, R., Jones, W. H., & Cheek, J. M. (1985). Socioanalytic theory: An alternative to armadillo psychology. In B. R. Schlenker (Ed.), *The self and social life* (pp. 175–198). New York: McGraw-Hill.

James, W. (1890). *The principles of psychology.* Cambridge, MA: Harvard University.

John, O. P., & Robins, R. W. (1992, August). *Method variance in self-perception: Self-enhancement, self-deception, and social desirability.* Paper presented in the Symposium "New Directions in Social Desirability Research" (M. Botwin, Chair), annual convention of the American Psychological Association, Washington, DC.

John, O. P., & Robins, R. W. (1993). Determinants of interjudge agreement on personality traits: The Big Five domains, observability, evaluativeness, and the unique perspective of the self. *Journal of Personality, 61,* 521–551.

John, O. P., & Robins, R. W. (1994). Accuracy and bias in self-perception: Individual differences in self-enhancement and the role of narcissism. *Journal of Personality and Social Psychology, 66,* 206–219.

Johnson, J. A. (1981). The "self-disclosure" and "self-presentation" views of item response dynamics and personality scale validity. *Journal of Personality and Social Psychology, 40,* 761–769.

Judd, C. M., & Park, B. (1993). Definition and assessment of accuracy in social stereotypes. *Psychological Review, 100,* 109–128.

Jussim, L. (1993). Accuracy in interpersonal expectations: A reflection-construction analysis of current and classic research. *Journal of Personality, 61,* 637–668.

Kelley, H. H. (1967). Attribution theory in social psychology. In D. Levine (Ed.), *Nebraska Symposium on Motivation* (Vol. 15, pp. 192–240). Lincoln: University of Nebraska Press.

Kelly, G. A. (1955). *The psychology of personal constructs.* New York: Norton.

Kenny, D. A. (1991). A general model of consensus and accuracy in interpersonal perception. *Psychological Review, 98,* 155–163.

Kenny, D. A. (1994). *Interpersonal perception: A social relations analysis.* New York: Guilford Press.

Kohut, H. (1971). *The analysis of self.* New York: International Universities Press.

Krueger, J., & Zeiger, J. S. (1993). Social categorization and the truly false consensus effect. *Journal of Personality and Social Psychology, 65,* 670–680.

Kruglanski, A. W. (1989). The psychology of being 'right': The problem of accuracy in social perception and cognition. *Psychological Bulletin, 106,* 395–409.

Lecky, P. (1945). *Self-consistency: A theory of personality.* New York: Island Press.

Lerner, J. S., Spranca, M. D., & Tetlock, P. E. (1994, June). *Accountability and allocating resources: Doing one thing but saying another.* Poster presented at the annual conference of the American Psychological Society, Washington, DC.

Lewinsohn, P. M., Mischel, W., Chaplin, W., & Barton, R. (1980) Social competence and depression: The role of illusory self-perceptions. *Journal of Abnormal Psychology, 89,* 203–212.

Lockard, J. S., & Paulhus, D. L. (1988). *Self-deception: An adaptive mechanism?* Englewood Cliffs, NJ: Prentice-Hall.

Markus, H., & Wurf, E. (1987). The dynamic self-concept: A social psychological perspective. *Annual Review of Psychology, 38,* 299–337.

McCrae, R. R. (1982). Consensual validation of personality traits: Evidence from self-reports and ratings. *Journal of Personality and Social Psychology, 43,* 293–303.

McCrae, R. R. & Costa, P. T. (1990). *Personality in adulthood.* New York: Guilford Press.

Millon, T. (1990). The disorders of personality. In L. A. Pervin (Ed.), *Handbook of personality: Theory and research* (pp. 339–370). New York: Guilford Press.

Mills, C., & Hogan, R. (1978). A role theoretical interpretation of personality scale item responses. *Journal of Personality, 46,* 778–785.

Morf, C. C., & Rhodewalt, F. (1993). Narcissism and self-evaluation maintenance: Explorations in object relations *Personality and Social Psychology Bulletin, 19,* 668–676.

Nisbett, R. E., & Ross, L. (1980). *Human inference: Strategies and shortcomings of social judgment.* Englewood Cliffs, NJ: Prentice-Hall.

Paulhus, D. L. (1984). Two-component models of socially desirable responding. *Journal of Personality and Social Psychology, 46,* 598–609.

Paulhus, D. L. (1990). Measurement and control of response bias. In J. P. Robinson, P. R. Shaver, & L. Wrightsman (Eds.), *Measures of personality and social-psychological attitudes* (pp. 17–59). San Diego, CA: Academic Press.

Robins, R. W. (1996). Unpublished data, University of California at Berkeley, Department of Psychology.

Robins, R. W., & John, O. P. (1996a) *A conceptual framework for the study of accuracy and bias in self-perception: Issues of definition and measurement.* Unpublished manuscript, University of California at Berkeley.

Robins, R. W., & John, O. P. (1996b). Toward a broader agenda for research on self and other perception. *Psychological Inquiry, 7,* 279–287.

Robins, R. W., & John, O. P. (1997). Self-perception, visual perspective, and narcissism: Is seeing believing? *Psychological Science* (in press).

Rogers, C. R. (1959). A theory of therapy, personality, and interpersonal relations, developed in the client-centered framework. In S. Koch (Ed.), *Psychology: A study of a science* (Vol. 3, pp. 185–256). New York: McGraw-Hill.

Rosenberg, M. (1979). *Conceiving the self.* New York: Basic Books.

Ross, M. (1989). Relation of implicit theories to the construction of personal histories. *Psychological Review, 96,* 341–357.

Schlenker, B. R. (1980). *Impression management: The self-concept, social identity, and interpersonal relations.* Monterey, CA: Brooks/Cole.

Schlenker, B. R. (1985). Introduction: Foundations of the self in social life. In B. R. Schlenker (Ed.), *The self and social life.* New York: McGraw-Hill.

Schlenker, B. R., Dlugolecki, D. W., & Doherty, K. (1994). The impact of self-presentations on self-appraisals and behavior: The power of public commitment. *Personality and Social Psychology Bulletin, 20,* 20–33.

Schlenker, B. R., & Leary, M. R. (1982). Audiences' reactions of self-enhancing, self-denigrating, and accurate self-presentations. *Journal of Experimental Social Pscyhology, 18,* 89–104.

Shedler, J., Mayman, M., & Manis, M. (1993). The *illusion* of mental health. *American Psychologist, 48,* 1117–1131.

Shrauger, J. S. (1975). Responses to evaluation as a function of initial self-perceptions. *Psychological Bulletin, 82,* 581–596.

Snyder, M. (1987). *Public appearances/private realities: The psychology of self-monitoring.* New York: Freeman.

Steele, C. (1993). Self-image resilience and dissonance: The role of affirmational resources. *Journal of Personality and Social Research, 64,* 885–896.

Storms, M. D. (1973). Videotape and the attribution process: Reversing actors' and observers' points of view. *Journal of Personality and Social Psychology, 27,* 165–175.

Swann, W. B., Jr. (1984). Quest for accuracy in person perception: A matter of pragmatics. *Psychological Review, 91,* 457–477.

Swann, W. B., Jr. (1990). To be adored or to be known: The interplay of self-enhancement and self-verification. In R. M. Sorrentino & E. T. Higgins (Eds.), *Motivation and cognition* (Vol. 2. pp. 33–66). New York: Guilford Press.

Swann, W. B., Jr., Pelham, B. W., & Krull, D. S. (1989). Agreeable fancy or disagreeable truth? Reconciling self-enhancement and self-verification. *Journal of Personality and Social Psychology, 57,* 782–791.

Taylor, S. E. (1989). *Positive illusions: Creative self-deception and the healthy mind.* New York: Basic Books.

Taylor, S. E., & Brown, J. (1988). Illusion and well-being: A social psychological perspective on mental health. *Psychological Bulletin, 103,* 193–210.

Taylor, S. E., & Brown, J. (1994). Positive illusions and well-being revisited: Separating fact from fiction. *Psychological Bulletin, 116,* 21–27.

Tesser, A. (1988). Toward a self-evaluation maintenance model of social behavior. In L. Berkowitz (Ed.), *Advances in experimental social psychology* (Vol. 21, pp 181–227). Orlando, FL: Academic Press.

Tetlock, P. E. (1992). The impact of accountability on judgment and choice: Toward a social contingency model. In M. P. Zanna (Ed.), *Advances in experimental social psychology* (Vol. 25, pp. 331–376). San Diego, CA: Academic Press.

Tetlock, P. E., & Kim, J. I. (1987). Accountability and judgment processes in a personality prediction task. *Journal of Personality and Social Psychology, 52,* 700–709.

Tetlock, P. E., & Levi, A. (1982). Attribution bias: On the inconclusiveness of the cognition-motivation debate. *Journal of Experimental Social Psychology, 18,* 68–88.

Trope, Y. (1979). Uncertainty-reducing properties of achievement tasks. *Journal of Personality and Social Psychology, 37,* 1505–1518.

Wells, L. E., & Marwell, G. (1976). *Self-esteem: Its conceptualization and measurement.* Beverly Hills, CA: Sage.

Westen, D. (1990). Psychoanalytic approaches to personality. In L. A. Pervin (Ed.), *Handbook of personality: Theory and research* (pp. 21–65). New York: Guilford Press.

Wills, T. A. (1991). Similarity and self-esteem in downward comparison. In J. Suls & T. A. Wills (Eds.), *Social comparison: Contemporary theory and research* (pp. 51–78). Hillsdale, NJ: Erlbaum.

CHAPTER 26

IDENTITY, SELF-CONCEPT, AND SELF-ESTEEM
THE SELF LOST AND FOUND

ROY F. BAUMEISTER

CASE WESTERN RESERVE UNIVERSITY

I. DEFINITIONS

The most obvious and common things are sometimes the most difficult to define. This certainly applies to the self. People use the word "self," especially with its many prefixes and suffixes, dozens of times each day, and yet it is difficult to pause and say what is meant by self.

For purposes of the present discussion, it seems best to define certain terms. The term *self* corresponds to its everyday usage in colloquial speech. As such, it encompasses the direct feeling each person has of privileged access to his or her own thoughts and feelings and sensations. It begins with the awareness of one's own body and is augmented by the sense of being able to make choices and initiate action. It also encompasses the more complex and abstract constructions that embellish the self. In everyday speech, the familiar expressions "to find yourself" or "to know yourself" do not ordinarily mean to locate one's body and be able to recognize it; rather, those expressions refer to some difficult act regarding complex, abstract knowledge.

The term *self-concept* refers to the totality of inferences that a person has made about himself or herself. These refer centrally to one's personality traits and schemas, but they may also involve an understanding of one's social roles and relationships.

Lastly, the term *identity* refers to the definitions that are created for and superimposed on the self. These definitions refer to concepts about who the person is and what the person is like. Identity can be analyzed as consisting of an interpersonal aspect (a set of roles and relationships), a potentiality aspect (a concept of who the person might become), and a values aspect (a set of values and priorities) (Baumeister, 1986). Identity differs from self-concept in that it is socially defined. That is, the self-concept is wholly contained in the person's own mind, whereas identity is often created by the larger society, although individuals typically have some opportunity to refine or negotiate the identities that society gives them.

Identity must be regarded as an aggregate definition of self. That is, a self can be defined in many ways—with many traits and many different roles. Identity is thus the product of the many definitions of self that exist. Likewise, the self-concept is a loose combination of the many ideas and inferences that the person has about him- or herself. The term *self-esteem* refers to the evaluative dimension of the self-concept.

II. FINDING THE SELF: CREATION OF IDENTITY

This section will examine how identity (and self-esteem) are constructed. It will begin with the role of culture, by considering how different historical periods have treated the single self. Then it will turn to how knowledge about the self is actually formed and organized. Next, it will take a closer look at the formation and maintenance of self-esteem. Lastly, it will consider briefly some of the ways people try to control the information about the self, usually in order to fit it into established or preconceived patterns.

A. The Self in Historical Perspective

Although the concept of self tends to seem so natural and normal as to be inevitable, it is in fact far from universal. Ideas about the nature of the self have varied widely across cultural and historical boundaries. Although more detailed accounts of these variations are available elsewhere (see Baumeister, 1986, 1987; Markus & Kitayama, 1991; Triandis, 1989), it is necessary to summarize briefly some of the factors that distinguish the sense of self in the modern Western world.

The sense of uniqueness is an appropriate starting point. Modern Western society treats each person as a special, unique individual and encourages people to regard themselves (and each other) that way. This is a fairly recent development, however. To be sure, the ancients recognized that people were not identical, but they placed relatively little importance on these differences. What mattered were the similarities in form and function. Similarly, in the Middle Ages people were regarded as having functions according to their place in society. The person's identity was intimately bound up with his or her social rank, family ties, and occupation, and people were not supposed to want to change any of these. More important, the models of human potential were essentially the same for the vast Christian majority: salvation in heaven, as a result of living a moral and pious life, was the goal for everyone. At most, people differed according to how well they served their functions, that is, whether they fulfilled their duties and obeyed the rules (see MacIntyre, 1981).

It was not until the early modern period (roughly 1500–1800) that people became fascinated with all the small characteristics that made one person different from another (e.g., Weintraub, 1978). One sign of this new interest was a great increase in biographical and autobiographical writing, including a greatly increased emphasis on accurate description of factual details about the person's life (Altick, 1965; Weintraub, 1978). This new interest was associated with a great social change toward an emphasis on individuality. Politically, economically, socially, philosophically, and in other ways, society came to treat each person as a unique, self-contained unit. People began to think of themselves as capable of changing roles, to search for their own unique traits and destiny, to campaign for individual rights and social equality, and to do other things that reflected this new sense of the individual.

The notion of an inner self expanded greatly during this same period. The inner self is a metaphor for one's private access to, or privileged possession of, one's thoughts and feelings and intentions. There is some evidence that the notion of an inner self began to gain in importance in our culture around the 16th century (e.g., Trilling, 1971). It may have been derived in some way from the Christian Gnostic notion of soul. At first, the inner self may have been simply a way of thinking about hypocrisy, deception, and insincerity: people were not always really the way they appeared on the surface to be.

Over time, however, the notion of an inner self expanded. People began to believe that their inner selves contained their true personality traits, the basis for creativity, and even their most strongly held values and opinions. Poets and other artists attracted great public attention because they were believed to lead rich inner lives (Altick, 1965). For example, instead of just enjoying Shakespeare's plays, people began to wonder seriously about what kind of person Shakespeare must have been (Altick, 1965). By the 19th century, the culture had come to regard each person as containing a vast inner realm of hidden material. The culture had also come to think that the path to personal fulfillment depended substantially on discovering this inner self and developing it (Baumeister, 1986; Sennett, 1974; Weintraub, 1978).

Two developments are associated with this shift toward an expanded concept of the inner self. First, self-knowledge had come to seem increasingly difficult. Confidence in self-knowledge eroded over the subsequent centuries through a series of developments that included the Puritan discovery of the pervasiveness of self-deception, the Victorian fascination with involuntary disclosure, and later the Freudian exploration of the unconscious.

The second development is the evolution of the idea of identity crisis. Erik Erikson (1968) claimed that he coined the term *identity crisis* in the 1940s and it immediately gained a wide usage. The instant popularity of the term suggests that there was already a broadly familiar phenomenon that it defined, so one must assume that identity crises were occurring before then. But the weight of the evidence suggests that the modern form of identity crisis only became generally apparent late in the 19th century. In the Middle Ages, for example, people had no term or concept for an identity crisis, nor did they apparently undergo the sort of experience to which it now refers.

The historical predecessors of identity crises were, first, the religious conversion experience, and, second, the belief that one did not belong in the role or life in which one found oneself. These experiences are important because they imply a separation of the person from his or her beliefs and actions (which are changed in religious conversion) and from his or her place in society. Thus, the self is conceived of as something that exists prior to and apart from its beliefs and roles (see MacIntyre, 1981, for elaboration). Undoubtedly, this new view of the self was encouraged by the rise in social, occupational, and geographical mobility, which showed how the same person could switch to a very different place in society.

The notion of identity crisis is based on the belief that a person is conceptually separate from his or her place in society, and on the belief that a person can find inside him or herself the basis for choosing an identity. These beliefs, as we have seen, are modern beliefs, and they would have been inconceivable to earlier eras. Identity crisis is thus a modern, Western phenomenon, reflecting the new ideas about the self. The modern notions of self are more complex and sophisticated than other notions, but they are not necessarily more accurate, and they also carry a variety of burdens and potential problems. The identity crisis is one symptom of the modern burden of selfhood.

Most cultures in the history of the world have not required people to create definitions of themselves that could serve as the basis for their adult lives, and so most cultures have not produced large numbers of identity crises. Indeed, even our own culture did not make such a requirement until recently. One's occupation was arranged by one's parents, who also took a leading role in arranging one's marriage, and so the individual did not have very many choices to make in determining his or her own adult identity. Now, however, parents at most provide advice, and the young person can (and must) choose from a bewildering variety of possible career opportunities and potential marriage partners (e.g., Kett, 1977).

Thus, although the modern self is associated with a great deal of freedom and opportunity and flexibility, it is also a problem. The 20th century has seen an expanding fascination with the problems of the self, as reflected in everything from the popular culture (e.g., books and movies in which people try to understand or find themselves) to scientific research (e.g., social science research on the self). What was once a simple, straightforward matter has now become something difficult, uncertain, and problematic.

Complicating the matter further is the fact that modern society has turned to selfhood to solve some of its more pressing problems. In particular, the main difficulty in finding meaning in life for modern Western individuals is that of finding a firm basis for values. In response to this value gap, modern society has placed an increasing emphasis on the self as a fundamental good and source of value. The rise of the self as a basic value is one of the most important cultural changes of the 20th century and has transformed the way people understand their identities and modern attitudes about work, family, love, and death (Baumeister, 1991b).

Partly as a result of this burden of selfhood, the modern self (along with its concepts and definitions) carries a substantial ambivalence. On the one hand, the modern self is a unique and special entity, a fascinating puzzle, and a presumed source of much that is valuable in life. On the other hand, the self can be a difficult and uncertain puzzle, a focus of fears and anxieties, and a burdensome source of demands and obligations. Whereas our ancestors had one word, "selfishness," to refer to orientation toward oneself (and to condemn it as morally undesirable), modern society has added a wide assortment of words that express many nuances of that orientation over a wide evaluative spectrum: individualism, individuality, egoism and egotism, self-confidence, self-centeredness, self-expression, and so forth. The modern psychology of self must be understood against the context of this ambivalence.

B. Self-Knowledge

Although the self may be understood as a unity, the self-concept is not really a single, unified concept so much as a loosely connected set of ideas, inferences, and illusions. Indeed, one recent thrust of research on self-knowledge has abandoned the notion of a single self-concept per se and focused instead on *self-schemas,* that is, specific concepts of various features of the self (Markus, 1977). The self-concept can be regarded as a collection of these particular schemas about its traits.

Developmental psychologists have addressed the question of how children accumulate knowledge about themselves (see Damon & Hart, 1982, for review). It appears that children begin early in life to form notions of who they are, but the formation of self-concept is dependent on a wide variety of factors, including the sources of feedback available from peers and the child's own developing ability to understand itself in abstract or complex ways.

Children are born with identities (insofar as they belong to particular families) but must develop self-concepts. The child's sense of self apparently begins with the discovery that some events are contingent on its own acts—perhaps most vividly, seeing one's image in the mirror and noticing that it moves whenever oneself moves (Lewis & Brooks-Gunn, 1979). The first contents of the self-concept appear to be as a member of a particular family, as being young and small, and as being male or female. Among older preschool children the self is understood especially in terms of capabilities and competencies (e.g., Keller, Ford, & Meacham, 1978). This emphasis continues through the early school years, although it becomes increasingly comparative; that is, the child evaluates competence relative to others' levels and relative to measured standards of competence (e.g., Erikson, 1950, 1968; Ruble, 1983). In adolescence, people increasingly come to think of themselves in terms of abstract and interpersonal traits, issues of choice, and values (e.g., Erikson, 1968; Montemayor & Eisen, 1977).

The development of self-knowledge is hardly a smooth or easy process. Indeed, a study by Rosenberg (1979) found that over half the preadolescents in his sample felt that their parents or other adults knew them better than they knew themselves. The notion that a person has privileged access to his or her inner states is one that children come to accept only after a long period of development.

Throughout life, an important source of self-knowledge is the social feedback people receive from each other. An extreme statement of this view was put forward by the symbolic interactionist George Herbert Mead, who proposed that self-knowledge is essentially distilled from feedback received from other people. But an extensive literature review by Shrauger and Schoeneman (1979) found the symbolic interactionist view of the self-concept to be inadequate. People's self-concepts do not correspond very closely to how they are regarded by others. On the other hand, there is considerable evidence that people are less than fully accurate in their perceptions of how others evaluate them (e.g., Greenwald, 1980; Taylor, 1989; Taylor & Brown, 1988). Self-deceptions enable people to sustain views of themselves that are more favorable than their actual feedback would tend to warrant.

Thus, the feedback people receive from others may be subject to substantial distortions. Shrauger and Schoeneman (1979) found that people's self-concepts were highly correlated with how they believed others regarded them, even though the self-concepts were not correlated with how others actually regarded them. Thus, it may be most accurate to suggest that the self-concept is the product of some negotiation between one's interpersonal feedback and one's preferred beliefs about oneself.

Swann and Hill (1982) demonstrated that the effects of social feedback depend on how people are able to respond to it. When subjects were given bogus personality feedback with no chance to respond to it, they tended to accept it and shift their private views of themselves to agree more with it. In contrast, when other subjects were given bogus feedback plus a chance to dispute it (which they did), they were not swayed by it. The implication is that the passive self may be shaped directly by external feedback, but the active self tends to take an aggressive and critical response to feedback so as to measure it against what it already knows. By responding actively to feedback, people can maintain their views of themselves despite contrary evidence.

By adolescence and certainly throughout adulthood, people have a collection of concepts about themselves. They have fairly detailed (although not necessarily coherent) concepts about who and what they are. They may also have fairly elaborate concepts about who and what they might become. Identity begins with an awareness of one's body, but in an adult human being identity is generally oriented toward goals (Baumeister, 1986). These goals include becoming a certain kind of person and not becoming another kind of person.

These concepts of what oneself might become have been termed *possible selves* by Markus and Nurius (1986, 1987). These researchers began with the older notion of an *ideal self* (e.g., Rogers & Dymond, 1954). People have some concept of themselves, not as they currently are, but rather as they would ideally like to be, and their efforts are often directed at becoming more like their ideal self. Markus and Nurius added, however, the important notion that people have concepts of what they fear becoming—such as overweight, unloved, or a failure. Often these undesirable possible selves are quite detailed and elaborate concepts, and people exert efforts to avoid becoming like these feared selves. Indeed, in many respects the undesired self becomes a major motivating factor (Ogilvie, 1987).

These conceptions of possible selves are not only important in shaping behavioral motivations, they also have a strong effect on emotions. Higgins (1987; also Higgins, Klein, & Strauman, 1987) has proposed that emotional patterns are strongly influenced by two sets of concepts about the self. In his view, people compare how they perceive themselves with an *ideal self* and with an *ought self*. The ideal self, again, is how one would like to be, and the ought self is the way one feels some obligation or duty to be. Agitated emotions, such as anxiety and guilt, arise when one sees a discrepancy between oneself and one's ought self. Dejected emotions, such as sadness, depressed mood, and disappointment, arise when one sees a discrepancy between oneself and one's ideal self.

People's efforts to become more like their ideal selves have been studied by Wicklund and Gollwitzer (1982). These researchers examined how people try to claim desired identities. When people's sense of being able to reach their goals is threatened, they try harder to achieve some success or even some symbolic gesture that will help them feel that they are reaching these goals.

An important category of symbolic gestures for claiming identity involves convincing others to see oneself as having that identity. Thus, it is not enough simply to believe privately that one is reaching one's ideal self; identity demands public recognition (e.g., Baumeister, 1982b; Schlenker, 1980, 1985, 1986). Wicklund and Gollwitzer found repeatedly that people will respond to an identity threat by trying to prove themselves to somebody. Interestingly, it seemed not to matter who this other person was. If you want to be an artist, and somehow that creative ability is questioned, you will tend to try to persuade someone of your artistic talent and accomplishments. Although one might think that other artists or art critics would be the most relevant audiences, empirically people seem to settle for whomever they can find and persuade (Gollwitzer, 1986). The important factor is thus the social validation of one's identity, almost regardless of who provides it.

C. The Basics of Self-Esteem

The importance of self-esteem may well begin early in life. Kagan (1981) reviews evidence that the words "good" and "bad" are among the most common ones spoken to young children, across many cultures. Moreover, by the second year of life, children compare their behavior to standards of goodness and badness, including standards of competent performance, and so the habit of self-evaluation is acquired early and is pervasive.

Self-esteem is a central trait, in the sense that it is one of the most important elements of the self-concept and that it affects many other elements (Greenwald, Bellezza, & Banaji, 1988). Indeed, when Wylie (1974, 1979) reviewed the research literature on self-concept, she found that the vast majority of it focused on self-esteem. To be sure, there are other aspects to how people think of themselves than the evaluative dimension, but the evaluative aspect is extremely important and has captured the primary interest of most researchers.

Despite the appeal of the symbolic interactionist arguments, most researchers have come to believe that there are two main sources of self-esteem. One is indeed the evaluative feedback the person receives from others (however distorted it may be). The other is direct experiences of efficacy and success (or failure). There is some evidence that these two aspects of self-esteem are not strongly related to each other (e.g., Franks & Marolla, 1976). People may be insecure about how others regard them but quite confident about their ability to do things right, or the reverse.

The study of individual differences in self-esteem typically features a questionnaire measure, which is used to sort people according to how favorably they regard themselves. There is a wide variety of such measures (see Wylie, 1974, 1979).

There have been several controversies about how to regard self-esteem. One controversy concerns the stability of self-esteem: does it fluctuate from day to day or remain stable? Most studies have found it to be quite stable across time. Some researchers are currently undertaking to revive the notion of self-esteem states that fluctuate rapidly, but this work has to overcome the stable tendencies of self-esteem (e.g., Heatherton & Polivy, 1991; Kernis, 1993). Baumeister (1991c) found a test–retest reliability of .904 across 2 weeks on a self-esteem scale, indicating very high stability. Harter (1993) has found that self-esteem can indeed change, particularly at major transition points in life (e.g., graduation), but still it tends to remain quite stable most of the time.

Another issue concerns whether self-esteem should be considered as a single quantity as opposed to a collection of independent (and uncorrelated) self-evaluations. That is, is it appropriate to think of people as having high or low self-esteem overall, or are people more likely to think well of themselves in some spheres (such as socially) while thinking poorly of themselves in others (such as athletically)? Current thinking on this issue has evolved toward a compromise. A hierarchical facet model has been proposed by Fleming and Courtney (1984; Fleming & Watts, 1980). This model says that there is indeed a global level of self-esteem that reflects a person's overall evaluation of self, but there are also specific levels of self-esteem with respect to various specific spheres. Researchers should therefore consider carefully whether they want to study global self-esteem or some particular dimension of self-esteem.

Self-esteem levels are centrally linked to differences in self-knowledge (Baumgardner, 1990; J. D. Campbell, 1990; J. D. Campbell & Lavallee, 1993). People with high self-esteem appear to have clear, consistent, and stable views about themselves. People with low self-esteem, in contrast, do not seem to know themselves well. Their self-concepts appear to be confused, contradictory, unstable, uncertain, and full of gaps.

Self-esteem has been shown to influence a variety of behaviors (see Baumeister, 1993, for such a compilation). People with low self-esteem appear to be more susceptible to influence than people with high self-esteem (Brockner, 1983; Cohen, 1959; Janis, 1954; Janis & Field, 1959). Initial failure is apparently quite aversive to people with high self-esteem, and they become determined to avoid repeating the experience. They respond either by trying harder on the second trial (e.g., Shrauger & Sorman, 1977; Silverman, 1964) or by avoiding the task if they can (e.g., Baumeister & Tice, 1985). People with low self-esteem respond to initial failure by remaining at about the same level of effort, although some researchers have interpreted this as a withdrawal of effort in comparison with the responses of people with high self-esteem (cf. Maracek & Mettee, 1972).

It is important to realize, however, that although self-esteem predicts responses to such feedback, there is very little evidence of any general tendency for people with low self-esteem to perform worse than people with high self-esteem; indeed, most laboratory studies have found the two groups to perform about the same (e.g., Brockner & Hulton, 1978; J. D. Campbell & Fairey, 1985). Thus, despite the occasional benefits of confidence, high self-esteem is not associated with large advantages in success or achievement. It is unwarranted to assume that low self-esteem is an accurate assessment of one's general lack of competence (see also A. Campbell, 1981).

However, there may be differences in success in life that do not depend on competence. Managing oneself effectively, such as by choosing appropriate tasks and making commitments that one can keep, can be just as important as overall competence in bringing success, and recent evidence indicates that people with high self-esteem are generally more effective at setting appropriate goals and living up to their commitments (Baumeister, Heatherton, & Tice, 1993), partly due to their superior self-knowledge (J. D. Campbell, 1990). On the other hand, ego threats produce extreme and irrational reactions from people with high self-esteem, and they become prone to respond in nonoptimal and even self-defeating ways to such threats. Their effective self-management seems to vanish in such circumstances (Baumeister et al., 1993).

People with low self-esteem are more likely than highs to say that their behavior varies across situations (e.g., Goldberg, 1981; Paulhus & Martin, 1988; see J. D. Campbell & Lavallee, 1993). This may reflect the greater plasticity or flexibility of people with low self-esteem (Brockner, 1983), and it may also reflect their general lack of firm self-knowledge (J. D. Campbell, 1990). Self-esteem also influences the way people respond to public situations. Many behavioral differences are found only in public situations (e.g., Archibald & Cohen, 1971; Shrauger, 1972; Wilson & Benner, 1971), which suggests that self-esteem is associated with important differences in self-presentational patterns (e.g., Arkin, 1981; Baumeister, 1982a).

For a long time, the evidence suggested that people with low self-esteem were more likely to hold negative stereotypes and prejudices than people with high self-esteem, but recent work has revealed a serious flaw in this evidence. People with low self-esteem are more critical of others and of themselves than are people with high self-esteem. The discrepancy between evaluation of self and evaluation of outgroups is about the same for people of all levels of self-esteem (Crocker & Schwartz, 1985).

D. Motivations Regarding the Self-Concept

We have already seen that the self-concept typically includes reference to certain goals, including trying to reach one's ideals and avoid certain undesirable possible selves. Beyond these broad goals, however, it appears that people spend a considerable amount of effort on their self-concepts. However, researchers have been sharply divided as to the nature and goal of these efforts.

The two main motivations regarding the self-concept are consistency and favorability. It is clear that once a person has formed a certain concept or evaluation of self, and if it is acceptable, people seek to maintain it, and they resist external influences designed to change it. But is this because the strive for consistency or because they desire favorability? The evidence is divided.

The view that people desire to hold positive views of themselves has a long history. It seems clear that the majority of people strive to sustain favorable views of themselves (Taylor, 1989; Taylor & Brown, 1988). They blame their failures externally but take credit for successes, they convince themselves that others like them, and they exaggerate their degree of control and efficacy (e.g., Greenwald, 1980). They persuade themselves that their abilities are unique but that their opinions are validated by most other people (J. D. Campbell, 1986).

On the other hand, there is evidence that people seek consistency. They strive to confirm their views of themselves, they dispute feedback that is discrepant from their self-concepts, and they will even avoid someone whose opinion of them differs from their self-concept (Swann, 1987).

The main test case, of course, is what happens when people have formed unfavorable opinions of themselves. In this case, if they desire consistency, they should prefer to receive unfavorable evaluations that confirm their low self-esteem. On the other hand, if they mainly desire favorable views of themselves, then they should prefer favorable evaluations.

An extensive review of the early research literature on this topic found some support for both predictions, but the preponderance of studies supported the favorability hypothesis (S. C. Jones, 1973). A later and more careful review by Shrauger (1975) found, however, that one could explain the discrepant findings by sorting the work according to how the response to evaluations had been measured. Shrauger found that when the measures were primarily affective, people showed a clear preference for favorable feedback, regardless of their level of self-esteem. However, when the measures were primarily cognitive, people seemed more inclined to believe and accept feedback that was consistent with their views of themselves. In short, people with low self-esteem are more likely to enjoy receiving favorable feedback but they are more likely to believe unfavorable feedback. Subsequent work has borne out Shrauger's conclusion (McFarlin & Blascovich, 1981; Swann, Griffin, Predmore, & Gaines, 1987).

The desire to think favorably of oneself can be placed in a broader context, especially if one accepts the view that the motivation is linked to emotional patterns. Becker (1973) proposed that self-esteem is a vital means of protecting oneself against anxiety. This hypothesis has recently been revived and elaborated by Greenberg, Pyszczynski, and Solomon (1986). According to this view, human beings are unique among animal species in that they know that they are going to die. This fear of death gives rise to an existential terror that is the main cause of anxiety in life. People therefore desperately need some defenses against this threat of death, or else they would be in a constant state of terror. Self-esteem furnishes a vital protection against anxiety, because it casts the individual as a valued participant in a cultural drama that will continue even after the individual dies. By regarding themselves as important, worthy individuals, people can begin to overcome the feelings of insignificance and ephemerality that are caused by the realization that they will die (Greenberg et al., 1986).

The terror management hypothesis has generated some controversy, mainly because there is some question as to whether the existential fear of death is really the central cause of all human anxiety. An alternative view has proposed that anxiety is a natural response to exclusion from social groups (Baumeister, 1990a; Baumeister & Leary, 1995; Baumeister & Tice, 1990). In other words, people feel anxiety when others reject them, dislike them, avoid them, and so forth, or even when there is merely some threat of rejection. The social exclusion view is nonetheless quite compatible with Becker's and Greenberg et al.'s hypothesis that self-esteem is an important defense against anxiety. People with high self-esteem consider themselves to be competent, virtuous, and attractive by definition, so they are less worried than others that they will be rejected or excluded. As a result, they are less troubled by anxiety. People with high self-esteem expect others to like them and to want to be associated with them, and they confidently pursue these outcomes.

III. LOSING THE SELF: PROBLEMS OF SELF-CONCEPT AND IDENTITY

At the beginning of this chapter, I proposed that the modern interest in self must be understood in the context of the tension between the great desire to know and express the self and the concomitant burdens and difficulties associated with the self. This section will examine some of the specific problems and difficulties that are associated with the self.

A. The Puzzle of Low Self-Esteem

Psychology has generally been sympathetic to people with high self-esteem. Indeed, studies of adjustment have often treated self-esteem as one measure of adjustment, such that the higher a person's self-esteem score, the better adjusted the person is assumed to be. If that were all there were to it, society should perhaps simply encourage everyone to be as conceited as possible! It is not difficult to understand the goals and motives of the people with high self-esteem. They want to succeed, to be loved and admired, and to enjoy their lives and accomplishments.

In contrast, the motives of people with low self-esteem have been a mystery. Their goals have been relatively uncertain. Indeed, as we saw in the precious section of this chapter, many psychologists have proposed that people with low self-esteem desire failure and rejection, because this feedback will confirm their negative opinions of themselves (e.g., Aronson & Carlsmith, 1962; Aronson & Mettee, 1968; Maracek & Mettee, 1972). The accumulated evidence has shown, however, that people with low self-esteem desire success just as much as anyone else (e.g., McFarlin & Blascovich, 1981).

The solution to the puzzle of low self-esteem may be somewhat complex. To perceive it, it is first necessary to realize that most research subjects who are classified as low in self-esteem are not low in an absolute sense. Baumeister, Tice, and Hutton (1989) reviewed the distributions of self-esteem scores for many different scales in many different studies, and they found that invariably there were only a few people whose scores were genuinely low. Many people score at the high end of the scale, and most of the rest score in the middle. Thus, in an absolute sense, most people should be labeled as either high or *moderate* in self-esteem. Low scores are only relatively low; in an absolute sense, they are moderate.

Next, it is vital to recognize that people with low self-esteem do not seem to have a firm sense of who and what they are, as already mentioned (Baumgardner, 1990; J. D. Campbell, 1990; J. D. Campbell & Lavallee, 1993). This pervasive "self-concept confusion" (J. D. Campbell & Lavallee, 1993) may underlie a broad range of their thoughts, feelings, and actions.

Furthermore, one must take into account the evidence that these "low" self-esteem individuals have mixed reactions to success, as already noted. They would like to succeed, but they do not expect to do so (McFarlin & Blascovich, 1981; Shrauger, 1975; Swann et al., 1987). Thus, they are somewhat insecure about achieving the outcomes they desire, in contrast to the people with high self-esteem who are confident that they can achieve whatever they try.

There is also some evidence suggesting that different levels of aspiration are associated with different levels of self-esteem. In a study by Baumeister and Tice (1985), people received initial success or failure and then had an opportunity to persist at the task or to devote their time to something else. Not surprisingly, people with high self-esteem showed great interest in the task when they initially succeeded, but they tended to avoid the task if they had initially failed. People with low self-esteem, however, showed the opposite pattern.

One way of interpreting these results is to suggest that people with high self-esteem are interested in achieving exceptional successes, whereas people with low self-esteem mainly want to avoid failures. When the person with low self-esteem receives failure feedback, it is discouraging, but the person will tend to work on this problem to try to remedy the deficit. That way, the likelihood of future failure is reduced. In contrast, initial success signifies to someone with low self-esteem that he or she is already performing at an adequate, passable level, so there is no need to work on it. Indeed, it may be prudent to avoid the task, so that there is no danger of ruining one's initial success by failing at it on a second try. Thus, people with low self-esteem may be oriented toward remedying their deficits and overcoming their faults, so as to reach an adequate or passable level.

A more general formulation has recently been put forward by Baumeister et al. (1989). This formulation distinguishes between the motive to *protect* one's self-concept and the motive to *enhance* it (i.e., make it more favorable). Self-enhancement requires seeking out opportunities to achieve, succeed, and stand out; self-protection involves avoiding chances of failure, rejection, or humiliation. Tice (1990) showed that even when similar behaviors are involved, they appear to be driven by different motivations: People with low self-esteem are mainly concerned with self-protection, whereas people with high self-esteem are mainly concerned with self-enhancement (see also Arkin, 1981; Baumeister et al., 1989; Wolfe, Lennox, & Cutler, 1986).

A final and important piece of the puzzle has been suggested by Steele (1988) and Spencer, Josephs, and Steele (1993). In their view, self-esteem is a resource, and people with low self-esteem simply do not have as much of it as people with high self-esteem. Accordingly, when stressed or threatened, they have less to draw upon, and they respond—and indeed approach life in general—in a more protective and defensive way.

Thus, a solution is slowly emerging to the puzzle of low self-esteem. People who score low on self-esteem measures typically lack a clear and definite stock of self-knowledge, and in particular they suffer from a lack of helpful, positive views about themselves. They desire and enjoy success, but their actions are influenced by their doubts that they will be able to achieve success on a regular or frequent basis. They focus on protecting themselves against failures and rejections, such as by presenting themselves in a cautious or modest fashion. They orient themselves toward finding out their shortcomings and inadequacies so as to remedy these. Unlike people with high self-esteem, who focus on their strengths and try to cultivate these so as to become outstanding, people with low self-esteem strive to be adequate by focusing on their weaknesses and overcoming them.

These are of course only broad, general patterns. People with high self-esteem dislike failure and will work hard to avoid humiliating experiences. But when they have a choice, their primary goal is to achieve great success rather than to avoid failure. People with low self-esteem will tend toward the opposite choice.

B. Self-Defeating Behavior

One of the greatest paradoxes of human behavior, and certainly in the study of the self, is self-defeating behavior. It is clear that people sometimes do things that cause themselves pain, harm, loss, and even death. Self-defeating behavior spans a wide spectrum, ranging from getting into debt or making poor investments to suicide. Self-preservation and the pursuit of self-interest are widely regarded as the essence of rational behavior, and so these self-defeating behaviors seem quintessentially irrational.

Considerable information is available about the ways people harm themselves and sabotage their projects (see Baumeister & Scher, 1988). To make sense of this information, it is first necessary to distinguish several possible categories of self-defeating behaviors. The purest form would be cases in which people engage in some action for the sake of the loss or suffering that it will bring them. In these cases of deliberately self-destructive behavior, the person both foresees and desires the harm to self. At the other extreme, people may harm themselves almost by accident; in these cases, people neither desire nor foresee the harm to self, but their efforts toward positive goals are undermined by counterproductive means or strategies. Lastly, an intermediate category includes cases in which the harm to self is perhaps foreseen but is not desired. In this category, typically, people are engaging in trade-offs, so they engage in the behavior for the sake of positive benefits and accept the risks and costs that accompany it.

There is very little evidence that normal adult human beings engage in the first kind of self-destructive behavior (i.e., deliberate self-destruction). However, there is considerable evidence of counterproductive strategies. People use various bargaining strategies (Pruitt, 1981) or ingratiation strategies (E. E. Jones & Wortman, 1973) that backfire and produce undesired results. They persist in failing endeavors far past the point at which they should rationally cut their losses and start over elsewhere (Rubin & Brockner, 1975; Staw, 1976; Teger, 1980). They respond to pressure situations by focusing on themselves, which tends to impair skilled performance (Baumeister, 1984). Even learned helplessness can be considered a maladaptive withdrawal of effort (Seligman, 1975; also Roth & Kubal, 1975).

Lastly, there is considerable evidence of self-defeating behavior that occurs as a result of trade-offs between competing, incompatible goals. People handicap their performances so as to give themselves an excuse for failure (e.g., E. E. Jones & Berglas, 1978). They use drugs and alcohol, which can cause considerable damage to one's health and relationships, in order to avoid realizing unpleasant things about themselves (Hull, 1981). They disregard and disobey medical advice from their physicians, even skipping important appointments and failing to take their medicines (e.g., Dunbar & Stunkard, 1979; Sackett & Snow, 1979). They sacrifice tangible rewards to avoid temporary embarrassment or to take revenge against others (Brown, 1968; Brown & Garland, 1971). Despite their desire to have friends, shy people avoid others and avoid social interactions, so they remain lonely and isolated (e.g., Cheek & Busch, 1981; W. H. Jones, Freemon, & Goswick, 1981; Maroldo, 1982; Schlenker & Leary, 1982).

One somewhat surprising conclusion that has emerged regarding self-defeating behavior is that it often appears to be motivated by states of high self-awareness (Baumeister & Scher, 1988). When attention is focused on the self, especially in an aversive fashion, people are more likely to do things that will produce harmful outcomes. In many cases, this appears to occur because people are eager to escape from an awareness of the self's shortcomings. The willingness to accept costs and risks for the sake of immediate relief is increased when the current state involves an aversive awareness of self.

It seems unwarranted, then, to infer that people have self-destructive urges or motivations. Self-defeating behavior occurs among normal people either as an unwanted by-product of some desirable outcome or as an unwanted result of poor judgment and ill-advised strategies.

C. Identity Crisis

The term *identity crisis* apparently originated in the 1940s (Erikson, 1950, 1968). Erikson's view was that an identity crisis is a normal, possibly universal stage of human development, typically associated with adolescence. The universality of identity crises has become an increasingly untenable hypothesis. For one thing, identity crises appear to be historically and culturally relative to some extent; as far as we can tell, people did not commonly have identity crises before the 19th century (e.g., Baumeister, 1986), although it is plausible that exceptional individuals occasionally had them (see Erikson, 1958). Furthermore, there is substantial evidence that many people today do not report anything resembling an identity crisis. In Erikson's view, identity crises could be unconscious, so people might not be aware of having them. Such a hypothesis is difficult to evaluate and perhaps impossible to disprove, but researchers have consistently found people who reveal no sign of identity crises even in response to in-depth interviews (e.g., Marcia, 1966, 1967).

The discovery that many people show no signs of identity crises has led researchers to formulate a taxonomy of *identity statuses* (Marcia, 1966, 1967; Orlofsky, Marcia, & Lesser, 1973). People are sorted according to whether they have had identity crises or not, and according to whether they have formed a secure identity with roles and commitments or not. The four statuses deserve some explanation and comment (for reviews, see Bernard, 1981; Bourne, 1978).

People who have had identity crises and resolved them successfully are classified as *identity achieved.* These people are typically mature, well adjusted, and flexible. Indeed, they score highest on most adjustment measures, suggesting that identity crises are generally beneficial in the long run.

People who have had identity crises but have not resolved them are classified as *moratoriums.* Typically, they are currently involved in the crisis. The term "crisis" carries a connotation of disaster and suffering, which is only partly accurate. Moratorium subjects often appear to be open to new experiences, actively exploring a wide range of ideas and lifestyles, and often exhilarated by some of what they find, although of course there are periods of confusion, depression, and dismay. Some researchers have recently come to prefer the term "exploration" rather than "crisis," simply to avoid the melodramatic implications of the latter term.

A third category, *foreclosures,* involves people who have commitments to adult identity patterns without having gone through a substantial period of crisis or exploration. Most children have foreclosed identities, for they tend to accept the beliefs, values, and goals that their parents instill in them. The adolescent identity crisis often begins with a rejection of these parental lessons. Hence, people who do not experience the adolescent crisis typically retain their allegiance to what their parents taught them. Foreclosures tend to seem mature earlier than their peers, and their lives often conform to a pattern of stable, continuous progress toward long-term goals. However, they tend to be inflexible and they do not adapt well to changing or stressful circumstances. There is some evidence suggesting that the foreclosure pattern is maladaptive for males but not for females (Marcia & Scheidel, 1983), although it would be premature to draw a broad conclusion.

The fourth category, *identity diffusion,* refers to people who have not formed the commitments to adult identity but are not engaged in any active search or effort to do so. This category is generally regarded as the most maladaptive and even pathological of the four. At a minimum, these individuals tend to resemble the "perpetual adolescent" who postpones the responsibilities, decisions, and commitments of adult life as long as possible.

The nature and processes of identity crisis have remained shrouded in mystery. The vagueness of the concept, combined with its multiple usages (including metaphorical and colloquial ones), has made it very difficult to study the process closely. One review of the available evidence concluded that there are actually two major types of identity crisis (Baumeister, Shapiro, & Tice, 1985; also Baumeister, 1986).

The first type of identity crisis can be called an *identity deficit.* This is the state created when the person's identity is inadequate to make the choices facing it. It is commonly associated with adolescence and midlife, arising especially when the person questions and then rejects the patterns of thinking and acting that have guided the person over the preceding years. In the adolescent, it is often associated with breaking away from parents and learning to think and act independently (e.g., Blos, 1962). At midlife, it may often be prompted by the sense that one's life is passing by and so one must reassess where best to devote one's time and efforts (see Levinson, 1978). The identity deficit is often accompanied by radical shifts in feelings and behaviors.

The other type of identity crisis can be called an *identity conflict.* It typically arises when the person has defined him or herself in terms of multiple commitments, and these make conflicting demands on the person. Examples of this type of identity crisis include conflicts between family ties and religious beliefs, and conflicts between occupational advancement and personal or home life. Unlike the wide mood swings of the identity deficit, the identity conflict is often characterized by a pervasive, oppressive sense of being trapped, guilty, or traitorous. These crises also do not show the exploratory openness to experience that characterizes the deficit crises. The person suffering from an identity conflict does not want new information or alternatives, for he or she already has too many commitments. Instead, there may be a tendency for the identity conflict to breed a passive attitude, as the person postpones making any irrevocable decision and hopes for a solution to emerge.

Thus identity crises are not universal but rather are associated with particular individuals, circumstances, and cultural or historical patterns. There are two broad types of identity crises, and research should distinguish between them. Identity deficits appear to be linked to particular stages in life, associated with the desire to reject and replace some definitions of the self, and associated with beneficial outcomes. Identity conflicts can occur at any age, they arise when the situation forces the person to choose between different definitions of self, and these crises do not apparently benefit the individual.

D. Escape from Self

If the self can be a burden or problem, then sometimes people may want to avoid self-awareness. Escapist motivations may be strongest when the self is linked to aversive emotional states. As Higgins (1987) has proposed, such states arise when people fall short of their standards, including ideals and moral obligations. Self-awareness is centrally concerned with comparing oneself with standards, so when the self falls short, it may be especially painful or unpleasant to focus attention on oneself (e.g., Duval & Wicklund, 1972; Wicklund, 1975). Research has shown a variety of circumstances that make self-awareness especially aversive and motivate people to try to avoid anything that would shift their attention inward. These circumstances include receiving a bad evaluation (Duval & Wicklund, 1972), hearing that one has personality problems that would be difficult to correct (Steenbarger & Aderman, 1979), receiving a rejection and putdown by an attractive member of the opposite sex (Gibbons & Wicklund, 1976), or performing actions that run counter to one's belief and values (Greenberg & Musham, 1981). Most of these studies measured escape from self-awareness by confronting the subject with a mirror and assessing the subject's attempts to avoid it, such as by choosing a seat facing away from the mirror or by finishing quickly and leaving the room.

In everyday life, of course, escape from aversive self-awareness is not always as easy as walking away from a mirror. When the self is cast in an unfavorable light, people may find themselves locked into undesirable emotional states and unable to distract themselves from the unpleasant thoughts about their failures and inadequacies.

Also, if the modern self is generally a source of burdensome demands and constraining definitions, people may find it exhilarating to escape from self-awareness even when nothing bad has happened. States of ecstasy appear to depend centrally on loss of ordinary awareness of self. Religious mystics speak of powerful experiences in which the ego is dissolved (see Goleman, 1988). "Peak" or "flow" experiences of ordinary individuals are often characterized by absorption in some activity, which may involve a suspension of one's normal awareness of self (e.g., Csikszentmihalyi, 1982). Thus, although escapist motivations may arise from specific, unhappy thoughts and feelings connected with the self, they may be attractive in their own right as appealing experiences.

How do people go about escaping from self-awareness? It is not easy to stop being aware of oneself. People generally find it difficult to prevent unwanted thoughts (Wegner, Schneider, Carter, & White, 1987), and the self may be especially difficult to suppress. After all, one cannot monitor one's success at not thinking about oneself, for in order to monitor oneself one must attend to oneself. A cognitive effort to avoid self-awareness may therefore be a paradoxical, impossible task.

What people appear to do instead, therefore, is to *deconstruct* the self. Identity is a *construct,* that is, an entity consisting of meaning and involving connections and relationships among many events, stimuli, and contexts. Deconstruction is a matter of breaking those connections and dissolving those relationships, thereby reducing the sense of self back to its bare minimum: a mere body. By focusing narrowly on physical movement and sensation, people can avoid broadly meaningful awareness, including awareness of implications about the self (Baumeister, 1989, 1990a, 1990b, 1991a; Vallacher & Wegner, 1985, 1987).

A variety of escapist behaviors can be understood on the basis of this process of shifting attention down to minimal levels. Cognitive deconstruction creates a state characterized by a narrow time frame (focused on the immediate present), concrete and rigid thinking, a rejection of meaningful thought, a focus on means and techniques rather than ends, a passive or impulsive style of behavior, and reduced or suppressed emotion. The deconstructed state may make the person's behavior more inconsistent, because it takes meaningful integration to recognize inconsistencies. It may also remove inhibitions, because inhibitions typically require high-level evaluations of the meanings of possible acts (see Baumeister, 1990a, 1990b, 1991a).

1. Alcohol Use

Hull (1981) proposed that alcohol use is often a means of escaping from self-awareness. Alcohol use impairs high-level cognitive processes and meaningful thought, focusing attention instead on sensations and movements. Even small doses have this effect, and so this view helps explain the appeal of having just a drink or two.

Experimental work has established the effectiveness of alcohol in escaping from unpleasant awareness of self. Alcohol makes people less likely to refer to themselves in speech and reduces the number of first-person pronouns they use (Hull, Levenson, Young, & Sher, 1983). People consume more alcohol after experiencing failure than after success (Hull & Young, 1983). Research on stress has failed to find that all forms of stress increase alcohol consumption, but people do increase consumption when the stress reflects unfavorably on the self (Hull, 1981). Indeed, one study examined the relapse rates for alcoholics who completed a detoxification program. People who experienced aversive life events tended to relapse more quickly than others, but only if they were inclined to reflect on themselves (Hull, Young, & Jouriles, 1986). When life stress was not accompanied by high self-awareness, there was presumably no drive to escape it by getting drunk.

Alcohol is a good illustration of both the positive and the negative aspects of deconstructing the self. As Hull's work has shown, people tend to consume alcohol to forget unpleasant implications about themselves. Undoubtedly, however, alcoholic intoxication is often an appealing state even in the absence of the need to escape from unpleasant emotions. By disconnecting certain aspects of the self and focusing narrowly on the immediate present, people are able to enjoy themselves more. Alcohol does appear to reduce inhibitions and make people more able to act in ways that are inconsistent with some of their abstract beliefs and values (e.g., Steele & Southwick, 1985). The uninhibited behaviors associated with wild parties are a familiar illustration of these effects of alcohol. These behaviors may involve the same escape from self-awareness and meaningful thought, for intoxicated people do things that are inconsistent with the way they normally regard themselves and want to be regarded by others. But in this case the impetus for consuming alcohol is not so much to end unpleasant feelings as the positive attractions of the intoxicated state.

2. Masochism

Masochism means obtaining sexual pleasure and arousal in connection with pain, bondage, and/or humiliation, and some theorists have extended the definition to nonsexual enjoyment of pain, helplessness, and humiliation as well. Masochism is one of psychology's long-standing puzzles. Most theorists who have written about masochism have worked from clinical observations and have regarded it as a variety of self-destructive behavior. Recent research has shown, however, that the majority of masochists appear to be normal, healthy, well-adjusted individuals who show no signs of mental illness apart from their deviant sexuality (e.g., Scott, 1983; T. Weinberg & Kamel, 1983). We saw earlier that normal people do not apparently engage in self-destructive behavior except in connection with positive, desirable goals (Baumeister & Scher, 1988). It is necessary, therefore, to furnish a new theory of masochism.

Based on current evidence, it seems reasonable to conclude that masochism is a set of techniques for removing one's ordinary identity from awareness (see Baumeister, 1988a, 1988b, 1989). Masochism deconstructs the self in multiple ways. To appreciate this, one must consider the common features of masochistic activity. These include humiliation and embarrassment, loss of control (especially through bondage), and pain.

Humiliation and embarrassment are a direct attack on the dignity of the self. Earlier in this chapter, it was noted that people are generally motivated to maintain favorable views of themselves; indeed, this is almost an axiom of the psychology of self. Masochists, however, seek out degrading experiences such as being dressed in embarrassing costumes, being kept on a leash like an animal, having to kiss another person's feet, being displayed naked, and so forth. These masochistic practices thus contradict one of the most pervasive functions of the self, and they make it impossible for the person to maintain his or her normal sense of identity.

A second pervasive motivation of the self is to gain and maintain control over the environment. People are relentlessly motivated to maintain control, and where real control is lacking they cultivate the illusion of control (e.g., Brehm, 1966; Langer, 1975; Rothbaum, Weisz, & Snyder, 1982; White, 1959). Masochists, however, seek the illusion of having lost all control. They desire to be tied up, blindfolded, gagged, and otherwise restrained. They seek a partner who will give them arbitrary commands and take over all initiative. Thus, the self as an active agent ceases to exist in masochism.

The desire for pain is perhaps the most puzzling feature of masochism, for it is hard to understand how pain could become pleasure. Evidence suggests that masochists do not actually come to enjoy the pain (e.g., M. S. Weinberg, Williams, & Moser, 1984; also Scott, 1983). Also, the masochistic desire for pain is not accompanied by any desire for injury, and in fact masochists appear to be very concerned with safety (e.g., Baumeister, 1988a; Scott, 1983; M. S. Weinberg et al., 1984). Pain is quite effective, however, at shifting attention to the immediate present. It deconstructs the world, preventing meaningful thought and focusing attention on immediate sensations (Scarry, 1985). Pain is thus a tool for manipulating awareness, to help bring about the escape from ordinary self-awareness.

3. Binge Eating

Another odd behavior pattern that appears to be on the rise in modern life is binge eating. Patterns of binge eating range from the temporary indulgences of dieters who, having broken their diets, feel that all rules are off and so eat large quantities of fattening foods, to the pathological patterns of bulimia nervosa.

There is some evidence that binge eating is associated with escape from self-awareness (Heatherton & Baumeister, 1991). First, eating binges are linked to negative views of self and awareness of the self's deficiencies (e.g., Garner, Olmsted, Polivy, & Garfinkel, 1984; Gross & Rosen, 1988; Katzman & Wolchik, 1984; Schlesier-Stropp, 1984). Second, manipulations that involve ego threat or aversive moods do increase the eating by obese or dieting subjects (i.e., those most prone to engage in eating binges), unlike control subjects (e.g., Baucom & Aiken, 1981; Frost, Goolkasian, Ely, & Blanchard, 1982; Ruderman, 1985; Slochower & Kaplan, 1980). Third, binges do not occur if people are kept in a state of high self-awareness, whereas the binge is associated with the loss of attention to self. In particular, people cease to monitor their eating during a binge (e.g., Polivy, 1976). This fits the view that inhibitions and restraints involve meaningful awareness of self, and so deconstruction removes them.

Eating binges may be pleasant and desirable in themselves, but the available evidence does suggest a powerful role of unpleasant emotions and aversive awareness of self. Self-awareness and aversive emotions are minimized, thinking becomes concrete and rigid, and the person focuses on immediate sensations (especially the food) rather than long-range considerations or goals. Such binges therefore appear to be more commonly motivated by the desire to get away from an unpleasant state than an attraction to the state of eating, although especially among dieters the eating may be intensely enjoyable.

4. Suicide

A last example of escaping the self is suicide. There are multiple patterns and causes of suicide, but escape appears to be the centrally important one (e.g., Baechler, 1975/1979; Baumeister, 1990b, 1991a). Indeed, some researchers have found escape to be more common than all other motives for suicide combined (e.g., Smith & Bloom, 1985).

The pattern of events preceding a suicide attempt appears to conform to the same process of escaping the self that was discussed in the preceding examples (see Baumeister, 1990b). Suicide is associated with a sense of falling short of one's goals and standards (including the expectations other people have for one), which produces an acute sense of self as incompetent, blameworthy, undesirable, and so forth. This awareness is initially accompanied by strong patterns of negative emotion, including depression and anxiety.

To escape from this aversive state, the person attempts to avoid meaningful thought. The mental state of the suicidal individual conforms very closely to the features of the deconstructed state. The person's sense of time is focused narrowly on the present (e.g., Greaves, 1971; Neuringer & Harris, 1974; Yufit & Benzies, (1973). Thinking is rigid and concrete (e.g., Henken, 1976; Perrah & Wichman, 1987). Initiative is stifled amid a general passivity (e.g., Henken, 1976; Ringel, 1976) or channeled into impulsive acts. Emotion is broadly stifled, so that even positive emotions are suppressed (Williams & Broadbent, 1986).

The suicide attempt itself may be a result of the person's inability to maintain the escape using less drastic methods. The person's mental state oscillates between periods of numbness (which are felt as boring and empty) and brief, intense doses of negative affect that arise whenever the person happens to resume meaningful thought. As the latter are felt as intolerable, the person is attracted to the presumed oblivion of death. The deconstructed state removes the person's normal inhibitions against taking his or her own life, and so a suicide attempt results (Baumeister, 1990a, 1990b, 1991a).

Suicide represents the most negative and maladaptive aspect of escapist motivations. It was suggested earlier that many common forms of self-defeating behavior are motivated by a desire to escape from an aversive state of high self-awareness (Baumeister & Scher, 1988). Suicide may often be an unfortunately extreme case of that principle. People attempt to take their own lives as a desperate strategy to bring an end to the emotional misery associated with an awareness of the self's failures and shortcomings.

IV. SUMMARY AND CONCLUSION

The self begins with simple and universal psychological experiences, such as having a body and being a distinct member of a social unit. From this crude beginning, however, the self can be defined and understood in a wide variety of ways, and different cultures and historical periods have indeed taken very different approaches to selfhood.

Our modern Western society constructs the self in a complex and elaborate fashion. The great cultural emphasis on cultivating a well-developed, unique, expressive, and successful self links the self to a variety of powerful motivations. These are both positive and negative. The opportunities for developing and fulfilling the self are greater in our modern culture than in nearly any other. At the same time, these patterns create demands, obligations, and threats that make the self especially problematic and burdensome. The self in some ways resembles the prize fish in Ernest Hemingway's novel *The Old Man and the Sea:* It is a great treasure and opportunity, and at the same time it is a source of dangers and difficulties.

On the positive side, people are very interested in self-knowledge. They desire to learn about themselves, although they have strong preferences regarding what they might find out. People seek to manage and control the information about themselves. Typically, people want to confirm their favorable opinions of themselves. People hold multiple conceptions of self, including possible future selves, images of how they ideally would like to be and how they ought to be, detailed (if inaccurate) concepts of how they really are and how they appear to others, and more. People with high self-esteem are guided by a desire to stand out, to excel, and to make strongly favorable impressions on others. People with low self-esteem are torn between a desire for favorable feedback and a tendency to distrust and disbelieve it. They appear to be guided by a desire to avoid failure, rejection, and humiliation, such as by remedying weaknesses and avoiding risks.

On the negative side, the self is associated with a variety of threats and problems. When people discover a discrepancy between how they are and how they want or ought to be, they suffer a variety of unpleasant emotions. Self-esteem may play an important role in defending the individual against anxiety, and so threats to self-esteem may trigger acutely aversive emotional states. It does not appear that people are generally motivated to suffer, but they do engage in a wide variety of self-destructive or self-defeating behaviors as a result of poor judgment or conflicting goals.

Identity crises appear to be one symptom of the modern emphasis on requiring each person to create and define his or her own identity. There are at least two major types of identity crisis. Identity deficits begin when the person rejects the values and behavior patterns that have shaped his or her life up to that point, and typically a period of exploration and experimentation follows, usually with long-term beneficial results. Identity conflicts arise in conflict situations that require the person to betray some personal commitments or self-definitions.

The modern burden of selfhood has fostered a great increase in the variety of means people use to escape from self-awareness. The most common process appears to involve deconstructing the identity by focusing narrowly on movements and sensations in the immediate situation. Alcohol use, sexual masochism, binge eating, suicide, and other patterns reflect this pattern of escape.

The modern fascination with self seems likely to endure, for it is deeply rooted in current social patterns that are probably going to continue. For the near future at least, defining the self is likely to continue to be a great source of challenge and satisfaction, as well as a great source of threat and difficulty. The construction of self is one of the major life tasks to confront the modern individual.

References

Altick, R. (1965). *Lives and letters: A history of literary biography in England and America.* New York: Knopf.

Archibald, W. P., & Cohen, R. L. (1971). Self-presentation, embarrassment, and facework as a function of self-evaluation, conditions of self-presentation, and feedback from others. *Journal of Personality and Social Psychology, 20,* 287–297.

Arkin, R. M. (1981). Self-presentational styles. In J. T. Tedeschi (Ed.), *Impression management theory and social psychological research* (pp. 311–333). New York: Academic Press.

Aronson, E., & Carlsmith, J. M. (1962). Performance expectancy as a determinant of actual performance. *Journal of Abnormal and Social Psychology, 65,* 178–182.

Aronson, E., & Mettee, D. (1968). Dishonest behavior as a function of differential levels of induced self-esteem. *Journal of Personality and Social Psychology, 9,* 121–127.

Baechler, J. (1979). *Suicides.* New York: Basic Books. (Original work published 1975)

Baucom, D. H., & Aiken, P. A. (1981). Effect of depressed mood on eating among obese and nonobese dieting persons. *Journal of Personality and Social Psychology, 41,* 577–585.

Baumeister, R. F. (1982a). Self-esteem, self-presentation, and future interaction. A dilemma of reputation. *Journal of Personality, 50,* 29–45.

Baumeister, R. F. (1982b). A self-presentational view of social phenomena. *Psychological Bulletin, 91,* 3–26.

Baumeister, R. F. (1984). Choking under pressure: Self-consciousness and paradoxical effects of incentives on skillful performance. *Journal of Personality and Social Psychology, 46,* 610–620.

Baumeister, R. F. (1986). *Identity: Cultural change and the struggle for self.* New York: Oxford University Press.

Baumeister, R. F. (1987). How the self became a problem. A psychological review of historical research. *Journal of Personality and Social Psychology, 52,* 163–176.

Baumeister, R. F. (1988a). Masochism as escape from self. *Journal of Sex Research, 25,* 28–59.

Baumeister, R. F. (1988b). Gender differences in masochistic scripts. *Journal of Sex Research, 25,* 478–499.

Baumeister, R. F. (1989). *Masochism and the self.* Hillsdale, NJ: Erlbaum.

Baumeister, R. F. (1990a). Anxiety and deconstruction: On escaping the self. In J. M. Olson & M. P. Zanna (Eds.). *Self-inference processes: The Ontario Symposium* (Vol. 6, pp. 259–291). Hillsdale, NJ: Erlbaum.

Baumeister, R. F. (1990b). Suicide as escape from self. *Psychological Review, 97,* 90–113.

Baumeister, R. F. (1991a). *Escaping the self: Alcoholism, spirituality, masochism, and other flights from the burden of selfhood.* New York: Basic Books.

Baumeister, R. F. (1991b). *Meanings of life.* New York: Guilford Press.

Baumeister, R. F. (1991c). On the stability of variability: Retest reliability of metatraits. *Personality and Social Psychology Bulletin, 17,* 633–639.

Baumeister, R. F. (Ed.). (1993). *Self-esteem: The puzzle of low self-regard.* New York: Plenum Press.

Baumeister, R. F., Heatherton, T. F., & Tice, D. M. (1993). When ego threats lead to self-regulation failure: Negative consequences of high self-esteem. *Journal of Personality and Social Psychology, 64,* 141–156.

Baumeister, R. F., & Leary, M. R. (1995). The need to belong: Desire for interpersonal attachments as a fundamental human motivation. *Psychological Bulletin, 117,* 497–529.

Baumeister, R. F., & Scher, S. J. (1988). Self-defeating behavior patterns among normal individuals: Review and analysis of common self-destructive tendencies. *Psychological Bulletin, 104,* 3–22.

Baumeister, R. F., & Senders, P. S. (1989). Identity development and the role structure of children's games. *Journal of Genetic Psychology, 150,* 19–37.

Baumeister, R. F., Shapiro, J. J., & Tice, D. M. (1985). Two kinds of identity crisis. *Journal of Personality, 53,* 407–424.

Baumeister, R. F., & Tice, D. M. (1985). Self-esteem and responses to success and failure: Subsequent performance and intrinsic motivation. *Journal of Personality, 53,* 450–467.

Baumeister, R. F., & Tice, D. M. (1990). Anxiety and social exclusion. *Journal of Social and Clinical Psychology, 9,* 165–195.

Baumeister, R. F., Tice, D. M., & Hutton, D. G. (1989). Self-presentational motivations and personality differences in self-esteem. *Journal of Personality, 57,* 547–579.

Baumgardner, A. H. (1990). To know oneself is to like oneself: Self-certainty and self-affect. *Journal of Personality and Social Psychology, 58,* 1062–1072.

Becker, E. (1973). *The denial of death.* New York: Free Press.

Bernard, H. S. (1981). Identity formation during late adolescence: A review of some empirical findings. *Adolescence, 16,* 349–357.

Blos, P. (1962). *On adolescence.* New York: Free Press.

Bourne, E. (1978). The state of research on ego identity: A review and appraisal. Part II. *Journal of Youth and Adolescence, 7,* 371–392.

Brehm, J. W. (1966). *A theory of psychological reactance.* New York: Academic Press.

Brockner, J. (1983). Low self-esteem and behavioral plasticity: Some implications. In L. Wheeler & P. Shaver (Eds.), *Review of personality and social psychology* (Vol. 4, pp. 237–271). Beverly Hills, CA: Sage.

Brockner, J., & Hulton, A. (1978). How to reverse the vicious cycle of low self-esteem: The importance of attentional focus. *Journal of Experimental Social Psychology, 15,* 564–578.

Brown, B. R. (1968). The effects of need to maintain face on interpersonal bargaining. *Journal of Experimental Social Psychology, 4,* 107–122.

Brown, B. R., & Garland, H. (1971). The effects of incompetency, audience acquaintanceship, and anticipated evaluative feedback on face-saving behavior. *Journal of Experimental Social Psychology, 7,* 490–502.

Campbell, A. (1981). *The sense of well-being in America.* New York: McGraw-Hill.

Campbell, J. D. (1986). Similarity and uniqueness: The effects of attribute type, relevance, and individual differences in self-esteem and depression. *Journal of Personality and Social Psychology, 50,* 281–294.

Campbell, J. D. (1990). Self-esteem and the clarity of the self-concept. *Journal of Personality and Social Psychology, 59,* 538–549.

Campbell, J. D., & Fairey, P. J. (1985). Effects of self-esteem, hypothetical explanations, and verbalization of expectancies on future performance. *Journal of Personality and Social Psychology, 48,* 1097–1111.

Campbell, J. D., & Lavallee, L. F. (1993). Who am I? The role of self-concept confusion in understanding the behavior of people with low self-esteem. In R. Baumeister (Ed.), *Self-esteem: The puzzle of low self-regard* (pp. 3–20). New York: Plenum Press.

Cheek, J. M., & Busch, C. M. (1981). The influence of shyness on loneliness in a new situation. *Personality and Social Psychology Bulletin, 7,* 572–577.

Cohen, A. R. (1959). Some implications of self-esteem for social influence. In C. I. Hovland & I. L. Janis (Eds.), *Personality and persuasibility* (pp. 102–120). New Haven, CT: Yale University Press.

Crocker, J., & Schwartz, I. (1985). Prejudice and ingroup favoritism in a minimal intergroup situation: Effects of self-esteem. *Personality and Social Psychology Bulletin, 11,* 379–386.

Crowne, D. P., & Marlowe, D. (1964). *The approval motive.* New York: Wiley.

Csikszentmihalyi, M. (1982). Toward a psychology of optimal experience. In L. Wheeler (Ed.), *Review of personality and social psychology* (Vol. 2, pp. 13–36) Beverly Hills, CA: Sage.

Damon, W., & Hart, D. (1982). The development of self-understanding from infancy through adolescence. *Child Development, 53,* 841–864.

Dunbar, J. M., & Stunkart, A. J. (1979). Adherence to diet and drug regimen. In R. Levy, B. Rifkind, B. Dennis, & N. Ernst (Eds.), *Nutrition, lipids, and coronary heart disease* (pp. 391–423). New York: Raven Press.

Duval, S., & Wicklund, R. A. (1972). *A theory of objective self-awareness.* New York: Academic Press.

Erikson, E. H. (1950). *Childhood and society.* New York: Norton.

Erikson, E. H. (1958). *Young man Luther.* New York: Norton.

Erikson, E .H. (1968). *Identity: Youth and crisis.* New York: Norton.

Fleming, J. S., & Courtney, B. E. (1984). The dimensionality of self-esteem: II. Hierarchical facet model for revised measurement scales. *Journal of Personality and Social Psychology, 46,* 404–421.

Fleming, J. S., & Watts, W. A. (1980). The dimensionality of self-esteem: Some results for a college sample. *Journal of Personality and Social Psychology, 39,* 921–929.

Franks, D. D., & Marolla, J. (1976). Efficacious action and social approval as interacting dimensions of self-esteem: A tentative reformulation through construct validation. *Sociometry, 39,* 324–341.

Freud, S. (1961). *Beyond the pleasure principle* (J. Strachey, Trans.). New York: Norton. (Original work published 1920).

Frost, R. O., Goolkasian, G. A., Ely, R. J., & Blanchard, F. A. (1982). Depression, restraint and eating behavior. *Behavior Research and Therapy, 20,* 113–121.

Garner, D. M., Olmsted, M. P., Polivy, J., & Garfinkel, P. E. (1984). Comparison between weight preoccupied women and anorexia nervosa. *Psychosomatic Medicine, 46,* 255–266.

Gibbons, F. X., & Wicklund, R. A. (1976). Selective exposure to self. *Journal of Research in Personality, 10,* 98–106.

Goldberg, L. R. (1981). Unconfounding situational attributions from uncertain, neutral, and ambiguous ones: A psychometric analysis of descriptions of oneself and others. *Journal of Personality and Social Psychology, 41,* 517–552.

Goleman, D. (1988). *The meditative mind: The varieties of meditative experience.* New York: St. Martin's Press.

Gollwitzer, P. M. (1986). Striving for specific identities: The social reality of self-symbolizing. In R. Baumeister (Ed.), *Public self and private self* (pp. 143–159). New York: Springer-Verlag.

Greaves, G. (1971). Temporal orientation in suicidals. *Perceptual and Motor Skills, 33,* 1020.

Greenberg, J., & Musham, C. (1981). Avoiding and seeking self-focused attention. *Journal of Research in Personality, 15,* 191–200.

Greenberg, J., Pyszczynski, T., & Solomon, S. (1986). The causes and consequences of self-esteem: A terror management theory. In R. Baumeister (Ed.), *Public and private self* (pp. 189–212). New York: Springer-Verlag.

Greenwald, A. G. (1980). The totalitarian ego: Fabrication and revision of personal history. *American Psychologist, 35,* 603–613.

Greenwald, A. G., Bellezza, F. S., & Banaji, M. R. (1988). Is self-esteem a central ingredient of the self-concept? *Personality and Social Psychology Bulletin, 14,* 34–45.

Gross, J., & Rosen, J. C. (1988). Bulimia in adolescents: Prevalence and psychosocial correlates. *International Journal of Eating Disorders, 7,* 51–61.

Harter, S. (1993). Causes and consequences of low self-esteem in children and adolescents. In R. Baumeister (Ed.), *Self-esteem: The puzzle of low self-regard* (pp. 87–116). New York: Plenum Press.

Heatherton, T. F., & Baumeister, R. F. (1991). Binge eating as escape from self-awareness. *Psychological Bulletin, 110,* 86–108.

Heatherton, T. F., & Polivy, J. (1991). Development and validation of a scale for measuring state self-esteem. *Journal of Personality and Social Psychology, 60,* 895–910.

Henken, V. J. (1976). Banality reinvestigated: A computer-based content analysis of suicidal and forced-death documents. *Suicide and Life-Threatening Behavior, 6,* 36–43.

Higgins, E. T. (1987). Self-discrepancy: A theory relating self and affect. *Psychological Review, 94,* 319–340.

Higgins, E. T., Klein, R. L., & Strauman, T. J. (1987). Self-discrepancies: Distinguishing among self-states, self-state conflicts, and emotional vulnerabilities. In K. Yardley & T. Honess (Eds.), *Self and identity: Psychosocial perspectives* (pp. 173–186). Chichester, England: Wiley.

Hull, J. G. (1981). A self-awareness model of the causes and effects of alcohol consumption. *Journal of Abnormal Psychology, 90,* 586–600.

Hull, J. G., Levenson, R. W., Young, R. D., & Sher, K. J. (1983). Self-awareness-reducing effects of alcohol consumption. *Journal of Personality and Social Psychology, 44,* 461–473.

Hull, J. G., & Young, R. D. (1983). Self-consciousness, self-esteem, and success-failure as determinants of alcohol consumption in male social drinkers. *Journal of Personality and Social Psychology, 44,* 1097–1109.

Hull, J. G., Young, R. D., & Jouriles, E. (1986). Applications of the self-awareness model of alcohol consumption: Predicting patterns of use and abuse. *Journal of Personality and Social Psychology, 51,* 790–796.

Janis, I. L. (1954). Personality correlates of susceptibility to persuasion. *Journal of Personality, 22,* 504–518.

Janis, I. L., & Field, P. (1959). Sex differences and personality factors related to persuasibility. In C. Hovland & I. Janis (Eds.), *Personality and persuasibility* (pp. 55–68, 300–302). New Haven, CT: Yale University Press.

Jones, E. E., & Berglas, S. C. (1978). Control of attributions about the self through self-handicapping strategies: The appeal of alcohol and the role of underachievement. *Personality and Social Psychology Bulletin, 4,* 200–206.

Jones, E. E., & Wortman, C. (1973). *Ingratiation: An attributional approach.* Morristown, NJ: General Learning Press.

Jones, S. C. (1973). Self- and interpersonal evaluations: Esteem theories vs. consistency theories. *Psychological Bulletin, 79,* 185–199.

Jones, W. H., Freemon, J. E. & Goswick, R. A. (1981). The persistence of loneliness: Self and other determinants. *Journal of Personality, 49,* 27–48.

Kagan, J. (1981). *The second year: The emergence of self-awareness.* Cambridge, MA: Harvard University Press.

Katzman, M. A., & Wolchik, S. A. (1984). Bulimia and binge eating in college women: A comparison of personality and behavioral characteristics. *Journal of Consulting and Clinical Psychology, 52,* 423–428.

Keller, A., Ford, L. H., & Meacham, J. A. (1978). Dimensions of self-concept in preschool children. *Developmental Psychology, 14,* 483–489.

Kernis, M. H. (1993). The roles of stability and level of self-esteem in psychological functioning. In R. Baumeister (Ed.), *Self-esteem: The puzzle of low self-regard* (pp. 167–182). New York: Plenum Press.

Kett, J. (1977). *Rites of passage: Adolescence in America 1790 to the present.* New York: Basic Books.

Langer, E. (1975). The illusion of control. *Journal of Personality and Social Psychology, 29,* 253–264.

Levinson, D. J. (1978). *The seasons of a man's life.* New York: Ballantine.

Lewis, M., & Brooks-Gunn, J. (1979). *Social cognition and the acquisition of self.* New York: Plenum Press.

MacIntyre, A. (1981). *After virtue.* Notre Dame, IN: University of Notre Dame Press.

Maracek, J., & Mettee, D. (1972). Avoidance of continued success as a function of self-esteem, level of esteem certainty, and responsibility for success. *Journal of Personality and Social Psychology, 22,* 98–107.

Marcia, J. E. (1966). Development and validation of ego-identity status. *Journal of Personality and Social Psychology, 3,* 551–558.

Marcia, J. E. (1967). Ego identity status: Relationship to change in self-esteem, "general maladjustment," and authoritarianism. *Journal of Personality, 35,* 118–133.

Marcia, J. E., & Scheidel, D. G. (1983). *Ego identity, intimacy, sex role orientation, and gender.* Presented at the annual meeting of the Eastern Psychological Association, Philadelphia.

Markus, H. (1977). Self-schemata and processing information about the self. *Journal of Personality and Social Psychology, 35,* 63–78.

Markus, H., & Nurius, P. S. (1986). Possible selves. *American Psychologist, 41,* 954–969.

Markus, H., & Nurius, P. S. (1987). Possible selves: The interface between motivation and the self-concept. In K. Yardley & T. Honess (Eds.), *Self and identity: Psychosocial perspectives* (pp. 157–172). Chichester, England: Wiley.

Markus, H. R., & Kitayama, S. (1991). Culture and the self: Implications for cognition, emotion, and motivation. *Psychological Review, 98,* 224–253.

Maroldo, G. K. (1982). Shyness and love on the college campus. *Perceptual and Motor Skills, 55,* 819–824.

McFarlin, D. B., & Blascovich, J. (1981). Effects of self-esteem and performance feedback on future affective preferences and cognitive expectations. *Journal of Personality and Social Psychology, 40,* 521–531.

Menninger, K. (1966). Man against himself. New York: Harcourt, Brace, & World. (Original work published 1938).

Montemayor, R., & Eisen, M. (1977). The development of self-conceptions from childhood to adolescence. *Developmental Psychology, 13,* 314–319.

Neuringer, C., & Harris, R. M. (1974). The perception of the passage of time among death-involved hospital patients. *Life-Threatening Behavior, 4,* 240–254.

Ogilvie, D. M. (1987). The undesired self: A neglected variable in personality research. *Journal of Personality and Social Psychology, 52,* 379–385.

Orlofsky, J. L., Marcia, J. E., & Lesser, I. M. (1973). Ego identity status and the intimacy versus isolation crisis of young adulthood. *Journal of Personality and Social Psychology, 27,* 211–219.

Paulhus, D. L., & Martin, C. L. (1988). Functional flexibility: A new conception of interpersonal flexibility. *Journal of Personality and Social Psychology, 55,* 88–101.

Perrah, M., & Wichman, H. (1987). Cognitive rigidity in suicide attempters. *Suicide and Life-Threatening Behavior, 17,* 251–262.

Polivy, J. (1976). Perception of calories and regulation of intake in restrained and unrestrained subjects. *Addictive Behaviors, 1,* 237–243.

Pruitt, D. G. (1981). *Negotiation behavior.* New York: Academic Press.

Ringel, E. (1976). The presuicidal syndrome. *Suicide and Life-Threatening Behavior, 6,* 131–149.

Rogers, C., & Dymond, R. (1954). *Psychotherapy and personality change.* Chicago: University of Chicago Press.

Rosenberg, M. (1979). *Conceiving the self.* New York: Basic Books.

Roth, S., & Kubal, L. (1975). Effects of noncontingent reinforcement on tasks of differing importance: Facilitation and learned helplessness. *Journal of Personality and Social Psychology, 32,* 680–691.

Rothbaum, F., Weisz, J. R., & Synder, S. (1982). Changing and world and changing the self: A two process model of perceived control. *Journal of Personality and Social Psychology, 42,* 5–37.

Rubin, J. Z., & Brockner, J. (1975). Factors affecting entrapment in waiting situations: The Rosencrantz and Guildenstern effect. *Journal of Personality and Social Psychology, 31,* 1054–1063.

Ruble, D. (1983). The development of social comparison processes and their role in achievement-related self-socialization. In E. T. Higgins, D. Ruble, & W. Hartup (Eds.), *Social cognition and social behavior: Developmental perspectives* (pp. 134–157). New York: Cambridge University Press.

Ruderman, A. J. (1985). Dysphoric mood and overeating: A test of restraint theory's disinhibition hypothesis. *Journal of Abnormal Psychology, 94,* 78–85.

Sackett, D. L., & Snow, J. C. (1979). The magnitude of compliance and noncompliance. In R. B. Haynes, D. W. Taylor, & D. L. Sackett (Eds.), *Complaince in health care* (pp. 11–22). Baltimore: Johns Hopkins University Press.

Scarry, E. (1985). *The body in pain: The making and unmaking of the world.* New York: Oxford University Press.

Schlenker, B. R. (1980). *Impression management.* Monterey, CA: Brooks/Cole.

Schlenker, B. R. (1985). *The self and social life.* New York: McGraw-Hill.

Schlenker, B. R. (1986). Self-identification: Toward an integration of the private and public self. In R. Baumeister (Ed.), *Public self and private self* (pp. 21–62). New York: Springer-Verlag.

Schlenker, B. R., & Leary, M. R. (1982). Social anxiety and self-presentation. A conceptualization and model. *Psychological Bulletin, 92,* 641–669.

Schlesier-Stropp, B. (1984). Bulimia: A review of the literature. *Psychological Bulletin, 95,* 247–257.

Schneider, D. J., & Turkat, D. (1975). Self-presentation following success or failure: Defensive self-esteem models. *Journal of Personality 43,* 127–135.

Scott, G. G. (1983). *Erotic power: An exploration of dominance and submission.* Secaucus, NJ: Citadel Press.

Seligman, M. E. P. (1975). *Helplessness: On depression, development, and death.* San Francisco: Freeman.

Sennett, R. (1974). *The fall of public man.* New York: Random House.

Shainess, N. (1984). *Sweet suffering: Woman as victim.* New York: Simon & Schuster.

Shrauger, J. S. (1972). Self-esteem and reactions to being observed by others. *Journal of Personality and Social Psychology, 23,* 192–200.

Shrauger, J. S. (1975). Responses to evaluation as a function of initial self-perceptions. *Psychological Bulletin, 82,* 581–596.

Shrauger, J. S., & Schoeneman, T. S. (1979). Symbolic interactionist view of the self-concept: Through the looking glass darkly. *Psychological Bulletin, 86,* 549–573.

Shrauger, J. S., & Sorman, P. B. (1977). Self-evaluations, initial success and failure, and improvement as determinants of persistence. *Journal of Consulting and Clinical Psychology, 45,* 784–795.

Silverman, I. (1964). Self-esteem and differential responsiveness to success and failure. *Journal of Abnormal and Social Psychology, 69,* 115–119.

Slochower, J., & Kaplan, S. P. (1980). Anxiety, perceived control, and eating in obese and normal weight persons. *Appetite, 1,* 75–83.

Smith, G. W., & Bloom, I. (1985). A study in the personal meaning of suicide in the context of Baechler's typology. *Suicide and Life-Threatening Behavior, 15,* 3–13.

Spencer, S. J., Josephs, R. A., & Steele, C. M. (1993). Low self-esteem: The uphill struggle for self-integrity. In R. Baumeister (Ed.), *Self-esteem: The puzzle of low self-regard* (pp. 21–36). New York: Plenum Press.

Staw, B. M. (1976). Knee-deep in the big muddy: A study of escalating commitment to a chosen course of action. *Organizational Behavior and Human Performance, 16,* 27–44.

Steele, C. M. (1988). The psychology of self-affirmation: Sustaining the integrity of the self. In L. Berkowitz (Ed.), *Advances in experimental social psychology* (Vol. 21, pp. 261–302). Orlando, FL: Academic Press.

Steele, C. M., & Southwick, L. (1985). Alcohol and social behavior I: The psychology of drunken excess. *Journal of Personality and Social Psychology, 48,* 18–34.

Steenbarger, B. N., & Aderman, D. (1979). Objective self-awareness as a nonaversive state: Effect of anticipating discrepancy reduction. *Journal of Personality, 47,* 330–339.

Swann, W. B. (1987). Identity negotiation: Where two roads meet. *Journal of Personality and Social Psychology, 53,* 1038–1051.

Swann, W. B., Griffin, J. J., Predmore, S. C., & Gaines, B. (1987). The cognitive-affective crossfire: When self-consistency confronts self-enhancement. *Journal of Personality and Social Psychology, 52,* 881–889.

Swann, W. B., & Hill, C. A. (1982). When our identities are mistaken: Reaffirming self-conceptions through social interaction. *Journal of Personality and Social Psychology, 43,* 59–66.

Taylor, S. E. (1989). *Positive illusions: Creative self-deception and the healthy mind.* New York: Basic Books.

Taylor, S. E., & Brown, J. (1988). Illusion and well-being: Some social psychological contributions to a theory of mental health. *Psychological Bulletin, 103,* 193–210.

Teger, A. I. (1980). *Too much invested to quit.* New York: Pergamon Press.

Tice, D. M. (1990). Esteem protection or enhancement? Self-handicapping motives and attributions differ by trait self-esteem. *Journal of Personality and Social Psychology, 60,* 711–725.

Triandis, H. C. (1989). The self and social behavior in differing cultural contexts. *Psychological Review, 96,* 506–520.

Trilling, L. (1971). *Sincerity and authenticity.* Cambridge, MA: Harvard University Press.

Vallacher, R. R., & Wegner, D. M. (1985). *A theory of action identification.* Hillsdale, NJ: Erlbaum.

Vallacher, R. R. & Wegner, D. M. (1987). What do people think they're doing: Action identification and human behavior. *Psychological Review, 94,* 3–15.

Wegner, D. M., Schneider, D. J., Carter, S. R., & White, T. L. (1987). Paradoxical effects of thought suppression. *Journal of Personality and Social Psychology, 53,* 5–13.

Weinberg, M. S., Williams, C. J., & Moser, C. (1984). The social constituents of sadomasochism. *Social Problems, 31,* 379–389.

Weinberg, T., & Kamel, W. L. (Eds.). (1983). *S and M: Studies in sadomasochism.* Buffalo, NY: Prometheus.

Weintraub, K. J. (1978). *The value of the individual: Self and circumstance in autobiography.* Chicago: University of Chicago Press.

White, R. W. (1959). Motivation reconsidered: The concept of competence. *Psychological Review, 66,* 297–333.

Wicklund, R. A. (1975). Objective self-awareness. In L. Berkowitz (Ed.), *Advances in experimental social psychology* (Vol. 8, pp. 233–275). New York: Academic Press.

Wicklund, R. A., & Gollwitzer, P. M. (1982). *Symbolic self-completion.* Hillsdale, NJ: Erlbaum.

Williams, J. M., & Broadbent, K. (1986). Autobiographical memory in suicide attempters. *Journal of Abnormal Psychology, 95,* 144–149.

Wilson, S. R., & Benner, L. A. (1971). The effects of self-esteem and situation upon comparison choices during ability evaluation. *Sociometry, 34,* 381–397.

Wolfe, R. N., Lennox, R. D., & Cutler, B. L. (1986). Getting along and getting ahead: Empirical support for a theory of protective and acquisitive self-presentation. *Journal of Personality and Social Psychology, 50,* 356–361.

Wylie, R. C. (1974). *The self-concept: Vol. 1. A review of methodological considerations and measuring instruments.* Lincoln: University of Nebraska Press.

Wylie, R. C. (1979). *The self-concept: Vol. 2. Theory and research on selected topics.* Lincoln: University of Nebraska Press.

Yufit, R. I., & Benzies, B. (1973). Assessing suicidal potential by time perspective. *Life-Threatening Behavior, 3,* 270–282.

CHAPTER 27

MENTAL REPRESENTATIONS OF PERSONS AND PERSONALITY

JOHN F. KIHLSTROM
YALE UNIVERSITY

REID HASTIE
UNIVERSITY OF COLORADO

The science of personality has long been troubled by the conflict between biosocial and biophysical conceptualizations of its subject matter (Allport, 1937). Empirical work on personality since Allport's time has emphasized the biophysical view. Thus, the traditional psychometric approach to personality has expressed its concern with individual differences in what might be called the Doctrine of Traits (Kihlstrom, 1988), in which persons are viewed as collections of intrapsychic dispositions, analogous to physical characteristics, which give surface behavior a high degree of coherence, stability across time, consistency across situations, and predictability. Still, the Doctrine of Traits has been under attack, off and on, for more than half a century (Hartshorne & May, 1928; Mischel, 1968; Nisbett, 1980; Peterson, 1968). According to its social-psychological critics, the correlations among topographically different behaviors, and among semantically related traits, are too low to provide more than the most abstract coherence: both observed behavior and inferred traits show at best only modest stability over even short periods of time and substantial variability from one situation to another; and the extent to which specific behavior can be predicted from generalized traits is very low, even when behavior is measured in the aggregate. Thus, coherence, stability, consistency, and predictability—the very *raison d'etre* for the Doctrine of Traits—appear to be more in the eye of the beholder than in the person beheld.

In this way, the social-psychological critique of the Doctrine of Traits leads naturally to an emphasis on the biosocial rather than biophysical aspects of personality—on *impressions* of personality, rather than personality per se. But, of course, one need not adopt the social-psychological critique of traditional psychometric approaches to personality in order to be interested in how people perceive, remember, and categorize themselves and others. In this chapter, we introduce contemporary research in social cognition which bears directly on the mental representation of other persons and their personalities (for a parallel review of people's mental representations of themselves, see Kihlstrom & Klein, 1994).

I. THE DOMAIN OF SOCIAL COGNITION

Cognitive psychology is concerned with mental representations of the world and the mental processes that operate on these representations in the course of acquiring manipulating, and utilizing knowledge stored in the mind. Cognitive psychology casts a very broad net; indeed, insofar as psychology is defined at "the science of mental life" (James, 1890/1981, p. 15), the idea of a cognitive psychology is almost redundant. Of course, there was a time when psychology was defined as the science of behavior and psychologists limited their work to tracing the functional relations between environmental stimuli and the organism's muscular and glandular responses to them. Cognitive psychology does not abjure an interest in behavior, but it does assume that a complete understanding of behavior requires an explication of the mental structures and processes that mediate between stimulus and response. Thus behavior is a window on the mind, and the visible expression of mind is intelligent action. Behavior that is not under cognitive control, what might be called reflexive or instinctual, is more properly the province of disciplines such as neuroscience and ethology.

Cognitive approaches to personality, social, and clinical psychology share the assumption that behavior is cognitively mediated—guided by our perceptions of the current situation, memories of similar situations encountered in the past, impressions of ourselves and other people in the current environment, attributions concerning their (and our own) experiences and actions, and other sorts of judgments and inferences that go beyond the information given in the stimulus situation. When we speak of *social* cognition, then, we speak of cognition in the social domain, both elements broadly construed. At one level, the study of social cognition is simply the study of our knowledge of social entities—of ourselves, other people, the situations in which we encounter them, and the interpersonal behaviors which are exchanged in those situations. At another level, it is concerned with the structure of mental representations of these social entities, as they are currently perceived or retrieved from memory, and the ways in which these representations are constructed, reconstructed, and used to guide our experience, thought, and action in social domains.

The formal study of social cognition is only about 50 years old. It had its beginnings in the work of Heider (1944) on phenomenal causality, Asch (1946) on impression formation, and Bruner and Tagiuri (1954) on implicit personality theory. Cognitive concerns are also represented in much of the classic work on cognitive consistency, balance, and dissonance, clinical judgment, and attribution theory produced during the "Golden Years" of experimental social psychology. But the cognitive concerns of social psychology during this period were relatively informal, perhaps because the field of modern cognitive psychology was also in its infancy.

This situation changed radically in the late 1960s, as social psychologists proposed formal models concerning the mental representation of persons and the judgments involved in causal attribution and impression formation. Of particular importance were Rosenberg's spatial models for the representation of persons (e.g., Rosenberg, Nelson, & Vivekananthan, 1968) and N. H. Anderson's (1965) algebraic models for social judgment processes. Through them, social cognition began to make closer contact with the emerging cognitive psychology. The connection has tightened since then, with many psychologists from both sides crossing the border frequently and effortlessly. The result has been that the study of social cognition is characterized by sophisticated concepts, theories, and methodologies, many of which are ripe for application in the fields of personality and clinical psychology.

II. Alternate Views of Social Cognition

At this point in time, several general approaches to social cognition have emerged that are coherent and distinctive enough to stand as identifiable theoretical paradigms (for a fuller discussion, see Hastie, 1983). Each of these differs from the others in terms of the completeness of its account of social cognition, and each offers a different budget of theoretical assets and liabilities.

Role theory (Sarbin, 1954) is based on a "dramaturgical metaphor" in which actors play out scripts before audiences. From this point of view, personal conduct is governed by social roles imposed by the context in which behavior takes place; socialization involves acquiring a repertoire of roles and understanding the roles required by various situations. In principle, role theory is ultimately a cognitive theory because roles are abstract ideas that an actor must learn in order to behave in conformity with social demands, expectations, and norms. In practice, however, Sarbin and his associates have not explored the sorts of mental structures and processes that are relevant to mainstream cognitive psychology. By focusing its analysis on the situational context in which social roles are enacted (Sarbin, 1982), role theory identifies itself as a version of situationism, and is more sociological than cognitive in its orientation to its subject matter.

The *cognitive algebra* approach is primarily associated with the research of Norman Anderson (1974, 1978, 1981) and his colleagues on the processes whereby information from several sources is integrated into a unitary impression of a single person. Unlike role theory, cognitive algebra provides a complete description of a cognitive system, including psychophysical relations governing perception, psycho-motor laws governing response generation, and a set of cognitive processes that mediate between stimulus and response. These mediating processes consist of algebraic rules for transforming stimulus values (usually according to a weighted averaging rule). A closely related program of research, labeled *social judgment theory* (Arkes & Hammond, 1986; Brunswik, 1956; Hammond, 1955), has also utilized algebraic models based on regression equations to capture the processes employed in social judgment tasks such as psychiatric diagnosis (Brehmer & Joyce, 1988; Slovic & Lichtenstein, 1971).

An alternative *judgment heuristics* approach is represented in the research and theory of Kahneman and Tversky (1974; Kahneman, Slovic, & Tversky, 1982), Nisbett and Ross (1980; Ross, 1977), and a collection of researchers who have studied causal attributions for behavior and predictions of social events (e.g., Heider & Simmel, 1944; Jones, 1979; Jones & Davis, 1965; Kelley, 1967, 1973). While the mental operations of cognitive algebra appear to require considerable effort, judgment heuristics invoke shortcuts that permit efficient judgments under conditions of uncertainty, but increase the likelihood of error. Thus, judgment heuristics account easily for the departures from normative rationality that are so frequently observed in social cognition.

From a bird's eye view, role theory has emphasized the contents of roles and their implications for action, but has neglected the manner in which these might be mentally represented and processed in the mind. The cognitive algebra and judgment heuristics approaches have both emphasized the manner in which information is processed, but have also neglected the manner in which it is represented. A fourth approach, *symbolic information processing theory,* provides a more thorough account of both the representation and the processing components of a complete cognitive theory. The information processing approach dominates the study of nonsocial cognition and provides the framework for the remainder of the present review (for a fuller description, see Hastie, 1986).

A. The Computer Metaphor

The information processing approach is derived from a computer metaphor of the mind and employs computer program simulations which are designed to provide "languages" in which to write cognitive theories. These simulation models are then tested to determine whether they mimic the actual behavior of people.

B. The Architecture of the Mind

Most current versions of the "architecture of cognition" (e.g., J. R. Anderson, 1983) provide for the movement of information "inward" from the sensory registers, "through" short-term memory, "toward" long-term memory, and "back" to short-term memory again. Recently there has been a shift toward a unitary conception of the memory store in which sensory registers are peripheral and a general long-term store is the locus of thinking in an activated portion described as short-term memory. A variant on this point of view distinguishes between merely active portions of memory and portions of memory that are in dynamic transformation, labeled the working memory.

C. A Taxonomy of Knowledge Structures

A useful conceptual distinction has been borrowed from computer science: *declarative* knowledge consists of general beliefs concerning the nature of the world and specific memories of events that have occurred in one's personal experience; *procedural* knowledge consists of the skills, strategies, and rules with which we manipulate and transform declarative knowledge as well as take action in the world (J. R. Anderson, 1983; Winograd, 1975). Within the domain of declarative knowledge it is common to distinguish between *semantic* knowledge, which comprises abstract, categorical information, perhaps best conceptualized as a combination dictionary and encyclopedia, and *episodic* knowledge, which consists of autobiographical memories of events encoded with reference to the self and experienced within a particular temporal, spatial, emotional, and motivational context (Tulving, 1983).

With respect to social cognition, declarative-semantic knowledge consists of the categories which we use to classify social stimuli—other people, ourselves, interpersonal actions, and the situations in which social interaction takes place. Declarative-episodic social knowledge has sometimes been studied in the form of an individual's memory for other persons, but it is more generally represented by the person's autobiographical memory. Procedural social knowledge consists of the social competencies, strategies, and rules by which we form impressions of others, make causal attributions and other judgments, encode and retrieve social memories, plan and execute social behaviors, and manage other people's impressions of us. At the boundary between declarative and procedural social knowledge are *scripts* for social interactions (Abelson, 1981; Schank & Abelson, 1977). As semantic knowledge structures, scripts are used to help categorize the situations that people find themselves in and to make inferences about what has happened in the past and what will happen in the future; as procedural knowledge structures, they guide the actor's behavior in the situation from start to finish.

D. The Activation of Ideas

A critical issue for research and theory has been to characterize the manner in which each of these structures is located and activated in its appropriate memory. The reigning principle, called "spreading activation," postulates that one activation of one concept in long-term memory, whether by perception or thought, activates closely related concepts according to the degree to which the new concepts share features or associative links to the initial concept. At some point, the idea becomes active enough to be accessed for utilization by the information processing system.

An important corollary to the spreading activation principle is that activation of any concept takes time to decay. If a concept retains an amount of activation, it can be more easily reactivated on a subsequent occasion. This "priming effect" diminishes quickly, but some systems of social nodes (such as personality concepts) have been hypothesized to be permanently activated (Bargh, Bond, Lombardi, & Tota, 1986; Higgins, King, & Mavin, 1982; Markus & Sentis, 1984). Chronic activation explains certain individual differences in sensitivity to types of information or habits in social comparison processes. For example, some perceivers seem to be "tuned to" channels of information about other people that have implications for their intelligence, while others are chronically concerned with attractiveness or with athletic ability.

E. Elementary Information Processes

The information processing approach is based on a reductionist theoretical method that assumes complex performances can be decomposed into a collection of elementary information processes. Thus, a complex achievement like the judgment of an applicant's suitability for a job or the response to a request for help from an acquaintance can be described ultimately as a chain of elementary processes that operate to activate, store, and transform information. This basic cognitive level is hypothesized to describe a level of organization just above the neural substrate.

F. Control of Thought

Working memory contains representations of a person's goals, including global goals and current subgoals that have to be achieved on the way to the ultimate goal, which join perceptual inputs as sources of activation of ideas in memory. Presumably there is an executive control structure that allocates priorities among multiple goals, coordinates goals when possible, and attempts to resolve competition among conflicting goals. From the point of view of social cognition, this executive control structure is an important component of the self.

G. Linking Mind and Body

Cognitive neuroscientists are beginning to fulfill some of the promises to link mind and body that were the subject of the earliest philosophical speculations about human psychology. This has led some psychologists to jump to the conclusion that theory at the cognitive level will soon be antiquated and that another level is more suitable closer to if not identical to the physical level of brain modeling. The most popular solution is to propose "neurally inspired" "connectionist" models that are intermediate between the cognitive level (frequently glimpsed through the lens of consciousness) and the neural level studied by anatomists.

III. PERSON PERCEPTION

For much of its early history, social cognition was defined as the study of person perception (Bruner & Tagiuri, 1954). The study of person perception begins with an analogy to the perception of nonsocial objects. The person exists as an object independent of the mind of the social perceiver, and the perceiver's task is to form an internal, mental representation of the person. In the same way that nonsocial perception extracts information from the array of physical energies impinging on sensory surfaces in order to address questions concerning the form, location, and activity of some object, social perception extracts information from the stream of behavior in order to address questions of the thoughts, moods, motives, and traits of other people.

The study of person perception begins with the work of Asch (1946, p. 207), who defined the general problem as follows:

> How do we organize the various data of observation into a single, relatively unified, impression? How do our impressions change with time and further experiences with the person? What effects on impressions do other psychological processes, such as needs, expectations, and established interpersonal relations, have?

In order to study this problem, Asch invented the impression-formation paradigm in which a subject is presented with an ensemble of traits describing another person (the target) and is asked to report an impression of the target by completing a free description, adjective checklist, or rating scales. He interpreted his findings (e.g., the discovery of *central traits*) as supporting the view, explicitly derived from Gestalt approaches to nonsocial perception, that the unified impression is greater than the sum of its individual elements.

Asch's experiments largely set the agenda for the next 20 years of research on person perception. For example, N. H. Anderson's (1965, 1974, 1978) work on cognitive algebra analyzed the mathematical rules (e.g., adding vs. averaging) that govern how trait information is combined. Wishner (1960) and Rosenberg et al. (1968) showed that central traits (e.g., Asch's "warm–cold" pair) have high loadings on the superordinate factors that summarize the trait lexicon. A major product of this line of research was the concept of *implicit personality theory* (IPT; for a review, see Schneider, 1970). Bruner and Tagiuri (1954) argued that perception of all kinds goes "beyond the information given" in the stimulus array, and depends on the perceiver's expectations and goals as well as general and specific world knowledge retrieved from memory. Thus, in the case of person perception, it is necessary to understand the "naive, implicit theories of personality" that people reason with, in order to understand how they form impressions of others. For Bruner and Tagiuri, IPT comprises the learned relations among various (biosocial) aspects of personality—relations that might be quite different from those present in actual, empirical (biophysical) database. Cronbach (1955) expanded the concept of IPT to include a list of the important dimensions of personality, estimates of population means and variances on each of these dimensions, and estimates of the covariances among them.

Later, Rosenberg and his colleagues (Kim & Rosenberg, 1980; Rosenberg & Sedlak, 1972) evaluated a three-factor semantic diffential model derived from Osgood's (Osgood, Suci, & Tannenbaum, 1957) connotative theory of meaning, and found that evaluation (social and intellectual) was the only perceptual dimension common to all subjects. More recently, Goldberg (1981) and others have proposed that Norman's (1963) "Big Five" model for the structure of personality (extraversion, agreeableness, conscientiousness, emotional stability, and culturedness) is a universally applicable structure of perceived personality—at least so far as Western, industrialized cultures are concerned.

A continuing debate concerns the origins of IPT. The question was initially raised by an early study by Passini and Norman (1966), who extracted the same five factors from personality ratings of strangers and of friends. Since the judges could not have known the actual covariation of features in the personalities of the target people, it seemed likely that the perceived correlations, as reflected in the factor structures, were contaminated by the judges' expectations and beliefs. This argument has been made most forcefully by Shweder and D'Andrade (1979; D'Andrade & Shweder, 1987; Shweder, 1982), and has been opposed by Weiss and his colleagues among others (Block, Weiss, & Thorne, 1979; Weiss & Mendelsohn, 1986).

A. The Ecological Approach to Social Perception

Asch (1946) described his stimulus persons in terms of lists of traits. This has the advantage of experimental convenience and mimics the ways in which people describe each other in social interaction (Fiske & Cox, 1979; Peevers & Secord, 1973; Shweder & Bourne, 1981). At the same time, it is clear that people do not really perceive each other as lists of traits (although much "secondhand" information is conveyed indirectly in third-person descriptions of a person; Gilovich, 1987). In the case of direct acquaintances, we perceive the physical characteristics and behaviors of other people. Trait lists may come close to the mental representation of personality stored in memory, but these abstractions are far from the faces, voices, and gestures that make up the actual array of stimulation encountered in the social environment. Accordingly, Ittelson and Slack (1958) raised the concern that analyses of person perception based on the Asch paradigm are incomplete, if not fundamentally misleading. Subsequently, McArthur and Baron (1983; Baron, 1981; Baron & Boudreau, 1987; Zebrowitz, 1990) have argued for an ecological approach to social perception inspired by the work of J. J. Gibson (1966, 1979), who asserted that phenomenal experience is the unmediated, *direct perception* of stimulation, qualitatively the same as perceiving the pitch of sound or the color of light. Ultimately, Gibson proposed that what we really perceive are *affordances:* the functional utilities of objects for organisms with certain action capabilities. In other words, we perceive the world in terms of the actions that we can take with respect to the objects in the world.

The Gibsonian approach has been applied to various topics in social perception. For example, one interpretation of attribution theory is that the environment supplies all the information needed to render a judgment of causal responsibility— that when the relevant information concerning consensus, consistency, and distinctiveness is available, causality "jumps out" at the perceiver (McArthur & Baron, 1983). While it might seem unlikely that specific neuronal structures have evolved to produce attributions of causality to actors, targets, and contexts, human beings do seem to possess some capacity for picking up the sorts of covariation information that lies at the core of Kelley's (1967, 1973) ANOVA model of causal attribution. That this apparently cognitive ability is part of our innate biological endowment is suggested by the fact that the ability to process covariations (or conditional probabilities) among environmental events is essential for classical conditioning to occur (Rescorla & Wagner, 1972)—a form of learning that is accessible to all vertebrate, and many invertebrate, organisms (Razran, 1971).

The manner in which perceivers respond to human faces seems to be especially conducive to analysis in terms of Gibsonian direct realism. For example, Ekman and Friesen (1971), following Darwin, have argued for an innate mechanism for perceiving another person's emotional states by extracting information from his or her face. Similarly, Rosenthal, Hall, DiMatteo, Rogers, and Archer (1979) have summarized the evidence for cross-cultural invariances in the perception of emotion from extralinguistic verbal cues. Age can be accurately perceived from such features as the ratio of head to body length, position of eyes with respect to the top of the head, size of eyes and length of nose and ears, and round versus pointed head shape (Shaw & Pittenger, 1977). Possession of "babyish" features lead adults to be perceived as low in strength and dominance (McArthur, 1982). A broad face or receding hairline increase perceptions of dominance (Keating, Mazur, & Segall, 1981).

Global perceptual properties of the body also seem to support some remarkably subtle conclusions about the person perceived. A number of such studies involve adaptations of the point-light technique of Johannsen (1973), in which target persons are clothed in black leotards to which point-light stimuli have been attached. When targets are photographed against a black background the resulting stimulus gives no clues to body morphology; yet Kozlowski and Cutting (1977) found that subjects were able to reliably discriminate between males and females on the basis of gait.

It is not yet clear how well the direct or ecological approach to perception will succeed, in either social or nonsocial domains. Still the Gibsonian concern with ecological validity is pushing researchers in social cognition to move from sterile stimulus materials such as still photographs, trait lists, and verbal descriptions of behavior to more life-like materials. Even if the direct/realist approach to person perception should prove to be misguided in its rejection of mental structures and processes, research within this tradition will lead a better description of the stimulus that is represented by internal mental structures and processes.

IV. Person Concepts

Forming mental representations of persons and other social stimuli is fundamentally a problem of perception, and, as Bruner (1957) noted, every act of perception is an act of categorization. We naturally sort stimuli into equivalence classes based on similarity of features, attributes, or properties, forming concepts—mental representations of categories of objects. The concepts that we use to guide social perception are basic components in the repertoire of social intelligence: they form the background against which we organize and make sense of our social world (Cantor & Kihlstrom, 1987, 1989; Kihlstrom & Cantor, 1989; Lingle, Altom, & Medin, 1984). They are also the cognitive basis for consistency in social behavior: people respond in a roughly equivalent fashion to persons, situations, and behaviors which belong to the same category. Thus, we cannot understand a person's social behavior unless we understand the person's repertoire of social concepts and how they are formed, organized, and used. As Kelly (1955, 1963) noted, individual differences in social behavior may arise from individual differences in the categories used to construe social objects and events.

There appear to be at least four major types of social categories. (1) Categories of *persons* are labeled by nouns that designate types of people—extraverts and neurotics, jocks and nerds, preppies and yuppies; there are also categories of social roles, such as parent, lover, teacher, and doctor. (2) Categories of *actions* are labeled by adjectives that designate qualities of behavior, for example, extraverted, agreeable, conscientious, emotionally stable, intelligent, cultured, or open. (3) Categories of *situations* are labeled by nouns designating the types of situations in which social behavior is displayed, for example, weddings, funerals, seminars, cocktail parties, interviews, and bar-mitzvahs. (4) Viewed as declarative knowledge structures, *scripts* are also concept-like, in that they contain bundles of features that various specific instances of a class of interactions have in common.

Although the content of social categories may differ from one individual or culture to another, the structure of these categories is probably pretty much the same for everyone (for comprehensive coverage, see E. E. Smith & Medin, 1981). Over the past two decades, the classical view of category structure, dominant from the time of Aristotle, has been replaced by a probabilistic or prototype view. This view, in turn, has been challenged by a new *exemplar* view of categorization. As an example of the difference among these views, consider Kant's (1798/1978) fourfold taxonomy of temperamental types: melancholic, choleric, sanguine, and phlegmatic. Kant described the melancholic individual as anxious, worried, unhappy, suspicious, serious, and thoughtful, and the phlegmatic individual as reasonable, high-principled, controlled, persistent, steadfast, and calm. Thus, under the classical view, all melancholics possess each of certain features in common, and any individual who possesses the entire set of features was thereby classified as a melancholic as opposed to a phlegmatic type of person. While such a scheme might fairly represent ideal personality types, they might not prove useful in the actual business of classifying people. For example, what would we do with Bob, who is anxious and worried but not serious and thoughtful? Or Tom, who is anxious and worried, serious and thoughtful, but also controlled and persistent? Proper-set definitions of categories seem to leave no room for the partial and combined expression of personality types (see Achenbach, 1980, for a related, empirically based critique of traditional psychodiagnostic categories). Probabilistic approaches solve this problem by classifying individuals in terms of the central tendencies of their traits. Bob would be labeled as melancholic if he displayed some critical number of central features of melancholia, even if he did not possess all of them and even if he possessed a few features normally associated with phlegmatics; alternatively, Tom would be labeled as melancholic if the average value of his melancholic traits were higher than that of his phlegmatic traits. Under the exemplar view, by contrast, Bob and Tom would be compared to specific individuals who exemplify melancholia or phlegmaticity, as opposed to summary prototypes. If Bob resembles Dave, and Dave has been labeled as a melancholic, then Bob will also be classified as a melancholic; if Tom does not resemble any known melancholic, then he will escape this particular label.

An extremely interesting application of probabilistic, fuzzy-set approaches to categorization has been in the area of psychiatric diagnosis (Cantor & Genero, 1986; Cantor, Smith, French, & Mezzich, 1980). Psychiatric diagnoses traditionally have been construed in terms of the classical view of categorization; a diagnostic category must be defined by the singly necessary and jointly sufficient features that define a *proper set*. In contrast, Cantor and her colleagues have argued cogently that the diagnostic categories are *fuzzy sets* of features that are correlated with, but not singly necessary or jointly sufficient for, category membership. The principal result of this situation is considerable heterogeneity among category members, such that they are related by family resemblance more than any set of common defining features. This probabilistic point of view was implicitly adopted in the 1987 revision of the Diagnostic and Statistical Manual of Mental Disorders, and is maintained in the fourth edition (American Psychiatric Association, 1994).

Certainly the probabilistic view has dominated studies of social categorization (Lingle et al., 1984). For example, Cantor and her colleagues (Cantor & Genero, 1986; Cantor & Mischel, 1979; Cantor, Mischel, & Schwartz, 1982; Genero & Cantor, 1987; Niedenthal & Cantor, 1984) performed seminal research on the role of feature list prototypes in the categorization of persons into types (see also Brown, 1980). Hampson (1982), Buss and Craik (1983), and John, Hampson, and Goldberg (1989) have offered similar analyses of the classification of specific behaviors by traits. By and large, this research has shown that our concepts of persons and their behaviors are organized probabilistically as fuzzy sets, imperfectly nested, heterogeneous, and summarized by category prototypes. However, there has been little research testing alternatives within the probabilistic view, and even less attention given to comparing the prototype view with the exemplar view.

Another outstanding issue concerns the nature of natural categories of persons. The question arises of whether there are natural categories of persons that have some degree of universality, regardless of the sociocultural affiliations of perceiver or target. Brown (1980) has proposed that social stereotypes based on race, sex, or nationality may serve the function of basic person categories. Consulting word frequency norms to determine which person categories are most frequently used in everyday discourse, and which might therefore represent the most psychologically salient and general categories, he turned up ethnic stereotypes such as Oriental and Jew, kinship terms such as mother and husband, and terms pertaining to culturally specific professions and social roles (teacher, lieutenant, poet, cook, nurse, etc.). Furthermore, Brown noted that college campuses, with their rich repertoire of labels relating to socioeconomic status (preppie, yuppie), political stance (hippie, eco-freak), and place of residence or voluntary association (Tri-Delt, Skull and Bones) provide another rich set of stereotype-based category labels. However, most of these categories of persons are specific to a particular culture or subculture.

Cantor (e.g., Cantor & Mischel, 1979) took a more theoretical tack and derived type labels, expressed as noun phrases, from Norman's (1963) "Big Five" structure of personality traits. Thus, extraversion was translated into "PR type" and "comic joker," conscientiousness into "religious devotee" and "social activist," and so forth. While Cantor's system has the advantage of a basis in current personality theories, it is not clear that either system captures universal distinctions in dispositions, temperament, emotion, and motivation that are inherent in our categorizations of personality.

Recently, researchers have noted a number of cracks in the empirical facade of the probabilistic prototype and exemplar models and have concluded that people carry more than feature lists around in their heads, and that classification processes involve more than similarity judgments (Medin, Goldstone, & Gentner, 1993). Just what this "What more?" comprises is a very open question, but theoreticians believe that important concepts are associated with common sense premises which serve as an explanatory theory to account for differential weights on features, feature intercorrelations, and the nature of the core features that seem to be the essence of concepts.

V. PERSON MEMORY

Perceptual activity leaves its traces in memory, to be retrieved at a later time and used to guide action. Concepts, with their prototypes, lists of characteristic features, and sets of exemplars, are one way to think about the long-term storage of abstract information about persons and personalities. But much of the social information in our memories is much more concrete. For example, we hold a voluminous store of memories of particular people and their behaviors—a domain known as *person memory* (for reviews, see Hastie & Carlston, 1980; Hastie, Park, & Weber, 1984).

The manner in which a person remembers and thinks about other people is of central importance in theories of personality. Many of the seminal schools of thought concerning the development and dynamics of personality put special emphasis on the person's relations with significant others and the manner in which others are conceptualized and remembered (Munroe, 1955). Even "modern" social learning theories of personality place a special emphasis on role models and vicarious learning and reinforcement processes that depend on the person's memories of other people (Bandura, 1977, 1986; Mischel, 1973). In addition, scientific analyses of clinical assessment methods and most types of psychotherapy require a theoretical understanding of the interviewer's, therapist's, and client's social perception and memory processes.

The earliest information processing theories tended to construe knowledge as represented by a verbal code—lists of features or instances associated with concepts or sentence-like propositional descriptions of objects and events. In the current descendants of these early models, concepts are the basic units from which knowledge structures are built. In the typical representation of an experienced event, nodes representing concepts are linked to other nodes representing the characteristic features of those concepts. Propositions consist of higher order networks built of concept nodes that represent the event in memory. For example, in J. R. Anderson's (1983) HAM and ACT structure system, a proposition consists of links between nodes representing subject and predicate; the predicate, in turn, consists of links representing relation and argument. These terms correspond, roughly, to the subject, verb, and object of seventh grade grammar class diagrams.

Other theorists have favored a dual-coding hypothesis, arguing that knowledge can be represented in an analogue as well as a propositional format. For some time, there was a lively debate among psychologists concerning the comparative merits of single-code and dual-code theories. However, there is now general agreement that information may be stored in the form of meaning-based abstract propositions, or as perception-based spatial images (preserving configural information), or as temporal strings (preserving order and contiguity information). In what follows, however, we focus on verbal representations of persons and personality.

There are various formal models of memory available in the information processing tradition, all variations on the theme of associative networks, and all implemented as computer simulations. Similarly, there are several information processing models of social memory (Hastie & Carlston, 1980; Hastie et al., 1984). Explicit proposals, within the information processing framework, have been made by Hamilton (Hamilton, Katz, & Leirer, 1980), Hastie (1980, 1981, 1988; Hastie & Kumar, 1979), Klein and Loftus (1993), Ostrom (Ostrom, Lingle, Pryor, & Geva, 1980; Ostrom, Pryor, & Simpson, 1981), and Wyer and Srull (1989; Wyer, 1974, 1989; Wyer & Carlston, 1979; Wyer & Gordon, 1984), among others.

The simplest representational structures that have been proposed for individuals are associative or semantic networks with unlabeled links, which can store varied types of information, including propositions, images, and emotional responses. An example is given in Figure 1A, where a particular person is represented by node P1, two of his or her traits by nodes T1 and T2, and six of his or her behaviors by nodes B1–B6. Hastie (1980, 1981, 1988), J. R. Anderson (1983; J. R. Anderson & Hastie, 1974), and Srull (1981) have been the primary advocates of these simple network structures. They assume that social memory is organized primarily by persons, who are represented as single nodes in the network. Events are represented by propositions which describe both the event and the context in which the event occurred. Nodes representing events are linked to the nodes representing the subjects of the propositions describing those events. There may also be episodic and semantic links to other events.

In addition to information about specific episodes, nodes representing abstract descriptive information can be linked to the person node. This would occur, for

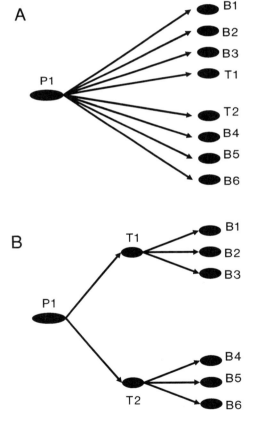

FIGURE 1 Two network representations of memory for a person's traits and behaviors. (A) Trait and behavioral information encoded independently. (B) Behavioral information organized by its trait implications.

example, when the subject forms an impression of a person as talkative or intelligent based on observations of behavior. An inferred abstraction serves as a background for processing new information about the person by providing category-based expectations that are compared with the implications of new experiences. However, research has shown that these abstract inferences are stored independent of the events on which they are based, at least for impressions of casual acquaintances (N. H. Anderson & Hubert, 1963; Hastie & Park, 1986). Furthermore, abstractions about a person like traits affect the encoding of new information because comparisons are made between new information and current salient abstractions. If the new information is surprising in the context of a salient trait (or other abstraction), Hastie (1980, 1981, 1984; Hastie & Kumar, 1979), Srull (1981), and others have hypothesized that it will receive extra attention and processing, and is likely to be associatively linked to other information about the person (Hastie, 1984). However, this on-line trait effect at encoding does *not* guarantee that behavioral information will be clustered in the memory representation "under" the trait attributed to the person (Hastie & Kumar, 1979).

Retrieval of person memory begins by activating the node corresponding to the person, and then activation spreads out along associative pathways emanating from that node. If activation reaches a node representing an event, that event is retrieved, that is, designated as part of working memory. The process continues until task goals are met (e.g., the desired fact has been found) or the process is exhausted (e.g., several attempts to retrieve new information have failed).

This model makes some subtle predictions that have been confirmed empirically. For example, surprising acts tend to be better remembered than expected acts, and a person who performs both expected and surprising acts will be better remembered than one who performs only expected acts. But, the current model is limited in several respects: it utilizes unlabeled, all-or-none links between nodes; search is random and undirected; and judgment is characterized as a simple anchor-and-adjust weighted averaging process. Hastie's model might be fruitfully complemented by another model, currently being developed by Smith, that also uses the architecture of ACT* production systems to generate inferences based on stored knowledge (E. R. Smith, 1984). The two models, combined and implemented as a computer simulation, would constitute a significant theoretical advance in social cognition.

A closely related structure in the form of a hierarchy with higher level "control elements" associated with traits of the remembered person's character has been proposed by Cantor and Mischel (1979), Hamilton (1989; Hamilton et al., 1980), Wyer and Gordon (1984), and others. The guiding precept is that the trait terms that are so prominent in people's spontaneous descriptions of one another (Allport, 1937; Fiske & Cox, 1979; Peevers & Secord, 1973) have a privileged status in social memory representations, serving to organize the other types of information that we have stored about a person (Hamilton, Driscoll, & Worth, 1989). Such a structure is illustrated in Figure 1B, where the trait nodes T1 and T2 fan out from the person node P1, and representations of events exemplifying these traits (B1–B3, B4–B6) fan out from their respective trait nodes.

However, the strong assumption that traits play a central role in memory representations of individuals has met with some opposition. Studies of the spontaneous self-concept find that personality traits play a much smaller role in self-descriptions than they do in descriptions of other people (McGuire & McGuire, 1988). And, from the beginning (Hastie & Kumar, 1979), many person memory studies have not found that recall memory is "clustered" by trait categories. Ostrom and his colleagues (1980, 1981) have proposed a model that relaxes the strong requirement of organization by traits. They hypothesize that memory for events is *usually* organized by persons when the participants are familiar to the subject, but that other "themes" such as temporal sequence, situational context, self-reference, or group membership dominate memory organization when the focal person is unfamiliar or the social goals of the perceiver do not foreground the other person as an individual.

Finally, Wyer and Srull (1989) have proposed a "bin" model, aimed at accounting for the results of impression-formation experiments, that also does not require that person memories be inevitably organized by traits. They simply combined the two basic models, scrambled associative network and trait organized hierarchy, and claimed that both representations are created, often with duplication of the specific information nodes in a dual representational structure. One part of a individual's representation in memory is hypothesized to be a scrambled collection of behaviors associated with a summary evaluative node, and another separate part is a hierarchical network of behaviors clustered under trait node elements. Long-term person memory is described as a warehouse of content-addressable storage bins, each tagged with the name of the object described by its contents. Within each bin, the contents are organized according to the temporal order in which they were experienced; otherwise, there is no inherent organization of bin contents.

Wyer and Srull (1989) have noted that a major weakness of all of the person memory models derives from the empirical and theoretical focus on information presented in the unnatural form of impression formation stimulus ensembles, rather than more representative social contexts. In everyday life, our experiences seem to be organized into temporally and causally structured episodes. Memory representations for social information organized into autobiographical episodes have been proposed by Kolodner (1984), Pennington and Hastie (1986), Wyer (Fuhrman & Wyer, 1988; Wyer, Shoben, Fuhrman, & Bodenhausen, 1985), and others. These structures are hypothesized to be more complex than simple networks in two regards: the embedded within-episode components organized to reflect our culturally shared expectations about the components of a well-formed episode and the links between episodes are labeled, with access to a link only permitted to memory probes that include the correct "key" features to "open" the link.

VI. PROSPECTS FOR THE INFORMATION PROCESSING APPROACH TO SOCIAL COGNITION

A minimal model for social cognition should include five elements common to all cognitive theories (Hastie & Carlson, 1980): (*a*) a vocabulary to describe the simulus; (*b*) a characterization of the processes by which stimuli are encoded in memory; (*c*) a description of the encoded mental representation of the stimulus event; (*d*) a characterization of the processes by which encoded representations are manipulated and transformed in the course of memory and judgment tasks; and (*e*) a vocabulary to describe the response to the stimulus. Of the four general approaches to social cognition discussed at the outset of this paper, information processing theory comes closest to satisfying these requirements. The information processing approach is general and it should apply to the cognition of almost anything, including entities in the social world such as other people and oneself. However, information processing theory, developed in a nonsocial laboratory domain, should not be applied uncritically, without modification to the social realm (Holyoak & Gordon, 1984; Ostrom, 1984).

One limit on information processing theory derives from its failure to thoroughly address emotional and motivational phenomena in everyday life. There have been preliminary discussions of the manner in which information processing models could handle these "hot" phenomena (Bower, 1981; Clark & Fiske, 1982; Leventhal, 1984; Mandler, 1984; Ortony, Clore, & Collins, 1988; Simon, 1967), but there has been relatively little laboratory research to adequately test theoretical models. We believe that the information processing approach will provide the best medium to develop hypotheses about interpersonal goals and other purposeful social behavior (Schank & Abelson, 1977; Showers & Cantor, 1985). But, again, more remains to be done than has been accomplished.

The information processing approach has not yet provided a full conceptualization of the conscious versus unconscious process distinction nor has it done justice to phenomena associated with unconscious processes that have been revealed through the history of research on personality and psychopathology (but see Kihlstrom, 1987, 1990). There is, of course, a long tradition of research on implicit (subliminal, preconscious) perception and perceptual defense and vigilance, but this activity has made little contact with the concerns of social cognition per se. Moreover, the analysis of unconscious phenomena in everyday social interaction is still virtually untouched (Bargh, 1994; Greenwald & Banaji, 1995; Kihlstrom, 1994).

Another challenge that exceeds current information processing treatments arises from the complexity of the social world. The properties of objects studied in experiments on nonsocial cognition tend to be stable over time and across contexts. However, people change considerably from situation to situation and even from moment to moment within a single situation (Mischel, 1968, 1973). This means that models that have been developed to characterize the formation and maintenance of mental representations of stable (laboratory) entities are bound to provide inadequate accounts of social cognition. A further complexity is introduced by the fact that many of the entities thought about in the social world are also sentient, independent, and likely to react to the belief that they are being thought about. Thus, a complex recursive sequence of inferences occurs when people wonder what other people are thinking about them and anticipate that the other people are wondering whether they are thinking about what the other person is thinking, and so forth. What this means is that theories of social cognition must take into account the representation of representations of representations within a single mind, where each mind is sensitive to other minds around it.

We do not believe that these difficulties imply that we should abandon the information processing approach to social cognition. To the contrary, we believe the information processing approach provides the best hope for a theory that is complex enough to handle emotion, motivation, the unconscious, and recursive self-conscious inferences about persons and personalities.

ACKNOWLEDGMENTS

The point of view represented herein is based on research supported in part by Grants MH-35856 and MH-44739 from the National Institute of Mental Health, Grants SES-9122154 and SBR-9308369 from the National Science Foundation, and Subcontract 1122SC from the Program on Conscious and Unconscious Mental Processes of the John D. and Catherine T. MacArthur Foundation, through the University of California, San Francisco. We thank Mahzarin Banaji, Terrence Barnhardt, Nancy Cantor, Lawrence Couture, Marilyn Dabady, Martha Glisky, Stanley Klein, Sheila Mulvaney, Paula Niedenthal, Nancy Pennington, Douglas Tataryn, Allison Titcomb, and Betsy Tobias for their comments during the preparation of this paper. Particular appreciation goes to James Cutting, William Epstein, and Mary Peterson for their help in understanding the implications of Gibson's work in perception for social cognition.

REFERENCES

Abelson, R. P. (1981). Psychological status of the script concept. *American Psychologist, 36,* 715–729.

Achenbach, T. M. (1980). DSM-III in light of empirical research on the classification of child psychopathology. *Journal of the American Academy of Child Psychiatry, 19,* 395–412.

Allport, G. W. (1937). *Personality: A psychological interpretation.* New York: Holt.

American Psychiatric Association. (1994). *Diagnostic and statistical manual of mental disorders* (4th ed.). Washington, DC: Author.

Anderson, J. R. (1983). *The architecture of cognition.* Cambridge, MA: Harvard University Press.

Anderson, J. R., & Hastie, R. (1974). Individuation and reference in memory: Proper names and definite descriptions. *Cognitive Psychology, 6,* 495–514.

Anderson, N. H. (1965). Averaging versus adding as a stimulus-combination rule in impression formation. *Journal of Experimental Psychology, 70,* 394–400.

Anderson, N. H. (1974). Cognitive algebra: Integration theory applied to social attribution. In L. Berkowitz (Ed.), *Advances in experimental social psychology* (Vol. 7, pp. 1–101). New York: Academic Press.

Anderson, N. H. (1978). Progress in cognitive algebra. In L. Berkowitz (Ed.), *Cognitive theories in social psychology* (pp. 103–126). New York: Academic Press.

Anderson, N. H. (1981). *Foundations of information integration theory.* New York: Academic Press.

Anderson, N. H., & Hubert, S. (1963). Effects of concomitant verbal recall on order effects in personality impression formation. *Journal of Verbal Learning and Verbal Behavior, 2,* 379–391.

Arkes, H. R., & Hammond, K. R. (Eds.). (1986). *Judgment and decision making: An interdisciplinary reader.* New York: Cambridge University Press.

Asch, S. E. (1946). Forming impressions of personality. *Journal of Abnormal and Social Psychology, 41,* 258–290.

Bandura, A. (1977). *Social learning theory.* Englewood Cliffs, NJ: Prentice-Hall.

Bandura, A. (1986). *Social foundations of thought and action: A social cognitive theory.* Englewood Cliffs, NJ: Prentice-Hall.

Bargh, J. A. (1994). The four horsemen of automaticity: Varieties of automatic influence in social perception and cognition. In J. S. Uleman & J. A. Bargh (Eds.), *Unintended thought* (pp. 3–51). New York: Guilford Press.

Bargh, J. A., Bond, R. N., Lombardi, W., & Tota, M. E. (1986). The additive nature of chronic and temporary sources of accessibility. *Journal of Personality and Social Psychology, 50,* 869–878.

Baron, R. (1981). Social knowing from an ecological event perspective: A consideration of the relative domains of power for cognitive and perceptual modes of knowing. In J. Harvey (Ed.), *Cognition, social behavior, and the environment* (pp. 61–92). Hillsdale, NJ: Erlbaum.

Baron, R., & Boudreau, L. A. (1987). An ecological perspective on integrating personality and social psychology. *Journal of Personality and Social Psychology, 53,* 1222–1228.

Block, J., Weiss, D. S., & Thorne, A. (1979). How relevant is a semantic similarity interpretation of personality ratings? *Journal of Personality and Social Psychology, 37,* 1055–1074.

Bower, G. H. (1981). Mood and memory. *American Psychologist, 36,* 129–148.

Brehmer, B., & Joyce, C. R. B. (1988). *Human judgment: The SJT view.* Amsterdam: North-Holland.

Brown, R. (1980). *Natural categories and basic objects in the domain of persons* (Katz-Newcomb Lecture). Ann Arbor: University of Michigan, Institute for Social Research.

Bruner, J. S. (1957). On perceptual readiness. *Psychological Review, 64,* 123–152.

Bruner, J. S., & Tagiuri, R. (1954). Person perception. In G. Lindzey (Ed.), *Handbook of social psychology* (Vol. 2, pp. 634–654). Reading, Ma.: Addison-Wesley.

Brunswik, E. (1956). *Perception and the representative design of psychological experiments.* Berkeley: University of California Press.

Buss, D. M. (1989). Sex differences in human mate preferences: Evolutionary hypotheses tested in 37 cultures. *Behavioral and Brain Sciences, 12,* 1–49.

Buss, D. M., & Craik, K. H. (1983). The act frequency approach to personality. *Psychological Review, 90,* 105–126.

Cantor, N., & Genero, N. (1986). Psychiatric diagnosis and natural categorization: A close analogy. In T. Millon & G. Klerman (Eds.), *Contemporary issues in psychopathology* (pp. 223–256). New York: Guilford Press.

Cantor, N., & Kihlstrom, J. F. (1987). *Personality and social intelligence.* Englewood Cliffs, NJ: Prentice-Hall.

Cantor, N., & Kihlstrom, J. F. (1989). Social intelligence and cognitive assessments of personality. In R. S. Wyer & T. K. Srull (Eds.), *Advances in social cognition* (Vol. 2, pp. 1–59). Hillsdale, NJ: Erlbaum.

Cantor, N., & Mischel, W. (1979). Prototypes in person perception. In L. Berkowitz (Ed.), *Advances in experimental social psychology* (Vol. 12, pp. 3–52). New York: Academic Press.

Cantor, N., Mischel, W., & Schwartz, J. (1982). A prototype analysis of psychological situations. *Cognitive Psychology, 14,* 45–77.

Cantor, N., Smith, E. E., French, R. DeS., & Mezzich, J. (1980). Psychiatric diagnosis as prototype categorization. *Journal of Abnormal Psychology, 89,* 181–193.

Clark, M. S., & Fiske, S. T. (1982). *Affect and cognition.* Hillsdale, NJ: Erlbaum.

Cronbach, L. J. (1955). Processes affecting scores on "understanding of others" and "assumed similarity." *Psychological Bulletin, 52,* 177–193.

D'Andrade, R. G., & Shweder, R. A. (1987). *The systematic distortion hypothesis: A clarification and update.* Unpublished manuscript, University of California, San Diego.

Ekman, P., & Friesen, W. V. (1971). Constants across culture in the face and emotion. *Journal of Personality and Social Psychology, 17,* 124–129.

Fiske, S. M., & Cox, M. G. (1979). The effect of target familiarity and descriptive purpose on the process of describing others. *Journal of Personality, 47,* 136–161.

Fuhrman, R. W., & Wyer, R. S. (1988). Event memory: Temporal-order judgments of personal life experiences. *Journal of Personality and Social Psychology, 54,* 365–384.

Genero, N., & Cantor, N. (1987). Exemplar prototypes and clinical diagnosis: Toward a cognitive economy. *Journal of Social and Clinical Psychology, 5,* 59–78.

Gibson, J. J. (1966). *The senses considered as perceptual systems.* Boston: Houghton-Mifflin.

Gibson, J. J. (1979). *The ecological approach to visual perception.* Boston: Houghton-Mifflin.

Gilovich, T. (1987). Secondhand information and social judgment. *Journal of Experimental Social Psychology, 23,* 59–74.

Goldberg, L. R. (1981). Language and individual differences: The search for universals in personality lexicons. In L. Wheeler (Ed.), *Review of personality and social psychology* (Vol. 2, pp. 141–165). Beverly Hills, CA: Sage.

Greenwald, A. G., & Banaji, M. R. (1995). Implicit social cognition: Attitudes, self-esteem, and stereotypes. *Psychological Review, 102,* 4–27.

Hamilton, D. L. (1989). Understanding impression formation: What has memory research contributed? In P. R. Solomon, G. R. Goethals, C. M. Kelleyy, & B. R. Stephens (Eds.), *Memory: Interdisciplinary approaches* (pp. 221–242). New York: Springer-Verlag.

Hamilton, D. L., Driscoll, D. M., & Worth, L. T. (1989). Cognitive organization of impressions: Effects of incongruency in complex representations. *Journal of Personality and Social Psychology, 57,* 925–939.

Hamilton, D. L., Katz, L. B., & Leirer, V. O. (1980). Organizational processes in impression formation. In R. Hastie, T. Ostrom, E. Ebbesen, R. Wyer, D. Hamilton, & D. Carlston (Eds.), *Person memory: The cognitive basis of social perception* (pp. 121–153). Hillsdale, NJ: Erlbaum.

Hammond, K. R. (1955). Probabilistic functioning and the clinical interview. *Psychological Review, 62,* 255–262.

Hampson, S. (1982). *The construction of personality: An introduction.* London: Routledge & Kegan Paul.

Hartshorne, H., & May, M. A. (1928). *Studies in the nature of character: I. Studies in deceit.* New York: Macmillan.

Hastie, R. (1980). Memory for behavioral information that confirms or contradicts a personality impression. In R. Hastie, T. M. Ostrom, E. B. Ebbesen, R. S. Wyer, D. L. Hamilton, & D. E. Carlston (Eds.), *Person memory: The cognitive basis of social perception* (pp. 155–177). Hillsdale, NJ: Erlbaum.

Hastie, R. (1981). Schematic principles in human memory. In E. T. Higgins, C. P. Herman, & M. P. Zanna (Eds.), *Social cognition: The Ontario Symposium* (Vol. 1, pp. 39–88). Hillsdale, NJ: Erlbaum.

Hastie, R. (1983). Social inference. *Annual Review of Psychology, 34,* 511–542.

Hastie, R. (1984). Causes and effects of causal attribution. *Journal of Personality and Social Psychology, 46,* 44–56.

Hastie, R. (1986). A primer of information processing theory for the political scientist. In R. Lau & D. O. Sears (Eds.), *Political psychology* (pp. 11–39). Hillsdale, NJ: Erlbaum.

Hastie, R. (1988). A computer simulation model of person memory. *Journal of Experimental Social Psychology, 24,* 423–447.

Hastie, R., & Carlston, D. (1980). Theoretical principles in person memory. In R. Hastie, T. M. Ostrom, E. B. Ebbesen, R. S. Wyer, D. L. Hamilton, & D. E. Carlston (Eds.), *Person memory: The cognitive basis of social perception* (pp. 1–53). Hillsdale, NJ: Erlbaum.

Hastie, R., & Kumar, P. A. (1979). Person memory: Personality traits as organizing principles in memory for behaviors. *Journal of Personality and Social Psychology, 37,* 25–38.

Hastie, R., & Park, B. (1986). The relationship between memory and judgment depends on whether the judgment task is memory-based or on-line. *Psychological Review, 93,* 258–268.

Hastie, R., Park, B., & Weber, R. (1984). Social memory. In R. S. Wyer & T. K. Srull (Eds.), *Handbook of social cognition* (Vol. 2, pp. 151–212). Hillsdale, NJ: Erlbaum.

Heider, F. (1944). Social perception and phenomenal causality. *Psychological Review, 51,* 358–374.

Heider, F., & Simmel, M. (1944). An experimental study of apparent behavior. *American Journal of Psychology, 57,* 243–259.

Higgins, E. T., King, G. A., & Mavin, G. H. (1982). Individual construct accessibility and subjective impressions and recall. *Journal of Personality and Social Psychology, 43,* 35–47.

Holyoak, K. J., & Gordon, P. C. (1984). Information processing and social cognition. In R. S. Wyer & T. K. Srull (Eds.), *Handbook of social cognition* (Vol. 1, pp. 39–70). Hillsdale, NJ: Erlbaum.

Ittelson, W. H., & Slack, C. W. (1958). The perception of persons as visual objects. In R. Tagiuri & L. Petrullo (Eds.), *Person perception and interpersonal behavior* (pp. 210–228). Stanford, CA: Stanford University Press.

James, W. (1981). *Principles of psychology* (2 vols.). In F. Burkhardt (Ed.), *The works of William James.* Cambridge, MA: Harvard University Press. (Origianl work published 1890)

Johannsen, G. (1973). Visual perception of biological motion and a model for its analysis. *Perception & Psychophysics, 14,* 201–211.

John, O. P., Hampson, S. E., & Goldberg, L. R. (1989). *Is there a basic level of personality description?* Unpublished manuscript, University of California, Berkeley.

Jones, E. E. (1979). The rocky road from acts to dispositions. *American Psychologist, 34,* 107–117.

Jones, E. E., & Davis, K. E. (1965). From acts to dispositions: The attribution process in person perception. In L. Berkowitz (Ed.), *Advances in experimental social psychology* (Vol. 2, pp. 219–266). New York: Academic Press.

Kahneman, D., Slovic, P., & Tversky, A. (1982). *Judgment under uncertainty: Heuristics and biases.* New York: Cambridge University Press.

Kant, I. (1978). *Anthropology from a pragmatic point of view.* Carbondale: Southern Illinois University Press. (Original work published 1798)

Keating, C. F., Mazur, A., & Segall, M. H. (1981). A cross-cultural exploration of physiognomic traits of dominance and happiness. *Ethology and Sociobiology, 2,* 41–48.

Kelley, H. H. (1967). Attribution theory in social psychology. In D. Levine (Ed.), *Nebraska Symposium on Motivation* (pp. 192–238). Lincoln: University of Nebraska Press.

Kelley, H. H. (1973). The processes of causal attribution. *American Psychologist, 28,* 107–128.

Kelly, G. (1955). *The psychology of personal constructs* (Vol. 1). New York: Norton.

Kelly, G. (1963). *The psychology of personal constructs* (Vol. 2). New York: Norton.

Kihlstrom, J. F. (1987). The cognitive unconscious. *Science, 237,* 1445–1452.

Kihlstrom, J. F. (1988). Personality. In E. R. Hilgard (Ed.), *Fifty years of psychology: Essays in honor of Floyd Ruch* (pp. 139–152). Glenview, IL: Scott, Foresman.

Kihlstrom, J. F. (1990). The psychological unconscious. In L. Pervin (Ed.), *Handbook of personality theory and research* (pp. 445–464). New York: Guilford Press.

Kihlstrom, J. F. (1994). Unconscious processes in social interaction. In S. Hameroof, A. W. Kaszniak, & A. C. Scott (Eds.), *Toward a scientific basis for consciousness* (pp. 93–104). Cambridge, MA: MIT Press

Kihlstrom, J. F., & Cantor, N. (1989). Social intelligence and personality: There's room for growth. In R. S. Wyer & T. K. Srull (Eds.), *Advances in social cognition* (Vol. 2, pp. 197–214). Hillsdale, NJ: Erlbaum.

Kihlstrom, J. F., & Klein, S. B. (1994). The self as a knowledge structure. In R. S. Wyer & T. K. Srull (Eds.), *Handbook of social cognition* (2nd ed., Vol. 1, pp. 153–208). Hillsdale, NJ: Erlbaum.

Kim, M. P., & Rosenberg, S. (1980). Comparison of two structural models of implicit personality theory. *Journal of Personality and Social Psychology, 38,* 375–389.

Klein, S. B., & Loftus, J. (1993). The mental representation of trait and autobiographical knowledge about the self. In T. K. Srull & R. S. Wyer, Jr. (Eds.), *Advances in social cognition* (Vol. 5, pp. 1–50). Hillsdale, NJ: Erlbaum.

Kolodner, J. L. (1984). *Retrieval and organizational strategies in conceptual memory: A computer model.* Hillsdale, NJ: Erlbaum.

Kozlowski, L. T., & Cutting, J. E. (1977). Recognizing the sex of a walker from a dynamic point-light display. *Perception & Psychophysics, 21,* 575–580.

Leventhal, H. (1984). A perceptual-motor theory of emotion. In L. Berkowitz (Ed.), *Advances in experimental social psychology* (Vol. 17, pp. 117–182). New York: Academic Press.

Lingle, J. H., Altom, M. W., & Medin, D. L. (1984). Of cabbages and kings: Assessing the extendibility of natural object concept models to social things. In R. S. Wyer & T. K. Srull (Eds.), *Handbook of social cognition* (Vol. 1, pp. 71–117). Hillsdale, NJ: Erlbaum.

Mandler, G. (1984). *Mind and body.* New York: Norton.

Markus, H., & Sentis, K. (1984). The self in social information processing. In J. Suls (Ed.), *Psychological perspectives on the self* (Vol. 1, pp. 41–70). Hillsdale, NJ: Erlbaum.

McArthur, L. Z. (1982). Judging a book by its cover: A cognitive analysis of the relationship between physical appearance and stereotyping. In A. Hastorf & A. Isen (Eds.), *Cognitive social psychology* (pp. 149–211). New York: Elsevier.

McArthur, L. Z., & Baron, R. (1983). Toward an ecological theory of social perception. *Psychological Review, 80,* 252–283.

McGuire, W. J., & McGuire, C. V. (1988). Content and process in the experience of the self. In L. Berkowitz (Ed.), *Advances in experimental social psychology* (Vol. 21, pp. 97–144). Orlando, FL: Academic Press.

Medin, D. L., Goldstone, R. L., & Gentner, D. (1993). Respects for similarity. *Psychological Review, 100,* 254–278.

Mischel, W. (1968). *Personality and assessment.* New York: Wiley.

Mischel, W. (1973). Toward a cognitive social learning reconceptualization of personality. *Psychological Review, 80,* 252–283.

Munroe, R. L. (1955). *Schools of psychoanalytic thought.* New York: Hole, Rinehart & Winston.

Niedenthal, P. M., & Cantor, N. (1984). Making use of social prototypes: From fuzzy concepts to firm decisions. *Fuzzy Sets and Systems, 14,* 5–27.

Nisbett, R. (1980). The trait construct in lay and professional psychology. In L. Festinger (Ed.), *Retrospections on social psychology* (pp. 109–130). New York: Oxford University Press.

Nisbett, R., & Ross, L. (1980). *Human inference: Strategies and shortcomings in social judgment.* Englewood Cliffs, NJ: Prentice-Hall.

Norman, W. (1963). Toward an adequate taxonomy of person attributes: Replicated factor structures in peer nomination personality ratings. *Journal of Abnormal and Social Psychology, 66,* 574–583.

Ortony, A., Clore, G. L., & Collins, A. (1988). *The cognitive structure of emotions.* New York: Cambridge University Press.

Osgood, C. E., Suci, G. J., & Tannenbaum, P. H. (1957). *The measurement of meaning.* Urbana: University of Illinois Press.

Ostrom, T. M. (1984). The sovereignty of social cognition. In R. S. Wyer & T. K. Srull (Eds.), *Handbook of social cognition* (Vol. 1, pp. 1–38). Hillsdale, NJ: Erlbaum.

Ostrom, T. M., Lingle, J. H., Pryor, J. B., & Geva, N. (1980). Cognitive organization of person impressions. In R. Hastie, T. M. Ostrom, E. B. Ebbesen, R. S. Wyer, D. L. Hamilton, & D. E. Carlston (Eds.), *Person memory: The cognitive basis of social perception* (pp. 55–88). Hillsdale, NJ: Erlbaum.

Ostrom, T. M., Pryor, J. B., & Simpson, D. D. (1981). The organization of social information. In E. T. Higgins, C. P. Herman, & M. P. Zanna (Eds.), *Social cognition: The Ontario Symposium* (pp. 3–38). Hillsdale, NJ: Erlbaum.

Passini, F. T., & Norman, W. T. (1966). A universal conception of personality structure? *Journal of Personality and Social Psychology, 4,* 44–49.

Peevers, B., & Secord, P. (1973). Developmental changes in attribution of descriptive concepts to persons. *Journal of Personality and Social Psychology, 27,* 120–128.

Pennington, N., & Hastie, R. (1986). Evidence evaluation in complex decision making. *Journal of Personality and Social Psychology, 51,* 242–258.

Peterson, D. R. (1968). *The clinical study of social behavior.* New York: Appleton-Century-Crofts.

Razran, G. (1971). *Mind in evolution.* Boston: Houghton-Mifflin.

Rescorla, R. A., & Wagner, A. R. (1972). A theory of Pavlovian conditioning: Variations in the effectiveness of reinforcement and non-reinforcement. In A. H. Black & W. F. Prokasy (Eds.), *Classical conditioning II* (pp. 64–99). New York: Appleton-Century-Crofts.

Rosenberg, S., Nelson, C., & Vivekananthan, P. S. (1968). A multidimensional approach to the structure of personality impressions. *Journal of Personality and Social Psychology, 9,* 283–294.

Rosenberg, S., & Sedlak, A. (1972). Structural representations of implicit personality theory. In L. Berkowitz (Ed.), *Advances in experimental social psychology* (Vol. 6, pp. 235–297). New York: Academic Press.

Rosenthal, R., Hall, J. A., DiMatteo, M. R., Rogers, P. L., & Archer, D. (1979). *Sensitivity to nonverbal communication.* Baltimore: Johns Hopkins University Press.

Ross, L. D. (1977). The intuitive psychologist and his shortcomings. In L. Berkowitz (Ed.), *Advances in experimental social psychology* (Vol. 10, pp. 173–220). New York: Academic Press.

Sarbin, T. R. (1954). Role theory. In G. Lindzey (Ed.), *Handbook of social psychology* (Vol. 1, pp. 223–258). Cambridge, MA: Addison-Wesley.

Sarbin, T. R. (1982). *The social context of conduct.* New York: Praeger.

Schank, R. C., & Abelson, R. P. (1977). *Scripts, plans, goals, and understanding.* Hillsdale, NJ: Erlbaum.

Schneider, D. (1970). Implicit personality theory: A review. *Psychological Bulletin, 79,* 294–309.

Shaw, R., & Pittenger, J. (1977). Perceiving the face of change in changing faces: Implications for a theory of object perception. In R. Shaw & J. Bransford (Eds.), *Perceiving, acting, knowing: Toward an ecological psychology* (pp. 103–132). Hillsdale, NJ: Erlbaum.

Showers, C. J., & Cantor, N. (1985). Social cognition: A look at motivated strategies. *Annual Review of Psychology, 36,* 275–305.

Shweder, R. A. (1982). Fact and artifact in trait perception: The systematic distortion hypothesis. In B. A. Maher (Ed.), *Progress in experimental personality research* (Vol. 11, pp. 65–100). New York: Academic Press.

Shweder, R. A., & Bourne, E. J. (1981). *Does the concept of the person vary cross-culturally?* (Cognitive Science Tech. Rep. No. 6). Ann Arbor and Chicago: University of Michigan and University of Chicago.

Shweder, R. A., & D'Andrade, R. G. (1979). Accurate reflection or systematic distortion? A reply to Block, Weiss, and Thorne. *Journal of Personality and Social Psychology, 37,* 1075–1084.

Simon, H. A. (1967). Motivational and emotional controls of cognition. *Psychological Review, 74,* 29–39.

Slovic, P., & Lichtenstein, S. (1971). Comparison of Bayesian and regression approaches to the study of information processing in judgment. *Organizational Behavior and Human Performance, 6,* 649–744.

Smith, E. E., & Medin, D. L. (1981). *Categories and concepts.* Cambridge, MA: Harvard University Press.

Smith, E. R. (1984). A model of social inference processes. *Psychological Review, 91,* 392–413.

Srull, T. K. (1981). Person memory: Some tests of associative storage and retrieval models. *Journal of Experimental Psychology: Human Learning and Memory, 7,* 440–463.

Tulving, E. (1983). *Elements of episodic memory.* Oxford: Oxford University Press.

Tversky, A., & Kahneman, D. (1974). Judgment under uncertainty: Heuristics and biases. *Science, 185,* 1124–1131.

Weiss, D. S., & Mendelsohn, G. A. (1986). An empirical demonstration of the implausibility of the semantic similarity explanation of how trait ratings are made and what they mean. *Journal of Personality and Social Psychology, 50,* 595–601.

Winograd, T. (1975). Frame representations and the procedural-declarative controversy. In D. Bobrow & A. Collins (Eds.), *Representation and understanding: Studies in cognitive science* (pp. 185–210). New York: Academic Press.

Wishner, J. (1960). Reanalysis of "Impressions of personality." *Psychological Review, 67,* 96–112.

Wyer, R. S. (1974). *Cognitive organization and change: An information-processing approach.* Potomac, MD: Erlbaum.

Wyer, R. S. (1989). Social memory and social judgment. In P. R. Solomon, G. R. Goethals, C. M. Kelley, & B. R. Stephens (Eds.), *Memory: Interdisciplinary approaches* (pp. 221–242). New York: Springer-Verlag.

Wyer, R. S., & Carlston, D. E. (1979). *Social cognition, inference, and attribution.* Hillsdale, NJ: Erlbaum.

Wyer, R. S., & Gordon, S. E. (1984). The cognitive representation of social information. In R. S. Wyer & T. K. Srull (Eds.), *Handbook of social cognition* (Vol. 2, pp. 73–150). Hillsdale, NJ: Erlbaum.

Wyer, R. S., Jr., Shoben, E. J., Fuhrman, R. W., & Bodenhausen, G. V. (1985). Event memory: The temporal organization of social action sequences. *Journal of Personality and Social Psychology, 49,* 857–877.

Wyer, R. S., & Srull, T. K. (1989). *Memory and cognition in its social context.* Hillsdale, NJ: Erlbaum.

Zebrowitz, L. A. (1990). *Social perception.* Pacific Grove, CA: Brooks/Cole.

CHAPTER 28

PERSONALITY STRUCTURE

THE RETURN OF THE BIG FIVE

JERRY S. WIGGINS AND PAUL D. TRAPNELL
UNIVERSITY OF BRITISH COLUMBIA

I. INTRODUCTION

The recent resurgence of interest in the venerable five-factor model of personality characteristics appears to reflect a "working consensus" among a substantial number of investigators on the primary importance of the dimensions of: (I) Surgency/Extraversion, (II) Agreeableness, (III) Conscientiousness, (IV) Neuroticism, and (V) Openness to Experience/Intellect. These dimensions have recently been the principal focus of *Annual Review of Psychology* chapters (e.g., Digman, 1990; Wiggins & Pincus, 1992), special issues of journals (e.g., Costa, 1991; McCrae, 1992), edited books (e.g., Costa & Widiger, 1993; Wiggins, 1996), and scores of articles in personality, clinical, and social psychology journals. In the present chapter, we will focus on earlier writers who have contributed, directly or indirectly, to the five-factor tradition and on current writers who have been associated with distinctive theoretical perspectives on the five-factor model.

In his historical review of the vicissitudes of personality research methods, Craik (1986) identified three trajectories of development: continuous, arrested, and interrupted, the last describing those methods that declined in prominence for a period of time and reemerged at a later date. If a similar type of historical analysis were made of the "Big Five" dimensions of personality, it would reveal several "interruptions" over time. These interruptions reflect, in part, the ambiguities of publication dates, the relative unavailability of unpublished and technical reports, and other artifacts. But it is fair to say that interest in the five-factor model of

TABLE I

Selected Citations from the History of the Five-Factor Model of Personality

Decade	Citations
1930s	Thurstone (1934); Allport and Odbert (1936)
1940s	Cattell (1943, 1945); Eysenck (1947); Guilford (1948); Fiske (1949)
1950s	Cronbach and Meehl (1955); Loevinger (1957); Cattell (1957); Guilford (1959)
1960s	Tupes and Christal (1961); Tupes and Kaplan (1961); Norman (1963, 1967); Borgatta (1964)
1970s	Adcock (1972); Eysenck (1972); Howarth (1976); Cattell (1973); Hofstee (1976); Goldberg (1977); Tomas (1977); Brokken (1978); Digman (1979)
1980s	Borkenau (1988); Botwin and Buss (1989); Conley (1985); McCrae and Costa (1985c); Digman and Takemoto-Chock (1981); Goldberg (1980, 1981, 1982); R. Hogan (1986); John, Goldberg, and Angleitner (1984); Peabody and Goldberg (1989); Trapnell and Wiggins (1990)

personality has waxed and waned over the past five decades for a variety of reasons, and that we are currently witnessing a waxing that seems likely to continue well into the future.

A. The 1930s

In Table I, we have selected a few, from among many, citations that are meant to highlight significant issues that have occured (and reoccured) in the evolution of the contempory five-factor model. The first citation is to a paper by L. L. Thurstone (1934), to which Goldberg (1993) has recently called attention because of its prescience with respect to the contemporary five-factor model. We cite Thurstone here as a seminal source of the multiple-factor methods which have played such an important role in multivariate models of personality traits. Thurstone (1934) also describes a study in which raters were provided with a list of 60 trait adjectives "in common use for describing people" and in which each rater was asked to indicate adjectives that might be used in describing someone he knew well. Thurstone found that five common factors sufficed in accounting for the intercorrelations among adjectives and he reached the optimistic conclusion that "the scientific description of personality might not be so hopelessly complex as it is sometimes thought to be" (p. 14). This may be the earliest example of Big Five enthusiasm for parsimony.

   Thurstone realized that his method of factor analysis was indeterminant in the sense that it did not identify a unique set of interpretable orthogonal axes.[1] In part, for this reason, he advocated the identification of clusters of synony-

---

[1] The issue of factor indeterminancy was subsequently to have an interesting "interrupted" development in the history of psychometrics (see Steiger, 1979).

mous adjectives on the surface of the sphere formed by the five basic factors, as he put it, "whatever be their nature." Since there are obviously hundreds of trait-descriptive terms "in common use," such an enterprise would benefit from a lexicon of trait-descriptive terms that would permit investigators to select and sample terms on a systematic basis. Allport and Odbert (1936) assembled such a lexicon by exhaustively examining the trait-descriptive terms in Webster's *New International Dictionary* (1925) and classifying them under the categories of personal traits, temporary states, social evaluations, and metaphorical terms. With reference to Thurstone's (1934) rating study, they observed,

> Theoretically it would be possible to apply this ingenious method to a complete list of trait-names, such as that contained in this monograph. One might determine the amount of overlap in meaning between all the terms as they are commonly understood and employed. The investigator might then declare that such and such trait-names are roughly synonymous and that only one of them needs to be retained if what is desired is a vocabulary of completely independent terms. The trait-names would be grouped, and only a single representative would be saved for each group.
>
> *(Allport & Odbert, 1936, p. 33).*

It was, of course, Cattell (1943) who responded to this suggestion in the forties.

Although related, it is important to distinguish between the tradition begun by Thurstone and that begun by Allport and Odbert. Thurstone's concern was with the development of multivariate models for capturing "vectors of mind" which, in the realm of personality, would reveal *personality structure* as manifested in individual differences. Historically, this tradition has been characterized by disagreements on a number of technical issues, such as the number of factors to retain, the appropriate method of factor rotation, and the nature of criteria for establishing the validity of factors. Such differences of opinion are evident in the contrasting systems of Cattell and Eysenck, for example.

The tradition begun by Allport and Odbert has been concerned with the development of taxonomies of *personality attributes* as reflected, for the most part, in ordinary language (John, Angleitner, & Ostendorf, 1988). In reviewing the taxonomies of trait-descriptive terms developed over the past 50 years, John, Goldberg, and Angleitner (1984) note that such taxonomies differ in: (a) sampling procedures, (b) extent of reduction, (c) degree of structure, (d) abstractness, and (e) criteria for evaluation. Allport and Odbert, for example, considered *all* terms in an unabridged dictionary, made no attempt to reduce their list, and listed terms alphabetically within four broad categories. Possible hierarchies were not considered and no attempt was made to evaluate the final lexicon. Goldberg (1982), in contrast, began with a reduced list from a previous dictionary search, reduced this list considerably, structured the taxonomy according to strict rules, generated a large number of categories which mapped onto higher-order dimensions, and evaluated the final taxonomy by several different criteria.

B. The 1940s

Taxonomies of trait-descriptive terms may be employed for a variety of purposes by lexicographers, psycholinguists, cognitive psychologists, and other students of language. They may also serve as a basis for the construction of instruments in the development of multivariate models of personality structure, as has been so ably demonstrated by Cattell. Cattell (1943) considered the Allport–Odbert lexicon to be a useful definition of the "language personality sphere." On the basis of judgments of semantic similarity, he reduced the lexicon of approximately 4500 terms to 171 synonym groups. Bipolar rating scales were constructed to represent the synonym groups, and from their intercorrelations in a peer-rating study, 35 clusters were identified as the "standard reduced personality sphere." In subsequent factor analytic studies, Cattell (1945) identified 12 primary factors underlying the 35 clusters.

   Cattell was a consultant to the Michigan VA Selection Research Project (E. L. Kelly & Fiske, 1951), in which procedures for the selection of graduate students in clinical psychology were investigated. The "basic data of assessment" in this project were a set of 22 bipolar rating scales selected from Cattell's 35 standard clusters. The rating scales were used to obtain self-ratings, teammate ratings, and staff assessment ratings for all trainees. This design allowed Fiske (1949) to perform the first study of the consistency of primary factor structures among ratings from different sources. Two important findings emerged from his study: (1) "a high degree of consistency exist[ed] between the factorial structures found in different rating sources" (p. 344), and (2) the data strongly suggested a 5 (not 12) factor solution. During this same decade the two major taxonomic research programs of J. P. Guilford and Hans J. Eysenck were beginning to take form. Guilford (1948) was instrumental in fostering a more widespread understanding of factor analytic approaches to test development and in applying these methods to the study of traits. Eysenck's (1947) first description of his two-factor structural model also appeared at this time, although in inchoate form.

C. The 1950s

The 1950s was a period of interrupted development in the history of the Big Five model and it was not until the end of that decade that the importance of Fiske's demonstration was recognized. Although there was little research of direct relevance to the five-factor model, there were two lines of development in personality assessment that laid the groundwork for a reemergence of the model in later years. The philosophy of science underlying the idea of construct validity (Cronbach & Meehl, 1955; Loevinger, 1957) encouraged a more substantive approach to test construction than did the widely held empirical perspective associated with the MMPI, and this substantive approach was compatible with dimensional assessment and theories of personality structure. The fifties was also a period in which factor analytic approaches to personality structure flourished. Cattell (1957) and Guilford (1959) presented major reviews of their structural research programs and numerous studies of the 16 PF and GZTS appeared.

D. The 1960s

Ernest Tupes was a member of the previously mentioned Michigan VA Assessment staff, and in his subsequent work at Lackland Air Force Base he used 20 of the 22 bipolar rating scales, from the earlier project, in the assessment of Air Force Academy cadets. In investigating the factor structure of peer ratings on these 20 variables, Tupes and Christal (1958) found a clear and generalizable five-factor solution which they identified as Surgency/Extraversion, Agreeableness, Conscientiousness, Emotional Stability, and Culture. Moreover, both the individual rating scales and the five personality factor scores were found to be related to important criterion variables, such as Cadet Effectiveness Reports (CER), which are ratings of leadership ability and officer potential based on a composite of peer ratings, upperclassmen ratings, and ratings by tactical officers. For example, the correlations between factor scores and CERs in three classes of cadets were as follows: Surgency (.24), Agreeableness (.35), Conscientiousness (.60), Emotional Stability (.58), and Culture (.53) (Tupes & Kaplan, 1961, p. 7).

In what we would classify as the first clear "advocacy" paper, Tupes and Christal (1961) investigated the "universal" nature of the five-factor solution by direct comparisons of factorial results from eight highly diverse samples of subjects. Four of these samples were military, two were Cattell's university student samples, and two were from the Kelly–Fiske study of graduate students. The trait-rating variables in all samples had been derived from Cattell's 35 clusters. The stability of the five-factor solution across diverse samples and conditions was "remarkable":

> In many ways it seems remarkable that such stability should be found in an area which to date has granted anything but consistent results. Undoubtedly the consistency has always been there, but it has been hidden by inconsistency of factorial techniques and philosophies, the lack of replication using identical variables, and disagreement among analysts as to factor titles. None of the factors identified in this study are new. They have been identified many times in previous analyses, although they have not always been called by the same names.
>
> *(Tupes & Christal, 1961, p. 12)*

No doubt, the impact of Tupes and Christal's advocacy on the psychometric community of the early sixties might have been limited by the fact that all of their reports were in the form of technical reports and technical notes issued from the Personnel Laboratory at Lackland AFB and circulated to a distinguished, but small, group of civilians. If it had not been for a published article by Warren Norman, a distinguished civilian whose research was supported by the Personnel Laboratory, there might well have been another "interruption" in the historical development of the Big Five.

Norman's (1963) paper is a milestone in the historical development of the five-factor model because it provided: (1) a clear statement of the rationale and procedures for developing a well-structured taxonomy of personality attributes; (2) psychometric criticisms of Cattell's earlier factorial work and an advocacy of analytic orthogonal rotation; (3) an analytic comparison of the generalizability of the five-factor solution within an appropriate experimental design; and (4) a call for the development of self-report measures of the five factors, using peer ratings as criteria.

Although clearly a five-factor enthusiast, Norman shared the skepticism of earlier investigators regarding the sufficiency of these factors and felt that "it is time to return to the total pool of trait names in the natural language—there to search for additional personality indicators not easily subsumed under one or another of these five recurrent factors" (p. 582). Acting on his own recommendations, Norman returned to the newly available *Webster's Third New International Dictionary* (1961) and developed a new master set of 18,125 terms which was rigorously reduced and classified (Norman, 1967) to provide the basis for most contemporary taxonomies of personality attributes, including those developed by Goldberg and his collaborators (see John et al., 1988, pp. 184–189).

E. The 1970s

Norman's contributions to the five-factor tradition led some to characterize the model as the "Norman Five" (e.g., Bouchard, Lalonde, & Gagnon, 1988). From a strictly historical perspective, one might be tempted to characterize the model as the "Cattell Five," but that would be a serious *faux pas.* For despite its origins in the clusters and rating scales that he developed, Cattell has never accepted the five-factor alternative to his 20 or more primary factors, nor has he been willing to accept the Big Five as useful approximations to five of his nine or more second strata factors (Cattell, 1973). Although Cattell's reasons for disowning the five-factor model may appear more methodological than substantive, one should bear in mind the close relation between method and content that exists in Cattell's theory of personality. More than any other theorist, Cattell relies upon specific methods of factor analytic investigation in his quest for the underlying determinants of phenotypic variables (Wiggins, 1984).

Cattell's (1973) objections to five-factor solutions, and to other solutions of relatively small dimensionality, are that: (1) correlation matrices have been underfactored; (2) factors have been mechanically, usually orthogonally, rotated through clusters of surface variables ("cluster chasing"); and (3) the resultant factors are often "pseudo second-order factors," rather than "true" or "grounded" second stratum factors: "We can distinguish between a *stratum,* which is a general psychological statement of the breadth and manner of influence of a factor, and an *order,* which is where it appears in a factor-analytic experiment" (pp. 132–133). Cattell's concern is that factors which are, in truth, secondary stratum factors may be mistakenly correlated into a set of primaries and appear at the primary level. This concern reflects his conceptual preference for primary factors: "the evidence is that the primaries . . . are scientifically more important and constant and that the secondaries are more elusive and above all related to the accidental circumstances of the particular group" (p. 107).

Cattell's conceptual and methodological preferences are far from universally shared, and the seventies was a period in which these preferences were increasingly challenged by workers from within and outside of the Cattellian tradition (e.g., Adcock, 1972; Digman, 1972; Eysenck, 1972; Goldberg, Norman, & Schwartz, 1972, 1980; Howarth, 1976; Howarth & Browne, 1971; Karson & O'Dell, 1974; Sells, Demaree, & Will, 1970). In response to these challenges, Cattell (1973) observed, "There has been a tendency to view these alternative possible conclusions as attacks on the establishment, and when that occurs positions which are themselves mutually incompatible are mistakenly seen as in alliance" (p. 289). Although it is true that these criticisms were too varied in nature to suggest a formal "alliance," there does appear to be the common theme that Cattell's earlier work was characterized by an *overextraction* of factors. During the next decade, the rather remarkable "return of the Big Five" signaled an era in which a new "establishment" threatened to replace the one to which Cattell referred.

F. The 1980s

From the relatively crude criterion of topical citation counts, it might appear that interest in, and advocacy of, the Big Five model suffered a number of false starts over the years and then exploded in the eighties. The development was more gradual, however, and much of it centered around the work and energy of Lewis R. Goldberg at the Oregon Research Institute (ORI). Since 1960, ORI has been a site to which scholars have been invited for periods ranging from a few days to several years. Since his early collaborations with Norman, Goldberg has had an enduring, and appropriately skeptical, interest in providing a firm lexical and psychometric base for the Big Five dimensions, and this interest has been widely communicated to others. In the latter respect, it is of interest to note some of the visitors to ORI over the past 30 years.[2] In chronological order of visits, they include Dean Peabody, Jerry Wiggins, Warren Norman, Willem Hofstee, Frank Brokken, Arend Tomas, Oliver John, Alois Angleitner, David Buss, James Conley, and Peter Borkenau (see Table I for citations).

During the eighties, Goldberg's published work served as an introduction to the Big Five for a younger audience and rekindled the interests of more experienced investigators:

> After our experience with these scales [Cattell's rating scales] our interest in the five-factor model waned, and returned only when Goldberg (1981, 1982,

---

[2] Goldberg, L. R., *Visits and vistors to ORI. Memo to colleagues* (March 2, 1990).

1983) renewed the search for universal dimensions in trait names, and developed
a better instrument.

(McCrae & Costa, 1985b, p. 165)

Continuity is also evident in the long-standing interest of John Digman in
the five-factor model of personality. Digman's (1963, 1972) early studies of child
personality ratings suggested that a relatively small number of factors were sufficient
for characterizing that domain, and subsequent reanalyses of these and adult studies
convinced him of the centrality of the Big Five dimensions (Digman, 1979), which
he has continued to advocate for 20 years (e.g., Digman, 1989; Digman & Inouye,
1986; Digman & Takemoto-Chock, 1981). In addition to his multivariate demonstrations of the ubiquitous nature of the five-factor structure, Digman (1985) has been
especially concerned with substantive interpretation of the factors themselves in
the light of earlier personality constructs. His previously mentioned chapter on
personality structure in the *Annual Review of Psychology* (Digman, 1990) is almost
exclusively concerned with the Big Five literature and reflects nicely the current
zeitgeist in the field.

II. THEORETICAL PERSPECTIVES ON THE BIG FIVE

In comparing and contrasting theoretical perspectives, it is often useful to do so in
terms of George Kelly's (1955) distinction between their differing foci and ranges
of convenience. The focus of convenience of a construct or set of constructs refers
to the events to which a construct is most conveniently applied, and typically
represents the particular events an author had in mind when devising a construct.
The range of convenience of constructs refers to the extent to which constructs
prove useful when applied to events outside their original focus of convenience.
We hope to make clear in this section that different theoretical perspectives on the
Big Five involve somewhat different foci and ranges of convenience. We would
also like to endorse Kelly's constructive-alternativistic philosophy that different
versions of the "truth" may coexist without chaos.

In comparing theoretical perspectives on *traits,* it is important to do so with
reference to an important distinction, first made by Allport (1937, pp. 299–300),
between the two different usages of that term which have resulted in conceptual
ambiguities in the trait literature. Rather than identifying these different usages
with a particular trait theory, we shall refer to them as "trait$_1$" and "trait$_2$" (Wiggins,
1984). The trait$_1$ concept denotes trait attributions, couched in ordinary language,
which are meant to *describe* or summarize the pattern of an individual's conduct
to date, from a normative perspective and with reference to the likely social outcome
of that conduct. The trait$_2$ concept denotes causal or generative mechanisms which
are meant to *explain* the behavior described in trait$_1$ language (Wiggins, this volume,
chap. 4). The importance and clarity of this distinction will be seen to vary among
different theoretical perspectives on the Big Five.

A. The Enduring Dispositional View of the Big Five: Costa and McCrae

> Somewhat surprisingly, the "breakthrough" that we feel has restored confidence
> in personality psychology was not the proposal of a new conceptual model or
> paradigm but a return to one of the oldest models: trait theory.
>
> *(Costa & McCrae, 1980, p. 67)*

1. Theoretical Orientation

The trait theory of Costa and McCrae was originally developed in the context of
longitudinal studies of personality and aging. Within that focus of convenience they
felt that a self-report, multivariate, trait model of personality would serve to clarify
and integrate the "bewildering variety of concepts and measures used in the field"
(Costa & McCrae, 1980, p. 68). Their subsequent research confirmed this expectation
and revealed an impressive degree of longitudinal stability (McCrae & Costa, 1990)
which further strengthened their commitment to the concept of traits as enduring
dispositions (Costa & McCrae, 1980).

Like other mainstream personality theories, the theoretical perspective of
Costa and McCrae places a heavy emphasis upon the trait concept. Within this
context, their position on the distinction between trait$_1$ and trait$_2$ concepts appears
to be closer to that of Allport and, to some extent, Murray than to that of Cattell
(see Wiggins, 1984): "The more of a trait people have [trait$_2$], the more likely they
are to show the behavior it disposes them toward, and thus the more frequently
we are likely to see it [trait$_1$]" (McCrae & Costa, 1990, p. 23). Although McCrae
and Costa (1990) explicitly "note that our definition of traits says nothing about
their origins" (p. 24), their use of the concept does not always distinguish the two:
"The trait names do not refer to the underlying physiology, but to the abstract
consistencies in the ways people act and experience [trait$_1$] and to whatever complex
underlying causes they may have [trait$_2$]" (p. 25)." For the most part, however, it
is the *enduring nature* of dispositions to behave and experience in particular ways
(trait$_1$) that makes them so central to, and predictive of, the ways in which emerging
lives develop.

Costa and McCrae rejected the "constructed consistency" view of traits
(e.g., Mischel, 1968) and adopted a "realist" position (e.g., Loevinger, 1957)
that received strong support from their demonstration of the convergent validity
(McCrae, 1982) and longitudinal stability (Costa & McCrae, 1988a) of both peer
and spouse ratings of self-reporting targets. Further, they adopted a generally
realist position on the veridicality of self-report and rejected both "social
desirability" (Costa & McCrae, 1988b; McCrae, 1986; McCrae & Costa, 1983)
and "impression management" (Costa & McCrae, in press; McCrae & Costa,
1984) conceptions, on impressive empirical grounds, in favor of a self-disclosure
model (Johnson, 1981).

McCrae and Costa (1984) maintain that a trait theory of individual differences
constitutes a legitimate and potentially comprehensive alternative to psychoanalytic,

behavioristic, and humanistic theories of personality, rather than being an append-age of or peripheral to those three conceptions of personality (pp. 32–33). Moreover, the demonstrated empirical comprehensiveness of the five-factor model should be viewed as a theoretical advance:

> The growing consensus on the five-factor model has led to great strides in integrating personality research; we hope the NEO-PI can be equally useful in integrating personality theory. The first step in this process is the recognition that the NEO-PI *does* reflect a theory of personality . . . .
>
> *(Costa & McCrae, in press)*

2. The NEO Personality Inventory (NEO-PI)

The NEO-PI (Costa & McCrae, 1985, 1989, 1992) is an extension of an earlier three-factor NEO model (*n*euroticism, *e*xtraversion, and *o*penness) that now includes the additional Big Five dimensions of Agreeableness and Conscientiousness. The earlier three-factor model evolved from a series of studies of the stability of trait structures across age groups (Costa & McCrae, 1976, 1978, 1980). Three age-invariant factors were first found in the 16 PF (Cattell, Eber, & Tatsuoka, 1970) and later identified in a conjoint factor analysis of the Eysenck Personality Inventory (Eysenck & Eysenck, 1964), the EASI Temperament Survey (Buss & Plomin, 1975), and the Experience Inventory (Coan, 1974). In the original NEO Inventory, each of the three age-invariant factors contained six facets which were chosen to be representative of previously identified substantive components and which were thought to provide "a useful level of generality" in representing these components (Costa & McCrae, 1986, p. 68).

Facet scales of Extraversion and Neuroticism were based, in part, on the structure and content of Buss and Plomin's (1975) EASI and on the results of structural analyses of other inventories (e.g., 16 PF, GZTS, EPI). The domain of Neuroticism comprised the facets of anxiety, hostility, depression, self-consciousness, vulnerability, and impulsiveness. The domain of Extraversion included the facets of gregariousness, attachment, assertiveness, activity, excite-ment-seeking, and positive emotions. Facet scales for Openness were based on three subscales from Coan's (1974) Experience Inventory—fantasy, aesthetics, and ideas—which were supplemented by three subscales developed by Costa and Mc-Crae—feelings, actions, and values.

The current five-factor NEO-PI had its origins in a study in which domain scales from the three-factor NEO Inventory were correlated with: (1) a set of adjectival markers of the Big Five developed by Goldberg (1983) and (2) factor scores derived from an extended set of Big Five adjectives which included the Goldberg markers. In this study, the N, E, and O domain scores converged on corresponding Goldberg scales and adjective factor scores, and were found to be uncorrelated with the adjectival measures of Agreeableness and Conscientiousness (McCrae & Costa, 1985c). These findings encouraged Costa and McCrae to extend their NEO Inventory by constructing brief questionnaire scales to index the domains of Agreeableness and Conscientiousness. Brief, preliminary markers (McCrae &

Costa, 1987) were later expanded into a full complement of facet scales for these two domains (Costa, McCrae, & Dye, 1991). A convenient 60-item short form of the NEO-PI has recently been published under the title "Five-Factor Inventory" (FFI; Costa & McCrae, 1989). These expansions and additions have been incorporated in a recent revision of the NEO (Costa & McCrae, 1992).

3. Comprehensiveness of the NEO-PI Model

Advocates of a "new" multivariate model, even one as long-standing as the five-factor model, should not be oblivious of the rich history of models in the personality assessment literature. Consider, for example, the following major research traditions: (1) Jung's (1923/1971) theory of psychological types was the first well-articulated typology and it has survived to this day in the Myers–Briggs Type Indicator (MBTI; Myers & McCaulley, 1985); (2) Murray's (1938) taxonomy of human needs has spawned more assessment instruments than any other perspective, and it is currently best represented by the Personality Research Form (PRF; Jackson, 1984); (3) Eysenck's (1947) long-standing system is among the most prominent on the contemporary scene, and it is operationalized in the Eysenck Personality Questionnaire (EPQ; Eysenck & Eysenck, 1975); (4) the empirical tradition in objective personality assessment (Meehl, 1945) is still very much alive in the most widely used and studied of all questionnaires, the Minnesota Multiphasic Personality Inventory (MMPI; Hathaway & McKinley, 1983); (5) the Institute for Personality Assessment and Research (IPAR; MacKinnon, 1948), both historically and currently, is a major center for personality assessment research, and the common descriptive language for assessment which evolved at that institution is represented by the California Q-Set (CQS; Block, 1961); (6) the interpersonal circumplex tradition (Freedman, Leary, Ossorio, & Coffey, 1951) has been revitalized in recent years and is implemented by instruments such as the Interpersonal Adjective Scales (IAS; Wiggins, 1995); (7) Holland's highly influential theory of vocational choice is based on the most extensively validated personality typology and is operationalized by the Self-Directed Search (SDS; Holland, 1985).

Costa and McCrae's claims to comprehensiveness of their five-factor model are largely, and justifiably, based on empirical studies of the relations between the NEO-PI and *all* of the above instruments, which, as we have noted, are representative of the major research traditions in personality assessment (Costa, Bush, Zonderman, & McCrae, 1986; Costa & McCrae, 1988a; Costa, McCrae, & Holland, 1984; McCrae & Costa, 1985a, 1989a, 1989b; McCrae, Costa, & Bush, 1986). Perusal of the just cited references suggests that predicted and meaningful convergences were found in all of these studies. This line of research has served to place the Big Five model in general, and the NEO-PI in particular, in the mainstream of both historical and contemporary research in personality assessment.

> It is of course possible that future research will discover other domains of personality not covered by the scales of the NEO-PI, but in the meantime, no other system has a better claim to comprehensiveness.
>
> *(Costa & McCrae, 1985, p. 27)*

B. The Dyadic Interactional View of the Big Five: Wiggins

The interpersonal tradition in personality assessment originated in a different research context than did the five-factor model and, until recently, developed quite independently of the Big Five tradition. The history of the interpersonal tradition spans some 40 years (LaForge, 1985) and, like the Big Five model, it has been characterized by both extended "interruptions" over time and a recent widespread resurgence of interest (Wiggins, 1985, 1996a). The focus of convenience of this tradition was upon dyadic interactions in psychotherapeutic settings (Leary, 1957) and, as a consequence, it has emphasized the two dimensions of personality that most clearly implicate interpersonal transactions: *dominance* (Surgency/Extraversion) and *nurturance* (Agreeableness). The dyadic-interactional perspective on the five-factor model is guided by the metatheoretical concepts of agency and communion (Wiggins, 1991). This perspective assigns a conceptual priority to the first two factors of the model and emphasizes the manifestations of agentic and communal concerns *within* the remaining three factors (Wiggins & Trapnell, 1996).

The interpersonal system of personality diagnosis (Leary, 1957) originated in an attempt to translate certain concepts of Harry Stack Sullivan (1953) into concrete measurement operations. The conceptual basis of the system was further enriched by incorporation of concepts from the social exchange literature (Carson, 1969; Foa & Foa, 1974) and by an explicit formulation of complementarity and similarity in interpersonal transactions (Kiesler, 1983). The conceptual continuity of the system has been maintained, in part, by the remarkable similarities between earlier Sullivanian concepts and recent developments in the field of cognitive psychology (Carson, 1991). The plausibility of measurement procedures associated with the interpersonal system has also increased with demonstrations of the fit between the conceptual model and the empirical data (e.g., Wiggins, Phillips, & Trapnell, 1989).

The structural model underlying the interpersonal system is a two-dimensional circumplex in which variables appear in a circular order around the bipolar, orthogonal coordinates of dominance/agency/status and nurturance/communion/love. The circumplex model provides an alternative to the simple-structure model of factor analysis in which all variables are expected to have their principal loadings on one or the other of two orthogonal factors. As a consequence, there is no optimal orientation of the principal axes of a circumplex, because any rotation is as good as any other. The placement of axes through dominance (PA) and nurturance (LM) in Figure 1 is not arbitrary, however, because it is based on a substantial body of theoretical writings and empirical findings that attest to the fundamental nature of agency and communion as conceptual coordinates for the understanding and measurement of interpersonal behavior (Wiggins, 1991).

Leary (1957) translated key Sullivanian concepts into measurement operations by placing them within a trait$_1$ perspective: "The basic units of personality come from the protocol language by which the subject's interpersonal behavior is described" (p. 34). The well-established circumplex structure of interpersonal trait attributions may thus be distinguished from their possible underlying causes (Wiggins, this volume, chap. 4).

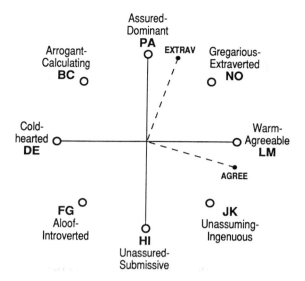

FIGURE 1   Circumplex model of interpersonal behavior.

Although the similarities between the interpersonal circumplex components of dominance and nurturance and the Big Five components of Surgency/Extraversion and Agreeableness have been recognized for some time (e.g., Goldberg, 1981), it is only recently that the relations between these two traditions have been considered in some detail. McCrae and Costa (1989b) examined the convergences between peer and self-ratings on the NEO-PI and self-ratings on the Interpersonal Adjective Scales (IAS; Wiggins, 1995). Combined factor analysis of the preceding sets of variables revealed a clear circumplex pattern of IAS variables around the orthogonal NEO-PI factors of Extraversion and Agreeableness (McCrae & Costa, 1989b, p. 589). As one might expect on substantive grounds, the obtained circumplex pattern of IAS variables was shifted from the standard orientations of dominance (PA) and nurturance (LM) toward the off-diagonal coordinates of extraversion (NO) and ingenuousness (JK). Another way of looking at this structure is provided in Figure 1, in which the NEO-PI domain scores of Extraversion and Agreeableness have been projected onto the IAS circumplex.

Although the optimal orientation of the two "interpersonal" axes of the five-factor model is likely to remain a contentious and nontrivial theoretical issue between interpersonalists and factor analysts, recognition that these two long-standing traditions are, in many senses, *complementary* to each other is certain to lead to advances in both traditions (McCrae & Costa, 1989b; Trapnell & Wiggins, 1990). For example, the interpersonal circumplex model lends itself well to the kinds of fine-grained distinctions required in the fields of psychodiagnosis (Wiggins, 1982) and psychotherapy (Kiesler, 1988). In the former field, Wiggins and Pincus

(1989) have demonstrated that the circumplex model captures nicely many of the distinctions made among six of the personality disorders of Axis II of DSM-III (American Psychiatric Association, 1980). However, these distinctions were further clarified and additional personality disorders illuminated when the full five-factor model of the NEO-PI was employed. In particular, despite the utility of the interpersonal circumplex for psychodiagnostic work, the full range of psycho-pathology represented by the personality disorders cannot be understood without taking into account the dimensions of Neuroticism, Conscientiousness, and, to some extent, Openness to Experience of the five-factor model (Wiggins & Pincus, 1989).

Because the interpersonal circumplex and the five-factor model are complementary to rather than competitive with each other, there is much to be said for an approach to personality assessment that combines the advantages of both models. To this end, Trapnell and Wiggins (1990) have extended the adjectival measure of the circumplex (IAS) to include the additional Big Five dimensions of Conscientiousness, Neuroticism, and Openness to experience. This flexible 124-item instrument (IAS-B5) has excellent structural properties and promising convergent and discriminant relations with the NEO-PI (Costa & McCrae, 1985) and the Hogan Personality Inventory (R. Hogan, 1986).

C. The Competency View of the Big Five: Hogan

> Although there are always individual differences, people need attention and approval; status; and predictability. These needs are largely satisfied through social interaction. The key to attaining status and approval is interpersonal competence. As observers, we think and talk about other people by using trait words to evaluate others in terms of their usefulness for our social groups; trait terms mark individual differences in social competence.
>
> *(R. Hogan, Carpenter, Briggs, & Hansson, 1984, p. 27)*

1. Theoretical Orientation

The distinction between trait$_1$ and trait$_2$ concepts is central to Hogan's theoretical orientation and stems, in part, from the focus of convenience of his theory upon the prediction of effective performance in work and social settings. Hogan equates this distinction with the different observational perspectives of actors and observers. Actors have needs for social approval, status, and predictability which cause them to seek social interactions with others. Such needs are clearly granted trait$_2$ status: ". . . these master motives cause and explain social action—why we do it and why it takes its prototypical forms" (R. Hogan, Jones, & Cheek, 1985, p. 195).

Approval, status, and predictability are sought through ritualized interactions with others. The actors's role in this social drama is scripted with reference to the dimensional coordinates of *sociability* (managing human resources of the group versus managing its technical resources) and *conformity*[3] (preserving the culture of

---

[3] This dimension is now labeled "prudence," but the earlier label might make more sense in the present context.

the group versus instigating cultural change). These coordinates appear to have the status of the metaconcepts of communion and agency in interpersonal theory (Wiggins, 1991). R. Hogan (1983) notes the similarity of his system to the typology provided by the interpersonal circumplex (e.g., gregarious-extraverted type). His own preference is for the vocational preference typology of Holland (1985) (e.g., social type).

Specialized occupational and social roles provide the vehicles through which an actor's needs for approval, status, and predictability may be pursued in interactions with others. In the course of these structured interactions, an actor attempts to communicate his underlying self-images (trait$_2$) to others through *self-presentations*. Unlike Goffman (1959), Hogan does not view these self-presentations as self-conscious efforts to foster a favorable impression, dictated by the situational demand of a particular role. Rather, he views these presentations as relatively self-conscious-free efforts to communicate one's self-view. To emphasize this difference in conceptualization, Cheek and Hogan (1982, p. 258) adopted the term "self-interpretation" as a more accurate representation of their position. Hogan also disagrees with Goffman's view that "personality" may be reduced to self-presentations across different situations. Instead, he postulates a number of stable trait$_2$ structures within the individual that are of both biological and social origins (R. Hogan, Jones, & Cheek, 1985).

Observers evaluate the potential contributions of an actor to a group by means of trait attributions, couched in ordinary language, which capture an actor's social reputation (trait$_1$). In R. Hogan's view, these evaluative trait descriptors evolved as a means of social control necessitated by the circumstances of group living. Further, they are, for the most part, well captured by the Big Five dimensions of personality. Thus, for Hogan, the Big Five are exclusively dimensions employed by *observers* in the evaluation of actors' contributions to groups or work organizations. This formulation is less radical than it might appear when it is recalled that the focus of convenience of the original Big Five work was on observer evaluations of fitness for the occupations of clinical psychologist (E. L. Kelly & Fiske, 1951) and Air Force officer (Tupes & Christal, 1958).

Hogan's competency perspective led him to formulate an alternative six-factor interpretation of the Big Five that is more directly focused on qualities related to successful performance. These factors (and their corresponding Norman numbers) are Sociability (Ia), Prudence (III), Likability (II), Ambition (Ib), Adjustment (IV), and Intellectance (V). Norman's Extraversion/Surgency factor was split apart because "sociability and assertiveness are conceptually distinct, and, in addition, they are not very highly correlated. . . . [They] have different psychological dynamics; assertiveness is associated with status-seeking, whereas sociability is associated with affiliativeness and popularity" (R. Hogan, 1983, p. 66).

2. Measurement Rationale

a. Structural model.   In Hogan's view, a typology of occupational or vocational specialization can be constructed from a circumplex model formed by the coordinates of sociability and conformity. Further, the remaining four orthogonal factors of Likability, Ambition, Adjustment, and Intellectance may be used to assess individual differences in competence *within* each of the occupational categories identified by the circumplex typology (R. Hogan, 1983; R. Hogan & Johnson, 1981). This combined circumplex–Big Five model is structurally, although not substantively, similar to that advocated by Trapnell and Wiggins (1990) in the interpretation of IAS-B5. However, Hogan does not recommend the use of his own dimensions of sociability and conformity for defining vocational personality types. Instead, he suggests that sociability and conformity, along with the other four factors of his system, be interpreted as dimensions of competence within the typology provided by Holland's (1985) hexagonal model (R. Hogan, 1986, pp. 22–33; see also Johnson, 1983).

     b. Item responding.   Unlike Costa and McCrae, Hogan adopts a strong self-presentational view of item responding:

> The processes involved in answering inventory items are formally identical to the processes underlying social interactions . . . responses to personality inventories are not self-reports . . . Rather, the responses reveal how the person wants to be regarded . . . scale scores derived from an aggregation of item responses do not necessarily reflect underlying traits [trait$_2$] in the respondent.
>
>   *(R. Hogan, 1986, p. 2).*

The implications of Hogan's theory of item responding for the construction and selection of items are less explicit than are those of some other test authors. For example, Jackson's (1986) theory of item responding serves as an explicit rationale for the innovative procedures he developed to minimize social desirability variance at the item level (Jackson, 1970). In this context, at least, it is clear that Hogan (Nicholson & Hogan, 1990) would *not* adopt these procedures for minimizing social desirability variance in test construction.

3. The Hogan Personality Inventory (HPI)

The HPI operationalizes Hogan's socioanalytic trait theory by means of a 310-item, self-report questionnaire. Consistent with that theory's observer-centered, competency interpretation of the Big Five dimensions, the HPI targets dimensions of reputation thought to possess "broad, general importance for personal and social effectiveness" (R. Hogan, 1986, p. 5). There are six HPI global or "primary" scales, Ambition, Sociability, Likability, Prudence, Adjustment, and Intellectance, each corresponding to a factor from Hogan's six-factor variant of the Big Five model. In addition, each primary scale may be decomposed into a number of small (3 to 6 items each) subscales called "homogeneous item clusters" (HICs). Each of the 43 HICs assesses a specific trait judged by Hogan and his research team to be most relevant to an individual's reputation with respect to one of the six HPI trait dimensions (e.g., "Math Ability" HIC for Intellectance, "Status-Seeking" HIC for Ambition).

Although the HPI purportedly spans the same universe of content as does the NEO-PI (i.e., the Big Five), the HPI apportions this universe into rather different content domains and facets than does the NEO-PI. For example, whereas the NEO-PI measures Factor V with six facets found empirically to define an "openness to experience" dimension, the HPI measures Factor V with nine HICs judged to exemplify the reputation of "intelligent." These nine HICs define two virtually orthogonal clusters, however, only one of which ("culture") bears a conceptual and empirical relation to NEO-PI Openness; the other cluster ("scholastic ability") correlates weakly with Conscientiousness and is essentially uncorrelated with Openness (Trapnell & Wiggins, 1990). Similarly, the HPI's eight Prudence HICs, selected to index the reputation of "prudential" (cautious/responsible), form two independent clusters. Only one of these clusters correlates with NEO-PI Conscientiousness; the other correlates substantially with an NEO-PI Extraversion facet ("excitement-seeking") (Trapnell & Wiggins, 1990). These and other substantive and structural differences between the HPI and the NEO-PI reflect the divergent trait theoretical positions held by R. Hogan and by Costa and McCrae in their conceptions of the Big Five dimensions: the NEO-PI reflects a "traditional" factor analytic (i.e., Eysenck, Cattell) orientation to the five factor model, while the HPI reflects an explicit socioanalytic orientation.

4. Applications of the HPI

As would be expected from its focus of convenience, the principal applications of the HPI have been in the prediction of organizational and occupational performance. Applied research with the HPI has typically involved: (1) development of a performance criterion for a general (e.g., salesperson) or specific (e.g., service operations dispatcher) occupational role, (2) correlation of the full set of HPI HICs with that criterion, and (3) selection of a subset of HICs that best predicts the criterion and scoring these items as an "occupational performance scale" for use in personnel selection and other practical assessment applications.

R. Hogan (1986) summarizes findings from 11 studies in which the HPI predicted such performance criteria as supervisor ratings, company commendations, fitness ratings (treadmill test), total dollar sales revenue, and training course completions. Findings from these and other studies (see J. Hogan & Hogan, 1986) have prompted development of HPI scales for clerical, sales, and managerial potential, employee reliability, stress tolerance, and service orientation (R. Hogan, 1986), as well as HPI personnel selection scales for occupations such as hospital service worker (Raza, Metz, Dyer, Coan, & Hogan, 1986), service operations dispatcher (R. Hogan, Jacobson, Hogan, & Thompson, 1987), line-haul driver (J. Hogan et al., 1985), combination driver (J. Hogan, Hogan, & Briggs, 1984), and habilitation therapist (J. Hogan, Arneson, Hogan, & Jones, 1986). Hogan has recently incorporated Hogan Assessment Systems to further develop and market applications of the HPI in government and industry.

D. The Lexical View of the Big Five: Goldberg

> The most promising of the empirical approaches to systematizing personality differences have been based on one critical assumption: *Those individual differences that are of the most significance in the daily transactions of persons with each other will eventually become encoded in their language.* . . . Moreover, this fundamental axiom has a highly significant corollary: *The more important is an individual difference in human transactions, the more languages will have a term for it.*
>
> *(Goldberg, 1981, pp. 141–142)*

Although there have been "interruptions" in the development of the Big Five model over time, there is one important line of research that has been continuous for 25 years. In the mid-sixties, Norman developed a hierarchical classification of approximately 1600 carefully selected trait-descriptive terms which were grouped into subordinate semantic categories within the broader classes provided by the Big Five model.[4] Norman's (1967) lexicon of trait descriptors and his preliminary Big Five classification system were the starting points for Goldberg's (1977) subsequent efforts to construct a common lexicon for the major characteristics of human personality.

1. Theoretical Orientation

Goldberg's conceptual approach to the study of individual differences, and the methods whereby he studies them, differs considerably from those of the enduring dispositional, dyadic interactional, and competency approaches. As a consequence, his work is not as easily classified with respect to distinctions between trait$_1$ and trait$_2$ or between range and focus of convenience. As is evident from the quotation above, Goldberg (1981) assumes that the most significant or fundamental dimensions of human interaction may be revealed through the study of language. The strongest form of this proposition is that "we should find a *universal order of emergence* of the individual differences encoded into the set of all the world's languages" (p. 142). Rigorous linguistic studies of the structure and function of ordinary trait language usage will identify the significant distinctions involved in person perception. The generalizability of these distinctions across different language groups will confirm (or disconfirm) their universal significance.

Goldberg does not appear to subscribe to any particular theory of traits. The distinction we made earlier in this chapter between the Allportian personality attributes tradition and the Thurstonian personality structure tradition is useful in the present context. Although each tradition may be pursued independently of the

---

[4] This unpublished research is succinctly summarized in John et al. (1988, pp. 184–189).

other, there is a growing consensus that taxonomic research should provide the basis for subsequent test construction procedures.

Most current approaches to inventory construction are based on some sort of classifications within the universe of content of special interest, although these classifications may be considerably less formal than those discussed by John et al. (1984). Costa and McCrae's NEO-PI is based on a review of the literature of earlier scales and inventories, with particular reference to the study of aging. Wiggins' IAS was developed from a theoretically based taxonomy of trait terms that was a direct offshoot of one of Goldberg's earlier taxonomies. Hogan's HPI was based on a review of the earlier Big Five literature from a competency perspective. Goldberg's taxonomies are based upon semantic relations uncovered in the natural language, rather than upon *a priori* distinctions from psychological theory. He hoped that such a semantic taxonomy "would serve to decode the Babel that has been created by researchers using their own labels for constructs, and speaking their own idiosyncratic tongues" (John et al., 1984, p. 4). To that end, his research efforts to date have been directed toward "the development of a compelling taxonomic structure for the personality-descriptive terms in the natural languages" (Goldberg, 1982, p. 203).

Goldberg's focus upon linguistic concepts does not itself restrict the potential range of application of results from his research program. Indeed, if lexical universals are found, and if they are related to fundamental dimensions of human interaction, the model would have an extraordinary degree of cross-cultural generalizability. Similarly, an exclusive focus on ordinary language usage (trait$_1$) is not without implications for the study of generative mechanisms (trait$_2$). In fact, Goldberg's (1970) main point is that linguistic analysis will reveal *which* phenotypical patterns are worthy of explanation and on that point he is in agreement with Allport, Cattell, and others.

2. *Taxonomic Research*

In his quest for a compelling taxonomic structure, Goldberg has strongly emphasized the importance of developing explicit criteria whereby such compellingness may be evaluated objectively. These criteria, in turn, have been the subject of extensive empirical investigations conducted by Goldberg and members of his research team. The issues to which these criteria are directed include those pertaining to: (1) grouping, (2) abstractness, (3) structure, (4) generalizability, and (5) comprehensiveness (John et al., 1984).

Within Goldberg's (1980, 1981, 1982) taxonomies, terms are *grouped* and organized in terms of their culturally shared meaning, as determined by meaning-similarity ratings of native speakers, dictionary definitions, and co-occurence of attributions in other and self-ratings. A distinction is made between internal structure (based on judges' ratings of semantic similarity) and external structure (based on observers' attributions to self and others). In general these two types of structure converge, although there is a tendency for internal structures to be simpler and more schematic than external structures (Peabody & Goldberg, 1989). Finer distinctions within semantic subcategories are achieved by Goldberg's extension of Peabody's (1967) model for separating the evaluative and descriptive components of trait terms.

The issue of *abstractness* concerns the breadth or generality of categories employed in a taxonomy and the manner in which differences in breadth among trait categories may be represented within a hierarchical structure, and this assumption has been closely examined by Goldberg and his co-workers (Goldberg, 1986; Hampson, Goldberg, & John, 1987; Hampson, John, & Goldberg, 1986). Their findings suggest that strict hierarchies are less frequent for personality traits than for categories of natural objects. Moreover, the preferred or "basic level" of personality description appears to differ from that found in other domains (John, Hampson, & Goldberg, 1991).

The issue of *structure* involves the choice between a dimensional and a categorical approach to trait classification. This is the same issue involved in the choice between dimensional and typological person classification and between dimensional and categorical psychiatric classification. Goldberg's preference is clearly for a dimensional approach which does justice to the continua implied by trait terms and their modifiers in most languages. A dimensional approach also permits rigorous quantification and the use of multivariate analysis in the construction and evaluation of taxonomies. In the latter respect, Goldberg's empirical analyses are unsurpassed in the field of trait taxonomic research.

The issue of cross-language *generalizability* of taxonomic structure is at the core of Goldberg's (1981) search for universals in personality lexicons. Although it is much too early to evaluate this aspect of his taxonomies, some very substantial first steps have been taken in this direction. Parallel taxonomies have been developed in the Dutch language (Brokken, 1978; Hofstee, 1976; Tomas, 1977) and in the German language (Angleitner, Ostendorf, & John, 1990; John & Angleitner, 1982). This international cooperative effort has provided rich data for the assessment of generalizability: "The use of identical procedures in three district but closely related languages (English, Dutch, German) produces a multilanguage–multimethod matrix for assessing the appropriateness of competing operations" (John et al., 1984).

The issue of *inclusiveness* has been characterized as "the degree to which the constructs from a particular domain of individual differences can be represented within the structure postulated for this domain" (John et al., 1984, pp. 9–10). An equally important aspect of inclusiveness is the extent to which a truly representative sample of terms from the natural language was ensured by initial search and culling procedures. As we will indicate further on, both of these aspects of inclusiveness appear to have been demonstrated for the Big Five model.

3. *Contributions to the Big Five*

Interest in the five-factor model derived mainly from the claim that five dimensions might provide an adequate preliminary taxonomy for *all* nontrivial personality traits—those whose importance in human interaction has resulted in a descriptive label in the natural language (e.g, dominant), as well as those reflected in the constructs of personality researchers (e.g., Machiavellianism). The demonstrations by Fiske, Tupes and Christal, Norman, Digman, and others of a recurrent five-factor structure among Cattell's 20–35 rating scales were important mainly because Cattell's method of deriving his rating scales appeared to provide a comprehensive sampling of traits. However, psychometric deficiencies of the Cattell rating scales themselves (McCrae & Costa, 1985b, p. 164), shortcomings of his taxonomic research procedures (John et al., 1988, pp. 183–184), and the repeated demonstrations of a five-factor structure on essentially the same set of variables (Waller & Ben-Porath, 1987) did little to advance the claim of comprehensiveness of the five-factor model.

Goldberg's (1980) factor analysis of adjective clusters derived from the Norman (1967) trait taxonomy provided the first persuasive evidence that five large factors provided a comprehensive account of trait description in the English language. Goldberg's results, which were remarkably similar to the earlier studies of the Cattell rating scales, were impressive because: (1) the Norman and Goldberg taxonomies used explicit and reasonably objective inclusion/exclusion criteria which permitted a more scientifically defensible claim to comprehensiveness than did the Cattell taxonomy; (2) Goldberg factored a much larger set of variables (75 and 133 scales) than did earlier researchers using the Cattell rating scales; (3) composites (small clusters of synonyms) were factored rather than single variables; (4) semantic consistency of the clusters was evaluated empirically; and (5) Goldberg demonstrated, in a psychometric tour de force, that the five-factor structure was invariant across varieties of factor extraction and rotation, number of factors extracted (6 through 12), method of variable selection, different samples, and different rating targets (self and peer). In a figure presented in this landmark paper, Goldberg also attempted a conceptual integration of alternative models of personality structure within a "Big Five" framework. Within such a framework, commonalities among semantic (Osgood, Peabody), interpersonal (Leary, Wiggins), lexical (Cattell, Norman), factor analytic (Guilford), temperament (Eysenck, Buss, & Plomin), and psychodynamic (Block) models of personality structure were made apparent. Goldberg offered the Big Five as a first step in "decoding [the] Babel" of personality constructs that had heretofore littered the field.

Goldberg's (1980) study strongly advanced the claim to comprehensiveness of the five-factor model, at least in regard to trait distinctions encoded in the natural language. The inclusiveness of a five-dimensional framework with respect to the constructs of personality researchers was later conclusively demonstrated by Costa and McCrae, as we discussed earlier. Goldberg's (1990, 1992) standard markers of the Big Five factor structure have facilitated both lexical and assessment research on these dimensions.

Most of Goldberg's research is directed toward providing a firmer linguistic basis for future assessment of the Big Five and other dimensions of personality. Current perspectives on the Big Five range from the "basic research" orientation of Goldberg to the "applied" interests of Hogan, and they are held by other investigators whose research interests involve different mixtures of these two orientations. Goldberg's empirical work has served to keep the rest of us honest and, at the same time, to illustrate that basic and applied research can be complementary in advancing the field of personality structure.

III. CONCLUSION

Although characterized by "interruptions," the history of the Big Five dimensions of personality structure suggests a cumulative convergence of thought that constitutes the longest, and quite possibly the most important, chapter to date in the history of personality structure research. It is clearly not the final chapter, however, and the most important developments may still lie ahead. Chief among these developments may be the incorporation of the structural model of the Big Five within an increasingly wide variety of theoretical perspectives (Wiggins, 1996). Perhaps the ultimate contribution of the Big Five model will be the increased opportunities it affords for communication among investigators of different theoretical persuasions in personality, social, and clinical psychology.

ACKNOWLEDGMENT

Preparation of this chapter was supported by Social Sciences and Humanities Research Council of Canada Grant 410-87-1322.

REFERENCES

Adcock, C. J. (1972). Multivariate measurement theory. In R. M. Dreger (Ed.), *Multivariate personality research* (pp. 1–50). Baton Rouge, LA: Claitor's Publishing.

Allport, G. W. (1937). *Personality: A psychological interpretation.* New York: Holt.

Allport, G. W., & Odbert, H. S. (1936). Trait-names: A psycho-lexical study. *Psychological Monographs, 47*(1, Whole No. 211).

American Psychiatric Association. (1980). *Diagnostic and statistical manual of mental disorders* (3rd ed.). Washington, DC: Author.

Angleitner, A., Ostendorf, F., & John, O. P. (1990). Towards a taxonomy of personality descriptors in German: A psycho-lexical study. *European Journal of Personality, 4,* 89–118.

Block, J. (1961). *The Q-sort method in personality assessment and psychiatric research.* Springfield, IL: Charles C. Thomas.

Borgatta, E. F. (1964). The structure of personality characteristics. *Behavioral Science, 9,* 8–17.

Borkenau, P. (1988). The multiple classification of acts and the Big Five factors of personality. *Journal of Research in Personality, 22,* 337–352.

Bouchard, M., Lalonde, F., & Gagnon, M. (1988). The construct validity of assertion: Contributions of four assessment procedures and Norman's personality factors. *Journal of Personality, 56,* 763–783.

Brokken, F. B. (1978). *The language of personality.* Meppel, Holland: Krips.

Buss, A. H., & Plomin, R. (1975). *A temperament theory of personality development.* New York: Wiley (Interscience).

Carson, R. C. (1969). *Interaction concepts of personality.* Chicago: Aldine.

Carson, R. C. (1991). The social-interactional viewpoint. In M. Hersen, A. E. Kazdin, & A. S. Bellack (Eds.), *The clinical psychology handbook* (2nd ed., pp. 185–199). New York: Pergamon Press.

Cattell, R. B. (1943). The description of personality. II. Basic traits resolved into clusters. *Journal of Abnormal and Social Psychology, 38,* 476–507.

Cattell, R. B. (1945). The principal trait clusters for describing personality. *Psychological Bulletin, 42,* 129–169.

Cattell, R. B., Eber, H. W., & Tatsuoka, M. M. (1970). *Handbook for the Sixteen Personality Factor Questionnaire (16 PF).* Champaign, IL: Institute for Personality and Ability Testing.

Cattell, R. B. (1957). *Personality and motivation structure and measurement.* Yonkers-on-Hudson, NY: World Book.

Cattell, R. B. (1973). *Personality and mood by questionnaire.* San Francisco: Jossey-Bass.

Cheek, J. M., & Hogan, R. (1982). Self-concepts, self-presentation, and moral judgments. In J. Suls & A. G. Greenwald (Eds.), *Psychological perspectives on the self* (Vol. 2, pp. 249–273). Hillsdale, NJ: Erlbaum.

Coan, R. W. (1974). *The optimal personality.* New York: Columbia University Press.

Conley, J. J. (1985). Longitudinal stability of personality traits: A multitrait-multimethod-multioccasion analysis. *Journal of Personality and Social Psychology, 49,* 1266–1282.

Costa, P. T., Jr. (Ed.). (1991). Clinical use of the five-factor model [Special Section]. *Journal of Personality Assessment, 57,*(3).

Costa, P. T., Jr., Bush, C. M., Zonderman, A. B., & McCrae, R. R. (1986). Correlations of MMPI factor scales with measures of the five-factor model. *Journal of Personality Assessment, 50,* 640–650.

Costa, P. T., Jr., & McCrae, R. R. (1976). Age differences in personality structure: A cluster analytic approach. *Journal of Gerontology, 31,* 564–560.

Costa, P. T., Jr., & McCrae, R. R. (1978). Objective personality assessment. In M. Storandt, I. C. Siegler, & M. F. Elias (Eds.), *The clinical psychology of aging* (pp. 119–143). New York: Plenum Press.

Costa, P. T., Jr., & McCrae, R. R. (1980). Still stable after all these years: Personality as a key to some issues in adulthood and old age. In P. B. Baltes & O. G. Brim, Jr. (Eds.), *Life span development and behavior* (Vol. 3, pp. 65–102). New York: Academic Press.

Costa, P. T., Jr., & McCrae, R. R. (1985). *The NEO Personality Inventory manual.* Odessa, FL: Psychological Assessment Resources.

Costa, P. T., Jr., & McCrae, R. R. (1986). Major contributions to personality psychology. In S. Modgil & C. Modgil (Eds.), *Hans Eysenck: Consensus and controversy* (pp. 63–72). Barcombe, Lewes Sussex, England: Falmer.

Costa, P. T., Jr., & McCrae, R. R. (1988a). Personality in adulthood: A six-year longitudinal study of self-reports and spouse ratings on the NEO Personality Inventory. *Journal of Personality and Social Psychology, 54,* 853–863.

Costa, P. T., Jr., & McCrae, R. R. (1988b). From catalogue to classication: Murray's needs and the five-factor model. *Journal of Personality and Social Psychology, 55,* 258–265.

Costa, P. T., Jr., & McCrae, R. R. (1989). *The NEO-PI/NEO-FFI manual supplement.* Odessa, FL: Psychological Assessment Resources.

Costa, P. T., Jr., & McCrae, R. R. (1992). *Revised NEO Personality Inventory (NEO PI-R) and NEO Five-Factor Inventory (NEO-FFI). Professional manual.* Odessa, FL: Psychological Assessment Resources.

Costa, P. T., Jr., & McCrae, R. R. (in press). The NEO Personality Inventory (NEO-PI). In S. R. Briggs & J. Cheek (Eds.), *Personality measures* (Vol. 1). Greenwich, CT: JAI Press.

Costa, P. T., Jr., McCrae, R. R., & Dye, D. A. (1991). Facet scales for Agreeableness and Conscientiousness: A revision of the NEO Personality Inventory. *Personality and Individual Differences, 12,* 887–898.

Costa, P. T., Jr., McCrae, R. R., & Holland, J. L. (1984). Personality and vocational interests in an adult sample. *Journal of Applied Psychology, 69,* 390–400.

Costa, P. T., Jr., & Widiger, T. A. (Eds.). (1993). *Personality disorders and the five-factor model of personality.* Washington, DC: American Psychological Association.

Craik, K. H. (1986). Personality research methods: An historical perspective. *Journal of Personality, 54,* 18–51.

Cronbach, L. J., & Meehl, P. E. (1955). Construct validity in psychological tests. *Psychological Bulletin, 52,* 281–302.

Digman, J. M. (1963). Principal dimensions of child personality as seen in teachers' judgments. *Child Development, 34,* 43–60.

Digman, J. M. (1972). The structure of child personality as seen in behavior ratings. In R. M. Dreger (Ed.), *Multivariate personality research* (pp. 587–611). Baton Rouge, LA: Claitor's Publishing.

Digman, J. M. (1979, November). *The five major domains of personality variables: Analysis of questionnaire data in light of the five robust factors emerging from studies of rated characteristics.* Paper presented at the annual meeting of the Society of Multivariate Experimental Psychology, Los Angeles.

Digman, J. M. (1985, November). *The Big Five factors of personality: Some efforts after meaning.* Paper presented at the annual meeting of the society of Multivariate Experimental Psychology, Berkeley, CA.

Digman, J. M. (1989). Five robust trait dimensions: Development, stability, and utility. *Journal of Personality, 57,* 195–214.

Digman, J. M. (1990). Personality structure: Emergence of the five-factor model. *Annual Review of Psychology, 41,* 417–440.

Digman, J. M., & Inouye, J. (1986). Further specification of the five robust factors of personality. *Journal of Personality and Social Psychology, 50,* 116–123.

Digman, J. M., & Takemoto-Chock, N. K. (1981). Factors in the natural language of personality: Reanalysis, comparison, and interpretation of six major studies. *Multivariate Behavioral Research, 16,* 149–170.

Eysenck, H. J. (1947). *Dimensions of personality.* London: Routledge & Kegan Paul.

Eysenck, H. J. (1972). Primaries or second order factors: A critical consideration of Cattell's 16 PF battery. *British Journal of Social and Clinical Psychology, 11,* 265–269.

Eysenck, H. J., & Eysenck, S. B. G. (1964). *The manual of the Eysenck Personality Inventory.* London: University of London Press.

Eysenck, H. J., & Eysenck, S. B. G. (1975). *Manual of the Eysenck Personality Questionnaire.* San Diego, CA: EdITS.

Fiske, D. W. (1949). Consistency of the factorial structures of personality ratings from different sources. *Journal of Abnormal and Social Psychology, 44,* 329–344.

Foa, U. G., & Foa, E. B. (1974). *Societal structures of the mind.* Springfield: Charles C Thomas.

Freedman, M., Leary, T., Ossorio, A. G., & Coffey, H. S. (1951). The interpersonal dimension of personality. *Journal of Personality, 20,* 143–161.

Goffman, E. (1959). *The presentation of self in everyday life.* Garden City, NY: Doubleday Anchor Books.

Goldberg, L. R. (1970). *Why measure that trait? An historical analysis of personality scales and inventories* (ORI Tech. Rep. 10, No. 3). Eugene: Oregon Research Institute.

Goldberg, L. R. (1977, August). *Language and personality: Developing a taxonomy of trait descriptive terms.* Invited address to the Division of Evaluation and Measurement at the annual meeting of the American Psychological Association, San Francisco.

Goldberg, L. R. (1980, May). *Some ruminations about the structure of individual differences: Developing a common lexicon for the major characteristics of human personality.* Paper presented at the annual meeting of the Western Psychological Assocation, Hono-lulu, HI.

Goldberg, L. R. (1981). Language and individual differences: The search for universals in personality lexicons. In L. Wheeler (Ed.), *Review of personality and social psychology* (Vol. 2, pp. 141–165). Beverly Hills, CA: Sage.

Goldberg, L. R. (1982). From Ace to Zombie: Some explorations in the language of personal-ity. In C. D. Spielberger & J. N. Butcher (Eds.), *Advances in personality assessment* (Vol. 1, pp. 203–234). Hillsdale, NJ: Erlbaum.

Goldberg, L. R. (1983, June). *The magic number five, plus or minus two: Some conjectures on the dimensionality of personality descriptors.* Paper presented at a research seminar, Gerontology Research Center, Baltimore.

Goldberg, L. R. (1986). The validity of rating procedures to index the hierarchical level of categories. *Journal of Memory and Language, 25,* 323–347.

Goldberg, L. R. (1990). An alternative "description of personality": The Big-Five factor structure. *Journal of Personality and Social Psychology, 59,* 1216–1229.

Goldberg, L. R. (1992). The development of markers for the Big-Five factor structure. *Psychological Assessment, 4,* 26–42.

Goldberg, L. R. (1993). The structure of phenotypic personality traits. *American Psychologist, 48,* 26–34.

Goldberg, L. R., Norman, W. T., & Schwartz, E. (1972). The comparative validity of question-naire data (16 PF scales) and objective test data (O-A Battery) predicting five peer-rating criteria. *Oregon Research Institute Research Bulletin, 12,* 1–18.

Goldberg, L. R., Norman, W. T., & Schwartz, E. (1980). The comparative validity of question-naire data (16 PF scales) and objective test data (O-A Battery) in predicting five peer-rating critera. *Applied Psychological Measurement, 4,* 183–194.

Guilford, J. P. (1948). Factor analysis in a test development program. *Psychological Review, 55,* 79–94.

Guilford, J. P. (1959). *Personality.* New York: McGraw Hill.

Hampson, S. E., Goldberg, L. R., & John, O. P. (1987). Category breadth and social desirabil-ity values for 573 personality terms. *European Journal of Personality, 1,* 241–258.

Hampson, S. E., John, O. P., & Goldberg, L. R. (1986). Category breath and hierarchical structures in personality: Studies of asymmetries in judgments of trait implications. *Journal of Personality and Social Psychology, 51,* 37–54.

Hathaway, S. R., & McKinley, J. C. (1983). *The Minnesota Multiphasic Personality Inventory manual.* New York: Psychological Corporation.

Hofstee, W. K. D. (1976). *Dutch traits: The first stages of the Groningen taxonomy study of personality descriptive adjectives.* Unpublished manuscript, University of Groningen, The Netherlands.

Hogan, J., Arneson, S., Hogan, R., & Jones, S. (1986). *Development and validation of personnel selection procedures for the job of habilitation therapist.* Tulsa, OK: Hogan Assessment Systems.

Hogan, J., & Hogan, R. (1986). *Hogan Personnel Selection Series manual.* Minneapolis, MN: National Computer Systems.

Hogan, J., Hogan, R., & Briggs, S. (1984). *Development and validation of an employee selection test for combination drivers.* Tulsa, OK: University of Tulsa.

Hogan, J., Peterson, S., Hogan, R., & Jones, S. (1985). *Development and validation of a line-haul driver selection inventory.* Tulsa, OK: University of Tulsa.

Hogan, R. (1983). A socioanalytic theory of personality. In M. M. Page (Ed.), *1982 Nebraska Symposium on Motivation: Personality—Current Theory and Research* (pp. 55–89). Lincoln: University of Nebraska Press.

Hogan, R. (1986). *Hogan Personality Inventory manual.* Minneapolis, MN: National Computer Systems.

Hogan, R., Carpenter, B. N., Briggs, S. R., & Hansson, R. O. (1984). Personnel assessment in personnel selection. In J. J. Bernardin & D. A. Bownas (Eds.), *Personality assessment in organizations* (pp. 21–52). New York: Praeger.

Hogan, R., Jacobson, G., Hogan, J., & Thompson, B. (1987). *Development and validation of a service operations dispatcher selection inventory.* Tulsa, OK: Hogan Assessment Systems.

Hogan, R., & Johnson, J. A. (1981, August). *The structure of personality.* Paper presented at the annual meeting of the American Psychological Association, Los Angeles.

Hogan, R., Jones, W., & Cheek, J. M. (1985). Socioanalytic theory: An alternative to armadillo psychology. In B. R. Schlenker (Ed.), *The self and social life* (pp. 175–198). New York: McGraw-Hill.

Holland, J. L. (1985). *Making vocational choices.* Englewood Cliffs, NJ: Prentice-Hall.

Howarth, E. (1976). Were Cattell's "personality sphere" factors correctly identified in the first instance? *British Journal of Psychology, 67,* 213–230.

Howarth, E., & Browne, J. A. (1971). An item factor analysis of the 16 PF. *Personality: An International Journal, 2,* 117–139.

Jackson, D. N. (1970). A sequential system for personality scale development. In C. D. Spielberger (Ed.), *Current topics in clinical and community psychology* (Vol. 2, pp. 61–96). New York: Academic Press.

Jackson, D. N. (1984). *Personality Research Form manual* (3rd ed.). Fort Huron, MI: Research Psychologists Press.

Jackson, D. N. (1986). The process of responding in personality assessment. In A. Angleitner & J. S. Wiggins (Eds.), *Personality assessment via questionnaires* (pp. 123–142). New York: Springer-Verlag.

John, O. P., & Angleitner, A. (1982). *Explorations into everyday person-descriptions: Some preliminary data* (Research Report of the Trait-Taxonomy Project, No. 1). Department of Psychology, University of Bielefeld, Bielefeld, Germany.

John, O. P., Angleitner, A., & Ostendorf, F. (1988). The lexical approach to personality: A historical reveiw of trait taxonomic research. *European Journal of Personality, 2,* 171–203.

John, O. P., Goldberg, L. R., & Angleitner, A. (1984). Better than the alphabet: Taxonomies of personality-descriptive terms in English, Dutch, and German. In H. C. J. Bonarius, G. L. M. Van Heck, & N. G. Smid (Eds.), *Personality psychology in Europe: Theoretical and empirical developments* (Vol. 1, pp. 83–100). Berwyn, PA: Swets North America.

John, O. P., Hampson, S. E., & Goldberg, L. R. (1991). The basic level in personality-trait hierarchies: Studies of trait use and accessibility in different contexts. *Journal of Personality and Social Psychology, 60,* 348–361.

Johnson, J. A. (1981). The "self-disclosure" and "self-presentation" views of item response dynamics and personality scale validity. *Journal of Personality and Social Psychology, 40,* 761–769.

Johnson, J. A. (1983). Criminality, creativity, and craziness: Structural similarities in three types of nonconformity. In W. S. Laufer & J. M. Day (Eds.), *Personality theory, moral development, and criminal behavior* (pp. 81–105). Lexington, MA: D. C. Heath.

Jung, G. C. (1971). *Psychological types* (H. G. Baynes, Trans., revised by R. F. C. Hull). Princeton, NJ: Princeton University Press. (Original work published 1923)

Karson, S., & O'Dell, J. W. (1974). Is the 16 PF factorially valid? *Journal of Personality Assessment, 38,* 104–114.

Kelly, E. L., & Fiske, D. W. (1951). *The prediction of performance in clinical psychology.* Ann Arbor: University of Michigan Press.

Kelly, G. A. (1955). *The psychology of personal constructs* (Vol. 1). New York: Norton.

Kiesler, D. J. (1983). The 1982 Interpersonal Circle: A taxonomy for complementarity in human transactions. *Psychological Review, 90,* 195–214.

Kiesler, D. J. (1988). *Therapeutic metacommunication: Therapist impact disclosure as feedback in psychotherapy.* Palo Alto, CA: Consulting Psychologist Press.

LaForge, R. (1985). The early development of the Freedman-Leary-Coffey Interpersonal System. *Journal of Personality Assessment, 49,* 613–625.

Leary, T. (1957). *Interpersonal diagnosis of personality.* New York: Ronald Press.

Loevinger, J. (1957). Objective tests as instruments of psychological theory. *Psychological Reports, 3,* 635–694.

Mackinnon, D. W. (1948). *Proposal for an institute for personality assessment and research.* Unpublished memo, University of California, Department of Psychology, Berkeley.

McCrae, R. R. (1982). Consensual validation of personality traits: Evidence from self-reports and ratings. *Journal of Personality and Social Psychology, 43,* 293–303.

McCrae, R. R. (1986). Well-being scales do not measure social desirability. *Journal of Gerontology, 41,* 390–392.

McCrae, R. R. (Ed.). (1992). The five-factor model: Issues and applications [Special issue]. *Journal of Personality, 60*(2).

McCrae, R. R., & Costa, P. T., Jr. (1983). Social desirability scales: More substance than style. *Journal of Consulting and Clinical Psychology, 51,* 882–888.

McCrae, R. R., & Costa, P. T., Jr. (1984). *Emerging lives, enduring dispositions: Personality in adulthood.* Boston: Little, Brown.

McCrae, R. R., & Costa, P. T., Jr. (1985a). Comparison of EPI and Psychoticism scales with measures of the five-factor model of personality. *Personality and Individual Differences, 6,* 587–597.

McCrae, R. R., & Costa, P. T., Jr. (1985b). Openness to experience. In R. Hogan & W. H. Jones (Eds.), *Perspectives in personality* (Vol. 1, pp. 145–172). Greenwich, CT: JAI Press.

McCrae, R. R., & Costa, P. T., Jr. (1985c). Updating Norman's "adequate taxonomy": Intelligence and personality dimensions in natural language and in questionnaires. *Journal of Personality and Social Psychology, 49,* 710–721.

McCrae, R. R., & Costa, P. T., Jr. (1987). Validation of the five-factor model of personality across instruments and observers. *Journal of Personality and Social Psychology, 52,* 81–90.

McCrae, R. R., & Costa, P. T., Jr. (1989a). Reinterpreting the Myers-Briggs Type Indicator from the perspective of the five-factor model of personality. *Journal of Personality, 57*, 17–40.

McCrae, R. R., & Costa, P. T., Jr. (1989b). The structure of interpersonal traits: Wiggins's circumplex and the five-factor model. *Journal of Personality and Social Psychology, 56*, 586–595.

McCrae, R. R., & Costa, P. T., Jr. (1990). *Personality in adulthood: Emerging lives enduring dispositions.* New York: Guilford Press.

McCrae, R. R., Costa, P. T., Jr., & Busch, C. M. (1986). Evaluating comprehensiveness in personality systems: The California Q-Set and the five-factor model. *Journal of Personality, 54*, 430–446.

Meehl, P. E. (1945). The dynamics of "structured" personality tests. *Journal of Clinical Psychology, 1*, 296–303.

Mischel, W. (1968). *Personality and assessment.* New York: Wiley.

Murray, H. A. (1938). *Explorations in personality.* New York: Oxford University Press.

Myers, I. B., & McCaulley, M. H. (1985). *Manual: A guide to the development and use of the Myers-Briggs Type Indicator.* Palo Alto, CA: Consulting Psychologists Press.

Nicholson, R. A., & Hogan, R. (1990). The construct validity of social desirability. *American Psychologist, 45*, 290–292.

Norman, W. T. (1963). Toward an adequate taxonomy of personality attributes: Replicated factor structure in peer nomination personality ratings. *Journal of Abnormal and Social Psychology, 66*, 574–583.

Norman, W. T. (1967). *2800 personality trait descriptors: Normative operating characteristics for a university population.* Ann Arbor: University of Michigan, Department of Psychology,

Peabody, D. (1967). Trait inferences: Evaluation and descriptive aspects. *Journal of Personality and Social Psychology Monograph, 7*(4, Whole No. 644).

Peabody, D., & Goldberg, L. R. (1989). Some determinants of factor structures from personality trait-descriptors. *Journal of Personality and Social Psychology, 57*, 552–567.

Raza, S., Metz, D., Dyer, P., Coan, T., & Hogan, J. (1986). *Development and validation of personnel selection procedures for hospital service personnel.* Tulsa, OK: University of Tulsa.

Sells, S. B., Demaree, R. G., & Will, D. P., Jr. (1970). Dimensions of personality: I. Conjoint factor structure of Guilford and Cattell trait markers. *Multivariate Behavioral Research, 5*, 391–422.

Steiger, J. H. (1979). Factor indeterminancy in the 1930's and 1970's: Some interesting parallels. *Psychometrika, 44*, 157–167.

Sullivan, H. S. (1953). *The interpersonal theory of psychiatry.* New York: Norton.

Thurstone, L. L. (1934). The vectors of mind. *Psychological Review, 41*, 1–32.

Tomas, A. (1977). *A lexicographical study of the personality domain* (Heymans Bulletins No. HB-77-296-EX). Groningen, The Netherlands: Psychologische Instituten R. U. Groningen.

Trapnell, P. D., & Wiggins, J. S. (1990). Extension of the Interpersonal Adjective Scales to include the Big Five dimensions of personality. *Journal of Personality and Social Psychology, 59*, 781–790.

Tupes, E. C., & Christal, R. E. (1958). Stability of personality trait rating factors obtained under diverse conditions. *USAF WADC Technical Note,* No. 58–61.

Tupes, E. C., & Christal, R. E. (1961). Recurrent personality factors based on trait ratings. *USAF ASD Technical Report,* No. 61–97.

Tupes, E. C., & Kaplan, M. N. (1961). Relationships between personality traits, physical proficiency, and cadet effectiveness reports of Air Force Academy Cadets. *USAF AFD Technical Report,* No. 61–53.

Waller, N. G., & Ben-Porath, Y. S. (1987). Is it time for clinical psychology to embrace the five-factor model of personality? *American Psychologist, 42,* 887–889.

Wiggins, J. S. (1982). Circumplex models of interpersonal behavior in clinical psychology. In P. C. Kendall & J. N. Butcher (Eds.), *Handbook of research methods in clinical psychology* (pp. 183–221). New York: Wiley.

Wiggins, J. S. (1984). Cattell's system from the perspective of mainstream personality theory. *Multivariate Behavioral Research, 19,* 176–190.

Wiggins, J. S. (1985). Symposium: Interpersonal circumplex models: 1948–1983 [Commentary]. *Journal of Personality Assessment, 49,* 626–631.

Wiggins, J. S. (1991). Agency and communion as conceptual coordinates for the understanding and measurement of interpersonal behavior. In W. Grove & D. Cicchetti (Eds.), *Thinking clearly about psychology: Essays in honor of Paul E. Meehl* (Vol. 2, pp. 89–113). Minneapolis: University of Minnesota Press.

Wiggins, J. S. (1995). *Interpersonal Adjective Scales: Professional Manual.* Odessa, FL: Psychological Assessment Resources.

Wiggins, J. S. (1996a). An informal history of the interpersonal circumplex tradition. *Journal of Personality Assessment, 66,* 217–233.

Wiggins, J. S. (Ed.). (1996b). *The five-factor model of personality: Theoretical perspectives.* New York: Guilford Press.

Wiggins, J. S., Phillips, N., & Trapnell, P. (1989). Circular reasoning about interpersonal behavior: Evidence concerning some untested assumptions underlying diagnostic classification. *Journal of Personality and Social Psychology, 56,* 296–305.

Wiggins, J. S., & Pincus, A. L. (1989). Conceptions of personality disorders and dimensions of personality. *Psychological Assessment: A Journal of Consulting and Clinical Psychology, 1,* 305–316.

Wiggins, J. S., & Pincus, A. L. (1992). Personality structure and assessment. *Annual Review of Psychology, 43,* 417–440.

Wiggins, J. S., & Trapnell, P. D. (1996). A dyadic-interactional perspective on the five-factor model. In J. S. Wiggins (Ed.). *The five-factor model of personality: Theoretical perspectives* (pp. 88–162). New York: Guilford Press.

CHAPTER 29

EXTRAVERSION AND ITS POSITIVE EMOTIONAL CORE

DAVID WATSON AND LEE ANNA CLARK
THE UNIVERSITY OF IOWA

I. INTRODUCTION

The extravert is a very familiar character. To most people, the term "extravert" quickly conjures up an image of one who seeks out and enjoys the companionship of others—one who is poised, confident, and facile in social situations. Other descriptors of the extravert that are perhaps less central, but nevertheless commonly recognized, include bold, assertive, lively, energetic, enthusiastic, and optimistic. Conversely, their characterological opposites—introverts—can be broadly sketched as more quiet and reserved, more socially aloof, and less interpersonally effective.

Introversion–Extraversion (which we will simply call "Extraversion") also is an extremely important concept in trait psychology. For example, an Extraversion factor can be identified in virtually every widely used multidimensional personality inventory, including the Multidimensional Personality Questionnaire (MPQ; Tellegen, 1982, 1985), the Personality Research Form (PRF; Jackson, 1984), and the Sixteen Personality Factor Questionnaire (16PF; Cattell, Eber, & Tatsuoka, 1980). Moreover, Extraversion factors have been isolated in many instruments not specifically designed to assess personality traits, including the California Psychological Inventory (CPI; Gough, 1987) and the Minnesota Multiphasic Personality Inventory (MMPI; Hathaway & McKinley, 1943; see Costa, Busch, Zonderman, & McCrae, 1986). Similarly, a general Extraversion dimension has been identified in an inventory designed to measure traits and behaviors relevant to personality disorder (Clark, 1993; Clark, Vorhies, & McEwen, 1994).

Furthermore, Extraversion has been included as a higher-order factor in every major taxonomic scheme of personality traits that has been developed during the past 50 years. For example, extensive interest has recently focused on a five-factor model of personality that invariably includes Extraversion as one of its constituent dimensions (e.g., Digman, 1990; Goldberg, 1993; McCrae & Costa, 1985, 1987). Other theorists (e.g., Eysenck & Eysenck, 1975; Tellegen, 1985) have instead proposed three-factor structures, but nevertheless retain Extraversion (or a conceptually comparable dimension) in their models. Thus, although we still lack a consensual taxonomy of personality traits, every model includes Extraversion as one of its constituent factors.

In the following sections we explore the nature, components, and correlates of Extraversion. Before doing so, however, we need to clarify two important points. First, this concept is often viewed typologically, with "extraverts" and "introverts" defining discrete and self-limited categories. However, research consistently shows that Extraversion is a *dimension* of individual differences. That is, although extreme cases can be found at both ends of the factor, scores can occur anywhere along a broad continuum. Moreover, most individuals obtain intermediate scores on the trait, and thus are not clearly identifiable as either introverts or extraverts.

Second, as noted earlier, extraversion consistently emerges as a higher-order disposition in taxonomic schemes of personality traits. Higher-order traits represent the broadest, most general level in the hierarchy of dispositions: this is the level at which personologists attempt to explain individual differences with the fewest possible, and most broadly applicable, dimensions. Extraversion is, therefore, a very general dimension that is itself composed of more specific, primary traits; its existence is inferred from empirically observed covariations among these primary traits. We will attempt to identify the most important components of this trait, but our focus will ultimately be on the higher-order disposition itself.

II. EARLY CONCEPTIONS OF EXTRAVERSION

A. Inconsistent and Contradictory Aspects of the Trait

Although the various theoretical conceptualizations of Extraversion all share some prominent component traits (e.g., talkativeness, sociability), a closer inspection of these models reveals some inconsistent and even contradictory features. For example, the description offered by Costa and McCrae (1985) closely resembles the popular conception of the extravert: "In addition to liking people and preferring large groups and gatherings, extraverts are also assertive, active, and talkative; they like excitement and stimulation, and tend to be cheerful in disposition. They are upbeat, energetic, and optimistic" (p. 10).

In contrast, consider the portrait offered by Eysenck and Eysenck (1975):

> The typical extravert is sociable, likes parties, has many friends, needs to have people to talk to, and does not like reading or studying by himself. He craves

excitement, takes chances, often sticks his neck out, acts on the spur of the moment, and is generally an impulsive individual. He is fond of practical jokes, always has a ready answer, and generally likes change; he is carefree, easy-going, optimistic, and likes to 'laugh and be merry' . . . . [A]ltogether his feelings are not kept under tight control, and he is not always a reliable person. (p. 5)

These two descriptions are entirely consistent in several important ways. Both emphasize that extraverts are sociable, talkative, cheerful, and optimistic, and that they enjoy change and excitement in their lives. Beyond that, however, there are some sharp divergences. Most notably, Eysenck and Eysenck—but not Costa and McCrae—argue that extraverts are impulsive, risk-taking, and somewhat unreliable. Generally speaking, the Eysenckian extravert seems more poorly socialized than does the individual described by Costa and McCrae.

An inspection of other relevant conceptualizations reveals even greater discrepancies. For example, both Hogan (1983) and Tellegen (1985) have emphasized that extraverts, in addition to being socially facile and influential, are ambitious, hardworking, and achievement-oriented individuals. Thus, despite their shared characteristics, these individuals ultimately seem somewhat removed from the unreliable, impulsive, and fun-loving person described by the Eysencks.

B. Origin of the Extraversion Concept

Why have these discrepancies emerged? In large part, they reflect how the Extraversion construct has evolved over time, a topic we consider shortly. They also reflect, however, the multifaceted nature of the original theoretical notion itself. The concept of introversion–extraversion was introduced by Jung (1921), although William James (1907) and others had earlier proposed somewhat similar typological schemes (see J. P. Guilford & Braly, 1930, for a review of these early models). In Jung's theory, introversion and extraversion are not personality traits per se, but instead represent differing attitudes or orientations toward the world. Introverts are oriented toward internal, subjective experience, focusing on their own thoughts, feelings, and perceptions. Consequently, they tend to be introspective, ruminative, and self-preoccupied, and appear aloof, quiet, unsociable, and reserved to others. In contrast, extraverts are more externally and objectively focused; they are more concerned with other people and the world around them, and oriented more toward action than thought. They are seen as active, outgoing, and sociable by others.

In modern dispositional terms this Jungian concept clearly is multidimensional, combining several essentially unrelated traits. As expected, extraverts are more sociable, but are also described as being more active and impulsive, less dysphoric, and as less introspective and self-preoccupied than introverts. This multidimensionality was quickly recognized by investigators seeking to measure the concept empirically (J. P. Guilford & Braly, 1930). Soon afterward, J. P. Guilford and Guilford (1934, 1936)—using the then-new technique of factor analysis—demonstrated that existing introversion–extraversion items could be factored into several distinct traits, including sociability, neuroticism, introspectiveness, impulsivity, and masculinity–femininity.

C. Guilford's Model

In succeeding studies, J. P. Guilford and his colleagues concentrated on devising scales to assess each of these specific traits; these efforts ultimately led to creation of the Guilford–Zimmerman Temperament Survey (GZTS; J. P. Guilford & Zimmerman, 1949; see also J. S. Guilford, Zimmerman, Guilford, 1976). The most important finding to emerge from these studies was that the sociability, negative emotionality, and introspectiveness/impulsivity items remained separate, even at the higher-order factor level. Thus, Guilford identified three higher-order factors in these data, two of which are especially relevant here. The first, which he calls Social Activity, is composed of three primary traits: Ascendance (dominance versus submissiveness), Sociability (social interest versus aloofness), and General Activity (energy versus sluggishness). This higher-order dimension clearly can be identified as the Extraversion construct that is the focus of our discussion.

Ironically, Guilford applied the term "Introversion–Extraversion" to his higher-order factor composed of the Rhathymia (restraint versus impulsivity) and Thoughtfulness (reflective versus unreflective) scales. Thus, Guilford viewed the impulsive and unreflective aspects of the original Jungian concept as the core of Extraversion. Ultimately, however, the factor names are less important than the finding that the sociability/energy and impulsivity/unreflective aspects of the Jungian concept ultimately define separate factors, even at the broadest level.

D. Eysenck's Model

It is in this context that we must view the evolution of H. J. Eysenck's model of Extraversion. Consistent with Guilford's interpretation of the construct's core, Eysenck used the Rhathymia scale as the starting point for the construction of his original Extraversion scale, which was contained in the Maudsley Personality Inventory (MPI; Eysenck, 1959). His analyses of 261 Guilford items ultimately led him to construct a scale that was largely composed of questions from Rhathymia and from the GZTS Sociability scale (see Eysenck & Eysenck, 1969; J. P. Guilford, 1975). This item composition was essentially retained in a later version of the scale, which was included in the Eysenck Personality Inventory (EPI; Eysenck & Eysenck, 1968).

Thus, Eysenck's Extraversion originally contained strong elements of both Sociability and Impulsivity. However, Guilford's finding that these components are largely independent of one another has since been replicated by several other investigators, and it is now generally acknowledged that Impulsivity should be split off from Sociability, Energy, and other aspects of Extraversion (e.g., J. P. Guilford, 1975; Zuckerman, Kuhlman, & Camac, 1988). Eysenck observed similar patterns in his own data, and so largely removed the Impulsivity component from his latest

Extraversion scale, which is contained in the Eysenck Personality Questionnaire (EPQ; Eysenck & Eysenck, 1975). Data to be presented subsequently, however, indicate that the EPQ Extraversion scale still taps impulsivity-related qualities to a greater extent than do other measures of the construct.

Unlike most of the other theoreticians in this area, Eysenck always has been primarily interested in the higher-order factor itself, and has never articulated a systematic structure at the primary-trait level. More recently, however, he has suggested that Extraversion is composed of nine primary traits, several of which clearly overlap with Guilford's (i.e., Sociable, Dominant, Assertive, Surgent, Active, Lively), but others of which continue to shade toward Impulsivity (i.e., Sensation-Seeking, Venturesome, Carefree) (Eysenck & Eysenck, 1985).

E. Cattell's Model

Cattell worked more or less independently from Guilford and Eysenck, but ultimately identified a very similar higher-order Extraversion dimension. This line of research originated in Allport and Odbert's (1936) effort to compile an exhaustive list of trait-related terms in the English language. Allport and Odbert eventually settled on a list of 4,504 terms that clearly represented trait dispositions. Cattell (1945, 1946) reduced this set to a more manageable pool of 35 clusters through rational content sortings and cluster analyses. Subsequent factorial studies led Cattell to construct his set of 16 primary traits (see Cattell et al., 1980).

Like Guilford, Cattell always was more interested in these primary traits than in higher-order dimensions. However, factor analyses of the 16PF consistently confirm the existence of a higher-order Extraversion factor that is largely defined by five primary traits (Cattell et al., 1980): A (warmhearted, easygoing versus reserved, detached), E (dominant, ascendant versus submissive), F (enthusiastic versus taciturn), H (bold, adventurous versus shy, timid), and Q_2 (socially enmeshed versus autonomous).

F. Summary and Integration of the Early Models

The higher-order dimensions identified by Guilford, Eysenck, and Cattell are strongly related to one another (e.g., Eysenck & Eysenck, 1969) and have several component traits in common. The most consistently recurring themes are those of Ascendance and Sociability—in all of these views, extraverts are gregarious, friendly, dominant, and socially facile. They enjoy being with other people and are confident and comfortable when interacting with them. Thus, all of these views strongly emphasize the social/interpersonal aspects of the construct.

Other common features may also be noted, however. For example, both Eysenck and Cattell view extraverts as bold and adventurous individuals who seek excitement and stimulation in their lives; this sensation-seeking further involves risk-taking in Eysenck's model. Furthermore, Guilford and Eysenck both argue that extraverts are active, lively, and full of energy. Finally, both Eysenck and

Cattell include a substantial affective component in their models—they describe extraverts as cheerful, optimistic, and enthusiastic. As we will see, these energy and affective components have become even more prominent in recent formulations.

III. CONTEMPORARY CONCEPTIONS OF EXTRAVERSION

A. Extraversion in Relation to Positive and Negative Affect

More recent formulations have retained many of the traditional primary traits, including a continued recognition of the social/interpersonal component. There have also been some significant changes, however, the most notable of these being an increased focus on the positive emotional aspect of the dimension.

To understand these changes, we must briefly examine the structure of subjective emotional experience. Studies have repeatedly demonstrated that self-rated mood is characterized by two dominant dimensions that reflect the crucial role of valence in affective experience (Mayer & Gaschke, 1988; Watson, 1988b; Watson & Tellegen, 1985). Specifically, negatively valenced mood terms strongly co-occur in individuals, and so combine to form a broad factor called "Negative Affect" (NA); similarly, positively valenced mood states also tend to co-occur, and so jointly compose the higher-order dimension of "Positive Affect" (PA). Both of these dimensions can be assessed either as a state (i.e., transient mood fluctuations) or as a trait (i.e., stable individual differences in general affective level).

NA represents one's level of subjective distress and dissatisfaction. High NA reflects a wide range of negative mood states, including fear, anger, sadness, guilt, contempt, disgust, and self-dissatisfaction. In contrast, PA represents a state of pleasurable arousal, and reflects feelings of being actively and effectively engaged. High PA is composed of terms reflecting enthusiasm (e.g., *excited, enthusiastic*), joy (*happy, delighted*), energy (*active, energetic*), mental alertness (*attentive, interested*), and confidence (*strong, confident*). Terms suggesting warm and affiliative feelings (e.g., *friendly, sociable, warmhearted*) are also strong markers of the PA factor, a point we consider in a later section. It is important to note, however, that these affiliative terms have been excluded from most PA measures, including all of our own scales. Thus, significant correlations between PA and various measures of social/interpersonal tendencies (e.g., social activity, Extraversion) cannot be explained by overlapping content.

Measures of NA and PA are largely independent, typically correlating from −.10 to −.25 with one another (e.g., Watson, 1988b). Moreover, they tend to have distinctly different correlates (e.g., Clark & Watson, 1988; Watson, 1988a). For our purposes, the most important findings concern their differential relations with personality: state PA scales are significantly correlated with Extraversion, but not with Neuroticism, whereas state NA scales are substantially correlated with Neuroticism, but are generally unrelated to Extraversion (Costa & McCrae, 1980, 1984; Emmons & Diener, 1986; Tellegen, 1985; Watson & Clark, 1984).

B. Costa and McCrae's Model

These findings have led researchers to explore more fully the relation between PA and Extraversion, and consequently to augment the affective component of the Extraversion construct. Costa and McCrae (1980, 1984) were the first investigators to explore these relations systematically, and they subsequently incorporated these findings into their model of Extraversion (Costa & McCrae, 1985, 1992). As outlined by Costa and McCrae (1985, 1992), Extraversion is composed of six primary traits or facets, several of which are very similar to those of the earlier models (Assertiveness, Excitement-Seeking, and Activity). One modest change is that Sociability is split into two strongly correlated facets, Gregariousness (desiring the company of others) and Warmth (feelings of affection toward others).

The most significant addition, however, is the inclusion of a facet called ''Positive Emotions.'' This facet reflects stable individual differences in the tendency to experience positive emotions; not surprisingly, it is significantly correlated with state PA scales. It is noteworthy, however, that all of the other Extraversion facets (especially Warmth, Activity, and Assertiveness) are also related to state PA, at least to some extent (Costa & McCrae, 1984). Moreover, our own data indicate that Positive Emotions does not necessarily have the strongest correlations with trait PA measures; in fact, we have found that the Activity, Assertiveness, and Positive Emotions facets all correlate similarly with trait PA.

C. Tellegen's View: Positive Emotionality

Although Costa and McCrae assign a more prominent role to individual differences in PA, they still view sociability—the preference for, and enjoyment of, others' company—as the core of the dimension (McCrae & Costa, 1987). Tellegen (1985; Tellegen et al., 1988), however, has proposed a more radical reformulation of the construct. In fact, individual differences in PA play such a prominent role in Tellegen's conceptualization that he has proposed that the higher-order disposition be renamed ''Positive Emotionality.''

In Tellegen's model, Positive Emotionality is divided into four primary facets. One component, Well-Being, represents the individual differences in PA that define the core of the construct. Two other facets reflect the interpersonal tendencies that are more traditionally associated with Extraversion: Social Potency is a measure of ascendance or dominance, whereas Social Closeness assesses sociability or affiliation. Tellegen's most interesting primary trait is Achievement: high scorers report that they are ambitious, perfectionistic, and willing to work long hours in pursuit of achievement-related goals. Thus, Tellegen's model also links this general trait with effectance motivation (White, 1959), feelings of competence and mastery (e.g., Bandura, 1977), and a style of effective engagement with one's environment. As noted earlier, this view of the construct emphasizes its adaptive, productive, and socialized qualities much more than the impulsive, reckless, and sensation-seeking individual of the old Eysenckian model.

D. Hogan's Bipartite Scheme

Tellegen et al. (1988) also note that Positive Emotionality splits into two subfactors in some of their analyses. One subfactor, which they call "Agentic Positive Emotionality," is best defined by the Achievement scale, and essentially reflects the dominance/competence/mastery aspects of the trait. The second subfactor is called "Communal Positive Emotionality," and is best defined by Social Closeness; this represents the warm, affiliative side of the disposition.

Interestingly, this bipartite scheme closely parallels the model proposed by Hogan (1983). Hogan argues that Extraversion ultimately should be divided into two distinct and separate dispositions, which he calls "Surgency" and "Sociability." Surgency primarily revolves around issues of status. Highly surgent individuals are ambitious, tenacious, and influential; they are leaders, and set high behavioral standards for themselves in work and other activities. In contrast, Sociability is centered around issues of popularity. Sociable individuals are friendly, expressive, and exhibitionistic, and enjoy being around other people.

It is noteworthy that these bipartite schemes produce factors that resemble the major dimensions of interpersonal theory. Wiggins (1979) has demonstrated that two dimensions consistently emerge in studies of interpersonal traits. One dimension can be called Status or Dominance, and is defined by *assertive* and *self-confident* at one end, versus *submissive* and *self-doubting* at the other; this can be identified with Surgency (Hogan) and Agentic Positive Emotionality (Tellegen). The second dimension can be termed Love or Affiliation. *Warm* and *agreeable* define one pole, with *cold* and *quarrelsome* at the other; this is obviously similar to Sociability (Hogan) and Communal Positive Emotionality (Tellegen).

These bipartite schemes have much merit and certainly warrant greater attention in the future. Ultimately, it may prove advantageous to decompose Extraversion into these two components. As we will see, however, although these subfactors are in some sense separate (i.e., they contain some unrelated elements), they also share some common features (most notably, the experience of positive affect) and ultimately recombine at a higher-order level. Thus, we will continue to treat Extraversion as a single, higher-order construct.

IV. AN INTEGRATIVE MODEL OF THE CONSTRUCT

A. A Schematic Model

Taken together, these models cover a very wide substantive range, and it is easy to lose a coherent sense of the underlying construct itself. Therefore, in order to summarize and clarify these views, we present an integrative model of the construct in Figure 1. This model is integrative in the sense that it captures the entire range of content that can be subsumed under this higher-order dimension; that is, it contains all of the major constituent elements that are included in all of the current formulations. We also should emphasize, however, that this model represents our

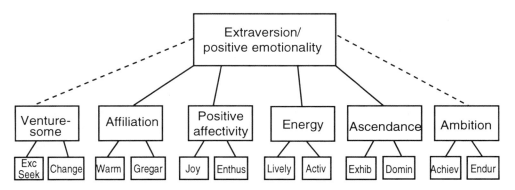

FIGURE 1 A schematic model of Extraversion showing its component traits and subtraits (Exc Seek, Excitement-Seeking; Warm, Warmth; Gregar, Gregariousness; Enthus, Enthusiasm; Lively, Liveliness; Activ, Activity; Exhib, Exhibitionism; Domin, Dominance; Achiev, Achievement; Endur, Endurance). See text for more details.

own understanding of the current literature, and does not necessarily reflect a consensual view of the construct.

Figure 1 schematically depicts three levels of the construct. At the highest level is the higher-order dimension itself. Here we have proposed two alternative labels. First, for purposes of historical continuity, we have retained the traditional name of "Extraversion." Second, we also have included Tellegen's proposed alternative, "Positive Emotionality," because it emphasizes the positive affective component that, in our view, forms the core of the construct. We explore this issue in more detail shortly.

At the next level, the higher-order dimension splits into six component traits. Four of these facets—Affiliation, Ascendance, Positive Affectivity, and Energy—are connected to the higher-order dimension by solid lines, indicating that they are viewed as central features of the construct. The remaining two components—Venturesomeness and Ambition—are conceived as less central, and so are connected by dotted lines. Consistent with our earlier discussion, Impulsivity is not included as a component trait of this dimension, although Venturesomeness contains some related qualities (Zuckerman et al., 1988).

The peripheral assignment of Venturesomeness and Ambition reflects several considerations. First, these components are completely absent from one or more of the major conceptualizations of the construct. Specifically, although Ambition plays an important role in Tellegen's and Hogan's models, it is omitted from all of the others. Similarly, Venturesomeness is included in the views of Eysenck, Costa and McCrae, and Cattell, but is absent from those of Hogan and Tellegen. Second, these traits are inconsistently related to the other components. For example, Venturesomeness and Ambition are essentially unrelated to each other, and neither is strongly or consistently correlated with Affiliation (e.g., Costa & McCrae, 1988). Third, both traits have been shown to load strongly on higher-order dimensions other than Extraversion. Zuckerman et al. (1988), for example, found that Excitement-Seeking scales loaded primarily on a higher-order Impulsivity/Sensation-Seeking dimension, although they tended to load secondarily on Extraversion as well. Similarly, Costa and McCrae (1988, 1992) have argued that Ambition actually is a component of Conscientiousness, rather than Extraversion.

At the lowest level of Figure 1, each of these six components is itself divided into two subtraits. It is important to emphasize that these subtraits almost inevitably are strongly correlated with one another. For example, Warmth and Gregariousness scales are typically highly correlated (e.g., Costa & McCrae, 1984), as are measures of Achievement and Endurance (e.g., Jackson, 1984). We have nevertheless listed these subtraits separately in order (1) to capture the entire range of content subsumed under each component, and (2) to suggest the types of scales that assess them.

Moreover, these subtraits sometimes show rather different associations with the other primary traits. For example, Costa and McCrae (1988) report a .40 correlation between NEO Gregariousness and PRF Exhibition, suggesting a moderate relation between Affiliation and Ascendance. However, they also report a .10 correlation between NEO Warmth and PRF Dominance, suggesting that these components are essentially unrelated. Furthermore, in Hogan's (1983) bipartite model the Dominance subtrait of Ascendance apparently combines with Ambition to form Surgency, whereas the Exhibitionism subtrait joins with Affiliation to comprise Sociability. These findings indicate the desirability of keeping these subtraits separate, at least provisionally.

B. Descriptions of the Component Traits

In order to clarify the range of content subsumed under this higher-order construct, we will briefly describe each of the component traits.

1. Venturesomeness reflects individual differences in boldness and adventurousness. High scorers desire change and variety in their lives, and become bored or dissatisfied when it is absent (Change). They also enjoy exciting activities and seek out intense, stimulating environments (Excitement-Seeking).

2. Affiliation represents the sociability component that has always been prominent in Extraversion models. Highly affiliative persons have warm and friendly feelings toward others, and place a high value on close interpersonal relationships (Warmth). Moreover, such individuals enjoy the company of others, and are strongly motivated toward frequent social interaction (Gregariousness).

3. Positive Affectivity represents stable individual differences in the frequency and intensity of positive mood states. High scorers frequently feel happy, cheerful, and optimistic about their future (Joy). Moreover, they find it easy to become excited and enthusiastic about events or activities in their lives (Enthusiasm).

4. The Energy component assesses individual differences in vigor. High scorers report having a great deal of energy, and that they move at a quick, rapid pace

(Liveliness). These individuals also have many interests and hobbies, and feel that they lead full, busy, and interesting lives (Activity).

5. Ascendance reflects differences in assertiveness and social visibility. High scorers are dramatic and entertaining, and like to be the center of attention in social situations (Exhibitionism). They are also forceful and decisive; they are good, strong leaders, and enjoy controlling and/or influencing others (Dominance).

6. Ambition reflects differences in success-, mastery-, or competence-related behaviors. Highly ambitious individuals enjoy meeting challenges and mastering difficult tasks; they prize excellence and maintain high standards for their own behavior (Achievement). They are also willing to work long hours in pursuit of their goals, and persevere even when they are tired or frustrated (Endurance).

V. EXPLORING THE CORE OF EXTRAVERSION

A. The Central Role of Positive Emotional Experience

Figure 1 demonstrates that the Extraversion construct subsumes a very wide range of psychological characteristics. What common factor do these diverse personality attributes share that leads them to be related at a higher-order level? Our reading of the literature suggests a model similar to that proposed by Tellegen (1985; Tellegen et al., 1988). That is, we believe that individual differences in positive emotionality form the core of the dimension, the unifying "glue" that holds these various aspects together. We should note, however, that in terms of Figure 1, we view this core as including both purely affective (i.e., Positive Affectivity) and Energy components. Although Positive Affectivity and Energy components can be distinguished conceptually (as in Figure 1) they tend to be strongly correlated empirically (see, for example, Table II). Moreover, as noted earlier, studies repeatedly have demonstrated that terms reflecting Joy (e.g., *happy, cheerful*), Enthusiasm (e.g., *excited, interested*), and Energy (e.g., *energetic, active*) are all strong markers of the PA factor.

To illustrate the central role of positive emotionality in the higher-order construct, Table I presents data collected from a mixed sample of 234 psychiatric patients. Shown are correlations among scales from Tellegen's MPQ that assess four of the components shown in Figure 1: the abbreviated, 11-item version of the Well-Being (WB) Scale (see Tellegen, 1982) is a marker of the Positive Affectivity component; Social Potency (SP) assesses Ascendance; Social Closeness (SC) measures Affiliation; and Achievement (Ach) taps Ambition.

Table I demonstrates that Positive Affectivity is significantly correlated with each of the other three Extraversion components. Moreover, the Ascendance, Affiliation, and Ambition scales all tend to be more highly related to trait PA than they are to each other: They have a mean correlation of .32 with Positive Affectivity (range = .22 to .37), but correlate, on average, only .16 among themselves (range = .00 to .31). For example, consistent with previous research (e.g., Hogan,

TABLE I
Correlations among Extraversion Component
Scales in a Mixed Psychiatric Patient Sample

Extraversion component	1	2	3
1. Positive Affectivity	—		
2. Ascendance	.36**	—	
3. Ambition	.22**	.31**	—
4. Affiliation	.37**	.17**	.00

Note. $N = 234$. Positive Affectivity = MPQ Well-
Being (abbreviated); Ascendance = MPQ Social
Potency; Ambition = MPQ Achievement; Affiliation = MPQ Social Closeness. See text for more details.
* $p < .05$, two-tailed.
** $p < .01$, two-tailed.

1983; Wiggins, 1979), Ascendance and Affiliation are significantly but only weakly related to one another ($r = .17$); both traits, however, are more strongly related to trait PA (for Ascendance, $r = .36$; for Affiliation, $r = .37$).

These data are consistent with the position that positive emotional experience forms the core of the higher-order construct. They further imply that removing this common affective element would lower (and perhaps eliminate) the correlations among the other component traits. To test this, we computed partial correlation coefficients, controlling for scores on Positive Affectivity. These results partially supported our view: the partial correlation between Ascendance and Ambition remained significant ($r = .26, p < .01$), but that between Ascendance and Affiliation dropped to near zero ($r = .05$, n.s.).

Table II presents data collected from 254 Southern Methodist University undergraduates. Again, the MPQ SP, SC, and Ach scales were used to assess Ascendance, Affiliation, and Ambition, respectively. In addition, three measures of Positive Affectivity/Energy were administered. First, subjects completed a trait form of the PA scale from the Positive and Negative Affect Schedule (PANAS; Watson, Clark, & Tellegen, 1988). The PANAS PA scale consists of 10 descriptors (*active, alert, attentive, determined, enthusiastic, excited, inspired, interested, proud, strong*) that have been shown to be excellent markers of high PA. In this sample, subjects rated the extent to which they generally experienced each of these affects on a five-point scale. Watson, Clark, and Tellegen (1988) present extensive evidence demonstrating that the PANAS PA scale is a highly reliable and valid measure of the underlying PA dimension.

We created two other measures from a large pool of true–false items that were used in the development of the General Temperament Survey, an inventory

TABLE II

Correlations among Extraversion Components
in an Undergraduate Sample

Component/scale	1	2	3	4	5
Positive Affectivity					
1. PANAS PA	—				
2. Posaff	.43**	—			
3. Energy	.44**	.64**	—		
4. Ascendance	.30**	.49**	.47**	—	
5. Ambition	.39**	.31**	.55**	.24**	—
6. Affiliation	.18**	.27**	.18**	.16**	.01

Note. $N = 254$. PANAS, Positive and Negative Affect Schedule; PA, Positive Affect; Posaff, Positive Affectivity Scale; Ascendance = MPQ Social Potency; Ambition = MPQ Achievement; Affiliation = MPQ Social Closeness. See text for more details.
* $p < .05$, two-tailed.
** $p < .01$, two-tailed.

that will be described subsequently. These scales were specifically designed to assess the Positive Affectivity and Energy components of Extraversion. The Positive Affectivity (Posaff) scale consists of 21 items directly relevant to the experience of PA; sample items include "I get excited when I think about the future," and "I enjoy nearly everything I do." The Energy scale is composed of 17 items assessing perceived energy and vigor; sample items are "People would describe me as a pretty energetic person," "I live a very full life," and "Other people sometimes have trouble keeping up with the pace I set."

Thus, the students were assessed on five of the six components shown in Figure 1. Table II presents correlations among these scales, and it can be seen that these results largely replicated those shown in Table I. Once again, Ascendance, Affiliation, and Ambition were weakly related to one another, with a mean intercorrelation of only .14 (range = .01 to .24). All three components were, however, more consistently related to the trait PA and Energy markers: Ascendance, Ambition, and Affiliation had mean correlations of .42, .42, and .21, respectively, with the three PA/Energy scales, which were themselves strongly interrelated (mean $r = .50$).

In Table II, we again see evidence that Ascendance, Affiliation, and Ambition are more highly related to trait PA/Energy than they are to each other. As before, we tested the centrality of PA by computing partial correlations, this time using the Posaff scale as the PA marker. When Posaff's influence was statistically eliminated, the correlations among the other components all became low and nonsignificant, ranging from .11 to −.08. Similar results were obtained when the other two PA/Energy scales were partialled out.

B. Relations between Measures of Positive Emotionality and Extraversion

As was discussed earlier, studies have consistently shown that Extraversion is significantly related to state PA scales. These correlations are only low to moderate in magnitude, however, typically ranging from .20 to .50 (Costa & McCrae, 1980, 1984; Emmons & Diener, 1986; Tellegen, 1985; Watson & Clark, 1984). These data confirm that Extraversion and state PA are related, but, by themselves, do not demonstrate that PA is a central feature of the construct.

To examine this issue, we must instead consider Extraversion in relation to trait PA measures. If, as we are arguing, stable individual differences in positive emotionality compose the core of Extraversion, then trait PA measures should be strongly related to more traditional measures of the higher-order disposition. Meyer and Shack (1989) report results that support this contention. In a sample of 231 students, the EPQ Extraversion scale correlated .66 with an eight-item trait PA scale. Moreover, as would be predicted from previous research (Tellegen, 1985; Watson & Clark, 1984) a parallel measure of trait NA correlated .63 with EPQ Neuroticism.

To explore these relations further, we administered markers of trait PA, trait NA, Extraversion, and Neuroticism to 528 undergraduates. Trait PA and NA were assessed using the general form of the PANAS scales. The PANAS PA scale has already been described. The PANAS NA scale was similarly derived, and also consists of 10 factor markers (*afraid, ashamed, distressed, guilty, hostile, irritable, jittery, nervous, scared, upset*).

Extraversion and Neuroticism were measured using scales developed by Goldberg (1983). On the basis of extensive analyses of English-language trait names (Goldberg, 1981, 1982), Goldberg selected eight adjectival pairs to assess each of the "Big Five" personality traits composing the prominent five-factor model of personality (see Digman, 1990; Goldberg, 1993; McCrae & Costa, 1985, 1987). In this sample, we used Goldberg's Surgency scale to measure Extraversion, and his Emotional Stability versus Neuroticism scale to assess Neuroticism. Subjects rated themselves on each of these trait pairs using a five-point scale, where 1 = very much like trait A, 3 = about average on this dimension, and 5 = very much like trait B (for more information regarding these scales, see McCrae & Costa, 1985).

Correlations among these measures are presented in Table III, and it can be seen that the expected pattern emerged: The PANAS PA scale correlated .61 with Goldberg's Surgency and only −.21 with Neuroticism, whereas the PANAS NA scale correlated .53 and −.26 with Neuroticism and Surgency, respectively.

Table III also presents correlations between the individual Goldberg trait pairs and the PANAS scales. For our purposes, the most noteworthy finding is that *all* of the Surgency items are significantly correlated with the PANAS PA scale. Thus, these data demonstrate that the association between trait PA and Extraversion is both strong and very broad based.

Mathews (1989) has examined these relations more thoroughly. In her study, 231 students completed a battery of tests related to the higher-order dimensions

TABLE III
Correlations between Trait PA and NA Scales and Goldberg's Measures of
Surgency and Neuroticism

Goldberg scale/item	Correlations with	
	PANAS PA	PANAS NA
Surgency	**.61****	−.21**
Unenergetic versus energetic	**.58****	−.22**
Passive versus active	**.48****	−.11*
Timid versus bold	**.43****	−.25**
Quiet versus talkative	**.37****	−.08
Retiring versus sociable	**.36****	−.14**
Submissive versus dominant	**.31****	−.09*
Conforming versus independent	**.26****	−.01
Humble versus proud	**.25****	−.15**
Neuroticism	−.26**	**.53****
At ease versus nervous	−.25**	**.46****
Secure versus insecure	−.38**	**.40****
Emotionally stable versus unstable	−.27**	**.38****
Not envious versus envious, jealous	−.16**	**.35****
Even-tempered versus temperamental	−.06	**.27****
Relaxed versus high-strung	−.01	**.22****
Unemotional versus emotional	.09*	**.17****
Objective versus subjective	**−.09***	.08

Note. $N = 528$. The stronger correlation for each item is in boldface. PANAS,
Positive and Negative Affect Schedule; PA, Positive Affect; NA, Negative Affect.
* $p < .05$, two-tailed.
** $p < .01$, two-tailed.

of Extraversion/PA, Neuroticism/NA, and Disinhibition versus Constraint. Subjects completed trait versions of the two PANAS scales, as well as Goldberg's (1983) measures of Surgency, Neuroticism, and Conscientiousness (e.g., reliable versus undependable, organized versus disorganized, and careful versus careless). In addition, they were assessed on the EPQ Extraversion, Neuroticism, and Psychoticism scales. It should be noted that, despite its name, EPQ Psychoticism is essentially a measure of Disinhibition, tapping individual differences in sensation-seeking, impulsivity, nonconformity, socialization, and behavioral restraint (see Tellegen, 1985; Zuckerman et al., 1988).

Finally, subjects completed a preliminary version of the General Temperament Survey (GTS; Clark & Watson, 1990). The GTS consists of three factor-analytically derived scales (answered in a true–false format) that assess higher-order dimensions similar to those identified by Eysenck and Eysenck (1975) and Tellegen (1985). Specifically, the Positive Temperament scale broadly assesses individual differences in positive emotionality; in terms of Figure 1, it taps content relevant to both the

TABLE IV
Varimax-Rotated Factor Loadings of the Personality
and Trait Affect Scales

Scale	Loading on		
	Factor 1	Factor 2	Factor 3
GTS Negative Temperament	.93		
EPQ Neuroticism	.90		
Goldberg Neuroticism	.84		
PANAS NA	.83		
GTS Positive Temperament		.87	
Goldberg Surgency		.86	
EPQ Extraversion		.83	
PANAS PA		.79	
GTS Disinhibition			.87
EPQ Psychoticism			.74
Goldberg Conscientiousness			−.83

Note. $N = 231$. Loadings below $|.30|$ are omitted. GTS, General Temperament Survey; EPQ, Eysenck Personality Questionnaire; PANAS, Positive and Negative Affect Schedule; NA, Negative Affect; PA, Positive Affect. Adapted from Mathews (1989).

Positive Affectivity and the Energy components. Sample items include "I get pretty excited when I'm starting a new project," and "I have more energy than most of the people I know." In contrast, the Negative Temperament and Disinhibition scales are general measures of trait NA and behavioral disinhibition versus control, respectively. (For details regarding the development, reliability, and validity of the GTS, see Watson & Clark, 1993; Watson, Clark, McIntyre, & Hamaker, 1992).[1]

Mathews (1989) subjected these personality and affect measures to a principal components analysis. As expected, three strong factors emerged with eigenvalues greater than 1.00; together, these factors accounted for 74.5% of the total variance. Three factors therefore were orthogonally rotated using varimax. The resulting loadings are presented in Table IV. The first and third factors clearly represent trait NA/Neuroticism and Disinhibition versus Constraint, respectively. The second factor is, however, of most interest for our present discussion: The trait PA and

[1] The data reported in this chapter and in Mathews (1989) are based on preliminary versions of the GTS Positive Temperament and Disinhibition scales, containing 19 and 30 items, respectively. The final version of Positive Temperament consists of 27 items, which includes two 12-item subscales that assess the Positive Affectivity and Energy components shown in Figure 1. The final version of Disinhibition includes 35 items. These preliminary versions are very highly correlated with the finalized scales and yield very similar results. The final Negative Temperament scale—which contains 28 items—was used in all analyses.

Extraversion scales were all highly related to one another, and so jointly compose a common dimension. It is notable, furthermore, that both types of scales load equally strongly on this factor.

Thus, we again see evidence that measures of Extraversion and positive emotionality are highly correlated with one another. Taken together, the data we have reviewed strongly affirm our contention that positive emotionality is a central core component of Extraversion (see also Watson & Clark, 1992; Watson et al., 1992).

C. Affective and Interpersonal Correlates of the Disposition

If positive emotionality truly forms the core of the higher-order disposition, then trait PA measures should have external correlates similar to those of more traditional Extraversion scales. That is, the two types of measures should be comparably related to nonpersonality variables. As a comprehensive discussion of this issue is beyond the scope of our review, we will focus instead on two types of variables that are especially relevant to our argument: (1) indices of social/interpersonal behavior (which are emphasized in more traditional conceptualizations of the construct) and (2) measures of positive emotional experience (which are highlighted in our model).

Watson (1988a) examined these relations in a sample of 71 students, each of whom completed a daily mood and activities questionnaire once per day over a 7-week period (M = 44.4 observations per subject). Mood was assessed using 24 items that yielded PA and NA factor scores. To measure social activity, the subjects indicated the number of hours (to the nearest half-hour) that they had spent with friends that day. Finally, they also completed personality measures both before and after the daily rating period.

Consistent with our model, various trait PA markers were significantly related not only to average levels of state PA, but also to social activity. For example, the abbreviated WB scale from the MPQ correlated .44 with mean PA, and .34 with mean social activity, over the rating period. It is also noteworthy that socially based traits showed the same pattern; for example, the MPQ SP scale (which, as noted earlier, is a measure of Ascendance) was equally related to both mean PA (r = .31) and mean social activity (r = .29). Given these results, it is not surprising that mean PA and social activity were significantly related to each other (r = .28).

Watson, Clark, and McIntyre (1990) conducted a more comprehensive analysis of these relations. In this study, 79 subjects completed a weekly mood and social activities questionnaire over a 13-week period (M = 12.3 assessments per subject). Mood was assessed using the PANAS PA and NA scales; respondents rated their feelings from the previous week. In addition, they indicated how frequently they had been involved in each of 15 categories of social activity during the past week, using a four-point scale (0 = not at all, 1 = once, 2 = twice, 3 = three or more times). The items sampled broad classes of social activity and tapped a wide range of interpersonal behavior (e.g., "romantic activity or dating," "going to/giving a party," "having a serious discussion"). Responses to these items were then summed to produce an overall index of social behavior.

Prior to the weekly rating period, subjects were assessed on various Extraversion/trait PA markers, including EPQ Extraversion, Goldberg Surgency, GTS Positive Temperament, and a General form of the PANAS PA scale. Table V presents correlations between these scales and mean PA, NA, and social activity scores computed over the 13-week rating period. Correlations among the mean scores are also shown in the table. Finally, Table V includes single markers of trait NA/Neuroticism (the General form of the PANAS NA scale) and Disinhibition versus Constraint (GTS Disinhibition) for comparison purposes.

These results closely replicate those of Watson (1988a). As before, mean social activity was significantly related to mean PA ($r = .35$). A more striking finding, however, was that the Extraversion/trait PA scales were similarly related to mean levels of both positive emotions and interpersonal behavior. It is especially noteworthy that EPQ Extraversion was no more highly correlated with social activity ($r = .31$) than with PA ($r = .30$). Similarly, the GTS Positive Temperament scale had virtually identical correlations with PA and social activity ($rs = .39$ and $.38$, respectively). Finally, note that the trait PA measures (Positive Temperament and PANAS PA) were more highly related to social activity (mean $r = .34$) than were the traditional Extraversion scales (EPQ Extraversion and Goldberg Surgency; mean $r = .24$). (These data are examined in a slightly revised form in Watson et al., 1992).

TABLE V

Correlations between Mean Affect and Social Activity Scores and Selected Markers of Extraversion, Neuroticism, and Disinhibition

Scale	Correlations with		
	M Positive Affect	M Social Activity	M Negative Affect
M Social Activity	.35**	—	—
M Negative Affect	.02	−.18	—
Extraversion/PA markers			
GTS Positive Temperament	.39**	.38**	−.15
PANAS PA	.67**	.30**	−.02
EPQ Extraversion	.30**	.31**	−.14
Goldberg Surgency	.35**	.17	−.09
Other personality scales			
PANAS NA	−.11	−.07	.47**
GTS Disinhibition	−.09	−.03	.05

Note. $N = 79$. GTS, General Temperament Survey; PANAS, Positive and Negative Affect Schedule; PA, Positive Affect, EPQ, Eysenck Personality Questionnaire; NA, Negative Affect. See Watson, Clark, McIntyre, and Hamaker (1992) for more details.
* $p < .05$, two-tailed.
** $p < .01$, two-tailed.

In addition to the personality and affect measures described previously (see Table IV), subjects in the Mathews (1989) study also answered a series of questions regarding various aspects of their current lifestyle, emphasizing in particular their social behavior and interpersonal relationships. Correlations between these items and several Extraversion/trait PA scales (GTS Positive Temperament, PANAS PA, EPQ Extraversion, Goldberg Surgency) are shown in Table VI. As before, single markers of trait NA/Neuroticism (GTS Negative Temperament) and Disinhibition (GTS Disinhibition) also are included for comparison purposes.

Consistent with earlier findings, the trait PA and Extraversion scales generally have similar lifestyle and behavioral correlates. For example, EPQ Extraversion and GTS Positive Temperament both are positively correlated with the number of leadership roles assumed, frequency of partying, number of close friends, and number of dating partners, and are (negatively) related to the percent of weekend time spent alone and the severity of speech anxiety. One interesting difference, however, is that the EPQ Extraversion scale—unlike the other markers of the higher-order construct—has low but significant correlations with alcohol, drug, and cigarette use. Furthermore, Table VI indicates that these variables are more strongly, broadly, and appropriately related to the Disinhibition dimension. It therefore appears that the impulsive/disinhibited component of the old Eysenckian model has not been entirely eliminated from the EPQ Extraversion scale.

TABLE VI

Correlations between Selected Extraversion, Neuroticism, and Disinhibition Markers and Various Measures of Current Lifestyle and Interpersonal Behavior

Item	Correlations with					
	GTS PosTemp	PANAS PA	EPQ Extra	Goldberg Surgency	GTS NegTemp	GTS Disinhibition
No. of leadership roles	.26**	.32**	.25**	.34**	−.07	.05
Frequency of partying	.19**	.17*	.33**	.24**	.05	.17*
% of weekend nights alone	−.19**	−.17*	−.17*	−.09	.09	−.12
No. of close friends	.20**	.18**	.30**	.14	−.07	.08
No. of dating partners	.19**	.15*	.19**	.13	−.18**	.01
Degree of speech anxiety	−.14*	−.11	−.21**	−.28**	.24**	−.11
Frequency of						
Alcohol consumption	.07	.09	.16*	.12	−.01	.26**
Drunkenness	−.01	.03	.21**	.13	.03	.38**
Drug use	.07	.04	.18**	.16*	−.08	.36**
Cigarette smoking	.02	−.01	.14*	.04	.06	.32**

Note. N = 217. GTS, General Temperament Survey; PosTemp, Positive Temperament; NegTemp, Negative Temperament; EPQ, Eysenck Personality Questionnaire; Extra, Extraversion; PANAS, Positive and Negative Affect Schedule; PA, Positive Affect. See text for more details.
* $p < .05$, two-tailed.
** $p < .01$, two-tailed.

VI. ORIGINS OF THE HIGHER-ORDER CONSTRUCT

A. Positive Affect as an Outcome Variable

We have demonstrated that positive emotional experience plays a central role in the Extraversion construct. This raises the further issue of *why* Extraversion has positive emotionality as its core. That is, why do these diverse primary traits all correlate with PA? Perhaps the most intuitively obvious explanation is that PA may represent a consistent *outcome* of Extraversion and its component primary traits. In other words, extraverts may behave in ways that are conducive to experiencing higher levels of PA. Compared to introverts, extraverts spend more time with other people (Affiliation), and because of their greater persuasiveness and social facility (Ascendance), are likely to derive greater reinforcements from their social interactions. Furthermore, extraverts are more active (Energy) and report being willing to work long hours in pursuit of their goals (Ambition); because of this, they may obtain more career- and competence-related rewards in their lives. Finally, extraverts actively seek out exciting and pleasurable experiences (Venturesomeness), which should further increase their general PA level.

This conceptual model guided most of the early research linking Extraversion and PA (e.g., Costa & McCrae, 1980, 1984), and it is surely true to a considerable extent. For example, our own research strongly suggests that certain types of social activity (especially physically active, informal, and epicurean activities) lead to transient increases in state PA (Clark & Watson, 1988; Watson, 1988a).

B. Positive Affect as a Motivating Force

However, PA cannot be viewed simply as a behavioral outcome. Considerable research also indicates that it is a powerful energizing force that motivates a broad range of activity. For instance, several studies have shown that high levels of state PA are associated with enhanced affiliative feelings and an increased preference for social, prosocial, and physically strenuous activities (Cunningham, 1988b; Rossi & Rossi, 1977). Moreover, increased PA levels are related to actual increases in social and prosocial behavior (Cunningham, 1988a; Cunningham, Steinberg, & Grev, 1980; Shaffer & Smith, 1985). Thus, it is not simply the case that social interaction and mastery experiences are pleasurable, and hence lead to higher PA levels; to some extent, PA also motivates one to pursue these activities. In other words, PA is both a cause and a result of behavior, especially social behavior.

C. Delineating a Common Biobehavioral System

Thus far, we have discussed PA and the other component traits of Extraversion as if they were distinct but related constructs that mutually influence one another. Another possibility is that these components are all reflections of a single integrated system. Tellegen (1985) has argued that this trait reflects individual differences in the behavioral activation system (BAS; Fowles, 1980; Gray, 1970), which is thought to control active approach and avoidance behaviors in response to signals of reward. According to Tellegen, Extraversion/trait PA levels may therefore represent individual differences in sensitivity to pleasurable stimuli. Furthermore, it is possible that the other components of Extraversion (e.g., gregariousness, dominance) also are under the control of the BAS. If so, then the affective and behavioral components of Extraversion both may be manifestations of common, underlying individual differences in active, pleasure-seeking behavior. In support of this idea, Depue, Luciana, Arbisi, Collins, and Leon (1994) have shown that Extraversion/Positive Emotionality is related to individual differences in the reactivity of the mesolimbic dopaminergic system.

Along these same lines, Depue and his colleagues (Depue & Iacono, 1989; Depue, Krauss, & Spoont, 1987) have proposed a compelling biobehavioral view of the construct. Depue et al. (1987) note that almost all of the component features of Extraversion systematically covary in bipolar disorder. That is, manic states are associated with heightened energy and hyperactivity; elated and euphoric mood; increased social interest, and more generally, elevations in interest level and hedonic capacity; enhanced excitement-seeking; and heightened feelings of confidence and optimism. Conversely, depressive episodes are characterized by sad and depressed mood; low levels of energy; social withdrawal and anhedonia; avoidance of strong stimulation; poor concentration; and feelings of pessimism and ineffectuality. In other words, mania and depression reflect strikingly different levels of Extraversion.

Depue et al. (1987) further demonstrate that these various traits covary within normal individuals as well. For example, subjects who are currently reporting high levels of perceived energy will also simultaneously report feeling alert, socially interested, confident, high in positive affect, and so on. This temporal covariation strongly suggests that these component traits all reflect the operation of a single, integrated biobehavioral system, which Depue and Iacono (1989) call the "behavioral facilitation system" (BFS). In their view, the BFS promotes enjoyable and efficacious interactions with the environment. It appears to do so in several related ways. First, the PA component provides a general motivation or incentive to engage in goal-directed behavior. Second, increased levels of energy and alertness/concentration provide the physical and mental resources necessary for competent performance. Finally, heightened feelings of self-confidence and optimism lead to an increased expectancy of successful outcomes.

Furthermore, variability is seen as an inherent feature of the BFS. Thus, individuals can be viewed in terms of both their mean BFS level and their characteristic degree of fluctuation around this central tendency. Most individuals exhibit fairly modest variations in their BFS level. Extraverts are those who generally show high BFS activity, whereas introverts typically display lower BFS levels. Individuals suffering from bipolar disorder, however, show much more extreme fluctuations on the BFS dimension (Depue et al., 1987).

The models proposed by Tellegen and Depue go beyond the existing data and are clearly somewhat speculative. Nevertheless, they have considerable value in terms of integrating the current findings and in directing future investigation in this area. More generally, models proposing integrative structures and systems offer a more sophisticated—and ultimately more satisfying—view of the construct.

VII. IMPLICATIONS AND CONCLUSIONS

A. Implications of the Changing View of Extraversion

Theoretical conceptualizations of Extraversion have gradually but systematically evolved over the past 75 years. This evolution necessarily involves elements of both continuity and change. The continuity is largely reflected in the interpersonal components of the trait: Whatever else has been included in their models, virtually all of the major theorists in the area have viewed—and continue to view—extraverts as gregarious and socially ascendant individuals.

At the same time, the construct has changed markedly over the years. Most notably, many of the older conceptualizations emphasized that extraverts were unreflective, reckless, impulsive, and unreliable. Generally speaking, these views tended to portray extraverts as somewhat unsocialized individuals who were poorly adapted to the restrictions of contemporary society. In contrast, recent models have tended to stress the more adaptive and productive aspects of the disposition. Thus, extraverts, in addition to their social facility and gregariousness, are increasingly viewed as being ambitious, hardworking, and dominant. Recent conceptualizations (including our own) have also stressed the positive affective component of the trait. These models emphasize that extraverts are happy, enthusiastic, confident, active, and energetic. More fundamentally, it now appears that Extraversion essentially taps individual differences in affectively rewarding performance: compared to introverts, extraverts view themselves as more effectively and pleasurably engaged in various aspects of their lives.

This reformulated view strongly suggests that Extraversion should play a more prominent role in clinical assessment and diagnosis. Meehl (1975) was one of the first theorists to recognize the potential clinical value of this trait. Meehl argued that significant, heritable individual differences exist in "hedonic capacity"—that is, in one's basic capacity for experiencing pleasure. According to Meehl, many patients who seek help will do so not because of excessive levels of anxiety or some other negative affect, but because of a general absence of joy and pleasure in their lives. Interestingly, Meehl suggested that Cattell's Surgency scale (which is an excellent marker of his higher-order Extraversion factor) was a likely candidate for assessing individual differences in hedonic capacity.

Subsequent research has supported Meehl's argument that Extraversion is an important dimension in clinical phenomena. For example, as noted earlier, Depue et al. (1987) have shown that this construct plays a central role in bipolar disorder. Similarly, several studies have shown that trait PA has important implications for understanding anxious and depressive phenomena (e.g., Clark & Watson, 1991;

Tellegen, 1985; Watson, Clark, & Carey, 1988). Specifically, measures of trait NA are strongly correlated with symptoms and diagnoses of both anxiety and depression, indicating that NA is an important general correlate of psychiatric disorder (see also Watson & Clark, 1984). In contrast, trait PA is clearly and consistently related only to symptoms and diagnoses of depression, suggesting that low PA may be a critical factor in distinguishing depressive from anxious states.

Other results corroborate Meehl's (1975) argument that low trait PA levels frequently motivate individuals to seek professional help. Clark et al. (1994) examined personality differences among three groups of subjects: (1) unselected college undergraduates, (2) students seeking counseling at a university counseling center, and (3) inpatients on the substance abuse and personality disorder units at a state hospital. The inpatients scored significantly higher on a trait NA factor than did the other two groups, again demonstrating that NA is a general concomitant of psychiatric disorder. Interestingly, however, both the inpatient and the counseling center groups scored lower than the normals on a trait PA factor.

This brief review is only meant to suggest some of the ways in which Extraversion/Positive Emotionality is related to important clinical phenomena. The critical point is that the clinical implications of this construct should be explored much more fully and systematically in the future. Furthermore, the available evidence strongly indicates that Extraversion/PA measures should be routinely included in clinical assessment.

B. Directions for Future Research

In this chapter we have attempted to summarize and integrate the major theoretical views of Extraversion. Clearly, however, many important questions currently remain unanswered. We will conclude our discussion by noting three areas that warrant special consideration. First, future research needs to explore the core of the construct in greater detail. We have argued that individual differences in positive emotionality constitute the central core of the disposition, but more research is obviously required on this issue. We believe that naturalistic studies examining how these components covary in the daily lives of individuals will prove particularly useful in this regard (see Depue et al., 1987).

Second, in constructing the schematic model shown in Figure 1, we were struck by the relative absence of research specifically investigating relations among the basic components of the trait. Needed are more systematic, data-based analyses of the interrelations among the primary facets of Extraversion. Further research along these lines may well indicate that some of the current components should be combined or dropped, and perhaps may also suggest that currently unrecognized facets be added. We emphasize, however, that such research necessarily must employ precise, valid, and specific measures of these facets. Many of the older facet scales (for example, those in the CPI and GZTS) were constructed without regard for discriminant validity, and as a consequence are simply too broad and heterogeneous to be useful in component-level research.

Finally, future research should explore the contention that Extraversion be divided into two distinct subfactors, one that involves successful adaptation through satisfying interpersonal relationships, and another that entails adaptation through dominance, mastery, and achievement (Hogan, 1983; Tellegen et al., 1988). These two modes of adaptation are conceptually quite distinct, and this bipartite scheme therefore has considerable appeal. Nevertheless, as noted earlier, both of these proposed subfactors contain a common positive affective element; consequently, they are ultimately (though not strongly) related to one another at a higher-order level. Because of this, we continue to believe that Extraversion remains viable as a single higher-order construct.

REFERENCES

Allport, G. W., & Odbert, H. S. (1936). Trait-names: A psycholexical study. *Psychological Monographs, 47*(1, Whole No. 211).

Bandura, A. (1977). Self-efficacy: Toward a unifying theory of behavioral change. *Psychological Review, 84,* 191–215.

Cattell, R. B. (1945). The principal trait clusters for describing personality. *Psychological Bulletin, 42,* 129–161.

Cattell, R. B. (1946). *The description and measurement of personality.* Yonkers-on-Hudson, NY: World Book.

Cattell, R. B., Eber, H. W., & Tatsuoka, M. M. (1980). *Handbook for the Sixteen Personality Questionnaire (16PF).* Champaign, IL: Institute for Personality and Ability Testing.

Clark, L. A. (1993). *Manual for the Schedule for Nonadaptive and Adaptive Personality (SNAP).* Minneapolis: University of Minnesota Press.

Clark, L. A., Vorhies, L., & McEwen, J. L. (1994). Personality disorder symptomatology from the five-factor model perspective. In P. T. Costa, Jr. & T. A. Widiger (Eds.), *Personality disorders and the five-factor model of personality* (pp. 95–116). Washington, DC: American Psychological Association.

Clark, L. A., & Watson, D. (1988). Mood and the mundane: Relations between daily life events and self-reported mood. *Journal of Personality and Social Psychology, 54,* 296–308.

Clark, L. A., & Watson, D. (1990). *The General Temperament Survey.* Unpublished manuscript, Southern Methodist University, Dallas, TX.

Clark, L. A., & Watson, D. (1991). Theoretical and empirical issues in differentiating depression from anxiety. In J. Becker & A. Kleinman (Eds.), *Advances in mood disorders: Vol. 1. Psychological aspects* (pp. 221–245). Hillsdale, NJ: Erlbaum.

Costa, P. T., Jr., Busch, C. M., Zonderman, A. B., & McCrae, R. R. (1986). Correlations of MMPI factor scales with measures of the five-factor model of personality. *Journal of Personality Assessment, 50,* 640–650.

Costa, P. T., Jr., & McCrae, R. R. (1980). Influence of extraversion and neuroticism on subjective well-being: Happy and unhappy people. *Journal of Personality and Social Psychology, 38,* 668–678.

Costa, P. T., Jr., & McCrae, R. R. (1984). Personality as a life-long determinant of wellbeing. In C. Z. Malatesta & C. E. Izard (Eds.), *Emotion in adult development* (pp. 141–157). Beverly Hills, CA: Sage.

Costa, P. T., Jr., & McCrae, R. R. (1985). *The NEO Personality Inventory manual.* Odessa, FL: Psychological Assessment Resources.

Costa, P. T., Jr., & McCrae, R. R. (1988). From catalog to classification: Murray's needs and the five-factor model. *Journal of Personality and Social Psychology, 55,* 258–265.

Costa, P. T., Jr., & McCrae, R. R. (1992). *Revised NEO Personality Inventory (NEO-PI-R) and NEO Five-Factor Inventory (NEO-FFI) professional manual.* Odessa, FL: Psychological Assessment Resources.

Cunningham, M. R. (1988a). Does happiness mean friendliness?: Induced mood and heterosexual self-disclosure. *Personality and Social Psychology Bulletin, 14,* 283–297.

Cunningham, M. R. (1988b). What do you do when you're happy or blue?: Mood, expectancies, and behavioral interest. *Motivation and Emotion, 12,* 309–331.

Cunningham, M. R., Steinberg, J., & Grev, R. (1980). Wanting to and having to help: Separate motivations for positive mood and guilt-induced helping. *Journal of Personality and Social Psychology, 38,* 181–192.

Depue, R. A., & Iacono, W. G. (1989). Neurobehavioral aspects of affective disorders. *Annual Review of Psychology, 40,* 457–492.

Depue, R. A., Krauss, S. P., & Spoont, M. R. (1987). A two-dimensional threshold model of seasonal bipolar affective disorder. In D. Magnusson & A. Öhman (Eds.), *Psychopathology: An interactional perspective* (pp. 95–123). Orlando, FL: Academic Press.

Depue, R. A., Luciana, M., Arbisi, P., Collins, P., & Leon, A. (1994). Dopamine and the structure of personality: Relation of agonist-induced dopamine activity to positive emotionality. *Journal of Personality and Social Psychology, 67,* 485–498.

Digman, J. M. (1990). Personality structure: Emergence of the five-factor model. *Annual Review of Psychology, 41,* 417–440.

Emmons, R. A., & Diener, E. (1986). Influence of impulsivity and sociability on subjective well-being. *Journal of Personality and Social Psychology, 50,* 1211–1215.

Eysenck, H. J. (1959). *Manual of the Maudsley Personality Inventory.* San Diego, CA: Educational and Industrial Testing Service.

Eysenck, H. J., & Eysenck, S. B. G. (1968). *Manual of the Eysenck Personality Inventory.* San Diego, CA: Educational and Industrial Testing Service.

Eysenck, H. J., & Eysenck, S. B. G. (1969). *Personality structure and measurement.* San Diego, CA: Knapp.

Eysenck, H. J., & Eysenck, S. B. G. (1975). *Manual of the Eysenck Personality Questionnaire.* San Diego, CA: Educational and Industrial Testing Service.

Eysenck, H. J., & Eysenck, M. W. (1985). *Personality and individual differences.* New York: Plenum Press.

Fowles, D. C. (1980). The three arousal model: Implications of Gray's two-factor learning theory for heart rate, electrodermal activity, and psychopathy. *Psychophysiology, 17,* 87–104.

Goldberg, L. R. (1981). Language and individual differences: The search for universals in personality lexicons. In L. Wheeler (Ed.), *Review of personality and social psychology* (Vol. 2, pp. 141–165). Beverly Hills, CA: Sage.

Goldberg, L. R. (1982). From ace to zombie: Some explorations in the language of personality. In C. D. Spielberger & J. N. Butcher (Eds.), *Advances in personality assessment* (Vol. 1, pp. 203–234). Hillsdale, NJ: Erlbaum.

Goldberg, L. R. (1983, June). *The magical number five, plus or minus two: Some conjectures on the dimensionality of personality descriptions.* Paper presented at a research seminar, Gerontology Research Center, Baltimore.

Goldberg, L. R. (1993). The structure of phenotypic personality traits. *American Psychologist, 48,* 26–34.

Gough, H. G. (1987). *California Psychological Inventory Administrator's Guide.* Palo Alto, CA: Consulting Psychologists Press.

Gray, J. A. (1970). The psychophysiological basis of introversion-extraversion. *Behaviour Research and Therapy, 8,* 249–266.

Guilford, J. P. (1975). Factors and factors of personality. *Psychological Bulletin, 82,* 802–814.

Guilford, J. P., & Braly, K. W. (1930). Extroversion and introversion. *Psychological Bulletin, 27,* 96–107.

Guilford, J. P., & Guilford, R. B. (1934). An analysis of the factors in a typical test of introversion-extroversion. *Journal of Abnormal and Social Psychology, 28,* 377–399.

Guilford, J. P., & Guilford, R. B. (1936). Personality factors S, E, and M and their measurement. *Journal of Psychology, 2,* 109–127.

Guilford, J. P., & Zimmerman, W. S. (1949). *The Guilford-Zimmerman Temperament Survey: Manual.* Beverly Hills, CA: Sheridan Supply.

Guilford, J. S., Zimmerman, W. S., & Guilford, J. P. (1976). *The Guilford-Zimmerman Temperament Survey Handbook.* San Diego, CA: Educational and Industrial Testing Service.

Hathaway, S. R., & McKinley, J. C. (1943). *The Minnesota Multiphasic Personality Inventory.* Minneapolis: University of Minnesota Press.

Hogan, R. T. (1983). A socioanalytic theory of personality. In M. Page (Ed.), *1982 Nebraska Symposium on Motivation* (pp. 55–89). Lincoln: University of Nebraska Press.

Jackson, D. N. (1984). *Personality Research Form Manual* (3rd ed.). Port Huron, MI: Research Psychologists Press.

James, W. (1907). *Pragmatism.* New York: Henry Holt.

Jung, C. G. (1921). *Psychological types.* New York: Harcourt, Brace.

Mathews, K. K. (1989). *Validating new trait scales in the context of three- and five-factor models of personality.* Unpublished master's thesis, Southern Methodist University, Dallas, TX.

Mayer, J. D., & Gaschke, Y. N. (1988). The experience and meta-experience of mood. *Journal of Personality and Social Psychology, 55,* 102–111.

McCrae, R. R., & Costa, P. T., Jr. (1985). Updating Norman's "adequate taxonomy": Intelligence and personality dimensions in natural language and in questionnaires. *Journal of Personality and Social Psychology, 49,* 710–721.

McCrae, R. R., & Costa, P. T., Jr. (1987). Validation of a five-factor model of personality across instruments and observers. *Journal of Personality and Social Psychology, 52,* 81–90.

Meehl, P. E. (1975). Hedonic capacity: Some conjectures. *Bulletin of the Menninger Clinic, 39,* 295–307.

Meyer, G. J., & Shack, J. R. (1989). The structural convergence of mood and personality: Evidence for old and new "directions." *Journal of Personality and Social Psychology, 57,* 691–706.

Rossi, A. S., & Rossi, P. E. (1977). Body time and social time: Mood patterns by menstrual cycle phase and day of the week. *Social Science Research, 6,* 273–308.

Shaffer, D. R., & Smith, J. (1985). Effects of preexisting moods on observers' reactions to helpful and nonhelpful models. *Motivation and Emotion, 9,* 101–122.

Tellegen, A. (1982). *Brief manual for the Differential Personality Questionnaire.* Unpublished manuscript, University of Minnesota, Minneapolis.

Tellegen, A. (1985). Structures of mood and personality and their relevance to assessing anxiety, with an emphasis on self-report. In A. H. Tuma & J. D. Maser (Eds.), *Anxiety and the anxiety disorders* (pp. 681–706). Hillsdale, NJ: Erlbaum.

Tellegen, A., Lykken, D. T., Bouchard, T. J., Jr., Wilcox, K. J., Segal, N. L., & Rich, S. (1988). Personality similarity in twins reared apart and together. *Journal of Personality and Social Psychology, 54,* 1031–1039.

Watson, D. (1988a). Intraindividual and interindividual analyses of positive and negative affect: Their relation to health complaints, perceived stress, and daily activities. *Journal of Personality and Social Psychology, 54,* 1020–1030.

Watson, D. (1988b). The vicissitudes of mood measurement: Effects of varying descriptors, time frames, and response formats on measures of positive and negative affect. *Journal of Personality and Social Psychology, 55,* 128–141.

Watson, D., & Clark, L. A. (1984). Negative affectivity: The disposition to experience aversive emotional states. *Psychological Bulletin, 96,* 465–490.

Watson, D., & Clark, L. A. (1992). On traits and temperament: General and specific factors of emotional experience and their relation to the five-factor model. *Journal of Personality, 60,* 441–476.

Watson, D., & Clark, L. A. (1993). Behavioral disinhibition versus constraint: A dispositional perspective. In D. M. Wegner & J. W. Pennebaker (Eds.), *Handbook of mental control* (pp. 506–527). New York: Prentice-Hall.

Watson, D., Clark, L. A., & Carey, G. (1988). Positive and negative affectivity and their relation to anxiety and depressive disorders. *Journal of Abnormal Psychology, 97,* 346–353.

Watson, D., Clark, L. A., & McIntyre, C. W. (1990). [General versus specific relations between temperament and social activity]. Unpublished raw data.

Watson, D., Clark, L. A., McIntyre, C. W., & Hamaker, S. (1992). Affect, personality, and social activity. *Journal of Personality and Social Psychology, 63,* 1011–1025.

Watson, D., Clark, L. A., & Tellegen, A. (1988). Development and validation of brief measures of positive and negative affect: The PANAS Scales. *Journal of Personality and Social Psychology, 54,* 1063–1070.

Watson, D., & Tellegen, A. (1985). Toward a consensual structure of mood. *Psychological Bulletin, 98,* 219–235.

White, R. W. (1959). Motivation reconsidered: The concept of competence. *Psychological Review, 66,* 297–333.

Wiggins, J. S. (1979). A psychological taxonomy of trait-descriptive terms: The interpersonal domain. *Journal of Personality and Social Psychology, 37,* 395–412.

Zuckerman, M., Kuhlman, D. M., & Camac, C. (1988). What lies beyond E and N? Factor analyses of scales believed to measure basic dimensions of personality. *Journal of Personality and Social Psychology, 54,* 96–107.

CHAPTER 30

AGREEABLENESS: A DIMENSION OF PERSONALITY

WILLIAM G. GRAZIANO
TEXAS A&M UNIVERSITY

NANCY EISENBERG
ARIZONA STATE UNIVERSITY

This chapter is devoted to agreeableness as a dimension of personality. This review is composed of three parts. First, we will briefly review conceptualizations and definitions of the dimension, and summarize the history of research on the dimension. Second, we will consider theoretical perspectives on agreeableness. Finally, we will focus on a special case of agreeableness, the prosocial personality.

I. CONCEPTUALIZATIONS OF AGREEABLENESS

A. Historical Review of Labels for Agreeableness

What is agreeableness? In the past, a basic dimension has been recognized, but it has received different labels from theorists. There may be disagreement on the origins and labels, but descriptions of the basic dimension for the phenomena of agreeableness show remarkable communalities. For example, Adler (1938/1964) suggested that successful resolution of all three problems requires *Gemeinschafts-gefühl,* or "social interest," manifested in such traits as cooperation and empathy, selflessness, and identification with others. In keeping with the psychoanalytic approach to attachment, Horney (1945) linked the positive approach to others as part of dependency in response to feelings of inadequacy.

Within the psychometric tradition, Fiske (1949) labeled the dimension "conformity." In their reanalysis of six major studies, Digman and Takemota-Chock (1981) suggested the label "friendly compliance vs. hostile noncompliance." Hogan (1983) offered the label "likability." Digman and Inouye (1986) later suggested that their dimension of friendly compliance is similar, if not identical, to the "love–hate" dimension in circumplex models of personality (e.g., Leary, 1957). More recently, Johnson and Ostendorf (1993) suggested that the meaning of agreeableness is probably determined by how a researcher chooses to rotate factor axes relative to other personality dimensions. Depending on the rotation, agreeableness may be meaningfully seen as either "possessing a pleasant disposition" or "conforming to others' wishes."

In the Wiggins circumplex model of personality (e.g., Wiggins, 1980; Wiggins & Broughton, 1985), the personality dimension of "warm-agreeable" is explicitly linked to the motivational orientation of altrusim, but the dimension is seen as not orthogonal to other motivational orientations (e.g., cooperation, martyrdom) and other dispositions, such as being gregarious and unassuming.

Given the scope of this particular dimension and the sweep of conceptualizations, the potentially relevant research literature is large. We were forced to establish restrictive criteria for inclusion in this review. The primary focus will be on more recent, empirically based work on "natural language" individual differences in adults (Goldberg, 1981). Special attention will be given to those differences associated with the "Big Five" bipolar dimension of agreeable–disagreeable, as formulated by Norman (1963) and Tupes and Cristal (1961).

B. Agreeableness in the Natural Language

A major source of information about personality comes from language. Cattell (1957) observed that over the centuries, the "pressure of urgent necessity" has induced people to generate verbal symbols for every important aspect of an individual person's behavior that is likely to affect interpersonal interaction. If agreeableness is an important dimension in the natural language of personality, then it should appear with some frequency in vocabulary and language use.

In 1936 Allport and Odbert published their monumental psycholexical analysis of trait names. These authors examined 17,953 terms in the 1925 edition of *Webster's New International Dictionary* that were descriptive of personality or personal behavior. The terms were divided into four separate lists, or columns. The major purpose of the columns was to separate "neutral" words (Column 1) from censorial, evaluative words (Column 3). Column 1 words symbolized what Allport and Odbert believed were "real" (quotes by Allport & Odbert) traits of personality.

By contrast, words in Columns 2, 3, and 4 were regarded as less value neutral and less control to personality. For present purposes, Column 3 is especially relevant. It was the longest of the four lists and contained character evaluations such as "agitating," "amiable," "agreeable," and "appealing." Allport and Odbert were uncertain about the status of these words as trait names; they appeared to be value estimates. The authors even went so far as to suggest that words in Column 3 "should be avoided by psychologists unless they are prepared to deal with the subject of social judgment . . ." (p. vii).

It is important to recognize one important point. The Allport–Odbert list is the major source of terms for linguistic analysis of personality terms. In their attempt to reduce the large number of Allport–Odbert trait words into a more manageable set, many subsequent researchers have largely limited themselves to the words in Column 1. This occurred despite the fact that the reliability of the original classification was not very high by modern standards (see Allport & Odbert, 1936, pp. 34–36). Consider, for example, Cattell's (1957) approach. Having limited himself to Column 1, Cattell proceeded to reduce the list to 171 terms by having subjects rate the words on meaning. Cluster analyses further shortened the list to a "standard reduced personality sphere" of 42–46 clusters. This reduced sphere has been used repeatedly (e.g., Bond & Forgas, 1984, Digman & Takemoto-Chock, 1981; Norman, 1963; Tupes & Cristal, 1961) and forms the foundation for much work on what is now known as the Big Five dimensions of personality. (Of course, not all studies rely on Cattell's reduced sphere; see John [1990] and John, Angleitner, & Ostedorf [1988] for reviews and thoughtful critiques; see also Peabody & Goldberg [1989] for a discussion of problems in Cattell's item selection.)

Given this state of affairs, one might not have expected factor-analytic studies of personality based on the standard reduced personality sphere to uncover a major dimension devoted primarily to "social evaluation." Nonetheless, when Digman and Takemoto-Chock (1981) reanalyzed data from six major, large-scale studies, the first factor to emerge was labeled "friendly compliance vs. hostile non-compliance."

II. THEORETICAL PERSPECTIVES ON AGREEABLENESS

A. Natural Language Perspectives on Agreeableness

1. Evolutionary Analyses

In his classic paper, Goldberg (1981) extended rigorously the analysis of personality language outlined earlier by Cattell. The heart of Goldberg's analysis can be captured in a single sentence: "Those individual differences that are of the most significance in the daily transactions of persons with each other will eventually become encoded in our language" (pp. 141–142). A corollary is that the more important an individual difference is in human transactions, the more languages will have a term for it. Goldberg suggests that each of the Big Five dimensions concerns answers to five universal questions individuals ask about strangers they are about to meet. One of the five questions is, "Is X *agreeable* (warm and pleasant) or disagreeable (cold and distant)?" (p. 161).

Also building on the Big Five, but employing a theoretical tack different from that used by Goldberg, Hogan (1983) takes a bioevolutionary approach. Hogan argues that personality languages has its origins in group processes. He argues that certain individual differences (e.g., cooperativeness) were more important in promoting the survival of the group than were others (e.g., aesthetic sensitivity) during the long period of human evolution. Survival-related individual differences should be especially conspicuous in the language of personality description. Hogan explicitly argues that the evolutionary acquisition of personality language terms is mediated through social consensus. It is reputational consensus in dispositional attribution that is important; that is, people who know or watch an individual will come to an agreement on the person's tendencies. In this analysis, the language of individual differences evolved as a vehicle for assessing social consensus about an individual's value to a group (cf. Baron's, 1988, ecological approach to social perception).

The pictures offered by Goldberg and Hogan are speculative; furthermore, they are painted with a broad brush. Evolutionary analyses can become complicated by many tangential issues (e.g., frequency-dependent selection); here we consider only the most direct issue, the evolution of sensitivity to a general dimension. For a more detailed analyses of heritability of individual differences in agreeableness-related behaviors, see Graziano (1994) and Loehlin (1992, pp. 56–64).

If we recognize that 99% of human evolution occurred when humans lived in hunting/gathering bands consisting of approximately 30 individuals, and if we recognize that cooperation is seen as an essential attribute in such groups (e.g., Konner, 1975), then it is plausible that an individual's agreeableness might be a dimension receiving special attention (Cosmides & Tooby, 1992; Graziano, Jensen-Campbell, Todd, & Finch, in press). It is not implausible that dispositioned disagreeableness and selfishness could lead to exclusion from social groups (Jensen-Campbell, Graziano, & West, 1995). Additional analyses of the dynamics of group inclusion and exclusion are offered by social psychologists.

2. Social Psychological Analyses

What might be the functional value of individual agreeableness to the group? One explanation is related to the need for group action. Groups ordinarily have tasks to accomplish, and the accomplishment is easier when group members hold a consensus on the task and a means for accomplishing it. In the language of the early group-dynamics researchers, group locomotion is more easily achieved the more cohesive the members of the group (e.g., Festinger, 1950).

If an individual holds a nonnormative viewpoint about group action, social pressures will be brought to bear on the deviant to induce group consensus, and thus cohesion. Pressure will appear first in communication patterns. Group members will direct many communications toward the deviant, with the intent of gaining conformity (e.g., Dabbs & Ruback, 1987; Schachter, 1951). If this kind of pressure fails to gain compliance, and the individual persists stubbornly in the nonnormative opinion, then there would be important consequences for both the individual and the group.

If a consensus forms that the deviant will not change toward the normative position, then communications to the deviant will drop off drastically. The deviant will no longer be viewed as a member of the group (e.g., Wilder, 1986). The ultimate consequence is that the individual will be effectively eliminated from the group. Such an outcome is clearly costly for both the group and the individual. From the group's perspective, the personal resources the individual might have provided to the group are now lost. Property might be confiscated and compliance might be forced, but these actions are costly compared with obtaining a "willing conversion." From the individual's perspective, rejection has occurred.

If an individual holds a deviant viewpoint and is cut off from the group, he or she may no longer be allowed to draw on group resources, and the individual's very survival may be questionable. As regards the group, it will now be smaller, and possibly poorer in resources, but the group as a whole will be more cohesive and will be better able to accomplish goals consensually defined as important. Thus group goal attainment, group cohesion, and individual influenceability are interconnected. One of the best documented conclusions in the groups' literature is that in high cohesive groups, individuals tend both to exert influence on other group members and to be susceptible to other individual's influence attempts (Collins & Raven, 1969).

If this line of theoretical speculation is valid, then it is possible to see how agreeableness might have evolved as an important dimension in determining an individual's value to a group. That is, norms for evaluating group members could be expected to include dimensions about agreeableness. If the norms were functional and had some adaptive significance, then they could be perpetuated through social transmission over very long periods (e.g., Campbell, 1988; Jacobs & Campbell, 1961). Individuals would be evaluated through the norms, and noncompliance with the norm could lead to exclusion. If there were a consensus that an individual was chronically unwilling to go along with others, was uncooperative, and gave few individual resources to the group, then that individual's potential contribution to the group would be small. Such an individual would be a force against cohesion and group locomotion. Outcomes of individual group members will not be maximized, at least in task-based groups, when cohesion is low (e.g., Bjerstedt, 1961; Schachter, 1951; cf. McGrath, 1964).

3. Convergence in Social Assessment of Agreeableness

For attributions of group members along a dimension of agreeableness to serve a useful function, members of the group must reach a consensus on such attributions. To assess convergence in attributions, one must measure concordance between two or more raters who view common targets. Norman and Goldberg (1966) provided clear evidence that peers do converge in their judgments. Costa, McCrae, and their colleagues have used older, nonstudent adults participating in the Baltimore Longitudinal Study to probe this hypothesis. In a paper focusing specifically on the agreeableness dimension, Costa, McCrae, and Dembroski (1989) found a .30 intraclass correlation among 884 pairs of 344 peers raters for 101 targets on the agreeableness dimension. The corresponding intraclass correlation for extraversion was .53. None of the divergent correlations exceeded .15 in absolute value. McCrae and Costa (1987) reported peer intraclass correlations on agreeableness ranging from .28 to .38 (NEO scale), and from .36 to .43 (adjective factor scores). The corresponding intraclass correlations for extraversion were .38 to .52 (NEO scale) and .37 to .59 (adjective factor scores).

A small number of studies, however, report fewer encouraging results for agreeableness. Albright, Kenny, and Malloy (1988) used the Social Relations Model approach to partition variance attributable to raters and targets. Albright et al. found that perceiver variance emerged on judgments of all traits, but the highest perceiver variance appeared on traits about agreeableness. Of the five dimensions assessed, the lowest proportion of target variance (4%) appeared on judgments of agreeableness. The highest proportion of target variance appeared on traits of extraversion (approximately 27%). Albright et al. concluded that the construct of agreeableness showed little or no interrater agreement. Watson (1989) computed peer rater convergence as a function of number of peer raters. The Spearman Brown reliability of peer rating of agreeableness ranged from a low of .21 for one rater to a high of .57 for five raters. The corresponding values for extraversion ranged from .36 (one rater) to .73 (five raters). One interpretation of these studies is that agreeableness is less easily seen than extraversion, particularly in minimally acquainted peers. Watson's data suggest, however, that as the number of raters used to form consensus increases, significant convergence can be achieved. We will return to the issue of salience and level of convergence in peer evaluation when we consider the Wiggins circumplex interpretation of agreeableness.

Smith and Kihlstrom (1987) conducted five rigorous laboratory social cognition studies to probe the hypothesis that the Big Five dimensions function as schemas. More specifically, each of the trait dimensions of the Big Five might be understood as a cognitive structure that organizes the lexicon of relevant but lower order traits. As a clear cognitive structure, agreeableness seemed to fare worse than the remaining dimensions of the Big Five.

Peabody and Goldberg (1989) reported research that is potentially relevant to the interpretation of the Smith and Kihlstrom program of research. These authors note that potential bias that can occur when samples are restricted to homogeneous targets, such as a rater and his or her friends. Peabody and Goldberg found that such restriction reduces the sizes of all factors, but especially that of agreeableness. From the perspective of Peabody and Goldberg, the tightly controlled program of laboratory studies conducted by Smith and Kihlstrom involved internal judgments; there was relatively little room for variations in stimulus materials involving agreeableness.

Taken together, the bulk of the evidence provides qualified support for the natural language approach articulated by Goldberg (1981) and expanded by Hogan (1983). The strongest support appears in more naturalistic studies with large samples provided with an adequate range of trait words (e.g., Costa et al., 1988; Graziano, Jensen-Campbell, & Hair, 1996; Graziano, Jensen-Campbell, Steele, & Hair, 1996; Norman & Goldberg, 1966). There is convergence across raters in the assessment of agreeableness, and the peer consensus correlates significantly with self-ratings of agreeableness. Weak or disconfirming evidence appears in less naturalistic laboratory studies (e.g., Smith & Kihlstrom, 1987). In both kinds of studies, agreeableness is less easy for naive perceivers to assess, particularly when the assessment is based on a small number of observations of strangers (e.g., Albright et al., 1988; Watson, 1989). The precise mechanism of social cognition that is responsible for judgments of agreeableness remains unclear. Agreeableness probably does not operate as an omnibus cognitive schema in perceivers through which the relevant lower order traits in others are organized (Smith & Kihlstrom, 1987).

It is interesting that agreeableness can be seen at all, given the obstacles it faces. Intuitively, one might think that agreeableness would be especially difficult to assess in strangers. The situational press surrounding interaction with strangers, or at least the kinds of interactions assessed in most psychological research, is one that requires mildly positive behavior. There is a very serious restriction in range on the relevant agreeableness cues. Other dimensions might be easier to assess. For example, conscientiousness might be assessed through the tidiness of a stranger's clothing or hair; extraversion might be assessed through the stranger's desire to talk over and beyond the demands of polite interaction. Furthermore, agreeableness may be predominantly an affective evaluation, and may be a broader, more diffuse reaction. As such, we might expect intuitively that it would be harder to identify reliably, especially in situations involving limited interaction. On the whole, these intuitions are off the mark: Agreeableness *can* be seen, even in strangers.

4. Circumplex Analysis of Agreeableness

Wiggins' (1991) approach to natural language and personality considers two major themes that appear to underlie many descriptions of interpersonal behavior. The first theme or dimension of interpersonal behavior is "agency," the condition of being a differential individual, and its manifestation in striving for mastery and power. The second theme is "communion," the condition of being part of a larger spiritual or social community, and its manifestation in striving for intimacy, union, and solidarity with that larger entity. For present purposes, we will restrict ourselves to the part of Wiggins' conceptualization that is most relevant to the dimension of agreeableness and its links to natural language and group processes.

Wiggins (1991) demonstrates that agency and communion are two distinct orthogonal dimensions, not bipolar ends of a single dimension. Within a given group, seeing all possible combinations of agency and communion should be possible, with interpersonal behaviors appearing as "blends." To illustrate, a sociable, exhibitionist person represents a blend of high agentic and high communal orientation, while a deferential, trusting person represents a blend of high communal and low agentic orientation.

Wiggins discusses ways in which natural language forms of address reflect the operation of agency and communion in different languages. One illustration involves a "nonreciprocal power semantic" (Brown & Gilman, 1960). Specifically, the singular form of address in many languages requires a socially important choice. If the person being addressed is a subordinate, the appropriate choice is T (e.g., "tu" in Latin, Italian, French, and Spanish; "tea" in Russian; and "du" in German). If the person is a superior, however, the appropriate choice is V (e.g., "vos" in Latin, "vous" in French, and "vea" in Russian). Choices of this sort are public acknowledgments of power and dominance, and within the framework of Wiggins' analysis reflect the interpersonal behaviors of agency.

Earlier forms of language apparently had no clear rules for differential use of T and V among equal status peers. Gradually, persons of equal status came to address each other with T as an expression of the "solidarity semantic." That is, language use evolved to allow expression of feelings of solidarity, intimacy, and similarity. In Wiggins' terms, language use evolved to reflect not only the dynamics of power and dominance ("agency"), but also the feelings of intimacy and group cohesiveness ("communion"). Apparently, this pattern is not restricted to Indo-European languages (e.g., White, 1980).

The approach taken by Wiggins may suggest some refinements to the natural language approach taken by Goldberg (1981) and Hogan (1983). Whether the agentic and communal differences appear in a single individual or are separated into a task leader and a socioemotional leader (e.g., Bales, 1958), both characteristics seem important to effective group functioning (Raven & Rubin, 1983, p. 501). Precisely where does agreeableness fit on the agency–communion circumplex?

McCrae and Costa (1989b) probed this question by jointly factoring the Wiggins revised Interpersonal Adjective Scales (IAS-R) with peer and spouse ratings on NEO-PI for a sample of 315 adults. Their analyses suggest that the Big Five dimensions of Extraversion and Agreeableness represent rotations of the agency and communion dimensions (or vice versa; factor analysis does not recognize the primacy of any particular rotational position of any axis.) If one visualizes agency as an axis running from north (high agency) to south (low agency) and communion from east (high communion) to west (low communion), agreeableness runs from southeast (agreeable) to northwest (disagreeable). In other words, agreeableness represents a low-agentic–high-communal orientation.

McCrae and Costa (1989b) claim certain advantages for the five-factor model over the circumplex. First, Wiggins' circumplex model and its dimensions are essentially interpersonal and describe the relations between two people. According to McCrae and Costa, concepts like love and warmth and communion may be adequate for research on social psychology, but may not be the best concepts for understanding enduring dispositions in individuals. More specifically, a dimension like agreeableness may include more than interpersonal elements (e.g., styles of cognition and affect). The relative diversity of interpersonal behaviors might be parsimoniously explained not by "blends" of interrelated dimensions but by a small set of orthogonal underlying causes.

There is an intuitive appeal to this reductionistic argument. Before it is accepted however, some problems should be noted. First, it is simply incorrect to assume that "the belief that most variables should load on a single factor follows from the parsimony principle that traits are more likely to have one cause than two" (McCrae & Costa, 1989b, p. 592). In fact, the principle of parsimony is conditional: Given an array of accounts, all of which are comparably adequate to explain a phenomenon, we should accept the simplest. At this juncture, it is premature to assume that the five-factor solution provides a simpler account of communal behavior or its cause than does the circumplex. Nor is it clear why "traits are more likely to have one cause than two," or for that matter 20 (cf. Ahadi & Diener, 1989). Causal identification is a complex business, dependent on such diverse variables as level of observation, mode of analysis, and substantive question being asked (Cook & Campbell, 1979, pp. 10–36; Houts, Cook, & Shadish, 1986). The principle of parsimony is irrelevant to the choice between the two approaches here.

Second, it may not be wise to attempt to partition a dimension like agreeableness into interpersonal and non-interpersonal components. It is true that the agreeableness dimension has correlations with such allegedly non-interpersonal variables as the Myers–Briggs dimension of feeling (e.g., McCrae & Costa, 1989a). Still, if we remove the interpersonal aspects of this dimension, then to what coherent set of processes or behaviors might this dimension predict? Furthermore, removing the interpersonal elements severs one promising link in the nomological network of agreeableness involving the evolution of natural language and group behavior (e.g., Cattell, 1957; Goldberg, 1981; Hogan, 1983; Johnson & Ostendorf, 1993). The basic rationale for the natural language approach focuses on the interpersonal aspects of personality; presumably, differences that are of the most significance in the daily transactions of persons with each other become encoded in language (Goldberg, 1981, p. 142).

Third, the circumplex approach might help explain outcomes of lab studies that raise troubling questions about the precise mechanisms underlying the operation of the Big Five. For example, the Smith and Kihlstrom (1987) studies suggested that agreeableness did not operate as an organizing cognitive schema for relevant lower order traits, and that the Big Five dimensions in general lacked "semantic coherence." If dimensions are conceptualized as a circumplex (i.e., not all dimensions are orthogonal), however, results like those reported by Smith and Kihlstrom become more explicable.

B. Biologically Based, Emotional-Motivational Perspectives on Agreeableness

1. Biological-Affect Perspective as a Complement to a Natural Language–Cognition Perspective

So far, we have considered agreeableness largely from a cognitive perspective. That is, we focused on agreeableness in terms of people's knowledge of agreeableness, in both themselves and others. The natural language approach is itself cognitive in orientation in that it emphasizes the interdependence among language, social perception, and personality. There are, however, three potential limitations to this perspective. First, the cognitive approach is primarily descriptive, not explanatory. That is, it describes how persons might organize impressions of agreeableness, but it is less clear on the mechanisms that induce some persons to be more chronically agreeable than others. Second, even within the framework of a natural language approach, the word "agreeable" connotes an affective element in the evaluation and the perception of motivational dispositions in the target of evaluation. Affective and motivational elements of agreeableness are probably not described (much less explained) adequately by models that focus on cognition, language, and rational evaluations (e.g., Adelmann & Zajonc, 1989; Zojonc & Markus, 1984).

Third, the cognitive approach has not established clear connections to the literature linking positive emotions to prosocial behavior. That literature focuses on relatively short-term effects and situationally induced emotions, but it is possible that chronic emotional states have a similar relation to positive social behavior (e.g., Cunningham, 1985, 1986; Eisenberg et al., 1989). Space limitations preclude a review of the literature on emotions and prosocial behavior here. Instead, we will focus on explanations of possible links between chronic emotions and individual differences in agreeableness. See Watson and Clark (this volume, Chap. 29) for a detailed analysis of positive emotional processes from a personality perspective. There is, of course, no reason to assume that cognitive and affective/motivational models of agreeableness-related behaviors are mutually exclusive alternatives, or even incompatible (e.g., Eisenberg, 1986; Eisenberg et al., 1989; Tellegen, 1985).

2. Temperament and Agreeableness

Individual differences in agreeableness in adults may have a temperamental basis. At the very least, there is evidence for the long term stability of disagreeable behavior across the life span. Ill-tempered boys become men who are described as undercontrolled, irritable, and moody (Caspi, Bem, & Elder, 1989). In discussing their temperamental dimension of emotionality, Buss and Plomin (1984) suggest that in comparison with unemotional people, emotional people become distressed when confronted with emotional stimuli, and they react with higher levels of emotional arousal. As a consequence, they may be harder to soothe when stressed. Rowe and Plomin (1977) found a correlation of −.42 between ratings of children's emotionality and those of their soothability. In one especially unpleasant form of disagreeableness, childhood aggression, chronic differences in emotional responding may play a key role. Perry and Perry (1974) found that chronically aggressive children react more aggressively when provoked and "require" more suffering from their victims before ending an attack than do nonaggressive children. Apparently, chronically aggressive children are not easy to placate or to soothe. Buss and Plomin (1984) suggest that the underlying arousal in emotionality is due to an overactive sympathetic division of the autonomic nervous system.

As a result of certain biological predispositions, individuals may be likely to follow a particular developmental trajectory leading to more or less agreeableness (for an excellent general review of the biological bases of temperament, see Rothbart, 1989). At this juncture, it is not clear how such mechanisms might operate, but individual differences in agreeableness may emerge as part of the ontogeny of systems of excitation and inhibition. If we can assume that agreeableness is associated with the inhibition of negative affect, then models linking brain lateralization and inhibition are relevant to this discussion.

3. Neurology and Agreeableness

Kinsbourne and Bemporad (1984) suggest a multiaxial, ontogenic model to explain the development of self-regulatory processes. In this model, the left frontotemporal cortex controls action over external change, including the planning and sequencing of acts (the "go" system). The right frontotemporal cortex controls internal emotional arousal (the "no go" system). The two systems operate synergistically, using information provided by posterior centers. Damage to the right orbital frontal cortex is associated with emotional disinhibition. Rothbart (1989) notes a parallel line of thinking in Luria's work in that the modulation of social behavior in accordance with the context is associated with the right frontal lobes. Damage to the left dorsolateral frontal area is associated with inaction and apathy. The normative evidence suggests that the right hemisphere develops sooner than the left.

Fox and Davidson (1984) suggest that there are differences in hemispheric specialization for affect. The left hemisphere is associated with positive affect and approach, while the right hemisphere is associated with negative affect and avoidance. Toward the end of the first year of life, development of commissural transfer permits left hemisphere inhibition of right hemisphere function. Two consequences are the inhibition of negative affect and the possibility of behavioral alternations between approach and avoidance.

The two models outlined here are normative-developmental in focus and describe a supposedly universal pattern of neurological ontogeny. However, if there were individual differences in the timing or completeness of any of these lateralization processes (as there surely must be), then there would be implications for origins of agreeableness. That is, during ontogeny individuals may differ in the strength or timing of their left hemispheric connections, or in commissural transfer. With these differences, there would be corresponding differences in emotional expression and in the inhibition of negative affect. Differences in expression in turn would lead to different socialization experiences. From a developmental perspective, even if the delayed ontogeny of inhibition were temporary, there could be long-term consequences. In one example, mothers report decreases in feelings of attachment for their 3-month-old infants if crying and other forms of negative affect do not decrease (i.e., come under inhibitory control), as they do in most infants (Robson & Moss, 1970). Longitudinal research on disruptions in mother–infant attachment has shown patterns of persistent disagreeableness such as aggression and noncompliance, particularly in boys (e.g., Renken, Egeland, Marvinney, Manglsdorf, & Sroufe, 1989).

A second speculative candidate involves neuroregulatory amines (Panskepp, 1986). These neurochemical systems apparently operate globally to influence shifts in vigilance and tendencies to act. For the present purposes, work by Cloninger is most relevant. Specifically, Cloninger (1987) speculates that norepinephrine functioning is related to reward dependence, which includes such behavior as being emotionally dependent (versus coolly detached), warmly sympathetic (versus tough-minded), sentimental, and sensitive to social cues. The bulk of the research on neuroregulatory amines has focused on psychiatric disorders, with relatively little work on normal adult personality processes (for a more detailed treatment, see Rothbart, 1989).

4. Approach–Avoidance and Agreeableness

Another explanation for agreeableness involves conflict between approach and avoidance motives (cf. Graziano, Jensen-Campbell, & Hair, 1996; Jensen-Campbell, Graziano, & Hair, 1996). Infante and Rancer (1982) offer a model of argumentativeness with two independent motives of approach and avoidance of arguments. That is, people differ in feelings of excitement in advocating positions on controversial issues, and in attacking others' positions (approach). People also differ in their motivation to avoid arguments. The motive to avoid arguments is seen as a debilitating factor, weakening the tendency to approach arguments by the anxiety associated with arguing. The motives to approach and to avoid arguments are independent, so that it is possible to be high on both motives, low on both, or high on one but low on the other.

In this approach, the chronically argumentative person experiences favorable excitement and has a strong tendency to approach arguments, while feeling no inhibition nor tendency to avoid arguments. The chronically nonargumentative person shows the opposite pattern of approach and avoidance. Infante and Rancer hypothesize that the expression of dispositional argumentativeness is moderated by the perceived probability of success in a particular argument and the importance (incentive value) of success in winning that argument. In this system, persons with similar levels of the two motives (e.g., high approach and high avoidance) should be more susceptible to situational influences than persons with different levels of the two motives. That is, persons high in approach but low in avoidance will be likely to argue across a range of incentive and probability of success conditions; persons high in both motives will be more responsive to variations in the incentives and probabilities of success in different situational contexts (see Perry, Williard, & Perry [1990] for a similar analysis of incentive and expectation effects in the selection of victims in children's aggression).

Infante and Rancer developed a 20-item scale and reported alpha reliabilities for the approach and avoidance components and resultant difference score ranging from .86 to .91. The correlation between self-ratings and friends' evaluations of argumentativeness (approach) was .54. The approach score component correlated .30 with a choice to participate in a debate and −.39 to avoid a debate. From the present perspective, it is possible that the individual differences identified by Infant and his colleagues are part of the larger construct of agreeableness.

5. Hostility and Agreeableness

Yet another explanation of agreeableness involves emotions associated with hostility. In their efforts to identify the "active ingredient" in the Type A link to coronary heart disease, Costa et al. (1988) consider the variable Potential of Hostility, as scored from Rosenman's (1978) Structured Interview (SI). This study also provided a wealth of information about correlates of agreeableness, as measured by the NEO-PI. Costa et al. note that much of the confusion surrounding the role of anger and hostility in cardiovascular disease is probably due to the fact that there are both neurotic and antagonistic forms of hostility. The experience of hostility is not the same as the expression of hostility. Across two replicating samples of college students ($N = 208$), self-reports of the experience of anger were correlated over +.60 with NEO-Neuroticism, but approximately −.33 with NEO-Agreeableness. Self-reports of anger expression, however, correlated .00 with Neuroticism, and approximately −.40 with Agreeableness. Peer ratings of the focal subjects showed essentially the same pattern, but correlations involving peer ratings of subjects' experience of anger were somewhat lower. In general, both the self-reported experience and the expression of hostility are negatively related to Agreeableness; this evaluation is corroborated in peer reports.

More interesting, perhaps, are the correlations of various forms of hostility taken from the SI with personality. Across both samples, all four forms of hostility (Hostile Content, Hostile Intensity, Hostile Style, and Potential for Hostility) had relatively small but significant negative correlations with Agreeableness. The correlations involving peer ratings, however, were generally nonsignificant. Costa et al. note that the college samples showed considerable restriction in range on the hostility variables; with a fuller range, larger correlations might have been seen (see Matthews, 1988). Costa et al. note that in 1988, there were no conclusive data linking agreeableness to coronary heart disease. At the very least, data from their study raise some intriguing questions. Costa et al. suggest that in their efforts to identify the "toxic component of Type A," researchers should not restrict themselves to a narrow view of antagonistic behaviors, and should supplement their use of the standard SI with measures of agreeableness.

The literature we have outlined in this section suggests that there are probably important links between emotional/motivational processes and individual differences in agreeableness. It also suggests that these emotional processes may have a biological base, and are further modified by life experiences as persons move through the life span. Differences in agreeableness are probably related to important socioemotional and health outcomes. Clearly, the interconnection among these variables is worthy of future research.

III. THE PROSOCIAL PERSONALITY

A. Definition of Prosociality and Scope of Analyses

In this section, we examine prosocial tendencies as one form of agreeableness. Prosocial behavior typically is defined as voluntary behavior intended to benefit another (regardless of whether the behavior is motivated by altruism or baser forms of motivation, such as rewards and social approval). Thus, it overlaps considerably with natural language trait words associated with agreeableness such as "sympathetic," "generous," "kind," "helpful," and "considerate" (see Goldberg, 1992). Because people may act in kind, considerate, and helpful ways for a variety of reasons and it is often impossible to assess individuals' motives for their prosocial actions, we focus on the broader category of prosocial behavior rather than solely on altruistic behavior (which is a type of prosocial behavior). However, it is possible that altruism and constructs such as sympathy, other-oriented moral reasoning, and perspective taking are more closely related to agreeableness than is prosocial behavior (Penner & Fritzsche, 1993).

In this section, we briefly summarize the literature concerning the existence of stable individual differences in prosocial proclivities. The evidence for the role of situational variables in prosocial behavior is persuasive (see Dovidio, 1984; Krebs & Miller, 1985) but is less central to this volume than are data concerning the role of personality variables; therefore, we do not review the enormous literature demonstrating that prosocial behavior varies as a function of a variety of situational factors. Rather, we focus primarily on the literature concerning stable individual differences in prosocial responding and the possible bases of those dispositions (much of which is developmental in focus).

To examine the role of dispositional factors in prosocial behavior, we review research concerning several issues: (1) the role of biology in prosocial tendencies; (2) the relation of prosocial tendencies to social learning variables believed to induce individual differences in prosocial responding; (3) consistency in prosocial responding across time; (4) consistency in prosocial responding across situations; and (5) the relation of prosocial behavior to various person/personality variables. Next we briefly sample studies stemming from an interactional perspective. Given our space constraints, our reviews are illustrative rather than detailed; nonetheless, we try to present an overview of the various types of data that are relevant to determining the role of personality in altruism.

B. The Biological Bases of Prosocial Behavior

1. Sociobiology

Recent interest in sociobiology has stimulated much discussion concerning the evolutionary bases of prosocial behavior. A variety of mechanisms for the evolution of altruism in humans have been proposed, including group selection (Wynne-Edwards, 1962), kin selection (Hamilton, 1964), reciprocal altruism (Trivers, 1971), and genetic similarity (Rushton, Russell, & Wells, 1984), all of which posit reasons why people who assist others would be more likely than less prosocial persons to ensure the survival of their genes in the gene pool (see Boorman & Leavitt, 1980; Cunningham, 1985–1986; Eisenberg, Fabes, & Miller, 1990). In recent variations on this theme, some psychologists and biologists have suggested that it is the interaction of cultural and biological factors that result in prosocial behavior being adaptive (in the reproductive sense; e.g., Batson, 1983; Hill, 1984; MacDonald, 1984).

2. Heritability

Evidence of innate, inherited differences in individuals' prosocial tendencies would provide strong support for the assertion that there is indeed a prosocial personality. However, most of the research and theorizing on the role of genetics in prosocial behavior concerns the existence of a genetic basis of prosocial behavior in the human species, not the existence of biologically based mechanisms that might be the source of individual differences in prosocial tendencies. Thus, the sociobiologists and psychologists interested in the genetic basis of altruism have done little work bearing directly on the issue of personality differences in prosocial tendencies.

Most of the limited work on inherited differences in prosocial tendencies concerns the construct of empathy. Stimulated by sociobiological ideas, Batson (1983) and M. Hoffman (1981) have proposed that the capacity for empathy is the biological substrate upon which human altruism is built. Empathy (and sympathy) has been empirically (Eisenberg Fabes, & Miller, in press) as well as conceptually (Batson, 1987; Blum, 1980; Feshbach, 1978; M. L. Hoffman, 1984; Staub, 1978) linked with prosocial behavior; therefore, if Hoffman and Batson are correct, genetically based individual differences in vicarious emotional responsivity to others could account for individual differences in prosocial behavior.

Consistent with the perspective that dispositional differences in both empathy and prosocial behavior have a biological basis, several groups of investigators have obtained high estimates of heritability (from .44 to .72) in studies of twins' self-reported empathy and prosocial behavior (Loehlin & Nichols, 1976; Matthews, Batson, Horn, & Rosenman, 1981; Rushton, Fulker, Neale, Nias, & Eysenck, 1986). These data must be interpreted with caution, however, because investigators frequently find higher relations between scores of identical twins than between scores to fraternal twins when self-report indices are used instead of other types of measures to assess aspects of personality (Plomin, 1986). However, recent work with very young children suggests that empathy-related responding is indeed partially genetically based, particularly the emotional components of empathy (Zahn-Waxler, Robinson, & Emde, 1992).

In summary, the few existing studies on the heritability of empathy and prosocial tendencies provide evidence consistent with the view that there are stable individual differences in prosocial responding. However, additional research involving behavioral indices of prosocial tendencies is needed.

C. The Social Learning Basis of Prosocial Behavior

The literature concerning the influence of cultural and specific child-rearing techniques is too voluminous to review in this chapter and has been reviewed extensively elsewhere (see Eisenberg & Mussen, 1989; Moore & Eisenberg, 1984; Radke-Yarrow, Zahn-Waxler, & Chapman, 1983). In general, however, researchers have found that prosocial responding is systematically related to both living in certain types of cultures and being exposed to specific types of socialization techniques.

Specifically, children who are routinely expected to assist in caring for others and in tasks important to the existence of the family are more prosocial than children from cultures in which such expectations are weak or absent (e.g., Whiting & Whiting, 1975). Moreover, people are relatively likely to engage in prosocial actions when they have been exposed to altruistic models, other-oriented preachings, and inductive (reasoning) modes of discipline; if they have been provided with high moral standards and opportunities to engage in prosocial activities; and if they have been exposed to such influences in a warm, supportive context. Findings supporting these conclusions have been obtained in laboratory studies and in correlational studies, and have been found in studies of real-life altruists (e.g., rescuers in Nazi Germany [Oliner & Oliner, 1988] and freedom riders in the southern part of the United States [Rosenhan, 1970]).

Although not all researchers have obtained this pattern of findings, the overall pattern is consistent enough to conclude that variations in the learning context are associated with relatively enduring individual differences in prosocial responding. Variations in learning experiences generally are believed to engender individual differences in values, motives, sociocognitive capacities, knowledge about helping, self-perceptions, and affective responses—differences associated with variations in prosocial tendencies.

D. Consistency of Prosocial Responding across Time and Situations

One of the most obvious ways to study the stability of individual differences in prosocial tendencies is to examine relative consistency in those tendencies over time and situations. If there are stable differences in individuals' characteristic levels of prosocial behavior over time and situations, it is likely that this stability is due in part to aspects of the individual's personality or sociocognitive functioning (see West & Graziano, 1989).

Those investigators who have obtained longitudinal data have frequently found evidence of modest stability in individuals' relative levels of prosocial tendencies. The evidence of stability is perhaps weakest in studies of young children. For example, Dunn and Munn (1986) found low, positive but nonsignificant correlations from 18 to 24 months of age for a composite of observed sharing/helping/comforting behaviors and for giving appropriately. Similarly, Eisenberg, Wolchik, Goldberg, Engel, and Pasternack (1992) examined consistency over 6 months in 1- to 2-year-olds' spontaneous and requested prosocial behaviors with mothers and fathers and obtained very modest evidence of consistency. The only correlations that were significant were for boys' (but not girls') requested prosocial behaviors with fathers and for boys' spontaneous behaviors with mothers.

The relatively sparse evidence of consistency in prosocial responding in the early years is not surprising given the major changes in sociocognitive capabilities (e.g., role taking, moral reasoning) and other skills, as well as socializers' behaviors, during the first years of life.

Stability in prosocial tendencies likely increases with age in childhood. Dunn and Munn (1986), in an observational study of siblings in their homes, found that older siblings (approximately 3 to 6 years of age) were more consistent over a 6-month period in their helping, sharing, and comforting behavior than were their 1- to 2-year-old siblings. Moreover, other researchers have obtained evidence of moderate stability in prosocial responding in the preschool and school years. Block and Block (1973) found that preschoolers who had been described by their nursery school teachers as generous, helpful and cooperative, empathic, considerate, dependable, and responsible at age 4 were more likely at age 5 than their peers to share a prize they had earned with another child who did not have time to earn a prize. Similarly, Baumrind (reported in Mussen & Eisenberg-Berg, 1977) found that social responsible, prosocial behavior in the preschool years (as rated by observers) was significantly correlated with similar behavior when in elementary school 5 to 6 years later.

In addition, Eisenberg et al. (1987) found that donating to charity was consistent from age 7–8 years to age 9–10 years, and from 9–10 to 11–12. Helping (e.g., helping pick up paper clips or spilled papers), which was assessed at ages 9 to 10 and 11 to 12, also was relatively stable over this 2-year period. Further, self-reported prosocial behavior and mothers' reports of children's prosocial behavior were both consistent over 4 years, as was helping by doing extra tasks for the experimenter (Eisenberg, Carlo, Murphy, & Van Court, 1993; Eisenberg, Miller, Shell, McNalley, & Shea, 1991). Finally, Bar-Tal and Raviv (1979) found that peers' and teachers' sociometric ratings of sixth graders' altruism were relatively stable over a 2-year period; however, sociometric ratings in sixth grade were not significantly related to self-reported willingness to help 2 years later.

An alternative index of stability in prosocial responding is the quality of the individual's reaction to a needy or distressed person (rather than simple quantity of a given behavior). In this regard, Radke-Yarrow and Zahn-Waxler (1984) obtained mothers' detailed reports of their 1- to 2-year-olds' naturally occurring reactions when they observed others in distress or need. They found that two-thirds of the children were stable over a 5-year period in mode of reaction. For example, if children responded emotionally, with avoidance, or with a cognitive, nonemotional response at age 2, they were likely to do so at age 7.

There are very few data concerning the stability of prosocial behavior in adolescents and adults. Oliner and Oliner (1988), in a retrospective study of Europeans who had previously rescued Jews from the Nazis in World War II, found that rescuers were more likely than peers who did not engage in rescuing activities to report involvement in several prosocial activities during the year before their interview (e.g., feeding the sick or aged or visiting the ill; making telephone calls for a group or cause; or helping raise money for a group or cause). Thus, using a sample of verified altruists, the Oliners obtained evidence of consistency in prosocial responding over 3 to 4 decades.

On a less grand scale, Small, Zeldin, and Savin-Williams (1983) found that peers' ratings of adolscents' prosocial behavior, as well as observed prosocial behaviors, were quite stable over a 3- to 4-week period (rs ranged from .48 to .99). In another study involving adolescents, Davis and Franzoi (1991) obtained fairly high correlations between high school students' self-reports of sympathetic concern over a 2- or 3-year period (rs for the total sample ranged from .48 to .64 or .64 to .81 when corrected for measurement error); similar findings have been obtained by Eisenberg and her colleagues (1991, 1993). Given the fact that sympathetic concern is positively related to behaviors that appear to be altruistic (Batson, 1987; Davis, 1983; see Eisenberg et al., in press) and is an index of other-oriented concern (cf. Jensen-Campbell et al., 1996), the Davis and Franzoi data also can be viewed as evidence of stability in altruistic responding.

Some of the strongest evidence of consistency in prosocial responding across settings comes from studies conducted by Savin-Williams and his colleagues. They observed four groups of adolescents at summer camping outings over periods of weeks (at wilderness travel programs and travel camp programs; see Savin-Williams, Small, and Zeldin, 1981; Small et al., 1983; Zeldin, Small & Savin-Williams, 1982; see Savin-Williams, 1987). Individual differences in prosocial behavior were clearly recognized by peers after only 4 days, and these perceptions remained stable over weeks (Zeldin et al., 1982). Moreover, observed levels of prosocial behavior were highly consistent across situations (Small et al., 1983).

Obtained correlations reported in studies of cross-situational or cross-time consistency are likely minimal estimates of the true correlations. As was evidenced in Rushton's (1980) reanalysis of the Hartshorne and May data, the use of aggregated indices would doubtless increase the size of the intercorrelations in relevant research (see Epstein, 1979). Moreover, the intercorrelations would be expected to be higher if all the indices of prosocial behavior were actually indices of altruism (and, consequently, were due to higher level motivations such as sympathy and internalized values).

In summary, the evidence suggests that there is moderate stability in individuals' prosocial responding after the preschool years. However, the correlations over time vary considerably in strength. It is impressive, nonetheless, that researchers often have obtained any evidence of consistency considering that children's interpretations and understandings of the nature of kindness change with age (see Eisenberg, 1986), as do their competencies with regard to helping (e.g., Peterson, 1983). Moreover, the evidence for consistency is strengthened by the fact that some of these studies involved observational indices of prosocial behavior rather than merely self-report indices (which may be affected by memory distortions and self-presentational concerns). In addition, it is likely that estimates of consistency in most studies were underestimated because few researchers have corrected stability coefficients for measurement error.

E. The Relation of Prosocial Responding to Person Variables

If there are stable individual differences in prosociality, one would expect prosocial persons to exhibit somewhat different personal characteristics than less prosocial persons. In particular, prosocial (and particularly altruistic) persons would be expected to exhibit high levels of those characteristics that have been conceptually linked to other-oriented, moral responding—for example, role taking, sympathy and empathy, high-level moral reasoning, valuing of others, feelings of responsibility toward others, and the tendency to ascribe responsibility for others to the self (see Eisenberg et al., in press; Schwartz & Howard, 1984; Staub, 1974, 1978, 1986; Underwood & Moore, 1982). Moreover, because prosocial behavior often involves not only an other-orientation but also the ability to enact helping actions, it is reasonable to expect correlations between indices of prosocial behavior and individual competence and control, including social competence and internal locus of control.

There do seem to be some associations between prosocial behavior and those personality characteristics conceptually linked to altruism, although these relations are often not strong or very consistent. For example, prosocial responding has been positively associated with a communal orientation (Clark, Ouellett, Powell, & Milberg, 1987), nurturance (e.g., Romer, Gruder, & Lizzardo, 1986; Rushton, Chrisjohn, & Fekken, 1981; Rushton, Littlefield, & Lumsden, 1986), social interest (Crandall & Harris, 1976; Rushton et al., 1981), social extensivity (Oliner & Oliner, 1988), social responsibility (Eisenberg et al., 1989; Oliner & Oliner, 1988), and ascription of responsibility for others to the self (Eisenberg et al., 1989; Staub, 1974; see review in Schwartz & Howard, 1981, 1984). Personal norms regarding helping, presumably constructed from internalized moral values, also have been linked with prosocial behavior in several studies (see Eisenberg, 1986; Pomazal & Jaccard, 1976; Schwartz & Howard, 1984; Zuckerman & Reis, 1978), as has endorsement of altruistic values (Larrieu & Mussen, 1986; Rushton et al., 1981). Moreover, in a review of the research on the personality correlates of community mental health volunteers, Allen and Rushton (cited by Krebs & Miller, 1985) found that the following personality traits were characteristic of the volunteers: internal locus of control, social responsibility, inner directedness, achievement via independence, self-control, flexibility, superego strength, self-acceptance, capacity for intimacy, and nurturance.

The relations of prosocial behavior to sociocognitive capabilities and affective aspects of responding are perhaps more consistent than relations for the traditionally studied personality characteristics. For example, individual differences in sympathy/ empathy (Eisenberg et al., in press) perspective-taking ability (Underwood & Moore, 1982), and level of moral reasoning (Blasi, 1980; Eisenberg, 1986; Underwood & Moore, 1982) have all been positively linked with prosocial responding in reviews of the literature. Moreover, this linkage might be stronger when one considers multiple sociocognitive and affective skills. For example, Knight, Johnson, Carlo, and Eisenberg (1994) found that children who were high in sympathy, perspective taking, and the understanding of money were highest in donating money to hospitalized children.

Sociability and assertiveness are personality characteristics that are more consistently related to prosocial behavior than are most traits. Specifically, they are positively associated with children's and adolescents' performance of prosocial acts that involve social initiative and direct interaction with others (e.g., Eisenberg, Cameron, Tryon, & Dodez, 1981; Eisenberg, Pasternack, Cameron, & Tryon, 1984; Hampson, 1984; Larrieu, 1984; Murphy, 1937). A certain level of assertiveness may be necessary for people to spontaneously approach others who need assistance (Midlarsky & Hannah, 1985). Given that high levels of spontaneous prosocial behavior have been associated with high sociability, moral reasoning, and other measures of competent social behavior, children who tend to perform helping and sharing behaviors spontaneously may fall into the group of agreeable people with high extraversion or emotional stability (as identified by Johnson & Ostendorf, 1993).

In contrast, low levels of assertiveness and dominance have been associated with children's compliant prosocial behavior (e.g., assisting in response to a request; Eisenberg et al., 1981, 1984; Eisenberg & Giallanza, 1984; Larrieu, 1984). Among preschoolers, nonassertive children are viewed as easy targets by their peers, and are asked to share or assist more often than are their more assertive peers (Eisenberg et al., 1981; Eisenberg, McCreath, & Ahn, 1988). Thus, the types of prosocial acts performed by persons varying in assertiveness and sociability probably differ somewhat in terms of their social significance and motivational bases, and are differentially performed depending on the social context. We now turn to this issue of the interaction between personal characteristics and environment.

F. The Interaction of Person and Environmental Variables

Situational variables appear to interact with person characteristics in a variety of ways (see Snyder & Ickes, 1985). Because this chapter's intent is to focus on agreeableness as a person variable, we do not attempt to describe all of the myriad possible person–situation interactions in prosociality. Rather, we acknowledge these interactions with illustrative examples.

Some researchers have found that specific types of helping contexts engender prosocial action in people with particular dispositional characteristics. For example, Gergen, Gergen, and Meter (1972) asked students to volunteer for a variety of prosocial activities ranging from counseling needy students to participating in an experiment involving unusual states of consciousness. They found that students with different dispositional characteristics and motives choose different helping activities, and that there seemed to be a match between students' dispositions and the ways in which they chose to help. It is likely that somewhat different personality traits are associated with planned versus informal helping.

In another particularly illustrative study, Romer et al. (1986) found that receptive givers, that is, people high in dispositional nurturance and need for succorance (the tendency to seek aid and support from others, especially when in need), were predisposed to help when compensation was expected. In contrast, adults who were high in nurturance and were more inner sustaining (independent) were more likely than receptive givers to help when compensation was not expected (and helped less than receptive givers when compensation was expected). People low in nurturance and high in succorance helped least, regardless of compensation. The results of studies such as these are consistent with other data suggesting that dispositional characteristics affect individuals' estimates of the costs and benefits of prosocial action in helping contexts (e.g., Penner, Michael & Brookmire, 1979).

The results of these and other studies suggest that the association between dispositional factors and prosocial behavior may be underestimated frequently by researchers who do not attend to moderating variables. Awareness of this problem is evident in theoretical work on heuristic models of prosocial behavior (e.g., Eisenberg, 1986, Figure 1). It is important to recognize, however, that the focus of most empirical work in the area has been on prosocial behavior, not solely altruistic behavior. Many dispositional and situational variables that affect nonaltruistic prosocial behaviors would not be expected to influence altruistic responding. The association between prosocial behavior and person-centered variables (e.g., moral reasoning, sympathetic tendencies) would increase if altruistic behavior only were considered (e.g., Rholes & Bailey, 1983).

IV. SUMMARY AND CONCLUSIONS

This chapter examined agreeableness as a dimension of personality. Agreeableness is probably best conceptualized as a general latent variable that summarizes more specific tendencies and behaviors (e.g., being kind, considerate, likable, cooperative, helpful). We used the natural language approach developed by Goldberg (1981) to organize the diverse findings in the literature. The central proposition of the natural language approach is that individual differences that are of the most significance in the daily transactions of persons with each other will eventually become encoded in our language. Agreeableness should certainly qualify as an individual difference having significance for people's daily transactions. We then discussed ways in which theoretical work by Hogan (1983) and Wiggins (1991) might be linked to the natural language approach. In particular, we noted how personality language may have its origins in the need for human groups to take concerted action (Hogan, 1983). Group action is most efficient when individual members are willing to conform to group norms and to suspend their own individual concerns for the good of the group.

With a few notable exceptions, the bulk of the literature is consistent with these theoretical ideas. Across a range of studies, agreeableness emerges in the natural language descriptions of the self and peers. Furthermore, there is evidence that self-rating and peer evaluations converge in assessing agreeableness. Such results are remarkable if we assume that the original research materials developed by Allport and Odbert and refined by Cattell probably biased outcomes against uncovering an agreeableness dimension. The precise mechanism linking assessments of agreeableness to specific behaviors remains unclear. Careful laboratory work suggests that agreeableness probably does not operate as an omnibus cognitive schema organizing lower level traits (Smith & Kihlstrom, 1987).

Other work suggests that agreeableness may be less salient as an individual difference, particularly among minimally acquainted people, than dimensions such as extraversion or dominance (e.g., Albright et al., 1988; Watson, 1989). Assessments of agreeableness may be more global, more affect-laden, or more diffuse than other kinds of assessments.

Promising lines of research have emerged linking agreeableness to motivational processes and affect. Wiggins (1991) suggests that individual differences in agreeableness might be part of a motivational system in which people strive for intimacy, union, and solidarity with the groups to which they belong (or seek to belong). Basic biobehavioral research suggests that individual differences in agreeableness in adults may have their origins in affective self-regulatory processes in childhood. In particular, individual differences in the pattern of inhibition of negative affect may be related to the development of agreeableness (e.g., Fox & Davidson, 1984), and these may be related to health, especially cardiovascular disease (Costa et al., 1988).

Prosocial behavior can be conceptualized as a form of agreeableness. Recent research suggests that there may be important dispositional components to prosocial behavior, and these may be seen even in young children. Precise identification of these dispositions has been inhibited by problems of differentiating among social motives, and by weak measures of altruism as an outcome and as a disposition. A further problem is that researchers have focused on main effects and not on moderated relations. Despite conceptual complexities and despite efforts to suppress its appearance, a construct approximated with the label agreeableness continually reappears in personality research. Its pervasiveness is best explained by its importance for understanding personality and interpersonal behavior.

ACKNOWLEDGMENT

Part of this work was supported by NSF Grant BNS 8705780 to William Graziano, and by NSF Grants BNS 8807784 and DBS-9208375, National Institute of Child Health & Development Career Development Award KO4 HD 00717, and National Institutes of Health Grant K02 MH00903 to Nancy Eisenberg. The authors express their appreciation to Steve Briggs,

Charles Halverson, Lauri Jensen Campbell, Delroy Paulhus, Louis Penner, Niels Waller, David Watson, and Steve West for comments on an earlier version of this chapter.

References

Adelmann, P. K., & Zajonc, R. B. (1989). Facial efference and the experience of emotion. *Annual Review of Psychology, 40,* 249–280.

Adler, A. (1964). *Social interest: A challenge to mankind.* New York: Capricorn. (Original work published 1938)

Ahadi, S., & Diener, E. (1989). Multiple determinants and effect size. *Journal of Personality and Social Psychology, 56,* 398–406.

Albright, L., Kenny, D. A., & Malloy, T. E. (1988). Consensus in personality judgments at zero acquaintance. *Journal of Personality and Social Psychology, 55,* 387–395.

Allen, N. J., & Rushton, J. P. (1983). Personality characteristics of community mental health volunteers: A review. *Journal of Voluntary Action Research, 12,* 36–49.

Allport, G. W., & Odbert, H. S. (1936). Trait names: A psycho-lexical study. *Psychological Monographs, 47*(1, Whole No. 211).

Bales, R. F. (1958). Task roles and social roles in problem solving groups. In E. E. Maccoby, T. M. Newcomb, & E. L. Hartley (Eds.), *Readings in social psychology* (3rd ed., pp. 437–447). New York: Holt, Rinehart.

Baron, R. M. (1988). An ecological framework for establishing a dual mode theory of social knowing. In D. Bar-Tal & A. W. Kruglanski (Eds.), *The social psychology of knowledge* (pp. 48–82). Cambridge, England: Cambridge University Press.

Bar-Tal, D., & Raviv, A. (1979). Consistency in helping-behavior measures. *Child Development, 50,* 1235–1238.

Batson, C. D. (1983). Sociobiology and the role of religion in promoting prosocial behavior: An alternative view. *Journal of Personality and Social Psychology, 45,* 1380–1385.

Batson, C. D. (1987). Prosocial motivation: Is it ever truly altruistic? In L. Berkowitz (Ed.), *Advances in experimental social psychology* (pp. 65–122). Orlando, FL: Academic Press.

Bjerstedt, A. (1961). Preparation, process, and product in small group interaction. *Human Relations, 14,* 183–189.

Blasi, A. (1980). Bridging moral cognition and moral action: A critical review of the literature. *Psychological Bulletin, 88,* 1–45.

Block, J., & Block, J. H. (1973, January). *Ego development and the provenance of thought: A longitudinal study of ego and cognitive development in young children* (Grant No. MH16080). Progress report for the National Institute of Mental Health.

Blum, L. A. (1980). *Friendship, altruism and morality.* London: Routledge & Kegan Paul.

Bond, M. H., & Forgas, J. P. (1984). Linking person perception to behavior intentions across cultures: The role of cultural collectivism. *Journal of Cross-Cultural Psychology, 15,* 337–352.

Boorman, S. A., & Levitt, P. R. (1980). *The genetics of altruism.* New York: Academic Press.

Brown, R., & Gilman, A. (1960). The pronouns of power and solidarity. In T. A. Sebreok (Ed.), *Style in language* (pp. 253–276). Cambridge: Technology Press.

Buss, A., & Plomin, R. (1984). *Temperament: Early developing personality traits.* Hillsdale, NJ: Erlbaum.

Campbell, D. T. (1988). Descriptive epistemology: Psychological, sociological, and evolutionary. In E. S. Overman (Ed.), *Methodology and epistemology for the social sciences: Selected papers* (pp. 435–486). Chicago: University of Chicago Press.

Caspi, A., Bem, D. J., & Elder, G. H., Jr. (1989). Continuities consequences of interactional styles across the life course [Special issue]. *Journal of Personality, 57,* 375–406.

Cattell, R. B. (1957). *Personality and motivation: Structure and measurement.* Yonkers-on-Hudson, NY: World Book.

Clark, M. S., Ouellette, R., Powell, M. C., & Milberg, S. (1987). Recipient's mood, relationship type, and helping. *Journal of Personality and Social Psychology, 53,* 94–103.

Cloninger, C. R. (1987). Neurogetic adaptive mechanisms in alcoholism. *Science, 236,* 410–416.

Collins, B. E., & Raven, B. H. (1969). Group structure: Attraction, coalitions, communication, and power. In G. Lindzey & E. Aronson (Eds.), *Handbook of social psychology* (2nd ed., Vol. 4, pp. 102–204). Reading, MA: Addison-Wesley.

Cook, T. D., & Campbell, D. T. (1979). *Quasi-experimentation: Design and analysis issues for field settings.* Chicago: Rand McNally.

Cosmides, L., & Tooby, J. (1992). Cognitive adaptations for social exchange. In J. H. Barkow, L. Cosmides, & J. Tooby (Eds.), *The adapted mind: Evolutionary psychology and the generation of culture* (pp. 163–228). New York: Oxford University Press.

Costa, P. T., Jr., McCrae, R. R., & Dembroski, T. M. (1989). Agreeableness versus Antagonism; Explication of a Potential Risk Factor for CHD. In A. Siegman & T. M. Dembroski (Eds.), *In search of coronary-prone behavior* (pp. 41–63). Hillsdale, NJ: Erlbaum.

Crandall, J. E., & Harris, M. D. (1976). Social interest cooperation and altruism. *Journal of Individual Psychology, 32,* 50–54.

Cunningham, M. R. (1985–1986). Levites and brother's keepers: A sociobiological perspective on prosocial behavior. *Humboldt Journal of Social Relations, 13,* 35–67.

Dabbs, J. M., Jr., & Ruback, R. B. (1987). Dimensions of group process: Amount and structure of vocal interaction. In L. Berkowitz (Ed.), *Advances in experimental social psychology* (Vol. 20, pp. 123–137). San Diego, CA: Academic Press.

Davis, M. H. (1983). Measuring individual differences in empathy: Evidence for a multidimensional approach. *Journal of Personality and Social Psychology, 44,* 113–126.

Davis, M. H., & Franzoi, S. (1991). Stability and change in adolescent self-consciousness and empathy. *Journal of Research in Personality, 25,* 70–87.

Digman, J. M., & Inouye, J. (1986). Further specification of the five robust factors of personality. *Journal of Personality and Social Psychology, 50,* 116–123.

Digman, J. M., & Takemoto-Chock, N. K. (1981). Factors in the natural language of personality: Re-analysis, comparison, and interpretation of six major studies. *Multivariate Behavioral Research, 16,* 149–170.

Dovidio, J. J. (1984). Helping behavior and altruism: An empirical and conceptual overview. In L. Berkowitz (Ed.), *Advances in experimental social psychology* (Vol. 17, pp. 361–427). New York: Academic Press.

Dunn, J., & Munn, P. (1986). Siblings and the development of prosocial behaviors. *International Journal of Behavioral Development, 9,* 265–284.

Eisenberg, N. (1986). *Altruistic emotion, cognition and behavior.* Hillsdale, NJ: Erlbaum.

Eisenberg, N., Cameron, E., Tryon, K., & Dodez, R. (1981). Socialization of prosocial behavior in the preschool classroom. *Developmental Psychology, 17,* 773–782.

Eisenberg, N., Carlo, G., Murphy, B., & Van Court, P. (1996). *Prosocial development in late adolescence and early adulthood: A longitudinal study.* Paper submitted for editorial review.

Eisenberg, N., Fabes, R. A., & Miller, P. A. (1990). The evolutionary and neurological roots of prosocial behavior. In L. Ellis & H. Hoffman (Eds.), *Crime in biological, social, and moral contexts* (pp. 247–260). New York: Praeger.

Eisenberg, N., Fabes, R. A., & Miller, P. A. (in press). The evolutionary and neurological roots of prosocial behavior. In L. Ellis & H. Hoffman (Eds.), *Evolution, the brain, and criminal behavior: Explorations in biosocial criminology.*

Eisenberg, N., & Giallanza, S. (1984). The relation of mode of prosocial behavior and other proprietary behaviors to toy dominance. *Child Study Journal, 14,* 115–121.

Eisenberg, N., McCreath, H., & Ahn, R. (1988). Vicarious emotional responsiveness and prosocial behavior: Their interrelations in young children. *Personality and Social Psychology Bulletin, 14,* 298–311.

Eisenberg, N., Miller, P. A., Schaller, M., Fabes, R. A., Fultz, J., Shell, R., & Shea, C. (1989). The role of sympathy and altruistic personality traits in helping: A re-examination. *Journal of Personality, 57,* 41–68.

Eisenberg, N., Miller, P. A., Shell, R., McNalley, S., & Shea, C. (1991). Prosocial development in adolescence: A longitudinal study. *Developmental Psychology, 27,* 849–857.

Eisenberg, N., & Mussen, P. (1989). *The roots of prosocial behavior in children.* Cambridge, England: Cambridge University Press.

Eisenberg, N., Pasternack, J. F., Cameron, E., & Tryon, K. (1984). The relation of quantity and mode of prosocial to moral cognitions and social style. *Child Development, 55,* 1479–1485.

Eisenberg, N., Shell, R., Pasternack, J., Lennon, R., Beller, R., & Mathy, R. M. (1987). Prosocial development in middle childhood: A longitudinal study. *Developmental Psychology, 23,* 712–718.

Eisenberg, N., Wolchik, S. A., Goldberg, L., Engel, I., & Pasternack, J. F. (1996). *Parental values, reinforcement, and young children's prosocial behavior: A longitudinal study.* Manuscript submitted for editorial review.

Epstein, S. (1979). The stability of behavior: 1. On predicting most of the people most of the time. *Journal of Personality and Social Psychology, 37,* 1097–1126.

Feshbach, N. D. (1978). Studies of empathic behavior in children. In B. A. Maher (Ed.), *Progress in experimental personality research* (Vol. 8, pp. 1–47). New York: Academic Press.

Festinger, L. (1950). Informal social communication. *Psychological Review, 57,* 271–292.

Fiske, D. W. (1949). Consistency of the factorial structure of personality ratings from different sources. *Journal of Abnormal and Social Psychology, 44,* 329–344.

Fox, N. A., & Davidson, R. J. (1984). Hemispheric substrates of affect: A developmental model. In N. A. Fox & R. J. Davison (Eds.), *The psychology of affective development* (pp. 353–382). Hillsdale, NJ: Erlbaum.

Gergen, K. J., Gergen, M. M., & Meter, K. (1972). Individual orientations to prosocial behavior. *Journal of Social Issues, 28,* 105–130.

Goldberg, L. R. (1981). Language and individual differences: The search for universals in personality lexicons. In L. Wheeler (Ed.), *Review of personality and social psychology* (Vol. 2, pp. 141–165). Beverly Hills, CA: Sage.

Goldberg, L. R. (1992). The development of markers for the big-five factor structure. *Journal of Personality and Social Psychology, 4,* 26–42.

Graziano, W. G. (1994). The development of agreeableness as a dimension of personality. In C. F. Halverson, G. A. Kohnstamm, & R. P. Martin (Eds.), *The developing structure of temperament and personality from infancy to adulthood* (pp. 339–354). Hillsdale, NJ: Erlbaum.

Graziano, W. G., Jensen-Campbell, L. A., & Hair, E. C. (1996). Perceiving interpersonal conflict and reacting to it: The case for agreeableness. *Journal of Personality and Social Psychology, 70*(4).

Graziano, W. G., Jensen-Campbell, L. A., Steele, R. G., & Hair, E. C. (1996, February 7). *Unknown words in self-reported personality: Lethargic and provincial in Texas.* Unpublished manuscript, Texas A&M University, College Station.

Graziano, W. G., Jensen-Campbell, L. A., Todd, M., & Finch, J. F. (in press). Interpersonal attraction from an evolutionary psychology perspective. In J. A. Simpson & D. T. Kenrick (Eds.), *Evolutionary social psychology.* Hillsdale, NJ: Erlbaum.

Hamilton, W. D. (1964). The genetical evolution of social behavior. *Journal of Theoretical Biology, 7,* 1–52.

Hampson, R. B. (1984). Adolescent prosocial behavior: Peer group and situational factors associated with helping. *Journal of Personality and Social Psychology, 46,* 153–162.

Hill, J. (1984). Human altruism and sociocultural fitness. *Journal of Social and Biological Structures, 7,* 17–35.

Hoffman, M. L. (1981). Is altruism part of human nature? *Journal of Personality and Social Psychology, 40,* 121–137.

Hoffman, M. L. (1984). Interaction of affect and cognition in empathy. In C. E. Izard, J. Kagan, & R. B. Zajonc (Eds.), *Emotions, cognition, and behavior* (pp. 103–131). Cambridge, MA: Cambridge University Press.

Hogan, R. T. (1983). A socioanalytic theory of personality. In M. Page (Ed.), *Nebraska Symposium on Motivation: Personality-Current theory and research* (pp. 58–89). Lincoln: University of Nebraska Press.

Horney, K. (1945). *Our inner conflicts.* New York: Norton.

Houts, A. C., Cook, T. D., & Shadish, W. R., Jr. (1986). The person-situation debate: A critical multiplist perspective [Special issue]. *Journal of Personality, 54,* 52–105.

Infante, D. A., & Rancer, A. S. (1982). A conceptualization and measure of argumentativeness. *Journal of Personality Assessment, 46,* 72–80.

Jacobs, R. C., & Campbell, D. T. (1961). The perpetuation of an arbitrary tradition through several generations of a laboratory micro-culture. *Journal of Abnormal and Social Psychology, 62,* 649–658.

Jensen-Campbell, L. A., Graziano, W. G., & Hair, E. C. (1996). Personality and relationships as moderators of interpersonal conflict in adolescence. *Merrill-Palmer Quarterly, 42,* 148–163.

Jensen-Campbell, L. A., Graziano, W. G., & West, S. G. (1995). Dominance, prosocial orientation, and female preferences: Do nice guys finish last? *Journal of Personality and Social Psychology, 68,* 427–440.

John, O. P. (1990). The big five-factor taxonomy: Dimensions of personality in the natural language and in questionnaires. In L. A. Pervin (Ed.), *Handbook of personality theory and research* (pp. 261–277). New York Guilford Press.

John, O. P., Angleitner, A., & Ostedorf, F. (1988). The lexical approach to personality: A historical review of trait taxonomic research. *European Journal of Personality, 2,* 171–203.

Johnson, J. A., & Ostendorf, F. (1993). Clarification of the five factor model with the abridged big five-dimensional circumplex. *Journal of Personality and Social Psychology, 55,* 824–835.

Kinsbourne, M., & Bemporad, B. (1984). Lateralization of emotion: A model and the evidence. In N. A. Fox & R. J. Davidson (Eds.), *The psychology of affective development* (pp. 259–292). Hillsdale, NJ: Erlbaum.

Knight, G. P., Johnson, L. G., Carlo, G., & Eisenberg, N. (1994). A multiplicative model of the dispositional antecedents of a prosocial behavior: Predicting more of the people more of the time. *Journal of Personality and Social Psychology, 66*(1), 178–183.

Konner, M. (1975). Relations among infants and juveniles in comparative perspective. In M. Lewis & L. A. Rosenblum (Eds.), *Friendship and peer relations* (pp. 100–130). New York: Wiley.

Krebs, D. L., & Miller, D. T. (1985). Altruism and aggression. In G. Lindzey & E. Aronson (Eds.), *Handbook of social psychology* (3rd ed., Vol. 2, pp. 1–71). New York: Random House.

Larrieu, J. A. (1984, March). *Prosocial values, assertiveness, and sex: Predictors of children's naturalistic helping.* Paper presented at the biennial meeting of the Southwestern Society for the Research in Human Development, Denver, CO.

Larrieu, J., & Mussen, P. (1986). Some personality and motivational correlates of children's prosocial behavior. *Journal of Genetic Psychology, 147,* 529–542.

Leary, T. (1957). *Interpersonal diagnosis of personality.* New York: Ronald Press.

Loehlin, J. C. (1992). *Genes and environment in personality development.* Newbury Park, CA: Sage.

Loehlin, J. C., & Nichols, R. C. (1976). *Heredity, environment, and personality.* Austin: University of Texas Press.

MacDonald, K. (1984). An ethological-social learning theory of the development of altruism. Implications for human sociobiology. *Ethology and Sociobiology, 5,* 97–109.

Matthews, K. A. (1988). Coronary heart disease and Type A behaviors: Update on an alternative to the Booth-Kewley and Friedman (1987) quantitative review. *Psychological Bulletin, 104,* 373–380.

Matthews, K. A., Batson, C. D., Horn, J., & Rosenman, R. H. (1981). "Principles in his nature which interest him in the fortune of others . . .": The heritability of empathic concern for others. *Journal of Personality, 49,* 237–247.

McCrae, R. R., & Costa, P. T., Jr. (1987). Validation of the five-factor model of personality across instruments and observers. *Journal of Personality and Social Psychology, 53,* 81–90.

McCrae, R. R., & Costa, P. T., Jr. (1989a). Reinterpreting the Myers-Briggs Type Indicator from the perspective of the five-factor model of personality. *Journal of Personality, 57,* 17–40.

McCrae, R. R., & Costa, P. T., Jr. (1989b). The structure of interpersonal traits: Wiggins' circumplex and the five-factor model. *Journal of Personality and Social Psychology, 56,* 586–595.

McGarth, J. E. (1964). *Social psychology: A brief introduction.* New York: Holt, Rinehart & Winston.

Midlarsky, E., & Hannah, M. E. (1985). Competence, reticence, and helping by children and adolescents. *Developmental Psychology, 21,* 534–541.

Moore, B. S., & Eisenberg, N. (1984). The development of altruism. In G. Whitehurst (Ed.), *Annals of child development* (pp. 107–174). Greenwich, CT: JAI Press.

Murphy, L. B. (1937). *Social behavior and child personality.* New York: Columbia University Press.

Mussen, P., & Eisenberg-Berg, N. (1977). *Caring, sharing, and helping: The development of prosocial behavior in children.* San Francisco: Freeman.

Norman, W. T. (1963). Toward an adequate taxonomy of personality attributes: Replicated factor structure in peer nomination personality ratings. *Journal of Abnormal and Social Psychology, 66,* 574–583.

Norman, W. T., & Goldberg, L. R. (1966). Raters, ratees, and randomness in personality structure. *Journal of Personality and Social Psychology, 4,* 681–691.

Oliner, S. P., & Oliner, P. M. (1988). *The altruistic personality: Rescuers of Jews in Nazi Europe.* New York: Free Press.

Panskepp, J. (1986). The neurochemistry of behavior. *Annual Review of Psychology, 37,* 77–107.

Peabody, D., & Goldberg, L. R. (1989). Some determinants of factor structure from personality-trait descriptors. *Journal of Personality and Social Psychology, 57,* 532–567.

Penner, L. A., & Fritzsche, B. A. (1993, August). *Measuring the prosocial personality: Four construct validity studies.* Paper presented at the annual meeting of the American Psychological Association, Toronto, Canada.

Penner, L. A., Michael, D. E., & Brookmire, D. A. (1979). Pre- and anti-social behavior as a function of cost estimates and personality and situational variables. *Multivariate Experimental Clinical Research, 4,* 111–124.

Perry, D. G., & Perry, L. C. (1974). Denial of suffering in the victim as a stimulus to violence in aggressive boys. *Child Development, 45,* 55–62.

Perry, D. G., Williard, J., & Perry, L. C. (1990). Peers perceptions of the consequences that victimized children provide aggressors. *Child Development, 61,* 1310–1325.

Peterson, L. (1983). Influences of age, task competence, and responsibility focus on children's altruism. *Developmental Psychology, 19,* 141–148.

Plomin, R. (1986). *Development, genetics, and psychology.* Hillsdale, NJ: Erlbaum.

Pomazal, R. J., & Jaccard, J. J. (1976). An information approach to altruistic behavior. *Journal of Personality and Social Psychology, 33,* 317–326.

Radke-Yarrow, M., & Zahn-Waxler, C. (1984). Roots, motives, and patterns in children's prosocial behavior. In E. Staub, D. Bar-Tal, J. Karylowski, & J. Reykowski (Eds.), *Development and maintenance of prosocial behavior: International perspectives* (pp. 81–99). New York: Plenum Press.

Radke-Yarrow, M., Zahn-Waxler, C., & Chapman, M. (1983). Children's prosocial dispositions and behaviors. In P. H. Mussen (Ed.), *Handbook of child psychology: Vol. 4. Socialization, personality, and social development* (pp. 469–545). New York: Wiley.

Raven, B. H., & Rubin, J. Z. (1983). *Social psychology* (2nd ed.). New York: Wiley.

Renken, B., Egeland, B., Marvinney, D., Manglsdorf, S., & Sroufe, L. A. (1989). *Early childhood antecedents of aggression and passive-withdrawal in early elementary school* [Special issue]. *Journal of Personality, 57,* 257–282.

Rholes, S. W., & Bailey, S. (1983). The effect of level of moral reasoning in consistency between moral attitudes and related behaviors. *Social Cognition, 2,* 32–48.

Robson, R. K., & Moss, H. A. (1970). Patterns and determinants of maternal attachment. *Journal of Pediatrics, 77,* 976–985.

Romer, D., Gruder, C. L., & Lizzardo, T. (1986). A person-situation approach to altruistic behavior. *Journal of Personality and Social Psychology, 51,* 1001–1012.

Rosenhan, D. L. (1970). The natural socialization of altruistic autonomy. In J. Macaulay & L. Berkowitz (Eds.), *Altruism and helping behavior* (pp. 251–268). New York: Academic Press.

Rosenman, R. H. (1978). The interview method of assessment of the coronary-prone behavior pattern. In T. M. Dembroski, S. M. Weiss, J. L. Shields, S. G. Haynes, & M. Feinleib (Eds.), *Coronary-prone behavior* (pp. 55–69). New York: Springer-Verlag.

Rothbart, M. K. (1989). Biological processes in temperament. In G. A. Kornstramm, J. Bates, & M. K. Rothbart (Eds.), *Handbook of temperament in childhood* (pp. 77–110). Sussex, England: Wiley.

Rowe, D., & Plomin, R. (1977). Temperament in early childhood. *Journal of Personality Assessment, 41,* 150–156.

Rushton, J. P. (1980). *Altruism, socialization, and society,* Englewood Cliffs, NJ: Prentice-Hall.

Rushton, J. P., Chrisjohn, R. D., & Fekken, G. C. (1981). The altruistic personality and the self-report altruism scale. *Personality and Individual Differences, 2,* 1–11.

Rushton, J. P., Fulker, D. W., Neal, M. C., Nias, D. K. B., & Eysenck, H. J. (1986). Altruism and aggression: The heritability of individual differences. *Journal of Personality and Social Psychology, 50,* 1192–1198.

Rushton, J. P., Littlefield, C. H., & Lumsden, C. J. (1986). Gene-culture coevaluation of complex social behavior: Human altruism and mate choice. *Proceedings of the National Academy of Sciences of the U.S.A., 83,* 7340–7343.

Rushton, J. P., Russell, R. J. H., & Wells, P. A. (1984). Genetic similarity theory: Beyond kin selection. *Behavior Genetics, 14,* 179–193.

Savin-Williams, R. C. (1987). *Adolescence: An ethological perspective.* New York: Springer-Verlag.

Savin-Williams, R. C., Small, S. A., & Zeldin, R. S. (1981). *Ethology and Sociobiology, 2,* 167–176.

Schachter, S. (1951). Deviation, rejection, and communication. *Journal of Abnormal and Social Psychology, 46,* 190–207.

Schwartz, S. H., & Howard, J. A. (1981). In J. P. Rushton & R. M. Sorrentino (Eds.), *Altruism and helping behavior* (pp. 189–211). Hillsdale, NJ: Erlbaum.

Schwartz, S. H., & Howard, J. A. (1984). Internalized values as motivators of altruism. In E. Staub, D. Bar-Tal, J. Karylowski, & J. Reykowski (Eds.), *International perspectives on positive development* (pp. 229–255). New York: Plenum Press.

Small, S. A., Zeldin, R. S., & Savin-Williams, R. C. (1983). In search of personality traits: A multimethod analysis of naturally occurring prosocial and dominance behavior. *Journal of Personality, 51,* 1–16.

Smith, S. S., & Kihlstrom, J. F. (1987). When is a schema not a schema? The Big Five traits as cognitive structures. *Social Cognition, 5,* 26–57.

Snyder, M., & Ickes, W. (1985). Personality and social behavior. In G. Lindzey & E. Aronson (Eds.), *Handbook of social psychology* (3rd ed. Vol. 2, pp. 1–71). New York: Random House.

Staub, E. (1974). Helping a distressed person: Social, personality, and stimulus determinants. In L. Berkowitz (Ed.), *Advances in experimental social psychology* (Vol. 7, pp. 293–341). New York: Academic Press.

Staub, E. (1978). Positive social behavior and morality: *Social and personal influences* (Vol. 1). New York: Academic Press.

Staub, E. (1986). A conception of the determinants and development of altruism and aggression: Motives, the self, and the environment. In C. Zahn-Waxler, E. M. Cummings, & R. Iannotti (Eds.), *Altruism and aggression: Biological and social origins* (pp. 135–164). Cambridge, England: Cambridge University Press.

Tellegen, A. (1985). Structures of mood and personality and their relevance to assessing anxiety, with an emphasis on self-report. In A. H. Tuma & J. D. Maser (Eds.), *Anxiety and anxiety disorders* (pp. 681–706). Hillsdale, NJ: Erlbaum.

Trivers, R. L. (1971). The evolution of reciprocal altruism. *Quarterly Review of Biology, 46,* 35–57.

Tupes, E. C., & Cristal, R. E. (1961). *Recurrent personality factors based on trait ratings* (USAF ASD Tech. Rep. No. 61–97). Lackland Air Force Base, TX: U.S. Air Force.

Underwood, B., & Moore, B. (1982). Perspective-taking and altruism. *Psychological Bulletin, 91,* 143–173.

Watson, D. (1989). Strangers' ratings of the five robust personality factors: Evidence of a surprising convergence with self-report. *Journal of Personality and Social Psychology, 57,* 120–128.

West, S. G., & Graziano, W. G. (1989). Long-term stability of personality: An introduction. *Journal of Personality, 57,* 175–193.

White, G. M. (1980). Conceptual universals in interpersonal language. *American Anthropologist, 82,* 759–781.

Whiting, B. B., & Whiting, J. W. M. (1975). *Children of six cultures.* Cambridge, MA: Harvard University Press.

Wiggins, J. S. (1980). Circumplex models of interpersonal behavior. In L. Wheeler (Ed.), *Review of personality and social psychology* (Vol. 2, pp. 265–294). Beverly Hills, CA: Sage.

Wiggins, J. S. (1991). Agency and communion as conceptual coordinates for the understanding and measurement of interpersonal behavior. In D. Cicchetti & W. Grove (Eds.), *Thinking critically in psychology: Essays in honor of Paul E. Meehl* (pp. 89–113). New York: Cambridge University Press.

Wiggins, J. S., Broughton, R. (1985). The Interpersonal Circle: A structural model for the integration of personality research. In R. Hogan & W. H. Jones (Eds.), *Perspectives in personality* (Vol. 1, pp. 1–47). Greenwich, CT: JAI Press.

Wilder, D. A. (1986). Social categorization: Implications for the creation and reduction of intergroup bias. In L. Berkowitz (Ed.), *Advances in experimental social psychology* (Vol. 19, pp. 293–356). Orlando, FL: Academic Press.

Wynne-Edwards, V. C. (1962). *Animal dispersion in relation to social behavior.* New York: Harper.

Zahn-Waxler, C., Robinson, J. L., & Emde, R. N. (1992). The development of empathy in twins. *Developmental Psychology, 28,* 1038–1047.

Zajonc, R. B., & Markus, H. (1984). Affect and cognition: The hard interface. In C. E. Izard, J. Kagan, & R. B. Zajonc (Eds.), *Emotions, cognition, and behavior* (pp. 73–102). Cambridge, England: Cambridge University Press.

Zeldin, R. S., Small, S. A., & Savin-Williams, R. C. (1982). Prosocial interactions in two mixed-sex adolescent groups. *Child Development, 53,* 1492–1498.

Zuckerman, M., & Reis, H. T. (1978). Comparison of three models for predicting altruistic behavior. *Journal of Personality and Social Psychology, 36,* 498–510.

CHAPTER 31

CONCEPTIONS AND CORRELATES OF OPENNESS TO EXPERIENCE

ROBERT R. McCRAE AND PAUL T. COSTA, JR.

GERONTOLOGY RESEARCH CENTER, NATIONAL INSTITUTE ON AGING,

NATIONAL INSTITUTES OF HEALTH, BALTIMORE, MARYLAND

Personality traits are normally defined as dimensions of individual difference, and they are often first recognized by noting groups of individuals who are conspicuously different. Much of personality psychology has been devoted to an attempt to understand psychopathology, because phobics, hypochondriacs, and suicides are so distressingly different from the rest of us.

Artists and poets form another group long held to be different, if not deviant. They are remarkable for their specific artistic talents, but they are also characterized by a set of mental, emotional, and attitudinal characteristics that set them apart (MacKinnon, 1962). Think of Leonardo da Vinci, of Beethoven, or of Whitman: They are all dreamers with keen imaginations, seeing possibilities that others miss. They are sensitive and passionate, with a wide and subtle range of emotional reactions. They are adventurous, bored by familiar sights, and stifled by routine. They have an insatiable curiosity, as if they retained into adulthood the child's wonder at the world. And they are unorthodox, free-thinking, and prone to flout convention.

As neurotics can be used as exemplars of high scorers on the dimension of Neuroticism, so artists can be considered prime examples of individuals high in Openness to Experience. Few people have the gifts needed to be a creative artist, but many people have the dispositions. Indeed, recent research suggests that Openness to Experience is one of the fundamental dimensions of personality (McCrae,

1993–1994, 1994), relevant not only to an understanding of the artistic temperament, but also to such diverse issues as social attitudes, hypnotizability, career changes, and moral reasoning. And although it is convenient to use the artist as an exemplar of Openness and to refer to "open" and "closed" individuals, it must be remembered that Openness refers to a continuum of individual differences in processing experience, and that the majority of people are intermediate in Openness.

In this chapter we review the empirical literature on Openness as a fundamental dimension of personality, but our major focus is on the conceptualization of Openness. We will argue that Openness cannot be understood as the culture that is acquired through education or good breeding, nor as intellect or any other cognitive ability. Instead, we will suggest that Openness must be viewed in both structural and motivational terms. Openness is seen in the breadth, depth, and permeability of consciousness, and in the recurrent need to enlarge and examine experience.

A caution to the reader is in order: The concept of Openness appears to be unusually difficult to grasp. Among personality psychologists, it is the most controversial of the five basic factors of personality (McCrae & John, 1992), and lay raters appear to have preconceptions about Openness that are inconsistent with psychological definitions (Funder & Sneed, 1993). But data provide abundant support for the construct, and an increasing number of psychologists have adopted it (e.g., John, 1990). Here is a construct that must be approached with an open mind and a willingness to learn new ways of thinking about people.

I. Openness as a Basic Dimension of Personality

Isolated parts of the broad domain of Openness have long been recognized in psychology. Authoritarianism (Adorno, Frenkel-Brunswik, Levinson, & Sanford, 1950/1969) was once a major research topic for personality psychologists; exploratory behavior has been a fixture of animal research since the 1950s (Berlyne, 1955); Rogers' (1961) theory of psychotherapy was based on generating conditions to enhance openness to feelings; private self-consciousness (Fenigstein, Scheier, & Buss, 1975) has recently attracted much attention. However, these traits have rarely been seen as aspects of a broader and more basic dimension of Openness. A few researchers have pointed to such a dimension, although with somewhat different labels. There appear to have been four relatively independent discoveries of the dimension we call Openness.

1. Working from Cattell's (1946) distillation of the personality sphere as represented in natural language traits and in psychological tests, Fiske (1949) and later Tupes and Christal (1961/1992) and Norman (1963) reported five robust factors which have come to be called the Big Five (John, Angleitner, & Ostendorf, 1988) and form the basis of the five-factor model of personality (McCrae & Costa, 1987). The fifth factor was called *Culture* by both Tupes and Christal and Norman; Fiske

had also considered the label *Cultured* before adopting the phrase *Inquiring Intellect.* As typically construed within the Big Five tradition, this factor is focused on intelligence or intellectual activity, but includes cultural sophistication and imagination. Goldberg (1981) found a similar factor in his analyses of English language adjectives and called it *Intellect;* Hogan (1986), strongly influenced by Big Five research, included a measure of *Intellectance* in his personality inventory.

2. Tellegen and Atkinson (1974) began with an analysis of measures which had been empirically linked to hypnotic susceptibility. In a joint analysis with measures of ego resiliency and control, they found three replicable factors which they interpreted as Stability (the opposite pole of Neuroticism), Introversion (versus Extraversion), and "openness to absorbing and self-altering experiences," or Absorption; only Absorption was related to hypnotic susceptibility. The Absorption factor was defined by scales measuring reality absorption, fantasy absorption, dissociation, devotion-trust, autonomy, and openness to experience. Tellegen and Atkinson explicitly noted the breadth of their Absorption factor: "it exemplifies the combination of *substantive divergence* and *structural convergence* that is suggestive of a major dimension" (p. 273), and they described cognitive and motivational-affective components. They concluded that Absorption was best interpreted as a capacity for absorbed and self-altering attention, found in peak and mystical experiences, hypnosis, and artistic creativity.

3. Coan (1974) was concerned with what he called the *optimal personality,* and he examined characteristics identified in a wide range of personality theories. He drew upon the work of Fitzgerald (1966) to measure the scope of awareness. Fitzgerald had been concerned with questionnaire assessment of the psychoanalytic concept of regression in service of the ego (Kris, 1952), and many of his items concerned regressive behavior and experience. Coan added other questions with a less pathological cast and found a general factor of openness in an analysis of the items. Coan reported that his Experience Inventory items were correlated with "measures that suggest emotional sensitivity, aesthetic interests, liberalism, and independence" and "a certain intellectual and emotional flexibility" (pp. 80–81). Because both Fitzgerald (1966) and Tellegen and Atkinson (1974) had drawn on the earlier work of Ås, O'Hara, and Munger (1962), these research lines are not strictly independent. It is noteworthy, however, that Tellegen and Atkinson focused on the depth and intensity of attention, whereas Coan was impressed by the scope of awareness in Open individuals.

4. Looking for age differences in personality structure, Costa and McCrae (1976) clustered the scales of the Sixteen Personality Factor Questionaire (16PF; Cattell, Eber, & Tatsuoka, 1970). In addition to Neuroticism and Extraversion clusters, they found that scales B (intelligence), I (tender-mindedness), M (imagination), and Q1 (liberal thinking) formed a loose cluster in some age groups. They interpreted this cluster as Openness to Experience, and continued research on the dimension using a modification of Coan's scales. An Experience Inventory (EI; Costa & McCrae, 1978) was created to measure Openness in the areas of fantasy, aesthetics, feelings, actions, ideas, and values. When jointly factored with 16PF

scales, a reasonably clear Openness factor was found, defined by 16PF B, M, and Q1 scales and Experience Inventory Fantasy, Aesthetics, Actions, Ideas, and Values scales. The EI scales were revised and ultimately incorporated in the Revised NEO Personality Inventory (NEO-PI-R; Costa & McCrae, 1992a), a questionnaire measure of the five-factor model. Factor analytic studies of the NEO-PI-R (Costa & McCrae, 1992b; Costa, McCrae, & Dye, 1991) show that the six Openness scales consistently define a separate factor in men and women, in young adults and old, and in self-reports and observer ratings.

Because the total NEO-PI Openness score is significantly and substantially related to Tellegen and Atkinson's Absorption, Goldberg's Intellect, and Norman's Culture (McCrae & Costa, 1985a), it appears that the lexical tradition and the ego regression traditions have converged in the identification of a broad and basic dimension of personality. Other studies of the five-factor model have also supported this conclusion. For example, when the 100 items of Block's (1961) California Q-Set (CQS) were factored, one of the five factors contrasted "Values intellectual matters," "Rebellious, non-conforming," and "Unusual thought processes" with "Favors conservative values," "Judges in conventional terms," and "Uncomfortable with complexities"; this factor correlated .62 with NEO-PI Openness scores (McCrae, Costa, & Busch, 1986). Similarly, Amelang and Borkenau (1982) found a factor they called *Unabhängigkeit der Meinungsbildung* (Independence of Judgment) in analyses of questionnaires and adjectives in a German sample. A wealth of more specific correlates of Openness have been identified; some of these are summarized in Table I (see also McCrae, 1993–1994).

II. Traditional Conceptions of Openness

Convergence on an empirical level has not been matched by convergence on a conceptual level. Indeed, there is not even widespread agreement on the label to use for this dimension (Saucier, 1992). Goldberg (1981) and Digman and Inouye (1986) preferred the term *Intellect;* Norman (1963) used *Culture;* and the corresponding factor (McCrae & Costa, 1989b) is identified as *Sensation versus Intuition* in the Myers–Briggs Type Indicator (MBTI; Myers & McCaulley, 1985). It is understandably difficult to sum up one of the broadest constructs in personality psychology in a single word, but the choice of labels is important. As Digman (1987) pointed out, researchers like Guilford, Eysenck, and Cattell assumed that intellectual interests were a reflection of intelligence and could best be measured by intelligence tests. Measures of the disposition of Openness were thus relatively neglected by these influential factorists.

The term *Openness to Experience* has its disadvantages, too. Especially when abbreviated as *Openness,* it may suggest the rather different trait of interpersonal openness or self-disclosure (Jourard, 1964). Openness may also suggest a passive or uncritical receptivity, which is clearly inappropriate. Open people actively seek

TABLE I

Selected Correlates of Self-reports on the NEO Personality Inventory (NEO-PI) Openness
Scale in Baltimore Longitudinal Study of Aging Samples

Criterion	N	r
Observer ratings		
Spouse-rated NEO-PI Openness	144	.60
Mean peer-rated NEO-PI Openness	213	.60
CQS items		
Aesthetically reactive	254	.40
Skilled in play and humor	254	.33
Judges in conventional terms	254	−.41
Favors conservative values	254	−.40
Bipolar Adjective Scales		
Uncurious–Curious	375	.30
Uncreative–Creative	375	.34
Imperceptive–Perceptive	375	.29
Simple–Complex	375	.35
SDS Occupations		
Anthropologist	275	.36
Author	275	.43
Journalist	275	.38
Sculptor/sculptress	275	.31
Revised CPI Scales[a]		
Social Presence	348	.42
Empathy	348	.43
Achievement via Independence	348	.41
Flexibility	348	.42
PRF Needs		
Change	296	.40
Sentience	296	.55
Understanding	296	.54
ACL Creative Personality Scale	310	.46
GZTS Thoughtfulness	275	.35
MBTI Sensation–Intuition	468	.73
Haan Coping Scales		
Intellectuality	348	.45
Logical Analysis	348	.48
Regression in Service of the Ego	348	.34
Suppression	348	−.12
Sensation Seeking Scales V		
Thrill and Adventure Seeking	312	.34
Experience Seeking	312	.55
Disinhibition of Impulses	312	.28
Boredom Susceptibility	312	.20

Note. All *p*s < .05. CQS, California Q-Set; CPI, California Psychological Inventory;
PRF, Personality Research Form; GZTS, Guilford–Zimmerman Temperament Survey;
MBTI, Myers–Briggs Type Indicator; SDS, Self-Directed Search. (Data adapted from Costa &
McCrae, 1988a, 1988b; Costa, McCrae, & Holland, 1984; McCrae, 1987, 1990; McCrae &
Costa, 1985b, 1987; McCrae, Costa, & Busch, 1986; McCrae, Costa, & Piedmont, 1993).
[a] Correlations are with Openness factor scores.

out experience and are apt to be particularly reflective and thoughtful about the ideas they encounter.

Whatever label we select will be insufficient to communicate the construct fully. For that we must rely on exemplars, like artists and poets; on an analysis of the elements or facets that combine to form the broad domain (cf. Briggs, 1989); and on a network of empirical correlates and outcomes associated with high or low standing on the dimension. In addition, however, it would be useful to have a conceptual definition, a theory of openness, that can help explain why people differ in Openness. Let us turn now to a consideration of some possible ways of construing Openness.

A. Openness as Culture

The term *Culture* was selected by Tupes and Christal (1961/1992) because it seemed to sum up the elements "intellectual, cultured," "esthetically fastidious," "imaginative," and "polished," in contrast to "boorish," "practical, logical," and "clumsy, awkward." Given these definers, the label seems apt; they have a peculiarly highbrow cast that suggests that the dimension may reflect differences in social class and breeding. If this characterization had been confirmed by subsequent research, the topic of Openness would perhaps have belonged in a handbook of sociology, not personality psychology. However, Tupes and Christal reported that this was the least clear of the five factors in their analyses, and subsequent studies have suggested that the elements of polish and sophistication are far less central to the dimension than intellectual and aesthetic interests and imagination (McCrae, 1990; McCrae & Costa, 1987; Peabody & Goldberg, 1989).

The label Culture suggests that this aspect of personality is the result of education—particularly the liberal education that has long been the central ideal of Western universities. Among the distinctive elements of this approach are exposure to a broad range of ideas, cultivation of both arts and sciences, and encouragement of a critical attitude with regard to accepted values and assumptions. Clearly, a liberal education will be most congenial to those who are by disposition open to experience.

The extent to which a liberal education is indeed broadening is an empirical question; there is some evidence in support of this premise (e.g., Webster, Freedman, & Heist, 1962). But education itself probably plays only a minor role in the development of Openness. In a national survey of nearly 10,000 men and women over the age of 35, a short scale measuring Openness showed only a modest correlation with years of education, $r = .28$, $p < .001$ (Costa et al., 1986). Education was neither necessary nor sufficient for Openness. About one-third of respondents with an eighth-grade education or less scored above the median on Openness; conversely, about one-third of respondents with some college education scored below the median. Individuals who are open without having had the benefits of formal education may be culturally unsophisticated—they may be deeply moved by the verses on greeting cards—but from a psychological perspective, they are open nonetheless.

Conversely, highly educated individuals may show the trappings of culture (attending museums, lectures, and concerts) without a deep appreciation of the experiences these events provide.

Formal education, of course, is not the only source of culture; family influences might also be important in modeling and encouraging breadth of interest and tolerant attitudes. As Rogerians might expect, loving and lenient parents tend to have children who are higher in Openness, but the association is very modest in magnitude (McCrae & Costa, 1988). By contrast, there was evidence of a strong heritable component of Openness in a study of adult Swedish twins (Bergeman et al., 1993), and Tellegen and his colleagues (1988) reported similar findings for Absorption in an American sample. These studies suggest that it may be wise to reverse the causal interpretation of the association of education with Openness: The intellectual interests of open men and women may lead them to seek higher levels of education.

B. Openness as Cognitive Ability

Perhaps the most popular alternative label for the dimension we have called Openness to Experience is some form of the word *Intellect,* which is defined as "the ability to learn and reason . . . [and the] capacity for knowledge and understanding" (Morris, 1976, p. 682). This definition suggests that the trait domain under consideration is best viewed as a set of cognitive abilities. Studies of trait adjectives show that such terms as *intelligent, perceptive, knowledgeable,* and *analytical* are among the definers of the factor—indeed, they are the chief definers in some studies (Angleitner & Ostendorf, 1989; Goldberg, 1989). The interest that open individuals have in a wide range of experiences might be understood as the result of their facility in handling information; certainly intellectual interests tend to follow abilities. Further, studies have shown that Openness, alone of the five factors, is positively related to psychometric measures of intelligence and other cognitive abilities (e.g., McCrae, 1987). The heritability of Openness might be explained by the heritability of intelligence. Psychologists have spent more time and effort studying intelligence than any other trait; by adopting the term Intellect, personality psychologists could claim this vast literature as their own. Openness could be construed as intelligence itself, or, as Cattell suggested, as the reflection of intelligence in the personality sphere.

Despite these temptations, there are five reasons to reject the label *Intellect* and the interpretation it suggests:

1. Factor analytic studies of natural language adjectives are inconclusive and suggest that rated intelligence may mark not one but two factors. As in all factor analyses, the nature of the factors depends chiefly on the variables included. Researchers like Borgatta (1964), convinced a priori of the interpretation of the factor as intelligence, included markers reflecting this interpretation (*intelligent, rational and logical, clear minded, alert, mature*). Researchers with a broader conception of

the factor included variables such as *imaginative, prefer variety, original,* and *artistic,* and found a correspondingly different factor (e.g., McCrae & Costa, 1985b). One way to avoid the possible biases of variable selection is to attempt to obtain a representative sample of adjectives. Goldberg's (1989) work in this regard has led him to a factor he characterizes as Intellect; Peabody's (1987) analyses of semantic similarity judgments recovered a factor he identified as Openness to Experience. Both these efforts were based on the assumption that the English language adequately represents all important personality traits in single adjectives, but that assumption has been questioned (McCrae, 1990). For example, the phrase "prefers variety," which corresponds to the widely researched trait of novelty-seeking or need for variety (Maddi & Berne, 1964), apparently has no counterpart in natural language adjectives.

Further, studies that include ability terms like *intelligent* typically find that these items have substantial secondary loadings on the Conscientiousness factor. Table II confirms this by showing loadings for variables related to rated intelligence on both Openness and Conscientiousness factors. Rated intelligence appears to be related to both factors in peer ratings, self-reports, and semantic similarity judgments. Conceptually, this is perfectly reasonable. Individuals may be considered intelligent for either (or both) of two reasons: they may be intellectually curious, imaginative, and inventive, or they may be efficient, well-organized, competent, and careful in their work. From this perspective, the label *Intellect* is too broad, because it encompasses and confounds aspects of two basically independent domains.

2. In another respect, *Intellect* is too narrow a label. Even if we include intellectual interests along with intellectual abilities, the range of phenomena known empirically to correlate with Openness would hardly be suggested by the term. Who would guess that individuals high in a factor labeled Intellect would be more easily hypnotized (Tellegen & Atkinson, 1974), more variable in mood (Wessman & Ricks, 1966), or more "skilled in play and humor" (cf. Table I)?

Open people are not only *able* to grasp new ideas, they *enjoy* doing so. The merely intelligent tend to have highly developed interests in specialized fields in which they excel; open people have a wide and ever-increasing range of interests. Further, these interests extend beyond intellectual pursuits. Open people want to taste different food, to see new sights, to reconsider their values, to develop elaborate fantasies. Cognitive abilities may in some degree facilitate this exploration of the world, but they are neither necessary nor sufficient for it.

Need for variety, tolerance of ambiguity, and preference for complexity all represent motivational aspects of Openness. In addition, open people can be characterized by their nontraditional attitudes, their rich and complex emotional lives, and their behavioral flexibility. Like the other four basic dimensions of personality, Openness is a broad constellation of traits with cognitive, affective, and behavioral manifestations. It cannot be reduced to a single underlying ability.

3. The empirical association of Openness with psychometric measures of intelligence is too weak to imply equivalence between the two constructs (McCrae,

TABLE II
Loadings of Rated Intelligence Variables on Openness and Conscientiousness
Factors in Selected Studies

| Study | N | Factor | |
		Openness	Conscientiousness
Norman (1963)			
Sample C ratings	215	74	47
Sample D ratings	241	84	10
Borgatta (1964)			
Female ratings	315	25	60
Male ratings	144	63	25
Conley (1985)			
Female self-reports	189	—	63
Male self-reports	189	—	25
McCrae & Costa (1985b, 1987)			
Self-reports	498	<40	44
Peer ratings	738	41	44
Peabody (1987)			
Internal analyses	—	66	54
Goldberg (1989)			
Self-reports (Table 6)	192	51	19
Self-reports (Table 7)	95	66	14
Self-reports (Table 8)	95	36	35
Self-reports (Table 9)	157	42	33
Self-reports, Study 6	215	59	18
Self-reports, Study 7	175	45	21
Median		51	33

Note. Decimal points are omitted. Conley (1985) did not report an Openness
factor. Peabody's (1987) data are based on similarity judgments made by four
raters.

1993–1994). In a sample of men from the BLSA, correlations of .22 and .20 were
found between NEO-PI Openness and WAIS Vocabulary and Total Army Alpha
scores, respectively; further, when measures of personality and cognitive ability are
factored jointly, six factors, not five, are recovered, with measured intelligence
forming a distinct factor (McCrae, 1994; McCrae & Costa, 1985a, 1985b). The
average participant in the BLSA receives high scores on measures of IQ, and
somewhat larger correlations would probably be seen in unselected samples. But
given the reliability of psychometric measures, even correlations of .30 or .40 would
mean that most of the valid variance in intelligence is *not* related to Openness
to Experience.

The one form of cognitive ability that does show somewhat stronger correlations with Openness is divergent thinking (McCrae, 1987). Correlations around .40
were consistently seen between a total divergent thinking score and a variety of

self-report and rating measures of Openness. We should not, however, discount the possibility that high scores on such tests may reflect motivational features of open people rather than ability: Curious and imaginative people may become more involved in tasks that require flexible and fluent thought. In any case, if an ability interpretation of Openness were to be advanced, Creativity would make a better label than Intellect.

The identification of Openness with Intellect may also be misleading with regard to assessment, because it suggests that Openness might be measured by psychometric tests. Given the relative reliabilities and validities of cognitive tests versus self-report questionnaires or ratings, this is a tempting alternative, and historically it has been extremely influential. Cattell, for example, included a measure of intelligence in his 16PF instead of asking questions about intellect. Eysenck (1991) also considered that this domain was adequately covered by cognitive measures. Of course, if Openness were equivalent to intelligence, this would be an appropriate decision. To the extent that Openness is something else, this approach ensures an incomplete assessment of personality.

Figure 1 summarizes the relations between Openness, Intellect, Intelligence, and Conscientiousness described in the preceeding sections. Both the breadth and

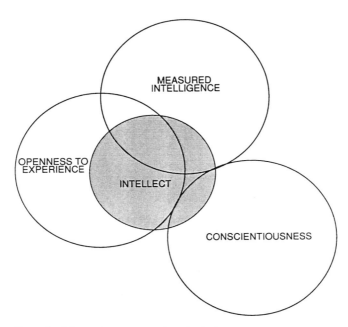

Figure 1 Schematic representation of relations among Openness to Experience, Measured Intelligence, Conscientiousness, and Intellect. Both Openness and Intellect are modestly related to Measured Intelligence. Some aspects of Intellect (*perceptive, curious*) are shared with Openness; others (*logical, foresighted*) are shared with Conscientiousness. Many elements in Openness (*liberal, adventurous, empathic*) are not included in Intellect.

the relatively greater independence of the Openness construct suggest its superiority to Intellect as a basic dimension of personality.

4. But there are also other, pragmatic reasons for preferring the term *Openness*. Intellect and Openness have very different evaluative connotations. Individuals who are closed to experience would probably accept this designation; they are content to be down-to-earth and may be proud of their traditionalism. By contrast, no one wants to be called *stupid*. The highly evaluative term Intellect presents difficulties when feedback on personality is provided, as in client-centered assessment (Costa & McCrae, 1989; McReynolds, 1985). It may also suggest to psychologists that Openness is superior to Closedness. In fact, there are many advantages—both to the individual and to society—to being closed to experience. Both innovation and conservation are necessary processes in any culture and any individual life.

5. Finally, the identification of Openness with Intellect effectively short circuits research on personality and intelligence. No one is likely to do research on the question of whether Intellect contributes to the development of intelligence, but if we distinguish Openness from intelligence, we can ask whether the former affects or is affected by the latter—a question that might have profound consequences for developmental and educational psychology. The heuristic value of distinguishing such concepts is seen in the work of Welsh (1975) on the related constructs of origence and intellectence.

On empirical, conceptual, and heuristic grounds, then, it seems that Openness is a better label for this factor than Intellect. This phrasing also spares us some empirical embarrassments. For example, open individuals frequently entertain ideas that we would not readily associate with intelligence. Epstein (Epstein & Meier, 1989) has developed a scale measuring "beliefs in esoteric and dubious phenomena, such as astrology and the existence of ghosts" (p. 51). In a college sample, this Esoteric Thinking scale was substantially correlated with NEO-PI Openness, $r = .47$, $N = 59$, $p < .001$. It is far easier to see these beliefs as an outcome of open-mindedness than as a reflection of intelligence.

III. ALTERNATIVE CONCEPTIONS: STRUCTURAL AND MOTIVATIONAL

A. Openness as Psychic Structure

As the consensual validation of Openness ratings across observers demonstrates, Openness is rather easily inferred from observable speech and behavior (McCrae & Costa, 1989a). But fundamentally Openness is a matter of inner experience, a mental phenomenon related to the scope of awareness or the depth and intensity of consciousness. It is therefore not surprising that much of the conceptual basis of this dimension comes from the work of dynamic psychologists, such as Adorno et al. (1950/1969), Kris (1952), and Rogers (1961), for whom the concept of consciousness was central.

As Coan (1974) noted, psychoanalysts have typically focused on psychopathology and on the restrictions in awareness brought about by the defensive processes of repression. A particular causal sequence is suggested by this model: intrapsychic conflicts lead to repression, which leads to limitations in the scope of awareness. Removing the conflicts should thus increase openness. This view is close to the one held by Rogers (1961), who viewed Openness as an outcome and reflection of mental health. Appealing as this formulation may be to both psychoanalysts and humanistic psychologists, it has two significant problems. First, Openness is unrelated to Neuroticism and most measures of mental health, meaning that poorly adjusted individuals are as likely to be open as are well-adjusted individuals (McCrae & Costa, 1985a). Second, it is difficult to explain the generality and pervasiveness of Openness from this perspective. In most psychoanalytic thought, defense mechanisms operate on specific conflicts or anxieties. It is understandable that an early trauma might leave a particular blind spot, but why should it also lead to conservative political views and indifference to art and beauty?

A more plausible dynamic model can be inferred from the writings of Frenkel-Brunswik in *The Authoritarian Personality* (Adorno et al., 1950/1969). This book was an ambitious—perhaps too ambitious—attempt to integrate political philosophy, social attitude research, and dynamic personality theory. Certainly no one today would advocate the use of the F Scale as a measure of Openness to Experience, but there can be little doubt that the high scorers on the Ethnocentrism and F scales studied by Adorno et al. were closed to experience (although they were also probably highly antagonistic). The CQS definers of low Openness (McCrae et al., 1986) in particular show an uncanny resemblance to authoritarian features: *favors conservative values; judges in conventional terms; uncomfortable with complexities; moralistic; sex-role stereotyped behavior;* and even *productive* (one of the few desirable characteristics attributed to authoritarians). Conversely, Frenkel-Brunswick noted that "there seems to be a general tendency on the part of low scores [nonauthoritarians] to expose themselves to broad experience—emotional, cognitive, and perceptual—even at the risk of having to modify [their] preconceived notions and of having to sustain conflicts" (p. 464). The hypothesis that Openness is inversely related to authoritarianism is supported by evidence that Altemeyer's (1981) Right-Wing Authoritarianism scale is related to total NEO-PI-R Openness, $r = -.57$, and all its facets, $rs = -.29$ to $-.63$, $N = 722$, $p < .001$ (Trapnell, 1994).

Frenkel-Brunswik interpreted her findings in terms of lower defensiveness on the part of open people, an ability to allow into consciousness unacceptable or undesirable impulses. It is the denial of these impulses and affects in authoritarians that leads to the development of prejudice, through the operation of projection and externalization. "The resultant break between the conscious and unconscious layers in the personality of the high scorers, as compared with the greater fluidity of transition and of intercommunication between the different personality strata in the low scorers, appears to have the greatest implications for their personality patterns" (p. 474).

However, Frenkel-Brunswik seems to have made a subtle but important distinction in the causal sequence envisioned. She did not suggest that authoritarians have more conflicts, but that they deal with conflicts in particular ways because of the structure of their consciousness. We might hypothesize that open men and women would intellectualize their conflicts, whereas closed men and women would repress or deny them. Projection may be used by closed individuals because they see the world simplistically in terms of good and bad, and it is easier to assume that others are bad and the self is good. Under this interpretation, authoritarianism (or closedness) is not the result of defense, but one of the determinants of the form of defense used. Repression and projection would then be seen not as causes of political conservativism and aesthetic insensitivity, but as correlates that share the same underlying cause: closedness to experience.

There is some empirical evidence for this position. Haan (1965) devised defense mechanism scales by empirically contrasting MMPI item responses of individuals clinically judged high or low in the use of various defenses; she created parallel coping mechanism scales from CPI items. Among the defense scales, Openness to Experience was positively related to Intellectualizing and negatively related to Denial (Costa, Zonderman, & McCrae, 1991). As Table I shows, Openness is also positively related to coping scales measuring Intellectuality and Logical Analysis, and negatively related to Suppression.

Table I shows that Openness is also related to Regression in Service of the Ego, a concept advanced by Kris (1952) to explain artistic creativity. Although described as a defense mechanism, it is clear that Regression in Service of the Ego is defined in structural rather than defensive terms. Kris suggested that some individuals can loosen the boundaries that separate mature, reality-oriented secondary process thinking from the prelogical, primary process thinking seen in dreams and psychotic delusions. This form of regression is adaptive, because primary process thinking is the source of creativity: the conventional associations between ideas and images are temporarily abandoned, leaving the mind free to try new associations. The artist then returns to secondary process thinking to select the useful products of this freer association and adapt them to the requirements of reality.

The consequences of permeable cognitive structures are not always adaptive. Hartmann, Russ, Oldfield, Siven, and Cooper (1987) studied chronic nightmare sufferers. They reported that their subjects were likely to be artists or students, and were described as being open, vulnerable, and defenseless "on the thin-boundary or permeable-boundary end of the continuum in all senses in which that term is used" (p. 56). (Hartmann, 1991, has gone on to develop his ideas about boundaries in the mind that provide a modern psychodynamic perspective on Openness.)

Similarly, recent studies have shown links between Openness and certain forms of cognitive aberration. West, Widiger, and Costa (1993) found that, among college students, NEO-PI-R Openness was associated with Perceptual Aberration and especially Magical Ideation scales (Chapman, Chapman, & Raulin, 1978; Eckblad & Chapman, 1983). Table III shows correlations of NEO-PI-R scales with measures of dissociation (Bernstein & Putnam's, 1986, DES; Riley's, 1988, QED)

TABLE III
Correlations between NEO-PI-R Openness
Scales and Measures of Dissociation and
Eccentric Perceptions

NEO-PI-R Scale	DES	QED	EP
O1: Fantasy	.37***	.58***	.42***
O2: Aesthetics	.24**	.32***	.47***
O3: Feelings	.22*	.33***	.30***
O4: Actions	.13	.14	.12
O5: Ideas	.15	.30***	.32***
O6: Values	−.04	.10	−.03
Total Openness	.30***	.49***	.47***

Note. N = 127. DES, Dissociative Experiences Scale;
QED, Questionnaire of Experiences of Dissociation;
EP, Eccentric Perceptions. Data cited by permission
from D. Watson, J. Harrison, and A. K. Slack, 1993,
[*Measures of dissociation and their relation to general
traits of personality*]. Unpublished raw data, University of Iowa.
*p < .05. **p < .01. ***p < .001.

and eccentric perceptions as measured by the Schedule for Non-Adaptive and Adaptive Personality (Clark, 1993). Very open people appear to have some of the characteristics of schizotypal thinking; whether these are adaptive or maladaptive will probably depend on other aspects of personality and on the individual's social environment.

Perhaps the most highly developed version of the structural model of Openness is found in the work of Rokeach (1960), who argued that ideas, beliefs, and attitudes were structured differently in open and closed individuals. Highly dogmatic individuals were thought to have compartmentalized thinking in which inconsistent beliefs were isolated and discrepant information was summarily rejected. Individuals low in dogmatism were able to tolerate ambiguity and could gradually shift attitudes as the weight of evidence accumulated. Using Coan's Openness scale, Wyrick (1969) showed that open individuals in fact acknowledged more frequent revisions in attitudes than did closed individuals.

It appears that one useful and important way to characterize Openness is in terms of the structure of consciousness. Open individuals have access to more thoughts, feelings, and impulses in awareness, and can maintain many of these simultaneously. Tolerance of ambiguity, emotional ambivalence, and perceptual synasthesia are all hallmarks of the open person. The capacity for absorption, for deeply focused attention, may be a result of this structure. For the closed individual, ideas, feelings, and perceptions are relatively isolated and must compete for full attention. For the open individual, all these elements may be simultaneously in awareness, providing a deeper and more intense experience.

B. Openness as Need for Experience

A structural account of Openness may be necessary, but it does not seem to be sufficient. Open people are not the passive recipients of a barrage of experiences they are unable to screen out; they actively seek out new and varied experiences. Openness involves motivation, needs for variety (Maddi & Berne, 1964), cognition (Osberg, 1987), sentience, and understanding (Jackson, 1984). This active pursuit of experience can be seen in all the facets of Openness. Closed individuals may have daydreams, but they are likely to be conventional and repetitive and serve the functions of escape from stress (McCrae, 1982) or mere wish fulfillment. The daydreams of open individuals are characterized by novelty and elaboration and are motivated by their intrinsic interest. The same is true for actions: Any reasonable adult (including some who are merely high in Agreeableness) would be willing to taste a new dish; the truly open go in quest of varied cuisines.

Fiske (1949) highlighted the active curiosity of open individuals by naming his corresponding factor *Inquiring* Intellect. Philosophical arguments are boring to closed individuals because they have no practical value; they are interesting to open people because they are intellectually challenging and because they may lead to new and surprising conclusions: Both the process of exploring and the novelty of discovery appeal to open people. Open individuals tend to endorse liberal political and social values (McCrae, in press) because questioning authority is a natural extension of their curiosity. The same willingness to pursue questions of value leads to higher moral development (Lonky, Kaus, & Roodin, 1984) and to the artist's bohemian rejection of convention.

Perhaps the clearest evidence of open individuals' need for experience per se is found in their appreciation of the arts. At least since Kant's *Critique of Judgment,* it has been generally recognized that the aesthetic experience is disinterested: There is no practical reason to be concerned with the fate of tragic heroes—no tangible benefit from listening to symphonies. The only function art serves is "to clarify, intensify, or otherwise enlarge our experience" (Canaday, 1980, p. 5), and this is the quintessential aim of open men and women.

Zuckerman's (1979, 1984) extensive research and theorizing on Sensation Seeking is surely relevant to an understanding of the motivational aspects of Openness. As Table I shows, all the Sensation Seeking scales are significantly related to Openness, particularly Experience Seeking. Zuckerman's (1984) suggestion that "novelty, in the absence of threat, may be rewarding through the activation of noradrenergic neurons" (p. 413), points to a possible neurochemical basis for Openness.

We have argued that open people are characterized both by a particular permeable structure of consciousness and by an active motivation to seek out the unfamiliar. It seems probable that the structure is the result of the motivation, rather than vice versa. In the absence of a need for new experience, an open structure would not provide any clear advantage; indeed, it would expose the individual to distracting thoughts, troubling impulses, and cognitive inconsistencies (cf. Maddi, 1968). The need for experience provides an incentive to tolerate ambiguity and dissonance, just as an animal's exploratory drive may overcome its need for security. In both cases, the evolutionary function seems clear: Greater experience ultimately provides a basis for better adaptation.

IV. Fᴜʀᴛʜᴇʀ Rᴇsᴇᴀʀᴄʜ ᴀɴᴅ Aᴘᴘʟɪᴄᴀᴛɪᴏɴs

It may seem odd to assert that Openness is the least researched and least understood of the five fundamental dimensions of personality. After all, there have been decades of research on psychological defenses, authoritarianism, hypnosis, creativity, and the need for variety. However, these diverse lines of research have not been integrated by the conception of Openness as a fundamental domain of personality which is reflected in each. As a result, there has been little cross-fertilization of ideas and the literature has been fragmented. The power of the construct of Openness in interpreting these areas can be seen in the explanations it provides for unanticipated results. Without it, how would we explain the curious finding that private self-consciousness is related to belief in paranormal phenomena (Davies, 1985)? Or the fact that the MBTI Sensation scale is *negatively* related to Zuckerman's Sensation Seeking, $r = -.43$, $N = 170$, $p < .001$, in BLSA participants? Once we understand that each of these variables reflects an aspect of Openness, the associations are clear.

Personality psychology is poised for a new round of research on these topics, guided by the concept of Openness. New instruments (e.g., Costa & McCrae, 1992a; Trapnell & Wiggins, 1990) provide validated measures of Openness and some of its facets in both self-report and observer rating formats. Scales measuring related traits such as absorption and private self-consciousness can be used more intelligently if they are understood as aspects of a broader and more fundamental construct.

A. Some Research Questions

Openness is so important and pervasive a dimension of individual difference that it should figure routinely in the research of personality psychologists. Researchers in other fields can also benefit by including measures of Openness in their studies (McCrae, in press). Social psychologists should assess openness in research on attitude formation and change. Educational psychologists should consider Openness as a moderator variable in assessing the value of different teaching methods. Industrial and organizational psychologists should include measures of Openness in their personnel selection batteries. Behavioral geneticists should study its heritability (Bergeman et al., 1993), and health psychologists should investigate its role in health information seeking and behavior change. Cognitive psychologists should examine the relation of Openness to field independence, cognitive complexity, and other cognitive styles (Tetlock, Peterson, & Berry, 1993).

In an earlier article (McCrae & Costa, 1985a), we argued that the future of Openness lay in the investigation of its effects across the life span in such areas as vocational career and family life. We know that open individuals have Artistic and Investigative interests (Costa, McCrae, & Holland, 1984) and that they make more midcareer shifts (McCrae & Costa, 1985a). There are characterizations of rigid and flexible managers (Kahn, Wolfe, Quinn, Snoek, & Rosenthal, 1964) that suggest how variations in Openness might be seen in organizational settings. But much remains to be learned about how Openness influences career paths, job satisfaction, and retirement planning. Similarly, we know little about the effects of Openness on the course of intimate and personal relationships. We know that Openness is stable in adulthood (Costa & McCrae, 1988a), so we should be able to approach many of these questions through retrospective studies; every prospective longitudinal study should certainly include baseline measures of Openness.

B. Applications in Psychiatry and Clinical Psychology

Personality traits have always been considered important for the diagnosis of psychiatric disorders, and extreme and maladaptive variants of some aspects of personality are classified as personality disorders in DSM-IV (American Psychiatric Association, 1994). Wiggins and Pincus (1989) have shown that scales measuring these disorders can be understood in terms of the five-factor model. Histrionics, for example, are extremely high in Extraversion; Avoidants are high in Neuroticism and low in Extraversion.

None of the DSM-IV personality disorders is uniquely associated with Openness, but a careful consideration of diagnostic criteria shows that aspects of Openness are relevant to several disorders (Costa & Widiger, 1994). The restricted affect of Schizoids, the self-aggrandizing fantasy of Narcissists, and the behavioral rigidity of Compulsives are all significant clinical features that may well be related to Openness. In his reconceptualization of personality disorders, Millon (1986) has suggested that each disorder is characterized by a particular intrapsychic structure, and as we have seen, Openness is a major determinant of psychic structure.

However, Openness has a history of being overlooked, and it is also worthwhile to consider that there may be personality disorders not identified in DSM-IV which represent pathological forms of Openness. Some individuals are so rigid in their adherence to tradition and so unwilling to accept change that they are unable to adapt to inevitable social changes. When combined with very low levels of Agreeableness, this closedness may take on an antisocial character. It is also possible that excessively high levels of Openness (particularly in the absence of comparably high levels of intelligence and Conscientiousness) may constitute a personality disorder. Such individuals may be so easily drawn to each new idea or belief that they are unable to form a coherent and integrated life structure.

Even where Openness is not relevant to the diagnosis of a psychiatric disorder, it may have important implications for psychotherapy (Miller, 1991). Open individuals may be more receptive to the idea of therapy itself and more tolerant of imaginative forms of therapy, such as Gestalt or hypnotherapy. Closed individuals are more likely to prefer concrete and practical suggestions. Biofeedback and directive therapies may prove more successful with them.

We began by suggesting that artists can be seen as exemplars of Openness, just as neurotics are exemplars of Neuroticism. People, however, are not one-dimensional exemplars; they are individuals who vary on at least five dimensions of personality. People who consult psychologists and psychiatrists about their problems bring more than these problems to the therapy; they also bring other dispositions that shape their lives and condition their responses to therapy. Individuals who are imaginative, sensitive, empathic, flexible, inquisitive, and tolerant will respond quite differently from those who are practical, down-to-earth, rigid, and dogmatic. Clinicians need to take Openness into account in designing the appropriate treatment for each client.

Rᴇꜰᴇʀᴇɴᴄᴇs

Adorno, T. W., Frenkel-Brunswik, E., Levison, D. J., & Sanford, R. N. (1969). *The authoritarian personality.* New York: Norton. (Original work published 1950)

Altemeyer, B. (1981). *Right-wing authoritarianism.* Winnipeg: University of Manitoba Press.

Amelang, M., & Borkenau, P. (1982). Über die faktorielle Struktur und externe Validität einiger Fragebogen-Skalen zur Erfassung von Dimensionen der Extraversion und emotionalen Labilität [On the factor structure and external validity of some questionnaire scales measuring dimensions of extraversion and neuroticism]. *Zeitschrift für Differentielle und Diagnostische Psychologie, 3,* 119–146.

American Psychiatric Association. (1994). *Diagnostic and statistical manual of mental disorders* (4th ed.). Washington, DC: Author.

Angleitner, A., & Ostendorf, F. (1989, July). *Personality factors via self- and peer-ratings based on a representative sample of German trait descriptive terms.* Paper presented at the First European Congress of Psychology, Amsterdam.

Ås, A., O'Hara, J. W., & Munger, M. P. (1962). The measurement of subjective experiences presumably related to hypnotic susceptibility. *Scandinavian Journal of Psychology, 3,* 47–64.

Bergeman, C. S., Chipuer, H. M., Plomin, R., Pedersen, N. L., McClearn, G. E., Nesselroade, J. R., Costa, P. T., Jr., & McCrae, R. R. (1993). Genetic and environmental effects on openness to experience, agreeableness, and conscientiousness: An adoption/twin study. *Journal of Personality, 61,* 159–179.

Berlyne, D. E. (1955). The arousal and satiation of perceptual curiosity in the rat. *Journal of Comparative and Physiological Psychology, 48,* 238–246.

Bernstein, E. M., & Putnam, F. W. (1986). Development, reliability, and validity of a dissociation scale. *Journal of Nervous and Mental Disease, 174,* 727–735.

Block, J. (1961). *The Q-sort method in personality assessment and psychiatric research.* Springfield, IL: Charles C. Thomas.

Borgatta, E. F. (1964). The structure of peronality characteristics. *Behavioral Science, 9,* 8–17.

Briggs, S. R. (1989). The optimal level of measurement for personality constructs. In D. M. Buss & N. Cantor (Eds.), *Personality research for the 1990's* (pp. 246–260). New York: Springer-Verlag.

Canaday, J. (1980). *What is art?* New York: Knopf.

Cattell, R. B. (1946). *The description and measurement of personality.* Yonkers-on-Hudson, NY: World Book.

Cattell, R. B., Eber, H. W., & Tatsuoka, M. M. (1970). *The handbook for the Sixteen Personality Factor Questionnaire.* Champaign, IL: Institute for Personality and Ability Testing.

Chapman, L. J., Chapman, J. P., & Raulin, M. L. (1978). Body image aberration in schizophrenia. *Journal of Abnormal Psychology, 87,* 399–407.

Clark, L. A. (1993). *The Schedule for Adaptive and Non-Adaptive Personality.* Minneapolis: University of Minnesota Press.

Coan, R. W. (1974). *The optimal personality.* New York: Columbia University Press.

Conley, J. J. (1985). Longitudinal stability of personality traits: A multitrait-multimethod-multioccasion analysis. *Journal of Personality and Social Psychology, 49,* 1266–1282.

Costa, P. T., Jr., & McCrae, R. R. (1976). Age differences in personality structure: A cluster analytic approach. *Journal of Gerontology, 31,* 564–570.

Costa, P. T., Jr., & McCrae, R. R. (1978). Objective personality assessment. In M. Storandt, I. C. Siegler, & M. F. Elias (Eds.), *The clinical psychology of aging* (pp. 119–143). New York: Plenum Press.

Costa, P. T., Jr., & McCrae, R. R. (1988a). Personality in adulthood: A six-year longitudinal study of self-reports and spouse ratings on the NEO Personality Inventory. *Journal of Personality and Social Psychology, 54,* 853–863.

Costa, P. T., Jr., & McCrae, R. R. (1988b). From catalog to classification: Murray's needs and the five-factor model. *Journal of Personality and Social Psychology, 55,* 258–265.

Costa, P. T., Jr., & McCrae, R. R. (1989). *The NEO-PI/NEO-FFI manual supplement.* Odessa, FL: Psychological Assessment Resources.

Costa, P. T., Jr., & McCrae, R. R. (1992a). *Revised NEO Personality Inventory (NEO-PI-R) and NEO Five-Factor Inventory (NEO-FFI) professional manual.* Odessa, FL: Psychological Assessment Resources.

Costa, P. T., Jr., & McCrae, R. R. (1992b). Trait psychology comes of age. In T. B. Sonderegger (Ed.), *Nebraska Symposium on Motivation: Psychology and aging* (pp. 169–204). Lincoln: University of Nebraska Press.

Costa, P. T., Jr., McCrae, R. R., & Dye, D. A. (1991). Facet scales for agreeableness and conscientiousness: A revision of the NEO Personality Inventory. *Personality and Individual Differences, 12,* 887–898.

Costa, P. T., Jr., McCrae, R. R., & Holland, J. L. (1984). Personality and vocational interests in an adult sample. *Journal of Applied Psychology, 69,* 390–400.

Costa, P. T., Jr., McCrae, R. R., Zonderman, A. B., Barbano, H. E., Lebowitz, B., & Larson, D. M. (1986). Cross-sectional studies of personality in a national sample: 2. Stability in neuroticism, extraversion, and openness. *Psychology and Aging, 1,* 144–149.

Costa, P. T., Jr., & Widiger, T. A. (Eds.). (1994). *Personality disorders and the five-factor model of personality.* Washington, DC: American Psychological Association.

Costa, P. T., Jr., Zonderman, A. B., & McCrae, R. R. (1991). Personality, defense, coping, and adaptation in older adulthood. In E. M. Cummings, A. L. Greene, & K. H.

Karraker (Eds.), *Life-span developmental psychology: Perspectives on stress and coping* (pp. 277–293). Hillsdale, NJ: Erlbaum.

Davies, M. F. (1985). Self-consciousness and paranormal belief. *Perceptual and Motor Skills, 60,* 484–486.

Digman, J. M. (1987, August). *Eysenck, Guilford, and Cattell and the Big Five factors of personality.* Paper presented at the American Psychological Association Convention, New York.

Digman, J. M., & Inouye, J. (1986). Further specification of the five robust factors of personality. *Journal of Personality and Social Psychology, 50,* 116–123.

Eckblad, M., & Chapman, J. L. (1983). Magical ideation as a measure of schizotypy. *Journal of Consulting and Clinical Psychology, 51,* 215–225.

Epstein, S., & Meier, P. (1989). Constructive thinking: A broad coping variable with specific components. *Journal of Personality and Social Psychology, 57,* 332–350.

Eysenck, H. J. (1991). Dimensions of personality: 16, 5, or 3?—Criteria for a taxonomic paradigm. *Personality and Individual Differences, 12,* 773–790.

Fenigstein, A., Scheier, M. F., & Buss, A. H. (1975). Public and private self-consciousness: Assessment and theory. *Journal of Consulting and Clinical Psychology, 43,* 522–528.

Fiske, D. W. (1949). Consistency of the factorial structures of personality ratings from different sources. *Journal of Abnormal and Social Psychology, 44,* 329–344.

Fitzgerald, E. T. (1966). Measurement of openness to experience: A study of regression in the service of the ego. *Journal of Personality and Social Psychology, 4,* 655–663.

Funder, D. C., & Sneed, C. D. (1993). Behavioral manifestations of personality: An ecological approach to judgmental accuracy. *Journal of Personality and Social Psychology, 64,* 479–490.

Goldberg, L. R. (1981). Language and individual differences: The search for universals in personality lexicons. In L. Wheeler (Ed.), *Review of personality and social psychology* (Vol. 2, pp. 141–165). Beverly Hills, CA: Sage.

Goldberg, L. R. (1989, June). *Standard markers of the Big Five factor structure.* Paper presented at an Invited Workshop on Personality Language, Groningen, The Netherlands.

Haan, N. (1965). Coping and defense mechanisms related to personality inventories. *Journal of Consulting Psychology, 29,* 373–378.

Hartmann, E. (1991). *Boundaries in the mind: A new psychology of personality differences.* New York: Basic Books.

Hartmann, E., Russ, D., Oldfield, M., Sivan, I., & Cooper, S. (1987). Who has nightmares? The personality of the lifelong nightmare sufferer. *Archives of General Psychiatry, 44,* 49–56.

Hogan, R. (1986). *Hogan Personality Inventory manual.* Minneapolis, MN: National Computer Systems.

Jackson, D. N. (1984). *Personality Research Form manual* (3rd ed.). Port Huron, MI: Research Psychologists Press.

John, O. P. (1990). The "Big Five" factor taxonomy: Dimensions of personality in the natural language and in questionnaires. In L. A. Pervin (Ed.), *Handbook of personality theory and research* (pp. 66–100). New York: Guilford Press.

John, O. P., Angleitner, A., & Ostendorf, F. (1988). The lexical approach to personality: A historical review of trait taxonomic research. *European Journal of Personality, 2,* 171–203.

Jourard, S. M. (1964). *The transparent self.* Princeton, NJ: Van Nostrand.

Kahn, R. L., Wolfe, D. M., Quinn, R. P., Snoek, J. D., & Rosenthal, R. A. (1964). *Organizational stress: Studies in role conflict and ambiguity.* New York: Wiley.

Kris, E. (1952). *Psychoanalytic explorations in art.* New York: International Universities Press.

Lonky, E., Kaus, C. R., & Roodin, P. A. (1984). Life experience and mode of coping: Relation to moral judgment in adulthood. *Developmental Psychology, 20,* 1159–1167.

MacKinnon, D. W. (1962). The nature and nurture of creative talent. *American Psychologist, 17,* 484–495.

Maddi, S. R. (1968). The pursuit of consistency and variety. In R. P. Abelson, E. Aronson, W. J. McGuire, T. M. Newcomb, M. J. Rosenberg, & P. H. Tannenbaum (Eds.), *Theories of cognitive consistency: A sourcebook* (pp. 267–274). Chicago: Rand McNally.

Maddi, S. R., & Berne, N. (1964). Novelty of productions and desire for novelty as active and passive forms of the need for variety. *Journal of Personality, 22,* 270–277.

McCrae, R. R. (1982). Age differences in the use of coping mechanisms. *Journal of Gerontology, 37,* 454–460.

McCrae, R. R. (1987). Creativity, divergent thinking, and openness to experience. *Journal of Personality and Social Psychology, 52,* 1258–1265.

McCrae, R. R. (1990). Traits and trait names: How well is openness represented in natural languages? *European Journal of Personality, 4,* 119–129.

McCrae, R. R. (1993–1994). Openness to experience as a basic dimension of personality. *Imagination, Cognition, and Personality, 13,* 39–55.

McCrae, R. R. (1994). Openness to experience: Expanding the boundaries of Factor V. *European Journal of Personality, 8,* 251–272.

McCrae, R. R. (in press). Social consequences of experiential openness. *Psychological Bulletin.*

McCrae, R. R., & Costa, P. T., Jr. (1985a). Openness to experience. In R. Hogan & W. H. Jones (Eds.), *Perspectives in personality* (Vol. 1, pp. 145–172). Greenwich, CT: JAI Press.

McCrae, R. R., & Costa, P. T., Jr. (1985b). Updating Norman's "adequate taxonomy": Intelligence and personality dimensions in natural language and in questionnaires. *Journal of Personality and Social Psychology, 49,* 710–721.

McCrae, R. R., & Costa, P. T., Jr. (1987). Validation of the five-factor model of personality across instruments and observers. *Journal of Personality and Social Psychology, 52,* 81–90.

McCrae, R. R., & Costa, P. T., Jr. (1988). Recalled parent-child relations and adult personality. *Journal of Personality, 56,* 417–434.

McCrae, R. R., & Costa, P. T., Jr. (1989a). Different points of view: Self-reports and ratings in the assessment of personality. In J. P. Forgas & M. J. Innes (Eds.), *Recent advances in social psychology: An international perspective* (pp. 429–439). Amsterdam: Elsevier.

McCrae, R. R., & Costa, P. T., Jr. (1989b). Reinterpreting the Myers-Briggs Type Indicator from the perspective of the five-factor model of personality. *Journal of Personality, 57,* 17–40.

McCrae, R. R., Costa, P. T., Jr., & Busch, C. M. (1986). Evaluating comprehensiveness in personality systems: The California Q-Set and the five-factor model. *Journal of Personality, 54,* 430–446.

McCrae, R. R., Costa, P. T., Jr., & Piedmont, R. L. (1993). Folk concepts, natural language, and psychological constructs: The California Psychological Inventory and the five-factor model. *Journal of Personality, 61,* 1–26.

McCrae, R. R., & John, O. P. (1992). An introduction to the five-factor model and its applications. *Journal of Personality, 60,* 175–215.

McReynolds, P. (1985). Psychological assessment and clinical practice: Problems and prospects. In J. N. Butcher & C. D. Spielberger (Eds.), *Advances in personality assessment* (Vol. 4, pp. 1–30). Hillsdale, NJ: Erlbaum.

Miller, T. (1991). The psychotherapeutic utility of the five-factor model of personality: A clinician's experience. *Journal of Personality Assessment, 57,* 415–433.

Millon, T. (1986). Personality prototypes and their diagnostic criteria. In T. Millon & G. L. Klerman (Eds.), *Contemporary directions in psychopathology: Towards the DSM-IV* (pp. 671–712). New York: Guilford Press.

Morris, W. (Ed.). (1976). *The American heritage dictionary of the English language.* Boston: Houghton-Mifflin.

Myers, I. B., & McCaulley, M. H. (1985). *Manual: A guide to the development and use of the Myers-Briggs Type Indicator.* Palo Alto, CA: Consulting Psychologists Press.

Norman, W. T. (1963). Toward an adequate taxonomy of personality attributes: Replicated factor structure in peer nomination personality ratings. *Journal of Abnormal and Social Psychology, 66,* 574–583.

Osberg, T. M. (1987). The convergent and discriminant validity of the Need for Cognition Scale. *Journal of Personality Assessment, 51,* 441–450.

Peabody, D. (1987). Selecting representative trait adjectives. *Journal of Personality and Social Psychology, 52,* 59–71.

Peabody, D., & Goldberg, L. R. (1989). Some determinants of factor structures from personality-trait descriptors. *Journal of Personality and Social Psychology, 57,* 552–567.

Riley, K. C. (1988). Measurement of dissociation. *Journal of Nervous and Mental Disease, 176,* 449–450.

Rogers, C. R. (1961). *On becoming a person: A therapist's view of psychotherapy.* Boston: Houghton-Mifflin.

Rokeach, M. (1960). *The open and closed mind.* New York: Basic Books.

Saucier, G. (1992). Openness versus intellect: Much ado about nothing? *European Journal of Personality, 6,* 381–386.

Tellegen, A., & Atkinson, G. (1974). Openness to absorbing and self-altering experiences ("absorption"), a trait related to hypnotic susceptibility. *Journal of Abnormal Psychology, 83,* 268–277.

Tellegen, A., Lykken, D. T., Bouchard, T. J., Jr., Wilcox, K. J., Segal, N. L., & Rich, S. (1988). Personality similarity in twins reared apart and together. *Journal of Personality and Social Psychology, 54,* 1031–1039.

Tetlock, P. E., Peterson, R. S., & Berry, J. M. (1993). Flattering and unflattering personality portraits of integratively simple and complex managers. *Journal of Personality and Social Psychology, 64,* 500–511.

Trapnell, P. D. (1994). Openness versus Intellect: A lexical left turn. *European Journal of Personality, 8,* 273–290.

Trapnell, P. D., & Wiggins, J. S. (1990). Extension of the Interpersonal Adjective Scales to include the Big Five dimensions of personality. *Journal of Personality and Social Psychology, 59,* 781–790.

Tupes, E. C., & Christal, R. E. (1992). Recurrent personality factors based on trait ratings. *Journal of Personality, 60,* 225–251. (Original work published 1961)

Webster, H., Freedman, M., & Heist, P. (1962). Personality changes in college students. In N. Sanford (Ed.), *The American college: A psychological and social interpretation of the higher learning* (pp. 811–846). New York: Wiley.

Welsh, G. S. (1975). *Creativity and intelligence: A personality approach.* Chapel Hill: University of North Carolina, Institute for Research in Social Science.

Wessman, A. E., & Ricks, D. F. (1966). *Mood and personality.* New York: Holt, Rinehart & Winston.

West, K. Y., Widiger, T. A., & Costa, P. T., Jr. (1993). *The placement of cognitive and perceptual abberations within the five-factor model of personality.* Unpublished manuscript, University of Kentucky, Lexington.

Wiggins, J. S., & Pincus, A. L. (1989). Conceptions of personality disorders and dimensions of personality. *Psychological Assessment: A Journal of Consulting and Clinical Psychology, 1,* 305–316.

Wyrick, L. C. (1969). *Correlates of openness to experience.* Unpublished master's thesis, University of Arizona, Tucson.

Zuckerman, M. (1979). *Sensation seeking: Beyond the optimal level of arousal.* Hillsdale, NJ: Erlbaum.

Zuckerman, M. (1984). Sensation seeking: A comparative approach to a human trait. *Behavioral and Brain Sciences, 7,* 413–471.

CHAPTER 32

CONSCIENTIOUSNESS AND INTEGRITY AT WORK

JOYCE HOGAN
UNIVERSITY OF TULSA

DENIZ S. ONES
UNIVERSITY OF MINNESOTA

I. OVERVIEW

Conscientiousness refers to conformity and socially prescribed impulse control. All comprehensive studies of natural-language personality descriptions—beginning with Allport and Odbert (1936)—identify a Conscientiousness dimension. Norman's (1963, 1967) peer rating studies of the structure of trait terms provide a taxonomic foundation for organizing contemporary inquiries about personality structure; Conscientiousness is one of five components of the taxonomy. Goldberg's (1990) analyses of Norman's trait lists repeatedly confirmed the five-factor structure; he coined the expression "Big Five" to describe this structure (see Goldberg, 1993, for a concise summary). Goldberg's research is persuasive; because we now know the structure of the trait lexicon, we can celebrate a major contribution to social science research.

Ironically, while personality psychologists were busy exploring the structure of the trait lexicon and identifying stable individual differences in interpersonal behavior, the use of personality assessment declined among applied psychologists. Skepticism regarding the usefulness of personality measurement reached a peak during the 1960s. Two critiques were particularly influential. The first was Mischel's

(1968) book, which claimed that (1) there is no evidence that personality is consistent across situations, and (2) personality measures explain only a trivial amount of variance in social behavior. The second, a review by Guion and Gottier (1965), concluded that there was no evidence for the validity of personality instruments. These claims spawned considerable research which ultimately resulted in a reversal of the critics' conclusions. Nevertheless, the shadow of skepticism stills exists and some applied psychologists continue to endorse these critiques of personality assessment.

The recent literature on the Big Five personality factors provides compelling evidence for its structural robustness; it is the basis for the resurgent interest in personality assessment. The evidence indicates that personality structure is consistent across different theoretical frameworks (Goldberg, 1981; Johnson & Ostendorf, 1993), using different assessments (e.g., Conley, 1985; Costa & McCrae, 1992; Lorr & Youniss, 1973), in different cultures (e.g., Bond, Nakazato, & Shiraishi, 1975; Borkenau & Ostendorf, 1989; Digman & Takemoto-Chock, 1981), and using ratings obtained from different sources (e.g., Digman & Inouye, 1986; McCrae & Costa, 1987; Norman, 1963; Norman & Goldberg, 1966; Watson, 1989). Substantial empirical evidence exists for the five-factor structure of peer descriptors (Cattell, 1943, 1946, 1947; Fiske, 1949; Norman, 1963; Tupes & Christal, 1961). Borgatta's (1964) research extends the robustness of the finding across five methods of data accumulation. We view the Big Five as a useful nosology, not as a theory nor an explanation. Nevertheless, there is some disagreement about the nature and meaning of the constructs, the scope of the taxonomy, and the degree to which the dimensions are fundamental and incisive (cf. Block, 1993; Hough, Eaton, Dunnette, Kamp, & McCloy, 1990; Johnson & Ostendorf, 1993; Waller & Ben-Porath, 1987). Among applied psychologists, renewed interest in personality assessment is based on qualitative (Goldberg, 1992; R. Hogan, 1991; Schmidt, Ones, & Hunter, 1992) and quantitative (Barrick & Mount, 1991; Hough et al., 1990; Ones, Viswesvaran, & Schmidt, 1993; Tett, Jackson, & Rothstein, 1991) reviews which conclude that when personality research is organized in terms of the Big Five factors, personality is consistently related to job performance criteria.

The Conscientiousness dimension led the personality assessment revival in applied psychology. There are at least two reasons for this. First, lack of conscientiousness is a major problem in the workplace. Conscientious employees are good organizational citizens; delinquent employees, in contrast, are nonproductive and erode the economic health of an organization. Employers beg the psychological community for effective assessments of "honesty" and "integrity"—which are their words. The demand persists and there is no sign that it will abate. Second, empirical findings support the validity of Conscientiousness measures for predicting counterproductive behavior and job performance. Some personality measures that were developed to predict organizational delinquency criteria are widely used (e.g., Gough, 1972; J. Hogan & Hogan, 1989; Paajanen, 1985). Meta-analyses including general measures of Conscientiousness show consistent and significant relations with all job performance criteria in the occupations studied (Barrick & Mount,

1991; Tett et al., 1991). These validity generalization studies indicate that the Big Five dimensions of personality, Conscientiousness is the *only* dimension of personality to show consistent validities across organizations, jobs, and situations.

In this chapter, we review three theoretical explanations of the Conscientiousness construct, including psychoanalytic theory, role-taking and folk concepts, and socioanalytic theory. We then describe the manner in which Conscientiousness has been assessed. We next review the empirical findings that support the validity of Conscientiousness measures. Finally, we offer some advice for thinking about Conscientiousness—in terms of measurement and interpretation.

II. CONCEPTUALIZING CONSCIENTIOUSNESS

A. Psychoanalytic Theory

In personality psychology, Freud provided an important early discussion of the Conscientiousness construct. He explained Conscientiousness in terms of the superego—conscience—the first structure to develop in personality. The superego determines one's attitude toward authority and, according to Freud, the superego is crucial because all of development concerns coming to terms with authority. Freud not only recognized the importance of the conscience, but he also anticipated a modern dilemma: that too much Conscientiousness can be as undesirable as too little. Although today's applied psychologists seem to be concerned only with too little, Freud was also concerned with the problems of too much—i.e., the problems caused by a rigid, omnipotent, and punitive superego that define the extreme high end of Conscientiousness.

Unlike the other personality structures, the superego depends on social relationships, and the fundamental determinant of a person's disposition toward authority is the resolution of the Oedipus complex. The Oedipus complex, a universal constellation of unconscious wishes and fantasies, involves interaction, conflict, and negotiation with one's parents. Whether its resolution is positive or negative depends on the relationship between the child and his or her parents. Further, Freud argued that the view of childhood as a period of innocence free of sexual corruption was mythical. Rather, children are primitive, undisciplined, and born in a state of "polymorphous perversity." Many of the child's pleasure-producing activities arouse parental disapproval and only a small number of behaviors are socially approved (Fancher, 1990, p. 374). Over time, the family or caretakers channel these primitive tendencies into acceptable expressions and civilized behavior. The nature of this long process of social development where the parents attempt to curb unruly childhood sexuality is fundamental to all subsequent relations with parents and authority.

The insights of Freud suggest that Conscientiousness is a product of the superego that develops from resolving conflict between childhood sexuality and parentally guided forces of socialization. One of Freud's more accurate theoretical insights is that Conscientiousness begins in the process of resolving conflicts with authority. Relations with the parents determine relations with other authority figures in life—military superiors, employers, mentors, and experts.

B. Role-Taking and Folk Concepts

The historic chasm between personality theory and personality measurement becomes particularly apparent in the 25 years between Freud's last writings and modern demonstrations of the validity of personality measures. Before 1950, the conventional wisdom of criminology (Sutherland, 1951) was that delinquents and nondelinquents could not be differentiated on the basis of personality. According to Gough and Peterson (1952), the most notable review of the time (Schuessler & Cressey, 1950) concluded, after examining 113 studies, that personality measures could not distinguish criminals from noncriminals. From a role-taking perspective and based on "intuitive grounds," Gough and Peterson developed a pool of 64 items that strongly differentiated delinquent from nondelinquent males, females, and army personnel, calling into question social science research findings from the previous 25 years.

Most interesting, however, was Gough's insight that four themes characterized the discriminating items—role-taking deficiencies, resentment, alienation, and rebelliousness. These themes were retained in the items included in the Socialization scale of the California Psychological Inventory (Gough, 1957, 1987), perhaps the most well-validated broad bandwidth measure of Conscientiousness available. From a role-taking theory of psychopathy and folk concepts, Gough (1960) proposed that people are normally distributed along a continuum of socialization so that some are unusually scrupulous and conscientious, most are normally rule-compliant, and some are hostile to society's rules and conventions. On empirical grounds, excessive hostility is associated with criminal and delinquent behavior. However, Gough's explanation for criminal and delinquent behavior is that the "psychopath" fails to anticipate social expectations and therefore exhibits a deficient role-taking capacity during social interaction. Insensitivity to expectations and rules seems to result from an egotistical inability to understand the effects of one's behavior on others. However, this argument does not explain why delinquents or psychopaths are insensitive to the rules in the first place.

C. Socioanalytic Theory

Socioanalytic theory (R. Hogan, 1983) also can account for the empirical relations while explaining the importance of and individual differences in the Conscientiousness dimension. Hogan's theory contends that (1) people evolved and still live in groups; (2) every group is characterized by a status hierarchy and those with status will make the rules for people living in the group; (3) people are consciously or unconsciously motivated by status and social acceptance, which are prerequisite for reproductive success in the group; (4) social interaction is the process by which all human needs and goals, including reproductive success, are met; and (5) the process of social interaction and social life is fundamental because the needs for status—getting ahead—and social acceptance—getting along—can cross purposes. People interact in terms of their identities, which are constructed unconsciously from attempts to achieve status and social acceptance in the peer group. Individual differences arise, in part, because some people are more skilled in their social performance and more attentive to processes that will support that identity than others.

Following socioanalytic theory, Conscientiousness is part of an identity choice—an interpersonal strategy for dealing with the members of one's group. In childhood, one might receive attention and approval for being tidy, compliant, and dependable; a child is likely to repeat activities that bring such approval from authority. However, by adulthood, the processes by which one supports a Conscientious identity are unconscious. It is easy to understand how Conscientiousness promotes survival in the group, and survival in today's organization. People engage in activities that are consistent with their identity; those who want others to see them as Conscientious will show up for work on time, complete assignments accurately, mow their lawns, and keep a balanced checkbook. People who earn the reputation of being Conscientious do not make waves, do not challenge authority, like rules, and avoid arguments, ambiguities, and altercations.

But how does socioanalytic theory explain individual differences in Conscientiousness, particularly deviancy? These may be only one strategy for supporting a Conscientious identity, and that is by complying with the rules, customs, norms, and expectations of the group; through such behavior, one is regarded by peers and co-workers as "conscientious." However, there are any number of behavioral predispositions that lead to a delinquent reputation. For example, among these are taking on a "tough guy" identity that facilitates status in a deviant group such as a gang. Others might be acts reflecting alienation, disaffection, dissolution, hostility toward authority, impulsiveness, and vengefulness. Still another source of individual variation is self-deception about the congruence between one's actions and group norms. Consider the employee who routinely lectures co-workers on business ethics, but continually steals time and resources from the company without any cognizance of the contradiction. As Freud suggested, some of us are unaware of the meanings of our actions, and in this case self-deception sets the stage for self-defeat.

How can we reconcile the socioanalytic theory of Conscientiousness with the Big Five model? Socioanalytic theory insists that two definitions of personality must be considered—personality from the view of the actor and personality from the view of the observer. Hogan suggests that personality from the view of the actor is a personal, intrapsychic evaluation of what a person is like "way down deep." It probably consists of goals, intentions, fears, motives, and beliefs; much of this content is not observable and therefore will not be easily amenable to scientific study. However, personality from the view of the observer is based on an actor's behavior and coded in terms of trait words which describe that person's reputation. Reputations are reasonably reliable across observers and time. Observers describe actors' behavior using trait terms—responsible, dependable, and careful, or, conversely, irresponsible, chaotic, and careless. Reputation is encoded in trait words, trait words have a well-defined mathematical structure, and these trait words are the substance of the Big Five model.

How do we get to Conscientiousness? Because people evolved in groups, there were pressures to get along as well as to get ahead. Trait words are the descriptive categories observers use to evaluate others during inevitable social interactions. As evaluative categories, these words reflect the amount of status and acceptance observers are willing to grant an actor; these trait descriptors become one's public reputation and have consequences for group success. Trait words can be organized in terms of the Big Five personality factors and these reflect the qualities and contributions which that person can be expected to bring to the group. The Big Five Conscientiousness dimension is concerned with a person seeming responsible and trustworthy, characteristics that are fundamental for maintaining a group.

III. ASSESSING CONSCIENTIOUSNESS

In the 50 years of personality research that began in the 1930s, all major inventories have contained some scale level assessment of the Conscientiousness construct, broadly defined. Although test authors had different agendas when constructing their instruments, it is noteworthy that, regardless of purpose, they included an assessment of Conscientiousness. In thinking about these scales, Cronbach's (1960) application of Shannon and Weaver's (1949) distinction between bandwidth and fidelity is appropriate. We began with the Socialization scale of the CPI which Gough and Peterson (1952) developed to distinguish delinquents and nondelinquents. The complexity of the scale's content gives it a broad bandwidth and an array of external correlates, from voting behavior to incarceration. Investigations of the internal structure of the CPI Socialization scale indicate that it is composed of four hierarchically ordered subfactors. These are hostility toward rules and authority, thrill-seeking impulsiveness, social insensitivity, and alienation (e.g., Rosen, 1977). The broad bandwidth of the Socialization scale necessarily reduces its fidelity in predicting any single relevant behavior. However, we contend that the richness and complexity of the Socialization scale is also appropriate for measurement of the broad Conscientiousness construct. Most criteria that applied psychologists aim to predict are complex in nature, with many factors interacting to cause the behavior of interest. A good example is the criterion of job performance in industrial/organizational psychology. To predict and explain such complex criteria, complex and rich predictors work best (Ones, Mount, Barrick, & Hunter, 1994).

The Big Five heuristic provides a systematic way to identify Conscientiousness measures included in omnibus personality inventories. Based on the work of Costa, McCrae, and their colleagues, a number of published studies report correlations between the NEO-PI (Costa & McCrae, 1992) and other well-known personality inventories published between 1930 and 1970. Table I presents selected correlational results for the NEO Conscientiousness scale and scales from other inventories. From this, it is apparent that the Conscientiousness construct is complex; there are at least three themes underlying the Table I correlations. Although these analyses use the NEO Conscientiousness scale as the factor marker, other researchers also have discovered the complex essence of this dimension (Barrick & Mount, 1991).

First, from the CPI Self-Control scale, Interpersonal Style Inventory Impulse Control scale, and Myers–Briggs Type Indicator Judging/Perceiving Type, a component of control emerges. These correlates suggest that Conscientiousness, in part, concerns a lack of impulsiveness and spontaneity, and a disposition toward cautiousness and criticality. Second, from the Order scales of the Edwards Personal Preference Schedule (EPPS) and the Personality Research Form (PRF), the component of orderliness, tidiness, and compulsiveness emerges. These relations suggest that Conscientiousness is also associated with being organized, neat, and methodical. Third, from the CPI Achievement via Conformity scale, the EPPS Endurance scale, and the PRF Orientation toward Work versus Play dimension (Skinner, Jackson, & Rampton, 1976), a component of hard work and perseverance emerges. These

TABLE I

Correlations between the NEO Conscientiousness Scale and Selected Personality Scales

Measure	Scale	NEO *r*
California Psychological Inventory (McCrae, Costa, & Piedmont, 1993)	Self-Control	.31
	Good Impression	.32
	Achievement via Conformance	.37
	Flexibility	−.40
	Norm Favoring (vector 2)	.39
Myers–Briggs (McCrae & Costa, 1989)	Judging/Perceiving (male)	−.49
	Judging/Perceiving (female)	−.46
Interpersonal Style Inventory (McCrae & Costa, 1991)	Impulse Control	.71
	Stability	.43
Edwards Personal Preference Schedule (Piedmont, McCrae, & Costa, 1992)	Order	.68
	Endurance	.63
Personality Research Form (Costa & McCrae, 1988)	Achivement	.46
	Cognitive Structure	.33
	Endurance	.42
	Harm Avoidance	−.39
	Order	.60
	Desirability	.46
Personality Research Form (Skinner scales: Skinner, Jackson, & Rampton, 1976)	Orientation toward Work versus Play	.60

correlates suggest that Conscientiousness concerns responsible work orientation, where a person works hard because it is the right thing to do—as opposed to a person who is ambitious but not necessarily conscientious.

In a joint factor analysis of the Comrey Personality Scales (CPS), the Eysenck Personality Inventory, and the Sixteen Personality Factors (16PF), Noller, Law, and Comrey (1987) interpreted the first factor as Conscientiousness. Although it contained components similar to control and orderliness identified above, the analysis also revealed the theme of conformity. The 16PF-G conformity scale defined the factor, with the CPS-C conformity scale loading .65 and the Eysenck lie scale loading .39. These results suggest that measures of the Conscientiousness construct also can reflect tendencies toward rule compliance, obedience, and conventional integrity. These same themes appear when interpreting scores on the CPI Socialization scale.

Since 1980, we have witnessed the development of a new generation of multidimensional personality inventories designed to assess some or all the Big Five factors as an explicit measurement goal. These inventories include the NEO-PI (Costa & McCrae, 1992), the Personal Characteristics Inventory (Barrick & Mount, 1993), Goldberg's adjective markers (Goldberg, 1992), the Hogan Personality Inventory (HPI; R. Hogan & Hogan, 1992), Lorr and Youniss's (1973) Interpersonal Style Inventory, the Multidimensional Personality Questionnaire (Tellegen, 1982), and the Interpersonal Adjective Scales-Revised (IAS-R; Wiggins, 1991). All of these inventories contain a scale of assess "conscientiousness." Given the different orientations of the inventory authors, it is not surprising that the interpretation of "conscientiousness" is inconsistent across instruments (Johnson & Ostendorf, 1993). For example, the NEO Conscientiousness scale reflects orderliness and persistence (McCrae & Costa, 1992), whereas the Goldberg adjectives concern dependability, responsibility, and carefulness (Goldberg, 1992), and the HPI Prudence scale reflects impulse control, professed probity, preference for predictability, and virtuousness (R. Hogan & Hogan, 1992).

A substantial body of evidence shows that many omnibus measures of personality contain a dimension of Conscientiousness. These measures have varying degrees of Conscientiousness saturation. Beyond a core interpretation that these measures concern conformity and dependability, there are nuances within each measure that can be interpreted only through their nomological network with other measures. Test–test correlates are useful, but they provide only a limited view of a construct and they are a necessary but insufficient condition for establishing validity. Analyses such as those reported in Table I need to be expanded to include evaluations of test–nontest relations, which permit broader understanding and interpretation of the Conscientiousness construct validity (R. Hogan & Nicholson, 1988; Landy, 1986). In a meta-analysis, examining the construct validity of the Big Five dimensions of personality, Ones, Schmidt, and Viswesvaran (1994) found that Conscientiousness-related scales from mainstream personality inventories correlate .47 among themselves ($N = 288,512$; $K = 226$). However, when the correlations between Conscientiousness scales from personality inventories explicitly based on the Big Five (HPI Prudence scale, Goldberg's Conscientiousness adjective checklist, and Personal Characteristics Inventory's Conscientiousness scale) were examined, the average disattenuated correlation was .71.

There are seemingly narrow bandwidth measures of Conscientiousness that serve a specific purpose in industrial psychology. These are measures of "integrity," where the assessment concerns honesty–dishonesty (Murphy, 1993, p. 115). Traditionally, a distinction is made between tests that inquire directly about honest behavior and attitudes (e.g., "I stole more than $5,000 from my last employer") and tests that use questions mapping onto the integrity construct. Questions on these measures are similar and, in some cases, identical to inventory items on Conscientiousness scales. Tests that inquire directly about honesty are labeled "overt" (Sackett, Burris, & Callahan, 1989) or "clear purpose" (Murphy, 1993, p. 117), while tests where items are used to make inferences about the candidate's honesty are labeled "personality-based" (Sackett et al., 1989) or "veiled purpose" (Murphy, 1993, p. 117) integrity tests. We will focus on the latter type.

Murphy (1993, p. 127) points out that it is difficult to distinguish veiled purpose integrity tests from personality inventories. He also contends that what these tests measure is not well established. We are less skeptical than Murphy because we believe that the meaning of these measures comes from the pattern of their external correlates. Examples of personality-based integrity measures used in workplace testing and in personnel research include the Personal Outlook Inventory (Science Research Associates, 1983), Personnel Reaction Blank (Gough, 1972), Personnel Decisions, Inc., Employment Inventory (Paajanen, 1985), and HPI Reliability scale (J. Hogan & Hogan, 1989).

Evidence for interpreting the validity of these integrity measures comes from external or nontest sources such as supervisor's reports of job behavior, records of employee behavior, self-reports of work incidents and biographical experiences, and peer or co-worker evaluations. In addition, the meaning of these measures can be inferred from the pattern of their relations with other well-validated instruments. Organizational users are interested in what tests mean in terms of predicting counterproductive job performance—that is, identifying persons whose scores suggest that they might behave in a dishonest or irresponsible way. For example, in a number of concurrent validation studies, scores on the HPI Reliability scale were associated with concentrations of blood alcohol levels of persons arrested for drunken driving ($r = -.62$; Y. Nolan, Johnson, & Pincus, 1994), excessive absences from work ($r = -.49$; R. Hogan, Jacobson, Hogan, & Thompson, 1987), work discharges ($r = -.28$; J. Hogan, Hogan, & Briggs, 1984), counseling for aberrant behavior ($r = -.18$; Raza, Metz, Dyer, Coan, & Hogan, 1986), and, conversely, commendations ($r = .51$; J. Hogan et al., 1984). Ones et al. (1993) conducted a comprehensive meta-analysis of integrity tests and found that the criterion-related validity for predicting supervisory ratings of job performance was .41 ($N = 7550$; $K = 23$). Ones et al. (1993) also found that personality-based integrity tests predict externally measured counterproductive behaviors with an operational validity of .29 ($N = 93,092$; $K = 62$). In terms of test–test relations, the HPI Reliability scale correlated with CPI Self-control, Good Impression, Socialization, and Achievement via Conformity scales with rs of .70, .49, .46, and .42, respectivley (J. Hogan & Hogan, 1989). Note the similarity in this pattern of relations to that found in correlations between the CPI scales and the NEO Conscientiousness scale. From peer ratings of persons ($N = 128$) who completed the HPI Reliability scale, the Adjective Checklist (Gough & Heilbrun, 1983) correlates of low Reliability scale scores included tense, moody, unstable, worrying, and self-pitying (R. Hogan & Hogan, 1992). J. Hogan and Hogan (1989) interpreted this scale as assessing tendencies toward organizational delinquency. Low scorers potentially engage in a wide variety of undesirable work behaviors, and high scorers tend to be commended and rated well by their supervisors. Correlations with other measures and peer evaluations suggest that persons with low Reliability scores are hostile, insensitive, impulsive, self-absorbed, and unhappy; conversely, persons with high scores are mature, thoughtful, responsible, and possibly somewhat inhibited. This scale and other personality-based integrity measures are broader than the narrowly focused overt measures of honesty, and, at the low end, they are capable of predicting a range of behaviors that make up a syndrome of organizational delinquency.

IV. EMPIRICAL EVIDENCE FOR THE VALIDITY OF CONSCIENTIOUSNESS

Meta-analyses evaluating the construct validity of Conscientiousness measures are beginning to be published. This is an important advance over earlier quantitative reviews of personality and job performance where measures of various constructs were aggregated (Ghiselli & Barthol, 1953; Schmitt, Gooding, Noe, & Kirsch, 1984).

For example, Barrick and Mount (1991) reviewed the published and unpublished literature from 1952 to 1988 to identify criterion-related validity studies of personality measures. They found 144 studies that met their inclusion criteria; these contained 162 samples and a total of 23,994 cases. They classified the studies by occupation and criterion type. The occupational groups consisted of professionals, police, managers, sales, and skilled/semiskilled workers, and these accounted for 5, 13, 41, 17, and 24% of the samples, respectively. The criterion types consisted of job proficiency, training proficiency, and personnel data, and these accounted for 68, 12, and 33% of the samples, respectively. There was some overlap in criterion type available for the samples.

Because there was no empirical means to classify the various personality scales into Big Five dimensions, Barrick and Mount asked six subject matter experts to classify the scales used in the 144 studies. Scales were placed into one of six categories labeled Neuroticism, Extraversion, Openness to Experience, Agreeableness, Conscientiousness, and Miscellaneous. Raters used information provided in test manuals or in research studies to make classification judgments. Agreement between four of six raters was used for final classification decisions, and as an example the

Conscientiousness classifications for 18 inventories and personality scales appear in Table II.

Barrick and Mount applied the meta-analytic procedures specified by Hunter and Schmidt (1990a) to examine the validity of the five personality dimensions for (1) each occupational group, (2) the three criterion types, and (3) objective versus subjective criteria. Focusing only on Conscientiousness, the results indicated that Conscientiousness scales were valid predictors for *all* occupational groups evaluated. The estimated true score correlations for professionals, police, managers, sales, and skilled/semiskilled occupations were .20, .22, .22, .23, and .21, respectively. Also, Conscientiousness was consistently valid across all criterion types with estimated

TABLE II

Conscientiousness Scale Classifications from the Barrick & Mount (1991) Meta-analysis

Inventory	Subscale
Gordon Personal Profile	Responsibility
Gordon Personal Inventory	Vigor
California Psychological Inventory	Achievement via Independence Conformance
	Status
	Responsibility
Edwards Personal Preference Schedule	Achievement
	Endurance
	Order
Adjective Checklist	Achievement
	Order
Guilford–Zimmerman Temperament Survey	Restraint
Self-Descriptive Inventory	Decisiveness
	Achievement Motivation
	Initiative
Thematic Apperception Test & Psychologist Ratings	Achievement
	Vigor
	Order
Jackson Personality Inventory	Organization
	Responsibility
Personality Research Form	Achievement
	Endurance
	Order
	Impulsivity
16 Personality Factor Questionnaire	Conscientious
Omnibus Personality Inventory	Impulse Expression
Multidimensional Personality Questionnaire	Hard Work
	Impulsiveness
Manifest Needs Questionnaire	Achievement
Hogan Personality Inventory	Prudence
	Ambition
Comfrey Personality Scales	Orderliness
Differential Personality Questionnaire	Control
	Achievement

true correlations of .23, .23, and .20 for job proficiency, training proficiency, and personal data, respectively. Finally, in evaluating the validity of personality measures for predicting objective versus subjective criteria, Barrick and Mount pointed out that subjective criteria are used about twice as frequently as objective criteria and, generally, true score correlations are higher for subjective ratings. Specifically, for Conscientiousness the estimated true correlation for subjective ratings was .26, whereas the correlation for various types of objective data was .14.

Barrick and Mount concluded that the most significant findings of their meta-analysis concerned the Conscientiousness dimension. It was consistently valid for the five occupational groups and the three criterion types evaluated. They interpret their findings to mean that at work, people who possess persistence and responsibility and who "exhibit a strong sense of purpose" will perform or be evaluated better than those who do not (p. 18). Barrick and Mount generalize to the larger world of work, stating that "it is difficult to conceive of a job in which the traits associated with the Conscientiousness dimension would not contribute to job success" (pp. 21–22). Their advice to practitioners is that when the goal is to predict job performance based on personality assessment, Conscientiousness measures are the ones most likely to yield valid predictions across all jobs. More recently, Barrick and Mount (1993) reported that as job autonomy increases, the criterion-related validity of Conscientiousness measures also increases. That is, Conscientiousness becomes more important for predicting job performance as autonomy becomes more prevalent in jobs. On a related note, Barrick, Mount, and Strauss (1993) used structural equations modeling to investigate the joint impact of goal setting and personality on job performance. They found that individuals high on Conscientiousness set goals and persist in attaining them, and, consequently, perform well on the job. So one reason why Conscientiousness predicts job performance is because Conscientious individuals plan to organize their work, spend more time on their job tasks, and persist at performance, all of which result in more job knowledge and superior supervisory ratings of job performance (Schmidt & Hunter, 1992).

Following Barrick and Mount, *Personnel Psychology* published a second meta-analysis of personality measures as predictors of job performance. This evaluation, conducted by Tett et al. (1991), concerned the same basic research questions raised by Barrick and Mount but included an investigation of relevant moderator variables. Tett et al. reviewed approximately 500 research abstracts published since 1968 concerning personality assessment and job performance. Using explicit criteria for inclusion, they identified 86 studies with 97 independent samples and 13,521 valid cases. Studies were coded by two trained raters according to 12 key objective characteristics (e.g., exploratory versus confirmatory research, applicant versus incumbent subjects), and their coding resulted in a 94% agreement. Personality measures used as predictors in these studies were classified using eight categories—Big Five dimensions, Locus of Control, Type A, and miscellaneous traits. Classifications of Big Five dimensions used factor analysis results from personality measures evaluated by Costa and McCrae (1988). Meta-analytic procedures specified by Hunter and Schmidt (1990a, 1990b) were used to estimate true correlations.

The results indicated a mean correlation, corrected for both predictor and criterion unreliability, of .24 between job performance and all personality. That means correlation increased to .29 when the analysis included only confirmatory research strategies. In addition, they found mean validities of .38, .30, .30, and .27 between personality measures and job performance studies that included job analyses, applicant subjects, military subjects, and published data, respectively. The corrected mean correlation between Conscientiousness measures and job performance was .18, with the 95% confidence interval ranging from −.11 to .35. Tett et al. reemphasized the validity of personality measures for predicting job performance, particularly where the research strategy is confirmatory and where measures chosen are based on job analysis results. Nevertheless, ongoing controversy exists about methodological and statistical variations introduced to their meta-analysis that make the precise estimates of criterion-related validities difficult (cf. Ones, Mount et al., 1994).

Ones's (1993) comprehensive analysis of personality measures, Conscientiousness measures, and integrity tests represents the most extensive research to date on the construct validity of measures of Conscientiousness. Ones's focus is on understanding measures of integrity, which she does through analyses of test–test as well as test–job performance measures. As suggested by Landy (1986) and R. Hogan and Nicholson (1988), these comparisons allow us to understand and interpret the Conscientiousness construct. Ones's primary research question concerned where the personality trait "integrity" falls under the Big Five factors. Most measures that assess integrity are preemployment integrity or honesty tests, which test publishers claim evaluate such characteristics as responsibility, long-term job commitment, consistency, proneness to violence, moral reasoning, hostility, work ethics, dependability, depression, and energy level (cf. O'Bannon, Goldinger, & Appleby, 1989). These descriptions suggest that Conscientiousness is the general construct underlying integrity tests and integrity tests are largely designed to identify the characteristics associated with the negative pole of the construct—irresponsibility, rule violation, and hostility.

Ones (1993) identified more than 100 studies reporting correlations between integrity tests and temperament measures. These studies suggest that integrity measures tend to correlate with each other and with personality-based measures of Conscientiousness. However, when other personality scales are included in the analyses, a pattern of relations with the Big Five Agreeableness and Emotional Stability factors also emerges (Collins & Schmidt, 1993; Nolan, 1991). So, integrity tests, evaluated in terms of the Big Five model, are primarily related to Conscientiousness and secondarily to Agreeableness. Also, integrity tests have substantial correlations with Emotional Stability.

To understand what is measured by integrity tests, Ones (1993) asked six specific research questions: (1) Are overt integrity tests correlated with each other? (2) Are personality-based integrity tests correlated with each other? (3) Do both overt and personality-based integrity tests measure the same underlying construct? (4) Do integrity tests correlate with Big Five measures? (5) Do integrity tests derive their criterion-related validity from the Conscientiousness dimension? (6) What is the estimated predictive validity of integrity tests? To answer these questions, Ones used two modes of data collection. The primary mode included test scores and demographic information from a student sample and job applicant sample (n = 1,365) on the London House Personnel Selection Inventory, Stanton Survey, and Reid Report (all overt integrity tests according to Ones, 1993); the PDI Inc. Employment Inventory, Hogan Personality Inventory (including the Reliability scale), Personnel Reaction Blank, and Inwald Personality Inventory (all personality-based integrity tests); and the Personal Characteristics Inventory and Goldberg's Adjective Checklist (both personality inventories). Between 300 and 500 students completed each inventory over 30 sessions of data collection. The secondary mode of data collection was a survey of published and unpublished reports of correlations between overt integrity tests, personality-based integrity tests, and measures of the Big Five dimensions. This resulted in more than 8,000 correlation coefficients. The personality scales were assigned to Big Five dimensions using the classifications developed by Barrick and Mount (1991) and Hough et al. (1990). These correlational data were analyzed using meta-analysis procedures developed by Hunter and Schmidt (1990a).

Using results from the primary data, Ones found that the true correlations between overt integrity tests averaged .85, and confirmatory factor analysis indicated that test intercorrelations were due to the presence of a single factor. Similarly, the true correlations between personality-based integrity tests averaged .75, which, after confirmatory factor analysis, also indicated that only a single factor explained the matrix. Ones formed a composite of the three overt integrity tests and correlated it with a composite of the four personality-based integrity measures; she found a true score correlation of .61. Confirmatory factor analysis of the intercorrelation matrix of the seven integrity tests indicated a shared general factor, with loadings ranging from .63 for the PDI Employment Inventory to .87 for the London House Personnel Selection Inventory. Further analysis suggested evidence for a hierarchical factor structure of integrity tests, with a general factor across tests and two group factors—one for overt tests and the other for personality-based tests, specific to test type. To determine the relation between integrity tests and Big Five dimensions, a linear composite of the seven integrity tests and linear composites for scales classified in Big Five dimensions were formed. True score correlations between the integrity composite and the Conscientiousness, Agreeableness, and Emotional Stability composites were .91, .61, and .50, respectively. This pattern of correlations were repeated for separate integrity composites of overt tests and personality-based measures.

Ones performed a meta-analysis of the secondary data to test the generalizability of the results from the primary analyses. Of interest are the correlations between integrity tests and the Big Five personality dimensions. For this analysis, 423 integrity–Conscientiousness correlations across 91,360 data points resulted in a true correlation of .42. True score correlations of integrity tests with Agreeableness and

Emotional Stability measures were .40 and .33, respectively. The correlations with Extraversion and Openness to Experience were −.08 and .12.

Meta-analysis was also used to determine the operational predictive validity of integrity tests and to determine whether their validity comes from the Conscientiousness dimension. Ones et al. (1993), in the most comprehensive meta-analysis ever reported, based on 665 validity coefficients across 576,460 data points, estimated the mean true score validity of integrity tests for predicting supervisory ratings of job performance to be .46. Using this correlation along with the true score correlation of .23 between individual scales of Conscientiousness and job performance (Barrick & Mount, 1991) and the true score correlation of .42 between integrity and Conscientiousness (Ones, 1993), Ones (1993) partialed Conscientiousness from the integrity–job performance relation, which reduced the true score correlation from .46 to .41. She determined that Conscientiousness as measured by individual personality scales only partially explains the validity of integrity tests for job performance. Conversely, when integrity test scores are partialed from the Conscientiousness–job performance relation, the true score correlation is reduced from .23 to .05. Ones concluded that measures of Conscientiousness, as assessed by Big Five personality inventories, are part of the broader construct measured by integrity tests. She suggests that integrity tests tap a higher order factor that includes Conscientiousness, Agreeableness, and Emotional Stability. It is interesting to note that these three Big Five are also those that Digman (1990) finds to be important for predicting delinquency and grades at school.

V. MEASUREMENT BREADTH AND THEORETICAL DYNAMICS

The Big Five structure emerged from the study of natural language, specifically adjectival peer descriptions. We view this taxonomy not as a theory but as a useful starting point for technical discussions. The Conscientiousness dimension of the Big Five structure concerns social conformity and impulse control. Questionnaire evaluations of this construct reflect one or both of these themes (John, 1990). Conscientiousness, as well as the other Big Five dimensions, has enormous bandwidth, and, of course, this is a source of criticism (Briggs, 1989). However, as broad as Conscientiousness descriptors are, it appears that the integrity construct is even broader. This is the point of our analysis and review. The earlier literature (Murphy, 1993) suggested that integrity assessments are narrow bandwidth, high-fidelity Conscientiousness measures. That is, in the hierarchical representation of Conscientiousness, integrity would appear at a low level and as such should be capable of predicting specific behaviors. Ones's (1993) analysis suggests that integrity is even broader (and psychologically more complex) than Conscientiousness.

How do we account for this? First, consider the derivation of the Big Five constructs. The natural language of personality description relied historically on rational and factor analytic methods. The lexical approach for identifying personality characteristics begins by listing relevant terms from dictionaries. Attributes were classified on conceptual grounds and later subjected to cluster and factor analytic techniques (Cattell, 1943). Confirmatory factor analysis is now the method of choice for Big Five researchers aligning personality scales with the five-factor taxonomy. From this analysis, Conscientiousness is interpreted though its network of other inventory correlates.

However, if we use an empirical approach to scale construction, either alone or in conjunction with rational and factor analytic methods, the results lead to a broader interpretation of the construct. Many integrity measures have been constructed empirically by comparing the item responses of persons known to be low in integrity with the responses of persons thought to be high in integrity. The criterion of interest (e.g., criminal versus noncriminal behavior (is defined first, and then inventory items are identified; those that discriminate between subjects on the criterion characteristic are retained because they are related to the behavior of interest. If the criterion is broad, then the empirical predictor also will be broad. Furthermore, it is not altogether clear why simple, factorially pure constructs should predict complex phenomena such as job performance and criminal behavior.

The CPI Socialization scale is a good example of the way in which broad criteria defined broad predictor measures. The criterion characteristic that Gough had in mind was the continuum of Socialization–Asocialization. As a way of establishing the validity of the scale, Gough tested groups that most people would agree differed in Socialization. Mean Socialization scale scores, which he views as a sociological continuum, range from high school "best citizens," bank officers, and school superintendents down to unmarried mothers, county jail inmates, and prison inmates (Gough, 1975). Similarly, in developing the HPI Reliability scale, the criterion of choice was antisocial behavior (J. Hogan & Hogan, 1989). The initial HPI item composites for the Reliability scale were chosen based on their correspondence with the structure of deviancy as revealed in earlier factor analytic studies of the CPI Socialization scale. In the case of the HPI, item composites that came from the personality scales of Conscientiousness, Agreeableness, Extraversion, and Emotional Stability empirically distinguished felons from nonfelons and delinquents from nondelinquents. This multifaceted measure of integrity, which is keyed against the delinquency criterion, has a broad range of antisocial behavioral correlates in the workplace—insubordination, excessive absences, tardiness, equipment sabotage, and negative supervisory ratings.

To summarize, Conscientiousness as assessed using rational or factor analytically derived measures necessarily will focus on a single well-defined construct. Conversely, if integrity measures are developed empirically and if the criterion characteristic to be predicted is broad (and reliable), then the resultant scale will be multifaceted and complex. These explanations are posed to account for the difference between measures of Conscientiousness and integrity.

How do we interpret Conscientiousness or integrity scores in terms of personality theory? Conscientiousness, defined as social conformity and impulse control, is the degree to which a person makes an effortless adaptation to authority. For Freud, a person cannot adapt fully to authority because there is always ambivalence in the relationship. From this developmental perspective, normally Conscientious behavior is a strategy designed to accommodate authority and to avoid guilt associated with critical superiors or their symbols. Individual differences in Conscientiousness form a continuum, from those who lack Conscientiousness—who are unable to resolve conflicts with authority—to those who are excessively Conscientious—who are compulsive, stingy, dependent, and stubborn.

However, recall the evolutionary features that characterize people. We evolved in groups, we live in groups, and we participate in a status hierarchy within our groups. To some degree, we are motivated to engage in social interaction, which is the process by which we achieve social status and social acceptance. People seek both social status, even if it is in the form of trying to avoid losing it, and social acceptance, even if it is in the form of trying to avoid criticism.

From R. Hogan's (1983) socioanalytic perspective, the vehicle for participating in the group process is one's identity. Identity is a repertoire of self-presentations that develop during youth and adolescence, and identity is the basis on which social status and social acceptance are granted—or withdrawn. We might develop the identity or vocational role of a scholar, counselor, minister, or person of integrity. When we interact and others observe us, their reactions to us become our reputations. Reputations are coded in trait words that reflect others' descriptions of the status and acceptance afforded our identities. And so we come full circle to the derivation of the trait lexicon—the content base for the Big Five.

Over time, a person who is described by others as conscientious develops the identity of a "person of integrity." Developmentally, conformity engenders social acceptance, and up to a point conformity also will facilitate social status. The Conscientious child probably enjoyed positive relations with parents, caretakers, and others of authority because of his or her tendency to conform and desire to get along. The Conscientious adolescent is reliable, gets things done for the group, goes along with the group, and is comfortable with adult authority. He or she develops the reputation for being dependable, responsible, and careful (Conscientious). Respect for others also will lead to a reputation for being kind and trusting (Agreeableness), as well as being consistently calm and content (Emotional Stability). This identity is reinforced through social acceptance and approval. In adulthood, the identity and the processes which support it normally will be outside of conscious awareness.

As for measurement, reputation is assessed through others' standardized appraisals. This can take the form of peer, spouse, or supervisors ratings using adjective checklists and observer reports. Although many applied psychologists attempt to have observers evaluate the particular behavior of actors, observers are rarely able to do this. Instead, they construct impressions of an actor's characteristics (Bartlett, 1932), and these impressions are what drive the evaluations (Murphy, Martin, & Garcia, 1982). On the other hand, we also consider a person's responses to a personality inventory to be a form of social interaction. The person endorses inventory items in the way that he or she would like to be regarded in social interactions. The respondent thinks about the question, considers the impression he or she would make with a particular response, and endorses the item to convey the desired image. R. Hogan (1983) points out that this process is not as conscious or deliberate as it is in this description. In fact, he contends that because identities are so well solidified in adulthood, little conscious effort goes into self-presentations. Moreover, this theoretical perspective on item response dynamics makes moot the issue of "faking" or item distortion (also see Hough et al., 1990).

The ubiquitous issue of faking also can be interpreted from a socioanalytic perspective, and this leads us to our final point. Persons who endorse such faking items as "I have never told a lie" or "I have never hated anyone" show excessive virtuousness in their interpersonal style. Conscientiousness is one of the normal dimensions of personality, measures of which lack item content at the extreme ends. Items, which may resemble faking items, at the low end of conscientiousness are absent because test takers find the content offensive or invasive (e.g., "I enjoy using illegal drugs"). Similarly, there are few items at the high end. If such items were used, we might have a very different view of high Conscientious people. Such persons are likely to have reputations as being inflexible, self-righteous, perfectionistic, judgmental, and evangelistic. Their private identities are likely to be that of a morally scrupulous, virtuous, upright, and characterologically superior person. Context is important for interpretation, so this person will also show relatively high scores for Emotional Stability and elevations for the other Big Five measures (Johnson, 1990). Persons who score low on Conscientiousness measures are and are seen as deviant—and this is their identity, too.

We are optimistic about the use of measures of Conscientiousness and integrity in applied psychology. In some ways, the Big Five has had the effect of pulling applied psychologists away from the retarding influences of behaviorism. Through meta-analyses, we begin to see the true potential of Conscientiousness and integrity measures for predicting important real world criteria such as job performance and counterproductivity on and off the job. As we learn more about this construct, we will better understand its nuances and measurement applications.

REFERENCES

Allport, G. W., & Odbert, H. S. (1936). Trait-names: A psycho-lexical study. *Psychological Monographs, 47* (No. 211).

Barrick, M. R., & Mount, M. K. (1991). The Big Five personality dimensions and job performance: A meta-analysis. *Personnel Psychology, 44,* 1–26.

Barrick, M. R., & Mount, M. K. (1993). Autonomy as a moderator of the relationships between the Big-Five personality dimensions and job performance. *Journal of Applied Psychology, 78,* 111–118.

Barrick, M. R., Mount, M. K., & Strauss, J. P. (1993). Conscientiousness and performance of sales representatives: Test of the mediating effects of goal setting. *Journal of Applied Psychology, 78,* 715–722.

Bartlett, F. C. (1932). *Remembering: A study in experimental and social psychology.* Cambridge, England: Cambridge University Press.

Block, J. (1993). *A contrarian view of the five-factor approach to personality description.* Unpublished manuscript, University of California, Berkeley.

Bond, M. H., Nakazato, H., & Shiraishi, D. (1975). Universality and distinctiveness in dimensions of Japanese person perception. *Journal of Cross-Cultural Psychology, 6,* 346–357.

Borgatta, E. F. (1964). The structure of personality characteristics. *Behavioral Science, 9,* 8–17.

Borkenau, P., & Ostendorf, F. (1989). Descriptive consistency and social desirability in self- and peer reports. *European Journal of Personality, 3,* 31–45.

Briggs, S. R. (1989). The optimum level of measurement for personality constructs. In D. M. Buss & N. Cantor (Eds.), *Personality psychology: Recent trends and emerging directions* (pp. 246–260). New York: Springer.

Cattell, R. B. (1943). The description of personality: Basic traits resolved into clusters. *Journal of Abnormal and Social Psychology, 38,* 476–506.

Cattell, R. B. (1946). *Description and measurement of personality.* Yonkers-on-Hudson, NY: World Book.

Cattell, R. B. (1947). Confirmation and clarification of primary personality factors. *Psychometrika, 12,* 197–220.

Collins, J. M., & Schmidt, F. L. (1993). Personality, integrity, and white-collar crime: A construct validity study. *Personnel Psychology 46,* 295–311.

Conley, J. J. (1985). Longitudinal stability of personality traits: A multitrait-multimethod-multioccasion analysis. *Journal of Personality and Social Psychology 49,* 1266–1282.

Costa, P. T., Jr., & McCrae, R. R. (1988). From catalog to classification: Murray's needs and the five-factor model. *Journal of Personality and Social Psychology, 55,* 258–265.

Costa, P. T., Jr., & McCrae, R. R. (1992). *NEO-PI-R professional manual.* Odessa, FL: Psychological Assessment Resources.

Cronbach, L. J. (1960). *Essentials of psychological testing* (2nd ed.). New York: Harper & Row.

Digman, J. M. (1990). Personality structure: Emergence of the Five Factor model. *Annual Review of Psychology, 41,* 417–440.

Digman, J. M., & Inouye, J. (1986). Further specification of the five robust factors of personality. *Journal of Personality and Social Psychology, 50,* 116–123.

Digman, J. M., & Takemoto-Chock, N. K. (1981). Factors in the natural language of personality: Re-analysis and comparison of six major studies. *Multivariate Behavioral Research, 16,* 149–170.

Fancher, R. E. (1990). *Pioneers of psychology.* New York: Norton.

Fiske, D. W. (1949). Consistency of the factorial structures of personality ratings from different sources. *Journal of Abnormal and Social Psychology, 44,* 329–344.

Ghiselli, E. E., & Barthol, R. P. (1953). The validity of personality inventories in the selection of employees. *Journal of Applied Psychology, 37,* 18–20.

Goldberg, L. R. (1981). Language and individual differences: The search for universals in personality lexicons. In L. Wheeler (Ed.), *Review of personality and social psychology* (Vol. 1, pp. 203–234). Hillsdale, NJ: Erlbaum.

Goldberg, L. R. (1990). An alternative "description of personality": The Big-Five factor structure. *Journal of Personality and Social Psychology, 59,* 1216–1229.

Goldberg, L. R. (1992). The development of markers of the Big-Five factor structure. *Psychological Assessment, 4,* 26–42.

Goldberg, L. R. (1993). The structure of phenotypic personality traits. *American Psychologist, 48,* 26–34.

Gough, H. G. (1948). A sociological theory of psychopathy. *American Journal of Sociology, 53,* 359–366.

Gough, H. G. (1957). *Manual for the California Psychological Inventory.* Palo Alto, CA: Consulting Psychologists Press.

Gough, H. G. (1960). Theory and measurement of socialization. *Journal of Consulting Psychology, 24,* 23–30.

Gough, H. G. (1972). *Manual for the Personal Reaction Blank.* Palo Alto, CA: Consulting Psychologists Press.

Gough, H. G. (1975). *Manual for the California Psychological Inventory.* Palo Alto, CA: Consulting Psychologists Press.

Gough, H. G. (1987). *California Psychological Inventory administrator's guide.* Palo Alto, CA: Consulting Psychologists Press.

Gough, H. G., & Heilbrun, A. B. Jr. (1983). *The Adjective Checklist manual: 1983 edition.* Palo Alto, CA: Consulting Psychologists Press.

Gough, H. G., & Peterson, D. R. (1952). The identification and measurement of predispositional factors in crime and delinquency. *Journal of Consulting Psychology, 16,* 207–212.

Guion, R. M., & Gottier, R. F. (1965). Validity of personality measures in personnel selection. *Personnel Psychology, 18,* 135–164.

Hogan, J., & Hogan, R. (1989). How to measure employee reliability. *Journal of Applied Psychology, 74,* 273–279.

Hogan, J., Hogan, R., & Briggs, S. R. (1984). *Development and validation of employee selection tests for combination drivers.* Tulsa, OK: University of Tulsa.

Hogan, R. (1983). A socioanalytic theory of personality. In M. M. Page (Ed.), *1982 Nebraska Symposium on Motivation* (pp. 55–89). Lincoln: University of Nebraska Press.

Hogan, R. (1991). Personality and personality measurement. In M. D. Dunnette & L. M. Hough (Eds.), *Handbook of industrial and organizational psychology* (Vol. 2, pp. 327–398). Palo Alto, CA: Consulting Psychologists Press.

Hogan, R., & Hogan, J. (1992). *Hogan Personality Inventory manual.* Tulsa, OK: Hogan Assessment Systems.

Hogan, R., & Nicholson, R. (1988). The meaning of personality test scores. *American Psychologist, 43,* 621–626.

Hogan, R., Jacobson, G., Hogan, J., & Thompson, B. (1987). *Development and validation of a service operations dispatcher selection inventory.* Tulsa, OK: Hogan Assessment Systems.

Hough, L. M., Eaton, N. K., Dunnette, M. D., Kamp, J. D., & McCloy, R. A. (1990). Criterion-related validities of personality constructs and the effect of response distortion on those validities. *Journal of Applied Psychology, 75,* 581–589.

Hunter, J. E., & Schmidt, F. L. (1990a). *Methods of meta-analysis: Correcting error and bias in research findings.* Newbury Park, CA: Sage.

Hunter, J. E., & Schmidt, F. L. (1990b). Dichotomization of continuous variables: The implications for meta-analysis. *Journal of Applied Psychology, 75,* 334–339.

John, O. P. (1990). The Big Five factor taxonomy: Dimensions of personality in the natural language and in questionnaires. In L. A. Pervin (Ed.), *Handbook of personality: Theory and research* (pp. 66–100). New York: Guilford Press.

Johnson, J. A. (1990, June). *Unlikely virtues provide multivariate substantive information about personality.* Paper presented at the 2nd annual meeting of the American Psychological Society, Dallas, TX.

Johnson, J. A., & Ostendorf, F. (1993). Clarification of the five factor model with the abridged Big-Five dimensional circumplex. *Journal of Personality and Social Psychology, 65,* 563–576.

Landy, F. J. (1986). Stamp collecting versus science: Validation as hypothesis testing. *American Psychologist, 41,* 1183–1192.

Lorr, M., & Youniss, R. P. (1973). An inventory of interpersonal style. *Journal of Personality Assessment, 37,* 165–173.

McCrae, R. R., & Costa, P. T., Jr. (1987). Validation of the five-factor model of personality across instruments and observers. *Journal of Personality and Social Psychology, 52,* 81–90.

McCrae, R. R., & Costa, P. T., Jr. (1989). Reinterpreting the Myers-Briggs Type Indicator from the perspective of the five-factor model of personality. *Journal of Personality, 57,* 17–40.

McCrae, R. R., & Costa, P. T., Jr. (1991, August). *Does Lorr's ISI measure the five-factor model?* Paper presented at the 99th annual Convention of the American Psychological Association, San Francisco.

McCrae, R. R., & Costa, P. T., Jr. (1992). Discriminate validity of NEO-PIR facet scales. *Educational and Psychological Measurement, 52,* 229–237.

McCrae, R. R., Costa, P. T., Jr., & Piedmont, R. L. (1993). Folk concepts, natural language, and psychological constructs: The California Psychological Inventory and the five-factor model. *Journal of Personality, 61,* 1–26.

Mischel, W. (1968). *Personality and assessment.* New York: Wiley.

Murphy, K. (1993). *Honesty in the workplace.* Pacific Grove, CA: Brooks/Cole.

Murphy, K., Martin, C., & Garcia, M. (1982). Do behavioral observations scales measure observation? *Journal of Applied Psychology, 67,* 562–567.

Nolan, K. A. (1991). *The relationship between socially desirable responding and personnel integrity testing: The unique effect of self-deception and impression management.* Unpublished master's thesis, Georgia State University, Atlanta.

Nolan, Y., Johnson, J. A., & Pincus, A. (1994). Personality and drunk driving: Identification of DUI types using the HPI. *Psychological Assessment, 6,* 33–40.

Noller, P., Law, H., & Comrey, A. L. (1987). Cattell, Comrey, and Eysenck personality factors compared: More evidence for the five robust factors? *Journal of Personality and Social Psychology, 53,* 77–782.

Norman, W. T. (1963). Toward an adequate taxonomy of personality attributes: Replicated factor structure in peer nomination personality ratings. *Journal of Abnormal and Social Psychology, 66,* 574–583.

Norman, W. T. (1967). *2,800 personality trait descriptors: Normative operating characteristics for a university population.* Ann Arbor: University of Michigan, Department of Psychology.

Norman, W. T., & Goldberg, L. R. (1966). Raters, ratees, and randomness in personality structure. *Journal of Personality and Social Psychology, 4,* 44–49.

O'Bannon, R. M., Goldinger, L. A., & Appleby, G. S. (1989). *Honesty and integrity testing.* Atlanta, GA: Applied Information Resources.

Ones, D. S. (1993). *The construct validity of integrity tests.* Unpublished doctoral dissertation, University of Iowa, Iowa City.

Ones, D. S., Mount, M. K. Barrick, M. R., & Hunter, J. E. (1994). Personality and job performance: A critique of Tett, Jackson, & Rothstein (1991) meta-analysis. *Personnel Psychology, 47,* 147–156.

Ones, D. S., Schmidt, F. L., & Viswesvaran, C. (1994). *Convergent and divergent validity evidence for the Big-Five dimensions of personality: A meta-analysis.* Unpublished manuscript.

Ones, D. S., Viswesvaran, C., & Schmidt, F. L. (1993). Comprehensive meta-analysis of integrity test validities: Findings and implications for personnel selection and theories of job performance. *Journal of Applied Psychology, 78,* 679–703.

Paajanen, G. E. (1985). *PDI Employment Inventory.* Minneapolis, MN: Personnel Decisions, Inc.

Piedmont, R. L., McCrae, R. R., & Costa, P. T., Jr. (1992). An assessment of the Edwards Personal Preference Schedule from the perspective of the five-factor model. *Journal of Personality Assessment, 58,* 67–78.

Raza, S., Metz, D., Dyer, P., Coan, T., & Hogan, J. (1986). *Development and validation of personnel selection procedures for hospital service personnel.* Tulsa, OK: University of Tulsa.

Rosen, A. S. (1977). On the dimensionality of the California Psychological Inventory socialization scale. *Journal of Consulting and Clinical Psychology, 45,* 583–591.

Sackett, P. R., Burris, L. R., & Callahan, C. (1989). Integrity testing for personnel selection: An update. *Personnel Psychology, 42,* 491–529.

Schmidt, F. L., & Hunter, J. E. (1992). Development of a causal model of processes determining job performance. *Current Directions in Psychological Science, 1,* 89–92.

Schmidt, F. L., Ones, D. S., & Hunter, J. E. (1992). Personnel selection. *Annual Review of Psychology, 43,* 627–670.

Schmitt, N., Gooding, R. Z., Noe, R. A., & Kirsch, M. (1984). Meta-analyses of validity studies published between 1964 and 1982 and the investigation of study characteristics. *Personnel Psychology, 37,* 407–422.

Schuessler, K. E., & Cressey, D. R. (1950). Personality characteristics of criminals. *American Journal of Sociology, 55,* 476–484.

Science Research Associates. (1983). *Personal Outlook Inventory.* Park Ridge, IL: Author.

Shannon, C., & Weaver, W. (1949). *The mathematical theory of communication.* Urbana: University of Illinois Press.

Skinner, H. A., Jackson, D. N., & Rampton, G. M. (1976). The Personality Research Form in a Canadian context: Does language make a difference? *Canadian Journal of Behavioral Science, 8,* 156–168.

Sutherland, E. H. (1951). Critique of Sheldon's 'Variety of Delinquent Youth.' *American Sociological Review, 16,* 10–23.

Tellegen, A. (1982). *Brief manual for the Differential Personality Questionnaire.* Unpublished manuscript, University of Minnesota, Minneapolis.

Tett, R. P., Jackson, D. N., & Rothstein, M. (1991). Personality measures as predictors of job performance: A meta-analytic review. *Personnel Psychology, 44,* 703–742.

Tupes, E. C., & Christal, R. C. (1961). *Recurrent personality factors based on trait ratings* (Tech. Rep. No. ASD-TR-61-97). Lackland Air Force Base, TX: U.S. Air Force.

Waller, N. G., & Ben-Porath, Y. S. (1987). Is it time for clinical psychologists to embrace the five-factor model of personality? *American Psychologist, 42,* 887–889.

Watson, D. (1989). Strangers' ratings of the five robust personality factors: Evidence of surprising convergence with self report. *Journal of Personality and Social Psychology, 57,* 120–128.

Wiggins, J. S. (1991). *Manual for the Interpersonal Adjective Scales.* Odessa, FL: Psychological Assessment Resources.

PART VIII

APPLIED PSYCHOLOGY

CHAPTER 33

PERSONALITY, INTERACTIVE RELATIONS, AND APPLIED PSYCHOLOGY

WILLIAM F. CHAPLIN

UNIVERSITY OF ALABAMA

The purpose of personality assessment is "the obtaining and evaluating of information regarding individual differences" (Cronbach, 1956, p. 173). Although the reasons for obtaining and evaluating such information are diverse (Fiske & Pearson, 1970), the prediction of useful criteria is a major one. In the preface to the most influential graduate text on personality assessment for the past two decades, *Personality and Prediction: Principles of Personality Assessment,* Wiggins (1973) writes, "An overriding emphasis on the prediction of socially relevant criteria has prompted me to adopt Donald W. Fiske's suggestion that the principle title . . . is the most appropriate characterization of the subject matter of this text" (p. iii). Certainly, the impetus for much of the work in the field of personality assessment has been the quest for large predictive validity coefficients (e.g., Ghiselli, 1956; Hase & Goldberg, 1967; Jackson, 1971; Sines, 1964).

I. PREDICTION MODELS

Contrary to popular belief, scientific predictions are nearly always inaccurate. "The government people didn't have a good sense of how science works. They couldn't come to grips with the fact that there are no absolute truths . . . that our data reflect closer and closer approximations of what might turn out to be true" (Richard Axel, quoted in Booth, 1989). Inaccuracy is a consequence of our necessary reliance on models of the phenomena we wish to predict—models that are generally fictitious in the sense that they are simplifications. "Astronomers did not achieve perfection and never would, not in a solar system tugged by the gravities of nine planets, scores of moons and thousands of asteroids, but calculations of planetary motion were so accurate that people forgot they were forecasts" (Gleick, 1987, p. 14). Thus, unless the phenomenon we wish to predict is as simple as the model—an especially unlikely circumstance when the phenomenon is human behavior—the predictions will be "approximate" (i.e., inaccurate).

A. The Bivariate Linear Model

The most basic model for predicting one variable from another is the well-known simple linear relation shown in Equation 1. In this equation, y is the criterion variable, x is the predictor variable, and b and a are constants reflecting the slope and intercept of the regression line, respectively. Typically, b and a are empirically derived to minimize the squared errors of prediction ("least-squares criterion"). The Pearson product–moment correlation coefficient provides an index of how well, again in a least-squares sense, the predictions match the observations.

$$y = bx + a. \tag{1}$$

This model is an extreme simplification of nearly all psychological phenomena. Even in the absence of measurement error, few criteria can be perfectly predicted from a linear model involving one predictor. One apparent tactic for improving predictions is to increase the complexity of the prediction models so that they more closely approximate the complexity of the criterion.

B. Multivariate Extension

The tactic that is most frequently used to increase the complexity of the prediction model is the introduction of more predictor variables into the equation. The rationale for this approach is that psychological criteria are multifaceted and multiply determined. Thus, combining variables that capture different aspects of the criterion should more completely model the criterion and, presumably, more accurately predict it. The general form of this multivariate model is

$$y = b_1x_1 + b_2x_2 + \cdots + b_ix_I + \cdots + b_kx_k + a, \tag{2}$$

where y is the criterion, x_i is the ith of k predictor variables, b_i is the ith of k weights, and a is the intercept.

The output of Equation 2 is a set of predicted values of y. The correlation between these predicted values and the actual values is called a "multiple correlation"; it indexes how well the model predicts (in a least-squares sense) the criterion.

This model has been the mainstay of statistical prediction for most of the history of personality assessment (Wiggins, 1973). Moreover, when the constants (i.e., b_is and a) in the model are optimally (least-squares criteria) derived, this model has a number of powerful features (Goldberg, 1991). In particular, it adjusts for (a) differences in the units of measurement, (b) redundancy among the predictors, (c) differential validities among the predictors, and (d) all regression effects. However, even in the unlikely event that this model included a comprehensive set of predictors, it would still be quite simplified. Specifically, this model is limited to a linear (additive) combination of the predictor variables. Psychological phenomena are almost certainly a more complicated, nonlinear function of a set of variables. One type of nonlinear relation that has been repeatedly proposed for personality predictions is an interaction or moderator effect.

C. Interactive Models

An interaction effect is usually discussed in the context of the analysis of variance. It is defined as occurring when the main effects of one independent variable are different at different levels of a second independent variable. One can then refer to the second variable as a "moderator variable" because it moderates the relation between the first independent variable and the dependent variable. However, the designation of one of the independent variables as a moderator variable is statistically, though perhaps not conceptually, arbitrary because interaction effects are symmetrical. It is equally legitimate (statistically) to refer to the first independent variable as a moderator of the relation between the second independent variable and the dependent variable.

As Cohen (1978) demonstrated some time ago, interaction effects can also be evaluated using a multiple regression paradigm. The general form of the two predictor interactive model is

$$y = b_1 x_1 + b_2 x_2 + b_3 x_1 x_2 + a, \tag{3}$$

where the terms are as defined in Equation 2.

Specifically, if the cross product of two independent variables is related to the dependent variable, after the effects of the two independent variables have been removed (partialed) from the cross product, then an interaction effect is present. Indeed, when the independent variables are qualitative, the value of F for the interaction in the analysis of variance and the value of F for the partialed cross product will be identical. However, when one or both of the independent variables are quantitative, the multiple regression procedure will have greater statistical power because it does not require that the independent variables be rendered, usually arbitrarily, into categories before the cross product is computed (Cohen, 1983). The multiple regression approach to modeling interactions has been most widely used within the context of prediction models. In this context it is typical to designate one independent variable as the "predictor" (e.g., scores on an aptitutde test) and the other as the "moderator" (e.g., an index of test anxiety). However, just as is the case in the analysis of variance, this designation is statistically arbitrary.

One important characteristic of interaction or moderator effects is that they are orthogonal to the main effects of the independent or predictor variables. Thus, in the analysis of variance the interaction effect is defined as a residual effect after the main effects of the independent variables have been removed. Indeed, the sum of squares used to assess the interaction effect can be obtained by subtracting the sum of squares of the two main effects from the cell sum of squares. Likewise, in the multiple regression paradigm it is the partial, not simple, correlation between the cross product and the dependent variable that indexes the moderator effect (Cohen, 1978). Failure to appreciate the independence of moderator effects has led to some erroneous proposals by Bobko (1986) and Morris, Sherman, and Mansfield (1986) for increasing the power of tests to detect interaction effects (Cronbach, 1987).

D. Summary

There is little doubt that multivariate and interactive equations are more faithful models of human behavior than either the bivariate or multivariate linear models. Moreover, the addition of further complexities, such as power polynomials (e.g., quadratic or cubic trends), nonlinear transformations (e.g., logarithmic or arcsine), and the higher order interactions of all these terms, might well further increase the correspondence between the equations and the phenomena they model. However, before beginning the unending task of considering more and more complex equations, let us consider how the increase in complexity entailed by interactive models has contributed to their power to predict human behavior.

II. Description and Evaluation of Some Interactive Models

In this section I will begin by briefly describing three different contexts—personality consistency, personnel selection, and education—in which it was widely believed that prediction models containing interaction terms would substantially increase predictive accuracy over that achieved with simpler models. However, I will note that in all three contexts the interactive models received dismal empirical support. Finally, I will consider the reasons for their poor showing—reasons that have important implications for the use of interactive models in applied settings.

A. Personality Consistency

During the 1960s and 1970s the field of personality assessment experienced a series of attacks on one of its most fundamental propositions, the consistency of personality characteristics. The perpetrators of this assault (cf. Mischel, 1968) marshalled evidence that human behaviors, even highly similar behaviors, varied substantially across different situations. Such variability, they argued, was incompatible with the existence of the stable dispositions (traits) that were the primary object of personality assessors' attention. In hindsight, this argument seems inconsequential because the variability of specific behaviors implies little about the consistency of the constructs indicated by those behaviors (Block, 1977; Golding, 1978; G. A. Kelly, 1955; Ozer, 1986). However, for some (e.g., Bem & Allen, 1974; Cheek, 1982; Kenrick & Stringfield, 1980; Turner, 1978), the only way to resurrect the concept of traits and reestablish the legitimacy of personality measurement appeared to be through the invocation of moderator variables.

In one of the most influential papers in that decade, Bem and Allen (1974) proposed that there are individual differences in personality consistency; for any one trait, some individuals will be consistent whereas others will not be. That is, these individual differences in consistency moderate the relation between two measures of the same trait. To support this proposition, Bem and Allen studied five personality traits and reported the results from two of them, friendliness and conscientiousness. For each trait, they divided a group of subjects into a high and low consistent group on the basis of a median split on two measures of cross-situational consistency. The high consistent group generally exhibited higher correlations among different measures of the target trait than the low consistent group, although this was true for each of the measures of cross-situational consistency for only one of the traits. Bem and Allen concluded that personality traits were sufficiently stable to warrant their continued study and measurement, but only within a subgroup of the population.

B. Differential Predictability

In the 1950s, the business of personnel prediction and selection was in desperate need of "new ideas" (McNemar, 1952). The results of several large-scale prediction studies (e.g., E. L. Kelly & Fiske, 1951; Office of Strategic Services Assessment Staff, 1948) were in, and the optimism with which these studies had been begun had been tempered by the general finding that the state-of-the-art, cross-validated, optimal, multiple predictor assessment model was not doing much better than chance at forecasting performance. We now know some of the reasons for the model's poor showing (Wiggins, 1973). These include (a) an inadequate specification of the criterion (the "criterion problem"), (b) the reliance on a single index, rather than a more generalizable aggregate index, of the predictor variables, and (c) the reduction in the power of a multiple regression equation when it is applied to new samples (the problem of "capitalization on chance"). However, one of the first responses was the introduction of the concept of *differential predictability* (Ghiselli, 1956; 1960a, 1960b, 1963).

The underlying premise of differential predictability, which explicitly violates one of the tenets of classical test theory, is that some individuals are more predictable than others. If there are systematic differences between predictable and unpredictable individuals, then those differences should in principle be identifiable with a third (moderator) variable. Predictive efforts can then be restricted to those people for whom those efforts will be rewarded. To develop an index for differentiating predictable individuals from unpredictable ones, Ghiselli (1956, 1960b) suggested computing correlations between items (usually from the predictor scales) and the absolute difference between the actual and predicted criterion scores of a group of individuals. Items that correlated with this discrepancy could then be combined into a scale that would index unpredictability. In a series of studies Ghiselli demonstrated that this approach significantly increased his ability to predict the performance of taxicab drivers (1956), sociability of college students (1960b), and the occupational level of adult men (1960a). Thus predictability appeared to moderate predictor–criterion relations.

C. Student Characteristics and Instructional Techniques

Perhaps the most pervasive belief in the field of education is that there are some techniques for teaching students that are more effective than others. This belief is illustrated by the large amount of time and effort that has been devoted to developing and evaluating instructional methods (e.g., Gage, 1963; Haines & McKeachie, 1967; Husband, 1954; Levine & Wang, 1983; Skinner, 1968). It is also illustrated by the soul-searching that many of us go through when it comes time to prepare our courses for the coming year. However, there is actually little evidence to suggest that this time, effort, and soul-searching have been well spent (Dubin & Taveggia, 1968). As Goldberg (1972) noted after reviewing the empirical literature on this issue, "the overwhelming finding that has emerged from hundreds of studies . . . is that differing college instructional procedures do *not* appear to produce any consistent differences in average course achievement" (p. 154).

One popular explanation for this surprising finding is that learning is more complicated than was first thought. Specifically, it was suggested that there was an interaction between student characteristics and instructional techniques such that techniques that work well with one type of student work poorly with other types, and vice versa (Cronbach, 1957, 1967; McKeachie, 1968; Snow, Tiffin, & Seibert, 1965). If this explanation is true, not only are past and future efforts to develop better teaching methods justified, but these efforts should be redoubled.

D. Empirical Evaluation

For each of these moderator variable solutions to the problems of personality consistency, performance prediction, and educational effectiveness, the initial empirical support for the interactive models seemed promising. However, following an initial period of optimism in which many investigators began to incorporate the interactive models into their research and practice, some disquieting results began to be reported. Specifically, researchers who tried to replicate the initial findings generally failed to do so. Following an extensive study of the moderating effects of cross-situational consistency, Chaplin and Goldberg (1984) concluded,

> The excitement that followed the publication of the Bem and Allen study now needs to be tempered. Not only did we fail to find any generalization of their findings to a larger and more representative sample of traits, but we even failed to replicate their findings for one of the two traits they investigated. (p. 1089)

This conclusion was echoed by other investigators (e.g., Mischel & Peake, 1982; Paunonen & Jackson, 1985). Even a more recent confirmatory report (Zuckerman et al., 1988) was not based on the discovery of substantial moderator effects. Rather it was based on demonstrating the statistical significance of small moderator effects with very large samples (Chaplin, 1991).

In the case of differential predictability, the ephemeral quality of the putative moderators was so widely documented (e.g., Brown & Scott, 1966, 1967; Goldberg, 1969; Kellogg, 1968; Stricker, 1967; Velicer, 1972; Wallach & Leggett, 1972) that Ghiselli himself concluded, "Furthermore, since the indications are that moderators are rather specific it might be that they, like suppressors, do not hold up well from sample to sample" (1963, p. 86). Finally, the search for "trait by treatment" interactions in education led to similar disappointments (e.g., Goldberg, 1964; Lublin, 1965; McKeachie, 1963; Tallmadge, 1968).

> These poignant findings, when coupled with those concerning the fate of attempts to construct new empirical interaction scales, suggest that the significant interactions discovered in this project . . . are unlikely to lead to differential predictions which are more valid than those achievable by general predictors alone.
>
> *(Goldberg, 1972, p. 200)*

Recently, a similar conclusion was reached by Dance and Neufeld (1988) about aptitude-by-treatment interaction research in clinical psychology.

E. What Went Wrong?

These examples all illustrate situations in which the existence of interaction effects was a foregone conclusion. Why, then, did the addition of interactive terms to prediction models fail to increase predictive validity? In answering this question I will consider some logical, statistical, psychometric, and conceptual issues that must be confronted by those who would venture into the moderator domain.

1. Logical Issues

The complexity of human behavior that makes the existence of interaction effects a certainty also makes it likely that the size of any given effect will be small. In writing about the discouraging failure of many studies to detect aptitude-by-treatment interactions, Cronbach (1975) noted, "Once we attend to interactions, we enter a hall of mirrors that extends to infinity. However far we carry our analysis—to third order or fifth order, or any other order—untested interactions of a still higher order can be envisioned" (p. 119). Likewise, in discussing the cross-situational consistency of behavior, Epstein (1983) wrote,

> Theoretically, any single instance of behavior can be predicted if all the right
> moderator variables are included. This is no more than to say that behavior is
> determined, and that if we knew everything that determined it, we could predict
> it. However, to do so might require the addition of so many moderator variables
> that they would generate interactions of such complexity as to make the proce-
> dure unfeasible and the results uninterpretable.
>
> *(p. 377)*

These statements lead to three related conclusions. First, the number of possible interaction effects for any dependent variable is very large, perhaps infinite.
Thus, within the context of any uncontrolled "naturalistic" system, any one effect
is almost certain to be small. If the effects are roughly equal, the proportional effect
of any one interaction is $1/k$ (where k is a very large number). Second, any interaction
effect is itself going to be moderated by a higher order interaction effect. Third, as
Nisbett (1977) noted, this renders the hypothesis that there exists some unspecified
moderator effect untestable (and also uninteresting), because any failure to detect
an effect can be attributed to an as yet undiscovered higher order interaction.

2. Statistical Issues

Even in the more limited domain of a specific study with a limited set of variables,
interaction effects will be statistically more difficult to detect than main effects
(Cohen, 1977; Keppel, 1982). First, statistical power is, in part, a function of sample
size. In a standard analysis of variance the number of observations on which each
cell mean is based will be less than the number of observations on which each
marginal mean is based, because the marginal means are a combination of cell
means. Interaction effects are based on cell means, whereas main effects are based
on marginal means.

Second, power is also a function of effect size. The larger the effect, the more
likely it is to be detected. The general linear model always expresses as much of
the systematic variance in any experiment in terms of main effects. Interaction
effects are, by definition, based on the residual systematic variance. Thus, even if
an interaction effect is present, especially if it is an ordinal interaction, it may
produce observations that are captured by the additive, linear terms of the model.
As always, a failure to reject the (null) hypothesis that there is no interaction effect
does not mean that an interactive process is not operating.

Third, the overall power of any analysis is generally decreased as one adds
terms to the model being tested. In their recommendations for testing interactions
within the framework of multiple regression analysis, Cohen and Cohen (1983)
suggested that investigators should be very selective about which variables and
their possible interactions they include in their analysis.

> For example, with 10 research factors (a not unusually large number outside
> the experimental laboratory), there are 45 two-way, 120 three-way interaction
> sets, and heaven knows how many individual IVs [independent variables] . . . .
> By omitting possible interaction sets carrying chance variance from the equation,

as many df [degrees of freedom] as there are omitted IVs become available to the error term, thereby increasing . . . the statistical power of the tests that are performed.

(Cohen & Cohen, 1983, p. 348)

3. Psychometric Issues

Measurement error has a deleterious impact on regression coefficients. Specifically, measurement error generally attenuates correlations between variables, and this introduces a negative bias in the regression coefficients associated with unreliably measured variables (Kenny, 1979). Because it is the product of variables, it might seem that the reliability of the term that carries the moderator effect would be a direct function of the reliability of its components. Unfortunately, the reliability of the cross product is, among other things, dependent on the scaling of its component variables. Thus, a cross product's reliability may not be easily discerned from the reliability of its components.

Bohrnstedt and Marwell (1977) derived the relation between the reliability of the product of two variables and the reliabilities of the components. This relation is

$$r_{xyxy} = \frac{(M_x^2/S_x^2)r_{yy} + (M_y^2/S_y^2)r_{xx} + 2(M_x/s_x)\,(M_y/s_y)r_{xy} + r_{xy}^2 + r_{xx}r_{yy}}{(M_x^2/S_x^2) + (M_y^2/S_y^2) + 2(M_x/s_x)\,(M_y/s_y)r_{xy} + r_{xy}^2 + 1.0}, \quad (4)$$

where r_{xyxy} is the reliability of the xy product; M_x and M_y are the means of x and y, respectively; S_x and S_y are the respective standard deviations; r_{xx} and r_{yy} are the respective reliabilities; and r_{xy} is the correlation between x and y.

As can be seen in Equation 4, the reliability of a product depends not only on the reliability of the component variables, but also on the correlation between the component variables and the ratios of their respective means to standard deviations. The ratio of means to standard deviations will be changed by any transformation that affects the origins of the variables (i.e., that contains an additive constant).

The scale dependence of cross-product reliabilities is certainly germane to recent discussions about the impact of scale transformations on the evaluation of moderator effects (e.g., Cronbach, 1987; Dunlap & Kemery, 1987; Morris et al., 1986). Moreover, as Bohrnstedt and Marwell (1977) have shown, it leads to certain anomalies in the estimation of cross-product reliabilities. For example, even if one of the component variables is completely unreliable, the reliability of the cross product will generally not be zero, and, under certain conditions, it will approach the reliability of the more reliable component variable. Also, when the correlation between the component variables is negative, the reliability of the cross product will be lower than if the correlation is positive, even if the component reliabilities are held constant.

More recently, Busemeyer and Jones (1983) have shown that these anomalies are eliminated if the component variables are converted to deviation scores. In this case, Equation 4 simplifies to

$$r_{xyxy} = \frac{r_{xy}^2 + r_{xx}r_{yy}}{r_{xy}^2 + 1.0}, \quad (5)$$

where the terms are as defined in Equation 4.

As is clear from Equation 5, the reliability of a cross product cannot exceed the reliability of its most reliable component. Typically, its reliability will be less. For example, consider two variables (in deviation score form), each with a reliability of .80. If those variables are uncorrelated, the reliability of their cross product will be .64. Even if the correlation between the two variables rises to the maximum allowed by their reliability (.80), the reliability of the cross product will be maximized at .78. As Busemeyer and Jones (1983) noted, "The presence of measurement error in the predictor variables will drastically reduce the power to detect a significant contribution from the product term" (p. 559).

In addition to the other handicaps, detecting interaction effects must generally be done in the presence of more measurement error than is present for main effects. Moreover, the extent of this measurement error cannot be directly estimated from the reliability of the component variables when the component variables are measured on scales that are not centered around zero. Indeed, it may be affected in anomalous ways by arbitrary scaling factors.

4. Conceptual Issues

In the three examples of personality consistency, personnel selection, and educational effectiveness, the primary hypothesis was that some moderator effect existed. However, in each of these examples, little effort was made to establish the construct validity of the proposed moderators, nor was any compelling theory for the specific moderator variable developed. Thus, Bem and Allen (1974) proposed that individuals who reported being cross-situationally consistent would be cross-situationally consistent; Ghiselli (1956) proposed that people who were more predictable would be more predictable; and numerous educators proposed that techniques that were better suited to a student would improve his or her academic performance. That these predictions sound trivial reflects the fact that they all are limited to asserting the mere existence (cf. Meehl, 1978) of a moderator variable; the nature of that variable and its operation are generally unspecified.

Standing in contrast to my pessimistic appraisal of the likelihood of a successful search for moderator variables are the many studies that have reported significant and replicable interactions. These include the moderating influence of self-efficacy on behavior change (Bandura, 1977), the interaction of personality variables with stressful situations (Friedman & Rosenman, 1974) or with arousal (Humphreys & Revelle, 1984), the divergent perspectives of actors and observers (Jones & Nisbett, 1972), the situational factors that influence bystander intervention (Darly & Latané, 1970), and the influence of family configurations on intelligence (Zajonc, 1976). However, unlike the studies reviewed at the beginning of this paper, these successful investigations all concerned specific moderator variables, and the conditions under which their effects would be observed had been predicted. Thus, the investigators were able to focus the full power of their design on those effects. In other words, they knew where to look.

By comparison, consider Goldberg's (1972) appraisal of the efforts to detect an interaction between teaching methods and student characteristics:

> While the directors of both research programs might argue that the personality measures they utilize are "theory-based" . . . it is doubtful whether either theory actually dictated these measurement decisions. For, at the moment, we have few theories in psychology—and none in college instruction—which specify the number and nature of those personality characteristics predisposing students to achieve differentially in different college courses . . . .
>
> *(p. 157)*

Tellegen, Kamp, and Watson (1982) made a similar point about the problem with moderators of cross-situational consistency, as did Wiggins (1973) with regard to differential predictability. "At present theories of personality structure do not appear to be sufficiently articulated to guide selection of appropriate mathematical prediction models from the myriad possibilities that exist" (Wiggins, 1973, p. 79).

III. Implications for Applied Psychology

Interactive models have not fared well in applied settings. Moderator variables are difficult to discover and are more difficult to replicate. In hindsight, these disappointing conclusions are not surprising: given the vast number of possible interaction effects, any one of them will generally be minuscule; the detection of such effects is further hampered by measurement unreliability and low statistical power; the replication of any effects that are detected will be difficult in the absence of a strong theory that predicted the effect. What, then, are the implications of this analysis for applied prediction?

A. The Importance of Theory

My prescription for finding moderator variables is to start with a clear specification of what the variables are and how they should be measured, as well as the conditions under, and the manner in which, their effects will be manifested. The paper by Humphreys and Revelle (1984) on the influence of individual differences and situational factors on information processing provides a sample script for these actions. In summarizing their program of research, they write, "We now can relate personality dimensions to situations and tasks and make specific predictions about the conditions under which people who differ in impulsivity, achievement motivation, or anxiety differ in their performance in a variety of situations" (p. 180). Once this has been done the usual procedures for increasing statistical power, including using large samples, reliable measures, and designs that maximize the size of the interaction effect, can be employed. However, although good experimental form may lead to the reliable detection of moderator effects, it will do so *despite* the relatively small size of those effects. Many efforts to find moderator variables have been motivated not by a theoretical interest, but by the desire to find variables that would substantially and "usefully" affect the relation between a predictor and a criterion. Bem and Allen (1974) sought to demonstrate that "personality coefficients" (Mischel,

1968) could greatly exceed the .30 barrier; Ghiselli (1956) intended his index of differential predictability to be of practical use; and the same goals are evident in the aptitude-by-treatment interaction literature. Given that interaction effects are in the "real world" generally small, I remain pessimistic about their practical impact.

B. Explanation versus Prediction

Prediction is the fundamental standard for scientifically evaluating a theoretical model. However, predictive accuracy does not imply a true model; rather, predictive inaccuracy implies a false model (Popper, 1962). This inferential asymmetry results because accurate predictions can be based on very inaccurate models (e.g., the model of the sun as a fiery chariot on a circular track did an excellent job of predicting the rising of the sun in the east). Thus, if the goal is efficient prediction, rather than explanation, the quest for highly accurate models may be unnecessary.

In 1974 Dawes and Corrigan published a review of the use of linear models in decision making. In this review they concluded that under a broad and reasonable set of conditions a linear combination of unit-weighted variables outperformed the same set of optimally (least-squares) weighted variables in predicting a criterion. The "robust beauty" of these unit-weighted models was further documented by Dawes in 1979. Neither Dawes nor Corrigan nor any other decision scientists has ever contended that these linear models, unit weighted or otherwise, are realistic portrayals of the phenomena they are predicting (e.g., Goldberg, 1968; Hoffman, 1960). Indeed, Hoffman introduced the expression "paramorphic models" to emphasize that distinction. "The true relationships need not be linear for linear models to work; they must merely be approximated by linear models" (Dawes, 1979, p. 573). Thus, although human behavior can only be understood and explained by appealing to very complex models, it can often be better predicted by relatively simple ones.

C. The Virtues of Simplicity

The development of increasingly complex prediction models has been guided by the seemingly straightforward assumption that complex phenomena will be better predicted by complex models. However, exactly the opposite conclusion is consistent with the evidence.

> In the derivation sample, it was clear that increases in the complexity of the prediction equations were associated with corresponding *increases* in predictive accuracy. However, . . . in a cross-validation sample, increases in complexity . . . were associated with corresponding *decreases* in predictive accuracy. With few exceptions, the usual multiple-regression equation outperformed the more complex models.
>
> *(Wiggins, 1973, pp. 78–79)*

Although complex relations can be modeled quite accurately, post hoc, in a given sample, the cost of accuracy is a sharp decrease in generality. There are at least two reasons for this.

1. Chance Disguised as Complexity

In any set of data it is likely that there will appear some intriguing patterns that are purely chance fluctuations. It is out of an appreciation for the clever way in which chance can disguise itself that we have developed statistical methods to evaluate sample results against chance distributions. However, the standard multiple regression equation is more easily seduced. Specifically, multiple regression equations rely heavily on any and all patterns of relations (chance or otherwise) among a set of variables in their single-minded pursuit of minimizing squared errors of prediction. Thus, multiple regression equations "capitalize" on chance fluctuations to derive optimal regression coefficients, and they do this all the more as terms are added to the equation (Wherry, 1931).

Within a sample of data it is not possible to distinguish random patterns from nonrandom ones. Thus, some of the complex terms that serve to characterize a given sample of data may be modeling "error." To separate chance patterns from systematic ones, one must cross validate (replicate) (Mosier, 1956) the model with a new set of data. In a new sample of data, the random patterns will be different and the terms that modeled these patterns in the original sample will no longer be accurate. Moreover, they will generally be counterproductive. One reason that simple models outperform complex ones in new samples is that the simple ones have been less influenced by chance patterns. Indeed, the basic bivariate linear model is largely impervious to capitalization on chance, and the unit-weighted multivariate linear model does not rely on a sample to derive its regression parameters. It is precisely these models that are typically the most accurate when they are applied to new samples (Dawes, 1979).

2. The Nomothetic Power of Simple Models

Certainly not all complexity is the result of random processes. However, even when complex terms reflect systematic relations, simple models may still outpredict complex ones. As we develop a more detailed and complex characterization of a phenomena, we place more conditions and qualifications on it. These conditions and qualifications necessarily restrict the generality of the model because in many situations all of the conditions may not be known or their operation may be further qualified by other variables. Moreover, each additional measure of a qualifying variable will bring with it more measurement error and a reduction in statistical power.

Simple models overcome these problems by aggregating the complexities into a smaller number of more reliable variables. For example, it is difficult to improve on the simple linear equation that uses high school grade-point average (GPA) to predict academic performance in college (APC). Certainly, an individual's academic performance is a complex function of ability, motivation, social skill, discipline, peer support, and a host of other factors. However, the simple model of APC = f(GPA) will typically outperform the more complicated model APC = f(ability, motivation, etc.). The reason is that GPA is an aggregate that reflects, assuming some consistency between high school and college, the personality, ability, and situational variables, combined in whatever complex way they combine. No one believes that the relation APC = GPA is, even remotely, an adequate *explanation* of academic performance in college. To explain performance we need a complex model, but to predict performance the simple model that sidesteps the complexity by aggregation works better. We do not need to know the idiographic variables and their relations for each student; we get that information for free, so to speak, when we obtain GPA.

IV. CONCLUSION

The conclusion that follows from this review is an old one that can best be expressed by those who invested considerable energy in the pursuit of moderators and other complex relations. "It is quite possible that the time and effort required to develop moderators might be more fruitfully spent in seeking improvements in reliability and validity of the sort that follow from classical psychometric theory" (Ghiselli, 1963, p. 86). "It still seems safe to assert that new predictions made on the basis of the most significant interaction effects are unlikely to be more valid than those made on the basis of general predictors alone" (Goldberg, 1972, p. 207). "The whole trick is to decide what variables to look at and then to know how to add" (Dawes & Corrigan, 1974, p. 105).

Models that are designed to increase our understanding of psychological phenomena need to reflect the conditional and nonlinear relations that are certainly operating among psychological variables. However, models that serve the more pragmatic goal of efficiently predicting important criteria are always handicapped by the inclusion of complex relations. Our efforts to improve predictions from personality variables should be devoted to the development of simple models that rely on higher order variables that automatically include the complexity that exists. Such models and variables will be of little scientific interest because they mask the processes we wish to understand. They may, however, be of great practical utility.

ACKNOWLEDGMENTS

Some of the ideas presented in this chapter were formulated while the author was a postdoctoral fellow at Stanford University, supported by Grant MH-15728 from the National Institute of Mental Health. Additional support was provided by Grant MH-39077 from the National Institute of Mental Health to the Oregon Research Institute. I thank Lewis R. Goldberg, Oliver P. John, Steven Prentice-Dunn, Stephen G. West, and Jennifer Wilson for their helpful reactions to initial drafts of this chapter.

REFERENCES

Bandura, A. (1977). Self-efficacy: Toward a unifying theory of behavioral change. *Psychological Review, 84,* 191–215.

Bem, D. J., & Allen, A. (1974). On predicting some of the people some of the time: The search for cross-situational consistencies in behavior. *Psychological Review, 81,* 506–520.

Block, J. (1977). Advancing the psychology of personality: Paradigmatic shift or improving the quality of research? In D. Magnusson & N. S. Endler (Eds.), *Personality at the crossroads: Current issues in interactional psychology* (pp. 37–63). Hillsdale, NJ: Erlbaum.

Bobko, P. (1986). A solution of some dilemmas when testing hypotheses about ordinal interactions. *Journal of Applied Psychology, 71,* 323–326.

Bohrnstedt, G. W., & Marwell, G. (1977). The reliability of products of two random variables. In K. F. Schuessler (Ed.), *Sociological methodology: 1978* (pp. 254–273). San Francisco: Jossey-Bass.

Booth, W. (1989). A clash of cultures at meeting on misconduct. *Science, 243,* 598.

Brown, F. G., & Scott, D. A. (1966). The unpredictability of predictability. *Journal of Educational Measurement, 3,* 297–301.

Brown, F. G., & Scott, D. A. (1967). Differential predictability in college admissions testing. *Journal of Educational Measurement, 4,* 163–166.

Busemeyer, J. R., & Jones, L. E. (1983). Analysis of multiplicative combination rules when causal variables are measured with error. *Psychological Bulletin, 93,* 549–562.

Chaplin, W. F. (1991). The next generation of moderator research in personality psychology. *Journal of Personality, 59,* 143–178.

Chaplin, W. F., & Goldberg, L. R. (1984). A failure to replicate the Bem and Allen study on individual differences in cross-situational consistencies. *Journal of Personality and Social Psychology, 47,* 1074–1090.

Cheek, J. M. (1982). Aggregation, moderator variables, and the validity of personality tests: A peer rating study. *Journal of Personality and Social Psychology, 43,* 1254–1269.

Cohen, J. (1977). *Statistical power analyses for the behavioral sciences* (Rev. ed.). New York: Academic Press.

Cohen, J. (1978). Partialed products *are* interactions; partialed powers *are* curve components. *Psychological Bulletin, 85,* 858–866.

Cohen, J. (1983). The cost of dichotomization. *Applied Psychological Measurement, 7,* 249–253.

Cohen, J., & Cohen, P. (1983). *Applied multiple regression/correlation analysis for the behavioral sciences* (2nd ed.). Hillsdale, NJ: Erlbaum.

Cronbach, L. J. (1956). Assessment of individual differences. *Annual Review of Psychology, 7,* 173–196.

Cronbach, L. J. (1957). The two disciplines of scientific psychology. *American Psychologist, 12,* 671–684.

Cronbach, L. J. (1967). How can instruction be adapted to individual differences? In R. M. Gagné (Ed.), *Learning and individual differences* (pp. 23–43). Columbus, OH: Merrill.

Cronbach, L. J. (1975). Beyond the two disciplines of scientific psychology. *American Psychologist, 30,* 116–127.

Cronbach, L. J. (1987). Statistical tests for moderator variables: Flaws in analyses recently proposed. *Psychological Bulletin, 102,* 414–417.

Dance, K. A., & Neufeld, R. W. J. (1988). Aptitude-treatment interaction research in the clinical setting: A review of attempts to dispel the "patient uniformity" myth. *Psychological Bulletin, 104,* 192–213.

Darley, J., & Latané, B. (1970). *Bystander intervention.* New York: Appleton-Century-Croft.

Dawes, R. M. (1979). The robust beauty of improper linear models in decision making. *American Psychologist, 34,* 571–582.

Dawes, R. M., & Corrigan, B. (1974). Linear models in decision making. *Psychological Bulletin, 81,* 95–106.

Dubin, R., & Taveggia, T. C. (1968). *The teaching-learning paradox: A comparative analysis of college teaching methods.* Eugene: University of Oregon Press.

Dunlap, W. P., & Kemery, E. R. (1987). Failure to detect moderating effects: Is multicollinearity the problem? *Psychological Bulletin, 102,* 418–420.

Epstein, S. (1983). Aggregation and beyond: Some basic issues on the prediction of behavior. *Journal of Personality, 51,* 360–392.

Fiske, D. W., & Pearson, P. H. (1970). Theory and techniques of personality measurement. *Annual Review of Psychology, 21,* 49–86.

Friedman, M., & Rosenman, R. (1974). *Type A behavior and your heart.* New York: Knopf.

Gage, N. L. (1963). *Handbook of research on teaching.* Chicago: Rand McNally.

Ghiselli, E. E. (1956). Differentiation of individuals in terms of their predictability. *Journal of Applied Psychology, 40* 374–377.

Ghiselli, E. E. (1960a). The prediction of predictability. *Educational and Psychological Measurement, 20,* 3–8.

Ghiselli, E. E. (1960b). Differentiation of tests in terms of the accuracy with which they predict a given individual. *Educational and Psychological Measurement, 20,* 675–684.

Ghiselli, E. E. (1963). Moderating effects and differential reliability and validity. *Journal of Applied Psychology, 47,* 81–86.

Gleick, J. (1987). *Chaos: Making a new science.* New York: Viking.

Goldberg, L. R. (1964). The effects of six teaching conditions on learning and satisfaction in a televised college course. *Psychology in the Schools, 2,* 366–375.

Goldberg, L. R. (1968). Simple models or simple processes? Some research on clinical judgments. *American Psychologist, 23,* 483–496.

Goldberg, L. R. (1969). The search for configural relationships in personality assessment: The diagnosis of psychosis and neurosis from the MMPI. *Multivariate Behavioral Research, 4,* 523–536.

Goldberg, L. R. (1972). Student personality characteristics and optimal college learning conditions: An extensive search for trait-by-treatment interaction effects. *Instructional Science, 1,* 153–210.

Goldberg, L. R. (1991). Human mind versus regression equation: Five contrasts. In D. Cicchetti & W. Grove (Eds.), *Thinking clearly about psychology: Essays in honor of Paul E. Meehl (Volume* 1: *Matters of public interest,* pp. 173–184). Minneapolis, MN: University of Minnesota Press.

Golding, S. L. (1978). Toward a more adequate theory of personality: Psychological organizing principles. In H. London (Ed.), *Personality: A new look at metatheories* (pp. 69–95). Washington, DC: Hemisphere.

Haines, D. B., & McKeachie, W. J. (1967). Cooperative versus competitive discussion methods in teaching introductory psychology. *Journal of Educational Psychology, 58,* 386–390.

Hase, H. D., & Goldberg, L. R. (1967). The comparative validity of different strategies of deriving personality inventory scales. *Psychological Bulletin, 67,* 231–248.

Hoffman, P. J. (1960). the paramorphic representation of clinical judgement. *Psychological Bulletin, 57,* 116–131.

Humphreys, M. S., & Revelle, W. (1984). Personality, motivation, and performance: A theory of the relationship between individual differences and information processing. *Psychological Review, 91,* 153–184.

Husband, R. W. (1954). Television versus classroom for learning general psychology. *American Psychologist, 9,* 181–183.

Jackson, D. N. (1971). The dynamics of structured personality tests: 1971. *Psychological Review, 78,* 229–248.

Jones, E. E., & Nisbett, R. E. (1972). The actor and the observer: Divergent perceptions of the causes of behavior. In E. E. Jones, D. E. Kanouse, H. H. Kelly, R. E. Nisbett, S. Valins, & B. Weiner (Eds.), *Attribution: Perceiving the causes of behavior* (pp. 79–94). Morristown, NJ: General Learning Press.

Kellogg, R. L. (1968). The Strong Vocational Interest Blank as a differential predictor of engineering grades. *Educational and Psychological Measurement, 28,* 1213–1217.

Kelly, E. L., & Fiske, D. W. (1951). *The prediction of performance in clinical psychology.* Ann Arbor: University of Michigan Press.

Kelly, G. A. (1955). *The psychology of personal constructs* (Vol. 1). New York: Norton.

Kenny, D. A. (1979). *Correlation and causality.* New York: Wiley.

Kenrick, D. T., & Stringfield, D. O. (1980). Personality traits and the eye of the beholder: Crossing some traditional boundaries in the search for consistency in all people. *Psychological Review, 87,* 88–104.

Keppel, G. (1982). *Design and analysis: A researcher's handbook* (2nd ed.). Englewood Cliffs, NJ: Prentice-Hall.

Levine, J. M., & Wang, M. C. (1983). *Teacher and student perceptions: Implications for learning.* Hillsdale, NJ: Erlbaum.

Lublin, S. C. (1965). Reinforcement schedules, scholastic aptitude, autonomy need, and achievement in a programmed course. *Journal of Educational Psychology, 56,* 295–302.

McKeachie, W. J. (1963). Research on teaching at the college and university level. In N. L. Gage (Ed.), *Handbook of research on teaching* (pp. 1118–1172). Chicago: Rand McNally.

McKeachie, W. J. (1968). Psychology at age 75: The psychology teacher comes into his own. *American Psychologist, 23,* 551–557.

McNemar, Q. (1952). Review of E. L. Kelly and D. W. Fiske, *The prediction of performance in clinical psychology. Journal of Abnormal and Social Psychology, 47,* 857–860.

Meehl, P. E. (1978). Theoretical risks and tabular asterisks: Sir Karl, Sir Ronald, and the slow progress of soft psychology. *Journal of Consulting and Clinical Psychology, 46,* 806–834.

Mischel, W. (1968). *Personality and assessment.* New York: Wiley.

Mischel, W., & Peake, P. (1982). Beyond déjà vu in the search for cross-situational consistency. *Psychological Review, 89,* 730–755.

Morris, J. H., Sherman, J. D., & Mansfield, E. R. (1986). Failures to detect moderating effects with ordinary least squares—moderated multiple regression: Some reasons and a remedy. *Psychological Bulletin, 99,* 282–288.

Mosier, C. I. (1951). Problems and designs of cross-validation. *Educational and Psychological Measurement, 11,* 5–11.

Nisbett, R. E. (1977). Interaction versus main effects as goals of personality research. In D. Magnusson & N. S. Endler (Eds.), *Personality at the crossroads: Current issues in interactional psychology* (pp. 235–241) New York: Wiley.

Office of Strategic Services Assessment Staff. (1948). *Assessment of men.* New York: Rinehart.

Ozer, D. J. (1986). *Consistency in personality: A methodological framework.* New York: Springer-Verlag.

Paunonen, S. V., & Jackson, D. J. (1985). Idiographic measurement strategies for personality and prediction: Some unredeemed promissory notes. *Psychological Review, 92,* 486–511.

Popper, K. R. (1962). *Conjectures and refutations.* New York: Basic Books.

Sines, J. O. (1964). Actuarial methods as appropriate strategy for the validation of psychological tests. *Psychological Review, 71,* 517–523.

Skinner, B. F. (1968). *The technology of teaching.* New York: Appleton-Century-Crofts.

Snow, R. E., Tiffin, J., & Seibert, W. F. (1965). Individual differences and instructional film effects. *Journal of Educational Psychology, 56,* 315–326.

Stricker, L. J. (1967). Compulsivity as a moderator variable: A replication and extension. *Journal of Applied Psychology, 50,* 331–335.

Tallmadge, G. K. (1968). Relationships between training methods and learner characteristics. *Journal of Educational Psychology, 59,* 32–36.

Tellegen, A., Kamp, J., & Watson, D. (1982). Recognizing individual differences in predictive structure. *Psychological Review, 89,* 95–105.

Turner, R. G. (1978). Consistency, self-consciousness, and predictive validity of typical and maximal personality measures. *Journal of Research in Personality, 12,* 117–132.

Velicer, W. F. (1972). Comment on the general inapplicability of Ghiselli's moderator system for two predictors. *Journal of Applied Psychology, 56,* 262–265.

Wallach, M. A., & Leggett, M. I. (1972). Testing the hypothesis that a person will be consistent: Stylistic consistency versus situational specificity in size of children's drawings. *Journal of Personality, 40,* 309–330.

Wherry, R. J. (1931). A new formula for predicting the shrinkage of the multiple correlation coefficient. *Annals of Mathematical Statistics, 2,* 440–457.

Wiggins, J. S. (1973). *Personality and prediction: Principles of personality assessment.* Reading, MA: Addison-Wesley.

Zajonc, R. B. (1976). Family configuration and intelligence. *Science, 192,* 227–236.

Zuckerman, M., Koestner, R., DeBoy, T., Garcia, T., Maresca, B. C., & Sartoris, J. M. (1988). To predict some of the people some of the time: A reexamination of the moderator variable approach in personality theory. *Journal of Personality and Social Psychology, 54,* 1006–1019.

CHAPTER 34

PERSONALITY AND HEALTH

PROGRESS AND PROBLEMS IN PSYCHOSOMATICS

DEBORAH J. WIEBE AND TIMOTHY W. SMITH
UNIVERSITY OF UTAH

The past few decades have witnessed a remarkable resurgence of interest in the potential influence of personality on health (Suls & Rittenhouse, 1987). Sparked by theory and research on the Type A behavior pattern (M. Friedman & Rosenman, 1974) and psychological hardiness (Kobasa, 1979), the study of personality and health has been an integral component of the developing fields of behavioral medicine and health psychology. Compared to their psychoanalytic predecessor, current approaches have been more closely tied to an expanding empirical base. As a result, such research has had a significant, growing impact on psychology and medicine. Yet despite these advances, work on personality and health has been the target of noteworthy criticism. Varying in degree from rejection (Angell, 1985) to careful discussion of methodological limitations (e.g., Holroyd & Coyne, 1987), the central theme of these critiques is that support for the basic psychosomatic hypothesis is tentative at best.

The purpose of this chapter is to provide: (1) an overview of conceptual models guiding research in this area, (2) brief summaries of several of the more developed areas of research, and (3) a discussion of common methodological limitations and challenges. We focus almost exclusively on the role of personality processes in the development and course of physical illness. However, personality is relevant to another central issue—psychological responses to physical illness and its treatment. For example, personality variables may moderate the emotional and behavioral effects of acute medical crises, as well as the adaptive demands of chronic physical illness. We focus on the contribution of personality to the development and course of physical illness, as it represents the oldest and most developed application of personality psychology to understanding disease.

I. Models of Associations between Personality and Health

This section provides an overview of four models that have been developed to explain the processes by which personality may influence health. Although the models are discussed separately, they are not clearly mutually exclusive or comprehensive explanations of the personality–health association. Multiple models are often utilized to explain how a specific personality dimension may be related to health.

A. Stress-Moderation Model

Many approaches to personality and health assign a central role to the concept of stress (for reviews, see Cohen, 1979; Contrada, Leventhal, & O'Leary, 1990; Houston, 1989; Suls & Rittenhouse, 1990). Although stress has been widely implicated in the development of disease, demonstrated stress–illness relations are quite weak (Rabkin & Struening, 1976). Such weak links have been hypothesized to reflect individual differences in susceptibility to stress. Thus, the stress-moderation model assumes that stress causes illness and that dispositional factors make one more or less vulnerable to its pathogenic effects.

Stress is generally hypothesized to affect health via several physiological pathways. Specifically, stress is believed to activate the sympathetic and neuroendocrine systems (i.e., the sympathetic adrenal–medullary and pituitary–adrenocortical systems), resulting in increased physiological arousal. Frequent and prolonged periods of arousal are presumed to place excessive strain on body organs and systems, eventually leading to illness (Krantz & Manuck, 1984; Menkes et al., 1989; Selye, 1956). Stress-induced neuroendocrine activation has also been reported to impair the effectiveness of the immune system, thereby increasing the risk of disease otherwise inhibited by immunological processes (e.g., infectious diseases and cancer; for reviews, see Herbert & Cohen, 1993; O'Leary, 1990).

The ways in which stress may influence these underlying pathogenic processes are illustrated in Figure 1. Although objective events vary in their potential to elicit arousal, it is generally the subjective appraisal of these events that activates the sympathetic and neuroendocrine systems. Hence, psychological stress and the concomitant physiological arousal have been theorized to occur when an event is appraised as threatening and presenting demands that cannot be met (Lazarus & Folkman, 1984). Cognitive and behavioral efforts for coping with stress also influence physiological arousal. Coping responses may exert effects by changing the intensity or duration of the current stressor, or by influencing the likelihood that similar events will occur or be appraised as stressful in the future.

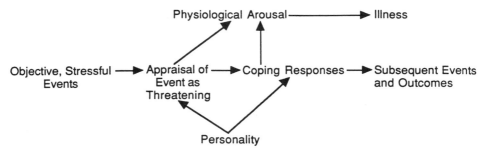

FIGURE 1   Interactional stress-moderation model.

Personality has been hypothesized to influence health at each point in this stress and coping process (see Figure 1). First, the cognitive and motivational aspects of personality are believed to exacerbate, attenuate, or prevent the appraisal of various stimuli as threatening, thereby affecting fluctuations in physiological arousal. Personality has also been theorized to influence pathogenic physiological arousal at the point of the coping response. If one believes that certain coping strategies influence the degree, duration, or frequency of experienced stress, then personality may impact health by determining whether more or less adaptive coping responses are utilized.

This basic stress-moderation model is limited in some respects. Although the straightforward approach is appealing, researchers have generally been unable to identify stable categories of coping responses that are consistently adaptive or maladaptive (Lazarus, 1990). There is growing recognition that coping and personality constructs must be conceptualized in process-oriented terms that consider interactions between personality, coping, and situational factors over time (Contrada et al., 1990; Houston, 1989; Lazarus, 1990; Lazarus & Folkman, 1984).

More recent stress-moderation models of personality and health move beyond this adherence to older, static interactional approaches to personality, and explicitly acknowledge the reciprocal relations between persons and situations (Smith, 1989; Suls & Sanders, 1989). The various *transactional* views of personality assert that people do not simply respond to situations—they also create the situations they encounter through their choices and actions (Buss, 1987; Cantor, 1990). For example, antagonistic individuals may create interpersonal conflicts through their argumentative social behavior, while agreeable persons might avoid such interpersonal strain.

As depicted in Figure 2, the transactional stress-moderation approach identifies three pathways through which personality may influence the pathophysiology of disease. In addition to impacting appraisal and coping responses to a given extent, personality is likely to influence the objective events themselves. More frequent, severe, and enduring exposure to stressful events is likely to contribute to disease. The reciprocal nature of these processes is reflected in the acknowledgment that personality dispositions may be strengthened and maintained by objective events

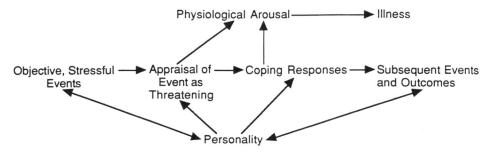

FIGURE 2 Transactional stress-moderation model.

and situational contexts, creating the short- and long-term cycles central to many transactional approaches to personality (e.g., Carson, 1969; Wachtel, 1977).

B. Health Behavior Models

In contrast to the direct physiological linkages of the stress-moderation model, the health behavior model proposes that personality affects health via the quality of one's health practices (Cohen, 1979; Contrada et al., 1990). It is well accepted that poor health practices (e.g., smoking, lack of exercise, high-fat diet) increase the risk of developing a variety of illnesses (Blair et al., 1989; Coyne & Holroyd, 1982; Paffenbarger & Hale, 1975). Further, personality variables such as hardiness (Wiebe & McCallum, 1986), neuroticism (Costa & McCrae, 1987b; McCrae, Costa, & Bosse, 1978), and hostility (Leiker & Hailey, 1988; Rask, 1990) are related to the tendency to engage in various healthy and unhealthy behaviors. Thus, according to this model, personality is linked to illness because it affects one's choice of health behaviors. This basic model is depicted in the upper portion of Figure 3. This is not a classic psychosomatic model since the direct physiological correlates of personality are not the identified mediators. However, health behaviors are increasingly recognized as contributing to the association between personality and disease.

Although personality dimensions have been associated with health behaviors, the causes of such associations are unclear. It is possible that psychological variables theorized to influence health practices are inherent aspects of some personality

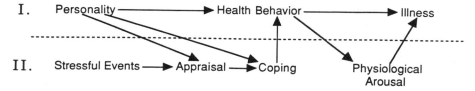

FIGURE 3 Health behavior model.

constructs. For example, self-efficacy (Bandura, 1989) and internal locus of control (Lau, 1988; Strickland, 1978) may be reasonably hypothesized to mediate various personality–health behavior relationships. It is also possible that the relationship between personality and health behaviors represents an additional form of stress moderation. Health practices often deteriorate during times of stress (Horowitz et al., 1979; Langlie, 1977; Shachter, Silverstein, Kozlowski, Herman, & Liebling, 1977). If dispositional traits affect the frequency and duration of appraised stress, then these personality dimensions may impact health by influencing stress-induced health behavior departures. Further, health behaviors such as smoking and alcohol and substance use have been characterized as regressive or avoidant coping behaviors. Personality may, thus, influence the likelihood that one will cope with appraised stress through health-damaging behaviors because one has fewer alternative coping resources. This more complex health behavior model is depicted in the lower portion of Figure 3.

Tests of the health behavior model are likely to be hampered by several inherent difficulties (Contrada et al., 1990). For example, personality appears to influence both health-enhancing and health-damaging behaviors. Because these behaviors are only weakly correlated with each other (Harris & Guten, 1979; Leventhal, Prohaska, & Hirschman, 1985) and fluctuate over time (Mechanic, 1979), it is unlikely that their aggregate will be strongly correlated with personality. It is, thus, improbable that global lifestyle factors will prove to be powerful mediators of the effects of personality on health.

C. Constitutional Predisposition Model

Some researchers have suggested that statistical associations between personality and health reflect the operation of a third variable rather than direct causal processes. This model, depicted in Figure 4, posits that individuals may be genetically predisposed to certain pathophysiological processes (e.g., enhanced sympathetic reactivity or reduced parasympathetic dampening of stress responses) which influence both the development of subsequent illness and the behavioral, cognitive, and emotional aspects of measured personality. Thus, although prospective studies may identify robust associations between personality and subsequent disease, the constitutional predisposition model characterizes this association as epiphenomenal. While this model has not been systematically studied across personality variables, evidence of the heritability of personality (Bouchard, Lylkken, McGue, Segal, &

FIGURE 4   Constitutional predisposition model.

Tellegen, 1990) suggests that it is important to understand the influence of genetic factors on personality–health associations.

D. Illness Behavior Model

In this model, personality is hypothesized to affect illness behavior rather than actual illness. Illness can be defined as the presence of objectively measured patho-physiological processes such as high blood pressure, documented organic disease, or death. Illness behavior, in contrast, refers to actions people take when they perceive themselves as ill. Such behaviors include reports of symptoms, work absenteeism, medical care utilization, and self-medication. Although illness behavior is clearly related to actual health status (Idler, Kasl, & Lemke, 1990; Kaplan & Camacho, 1983; Kaplan & Kotler, 1985; Maddox & Douglas, 1973), this correlation is far from perfect. Stoical individuals may display less illness behavior than their actual health warrants, while hypochondriacs typically display excessive illness behavior. Illness behavior is heavily influenced by psychological factors such as the tendency to perceive physiological sensations and to label them as illness (see Cioffi, 1991; Cohen, 1979; Pennebaker, 1982; Watson & Pennebaker, 1989, for reviews). Thus, from the illness behavior perspective, personality–health relationships are potentially artifactual.

Figure 5 illustrates how psychological factors might influence illness behavior in the absence of underlying pathophysiology. Research on a commonly used illness behavior measure—self-reported physical symptoms—suggests that symptom reports are strongly affected by situational and dispositional differences in focus of attention and by health beliefs and related cognitive processes (Pennebaker, 1982). As discussed later, the personality dimension of neuroticism includes a high level of somatic concern, which in turn increases symptom reporting. Actions such as staying home from work and visiting a physician are also likely to be affected by the manner in which an individual perceives and labels ongoing physiological sensations. Thus, these seemingly more objective health measures may be heavily influenced by psychological factors.

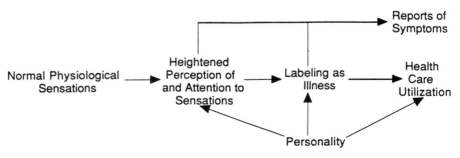

FIGURE 5   Illness behavior model.

II. PERSONALITY CONSTRUCTS IN CURRENT RESEARCH

A great variety of personality dimensions have been examined in the most recent cycle of research on personality and health. Although we cannot provide the depth and range of discussion needed for a comprehensive review, this section summarizes research concerning the most important personality constructs examined to date. In each case, we address four issues—conceptual frameworks, assessment procedures, evidence of associations with health, and methodological limitations.

A. Type A Behavior and Hostility

M. Friedman and Rosenman's (1959) description of the Type A pattern—competitiveness, hostility, impatience, achievement striving, job involvement, and a loud, explosive speech style—represents the beginning of the current resurgence of personality and health research. They described the Type A pattern as an action–emotion complex and a style of response to environmental challenges and demands.

Subsequent conceptual approaches to the Type A pattern have extended descriptions and explanations of this behavioral style. Glass (1977) suggested that the Type A pattern represents a style of responding to perceived threats to one's control over the environment. Compared to the more relaxed, easygoing Type B's, Type A's are more concerned with control, have a lower threshold for perceiving threats to control, and respond with more vigorous attempts to exert control. Price (1982) described the Type A pattern as the overt manifestation of an underlying tentative sense of self-esteem and beliefs concerning the necessity and difficulty of demonstrating self-worth through success and achievement. Several variations of these basic conceptual approaches have been offered.

The major conceptual descriptions of Type A behavior and its association with coronary disease identify physiological reactivity as the underlying pathophysiological mechanism. Consistent with an interactional stress-moderation model, Type A's are hypothesized to display larger stress-induced increases in cardiovascular and neuroendocrine parameters (e.g., blood pressure, heart rate, circulating catecholamines) than their Type B counterparts. Quantitative and qualitative reviews have supported the hypothesis that Type A's exhibit more pronounced reactivity (Harbin, 1989; Houston, 1988).

Other approaches to the issue of mechanisms linking Type A behavior and health have adopted a *transactional* stress-moderation model. From this perspective, Type A's not only respond to challenges with more pronounced reactivity, they also create more severe, frequent, and enduring stressors through their thoughts and actions (Smith, 1989; Smith & Anderson, 1986). The physiological consequences of this greater exposure to stressors contribute, in turn, to the development of disease. Finally, some authors have proposed a constitutional predisposition model (Krantz & Durel, 1983). From this perspective, the overt behavioral manifestations of the Type A pattern reflect an underlying constitutional predisposition, specifically a more responsive or reactive sympathetic nervous system. This autonomic responsivity not only produces the Type A behavioral style, but also contributes to the development of cardiovascular disease.

Three assessment devices have been used in the bulk of the research on the Type A pattern and are considered primary by virtue of their inclusion in large, prospective studies of coronary risk: the Type A Structured Interview (SI; Rosenman, 1978), the Jenkins Activity Survey (Jenkins, Rosenman, & Zyzanski, 1974), and the Framingham Type A Scale (Haynes, Feinleib, & Kannel, 1980). Although initially intended to assess the same construct, these measures are quite modestly intercorrelated (Chesney, Black, Chadwick, & Rosenman, 1981; Matthews, Krantz, Dembroski, & MacDougall, 1982) and exhibit distinct patterns of correlations with other personality traits (e.g., Chesney et al., 1981; Smith, O'Keefe, & Allred, 1989). Thus, the convergent and discriminant validity of measures of Type A behavior is questionable. This inequivalence of measures intended to assess the same construct has contributed to confusion and controversy surrounding the Type A concept.

Research on the association between the Type A pattern and subsequent coronary disease has produced inconsistent findings. After two decades of generally supportive data, a panel of experts convened by the American Heart Association concluded that the Type A pattern was a robust coronary risk factor (Cooper, Detre, & Weiss, 1981). Several widely published failures to replicate this association have recently raised doubts about the previous conclusion (e.g., Case, Heller, Case, & Moss, 1985; Ragland & Brand, 1988; Shekelle, Gale, & Norusis, 1985). This controversy has been reduced to some extent by recent meta-analyses of the available prospective studies (Matthews, 1988; Miller, Turner, Tindale, Posovac, & Dugoni, 1991). In previously healthy populations, the Type A pattern is associated with increased risk of initial, premature development of coronary disease. However, this is true only of the Type A pattern when quantified by the SI, and is not true in high-risk groups (e.g., high levels of traditional coronary risk factors, or patients with preexisting disease). The study of high-risk populations appears to account for much of the recent inconsistencies.

One result of the inconsistency of findings in this area has been increased attention on the health risks associated with the individual elements within the array of Type A characteristics. Prospective studies using the SI and scoring components separately have identified hostility as the "toxic" element within the Type A pattern (Dembroski, MacDougall, Costa, & Grandits, 1989; Hecker, Chesney, Black, & Frautchi, 1988; Matthews, Glass, Rosenman, & Bortner, 1977). These findings have prompted considerable interest in the health consequences of hostility (see Smith, 1992, for review). Because of its use in an early cross-sectional study of coronary disease (R. B. Williams et al., 1980) and its availability in archival MMPI data sets, the Cook and Medley (1954) Hostility (Ho) Scale has been pressed into service in several longitudinal studies. Although an equal number of studies have supported and failed to support an association between Ho scale scores and subsequent health (e.g., Barefoot, Dodge, Peterson, Dahlström, & Williams, 1989; Hearn, Murray, & Leupker, 1989; Leon, Finn, Murray, & Bailey, 1988; Shekelle, Gale, Ostfeld, & Paul, 1983), other prospective studies using different self-report measures of hostility have found this trait to predict subsequent illness (Barefoot et al., 1987; Koskenvuo et al., 1988).

A recent meta-analysis of this literature indicates that both behavioral ratings of hostility and the Ho scale are reliable predictors of coronary heart disease (CHD), although the latter association is smaller than the former (Miller, Smith, Turner, Guijarro, & Hallett, 1993). Further, hostility as measured by the Ho scale and other self-report instruments predicts all-cause mortality. That is, hostile persons are likely to die at an earlier age from both CHD and other illnesses.

As in the case of the broader Type A pattern, models of the mechanisms linking hostility and health have focused primarily on physiological reactivity to environmental stressors (Smith, 1994; R. B. Williams, Barefoot, & Shekelle, 1985). Several studies have found that hostile persons respond to social stressors such as interpersonal conflict and provocation with larger increases in blood pressure than is exhibited by comparatively friendly, agreeable subjects (Christensen & Smith, 1993; Hardy & Smith, 1988; Smith & Allred, 1989; Suarez & Williams, 1989). In addition to these stress-moderation studies, several studies suggest that hostile persons experience more frequent and severe interpersonal stressors and have fewer and less satisfactory social supports (Blumenthal, Burg, & Williams, 1987; Houston & Kelley, 1989; Smith & Frohm, 1985; Smith, Pope, Sanders, Allred, & O'Keefe, 1988). This pattern of psychosocial correlates of hostility may reflect the impact of hostile stress-engendering behavior on the interpersonal environment. Thus, transactional stress-moderation models may also be useful in explicating the health consequences of hostility (Smith & Pope, 1990).

One recent component analysis suggests that hostility may not be the only coronary-prone aspect of the Type A pattern. Houston, Chesney, Black, Cates, & Hecker (1992) found that both hostility and social dominance are independent predictors of subsequent CHD. Interestingly, the act of exerting social influence and control elicits heightened cardiovascular reactivity, and social dominance is associated with CHD in animal models (see Smith & Christensen, 1992, for review). Thus, both socially controlling and hostile persons might be at increased coronary risk.

B. Neuroticism

Neuroticism is a broad dimension of normal personality characterized by a tendency to experience chronic negative emotions and to display related behavioral and cognitive characteristics (Costa & McCrae, 1980, 1987b; McCrae & Costa, 1984). Highly neurotic individuals thus have generally negative views of themselves and the world regardless of the objective reality. Neuroticism is quite stable (McCrae & Costa, 1984) and there is growing evidence that it is heritable (Pedersen, Plomin, McClearn, & Friberg, 1988; Rose, Koskenvuo, Kaprio, Sarna, & Langinvainio, 1988; Tellegen et al., 1988).

Many instruments exist for measuring neuroticism (McCrae, 1982). Familiar scales include the Eysenck Personality Inventory Neuroticism Scale (Eysenck &

Eysenck, 1968) and the Neuroticism factor of the NEO Personality Inventory (Costa & McCrae, 1985). Watson and Clark (1984), however, have argued that many scales developed to measure seemingly different dimensions of negative affects (e.g., depression, trait anxiety, and neuroticism) correlate so strongly that they can be interpreted as measuring the same latent construct.

Neuroticism correlates significantly with various measures of illness (see Costa & McCrae, 1987b; H. S. Friedman & Boothe-Kewley, 1987; Watson, 1988; Watson & Pennebaker, 1989, for reviews). Because negative emotions are associated with both autonomic fluctuations and hazardous health behaviors (e.g., smoking, alcohol or substance use; Costa & McCrae, 1987b), such associations suggest that neuroticism may contribute to the development of disease. There is reason to be skeptical, however, since the majority of studies have utilized subjective illness behavior indices (e.g., self-report symptom checklists; Stone & Costa, 1990). As already argued, such measures may reflect tendencies to perceive or report physical sensations as illness symptomology rather than any pathophysiological process. Recent research has, thus, attempted to distinguish between the illness behavior and the psychosomatic effects of neuroticism.

There is evidence that neuroticism is associated with the psychological processes articulated in the illness behavior model (e.g., exaggerated encoding and recall of symptoms; Larsen, 1992). Further, although there are inconsistencies (Persky, Kempthorne-Rawson, & Shekelle, 1987; Shekelle et al., 1981; Somervell et al., 1989), data generally indicate that neuroticism does not predict the objective health measure of mortality (e.g., Almada et al., 1991; Costa & McCrae, 1987b; Dattore, Shontz, & Coyne, 1980; Kaplan & Reynolds, 1988; Keehn, Goldberg, & Beebe, 1974; Zonderman, Costa, & McCrae, 1989). One exception to this pattern is that depression may hasten death in high-risk populations, such as patients with chronic disease (Burton, Kline, Lindsay, & Heidenheim, 1986; Carney, Rich, & Freedland, 1988; Frasure-Smith, Lesperance, & Talajic, 1993). Although neuroticism may be associated with increased behaviorally mediated mortality (e.g., suicide or accidents; Keehn et al., 1974), it does not appear to be a robust risk factor for disease in the general population.

In support of the illness behavior hypothesis, patients complaining of chest pain who have been objectively shown to have healthy arteries score higher on neuroticism than do patients with actual disease or noncomplaining disease-free controls (Costa, Fleg, McCrae, & Lakatta, 1982). Further, some researchers have reported a negative association between indices of neuroticism and arterial occlusion (Barefoot, Beckham, Peterson, Haney, & Williams, 1992; Bass & Wade, 1984; Elias, Robbins, Blow, Rice, & Edgecomb, 1982). Prospective studies indicate that the dispositional tendency to report physical symptoms is associated with increased risk of developing angina-like chest pain syndromes, but not with objective evidence of CHD such as documented myocardial infarction (Shekelle, Vernon, & Ostfeld, 1991). Thus, neuroticism and related traits appear to be associated with cardiac symptom reporting, but not with the development of actual cardiac disease. In summary, available data suggest that neuroticism increases the tendency to perceive, report, or act upon general physical sensations rather than the development of physical illness itself.

The relationship between neuroticism and illness behavior has specific implications for personality and health research. As mentioned above, this area of research has often utilized subjective health measures that are clearly contaminated with neuroticism. Although this approach may provide useful information in the beginning stages of research, investigators must progress beyond this and clearly distinguish the psychological causes of illness behavior from those of actual disease. Second, many personality variables that are commonly studied in the personality and health literature are either conceptually similar to neuroticism or have been found to be associated with neuroticism (e.g., Funk & Houston, 1987; Smith, Pope, Rhodewalt, & Poulton, 1989). Any association between such personality variables and subjective health measures may, therefore, reflect the common influence of neuroticism. Personality and health researchers would benefit from more precisely assessing the personality variables of interest and demonstrating their distinction from broad constructs such as neuroticism. Finally, at a more complex level, many of the variables hypothesized to mediate the effects of personality on health (e.g., stressful life events, social support, and health behaviors) are also correlated with neuroticism (Depue & Monroe, 1986; Schroeder & Costa, 1984). This potential overlap of theoretically different constructs impedes accurate explication of personality–health relationships.

C. Hardiness

The construct of hardiness represents the aggregate of beliefs that life is meaningful, controllable, and challenging rather than threatening (Kobasa, 1979). Such beliefs are theorized to reduce the likelihood that an encountered life event is appraised as stressful, thereby diminishing the potential of that event to induce adverse autonomic arousal (Kobasa, Maddi, Puccetti, & Zola, 1985). Thus, hardiness theory relies heavily on the interactional stress-moderation model.

A variety of hardiness measures have appeared in the literature (see Funk, 1992; Orr & Westman, 1990, for reviews). As discussed below, each has been criticized and there is currently no accepted standard hardiness scale. The initial assessment devices were developed by selecting a battery of existing personality scales that discriminated between high-stress–high-illness and high-stress–low-illness male executives (Kobasa, 1979; Kobasa, Maddi, & Kahn, 1982). Several shortened versions of this battery have appeared in the literature, and a revised 50-item scale is currently being marketed (Personal Views Survey, The Hardiness Institute).

Hardiness has been primarily studied by examining its relationship with self-reported physical symptoms. Most studies indicate that high-hardy subjects report lower levels of concurrent symptoms (Banks & Gannon, 1988; Kobasa et al., 1982; Kobasa & Puccetti, 1983; Rhodewalt & Zone, 1989; Roth, Wiebe, Fillingim, & Shay, 1989; P. W. Williams, Wiebe, & Smith, 1992) and subsequent symptoms than do low-hardy subjects (Banks & Gannon, 1988; Kobasa et al., 1982, 1985; Wiebe & McCallum, 1986).

While these main effects appear consistent with hardiness theory, this interpretation may be misleading for at least two reasons. First, hardiness theory is based on the stress-moderation model, which implies the presence of a statistical interaction between hardiness and stress. Some studies have reported this necessary interaction (Banks & Gannon, 1988; Kobasa et al., 1982; Rhodewalt & Zone, 1989), but others have not (Funk & Houston, 1987; Roth et al., 1989; Schmied & Lawler, 1986; Wiebe & McCallum, 1986). Second, these data are based upon subjective measures of physical symptoms and are open to the interpretation that hardiness influences illness behavior rather than actual illness. This possibility takes on added significance when one considers that the hardiness scales appear heavily contaminated with neuroticism (Allred & Smith, 1989; Funk & Houston, 1987).

In a test of the convergent and discriminant validity of the hardiness scales, Wiebe, Williams, and Smith (1990) found that separate measures of hardiness correlated more strongly with each other than they did with measures of neuroticism. Despite such discrimination, however, hardiness and neuroticism were strongly correlated. This overlap makes it possible that demonstrated associations between hardiness and illness behavior occur as a function of the common influence of neuroticism rather than of the portion of hardiness that is distinct from neuroticism. Direct tests of this possibility indicate that this does occur to some extent (Funk & Houston, 1987; Rhodewalt & Zone, 1989; P. W. Williams et al., 1992).

The physiological mechanisms hypothesized to link hardiness and health have also been studied. Several studies have reported that, in response to laboratory stressors, high-hardy subjects display lower cardiovascular arousal than low-hardy subjects (Contrada, 1989; Wiebe, 1991; Wiebe & Williams, 1992). Allred and Smith (1989), however, reported that high hardiness was associated with increased, rather than decreased, systolic blood pressure responses to evaluative threat.

In addition to such broad tests of hardiness and stress moderation, attempts have been made to identify the specific cognitive mechanisms by which hardiness is theorized to attenuate responses to stress. These studies have primarily focused on the mediating effects of stress appraisal. In support of hardiness theory, low-hardy subjects have been found to make fewer positive self-statements after an evaluative threat task than do high-hardy subjects (Allred & Smith, 1989). These individuals have also been reported to rate the same life experiences (Rhodewalt & Agustsdottir, 1984; Rhodewalt & Zone, 1989) and laboratory stressors (Wiebe, 1991; Wiebe & Williams, 1992) as less positive and controllable than do high-hardy individuals. Finally, some data suggest that such appraisals mediate the relationship between hardiness and health outcomes (Rhodewalt & Zone, 1989; Roth et al., 1989; Wiebe, 1991). Subjectively appraised stress has also been reported to mediate the relationship between hardiness and health behaviors (Wiebe & McCallum, 1986), suggesting that adaptive stress appraisals may impact health by reducing stress-induced health behavior departures.

Although research on the cognitive aspects of hardiness is fairly supportive, the complete body of literature is highly inconsistent. This may reflect problems in the measurement of hardiness. In addition to the documented overlap with neuroticism, the more commonly used hardiness scales have been criticized because they combine three different component scores (commitment, control, and challenge) into one composite index. However, the accuracy of viewing hardiness as a unidimensional construct has been questioned due to inconsistent findings from factor analyses of the hardiness scale and to reports that the commitment and control components predict health outcomes while challenge does not (see Carver, 1989; Funk & Houston, 1987; Hull, Lehn, & Tedlie, 1991; Hull, VanTreuren, & Virnelli, 1987, for reviews). Progress on the health consequences of hardiness is likely to be hampered until such psychometric issues are resolved.

D. Optimism and Explanatory Style

Scheier and Carver (1985, 1992) propose that the personality trait of optimism has beneficial effects on health. They define dispositional optimism as a stable, generalized expectation that good things will happen. In the context of their Control Theory approach to adaptation and self-regulation (Carver & Scheier, 1982), these authors argue that individual differences in optimism are central to the process of adjustment. When individuals recognize a discrepancy between their behavioral goals or standards and their present situation, individual differences in optimism–pessimism influence subsequent actions. Optimists, anticipating positive outcomes, will persist in attempts to reduce the discrepancy between goals and the present situation. That is, optimists should strive to solve problems and cope actively. In contrast, pessimists, anticipating bad outcomes, are likely to exhibit passive or fatalistic responses. Further, the more adaptive coping of optimists should lessen the otherwise deleterious effects of stressors on emotional adjustment and physical health. Thus, this approach clearly conforms to the general interactional stress-moderation model, with an emphasis on individual differences in secondary appraisal and subsequent coping.

To assess individual differences in optimism–pessimism, Scheier and Carver (1985) developed an eight-item Life Orientation Test (LOT). Consistent with predictions, high LOT scores have been found to be associated with reduced reports of physical illness (Scheier & Carver, 1985), higher levels of problem-focused coping, and less use of passive coping strategies such as avoidance (Scheier, Weintraub, & Carver, 1986). In other interesting tests of predictions derived from the model, expectant mothers with high LOT scores are less likely to experience postpartum depression (Carver & Gaines, 1987), and alcoholics with high LOT scores are more likely to complete treatment (Strack, Carver, & Blaney, 1987). Scheier et al. (1989) found that, compared to their pessimistic counterparts, optimistic cardiac surgery patients exhibited more rapid postoperative recoveries and less likelihood of an intraoperative myocardial infarction. Optimism has also been found to predict improved emotional adjustment to breast cancer, an effect that is apparently mediated by adaptive coping responses (Carver et al., 1993).

To evaluate the overlap of neuroticism and optimism, Smith, Pope, Rhodewalt, & Poulton (1989) conducted a convergent-discriminant validity analysis. In three independent samples, the LOT was as closely correlated with two measures of neuroticism as it was with a second measure of optimism—the Generalized Expectancy for Success Scale (Fibel & Hale, 1978). As a result, the LOT could be construed as a measure of neuroticism (i.e., scored in the opposite direction), and at the very least is clearly contaminated with this trait. Such contamination raises the question of whether or not shared variance with neuroticism underlies the correlations of optimism with various indices of coping and adjustment. In two independent samples, statistical control of neuroticism scores eliminated the otherwise significant correlation between optimism and physical symptoms and coping behaviors (Smith, Pope, Rhodewalt, & Poulton, 1989, Studies 1 and 2). These results and others (e.g., Mroczek, Spiro, Aldwin, Ozer, & Bosse, 1993) suggest that some of the findings consistent with the optimism model can be interpreted as reflecting the more basic, established dimension of neuroticism.

From a different conceptual background, Peterson and Seligman (1987) have described a construct similar to optimism. Explanatory style refers to stable patterns of causal attributions individuals make for positive and negative events in their lives. Derived from the learned helplessness framework, an optimistic explanatory style refers to the characteristic tendency to make internal, stable, and global attributions for positive events, and external, unstable, and specific attributions for negative events. The pessimistic explanatory style is characterized by the opposite pattern of causal attributions.

Explanatory style can be assessed with either structured questionnaires or a rating technique using written or verbal descriptions of events. The questionnaire presents a series of hypothetical positive and negative events, and requires causal attribution in response to an open-ended question as well as ratings of the stated cause on the three dimensions. The text-based system is an independent rater-based approach, though it relies on the same attribution dimensions.

Although this approach has not been used extensively in health research, some results suggest that explanatory style may be related to subsequent health (for a review, see Peterson & Seligman, 1987). For example, a pessimistic explanatory style is prospectively related to increased reports of illness, as well as visits to a physician. The interpretive ambiguities of research using illness behavior as an outcome apply to these findings. However, Peterson, Seligman, and Valliant (1988) found that a pessimistic explanatory style was associated with physicians' ratings of subjects as less healthy over a 35-year follow-up. Given the somewhat more objective nature of this health index, this finding is more compelling.

One limitation of these provocative findings concerns assessment procedures. The convergence of the questionnaire and rating approaches is not established, and independent evidence of construct validity is lacking. Thus, something assessed by these techniques may be useful in predicting health outcomes, but just what that dimension is has not been clearly identified. Further, potential mechanisms linking explanatory style and health have not been extensively explored. Preliminary findings, however, suggest that pessimists are less likely to take active steps to treat their illnesses than are optimists (Lin & Peterson, 1990). Thus, maladaptive, passive health behavior in response to initial illness may exacerbate disease, contributing to the associations between explanatory style and health observed in some studies.

E. Inhibited Power Motivation

Power motivation is defined as the desire to have an impact on others by controlling, influencing, aggressing against, or even helping them (McClelland, 1975, 1985). The general conceptual model states that when inhibited or frustrated by psychological processes such as self-restraint or situational factors, power motivation contributes to the development of physical illness. Thus, this is another interactional stress-moderation approach: a motivationally based personality trait interacts with situational factors to influence health.

Inhibited power motivation is assessed through the use of projective techniques, specifically the Thematic Apperception Test. Ratings of responses can be made reliably and are fairly stable over time (see Jemmott, 1987, for review). Independent, thorough evaluations of construct validity, however, have not been reported to date.

Inhibited power motivation has been linked to a variety of health outcomes and pathophysiological mechanisms. In two cross-sectional studies, individuals high in inhibited power motivation were more likely to have high blood pressure (McClelland, 1979). A prospective study found that inhibited power motivation was associated with increased risk of developing hypertension over a 20-year follow-up. Individuals with this motivational dynamic have also been found to report more physical illness (McClelland & Jemmott, 1980). Further, inhibited power motivation has been linked to a reduced immunocompetence that could place such individuals at greater risk for a variety of infections and neoplastic diseases (Jemmott et al., 1983, 1990; McClelland, Alexander, & Marks, 1982; McClelland, Floor, Davidson, & Saron, 1980).

Associations between this personality trait and high blood pressure and suppressed immune functioning suggest plausible pathophysiological mechanisms. Lacking from the available evidence, however, are larger, prospective studies evaluating the utility of this trait in predicting death or objective indications of serious illness. Nevertheless, there are interesting parallels between this model and interactional stress-moderation research with both humans and animals. In humans, the attempt to assert influence or control over others is associated with heightened cardiovascular reactivity (Brown & Smith, 1992; Smith, Baldwin, & Christensen, 1990). Thus, the social behaviors likely to be associated with power and dominance are related to physiological stress responses hypothesized to increase disease risk. In a series of studies by Kaplan, Manuck, and their colleagues (see Manuck, Kaplan, Adams, & Clarkson, 1988, for review), chronic stress induced by repeated reorganization of social groups produced accelerated atherosclerosis in dominant—but not subordinate—male monkeys. The stable individual difference variable of dominance–submission in this animal model is clearly similar to the human motivational variable described by McClelland, and the social reorganization stressor is similar to the situational factors in the power motivation model. Although highly speculative, the elegant and compelling findings from these animal studies suggest that social dominance and power motivation may be useful traits in future personality and health research.

III. LIMITATIONS AND CHALLENGES IN PERSONALITY AND HEALTH RESEARCH

The preceding overview of selected topics in personality and health research clearly documents a flurry of recent activity. Although several areas have produced potentially important findings, recurring limitations are readily apparent. They can be grouped into three categories—personality assessment, model testing, and description versus explanation.

A. Personality Assessment

In each of the previous summaries, the issue of valid personality assessment was raised. In all cases, there was either a lack of sufficient evidence of construct validity or clear evidence of questionable validity. If the only intent of personality and health research was the improved prediction of health outcomes, construct validity would be irrelevant. For example, it would not matter if a scale that was intended to assess Type A behavior actually measured intelligence, because the sole concern regarding the personality measures would be their incremental predictive utility. Research in this field, however, is clearly more ambitious than improved statistical prediction alone. The efforts are intended to test specific conceptual hypotheses about the contribution of personality *constructs* to subsequent health. Yet the task of establishing the construct validity of personality assessments is all too often overlooked.

A related problem is the failure to evaluate the relation of newly proposed scales and constructs to established dimensions of personality. Overlap with neuroticism was a common concern, despite the fact that this dimension has a long history in personality taxonomies. Failure to address this concern creates the possibility of reinventing old traits under new labels (Holroyd & Coyne, 1987). The potential result is an ever-expanding set of unintegrated and misleading literatures.

Both of these assessment problems could be rectified to a large extent by greater use of existing tools in the broader field of personality. Rich and continually refined approaches to measurement are a keystone of personality research, and the emerging consensus regarding the five-factor model as an adequate trait taxonomy (Digman, 1990) would provide an important anchor for integrative efforts. As several authors have argued (Costa & McCrae, 1987a; Smith & Williams, 1992), examining the association between measures used in the personality and health literature and inventories based on the five-factor model of personality structure may be quite useful in this regard.

B. Testing Models of Personality and Health

Even with careful validation of measures, other problems may limit the correspondence between the statistical hypothesis that is tested and the conceptual model that guides it. As has been described, the operational definitions of health and illness have enormous implications for the interpretation of research results. Because of ease and low cost, symptom reports are commonly used to measure illness. Given the interpretive ambiguity resulting from this strategy, this approach is unlikely to produce important increments over existing knowledge.

Even if valid personality assessments are utilized and objective health outcomes are assessed, it is important to recognize which features of the guiding conceptual models have been tested and which have not. For example, despite the fact that the predominant model of the cardiovascular effects of hostility is a person by situation, stress-moderation approach, the major prospective studies of this trait have only examined the main effect of hostility. The predicted interactive effects of individual differences and situational parameters cannot be tested, because no assessments of situational factors are included (Matthews, 1983; Smith, 1989). If the model is correct, the predictive power of the interaction is diluted by collapsing across situation factors.

Similarly, most of these models specify some sort of physiological mechanism linking personality traits and illness. To date, no studies have evaluated the complete path model in which the association between personality and actual physical disease is mediated by a physiological or health behavior mechanism (Krantz & Hedges, 1987). Intermediate strategies of associating personality with psychophysiological reactivity and immune functioning are becoming more common and sophisticated. However, the association between these processes and subsequent illness is far from established. That is, the overall significance of the short-term immunological, neuroendocrine, or cardiovascular correlates of personality in experimental studies is simply not known (Blascovich & Katkin, 1993; Herbert & Cohen, 1993). Thus, the final common pathway in these models is not an established strand in the surrounding nomological net.

In addition to not testing the complete model of personality–health associations, research designs often do not rule out competing explanations of documented relationships. For example, one common approach to testing associations between personality traits and health is the cross-sectional, group comparison design where personality characteristics are contrasted in currently ill and healthy groups. Although useful in preliminary hypothesis testing, significant group differences may actually reflect *somatopsychic* processes rather than psychosomatic effects. That is, personality differences may be the result, rather than the cause, of physical illness.

C. Description versus Explanation

It is clear that many of the most important and formidable challenges in this field involve description. Which measures are reliably related to substantive health outcomes, and which traits do these measures assess? Once such associations are documented, knowledge of *how* personality influences health becomes important. This more explanatory information is likely to be useful in guiding the development of primary and secondary interventions.

In cases where descriptive research supports the pursuit of explanation, developments in personality research could again prove useful. Cognitive and social approaches to personality provide conceptual and methodological tools for understanding dynamic personality processes through which people interpret life tasks and their social environment, regulate and evaluate their behavior, and devise and implement problem-solving strategies. This more recent focus on the "doing" aspects of personality is an important complement to the recent advances in understanding taxonomies and structure, or the "having" side of personality (Cantor, 1990). Thus, once again a more complete use of the larger field of personality research could lead to important progress in understanding psychological influences on health.

IV. CONCLUDING THOUGHTS

The study of personality and health currently confronts both daunting and exciting challenges. The advances in several areas are sufficient to support continued efforts, but simple methodological approaches and incomplete tests of the underlying models threaten the longevity of this psychosomatic renaissance. Evolving medical technologies now provide opportunities for more compelling evaluations of health outcomes and pathophysiological mechanisms than were previously available. Current personality theory, research, and methods contain avenues for addressing critical limitations in research on the psychological side of the psychosomatic equation. Thus, lasting advances in the long-standing issue of the impact of personality on physical health may now be possible through the creative application of recent developments in personality psychology and medicine. We eagerly await such advances.

REFERENCES

Allred, K. D., & Smith, T. W. (1989). The hardy personality: Cognitive and physiological responses to evaluative threat. *Journal of Personality and Social Psychology, 56*, 257–266.

Almada, S. G., Zonderman, A. B., Shekelle, R. B., Dyer, A. R., Daviglus, M. L., Costa, P. T., Jr., & Stamler, J. (1991). Neuroticism and cynicism and risk of death in middle-aged men: The Western Electric Study. *Psychosomatic Medicine, 53*, 165–175.

Angell, M. (1985). Disease as a reflection of the psyche. *New England Journal of Medicine, 312,* 1570–1572.

Bandura, A. (1989). Human agency in social cognitive theory. *American Psychologist, 44,* 1175–1184.

Banks, J. K., & Gannon, L. R. (1988). The influence of hardiness on the relationship between stressors and psychosomatic symptomatology. *American Journal of Community Psychology, 16,* 25–37.

Barefoot, J. C., Beckham, J. C., Peterson, B. L., Haney, T. L., & Williams, R. B. (1992). Measures of neuroticism and disease status in coronary angiography patients. *Journal of Consulting and Clinical Psychology, 60,* 127–132.

Barefoot, J. C., Dodge, K. A., Peterson, B. L., Dahlström, W. G., & Williams, R. B., Jr. (1989). The Cook-Medley Hostility Scale: Item content and ability to predict survival. *Psychosomatic Medicine, 51,* 46–57.

Barefoot, J. C., Siegler, I. C., Nowlin, J. B., Peterson, B., Haney, T. L., & Williams, R. B., Jr. (1987). Suspiciousness, health, and mortality: A follow-up study of 500 older adults. *Psychosomatic Medicine, 49,* 450–457.

Bass, C., & Wade, C. (1984). Chest pain with normal coronary arteries: A comparative study of psychiatric and social morbidity. *Psychological Medicine, 14,* 51–61.

Blair, S. H., Kohl, H. W., Paffenbarger, R. S., Clark, M. S., Cooper, K. H., & Gibbons, L. W. (1989). Physical fitness and all-cause mortality: A prospective study of healthy men and women. *JAMA, Journal of the American Medical Association, 262,* 2395–2401.

Blascovich, J., & Katkin, E. S. (1993). *Cardiovascular reactivity to psychological stress and disease.* Washington, DC: American Psychological Association.

Blumenthal, J. A., Barefoot, J. C., Burg, M. M., & Williams, R. B. (1987). Psychological correlates of hostility among patients undergoing coronary angiography. *British Journal of Medical Psychology, 60,* 349–355.

Bouchard, T. J., Jr., Lylkken, D. T., McGue, M., Segal, B. L., & Tellegen, A. (1990). Sources of human psychological differences: The Minnesota study of twins reared apart. *Science, 250,* 223–228.

Brown, P. C., & Smith, T. W. (1992). Social influence, marriage, and the heart: Cardiovascular consequences of interpersonal control in husbands and wives. *Health Psychology, 11,* 88–96.

Burton, H. J., Kline, S. A., Lindsay, R. M., & Heidenheim, A. P. (1986). The relationship of depression to survival in chronic renal failure. *Psychosomatic Medicine, 48,* 261–269.

Buss, D. M. (1987). Selection, evocation, and manipulation. *Journal of Personality and Social Psychology, 53,* 1214–1221.

Cantor, N. (1990). From thought to behavior: "Having" and "doing" in the study of personality and cognition. *American Psychologist, 45,* 735–750.

Carney, R. M., Rich, M. W., & Freedland, K. E. (1988). Major depressive disorder predicts cardiac events in patients with coronary-artery disease. *Psychosomatic Medicine, 50,* 627–633.

Carson, R. C. (1969). *Interaction concepts in personality.* Chicago: Aldine.

Carver, C. S. (1989). How should multifaceted personality constructs be tested? Issues illustrated by self-monitoring, attributional style, and hardiness. *Journal of Personality and Social Psychology, 56,* 577–585.

Carver, C. S., & Gaines, J. G. (1987). Optimism, pessimism, and post-partum depression. *Cognitive Therapy and Research, 11,* 449–462.

Carver, C. S., Pozo, C., Harris, S. D., Noriega, V., Scheier, M. F., Robinson, D. S., Ketcham, A. S., Moffat, F. L., & Clark, K. L. (1993). How coping mediates the effect of optimism on distress: A study of women with early stage breast cancer. *Journal of Personality and Social Psychology, 65,* 375–390.

Carver, C. S., & Scheier, M. F. (1982). Control theory: A useful conceptual framework for personality—social, clinical, and health psychology. *Psychological Bulletin, 92,* 111–135.

Case, R. B., Heller, S. S., Case, N. B., & Moss, A. J. (1985). Type A behavior and survival after acute myocardial infarction. *New England Journal of Medicine, 312,* 737–741.

Chesney, M. A., Black, G. W., Chadwick, J. H., & Rosenman, R. H. (1981). Psychological correlates of the Type A behavior pattern. *Journal of Behavioral Medicine, 4,* 217–229.

Christensen, A. J., & Smith, T. W. (1993). Cynical hostility and cardiovascular response during self-disclosure. *Psychosomatic Medicine, 55,* 193–202.

Cioffi, D. (1991). Beyond attentional strategies: A cognitive-perceptual model of somatic interpretation. *Psychological Bulletin, 109,* 25–41.

Cohen, F. (1979). Personality, stress, and the development of physical illness. In G. C. Stone, F. Cohen, & N. E. Adler (Eds.), *Health psychology: A handbook* (pp. 77–111). San Francisco: Jossey-Bass.

Contrada, R. J. (1989). Type A behavior, personality hardiness, and cardiovascular response to stress. *Journal of Personality and Social Psychology, 57,* 895–903.

Contrada, R. J., Leventhal, H., & O'Leary, A. (1990). Personality and health. In L. A. Pervin (Ed.), *Handbook of personality: Theory and research* (pp. 638–669). New York: Guilford Press.

Cook, W., & Medley, D. (1954). Proposed hostility and pharisaic virtue scales for the MMPI. *Journal of Applied Psychology, 38,* 414–418.

Cooper, T., Detre, T., & Weiss, S. M. (1981). Coronary-prone behavior and coronary heart disease: A critical review. *Circulation, 63,* 1199–1215.

Costa, P. T., Jr., Fleg, J. L., McCrae, R. R., & Lakatta, E. G. (1982). Neuroticism, coronary artery disease, and chest pain complaints: Cross-sectional and longitudinal studies. *Experimental Aging Research, 8,* 37–44.

Costa, P. T., Jr., & McCrae, R. R. (1980). Somatic complaints in males as a function of age and neuroticism: A longitudinal analysis. *Journal of Behavioral Medicine, 3,* 245–257.

Costa, P. T., Jr., & McCrae, R. R. (1985). *The NEO Personality Inventory manual.* Odessa, FL: Psychological Assessment Resources.

Costa, P. T., Jr., & McCrae, R. R. (1987a). Personality assessment in psychosomatic medicine. In T. M. Wise (Ed.), *Advances in psychosomatic medicine* (pp. 71–82). Basel: Karger.

Costa, P. T., Jr., & McCrae, R. R. (1987b). Neuroticism, somatic complaints, and disease: Is the bark worse than the bite? *Journal of Personality, 55,* 299–316.

Coyne, J., & Holroyd, K. (1982). Stress, coping, and illness: A transactional perspective. In T. Millon, C. Green, & R. Meagbee (Eds.), *Handbook of clinical health psychology* (pp. 105–127). New York: Plenum Press.

Dattore, P. J., Shontz, F. C., & Coyne, L. (1980). Premorbid personality differentiation of cancer and non-cancer groups: A test of the hypothesis of cancer proneness. *Journal of Consulting and Clinical Psychology, 48,* 388–394.

Dembroski, T. M., MacDougall, J. M., Costa, P. T., Jr., & Grandits, G. A. (1989). Components of hostility as predictors of sudden death and myocardial infarction in the Multiple Risk Factor Intervention Trial. *Psychosomatic Medicine, 51,* 514–522.

Depue, R. A., & Monroe, S. M. (1986). Conceptualization and measurement of human disorder in life stress research: The problem of chronic disturbance. *Psychological Bulletin, 99,* 36–51.

Digman, J. M. (1990). Personality structure: Emergence of the five-factor model. *Annual Review of Psychology, 41,* 417–440.

Elias, M. F., Robbins, M. A., Blow, F. C., Rice, A. P., & Edgecomb, T. L. (1982). Symptom reporting anxiety, and depression in arteriographically classified middle-aged chest pain patients. *Experimental Aging Research, 8,* 45–51.

Eysenck, H. J., & Eysenck, S. B. (1968). *Eysenck Personality Questionnaire manual.* San Diego, CA: Educational and Industrial Testing Service.

Fibel, B., & Hale, W. D. (1978). The Generalized Expectancy for Success Scale—A new measure. *Journal of Consulting and Clinical Psychology, 46,* 924–931.

Frasure-Smith, N., Lesperance, F., & Talajic, M. (1993). Depression following myocardial infarction: Impact on six-month survival. *JAMA, Journal of the American Medical Association, 270,* 1819–1825.

Friedman, H. S., & Booth-Kewley, S. (1987). The "disease-prone personality": A meta-analytic view of the construct. *American Psychologist, 42,* 539–555.

Friedman, M., & Rosenman, R. H. (1959). Association of a specific overt behavior pattern with increases in blood cholesterol, blood clotting time, incidence of arcus senilis and clinical coronary artery disease. *JAMA, Journal of the American Medical Association, 169,* 1286–1296.

Friedman, M., & Rosenman, R. H. (1974). *Type A behavior and your heart.* New York: Knopf.

Funk, S. C. (1992). Hardiness: A review of theory and research. *Health Psychology, 11,* 335–345.

Funk, S. C., & Houston, B. K. (1987). A critical analysis of the Hardiness Scale's validity and utility. *Journal of Personality and Social Psychology, 53,* 572–578.

Glass, D. C. (1977). *Behavior patterns, stress, and coronary disease.* Hillsdale, NJ: Erlbaum.

Harbin, T. J. (1989). The relationship between Type A behavior pattern and physiological responsivity: A quantitative review. *Psychophysiology, 26,* 110–119.

Hardy, J. D., & Smith, T. W. (1988). Cynical hostility and vulnerability to disease: Social support, life stress, and physiological response to conflict. *Health Psychology, 7,* 447–459.

Harris, D. M., & Guten, G. (1979). Health protective behavior: An exploratory study. *Journal of Health and Social Behavior, 20,* 17–29.

Haynes, S. G., Feinleib, M., & Kannel, W. B. (1980). The relationship of psychosocial factors to coronary heart disease in the Framingham Study: III. Eight-year incidence of coronary heart disease. *American Journal of Epidemiology, 111,* 37–58.

Hearn, M. D., Murray, D. M., & Leupker, R. V. (1989). Hostility, coronary heart disease, and total mortality: A 33-year follow-up study of university students. *Journal of Behavioral Medicine, 12,* 105–121.

Hecker, M. H. L., Chesney, M. A., Black, G. W., & Frautchi, N. (1988). Coronary-prone behaviors in the Western Collaborative Group Study. *Psychosomatic Medicine, 50,* 153–164.

Herbert, T. B., & Cohen, S. (1993). Stress and immunity: A meta-analytic review. *Psychosomatic Medicine, 55,* 364–379.

Holroyd, K. A., & Coyne, J. C. (1987). Personality and health in the 1980s: Psychosomatic medicine revisited? *Journal of Personality, 55,* 359–375.

Horowitz, M. J., Berfari, R., Hulley, S., Blair, S., Alvarez, W., Borhani, N., Reynolds, A., & Simon, N. (1979). Life events, risk factors, and coronary disease. *Psychosomatics, 20,* 586–592.

Houston, B. K. (1988). Cardiovascular and neuroendocrine reactivity, global Type A, and components of Type A behavior. In B. K. Houston & C. R. Snyder (Eds.), *Type A behavior pattern: Research, theory, and intervention* (pp. 212–253). New York: Wiley.

Houston, B. K. (1989). Personality dimensions in reactivity and cardiovascular disease. In N. Schneiderman, S. M., Weiss, & P. G. Kaufman (Eds.), *Handbook of research methods in cardiovascular behavioral medicine* (pp. 495–509). New York: Plenum Press.

Houston, B. K., Chesney, M. A., Black, G. W., Cates, D. S., & Hecker, M. H. L. (1992). Behavioral clusters and coronary heart disease risk. *Psychosomatic Medicine, 54,* 447–461.

Houston, B. K., & Kelley, K. E. (1989). Hostility in employed women: Relation to work and marital experiences, social support, stress, and anger expression. *Personality and Social Psychology Bulletin, 15,* 175–182.

Hull, J. G., Lehn, D. A., & Tedlie, J. C. (1991). A general approach to testing multifaceted personality constructs. *Journal of Personality and Social Psychology, 61,* 932–945.

Hull, J. G., VanTreuren, R. R., & Virnelli, S. (1987). Hardiness and health: A critique and alternative approach. *Journal of Personality and Social Psychology, 53,* 518–530.

Idler, E. L., Kasl, S. V., & Lemke, J. H. (1990). Self-evaluated health and mortality among the elderly in New Haven, Connecticut and Iowa and Washington Counties, Iowa, 1982–1986. *American Journal of Epidemiology, 131,* 91–103.

Jemmott, J. B., III. (1987). Social motives and susceptibility to disease: Stalking individual differences in health risks. *Journal of Personality, 55,* 267–298.

Jemmott, J. B., III, Borysenko, J. Z., Boresenko, M., McClelland, D. C., Chapman, R., Meyer, D., & Benson, H. (1983). Academic stress, power motivation, and decrease in salivary secretory immunoglobulin A secretion rate. *Lancet, 1,* 1400–1402.

Jemmott, J. B., III, Hellman, C., McClelland, D. C., Locke, S. E., Kraus, L., Williams, R. M., & Valeri, C. R. (1990). Motivational syndromes associated with natural killer cell activity. *Journal of Behavioral Medicine, 13,* 53–73.

Jenkins, C. D., Rosenman, R. H., & Zyzanski, S. J. (1974). Prediction of clinical coronary heart disease by a test for the coronary-prone behavior pattern. *New England Journal of Medicine, 23,* 1271–1275.

Kaplan, G. A., & Camacho, T. (1983). Perceived health and mortality: A nine-year follow-up of the Human Population Laboratory cohort. *American Journal of Epidemiology, 117,* 292–304.

Kaplan, G. A., & Kotler, P. L. (1985). Self-reports predictive of mortality from ischemic heart disease: A nine-year follow-up of the Human Population Laboratory cohort. *Journal of Chronic Diseases, 38,* 195–201.

Kaplan, G. A., & Reynolds, P. (1988). Depression and cancer mortality and morbidity: Prospective evidence from the Marneda County Study. *Journal of Behavioral Medicine, 11,* 1–13.

Keehn, R. J., Goldberg, I. D., & Beebe, G. W. (1974). Twenty-four-year mortality follow-up of army veterans with disability separations for psychoneurosis in 1944. *Psychosomatic Medicine, 36,* 27–46.

Kobasa, S. C. (1979). Stressful life events, personality and health: An inquiry into hardiness. *Journal of Personality and Social Psychology, 37,* 1–11.

Kobasa, S. C., Maddi, S. R., & Kahn, S. (1982). Hardiness and health. A prospective study. *Journal of Personality and Social Psychology, 42,* 168–177.

Kobasa, S. C., Maddi, S. R., Puccetti, M. C., & Zola, M. A. (1985). Effectiveness of hardiness, exercise, and social support as resources against illness. *Journal of Psychosomatic Research, 29,* 525–533.

Kobasa, S. C., & Puccetti, M. C. (1983). Personality and social resources in stress resistance. *Journal of Personality and Social Psychology, 45,* 839–850.

Koskenvuo, M., Kapiro, J., Rose, R. J., Kesaniemi, A., Sarna, S., Heikkila, K., & Langinvainio, H. (1988). Hostility as a risk factor for mortality and ischemic heart disease in men. *Psychosomatic Medicine, 50,* 330–340.

Krantz, D. S., & Durel, L. A. (1983). Psychobiological substrates of the Type A behavior pattern. *Health Psychology, 2,* 393–411.

Krantz, D. S., & Hedges, S. M. (1987). Some cautions for research on personality and health. *Journal of Personality, 55,* 351–357.

Krantz, D. S., & Manuck, S. B. (1984). Acute psychophysiologic reactivity and risk of cardiovascular disease: A review and methodological critique. *Psychological Bulletin, 96,* 435–464.

Langlie, J. K. (1977). Social networks, health beliefs, and preventive health behavior. *Journal of Health and Social Behaviors, 18,* 244–260.

Larsen, R. J. (1992). Neuroticism and selective encoding and recall of symptoms: Evidence from a combined concurrent-retrospective study. *Journal of Personality and Social Psychology, 62,* 480–488.

Lau, R. R. (1988). Beliefs about control and health behavior. In D. S. Gochman (Ed.), *Health behavior: Emerging research perspectives* (pp. 43–63). New York: Plenum Press.

Lazarus, R. S. (1990). Stress, coping, and illness. In H. S. Friedman (Ed.), *Personality and disease* (pp. 97–120). New York: Wiley.

Lazarus, R. S., & Folkman, S. (1984). *Stress, appraisal, and coping.* New York: Springer.

Leiker, M., & Hailey, B. J. (1988). A link between hostility and disease: Poor health habits? *Behavioral Medicine, 3,* 129–133.

Leon, G. R., Finn, S. E., Murray, D., & Bailey, J. M. (1988). The inability to predict cardiovascular disease from hostility scores or MMPI items related to Type A behavior. *Journal of Consulting and Clinical Psychology, 56,* 597–600.

Leventhal, H., Prohaska, T. R., & Hirschman, R. S. (1985). Preventive health behavior across the life span. In J. C. Rosen & L. J. Solomon (Eds.), *Prevention in health Psychology* (Vol. 8, pp. 199–235). Hanover, NH: University Press of New England.

Lin, E. H., & Peterson, C. (1990). Pessimistic explanatory style and response to illness. *Behaviour Research and Therapy, 28,* 243–248.

Maddox, G. L., & Douglas, E. B. (1973). Self-assessment and health: A longitudinal study of elderly subjects. *Journal of Health and Social Behavior, 14,* 87–93.

Manuck, S. B., Kaplan, J. R., Adams, M. R., & Clarkson, T. B. (1988). Effects of stress and the sympathetic nervous system on coronary artery disease in the cynomolgus macaque. *American Heart Journal, 116,* 328–333.

Matthews, K. A. (1983). Assessment issues in coronary-prone behavior. In T. M. Dembroski, T. H. Schmidt, & G. Blumchen (Eds.), *Biobehavioral bases of coronary heart disease* (pp. 62–78). Basel: Karger.

Matthews, K. A. (1988). CHD and Type A behavior: Update on and alternative to the Booth-Kewley and Friedman quantitative review. *Psychological Bulletin, 104,* 373–380.

Matthews, K. A., Glass, D. C., Rosenman, R. H., & Bortner, R. W. (1977). Competitive drive, Pattern A, and coronary disease: A further analysis of some data from the Western Collaborative Group Study. *Journal of Chronic Diseases, 30,* 489–498.

Matthews, K. A., Krantz, D. S., Dembroski, T. M., & MacDougall, J. M. (1982). Unique and common variance in structured interview and Jenkins Activity Survey measures of the Type A behavior pattern. *Journal of Personality and Social Psychology, 42,* 303–313.

McClelland, D. C. (1975). *Power: The inner experience.* New York: Irvington-Halsted.

McClelland, D. C. (1979). Inhibited power motivation and high blood pressure in men. *Journal of Abnormal Psychology, 88,* 182–190.

McClelland, D. C. (1985). *Human motivation.* Glenview, IL: Scott-Foresman.

McClelland, D. C., Alexander, C., & Marks, E. (1982). The need for power, stress, immune function, and illness among male prisoners. *Journal of Abnormal Psychology, 91,* 61–70.

McClelland, D. C., Floor, E., Davidson, R. J., & Saron, C. (1980). Stressed power motivation, sympathetic activation, immune function, and illness. *Journal of Human Stress, 6*(2), 11–19.

McClelland, D. C., & Jemmott, J. B., III. (1980). Power motivation, stress, and physical illness. *Journal of Human Stress, 6*(4), 6–15.

McCrae, R. R. (1982). Consensual validation of personality traits: Evidence from self-reports and ratings. *Journal of Personality and Social Psychology, 43,* 293–303.

McCrae, R. R., & Costa, P. T., Jr. (1984). *Emerging lives, enduring dispositions: Personality in adulthood.* Boston: Little, Brown.

McCrae, R. R., Costa, P. R., Jr., & Bosse, R. (1978). Anxiety, extraversion, and smoking. *British Journal of Social and Clinical Psychology, 17,* 269–273.

Mechanic, D. (1979). The stability of health and illness behavior: Results from a 16-year follow-up. *American Journal of Public Health, 69,* 1142–1145.

Menkes, M. S., Matthews, K. A., Krantz, D. S., Lundberg, U., Mead, L. A., Qaqish, B., Liang, K., Thomas, C. B., & Pearson, T. A. (1989). Cardiovascular reactivity to the cold pressor test as a predictor of hypertension. *Hypertension, 14,* 524–530.

Miller, T. Q., Smith, T. W., Turner, C. W., Guijarro, M. L., & Hallett, A. J. (1996). *A meta-analytic review of research on hostility and physical health. Psychological Bulletin, 119,* 322–348.

Miller, T. Q., Turner, C. W., Tindale, R. S., Posovac, E. J., & Dugoni, B. (1991). Reasons for the trend toward null findings in research on Type A behavior. *Psychological Bulletin, 110,* 469–485.

Mroczek, D. K., Spiro, A., Aldwin, C. M., Ozer, D. J., & Bosse, R. (1993). Construct validation of optimism and pessimism in older men: Findings from the Normative Aging Study. *Health Psychology, 12,* 406–409.

O'Leary, A. (1990). Stress, emotion, and human immune function. *Psychological Bulletin, 108,* 363–382.

Orr, E., & Westman, M. (1990). Does hardiness moderate stress, and how?: A review. In M. Rosenbaum (Ed.), *Learned resourcefulness: On coping skills, self control, and adaptive behavior* (pp. 64–94). New York: Springer.

Paffenbarger, R. S., & Hale, W. E. (1975). Work activity and coronary heart mortality. *New England Journal of Medicine, 292,* 545–550.

Pedersen, N. L., Plomin, R., McClearn, G. E., & Friberg, L. (1988). Neuroticism, extraversion, and related traits in adult twins reared apart and reared together. *Journal of Personality and Social Psychology, 55,* 950–957.

Pennebaker, J. W. (1982). *The psychology of physical symptoms.* New York: Springer-Verlag.

Persky, V. W., Kempthorne-Rawson, J., & Shekelle, R. B. (1987). Personality and risk of cancer: 20-year follow-up of the Western Electric Study. *Psychosomatic Medicine, 49*, 435–449.

Peterson, C., & Seligman, M. E. P. (1987). Explanatory style and illness. *Journal of Personality, 55*, 237–265.

Peterson, C., Seligman, M. E. P., & Vaillant, G. E. (1988). Pessimistic explanatory style is a risk factor for physical illness: A thirty-five-year longitudinal study. *Journal of Personality and Social Psychology, 55*, 23–27.

Price, V. A. (1982). *Type A behavior pattern: A model for research and practice.* New York: Academic Press.

Rabkin, J. G., & Struening, E. H. (1976). Life events, stress, and illness. *Science, 194*, 1013–1020.

Ragland, D. R. & Brand, R. J. (1988). Type A behavior and mortality from coronary heart disease. *New England Journal of Medicine, 318*, 65–69.

Rask, M. K. (1990). *Mediating variables in the cynical hostility and health relationship.* Unpublished doctoral dissertation, University of Utah, Salt Lake City.

Rhodewalt, F., & Agustsdottir, S. (1984). On the relationship of hardiness to the Type A behavior pattern: Perception of life events versus coping with life events. *Journal of Research in Personality, 18*, 212–223.

Rhodewalt, F., & Zone, J. B. (1989). Appraisal of life change, depression, and illness in hardy and nonhardy women. *Journal of Personality and Social Psychology, 56*, 81–88.

Rose, R. J., Koskenuvo, M., Kaprio, J., Sarna, S., & Langinvainio, H. (1988). Shared genes, shared experiences, and similarity of personality: Data from 14,288 adult Finnish 10-twins. *Journal of Personality and Social Psychology, 54*, 161–171.

Rosenman, R. H. (1978). The interview method of assessment of the coronary-prone behavior pattern. In T. M. Dembroski, S. M. Weiss, J. L. Shields, S. G. Haynes, & M. Feinleib (Eds.), *Coronary-prone behavior* (pp. 55–70). New York: Springer-Verlag.

Roth, D. L., Wiebe, D. J., Fillingim, R. B., & Shay, K. A. (1989). Life events, fitness, hardiness, and health: A simultaneous analysis of proposed stress-resistance effects. *Journal of Personality and Social Psychology, 57*, 136–142.

Schachter, S., Silverstein, B., Kozlowski, E. T., Herman, L. P., & Liebling, B. (1977). Effects of stress on cigarette smoking and urinary pH. *Journal of Experimental Psychology: General, 106*, 24–30.

Scheier, M. F., & Carver, C. S. (1985). Optimism, coping, and health: Assessment and implications of generalized outcome expectancies. *Health Psychology, 4*, 219–247.

Scheier, M. F., & Carver, C. S. (1992). Effects of optimism on psychological and physical well-being: Theoretical overview and empirical update. *Cognitive Therapy and Research, 16*, 201–228.

Scheier, M. F., Matthews, K. A., Owens, J. F., Magovern, G. J., Lefebvre, R. C., Abbott, R. A., & Carver, C. S. (1989). Dispositional optimism and recovery from coronary artery bypass surgery: The beneficial effects on physical and psychological well-being. *Journal of Personality and Social Psychology, 57*, 1024–1040.

Scheier, M. F., Weintraub, J. K., & Carver, C. S. (1986). Coping with stress: Divergent strategies of optimists and pessimists. *Journal of Personality and Social Psychology, 51*, 1257–1264.

Schmied, L. A., & Lawler, K. A. (1986). Hardiness, Type A behavior, and the stress-illness relationship in working women. *Journal of Personality and Social Psychology, 51*, 1218–1223.

Schroeder, D. H., & Costa, P. T., Jr. (1984). Influence of life event stress on physical illness: Substantive effects on methodological flaws? *Journal of Personality and Social Psychology, 46,* 853–863.

Selye, H. (1956). *The stress of life.* New York: McGraw-Hill.

Shekelle, R. B., Gale, M., & Norusis, M. (1985). Type A score (Jenkins Activity Survey) and risk of recurrent coronary heart disease in the Aspirin Myocardial Infarction Study. *American Journal of Cardiology, 56,* 221–225.

Shekelle, R. B., Gale, M., Ostfeld, A. M., & Paul, O. (1983). Hostility, risk of coronary heart disease, and mortality. *Psychosomatic Medicine, 45,* 109–114.

Shekelle, R. B., Raynor, W. J., Ostfeld, A. M., Garron, D. C., Bieliauskas, L. A., Liu, S. C., Maliza, C., & Paul, O. (1981). Psychological depression and 17-year risk death from cancer. *Psychosomatic Medicine, 43,* 117–125.

Shekelle, R. B., Vernon, S. W., & Ostfeld, A. M. (1991). Personality and coronary heart disease. *Psychosomatic Medicine, 53,* 176–184.

Smith, T. W. (1989). Interactions, transactions, and the Type A pattern: Additional avenues in the search for coronary-prone behavior. In A. W. Siegman & T. M. Dembroski (Eds.), *In search for coronary-prone behavior* (pp. 91–116). Hillsdale, NJ: Erlbaum.

Smith, T. W. (1992). Hostility and health: Current status of a psychosomatic hypothesis. *Health Psychology, 11,* 88–96.

Smith, T. W. (1994). Concepts and methods in the study of anger, hostility, and health. In A. W. Siegman & T. W. Smith (Eds.), *Anger, hostility, and the heart* (pp. 23–42). Hillsdale, NJ: Erlbaum.

Smith, T. W., & Allred, K. A. (1989). Blood pressure responses during social interaction in high and low cynically hostile males. *Journal of Behavioral Medicine, 12,* 135–143.

Smith, T. W., & Anderson, N. B. (1986). Models of personality and disease: An interactional approach to Type A behavior and cardiovascular risk. *Journal of Personality and Social Psychology, 50,* 1166–1173.

Smith, T. W., Baldwin, M., & Christensen, A. J. (1990). Interpersonal Influence as active coping: Effects of task difficulty on cardiovascular reactivity. *Psychophysiology, 27,* 429–437.

Smith, T. W., & Christensen, A. J. (1992). Cardiovascular reactivity and interpersonal relations: Psychosomatic processes in social context. *Journal of Social and Clinical Psychology, 11,* 279–301.

Smith, T. W., & Frohm, K. D. (1985). What's so unhealthy about hostility? Construct validity and psychosocial correlates of the Cook and Medley Ho Scale. *Health Psychology, 4,* 503–520.

Smith, T. W., O'Keeffe, J. L., Allred, K. D. (1989). Neuroticism, symptom reports, and Type A behavior: Interpretive cautions for the Framingham scale. *Journal of Behavioral Medicine, 12,* 1–11.

Smith, T. W., & Pope, M. K. (1990). Cynical hostility as a health risk: Current status and future directions. *Journal of Social Behavior and Personality, 5,* 77–88.

Smith, T. W., Pope, M. K., Rhodewalt, F., & Poulton, J. L. (1989). Optimism, neuroticism, coping, and symptom reports: An alternative interpretation of the Life Orientation Test. *Journal of Personality and Social Psychology, 56,* 640–648.

Smith, T. W., Pope, M. K., Sanders, J. D., Allred, K. D., & O'Keeffe, J. L. (1988). Cynical hostility at home and work: Psychosocial vulnerability across domains. *Journal of Research in Personality, 22,* 525–548.

Smith, T. W., & Williams, P. G. (1992). Personality and health: Advantages and Limitations of the Five Factor Model. *Journal of Personality, 60,* 395–423.

Somervell, P. D., Kaplan, B. H., Heiss, G., Tyroler, H. A., Kleinbaum, D. G., & Obrist, P. A. (1989). Psychologic distress as a predictor of mortality. *American Journal of Epidemiology, 130,* 1013–1023.

Stone, S. V., & Costa, P. T., Jr. (1990). Disease-prone personality or distress-prone personality? The role of neuroticism in coronary heart disease. In H. S. Friedman (Ed.), *Personality and disease* (pp. 178–200). New York: Wiley.

Strack, S., Carver, C. S., & Blaney, P. H. (1987). Predicting successful completion of an aftercare program following treatment for alcoholism: The role of dispositional optimism. *Journal of Personality and Social Psychology, 53,* 579–584.

Strickland, B. R. (1978). Internal-external expectancies and health-related behaviors. *Journal of Consulting and Clinical Psychology, 46,* 1192–1211.

Suarez, E. C., & Williams, R. B., Jr. (1989). Situational determinants of cardiovascular and emotional reactivity in high and low hostile men. *Psychosomatic Medicine, 51,* 404–418.

Suls, J., & Rittenhouse, J. D. (1987). Personality and health: An introduction. *Journal of Personality, 55,* 155–167.

Suls, J., & Rittenhouse, J. D. (1990). Models of linkages between personality and disease. In H. S. Friedman (Ed.), *Personality and disease* (pp. 38–64). New York: Wiley.

Suls, J., & Sanders, G. S. (1989). Why do some behavioral styles place people at coronary risk? In A. W. Siegman & T. M. Dembroski (Eds.), *In search of coronary-prone behavior* (pp. 1–20). Hillsdale, NJ: Erlbaum.

Tellegen, A., Lykken, D. T., Bouchard, T. J., Jr., Wilcox, K. J., Segal, N. L., & Rich, S. (1988). Personality similarity in twins reared apart and together. *Journal of Personality and Social Psychology, 54,* 1031–1039.

Wachtel, P. L. (1977). *Psychoanalysis and behavior therapy.* New York: Basic Books.

Watson, D. (1988). Intraindividual and interindividual analyses of positive and negative affect: Their relation to health complaints, perceived stress, and daily activities. *Journal of Personality and Social Psychology, 54,* 1020–1030.

Watson, D., & Clark, L. A. (1984). Negative affectivity: The disposition to experience aversive emotional states. *Psychological Bulletin, 96,* 465–490.

Watson, D., & Pennebaker, J. W. (1989). Health complaints, stress, and distress: Exploring the central role of negative affectivity. *Psychological Review, 96,* 234–254.

Wiebe, D. J. (1991). Hardiness and stress moderation: A test of proposed mechanisms. *Journal of Personality and Social Psychology, 60,* 89–99.

Wiebe, D. J., & McCallum, D. M. (1986). Health practices and hardiness as mediators in the stress-illness relationship. *Health Psychology, 5,* 425–438.

Wiebe, D. J., & Williams, P. G. (1992). Hardiness and health: A social psychophysiological perspective on stress and adaptation. *Journal of Social and Clinical Psychology, 11,* 238–262.

Wiebe, D. J., Williams, P. W., & Smith, T. W. (1990). *Hardiness and neuroticism: Overlapping constructs?* Paper presented at the 11th annual meeting of the Society of Behavioral Medicine, Chicago.

Williams, P. W., Wiebe, D. J., & Smith, T. W. (1992). Coping processes as mediators of the relationship between hardiness and health. *Journal of Behavioral Medicine, 15,* 237–255.

Williams, R. B., Jr., Barefoot, J. C., & Shekelle, R. B. (1985). The health consequences of hostility. In M. A. Chesney & R. H. Rosenman (Eds.), *Anger and hostility in cardiovascular and behavioral disorders* (pp. 173–185). New York: Hemisphere.

Williams, R. B., Jr., Haney, T. L., Lee, K. L., Kong, Y., Blumenthal, J., & Whalen, R. (1980). Type A behavior, hostility, and coronary atherosclerosis. *Psychosomatic Medicine, 42,* 539–549.

Zonderman, A. B., Costa, P. T., & McCrae, R. R. (1989). Depression as a risk for cancer mortality in a nationally representative sample. *JAMA, Journal of the American Medical Association, 262,* 1191–1195.

PERSONALITY DIAGNOSIS AND PERSONALITY DISORDERS

LESLIE C. MOREY

VANDERBILT UNIVERSITY

I. INTRODUCTION

The conceptualization of personality disorder represents a particular challenge to research in the areas of personality and abnormal psychology. In part, this difficulty stems from the puzzling and inconsistent behavior of individuals bearing this diagnosis, but it also reflects the vague and ill-defined nature of the very concept of personality disorder. As a further complication, the very definition of personality disorder has undergone changes in recent years.

At present, there are a number of competing approaches for the understanding and representation of personality disorder. Some of these models are tied to specific etiological theories, while other are more descriptive in nature. This chapter provides an overview of the major approaches that have been proposed for conceptualizing these disorders. In addition, important controversies in the area will be explored, including issues pertaining to the diagnosis, temporal and cross-situational stability, and validity of these concepts.

II. THE HISTORY OF PERSONALITY DISORDER

The concept of personality disorder likely has a history as lengthy as the conceptual history of personality. The ancient appreciation of undesirable and maladaptive character traits was apparent in the works of many classical dramatists and authors as well as in the doctrine of the four humors and their corresponding temperaments. Modern psychiatric concepts of personality disorder probably had their roots in Pinel's concept of *manie sans delire,* or madness without loss of reason. These individuals were thought to typically present with disordered behavior and emotional instability, but with no corresponding loss of contact with reality. Prichard further expanded upon this concept by elaborating the features of what he called *moral insanity* (Mack, 1975). Prichard emphasized that these cases of insanity did not suffer from a deterioration of the intellectual faculties, but rather were impaired in "feelings, temper, or habits." Furthermore, these impairments were seen as variations of "natural" behaviors, rather than as qualitatively distinct or "unnatural" behaviors. In proposing this idea. Prichard greatly expand the boundaries of the concept of insanity, which under his writings included current notions such as personality disorder and substance dependence. Prior to this time, conduct of this sort would have largely been considered a moral shortcoming, to be dealt with by religious and/or legal authorities.

Toward the end of the 19th century, Koch (1891) introduced the term "psychopathic" as a personality descriptor. This personality style tended to be an affliction of the community, typically criminal or other antisocial behavior. This label became popular within European psychiatric schools, and many writers of the time speculated that the psychopathic character resulted from some abnormal hereditary disposition. Emil Kraepelin, the preeminent nosographer of his day, described different varieties of psychopathic personalities (e.g., "born criminals") that he felt represented individuals in undeveloped stages of psychosis, which were largely constitutional in origin (Kraepelin, 1902). Similarly, Birnbaum and Gruhle also proposed genetic mechanisms underlying such character defects (Schneider, 1923/1958).

Kurt Schneider's approach to personality disorder was noteworthy in that his concept was both broader and more precisely demarcated from other forms of mental disorder. Schneider (1923/1958) described two concepts, *abnormal personality* and *psychopathic personality.* Abnormal personality was defined as

> a variation upon an accepted yet broadly conceived range of average personality. The variation may be expressed as an excess or deficiency of certain personal qualities and whether this is judged good or bad is immaterial to the issue. The saint and the poet are equally abnormal as the criminal. All three of them fall outside the range of average personality as we conceive it so that all persons of note may be classed as abnormal personalities.
>
> *(Schneider, 1923/1958, pp. 2–3)*

Schneider's *psychopathic personality* concept was analogous to what is currently called personality disorder (the term "psychopathic" was used in reference to "psychopathological," rather than referring to antisocial behavior). For Schneider, abnormal personality becomes personality disorder when it either (1) causes a person to suffer because of his or her abnormality or (2) causes the community to suffer because of one's abnormality. Thus, Schneider's definition of disordered personality was based upon two criteria, one being statistical rarity and the other being the impact of the personality upon the person and upon society. In doing so, Schneider sought to remove the "moral judgment" implicit in definitions such as that offered by Prichard. Furthermore, Schneider was dissatisfied with the biological definition offered by investigators such as Kraepelin. According to Schneider,

> Abnormal (psychopathic) personality may apparently be based upon some specific bodily condition but the antecedents are not morbid organic processes. They are morphological and functional variations which it would strain reasonable conjecture to suppose are not in some way formative of the condition. The associated psychic abnormalities cannot therefore be regarded rightly as morbid phenomena and there seems to be no logical ground for calling the resultant personalities sick ones.
>
> *(Schneider, 1923/1958, pp. 9–10)*

Schneider identified a number of distinct types of personality which were precursors to many contemporary concepts. His classification of 10 psychopathic personality types provided the first widely used descriptive scheme for personality disorder in psychiatry (Vaillant, 1987). Schneider's personality types have been found to have significant relationships to current personality disorder concepts (Standage, 1986). In fact, certain writers have proposed that the few Schneiderian types which do not have direct contemporary equivalents, such as *hyperthymic personality,* should also be included due to their theoretical importance and clinical utility.

A. Early Psychoanalytic Models of Personality Disorder

Freud's 1908 paper entitled "Character and Anal Eroticism" stimulated thinking about the development of personality traits and development, in contrast to the development of symptomatic features with which psychoanalysis had been primarily concerned prior to that time. However, Freud's interests along this line seemed limited to identifying derivatives of instinctual drives, and his writings on broader forms of personality functioning were not extensive. In contrast, Jung paid particular attention to personality and individual differences, most notably in his well-known personality typology (Jung, 1923). Jung identified certain dichotomous attitude types and function types which accounted for important individual differences, with the most fundamental of these involving the difference between the *introverted* and the *extroverted* attitude types. Interestingly, despite Jung's close association with the developmental theory of Freud, he felt that such fundamental differences were likely to be inborn, writing, "two children of the same mother may exhibit contrary attitudes at an early age, though no change in the mother's attitude can be demonstrated. Although nothing would induce me to underrate the incalculable importance of parental influence, this familar experience compels me to conclude that the decisive factor must be looked for in the disposition of the child" (Jung, 1923, p. 415).

Of Freud's followers, Franz Alexander and Wilhelm Reich were of particular importance in the development of psychoanalytic concepts of personality disorder. Alexander drew the distinction between symptomatic neuroses and character neuroses (i.e., personality disorder) on the basis of the primary mode of instinct gratification and the type of conflicts typically noted with these types of patients. According to Alexander, instinctual gratification could be differentiated into the *autoplastic* mode, where the locus of gratification was internal to the patient and impulses were gratified symbolically, and the *alloplastic* mode, where gratification results primarily from external objects and impulses were acted out. The former mode was characteristic of the symptomatic neuroses, while the latter defined personality disorder.

Among the psychoanalytic theorists, Wilhelm Reich also was one of the most important writers in the area of personality and character. Reich extended Freud's writings in the area of character formation and delineated a number of character disorders, including among others the impulsive, hysterical, and masochistic types. Reich's discussions were central in the development of the concept of character disorders as ego syntonic (as opposed to ego dystonic) disturbances. In early psychoanalytic writings, those disorders amenable to psychoanalysis were *ego-dystonic* in that the symptoms represented manifestations of impulses unacceptable to the ego. In contrast, *ego-syntonic* experiences were those phenomena consistent with the goals of the ego. For Reich, this distinction could be used to identify the difference between neurotic symptoms and character disorders. In his words,

> The neurotic symptom is experienced as a foreign body and creates a feeling of being ill. The neurotic character trait, on the other hand, such as the exaggerated orderliness of the compulsive character or the anxious shyness of the hysterical character, are organically built into the personality. One may complain about being shy but does not feel ill for this reason.
>
> *(W. Reich, 1949, p. 42).*

Reich pointed out that character represents a specific way of being for an individual, an expression of his or her total past, while a symptomatic disorder generally corresponds to a single experience.

III. CONTEMPORARY APPROACHES TO PERSONALITY DISORDER

A. Standard Nomenclature: The Diagnostic and Statistical Manual of Mental Disorder

As can be seen from the preceding history, there have been many widely differing conceptual models for personality disorders. Historically, this has led to a bewildering array of different classifications of mental disorder (Menninger, 1963), resulting in a conceptual Tower of Babel where mental health workers use different words to designate the same concept and identical words to connote different concepts (the term "borderline" is a good example of the latter phenomenon). During the period following the end of World War II, there were at least four major competing classification systems for mental disorder (Raines, 1952). In an attempt to standardize mental health terminology, the American Psychiatric Association published the first edition of the *Diagnostic and Statistical Manual of Mental Disorder* (DSM-I) in 1952. The second edition of this manual (the DSM-II) was published in 1968 and was relatively similar in content and format to its predecessor (American Psychiatric Association, 1968).

In 1980, the American Psychiatric Association published the DSM-III, which was a substantial revision of the earlier classification systems. These revisions came in response to a period of intense criticism of psychiatric diagnosis. The DSM-III (American Psychiatric Association, 1980) contained a number of innovations designed to improve the utility of diagnosis. To address the difficulties associated with diagnostic reliability, the DSM-III incorporated the use of relatively specific criteria which a person must meet in order to receive a diagnosis, which led to greater agreement between different diagnosticians than had been noted in the past (Spitzer, Forman, & Nee, 1979).

However, it should be noted that the criteria used in the DSM will not guarantee that all persons with a particular diagnosis will share critical features. Many of the definitions provided in the DSM (including all of the personality disorder definitions) are set up in a format where an individual must have a subset of several features in order to be diagnosed. This approach to diagnostic classification is called *polythetic,* meaning that there are no "necessary and sufficient" conditions which all persons in a particular diagnostic category must share. Thus, for the nine DSM-IV (American Psychiatric Association, 1994) diagnostic features of Borderline Personality, at least five of which are required for diagnosis, there are 256 different criteria combinations that can result in this diagnosis. Such an approach to classification acknowledges the heterogeneity of personality disorder manifestations, but at the same time makes the development of diagnostic instrumentation quite difficult.

The DSM-IV, consistent with previous major medically oriented nosologies, represents a categorical approach to taxonomy. In such a system, a person conceptually either has a disorder or does not. However, the use of a categorical approach in DSM-IV did not necessarily mandate that all category members would be strictly homogeneous, as the use of polythetic criteria illustrates. This aspect suggests the adoption of a *prototype* model of categorization (e.g., Smith & Medin, 1981). Prototype classes may be contrasted to classically defined categories, where class membership is defined by the presence of necessary and sufficient conditions; for example, members of the classically defined concept "even numbers" are those numbers evenly divisible by two. Under the assumptions of the prototype model, the set of defining features represents an "ideal type" or best example of class members (i.e., the prototype), and decisions regarding class membership are made on the basis of similarity comparison to this prototype (Smith & Medin, 1981). As a result, some class members are clearly better exemplars of the concept than others (Rosch, 1973); for example, a robin is a better exemplar of the class "bird" than is a penguin, yet each are members of this discrete category. Among the categories of mental disorders represented in DSM-IV, the personality disorders have been singled out as concepts which are best modeled as prototypes (Blashfield, Sprock, Pinkston, & Hodgin, 1985). In fact, some revisions to the DSM were intended to make the personality disorders more representative of a prototype model by removing any single necessary features from the definitions (Widiger, Frances, Spitzer, & Williams, 1988). Thus, the use of prototype categorization allows an introduction of some dimensionality into an essentially categorical personality diagnostic system. For example, although two patients may both share the DSM-IV diagnosis of Borderline Personality Disorder, this does not imply that they are equally good examples of the category, nor that they will present with the same number or severity of borderline personality features.

Another important aspect of the DSM-IV system is the use of a multiaxial approach to diagnosis. Rather than receiving one diagnosis (as was the case prior to the DSM-III), five separate evaluations are to be made. Axis I, which composes most of the instrument, describes the *clinical syndromes,* while Axis II is used to code *personality disorders* and certain developmental disorders. Axis III reflects *physical conditions* that are judged to be in some way related to a behavior disorder. Axis IV includes *psychosocial stressors* which may have been related to the onset of current difficulties. Finally, Axis V codes the current or recent level of the person's *adaptive functioning.*

The multiaxial approach introduced in DSM-III represented what was perhaps one of the most important developments in the recent history of the personality disorders. This classification system attempted to make explicit the qualitative differences between personality disorders and traditional psychiatric diagnoses such as schizophrenia. In particular, the personality disorders were seen as *trait* disturbances; that is, in this system a personality disorder reflects a long-standing personality trait (or traits) which came to be inflexible, maladaptive, and causally related to subjective distress or impairment in functioning. These disturbances were thought to be first evident in childhood or adolescence, continuing without periods of remission or exacerbation throughout adulthood. By implication, the clinical syndromes such as schizophrenia and depression could be differentiated from personality disorders in that they involve *state* (i.e., more temporary) manifestations. A total of 10 trait disturbances are defined using operational criteria in DSM-IV. These disorders were arranged into three "clusters" or superordinate groupings of disorders: Cluster A (including Schizotypal, Schizoid, and Paranoid Personality Disorders), Cluster B (Histrionic, Narcissistic, Antisocial, and Borderline), and Cluster C (Dependent, Avoidant, and Obsessive-Compulsive).

However, in practice the conceptual approach taken in DSM-IV for separating personality disorders from clinical syndromes continues to be unclear. The distinctions drawn between these two axes of diagnosis are inconsistent and often puzzling. For example, dysthymic disorder, characterized by a long-standing, relatively mild depression, has been thought by some to represent a personality style, in contradistinction to the mood disorder it is conceptualized as in the DSM-IV. Furthermore, the DSM approach to personality disorder has been criticized for many reasons aside from conceptual ambiguity. The selection of the particular personality disorder constructs has been criticized for both lack of theoretical coherence (Millon, 1981) and clinical verisimilitude (Gunderson, 1983). DSM-based personality disorder diagnoses invariably have been found to have relatively low reliability (Mellsop, Varghese, Joshua, & Hicks, 1982; Spitzer et al., 1979), among the lowest of any of the categories in the entire diagnostic manual. The categories also overlap extensively (Morey, 1988b; Pfohl, Coryell, Zimmerman, & Stangl, 1986), such that an individual receiving any particular personality disorder diagnosis has at least a 50% chance of meeting criteria for another personality disorder. Finally, the coverage of personality disorder has been criticized (Peele, 1986), suggesting that there are many patients with a personality disorder who do not meet criteria for any of the Axis II disorders. The data addressing the DSM-III-R revisions indicate that these changes had limited success in addressing such shortcomings (Morey, 1988b), and the DSM-IV modifications also seem to have had limited impact on some of these issues.

On the positive side, the approach to personality disorder taken in the DSM has been of tremendous heuristic importance. For example, the greater specificity of personality disorder definitions beginning with the DSM-III fostered the development of several assessment devices with which to ascertain these diagnoses with far geater reliability than had been previously possible. These efforts made possible an unprecedented amount of research on the personality disorders (Blashfield & McElroy, 1987). Furthermore, the DSM classification of personality disorders is a reasonable reflection of the empirical covariation of commonly encountered personality problems, under the assumptions upon which the DSMs were founded (Morey, 1988a).

Despite these important aspects, there are shortcomings in the DSM taxonomy of personality disorder that create difficulties for all scientific efforts directed at investigating the etiology or treatment of these conditions. Such shortcomings have led a number of investigators to propose alternative approaches to personality disorder conceptualization, many of them dimensional ones. The following sections review a few of the most promising models that have garnered attention in recent years.

B. Millon's Biosocial Learning Typological Model

Theodore Millon (1969, 1981) has developed a personality model that roughly parallels the typological organization of the DSM-III personality disorders, and Millon (1983) was active in the development of the DSM-III conceptualization of some of the personality disorders. However, Millon's organization reflects a conceptually based approach not mirrored in DSM-III. Millon views personality as a habitual coping pattern which represents a particular way of achieving positive reinforcements and avoiding punishment. In Millon's system, reinforcement lies at the core of the personality model; personality styles are seen as differing primarily in the ways in which reinforcement is pursued and obtained.

Millon (1969) originally identified personality coping patterns based upon three dichotomies of instrumental behavior. The first dichotomy involves the *active–*

passive dimension, which refers to whether the individual takes the initiative in pursuing reinforcement or alternatively such behavior is largely reactive to environmental events. The second distinction involves the *pleasure–pain* dimension, referring to a tendency to be primarily motivated either by the pursuit of pleasure or instead by the avoidance of aversive events. The third dimension refers to *self–other,* or the relative importance of subjective and objective modes of experience.

Millon utilized these dichotomies in creating a 10-fold (originally an 8-fold, and revised to be consistent with DSM-III-R) typology of personality styles. These styles may be placed in a "reinforcement matrix" similar to that presented in Table I. The rows of this matrix address what Millon calls the "instrumental polarity," or the manner in which a person seeks reinforcement (*actively* or *passively*). The columns of this table refer to the "source polarity," or the sources from which reinforcement will primarily be sought. With respect to sources, Millon outlines five types: *independent,* or seeking reinforcement from the self; *dependent,* or seeking reinforcement from others; *ambivalent,* or uncertainty and vacillation in reinforcement seeking; *detached,* a seeming failure to seek or at least experience reinforcement by any source; and *discordant,* or a seeming reversal of the experience of reinforcement and punishment.

According to Millon, the personality disorders represent the maladaptive poles of these 10 basic personality styles that may have self-destructive consequences of which the individual is unaware. Under persistent environmental adversity, however, Millon proposes that the personality functioning will decompensate toward one of three pathological personality syndromes, depending upon the person's basic sources of reinforcement. According to Millon (1987), those with an independent style of reinforcement deteriorate to a Paranoid personality syndrome, those with

TABLE I
Millon's Typological Model of Personality and Personality Disorders

Instrumental pattern	Preferred source of reinforcement				
	Dependent	Independent	Ambivalent	Discordant	Detached
Passive[a]					
Normal	Cooperative	Confident	Respectful	Self-abasing	Introversive
Mild	Dependent	Narcissistic	Compulsive	Self-defensive	Schizoid
Severe	Borderline	Paranoid	Paranoid	Borderline	Schizotypal
Active[a]					
Normal	Sociable	Forceful	Sensitive	Antagonistic	Inhibited
Mild	Histrionic	Antisocial	Passive-aggressive	Sadistic	Avoidant
Severe	Borderline	Paranoid	Borderline	Paranoid	Schizotypal

Note. Adapted from Millon (1987).
[a] The first type mentioned indicates normal personality pattern; the second indicates mild personality disorder pattern; and the third indicates severe personality disorder pattern.

a dependent style will become Borderline, and those with a detached style develop a Schizotypal personality, while the ambivalent and discordant types may become either Paranoid or Borderline. Millon's typology incorporates a number of constructs central to personality theory, and its parallels to the DSM offer a number of research and clinical advantages. However, it should be noted that the relationship of Millon's ideas to DSM constructs has been controversial (Millon, 1985, 1986; Widiger, Williams, Spitzer, & Frances, 1986).

C. Interpersonal Models of Personality Disorder

Within the broad rubric of psychodynamic theories, a school of thought emerged which viewed personality as shaped by social and cultural circumstances to a greater extent than by biological or instinctual factors. Harry Stack Sullivan proposed a systematic interpersonal theory that viewed personality as "the relatively enduring pattern of recurring interpersonal situations which characterize a human life" (Sullivan, 1953, p. 111). Sullivan's ideas were futher systematized by Timothy Leary, a young academic psychologist who later pursued other interests. Leary, in appraising the impact of Sullivan, felt that Sullivan "convincingly buried the much-berated remains of descriptive, Kraepelinian, and negatively-value-toned psychiatry, but provided no substitute classification system" (Leary, 1957, p. 10). Leary attempted to provide a classification scheme which would allow an interpersonally based appraisal of personality function and dysfunction. In his influential 1957 book *Interpersonal Diagnosis of Personality,* Leary presented a two-dimensional model of interpersonal behavior in which the variables were arrayed in a circular manner. This circular array is divided into quadrants through the use of two orthogonal dimensions, one representing *affiliation* (the horizontal axis), and the other involving interpersonal *dominance* (the vertical axis). As a result, 16 sections of the circumplex could be described that represented different blends of affiliation and dominance.

Leary's book stimulated a great deal of interest and research in an interpersonal circumplex model of personality. Some of this research pointed to various shortcomings of the Leary model (Wiggins, 1982). For example, there seemed to be a noticeable gap between octants PA (Autocratic) and NO (Hypernormal) suggesting that persons in these adjoining octants were more different than portrayed by the model. Furthermore, certain variables hypothetically at opposing ends of the circle did not seem to be inversely related, as would be expected under the model. As a result, a number of investigators have proposed revisions to the original Leary formulation. Many of these revisions, such as those proposed by Schutz (1958), Lorr Bishop, and McNair (1965), Wiggins (1979), Kiesler (1983), and Benjamin (1974), have attracted significant research attention in their own right.

A number of authors have argued that an interpersonal taxonomy is crucial for an adequate conceptualization of personality disorder (Benjamin, 1993). McLemore and Benjamin (1979) proposed that the interpersonal approach represents a potential improvement upon traditional psychiatric classification systems. In their view, the primary advantage of the interpersonal approach to diagnosis is that it is prescriptive as well as descriptive; in other words, it specifies steps to take in implementing a successful treatment. This system has been seen as particularly relevant as a descriptive scheme for personality disorder (McLemore & Brokaw, 1987). According to McLemore and Brokaw, there are four basic assumptions underlying an interpersonal approach to the conceptualization of personality disorder:

1. Deeply ingrained behavioral styles are much more psychologically significant than discrete "symptoms." This assumption implies that the interpersonal style tends to be consistent over time, potentially giving rise to varying symptomatic patterns. Thus, the interpersonal style must be addressed if the symptomatic presentation is to be permanently ameliorated.

2. Personality disorders reflect disordered relationships with other people. McLemore and Brokaw note that these relationships need not be with people in the immediate social milieu, but may also include relations with individuals no longer present, or even deceased.

3. Effective treatment of personality disorder requires the interruption of self-defeating interpersonal cycles. As such, the interpersonal diagnostic approach leads to an understanding of: (*a*) what other people have done to the patient; (*b*) how others' behavior pulls maladaptive behavior from the patient; (*c*) how the patient may engineer interpersonal circumstances which may maintain the disordered pattern; and (*d*) what the patient must do to break out of this cyclical maladaptive pattern (Strupp & Binder, 1984).

4. The establishment of an interpersonal relationship is a prerequisite to personality disorder treatment. It is through this relationship that the self-defeating cycles described above may be experientially observed by both therapist and patient, allowing for some intervention.

It has been noted that there are several conceptual and empirical relationships between DSM personality disorder categories and the interpersonal circumplex model (Frances, 1982; Kiesler, 1986; Morey, 1985; Widiger & Kelso, 1983; Wiggins, 1982; Wiggins & Pincus, 1994). However, the interpersonal domains also taps many aspects of behavior not well represented in traditional personality diagnostic systems. In fact, a study conducted by Morey (1985) and replicated by DeJong, van den Brink, Jansen, and Schippers (1989) suggested that the DSM personality disorders may not adequately tap many facets of interpersonal behavior, particularly the affiliative components. The interpersonal model of personality is clearly pertinent to personality disorder classification and should be considered as a promising alternative.

D. Dimensional Conceptualizations of Personal Disorder

In contrast to the categorical models historically proposed within psychiatry, a somewhat different approach to the conceptualization of personality disorder has been most prominent within academic psychology. This approach views personality disorder as the extreme of a continuous dimension of normal personality functioning. The dimensional perspective has gained popularity in psychology for a number of reasons (Widiger, 1993; Widiger & Frances, 1985). For example, it has been suggested that dimensional personality models are more precise (Frances, 1982). Furthermore, dimensional clinical judgments of personality disorder are far more reliable than categorical judgments (Heumann & Morey, 1990). Categorical classifications with high overlap such as Axis II of the DSM (Morey, 1998b) make the identification of "pure" diagnostic groups very difficult, with the resulting subjects probably not representative of the majority of patients presenting in routine clinical practice. Also, in general, psychometric research on personality traits has failed to identify sharp distinctions between adaptive and maladaptive personality characteristics (Eysenck, Wakefield, & Friedman, 1983).

The dimensional psychometric tradition in modern psychology dates back to the research in individual differences performed in Great Britain by Sir Francis Galton. The British tradition produced a number of important scholars in the area of personality and individual differences. Perhaps the two best known are Hans Eysenck (e.g., Eysenck & Eysenck, 1985) and Raymond Cattell (e.g., Cattell, 1965), each of whom developed models of personality structure utilizing dimensional statistical methods of factor analysis. Cattell originally identified 16 "source" traits which he believed operated as the underlying source of observed behavior; subsequent studies from Cattell's laboratory discovered as many as 9 additional source traits. For Cattell, different maladaptive personality variants could be represented as different constellations of these source personality traits, each of which tend to share relatively low scores on a trait described as "ego strength."

Eysenck has proposed that personality is best modeled as consisting of three independent dimensions, which he has label *neuroticism, psychoticism,* and *extroversion–introversion.* The neuroticism trait refers to a tendency to be emotionally reactive; the psychoticism trait involves emotional independence (i.e., impersonal, unempathic); and the extroversion trait refers to sociability and venturesomeness. In contrast to Cattell's personality dimensions, Eysenck maintains that these major dimensions are uncorrelated in the general population, such that each reflects an independent aspect of personality style. In his theoretical writings, Eysenck has proposed that these traits reflect heritable biological mechanisms, with neuroticism representing a highly reactive autonomic nervous system, extroversion involving low resting cortical activation, and psychoticism involving hormonal mechanisms (Eysenck & Eysenck, 1985).

For Eysenck, personality disorders are viewed as extreme positions along these personality dimensions. In his words, "the concept of personality disorders is not seen as a categorical diagnosis, but as behavior characterized by the confluence of three major dimensions of personality, determined in its precise operation by the predominance of one or another of these, and shading gradually and imperceptibly into more normal types of behavior" (Eysenck, 1987, p. 215). Because of this emphasis upon the dimensionality of behavior, Eysenck has been a leading critic of the traditionally categorical psychiatric approach to personality disorder (Eysenck et al., 1983).

Another dimensional approach to personality conceptualization which has recently attracted research attention is the so-called "five-factor" model of personality. The five-factor model, proposed initially by Tupes and Christal (1961) and refined by Norman (1963), has a number of elements in common other popular dimensional approaches; in fact, it resembles an integration of the Eysenck model, the higher order factors of Cattell's theory, and the two interpersonal dimensions described by Leary (1957) and his successors as described earlier. The five factors may be described as follows (McCrae & Costa, 1984): *Neuroticism,* characterized by worry, insecurity, and self-pity, as opposed to a calm and self-satisfied nature; *Extroversion,* referring to a sociable and affectionate person in contrast to a sober, reserved individual; *Openness,* implying an imaginative, independent personality contrasted to a conforming, orderly nature; *Agreeableness,* characterized by a trusting, helpful attitude in contrast to a suspicious, exploitative orientation; and *Conscientiousness,* denoting a well-organized, careful, disciplined person as opposed to a careless, weak-willed individual.

As pointed out by Costa and McCrae (1986), the utility and robust nature of the five-factor model have been supported in a number of research studies. In addition, there is substantial evidence to suggest that these five factors reflect enduring characteristics which persist throughout much of adult life (McCrae & Costa, 1984). It has been suggested by McCrae and Costa that the personality disorders may be well represented by the five factors, with all such disorders tending to be high on Neuroticism and specific disorders reflecting particular constellations of the remaining four factors. Widiger, Trull, Clarkin, Sanderson, and Costa (1994) specify hypothetical patterns for each of the DSM personality disorders on the five factors and their subfacets, with many of the disorders displaying facets of Neuroticism. The robustness of these five factors of personality across many diverse empirical studies highlights their potential as a useful model of the structure of personality.

E. Assessment and Diagnosis of Personality Disorder

As mentioned earlier, the introduction of the DSM-III did not ameliorate problems associated with personality disorder diagnosis, which continued to be among the least reliable of all mental disorders (Mellsop et al., 1982). Some authors have speculated that possible explanations for this relative lack of reliability may in part be attributed to idiosyncratic interviewing styles by clinicians. Other studies suggested that systematic biases, perhaps related to demographic features such as the gender or race of the client, may be occurring in the assignment of certain personality disorder diagnoses (Morey & Ochoa, 1989; Warner, 1978). For numerous reasons, it soon became clear that advances in diagnostic instrumentation for the personality disorders were required if substantive research was to be performed.

As noted by several reviews, this need led to the development of several new diagnostic techniques for use with personality disorders. In addition, a number of the more time-honored personality assessment instruments have been adapted for use with this aim. The reader is encouraged to peruse the several reviews of instrumentation in this area, such as those by Widiger and Frances (1987), J. H. Reich (1987), or Zimmerman (1994).

There are a number of thorny issues to resolve in evaluating personality disorder assessment instruments. The definition of criterion groups for research is a perennial problem, since there are no well-validated markers for these concepts. For the most part, the described instruments follow some approximation of the DSM format since it is currently the standard nomenclature in mental health. However, the DSM concepts themselves are ill defined and unreliably identified. As such, negative results in assessment validity studies are difficult to interpret: Are the instruments not useful for diagnosing DSM personality disorder constructs, or are the constructs themselves not useful? As noted by Stangl, Pfohl, Zimmerman, Bowers, and Corenthal, (1985), this creates a "catch-22" for diagnostic researchers that is not easily resolved.

Another difficulty besetting diagnostic research with the personality disorders involves diagnostic overlap. It has been well established that there is a great deal of overlap among the personality disorders (Morey, 1988b; Pfohl et al., 1986); consequently, it is typical to find patients presenting with features of a number of different personality disorders. As a result, identifying a relatively pure "criterion group" in this area becomes exceedingly difficult. Furthermore, even if such groups are obtained, they may be somewhat artificial in that they are not representative of usual patient populations. This high diagnostic overlap suggests that differentiating among these disorders will be very difficult for any instrument.

A final consideration in assessing these conditions involves modes of data gathering. Self-report data collection is subject to distortion arising from several sources, such as impression management efforts, and personality disordered individuals are notorious in this regard. For example, when "frequent lying" is one of the definitional criteria (as it is for antisocial personality), it is safe to assume that self-report information provided by these individuals may be suspect. Futhermore, individuals with personality disorders often do not come into contact with mental health professionals in an entirely voluntary fashion; typically, there are situational elements that provide motivation for distorting their self-presentation. Hare (1985) gives the example of one highly psychopathic prisoner who had his own MMPI scoring keys and an MMPI research library that he used as the basis for a consulting service of "manufacturing" profiles for other inmates. Such concerns have led some researchers to caution against a reliance upon self-report information in establishing personality disorder diagnoses.

However, the use of structured interviews, touted as an alternative to self-report data that may circumvent such distortions through the use of clinical judgment, is also problematic. A primary consideration is that many of the traits which must be identified to establish personality disorder diagnoses may defy direct inquiry. For example, one of the DSM-III criteria for Paranoid Personality Disorder involved the lack of a true sense of humor; it is not easy to imagine a structured interview question which would yield meaningful information about this attribute.

In contrast to many of the Axis I disorders, diagnosis of personality disorder does not solely involve gathering information about the patient, but also entails developing a sense of the patient as a person. The constraints imposed by the comparatively rigid format of structured interviews may in fact be a hindrance to such efforts. Another formidable problem with such interviews is that they are based upon the assumption that personality judgments can be made with uniform ease by mental health professionals, an assumption that has long been suspect (e.g., Taft, 1955). In general, it is advised that personality disorder assessment involve some combination of self-report and interview contact in order to maximize available information.

IV. THE NATURE OF PERSONALITY DISORDER: CURRENT CONTROVERSIES

In the majority of instances, the term *personality disorder* is employed to refer to a collection of conditions that may not seem to have much in common. The DSM manuals, which attempt to provide explicit diagnostic criteria for a number of specific personality disorders, is unfortunately vague when called upon to provide a definition of superordinate construct. Without such a definition, the line between personality disorder and other clinical phenomena, as well as that between personality disorder and normal personality, becomes quite murky. The remainder of this chapter is devoted to exploring facets of such a definition.

As used here, a personality disorder denotes a maladaptive personality constellation which: (1) is evident early in life; (2) is stable over time; (3) is manifest across diverse situations; (4) is an ego-syntonic condition; (5) is particularly evidenced by interpersonal disruption; (6) represents an extreme of normal variation among people; and (7) may arise as a result of multiple influences. Each of these assumptions represents an area of some controversy, and there is often minimal evidence that can be offered in support of these claims. The following sections briefly examine the evidence and the implications of each of these assumptions for the conceptualization of personality disorder.

A. The Seven Assumptions

1. Personality Disorders Are Evident Early in Life

There are a number of follow-back studies which demonstrate that adults with psychological disorders tend to have had childhoods characterized by relatively poor adjustment (Parker & Asher, 1987). Although much of this literature focused upon psychotic patients (e.g., Rolf, Knight, & Wertheim, 1976), for certain personality constructs the research evidence supporting the early appearance of personality problems is fairly compelling. Perhaps the most thoroughly examined area has involved antisocial personality characteristics. A well-known study in this domain was conducted by Robins (1966), who prospectively followed children who exhibited antisocial behavior and found that such behavior was predictive of sociopathic actions during adulthood. Subsequent research has also shown that adult antisocial behavior can be predicted from childhood features, such as aggressiveness and stealing, manifest as early as ages 6 to 9 years (Loeber & Dishion, 1983). In fact, the predictive utility of childhood behavior in predicting adult antisocial personality led to an incorporation of such material into the DSM-III and DSM-III-R diagnostic criteria for this disorder.

For other personality constellations, there is relatively little information on how early in life such features may be identified. One longitudinal study of personality disordered males demonstrated that adaptive difficulties were evident by age 14 (Drake & Vaillant, 1985). There is isolated evidence to suggest that adult deficits in interpersonal skills, which are prominent in personality disorder, can be observed at an early age (Havighurst, Bowman, Liddle, Matthews, & Pierce, 1962; Robins, 1966). Although a childhood behavioral style of shyness and withdrawal is of little predictive value for later psychopathology (Parker & Asher, 1987), most follow-back studies of schizophrenia-spectrum patients indicate that a childhood characterized by a withdrawn interpersonal style was common (e.g., Ricks & Berry, 1970). As such, Schizoid and Schizotypal Personality Disorders might be expected to demonstrate observable manifestations at an early age. However, research on other personality disorders constructs is either lacking or yields unimpressive results. For example, the Fels Longitudinal Study (Kagan & Moss, 1962) reported only minor associations between dependency behaviors identified during childhood and adult dependency.

A major study of personality stability within the normal range was conducted by Block (1971), who examined personality characteristics during early adolescence (junior high school), middle adolescence (senior high school), and adulthood (generally in their thirties) for 171 subjects studied at the Institute of Human Development at University of California, Berkeley. The average correlation between personality configuration during junior high school and senior high school was .77 and .75, while between senior high school and adulthood the average correlation was .56 and .54 for men and women, respectively (Block, 1971). These data indicate that, on average, there appears to be appreciable personality consistency across the time intervals examined by Block, even for personality within the normal range. As a result, one would expect that most personality disorders, which are distinguished by rigidity and inflexibility, would begin to be evidenced by early adolescence if not earlier. However, there is clearly a significant amount of research which needs to be done in order to better substantiate this assumption.

2. Personality Disorders Are Reasonably Stable over Time

In general, it is assumed that personality disorders tend to be fairly stable over the adult years, although the nature of the difficulties which these individuals experience may vary across time. The evidence cited above suggests that personality difficulties in adulthood tend to be evident fairly early in life, supporting the contention that such disorders are stable over time. Furthermore, there is considerable evidence which indicates that personality stability is evident well into older age (McCrae & Costa, 1984). As such, one should not expect that personality disorders will be confined to a relatively youthful segment of the population.

Unfortunately, the temporal persistence of personality disorders has been further demonstrated in a number of studies of treatment samples, which supports the clinical observation that these disorders are fairly refractory to treatment. For example, Pope, Jonas, Hudson, Cohen, and Gunderson (1983) followed a cohort of patients diagnosed as having Borderline Personality Disorder over periods ranging from 4 to 7 years; this period included at least one hospitalization and numerous treatment contacts. They found that 67% of these patients continued to meet criteria for Borderline Personality at follow-up despite treatment efforts. Similarly, McGlashan (1983) conducted a long-term follow-up study of roughly 100 inpatients diagnosed with Borderline Personality Disorder at admission to the index hospitalization. Outcome data on these patients were collected an average of 15 years following the discharge from this hospitalization. Between 44 and 50% of these individuals were diagnosed as Borderline Personality at follow-up, depending upon the particular criteria used for diagnosis. Additionally, 46% of Borderline patients were still in some form of treatment at the time of follow-up contact. Such results support the contention that the problems associated with personality disorders tend to be stable over lengthy time periods.

One widely believed bit of clinical lore concerning the personality disorders involves the belief that they tend to "burn-out" during later years; that is, the personality difficulties are thought to abate sometime during ages 40 to 55. Although longitudinal studies of patients with personality disorder are often difficult to conduct, there is evidence that these problems seem to decrease over time (Glueck & Glueck, 1968; McGlashan, 1986; Robins, 1966). However, in McGlashan's longitudinal study of borderline personality, a curvilinear trend was observed with reemergence of difficulties noted after age 60. According to McClashan, "many middle-aged borderline patients develop stable instrumental functioning but not close social and personal relationships. The latter deficit appears not to change with time and may 'haunt' these patients in a symptom-exacerbating fashion as they age and lose their work capacities and opportunities with the attendant structure and gratifications" (McGlashan, 1986, p. 29).

In assessing personality disorder, the assumption of temporal stability is an important consideration. To firmly establish these diagnoses, it is important to make a careful determination of the person's life history without being unduly influenced by immediate situational circumstances or concurrent Axis I psychopathology. With careful questioning, a life pattern will emerge which often will be telling with respect to personality difficulty. As such, interviews should not neglect historical information which may be buried in discussions of current precipitating circumstances.

3. Personality Disorders Are Reasonably Stable across Different Situations

The assumption that people behave consistently across diverse situations is one which has generated a great deal of controversy within personality psychology (e.g.,

Epstein & O'Brien, 1985; Kenrick & Funder, 1988; Mischel, 1968, 1983). Walter Mischel, for example, created a furor with his 1968 book on this topic, entitled *Personality and Assessment.* In that volume Mischel pointed out that much psychological research has not supported the contention that individual differences in behavior are very stable across situations. As a result, Mischel and others have suggested that the situation in which the person finds her or himself is a much stronger determinant of behavior than internal personality dispositions.

However, according to the DSM, personality disorders reflect traits which by definition are stable across different situations, even though this "stability" may well be maladaptive. Block and Block (1980) have described the construct of *ego resiliency,* which refers to an individual's capacity to modify his or her behavior as a function of the demands of the environment. Presumably, resilient individuals have the capacity to vary their behavior according to the demands of different situations; as such, situations may seem to be powerful mediators of behavior in relatively resilient individuals. Block and Block have demonstrated that this resiliency is a stable and consistent differentiator of people; individuals with personality disorders would characterized in their scheme as nonresilient personalities. In other words, a personality disorder represents a failure of the adaptation mechanism described by Block and Block, whereby the personality is stable to a problematic extent.

However, this assumption must not be interpreted to mean that personality disordered individuals will always behave in a manner consistent with their diagnosis. In general, it is important to recognize that the stability of personality across situations is evident when one considers aggregates of behavior rather than single behavioral instances (Epstein & O'Brien, 1985). In other words, a trend suggestive of a personality disorder only becomes apparent over a number of observations of a particular individual. Even with the most rigid personality disorder that a clinician is likely to encounter, it is unlikely that we can predict precisely what that individual will do in a given situation with a high degree of accuracy. It is for this reason that judgments of relatively specific behavioral instances, such as immediate dangerousness, are so difficult to make (Ewing, 1983). The concept of personality disorder implies that such individuals act in a certain way with much greater frequency and in more situations than is expected of most people. However, it does not imply that these people will behave in this manner at all times and in all situations.

An important implication of this assumption is that the diagnostician should not assume that the personality-relevant behavior a person demonstrates during an initial interview is necessarily representative of their typical functioning. Unfortunately, many explanatory models of mental disorder include theoretical constructs such as transference (e.g., Zetzel, 1956) or stimulus generalization (e.g., Dollard & Miller, 1950), which imply that the examinee's behavior in such an interview situation should be typical of their personality style. However, this conclusion is inconsistent with a large body of research evidence in the personality field. A 1-hr interview with a mental health professional hardly constitutes a representative sample of behavior, and a personality disorder diagnosis cannot be assigned with much confidence following such a contact. It is essential that such judgments be based on information gathered across repeated observations. Although the gathering of these details is often not feasible for the diagnostician, it is frequently possible to gain such information from relatives or other peers who indeed have had repeated contacts with the examinee.

4. Personality Disorders Are Ego-Syntonic Conditions

This assumption addresses the experience of the individual with a personality disorder. Consistent with the descriptions provided by psychoanalytics such as Alexander and Reich, it is assumed that personality disorders involve traits which are an essential part of the personality, rather than symptoms which are experienced by the person as alien to the personality. As such, patients with these disorders are often portrayed as having little insight into the nature of their difficulties. However, this characterization is a bit unfair given that the nature of the difficulties experienced by individuals with personality disorders tend to be somewhat different than those associated with symptomatic disorders. For example, Reich points out that personality problems are more readily rationalized than symptoms: "A reason is often given for neurotic character traits which would be immediately rejected as absurd if it were given for symptoms: 'he is just that way'" (W. Reich, 1949, p. 43). In other words, a "way of being" is less likely to be seen as an immediate source of distress than would be ego-alien symptoms such as anxiety or obsessions.

The assumption that personality disorders are by nature ego-syntonic creates a host difficulties for their assessment. For the most part, the presenting problems with which most individuals with Axis I disorders present involve experiences directly pertinent to establishing a diagnosis. For example, a person with panic disorder is likely to rapidly identify his or her problems as associated with transient episodes of severe, debilitating anxiety; his or her experience is directly pertinent to the criteria required for diagnosis. On the other hand, the presenting problems of the personality disordered individual are rarely so straightforward. They are often seeking evaluation at someone else's request. Their presenting complaints often involve the behavior of other people, rather than their own experiences. Almost by definition, they do not see the phenomena most pertinent to the establishment of the diagnosis as being problematic; at best, they recognize that the consequences of these phenomena lead to some difficult circumstances. As such, the self-reported problems of such persons will often obscure rather than clarify the clinical picture.

5. Personality Disorders Are Primarily Distinguished by Interpersonal Disruption

Over the past several decades, a number of writers have identified interpersonal behavior as an important focus for the study of personality and psychopathology (Adams, 1964; Horney, 1945; Kiesler, 1986; Leary, 1957; McLemore & Benjamin, 1979; Sullivan, 1953; Wiggins, 1982). One focus of such attention has concerned the utility of the interpersonal approach as a foundation for the diagnosis and classification of all functional mental disorders. For example, Adams (1964) identi-fied a large degree of overlap between most measures of psychopathology and social behavior, and he concluded that what has traditionally been considered "mental illness" is actually more accurately represented as a maladaptive variant of interpersonal behavior.

More recently, McLemore and Benjamin (1979) proposed a taxonomy of social behavior which they felt had the potential to serve as a "psychosocial alternative" to the DSM system. These authors claimed that "DSM-III shows near total neglect of social psychological variables and interpersonal behavior" (McLemore & Benjamin, 1979, p. 18). Other authors (i.e., Frances, 1980; Widiger & Kelso, 1983) have sug-gested that interpersonal models, while not likely to replace the entire DSM-III classification, have a great deal of potential to serve as a taxonomy for personality functioning. Each of these writers has observed that many psychiatric diagnoses are frequently based upon reports or observations of interpersonal behavior.

The assumption made here is that personality disorders, unlike certain other forms of mental disorder, are dysfunctional primarily through their expression in the social milieu. Even though this interpersonal disruption may well be a manifesta-tion of some intrapsychic difficulties, the maladaptiveness which qualifies personality disorders as mental disorders can only be evident in an interpersonal context. For example, traits like passive-aggressiveness or avoidant behavior are unlikely to be very maladaptive for a person stranded on a desert island without other persons present. In contrast, conditions such as schizophrenia or panic disorder will tend to cause problems for our hypothetically stranded person, even without another individual to whom such symptoms can be reported. As described by McLemore and Brokaw (1987), personality disorders are "disturbances" in the sense that the behavior of such people is disturbing to someone else.

This interpersonal assumption has unique implications for the assessment of personality disorder. Most significantly, it calls into question the utility of relying upon self-reported information in establishing diagnoses. Traditionally, assessment in clinical psychology and psychiatry has relied heavily upon information provided directly by the patient, whether gathered in the form of an interview or through the use of questionnaires. An assumption that personality disorders are inherently interpersonal problems requires that this interpersonal field should be sampled in some way.

One manner in which important information concerning interpersonal rela-tionships may be obtained is through the use of peer ratings or other sociometric strategies. The use of peers in obtaining assessment information has long been seen as a powerful technique in research with children and adolescents (e.g., Ausubel, 1955), but it has been applied to adults with relative infrequency. This neglect is unfortunate since, as Wiggins (1973) has stated, "in general, peer ratings have been shown to have substantial generalizability in terms of inter-observer agreement, generalizability of external structure across diverse rating groups and conditions, and generalizability to criterion situations of social importance" (Wiggins, 1973, p. 378). For the personality disorders, an informant such as a close friend or relative may be an ideal source of information about the long-standing behavior patterns of the examinee. Self-reported information about personality functioning in patients with these disorders is often distorted by situational circumstances; it should be noted that this distortion may be either in a positive/idealized (Tyrer et al., 1984) or a negative/pathological (Edell, 1984) direction. Although the reports of any particular information may contain some bias, the use of multiple informants should provide a pattern that is likely to be an accurate portrayal of the subject's pertinent characteristics. To the greatest extent possible, information from peers, friends, and relatives should be considered in the establishment of personality disorder diagnoses.

6. *Personality Disorders Reflect Extremes of Normal Personality Variation*

This assumption, which is a rather controversial point of debate among contemporary classification researchers, holds that the difference between those individuals with personality disorders and those with "normal" personalities is a difference of degree rather than a difference of kind. In other words, it is assumed that there is no natural boundary or discontinuity between the normal and the abnormal ranges of personality. Although the DSM calls for a discrete categorical decision whereby the person either has a personality disorder or they do not, there is little evidence in support of considering personality disorder as a categorical "disease entity." In fact, there is little evidence to suggest that any functional psychiatric disorder has been identified as such (Kendell, 1975), but those considerations are beyond the scope of this book. Here, a personality disorder is assumed to represent the extreme end of a normally distributed personality constellation. As a result, any boundary drawn between normal personality disorder is inherently arbitrary.

The distinction between "personality disorder" and "psychiatric disturbance" is also not one which is easily drawn. One interesting approach to drawing this distinction was taken by Foulds (1971). Foulds separated what he called personality deviance (i.e., personality disorder) from personal illness (i.e., clinical syndrome), and he proposed a model of the relationship between these conditions whereby they were viewed as overlapping but conceptually independent domains. In making this distinction, he focused upon quantitative aspects of these conditions, namely, the distributions of symptoms (features of personal illness) and traits (features of personality deviance) in various populations.

Expanding upon this approach, Morey and Glutting (1994) identified four quantitative features that could be used to distinguish normal personality traits from features of psychopathology.

a. Normal and Abnormal Personality Constructs Differ in the Distribution of Their Related Features in the General Population. Foulds hypothesized that abnormal symptoms should have distributions which have a marked positive skew (i.e., occur infrequently) in normal samples but are roughly normally distributed in clinical samples. In contrast, normative personality traits should be distributed in a roughly Gaussian (i.e, bell-shaped) manner in the general population; a sample of individuals with "deviant" personalities are distinguished by the personality trait being manifest to a degree rarely encountered in the general population. It should be noted that both types of constructs may be of clinical interest. Various regions of each type of construct may represent an area of concern; a person can be having difficulties because he or she manifests a particular normative trait to an extreme degree (e.g., introversion), or because he or she manifests an abnormal construct to even a slight degree (e.g., suicidal ideation). The primary difference is in the nature of the construct; the individual with a clinical trait (i.e., psychopathology) may be somehow qualitatively different from normals, while individuals with an "abnormal amount" of a normative personality trait are quantitatively distinct; that is, a difference of degree rather than kind.

   b. Normal and Abnormal Personality Constructs Differ Dramatically in Their Social Desirability. Assessment investigators have long recognized that self-report personality tests can be vulnerable to efforts at impression management. In particular, much concern has been expressed about the influence of efforts to respond in a socially desirable fashion on such tests. Various diverse and creative efforts have been directed at resolving this dilemma, including the empirical keying strategy behind the development of the original MMPI as well as the subsequent use of the "k-correction" and the forced choice matched item alternatives employed in the Edwards Personal Preference Schedule. However, for self-report tests that focus on "abnormal" constructs, these strategies tend not to work very well. It is suggested that the reason for these problems is that abnormal constructs are inherently socially undesirable. As such, most measures of social desirability responding will correlate quite highly with measures of abnormal constructs. In contrast, the social desirability of normative personality features is more ambiguous, less evaluative, and more likely to be tied to a specific context. For example, the trait adjective "talkative" might be a socially desirable characteristic in a salesperson but not in a librarian. There is likely to be little consensus among people as to whether being "talkative" is a desirable or undesirable characteristic, whereas characteristics such as "depressed" or "delusional" will invariably be viewed consensually as undesirable. This implies that the social desirability of a construct may be useful as an indicator of its status in capturing normal or abnormal variation between people.

   c. Scores on Measures of Abnormal Personality Constructs Differ Dramatically between Clinical and Community Samples, While Scores of Normal Constructs Do Not. This criterion is based upon the assumption that, in dealing with an abnormal personality construct, "more" is worse; that is, the more of the construct a person has, the greater the impairment the person manifests and the more likely the person is to come to the attention of mental health professionals. For example, when considering disordered thinking as a personal characteristic, greater amounts of thought disorder will be associated with greater impairment and need for intervention. Thus, a clinical population should invariably obtain higher scores on measures of such constructs than a community sample. In contrast, for a normative personality trait, the adaptive direction of scores is less clear-cut. Given the assumption that such traits are normally distributed, then the traits are inherently bipolar, and extreme scores at *either* end of the trait may be maladaptive. Thus, even if clinical samples were restricted to persons with problems on a particular normative trait (e.g., extreme scores on Introversion–Extraversion), there would still be no reason to suspect mean differences between clinical and community subjects, as the extreme scores of the clinical subjects at either end of the continuum would be expected to balance out.

   d. Measures of Normative Personality Traits Should Demonstrate Factorial/ Correlational Invariance across Clinical and Community Samples, While Measures of Abormal Traits May Not.   The basic assumption behind this criterion is that the correlation pattern that gives abnormal constructs their syndromal coherence should only emerge in samples where there is adequate representation of individuals manifesting the syndrome (i.e., clinical samples). In community samples, which may include relatively few individuals who have a clinical syndrome, the association between features of the same syndrome may be no greater than that between any two features selected randomly. As an example, if depression were defined by five necessary and sufficient criteria, and these five criteria were intercorrelated in a community sample that contained no depressed subjects, the average correlation between these features might well be zero. In a sample of nondepressed individuals, sleep problems and low self-esteem may only be associated at chance levels since individuals who share the putative causal process that underlies the clinical association of these features have been removed from the sample. It is the covariation of these features in individuals considered to be depressed that lends a correlation pattern to these features. Thus, highly intercorrelated sets of features (i.e., syndromes) might emerge from a factor analysis of clinical subjects that would not be identified in a sample of subjects from the community.

   In contrast, those traits that describe normal variation in personality would be expected to capture this variability among clinical as well as normal subjects. Even though the clinical subjects may be, as a group, more extreme on normal personality traits, similar correlational patterns among elements of the trait should be obtained. For example, the construct of Extroversion–Introversion should identify meaningful differences among clinical subjects as well as normal subjects, and the intercorrelation of the behaviors that make up this construct should be similar in the two populations. This should yield predictable empirical results with respect to the factor structure (for multifaceted scales/constructs) and the average item intercorrelation (i.e., coefficient alpha, for unidimensional constructs); for a normative trait, these results should be similar in clinical and nonclinical samples. In contrast, these values may well differ if an "abnormal" construct is being examined.

   Empirical work has supported this assumption with respect to many features of personality disorder. For example, Tyrer and Alexander (1979) examined a personality disorder classification scheme similar to the system by Schneider that was described earlier. Their factor analyses found no qualitative difference between the personalities of individuals with personality disorder and those of individuals without such disorders. In their words, "the results of the factor analysis reveal that the underlying structure of variables is similar in both those with and those without primary personality disorder and hence supports the concept of personality disorders as being at the extreme of a multidimensional continuum" (Tyrer & Alexander, 1979, p. 166).

7. Personality Disorders Are Multiply Determined

This assumption proposes that there is no single specific etiology for the personality disorders. Rather, personality traits are seen as evolving from a number of different origins, including constitutional, developmental, and environmental/situational influences. Futhermore, within each of these domains it is assumed that there are different routes to the same personological presentation. For example, it is not difficult to imagine that dependency behaviors may arise out of constitutional limitations, or from early development (e.g., parental overinvolvement), or from prolonged situational pressures (e.g., an abusive spouse).

V. CONCLUSION

It is important to note that all of the seven assumptions just described represent areas of considerable controversy within both psychology and psychiatry. The above discussions should not be interpreted as indicating that these issues are resolved; rather, they may be viewed as a guide to major conceptual issues in this area in need of resolution. It is important to understand that the conceptualization of personality disorder presented here is not necessarily consonant with the viewpoint expressed in the DSM. However, they do represent an attempt to make explicit, in a way which the American Psychiatric Association manuals do not, the domain of phenomena denoted by the concept of "personality disorder."

REFERENCES

Adams, H. B. (1964). 'Mental illness' or interpersonal behavior? *American Psychologist,* *19,* 191–197.

American Psychiatric Association. (1952). *Diagnostic and statistical manual of mental disorder.* Washington, DC: Author.

American Psychiatric Association. (1968). *Diagnostic and statistical manual of mental disorder* (2nd ed.). Washington, DC: Author.

American Psychiatric Association. (1980). *Diagnostic and statistical manual of mental disorder* (3rd ed.). Washington, DC: Author.

American Psychiatric Association. (1987). *Diagnostic and statistical manual of mental disorder* (3rd rev. ed.). Washington, DC: Author.

American Psychiatric Association. (1994). *Diagnostic and statistical manual of mental disorder* (4th ed.). Washington, DC: Author.

Ausubel, D. P. (1955). Sociempathy as a function of sociometric status in an adolescent group. *Psychological Review, 62,* 378–390.

Benjamin, L. S. (1974). Structural analysis of social behavior. *Psychological Review, 81,* 392–425.

Benjamin, L. S. (1993). Dimensional, categorical, or hybrid analyses of personality: A response to Widiger's proposal. *Psychological Inquiry, 4,* 91–134.

Blashfield, R. K., & McElroy, R. A. (1987). The 1985 journal literature on the personality disorders. *Comprehensive Psychiatry, 28,* 536–546.

Blashfield, R. K., Sprock, J., Pinkston, K., & Hodgin, J. (1985). Exemplar prototypes of personality disorder diagnoses. *Comprehensive Psychiatry, 26,* 11–21.

Block, J. (1971). *Lives through time.* Berkeley, CA: Bancroft.

Block, J. & Block, J. H. (1980). The role of ego-control and ego-resiliency in the organization of behavior. In W.A. Collins (Ed.), *Minnesota Symposium on Child Psychology* (Vol. 13) pp 39–101.) Hillsdale, NJ: Erlbaum.

Cattell, R. B. (1965) *The scientific analysis of personality.* Baltimore: Penguin Books.

Costa, P. T., & McCrae, R. R. (1986). Personality stability and its implications for clinical psychology. *Clinical Psychology Review, 6,* 407–423.

DeJong, C. A. J., van den Brink, W., Jansen, J. A. M., & Schippers, G. M. (1989). Interpersonal aspects of DSM-III axis II: Theoretical hypotheses and empirical findings. *Journal of Personality Disorders, 3,* 135–146.

Dollard, J., & Miller, N. E. (1950). Personality and psychotherapy. New York: McGraw–Hill.

Drake, R. E., & Vaillant, G. E. (1985). A validity study of Axis II of DSM-III. *American Journal of Psychiatry, 142,* 553–558.

Edell, W. S. (1984). The Borderline Syndrome Index: Clinical validity and utility. *Journal of Nervous and Mental Disease, 172,* 254–263.

Epstein, S., & O'Brien, E. J. (1985). The person-situation debate in historical and current perspective. *Psychological Bulletin, 98,* 513–537.

Ewing, C. P. (1983). "Dr. Death" and the case for an ethical ban on psychiatric and psychological predictions of dangerousness in capital sentencing proceedings. *American Journal of Law and Medicine, 8,* 407–428.

Eysenck, H. J. (1987). The definition of personality disorder and criteria appropriate for their description. *Journal of Personality Disorders, 1,* 211–219.

Eysenck, H. J., & Eysenck, M. W. (1985). *Personality and individual differences.* New York: Plenum Press.

Eysenck, H. J., Wakefield, J. A., & Friedman, A. F. (1983). Diagnosis and clinical assessment: The DSM-III. *Annual Review of Psychology, 34,* 167–193.

Foulds, G. A. (1971). Personality deviance and personal symptomatology. *Psychological Medicine, 1,* 222–233.

Frances, A. (1980). The DSM-III personality disorders section: A commentary. *American Journal of Psychiatry, 137,* 1050–1054.

Frances, A. (1982). Dimensional and categorical systems of personality diagnosis: A comparison. *Comprehensive Psychiatry, 23,* 516–527.

Glueck, S., & Glueck, E. T. (1968). *Non-delinquents in perspective.* Cambridge, MA: Harvard University Press.

Gunderson, J. G. (1983). DSM-III diagnoses of personality disorders. In J. P. Frosch (Ed.), *Current perspectives on personality disorders* (pp. 20–39). Washington, DC: American Psychiatric Press.

Hare, R. D. (1985). Comparison of procedures for the assessment of psychopathy. *Journal of Consulting and Clinical Psychology, 53,* 7–16.

Havighurst, R. J., Bowman, P. H., Liddle, G. P., Matthews, C. V., & Pierce, J. V. (1962). *Growing up in River City.* New York: Wiley.

Heumann, K. A., & Morey, L. C. (1990). Reliability of categorical and dimensional judgments of personality disorder. *American Journal of Psychiatry, 147,* 498–500.

Horney, K. (1945). *Our inner conflicts.* New York: Norton.

Jung, C. G. (1923). *Psychological types.* New York: Harcourt, Brace.

Kagan, J., & Moss, H. A. (1962). *Birth to maturity: A study in psychological development.* New York: Wiley.

Kendell, R. E. (1975). *The role of diagnosis in psychiatry.* London: Blackwell Scientific.

Kenrick, D. T., & Funder, D. C. (1988). Profiting from controversy: Lessons from the person-situation debate. *American Psychologist, 43,* 23–34.

Kiesler, D. J. (1983). The 1982 interpersonal circle: A taxonomy for complementarity in human transactions. *Psychological Review, 90,* 185–214.

Kiesler, D. J. (1986). Interpersonal methods of diagnosis and treatment. In J. O. Cavender (Ed.), *Psychiatry* (Vol. 1, No. 4, pp. 1–23). New York: Lippincott.

Koch, J. L. (1981). *Die psychopathischen minderwertigkeiten.* Ravensburg: Maier.

Kraepelin, E. (1902). *Clinical psychiatry: A textbook for students and physicians* (A. R. Diefendorf, Trans.) (6th ed.). London: Macmillan.

Leary, T. (1957). *Interpersonal diagnosis of personality.* New York: Ronald.

Loeber, R., & Dishion, T. (1983). Early predictors of male delinquency: A review. *Psychological Bulletin, 94,* 8–99.

Lorr, M., Bishop, P. F., & McNair, D. M. (1965). Interpersonal types among psychiatric patients. *Journal of Abnormal Psychology, 70,* 468–472.

Mack, J. E. (1975). Borderline states: An historical perspective. In J. E. Mack (Ed.), *Borderline states in psychiatry* (pp. 1–21). New York: Grune & Stratton.

McCrae, R. R., & Costa, P. T. (1984). *Emerging lives, enduring dispositions: Personality in adulthood.* Boston: Little, Brown.

McGlashan, T. H. (1983). The borderline syndrome. I. Testing three diagnostic systems. *Archives of General Psychiatry, 40,* 1311–1318.

McGlashan, T. H. (1986). The Chestnut Lodge follow-up study: III. Long-term outcome of borderline personalities. *Archives of General Psychiatry, 43,* 20–30.

McLemore, C. W., & Benjamin, L. S. (1979). Whatever happened to interpersonal diagnosis? A psychosocial alternative to DSM-III. *American Psychologist, 34,* 17–34.

McLemore, C. W., & Brokaw, D. W. (1987). Personality disorders as dysfunctional interpersonal behavior. *Journal of Personality Disorders, 1,* 270–285.

Mellsop, C., Varghese, F., Joshua, S., & Hicks, A. (1982). The reliability of Axis II of DSM-III. *American Journal of Psychiatry, 139,* 1360–1361.

Menninger, K. (1963). *The vital balance.* New York: Viking Press.

Millon, T. (1969). *Modern psychopathology.* Philadelphia: Saunders.

Millon, T. (1981). *Disorders of personality: DSM-III Axis II.* New York: Wiley.

Millon, T. (1983). The DSM-III: An insiders perspective. *American Psychologist, 38,* 804–814.

Millon, T. (1985). The MCMI provides a good assessment of DSM-III disorders: The MCMI-II will prove even better. *Journal of Personality Assessment, 49,* 379–392.

Millon, T. (1986). The MCMI and DSM-III: Further commentaries. *Journal of Personality Assessment, 49,* 205–207.

Millon, T. (1987). Millon clinical multiaxial inventory-II manual. Minneapolis, MN: National Computer Systems.

Mischel, W. (1968). *Personality and assessment.* New York: Wiley.

Mischel, W. (1983). Alternatives in the pursuit of predictability and consistency of persons: Stable data that yield unstable interpretations. *Journal of Personality, 51,* 578–604.

Morey, L. C. (1985). An empirical comparison of interpersonal and DSM-III approaches to classification of personality disorders. *Psychiatry, 48,* 358–364.

Morey, L. C. (1988a). The categorical representation of personality disorder: A cluster analysis of DSM-III-R personality features. *Journal of Abnormal Psychology, 97,* 314–321.

Morey, L. C. (1988b). Personality disorders under DSM-III and DSM-III-R: An examination of convergence, coverage, and internal consistency. *American Journal of Psychiatry, 145,* 573–577.

Morey, L. C., & Glutting, J. H. (1994). The Personality Assessment Inventory: Correlates with normal and abnormal personality. In S. Strack & M. Lorr (Eds), *Differentiating normal and abnormal personality* (pp. 402–420). New York: Springer.

Morey, L. C., & Ochoa, E. S. (1989). An investigation of adherence to diagnostic criteria: Clinical diagnosis of the DSM-III personality disorders. *Journal of Personality Disorders, 3,* 180–192.

Norman, W. T. (1963). Toward an adequate taxonomy of personality attributes: Replicated factor structure in peer nomination personality ratings. *Journal of Abnormal and Social Psychology, 66,* 574–583.

Parker, J. G., & Asher, S. R. (1987). Peer relations and later personal adjustment: Are low-accepted children at risk? *Psychological Bulletin, 102,* 357–389.

Peele, R. (1986). Report of the Speaker-Elect. *American Journal of Psychiatry, 143,* 1348–1353.

Pfohl, B., Coryell, W., Zimmerman, M., & Stangl, D. (1986). DSM-III personality disorders: Diagnostic overlap and internal consistency of individual DSM-III criteria. *Comprehensive Psychiatry, 27,* 21–34.

Pope, H. G., Jonas, J. M., Hudson, J. I., Cohen, B. M., & Gunderson, J. G. (1983). The validity of DSM-III borderline personality disorder: A phenomenologic, family history, treatment response, and long-term follow-up study. *Archives of General Psychiatry, 40,* 23–30.

Raines, G. N. (1952). Foreword. In *Diagnostic and statistical manual of mental disorder.* Washington, DC: American Psychiatric Association.

Reich, J. H. (1987). Instruments measuring DSM-III and DSM-III-R personality disorders. *Journal of Personality Disorders. 1,* 220–240.

Reich, W. (1949). *Character analysis.* New York: Orgone Institute.

Ricks, D. F., & Berry, J. C. (1970). Family and symptom patterns that precede schizophrenia. In M. Roff & D. Ricks (Eds.), *Life history research in psychopathology,* (pp. 31–39). Minneapolis: University of Minnesota Press.

Robins, L. N. (1966). *Deviant children grown up: A sociological and psychiatric study of sociopathic personality.* Baltimore: Williams & Wilkins.

Rolf, J. E., Knight, R., & Wertheim, E. (1976). Disturbed preschizophrenics: Childhood symptoms in relation to adult outcomes. *Journal of Nervous and Mental Disease, 162,* 274–279.

Rosch, E. (1973). On the internal structure of perceptual and semantic categories. In T. E. Moore (Ed.), *Cognitive development and the acquisition of language* (pp. 27–48). New York: Academic Press.

Schneider, K. (1958). *Psychopathic personalities.* London: Cassell. (Original work published 1923).

Schutz, W. C. (1958). *FIRO-B: A three dimensional theory of interpersonal behavior.* New York: Rinehart.

Smith, E. E., & Medin, D. L. (1981). *Categories and concepts.* Cambridge, MA: Harvard University Press.

Spitzer, R. L., Forman, J. B., & Nee, J. (1979). DSM-III field trials: I. Initial interviewer diagnostic reliability. *American Journal of Psychiatry, 36,* 815–817.

Standage, K. (1986). A clinical and psychometric investigation comparing Schneider's and the DSM-III typologies of personality disorders. *Comprehensive Psychiatry, 27,* 35–46.

Stangl, D., Pfohl, B., Zimmerman, M., Bowers, W., & Corenthal, C. (1985). A structured interview for the DSM-III personality disorders. *Archives of General Psychiatry, 42,* 591–596.

Strupp, H. H., & Binder, J. (1984). *Psychotherapy in a new key.* New York: Basic Books.

Sullivan, H. S. (1953). *The interpersonal theory of psychiatry.* New York: Norton.

Taft, R. (1955). The ability to judge people. *Psychological Bulletin, 52,* 1–23.

Tupes, E. C., & Christal, R. E. (1961). *Recurrent personality factors based on trait ratings.* (USAF ASD Tech. Rep. No. 61–97). Lockland Air Force Base, TX: U.S. Air Force.

Tyrer, P., & Alexander, J. (1979). Classification of personality disorder. *British Journal of Psychiatry, 135,* 163–167.

Tyrer, P., Cicchetti, D. V., Casey, P. R., Fitzpatrick, K., Oliver, R., Balter, A., Giller, E., & Harkness, L. (1984). Cross-national reliability study of a schedule for assessing personality disorders. *Journal of Nervous and Mental Disease, 172,* 718–721.

Vaillant, G. E. (1987). A developmental view of old and new perspectives on personality disorder. *Journal of Personality Disorders, 1,* 146–156.

Warner, R. (1978). The diagnosis of antisocial and hysterical personality disorders: An example of sex bias. *Journal of Nervous and Mental Disease, 166,* 839–845.

Widiger, T. A. (1993). The DSM-III-R categorical personality disorder diagnoses: A critique and an alternative. *Psychological Inquiry, 4,* 75–90.

Widiger, T. A., & Frances, A. (1985). The DSM-III personality disorders: Perspectives from psychology. *Archives of General Psychiatry, 42,* 615–623.

Widiger, T. A., & Frances, A. (1987). Instruments and inventories for the measurement of personality disorders. *Clinical Psychology Review, 7,* 49–76.

Widiger, T. A., Frances, A., Spitzer, R. L., & Williams, J. B. W. (1988). The DSM-III-R personality disorders: An overview. *American Journal of Psychiatry, 145,* 786–795.

Widiger, T. A., Trull, T. J., Clarkin, J. F., Sanderson, C., & Costa, P. T. (1994). A description of the DSM-III-R and DSM-IV personality disorders with the five-factor model of personality. In P. T. Costa T. A. Widiger (Eds.), *Personality disorders and the five-factor model of personality,* (pp. 41–56). Washington, DC: American Psychological Association.

Widiger, T. A., Kelso, K. (1983). Psychodiagnosis of Axis II. *Clinical Psychology Review, 3,* 491–510.

Widiger, T. A., Williams, J. B., Spitzer, R. L., & Frances, A. (1986). The MCMI and DSM-III: A brief rejoinder to Millon. *Journal of Personality Assessment, 50,* 198–204.

Wiggins, J. S. (1973). *Personality and prediction: Principles of personality assessment.* New York: Wiley.

Wiggins, J. S. (1979). A psychological taxonomy of trait-descriptive terms: The interpersonal domain. *Journal of Personality and Social Psychology, 37,* 395–412.

Wiggins, J. S. (1982). Circumplex models of interpersonal behavior in clinical psychology. In P. Kendall & J. Butcher (Eds.), *Handbook of research methods in clinical psychology* (pp. 183–221). New York: Wiley.

Wiggins, J. S., & Pincus, A. L. (1994). Personality structure and the structure of personality disorders. In P. T. Costa and T. A. Widiger (Eds.), *Personality disorders and the five-factor model of personality* (pp. 73–93). Washington, DC: American Psychological Association.

Zetzel, E. (1956). Current concepts of transference. *International Journal of Psycho-Analysis, 37,* 369–375.

Zimmerman, M. (1994). Diagnosing personality disorders: A review of issues and research methods. *Archives of General Psychiatry, 51,* 225–245.

CHAPTER 36

TRENDS AND PRACTICES IN PSYCHOTHERAPY OUTCOME ASSESSMENT AND THEIR IMPLICATIONS FOR PSYCHOTHERAPY AND APPLIED PERSONALITY

MICHAEL J. LAMBERT

BRIGHAM YOUNG UNIVERSITY

EDWIN C. SUPPLEE

TRIPLER REGIONAL MEDICAL CENTER

In this chapter we will focus on research in personality and psychotherapy. There are many ways in which personality has been discussed and analyzed in psychotherapy. These include studies on the effects of therapist personality on clients from different diagnostic groupings; for example Whitehorn and Betz (1954) hypothesized that A and B therapist types had differential outcomes with schizophrenic and neurotic patients. Also present are studies of patient personality and its relationship to both therapy outcome and the manner in which therapists and patients participate in therapy sessions. This work is characterized by studies of the relationship between patient ego strength (as measured by the Rorschach, MMPI, or judges ratings) and indices of improvement (Garfield, 1978). The effect of similarities between therapist and client personality, as well as other matching strategies based upon numerous personality dimensions, has also been the subject of considerable research (Berzins, 1977). Typical of this research is Carson's (1969) *Interaction Concepts of Personality,* in which it is argued that complementary and incompatible personality styles can be identified and will lead to differential outcome.

Although research on therapist and patient personality could form the basis of this chapter, we would be writing mostly about the history of psychotherapy and not about contemporary research issues. To a large extent personality variables have not been used successfully to ideally match therapists and patients, to select patients for treatments, or to predict therapy outcome. It has proved difficult to identify salient personality characteristics and to effectively measure those that have been hypothesized to be important in the therapeutic process. While it would be interesting to discuss past and present attempts to facilitate therapy through personality research and the reasons for our failures, we have chosen a different focus. The particular vantage point for our analysis is the myriad ways in which changes in patients who have undergone psychotherapy have been assessed, and how assessment practices interact with the study of personality. First, the assessment of outcome will be put in an historical perspective. This will be followed with a discussion of current assessment practices and their relation to personality. Finally, we will discuss the implications of current practices for personality and psychotherapy and suggest directions for future research.

Byrne (1964) noted that in the early days of personality test construction, experiments and psychometricians were advancing independent of each other, leaving "the former short on measurement and the latter short on theory." The two have since been wedded, with mutual advancement. In contrast, treatment outcome research and personality research continue to develop in completely separate spheres. Personality researchers regard the advancement and usefulness of personality measurement more optimistically (Craik, 1986) than psychotherapy researchers (Lambert, Shapiro, & Bergin, 1986). As we shall point out, there is an urgent need for psychotherapy researchers and those interested in measurement and personality to join forces if significant advances are to be made.

I. HISTORICAL OVERVIEW

Research into the effects of psychotherapy has a relatively short history, dating back to the 1930s. The psychotherapy of the day was, of course, psychoanalytically oriented. And quite naturally, theoreticians and practitioners were ambitiously engaged in changing the "structure of personality" as well as the prominent disturbing symptoms of central concern to the client. Freud contended that the analyst was the prime, and perhaps the only, medium for assessing the outcome of therapy.

This appears to be because of the multifarious and complex dimensions present in each case and in each session, and the traditional scientific research conducted in that day did not account for all of those variables, at least to Freud's satisfaction. Most reports of outcome were of a qualitative nature and single case studies, although there were also quantitative studies produced (Rachman, 1971; Luborksy & Spence, 1978).

In those early quantitative studies, outcome was reported in terms of percentage of those improving, without much detail on the type or quality of outcome and without the use of reliable rating scales based on patient reports or objective observer ratings.

In the Berlin Psychoanalytic Institute's report (ca. 1930), the criteria that Fenichel used to determine success were an "analytically acceptable personality change" and an improvement of symptoms (Bergin & Lambert, 1978). The interpretations of the results have been contended since Eysenck's 1952 survey (Bergin, 1971; Bergin & Lambert, 1978), with the controversy left largely unresolved (Garfield & Bergin, 1986); depending on how one views the data, the improvement rate was either 31 or 91% (Bergin, 1971). Here, the means of determining personality change is reasonably assumed to be the analyst's judgement, but the specifics of how the judgement is arrived at are not attended to. In this study, as well as many others of this period, personality functioning was reported as global improvement in gross functioning as viewed by the therapist (Luborsky & Spence, 1978). This observation appears to hold true for other schools in the early half of this century, including behaviorism (Eysenck & Beech, 1971) and humanism (Rogers, 1942).

Historically, one of the most important landmarks of psychotherapy, and of research on outcome, was the body of studies produced by Rogers and his associates starting in the early 1950s (Rogers & Dymond, 1954). This research continued to emphasize personality change but deviated in important ways from research on psychoanalysis. In their early volume of research studies (Rogers & Dymond, 1954), Rogers and his associates stated that, given the facilitative therapeutic conditions,

> the client will reorganize himself at both the conscious and the deeper levels of his personality in such a manner as to cope with life more constructively, more intelligently, and in a more socialized as well as a more satisfying way. More specifically it is hypothesized that the client will change in his perception of self, will become more understanding of self and others, more accepting of self and others, more creative, more adaptive, more self-directing and autonomous, more mature in his behavior, less defensive, and more tolerant of frustrations.
>
> *(p. 4)*

The outcome measure did not rely solely on clinical observation, but the clients' views of successful therapy were objectified by the use of the Q-sort routine. They outlined from their research "necessary and sufficient" therapist characteristics, client characteristics, and therapeutic outcome (Truax & Mitchell, 1971).

While in the early 1950s most therapy outcome research on personality was (or was striving to be) a nomothetic endeavor, there were some who proposed research with the individual and with personality. George Kelly's (1955) personal-construct psychology is an example. In order for the therapist to better understand a client's personal-construct system, Kelly devised the Role Construct Repertory (Rep) Test. The Rep Test could also be used as an outcome measure, to see if and how a person's core constructs may have changed via therapy. Gordon Allport advocated quantitative methods in single case studies as important for understanding the individual's personality structure, although his methods were not applied systematically in behavior change research (Kiesler, 1971).

With this growing popularity of applied behaviorism in the 1960s and 1970s, there was a drastic change in the methods used to assess outcome and in the status and importance of personality-based treatment. The behaviorally oriented theorists were interested in measuring readily observable change. Wolpe was primarily concerned with anxiety as the antecedent of neurotic behavior and the control (reduction) of anxiety as the measure of outcome of desensitization (Eysenck & Beech, 1971). The criterion for success of Lazarus's adaptation of desensitization, behavior rehearsal, was behavioral change primarily regarding assertiveness (Lazarus, 1971). Hans Eysenck postulated that personality could be divided into two major factors. Persons were seen as varying on the dimensions of instability–stability and on an extroversion–introversion continuum. These factors were hypothesized to be based on neurophysiological structures, with a predisposition to neurosis dependent upon both genetic and environmental influence. Understanding to what extent these factors exist within an individual should determine the therapeutic approach. He did not, however, expound on how these factors might or might not change as a result of treatment, and in fact seemed to view them as rather stable traits that therapy was not aimed at modifying (Eysenck, 1987; Eysenck & Beech, 1971).

Operant conditioning, as studied by Skinner and others, has been used to elicit changes in component behaviors of a wide variety of divergent disorders: with schizophrenics, improvement in disorganized thinking, apathy, social withdrawal, and bizarre verbalizations; modification of delinquent behavior in children; and treatment of marital problems. Here again we have some strong positive findings for the efficacy of a technique, as with most behavioral techniques and as per the measurement criteria, but it is difficult to define changes in personality per se (Krasner, 1971). Of course, this is irrelevant for most behaviorists and even behavioral therapists.

However, there are some theorists from the behavioral tradition who, early on, measured more than changes in the frequency of specific behaviors. Bandura (1971), using multiple outcome measures (i.e., a behavioral test of avoidance, a fear inventory, and a semantic differential technique to obtain attitudinal ratings), reported changes through modeling that lie not only in behavior but in affect and attitude. But even Bandura placed relatively little attention on integrated personality change, focusing more on limited aspects of personality.

Despite the radical shift from personality-based therapies to behaviorally based therapies, there continued to be a pocket of research and theory that espoused an interest in, and in fact concentrated on, assessing more integrated and less reductionistic aspects of people. For example, Albert Ellis (1973) described rational-emotive therapy as a

> method of personality change that quickly and efficiently helps the individual to foster and implement his natural human tendencies to gain more individuality, freedom of choice, and enjoyment and also helps him to discipline himself so that he minimizes his natural human tendencies to be conforming, suggestible, and unenjoying. It actively and didactically, as well as emotively and behaviorally, shows him how to abet and enhance one side of his humanness while simultaneously changing and living more happily with (and not repressing or squelching) another side of his humanity.
>
> *(p. 200)*

Even more recently Robert Wallerstein (1989) summarized findings from the Psychotherapy Research Project of the Menninger Foundation and reiterated the psychoanalytic position on change in psychotherapy by drawing a distinction between two basic types of change,

> structural change, which is based on the interpretive resolution of unconscious intrapsychic conflicts, and behavioral change, or change in manifest behavior patterns that represents nothing more than altered techniques of adjustment. It is presumed that only behavioral change can result from supportive psychotherapeutic techniques and implementations. Intrinsic to this dichtomizing between kinds of change has been the assumption that only structural change, as brought about through conflict resolution and appropriately achieved insight, has a guarantee of stability and durability.
>
> *(p. 203)*

This longitudinal study was started in 1954 and still continues. Among the quantitative measures used was Luborsky's Health–Sickness Rating Scale (Wallerstein, 1989). Qualitatively measured patients, treatment, and situational variables were taken as well. Positive "structural" change, which occurred in all three of the therapeutic modes, was defined, as "changes in specific intrapsychic configurations, in the patterning of defenses, in thought and affect organization, in anxiety tolerance, and in ego strength" (p. 203). Projective testing provided support for the clinical evaluation of structural change; however, the reports have not discussed the nature of the projective tests again. A finding that was not predicted by the initial study group was that significant structural change was found in the supportive psychotherapy group, a group that received a mode of psychotherapy in which attempts to foster analytically relevant insight was minimal or nonexistent.

The Menninger study is typical of early studies of psychotherapy that applied devices developed from Freudian dynamic psychology. Not at all uncommon was the use of projective methodologies, including the Rorschach Inkblot Test, the Thematic Apperception Test (TAT), drawing a person, and sentence-completion methods. Problems with the psychometric qualities of these tests, their reliance on inference, and derivation from a theoretical position based on the unconscious have resulted in their waning use as indices of outcome. Rarely today does one hear the virtues of such tests for outcome measurement. Changes in the quality of fantasy material as produced on the TAT and other projective tests simply do not convince most researchers and observers that significant improvement has occurred in the actual lives of patients, let alone their personality integration.

Although the espoused goal of many different therapies is to reconstruct the personality (e.g., RET, analytic), the major effects reported by those researching outcome are in the areas of decreased anxiety and pain, increased freedom of action, and so forth. Currently, change in personality, that is, core personality, as a result of therapy is seldom measured and is even considered irrelevant to the goals of many treatment studies (Lambert et al., 1986). Currently there is considerable skepticism about the value of personality assessment. This skepticism comes from various quarters, including: (1) the popularity of behavioral approaches and the corresponding lack of interest in standard assessment methods that elaborate on internal dynamics; (2) the humanistically derived belief that the testing and diagnostic enterprise is itself an unhelpful way of relating to persons seeking help; (3) the growing popularity of cognitive methods with their emphasis on self-talk, irrational beliefs, and similar limited constructs; (4) the belief that personality tests do not work very well and have unimpressive validity coefficients because they largely measure personality traits to the exclusion of situational variables; (5) the excessive time required by measures such as the TAT, Rorschach, and MMPI; and (6) the current emphasis on brief, crisis-oriented treatments that are short term and merely restore a person to prior levels of functioning or focus on other limited goals (Lambert et al., 1986).

Figure 1 may help the reader grasp the changes in outcome assessment that have occurred over the past 50 years, including those just discussed. Figure 1 suggests

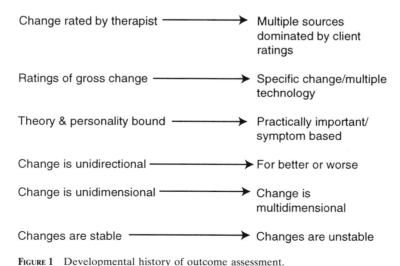

Change rated by therapist	→ Multiple sources dominated by client ratings
Ratings of gross change	→ Specific change/multiple technology
Theory & personality bound	→ Practically important/symptom based
Change is unidirectional	→ For better or worse
Change is unidimensional	→ Change is multidimensional
Changes are stable	→ Changes are unstable

FIGURE 1 Developmental history of outcome assessment.

several dimensions upon which assessments have varied since the focus of initial research to the present. The field has gradually moved from complete reliance on therapist ratings of gross/general improvement to the use of outcome indices of specific symptoms that are quantified from a variety of viewpoints, including the patient, outside observers, relatives, physiological indices, and environmental data such as employment records. Assessment *procedures* are becoming more complex and are also relying more heavily on standardized instruments that deal with specific kinds of change rather than theory-based measures such as projective tests. Researchers are more sensitive to the possibility of both positive and negative change and construct outcome assessment devices that tap both kinds of change. There has been a growing awareness that change is multidimensional and that many facets of the person change simultaneously and sometimes dyschronisticly. There is an intuitive awareness as well as empirical support for the ideas that changes come about on multiple levels, that a small intervention may generate multiple changes, and that a singular aspect of human behavior may be effected by multiple approaches (Luborsky & Schimek, 1964). Changes are not permanent and researchers are making greater efforts to understand the patterns of change over time rather than viewing change as stable or final. It is difficult, however, to ferret out whether changes measured are due to the person, the test, or the situation (Kenny & Campbell, 1989).

II. PERSONALITY CHANGE MEASUREMENT INSTRUMENTS: CURRENT STATUS OF KNOWLEDGE AND PATTERN OF USE

Although outcome research has divorced itself from the sole use of theoretically based, single measures of change, the result has been great divergence in the criteria used. Froyd and Lambert (1989), after reviewing assessment practices in outcome studies published in 20 major journals between the years of 1983 and 1988, found that no less than 1,430 measures were applied in 348 outcome studies, and of these, 840 were used only once! The type, number, and quality of measures varied greatly across journals, disorders, and treatment methods. Some data from this literature review are presented in Table I. By far, the most frequently used instrument was the Beck Depression Inventory (BDI), followed by the State–Trait Anxiety Inventory, weight, and the Hamilton Rating Scale for Depression (HRSD). Of the multitude of remaining diverse instruments, many yield indices of depression, anxiety, global symptoms, marital/family relations, cognitions, and self-concept, while personality measurement, in the traditional sense, was rare.

In the Froyd and Lambert (1989) review only two projective measures were readily recognizable, the Rorschach (seen twice) and a human figures drawing test (seen once). Similarly, in an earlier review of outcome studies published in the *Journal of Clinical and Consulting Psychology* (*JCCP*) between 1978 and 1982, projective techniques were not mentioned at all as outcome measures (Lambert, 1983). It appears that even those who espouse psychoanalytic and psychodynamic

TABLE I

Frequency and Percentage of Measures Used
in 348 Outcome Studies According to
Their Content[a]

Content	Frequency	%
Intrapersonal	1,053	74
Interpersonal	240	17
Social role performance	132	9
Total	1,430	

Most frequently used measures in a broad sample of outcome studies[a]

Outcome measure	Frequency
Beck Depression Inventory	42
Weight	23
State–Trait Anxiety Inventory (State & Trait Forms)	18
Hamilton Rating Scale for Depression	18
Symptom Checklist-90 (R)	14
Self-Efficacy Rating Scales	14
Locke–Wallace Marital Adjustment Scale	13
Blood pressure	12
Heart rate	11
MMPI (all forms)	10

[a] Based on a review of all outcome studies published in 20 exemplary
journals over a 5-year period. Reprinted by permission of the authors
Froyd and Lambert (1989).

orientations utilize more readily interpretable measures such as the HRSD, BDI,
and Symptoms Checklist-90(R). As can be seen from the Froyd and Lambert (1989)
and Lambert (1983) reviews, many of the outcome devices used in recent times
are atheoretical measures of symptoms, behavioral checklists, and the direct observation of target behaviors.[1]

The same general trend found in broad reviews of psychotherapy research is
also reflected in measurement practices in reviews of single disorders. For example,
Ogles, Lambert, Weight & Payne (1990) studied the assessment practices used in
controlled outcome studies of agoraphobia published between 1966 and 1988. Some
of the results of this review are shown in Tables II and III.

[1] It is interesting to note, however, that although projective personality measures may have fallen
out of favor with psychotherapy outcome researchers, the Rorschach, TAT, and sentence-completion
tests are still among the assessment instruments most widely utilized by psychotherapists (Rychlak, 1981).

TABLE II
Number of Agoraphobia Instruments Used in 170 Outcome Studies by Category of Measure

Category	Number of specific scales/measures
Fear and anxiety measures	27
Behavioral measures	10
Depression	9
Mental evaluation	8
Unstandardized rating scales (symptom-based anxiety ratings)	39
Physiological	6
Personality and general symptoms[a]	14
Others	22
Total	135

[a] Specific scales and their frequency of use are listed in Table III. Based on Ogles, Lambert, Weight, & Payne (1990).

Inspection of these data shows that over 135 separate measures were employed in the 170 studies analyzed. This is an amazing diversity when one considers that the focus of treatment (agoraphobia), the goals of treatment (anxiety reduction and behavior change), and the interventions employed (mostly behavioral and

TABLE III
Personality/General Symptom Instruments[a]

Instruments	Frequency of use in 170 studies
Personality	
Eysenck Personality Inventory	13
16 Personality Factor Questionnaire	3
Minnesota Multiphasic Personality Inventory	3
Maudsley Personality Inventory	2
Willoughby Personality Inventory	2
Total	23
Symptoms	
Hopkins Symptom Checklist-90	17
Middlesex Hospital Questionnaire	12
Brief Psychiatric Rating Scale	3
Cornell Medical Index	2
Tavistock Self-Assessment	2
Treatment Emergent Signs and Symptoms	2
Wittenborn Psychiatric Rating Scale	1
Total	39

[a] Based on Ogles, Lambert, Weight, & Payne (1990).

cognitive therapies) were very limited in scope. It is also surprising that only five personality measures were used (Table III) in the 170 studies examined. There is little evidence for strong interest in personality and changes in personality dimensions reflected in the traditional measures of the core personality traits of persons who have the symptoms of agoraphobia.

Of central interest to the psychotherapy researchers is the degree to which different measures and different types of measures reflect the size of changes that are occuring as a result of therapy. As part of the analysis undertaken by Ogles et al (1990), the effect size of various measures and classes of measures was estimated. This analysis combined the results of several studies that assessed patients with the same measures (or classes of measures) so that comparisons reflected the differences between measures rather than differences in treatment type, patient population, and procedural differences, such as the time lapse between pre- and post-testing.

The results of this analysis are presented in Table IV. The data in Table IV suggest that the more that dependent measures assess the limited and actual targets of treatment, the larger the treatment effects. Thus, measures that tap changes in anxiety and avoidance in high-stress agoraphobic situations resulted in larger treatment effects than measures that tap fear generally (such as the Fear Survey Schedule) or personality in the broad sense.

This finding is not unique to agoraphobia and can be seen in other meta-analytic comparisons of various disorders. Tables V and VI suggest this trend, although they are not based on within-group comparisons and are thus less sound methodologically than the within-group data on agoraphobia.

To the psychotherapy researcher, data like these further reinforce the value of employing symptom-specific measures prior to or instead of general symptom

TABLE **IV**
Overall Effect Size (ES) Means and Standard Deviations by Scale

Scale	N^a	M_{ES}	SD_{ES}
Phobic Anxiety & Avoidance	65	2.66	1.83
Global Assessment Scale	31	2.30	1.14
Self-Rating Severity	52	2.12	1.55
Fear Questionnaire	56	1.93	1.30
Anxiety during BAT	48	1.36	.85
Behavioral Approach Test (BAT)	54	1.15	1.07
Depression measures	60	1.11	.72
Fear Survey Schedule	26	.99	.47
Heart rate	21	.44	.56

[a] N represents the number of treatments whose effects were measured by each scale. A study may contribute more than one treatment. Reprinted from Ogles, Lambert, Weight, & Payne by permission of the American Psychological Association.

TABLE V

The Relationship of Assessment Content to Psychotherapy Outcome:
The Result of Choosing a Target Problem on Outcome across Therapies

Target problem	Number of effect sizes	Resulting effect size
Fear/Anxiety	719	1.06
Adjustment	66	.96
Social Behavior	391	.95
Self-Esteem	164	.95
Personality traits	30	.52
Achievement	139	.28

Note. Based on Shapiro and Shapiro (1982).

measures and personality inventories. If you want to demonstrate the power of a treatment, do not measure outcome with personality tests or inventories that tap underlying styles, attitudes, or the patterns that are usually sought in personality assessment. These results do suggest that the personality measures often applied in psychotherapy research may measure what they sometimes purport to measure: the relatively enduring attitudes, interests, needs, preferences, and patterns that make personality stable. Alternatively, traditional personality measures may not be sensitive to "stable" attributes that do change through psychotherapy.

TABLE VI

Average, Standard Deviation, and Number of Effect Sizes Classified by Type of Outcome Measure[a]

Outcome measure category	Average effect	Standard deviation	Number of effects
Fear-anxiety	1.12	1.72	647
Vocational or personal development	0.85	1.13	59
Emotional-somatic complaint	0.84	0.56	70
Measures and ratings of global adjustment	0.80	0.86	383
Addiction	0.77	0.52	55
Physiological stress	0.71	1.08	50
Self-esteem	0.69	0.97	99
Sociopathic behaviors	0.64	0.82	94
Work or school achievement	0.49	0.76	215
Life indicators of adjustment	0.46	0.43	35
Personality traits	0.31	0.56	18

[a] Based on Smith, Glass, and Miller (1980), p. 109.
Note. Reprinted by permission Johns Hopkins University Press.

III. WHAT ASPECTS OF PERSONALITY ARE BEING MEASURED IN PSYCHOTHERAPY OUTCOME RESEARCH?

It is abundantly clear from our review of psychotherapy outcome research that the field, in general, has moved a long way from interest in *personality* change per se. The common practice in contemporary research is to offer specific treatments for specific disorders and measure change with three to six scales rather closely related to the targets (symptoms and symptom complexes) of treatment. As may be expected when researchers study variables that move further into the abstract domain of personality functioning, they are less likely to see large changes, although the small changes that do occur in the personality domain may be of theoretical interest. There remains some research interest in tapping the more general and abstract dimensions of persons that are often thought of as part, if not central aspects, of personality. We turn now to a discussion of some of these personality dimensions and to inferences about personality that can be drawn from current psychotherapy research.

A. Depression

Depression is a clear example of a disorder that has been popularly characterized and diagnosed from a symptomatic perspective. The DSM-IV and DSM-III-R have provided relatively comprehensive, atheoretical, and concrete criteria for diagnosing depression, and many of the methods used to define depression reflect that some orientation (Moran & Lambert, 1983). The theoretical orientations from which these measures have been derived have also been the foundation of the most widely studied forms of therapy with depression, that is, the cognitive, behavioral, cognitive-behavioral, and pharmacological therapies (Hollon & Beck, 1994; Shapiro & Shapiro, 1982).

Depression has been one of the more popular topics of treatment outcome research and is measured both in studies of depression and as a variable of interest in other studies of psychotherapy such as marital distress (Jacobson, Follete, & Pagel, 1986), anxiety (Borkovec & Mathews, 1988), and substance abuse (Alden, 1988). The Beck Depression Inventory was the most widely used instrument in Froyd and Lambert's (1989) survey. From the time of Lambert's 1976–1980 survey to a 5-year survey undertaken in the late eighties, use of the instrument has risen from 5 times to over 25 times in *JCCP* alone.

Depression was also frequently measured with the Hamilton Depression Rating Scale based on an assessment interview. Both instruments tap the cardinal signs of depression but do not attempt (an in fact avoid) measuring broader aspects of personality. Most of the depression measures have been described as "state" measures (Moran & Lambert, 1983), sampling signs, and symptoms from 2 weeks to a couple of months in the past. Scores from these measures can certainly be interpreted to be an indication of certain active personality variables as they tap physiological functioning in the form of sleep, gastrointestinal symptoms, and sexual interests, as well as thoughts and mood. Changes in any of these dimensions would indicate a change in some aspect of a person's personality. But little is known about the degree to which these scales tap deeper, more stable personality dimensions. They correlate highly with other symptomatic measures of depression and anxiety, as well as other measures of psychopathology (Moran & Lambert, 1983). There is a clear need for research on such personality correlates as dependency, passivity, and overreliance on certain psychological defense mechanisms or coping strategies.

These comments are equally true for instruments that have been devised directly from cognitive theories and the treatment of depression. Cognitive constructs differ on a number of important aspects, including the level of inference and depth of awareness tapped by various measures. Psychologists interested in cognitive interventions have focused on such surface concepts as positive and negative self-statements, irrational beliefs, and cognitive distortions. These concepts have been measured with tests such as the Automatic Thoughts Questionnaire without reference to deeper personality dimensions. There is a high correlation between these cognitive scales and measures such as the BDI. But much less is known about changes on these dimensions and their relationship to changes in deeper cognitive personality dimensions such as depressive schemata. The failure to understand the deeper meanings (if any) of scores on scales like the HRSD and Beck Inventory have several implications for psychotherapy research and for appropriate selection and treatment assignment.

There is reason to believe that the assessment of personality dimensions in addition to symptoms could have a positive effect on clients who suffer with depression. There is a movement toward classifying some forms of mood disorders (e.g., dysthymia) as a character disorder (Kocsis & Francis, 1987), drawing parallels between dysthymia and personality disorders. Akiskal (1983) has delineated several forms of depression, including a "character-spectrum dysphoric pattern" which has a slow, early onset and is particularly resistant to pharmacotherapy and psychotherapy. In addition there appears to be growing consensus among clinicians that depressive symptoms often mask underlying personality disorders that are not addressed in many treatments. The presence of a personality disorder that goes unassessed and untreated probably leads to the high level of relapse in depressed patients. Thus the undue emphasis of symptoms, characteristic of contemporary research on depression, fails to deal with the complexity of persons with this disorder and often leads to limited understanding of treatment-by-patient interactions. We see a similar pattern in the assessment of changes in anxiety.

B. Anxiety

Related to and often coexisting with depression is anxiety. In recent years anxiety has been the second most frequently measured symptom complex. The instrument most often used is the State–Trait Anxiety Inventory (STAI; Spielbeger, Gorsuch, & Lushène, 1970), which attempts to deliver an index of both lasting (trait) and transient (state) anxiety; a composite score may also be obtained. Most of the studies have found change to occur in both the state and the trait anxiety scores of the STAI. These changes are frequently noted along with changes in other psychological variables such as depression, abstinence from drinking (Alden, 1988), Type A behavior pattern (K. R. Kelly & Stone, 1987), and specific phobic anxiety (Borkovec & Mathews, 1988). Maintenance of decreased anxiety scores on follow-up may indicate alteration in one's behavior pattern; however, it is questionable whether trait anxiety is actually being measured, particularly with the STAI, as the construct validity of the Trait scale has been called into question (Chaplin, 1986). So even the Trait scale may be tapping more superficial and transient aspects of personality. Like depression, research on anxiety-based disorders suggests an emphasis on the most symptomatic aspects of the person with little regard for the personality dynamics or patterns that bring anxiety into play. As with depression, emphasis in future research might profitably be placed on these patterns, dynamics, or structures to increase the likelihood that more permanent change will result from psychological interventions.

There are numerous personality traits and patterns that can be identified as underlying anxiety and related disorders. One area of contemporary concern that can serve as an illustration is research into the interaction between personality and premenstrual syndrome (PMS). Interest in this syndrome is evident in its inclusion as a narrow classification, Premenstrual Dysphoric Disorder, under consideration as a diagnosis in the Diagnostic and Statistical Manual (American Psychiatric Association, 1994). Although pharmacological and psychological interventions focus on the symptoms present during the acute phase of the disorder, there is considerable interest in the personality and life event factors that may predict and exacerbate this disorder. Keye, Hammond, and Strong (1986) as well as Palmer (1986) have outlined several personality traits of at least a portion of women with severe PMS. This personality pattern suggests that the subtype demonstrates a stable personality pattern, even in the postmenstrual phase, that is characterized by verbal acting out, undercontrol with insufficient thinking and deliberation, observer-perceived drama and self-centeredness, and strong needs for affection but with conflicts over dependency. They were also described as being demanding yet sensitive to the demands of others as well as crying easily and being depressed.

Given this personality configuration, these women are especially vulnerable to the extremely distressing premenstrual episode as well as to environmental stressors related to their pattern of interacting with family members. Thus treatment aimed at and assessments targeted only toward the acute symptoms may have little lasting effect. Although a demanding request, psychotherapy and psychotherapy research may be most productive, in the long run, by attending to personality dimensions in assessing changes in patients.

C. Self-Concept

In Froyd and Lambert's (1989) review, there are several dimensions that were assessed and can be identified as reflecting aspects of traditional personality functioning that date back to the original client-centered research and social-learning theory. One such aspect is people's views of themselves as measured by self-concept scales, measures of self-esteem, and self-efficacy ratings. Measures of self-concept have been used in such diverse research areas as eating disorders (Dworkin & Kerr, 1987; Leitenberg, Rosen, Gross, Nudelman, & Vara, 1988), depression (Graff, Whitehead, & LeCompte, 1986), marital therapy (Snyder & Wills, 1989), and crisis intervention (Viney, Clarke, Bunn, & Benjaman, 1985). For example, Williams, Turner, and Peer (1985), comparing guided mastery and performance desensitization, found that perceived self-efficacy "was a uniformly accurate predictor of treatment effects regardless of the treatment received."

Like depression and anxiety, self-concept appears to be an important dimension in a wide variety of disorders and to more closely resemble traditional personality/theoretical concerns. An example with a disorder of contemporary concern might be bulimia nervosa. In this disorder, compensation for low self-esteem and fears of rejection have been proposed as reasons behind the bulimic's wishes and compulsive attempts to achieve an idealized body. Dworkin and Kerr (1987), in a study of women with body image problems, found self-cathexis (self-concept) to be related to body cathexis. Despite the fact that self-concept could be considered central in eating disorder research, it is more common for researchers to study weight and possibly eating attitudes than self-concept per se.

In a study by Leitenberg et al. (1988) comparing exposure plus response prevention with cognitive-behavioral therapy for bulimics, all treatment groups were found to experience increases in self-esteem. The authors, however, found no significant difference in weight increase or decrease for any of the groups. Similarly, in a review of anorexia nervosa therapy outcome research (reporting on more than 100 studies), Qualls and Berman (1988) also found a lack of relationship between weight gains and psychological improvement. The lack of concordance between these measures of outcome suggests the need to measure both and to remain cautious about the common-sense link between them. While the targets of treatment often reflect both symptoms and self-perception, treatment outcome more often is limited to weight gain or eating attitudes. Again, changes in personality structure seem an important but neglected topic even in outcome studies that use measures of self-concept.

D. General Issues

Beyond the three broad areas already outlined (depression, anxiety, and self-concept), there is little cohesion between the remaining measures that is particularly meaningful for the study of personality. Direct observation of behaviors and physiological measures, such as weight loss, skin conductance, heart rate, and number of times behaviors occurred, represent about 25% of the outcome measures used (Froyd & Lambert, 1989; Lambert, 1983). These measures do not readily translate into personality indices, although one can infer that lasting change in weight loss, smoking, or even physiological measures such as skin conductance and blood catecholamine levels indicates a change in some pattern of psychological functioning (i.e., in personality). Linking changes in these behaviors to changes in personality is a difficult task.

Within the trend of measuring specific rather than global improvement is the effort to tailor change criteria to the individual client. In other words, if a client seeks help for severe depression and shows little evidence of pathological anxiety, the emphasis would be on changes in depression rather than changes in anxiety. Attempts to clarify the specific complaints and create specific therapeutic goals are reflected in measures such as the Goal Attainment Scaling, the Battle Target Complaints, and other "homemade" measures (Froyd & Lambert, 1989; Lambert, 1983). The problems with these measures are that as a means of structuring the patient's goals they leave open the possibility that the individualized goals will become or remain poorly defined subjective decisions created by the patient or the clinician. Though they undoubtedly reflect personality, they are attempts to eliminate personality factors and focus on observable behaviors.

Measures of relationships and social role performance have been occasionally used in outcome research. Several procedures have been found to be useful in measuring how the individual functions in the world, from the view of significant others (e.g., the Personal Adjustment and Role Skills, The Katz Ajustment Scale, and the Social Adjustment Scale), from self-report (e.g., the Social Adjustment Scale, SR version), and from trained observers (e.g., the Structural Analysis of Social Behavior Observations). These scales provide factors from which variables, directly and indirectly tied to personality, can be derived, such as anxiety, helplessness, suspiciousness, and negativism (Lambert, Christensen, and DeJulio, 1983; Lambert et al., 1986).

Rather than inferring changes in personality from symptom scales and behavioral observations, one might think that outcome researchers would employ multidimensional personality inventories to make this task unnecessary. However, there is a decidedly clear lack of interest in including such scales in outcome studies. Although multidimensional personality inventories such as the MMPI, Edwards Personal Preference Schedule, and California Psychological Inventory continue to be used in clinical practice, they are not used in outcome research. The Edwards Personal Preference Schedule was used once over a 5-year span, utilizing only (and finding changes in) the Affiliation and Independence scales (Jacobson et al., 1986). While in times past the MMPI has been the most popular objective personality measure in outcome research (Beutler & Crago, 1983), it is used today far less than specific symptom indices (Lambert, 1983). In a 5-year review the MMPI was found only 10 times, and only then with selected scales (i.e., depression) or the sum of the clinical scales used (Froyd & Lambert, 1989).

The Eysenck Personality Inventory, while recommended as having a more reliable factorial structure and as being a better general measure of change in personality than the MMPI (Beutler & Crago, 1983), was used once in a 5-year review (Graff et al., 1986), with less neuroticism found as a result of therapy. The same can be said for the ipsative measures that came from Kelly and Allport

(Kiesler, 1971), whose theories have been influential in American psychology: the instruments they created are rarely seen. Kelly's repertory grid is virtually nonexistent in outcome research literature in the United States. The authors's experience has been that, although subjects find the Rep grid an interesting and often enlightening instrument, it is quite arduous to complete. And although computer programs are available for scoring, researchers have continued to eschew its use.

A paradox of psychotherapy research is that while theoretical interest in *personality change* remains high, its measurement is either not undertaken or, when it is, changes in personality dimensions are small in comparison to symptomatic changes. These smaller changes may actually be more clinically meaningful and suggest reorganizations that could be important for relapse prevention and the maintenance of treatment gains, yet they are increasingly eschewed by psychotherapy researchers who fear that broad personality measures may not reflect some of the practical outcomes of therapy interventions and patient change. At least for the present, psychotherapy researchers in the United States are content to assess for the most part micro changes in the form or discrete symptoms and limited behaviors.

Medard Boss, in a discussion on reality, posited, "What makes a rock a rock?" Is it its shape? Is it its texture? Its color? Its weight? The answer to all of these questions is no, but take them away and there is no rock (Rychlak, 1981). What then is personality? Is it a reaction to stress in terms of anxiety, or anger, or compliance? Is it weight change, or number of cigarettes smoked, or BDI score? Again we might answer, "No, but take them away and there is no concept—no personality." The purpose here is not to resurrect the Kantian/Lockean debate, but to emphasize the fact that there is no easy way to include or exclude any psychological variable when discussing the nature of personality. But if anything is clear from our review of the way change in psychotherapy is measured, it is that the way persons are studied today is highly different than the way persons were studied in the first therapy outcome research. It is more practical, yet it appears more fragmented and even chaotic, and it is based only peripherally on personality theory. Traditional personality measures have proved to be ill suited to the demands of psychotherapy research and, perhaps, even more ill suited to the social, political, and academic climate in which research is undertaken today. What implications does this have for psychotherapy outcome and personality?

IV. Summary, Conclusions, and Future Directions

Our review of psychotherapy research and personality change suggests a number of conclusions and recommendations:

1. Psychotherapy research has changed a great deal from its origins as intensive examination or individual cases through the lenses of psychoanalytically oriented therapists who both conceptualized and rated change from an integrated framework in which personality theory was central.

2. The movement from a theory-based analysis has been gradual and incomplete but owes its impetus to several identifiable forces—the emergence of behaviorism, the failure of traditional personality assessment devices to reflect patient change, changes in the Diagnostic and Statistical Manual with its greater emphasis on observable symptoms, the emergence of short-term therapies, the political and financial pressure to demonstrate practically important changes, and the proliferation of competing therapies, many of which are only loosely tied to personality theory. We live in a practical world—a world less willing to tolerate academic endeavors unless they show some immediate benefit for the "consumer" of services.

3. The proliferation of theories, and the diversity of thought on behavior change, has resulted in an exponential rise in methods and devices for assessing changes in patient status. Very few of these measures can be accurately called measures of personality change, personality integration, or even personality.

4. In many ways this appears to be a positive development for the patient receiving treatment. We can manage to identify and measure discrete aspects of personal functioning and we can test the effects of interventions on these discrete areas of functioning. The treatment situation is a competitive market place, and the diversity enhances and broadens the search for causal relationships and effective interventions.

5. Despite the positive side of the current status of treatment outcome assessment, we have a sense that the field is in chaos. With large numbers of new assessment instruments created every year and few being used more than once, it is hard to believe that the empirical side of psychotherapy will advance at a fast pace (if at all) as a whole. There will undoubtedly be pockets of rapid development, but as a discipline psychotherapy and behavior change seems to lack orderly progress toward the goal of empirically based practice with a clear understanding of mechanisms of change.

6. As the crisis grows and becomes apparent, it seems possible that it will provide the opportunity, if not the necessity, for reorganization. This propitious moment cannot be far off. We cannot predict or imagine the theory of personality change that can unify even a small section of the field. Eclectic approaches perhaps come the closest to forcing an integration. But as any reader of *The Handbook of Eclectic Psychotherapy* (Norcross, 1986) or the *Journal of Integrative and Eclectic Psychotherapy* can see, eclectic theories themselves are being developed with lightening quickness but little impact.

7. Nevertheless, we remain optimistic about the future and call for the interested theorist or dedicated student to lend a hand. It does seem that personality theory combined with continued research may eventually result in dramatic improvements in the way we work with people who are suffering and need our expertise. A beginning point may be to attempt a more thorough understanding of the meaning of symptomatic change for personality organization.

REFERENCES

Akiskal, H. S. (1983). Dysthymic disorder: Psychopathology of proposed chronic depressive subtypes. *American Journal of Psychiatry, 140,* 11–20.

Alden, L. E. (1988). Behavior self-management and controlled-drinking strategies in a context of secondary prevention. *Journal of Consulting and Clinical Psychology, 56,* 280–286.

American Psychiatric Association. (1994). *Diagnostic and stastical manual of mental disorders* (4th Rev. ed.) Washington, DC: Author.

Bandura, A. (1971). *Behavior modification.* New York: Holt, Rinehart & Winston.

Bergin, A. E. (1971). The evaluation of psychotherapeutic outcomes. In S. L. Garfield & A. E. Bergin (Eds.), *The handbook of psychotherapy and behavior change* (1st ed., pp. 217–270). New York: Wiley.

Bergin, A. E., & Lambert, M. J. (1978). the evaluation of therapeutic outcomes. In S. L. Garfield & A. E. Bergin (Eds.), *The handbook of psychotherapy and behavior change* (2nd ed., pp. 139–190). New York: Wiley.

Berzins, J. I. (1977). Matching therapists and patients in psychotherapy. In A. S. Gurman & A. M. Razin (Eds.), *Effective psychotherapy: A handbook of research* (pp. 442–481). New York: Pergamon Press.

Beutler, L. E., & Crago, M. (1983). Self-report measures of psychotherapy outcome. In M. J. Lambert, E. R. Christensen, R. Edwin, & S. S. DeJulio (Eds.), *The assessment of psychotherapy outcome* (pp. 453–497). New York: Wiley.

Borkovec, T. D., & Mathews, A. M. (1988). Treatment of nonphobic anxiety disorders: A comparison of nondirective, cognitive, and coping desensitization therapy. *Journal of Consulting and Clinical Psychology, 56,* 877–884.

Byern, D. (1964). Assessing personality variables and their alteration. In P. Worchel & D. Byrne (Eds.), *Personality change* (pp. 38–68). New York: Wiley.

Carson, R. C. (1969). *Interaction concepts of personality.* Chicago: Aldine.

Chaplin, W. F. (1986). Strait-trait Anxiety Inventory. *Test Reviews, 1,* 626–632.

Craik, K. H. (1986). Personality research methods: An historical perspective, *Journal of Personality, 54,* 19–51.

Dworkin, S. H., & Kerr, B. A. (1987). Comparison of interventions for women experiencing body image problems. *Journal of Counseling Psychology, 34,* 136–140.

Ellis, A. (1973). Rational-emotive therapy. In R. Corsini (Ed.), *Current psychotherapies* (pp. 167–206). Itasca, IL: F. E. Peacock.

Eysenck, H. J. (1987). The role of heredity, environment, and "preparedness" in the genesis of neurosis. In H. J. Eysenck & I. Martin (Eds.), *Theoretical foundations of behavior therapy* (pp. 78–97). New York: Plenum Press.

Eysenck, H. J., & Beech, R. (1971). Counterconditioning and related methods. In S. L. Garfield & A. E. Bergin (Eds.), *The handbook of psychotherapy and behavior change* (1st ed., pp. 543–611). New York: Wiley.

Froyd, J. D., & Lambert, M. J. (1989, April). *A survey and critique of psychotherapy outcome measurement.* Poster presented at the Western Psychological Association, Reno, NV.

Garfield, S. L. (1978). Research on client variables in psychotherapy. In S. L. Garfield & A. E. Bergin (Eds.), *Handbook of psychotherapy and behavior change: An empirical analysis* (2nd ed., pp. 191–232). New York: Wiley.

Garfield, S. L., & Bergin, A. E. (Eds.). (1986). *The handbook of psychotherapy and behavior change* (3rd ed.). New York: Wiley.

Graff, R. W., Whitehead, G. I., III, & LeCompte, L. (1986). Group treatment with divorced women using cognitive-behavioral and supportive-insight methods. *Journal of Counseling Psychology, 33,* 276–281.

Hollon, S., & Beck, A. T. (1994). Research on cognitive therapies. In A. E. Bergin & S. L. Garfield (Eds.), *Handbook of psychotherapy and behavior change* (4th ed., pp. 428–466). New York: Wiley.

Jacobson, N. S., Follete, W. C., & Pagel, M. (1986). Predicting who will benefit from behavioral marital therapy. *Journal of Consulting and Clinical Psychology, 54,* 518–522.

Kelly, G. A. (1955). *The psychology of personal constructs: Vol. 1. A theory of personality.* New York: Norton.

Kelly, K. R., & Stone, G. L. (1987). Effects of three psychological treatments and self-monitoring on the reduction of type A behavior. *Journal of Counseling Psychology, 34,* 46–54.

Kenny, D. A., & Campbell, D. T. (1989). On the measurement of stability in over-time data. *Journal of Personality, 57,* 445–481.

Keye, W. R., Hammond, D. C., & Strong, T. (1986). Medical and psychological characteristics of women presenting with premenstrual symptoms. *Obstetrics and Gynecology, 68,* 634–637.

Kiesler, D. J. (1971). Experimental designs in psychotherapy research. In A. E. Bergin & S. L. Garfield (Eds.), *The handbook of psychotherapy and behavior change* (1st ed., pp. 36–74). New York: Wiley.

Kocsis, J. H., & Francis, A. J. (1987). A critical discussion of DSM-III dysthymic disorder. *American Journal of Psychiatry, 144,* 1534–1542.

Krasner, L. (1971). The operant approach in behavior therapy. In A. E. Bergin & S. L. Garfield (Eds.), *The handbook of psychotherapy and behavior change* (1st ed., pp. 612–652). New York: Wiley.

Lambert, M. J. (1983). Introduction to assessment of psychotherapy outcome: Historical perspective and current issues. In M. J. Lambert, E. R. Christensen, & S. S. DeJulio (Eds.), *The assessment of psychotherapy outcome* (pp. 3–32). New York: Wiley.

Lambert, M. J., Christensen, E. R., & DeJulio, S. S. (1983). *The assessment of psychotherapy outcome.* New York: Wiley.

Lambert, M. J., Shapiro, D. A., & Bergin, A. E. (1986). The effectiveness of psychotherapy. In S. L. Garfield & A. E. Bergin (Eds.), *The handbook of psychotherapy and behavior change* (3rd ed., pp. 157–212). New York: Wiley.

Lazarus, A. A. (1971). *Behavior therapy and beyond.* New York: McGraw-Hill.

Leitenberg, H. Rosen, J. C., Gross, J., Nudelman, S., & Vara, L. S. (1988). Exposure plus response-prevention treatment of bulimia nervosa. *Journal of Consulting and Clinical Psychology, 56,* 535–541.

Luborsky, L., & Schimek, J. (1964). Psychoanalytic theories of therapeutic and developmental change: Implications for assessment. In P. Worchel & D. Byrne (Eds.), *Personality change* (pp. 73–99). New York: Wiley.

Luborsky, L., & Spence, D. P. (1978). Quantitative research on psychoanalytic therapy. In S. L. Garfield & A. E. Bergin (Eds.), *The handbook of psychotherapy and behavior change* (2nd ed., pp. 331–368). New York: Wiley.

Moran, P. W., & Lambert, M. J. (1983). A review of current assessment tools for monitoring changes in depression. In M. J. Lambert, E. R. Christensen, & S. S. DeJulio (Eds.), *The assessment of psychotherapy outcome* (pp. 263–303). New York: Wiley.

Norcross, J. (1986). *Handbook of eclectic psychotherapy.* New York: Guilford Press.

Ogles, B. M., & Lambert, M. J., Weight, D. G., & Payne, I. R. (1990). *Agoraphobia outcome measurement: A review and meta-analysis. Psychological Assessment, 2,* 317–325.

Palmer, S. (1986). *MMPI profiles of women with premenstrual syndrome.* Unpublished doctoral dissertation, Brigham Young University, Provo, UT.

Qualls, R. C., & Berman, J. S. (1988, August). *Anorexia nervosa: A quantitative review of the treatment outcome literature.* Paper presented at the symposium of the 96th annual Convention of the American Psychological Association in Atlanta, GA.

Rachman, S. (1971). *The effects of psychotherapy.* Oxford, England: Pergamon Press.

Rogers, C. R. (1942). *Counseling and psychotherapy.* Boston: Houghton-Mifflin.

Rogers, C. R., & Dymond, R. F. (1954). *Psychotherapy and personality change.* Chicago: University of Chicago Press.

Rychlak, J. F. (1981). *Personality and psychotherapy.* Boston: Houghton-Mifflin.

Shapiro, D. A., & Shapiro, D. (1982). Meta-analysis of comparative therapy outcome studies: A replication and refinement. *Psychological Bulletin, 92,* 605–640.

Smith, M. L., Glass, G. V., & Miller, T. I. (1980). *The benefits of psychotherapy.* Baltimore: Johns Hopkins University Press.

Snyder, D. E., & Wills, R. M. (1989). Behavioral versus insight-oriented marital therapy: Effects on individual and interspousal functioning. *Journal of Consulting and Clinical Psychology, 57,* 39–46.

Spielberger, C. D., Gorsuch, R. L., & Lushène, R. E. (1970). *State-Trait Anxiety Inventory.* Palo Alto, CA: Consulting Psychologists' Press.

Truax, C. B., & Mitchell, K. M. (1971). Research on certain therapist interpersonal skills in relation to process and outcome. In S. L. Garfield & A. E. Bergin (Eds.), *The handbook of psychotherapy and behavior change* (1st ed., pp. 299–344). New York: Wiley.

Viney, L. L., et al. (1985). Crisis-intervention counseling: An evaluation of long- and short-term effects. *Journal of Counseling Psychology, 32,* 29–39.

Wallerstein, R. S. (1989). The Psychotherapy Research Project of the Menninger Foundation: An overview. *Journal of Consulting and Clinical Psychology, 57,* 195–205.

Whitehorn, J. C., & Betz, B. (1954). A study of psychotherapeutic relationships between physicians and schizophrenic patients. *American Journal of Psychiatry, 3,* 321–331.

Williams, L. S., Turner, S. M., & Peer, D. F. (1985). Guided mastery and performance desensitization treatments for severe acrophobia. *Journal of Consulting and Clinical Psychology, 53,* 237–247.

INDEX

HANDBOOK OF PERSONALITY PSYCHOLOGY

Edited by

ROBERT HOGAN
University of Tulsa, Oklahoma

JOHN JOHNSON
Pennsylvania State University, DuBois

STEPHEN BRIGGS
University of Tulsa, Oklahoma

The most comprehensive single volume ever published on the subject, the *Handbook of Personality Psychology* is the end-all, must-have reference work for personality psychologists. This handbook discusses the development and measurement of personality as well as biological and social determinants, dynamic personality processes, the personality's relation to the self, and personality in relation to applied psychology.

Authored by the field's most respected researchers, each chapter provides a concise summary of the subject to date. Topics include such areas as individual differences, stability of personality, evolutionary foundations of personality, cross-cultural perspectives, emotion, psychological defenses, and the connection between personality and health. Intended for an advanced audience, the *Handbook of Personality Psychology* will be your foremost resource in this diverse field.

Academic Press
Harcourt Brace & Company, Publishers
San Diego, London, Boston, New York, Sydney, Tokyo, Toronto
Printed in the United States of America

ISBN 0-12-134646-3

90018

9 780121 346461